Contemporary Authors ®
NEW REVISION SERIES

ISSN 0275-7176

Contemporary Authors®

A Bio-Bibliographical Guide to Current Writers in Fiction, General Nonfiction, Poetry, Journalism, Drama, Motion Pictures, Television, and Other Fields

NEW REVISION SERIES
volume 148

THOMSON

GALE

Detroit • New York • San Francisco • San Diego • New Haven, Conn. • Waterville, Maine • London • Munich

THOMSON

GALE

Contemporary Authors, New Revision Series, Vol. 148

Project Editor
Tracey L. Matthews

Editorial
Michelle Kazensky, Julie Mellors, Joshua Kondek, Lisa Kumar, Mary Ruby

Composition and Electronic Capture
Carolyn Roney

Manufacturing
Drew Kalasky

LIBRARY OF CONGRESS CATALOG CARD NUMBER 81-640179

ISBN 0-7876-7902-X
ISSN 0275-7176

This title is also available as an e-book.
ISBN 1-4144-1012-3
Contact your Thomson Gale sales representative for ordering information.

Printed in the United States of America
10 9 8 7 6 5 4 3 2 1

Contents

Indexing note: All *Contemporary Authors* entries are indexed in the *Contemporary Authors* cumulative index, which is published separately and distributed twice a year.

As always, the most recent Contemporary Authors cumulative index continues to be the user's guide to the location of an individual author's listing.

Preface

Contemporary Authors (*CA*) provides information on approximately 120,000 writers in a wide range of media, including:

- Current writers of fiction, nonfiction, poetry, and drama whose works have been issued by commercial publishers, risk publishers, or university presses (authors whose books have been published only by known vanity or author-subsidized firms are ordinarily not included)

- Prominent print and broadcast journalists, editors, photojournalists, syndicated cartoonists, graphic novelists, screenwriters, television scriptwriters, and other media people

- Notable international authors

- Literary greats of the early twentieth century whose works are popular in today's high school and college curriculums and continue to elicit critical attention

A *CA* listing entails no charge or obligation. Authors are included on the basis of the above criteria and their interest to *CA* users. Sources of potential listees include trade periodicals, publishers' catalogs, librarians, and other users.

How to Get the Most out of *CA*: Use the Index

The key to locating an author's most recent entry is the *CA* cumulative index, which is published separately and distributed twice a year. It provides access to *all* entries in *CA* and *Contemporary Authors New Revision Series* (*CANR*). Always consult the latest index to find an author's most recent entry.

For the convenience of users, the *CA* cumulative index also includes references to all entries in these Thomson Gale literary series: *African-American Writers, African Writers, American Nature Writers, American Writers, American Writers: The Classics, American Writers Retrospective Supplement, American Writers Supplement, Ancient Writers, Asian American Literature, Authors and Artists for Young Adults, Authors in the News, Beacham's Encyclopedia of Popular Fiction: Analyses, Beacham's Encyclopedia of Popular Fiction: Biography and Resources, Beacham's Guide to Literature for Young Adults, Beat Generation: A Gale Critical Companion, Bestsellers, Black Literature Criticism, Black Literature Criticism Supplement, Black Writers, British Writers, British Writers: The Classics, British Writers Retrospective Supplement, British Writers Supplement, Children's Literature Review, Classical and Medieval Literature Criticism, Concise Dictionary of American Literary Biography, Concise Dictionary of American Literary Biography Supplement, Concise Dictionary of British Literary Biography, Concise Dictionary of World Literary Biography, Contemporary American Dramatists, Contemporary Authors Autobiography Series, Contemporary Authors Bibliographical Series, Contemporary British Dramatists, Contemporary Canadian Authors, Contemporary Dramatists, Contemporary Literary Criticism, Contemporary Novelists, Contemporary Poets, Contemporary Popular Writers, Contemporary Southern Writers, Contemporary Women Dramatists, Contemporary Women Poets, Contemporary World Writers, Dictionary of Literary Biography, Dictionary of Literary Biography Documentary Series, Dictionary of Literary Biography Yearbook, DISCovering Authors, DISCovering Authors 3.0, DISCovering Authors: British Edition, DISCovering Authors: Canadian Edition, DISCovering Authors Modules, Drama Criticism, Drama for Students, Encyclopedia of World Literature in the 20th Century, Epics for Students, European Writers, Exploring Novels, Exploring Poetry, Exploring Short Stories, Feminism in Literature, Feminist Writers, Gay & Lesbian Literature, Guide to French Literature, Harlem Renaissance: A Gale Critical Companion, Hispanic Literature Criticism, Hispanic Literature Criticism Supplement, Hispanic Writers, International Dictionary of Films and Filmmakers: Writers and Production Artists, International Dictionary of Theatre: Playwrights, Junior DISCovering Authors, Latin American Writers, Latin American Writers Supplement, Latino and Latina Writers, Literature and Its Times, Literature and Its Times Supplement, Literature Criticism from 1400-1800, Literature of Developing Nations for Students, Major Authors and Illustrators for Children and Young Adults, Major Authors and Illustrators for Children and Young Adults Supplement, Major 21st Century Writers (eBook version), Major 20th-Century Writers, Modern American Women Writers, Modern Arts Criticism, Modern Japanese Writers, Mystery and Suspense Writers, Native North American Literature, Nineteenth-Century Literature Criticism, Nonfiction Classics for Students, Novels for Students, Poetry Criticism, Poetry for Students, Poets: American and British, Reference Guide to American Literature, Reference Guide to English Literature, Reference Guide to Short Fiction, Reference Guide to World Literature, Science Fiction Writers, Shakespearean Criticism, Shakespeare for Students, Shakespeare's Characters for Students, Short Stories for Students, Short Story Criticism, Something About the Author, Something About the Author Autobiography Series, St. James Guide to Children's Writers, St. James Guide to Crime & Mystery Writers, St. James Guide to Fantasy Writers, St. James Guide to Horror, Ghost & Gothic Writers, St. James Guide to Science Fiction Writers, St. James Guide to Young Adult Writers, Supernatural Fiction*

Writers, Twayne Companion to Contemporary Literature in English, Twayne's English Authors, Twayne's United States Authors, Twayne's World Authors, Twentieth-Century Literary Criticism, Twentieth-Century Romance and Historical Writers, Twentieth-Century Western Writers, William Shakespeare, World Literature and Its Times, World Literature Criticism, World Literature Criticism Supplement, World Poets, World Writing in English, Writers for Children, Writers for Young Adults, and *Yesterday's Authors of Books for Children.*

A Sample Index Entry:

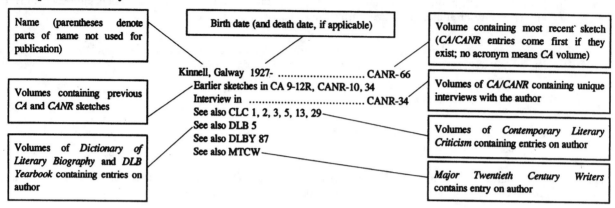

How Are Entries Compiled?

The editors make every effort to secure new information directly from the authors; listees' responses to our questionnaires and query letters provide most of the information featured in *CA*. For deceased writers, or those who fail to reply to requests for data, we consult other reliable biographical sources, such as those indexed in Thomson Gale's *Biography and Genealogy Master Index,* and bibliographical sources, including *National Union Catalog, LC MARC,* and *British National Bibliography.* Further details come from published interviews, feature stories, and book reviews, as well as information supplied by the authors' publishers and agents.

An asterisk (*) at the end of a sketch indicates that the listing has been compiled from secondary sources believed to be reliable but has not been personally verified for this edition by the author sketched.

What Kinds of Information Does An Entry Provide?

Sketches in *CA* contain the following biographical and bibliographical information:

- **Entry heading:** the most complete form of author's name, plus any pseudonyms or name variations used for writing

- **Personal information:** author's date and place of birth, family data, ethnicity, educational background, political and religious affiliations, and hobbies and leisure interests

- **Addresses:** author's home, office, or agent's addresses, plus e-mail and fax numbers, as available

- **Career summary:** name of employer, position, and dates held for each career post; resume of other vocational achievements; military service

- **Membership information:** professional, civic, and other association memberships and any official posts held

- **Awards and honors:** military and civic citations, major prizes and nominations, fellowships, grants, and honorary degrees

- **Writings:** a comprehensive, chronological list of titles, publishers, dates of original publication and revised editions, and production information for plays, television scripts, and screenplays

- **Adaptations:** a list of films, plays, and other media which have been adapted from the author's work

- **Work in progress:** current or planned projects, with dates of completion and/or publication, and expected publisher, when known

- **Sidelights:** a biographical portrait of the author's development; information about the critical reception of the author's works; revealing comments, often by the author, on personal interests, aspirations, motivations, and thoughts on writing

- **Interview:** a one-on-one discussion with authors conducted especially for *CA*, offering insight into authors' thoughts about their craft

- **Autobiographical essay:** an original essay written by noted authors for *CA*, a forum in which writers may present themselves, on their own terms, to their audience

- **Photographs:** portraits and personal photographs of notable authors

- **Biographical and critical sources:** a list of books and periodicals in which additional information on an author's life and/or writings appears

- **Obituary Notices** in *CA* provide date and place of birth as well as death information about authors whose full-length sketches appeared in the series before their deaths. The entries also summarize the authors' careers and writings and list other sources of biographical and death information.

Related Titles in the *CA* Series

Contemporary Authors Autobiography Series complements *CA* original and revised volumes with specially commissioned autobiographical essays by important current authors, illustrated with personal photographs they provide. Common topics include their motivations for writing, the people and experiences that shaped their careers, the rewards they derive from their work, and their impressions of the current literary scene.

Contemporary Authors Bibliographical Series surveys writings by and about important American authors since World War II. Each volume concentrates on a specific genre and features approximately ten writers; entries list works written by and about the author and contain a bibliographical essay discussing the merits and deficiencies of major critical and scholarly studies in detail.

Available in Electronic Formats

GaleNet. *CA* is available on a subscription basis through GaleNet, an online information resource that features an easy-to-use end-user interface, powerful search capabilities, and ease of access through the World-Wide Web. For more information, call 1-800-877-GALE.

Licensing. *CA* is available for licensing. The complete database is provided in a fielded format and is deliverable on such media as disk, CD-ROM, or tape. For more information, contact Thomson Gale's Business Development Group at 1-800-877-GALE, or visit us on our website at www.galegroup.com/bizdev.

Suggestions Are Welcome

The editors welcome comments and suggestions from users on any aspect of the *CA* series. If readers would like to recommend authors for inclusion in future volumes of the series, they are cordially invited to write the Editors at *Contemporary Authors*, Thomson Gale, 27500 Drake Rd., Farmington Hills, MI 48331-3535; or call at 1-248-699-4253; or fax at 1-248-699-8054.

Contemporary Authors Product Advisory Board

The editors of *Contemporary Authors* are dedicated to maintaining a high standard of excellence by publishing comprehensive, accurate, and highly readable entries on a wide array of writers. In addition to the quality of the content, the editors take pride in the graphic design of the series, which is intended to be orderly yet inviting, allowing readers to utilize the pages of *CA* easily and with efficiency. Despite the longevity of the *CA* print series, and the success of its format, we are mindful that the vitality of a literary reference product is dependent on its ability to serve its users over time. As literature, and attitudes about literature, constantly evolve, so do the reference needs of students, teachers, scholars, journalists, researchers, and book club members. To be certain that we continue to keep pace with the expectations of our customers, the editors of *CA* listen carefully to their comments regarding the value, utility, and quality of the series. Librarians, who have firsthand knowledge of the needs of library users, are a valuable resource for us. The *Contemporary Authors* Product Advisory Board, made up of school, public, and academic librarians, is a forum to promote focused feedback about *CA* on a regular basis. The seven-member advisory board includes the following individuals, whom the editors wish to thank for sharing their expertise:

- **Anne M. Christensen,** Librarian II, Phoenix Public Library, Phoenix, Arizona.

- **Barbara C. Chumard,** Reference/Adult Services Librarian, Middletown Thrall Library, Middletown, New York.

- **Eva M. Davis,** Youth Department Manager, Ann Arbor District Library, Ann Arbor, Michigan.

- **Adam Janowski, Jr.,** Library Media Specialist, Naples High School Library Media Center, Naples, Florida.

- **Robert Reginald,** Head of Technical Services and Collection Development, California State University, San Bernadino, California.

- **Stephen Weiner,** Director, Maynard Public Library, Maynard, Massachusetts.

International Advisory Board

Well-represented among the 120,000 author entries published in *Contemporary Authors* are sketches on notable writers from many non-English-speaking countries. The primary criteria for inclusion of such authors has traditionally been the publication of at least one title in English, either as an original work or as a translation. However, the editors of *Contemporary Authors* came to observe that many important international writers were being overlooked due to a strict adherence to our inclusion criteria. In addition, writers who were publishing in languages other than English were not being covered in the traditional sources we used for identifying new listees. Intent on increasing our coverage of international authors, including those who write only in their native language and have not been translated into English, the editors enlisted the aid of a board of advisors, each of whom is an expert on the literature of a particular country or region. Among the countries we focused attention on are Mexico, Puerto Rico, Spain, Italy, France, Germany, Luxembourg, Belgium, the Netherlands, Norway, Sweden, Denmark, Finland, Taiwan, Singapore, Malaysia, Thailand, South Africa, Israel, and Japan, as well as England, Scotland, Wales, Ireland, Australia, and New Zealand. The sixteen-member advisory board includes the following individuals, whom the editors wish to thank for sharing their expertise:

- **Lowell A. Bangerter,** Professor of German, University of Wyoming, Laramie, Wyoming.

- **Nancy E. Berg,** Associate Professor of Hebrew and Comparative Literature, Washington University, St. Louis, Missouri.

- **Frances Devlin-Glass,** Associate Professor, School of Literary and Communication Studies, Deakin University, Burwood, Victoria, Australia.

- **David William Foster,** Regent's Professor of Spanish, Interdisciplinary Humanities, and Women's Studies, Arizona State University, Tempe, Arizona.

- **Hosea Hirata,** Director of the Japanese Program, Associate Professor of Japanese, Tufts University, Medford, Massachusetts.

- **Jack Kolbert,** Professor Emeritus of French Literature, Susquehanna University, Selinsgrove, Pennsylvania.

- **Mark Libin,** Professor, University of Manitoba, Winnipeg, Manitoba, Canada.

- **C. S. Lim,** Professor, University of Malaya, Kuala Lumpur, Malaysia.

- **Eloy E. Merino,** Assistant Professor of Spanish, Northern Illinois University, DeKalb, Illinois.

- **Linda M. Rodríguez Guglielmoni,** Associate Professor, University of Puerto Rico—Mayagüez, Puerto Rico.

- **Sven Hakon Rossel,** Professor and Chair of Scandinavian Studies, University of Vienna, Vienna, Austria.

- **Steven R. Serafin,** Director, Writing Center, Hunter College of the City University of New York, New York City.

- **David Smyth,** Lecturer in Thai, School of Oriental and African Studies, University of London, England.

- **Ismail S. Talib,** Senior Lecturer, Department of English Language and Literature, National University of Singapore, Singapore.

- **Dionisio Viscarri,** Assistant Professor, Ohio State University, Columbus, Ohio.

- **Mark Williams,** Associate Professor, English Department, University of Canterbury, Christchurch, New Zealand.

CA Numbering System and Volume Update Chart

Occasionally questions arise about the *CA* numbering system and which volumes, if any, can be discarded. Despite numbers like "29-32R," "97-100" and "240," the entire *CA* print series consists of 316 physical volumes with the publication of *CA* Volume 241. The following charts note changes in the numbering system and cover design, and indicate which volumes are essential for the most complete, up-to-date coverage.

***CA* First Revision**	• 1-4R through 41-44R (11 books) *Cover:* Brown with black and gold trim. There will be no further First Revision volumes because revised entries are now being handled exclusively through the more efficient *New Revision Series* mentioned below.
***CA* Original Volumes**	• 45-48 through 97-100 (14 books) *Cover:* Brown with black and gold trim. 101 through 241 (141 books) *Cover:* Blue and black with orange bands. The same as previous *CA* original volumes but with a new, simplified numbering system and new cover design.
***CA* Permanent Series**	• *CAP*-1 and *CAP*-2 (2 books) *Cover:* Brown with red and gold trim. There will be no further Permanent Series volumes because revised entries are now being handled exclusively through the more efficient *New Revision Series* mentioned below.
***CA* New Revision Series**	• CANR-1 through CANR-148 (148 books) *Cover:* Blue and black with green bands. Includes only sketches requiring significant changes; **sketches are taken from any previously published CA, CAP, or CANR volume.**

If You Have:	You May Discard:
CA First Revision Volumes 1-4R through 41-44R and *CA* Permanent Series Volumes 1 and 2	*CA* Original Volumes 1, 2, 3, 4 and Volumes 5-6 through 41-44
CA Original Volumes 45-48 through 97-100 and 101 through 241	**NONE:** These volumes will not be superseded by corresponding revised volumes. Individual entries from these and all other volumes appearing in the left column of this chart may be revised and included in the various volumes of the *New Revision Series*.
CA New Revision Series Volumes *CANR*-1 through *CANR*-148	**NONE:** The *New Revision Series* does not replace any single volume of *CA*. Instead, volumes of *CANR* include entries from many previous *CA* series volumes. All *New Revision Series* volumes must be retained for full coverage.

A Sampling of Authors and Media People
Featured in This Volume

Betsy Byars

Over the course of her long and productive career, Byars has received extensive critical praise for her insightful portrayals of adolescents suffering from feelings of isolation and loneliness. She has produced books for children of several different ages, including chapter books for beginning readers and novels aimed at an early adolescent audience. Though her works are intended for children, Byars does not shy away from controversial subjects, and her skillful handling of the material has helped convince critics that such issues can be effectively portrayed in juvenile literature.

Sarah Dunant

British author Dunant has written numerous mystery novels, most famously the "Hannah Wolfe" mystery series. Dunant has branched out into writing historical fiction as well with *The Birth of Venus,* and she has contributed to *The War of the Words: The Political Correctness Debate,* a collection of essays that argues the relevance of gender and ethnic issues in any contemporary political debate. Also the author of novels with Peter Busby, Dunant and her coauthor publish under the joint pseudonym Peter Dunant.

Nicholas Evans

Evans, originally a screenwriter, is best known for his bestselling book *The Horse Whisperer,* which was also made into a successful film. While not a critical favorite, *The Horse Whisperer,* along with *The Smoke Jumper* and his other works, has given Evans a large following among the general public.

Nuruddin Farah

An African writer best known for novels that champion the oppressed, particularly women, Farah sets his plots in twentieth-century Somalia, with most of the action occurring in the capital, Mogadishu. He is best known for his "Variations on the Theme of an African Dictatorship," a trilogy about a dictatorship led by the fictional Major General Muhammad Siyad, and the subsequent demise of democracy in Somalia. Though sometimes criticized for substandard stylistic and technical writing, Farah is generally acknowledged as one of the African writers who have gone to the greatest lengths to promote human rights.

Liu Heng

Screenwriter and novelist Heng's career rose alongside that of Chinese director Zhang Yimou. Heng joined the highly regarded director to write screenplays for the films *Red Sorghum, Ju Dou* (the first Chinese film ever nominated for an Academy Award), and *The Story of Qiu Ju.* He is often caught between his creative principles and the expectations of the Chinese communist government, which frequently denounces his work for focusing on unpleasant issues in modern Chinese life. Heng is part of a development in Chinese literature in which writers contradict the official portrayal of Chinese society and explore aspects of Chinese life that were previously censored or forbidden.

Eric Idle

Idle is one of six members of Monty Python, a group of British comedians whose absurd humor earned them a large following in Europe and North America. Idle has also undertaken a number of successful solo projects, writing novels, short films, and *Monty Python's Spamalot,* a Tony-winning stage adaptation of the film *Monty Python and the Holy Grail.*

Cheech Marin

Comedy writer and performer Marin is famous for his albums and films with early comedic partner Tommy Chong. Together, Cheech and Chong became renowned for their drug-related humor, included in movies such as *Up in Smoke,* and *The Corsican Brothers.* Marin has also done solo projects; he wrote, directed, and appeared in the film *Born in East L.A.* In addition to his comedy work, Marin is known for his large collection of Chicano art, which he discusses in the art book *Chicano Visions: American Painters on the Verge.*

Bill Moyers

Retired White House press secretary and broadcast journalist Moyers is well known for the decades he has spent providing American television audiences with "news of the mind." His erudite political commentaries, historical essays, and series on such subjects as myth and evil challenged the limits of television programming and offered educational alternatives to standard prime-time fare. Moyers is the author of several books, including the collection of critical essays *Moyers on America: A Journalist and His Times.*

A

ACKERMAN, Diane 1948-

PERSONAL: Born October 7, 1948, in Waukegan, IL; daughter of Sam (a restaurant owner) and Marcia (Tischler) Fink. *Education:* Attended Boston University, 1966-67; Pennsylvania State University, B.A., 1970; Cornell University, M.F.A., 1973, M.A., 1976, Ph.D., 1978. *Hobbies and other interests:* Gardening, bicycling.

ADDRESSES: Home—Ithaca, NY. *Agent*—c/o Author Mail, BrownTrout Publishers, Inc., P.O. Box 280070, San Francisco, CA 94128-0070. *E-mail*—inkdream@ hotmail.com.

CAREER: Writer. Social worker in New York, NY, 1967; Pennsylvania State University, University Park, government researcher, 1968; *Library Journal,* New York, NY, editorial assistant, 1970; *Epoch,* Ithaca, NY, associate editor, 1971-77; Cornell University, Ithaca, NY, teaching assistant, 1971-78, lecturer, 1978-79; University of Pittsburgh, Pittsburgh, PA, assistant professor of English, 1980-83; Washington University, St. Louis, MO, director of writers program and writer-in-residence, 1984-86; *New Yorker,* New York, NY, staff writer, 1988-94. Host, *Mystery of the Senses,* Public Broadcasting System (PBS), 1995. Writer-in-residence, William and Mary College, Williamsburg, VA, 1983, Ohio University, Athens, 1983; visiting writer, Columbia University, New York, NY, 1986, New York University, New York, NY, 1986; Cornell University, visiting writer, 1987, visiting professor at Society for the Humanities, 1998-99; Atlantic Center for the Arts, New Smyrna Beach, FL, master artist-in-residence, 1988; University of Richmond, Richmond, VA, National Endowment for the Humanities Distinguished Professor. Member of literature panels, including New York State Council on the Arts, 1980-83; member of advisory board, Planetary Society, Pasadena, CA, 1980—. Has participated in readings, residencies, and workshops. Produced the recordings *The Naturalists,* Gang of Seven Inc., 1992, and *A Natural History of Love,* 1994.

AWARDS, HONORS: Poetry Prize, Academy of American Poets, Cornell University, 1972; Corson Bishop French Prize, Cornell University, 1972, 1977; Abbie Copps Prize, Olivet College, 1974; Rockefeller graduate fellowship, 1974-76; Heermans-McCalmon Playwriting Prize, Cornell University, 1976; National Endowment for the Arts, creative writing fellowships, 1976 and 1986; Creative Artists Public Service fellowship, 1980; Poetry Prize, *Black Warrior Review,* 1981; Associated Writing Programs, member of board of directors, 1982-85; Pushcart Prize VIII, 1984; Peter I.B. Lavan Younger Poet Award, Academy of American Poets, 1985; Lowell Thomas Award, Society of American Travel Writers, 1990; National Endowment for the Arts, member of Poetry Panel, 1991; National Book Critics Circle Award nomination, 1991; Wordsmith Award, 1992; "New and Noteworthy Book of the Year," *New York Times Book Review,* for *The Moon by Whale Light,* 1992, and for *Jaguar of Sweet Laughter,* 1993; Golden Nose Award, Olfactory Research Fund, 1994; named a "Literary Lion" by the New York Public Library, 1994; Journalist-in-Space Project semifinalist; John Burroughs Nature Award, 1998; Guggenheim fellowship, Guggenheim Memorial Foundation, 2003.

WRITINGS:

POETRY

(With Jody Bolz and Nancy Steele) *Poems: Ackerman, Bolz, and Steele* (chapbook), Stone Marrow Press (Cincinnati, OH), 1973.
The Planets: A Cosmic Pastoral, Morrow (New York, NY), 1976.
Wife of Light, Morrow (New York, NY), 1978.
Lady Faustus, Morrow (New York, NY), 1983.
Jaguar of Sweet Laughter: New and Selected Poems, Random House (New York, NY), 1991.
(Editor, with Jeanne Mackin) *The Book of Love,* Norton (New York, NY), 1998.
I Praise My Destroyer, Random House (New York, NY), 1998.
Origami Bridges: Poems of Psychoanalysis and Fire, HarperCollins (New York, NY), 2002.
Animal Sense (juvenile), illustrated by Peter Sís, Knopf (New York, NY), 2003.

NONFICTION

Twilight of the Tenderfoot: A Western Memoir, Morrow (New York, NY), 1980.
On Extended Wings (memoir), Atheneum (New York, NY), 1985, published as *On Extended Wings: An Adventure in Flight,* Scribner (New York, NY), 1987.
A Natural History of the Senses, Random House (New York, NY), 1990.
The Moon by Whale Light, and Other Adventures among Bats, Penguins, Crocodilians, and Whales, Random House (New York, NY), 1991.
A Natural History of Love, Random House (New York, NY), 1994.
The Rarest of the Rare: Vanishing Animals, Timeless Worlds, Random House (New York, NY), 1995.
Monk Seal Hideaway (juvenile), Crown (New York, NY), 1995.
Bats: Shadows in the Night (juvenile), photographs by Merlin Tuttle, Crown (New York, NY), 1997.
A Slender Thread: Crisis, Healing, and Nature, Random House (New York, NY), 1997.
Deep Play, illustrated by Peter Sís, Random House (New York, NY), 1999.
Cultivating Delight: A Natural History of My Garden, HarperCollins (New York, NY), 2001.
An Alchemy of Mind: The Marvel and Mystery of the Brain, Scribner (New York, NY), 2004.

OTHER

Reverse Thunder: A Dramatic Poem (play; produced in New Brunswick, NJ, 1982), Lumen (Cambridge, MA), 1988.
Ideas (television documentary), 1990.
Mystery of the Senses (television documentary), Public Broadcasting System, 1995.

Also author of the play *All Seasons Are Weather,* in *Texas Arts Journal* (Dallas, TX), fall, 1979. Contributor to books and anthologies, including *The Morrow Anthology of Younger Poets,* edited by Dave Smith and David Bottoms, Morrow, 1985; *Norton Introduction to Literature,* edited by Jerome Beaty and J. Paul Hunter, 4th edition, Norton, 1986; *Norton Introduction to Poetry,* edited by Hunter, 3rd edition, Norton, 1986; *The Paris Review Anthology,* edited by George Plimpton, Norton, 1989; *Beyond the Map,* ELM Press, 1995; *Going on Faith: Writing as a Spiritual Quest,* edited by William Zinsser, Marlowe, 1999; (with others) *Food and Faith: Justice, Joy, and Daily Bread,* edited by Michael Schut, 2002; *Within the Stone,* 2004; and numerous other poetry and prose anthologies.

Contributor of poems and nonfiction to literary journals, periodicals, and newspapers, including *New Yorker,Poetry, Life,Omni, Kenyon Review,American Poetry Review, Parnassus, Michigan Quarterly Review,Paris Review, Parnassus: Poetry in Review, Discover, World Magazine,* and *New York Times.* Contributor of reviews to *New York Times Book Review.*

ADAPTATIONS: *On Extended Wings: An Adventure in Flight* was adapted for the stage in 1987 by Norma Jean Griffin.

SIDELIGHTS: Diane Ackerman has been hailed by several critics not only for her poetry but for her prose explorations into the world of science and natural history. She once said in *Contemporary Poets:* "People sometimes ask me about all of the science in my work, thinking it odd that I should wish to combine science and art, and assuming that I must have some inner pledge or outer maxim I follow. But the hardest job for me is trying to keep science out of my writing. We live in a world where amino acids, viruses, airfoils, and such are common ingredients in our daily sense of

Nature. Not to write about Nature in its widest sense, because quasars or corpuscles are not 'the proper realm of poetry,' as a critic once said to me, is not only irresponsible and philistine, it bankrupts the experience of living, it ignores much of life's fascination and variety."

Ackerman's voracious appetite for knowledge and her eager appreciation of the natural world are evident in *Jaguar of Sweet Laughter: New and Selected Poems,* according to *New York Times Book Review* contributor David Kirby. He asserted, "Diane Ackerman's poems not only operate in the present but press toward the future. . . . Just about everything Ms. Ackerman writes, prose or poetry, is exploratory. . . . [Her] speakers push ahead; they probe, open, take off lids, peel back covers, inspect, taste, sniff." Her constant sense of wonder is the key to the appeal of her work, concluded Kirby: "Ms. Ackerman trains her telescope on the bend in the river, all but pitching over the rail as she strains toward the next surprise."

In his essay in *Parnassus,* Mark Doty compared Ackerman's work to that of another, more "metaphysical" nature poet, Mary Oliver, whose poetic quest remains a search for meaning in what she finds in the natural world. In contrast, Doty maintained, Ackerman "does not look for an overarching metaphysic, a coherence, because she fundamentally doesn't believe there is such a thing. . . . Where Darwin amassed a lifetime's worth of observed detail in order to generalize and arrive at evolutionary patterns, Ackerman prefers the sensuous, puzzling, intractable particular."

Ackerman has also been praised for her skill at observing and then eloquently describing the details of the natural world, and nowhere is that more evident than in *The Moon by Whale Light, and Other Adventures among Bats, Penguins, Crocodilians, and Whales,* a collection of four essays expanded from articles previously published in the *New Yorker.* Allying herself with experts on each species, Ackerman went into the field to gain firsthand experience with these animals. She recorded her observations in detail, along with her thoughts on the folklore of each animal. Fraser Harrison noted in *New Statesman and Society:* "Ackerman . . . is a hands-on journalist in a very literal sense, for, as befits the author of *A Natural History of the Senses,* she always insists on touching her subjects, even the whales. Especially vivid is her account of sitting astride an alligator, its mouth bound with tape,

and feeling her way round its 'beautiful, undulating skin.'" Harrison found Ackerman's portrayal of penguins "shamelessly anthropomorphic" yet justifiable. Her depiction of their habitat, he added, is poetic, "and it is this quality that makes her a considerable nature writer as well as an intrepid, sharp-eyed journalist, for she has the imaginative gift to identify with the character of her animals and the intelligence to keep them in their ecological place."

Michiko Kakutani, writing in the *New York Times,* offered similar praise, writing that Ackerman "has a gift for sparkling, resonant language, and her descriptions of various animals and their habitats are alive with verbal energy and delight. She describes bats as delicately assembled packages of 'fur and appetite' and characterizes their high-pitched cries as 'vocal Braille.'" Kakutani further praised the author for providing a great deal of "fascinating" information about the lives of each species. In addition, Franklin Burroughs, writing in the *Southern Review,* enthusiastically endorsed Ackerman's "fine eye for detail, her adventurousness, and her humor" and noted: "When these essays first appeared in the familiar milieu of the *New Yorker,* they seemed to fall within its civilized, flexible conception of an American middle voice: informative, engaging, modest, witty, and thoroughly *professional,* not subject to the enthusiasms, large claims, and idiosyncrasies of the writer for whom writing itself remains the central, animating adventure."

Ackerman shifted her focus from the animal world to the human province of romantic love with her 1994 collection of essays *A Natural History of Love. Washington Post Book World* contributor Barbara Raskin characterized this volume as "an audaciously brilliant romp. . . . Using an evolutionary history as her launchpad, Ackerman takes off on a space flight in which she describes, defines, theorizes, analyzes, analogizes, apologizes, generalizes, explains, philosophizes, embellishes, codifies, classifies, confesses, compares, contrasts, speculates, hypothesizes and generally carries on like a hooligan about amatory love. It's a blast." Ackerman follows a quick survey of two thousand years of love with an analysis of famous literary passages on romance, the chemistry of love, the effects of lovelessness on children and cultures, and many more subjects. Some critics believed that she included too many topics in the collection and used too many different writing styles. Chris Goodrich, writing in the *Los Angeles Times,* praised *A Natural History of Love* as an enjoyable read but found it "surprisingly shapeless," with contents "that vary between the arresting and the superficial, the illuminating and the irksome. Reading the book, you spend half your time wishing it were better, and the other half captivated by those passages in which Ackerman . . . has found a particularly good lens through which to view her subject." Still, he acknowledged that the book was "a pleasure" and described Ackerman as "a beguiling, even seductive writer." Raskin also emphasized the author's power with words, stating: "Of all the loves Ackerman describes, none is greater than her own love of language. . . . She produces hard-hitting metaphors and sweet constellations of similes that are like confectionery recipes for fresh insights."

In the mid-1990s Ackerman wrote up her observations from two research expeditions to produce her first books for children: *Monk Seal Hideaway,* about monk seals at the Hawaiian Island National Wildlife Refuge, and *Bats: Shadows in the Night,* an account of her trip to Big Bend National Park in Texas accompanied by Merlin Tuttle, a bat expert and photographer. *Bulletin of the Center for Children's Books* contributor Roger Sutton found the tone of *Monk Seal Hideaway* to be "amiable and engaging" and noted that "budding naturalists will appreciate the eyewitness report." *Bats* also won praise as "natural history writing at its best," in the words of Sally Estes in *Booklist.*

Even as Ackerman has branched out into writing children's books, she continues to write poetry. Without the guidance and comfort of religious dogma, Ackerman asks in *I Praise My Destroyer,* how does an agnostic face up to the "horror lesson" of death? As John Taylor points out in his *Poetry* review, the agnostic's "only certitude is eschatological uncertainty." He praised Ackerman for the "precision and enthusiasm" with which she confronts this dilemma by "exalting the organic processes whereby entities such as ourselves come into existence, exist, then perish." Moreover, the "gently erotic love poems" included in this collection, Taylor observed, "show that we must come to terms not only with our demise, but also sometimes—and no less intensely—with the lover who fled 'the love-brightened room. ' . . . We also die . . . several times in the midst of life through amorous leave-takings and unrequited attractions."

Death plays an altogether different role in *A Slender Thread: Crisis, Healing, and Nature,* Ackerman's ac-count of working the night shift of a suicide prevention hotline for one year. Antoinette Brinkman described the book in the *Library Journal* as "intensely interdisciplinary," noting that Ackerman "deftly interweaves moving stories of battered women, the lonely middle-aged, and suicidal teens with observations of nature by day and human nature in the later hours." *New York Times Book Review* critic Kate Jennings noted that the author comes across "as a thoroughly nice person," but pointed out that sentimentality can be "an occupational hazard" among those who write in the first person. In this regard, Jennings cited May Sarton, M.F.K. Fisher, and Annie Dillard, all critically acclaimed authors whose first-person writings nonetheless, like Ackerman's, "walk a fine line, risking self-regard and preciousness as well as sentimentality."

Ackerman's 1999 title, *Deep Play,* deals with transcendence of the daily norm through forms of "play" such as art, religion, and other human practices that lead to a heightened state of being. Winifred Gallagher observed in the *New York Times Book Review* that Ackerman "writes best when she balances her impressions with objective knowledge, like research on the functions of play in various species or the utility of color in nature." A *Publishers Weekly* reviewer noted that Ackerman's best writing emerges when her subject is "something observable" and she "beguile[s] readers with fine turns of phrase." The *Publishers Weekly* reviewer was less impressed when Ackerman "indulges her weakness for abstraction," but *Booklist* contributor Donna Seaman found that "the very act of reading this original, exultant, sage, poetic, and generous meditation on the importance of enchantment is deep play."

In *Cultivating Delight: A Natural History of My Garden,* Ackerman takes the reader on a philosophical jaunt through the four seasons as observed in her own backyard landscape. This book is not a gardening manual; Ackerman's interest is not so much in how things grow as in what the natural world does for the human soul and spirit. From this perspective, "Ackerman buzzes productively from idea to revelation to insight," a *Publishers Weekly* reviewer noted, as she "reprises her role as an enchanting intellectual sensualist."

Ackerman's *Origami Bridges: Poems of Psychoanalysis and Fire* documents a year and a half of psychoanalysis with an analyst the poems refer to as "Dr. B."

Written in free verse and loose rhyme, the poems are divided into four sections. Christina Pugh, a contributor to *Poetry* magazine, reported that in the introduction to the collection, Ackerman explains that the book was written to "corral the unruly emotions that arose during intense psychotherapy." Pugh also suggested that good literature "ultimately has to separate from its therapeutic origins in order to stand as viable art. This separation is not quite achieved in *Origami Bridges*." Interestingly, no clear reason for the psychotherapy is revealed. As a result, Pugh cited "an uncomfortable combination of exhibition and withholding." However, in a review for the *Library Journal*, Barbara Hoffert commented on the book's "down to the essence" diction.

One year after *Origami Bridges* was released, Ackerman published *Animal Sense*, a collection of poetry for children. *Animal Sense* contains fifteen poems in five sections, each section focusing on a certain sense, each poem focusing on a different animal. In this collection, Ackerman intertwines her poetry with scientific facts about animals. A *Publishers Weekly* critic noted the beauty of the artwork, but had some reservations regarding the poetry, calling the book "a beautifully designed but unfortunately flawed collection." However, Lauralyn Persson, writing in the *School Library Journal,* noted that "readers who want to go beyond the obvious will savor it."

Published in 2004, *An Alchemy of Mind: The Marvel and Mystery of the Brain* employs Ackerman's flair for metaphor to explain the complex workings of the brain. One *Publishers Weekly* contributor acknowledged, "Even brain buffs used to a more detached approach should be won over by her uniquely personal perspective." Combining experience, history, literature, and science, Ackerman produces a new sort of study on how and why we think by infusing her trademark poetic language into scientific writing. *Booklist* critic Donna Seaman called the writing "agile, involving and uniquely far-ranging and insightful." On the other hand, the differences between the book and most scientific writing are also what might discourage some readers. "Ackerman has a tendency to wander, dazed and marveling," wrote a contributor to *Kirkus Reviews,* who continued, "this is at once her greatest strength and besetting weakness . . . her reveries can seem like extended diary entries, or plain old wheel-spinning."

According to Ackerman *An Alchemy of Mind* is the natural next step following her previous work. In an interview with Ron Hogan of *Publishers Weekly,* she maintained: "All of my books are an effort to discover a little better what it once was like to be alive on the planet: what the passions felt like, what it tasted like, what it smelt like, the whole experience of being alive." Ackerman's wonder at every aspect of life makes up the thread that runs through all of her work. In an interview with Barbara Adams of *Writer's Digest,* Ackerman reflected, "Sometimes people think that I write different kinds of books—some about animals and some about people. But to my mind, it's all part of the same quest, to understand the human condition and what life on Earth feels like."

BIOGRAPHICAL AND CRITICAL SOURCES:

BOOKS

Ackerman, Diane, *Twilight of the Tenderfoot: A Western Memoir,* Morrow (New York, NY), 1980.
Ackerman, Diane, *On Extended Wings,* Atheneum (New York, NY), 1985.
Contemporary Poets, 6th edition, St. James Press (Detroit, MI), 1996.
Contemporary Women Poets, St. James Press (Detroit, MI), 1998.
Dictionary of Literary Biography, Volume 120: *American Poets since World War II,* Third Series, Gale (Detroit, MI), 1992.

PERIODICALS

Affilia Journal of Women and Social Work, summer, 1998, Catherine Hiersteiner, review of *A Slender Thread: Crisis, Healing, and Nature,* pp. 255-256.
American Biology Teacher, May, 1992, Rita Hoots, *The Moon by Whale Light, and Other Adventures among Bats, Penguins, Crocodilians, and Whales,* pp. 314-315.
Appraisal: Science Books for Young People, fall, 1998, review of *Bats: Shadows in the Night,* p. 5.
Book, May, 1999, review of *Deep Play,* p. 82; November-December, 2002, Stephen Whited, review of *Origami Bridges: Poems of Psychoanalysis and Fire,* p. 89.
Booklist, October 1, 1997, Sally Estes, review of *Bats,* p. 320; March 15, 1998, Donna Seaman, review of *I Praise My Destroyer,* p. 1197; March 1, 1999, Donna Seaman, review of *Deep Play,* p. 1099;

September 1, 2001, Donna Seaman, review of *Cultivating Delight: A Natural History of My Garden,* p. 26; September 1, 2002, Donna Seaman, review of *Origami Bridges,* p. 48; February 15, 2003, Gillian Engberg, review of *Animal Sense,* p. 1068; April 1, 2003, review of *Animal Sense,* p. 1407; May 1, 2004, Donna Seaman, review of *An Alchemy of Mind: The Marvel and Mystery of the Brain,* p. 1533; January 1, 2005, review of *An Alchemy of Mind,* p. 768.

BookPage, October, 2001, review of *Cultivating Delight,* p. 4; April, 2003, review of *Animal Sense,* p. 28.

Bookworld, July, 18, 1999, review of *Deep Play,* p. 7; October 7, 2001, review of *Cultivating Delight,* p. 13; April 27, 2003, review of *Animal Sense,* p. 12; June 13, 2004, Carl Zimmer, review of *An Alchemy of Mind,* p. 13.

Bulletin of the Center for Children's Books, June, 1995, Roger Sutton, review of *Monk Seal Hideaway,* p. 337; September, 1997, review of *Bats,* p. 4.

Catholic Library World, February 23, 1998, review of *I Praise My Destroyer,* p. 70.

Choice, October, 1997, review of *A Slender Thread,* p. 327.

Christian Science Monitor, October 24, 2001, review of *Cultivating Delight,* p. 19.

Discover, May, 2002, review of *Cultivating Delight,* p. 76; March, 2003, review of *Animal Sense,* p. 73.

Entertainment Weekly, January 17, 1997, Vanessa V. Friedman, review of *A Slender Thread,* p. 58; June 11, 2004, Tina Jordan, review of *An Alchemy of Mind,* p. 128.

Globe & Mail (Toronto, Ontario, Canada), June 12, 1999, review of *Deep Play,* p. D11; December 1, 2001, review of *Cultivating Delight,* p. 1.

Good Housekeeping, December, 1999, Kathleen Powers, "Lovers: Great Romances of Our Time through the Eyes of Legendary Writers," p. BIH8.

Horn Book Magazine, January, 2003, review of *Animal Sense,* p. 88.

Kirkus Reviews, April 1, 1998, review of *I Praise My Destroyer,* p. 441; April 1, 1999, review of *Deep Play,* p. 497; August 1, 2001, review of *Cultivating Delight,* p. 1077; December 15, 2002, review of *Animal Sense,* p. 1844; February 15, 2004, review of *An Alchemy of Mind,* p. 161.

Library Bookwatch, November, 2004, review of *An Alchemy of Mind.*

Library Journal, January, 1997, Antoinette Brinkman, review of *A Slender Thread,* p. 125; February 1,

1998, Richard K. Burns, review of *The Book of Love,* p. 84; March 15, 1998, Ann Van Buren review of *I Praise My Destroyer,* p. 67; June 1, 1998, review of *A Slender Thread,* p. 75; September 1, 2001, Daniel Starr, review of *Cultivating Delight,* p. 215; October 15, 2002, Barbara Hoffert, review of *Origami Bridges,* p. 77; April 15, 2003, Barbara Hoffert, review of *Origami Bridges,* p. 90; March 15, 2004, Laurie Bartolini, review of *An Alchemy of Mind,* p. 103.

Library Media Connection, October, 2003, Judith Beavers, review of *Animal Sense,* p. 63.

Los Angeles Times, July 8, 1994, Chris Goodrich, review of *A Natural History of Love,* p. E8; October 30, 2001, Michael Harris; review of *Cultivating Delight,* p. E3.

Michigan Quarterly Review, winter, 2000, Carolyn Kizer, "Four Smart Poets," pp. 167-172; winter, 2004, "The Personal Lyric and the Physical World," review of *Origami Bridges,* pp. 117-132.

New Leader, September, 2002, review of *Origami Bridges,* p. 33.

New Statesman and Society, May 21, 1993, Fraser Harrison, review of *The Moon by Whale Light, and Other Adventures among Bats, Penguins, Crocodilians, and Whales,* p. 35.

Newsweek, February 10, 1997, Jeff Giles, review of *A Slender Thread,* p. 66.

New Yorker, March 24, 1997, review of *A Slender Thread,* p. 83.

New York Times Book Review, November 3, 1991, David Kirby, review of *Jaguar of Sweet Laughter: New and Selected Poems,* p. 14; December 29, 1991, Michiko Kakutani, review of *The Moon by Whale Light, and Other Adventures among Bats, Penguins, Crocodilians, and Whales,* p. 7; February 16, 1997, review of *The Rarest of the Rare: Vanishing Animals, Timeless Worlds,* p. 32; March 2, 1997, Kate Jennings, "Calling out for Help," p. 11; December 7, 1997, review of *A Slender Thread,* p. 76; April 19, 1998, review of *A Slender Thread,* p. 40; June 20, 1999, Winifred Gallagher, "May the Force Be with You," p. 10; October 21, 2001, Miranda Seymour, "A Poet's Green Plot," review of *Cultivating Delight,* p. 17; October 28, 2001, review of *Cultivating Delight,* p. 30; November 4, 2001, review of *Cultivating Delight,* p. 34; December 2, 2001, review of *Cultivating Delight,* p. 68; October 13, 2002, Scott Veale, review of *Cultivating Delight,* p. 32; December 8, 2002, review of *Cultivating Delight,* p. 32; June 1, 2003, review of *Animal Sense,* p. 24; August 29, 2004, Marina Warner, "Circuits," p. 15.

North American Review, November-December, 2003, Vincent F. Gotera, review of *Animal Sense,* p. 58.

Parnassus, fall, 1995, Mark Doty, "Horsehair Sofas of the Antarctic: Diane Ackerman's Natural Histories."

People, March 10, 1997, Thomas Curwin, review of *A Slender Thread,* p. 31; October 29, 2001, review of *Cultivating Delight,* p. 56; July 12, 2004, Moira Bailey, review of *An Alchemy of Mind,* p. 46.

Poetry, December, 1998, John Taylor, review of *I Praise My Destroyer,* p. 182; August, 2003, Christina Pugh, review of *Origami Bridges,* p. 291.

Psychology Today, May-June, 2004, review of *An Alchemy of Mind,* p. 82.

Publishers Weekly, December 15, 1997, review of *The Book of Love,* p. 51; March 1, 1999, review of *Deep Play,* p. 47; July 23, 2001, review of *Cultivating Delight,* p. 58; September 23, 2002, review of *Origami Bridges,* p. 68; December 16, 2002, review of *Animal Sense,* p. 67; May 31, 2004, review of *An Alchemy of Mind,* p. 68.

Reference and Research Book News, November, 2004, review of *Within the Stone,* p. 249.

Roundup Magazine, April, 2003, review of *Twilight of the Tenderfoot,* p. 23.

School Library Journal, October, 1997, Patricia Manning, review of *Bats,* p. 141; February, 2003, Lauralyn Persson, review of *Animal Sense,* p. 126.

Science Books and Films, January, 1998, review of *Bats,* p. 20; May-June, 2004, Nancy A. Ridenour, review of *An Alchemy of Mind,* p. 117; May-June, 2005, review of *An Alchemy of Mind,* p. 95.

Science News, March 16, 2002, review of *Cultivating Delight,* p. 175.

Smithsonian, October, 2001, Kathryn Brown, review of *Cultivating Delight,* p. 138.

Southern Review, October, 1992, Franklin Burroughs, review of *The Moon by Whale Light, and Other Adventures among Bats, Penguins, Crocodilians, and Whales,* p. 928.

Tribune Books, December 1, 2002, review of *Cultivating Delight,* p. 6.

Underwater Naturalist, 2002, review of *The Moon by Whale Light and Other Adventures among Bats, Penguins, Crocodilians, and Whales,* p. 47.

Washington Post Book World, Barbara Raskin, review of *A Natural History of Love,* June 19, 1994, p. 2; October 7, 2001, "As Someone Who Has Yet to Be . . .," p. T13.

Women's Review of Books, December, 2004, Peg Aloi, review of *An Alchemy of Mind,* pp. 11-12.

Writer's Digest, September, 1997, Barbara Adams, "Diane Ackerman: Tight Focus in Small Spaces," author interview, p. 29.

ONLINE

Diane Ackerman Home Page, http://www.diane ackerman.com (October 17, 2005).

HarperCollins Web site, http://www.harpercollins.com/ (October 17, 2005).*

* * *

ALAMEDDINE, Rabih 1959-

PERSONAL: Born 1959, in Jordan (some sources say Beirut, Lebanon).

ADDRESSES: Home—San Francisco, CA; Beirut, Lebanon. *Agent*—c/o Author Mail, W.W. Norton & Co., Inc., 500 5th Ave., New York, NY 10110.

CAREER: Began career as engineer; writer and painter, 1998—; has exhibited his works in galleries in the United States, Europe, and the Middle East.

WRITINGS:

Koolaids: The Art of War (novel), Picador (New York, NY), 1998.

The Perv: Stories, edited by Michael Denneny, Picador USA (New York, NY), 1999.

I, the Divine: A Novel in First Chapters (novel), W.W. Norton & Co. (New York, NY), 2001.

Also contributor of stories to *Zoetrope: All-Story.*

SIDELIGHTS: Already a respected painter, Rabih Alameddine began writing in the late 1990s, often weaving his Middle Eastern background into his stories. His first novel, *Koolaids: The Art of War,* interweaves the long-running war in Lebanon with the Acquired Immune Deficiency Syndrome (AIDS) crisis in the United States through the use of four characters. Samia is a mother in Beirut whose diary entries bring the terror of the random incidents of war home to

Alameddine's readers. Mohammed, like the novelist himself, is a painter working in the United States—his works of art are celebrated in his adopted country as wonderful abstractions, while his fellow Lebanese immigrants "recognize them as visual representations of their home country's horrors," according to a *Publishers Weekly* critic. Samir is a gay man whose sexuality has forced him to leave Lebanon for the United States; and Mark is a gay American who is HIV-positive and has sat through many a bedside vigil for friends dying of the same disease. Throughout his novel, Alameddine intersperses his fictional characters' viewpoints with excerpts from actual news stories and quotations from famous people.

Koolaids met with a positive response from many critics. Though Mark Lindquist, reviewing the novel in the *New York Times Book Review,* felt that "despite some interesting ideas and memorable imagery, [Alameddine's] book demonstrates little feel for narrative," Roger W. Durbin hailed *Koolaids* in the *Library Journal* as "fascinating reading . . . immediate, pitched, and frightening." A contributor to *Publishers Weekly* summed up the novel as "a graphic portrait of two cultures torn from the inside."

Alameddine followed *Koolaids* with the collection *The Perv: Stories.* Most of the tales here feature characters who lived in Lebanon during that country's civil war. The stories share a commonality: many of the characters have been deeply affected by the conflict and cannot be at peace, whether they still live there or have moved abroad. A number of them have gay men as main characters, exploring how their homosexuality has left them isolated from their culture. A reviewer in *Publishers Weekly* wrote of *The Perv:* "These stinging narratives vibrate with an electrical tension that comes partly from Alameddine's penchant for the outrageous, partly from his unflinching view of a society in chaos."

Alameddine's second novel also explores a cultural divide similar to the author's experiences. *I, the Divine: A Novel in First Chapters* is the main character's attempt to write a memoir. However, each time Sarah Nour El-din starts, she can only make it through the first chapter. The novel includes her nearly sixty tries at the first chapter, many quite incomplete. *Guardian* reviewer Maya Jaggi noted: "While it lacks the compelling immediacy of *Koolaids,* it confirms Alameddine as a captivating storyteller who can move and amuse even in fragments."

Over the course of *I, the Divine,* it is revealed that Sarah was born of a Lebanese father and American mother in Beirut. After her parents' marriage ended, she and her sisters were raised in Lebanon by her father and stepmother. She is the victim of a rape, becomes pregnant as a result and has an abortion. As an adult, Sarah moves to the United States to elope with her first husband, goes to college, and loses custody of their son to him when he returns to Lebanon. Returning occasionally to Lebanon herself to deal with family situations, Sarah chooses to live primarily in the United States. There, her relationships with men are difficult at best. For example, the mother she is trying to get to know again kills herself. Yet Sarah still finds her own voice, becoming a successful painter. Although a *Publishers Weekly* critic worried that the novel's narrative style borders on being just as confusing as Sarah's distressed state of mind, the reviewer added that "Sarah is a compelling, believable character who struggles to establish an identity as she navigates between cultures."

BIOGRAPHICAL AND CRITICAL SOURCES:

PERIODICALS

Guardian (London, England), September 21, 2002, Maya Jaggi, "The Discomfort of Families: Maya Jaggi on an Accomplished Tale of Traumatic Lives Spanning Beirut and America," review of *I, the Divine: A Novel in First Chapters,* p. 29.
Library Journal, May 1, 1998, Roger W. Durbin, review of *Koolaids: The Art of War,* p. 135.
New York Times Book Review, July 26, 1998, Mark Lindquist, review of *Koolaids,* p. 19.
Publishers Weekly, March 30, 1998, review of *Koolaids,* p. 69; May 17, 1999, review of *The Perv: Stories,* p. 54; October 29, 2001, review of *I, the Divine,* p. 37.

ONLINE

Mississippi Review, http://www.mississippireview.com/ (October 4, 2005), Kieron Devlin, interview with Rabih Alameddine.

*   *   *

ANDERSON, Fred 1949-

PERSONAL: Born April 11, 1949, in Omaha, NE; son of Wayne W. and Melva D. (Torrens) Anderson; married Virginia Ann DeJohn (a professor of history), August 16, 1980. *Education:* Colorado State University, B.A. (with highest honors), 1971; Harvard University, A.M., 1973, Ph.D., 1981. *Religion:* Roman Catholic.

ADDRESSES: Home—200 Agate Way, Broomfield, CO 80020. *Office*—Department of History, University of Colorado—Boulder, Boulder, CO 80309. *Agent*— Lisa Adams, Garamond Agency, 12 Horton St., Newburyport, MA 01950. *E-mail*—fred.anderson@ colorado.edu.

CAREER: Harvard University, Cambridge, MA, lecturer in history and literature, 1981-83; University of Colorado at Boulder, assistant professor, 1983-89, associate professor, 1989-2001, professor of history, 2001—. Co-director, National Endowment for the Humanities Summer Institute, "The Young Republic," 1986-89; War for Empire Consortium, Pittsburgh, PA, consultant, 2000—historical advisor, *The War That Made America* (film), 2000. Lecturer at numerous symposia and universities. *Military service:* U.S. Army, Signal Corps, 1973-75; U.S. Army Reserve, 1975-81, became captain.

MEMBER: American Historical Association, Organization of American Historians, Society of American Historians, Phi Beta Kappa.

AWARDS, HONORS: Jamestown Prize, Institute of Early American History and Culture, 1982, for *A People's Army;* citation of honor, Society of Colonial Wars, 1987, for *A People's Army;* National Book Critics Circle Award nomination, Colorado Book Award, Francis Parkman Prize, Mark Lynton History Prize, all 2001, all for *The Crucible of War.*

WRITINGS:

A People's Army: Massachusetts Soldiers and Society in the Seven Years' War, University of North Carolina Press (Chapel Hill, NC), 1984.
(Illustrator) Richard Balkwill, *Trafalgar,* New Discovery (New York, NY), 1993.
The Crucible of War: The Seven Years' War and the Fate of Empire in British North America, 1754-1766 (contains illustrations from the William L. Clements Library), Alfred A. Knopf (New York, NY), 2000.

(Editor) George Washington, *George Washington Remembers: Reflections on the French and Indian War,* Rowman & Littlefield Publishers (Lanham, MD), 2004.
(With Andrew Cayton) *The Dominion of War: Empire and Liberty in North America, 1500-2000,* Viking Press (New York, NY), 2005.
The War that Made America: A Short History of the French and Indian War, Viking Press (New York, NY), 2005.

Section editor and contributor, *The Oxford Companion to American Military History,* Oxford University Press (New York, NY), 1999. Contributor to *William and Mary Quarterly, Massachusetts Historical Review,* and *Reviews in American History.* Contributor of book reviews to numerous periodicals.

SIDELIGHTS: Fred Anderson served in the U.S. Army Signal Corps from 1973 to 1975, remaining in the Army Reserve until 1981. Anderson once told *CA:* "My own experience of military service, humdrum and ordinary in every respect, alerted me to what became the subject of my first book [*A People's Army: Massachusetts Soldiers and Society in the Seven Years' War*], the effects of army life on the participants. My interests have since widened to include concern with the effects of war on society, and particularly with the influence of wars in the formation of generations as self-conscious entities."

Anderson is best known for his award-winning history, *The Crucible of War: The Seven Years' War and the Fate of Empire in British North America, 1754-1766,* published in 2000. The work combines scholarly detail with a writing style easily accessible by the general reader, and it portrays—often through vignettes of famous generals and notable Native American warriors—the entirety of the Seven Years' War as it was fought on North American soil. Better known as the French and Indian War, the Seven Years' War was fought on a much more global scale, with England and France vying for supremacy in regions as varied as Europe, the Far East, and Africa. In some respects, Anderson sees the conflict as the first "world war," and of far greater consequence to American history than most students believe.

The Crucible of War was nominated for the National Book Critics Circle Award, and it won the Colorado Book Award, the Francis Parkman Prize, and the Mark

Lynton History Prize. Generally, the book was praised by critics not only for its thorough coverage of the conflict as conducted in North America, but also for its accessible style and original conclusions. "Fred Anderson offers a compelling and well-written narrative, full of rich characterizations and fascinating detail, driven by a sustained and sophisticated analysis," wrote Michael A. Bellesiles in the *Journal of British Studies.* "This book will permanently place the Seven Years' War where it belongs, at the center of our understanding of American development in the eighteenth century." Colin Nicolson, in the *English Historical Review,* called the work "magnificent," adding that it "is a beautifully written and illustrated narrative, interspersed with concise analyses." In his *New Republic* essay on the book, Alan Taylor suggested: "Readers who plunge into the text will discover [Anderson's] flair for narrating dramatic events and describing vivid characters. And he has a great, sprawling tale to tell."

Because the Seven Years' War affected the boundaries of both the United States and Canada, Anderson's *The Crucible of War* also found readers in Canada and the United Kingdom. The *Canadian Journal of History* devoted five reviews to the book in its December, 2000 issue and also allowed Anderson to respond to the reviewers' comments. In his introduction to the selection of reviews, Ian K. Steele noted, "All five reviewers here confirm what the popular press and book club adoptions suggest: Anderson has written a masterful narrative." In his review in the same periodical, John Shy stated: "The story is familiar . . . yet Anderson makes it crisp and original, in part with very good writing but also by bringing to each episode a rare grasp of both difficulties and context." Also in the *Canadian Journal of History,* Gregory Evans Dowd concluded: "Whatever one's tastes, Anderson's mastery of detail, narrative, and breadth of action invite both deep admiration and serious attention."

Anderson coauthored *The Dominion of War: Empire and Conflict in America, 1500-2000* with Andrew Cayton. This title examines how the United States evolved from a quarrelsome group of colonies into a global superpower, using war as the "engine of change," to quote *New Statesman* reviewer Michael Lind. The authors focus on several notable historical figures, including Samuel de Champlain, William Penn, George Washington, Andrew Jackson, Antonio de Lopez de Santa Anna, Ulysses S. Grant, Douglas

MacArthur, and Colin Powell. Through individual chapters on these men, Anderson and Cayton explore the importance of military action in the expansion of American global influence. Ruud Janssens in *History: Review of New Books* deemed the work "well researched and insightful," especially in its "excellent chapters on individual political and military leaders." A *Publishers Weekly* critic cited *The Dominion of War* as an "enterprising, readable work. . . . It's solid corrective history." *Booklist* contributor Jay Freeman found the work "an incisive, provocative account of the U.S. rise to global preeminence."

BIOGRAPHICAL AND CRITICAL SOURCES:

PERIODICALS

Atlantic Monthly, December, 2000, review of *Crucible of War: The Seven Years' War and the Fate of Empire in British North America, 1754-1766,* p. 122.

Booklist, January 1, 2000, Gilbert Taylor, review of *Crucible of War,* p. 865; November 15, 2004, Jay Freeman, review of *The Dominion of War: Empire and Liberty in North America, 1500-2000,* p. 547.

Canadian Journal of History, December, 2000, Ian K. Steele, "Narrative as Master: A Forum on Fred Anderson's *Crucible of War,* p. 473; December, 2000, John Shy, "Crucible of Revolution," p. 479; December, 2000, Gregory Evans Dowd, "North American Baroque," p. 483; December, 2000, Jonathan R. Dull, "The French and Indian War without the French," p. 491; December, 2000, P. J. Marshall, "Fred Anderson's Seven Years' War in Imperial Perspective," p. 495.

English Historical Review, June, 2001, Colin Nicolson, review of *Crucible of War,* p. 736.

Foreign Affairs, May-June, 2005, Walter Russell Mead, review of *The Dominion of War,* p. 138.

History: Review of New Books, spring, 2005, Ruud Janssens, review of *The Dominion of War,* p. 92.

Journal of American History, September, 1985, p. 390.

Journal of British Studies, October, 2001, Michael A. Bellesiles, review of *Crucible of War,* p. 585.

Journal of Southern History, May, 2002, Robert M.S. McDonald, review of *Crucible of War,* p. 436.

Kirkus Reviews, November 1, 2004, review of *The Dominion of War,* p. 1033.

Library Journal, February 1, 2000, Thomas J. Schaeper, review of *Crucible of War,* p. 100.

New Republic, August 14, 2000, Alan Taylor, "The Forgotten War," p. 40.

New Statesman, July 25, 2005, Michael Lind, review of *The Dominion of War,* p. 52.

Parameters, winter, 2001, Robert Major Bateman, review of *Crucible of War,* p. 167.

Publishers Weekly, December 20, 1999, review of *Crucible of War,* p. 64; November 22, 2004, review of *The Dominion of War,* p. 52.

Washington Monthly, September, 2000, Thomas E. Ricks, review of *Crucible of War,* p. 57.*

*   *   *

APTER, T.E.
See APTER, Terri

*   *   *

APTER, Terri 1949-
(T.E. Apter, Terri E. Apter)

PERSONAL: Born February 28, 1949, in Chicago, IL; daughter of Nathaniel (a psychoanalyst) and Julia (an ophthalmologist; maiden name, Tutleman) Apter; married David Newbery (an economist), July 5, 1975; children: Miranda, Julia. *Education:* University of Edinburgh, M.A., 1969; Cambridge University, Ph.D., 1987.

ADDRESSES: Home—9 Huntingdon Rd., Cambridge CB3 0HH, England. *Agent*—Michael Thomas, A.M. Heath & Co. Ltd., 79 St. Martin's Lane, London WC1N 4DD, England. *E-mail*—tea20@cam.ac.uk.

CAREER: Cambridge University, Cambridge, England, English and American literature teacher; professor of social psychology; writer.

AWARDS, HONORS: Notable book of the year selection, *New York Times,* 1990, for *Altered Loves: Mothers and Daughters during Adolescence;* Delta Kappa Gamma International Educators' Award, 1998.

WRITINGS:

Why Women Don't Have Wives: Professional Success and Motherhood, Schocken (New York, NY), 1985.

Loose Relations: Your In-Laws and You, Macmillan (Hampshire, England), 1986.

Altered Loves: Mothers and Daughters during Adolescence, St. Martin's Press (New York, NY), 1990.

Working Women Don't Have Wives: Professional Success in the 1990s, St. Martin's Press (New York, NY), 1993.

Secret Paths: Women in the New Midlife, Norton (New York, NY), 1995.

The Confident Child: Raising a Child to Try, Learn, and Care, Norton (New York, NY), 1997.

(With Ruthellen Josselson) *Best Friends: The Pleasures and Perils of Girls' and Women's Friendships,* Crown (New York, NY), 1998.

The Myth of Maturity: What Teenagers Need from Parents to Become Adults, Norton (New York, NY), 2001.

You Don't Really Know Me: Why Mothers & Daughters Fight and How Both Can Win, Norton (New York, NY), 2004.

AS T.E. APTER

Silken Lines and Silver Hooks, Heinemann (London, England), 1976.

Adonis' Garden, Heinemann (London, England), 1977.

Thomas Mann: The Devil's Disciple, New York University Press (New York, NY), 1978.

Virginia Woolf: A Study of Her Novels, New York University Press (New York, NY), 1979.

Fantasy Literature: An Approach to Reality, Indiana University Press (Bloomington, IN), 1982.

Also contributor to periodicals, including *Mother* and *Cosmopolitan.*

SIDELIGHTS: In her 1990 book, *Altered Loves: Mothers and Daughters during Adolescence,* Terri Apter questions the validity of the view that mothers and teenaged daughters have volatile relationships. Previous familial theories suggested the inevitability of frequent conflicts between an overbearing, critical, jealous mother and a hostile, surly, rebellious adolescent trying to break ties with her parent. However, through interviews with sixty-five pairs of mothers and daughters, Apter unearthed a more positive hypothesis. Although the author admits this relationship involves unavoidable arguments, she discovered both parties downplayed the seriousness of such squabbles. Apter found that most daughters she spoke to complimented their mothers for their continual emotional support, while mothers mentioned that, in contrast to a popular assumption, their daughters' adolescent years were not marked by excessive turmoil and attempts at separation. Apter argues that teenagers distance themselves to work out their own individuality, not to back away from the affection and guidance of their parents. Carol Tavris, reviewing *Altered Loves* in the *New York Times Book Review,* remarked that Apter's "analysis of mothers and daughters during adolescence is simply wonderful—a fresh vision that blows away old stereotypes. . . . It is a model of lucid research and writing."

Apter has also challenged the notion that women lose more than they gain as they age in *Secret Paths: Women in the New Midlife.* Instead of emotionally declining as they approach menopause, Apter argues that women in their forties are stepping over the threshold of a new personal awakening, and that they come out on the other side with a self-awareness that causes them to view themselves not as who they are, but as who they have become. Remarking on the lack of constructive literature on "women and aging," Deborah Anna Luepnitz, contributor to *Women's Review of Books,* stated that "Terry Apter's nimble prose sets her book apart from the rest." While Luepnitz faulted the author for failing to delve further into the lives of unmarried women and lesbians ("The word 'lesbian' does not appear anywhere in this book."), the reviewer felt that "Apter succeeds admirably in avoiding the twin misconceptions of midlife as partial death or no big deal," and commented that "*Secret Paths* is a valuable book." In further praise for the book, *Booklist* contributor Patricia Monaghan wrote: "Not only carefully theorized, Apter's work is also written in a vigorous and provocative manner that makes it a pleasure to read."

For her *Best Friends: The Pleasures and Perils of Girls' and Women's Friendships,* Apter collaborated with writer and psychotherapist Ruthellen Josselson to study female friendships and how they effect the sense of self in girls and young women as they grow into adults. *Best Friends* affirms that female friendships are integral to the development of confidence and individuality in young women, and that while such unions often result in painful confrontations and betrayals, these habitual interactions are vital if young women are to achieve emotional stability. One *Publishers*

Weekly contributor regarded the book as an "interesting and accessible analysis." *Library Journal* contributor Elizabeth Goeters also found value in the book, defining it as a "very well documented and interesting study."

In her next assessment of relationships and their social correlations, *The Myth of Maturity: What Teenagers Need from Parents to Become Adults,* Apter shifts her focus to parents and their twenty-something children. Apter theorizes that young adults often suffer from their parents' eagerness to cut them loose during college and after graduation. While she recognizes that parents do this not to be malicious, but to allow their children some "real world" experience, Apter feels that this is a mistake, often leading to depression and anxiety—sometimes severe—in young adults who feel they have been abandoned by their parents.

The examination of the mother-daughter relationship resurfaces in *You Don't Really Know Me: Why Mothers & Daughters Fight and How Both Can Win.* In this book, Apter scrutinizes relationships between adolescent girls and their mothers to determine the root of the communication issues and tensions that are common to mother-daughter relationships, as well as to formulate a solution to these problems. She told an interviewer for *People:* "There is a strong theory of adolescence that girls want a kind of psychological divorce from their parents—that they want to cut ties." After interviewing several girls and their mothers, the author concludes that this is not the case. Instead, Apter finds that daughters are constantly challenging their mothers, and that mothers who refrain from yelling at, judging, or forcing upset daughters into unsolicited conversations will have more effective communications with their daughters. One *Publishers Weekly* reviewer wrote that Apter's advice in *You Don't Really Know Me* is "sound, if not revolutionary."

Apter told *CA:* "As the daughter of a psychoanalyst, I grew up with a fascination for the study of mind, but also with a keen awareness of how traditional theory can limit and frustrate a child's self-understanding. In my writing, I try to underline the enormous variety of human responses, and hence I often challenge the narrowness of established views. Human development at its best is flexible, and writers discussing development should exhibit a complementary flexibility."

BIOGRAPHICAL AND CRITICAL SOURCES:

PERIODICALS

Affilia: Journal of Women and Social Work, fall, 1992, Mary Lou Balassone, review of *Altered Loves: Mothers and Daughters during Adolescence,* p. 115.

Booklist, June 1, 1995, Patricia Monaghan, review of *Secret Paths: Women in the New Midlife,* p. 1698; May 15, 2001, Vanessa Bush, review of *The Myth of Maturity,* p. 1712.

Books & Bookman, March, 1979, review of *Thomas Mann: The Devil's Disciple,* p. 61.

Books & Culture, May, 2002, review of *The Myth of Maturity: What Teenagers Need from Parents to Become Adults,* p. 27.

Book World, August 13, 1995, review of *Fantasy Literature: An Approach to Reality,* p. 6; June 3, 2001, review of *The Myth of Maturity,* p. 4.

British Book News, October, 1985, review of *Why Women Don't Have Wives: Professional Success and Motherhood,* p. 593.

Choice, September, 1979, review of *Thomas Mann,* p. 842; February, 1980, review of *Virginia Woolf: A Study of Her Novels,* p. 1578; December, 1982, review of *Fantasy Literature,* p. 575; December, 1985, review of *Why Women Don't Have Wives,* p. 633; May, 1994, M. M. Ferree, review of *Working Women Don't Have Wives: Professional Success in the 1990s,* p. 1508; January, 1996, C. Adamsky, review of *Secret Paths,* p. 877.

Clinical Social Worker Journal, winter, 1997, Sharon McQuaide, review of *Secret Paths,* p. 471.

Entertainment Weekly, October 16, 1998, Alexandra Jacobs, review of *Best Friends: The Pleasures and Perils of Girl's and Women' Friendships,* p. 82.

Kirkus Reviews, October 15, 1985, review of *Why Women Don't Have Wives,* p. 1109; November 15, 1993, review of *Working Women Don't Have Wives,* p. 1428; April 15, 1995, review of *Secret Paths,* p. 519; June 15, 1998, review of *Best Friends,* p. 859.

Kliatt, April, 1992, review of *Altered Loves,* p. 31.

Library Journal, November 15, 1985, Suzanne Druehl, review of *Why Women Don't Have Wives,* p. 106; February 1, 1994, Patty Miller, review of *Working Women Don't Have Wives,* p. 90; June 1, 1995, Kathleen L. Atwood, review of *Secret Paths,* p. 144; October 15, 1998, Elizabeth Goeters,

review of *Best Friends,* p. 85; June 15, 2001, Linda Beck, review of *The Myth of Maturity,* p. 96; October 1, 2001, review of *The Myth of Maturity,* p. 70; April 15, 2004, Mirela Roncevic, "The Mother Knot," review of *You Don't Really Know Me: Why Mothers & Daughters Fight and How Both Can Win,* p. 110.

Listener, February 17, 1977, review of *Adonis' Garden,* p. 221.

Modern Fiction Studies, summer, 1980, review of *Virginia Woolf,* p. 282; summer, 1981, review of *Thomas Mann,* p. 406; summer, 1983, review of *Fantasy Literature,* p. 350.

New Statesman, February 4, 1977, Paddy Beesley, review of *Adonis' Garden,* p. 163.

New York Times Book Review, July 1, 1990, Carol Tavris, review of *Altered Loves,* p. 64; January 30, 1994, Alice Kessler-Harris, review of *Working Women Don't Have Wives,* p. 63; March 30, 1997, review of *Fantasy Literature,* p. 24.

Observer (London, England), January 11, 1976, review of *Silken Lines and Silver Hooks,* p. 21; February 6, 1977, review of *Adonis' Garden,* p. 31.

Publishers Weekly, May 15, 1995, review of *Secret Paths,* p. 66; December 30, 1996, review of *Fantasy Literature,* p. 64; March 24, 1997, review of *The Confident Child: Raising a Child to Try, Learn, and Care,* p. 78; June 15, 1998, *Best Friends,* p. 47; May 21, 2001, review of *The Myth of Maturity,* p. 104; February 23, 2004, review of *You Don't Really Know Me,* p. 61.

Reference & Research Book News, November, 2001, review of *The Myth of Maturity,* p. 131.

Review of English Studies, May, 1981, review of *Virginia Woolf,* p. 237.

Science Fiction & Fantasy Book Review, July, 1983, review of *Fantasy Literature,* p. 19.

Times Literary Supplement, January 16, 1976, review of *Silken Lines and Silver Hooks,* p. 51; March 18, 1977, review of *Adonis' Garden,* p. 325; October 5, 2001, review of *The Myth of Maturity,* p. 35; June 4, 2004, Katherine Duncan-Jones, "Forever Embedded," review of *You Don't Really Know Me,* p. 36.

Tribune Books, March 3, 1997, review of *Fantasy Literature,* p. 8; May 26, 2002, review of *The Myth of Maturity,* p. 7.

Women's Review of Books, February, 1996, review of *Secret Paths,* p. 15.

World Literature Today, spring, 1980, review of *Thomas Mann,* p. 279; summer, 1983, review of *Fantasy Literature,* p. 517.

ONLINE

Terri Apter Home Page, http://www.motherinlaw stories.com (October 21, 2005).*

*   *   *

APTER, Terri E.
See APTER, Terri

*   *   *

ARJOUNI, Jakob 1964-

PERSONAL: Born October 8, 1964, in Frankfurt am Main, Hesse, Germany. *Ethnicity:* "Turkish."

ADDRESSES: Home—6 Avenue des corbieres, 11120 Ginestas, France. *Agent*—c/o Author Mail, Diogenes Verlag, Sprecherstrasse 8, CH-8032 Zürich, Switzerland. *E-mail*—jakob.arjouni@noexit.co.uk.

CAREER: Author of novels, stage plays, radio plays, and short stories.

AWARDS, HONORS: German Thriller Prize, 1992, for *Ein Mann, ein mord.*

WRITINGS:

"KEMAL KAYANKAYA" MYSTERY NOVELS

Happy Birthday, Türke!, Diogenes Verlag (Zürich, Switzerland), 1987, translation by Anselm Hollo published as *Happy Birthday, Turk!,* Fromm International (New York, NY), 1993.
Mehr Bier (title means "More Beer"), Diogenes Verlag (Zürich, Switzerland), 1987, translation by Anselm Hollo published as *And Still Drink More!,* Fromm International (New York, NY), 1994, published in England as *More Beer,* No Exit (London, England), 2000.
Ein Mann, ein mord, Diogenes Verlag (Zürich, Switzerland), 1991, translation by Anselm Hollo published as *One Death to Die,* Fromm Interna-

tional (New York, NY), 1997, published in England as *One Man, One Murder,* No Exit (London, England), 1997.
Kismet (title means "Fate"), Diogenes Verlag (Zürich, Switzerland), 2001.

OTHER

Edelmanns Tochter: Theaterstück (play; title means "Edelmann's Daughter"), Diogenes Verlag (Zürich, Switzerland), 1996.
Magic Hoffmann (novel), Diogenes Verlag (Zürich, Switzerland), 1996.
Ein Freund: Geschichten (short stories; title means "A Friend"), Diogenes Verlag (Zürich, Switzerland), 1998.
Nazim schiebt ab (play; title means "Nazim Goes Away"), Diogenes Verlag (Zürich, Switzerland), 1998.
Die Garaden (play; title means "The Garages"), Diogenes Verlag (Zürich, Switzerland), 1998.
Idioten: Fünf Märchen, Diogenes Verlag (Zürich, Switzerland), 2003, translation by Anthea Bell published as *Idiots: Five Fairy Tales and Other Stories,* Other Press (New York, NY), 2005.

Also author of *Hausaufgaben* (title means "Homework").

SIDELIGHTS: Jakob Arjouni is a German-born author of Turkish descent who has realized success as a mystery novelist and short story writer. Arjouni's detective novels feature hardened private investigator Kemal Kayankaya, a disillusioned Turk living in Germany and suffering that nation's subtle prejudices. Arjouni introduced Kayankaya in *Happy Birthday, Türke!* (published in translation as *Happy Birthday, Turk!*), in which the character probes the mysterious death of a Turkish immigrant who had apparently been stabbed while he visited the seamy prostitution section of Frankfurt. Upon being hired by the victim's widow, Kayankaya soon finds himself the target of vicious thugs. But he perseveres in his investigation and eventually uncovers the existence of a drug ring that profits from the plight of Frankfurt's Turkish inhabitants. A contributor reviewing *Happy Birthday, Turk!* in *Publishers Weekly* reported that "every genre cliché about the hard-drinking, smart-mouthed gumshoe is shamelessly overemployed." in the novel. However, a *Kirkus Reviews* critic called *Happy*

Birthday, Turk! "a blistering debut" and described Kayankaya as "a perfect hardboiled detective." Another reviewer, Pat Dowell, wrote in the *Washington Post Book World* of Arjouni's "poetic hardboiled patter."

Subsequent Kayankaya novels cover similar ground, with emphasis on the bias shown by Germans to immigrants from many nations. *Mehr Bier* (published in translation in the United States as *And Still Drink More!* and in England as *More Beer*) concerns eco-terrorism and conspiracy centered upon a chemical plant. In the tale *Ein Mann, ein mord* (published in translation in the United States as *One Death to Die* and in England as *One Man, One Murder*), the private investigator undertakes a search for an artist's missing girlfriend. Kayankaya's quest leads him into Frankfurt's sordid underworld, where he learns that immigrant women—including, perhaps, his client's girlfriend, who is of Asian descent—are being kidnapped and forced into prostitution. Neil Spencer, writing in the London *Observer,* noted that the novel is "sparingly . . . written in Dashiell Hammett's style," and *Booklist* reviewer Bill Ott commented on Arjouni's "eye-opening view of the underside of German society." A *Publishers Weekly* critic described the Kayankaya novels as a "pungent series" and observed that in *One Death to Die* Arjouni shows "a light touch for pithy description." Likewise, Dick Adler wrote in Chicago *Tribune Books* of the novel's "twisty surprises." The reviewer also considered Anselm Hollo's translation "fine" work. Still another reviewer, Marilyn Stasio, maintained in the *New York Times Book Review* that *One Death to Die* constitutes an "acidly funny escapade" and Kayankaya a "cocky gumshoe."

Arjouni's collection of short stories, *Idioten: Fünf Märchen,* translated as *Idiots: Five Fairy Tales and Other Stories,* updates the fantastic and applies it to modern-day circumstances. In the first five stories, hapless egotists are allowed one wish by helpful—if not always capable—fairies. The other pieces likewise include magical realism as they confront modern nihilism and torpor. A *Publishers Weekly* contributor observed that Arjouni "weaves lively, ironic tales about desperate folk at the edges of contemporary German society." A *Kirkus Reviews* critic liked the "crafty, contemporary tales," observing that in them, Arjouni" shifts his creative talents and humor into overdrive."

BIOGRAPHICAL AND CRITICAL SOURCES:

PERIODICALS

Booklist, November 1, 1993, Jay Freeman, review of *Happy Birthday, Turk!,* p. 504; March 15, 1997, Bill Ott, review of *One Death to Die,* p. 1228.

Kirkus Reviews, August 15, 1993, review of *Happy Birthday, Turk!,* p. 1029; March 1, 2005, review of *Idiots: Five Fairy Tales and Other Stories,* p. 241.

New York Times Book Review, March 30, 1997, Marilyn Stasio, review of *One Death to Die,* p. 23.

Observer (London, England), April 20, 1997, Neil Spencer, "OK, Somerset Is Not an Obvious Setting for a Car Chase, but at Least We've Moved On from Dixon of Dock Green," p. 18.

Publishers Weekly, September 6, 1993, review of *Happy Birthday, Turk!,* p. 86; February 10, 1997, review of *One Death to Die,* p. 71; April 11, 2005, review of *Idiots,* p. 32.

Tribune Books (Chicago, IL), March 2, 1997, Dick Adler, "A World of Sleuths," p. 5.

Washington Post Book World, October 17, 1993, Pat Dowell, "Turkish Attitude," p. 8.

ONLINE

No Exit, http://www.noexit.co.uk/ (October 25, 2005).*

*   *   *

AVISE, John C. 1948-
(John Charles Avise)

PERSONAL: Born September 19, 1948, in Grand Rapids, MI; son of Reginald Dean and Edith Dorothy (Johnson) Avise; married Joan Marie Yanov, December 24, 1979; children: Jennifer Ann. *Education:* University of Michigan, B.S., 1970; University of Texas—Austin, M.A., 1971; University of California—Davis, Ph.D., 1975. *Hobbies and other interests:* Nature study, sports.

ADDRESSES: Office—Department of Genetics, University of Georgia, Life Sciences Building, Athens, GA 30602. *E-mail*—javise@uci.edu.

CAREER: University of Georgia, Athens, assistant professor of zoology, 1975-79, associate professor, 1979-84, professor of genetics, beginning 1984, currently distinguished research professor emeritus.

MEMBER: American Association for the Advancement of Science (fellow), National Academy of Science (fellow), American Ornithologists' Union (fellow), Society for the Study of Evolution (president, 1994), American Academy of Arts and Sciences (fellow), American Genetic Association (president, 2000), Society of Molecular Biology and Evolution (president, 2004).

AWARDS, HONORS: Brewster Award, American Ornithological Union, 1997; Pew Fellowship in Marine Conservation, Pew Foundation, 1998; Lamar Dodd Award, University of Georgia.

WRITINGS:

NONFICTION

Molecular Markers, Natural History and Evolution, Chapman & Hall (New York, NY), 1994, second edition, Sinaur (Sunderland, MA), 2004.
(Editor, with J.L. Hamrick) *Conservation Genetics: Case Histories from Nature,* Chapman & Hall (New York, NY), 1996.
The Genetic Gods: Evolution and Belief in Human Affairs, Harvard University Press (Cambridge, MA), 1998.
Phylogeography: The History and Formation of Species, Harvard University Press (Cambridge, MA), 2000.
Captivating Life: A Naturalist in the Age of Genetics (memoir), Smithsonian Institution Press (Washington, DC), 2001.
Genetics in the Wild, Smithsonian Institution Press (Washington, DC), 2002.
The Hope, Hype, & Reality of Genetic Engineering, Oxford University Press (New York, NY), 2004.

Contributor of articles to scientific journals. Has served as member of editorial board, *Systematic Zoology, Paleobiology, Genetica, Genetics, Molecular Biology and Evolution, Journal of Molecular Evolution, Annual Review of Ecology and Systematics, Oxford Surveys in Evolutionary Biology, Molecular Phylogenetics and Evolution, Proceedings of the National Academy of Sciences,* and *Molecular Ecology.*

SIDELIGHTS: Known as the father of phylogeography (the study of how geography plays a role in the distribution of genealogical lineages of animals, primarily through the study of mitochondrial deoxyribonucleic acid, or DNA), evolutionary geneticist John C. Avise has published a number of books on this subject as well as other topics in genetics, zoology, and natural history. He has written books for both scholars and general audiences.

Two books written by Avise that are intended for a general audience are *The Genetic Gods: Evolution and Belief in Human Affairs* and *Genetics in the Wild. The Genetic Gods* is Avise's overview of genetics, its history, the genetic proof for evolution, and the process of evolution in terms of genetics. "Avise does a superb job of discussing many of the ethical implications that have arisen from our growing knowledge of human genetics," commented a *Publishers Weekly* reviewer. For its intended audience, "the book is an excellent distillation of a broad and increasingly important field," according to David W. Hodo in the *Journal of the American Medical Association.*

Genetics in the Wild contains Avise's accessible explanations for the many previously unexplainable questions in nature and natural history. Divided into sections to individually address each question, the book tells related stories and draws on the author's scientific background to provide the answers. Some of the mysteries he discusses include the migration patterns of whales and the relationship of Neanderthals to humans.

Intended for an audience of scientists and graduate students are Avise's *Phylogeography: The History and Formation of Species* and *Molecular Markers, Natural History, and Evolution.* The former is an evolutionary biology textbook that provides concrete examples of phylogeography, such as where humans evolved in a geographic sense and how the African cichlid fish quickly evolved into many new species.

The updated and expanded second edition of Avise's *Molecular Markers, Natural History, and Evolution* was published in 2004. The first edition became a primary reference book for scientists and graduate students on molecular evolutionary biology. The second edition was expected to serve the same purpose. In a review published in the *Quarterly Review of Biology,* Axel Meyer found the new edition praiseworthy. Meyer wrote, "With admirable clarity and astonishing breadth and depth, Avise authoritatively reviews the seemingly exponentially increasing literature in fields ranging from molecular phylogenetics and phylogeography to conservation biology and population genetics."

In 2001 Avise published a book that crosses popular and academic lines. *Captivating Life: A Naturalist in the Age of Genetics* is his scientific memoir about his life and work, beginning from his childhood interest in natural history and going through his own evolution as a scientist and the methods he has used to come to his conclusions. In *Captivating Life,* Avise discusses both the development of his methods for studying molecular genetics and the application of his methodology, including his field work studying various species such as the nine-banded armadillo and horseshoe crab. He also includes his ideas about conservation and the evolution of his own theories. While some critics found the book difficult for a general audience, a reviewer in *Publishers Weekly* commented, "On occasion the author's ego obscures his sturdy prose, though these lapses are overcome by guileless confessions of personal and professional faults."

Avise once told *CA:* "My laboratory is interested in the study of the natural history, phylogeography, and evolution of natural populations through the use of molecular genetic markers. Laboratory methods include a variety of protein and DNA assays, with particular emphasis on restriction site and sequence analyses of mitochondrial DNA, alone or in conjunction with allozymes, microsatellites, and other nuclear gene markers. Topics studied range from micro-to macro-evolutionary, and research has been conducted on all major vertebrate groups and selected invertebrates. In most cases, the primary focus is on understanding the natural histories and evolution of organisms through application of molecules as genetic markers, but a secondary concern includes the elucidation of features of the protein and DNA molecules themselves. Effort in the laboratory has also been devoted to concepts and theories of population genetics and speciation. The theory and practice of evolutionary genetics are highly relevant to conservation biology, an area that provides an underlying theme to most of our research. I am also interested in evolutionary-genetic findings as applied to the human species, and that is the topic of my book *The Genetic Gods: Evolution and Belief in Human Affairs.*"

BIOGRAPHICAL AND CRITICAL SOURCES:

BOOKS

Avise, John C., *Captivating Life: A Naturalist in the Age of Genetics,* Smithsonian Institution Press (Washington, DC), 2001.

PERIODICALS

Journal of the American Medical Association, December 8, 1999, David W. Hodo, review of *The Genetic Gods: Evolution and Belief in Human Affairs,* p. 2179.

Library Journal, September 1, 1998, Eric D. Albright, review of *The Genetic Gods,* p. 208, September 1, 2001, Margaret Henderson, review of *Captivating Life,* p. 219.

Natural History, October, 1998, review of *The Genetic Gods,* p. 14.

Nature, August 4, 1994, John F. Y. Brookfield, review of *Molecular Markers, Natural History, and Evolution,* p. 338.

Publishers Weekly, July 13, 1998, review of *The Genetic Gods,* p. 70; July 23, 2001, review of *Captivating Life,* p. 62.

Quarterly Review of Biology, December, 2004, Axel Meyer, review of *Molecular Markers, Natural History, and Evolution,* p. 414.

Science, January 6, 1995, Allan Larson, review of *Molecular Markers, Natural History, and Evolution,* p. 115, January 29, 1999, review of *The Genetic Gods,* p. 645.

Times Literary Supplement, August 2, 2002, John Tyler Bonner, "Down to the Cells," review of *Captivating Life,* p. 7.

ONLINE

2think.org, http://www.2think.org/ (January 1, 2003), review of *Phylogeography: The History and Formation of Species.*

University of Georgia Genetics Web site, http://www.genetics.uga.edu/ (October 4, 2005), biography of John C. Avise.*

*   *   *

AVISE, John Charles
  See AVISE, John C.

B

BARBER, Antonia 1932-
[A pseudonym]
(Barbara Barber)

PERSONAL: Born Barbara Barber, December 10, 1932, in London, England; daughter of Derek (a box-office manager) and Julie (a landscape gardener; maiden name, Jeal) Wilson; married Kenneth Charles Barber (a structural engineering consultant), August 6, 1956 (died December, 1981); children: Jonathan Charles, Nicholas James, Gemma Thi-Phi-Yen. *Education:* University College, London, B.A. (with honors), 1955. *Hobbies and other interests:* Walking, reading, theatre, gardening.

ADDRESSES: Home—Horne's Place Oast, Appledore, Kent TN26 2BS, England. *Agent*—David Higham Associates, 5-8 Lower John St., Golden Square, London W1R, 4HA, England.

CAREER: Writer, beginning 1966.

MEMBER: British Society of Authors, Friends of the Earth, Amnesty International, Greenpeace.

AWARDS, HONORS: Carnegie Award runner-up, for *The Ghosts,* and shortlist, for *The Ring in the Rough Stuff;* Nestle Smarties Book Prize Children's Choice, Kate Greenaway Medal Commendation, and British Book Award for Illustrated Book of the Year, all for *The Mousehole Cat.*

WRITINGS:

The Affair of the Rockerbye Baby, J. Cape (London, England), 1966, Delacorte (New York, NY), 1970.

The Ghosts, Farrar, Straus (New York, NY), 1969, published as *The Amazing Mr. Blunden,* Penguin (Harmondsworth, England), 1972.

The Ring in the Rough Stuff, J. Cape (London, England), 1983.

The Enchanter's Daughter, illustrated by Errol le Cain, J. Cape (London, England), 1987.

Satchelmouse and the Dinosaurs, Walker Books (London, England), 1987.

Satchelmouse and the Doll's House, Walker Books (London, England), 1987.

The Mousehole Cat, illustrated by Nicola Bayley, Macmillan (New York, NY), 1990.

Gemma the Broody Hen, illustrated by Karin Littlewood, ABC (London, England), 1992, published as *Gemma and the Baby Chick,* Scholastic (New York, NY), 1993.

(Adaptor) *Tales from Grimm,* illustrated by Margaret Chamberlain, Frances Lincoln (London, England), 1992.

Catkin, illustrated by P.J. Lynch, Candlewick Press (Cambridge, MA), 1994.

The Monkey and the Panda, illustrated by Meilo So, Macmillan Books for Young Readers (New York, NY), 1995.

Shoes of Satin, Ribbons of Silk: Tales from the Ballet, illustrated by Diz Wallis, Kingfisher (New York, NY), 1995, published as *Tales from the Ballet,* 1999.

(Reteller) *Snow White and Rose Red,* MacDonald Young (London, England), 1997.

Apollo and Daphne: Masterpieces of Greek Mythology, J. Paul Getty Museum, 1998, published as *Apollo and Daphne: Masterpieces of Mythology,* Frances Lincoln (London, England), 1998.

Noah and the Ark, Corgi (London, England), 1998.

Hidden Tales from Eastern Europe, illustrated by Paul Hess, Frances Lincoln (London, England), 2002.
The Frog Bride, Frances Lincoln (London, England), 2006.

Contributor to books, including Pamela Oldfield, editor, *Hurdy Gurdie,* Blackie & Son, 1984; and Jean Richardson, editor, *Cold Feet,* Hodder & Stoughton (London, England), 1985.

Barber's books have been translated into Gaelic.

"DANCING SHOES" SERIES

Friends and Rivals, Puffin (London, England), 1998.
Into the Spotlight, Puffin (London, England), 1998.
Lessons for Lucy, Puffin (London, England), 1998.
Out of Step, Puffin (London, England), 1998.
Making the Grade, Puffin (London, England), 1999.
Time to Dance, Puffin (London, England), 1999.
Lucy's Next Step, Puffin (London, England), 1999.
Best Foot Forward, Puffin (London, England), 1999.
Model Dancers, Puffin (London, England), 2000.
In a Spin, Puffin (London, England), 2000.
In the Wings, Puffin (London, England), 2000.
Dance to the Rescue, Puffin (London, England), 2000.
The Big Book of Dancing Shoes, Volume 1, Puffin (London, England), 2000.
The Big Book of Dancing Shoes, Volume 2, Puffin (London, England), 2001.

ADAPTATIONS: The Ghosts was adapted for film as *The Amazing Mr Blunden,* 1971, and later adapted for television by the British Broadcasting Corporation (BBC-TV); *The Ring in the Rough Stuff* was adapted for television by BBC-TV; *The Mousehole Cat* was adapted as an animated film, a concert production, music by Ian Hughes, 1995, and as a musical stage play.

SIDELIGHTS: British writer Antonia Barber has gained widespread praise for her fanciful stories for young children as well as for her retellings of traditional folklore and mythology. Beginning her writing career in the mid-1960s, Barber has produced the award-winning novel *The Ghosts,* and the popular picture books *The Mousehole Cat* and *Gemma and the Baby Chick,* as well as story collections that include *Tales from the Ballet* and *Hidden Tales from Eastern*

Europe. Noting that the seven stories in *Hidden Tales from Eastern Europe* combine traditional story elements "in unusual combinations," a *Publishers Weekly* contributor wrote that, "with economy and restraint," Barber "renders even miraculous moments simply, allowing the luster of these stories to shine forth."

Barber's second published book, the novel *The Ghosts,* combines suspense and the supernatural. A young brother and sister, James and Lucy Allen, are confronted by the ghosts of two children killed a hundred years earlier in a fire. The apparitions seek aid, and the Allen children are required to travel back in time in order to change the course of history. A *Horn Book* reviewer called *The Ghosts* "a good English time fantasy, filled with surprising twists and ingeniously resolved mysteries." Popular with readers, the novel was later released as the feature film *The Amazing Mr Blunden.*

Despite the success of her first two books—particularly *The Ghosts,* which was honored by the Carnegie Award committee—Barber credits her experiences as a mother with enhancing her work as a children's writer. As she once commented: "I am an example of a contemporary phenomenon: the professional woman writer who takes a few years out for the fascinating experience of raising young children. After two successful children's books, both widely published and translated, I gave up writing for a while to bring up two adopted sons, intending to return to work when they reached school age. The chance to add a baby daughter, a Vietnamese war orphan, to our family delayed me again; but [after] she . . . joined the boys in school, I . . . returned to writing full time. The marvelous years in between have been of inestimable value to me as a writer. Having seen childhood . . . from the outside as well as the inside, and knowing what it is to be a parent as well as to have parents, I have a much deeper understanding of human character and relationships."

The Mousehole Cat is one of many books Barber has written since taking a break to raise her family. Taking place in the Cornish fishing village of Mousehole—pronounced "Mowzel"—the story follows the efforts of Mowzer, a wise old cat, to protect her human companion, fisherman Tom, when a vicious storm forces the villagers to stay indoors and food becomes scarce. Mowzer's caterwauling and soothing purr appeases the Great Storm Cat and allows Tom to cast his nets and bring food to the town. Praising the book for its "captivating" story, a *Publishers Weekly* contributor added that Barber's text is "by turns funny, dramatic and touching" and her story's resolution "comforting." Also cited for its artwork by Nicola Bayley, *The Mousehole Cat* earned the British Book Award for Best Illustrated Book, among other honors. It has been adapted as an animated film as well as a concert production and a stage musical.

A caretaker cat also plays a starring role in Barber's *Catkin,* which, like *The Mousehole Cat,* contains an element of fantasy. In this tale a fortune-teller seeing danger in young Carrie's future gives the girl a clever cat to watch over her. The fortune-teller's vision proves accurate, however, when Catkin is distracted by some passing butterflies and Carrie is abducted into the underworld by the Little People. In tracing Catkin's journey to free her charge, Barber spins a tale that "rings with the . . . nostalgia of the best fairy stories and the primacy of myth," according to a reviewer for *Publishers Weekly.*

After Barber's husband passed away in 1991, the author "joined the growing band of single parents," as she once explained. "Single parents do not have much time for writing, so I . . . turned for a while to shorter books for younger children." Drawing on her love of the ballet, Barber produced twelve volumes in the "Dancing Shoes" series, a group of books inspired by her 1995 story collection *Tales from the Ballet. Tales from the Ballet* retells the story of nine popular ballets in what *Booklist* reviewer April Judge described as "crisp, dramatic, and action-packed prose." Enchanters, princes and princesses, nutcrackers, nightingales, and firebirds, together with comments about the actual ballet, all find their way into the book, which features engaging pastel illustrations by Diz Wallis.

Commenting on the inspiration for her fiction, Barber once said: "The question children ask me most often in their letters is: 'What made you write the book *The Ghosts?*' My answer is: J.W. Dunne's book *An Experiment with Time,* which I read when I was seventeen; T S. Eliot's poem 'Four Quartets,' which I read when I was seventeen; a story about a real apparition, told to me by an elderly man when I was twenty-six; and an old house I visited for a furniture auction when I was thirty-two, which made all the other memories come together to make a story. The moral is: You never know what may be useful if you are a writer."

BIOGRAPHICAL AND CRITICAL SOURCES:

PERIODICALS

Booklist, November 15, 1995, April Judge, review of *Shoes of Satin, Ribbons of Silk: Tales from the Ballet,* p. 594; October 15, 1998, Susan Dove Lempke, review of *Apollo and Daphne: Masterpieces of Greek Mythology,* p. 409.
Publishers Weekly, August 31, 1990, review of *The Mousehole Cat,* p. 65; January 18, 1993, review of *Gemma and the Baby Chick,* p. 468; November 21, 1994, review of *Catkin,* p. 76; March 15, 2004, review of *Hidden Tales from Eastern Europe,* p. 75.
Teacher Librarian, June, 2000, Jessica Higgs, review of *Apollo and Daphne,* p. 53.
Times Literary Supplement, June 26, 1969.

ONLINE

David Higham Associates Web site, http://www.david higham.co.uk/ (June 20, 2005), "Antonia Barber."*

*   *   *

BARBER, Barbara
    See BARBER, Antonia

*   *   *

BARICCO, Alessandro 1958-

PERSONAL: Born 1958, in Turin, Italy.

ADDRESSES: Home—Italy. *Agent*—c/o Author Mail, Knopf, 1745 Broadway, New York, NY 10019.

CAREER: La Stampa, Turin, Italy, cultural correspondent; *La Repubblica,* Italy, music critic; Holden School of Writing, Turin, founder. Producer of *L'amore X un dardo* (title means "Love Is a Dart") for Italian public television channel RAI3, 1993, and *Pickwick, del leggere e dello scrivere* (title means "Pickwick: Of Reading and Writing").

AWARDS, HONORS: Prix Midicis, France, for *Castelli di rabbia;* Selezione Campiello Prize, Italy, for *Castelli di rabbia;* Viareggio Prize, for *Ocean Sea;* Palazzo del Bosco Prize, for *Ocean Sea.*

WRITINGS:

NOVELS

Castelli di rabbia, Rizzoli (Milan, Italy), 1991.
Oceano Mare, Rizzoli (Milan, Italy), 1993, translated by Alastair McEwan as *Ocean Sea,* Knopf (New York, NY), 1999.
Seta, 1996, translated by Guido Waldman as *Silk,* Harvill (London, England), 1997.
City, Rizzoli (Milan, Italy), 1999 translated by Amy Goldstein as *City: A Novel,* Knopf (New York, NY), 2002.
Senza Sangue, Rizzoli (Milan, Italy), 2002, translated by Ann Goldstein as *Without Blood,* Knopf (New York, NY), 2004.

OTHER

Novecento (stage monologue), Feltrinelli (Milan, Italy), 1994.
Punteggiartura, Scuola Holden (Turin, Italy), 2001.
Next: Piccolo Libro sulla Globalizzazione e sul mondo che verrà (essays), Feltrinelli (Milan, Italy), 2002.
(With Lucia Moisio) *Partita spagnola* (drama), D. Audino (Rome, Italy), 2003.
La Fenice: Splendidezza di Ornamenti e Dorature (nonfiction), De Luca (Rome, Italy), 2004.
An Iliad (drama), translated by Ann Goldstein, Knopf (New York, NY), 2006.

ADAPTATIONS: Baricco's stage monologue *Novecento* was adapted as the film *Laleggenda del pianista sull'Oceano* (title means "The Legend of the Pianist on the Ocean"), renamed *The Legend of 1900* for international release, and released by Fine Line Features, 1999; the novel *Silk* served as the basis for a forthcoming opera by André Previn and a film to be produced by Miramax.

SIDELIGHTS: Italian novelist Alessandro Baricco gained considerable critical attention for his book *Silk.* The story begins in 1861 and follows Herve Joncour, a young French silkworm merchant who travels to Japan in search of uncontaminated eggs after an epidemic affects the usual supplies from Africa and the Middle East. The Japanese will sell their silk, but there is a ban on the export of Japanese silkworm eggs, and Joncour is in danger of being prosecuted if discovered. Joncour is married to, and loves, Helene; however, during his first trip he encounters a young concubine with whom he becomes obsessed, but who is the mistress of Japanese trader Hara Kei. "Although the two have virtually no contact beyond glances, and speak no common language, the passion that springs from this encounter provides a further elegiac air for the narrative," wrote Caroline Moorehead in the *Times Literary Supplement.* Joncour returns several times for the precious eggs, which he carefully wraps and packs in crates, always arriving back in his home of Lavilledieu during the Easter season in time for high mass. Each four-month journey takes him through Europe and Russia as he travels to Japan. London *Independent* contributor, Lilian Pizzichini, asserted that the story "has absence at its core," not only because the woman Joncour desires is off-limits, but also because it is "about a man who crosses continents and notices nothing."

Joncour makes a total of four trips to Japan and finally consummates his love with the concubine. His last trip is a failure when the eggs hatch before he reaches France. While home, he receives letters in Japanese which he believes to be from his lover; he has them translated by a Japanese woman in a neighboring village. "These letters and a surprising ending to this intriguing tale confirm Mr. Baricco's gift as a story-teller," wrote an *Economist* contributor. In *World Literature Today,* Luigi Monga called Baricco's style "deliberately simple, almost awkward, and at times dull." Monga concluded that the narrative is "a metaphor for human life" that leaves us "guessing. Life as what? As a voyage? As a dream?" Baricco's story "weaves a fine, tight fabric of recurrent phrases and motifs, a novel as delicate and strong as its subject," commented a contributor to *Publishers Weekly.*

Baricco followed *Silk* with *City: A Novel,* his first novel set in contemporary times. Like many of Baricco's books, *City* has a very unique, individual, experimental style that is both lyrical and impressionistic. This novel is a complicated experimental satire about the United States and the very nature of storytelling. Baricco has his two main characters, a thirteen-year-old mathematical genius named Gould and Shatzy Shell, Gould's thirty-something caregiver and surrogate mother, spend most of their time fixated on complex fantasy stories they have been working on for years. Gould's tale focuses on a Horatio Alger-type boxer, while Shell has devised a number of vignettes set in the Wild West intended for a film. Both characters are looking for connection and comfort from the cold world as they live primarily in their imaginations. Paul Haacke noted in the *Review of Contemporary Fiction* that "they give us a hilarious impression of 'metropolitan' America: center of precociousness and immaturity, rich in boredom, desire, and possiblity."

Senza Sangue, which was translated into English as *Without Blood,* is a brief, poetic novel of only about one hundred pages. Touching on the theme of the end-less nature of revenge by the use of a circular structure, the narrative is driven by the pointless murder of a family—a doctor who committed war-time atrocities, Manuel Roca, and his son—by a group of assassins after the end of a brutal armed conflict. Only Roca's daughter, Nina, survives, because one of the men who commits the crime, Tito, finds her hiding and chooses not to kill her. In the second half of *Without Blood,* Tito and Nina have an encounter about a half century later. They discuss what happened fifty years earlier and the greater meaning of war. Praising Baricco's elegant construction of character and the meditative quality of the book, Brian Budzynski remarked in the *Review of Contemporary Fiction,* "Baricco is a writer of great intuition, able to transform the simplest language, which perhaps at first reading is plain, into a kind of poetry of experience."

BIOGRAPHICAL AND CRITICAL SOURCES:

PERIODICALS

Economist, May 18, 1996, review of *Seta,* pp. S16-18.

Independent (London, England), May 17, 1998, Lilian Pizzichini, review of *Silk.*

Kirkus Reviews, March 15, 2004, review of *Without Blood,* p. 235.

Publishers Weekly, September 1, 1997, review of *Silk,* p. 96.

Review of Contemporary Fiction, fall, 2002, Paul Haacke, review of *City,* p. 164; summer, 2004, Brian Budzynski, review of *Without Blood,* p. 147.

Times Literary Supplement, April 18, 1997, Caroline Moorehead, review of *Silk,* p. 20.

World Literature Today, spring, 1997, Luigi Monga, review of *Seta,* p. 368.*

*   *   *

BARKER, Pat 1943-
(Patricia Barker)

PERSONAL: Born May 8, 1943, in Thornaby-on-Tees, England; married David Barker (a professor of zoology), January 29, 1978; children: John, Annabel. *Education:* London School of Economics and Political Science, London, B.Sc., 1965.

ADDRESSES: Home—10th Ave., Durham DH1 4ED, England. *Agent*—Aitken Associates, 29 Fernshaw Rd., London SW10 OTG, England.

CAREER: Writer. Worked as teacher in England, 1965-70.

MEMBER: Society of Authors, PEN.

AWARDS, HONORS: Named one of Britain's twenty best young writers by Book Marketing Society, 1982; Fawcett Prize, Fawcett Society, 1982, for *Union Street;* Special Award, Northern Electric Arts Awards, 1993; *Guardian* Fiction Prize, 1993, for *The Eye in the Door;* Booker Prize for fiction, 1995, for *The Ghost Road;* honorary M.Litt., University of Teesside, 1993; honor-ary fellow, L.S.E., 1996; honorary D. Litt., Napier, 1996, Hertfordshire, 1998, and Durham, 1998; honor-ary doctorate, Open University, 1997; decorated Com-mander of the British Empire, 2000.

WRITINGS:

NOVELS

Union Street, Virago Press (London, England), 1982, Putnam (New York, NY), 1983.

Blow Your House Down, Putnam (New York, NY), 1984.

The Century's Daughter, Putnam (New York, NY), 1986, also published as *Liza's England,* 1996.

The Man Who Wasn't There, Virago Press (London, England), 1989, Ballantine (New York, NY), 1990.

Regeneration, Viking (London, England), 1991, Dutton (New York, NY), 1993.

The Eye in the Door, Viking (London, England), 1993, Dutton (New York, NY), 1994.

The Ghost Road, Viking (London, England), 1995, Dutton (New York, NY), 1996.

The Regeneration Trilogy, Viking (London, England), 1996.

Another World, Viking (London, England), 1998.

Border Crossing, Farrar, Straus (New York, NY), 2001.

Double Vision Farrar, Straus (New York, NY), 2003.

Life Class, Penguin (London, England), 2006.

ADAPTATIONS: Union Street was adapted as the feature film *Stanley & Iris,* Metro-Goldwyn-Mayer, 1989, starring Robert De Niro and Jane Fonda; *Regeneration* was adapted as a film of the same title, 1997, directed by Gillies MacKinnon, starring Jonathan Pryce, James Wilby, and Jonny Lee Miller.

SIDELIGHTS: Pat Barker is among the most acclaimed writers to emerge from England in the 1980s. Her novels—among them *Union Street, Blow Your House Down, Double Vision,* and a trilogy of novels concerning World War I that includes 1995's *The Ghost Road*—have earned praise for both their spare, direct prose and their depictions of working-class life. Once in danger of being labeled merely a feminist writer for her stories of struggling women in industrial England, Barker has since earned praise as a voice for the human condition in general. "It has been Pat Barker's accomplishment to enlarge the scope of the contemporary English novel," noted Claudia Roth Pierpont in the *New Yorker.* Pierpont further described Barker as "an energetic writer who achieves much of her purpose through swift and easy dialogue and the bold etching of personality—effects so apparently simple and forthright that the complications of feeling which arise seem to do so unbidden."

Barker's first three published novels draw upon her memories of working-class women of her mother's and grandmother's generations. She herself grew up in Thornaby-on-Tees, an industrial town in the north of England. In an interview with *CA,* the author recalled that she turned to writing her "gritty" and "realistic"

works after failing to sell a series of middle-class novels of manners. She was encouraged to explore her own background by the author Angela Carter, who read a Barker work-in-progress during a writer's conference. Barker once told *CA:* "I think along with the desire to write about the sort of environment I'd grown up with came a desire to write, initially at least, more about women because I felt that, although the men in that environment had also been deprived of a voice, and were not being given any kind of public recognition of their experiences of life, the women had been in a way still more deprived. . . . I was writing about the most silenced section of our society."

Union Street, Barker's first novel, concerns seven neighboring women near a factory in northeast England. Life for these women is trying and unrewarding. Some of them are married to alcoholics; some of them are victims of spousal abuse; all of them seem resigned to suffering. Meredith Tax, writing in the *Village Voice,* described the novel's characters as "women who have given up on love." Tax added, however, that Barker "dramatizes the strength of her working-class people without sentimentality, for she knows the way they participate in their own victimization." Tax also added that the various women in *Union Street* experience growth and strength through their suffering, noting that the novel's "point is life, and how rich and hard it is, and the different ways people have of toughing it through the pain without being crushed."

Many critics praised *Union Street.* Ivan Gold, who wrote in the *New York Times Book Review* that Barker's "pungent, raunchy . . . dialogue" alternates "with passages of fine understated wit," called *Union Street* a "first-rate first novel." Likewise, Eileen Fairweather wrote in the *New Statesman* that "Barker may have written the latest, long over-due working-class masterpiece," and Elizabeth Ward wrote in the *Washington Post Book World* that "Barker achieves immediate distinction with *Union Street.*" Ward added that though "the book's vision . . . is of a life brutal and scabrous in the extreme," Barker nonetheless includes "a flicker of affirmation" for each of the main characters. Ward called *Union Street* "a singularly powerful achievement." A film version of the book, released as *Stanley & Iris,* was produced in 1989.

Barker enjoyed further acclaim with her next novel, *Blow Your House Down.* Like *Union Street,* the second novel details events in the lives of several women in working-class, industrial England. Unlike the women in *Union Street,* though, the characters in *Blow Your House Down* are prostitutes, and their problems include not only those of the women in *Union Street*— notably abuse and financial insecurity—but one of survival in a red-light district frequented by a vicious, Jack the Ripper-style killer. Many reviewers praised *Blow Your House Down* as a gripping account of life in a gloomy industrial town. *Encounter* critic James Lasdun noted: "Pat Barker has an impressive feel for the starkness of English working-class existence at its roughest end." Lasdun cited Barker's "perfect ear for dialogue" and called her second novel "disturbingly convincing."

The Century's Daughter, Barker's third novel, offered further insights into the hardships of being a woman in industrial England. The story's protagonist is Liza Jarrett Wright, an octogenarian who recounts her life to Steven, a homosexual social worker who befriends her while trying to move her from a doomed neighborhood. Liza tells Steven of her childhood spent in poverty and neglect. She also recalls her son, killed during World War II, and her promiscuous daughter, whose child Liza raised herself. Comparing *The Century's Daughter* to Barker's preceding novels, reviewers found it more sentimental but equally compelling.

In a 1992 *Village Voice* interview, Barker admitted that the success of her first three novels led her to fear that she was being "boxed in" by public expectations. "I had become strongly typecast as a northern, regional, working-class feminist . . . label, label, label," she commented. "You get to the point where people are reading the label instead of the book." Not one to accept such limitations, Barker extended her imaginative reach and entered the world of the male psyche. *The Man Who Wasn't There* tells the story of Colin, a fatherless teenager who concocts fantasies about himself and his absent parent in an effort to alleviate the silent grief he feels. *Times Literary Supplement* reviewer Kathleen Jamie praised the book for its authentic vision of post-war Britain. "Pat Barker's talent is for people, period and dialogue; and in Colin she perfectly creates the mind of a 1950s twelve-year-old, a latch-key kid," the critic wrote.

Additionally, Barker turned to the history of World War I and wrote a trilogy of novels about mentally ill soldiers and the therapist who struggles with his own

moral values while treating them. The first volume of the trilogy, 1992's *Regeneration,* drew a wealth of acclaim on both continents. Based on actual people and events, the novel follows Royal Welch Fusiliers hero Siegfried Sassoon through his "treatment" at Craiglockhart War Hospital in Edinburgh in 1917. Sassoon has been sent to Craiglockhart after writing a letter denouncing his country's political motives in the conflict and refusing to suffer any more agonies on behalf of an ungrateful nation. His case is taken up by Dr. William H.R. Rivers, an army psychologist who soon realizes the similarities between the stresses suffered by trench soldiers and those experienced by poor women on the home front.

The Eye in the Door continues the saga of Dr. Rivers and his shell-shocked patients, this time focusing on a bisexual lieutenant named Billy Prior—a wholly fictional creation of Barker's—who suffers from "bouts of amnesia." Voiceless as well as without any memory of a six-day period during which he was injured at the front and taken to a military hospital, Prior nonetheless exhibits a raw intelligence that belies his working-class roots. Familiar with Rivers' work, Prior asks the noted psychologist to hypnotize him, a request that results in the shell-shocked officer's recall of the destruction of his fellow soldiers—the result of an enemy shell—and his futile attempts to gather their scattered remains back inside the trench. During the healing process that follows the return of his memory, Prior works in the London Intelligence Office, awaiting his return to the front as a test-case for Rivers— will the glue hold? Will he be able to withstand yet another glimpse of such horror? Meanwhile, through their interaction during Prior's therapy, Rivers and his patient begin to change roles: the psychologist becomes patient, gradually allowing himself to experience feelings of caring and empathy with regard to his patient that he had previously closed off out of necessity.

The Eye in the Door "succeeds as both historical fiction and as sequel," wrote Jim Shepard in the *New York Times Book Review.* "Its research and speculation combine to produce a kind of educated imagination that is persuasive and illuminating about this particular place and time."

The third novel in the World War I trilogy, *The Ghost Road,* was published in 1995 and received that year's Booker Prize for fiction. Both Rivers and Prior return, with Rivers now employed at a hospital in London and Prior, now fully recovered, on his way back to the battle front. Interspersed with his current activities at the hospital are the doctor's recollections of a period, a decade before the war, that he spent on Eddystone Island, in Melanesia. There, he recalls while looking around him now at a country peopled by shattered souls and battered bodies, its buildings bombed, and a sense of despair permeating the air, the old, sick, and infirm were no longer grouped with the living, but rather were said to be traveling the "ghost road." Prior, the reader soon realizes, is also traveling such a road; his trip back to the front will ultimately prove fatal. The journey back into the trenches is somehow preordained, its inexorableness juxtaposed by Barker with a meeting with poet Wilfred Owen—himself an actual casualty of the Great War—when she gives the poet voice: "At night you get the sense of something *ancient*. . . . It's as if all other wars had somehow . . . distilled themselves into this war, and that makes it something you . . . almost can't challenge."

The brutal, sometimes graphically unpleasant, aspects of the novel fascinated several critics, particularly because they had come from the pen of a female author. Commenting on Barker's self-confessed bluntness in dealing with the "masculine" facets of human behavior that reflect the violence of war, *New Yorker* contributor Blake Morrison noted that "there is at times something very 1990s and predictable about her preoccupation with gender, emasculation, bisexuality, and role reversals." However, the critic concluded, Barker's ultimate focus on the parallels drawn by Rivers between primitive Melanesian society and civilized England draws the novel—the close of the trilogy—toward the timeless. "Whatever the waste of human life," Morrison posited, "isn't war fundamental to the human spirit? It's a dark and distinctly un-nineties thought with which to end this complex trilogy." *Times Literary Supplement* reviewer Peter Parker noted that *The Ghost Road* "amply fulfills the high expectations raised by its predecessors," and concluded of the novel that it is "startlingly good . . . in its own right."

"Here is another of [Barker's] descents into hell," wrote *Spectator* critic Jane Gardam of the author's 2001 offering *Border Crossing*. In this novel, Barker explores what Gardam termed "the genesis of evil," through the development of the relationship between doctor and patient. Tom Seymour, one of the book's two protagonists, is an unhappily married psychologist who specializes in children's issues. During a walk along the banks of the Tyne River, Tom and his wife witness a man attempting to kill himself by jumping into the water. After he rescues the man, Tom learns that he is in fact a former patient: Danny Miller, who, after murdering an elderly woman at age ten, was sent to prison based on Tom's expert testimony at trial. Danny has emerged from prison thirteen years later as "a successful product of the system," according to *New Criterion* reviewer Brooke Allen, "startlingly attractive and intelligent" but "also clearly damaged" by his experiences. Danny asks Tom to take him on as a patient, in order to help the younger man analyze and resolve his childhood traumas. Once the sessions begin, however, Tom becomes too close to his patient, and, as Gardam noted, their relationship "crystallises into a confrontation, a duet, between good and evil." While the *Library Journal* contributor Wilda Williams felt that "the novel falls flat at the end, leaving the reader disappointed and dissatisfied," Allen commented that "*Border Crossing* is emotionally affecting and sophisticated, and poses, as well, a tormenting and almost insoluble philosophical challenge."

In Barker's tenth novel, *Double Vision,* the characters grapple with personal grief and loss caused by violence. The novel's protagonist, Kate Frobisher, is a sculptor and recent widow suffering from injuries caused by a car accident. Her husband, Ben, a photojournalist, was killed by a sniper bullet in Afghanistan. Stephen Sharkey, a journalist and friend of her husband, discovers that his wife is having an affair as he watches the Twin Towers collapse. Stephen is also suffering from post-traumatic stress syndrome from covering conflicts in Bosnia and Rwanda. After his divorce, Stephen moves in with his brother, whose home is not far from Kate's. "This may all sound too neat, but it's not," remarked *Library Journal* reviewer Barbara Hoffert. She concluded that Barker "shows how tightly bound we are and how our actions reverberate; every step is fraught with consequence."

BIOGRAPHICAL AND CRITICAL SOURCES:

BOOKS

Contemporary Literary Criticism, Volume 32, Gale (Detroit, MI), 1985.

PERIODICALS

American Prospect, April 9, 2001, Mark Greif, review of *Border Crossing,* pp. 36-39.

Book, March, 2001, Chris Barsanti, review of *Border Crossing,* p. 81.

Booklist, March 1, 1999, Brad Hooper, review of *Another World,* p. 1150; March 1, 2001, Nancy Pearl, review of *Border Crossing,* p. 1225; December 1, 2003, Joanne Wilkinson, review of *Double Vision,*.

Economist, March 10, 2001, review of *Border Crossing,* p. 7; August 23, 2003, review of *Double Vision,* p. 69.

Encounter, September-October, 1984, James Lasdun, review of *Blow Your House Down.*

English Review, September, 1999, Philippa Caldicott, review of *Another World,* p. 18.

Entertainment Weekly, Lisa Schwarzbaum, "Mourning After," p. 103.

Esquire, April, 2001, Sven Birkets, review of *Border Crossing,* p. 56.

Globe & Mail (Toronto, Ontario, Canada), August 23, 2003, review of *Double Vision,* p. D3.

Hudson Review, winter, 2000, Dean Flower, review of *Another World,* p. 657.

Kirkus Reviews, October 15, 2003, review of *Double Vision,* pp. 1237-1239.

Library Journal, April 15, 1999, Wilda Williams, review of *Another World,* p. 142; April 1, 2001, Wilda Williams, review of *Border Crossing,* p. 131; November 1, 2003, Barbara Hoffert, review of *Double Vision,* p. 121.

New Criterion, May, 1999, Brooke Allen, review of *Another World,* p. 74; May, 2001, Brooke Allen, "Blurring the Borders," pp. 62-66.

New Statesman, May 14, 1982, Eileen Fairweather, review of *Union Street;* June 8, 1984; September 8, 2003, Christina Lamb, "Battle Scars," review of *Double Vision,* p. 53.

New Yorker, August 10, 1992, Claudia Roth Pierpoint, review of *Regeneration,* pp. 74-76; January 22, 1996, Blake Morrison, review of *The Ghost Road,* pp. 78-82.

New York Review of Books, February 15, 1996, pp. 19-21; May 20, 1999, Gabriele Annan, review of *Another World,* p. 28; May 17, 2001, Gabriele Annan, review of *Border Crossing,* p. 44.

New York Times Book Review, October 2, 1983, Ivan Gold, review of *Union Street;* May 15, 1994, Jim Shepard, review of *The Eye in the Door,* p. 9; December 14, 2003, Neil Gordon, review of *Double Vision,* p. 12; December 18, 2003, Joyce Carol Oates, review of *Double Vision,* p. 78.

Observer (London, England), May 5, 2002, review of *Border Crossing,* p. 18.

Publishers Weekly, February 15, 1999, review of *Another World,* p. 83; January 22, 2001, review of *Border Crossing,* p. 300; August 17, 2003, review of *Double Vision,* p. 18.

Spectator, November 21, 1998, Helen Osborne, review of *Another World,* p. 49; March 31, 2001, Jane Gardam, review of *Border Crossing,* p. 47; August 20, 2003, Anita Brookner, "Calm after the Storm," review of *Double Vision,* p. 29; November 10, 2003, review of *Double Vision,* p. 42.

Time, June 7, 1999, Elizabeth Gleick, review of *Another World,* p. 82.

Times Literary Supplement, April 14, 1989, Kathleen Jamie, review of *The Man Who Wasn't There,* p. 404; September 8, 1995, Peter Parker, review of *The Ghost Road;* October 23, 1998, Carol Birch, review of *Another World,* p. 25; March 30, 2001, Robert MacFarlane, review of *Border Crossing,* p. 24; August 29, 2003, Michael Caines, "News from the Burning City: Pat Barker's Vivid Variations on War, Memory, and Present Suffering," review of *Double Vision,* p. 19.

Village Voice, December 6, 1983, Meredith Tax, review of *Union Street;* July 14, 1992, interview and review of *Regeneration,* p. 91.

Washington Post Book World, September 18, 1983, Elizabeth Ward, review of *Union Street.*

Women's Review of Books, September, 1999, E.J. Graff, review of *Another World,* p. 5.

*   *   *

BARKER, Patricia
   See BARKER, Pat

*   *   *

BELLER, Thomas 1965-

PERSONAL: Born May 23, 1965. *Education:* Vassar College, B.A.; Columbia University, M.F.A.

ADDRESSES: Home—New York, NY. *Office*—Open City, 270 Lafayette St., Ste. 1412, New York, NY, 10012. *Agent*—Mary Evans Inc., 242 E. 5th St., New York City, 10003. *E-mail*—tom@opencity.org.

CAREER: Open City (magazine), Manhattan, NY, cofounder and coeditor; creator of the Web sites, *Mr.*

Beller's Neighborhood, and *Mapsites.net.* Has worked in a bagel factory and as a bike messenger.

WRITINGS:

Seduction Theory: Stories, Norton (New York, NY), 1995.

(Editor) *Personals: Dreams and Nightmares from the Lives of Twenty Young Writers,* Houghton Mifflin (Boston, MA), 1998.

The Sleep-Over Artist (stories), Norton (New York, NY), 2000.

(Editor, with Kip Kotzen) *With Love and Squalor: Fourteen Writers Respond to the Work of J.D. Salinger,* Broadway Books (New York, NY), 2001.

Before and After: Stories from New York, Norton (New York, NY), 2002.

How To Be a Man: Scenes from a Protracted Boyhood (essays), Norton (New York, NY), 2005.

Also author of *Cabinet 9: Childhood,* and contributor to several anthologies. Contributor of short stories to *New Yorker, Ploughshares, Mademoiselle, Southwest Review, Cambodia Daily,* and *New York;* contributor of articles to *Mademoiselle, New Yorker, New York Times* and *Harper's Bazaar;* contributing editor of *Cambodia Daily.*

The story *"A Different Kind of Imperfection,"* is included in *Best American Short Stories 1992,* edited by Robert Stone.

SIDELIGHTS: Thomas Beller is a New York writer whose short stories portray the plight of young, middle-class urbanites. Reviewers warmed to Beller's first collection, *Seduction Theory: Stories,* with its depictions of characters trying to connect with one another but invariably failing. According to Lucy Atkins of the *Times Literary Supplement,* the stories portray a "society teeming with desperate characters who long to bond with others, yet fear for their self-preservation."

Half the stories in *Seduction Theory* feature Alex Fader, a character critics generally identify with the author himself, as he grows from pre-adolescence to young adulthood. "The [Alex] Fader stories are the most memorable and show off Beller's true talent," observed Elizabeth Manus in the *San Francisco Review of Books.* A contributor to *Publishers Weekly* described the collection's last story, in which Alex introduces his lover to his overprotective mother during a family Hanukkah gathering, as "aglow with wise humor and heartfelt compassion."

Time critic Gina Bellafante observed that *Seduction Theory*'s setting and subject—"a hyperexposed world of young, well-bred New Yorkers" looking for love but afraid of commitment—is familiar, but maintained that Beller had created "touching and exceptionally memorable tales" from his material. Other critics similarly proclaimed themselves charmed by Beller's carefully crafted stories and rueful but precise observations on young urban love. Beller's stories "recall . . . the poignant nostalgia of Cheever, and the earnest but confused innocence of Salinger," Albert E. Wilhelm wrote in the *Library Journal.*

Beller was working in a bagel factory when "A Different Kind of Imperfection," one of the stories collected in *Seduction Theory,* was published in *Best American Short Stories 1992.* In an interview with Manus, the author discussed the uncertainties and ironies of the life of a writer. "I am constantly having misgivings about this profession. . . . The world at large is unfriendly to fiction writers," said Beller. During the interview, the author also noted each of the stories in *Seduction Theory* was subjected to his practice of completing a piece, putting it away for a time, and reworking it again before he considered it finished. "Fiction has a cleaner, more candid world view," he told Manus. "It's more honest because it's had time to be."

In *Personals: Dreams and Nightmares from the Lives of Twenty Young Writers,* Beller compiles twenty short memoirs. As editor, Beller's only direction to the writers was to "find something that matters . . . and write a story about it," reported a *Publishers Weekly* contributor. Yet Paula Friedman of *New Criterion* felt that "the relative youth of these writers probably accounts for some for their difficulties." According to Friedman, the writers are too self-conscious in their art. She commented: "Too often these writers seem so bent on eschewing sentimentality that they end up squelching all sentiment." On the other hand, Katherine K. Koenig of the *Library Journal* said that the collection contains an honest portrayal of young people. She noted that the book "taps the angst of new and aspiring twentysomething writers."

Beller's collection *The Sleep-Over Artist* reunites readers with Alex Fader from *Seduction Theory.* This short story collection follows him from age six through adulthood. Erin Doyle, a reviewer for *Book,* commented: "Beller's prose is often sharp and funny;" however, she then pointed out that both the book's writer and protagonist are "distractingly self-aware for too much of the book." Other reviewers also acknowledged that the book might be a bit too focused on its central character. Nevertheless, a *Publishers Weekly* reviewer called *The Sleep-Over Artist* "carefully crafted," and called Alex "curious and keenly observant."

In 2001 Beller coedited *With Love and Squalor: Fourteen Writers Respond to the Work of J.D. Salinger.* The essays in the collection range from serious to hilarious and serve as a tribute to Salinger's immense influence on adolescent readers. Some reviewers took issue with the youthful feel of the book. However, Kristine Huntley, writing in *Booklist,* stated, "These intelligent and reflective essays will have readers eagerly reaching for their copies of Salinger's books." According to a contributor to *Kirkus Reviews,* the book offers "some humdinging stuff, as much tortured fun as their subject."

Beller published *Before and After: Stories from New York,* which contains sixty stories collected from his Web site, *Mr. Beller's Neighborhood.* Half of the stories in the book take place before the September 11 attacks, and half of the book takes place after them. Of the tone of the first half, a *Publishers Weekly* reviewer pointed out that "the feel is definitively late '90s, and the city seems full of promise, romance and cash." A *Kirkus Reviews* contributor noted, "The writers knew they were onto something good, fleeting, and worth the telling," and then went on to compare each story to a crab apple: "Bite into it and it bites you back."

How to Be a Man: Scenes from a Protracted Childhood is also a collection, but this time of personal essays. Many of the essays were previously published in the *New Yorker* and the *New York Times.* Together, they chronicle the relationships of an aging New Yorker. Some reviewers commented on the lack of structure and cohesiveness in the organization of the collection. A *Kirkus Reviews* contributor called the book a "loose assemblage of Beller's nonfiction pieces." Yet a contributor to *Publishers Weekly* noted

the "spare, crisp language" and stated that the essays are reminiscent of "Raymond Carver in their clarity of language and subdued emotion."

BIOGRAPHICAL AND CRITICAL SOURCES:

PERIODICALS

Book, September, 2000, review of *The Sleep-Over Artist,* p. 81.
Booklist, May 1, 2000, Mary Ellen Quinn, review of *The Sleep-Over Artist,* p. 1648; October 1, 2001, Kristine Huntley, review of *With Love and Squalor: Fourteen Writers Respond to the Work of J.D. Salinger,* p. 294.
Entertainment Weekly, August 7, 1998, review of *Personals: Dreams and Nightmares from the Lives of Twenty Young Writers,* p. 67; August 12, 2005, Gilbert Cruz, review of *How to Be a Man: Scenes from a Protracted Boyhood,* p. 82.
Kirkus Reviews, June 1, 1998, review of *Personals,* p. 787; April 15, 2000, review of *The Sleep-Over Artist,* p. 492; August 1, 2001, review of *With Love and Squalor,* p. 1093; December 15, 2001, review of *Before and After: Stories from New York,* p. 1729; May 1, 2005, review of *How to Be a Man,* p. 519-520.
Library Journal, May 15, 1995, Albert E. Wilhelm, review of *Seduction Theory: Stories,* p. 98; July, 1998, Katherine K. Koenig, review of *Personals,* p. 91; August 1, 2005, Audrey Snowden, review of *How to Be a Man,* p. 84.
Los Angeles Times, July 9, 2000, review of *The Sleep-Over Artist,* p. 11.
M2 Best Books, February 12, 2002, review of *Before and After.*
New Criterion, January, 1999, Paula Friedman, review of *Personals,* p. 76.
New Yorker, October 5, 1998, Daphne Merkin, review of *Personals,* p. 108.
Publishers Weekly, April 17, 1995, review of *Seduction Theory,* p. 39; June 29, 1998, review of *Personals,* p. 48; April 17, 2000, review of *The Sleep-Over Artist,* p. 46; January 21, 2002, review of *Before and After* p. 78; May 16, 2005, review of *How to Be a Man,* p. 51; August 15, 2005 David Bahr, "He Got Game: Thomas Beller Does it All," p. 18.
San Francisco Review of Books, May-June, 1995, Elizabeth Manus, interview and review of *Seduction Theory,* p. 11.

Time, July 10, 1995, Gina Bellafante, review of *Seduction Theory,* p. 46.

Times Literary Supplement, September 1, 1995, Lucy Atkins, review of *Seduction Theory,* p. 21.

Tribune Books, November 25, 2001, review of *The Sleep-Over Artist,* p. 6.

ONLINE

Mr. Beller's Neighborhood, http://mrbellers neighborhood.com (October 25, 2005).

Thomas Beller Home Page, http://thomasbeller.com (October 25, 2005).*

*   *   *

BINGHAM, Jane M. 1941-
(Jane Marie Bingham)

PERSONAL: Born September 21, 1941, in Huntington, WV; daughter of Ferrell Jeff and Nora Lucille (Stephenson) Bingham. *Education:* Flint Junior College, A.A., 1961; Central Michigan University, B.A., 1964; Michigan State University, M.A., 1966, Ph.D., 1970.

ADDRESSES: Home—Rochester, MI. *Office*—Department of Education, Oakland University, 501 O'Dowd Hall, Rochester, MI 48309-4401. *E-mail*—bingham@ oakland.edu.

CAREER: Elementary school teacher at public schools in Flint, MI, 1961-65; Michigan State University, East Lansing, assistant instructor in education, 1965-66; Flint Junior College, Flint, instructor in children's literature, summer, 1967; Oakland University, Rochester, MI, instructor, 1969-70, assistant professor, 1970-75, associate professor of children's literature, 1975-c. 2001. Member of Friends of Flint Public Library, Detroit Public Library, Avon Township Library, Kerlan Collection at University of Minnesota, Osborne Collection at Toronto Public Library, De-Grummond Collection at University of Mississippi, and Detroit Institute of Art.

MEMBER: International Reading Association, International Research Society for Children's Literature, Association for Childhood Education International,

National Council of Teachers of English (treasurer of Children's Literature Assembly, 1973-75; chairperson, 1976-78), American Library Association (member of Laura Ingalls Wilder and Caldecott Medal awards committees; chairperson of national planning for special collections committee), Children's Literature Association (board member, 1975-78; secretary, 1975-76).

WRITINGS:

NONFICTION FOR CHILDREN

(Editor, with Fiona Chandler and Sam Taplin) *The Usborne Internet-linked Encyclopedia of World History,* Usborne, 2001.

Tiananmen Square: June 4, 1989, Raintree (Chicago, IL), 2004.

The Red Cross Movement, Raintree (Chicago, IL), 2004.

The Human Body: From Head to Toe, Heinemann Library (Chicago, IL), 2004.

A History of Fashion and Costume, Volume 1: *The Ancient World,* Facts on File (New York, NY), 2005.

Johnny Depp, Raintree (Chicago, IL), 2005.

Sikh Gurdwaras, Raintree (Chicago, IL), 2005.

Why Do Families Break Up?, Raintree (Chicago, IL), 2005.

"WHAT'S THE DEAL?" SERIES; NONFICTION FOR CHILDREN

Heroin, Heinemann Library (Chicago, IL), 2005.

Alcohol, Heinemann Library (Chicago, IL), 2005.

Marijuana, Heinemann Library (Chicago, IL), 2005.

Smoking, Heinemann Library (Chicago, IL), 2005.

"WORLD ART AND CULTURE" SERIES; NONFICTION FOR CHILDREN

Indian Art and Culture, Raintree (Chicago, IL), 2004.

African Art and Culture, Raintree (Chicago, IL), 2004.

Aboriginal Art and Culture, Raintree (Chicago, IL), 2005.

FOR ADULTS

(With Grayce Scholt) *Fifteen Centuries of Children's Literature: An Annotated Chronology of British and American Works in Historical Context,* Greenwood Press (Westport, CT), 1980.

Author of "Children's Literature: Views and Reviews," a quarterly column written with Grayce Scholt for *Michigan Reading Journal,* 1971-76. Contributor of articles and reviews to education, library, and women's studies journals. Editor of *Children's Literature in Review* and *The Three R's: Reading, Writing and Radio* (children's magazine).

SIDELIGHTS: Jane M. Bingham spent most of her adult life teaching college students about children's literature at Oakland University, collecting and studying children's books from across history and around the world, and campaigning for better materials for children to read. After she retired from that career, she began writing children's books of her own. Bingham has since authored several nonfiction books that seek to explain contemporary issues to children, including divorce, the dangers of drug abuse, and the art and culture of civilizations around the world.

Tiananmen Square: June 4, 1989 examines the student-led protest against China's Communist rulers that occurred there, in the middle of Beijing, in the spring of 1989. On June 4, the government mobilized the army, including tanks, to disperse the demonstrators, killing several of them in the process. "The excellent illustrations and clear narrative," Elizabeth Talbot wrote in the *School Library Journal,* make *Tiananmen Square* a "good introduction" to the protest and its aftermath.

In *Why Do Families Break Up?* Bingham attempts to demystify the process of divorce for middle-school students. The book begins by examining some of the reasons a couple might decide to divorce, then moves on to explain the process of coping and moving on after a family separates. *School Library Journal* contributor Sharon A. Neal described the book as "supportive [and] unbiased" and noted: "Despite the nature of the topic, the book is hopeful."

Bingham is the author of three installments in the "World Art and Culture" series, examining India, Africa, and Aboriginal Australia. Each book is brief, only fifty-six pages long, and "the texts are straightforward and concise," Gillian Engberg noted in a review of *African Art and Culture* for *Booklist.* Despite this brevity, much information is packed into each volume. Bingham opens each book with a chapter about the history of the region, from thousands of years ago to the present day, and follows with chapters about the

art forms practiced in that area. These include architecture, basket-weaving, musical instruments, dance, and body modification (tattoos, piercings, and the like), among others. *Indian Art and Culture* also includes a chapter on one of that country's modern art forms, the "Bollywood" movie industry. As Donna Cardon noted in the *School Library Journal:* "The texts not only describe the art forms and how they are created, but also explain the role that art plays in the cultures."

Bingham once wrote: "In 1981 I completed a trip which took me to American Samoa, New Zealand, Australia, Hong Kong, China, Thailand, Bangladesh, India, Kenya, South Africa, and Swaziland. I collected examples of children's books along the way and became acutely aware of the need for books and other teaching resources in many developing countries. I was especially impressed with the variety of India's and Bangladesh's children's books—in spite of the difficulties their creators often encounter in publishing and promoting them. I also found that becoming aware of and enjoying the literature from other countries enriched my appreciation of American children's books. I found myself asking over and over why we, with the plethora we have to choose from, too often opt for the mediocre rather than the 'rarest kind of best.' As educators, creators, and consumers, we all too often forget to think of children's books as real literature because we fail to apply critical literary standards. It is my hope that my teaching and writing will draw attention to the continuing need for quality books in our own country and will also encourage American students and teachers to adopt a wider, world view of children's literature."

BIOGRAPHICAL AND CRITICAL SOURCES:

PERIODICALS

Booklist, April 1, 2004, Gillian Engberg, review of *African Art and Culture,* p. 1373.

Oakland University Post (Oakland, MI), March 27, 2002, Ashlyn Cates, "Bingham Gives Kresge Books."

School Arts, February, 2005, Ken Marantz, review of *Indian Art and Culture,* p. 55.

School Library Journal, November, 2001, review of *The Usborne Internet-linked Encyclopedia of World History,* p. 86; February, 2004, Donna

Cardon, review of *African Art and Culture,* p. 156; April, 2004, Wendy Lukehart, review of *African Art and Culture,* p. 63; June, 2004, Marilyn Ackerman, review of *The Red Cross Movement,* p. 157; October, 2004, Elizabeth Talbot, review of *Tiananmen Square: June 4, 1989,* p. 186; February, 2005, Sharon A. Neal, review of *Why Do Families Break Up?,* p. 145.*

*   *   *

BINGHAM, Jane Marie
  See BINGHAM, Jane M.

*   *   *

BLACKBURN, Simon 1944-

PERSONAL: Born July, 1944, in England; son of Cuthbert Walter and Edna (Walton) Blackburn; married Angela Margaret Bowles (an editor), 1968; children: Gwendolen, James. *Education:* Attended Clifton College, Bristol, 1957-62; Trinity College, Cambridge, B.A., 1963; Churchill College, Cambridge, Ph.D., 1969. *Politics:* "Middle." *Hobbies and other interests:* Mountaineering, photography, sailing.

ADDRESSES: Home—313 Woodhaven Rd., Chapel Hill, NC 27514. *Office*—Faculty of Philosophy, University of Cambridge, Sidgwick Ave., Cambridge, CB3 9DA, England. *E-mail*—swb24@cam.ac.uk.

CAREER: Oxford University, Pembroke College, Oxford, England, fellow and tutor in philosophy, 1969-90; University of North Carolina, Chapel Hill, Edna J. Koury Distinguished Professor of Philosophy, beginning 1990; University of Cambridge, Cambridge, England, professor of philosophy. Adjunct professor, Australian National University, Canberra, 1993-2003. Visiting appointments at the University of Melbourne, the University of British Columbia, Oberlin College, Princeton University, Ohio State University, and the Universidad Autonomia de Mexico. Churchill College junior research fellow, 1967-69; Pembroke College fellow, 1969-90; Trinity College fellow; British Academy fellow, 2001—.

WRITINGS:

Reason and Prediction, Cambridge University Press (Cambridge, England), 1973.

(Editor) *Meaning, Reference, and Necessity,* Cambridge University Press (Cambridge, England), 1975.

Spreading the Word: Groundings in the Philosophy of Language, Oxford University Press (New York, NY), 1984.

Knowledge, Truth, and Reliability, Longwood, 1986.

Essays in Quasi-Realism, Oxford University Press (New York, NY), 1993.

The Oxford Dictionary of Philosophy, Oxford University Press (New York, NY), 1994.

Ruling Passions: A Theory of Practical Reasoning, Oxford University Press (New York, NY), 1998.

(Editor, with Keith Simmons) *Truth,* Oxford University Press (New York, NY), 1999.

Think: A Compelling Introduction to Philosophy, Oxford University Press (New York, NY), 1999.

Being Good: An Introduction to Ethics, Oxford University Press (New York, NY), 2001.

Ethics: A Very Short Introduction, Oxford University Press (New York, NY), 2003.

Lust (part of "The Seven Deadly Sins"series), Oxford University Press (New York, NY), 2004.

Liberalism, Religion, and the Sources of Value (Lindley lecture series), Department of Philosophy, University of Kansas (Lawrence, KS), 2005.

Truth: A Guide for the Perplexed, Oxford University Press (New York, NY), 2005.

Editor, *Mind,* 1984-90.

SIDELIGHTS: Simon Blackburn's *The Oxford Dictionary of Philosophy* has been praised by numerous reviewers as an engrossing book to read, as well as a valuable and notably thorough reference work for students of philosophy and anyone else interested in general intellectual movements. The author, an esteemed professor of philosophy, "operates in the Anglo-American analytic philosophical tradition, as opposed to the existentialist or phenomenological traditions of Europe," noted one *Booklist* reviewer.

The Oxford Dictionary of Philosophy contains nearly 3,000 entries, including mini-biographies of some 500 notable individuals from Plato and Thomas Aquinas to more modern individuals such as Nietzsche and Albert Einstein. Baffling philosophical terms such as "the Dirty Hands Argument" and "Wittgenstein's Beetle in the Box" are also illuminated in a "concise, focused" manner, according to the *Booklist* contributor. The origins of Eastern and Western philosophy are thoroughly discussed, as are more unusual topics such as philosophical insights or approaches to dreams, love, and biology. "Blackburn writes in an interesting and easy-to-follow style," concluded the reviewer.

Blackburn has also authored the philosophy primer *Think: A Compelling Introduction to Philosophy.* In it, Blackburn familiarizes readers with famous figures in philosophy and their ideas about knowledge, truth, morality, destiny, logic, free will, religion, sensory perception, identity, and goodness, among other topics. He explains philosophical concepts by offering readers simple analogies. Gilbert Taylor, contributor to *Booklist,* felt that *Think* is "unintimidating" and "written with exemplary concision and with conviction that philosophy needn't be an ethereal subject, alienated from practical concerns." *Library Journal* contributor Leon H. Brody observed: "To read this book is to sit down with an engaging, highly learned conversationalist."

In a contribution to the Oxford University Press series "The Seven Deadly Sins," Blackburn argues in his book *Lust* that sexual lust has been historically misrepresented as a sin. For this error, Blackburn blames historical Christian figures for associating lust with guilt, as well as psychologist Sigmund Freud and philosopher Jean Paul Sartre for creating a false understanding of lust. Blackburn feels that lust is essential and enjoyable, and he concludes by categorizing it as a virtue rather than a sin.

In a review of *Lust* for the *Library Journal,* Gary P. Gillum wrote that Blackburn "amuses us with his provocative defense of lust," commenting, "While religious conservatives could regard Blackburn's *Lust* as outrageous, it thoughtfully balances the other books in the series." Indeed, some religious-minded readers found the book to be invalid. W. Jay Wood, contributor to *Books & Culture,* praised the author as "a prolific writer . . ., an outstanding essayist, and an insightful reviewer of books whose sparkling prose customarily displays philosophical skill and evident wit." However, Wood felt that while "*Lust* doesn't lack in stylistic grace and wit . . . its ground note is a smirking

satisfaction with its own provocations." Wood went on to warn that "Christians . . . need to think carefully to determine when healthy sexual desires and amorous inclinations veer off into unhealthiness and sin. Unfortunately, they'll get little or no help . . . [from] Blackburn's *Lust.*" On the other hand, a *Publishers Weekly* reviewer wrote: "Because lust is broadly condoned in our culture, most readers will find that Blackburn's condescension comes across quite sympathetically." The reviewer depicted Blackburn as a "witty writer," praising the author for being "particularly adept at pitting temporally disparate thinkers . . . against each other."

Published in 2005, Blackburn's book *Truth: A Guide for the Perplexed* examines the scientific, reason-based definitions of truth, tracing the history of its philosophy since ancient times and contesting many theories of some of the world's most revered philosophers. He encourages readers to look not to philosophical figures such as Nietzsche for the truth, but instead to seek truth in the personal judgments and assessments that facilitate everyday life. Blackburn does not disavow absolutist and relativist philosophies, but rather finds a common ground between the two, a place where truth emerges out of individual actions. While *New Statesman* contributor Edward Skidelsky agreed with the author that "we must not let our confidence be sapped by the 'aprés-truth chit-chat' of coffee-house intellectuals," Skidelsky further commented that the author is "over-optimistic . . . in his assumption that our intellectual practices are in themselves perfectly healthy, that the virus of doubt enters only from without." Nonetheless, one *Publishers Weekly* contributor commented: "Blackburn considers truth 'the most exciting and engaging issue in the whole of philosophy,' and with wit and erudition, he succeeds in proving that point."

BIOGRAPHICAL AND CRITICAL SOURCES:

PERIODICALS

Booklist, January 15, 1995, review of *The Oxford Dictionary of Philosophy,* p. 962; October 1, 1999, Gilbert Taylor, review of *Think: A Compelling Introduction to Philosophy,* p. 309; February 1, 2004, Ray Olson, review of *Lust,* p. 936.

Books & Culture, May-June, 2005, W. Jay Wood, "The 'Virtue' of Lust?," pp. 18-19.

Bookseller, February 4, 2005, review of *Truth: A Guide for the Perplexed,* p. 37.

Cambridge Quarterly, December, 2001, Michael Bell, review of *Ruling Passions: A Theory of Practical Reasoning,* pp. 363-366.

Ethics, July, 2001, Russell Shafer-Landau, review of *Ruling Passions,* p. 799.

Globe & Mail (Toronto, Ontario, Canada), May 20, 2000, G.J. Dalcourt, review of *Think,* p. D5; June 23, 2001, review of *Being Good: An Introduction to Ethics,* p. D2; February 14, 2004, "Lust Horizons," p. D4; July 30, 2005, "That's So True . . . Isn't It?," p. D6.

Harper's, January, 2005, Arthur Krystal, "The Pages of Sin: Indulging in the Seven Deadlies," review of *Lust,* pp. 96-101.

International Philosophical Quarterly, September, 2000, Corey W. Beals, review of *Ruling Passions,* p. 402; June, 2002, review of *Being Good,* pp. 262-265.

Journal of American Culture, September, 2004, Marshall Fishwick, review of *Lust,* pp. 344-345.

Kirkus Reviews, May 15, 2001, review of *Being Good,* p. 718; December 1, 2003, review of *Lust,* p. 1400.

Library Journal, November 1, 1994, p. 66; September 15, 1999, Leon H. Brody, review of *Think,* p. 86; February 15, 2004, Gary P. Gillum, review of *Lust,* p. 131; May 15, 2005, Leon H. Brody, review of *Truth,* p. 121.

Mind, April, 2001, Mark Sainsbury, review of *Think,* pp. 430-432; December, 2001, Max Kolbel, review of *Ruling Passions,* pp. 373-380.

New Scientist, December 15, 2001, review of *Think,* p. 51.

New Statesman, May 23, 2005, Edward Skidelsky, "Why Practice Doesn't Make Perfect," review of *Truth,* pp. 48-49.

New Yorker, August 13, 2001, review of *Being Good,* p. 78.

New York Times Book Review, July 24, 2005, Anthony Gottlieb, "The Truth Wars," review of *Truth,* p. 20(L).

Philosophical Quarterly, January, 2001, Bruce Russell, review of *Ruling Passions,* pp. 110-114.

Philosophical Review, October, 2000, Michael E. Bratman, review of *Ruling Passions,* p. 586.

Philosophy, July, 2000, Piers Benn, review of *Ruling Passions,* pp. 454-458.

Publishers Weekly, June 11, 2001, review of *Being Good,* p. 73; January 19, 2004, review of *Lust,* p. 65; May 16, 2005, review of *Truth,* p. 48.

Religious Studies Review, October, 1999, review of *Ruling Passions,* p. 394.

Res Publica, spring, 2000, Phillip Stratton-Lake, review of *Ruling Passions,* pp. 117-125.

School Library Journal, May, 1995, p. 137.

Skeptical Inquirer, September-October, 2005, review of *Truth,* p. 54.

Time, October 4, 1999, Walter Isaacson, review of *Think,* p. 108.

Times Higher Education Supplement, February 19, 1999, Alex Klaushofer, review of *Ruling Passions,* p. 38; September 14, 2001, Mary Midgely, review of *Being Good,* p. 27.

Times Literary Supplement, June 25, 1999, Samuel Scheffler, review of *Ruling Passions,* p. 6; April 27, 2001, Maximillian De Gaynesford, review of *Think,* p. 31; July 6, 2001, Adam Morton, review of *Being Good,* pp. 3-4.

ONLINE

University of Cambridge, Department of Philosophy Web site, http://www.phil.cam.ac.uk/ (October 25, 2005), author profile.*

*   *   *

BOELTS, Maribeth 1964-

PERSONAL: Born January 19, 1964, in Waterloo, IA; daughter of Gerald Clifford (a machinist) and Dorothy Angela (a registered nurse; maiden name, Shimek) Condon; married Darwin Dale Boelts (a firefighter), August 1, 1983; children: three. *Education:* University of Northern Iowa, B.A., 1987; Hawkeye Institute of Technology, emergency medical technician certification, 1988. *Politics:* Democrat. *Religion:* Christian Reformed. *Hobbies and other interests:* Reading, exercise, spending time with husband and children.

ADDRESSES: Home—3815 Clearview Dr., Cedar Falls, IA 50613. *E-mail*—maribeth@cfu.net.

CAREER: Author. St. John/St. Nicholas School, Evansdale, IA, preschool teacher, 1988-91, has also worked as a substitute teacher; *Waterloo Courier,* Waterloo, IA, freelance feature writer, 1992-94.

MEMBER: Society of Children's Book Writers and Illustrators.

WRITINGS:

FICTION

With My Mom, with My Dad (also see below), Pacific Press (Boise, ID), 1992.

Tornado, Paulist Press (Mahwah, NJ), 1993.

Grace and Joe, Albert Whitman (Morton Grove, IL), 1994.

Lullaby Babes, Albert Whitman (Morton Grove, IL), 1994.

Summer's End, illustrated by Ellen Kandoian, Houghton Mifflin (Boston, MA), 1995.

Big Daddy, Frog Wrestler, illustrated by Benrei Huang, Albert Whitman (Morton Grove, IL), 2000.

Lullaby Lullabook, illustrated by Bruce Whatley, HarperFestival (New York, NY), 2002.

The Sloths Get a Pet, illustrated by Jan Gerardi, Random House (New York, NY), 2003.

Looking for Sleepy, illustrated by Bernadette Pons, Albert Whitman (Morton Grove, IL), 2004.

When It's the Last Day of School, illustrated by Hanako Wakiyama, Putnam (New York, NY), 2004.

The Firefighters' Thanksgiving, illustrated by Terry Widener, Putnam (New York, NY), 2004.

"LITTLE BUNNY" SERIES

Dry Days, Wet Nights, Albert Whitman (Morton Grove, IL), 1994.

Little Bunny's Preschool Countdown, illustrated by Kathy Parkinson, Albert Whitman (Morton Grove, IL), 1996.

Little Bunny's Cool Tool Set, illustrated by Kathy Parkinson, Albert Whitman (Morton Grove, IL), 1997.

Little Bunny's Pacifier Plan, illustrated by Kathy Parkinson, Albert Whitman (Morton Grove, IL), 1999.

You're a Brother, Little Bunny!, illustrated by Kathy Parkinson, Albert Whitman (Morton Grove, IL), 2001.

NONFICTION

(With husband, Darwin Boelts) *Kids to the Rescue!: First Aid Techniques for Kids,* Parenting Press (Seattle, WA), 1992, revised edition, illustrated by Marina Megale, Parenting Press (Seattle, WA), 2003.

A Kid's Guide to Staying Safe on the Streets, PowerKids Press (New York, NY), 1997.

A Kid's Guide to Staying Safe in the Water, PowerKids Press (New York, NY), 1997.

A Kid's Guide to Staying Safe on Bikes, PowerKids Press (New York, NY), 1997.

A Kid's Guide to Staying Safe at School, PowerKids Press (New York, NY), 1997.

A Kid's Guide to Staying Safe at Playgrounds, PowerKids Press (New York, NY), 1997.

A Kid's Guide to Staying Safe around Fire, PowerKids Press (New York, NY), 1997.

"HELPING KIDS HEAL" SERIES

Sometimes I'm Afraid: A Book about Fear, illustrated by Cheri Bladholm, Zonderkidz (Grand Rapids, MI), 2004.

Sarah's Grandma Goes to Heaven: A Book about Grief, illustrated by Cheri Bladholm, Zonderkidz (Grand Rapids, MI), 2004.

With My Mom, with My Dad, illustrated by Cheri Bladholm, Zonderkidz (Grand Rapids, MI), 2004.

Why Did You Bring Home a New Baby?, illustrated by Cheri Bladholm, Zonderkidz (Grand Rapids, MI), 2005.

SIDELIGHTS: Maribeth Boelts is the author of a number of works for children, including picture books such as *When It's the Last Day of School* and *Big Daddy, Frog Wrestler,* and nonfiction titles such as *Kids to the Rescue!: First Aid Techniques for Kids,* cowritten with her husband, Darwin Boelts, a firefighter. The mother of three children, Boelts often draws on her experiences as a parent for inspiration.

A former preschool teacher, Boelts once explained her decision to write children's books: "I grew up in a family of readers, spending long hours at the Waterloo Public Library, filling my backpack every Saturday with Beverly Cleary, Laura Ingalls Wilder, and *Boy's Life* magazine (much more exciting, I thought, than anything out for girls at the time.) The writing joined the reading when I was in first grade, and from that [first] poem on, I was hooked on words. I continued to write through high school and into college, but as a twenty-year-old married college student with a newborn baby, pursuing an actual writing career seemed like a frivolous dream. I needed a job, and because I liked kids and had always liked school, teaching seemed a reasonable choice. After three years of teaching, however, I realized that the writing, like an impatient child, wouldn't wait. I quit my job, taking with me a file folder of ideas from the children I taught and the two young children I had at home. I wrote a few really bad children's stories, received a lot of rejections, did some more research, spent hours reading children's books, and then wrote some more. Eventually, I got some good news from a publisher, and that was all I needed for fuel."

Shortly after publishing her debut work, Boelts was hired to write *Kids to the Rescue!*, a first aid book for children. "It was a great fit for me," Boelts stated on the Parenting Press Web site. "I took the Emergency Medical Technician certification course at my local community college and worked on *Kids to the Rescue!* with my husband, who was completing paramedic training for his new job with the fire department." Boelts has since published several other easy-to-read advice books for children, including *A Kid's Guide to Staying Safe in the Water* and *A Kid's Guide to Staying Safe on Bikes*.

Boelts's "Little Bunny" series of picture books for toddlers explores familiar family situations. In *Little Bunny's Pacifier Plan*, the title character attempts to wean himself from his source of comfort. "The situation is never defined as a problem, just a normal part of growing up," remarked Carolyn Phelan in *Booklist*. The arrival of a new sibling is the subject of *You're a Brother, Little Bunny!* Little Bunny believes he is well prepared for baby Kale, but the newborn's constant crying and smelly diapers prove to be quite a challenge. "Boelts has a good ear for the feelings of a preschooler," Phelan observed.

In *Big Daddy, Frog Wrestler*, a young frog named Curtis discovers his father had once been a champion grappler. Though Curtis is elated when his father is offered a world tour, Big Daddy quickly realizes that he prefers time with his family to life on the road. "The father-son relationship glows with affection," noted Gay Lynn Van Vleck in the *School Library Journal*. An energetic class clown decides to rein in his antics in *When It's the Last Day of School*, "a story that radiates the lighter side—or anyway more rascally side—of schooling," according to a critic in *Kirkus Reviews*. James is on his best behavior, stifling burps, thanking a grumpy lunch lady, and earning a gold star. As the last bell rings, "James literally explodes off the

final page, ready for a long, hot summer of frolicking with his friends," wrote *School Library Journal* contributor Lisa Gangemi Kropp.

Boelts again used her knowledge of rescue workers in the rhyming picture book *The Firefighters' Thanksgiving*. On Thanksgiving Day, fireman Lou volunteers to cook a big meal for his coworkers, but his plans are interrupted by several calls to duty. When Lou has to be hospitalized after fighting a blaze, the grateful people he helped that day pitch in to deliver a wonderful feast to the station. A contributor in *Kirkus Reviews* called the work "a satisfying holiday story with an unusual perspective."

BIOGRAPHICAL AND CRITICAL SOURCES:

PERIODICALS

Booklist, April 1, 1995, Hazel Rochman, review of *Summer's End*, p. 1422; September 15, 1996, Carolyn Phelan, review of *Little Bunny's Preschool Countdown*, p. 245; September 15, 1997, April Judge, review of *Little Bunny's Cool Tool Set*, p. 239; March 1, 1999, Carolyn Phelan, review of *Little Bunny's Pacifier Plan*, p. 1218; March 1, 2000, Gillian Engberg, review of *Big Daddy, Frog Wrestler*, p. 1249; December 1, 2001, Carolyn Phelan, review of *You're a Brother, Little Bunny!*, p. 647; April 15, 2004, Carolyn Phelan, review of *When It's the Last Day of School*, p. 1445; May 15, 2004, Ilene Cooper, review of *Looking for Sleepy*, p. 1624; August, 2004, Gillian Engberg, review of *The Firefighters' Thanksgiving*, p. 1940.

Kirkus Reviews, September 15, 2001, review of *You're a Brother, Little Bunny!*, p. 1354; January 15, 2004, review of *When It's the Last Day of School*, p. 80; July 1, 2004, review of *The Firefighters' Thanksgiving*, p. 625.

Publishers Weekly, September 27, 2004, review of *The Firefighters' Thanksgiving*, p. 59.

School Library Journal, March, 2000, Gay Lynn Van Vleck, review of *Big Daddy, Frog Wrestler*, p. 189; January, 2002, Doris Gebel, review of *You're a Brother, Little Bunny!*, p. 95; April, 2004, G. Alyssa Parkinson, review of *Looking for Sleepy*, and Lisa Gangemi Kropp, review of *When It's the Last Day of School*, pp. 102-103; January, 2005, James K. Irwin, review of *The Firefighters' Thanksgiving*, p. 86.

ONLINE

Maribeth Boelts Home Page, http://maribethboelts. com (July 15, 2005).
Parenting Press Web site, http://www.parentingpress. com/ (fall, 2002), "Maribeth Boelts Launched Writing Career Three Months into Sabbatical from Teaching."

*　　*　　*

BOGOSIAN, Eric 1953-

PERSONAL: Born April 24, 1953, in Boston, MA; son of Henry and Edwina Bogosian; married Jo Anne Bonney (a graphic designer and theater director), October, 1980; children: Harris Wolf. *Education:* Attended University of Chicago; Oberlin College, B.A., 1976.

ADDRESSES: Home—New York, NY. *Agent*—Philip Rinaldi Public Relations, Lincoln Center Theater, 150 W. 65th St., New York, NY 10023. *E-mail*—blastula1953@yahoo.com.

CAREER: Actor and writer. Cofounder of Woburn Drama Guild, Woburn, MA; director and founder of dance program at the Kitchen in New York, NY. Actor in stage productions, including *Careful Moment, Drinking in America,* 1987, *Talk Radio,* 1988, *Sex, Drugs, and Rock 'n' Roll,* 1990, *SubUrbia,* 1994, *Pounding Nails in the Floor with My Forehead,* 1994, *Griller,* 1998, *Wake Up and Smell the Coffee,* 2000, *Humpty Dumpty,* 2004, *The Worst of Eric Bogosian,* 2005, and *The Last Days of Judas Iscariot,* 2005. Actor in television shows, including *The Twilight Zone, Tales from the Dark Side, Miami Vice, Last Flight Out, Law & Order, The Larry Sanders Show, Witchhunt, A Bright Shining Lie, The Wedding Toast, Beggars and Choosers, Welcome to New York, Blonde, Shot in the Heart, Third Watch, Love Monkey,* and *Crime Story.* Actor in motion pictures, including *Caine Mutiny Court Martial, Talk Radio, Dolores Claiborne, Confessions of a Porn Star, Under Siege 2, Beavis and Butthead Do America* (voice-over), *Deconstructing Harry, Wonderland, Gossip, Ararat,* and *Charlie's Angels: Full Throttle.* Co-creator of television series *High Incident.*

AWARDS, HONORS: Obie Award for playwriting, *Village Voice,* and Drama Desk Award for outstanding solo performance, both 1986, both for *Drinking in America;* Silver Berlin Bear for Outstanding Single Achievement, Berlin International Film Festival, 1989, for *Talk Radio;* Obie Award special citation, 1990, for *Sex, Drugs, and Rock 'n' Roll;* Obie Award for playwriting, 1994, for *Pounding Nails in the Floor with My Forehead;* National Endowment for the Arts theatre residency, 2001; Guggenheim fellowship, 2004.

WRITINGS:

STAGE PLAYS

Careful Moment, produced in New York, NY, 1977.
Slavery, produced in New York, NY, 1977.
Garden, produced in New York, NY, 1978.
Heaven, Heaven, Heaven, produced at Eventworks (Boston, MA), 1978.
Sheer Heaven, produced in New York, NY, 1980.
That Girl, produced in Chicago, IL, 1981.
Men Inside [and] *Voices of America* (double bill), produced Off-Broadway, 1982.
Advocate, produced in New York, NY, 1983.
FunHouse, produced Off-Broadway, 1983.
(With Michael Zwack) *I Saw the Seven Angels,* produced in New York, NY, 1984.
Drinking in America, (produced Off-Broadway, 1986; also see below), Vintage (New York, NY), 1987.
Talk Radio (produced Off-Broadway, 1987; also see below), Samuel French (New York, NY), 1988.
Sex, Drugs, and Rock 'n' Roll (produced Off-Broadway, 1988; also see below), HarperCollins (New York, NY), 1991.
Pounding Nails in the Floor with My Forehead (produced Off-Broadway, 1994; produced on CD, Blackbird, 1998), Theatre Communications Group (New York, NY), 1994.
SubUrbia (produced at Lincoln Center, New York, NY, 1994; also see below), Theatre Communications Group (New York, NY), 1995.
(With others) *Love's Fire: Seven New Plays Inspired by Shakespearean Sonnets* (produced at Public Theater, New York, NY, 1998), William Morrow (New York, NY), 1998.
Griller, produced at Goodman Theatre, Chicago, IL, 1998.
Wake Up and Smell the Coffee (produced Off-Broadway, 2000), Theatre Communications Group (St. Paul, MN), 2001.
Humpty Dumpty, produced at the McCarter Theater Center, Princeton, NJ, 2002.

The Worst of Eric Bogosian, produced at Freud Playhouse, University of California, Los Angeles, 2002.

Humpty Dumpty and Other Plays, Theatre Communications Group (New York, NY), 2005.

Author of numerous other plays, including *The Ricky Paul Show, The New World, Men Inside,* and *Chasing the Dragon.*

OTHER

Eric Bogosian Takes a Look at Drinking in America (television production; adapted from *Drinking in America*), HBO/Cinemax, 1986.

(With Oliver Stone) *Talk Radio* (screenplay; adapted from Bogosian's play of the same title), Universal, 1988.

Sex, Drugs, and Rock 'n' Roll (screenplay; adapted from Bogosian's play of the same title), Avenue Entertainment, 1991.

Notes from Underground (contains novella *Notes from Underground* and play *Scenes from the New World*), Hyperion (New York, NY), 1993.

The Essential Bogosian, Theatre Communications Group (New York, NY), 1994.

SubUrbia (screenplay; adapted from Bogosian's play of the same title), Castle Rock Entertainment, 1997.

(Author of introduction) *Physiognomy: The Mark Seliger Photographs,* Little, Brown (Boston, MA), 1999.

Mall (novel), Simon & Schuster (New York, NY), 2000.

Wasted Beauty (novel), Simon & Schuster (New York, NY), 2005.

Contributor to periodicals, including *New York Times* and *Esquire.*

SIDELIGHTS: Eric Bogosian is an actor and writer who has garnered acclaim for his various stage productions, including several solo works. After graduating from Oberlin College in 1976, he worked odd jobs at a Westside theater in New York City and then went on to direct dance productions at the Kitchen, a forum for avant-garde works in New York. In 1977 he made his acting and writing debut with *Careful Moment,* a one-man show in which he played a range of characters, including a game-show host and a dancer. Throughout the next several years and into the 1980s, Bogosian developed and performed in similar works, each featuring him as a number of different characters. Among the more memorable of his characterizations, according to some critics, is his portrait of Ricky Paul, a particularly obnoxious comedian who harangues and humiliates his audience.

Bogosian eventually grew weary of performing in his solo, multi-character works, particularly those featuring the exhaustingly abusive Ricky Paul. In the early 1980s he wrote and directed *The New World,* a play in which he appeared, for the first time, with other actors. Bogosian followed *The New World* with another one-man production, *Men Inside,* featuring entirely new characters. That show, in which Bogosian plays a carnival barker and a success-seminar conductor, among others, was his first work to draw substantial attention from the New York press.

In 1983 Bogosian created *FunHouse,* in which he played such characters as a bum, a man with a rubber fetish, and a convicted killer awaiting execution. With this work Bogosian drew further recognition from reviewers. *New York* critic John Simon, though harboring reservations about *FunHouse,* observed that Bogosian possesses "imagination, wit . . . and a good ear for the rumblings of society's underbelly and the burblings of our brain-damaged media." *Dance* reviewer Kevin Grubb noted that Bogosian manages the difficult task of producing "an engrossing, though difficult-to-digest, brand of performance art." Grubb added that Bogosian's unsparing vision—which is sometimes horrific, sometimes humorous—makes him "one of our most important performing artists."

Bogosian impressed critics once again with *Drinking in America,* a fast-paced examination of life's more sordid denizens. In this self-authored production, he performed as a fatuous hippie; a manic, substance-abusing Hollywood agent; an empty-headed young vandal; and a pathetic wino. Frank Rich, in his *New York Times* review, described *Drinking in America* as "a breakneck, hair-raising comic tour of the contemporary American male psyche," while *New York* contributor Simon praised the production as "sardonic and uncompromising social commentary." Most of the skits, Simon added, "are precise, sharp, witty, and disturbing." This work, among Bogosian's most popular, ran Off-Broadway for sixteen weeks and was published in 1987. In addition, it was adapted by Bogosian and broadcast on cable television as *Eric Bogosian Takes a Look at Drinking in America.*

In his next work, the play *Talk Radio,* Bogosian limited himself to one characterization, that of a misanthropic, hyper-energetic radio talk-show host who regularly degrades those listeners foolhardy enough to phone in questions and comments to the show. *Talk Radio* drew the attention of filmmaker Oliver Stone, who collaborated with Bogosian on the script for a broader, multi-character film version that retained Bogosian in the lead role. Some reviewers thought the adaptation overwhelming in nature but unenlightening in effect, but other critics found it a bold, invigorating portrait of haywire America. *Washington Post* contributor Michael Wilmington, for instance, deemed it a "savagely audacious" work that "makes you laugh, makes you mad, and keeps you edgily watching for the killers in the shadows."

Sex, Drugs, and Rock 'n' Roll, Bogosian's next solo stage work, features the actor-writer's familiar gallery of street people and introduces several others, notably a blowhard rock star who seems to be exploiting the save-the-rainforest groundswell to further his own stardom, and a spiteful old man railing against the Industrial Revolution's repercussions of widespread, life-threatening pollution. Bogosian ended his performance with what *New York Times* reviewer Frank Rich described as a "chilling soliloquy," one in which a former hippie argues that the United States has become a nation enslaved by computers and other technological devices. Rich called *Sex, Drugs, and Rock 'n' Roll* a "brilliant show, [Bogosian's] funniest and scariest yet," and he praised Bogosian as "a great talent, a chameleon actor and penetrating social observer."

Pounding Nails in the Floor with My Forehead, another solo work, features Bogosian playing several bizarre and disturbing characters, including a drug dealer, a bigoted suburbanite, a platitude-mouthing pop psychologist, an arrogant doctor, and an ordinary man whose complacency is shattered by televised images of people starving in Africa. The production, like many of Bogosian's works, was directed by his wife, Jo Anne Bonney, who also served as dramaturge, with input into "what actually happens in the tone of the show," Bogosian told *Back Stage* interviewer Hettie Lynne Hurtes. William A. Henry III, reviewing the show for *Time,* called Bogosian "the subtlest and most

daring" of solo performers. *Back Stage* critic David Lefkowitz pointed to Bogosian's "enthralling stage presence," but saw a "creeping familiarity" in the script. "Are Bogosian's losers all starting to sound the same?" asked Lefkowitz in his review. In addition to being performed on stage and published, *Pounding Nails in the Floor with My Forehead* was Bogosian's first performance work to be produced in a CD version.

Bogosian did not appear in his play *SubUrbia,* about aimless young people in a blue-collar suburb who spend most of their time hanging out in a convenience-store parking lot, eating junk food, drinking beer, and using recreational drugs. The promise of some excitement, however, comes with the return to town of a friend who has achieved some degree of fame, if not the top echelon of success, as a rock musician. When he arrives, the characters are drawn into sexual power games and violent struggles. *New Republic* contributor Robert Brustein found "structural imperfections" in the play but called it "a considerably more ambitious effort" than Bogosian's one-man shows. Bogosian is a "potentially strong, gritty playwright," Brustein added. *Back Stage* correspondent David Sheward deemed Bogosian's work "promising," although he suggested that the characters were underdeveloped. The film version of *SubUrbia* was released in 1997. John Simon, critiquing it for the *National Review,* termed the material "theatrical, not cinematic." He explained: "Transposed to the screen, it works about as well as a poem in a prose translation." *Nation* commentator Stuart Klawans, though, praised Bogosian's screenplay as being "well constructed in plot and frequently sharp in its dialogue."

Bogosian returned to solo performance work with *Wake Up and Smell the Coffee,* portraying characters that include a self-help guru, an unscrupulous film producer, and a fawning actor reflecting on his discomfort with being a celebrity. The show is "a commentary on two recent trends in American culture, a taste for pop spirituality and the quest for lots and lots of money, and it's strongest when it's tackling those two subjects directly and making connections between them," remarked Charles Isherwood in *Variety.* Isherwood found "plenty of bitter truth" in the monologues, but thought "the unremitting bleakness of Bogosian's work here grows somewhat monotonous." However, the critic noted that no matter what the material, "Bogosian is an amazingly magnetic live performer."

Bogosian's first novel, *Mall,* features the quirky characters one might expect from the playwright, such as a businessman with a penchant for voyeurism, a homemaker looking for sexual fulfillment, and a drug-addled teenager. One night at their local mall, they experience no ordinary shopping trip, but events of shocking violence as a gunman roams the building. In the *New York Times,* Janet Maslin stated that the book's characters "feel as if they need actors to make them complete," while allowing that Bogosian "manages to sketch, propel, and intermingle them with a Satirist's sure hand." *Entertainment Weekly* reviewer L.S. Klepp commented on Bogosian's "merciless, satirical vision" but saw the plot as lacking in credibility. *Mother Jones* contributor Ben Ehrenreich felt Bogosian's subject matter was overly familiar and his writing often cliched, "despite a few sharp, satiric moments." A *Publishers Weekly* critic, though, commended the author for his "droll remarks and dramatic pacing" and termed *Mall* "a typically Bogosian experience—lively and unique." *Library Journal* contributor Jeff Ayers called the book "an entertaining success," with well-conceived characters and effective flashes of humor even in terrifying scenes. Ted Leventhal, writing in *Booklist,* described Bogosian's writing style as "clever, vivid, and infused with very dark humor," and called the novel an "impressive, frightful work."

Bogosian continues to craft works for the stage, including *Humpty Dumpty,* a drama about two upper-class couples caught helpless in a power failure during a vacation in the country, and *The Worst of Eric Bogosian,* a solo piece that reprises some of his older material and adds new sketches. Bogosian also received praise from some critics for his performance as Satan in Stephen Adly Guirgis's 2005 play *The Last Days of Judas Iscariot.*

Bogosian's 2005 novel *Wasted Beauty* reflects the sordid underpinnings not only of urban life in New York, but of rural and suburban lifestyles as well. The novel's characters include a fresh-faced farm girl who loses her balance when she becomes a supermodel, the girl's desperate brother, and a seemingly happy married family man who meets the siblings during a hospital visit. A *Kirkus Reviews* contributor called the work a "dark, raunchy second novel . . . about sex and drugs in the big city." The reviewer concluded that the last third of the book is "gripping." A *Publishers Weekly* reviewer similarly characterized the novel as "a vicarious walk on the wild side," while praising the "great guilty pleasure of a story line." In the *Library Journal,* Bob Lunn likened *Wasted Beauty* to the nihilistic works of Bret Easton Ellis and Chuck

Palahniuk, noting that Bogosian's plot "captures all the fascination of watching a train wreck unfold."

On his Web site, Bogosian made clear that he does not consider himself a performance artist. He called himself "a writer and actor who spent time around the art scene." He considers himself "a creator of monologues and solo shows . . . a playwright."

BIOGRAPHICAL AND CRITICAL SOURCES:

BOOKS

Contemporary Literary Criticism, Volume 45, Gale (Detroit, MI), 1987.
Newsmakers 90, Gale (Detroit, MI), 1990.

PERIODICALS

Art in America, April, 1986, pp. 189-190.
Back Stage, October 29, 1993, Hettie Lynne Hurtes, "Eric Bogosian Hits Hard by 'Driving Nails,'" p. 6W; February 25, 1994, David Lefkowitz, review of *Pounding Nails in the Floor with My Forehead,* p. 48; May 27, 1994, David Sheward, review of *SubUrbia* (play), p. 32; May 12, 2000, David A. Rosenberg, review of *Wake Up and Smell the Coffee,* p. 44.
Back Stage West, February 14, 2002, Scott Proudfit, review of *The Worst of Eric Bogosian,* p. 11.
Book, November, 2000, Don McLeese, review of *Mall,* p. 75.
Booklist, October 1, 2000, Ted Leventhal, review of *Mall,* p. 323; March 1, 2005, Jerry Eberle, review of *Wasted Beauty,* p. 1101.
Chicago Tribune, May 8, 1987; June 28, 1987; December 20, 1988; December 22, 1988.
Daily Variety, March 8, 2005, Robert Hofler, "Sinners & 'Scoundrels,'" p. 15.
Dance, January, 1984, Kevin Grubb, review of *FunHouse,* pp. 78-83.
Entertainment Weekly, December 1, 2000, L. S. Klepp, review of *Mall,* p. 92.
Kirkus Reviews, January 15, 2005, review of *Wasted Beauty,* p. 65.
Library Journal, September 15, 2000, Jeff Ayers, review of *Mall,* p. 111; April 1, 2005, Bob Lunn, review of *Wasted Beauty,* p. 83.
Listener, June 16, 1988, p. 34.
Los Angeles Times, April 10, 1985; December 21, 1988.
Los Angeles Times Book Review, July 19, 1987, p. 3.

Mother Jones, November, 2000, Ben Ehrenreich, review of *Mall.*

Nation, March 3, 1997, Stuart Klawans, review of *SubUrbia* (film), p. 35.

National Review, March 10, 1997, John Simon, review of *SubUrbia* (film), p. 53.

New Criterion, June, 2000, Mark Steyn, "Waddling toward the Edge," p. 41.

New Republic, June 27, 1994, Robert Brustein, review of *SubUrbia* (play), p. 28.

Newsweek, March 24, 1986, p. 69; February 16, 1997, Jack Kroll, review of *SubUrbia* (film), p. 66.

New York, October 31, 1983, p. 60; February 3, 1986, p. 57; December 12, 1988, pp. 50-56.

New Yorker, February 3, 1986, p. 85.

New York Times, July 8, 1983; September 30, 1983; January 21, 1986, p. 15; July 30, 1987; December 21, 1988; February 4, 1990; February 9, 1990; November 20, 2000, Janet Maslin, "Attention, Shoppers: Gallows Humor."

New York Times Magazine, May 24, 1987.

People, May 16, 2005, Jonathan Durbin, review of *Wasted Beauty,* p. 60.

Publishers Weekly, October 2, 2000, review of *Mall,* p. 57; March 7, 2005, review of *Wasted Beauty,* p. 48.

Rolling Stone, February 9, 1989, pp. 95-97.

Time, February 15, 1994, William A. Henry III, review of *Pounding Nails in the Floor with My Forehead,* p. 67; March 7, 1994, W.A. Henry III, "One and Only," p. 66.

Tribune Books (Chicago, IL), January 6, 1991.

Variety, May 8, 2000, Charles Isherwood, review of *Wake Up and Smell the Coffee,* p. 88; April 15, 2002, Robert L. Daniels, review of *Humpty Dumpty,* p. 37.

Washington Post, December 20, 1988; December 21, 1988; December 23, 1988.

ONLINE

Eric Bogosian's Home Page, http://www.ericbogosian.com (October 4, 2005).*

*   *   *

BORSOOK, Eve 1929-

PERSONAL: Born October 3, 1929 in Toronto, Ontario, Canada; daughter of Henry and Lisl Hummel. *Education:* Vassar College, B.A.; New York University, M.A.; Courtauld Institute of Art, London, Ph.D. *Hobbies and other interests:* Mural conservation, pottery, arts and crafts, reverse paintings on glass, history of glass techniques.

ADDRESSES: Office—Villa I Tatti, Via di Vincigliata 26, Florence 50135, Italy.

CAREER: Art historian, teacher and writer.

WRITINGS:

The Mural Painters of Tuscany, from Cimabue to Andrea del Sarto, Phaidon Press (London, England), 1960, 2nd edition, Oxford University Press (New York, NY), 1980.

(With Leonetto Tintori) *Giotto: The Peruzzi Chapel,* Harry N. Abrams (New York, NY), 1965.

Ambroglio Lorenzetti, Sadea/Sansoni (Florence, Italy), 1966.

The Companion Guide to Florence, Harper & Row (New York, NY), 1966, 8th edition, Companion Guides (Rochester, NY), 1998.

Gli affreschi di Montesiepi, EDAM (Florence, Italy), 1969.

(With Johannes Offerhaus) *Francesco Sassetti and Ghirlandaio at Santa Trinita, Florence: History and Legend in a Renaissance Chapel,* Davaco Publishers (Doornspijk, Netherlands), 1981.

(Editor, with A. Morrogh, F. Superbi Gioffredi, and P. Morselli) *Renaissance Studies in Honor of Craig Hugh Smyth,* two volumes, Barbéra (Florence, Italy), 1985.

(Editor, with Fiorella Superbi Gioffredi) *Tecnica e stile: esempi di pittura murale del Rinascimento italiano* (papers from Harvard Center for Italian Renaissance Studies convention), two volumes, Silvana (Milan, Italy), 1986.

Messages in Mosaic: The Royal Programmes of Norman Sicily, 1130-1187, Oxford University Press (New York, NY), 1990.

(Editor, with Fiorella Superbi Gioffredi) *Italian Altarpieces, 1250-1550: Function and Design,* Clarendon Press (New York, NY), 1994.

(Editor, with Fiorella Gioffredi Superbi and Giovanni Pagliarulo, and author of introduction) *Medieval Mosaics: Light, Color, Materials,* Silvana Editoriale (Milan, Italy), 2000.

(Coeditor and coauthor of introduction) *L'oro dei poveri: La paglia nell'arredo liturgico e nelle immagini devozionali dell'Italia centrale fra il 1670e il 1870,* Polistampa (Florence, Italy), 2000.

Contributor to books, including *Festschrift: Ulrich Middeldorf,* edited by A. Kosegarten and P. Tigler, de Gruyter (Berlin, Germany), 1968; *Art the Ape of Nature: Studies in Honor of H.W. Janson,* edited by M. Barasch and L. F. Sandler, Harry N. Abrams (New York, NY), 1981; *Santa Maria del Fiore: The Cathedral and Its Sculpture,* edited by M. Haines, Cadmo (Fiesole, Italy), 2001. Contributor of articles and reviews to periodicals around the world, including *Portfolio and Art News Annual, Journal of the Society of Architectural Historians, Arte medievale, Studi Medievali,* and *Burlington.*

SIDELIGHTS: Art historian Eve Borsook has devoted her professional life to the study of murals and mosaics from the Middle Ages and the Italian Renaissance. She has written books on individual painters as well as matters of technique, function, and design. She has also edited volumes of scholarly essays. In addition, her guidebook to the city of Florence has remained in print for over thirty years and has undergone eight editions to date.

Borsook's first published book, *The Mural Painters of Tuscany, from Cimabue to Andrea del Sarto,* was a revision of her doctoral dissertation. This book was welcomed as a groundbreaking survey of mural painting and was revered as basically the sole comprehensive study on the subject until flooding in Florence in 1966 threatened to damage the city's artistic heritage and new interest arose in preserving mural art. Indeed, the restorations that took place after this flood enabled Borsook to conduct new observations and research that culminated in the book's extensive enlargement and revision in 1980. Though the book's first edition had been highly praised, the revised edition received even more lavish accolades. A *Choice* reviewer commented that the book "should be made available to every student and scholar," and praised Borsook's exceptionally thorough, scholarly, and succinct catalog notes. In *Apollo,* however, reviewer Cecil Gould found that Borsook's comments on Leonardo's "Last Supper" suggested that she was "rather out of her depth" on this subject; he also pointed out some factual errors. Although he criticized Borsook for failing to include a detailed discussion of the technical problem of the "eye level," he concluded that the book was informative and thorough on several matters and "is probably the most convenient work of reference now available."

Before and after *The Mural Painters of Tuscany,* Borsook worked with Leonetto Tintori (between 1952 and 1982) on *Giotto: The Peruzzi Chapel,* a study of the murals in the Peruzzi Chapel in Florence's Santa Croce church. A *Kirkus Reviews* critic admired the historical context provided in the book and its analysis of the restoration of individual murals. With her reputation by this time established as an expert in Florentine art, Borsook was next asked to write a new guidebook to the city. *The Companion Guide to Florence* received mixed reviews. A *Choice* contributor praised Borsook's aesthetic sensibility, insight, and warmth, and observed that each chapter contained "a useful summary of monuments." But the reviewer also noted the book's "utterly romantic and adulatory" tone and its disorganized structure. In *Books and Bookmen,* a critic called the book an excellent companion guide distinguished by its "taste." Marghanita Laski, however, wrote in the *Listener* that *The Companion Guide to Florence* was "disappointing." Though she found the book adequately informative, she observed that it remained "somehow incapable of rousing enthusiasm." A *Times Literary Supplement* critic dismissed Borsook's organization as "thoroughly unpractical" and her information "inaccurate" and "careless." The critic pointed out several mistakes in the walking and biking tours Borsook described in the book and criticized the inclusion of personal encounters as an embarrassment. The critic concluded that, though the book was likely to be popular, tourists "will not be greatly aided in choosing what to look at or in understanding what they see" by the work.

Though *The Companion Guide to Florence* was not an unqualified critical success, Borsook's more specialized works met with more consistent praise. Her study of the murals in the Sassetti chapel of St. Francis in Florence's Vallombrosan church, *Francesco Sassetti and Ghirlandaio at Santa Trinita, Florence: History and Legend in a Renaissance Chapel,* written with Johannes Offerhaus, according to *Burlington* contributor Amanda Lillie, "is not the comprehensive monograph" that it could have been but acknowledged its informative appendix of new documents and its "well-chosen" and well-reproduced illustrations.

In *Messages in Mosaic: The Royal Programmes of Norman Sicily, 1130-1187,* Borsook departed from the Renaissance and mural painting to consider the medieval mosaics at Cefalu, the Cappella Palatina at Palermo, and Monreale. These were created during the rule of the Norman kings in Sicily, and Borsook argues that the mosaic cycles were created "to legitimize and fortify a new monarchy" over the Papacy. Paul Williamson in *Apollo* found this book "consistently thought-provoking" but took issue with several of Borsook's theories, commenting that the author "has both gone too far and not far enough in her interpretations." Williamson was particularly disappointed that Borsook chose not to discuss in detail the mosaics of the Martorana, which contain a panel that shows Roger II being crowned by Christ—a subject Williamson believed would shed light on Borsook's thesis about the monarchy's claims. While *Choice* reviewer E. Kosmer found the book "densely written" and "often difficult to follow," the critic also admired its scope and wealth of information.

Both *Burlington* contributor George Zarnecki and *Times Literary Supplement* reviewer Raleigh Trevelyan found Borsook's arguments in *Messages in Mosaic* provocative and persuasive. Calling the author's analysis of individual works "masterly," Zarnecki called Borsook's study "a stimulating book, full of challenging and, on the whole, convincing ideas." Trevelyan, too, enjoyed what he called the book's sometimes "controversial" but well-reasoned and well-documented arguments. And both reviewers particularly noted Borsook's insights on the mosaics' theological symbolism of light.

In addition to her own monographs, Borsook has also served as editor for two collections of symposium papers. *Tecnica e stile: esempi di pittura murale del Rinascimento italiano,* edited with Fiorella Superbi Gioffredi, presents papers from a conference sponsored by the Harvard University Center for Italian Renaissance Studies in May 1983. Contributors included art historians, curators, and fresco restoration professionals. John Pope-Hennessy observed in *Apollo* that the collection's "careful editing" and excellent photographs make it "an eye-opening book." Borsook again worked with Superbi Gioffredi in editing *Italian Altarpieces, 1250-1550: Function and Design,* a collection of eight papers from a symposium held at Villa I Tatti in 1988. *London Review of Books* critic Nicholas Penny observed that the book "is little more than the sum of its parts," but added that its surfeit of information would make it a welcome study for historians of the Renaissance.

BIOGRAPHICAL AND CRITICAL SOURCES:

BOOKS

Borsook, Eve, *Messages in Mosaic: The Royal Programmes of Norman Sicily, 1130-1187,* Oxford University Press, 1990.

Osti, Ornella Francisco, editor, *Mosaics of Friendship: Studies in Art and History for Eve Borsook,* Centro Di (Florence, Italy), 1999.

PERIODICALS

Apollo, July, 1981, Cecil Gould, review of *The Mural Painters of Tuscany, from Cimabue to Andrea del Sarto,* p. 68; March, 1987, John Pope-Hennessy, review of *Tecnica e stile: esempi di pittura murale del Rinascimento italiano,* pp. 240-241; December, 1990, p. 433.

Books and Bookmen, August, 1973, review of *The Companion Guide to Florence,* p. 140.

Burlington, Amanda Lillie, review of *Francesco Sassetti and Ghirlandaio at Santa Trinita, Florence: History and Legend in a Renaissance Chapel;* May, 1984, pp. 293-295; February, 1990, George Zarnecki, review of *Messages in Mosaic: The Royal Programmes of Norman Sicily, 1130-1187,* pp. 132-133; March, 1991, pp. 198-199.

Choice, April, 1967, review of *The Companion Guide to Florence,* p. 147; October, 1981, review of *The Mural Painters of Tuscany, from Cimabue to Andrea del Sarto,* p. 227; October, 1991, p. 268; May, 1995, p. 1438.

Connoisseur, February, 1982, p. 89.

Kirkus Reviews, July 1, 1965, review of *Giotto: The Peruzzi Chapel,* p. 670.

Listener, January 12, 1967, Marghanita Laski, review of *The Companion Guide to Florence,* p. 64.

London Review of Books, April 6, 1995, Nicholas Penny, review of *Italian Altarpieces, 1250-1550: Function and Design,* p. 17.

Renaissance Quarterly, autumn, 1983, pp. 413-418; summer, 1988, pp. 308-310; winter, 1997, p. 1259.

Times Literary Supplement, July 21, 1966, review of *The Companion Guide to Florence,* p. 630; September 25, 1998, Raleigh Trevelyan, review of *Messages in Mosaic,* p. 32.

*   *   *

BOWEN, Michael 1951-
(Michael Anthony Bowen)

PERSONAL: Born July 16, 1951, in Fort Monroe, VA; son of Harold (a medical photographer) and Judith (an office worker; maiden name, Carter-Waller) Bowen; married Sara Armbruster (a lawyer), August 30, 1975;

children: Rebecca, Christopher, John, Marguerite, James. *Education:* Rockhurst College, A.B. (summa cum laude), 1973; Harvard University, J.D. (cum laude), 1976. *Politics:* Democrat. *Religion:* Roman Catholic.

ADDRESSES: Home—Fox Point, WI. *Office*—Foley & Lardner, 777 East Wisconsin Ave., Ste. 3900, Milwaukee, WI 53202-5367. *E-mail*—mbowen@foley. com.

CAREER: Admitted to the Bars of Wisconsin and the United States Court of Appeals for the Fifth, Seventh, and Tenth Circuits; Foley & Lardner (law firm), Milwaukee, WI, partner, 1976—. Member of Milwaukee Archdiocese Medical Ethics Committee and Wisconsin Right to Life Legal Committee.

MEMBER: St. Thomas More Lawyers' Society, Milwaukee Bar Association, Milwaukee Young Lawyers Association.

AWARDS, HONORS: Award for provision of pro bono legal services, Milwaukee Young Lawyers Association.

WRITINGS:

MYSTERY NOVELS

Badger Game, St. Martin's (New York, NY), 1989.
Fielder's Choice, St. Martin's (New York, NY), 1991.
Act of Faith, St. Martin's (New York, NY), 1993.
The Fourth Glorious Mystery, Branden Publishing (Boston, MA), 2000.

"RICHARD MICHAELSON AND MAJORIE RANDOLPH" SERIES; MYSTERY NOVELS

Washington Deceased, St. Martin's (New York, NY) 1990.
Faithfully Executed, St. Martin's (New York, NY), 1992.
Corruptly Procured, St. Martin's (New York, NY), 1994.
Worst Case Scenario: A Washington, D.C. Mystery, Crown Publishers (New York, NY), 1996.
Collateral Damage, St. Martin's (New York, NY), 1999.

"REP AND MELISSA PENNYWORTH" SERIES; MYSTERY NOVELS

Screenscam, Poisoned Pen Press (Scottsdale, AZ), 2001.
Unforced Error: A Rep and Melissa Pennyworth Mystery, Poisoned Pen Press (Scottsdale, AZ), 2001.

OTHER

(With Gary Marshall and Kay Freeman) *Passing By: The United States and Genocide in Burundi* (monograph), Carnegie Endowment for International Peace (Washington, DC), 1973.
Can't Miss, Harper (New York, NY), 1987.
(With Brian E. Butler) *The Wisconsin Fair Dealership Law,* State Bar of Wisconsin (Madison, WI), 1988, third edition, 2003.
(With Denis Fox) *The Law of Private Companies,* Sweet & Maxwell (London, England), 1991.
Hillary!: How America's First Woman Won the White House (novel), Braden Books (Boston, MA), 2003.

Contributor to law journals, including *Harvard Law Review.*

SIDELIGHTS: Michael Bowen is a practicing lawyer who specializes in commercial litigation and arbitration, and lender liability. In addition to writing legal-related books, he is also the author of a number of mystery novels, many of which draw on his legal and political knowledge. Several novels by Bowen feature Richard Michaelson, a retired Foreign Service diplomat, and his friend Marjorie Randolph. In one title in the series, *Worst Case Scenario: A Washington D.C. Mystery,* Michaelson investigates the murder of a young woman retaining a piece of paper that has the potential to cause a major political scandal in Washington, DC. While Dick Lochte, writing in the *Los Angeles Times,* found the dialogue to be sharp but overwhelming in quantity, he also noted that "Bowen seems to have the real stuff. He's funny and cynical and is capable of conjuring up a credible scenario."

Michaelson investigates another case in *Collateral Damage.* This novel focuses on the sale of a mansion owned by a recently deceased Central Intelligence Agency (CIA) agent. The agent's daughters, Cindy and Catherine Shepherd, are odd at best and want the house sold quickly. The sale takes an unusual turn because the property itself is at the center of a secret. Michaelson takes charge of the mansion's sale as well as the investigation of the unexpected death of Catherine's fiancé on the property. Budd Arthur praised Bowen's development as a writer in *Booklist,* acknowledging that "solid research and sharp writing make for an excellent read."

Another series of Bowen's mysteries follows Repper "Rep" Pennyworth, an intellectual property lawyer based in Indianapolis, Indiana. He wants to live a simple, quiet life, spending time with his wife, Melissa, and their family, but he and his wife get caught up in investigations which pull them away from home. One of their adventures, *Screenscam,* is a book that a *Kirkus Review* critic called "the first mystery in many a day that should have been longer." In the novel, Pennyworth is assigned the case of Charlotte Buchanan, the author of a poorly written novel and the daughter of a wealthy client of his firm's. Charlotte believes the idea behind her abysmal novel has been stolen to be made into a movie, and she instructs Pennyworth to take the studio to court. Though they doubt the validity of her claim at first, Pennyworth and his wife realize that she might be right. During the course of his investigation, Pennyworth discovers the case is more complicated than it appears; Charlotte herself has sinister intentions. A *Publishers Weekly* reviewer commented, "Bowen writes with knowledge and wit, tongue in cheek or rudely protruding. His cat-and-mouse corporate thriller zips merrily to a high-speed conclusion."

The Pennyworths return in *Unforced Error: A Rep and Melissa Pennyworth Mystery.* Here the couple travels to Kansas City, Missouri, to participate in a reenactment of a Civil War battle and spend time with a school friend of Melissa's, Laura Damon, and her husband, Peter. Laura works for a publisher that Rep would like for a client. Rep and Melissa end up investigating the death of Laura's co-worker and lover, Thomas Quinlan, during the battle and the subsequent disappearance of Peter. *Unforced Error* is "well-crafted" and "well-researched," according to a *Publishers Weekly* writer, who concluded that "fans of more literate mysteries have good reason to cheer."

Bowen once told *CA:* "My readers are elite in the sense that the British Parliament is elite—they are not particularly distinguished, but there are only about 600

of them! I like to think of myself as the last novelist in America who hasn't been ripped off for an Eddie Murphy movie. My two driving ambitions are to make it to the U.S. Supreme Court and to appear on the French television program *Apostrophes.*"

BIOGRAPHICAL AND CRITICAL SOURCES:

PERIODICALS

Booklist, May 15, 1999, Budd Arthur, review of *Collateral Damage,* p. 1672.
Kirkus Reviews, September 1, 2001, review of *Screenscam,* p. 1246.
Los Angeles Times, December 15, 1996, Dick Lochte, "Murder, He Wrote," review of *Worst Case Scenario,* p. 3.
Publishers Weekly, September 24, 2001, review of *Screenscam,* p. 70; March 22, 2004, review of *Unforced Error: A Rep and Melissa Pennyworth Mystery,* p. 66.

ONLINE

Foley & Lardner LLP Web site, http://www.foley.com/ (October 4, 2005), biography of Michael Bowen.*

*   *   *

BOWEN, Michael Anthony
See BOWEN, Michael

*   *   *

BRIGGS, Raymond 1934-
  (Raymond Redvers Briggs)

PERSONAL: Born January 18, 1934, in London, England; son of Ernest Redvers (in milk delivery) and Ethel (Bowyer) Briggs; married Jean Taprell Clark (a painter), 1963 (died 1973). *Education:* Wimbledon School of Art, national diploma in design, 1953; attended Slade School of Art, 1955-57; University of London, diploma in fine art, 1957. *Politics:* "Green."

Religion: "None—Atheist." *Hobbies and other interests:* Reading, second-hand books, gardening, growing fruit, and modern jazz.

ADDRESSES: Home—Weston, Underhill Ln., Westmeston, Hassocks, Sussex BN6 8XG, England.

CAREER: Illustrator and writer of books for children, 1957—. Brighton College of Art (part of Brighton Polytechnic after 1970), Sussex, England, part-time faculty member, 1961-87; Slade School of Fine Art, London, England, teacher; Central Art School, London, England, teacher. Set designer and playwright. Member, British Campaign for Nuclear Disarmament, 1982—. *Military service:* British Army, 1953-55.

MEMBER: Chartered Society of Designers (fellow), Society of Industrial Artists, Dairy Farmer's Association, Groucho Club.

AWARDS, HONORS: Kate Greenaway Medal commendation, Library Association, 1964, for *Fee Fi Fo Fum: A Picture Book of Nursery Rhymes;* Kate Greenaway Medal, Library Association, 1966, for *Mother Goose Treasury,* 1973, for *Father Christmas;* Spring Book Festival Picture Book Honor, *Book World,* 1970, for *The Elephant and the Bad Boy;* Children's Book Showcase, Children's Book Council, 1974, for *Father Christmas;* Art Books for Children Citation, Brooklyn Museum and Brooklyn Public Library, 1975, for *Father Christmas,* 1979, for *The Snowman;* Francis Williams Illustrations Award, Book Trust, 1977, for *Father Christmas;* Kate Greenaway Medal high commendation, Library Association, 1978, for *The Snowman; Boston Globe-Horn Book* Award for Illustration, *Boston Globe,* 1979, for *The Snowman;* Premio Critici in Erba, Bologna (Italy) Book Festival, 1979, for *The Snowman;* Lewis Carroll Shelf Award, 1979, for *The Snowman;* Dutch Silver Pen Award, the Netherlands, 1979, for *The Snowman;* British Academy of Television Arts & Sciences Award, best children's program—drama, 1982, for *The Snowman* (film); Academy Award nomination, Academy of Motion Picture Arts and Sciences, best animated short film, 1982, for *The Snowman* (film); Francis Williams Illustrations Award, Book Trust, 1982, for *The Snowman;* Francis Williams Illustration Award, Victoria & Albert Museum, 1982; Other Award, Children's Rights Workshop, 1982, for *When the Wind Blows;* Broadcasting Press Guild Radio Award, most outstanding radio program, 1983, for *When the Wind Blows* (radio play); Broadcasting Press Guild Award, 1984, for radio play; *Redbook* Award, 1986, for *The Snowman;* Children's Author of the Year, 1992; Kurt Maschler Award, Booktrust, 1992; Best Illustrated Book of the Year Award, British Book Awards, 1998, for *Ethel and Ernest.*

WRITINGS:

CHILDREN'S BOOKS; AND ILLUSTRATOR

Midnight Adventure, Hamish Hamilton (London, England), 1961.

The Strange House, Hamish Hamilton (London, England), 1961.

Ring-a-Ring o' Roses (poetry), Coward (New York, NY), 1962.

Sledges to the Rescue, Hamish Hamilton (London, England), 1963.

(Editor) *The White Land: A Picture Book of Traditional Rhymes and Verses,* Coward (New York, NY), 1963.

(Editor) *Fee Fi Fo Fum: A Picture Book of Nursery Rhymes,* Coward (New York, NY), 1964.

(Editor) *The Mother Goose Treasury,* Coward (New York, NY), 1966.

Jim and the Beanstalk, Coward (New York, NY), 1970.

Father Christmas, Coward (New York, NY), 1973.

Father Christmas Goes on Holiday, Coward (New York, NY), 1975.

Fungus the Bogeyman, Hamish Hamilton (London, England), 1977.

Gentleman Jim (also see below), Hamish Hamilton (London, England), 1980.

When the Wind Blows (also see below), Schocken Books (New York, NY), 1982.

The Tin-Pot Foreign General and the Old Iron Woman, Hamish Hamilton (London, England), 1984.

The Party, Little, Brown (Boston, MA), 1985.

(With Mitsumasa Anno) *All in a Day,* Philomel Books (New York, NY), 1986.

Unlucky Wally, Hamish Hamilton (London, England), 1987.

Unlucky Wally Twenty Years On, Hamish Hamilton (London, England), 1989.

Father Christmas Having a Wonderful Time, Hamish Hamilton (London, England), 1993.

The Bear, Random House (New York, NY), 1994.

The Man, Random House (New York, NY), 1995.

Ethel and Ernest: A True Story, Knopf (New York, NY), 1999.

Ug: Boy Genius of the Stone Age and His Search for Soft Trousers, Knopf (New York, NY), 2002.

"SNOWMAN" SERIES

The Snowman, Random House (New York, NY), 1978.

Building the Snowman, Little, Brown (Boston, MA), 1985.

Dressing Up, Hamish Hamilton (London, England), 1985.

Walking in the Air, Little, Brown (Boston, MA), 1985.

Snowman Pop-up, Hamish Hamilton (London, England), 1986.

The Snowman Storybook, Random House (New York, NY), 1990.

The Snowman Flap Book, Random House (New York, NY), 1991.

The Snowman Tell-the-Time Book, Hamish Hamilton (London, England), 1991.

The Snowman Clock Book, Random House (New York, NY), 1992.

Snowman: Songbook, Hal Leonard (Milwaukee, WI), 1993.

The Snowman: Things to Touch and Feel, See and Sniff, Random House (New York, NY), 1994.

The Snowman: A Fun-shaped Play Book, Random House (New York, NY), 1999.

ILLUSTRATOR

(With others) Julian Sorell Huxley, *Wonderful World of Life,* Doubleday (New York, NY), 1958.

Barbara Ker Wilson, *The Wonderful Comet,* 1958.

Ruth Manning-Sanders, *Peter and the Piskies,* Oxford University Press (London, England), 1958, Roy (New York, NY), 1966.

A. Stephen Tring, *Peter's Busy Day,* 1959.

Alfred Leo Duggan, *Look at Castles,* Hamish Hamilton (London, England), 1960, published as *The Castle Book,* Pantheon (New York, NY), 1961.

Alfred Duggan, *Look at Churches,* 1961.

A.L. Duggan, *Arches and Spires,* Hamish Hamilton (London, England), 1961, Pantheon (New York, NY), 1962.

Meriol Trevor, *William's Wild Day Out,* 1963.

Jacynth Hope-Simpson, editor, *Hamish Hamilton Book of Myths and Legends,* Hamish Hamilton (London, England), 1964.

William Mayne, editor, *Whistling Rufus,* Hamish Hamilton (London, England), 1964, Dutton (New York, NY), 1965.

Elfrida Vipont, *Stevie,* 1965.

Ruth Manning-Sanders, editor, *Hamish Hamilton Book of Magical Beasts,* Hamish Hamilton (London, England), 1965, published as *A Book of Magical Beasts,* Thomas Nelson (Camden, NJ), 1970.

James Aldridge, *The Flying 19,* Hamish Hamilton (London, England), 1966.

Mabel Esther Allen, *The Way over Windle,* 1966.

Bruce Carter, *Jimmy Murphy and the White Duesenberg,* Coward (New York, NY), 1968.

Bruce Carter, *Nuvolari and the Alpha Romeo,* Coward (New York, NY), 1968.

Nicholas Fisk, *Lindbergh: The Lone Flier,* Coward (New York, NY), 1968.

Nicholas Fisk, *Richtofen: The Red Baron,* Coward (New York, NY), 1968.

William Mayne, editor, *The Hamish Hamilton Book of Giants,* Hamish Hamilton (London, England), 1968, published as *William Mayne's Book of Giants,* Dutton (New York, NY), 1969.

Michael Brown, *Shackleton's Epic Voyage,* Coward (New York, NY), 1969.

Elfrida Vipont Foulds, *The Elephant and the Bad Baby,* Coward (New York, NY), 1969.

Showell Styles, *First up Everest,* Coward (New York, NY), 1969.

James Reeves, editor, *The Christmas Book,* Dutton (New York, NY), 1970.

Ian Serraillier, *The Tale of Three Landlubbers,* Hamish Hamilton (London, England), 1970, Coward (New York, NY), 1971.

Virginia Haviland, *The Fairy Tale Treasury,* Coward (New York, NY), 1972.

Ruth Manning-Sanders, editor, *Festivals,* Heinemann (London, England), 1972, Dutton (New York, NY), 1973.

James Reeves, editor, *The Forbidden Forest,* 1973.

Mitsumasa Anno, *All in Day,* 1986.

Allan Ahlberg, *The Adventures of Bert,* Farrar, Straus & Giroux (New York, NY), 2001.

Allan Ahlberg, *A Bit More Bert,* Farrar, Straus & Giroux (New York, NY), 2002.

OTHER

The Snowman (screenplay; based on Briggs' book of the same title), Weston Woods, 1982.

When the Wind Blows (play; based on Briggs' book of the same title), broadcast on British Broadcasting Corp. radio, and produced on stage in Bristol, England, and London, England, 1983, and Washington, DC, 1985.

Gentleman Jim (stage play; based on Briggs' book of the same title), produced in Nottingham, England, at Nottingham Playhouse, 1985.

When the Wind Blows (screenplay; based on Briggs' book of the same title), Film Four, 1986.

Blooming Books, commentaries by Nicolette Jones, Jonathan Cape (London, England), 2003.

Also adaptor of *Father Christmas* for film, as well as *The Bear,* 1999, and *Ivor the Invisible,* 2001.

ADAPTATIONS: The Snowman was adapted into a book written by Michelle Knudsen, illustrated by Maggie Downer, and published as *Raymond Briggs' The Snowman,* Random House (New York, NY), 1999.

SIDELIGHTS: Children's book author and illustrator Raymond Briggs uses the medium of picture books for his often radical social commentary. Focusing on such subjects as nuclear war, nationalism, racial intolerance, and government wrong-doing, Briggs offsets the harsh, controversial messages of his stories with cartoon-like formats and visual humor. Among Briggs' most popular books are those in the "Snowman" series, in which the author presents a snowman who comes to life and his adventures with the little boy who created him. A *Publishers Weekly* critic found the first book in the series, the award-winning *The Snowman,* to be "incomparably sweet, touching and funny . . . with all the depth and breadth of a novel." A reviewer for the *Economist* called it Briggs' "great classic."

In *Fungus the Bogeyman,* Briggs creates an entire imaginary world alternative to the everyday world. As Geoff Fox described it in the *Times Educational Supplement,* "the story of *Fungus the Bogeyman* is little more than a thread we follow through the underworld which is Bogeydom. Here live Fungus, his wife Mildew, little Mould and the whole bogey community, relishing the 'fetid darkness,' dirt, slime and smells." Russell Davies, writing in the *Times Literary Supplement,* noted that *Fungus the Bogeyman* is "an obsessive monologue on decay" and found it "peculiarly disgusting" for its "anal-erotic preoccupa-

tions." However, Margery Fisher, writing in *Growing Point,* concluded that *Fungus the Bogeyman* "is in fact a highly intellectual book."

Briggs' turns to the grim subject of nuclear holocaust in *When the Wind Blows,* the story of a quiet retired couple, the Bloggs, as they face atomic war. As Christopher Lehmann-Haupt put it in his review for the *New York Times,* "Armageddon comes, and we are in a place to which no picture book has ever taken us before." The Bloggs carry on gamely in the face of societal breakdown following a nuclear strike by the Soviet Union, seemingly oblivious to both the disaster's source or consequences. Penelope Mesic commented in the *Bulletin of the Atomic Scientists* that "it would make devastating reading for anyone so young or innocent as to lack a protective cynicism. . . . The tone of the narrative is bitterly ironic."

In *The Man* Briggs presents the story of a young boy confronted by an unwanted guest—a miniature man, naked, cold, and hungry, who demands to be cared for. While young John seeks to please his demanding, rude guest, and keep him secret from his parents, the man disrupts his life with his thoughtless behavior. The visitor, wrote Peter F. Neumeyer in the *Horn Book,* "arrives, says he's cold, demands food, urinates, warms himself, bathes, eats again, demands toilet paper, and climbs to the roof to defecate. . . . Aside from his stench of carnality, Briggs's Man is by turns arrogant, vain, peremptory, maudlin, whining, frightened. He is xenophobic . . . and racist." The story, Susan Dove Lempke explained in *Booklist,* "touches on subjects ranging from politics and religion to philosophy." "Though the characters' conversations touch on some worthy issues (self-image, identity, tolerance and diversity), it's a lot for kids to sort out," observed a critic for *Publishers Weekly.*

Briggs received a much different reaction from critics for *Ethel and Ernest: A True Story.* This book, primarily intended for adults, is a pictography with short vignettes to form a biography of his parents' life, from their first meeting through their deaths within weeks of each other. *Bookseller* critic Nicolette Jones wrote: "Many regard *Ethel and Ernest* as Briggs' masterpiece. It elevated the strip illustration to the stature of literature." The book is a loving tale told by their only child, which also touches on changes in the world from the Great Depression until the early 1970s.

A *Publishers Weekly* reviewer commented: "The dialogue is heartbreakingly accurate, the pictures cinematic in their conveyance of delight and drama; the whole book is . . . a deeply moving testament to 'ordinary' folk."

Briggs followed *Ethel and Ernest* with the satirical, witty *Ug: Boy Genius of the Stone Age and the Search for Soft Trousers,* another story drawn in Briggs' distinctive comic-like style. Ug's quest for pants made of something comfortable in a world where everything is carved from stone, as well as his many other modern ideas, befuddle his parents, father Dug and mother Dugs, and local villagers. As Ug questions everything in an attempt to better the world around him, only Dug tries to understand and help Ug make his notions become real. Briggs contrasts Ug's point of view with his parents' through use of language. *New York Times Book Review* contributor Rika Leser noted Dug and Dugs "speak in forward-looking anachronisms like 'hard as nails' which Briggs takes the trouble to point out in amusing—at times hilariously inaccurate—footnotes."

While *Booklist* reviewer Michael Cart praised the look of *Ug,* he also felt that "Briggs' famous misanthropy spills over into misogyny." In contrast, *Horn Book* writer Sarah Ellis found the book had qualities which many parents and children could relate to. "All will warm to the tenderness of a story in which the author-illustrator champions the tentative, sympathizes with the perplexed, and persuades of the heroism of a failed vision," she asserted.

In addition to writing and illustrating his own books, Briggs also has illustrated many books by other authors. One series for which Briggs more recently provided drawings is centered around a character named Bert. Written by Allan Ahlberg, *The Adventures of Bert* and *A Bit More Bert* are humorous stories about the simple yet odd experiences Bert has in his everyday life. Reviewing *The Adventures of Bert* in *Horn Book,* Martha V. Parravano suggested that "readers will feel . . . hurtled through the book by the enormous energy of Brigg's vivid, mostly-colored-pencil illustrations."

BIOGRAPHICAL AND CRITICAL SOURCES:

BOOKS

St. James Guide to Children's Writers, fifth edition, St. James Press (Detroit, MI), 1999.

PERIODICALS

Booklist, February 1, 1996, Susan Dove Lempke, review of *The Man,* p. 931; November 15, 2002, Michael Cart, review of *Ug: Boy Genius of the Stone Age and the Search for Soft Trousers,* p. 600.
Bookseller, July 18, 2003, Nicolette Jones, "Briggs' Blooming Books: Raymond Briggs Has Elevated the Standing of Cartoon Strips and Children's Books," biography of Raymond Briggs, p. 22.
Bulletin of the Atomic Scientists, February, 1983, Penelope Mesic, review of *When the Wind Blows,* pp. 39-40.
Economist, December 1, 1984, review of *The Tin-Pot Foreign General and the Old Iron Woman,* p. 110; November 26, 1994, review of *The Snowman,* p. 101.
Growing Point, July, 1978, Margery Fisher, review of *Fungus the Bogeyman,* pp. 3368-3369.
Horn Book, May-June, 1996, Peter F. Neumeyer, review of *The Man,* p. 315; July, 2001, Martha V. Parravano, review of *The Adventures of Bert,* p. 548; November-December, 2002, Sarah Ellis, review of *Ug,* p. 734.
New York Times, September 14, 1982, Christopher Lehmann-Haupt, review of *When the Wind Blows,* p. C7.
New York Times Review of Books, November 17, 2002, Rika Lesser, "Ahead of His Time: Thinking and Inventing Are What Ug Does Best—Which Makes Him an Unusual Stone Age Boy," review of *Ug,* p. 35.
Publishers Weekly, October 9, 1978, review of *The Snowman,* p. 76; October 2, 1995, review of *The Man,* p. 73; August 9, 1999, review of *Ethel and Ernest: A True Story,* p. 328.
Times Educational Supplement, November 18, 1977, Geoff Fox, review of *Fungus the Bogeyman,* p. 35.
Times Literary Supplement, December 2, 1977, Russell Davies, review of *Fungus the Bogeyman,* p. 1412.

ONLINE

Absoluteastronomy.com, http://www.absolute astronomy.com/ (October 5, 2005), biography of Raymond Briggs.*

*   *   *

BRIGGS, Raymond Redvers
See BRIGGS, Raymond

BRIMELOW, Peter 1947-

PERSONAL: Born October 13, 1947, in Warrington, England; naturalized U.S. citizen; son of Frank Sanderson (a transport executive) and Bessie (Knox) Brimelow; married Margaret Alice Laws (an investment banker), September 20, 1980 (died, 2004); children: Alexander James Frank, Hannah Claire Catherine. *Education:* University of Sussex, B.A. (with honors), 1970; Stanford University, M.B.A., 1972. *Religion:* Episcopalian.

ADDRESSES: Office—Center for American Unity, P.O. Box 910, Warrenton, VA 20188. *E-mail*—pbrimelow@ vdare.com.

CAREER: Richardson Securities of Canada, Winnipeg, Manitoba, Canada, investment analyst, 1972-73; *Financial Post,* Toronto, Ontario, Canada, assistant editor, 1973-76; *Maclean's,* Toronto, business editor and columnist, 1976-78; *Financial Post,* Ontario, Canada, columnist and contributing editor, 1978-80; U.S. Senate Staff, Washington, DC, economic counsel to Senator Orrin G. Hatch, 1980-81, 1988-90; *Toronto Sun,* Toronto, columnist, 1980-82; *Barron's,* New York, NY, associate editor, 1981-83, contributing editor, 1984-86; *Fortune,* New York, NY, associate editor, 1983-84; *Chief Executive Magazine,* New York, NY, columnist and contributing editor, 1984-86; *Influence,* Toronto, contributing editor, 1984-86; *Times,* London, England, 1986-90; *Forbes,* New York, NY, senior editor, 1986-2002; *National Review,* New York, NY, senior editor, 1993-98; *VDARE.com,* editor, 1999—. Center for American Unity (nonprofit organization), Warrenton, VA, president, 1999—. Pacific Research Institute, San Francisco, CA, senior fellow, c. 2002.

MEMBER: Philadelphia Society.

AWARDS, HONORS: Fulbright Fellowship, United States Department of State, 1970; Commonwealth Universities scholar, 1970; National Business Writing Award, Royal Bank of Canada and Toronto Press Club, 1976; National Business Writing Citations, Royal Bank of Canada and Toronto Press Club, 1977, 1978; Gerald Loeb Award, Anderson School at the University of California at Los Angeles, 1990.

WRITINGS:

NONFICTION

The Wall Street Gurus: How You Can Profit from the Investment Newsletters, Random House (New York, NY), 1986.

The Patriot Game: National Dreams and Political Realities, Key Porter (Toronto, Ontario, Canada), 1986, published as *The Patriot Game: Canada and the Canadian Question Revisited,* Hoover Institution Press (Stanford, CA), 1987.

The Enemies of Freedom, Citizens for Foreign Aid Reform (Toronto, Ontario, Canada), 1990.

Alien Nation: Common Sense about America's Immigration Disaster, Random House (New York, NY), 1995.

The Worm in the Apple: How the Teacher Unions Are Destroying American Education, HarperCollins (New York, NY), 2003.

Contributor to *The Debate in the United States over Immigration,* Hoover, 1997. Also contributor of articles and reviews to magazines, including *Harper's, Canadian Business, National Review, Human Events, Policy Review,* and *Saturday Night.* Columnist, *CBS MarketWatch,* columnist, 2002. Guest writer for editorial page, *Wall Street Journal,* 1978.

SIDELIGHTS: In 1995 financial journalist Peter Brimelow published *Alien Nation: Common Sense about America's Immigration Disaster.* The book represents Brimelow's expansion of his "powerful and elegant article, published in the *National Review,* in which he argues that current American immigration policies were leading to disaster," explained Richard Bernstein in the *New York Times.* Timed to become a part of the national debate preceding the 1996 presidential election, *Alien Nation* continues to offer "a highly cogent presentation of what is going to be the benchmark case against immigration as it is currently taking place," Bernstein observed.

In *Alien Nation,* Brimelow argues that "the mistaken belief that large-scale legal immigration to the United States is a purely natural phenomenon should first be corrected," Jack Miles commented in the *Atlantic Monthly.* "Heavy immigration has not just happened. It has come about through political decisions." Among the most important of these decisions, in Brimelow's view, is the Immigration and Nationality Act Amendments of 1965. The result over the last thirty years, Brimelow maintains, has been too much immigration, especially by those with few job skills and by those with cultures vastly different from the American norm. And, because there has been no interruption in the immigrant flow, there has been no time for the new groups to assimilate. Just as the current situation has been caused by political decisions, so political decisions can solve the problem, Brimelow believes. He suggests a number of approaches, including eliminating family reunification as a priority; increasing the number of border patrol officers and the case workers in the Immigration and Naturalization Service; issuing Americans a national identity card; imposing an English-language proficiency requirement; ending automatic citizenship for everyone born on U.S. soil; and reducing legal immigration to less than half of current levels.

"Brimelow marshals an impressive array of demographic and economic data to press this case," Peter Skerry wrote in *Commentary,* "stressing in particular that today's immigrants differ significantly—for the worse—from those who came in earlier days." These new immigrants are more poorly prepared for American life than their predecessors, Nicholas Lemann explained in the *New York Times Book Review,* and for this reason they "are a net drain on the country, crowding public schools, welfare rolls, jails and hospitals. And by their mere presence they exacerbate ethnic tension." While recognizing the support he offers for his arguments, a number of reviewers have challenged Brimelow's conclusions. "His discussion of the economic effects of immigration is one-sided," commented Skerry, "and ignores evidence that contradicts his case. . . . Of those professional economists who have examined the question, most do not share Brimelow's negative appraisal of the contribution immigration makes to the national balance sheet." Moreover, in Bernstein's opinion, "Mr. Brimelow does very little on-the-scene reporting, which makes his stress on statistics seem not only abstract but also detached from the concrete human and spiritual reality involved in immigration." "To engage its topic seriously," John J. Miller maintained in *Reason,* "*Alien Nation* would have to dispense with its ad hominem cynicism and deliver a full-blown discussion of the good, bad, and unquantifiable impacts of immigrants on our economy, culture, and society. It never does."

Other reviewers have disagreed with the vision of America that Brimelow, himself an immigrant from England, offers in support of his argument against immigration. In suggesting that the bulk of current immigration is vastly different from previous groups in its closeness to traditional American culture, Brimelow reveals that his "view of American culture from its very origins is almost truculently Anglocentric," observed Miles. He continued, "This nation is not now *and never has been* culturally as English as Brimelow wants to believe." Brimelow also focuses on the ethnic and racial disparity between new immigrant groups and established Americans as a source of conflict and concern. Yet, Lemann believed that because of Brimelow's background as an Englishman, he overlooks the force that unifies Americans. "At bottom he just doesn't believe in the 'American idea' that people here can transcend ethnicity through allegiance to abstract national principles like democracy and opportunity."

Even with such reservations, reviewers have recognized the value of Brimelow's perspective on this national issue. "Brimelow deserves much credit for getting discussion of these issues under way," Skerry wrote, "even if immigration and the heterogeneity it brings are much more woven into the warp and woof of American society than he seems to understand or is ready to concede." For Miles, "At his best, Peter Brimelow is an inspired controversialist, determined to storm the enemy's redoubt where it is strongest, not where it is weakest." The reviewer concluded that "he makes a powerful—indeed, nearly overwhelming—case against the status quo. And if his book is at times uncomfortably personal, it is also painfully honest."

As Brimelow's career transitioned into serving as president of his nonprofit organization, Center for American Unity, and editing an online journal, *VDARE. com,* he continued to address controversial topics in book form. *The Worm in the Apple: How the Teacher Unions Are Destroying Education* offers his take on how American students are being ill served by public education and teachers's unions in the United States. While teachers are part of the problem, he believes the powerful teacher unions, such as the National Education Association and American Federation of Teachers, are the bigger issue. Brimelow argues that the unions are hurting schools and education. For him, teacher unions turn public education into a political game. They foster bureaucracy and keep unskilled teachers employed. Brimelow also outlines his suggestions for improving the situation, including making public education into a free market commodity in the United States. While some reviewers noted that the arguments and comments Brimelow makes in *The Worm in the Apple* are one-sided and intended to be controversial, they also saw significant truths. *Booklist* contributor

Ray Olson, for example, characterized the book as "rougher reading than *Alien Nation* but just as bracing."

BIOGRAPHICAL AND CRITICAL SOURCES:

PERIODICALS

Atlantic Monthly, April, 1995, Jack Miles, review of *Alien Nation: Common Sense about America's Immigration Disaster,* p. 130.
Booklist, February 1, 2003, Ray Olson, review of *The Worm in the Apple: How Teacher Unions Are Destroying American Education,* p. 959.
Commentary, May, 1995, Peter Skerry, review of *Alien Nation,* p. 70.
New York Times, April 19, 1995, Richard Bernstein, review of *Alien Nation,* p. B2.
New York Times Book Review, April 16, 1995, Nicholas Lemann, review of *Alien Nation,* p. 3.
Reason, June, 1995, John J. Miller, review of *Alien Nation,* p. 50.

ONLINE

VDARE.com, http://www.vdare.com/ (October 22, 2005), includes articles written by Brimelow.*

*   *   *

BROOKS, Geraldine 1956(?)-

PERSONAL: Born c. 1956, in Sydney, Australia; married Tony Horowitz (a journalist), 1984; children: Nathaniel. *Education:* Columbia University, M.J., 1983; Sydney University, graduate. *Religion:* Jewish.

ADDRESSES: Home—Waterford, VA; Sydney, Australia. *Agent*—c/o Author Mail, Viking Publicity, 375 Hudson St., New York, NY 10014.

CAREER: Sydney Morning Herald, Sydney, Australia, former reporter; *Wall Street Journal,* London, England, Middle Eastern correspondent, 1988-c. 1997; United Nations, New York, NY, correspondent, 1993-94; writer, c. 1997—.

AWARDS, HONORS: Hal Boyle Award, Overseas Press Club of America, 1990, for the best daily newspaper or wire service reporting from abroad; Kibble Award, Australia, 1998, for *Foreign Correspondence: A Pen Pal's Journey from Down Under to All Over;* Impac Award shortlist for *Year of Wonder.*

WRITINGS:

Nine Parts of Desire: The Hidden World of Islamic Women (nonfiction), Anchor Books (New York, NY), 1995.
(With Margaret Courtney-Clarke) *Imazighen: The Vanishing Traditions of Berber Women,* Clarkson Potter Publishers (New York, NY), 1996.
Foreign Correspondence: A Pen Pal's Journey from Down Under to All Over (memoir), Anchor Books/ Doubleday (New York, NY), 1998.
Year of Wonders: A Novel of the Plague, Viking (New York, NY), 2001.
March (novel), Viking (New York, NY), 2005.

SIDELIGHTS: Author and journalist Geraldine Brooks (not to be confused with Geraldine Brooks the film and stage actress) has won awards for her coverage of the Middle East for the *Wall Street Journal,* including reports on the Persian Gulf War. She channels a unique part of that experience into her first nonfiction book, *Nine Parts of Desire: The Hidden World of Islamic Women.* When Brooks first arrived in the Middle East she felt cut off, as a female correspondent, from much of Muslim society. She turned that liability into an advantage when she donned the *hijab* (the black veil worn by most Muslim women in the Middle East) and thereby enabled herself to penetrate the cloistered world of Muslim women.

The title of *Nine Parts of Desire* comes from an interpretation of the Q'uran offered by the Shiite branch: "Almighty God created sexual desires in ten parts; then he gave nine parts to women and one to men." As Laura Shapiro, writing for *Newsweek,* commented: "Good enough reason to keep women under wraps." Brooks uncovers a complex picture in her investigation of Muslim women's lives that goes beyond the Western assumption of women's oppression and isolation from public life.

Brooks interviewed a wide range of Muslim women, from belly dancers to housewives, and from activists to female army recruits; her list of interviewees includes Queen Noor of Jordan and Ayatollah Khomeini's daughter. Her discoveries are fascinating and wide-ranging, if sometimes contradictory, according to reviewers. *Booklist* contributor Mary Ellen Sullivan wrote that, according to Brooks, sexual gratification is considered "an inherent right" for Muslim women, but genital mutilation is still a common practice. It may surprise some Americans to read that women fare better in Iran than in the rest of the Middle East. Brooks explains: "To Muslim women elsewhere . . . the Iranian woman riding to work on her motorbike, even with her billowing *chador* gripped firmly in her teeth, looks like a figure of envy." By wearing the *chador* herself, Brooks discovers a camaraderie among the women that she has experienced elsewhere, as when she bakes bread with Kurdish women. But when she notices a young boy sampling bits of bread that his sister sweats to make, she sees the negative side of strict sexual divisions as well: "His sister, not much older, was already part of our bread-making assembly line. Why should he learn so young that her role was to toil for his pleasure?"

Sullivan called Brooks "a wonderful writer and thinker," noting that her study gives readers new insight into the lives of Muslim women. A *Publishers Weekly* reviewer called the book a "powerful and enlightening report" that brings Westerners much closer to the reality of Muslim life for women. Shapiro admired the firsthand reporting that led Brooks to an "intimacy with these women [that] made it impossible either to romanticize or to demonize the tradition that ruled them."

A few years later, Brooks followed her first book with *Foreign Correspondence: A Pen Pal's Journey from Down Under to All Over,* a memoir of her childhood that focuses on the importance of foreign pen pals to her sense of an independent identity and freedom from what she then considered the boring backwater of her hometown, Sydney, Australia. The frame of the narrative is the approaching death of Brooks's father, which brings her back to Sydney from her life as a foreign correspondent for the *Wall Street Journal.* While going through family papers, she finds letters from pen pals—from as far as the United States, France, and Israel—she had long ago forgotten. Rereading these letters brings her back to her youthful sense of restlessness and early belief that "real life happened in far-off lands." During her childhood and adolescence, the pen pals fulfilled her yearning for the exotic, and gave a

sense of breaking away, as Donna Seaman commented in *Booklist,* from "Australia's mid-century, Anglo-focused insularity." The experience was formative in bringing Brooks to her position as a traveling journalist and "fireman" for the *Wall Street Journal* (the term identifies journalists who can report on controversial subjects and issues). Brooks's rereading of the letters inspired her to look up her old pen pals, among them Joannie, her pen pal from the United States who spent the summer in Switzerland and Martha's Vineyard, but whose glamorous-sounding life ended early from the ravages of anorexia. Seaman termed the book a "magnetic memoir," while a reviewer in *Publishers Weekly* deemed it "competent but unexciting." A critic for *Kirkus Reviews,* however, offered unadulterated praise, calling it an "evocative, superbly written tale of a woman's journey to self-understanding."

In addition to her nonfiction works, Brooks has also written two novels. The first was shortlisted for the Impac Award. *Year of Wonders: A Novel of the Plague* is a work of historical fiction set in Great Britain in the 1660s. *Year of Wonders* is based on the true story of the English village of Eyam after the bubonic plague has arrived. The people who live in the village make a difficult decision to quarantine their community from the outside in an effort to stop the plague in its tracks. Writing in *Publishers Weekly,* a critic commented that "Brooks keeps readers glued through the starkly dramatic episodes and a haunting story of flawed, despairing human beings. This poignant and powerful account carries the pulsing beat of a sensitive imagination and the challenge of moral complexity."

Narrating *Year of Wonders* is the fictional Anna Frith, a young mother, shepherdess, and servant to the town's pastor. She outlives her immediately family and helps with the sickness in Eyam. Brooks uses her to relate the devastating effects of the disease on Anna and those around her, and also allows the character to experience personal growth from the experience. Of Brooks' characterization of Frith, Liz Doran wrote in *Geelong Small Press Publishing:* "The voice of Anna is a charming blend of innocence and natural intelligence with enough historical dialect to resonate the period without being tedious."

A chance discovery inspired Brooks to research Louis May Alcott and her father, A. Bronson Alcott, which led her to write *March.* This novel focuses on what happened to John March, the father character in Alcott's *Little Women,* the year he was away from his wife and four daughters. March was based on Alcott's own father, an educator, abolitionist, and progressive thinker. During the course of the novel, March serves as a chaplain for the Union Army during the U.S. Civil War, primarily away from the front lines, and encounters many challenges on and off the battlefield. Brooks depicts him as a complex character, idealistic and full of conviction yet disheartened by his experiences. Critics responded positively to her creation of March. For example, Christina Schwarz wrote in the *Atlantic Monthly* that "the naive earnestness and ready affection with which Brooks endows him, the high standards he sets for himself, and his remarkable willingness to admit mistakes make him wonderfully likable, even when he is egregiously in the wrong." A number of reviewers felt that *March* was a respectful tribute to Alcott's original novel. As an *Economist* contributor noted, "Ms. Brooks merely imbues her pages with the same perfume that rises from Alcott's account of the saintly Marches."

BIOGRAPHICAL AND CRITICAL SOURCES:

BOOKS

Brooks, Geraldine, *Nine Parts of Desire: The Hidden World of Islamic Women,* Anchor Books (New York, NY), 1995.
Brooks, Geraldine, *Foreign Correspondence: A Pen Pal's Journey from Down Under to All Over,* Anchor Books/Doubleday (New York, NY), 1998.

PERIODICALS

Atlantic Monthly, April, 2005, Christina Schwarz, review of *March,* p. 115.
Booklist, September 15, 1994, Mary Ellen Sullivan, review of *Nine Parts of Desire,* p. 88; November 1, 1997, Donna Seaman, review of *Foreign Correspondence,* p. 436.
Economist March 26, 2005, review of *March,* p. 84.
Kirkus Reviews, November 1, 1997, review of *Foreign Correspondence,* pp. 1616-1617.
Newsweek, February 13, 1995, Laura Shapiro, review of *Nine Parts of Desire,* p. 81.
Publishers Weekly, November 21, 1994, review of *Nine Parts of Desire,* p. 64; October 27, 1997, review of *Foreign Correspondence,* p. 57; June 25, 2001, review of *Year of Wonders,* p. 43.

ONLINE

Geelong Small Press Publishing Web site, http://www.gspp.com.au/ (September 21, 2003), Liz Doran, review of *Year of Wonders.*
Geraldine Brooks Home Page, http://www.geraldinebrooks.com (October 23, 2005).
Powell's, http://www.powells.com/ (October 23, 2005), interview with Geraldine Brooks.
Sunday Morning Herald Online, http://www.smh.com.au/ (October 5, 2005), Catherine Keenan, "March to the Front," interview with Geraldine Brooks.*

*   *   *

BUNCH, Chris 1943-2005
(Christopher R. Bunch)

PERSONAL: Born 1943, in Fresno, CA; died of a lung ailment, July 4, 2005, in Ilwaco, WA.

CAREER: Novelist and television writer. *Military service:* Served in the Vietnam War.

WRITINGS:

FANTASY AND SCIENCE-FICTION NOVELS

The Seer King, Aspect/Warner (New York, NY), 1997.
The Darkness of God, Random House (New York, NY), 1997.
The Demon King, Aspect/Warner (New York, NY), 1998.
The Warrior King, Aspect/Warner (New York, NY), 1999.
Firemask, Roc (New York, NY), 2000.
Stormforce, Roc (New York, NY), 2000.
The Empire Stone, Aspect/Warner (New York, NY), 2000.
Homefall, Roc (New York, NY), 2001.
Corsair, Aspect/Warner (New York, NY), 2001.
Star Risk, Ltd., Roc (New York, NY), 2002.
The Scoundrel Worlds: A Star Risk, Ltd., Novel, Roc (New York, NY), 2003.
The Doublecross Program: A Star Risk, Ltd., Novel, Roc (New York, NY), 2004.

Storm of Wings, Aspect/Warner (New York, NY), 2005.
Knighthood of the Dragon, Roc (New York, NY), 2006.

FANTASY NOVELS; WITH ALLAN COLE

The Far Kingdoms, Del Rey (New York, NY), 1993.
The Warrior's Tale, Del Rey (New York, NY), 1994.
Kingdoms of the Night, Del Rey (New York, NY), 1995.

NOVELS; WITH ALLAN COLE

Sten, Del Rey (New York, NY), 1982.
The Wolf Worlds, Del Rey (New York, NY), 1984.
The Court of a Thousand Suns, Del Rey (New York, NY), 1986.
A Reckoning for Kings, Atheneum (New York, NY), 1987.
Fleet of the Damned, Del Rey (New York, NY), 1988.
Revenge of the Damned, Del Rey (New York, NY), 1989.
The Return of the Emperor, Del Rey (New York, NY), 1990.
Vortex, Del Rey (New York, NY), 1992.
Empire's End, Del Rey (New York, NY), 1993.
A Daughter of Liberty, Ballantine (New York, NY), 1993.

TELEVISION EPISODES

Kate Loves a Mystery, National Broadcasting Co. (NBC), 1979.
The Incredible Hulk, Columbia Broadcasting Sysytem (CBS), 1979–80.
The Misadventures of Sheriff Lobo, NBC, 1979–81.
Buck Rogers, NBC, 1980.
Code Red, American Broadcasting Co. (ABC), 1981.
Gavilan, NBC, 1982.
The Master, NBC, 1984.
The A-Team, NBC, 1984.
Jessie, ABC, 1984.
Hunter, NBC, 1984.
MacGruder and Loud, ABC, 1985.

TELEVISION EPISODES; WITH ALLAN COLE

Quincy, NBC, 1979–81.
Magnum, P.I., CBS, 1981.

Also author, with Allan Cole, of television scripts for *The Rockford Files.* Served as combat correspondent, *Stars & Stripes.* Contributor to periodicals, including *Look* and *Rolling Stone.*

SIDELIGHTS: Author Chris Bunch, who died in 2005, made a name for himself as a novelist and television scriptwriter. On his own, he wrote episodes for series such as *The A-Team* and the *Incredible Hulk* in the 1980s. His first solo fantasy novel, *The Seer King,* was published in 1997. More than a dozen other novels followed, including the "Star Risk, Ltd.," science fiction series and other fantasy series. With frequent writing partner Allan Cole, Bunch also worked on popular television shows such as *Magnum P.I., Quincy,* and *The Rockford Files.* In addition, Bunch collaborated with Cole on a series of science fiction novels featuring the hero Sten, a fantasy series that follows the adventures of Amalric Antero and his family, and a novel of the Vietnam War entitled *A Reckoning for Kings.*

Sten first appeared in 1982's eponymous *Sten.* In subsequent novels such as *Fleet of the Damned,*, the character has had to fight the enemy Tahn in defense of the Emperor. In *Revenge of the Damned,* Sten must overcome a stint as a slave in a labor camp. In 1992's *Vortex,* Sten's long-sleeping Emperor finally awakes and attempts to regain his power. Sten must pave the way and keep civil war from breaking out in Alai. Roland Green, reviewing *Vortex* in *Booklist,* cited the tale's fast pace and "as many original touches with the main character as can reasonably be expected," in recommending the novel. The suitably titled *Empire's End* finished Sten's adventures in 1993.

The Far Kingdoms, the first book in Bunch and Cole's fantasy trilogy, appeared in 1994. The novel's protagonist is Amalric Antero, a young man of Orissa about to be sent on his rite-of-passage journey as the tale opens. In the course of his adventures, he is rescued by Janos Greycloak, a student of illegal magic. The two pair up in an attempt to search for the fabled "far kingdoms." The novel is epic and encompasses several journeys involving Antero and Greycloak, as well as the former's marriage and subsequent loss of his wife. On the third journey, Greycloak is corrupted by an evil sorcerer, and Antero must face and fight his old friend in order to save his country. A *Publishers Weekly* reviewer hailed *The Far Kingdoms* as "thoughtful and well-crafted," while Vicky Burkholder in the *Voice of Youth Advocates* warned readers about graphic sex and violence. Still, Burkholder concluded: "It starts slowly, but by the end, you find yourself turning the pages to find out what happens next."

The Warrior's Tale focuses on the character of Amalric Antero's sister, Rali. She is the leader of the all-female Maranon Guard—a band of warriors who have more-or-less contentedly sworn off sexual relations with men. Treated as something of a joke by the male warriors of Orissa, they eventually gain respect by destroying one of two attacking evil wizards and are assigned to track down the survivor. In the course of this quest, which is spent much of the time at sea, Rali rescues a princess with whom she proceeds to have a lesbian affair. In another *Booklist* piece, Green declared that *The Warrior's Tale* "lacks absolutely nothing to thoroughly grip fantasy readers," adding that "Rali is a superior entry in the ranks of martial women." A *Publishers Weekly* reviewer declared the novel to be "a charmingly subversive lesbian feminist romp." Kathleen Beck in the *Voice of Youth Advocates* noted, "that the warrior of the title is female is an interesting twist that may attract new readers to the genre."

Kingdoms of the Night rounds out the trilogy. Amalric Antero is a prematurely aged man who is lured back into the world of quest by a young woman, Janela, who claims to be Janos Greycloak's granddaughter. She contends that Antero and Greycloak did not actually discover the "far kingdoms" they sought in the first novel; instead, these kingdoms lie even farther beyond the path of their former journeys. Though in the course of their present quest they manage to free the Kingdoms of Night from the king of demons, they must eventually, according to a *Kirkus Reviews* critic, "shrug off their bodies to go traveling on the psychic plane." A *Publishers Weekly* reviewer complained that "sequel-itis takes hold of Cole and Bunch" in this novel, but Green "highly recommended" *Kingdoms of the Night* in *Booklist,* concluding that the three books together made "one of the most satisfactory recent fantasy trilogies."

Bunch, with his coauthor Cole, took a departure from the worlds of fantasy and science fiction for their 1987 collaboration, *A Reckoning for Kings.* Though this novel utilizes as its setting a fictional Vietnamese province, it tells the story of the Tet Offensive, which helped determine the outcome of the Vietnam War.

The authorial pair uses a variety of viewpoints to relate their tale, including that of a North Vietnamese general named Duan, American Major Shannon, and a lowly private trying to survive. Larry Heinemann gave *A Reckoning for Kings* a positive notice in the *Los Angeles Times Book Review,* remarking that "Bunch and Cole's combined knowledge of the war in Southeast Asia is encyclopedic—how to rig your pack, what a starlight scope is, what is the sound of a company-size air assault, what it is to wallow in the squalor of the aftermath of a fire fight, on and on." Heinemann concluded that "overall, what the story gives you is a sense of the inevitable chaos of a military campaign; the incredible personal, physical pain; the extreme ugliness of the death that awaits even the most savvy *line animal*—as grunts are called here." A *Publishers Weekly* critic praised the book as well, citing its "excitement and suspense" and calling it "a compelling, if conventional, story of men at war."

Bunch struck out on his own for the 1997 fantasy novel *The Seer King.* The narrator of this tale, Damastes, is a member of the former kingdom of Numantia's cavalry. Assigned to a diplomatic mission, he teams up with a seer called Tenedos in order to fight the powers of neighboring Kait—powers that include the avaricious Baber Fergana, the evil sorcerer Irshad, and a demon answering to Thak who heads a cult of assassins. Thak pursues the pair back to Numantia accompanied by his loyal stranglers, and with the help of Chardin Sher, a wizard more powerful than Tenedos, sets off a civil war in Damastes' homeland. In order to quell this conflict, Damastes and Tenedos must attempt to take over Numantia themselves. During this process, they are beset by further military and magical problems. As in the case of *A Reckoning for Kings,* critics noticed what a *Kirkus Reviews* contributor termed "Bunch's sure grasp of military history and organization." A *Publishers Weekly* reviewer pointed to the "glaringly modern dialogue" for a fantasy novel but conceded that "Bunch knows how to mold heroes, how to keep the pace fast and how to create exciting scenes."

Bunch wrote two sequels to *The Seer King—The Demon King* and *The Warrior King.* The finale finds Damastes still fighting, even after he manages to free himself from prison. He falls in love with a sorceress named Cymea, and they team up against Tenedos, whom Damastes betrayed in the second volume of the trilogy. Reviewing *The Warrior King,* a contributor for

Publishers Weekly found the novel a "brawny story of war and power," and went on to praise Bunch's writing as "clear and vivid."

Bunch turned to military science fiction with *Star Risk, Ltd.,* the first title in a sequence of novels following the adventures and misadventures of a "motley crew of spacefaring mercenaries," as Roland Green described the protagonists in *Booklist.* Former members of the military, the Star Risk crew hires out to the highest payers for dangerous intergalactic missions. In their debut, they are joined by marine major M'chel Riss, who has left the service after eight years of duty and is looking for a way to better her ailing finances. Joining Star Risk, Ltd., she and the other members set off on an attempt to free another soldier from a high-security prison. This debut title demonstrated, according to Green, "superior" pacing. *The Scoundrel Worlds* continues the adventures of the Star Risk team. Here they are at first hired to give security to referees at a skyball tournament, for the fans—who come from many different planets—have pushed rowdy behavior into murderous action. After successfully completing this mission, the team sets about gathering evidence to prove that another man is innocent of treason charges. *Booklist* contributor Frieda Murray found this novel "lightweight action sf that sometimes reads like a novelized TV script."

The prolific Bunch was also writing a fantasy series, "Dragonmaster," at the same time as his "Star Risk, Ltd.," series. The fantasy sequence was initiated with *Storm of Wings,* which follows the development of Hal Kailis from a teenager enchanted with the dragons that inhabit the rocky regions near his village to the mature warrior and Dragonmaster he becomes. Conscripted into the Derain army, Hal survives a bloody battle against the Roche, the only one of his outfit to make it. Thereafter, he seeks revenge for his fallen comrades, becoming a dragon flier and quickly earning promotion. Sally Estes, reviewing *Storm of Wings* in *Booklist,* noted that the action is "nonstop and violent" in this first book in the series, and that "Bunch's military background stands him in good stead." Reviewing the same title in the *Library Journal,* Jackie Cassada felt "fans of military fantasy and dragon lore should enjoy this fantasy adventure." The action is carried forward in *Knighthood of the Dragon,* in which the Derain-Roche war continues. Hal, now a Dragonmaster, is lingering in a Roche prison and must escape somehow to rejoin his men

and fight on. Cassada, writing in the *Library Journal,* commented that Bunch had created "a tale of epic war and sorcery with a strong appeal to dragon lovers." Bunch died shortly after completing *Knighthood of the Dragon.*

BIOGRAPHICAL AND CRITICAL SOURCES:

PERIODICALS

Booklist, April 15, 1992, Roland Green, review of *Vortex,* p. 1509; October 15, 1994, Roland Green, review of *The Warrior's Tale,* p. 405; May 15, 1995, Roland Green, review of *Kingdoms of the Night,* p. 1635; August, 2002, Roland Green, review of *Star Risk, Ltd.,* p. 1936; September 1, 2002, Sally Estes, review of *Storm of Wings,* p. 70; August, 2003, Frieda Murray, review of *The Scoundrel Worlds: A Star Risk, Ltd., Novel,* p. 1967; September 15, 2003, Frieda Murray, review of *Knighthood of the Dragon,* p. 217.

Kirkus Reviews, August 15, 1993, review of *The Far Kingdoms;* September 1, 1994, review of *The Warrior's Tale;* April 15, 1995, review of *Kingdoms of the Night;* December 1, 1996, review of *The Seer King.*

Library Journal, March 15, 1984, review of *The Wolf Worlds,* p. 600; March 15, 1987, Robert H. Donahugh, review of *A Reckoning for Kings,* p. 88; October 15, 1994, Jackie Cassada, review of *The Warrior's Tale,* p. 90; September 15, 2002, Jackie Cassada, review of *Storm of Wings,* p. 97; September 15, 2003, Jackie Cassada, review of *Knighthood of the Dragon,* p. 96.

Locus, July, 1993, Farin Miller, review of *The Far Kingdoms,* pp. 19, 47-48.

Los Angeles Times Book Review, April 26, 1987, Larry Heinemann, review of *A Reckoning for Kings,* p. 6.

Publishers Weekly, February 3, 1984, review of *The Wolf Worlds,* p. 40; November 28, 1986, Sybil Steinberg, review of *A Reckoning for Kings,* p. 67; November 20, 1987, review of *A Reckoning for Kings,* p. 66; August 30, 1993, review of *The Far Kingdoms,* p. 80; October 24, 1994, review of *The Warrior's Tale,* p. 56; May 22, 1995, review of *Kingdoms of the Night,* p. 52; January 20, 1997, review of *The Seer King,* p. 399; January 25, 1999, review of *The Warrior King,* p. 77.

Voice of Youth Advocates, February, 1994, Vicky Burkholder, review of *The Far Kingdoms;* May, 1995, Kathleen Beck, review of *The Warrior's Tale.**

BUNCH, Christopher R.
    See BUNCH, Chris

*   *   *

BYARS, Betsy 1928-
    (Betsy Cromer Byars)

PERSONAL: Born August 7, 1928, in Charlotte, NC; daughter of George Guy and Nan (Rugheimer) Cromer; married Edward Ford Byars (an engineering professor and writer), June 24, 1950; children: Laurie, Betsy Ann, Nan, Guy. *Education:* Attended Furman University, 1946-48; Queens College, B.A., 1950. *Hobbies and other interests:* Flying (licensed pilot).

ADDRESSES: Home—401 Rudder Ridge, Seneca, SC 29678.

CAREER: Writer.

AWARDS, HONORS: America's Book of the Year selection, Child Study Association, 1968, for *The Midnight Fox,* 1969, for *Trouble River,* 1970, for *The Summer of the Swans,* 1972, for *The House of Wings,* 1973, for *The Winged Colt of Casa Mia* and *The 18th Emergency,* 1974, for *After the Goat Man,* 1975, for *The Lace Snail,* 1976, for *The TV Kid,* and 1980, for *The Night Swimmers;* Notable Book Award, American Library Association (ALA), 1969, for *Trouble River,* 1970, for *The Summer of the Swans,* 1972, for *The House of Wings,* 1977, for *The Pinballs,* and 1996, for *My Brother Ant;* Lewis Carroll Shelf Award, 1970, for *The Midnight Fox;* John Newbery Medal, ALA, 1971, for *The Summer of the Swans;* Best Books for Spring selection, *School Library Journal,* 1971, for *Go and Hush the Baby; Library Journal* Booklist, 1972, and National Book Award finalist, 1973, both for *House of Wings; New York Times* Outstanding Book of the Year, 1973, for *The Winged Colt of Casa Mia* and *The 18th Emergency,* 1979, for *Good-bye Chicken Little,* and 1982, for *The Two-Thousand-Pound Goldfish;* Dorothy Canfield Fisher Memorial Book Award, Vermont Congress of Parents and Teachers, 1975, for *The 18th Emergency;* Woodward Park School Annual Book Award, 1977; Children's Book Award, Child Study Children's Book Committee at Bank Street College of Education, 1977; Hans Christian Andersen Honor List for Promoting Concern for the Disadvantaged and Handicapped, 1979; Georgia Children's Book Award, 1979; Charlie May Simon Book Award, Arkansas Elementary School Council, 1980 and 1987; Surrey School Book of the Year Award, School Librarians of Surrey, British Colombia, 1980; Mark Twain Award, Missouri Library Association, 1980, William Allen White Children's Book Award, Emporia State University, 1980, Young Readers Medal, California Reading Association, 1980, Nene Award runner-up, 1981 and 1983, and Golden Archer Award, Department of Library Science, University of Wisconsin—Oshkosh, 1982, all for *The Pinballs;* Best Book of the Year, *School Library Journal,* 1980, and National Book Award for Children's Fiction, 1981, both for *The Night Swimmers;* Children's Choice, International Reading Association, 1982, Tennessee Children's Choice Book Award, Tennessee Library Association, 1983, and Sequoyah Children's Book Award, 1984, all for *The Cybil War;* Parent's Choice Award for Literature, Parent's Choice Foundation, 1982, Best Children's Books, *School Library Journal,* 1982, CRABbery Award, Oxon Hill Branch of Prince George's County Library, 1983, and Mark Twain Award, 1985, all for *The Animal, the Vegetable, and John D. Jones;* Notable Book of the Year, *New York Times,* 1982, for *The Two-Thousand-Pound Goldfish;* Regina Medal, Catholic Library Association, 1987; Charlie May Simon Award, 1987, for *The Computer Nut;* South Carolina Children's Book Award, William Allen White Award, and Maryland Children's Book Award, all 1988, all for *Cracker Jackson;* Edgar Alan Poe Award, Mystery Writers of America, 1992, for *Wanted . . . Mud Blossom;* Texas Bluebonnet Award and Sunshine State Young Readers Award, both 1998, both for *Tornado;* Nevada Young Readers Award, 1998, for *Tarot Says Beware.*

WRITINGS:

FOR CHILDREN

Clementine, illustrated by Charles Wilton, Houghton (Boston, MA), 1962.
The Dancing Camel, illustrated by Harold Berson, Viking (New York, NY), 1965.
Rama, the Gypsy Cat, illustrated by Peggy Bacon, Viking (New York, NY), 1966.
(And illustrator) *The Groober,* Harper (New York, NY), 1967.

The Midnight Fox, illustrated by Ann Grifalconi, Viking (New York, NY), 1968.

Trouble River, illustrated by Rocco Negri, Viking (New York, NY), 1969.

The Summer of the Swans, illustrated by Ted CoConis, Viking (New York, NY), 1970, reprinted, Puffin Books (New York, NY), 2004.

Go and Hush the Baby, illustrated by Emily A. McCully, Viking (New York, NY), 1971.

The House of Wings, illustrated by Daniel Schwartz, Viking (New York, NY), 1972.

The 18th Emergency, illustrated by Robert Grossman, Viking (New York, NY), 1973.

The Winged Colt of Casa Mia, illustrated by Richard Cuffari, Viking (New York, NY), 1973.

After the Goat Man, illustrated by Ronald Himler, Viking (New York, NY), 1974.

(And illustrator) *The Lace Snail,* Viking (New York, NY), 1975.

The TV Kid, illustrated by Richard Cuffari, Viking (New York, NY), 1976.

The Pinballs, Harper (New York, NY), 1977.

The Cartoonist, illustrated by Richard Cuffari, Viking (New York, NY), 1978.

Good-bye Chicken Little, Harper (New York, NY), 1979.

The Night Swimmers, illustrated by Troy Howell, Delacorte (New York, NY), 1980.

The Cybil War, illustrated by Gail Owens, Viking (New York, NY), 1981.

The Animal, the Vegetable, and John D. Jones, illustrated by Ruth Sanderson, Delacorte (New York, NY), 1982.

The Two-Thousand-Pound Goldfish, Harper (New York, NY), 1982.

The Glory Girl, Viking (New York, NY), 1983.

The Computer Nut, illustrated with computer graphics by son Guy Byars, Viking (New York, NY), 1984.

Cracker Jackson, Viking (New York, NY), 1985.

The Not-Just-Anybody Family, illustrated by Jacqueline Rogers, Delacorte (New York, NY), 1986.

The Golly Sisters Go West, illustrated by Sue Truesdale, Harper (New York, NY), 1986.

The Blossoms Meet the Vulture Lady, illustrated by Jacqueline Rogers, Delacorte (New York, NY), 1986.

The Blossoms and the Green Phantom, illustrated by Jacqueline Rogers, Delacorte (New York, NY), 1987.

A Blossom Promise, illustrated by Jacqueline Rogers, Delacorte (New York, NY), 1987.

Beans on the Roof, illustrated by Melodye Rosales, Delacorte (New York, NY), 1988.

The Burning Questions of Bingo Brown, illustrated by Cathy Bobak, Viking (New York, NY), 1988.

Bingo Brown and the Language of Love, illustrated by Cathy Bobak, Viking (New York, NY), 1988.

Hooray for the Golly Sisters, illustrated by Sue Truesdale, Harper (New York, NY), 1990.

Bingo Brown, Gypsy Lover, Viking (New York, NY), 1990.

The Seven Treasure Hunts, Harper (New York, NY), 1991.

Wanted . . . Mud Blossom, Delacorte (New York, NY), 1991.

Bingo Brown's Guide to Romance, Viking (New York, NY), 1992.

Coast to Coast, Delacorte (New York, NY), 1992.

McMummy, Viking (New York, NY), 1993.

The Golly Sisters Ride Again, illustrated by Sue Truesdale, HarperCollins (New York, NY), 1994.

The Dark Stairs: A Herculeah Jones Mystery, Viking (New York, NY), 1994.

(Compiler) *Growing up Stories,* Kingfisher (New York, NY), 1995.

Tarot Says Beware, Viking (New York, NY), 1995.

My Brother, Ant, illustrated by Marc Simont, Viking (New York, NY), 1996.

The Joy Boys, illustrated by Frank Remkiewicz, Yearling First Choice Chapter Book (New York, NY), 1996.

Tornado, illustrated by Doron Ben-Ami, HarperCollins (New York, NY), 1996.

Dead Letter, Viking (New York, NY), 1996.

Ant Plays Bear, illustrated by Marc Simont, Viking (New York, NY), 1997.

Death's Door, Viking (New York, NY), 1997.

Disappearing Acts, Viking (New York, NY), 1998.

Me Tarzan, HarperCollins (New York, NY), 2000.

(With Betsy Duffey and Laurie Myers) *My Dog, My Hero,* illustrated by Loren Long, Holt (New York, NY), 2000.

Little Horse, illustrated by David McPhail, Henry Holt (New York, NY), 2001.

The Keeper of the Doves, Viking (New York, NY), 2002.

(Compiler) *Top Teen Stories,* illustrated by Robert Geary, Kingfisher (Boston, MA), 2004.

Little Horse on His Own, illustrated by David McPhail, Henry Holt (New York, NY), 2004.

(With Betsy Duffey and Laurie Myers) *The SOS File,* illustrated by Arthur Howard, Henry Holt (New York, NY), 2004.

King of Murder, Sleuth/Viking (New York, NY), 2006.

OTHER

Contributor of "Taking Humor Seriously," to *The Zena Sutherland Lectures,* Clarion (New York, NY), 1983-92. Contributor of articles to numerous magazines, including *Saturday Evening Post, TV Guide,* and *Look.* Byars's works have been translated into nine languages.

ADAPTATIONS: The following books have been adapted for ABC-TV and broadcast as episodes of the *ABC Afterschool Special: The 18th Emergency,* broadcast as "Psst! Hammerman's after You," 1973; *The Summer of the Swans,* broadcast as "Sara's Summer of the Swans," 1974; *The Pinballs,* 1977; and *The Night Swimmers,* broadcast as "Daddy, I'm Their Mamma Now," 1981. *Trouble River,* 1975, and *The Winged Colt of Casa Mia* (adapted as "The Winged Colt"), 1976, were broadcast as *Saturday Morning Specials,* ABC-TV; *The Lace Snail* was adapted as a filmstrip and cassette by Viking; *The Midnight Fox, The Summer of the Swans, Go and Hush the Baby,* and *The TV Kid* were adapted as record/audio cassette recordings by Miller-Brody; *The Pinballs* was adapted as a play, published in *Around the World in 21 Plays: Theatre for Young Audiences,* edited by Lowell Swortzell, Applause (New York, NY), 1997.

SIDELIGHTS: Over the course of her long and productive career, Betsy Byars has received extensive critical praise for her insightful portrayals of adolescents suffering from feelings of isolation and loneliness. "In a succession of psychologically-sound stories," wrote a *New York Times Book Review* critic, "she has developed her theme: that the extreme inward pain of adolescence lessens as a person reaches outward." Byars has produced books for children of several different ages, including chapter books for beginning readers and novels aimed at an early adolescent audience. Though her works are intended for children, Byars does not shy away from controversial subjects. Mental retardation, teenage sexuality, and physical abuse are among the volatile topics considered in Byars's work, and her skillful handling of the material has helped convince critics that such issues can be effectively portrayed in juvenile literature.

Raised in North Carolina, Byars entered college as a math major but soon found English more to her liking. After marrying and starting a family, she turned to writing. She got her start by penning magazine articles, but eventually devoted her talents to children's literature. Her first published book, *Clementine,* appeared in 1962, but the negative reviews it received caused Byars to turn away from the personal material she had included in the book. "I went back to writing books that anyone could have written," Byars related in an interview for *Children's Literature in Education,* "like *Rama the Gypsy Cat*—very impersonal." Though she continued to publish regularly throughout the 1960s, it was not until she wrote *The Midnight Fox* that Byars again returned to events from her own life as a source of her fiction.

The Summer of the Swans, Byars's next effort, was drawn from the author's work with mentally retarded children. *The Summer of the Swans* tells the story of Sara, an awkward adolescent who struggles both with doubts about herself, and with the mixed feelings she has for her mentally impaired brother, Charlie. When Charlie wanders away from the house and becomes lost in a forest, Sara understands how valuable her brother is to her. In the end, Sara locates Charlie, and in the process she gains a new and positive sense of herself.

In a *Horn Book* review of *The Summer of the Swans,* Ethel L. Haines stated: "Seldom are the pain of adolescence and the tragedy of mental retardation presented as sensitively and unpretentiously as in the story of Sara and Charlie." A *Top of the News* reviewer also lauded the book: "Betsy Byars, a sensitive writer with an ear and heart attuned to the subtleties of growing up, has created a story of extraordinary understanding and warmth." Barbara H. Baskin and Karen H. Harris, writing in *Notes from a Different Drummer: A Guide to Juvenile Fiction Portraying the Handicapped,* attributed the book's strengths, in part, to the way in which Byars handled the sentimental aspects of the story. "The descriptions of behavior are both tender and accurate," the authors wrote. "[Byars] can describe scenes revealing limitations in ways that reflect reality and avoid maudlin pity." Byars's ability to avoid an overly sentimental treatment of her subjects has been praised frequently by reviewers of her work. Another factor contributing to the author's critical success is her use of comedy. In *Children and Books,* Zena Sutherland, Dianne L. Monson, and May Hill Arbuthnot wrote that Byars's writing exhibits a "quiet, understated sense of humor that children quickly recognize and enjoy."

An example from a more recent Byars work, *Cracker Jackson,* also demonstrates how the author uses humor effectively. In the course of the book, eleven-year-old Jackson discovers that his former baby sitter, Alma, is being physically abused by her husband. When the abuse includes Alma's baby, Jackson and a friend take action. Their attempt to drive Alma to a shelter for battered women is related as a humorous adventure, and the comedy of Jackson's day-to-day mischief is also woven throughout the story. *Horn Book* reviewer Ethel R. Twichell noted that this combination of humor with a serious situation "would be an audacious undertaking in the hands of a less-skilled storyteller," but found Byars's effort to be an "expert blend of humor and compassion." *New York Times Book Review* contributor Mary Louise Cuneo registered a minor complaint about the characterization of Goat, Jackson's friend. "Goat regularly acts so much like a standard free spirit," Cuneo wrote, "that a reader could tire or disbelieve him." However, Cuneo also cited Byars's ability to "write low-key humor deftly."

Such criticism of Byars's characterization is rare. Her books have often been hailed for containing vivid characters that appeal to young readers. For instance, critic Jean Fritz wrote in the *New York Times Book Review* that Byars "has always had the capacity to create unique and believable characters." This ability is demonstrated in her series of novels featuring the Blossom family. Junior Blossom has a knack for unsuccessful inventions such as his subterranean hamster resort. Junior's sister, Maggie, wants to be a trick horseback rider like her mother and deceased father; and Vicki, the mother, occasionally leaves her children to rejoin the professional rodeo circuit. The family's acquaintances are also unusual, including Ralphie, a boy with an artificial leg, and Mad Mary, who lives in a cave and makes her dinner from the dead animals that she finds on the road.

In her review of *A Blossom Promise, Los Angeles Times Book Review* contributor Kristiana Gregory wrote that Byars's "perception of kids' feelings is keen." She also praised the author for creating a "cast so memorably quirky that you hate to say good-bye." However, Elizabeth-Ann Sachs's review of *Wanted . . . Mud Blossom* in the *New York Times Book Review* sounded a cautionary note regarding the bizarre characters. "The adults are atypical," Sachs wrote, "more flawed than it is comfortable to think about—indeed somewhat alarming in their eccentricity."

Despite this reservation, Sachs found that "Ms. Byars's dialogue rings true. She captures the whining and the teasing and the playfulness of children."

The Blossom series also demonstrates Byars's attempt to create a detailed view of her protagonists by devoting several books to their adventures. She has applied this approach to other characters as well, including Bingo Brown. In the first installment of this series, *The Burning Questions of Bingo Brown,* the title character grapples with uncertainty by writing down his questions about various adolescent concerns. Many of Bingo's questions deal with the three girls he has fallen in love with simultaneously. There are also questions regarding Bingo's English teacher, Mr. Markham, who has begun to give the class strange lectures on suicide and the woman that he loves. When Mr. Markham is involved in a motorcycle crash, Bingo wonders if the teacher was attempting to take his own life.

Ellen Fader, reviewing the book in the *School Library Journal,* called *The Burning Questions of Bingo Brown* a "humorous and poignant novel," but also warned readers about the book's consideration of suicide. "Byars's light handling of a serious subject may disturb some adults," the critic wrote. Despite this reservation, Fader ultimately judged the book a success: "Accurate characterization developed through believable dialogue and fresh language, give this tremendous child appeal and read-aloud potential." A *Publishers Weekly* reviewer also praised the book: "Byars relays Bingo's questions and his answers in a way that is so believable that readers may wonder if there isn't a Bingo Brown in their classrooms."

In 1994 Byers published *The Dark Stairs: A Herculeah Jones Mystery,* the first of a new series. The well-received series revolves around thirteen-year-old Herculeah, whose father is a police officer and whose mother is a private investigator. A *Publishers Weekly* reviewer called Herculeah a "distinctive and engaging heroine," and a *Booklist* reviewer lauded this "delightful middle-grade" mystery. Byers continued the series with *Dead Letter, Death's Door, Tarot Says Beware,* and *Disappearing Acts.* Many critics have offered positive assessments of this series, and *Tarot Says Beware* garnered the Nevada Young Readers Award in 1998.

Byars wrote of a young girl confronting life's biggest issues in her novel *The Keeper of the Doves.* Birth, death, the process of change and the mysteries of human behavior are all on the mind of Amen McBee (also called Amie), the youngest girl growing up in the late 1800s in a well-to-do family with five daughters. Ever since Amen can remember, her older sisters have frightened her with stories about Mr. Tominski, a mysterious and reclusive Polish immigrant who lives in the chapel behind their house. Amen knows that Tominski once saved her father's life and she believes he is really harmless, but it is true that his behavior can be strange and frightening. When the family pet is killed, her sisters accuse Mr. Tominski, but as Caroline Ward reported in a *School Library Journal* review, "The surprising climax presents provocative questions about judging others and the nature of truth." Ward also praised Byars's skillful evocation of both major and minor characters. *Booklist* reviewer Ilene Cooper noted that while the story elements are sometimes handled "abruptly," the book is a success due to "the mood Byars creates in short, short chapters in which every word is important." *The Keeper of the Doves* is presented in twenty-six chapters that are tied to the letters of the alphabet. The "echo of alpha and omega, source and ending," was effective, in the estimation of Joanna Rudge, a reviewer for *Horn Book*. She considered the book "Byars at her best—witty, appealing, thought-provoking." Byars's love of language is reflected in the character of Amen, who seeks to express her feelings about the events taking place through poetry. The family's life is depicted "in a prose that ripples with clarity and sweetness and an underlying evolution of spirit," stated a *Kirkus Reviews* writer. High praise for the author's skills also came from the *Publishers Weekly* reviewer, who stated: "Byars effortlessly links subtle images into a cycle of life. . . . The snippets of Amie's and her family's lives add up to an exquisitely complete picture."

Byars has collaborated with two of her daughters in writing the books *My Dog, My Hero* and *The SOS File.* The latter is a collection of narratives taken from the fictional Mr. Magro's class, for which students did writing assignments for extra credit. These short pieces cover a wide range of personalities and situations, from one child's account of being rescued from a dumpster as a newborn to another's dilemma of eating all the candy that was intended for a fundraising project. *Booklist* reviewer Shelle Rosenfeld predicted that the anecdotes in this volume would "inspire thought and discussion," and she praised the "lively" writing style. "Some tales are poignant, others are humorous; all are as credible as the characters sketched," affirmed Maria

B. Salvadore in the *School Library Journal.* In addition to the quality of the stories, some reviewers noted that their short length and variety made this book "perfect for encouraging reluctant readers," in the words of a *Kirkus Reviews* contributor.

Over the course of her career, Byars has gained a great respect for her young readers. "Boys and girls are very sharp today," Byars told Rachel Fordyce in an interview for *Twentieth-Century Children's Writers.* "When I visit classrooms and talk with students I am always impressed to find how many of them are writing stories and how knowledgeable they are about writing." Her personal contact with children has also affected the way she shapes her stories. "Living with my own teenagers has taught me that not only must I not write down to my readers," Byars said, "I must write up to them."

BIOGRAPHICAL AND CRITICAL SOURCES:

BOOKS

Baskin, Barbara H., and Karen H. Harris, *Notes from a Different Drummer: A Guide to Juvenile Fiction Portraying the Handicapped,* Bowker (New York, NY), 1977.
Children's Literature Review, Volume 1, Gale (Detroit, MI), 1976.
Contemporary Literary Criticism, Volume 32, Gale (Detroit, MI), 1985.
Kirkpatrick, D.L., editor, *Twentieth-Century Children's Writers,* St. Martin's Press (New York, NY), 1978.
Rees, David, *Painted Desert, Green Shade: Essays on Contemporary Writers of Fiction for Children and Young Adults,* Horn Book (Boston, MA), 1984.
Something about the Author Autobiography Series, Volume 1, Gale (Detroit, MI), 1986.
Sutherland, Zena, Dianne L. Monson, and May Hill Arbuthnot, editors, *Children and Books,* sixth edition, Scott Foresman (New York, NY), 1981.
Usrey, Malcolm, *Betsy Byars,* Twayne (New York, NY), 1995.

PERIODICALS

Book, September, 2000, Kathleen Odean, review of *Me Tarzan,* p. 86.

Booklist, April 1, 1994, Stephanie Zvirin, review of *The Golly Sisters Ride Again,* p. 1465; August, 1994, Stephanie Zvirin, review of *The Dark Stairs: A Herculeah Jones Mystery,* p. 2042; July, 1995, Stephanie Zvirin, review of *Tarot Says Beware,* p. 1878; January 1, 1996, review of *My Brother, Ant,* p. 828; September 15, 1996, Carolyn Phelan, review of *Tornado,* p. 238; March 1, 1997, Stephanie Zvirin, review of *Death's Door,* p. 1162; September 1, 1997, Hazel Rochman, review of *Ant Plays Bear,* p. 116; March 1, 1998, Stephanie Zvirin, review of *Disappearing Acts,* p. 1134; March 15, 2000, Hazel Rochman, review of *Me Tarzan,* p. 1376; January 1, 2001, Ellen Mandel, review of *My Dog, My Hero,* p. 954; October 1, 2002, Ilene Cooper, review of *The Keeper of the Doves,* p. 322; June 1, 2004, Shelle Rosenfeld, review of *The SOS File,* p. 1725; September 1, 2004, Jennifer Mattson, review of *Little Horse on His Own,* p. 120.

Children's Literature in Education, winter, 1982, interview with Betsy Byars.

Horn Book, February, 1971, Ethel L. Haines, review of *The Summer of the Swans;* May-June, 1985, Ethel R. Twichell, review of *Cracker Johnson,* p. 310; May-June, 1998, Elizabeth S. Watson, review of *Disappearing Acts,* p. 341; May, 2000, review of *Me Tarzan,* p. 309; September-October, 2002, Joanna Rudge, review of *The Keeper of the Doves,* p. 567.

Kirkus Reviews, July 15, 2002, review of *The Keeper of the Doves,* p. 1028; May 1, 2004, review of *The SOS File,* p. 439; August 15, 2004, review of *Little Horse on His Own,* p. 803.

Los Angeles Times Book Review, January 31, 1988, Kristiana Gregory, review of *A Blossom Promise,* p. 7.

NEA Today, September, 2004, review of *The SOS File,* p. 59.

New York Times, December 5, 1980, George A. Woods, review of *The Night Swimmers,* p. 19; November 30, 1982, George A. Woods, review of *The Two-Thousand-Pound Goldfish,* p. 23.

New York Times Book Review, May 4, 1980, Jean Fritz, review of *The Night Swimmers,* p. 26; July 19, 1981, Patricia Lee Gauch, review of *The Cybil War,* p. 21; May 30, 1982, Michele Slung, review of *The Animal, the Vegetable, and John D. Jones,* p. 14; November 28, 1982, George A. Woods, review of *The Two-Thousand-Pound Goldfish,* p. 24; November 27, 1983, Marilyn Kaye, review of *The Glory Girl,* p. 34; August 4, 1985, Mary Louise Cuneo, review of *Cracker Jackson,* p. 21; December 15, 1991, Elizabeth-Ann Sachs, review of *Wanted . . . Mud Blossom,* p. 29.

Publishers Weekly, April 8, 1988, Kimberly Olson Fekih, review of *The Burning Questions of Bingo Brown,* p. 95; July 19, 1991, review of *Wanted . . . Mud Blossom,* p. 56; April 20, 1992, review of *The Moon and I,* p. 58; May 18, 1992, review of *Bingo Brown's Guide to Romance,* p. 71; October 12, 1992, review of *Coast to Coast,* p. 79; August 16, 1993, review of *McMummy,* p. 105; July 18, 1994, review of *The Dark Stairs,* p. 246; May 22, 2000, review of *Me Tarzan,* p. 93; August 19, 2002, review of *The Keeper of the Doves,* p. 90; May 17, 2004, review of *The SOS File,* p. 50.

School Library Journal, May, 1988, Ellen Fader, review of *The Burning Questions of Bingo Brown,* pp. 95-96; April, 1992, Phyllis Graves, review of *The Moon and I,* p. 112; January, 1998, review of *Bingo Brown, Gypsy Lover;* March, 1998, Linda L. Plevak, review of *Disappearing Acts,* p. 211; July, 2000, Janet Gillen, review of *Me Tarzan,* p. 68; January, 2001, Pat Leach, review of *My Dog, My Hero,* p. 92; October, 2002, Caroline Ward, review of *The Keeper of the Doves,* p. 158; June, 2004, Maria B. Salvadore, review of *The SOS File,* p. 103.

Top of the News, April, 1971, review of *The Summer of the Swans.*

Washington Post Book World, January 13, 1985, Carolyn Banks, review of *The Computer Nut,* p. 9.*

*   *   *

BYARS, Betsy Cromer
See BYARS, Betsy

C

CAMAZINE, S. 1952-
(Scott Camazine)

PERSONAL: Born August 4, 1952, in Rochester, NY; son of Murray (a builder) and Ruth (a social worker; maiden name, Widelitz) Camazine; married Sue Trainor (a cardiac care nurse); children: Caela. *Education:* Harvard University, B.A., 1974, M.D., 1978; Cornell University, Ph.D., 1993. *Hobbies and other interests:* Woodturning.

ADDRESSES: Office—310 West Main St., Boalsburg, PA 16827. *E-mail*—camazine@adelphia.net; scott_camazine@agcs.cas.psu.edu.

CAREER: University Hospital, University of California, San Diego, CA, intern, 1979-80; St. Joseph's Hospital, Elmira, NY, emergency room physician, 1980-88; Cornell University, Section of Neurobiology and Behavior, Ithaca, NY, research associate, 1980-83, 1986-87, visiting fellow in department of entomology, 1983-86; Ithaca College, Ithaca, NY, lecturer, 1985; Tompkins Community Hospital, Ithaca, NY, emergency room physician, beginning 1989; Penn State University, Happy Valley, PA, assistant professor of entomology. Medical, science, and nature photographer for clients including the United States Postal Service, Microsoft, Time, Inc., Audubon, *Natural History* magazine, *Life, New York Times Magazine,* and *Scientific American;* lecturer. Consultant to South Korea for United Nations Food and Agriculture Organization, 1987.

MEMBER: American College of Emergency Physicians, Entomological Society of America, Phi Beta Kappa.

AWARDS, HONORS: Bache Fund grant, National Academy of Sciences, 1982; British Broadcasting Corporation Wildlife Photography Award, 1987; Children's Science Book Award, New York Academy of Sciences, 1988, for *Naturalist's Year;* named Kodak Wildlife Photographer of the Year, 1988; John M. Olin Graduate Fellowship, 1989; National Science Foundation Graduate Research fellowship, 1989; Association of American Publishers Award, Professional/Scholarly Publishers Division, 2002.

WRITINGS:

Naturalist's Year (nonfiction), illustrations by stepmother, Cynthia Camazine, John Wiley & Sons (New York, NY), 1988.
Velvet Mites and Silken Webs: The Wonderful Details of Nature in Photographs and Essays (essays and photographs), John Wiley & Sons (New York, NY), 1991.
(With Jean-Louis Deneubourg, Nigel R. Franks, James Sneyd, Guy Theraulaz, and Eric Bonabeau) *Self-Organization in Biological Systems* (nonfiction), original line drawings by William Ristine and Mary Ellen Didion, StarLogo programming by William Thies, Princeton University Press (Princeton, NJ), 2001.

Contributor of articles to scientific journals and nature magazines, including *Bee World, Behavioral Ecology* and *Sociobiology.*

SIDELIGHTS: After a career that included working as an emergency room physician while earning his Ph.D. in biology from Cornell University, S. Camazine became a professor in entomology at Penn State University. He has also worked as a professional photographer, specializing in nature, and has had a long-standing interest in nature. His 1988 book, *Naturalist's Year,* is an illustrated guide to the plant, animal, bird, and insect life in common American natural wildlife habitats. He encourages his readers to carry out their own investigations into natural phenomena in chapters discussing such topics as herbal medicines, edible plants and fungi, and bird migration patterns. Camazine hopes his work will help to cultivate increased awareness of and appreciation for the natural environment.

In 2002 he coauthored *Self-Organization in Biological Systems,* an overview of a budding area of research known as self-organization theory. Focusing primarily on behavior, scientists working in this discipline look at how organisms create patterns and structures that are often complex yet seem spontaneous. Camazine and his collaborators provide an overview of the subject and provides detailed studies of several examples of this behavior in certain organisms such as fish, bees, termites, and ants. Some reviewers, such as Diane Lipscomb in *Science Books & Films,* criticized several areas lacking in the book, including an exploration of alternative explanations for the animals' behaviors and a discussion of the history of self-evolution. Reviewing *Self-Organization in Biological Systems* in *Science,* however, John W. Pepper and Guy Hoelzer noted that the book"presents a unique opportunity to watch a group of active researchers apply these intriguing concepts to formerly mystifying feats of social organization in animals. We know of no better guide."

BIOGRAPHICAL AND CRITICAL SOURCES:

PERIODICALS

Science, November 16, 2001, John W. Pepper and Guy Hoelzer, review of *Self-Organization in Biological Systems,* p. 14666.
Science Books & Films, September/October 2002, Diane Lipscomb, review of *Self-Organization in Biological Systems,* p. 500.

ONLINE

Penn State Agriculture Magazine Web site http://aginfo.psu.edu/ (winter/spring, 1998), John Wall,

"At Play in Fields Filled with Bees," biography of Scott Camazine.
Scott Camazine Home Page, http://www.scott camazine.com (October 22, 2005).*

*   *   *

CAMAZINE, Scott
See CAMAZINE, S.

*   *   *

CARCATERRA, Lorenzo 1954-

PERSONAL: Born October 16, 1954, in New York, NY; son of Mario (a butcher) and Raffaela (a homemaker) Carcaterra; married Susan J. Toepfer (a magazine editor), May 16, 1981; children: Katherine, Nicholas. *Education:* St. John's University, B.S., 1976. *Politics:* "Moderate." *Religion:* Catholic.

ADDRESSES: Home—498 Manor Ln., Pelham Manor, NY 10803. *Office*—1600 Broadway, Ste. 701, New York, NY 10020. *Agent*—Loretta Fidel, Weingel-Fidel Agency, 310 E. 46th St., New York, NY 10017.

CAREER: New York Daily News, New York, NY, reporter and editor, 1976-83; *TV-Cable Week,* staff writer, 1983; freelance writer, 1983—; Columbia Broadcasting System (CBS), New York, NY, managing editor of *Top Cops,* 1990-c. 1994. Has also worked for TimeWarner; writer and producer for *Law and Order* television series aired by the National Broadcasting Company, Inc. (NBC).

MEMBER: International Association of Crime Writers, Authors Guild, Authors League of America.

AWARDS, HONORS: Leone Di San Marco award, Italian Heritage and Culture Committee, 1993, for *A Safe Place: The True Story of a Father, a Son, a Murder.*

WRITINGS:

A Safe Place: The True Story of a Father, a Son, a Murder, Villard (New York, NY), 1993.

Sleepers (novel), Ballantine (New York, NY), 1995.

Apaches (novel), Ballantine (New York, NY), 1997.

Gangster (novel), Ballantine (New York, NY), 2001.

Street Boys (novel), Ballantine (New York, NY), 2002.

Paradise City (novel), Ballantine (New York, NY), 2004.

(Contributor) *Dangerous Women: Original Stories from Today's Greatest Suspense Writers*, edited by Otto Penzler, Mysterious Press (New York, NY), 2005.

Also author of filmscripts, including *Street Boys, Dreamer,* and *Doubt.*

Contributor to periodicals, including *People, Life, Us, Cop Talk,* and *National Geographic Traveler* magazine.

ADAPTATIONS: Sleepers was adapted into a major motion picture starring Kevin Bacon, Robert DeNiro, Jason Patric, Brad Pitt, and Minnie Driver, directed by Barry Levinson, Warner Bros., 1996; *Gangster* is being developed as a feature film by Revolution Studios; *Street Boys* was purchased by Warner Bros.; *Apaches* has been optioned for film by producer Jerry Bruckheimer.

WORK IN PROGRESS: Two novels, *Chasers* and *Midnight Angels;* a pilot for Touchstone titled *The Ghost;* a video game for Atari/Eden titled *Alone in the Dark: Near Death Investigation,* expected 2006.

SIDELIGHTS: Journalist and scriptwriter Lorenzo Carcaterra began his career as an author when he took a leave from writing for the television series *Top Cops* to write his own life story. His first book, *A Safe Place: The True Story of a Father, a Son, a Murder,* is Carcaterra's memoir of life with his father, a violent man whose temper had resulted not only in the death of his first wife but in the repeated abuse of his second, Carcaterra's mother. Reviewing the book for *People,* Joseph Olshan called it "haunting" and "remarkable," and commended the author's believable, well-rounded portrait of his father. Martha Southgate, a writer for *Entertainment Weekly,* felt that Carcaterra had set himself up for an almost "impossible" task by attempting to show the humanity in his brutal father; she noted that the author tried "valiantly" to tell his terrible story.

With the success of *A Safe Place,* other books followed from Carcaterra, among them *Sleepers,* the story of a group of childhood friends who become involved in murder. Upon its publication in 1995, *Sleepers* became newsworthy not only because of its bestseller status, but because it was released as a work of nonfiction. While Carcaterra claimed that the only fictionalized aspects of the book were done to protect the identities of its subjects, some critics were skeptical. The book follows a group of four young people raised in the Hell's Kitchen area of New York City—where the author himself was raised—and details their brush with the law, their resulting incarceration in an upstate New York reform school, and their ultimate, violent revenge on the school guards responsible for torturing them during that incarceration. The book was adapted into a major motion picture in 1996.

Despite the popularity of the book, critical reaction to *Sleepers* was mixed for a variety of reasons. In a *Spectator* review, contributor Michael Carlson called Carcaterra "a fine writer and facile stylist," but found "more worrying than the question of the book's veracity . . . the moral dilemma at its centre," a dilemma that involves a Roman Catholic priest's complicity in a lie. Trey Graham concluded in the *Washington Post Book World:* "*Sleepers* is undeniably powerful, an enormously affecting and intensely human story."

Carcaterra followed *Sleepers* with a fictional work titled *Apaches.* Even more violent than its predecessor, *Apaches* details, with a great deal of blood and gore, a scheme whereby some ruthless drug runners transport their product in the bodies of murdered infants. While noting that the author "is good at creating an obscenity-laced, gallows humor dialogue" for his characters, *New York Times* contributor Richard Bernstein was less enthusiastic about the novel as a whole. Rife with brutal murder sequences, sadistic villains, and heroic city cops prepared to lay down their lives to save a child, *Apaches* "relies on just about every stale, manipulative device of the pulp thriller genre as it slogs toward its predictably noisy climax," according to the critic. *Newsweek* reviewer Jeff Giles called Carcaterra "one of the most intriguing writers around," yet he found *Apaches* flawed. Drug-filled baby corpses are "the strongest metaphor imaginable for the corruption of innocence," wrote Giles.

Crime is again at the heart of Carcaterra's next novel, *Gangster,* which tells the story of two generations of a Mafia family. Angelo Vestieri, an underworld kingpin, takes a paternal interest in Gabe, a ten-year-old boy who flees his foster home in the early 1960s. Doing small jobs for Angelo, Gabe learns all about life inside the mob, but he ultimately rejects that lifestyle when Angelo offers him a powerful position within it. "Carcaterra shows dexterity in humanizing the denizens of the urban underbelly," commented a *Publishers Weekly* reviewer, who added: "Through a fine characterization of the enigmatic Vestieri, he provides a stirring perspective on the ways of mobsters and their history." *Library Journal* contributor Craig L. Shufelt predicted that the book would find an enthusiastic audience "among readers who enjoy gangster novels." Brad Hooper, a writer for *Booklist,* pointed to "the author's psychological fathoming of the kind of character that turns to a life of organized crime" and called *Gangster* "a very compelling drama."

Street Boys recounts a World War II-era story. The plot revolves around a band of children orphaned by war and hiding from the Nazis in their hometown of Naples. Enter Steve Connors, an American soldier who goes to Naples on a mission and begins helping the children with their makeshift army. Before long the children and their mentor are causing the Nazis embarrassing problems. Robert Conroy, writing in the *Library Journal,* felt the author told a "gripping story." Mary Frances Wilkens commented in *Booklist* that "the syrupy plot is endearing." A *Kirkus Reviews* contributor wrote "there's a great story here."

In the 2004 novel *Paradise City,* Carcaterra tells the story of Italian cop Giancarlo Lo Manto, who has come to America to hunt down his kidnapped niece. Lo Manto soon encounters a crime gang based in his hometown of Naples and finds himself attracted to his assigned American partner, Jennifer Fabini. A contributor to *Publishers Weekly* noted that "readers unafraid of a little purple in their prose . . . will have a perfectly good time." Mary Frances Wilkins, writing in *Booklist,* found that "Lo Manto's characterization displays a bit more depth than many of the author's other swashbuckling leading men."

Carcaterra once told *CA:* "I was raised in a violent world, but one which I found great comfort in. I didn't own a book until I was twenty, though I always thought of writing. Since then it's been one lesson after another, all learned in the hopes of making myself a better writer. Some of the lessons were enjoyable (such as my years spent as a reporter for the *New York Daily News,* a tabloid that proved to be a great place

for a young writer to grow up), while some of the lessons were stark and difficult (a number of lean freelance years, for example). I have written for all types of magazines, some well known (*People, Life*), and others less so. Then, in 1990, I got lucky when a producer put me in charge of *Top Cops,* a television show that found an audience."

BIOGRAPHICAL AND CRITICAL SOURCES:

BOOKS

Carcaterra, Lorenzo, *A Safe Place: The Story of a Father, a Son, a Murder,* Villard (New York, NY), 1993.

PERIODICALS

America, November 16, 1996, Edward J. Mattimoe, "True and Truth," discusses film adaptation of *Sleepers,* p. 17.

Antioch Review, winter, 1996, review of *Sleepers,* p. 120.

Booklist, May 1, 1995, Brad Hooper, review of *Sleepers,* p. 1530; October 15, 2000, Brad Hooper, review of *Gangster,* p. 388; August, 2002, Mary Frances Wilkens, review of *Street Boys,* p. 1884; August, 2004, Mary Frances Wilkens, review of *Paradise City,* p. 1868.

Business Wire, March 20, 2001, "Warner Bros. Pictures and Bel-Air Entertainment Acquire Rights to New Novel by Lorenzo Carcaterra," p. 0742.

Detroit Free Press (via *Knight-Ridder/Tribune News Service*), February 21, 2001, John Smyntek, review of *Gangster.*

Entertainment Weekly, January 22, 1993, Martha Southgate, review of *A Safe Place,* p. 52; March 17, 1995, "Big Deal," discusses film rights to *Sleepers,* p. 81; July 14, 1995, Tom De Haven, review of *Sleepers,* p. 46; November 1, 1996, Owen Gleiberman, review of *Sleepers,* p. 40.

Kirkus Reviews, May 1, 1995, review of *Sleepers,* p. 600; July 15, 2002, review of *Street Boys,* p. 972; July 1, 2004, review of *Paradise City,* p. 589.

Kliatt Young Adult Paperback Book Guide, May, 1996, review of *Sleepers* (audio version), p. 48; November 15, 2000, review of *Gangster,* p. 1559.

Library Journal, February 1, 1993, Gregor A. Preston, review of *A Safe Place,* p. 98; July, 1995, Robert H. Donahugh, review of *Sleepers,* p. 89; September 15, 1997, Stephen L. Hupp, review of *Apaches* (audio version), p. 118; November 15, 2000, Craig L. Shufelt, review of *Gangster,* p. 95; September 1, 2002, Robert Conroy, review of *Street Boys,* p. 210; May 1, 2004, Barbara Hoffert, review of *Paradise City,* p. 86.

Maclean's, August 28, 1995, Barbara Wickens, review of *Sleepers,* p. 48.

New Statesman & Society, December 15, 1995, review of *Sleepers,* p. 66.

Newsweek, February 8, 1993, review of *A Safe Place,* p. 67; December 9, 1996, Jeff Giles and Ray Sawhill, "Hollywood's Dying for Novel Ideas," discusses *Sleepers,* p. 80; August 11, 1997, Jeff Giles, review of *Apaches,* p. 75.

New York, November 4, 1996, David Denby, review of *Sleepers,* p. 84.

New Yorker, November 4, 1996, Terrence Rafferty, review of *Sleepers,* p. 117.

New York Times, July 7, 1995, p. B2; August 3, 1995, Christopher Lehmann-Haupt, review of *Sleepers,* p. C16; August 13, 1997, Richard Bernstein, review of *Apaches,* p. 2.

Observer (London, England), April 21, 1996, review of *Sleepers,* p. 16.

People, January 18, 1993, Joseph Olshan, review of *A Safe Place,* p. 30; July 31, 1995, William Plummer, review of *Sleepers,* p. 30.

Publishers Weekly, March 6, 1995, Paul Nathan, "Peak Market," about optioning of author's novel *Sleepers,* p. 23; June 5, 1995, review of *Sleepers,* p. 45; March 11, 1996, review of *Sleepers,* p. 58; December 11, 2000, review of *Gangster,* p. 61; July 15, 2002, review of *Street Boys,* p. 53; July 5, 2004, review of *Paradise City,* p. 34.

Rolling Stone, October 31, 1996, Peter Travers, review of *Sleepers,* p. 75.

Spectator, October 7, 1995, review of *Sleepers,* p. 45.

Time, July 31, 1995, Paul Gray, review of *Sleepers,* p. 69.

Tribune Books (Chicago), August 6, 1995, p. 5.

Washington Post, July 26, 1995, Peter Streitfeld, "'Sleepers': A Rude Awakening? Editor Denies That Nonfiction Bestseller Played Loose with Facts," p. D1.

Washington Post Book World, February 7, 1993, review of *A Safe Place,* p. 1; July 30, 1995, review of *Sleepers,* p. 6; August 24, 1997, review of *Apaches,* p. 5.

ONLINE

AllReaders.com, http://www.allreaders.com/ (September 24, 2005), Harriet Klausner, reviews of *Street Boys, Sleepers, Paradise City,* and *Gangster.*

BookReporter.com, http://www.bookreporter.com/ (September 24, 2005), Joe Hartlaub, review of *Paradise City.*

Lorenzo Carcaterra Home Page, http://www.lorenzo carcaterra.com (October 19, 2005).

Mystery Reader, http://www.themysteryreader.com/ (September 24, 2005), Dede Anderson, review of *Apaches;* Lesley Dunlap, review of *Paradise City.*

Shots Ma, http://www.shotsmag.co.uk/ (September 24, 2005), Keith Miles, review of *Paradise City.**

*   *   *

CHISHOLM, P.F.
See FINNEY, Patricia

*   *   *

CLARKSON, John 1947-

PERSONAL: Born 1947; married.

ADDRESSES: Office—Clarkson Cogen Inc., 72 Spring St., New York, NY 10012.

CAREER: Has worked as a copywriter for advertising agencies in New York, NY; Clarkson/Cogen, Inc. (advertising agency), New York, NY, founder; coproducer of five episodes of the television series *Land's End.*

MEMBER: Authors' Guild, Authors League of America, Writers' Guild of America East.

WRITINGS:

NOVELS

And Justice for One, Crown (New York, NY), 1992.
One Man's Law, Berkeley (New York, NY), 1994.

One Way Out, Jove (New York, NY), 1995.
New Lots, Forge (New York, NY), 1998.
Reed's Promise, Forge (New York, NY), 2001.

OTHER

And Justice for One (screenplay), Paramount Pictures, c. 1999.

Also author of plays, one of which has been produced at the Ensemble Studio Theater, New York, NY. Head writer and author of five episodes of the television series *Land's End.* Contributor of short stories to periodicals, including *Smoke.*

SIDELIGHTS: John Clarkson is a novelist with a flair for thrilling stories. His first novel, 1992's *And Justice for One,* begins with brothers Jack and George Devlin drinking away their sorrows in Manhattan bars after their father's funeral. Jack, who is single, finds a beautiful woman to comfort him, while George, who is married, has kids, and lives in the suburbs, visits an illegal after-hours nightclub. George is beaten by employees of the nightclub's evil, sadistic owner, Robert Wexler.

Jack finds his brother lying comatose in the hospital, and he also learns that the police have no leads in the crime and have little intention of pursuing the case. The attack becomes Jack's problem to solve, and he has almost nothing to go on. Jack encounters a couple of love interests en route to answering such questions as whether Does Wexler have friends in high places, including the police department. A critic for *Kirkus Reviews* called *And Justice for One* "dark, sexy, tough, and fast. Reminiscent of the best early Lawrence Sanders." Marilyn Stasio commented in the *New York Times Book Review* that Clarkson's first novel "packs a savage punch." Clarkson is also the author of two other novels featuring Jack Devlin, *One Man's Law* and *One Way Out.*

In addition, Clarkson has published stand-alone novels outside the Devlin series. In *New Lots* Lloyd Shaw is a struggling New York City detective who is assigned to "New Lots," a housing project in Brooklyn. Shaw must keep the residents of New Lots safe from dangerous drug dealers who live in the project. To accomplish

his task, he must put together a team of rogue cops to take on the drug dealers. David Pitt recommended *New Lots* in his *Booklist* article to "fans of gritty crime dramas."

Another stand-alone novel by Clarkson is the mystery thriller *Reed's Promise,* a book that a *Kirkus Reviews* critic called "well-researched." The books's primary character is Bill Reed, a retired Federal Bureau of Investigation (FBI) agent who has recently become an amputee. When Johnny Boy Reed, Bill Reed's mentally challenged cousin, calls him in distress, Bill becomes engrossed in a mystery surrounding illegal funds passing through the institution housing his cousin. A reviewer for *Publishers Weekly* wrote: "This engaging thriller is equipped with psychological depth and a solidly believable center."

BIOGRAPHICAL AND CRITICAL SOURCES:

PERIODICALS

Booklist, September 1, 1998, David Pitt, review of *New Lots,* p. 69.
Kirkus Reviews, November 15, 1991, review of *And Justice for One,* p. 1419; October 1, 2001, review of *Reed's Promise,* p. 1381.
New York Times Book Review, March 1, 1992, Marilyn Stasio, review of *And Justice for One,* p. 25.
Publishers Weekly, November 19, 2001, review of *Reed's Promise,* p. 50.*

*   *   *

CLEAGE, Pearl 1948-
(Pearl Michelle Cleage, Pearl Lomax, Pearl Cleage Lomax)

PERSONAL: Surname is pronounced "cleg"; born December 7, 1948, in Springfield, MA; daughter of Albert Buford (a minister) and Doris (a teacher; maiden name, Graham) Cleage; married Michael Lucius Lomax (an elected official of Fulton County, GA), October 31, 1969 (divorced, 1979); married Zaron W. Burnett, Jr.; children: (first marriage) Deignan Njeri. *Ethnicity:* "Black." *Education:* Attended Howard University, 1966-69, Yale University, 1969, and University of the West Indies, 1971; Spelman College, B.A., 1971; graduate study at Atlanta University, 1971.

ADDRESSES: Home—1665 Havilon Dr. S.W., Atlanta, GA 30311. *Office*—Just Us Theater Co., P.O. Box 42271, Atlanta, GA 30311-0271. *Agent*—c/o Author Mail, Ballantine, 1745 Broadway, New York, NY 10019.

CAREER: Playwright, poet, novelist, and educator. Just Us Theater Co., Atlanta, GA, playwright-in-residence, 1983-87, artistic director, 1987—; Spelman College, Atlanta, instructor in creative writing, 1986-91, playwright-in-residence, 1991—. Martin Luther King, Jr. Archival Library, member of field collection staff, 1969-70; Southern Education Program, Inc., assistant director, 1970-71; WETV, Atlanta, "Black Viewpoints" (produced by Clark College), host and interviewer, 1970-71; WQXI, Atlanta, staff writer and interviewer for *Ebony Beat Journal,* 1972, writer and associate producer, 1972-73; WXIA, Atlanta, executive producer, 1972-73; City of Atlanta, director of communications, beginning 1973; Brown/Gray, Ltd., writer, beginning 1976. Member of board of directors, Atlanta Center for Black Art, 1970-71.

MEMBER: Writers Guild of America (East).

AWARDS, HONORS: First prize for poetry, *Promethean Literary Magazine,* 1968; Georgia Council for the Arts residency grants from the city of Atlanta, 1982 and 1984; National Endowment for the Arts residency grants through Just Us Theater Co., 1983-87; Audience Development Committee (AUDELCO) Recognition Awards for Best Play and Best Playwright, 1983, for *Hospice;* Bronze Jubilee Award for Literature, Atlanta, Georgia, 1983; Mayor's fellowship in the arts, Atlanta Bureau of Cultural Affairs, 1986; seed grant from Coordinating Council of Literary Magazines, 1987, for *Catalyst;* AT&T New Work Development Grant, 1990; outstanding columnist award, Atlanta Association of Black Journalists, 1991; individual artist grant, Georgia Council on the Arts, 1991; grant from AT&T Onstage program, 1992, for *Flyin' West;* outstanding columnist award, Atlanta Association of Media Women, 1993; grants from the Coca-Cola Company, the Coca-Cola Foundation, and the Whitter-Bynner Foundation for Poetry; Oprah Book Club Selection, 1998, for *What Looks Like Crazy on an Ordinary Day..*

WRITINGS:

We Don't Need No Music (poetry), Broadside Press, 1971.

(Author of essay, under name Pearl Cleage Lomax) *P.H. Polk, Photographs,* Nexus Press (Atlanta, GA), 1980.

Dear Dark Faces: Portraits of a People (poetry), Lotus Press, 1980.

One for the Brothers (chapbook), privately printed, 1983.

Mad at Miles: A Blackwoman's Guide to Truth, Cleage Group (Southfield, MI), 1990.

The Brass Bed and Other Stories (young adult short fiction and poetry), Third World Press (Chicago, IL), 1991.

Deals with the Devil: And Other Reasons to Riot (essays), Ballantine (New York, NY), 1993.

What Looks like Crazy on an Ordinary Day (novel), Avon Books (New York, NY), 1997.

I Wish I Had a Red Dress (novel), William Morrow (New York, NY), 2001.

Some Things I Never Thought I'd Do (novel), One World/Ballantine Books (New York, NY), 2003.

(With Zaron W. Burnett, Jr.) *We Speak Your Names: A Celebration* (poetry), One World/Ballantine Books (New York, NY), 2005.

Babylon Sisters (novel), One World/Ballantine Books (New York, NY), 2005.

PLAYS

Hymn for the Rebels (one-act), first produced in Washington, DC, at Howard University, 1968.

Duet for Three Voices (one-act), first produced in Washington, DC, at Howard University, 1969.

The Sale (one-act), first produced in Atlanta, GA, at Spelman College, 1972.

puppetplay, first produced in Atlanta, GA, by Just Us Theater Co., 1983.

Hospice (first produced Off-Broadway at the New Federal Theatre, New York, 1983; first international production, the MAMU Players, South Africa, 1990), published in *New Plays for the Black Theater,* edited by Woodie King, Jr., Third World Press (Chicago, IL), 1989.

Good News, first produced in Atlanta, GA, by Just Us Theater Co., 1984.

Essentials, first produced in Atlanta, GA, by Just Us Theater Co., 1985.

Banana Bread (two-character piece), videotaped and premiered as part of the PBS series *Playhouse 30,* Atlanta, GA, 1985.

(With Walter J. Huntley) *PR: A Political Romance,* first produced by Just Us Theater Co., Atlanta, GA, 1985.

Porch Songs, first produced at the Phoenix Theater, Indianapolis, IN, 1985.

Come and Get These Memories, first produced at the Billie Holiday Theater, Brooklyn, NY, 1988.

Chain (one-act; first produced off-Broadway by the Women's Project and Productions and the New Federal Theater, 1992), published in *Playwrighting Women: Seven Plays from the Women's Project,* edited by Julia Miles, Heinemann Press, 1993.

Late Bus to Mecca (one-act; first produced Off-Broadway by the Women's Project and Productions and the New Federal Theater, 1992), published in *Playwrighting Women: Seven Plays from the Women's Project,* edited by Julia Miles, Heinemann Press, 1993.

Flyin' West, (produced by Alliance Theater Company, Atlanta, GA, 1992), Dramatists Play Service (New York, NY), 1995.

Blues for an Alabama Sky (produced by Alliance Theater Company, Atlanta, GA, 1995), Dramatists Play Service (New York, NY), 1999.

Flyin' West and Other Plays (includes *Flyin' West, Blues for an Alabama Sky, Bourbon Border, Chain,* and *Late Bus to Mecca*), Dramatists Play Service (New York, NY), 1999.

Also author of *Christmas, 1967* and *Christmas, 1981* (short fiction). Author, with Zaron Burnett, of *Live at Club Zebra!: The Book,* Volume 1, Just Us Theater Press (Atlanta, GA). Author of and performer in *The Jean Harris Reading,* 1981; *The Pearl and the Brood of Vipers,* 1981; *Nothin' but a Movie,* 1982; *My Father Has a Son,* 1986; *A Little Practice,* 1986; *Love and Trouble,* with Burnett, 1987; *Live at Club Zebra!* with Burnett; *The Final Negro Rhythm and Blues Revue,* with Burnett, 1988; *Clearing the Heart,* 1989; and *Mad at Miles,* 1990.

Work represented in numerous anthologies, including *The Insistent Present, We Speak as Liberators: Young Black Poets, A Rock against the Wind, The Poetry of Black America, Proverbs for the People: Contemporary African American Fiction,* and *Mending the World: Stories of Family by Contemporary Black Writers.*

Columnist for the *Atlanta Gazette,* 1976—, *Atlanta Constitution,* 1977, and *Atlanta Tribune,* 1988-1998. Contributor to various periodicals and journals, including *Essence, Readers and Writers, Promethean, Afro-American Review, Journal of Black Poetry, Dues, Essence, Pride, Black World, Ms., Atlanta Magazine, New York Times Book Review, Southern Voices,* and *Black Collegian.* Founding editor, *Catalyst,* 1987—.

ADAPTATIONS: What Looks like Crazy on an Ordinary Day was adapted for audiobook, read by the author, Simon and Schuster Audio, 1998; *I Wish I Had a Red Dress* was adapted for audiobook, read by the author, Harper Audio, 2001; *Some Things I Never Thought I'd Do* was adapted for audiobook, BBC Audiobooks America, 2003; *Babylon Sisters* was adapted for audiobook, read by the author, Audio Partners, 2005.

SIDELIGHTS: A poet, essayist, playwright, performer, and novelist, Pearl Cleage has been hailed by critics as a multitalented voice for the African American community. As Samiya A. Bashir commented in *Black Issues Book Review,* "Cleage has firmly cemented her place in African American literary history as a woman of many talents and a strong vision for social change." Cleage once commented: "As a black female writer living and working in the United States, my writing of necessity reflects my blackness and my femaleness. I am convinced that this condition of double-oppression based on race and sex gives me a unique perspective that, hopefully, adds energy and certain creative tension to my work. Here's hoping." Cleage worked for many years in the theater, writing plays including *Flyin' West,* about black women pioneers homesteading in the early nineteenth century, before publishing her first novel, *What Looks Like Crazy on an Ordinary Day,* in 1997. That novel was chosen for the Oprah Book Club and climbed to the top of the *New York Times* bestseller list, where it remained for nine weeks. Since then, Cleage has published several other novels featuring strong female protagonists facing difficult life decisions.

What Looks like Crazy on an Ordinary Day, traces the arc of experience of Ava Johnson, the owner of a hair salon in Atlanta, Georgia, who discovers she has AIDS. Ava decides to move to San Francisco and build a new life with the time left to her. First, she visits her Michigan hometown, where her sister has just adopted a crack baby. Ava grows attached to the baby and joins in the battle against church conservatives who want to prevent teens from getting AIDS-prevention information. She also falls in love with a local man, Eddie Jefferson, but thinks happiness has come too late in life for her. However, Eddie has a different way of looking at things. Reviewing the novel in *People,* Laura Jamison found it "uplifting" and felt that Cleage presented her message "with a deft and joyful touch." Cleage told Bashir in a *Black Issues Book Review* interview that her inspiration to write a novel grew out of personal experience: "I had an idea for a black woman character who'd been living her life, went in for a regular physical and found out she was HIV positive. . . . I was struck by how many people I knew who were still in denial about HIV/AIDS. I wanted to write about someone who was diagnosed and then had to figure out what to do with the rest of her life."

Cleage's second novel, *I Wish I Had a Red Dress,* is set in the same Michigan town, Idlewild, a former resort, as was her first novel. She also reprises characters from that book for a sequel of sorts. Here the story focuses on Ava's older sister, Joyce, who never lived an exciting life like her younger sister. A widow, Joyce also lost her son and daughter and now runs a social club and counseling center for young women and unmarried mothers. After giving of herself for so many years, Joyce finds romance with tall Nate and thinks it might be time for a bit of high-living for a change. Cleage's book "suffers from second-novelitis," in the opinion of *American Theatre* contributor Frank J. Baldaro. While Baldaro thought the novel would be a "crowd pleaser," he also felt it "wears thin as it ham-fistedly scores its points."

For her third novel, *Some Things I Never Thought I'd Do,* Cleage leaves Michigan behind but again focuses on an African American woman in crisis. Ambitious Regina Burns is trying to reconstruct her life after a rehab program for drug addition. She desperately needs money to save the family home and takes a job with the mother of her former betrothed, Son Davis, who died in the 9/11 terrorist attack on New York City. Davis's mother hires Regina to help organize a memorial for her son. This position, in turn, takes Regina back to Atlanta, where, reading through her former lover's papers, she uncovers a secret past. She also meets Blue Hamilton, a black man so-named after his blue eyes. He is the local gentleman and protector of women, and Regina finds herself drawn to him. However, complications soon arise with neighborhood tensions and local criminals who threaten to destroy

Regina's newfound happiness. *Library Journal* contributor Joyce Kessel felt this third novel was "not quite as engaging" as Cleage's earlier two, but that its "secrets and characters are compelling enough to sustain the tale." Higher praise came from Melissa Ewey Johnson in *Black Issues Book Review.* Johnson wrote, "Cleage's third novel sets the standard for fiction that not only entertains but raises important issues relevant in the real world."

Babylon Sisters, Cleage's fourth novel, is once again set in Atlanta, Cleage's home. Catherine Sanderson must decide whether or not to tell her daughter Phoebe the identity of her father. Always close, mother and daughter are being pulled apart by Phoebe's desire to know who her father is. Added to this is another plot dealing with the business Catherine runs that helps establish migrant women in their new country. Tensions mount when Phoebe's father—a journalist covering a story on immigrants who are being forced into prostitution—comes to town. Catherine realizes she is still attracted to him, but he has yet to learn that Phoebe is his daughter. Writing in *Black Issues Book Review,* Johnson deemed the novel both "suspenseful and engaging."

BIOGRAPHICAL AND CRITICAL SOURCES:

BOOKS

Contemporary Black Biography, Gale (Detroit, MI), 1998.
In Black and White, third edition, two volumes, Gale (Detroit, MI), 1980, third edition, supplement, 1985.
Notable Black American Women, Gale (Detroit, MI), 1996.

PERIODICALS

African American Review, winter, 1997, Freda Scott Giles, "The Motion of Herstory: Three Plays by Pearl Cleage," p. 709.
American Theatre, December, 1992, Cathy Madison, "Home Sweet Homestead," review of *Flyin' West,* p. 11; July-August, 1996, Douglas Langworthy, interview with Pearl Cleage, p. 21; November, 2002, Frank J. Baldaro, review of *I Wish I Had a Red Dress,* p. 77.

American Visions, October-November, 1994, Steve Monroe, "Black Women as Pioneers," review of *Flyin' West,* p. 31.

Belle Lettres, spring, 1994, Jeanette Lambert, review of *Deals with the Devil: And Other Reasons to Riot,* p. 84.

Black Issues Book Review, July, 2001, Samiya A. Bashir, "Pearl Cleage's Idlewild Idylls," p. 16; January-February, 2004, Melissa Ewey Johnson, review of *Some Things I Never Thought I'd Do,* p. 51; March-April, 2005, Melissa Ewey Johnson, review of *Babylon Sisters,* p. 49.

Booklist, August, 1999, review of *What Looks like Crazy on an Ordinary Day,* p. 2024; September 15, 2001, Whitney Scott, review of *I Wish I Had a Red Dress* (audiobook), p. 243; February 14, 2004, Mary McCay, review of *Some Things I Never Thought I'd Do* (audiobook), p. 1081.

Kliatt, July, 2005, Nola Theiss, review of *Babylon Sisters* (audiobook), p. 47.

Library Journal, February 1, 1999, Adrienne Furness, review of *What Looks like Crazy on an Ordinary Day,* p. 138; September 15, 2004, Joyce Kessel, review of *Some Things I Never Thought I'd Do* (audiobook), p. 88; June 1, 2005, Gwendolyn Osborne, review of *Babylon Sisters,* p. 186.

People, February 2, 1998, Laura Jamison, review of *What Looks like Crazy on an Ordinary Day,* p. 30.

Publishers Weekly, June 7, 1993, review of *Deals with the Devil: And Other Reasons to Riot,* p. 59.

ONLINE

Pearl Cleage Home Page, http://www.pearlcleage.net (November 22, 2005).*

*   *   *

**CLEAGE, Pearl Michelle
See CLEAGE, Pearl**

*   *   *

**COLLINS, Joan 1933-
(Joan Henrietta Collins)**

PERSONAL: Born May 23, 1933, in London, England; daughter of Joseph William (a talent agent) and Elsa (Bessant) Collins; married Maxwell Reed (an actor), 1952 (divorced, 1956); married Anthony New-ley (an entertainer), 1963 (divorced, 1971); married Ron Kass (a record producer), 1972 (divorced, 1984); married Peter Holm, 1985 (divorced, 1987); married Percy Gibson, February 17, 2002; children: (second marriage) Tara Newley, Alexander Newley; (third marriage) Katyana Kass. *Education:* Attended the Royal Academy of Dramatic Arts. *Hobbies and other interests:* Traveling, collecting eighteenth-century antiques, cinema, and reading.

ADDRESSES: Office—c/o Paul Keylock, 16 Bulbecks Walk, South Woodham Ferrers, Chelmsford, Essex CM3 5ZN, England. *Agent*—(theatrical) Peter Charlesworth, Peter Charlesworth & Associates, 68 Old Brompton Rd., London SW7 3LZ, England; (publicity) Stella Wilson Publicity, 293 Faversham Rd., Seasalter, Whitstable, Kent CT5 4BN, England; (literary) Jonathan Lloyd, Curtis Brown & Associates, Haymarket House, 28/29 Haymarket, London SW1Y 4SP, England; (U.S. agent) Jack Gilardi, 8942 Wilshire Blvd., Beverly Hills, CA 90211.

CAREER: Actress in stage productions, including *A Doll's House,* Arts Theatre, London, England, 1946; *Last of Mrs. Cheyne,* London, England, 1979-80; *Private Lives,* Aldwych Theatre, London England, 1990, then Broadhurst Theatre, New York, NY, 1992, and U.S. cities; *Love Letters,* U.S. cities, 2000; and *Over the Moon,* Old Vic, London, England, c. 2002. Actress in films, including *I Believe in You,* 1952; *The Woman's Angle,* Stratford, 1952; *Judgment Deferred,* Associated British, 1952; *Decameron Nights,* Film Locations, 1952; *I Believe in You,* Universal, 1953; *Cosh Boy,* Lippert, 1953; *Turn the Key Softly,* Arvis, 1953; *The Square Ring,* Republic, 1953; *Our Girl Friday,* Twentieth Century-Fox, 1953; *The Adventures of Sadie,* 1953; *The Good Die Young,* Independent Film Distributors, 1954; *Land of the Pharaohs,* Warner Bros., 1955; *The Virgin Queen,* Twentieth Century-Fox, 1955; *The Girl in the Red Velvet Swing,* Twentieth Century-Fox, 1955; *Lady Godiva Rides Again,* Carroll, 1955; *The Opposite Sex,* Metro-Goldwyn-Mayer, 1956; *The Wayward Bus,* 1957; *Island in the Sun,* Twentieth Century-Fox, 1957; *Sea Wife,* Twentieth Century-Fox, 1957; *Stopover Tokyo,* Twentieth Century-Fox, 1957; *The Bravados,* Twentieth Century-Fox, 1958; *Rally 'Round the Flag Boys!,* Twentieth Century-Fox, 1958; *Seven Thieves,* Twentieth Century-Fox, 1960; *Esther and the King,* 1960; *Road to Hong Kong,* United Artists, 1962; *One Million Dollars,* Columbia, 1965; *Warning Shot,* Paramount, 1967; *Subterfuge,* Commonwealth United Entertainment, 1969; *If It's Tuesday, This Must Be Belgium,* United Artists, 1969; *Can Heironymus Merkin Ever Forget Mercy Humppe and Find True Happiness?,* Regional, 1969; *Up in the Cellar,* American International, 1970; *The Executioner,* Columbia, 1970; *Tough Guy,* 1970; *Terror from under the House,* Hemisphere, 1971; *The Quest for Love,* Rank, 1971; *Revenge,* 1971; "All through the House," *Tales from the Crypt,* 1972; *Fear in the Night,* International, 1972; *The Aquarian,* 1972; *Tales that Witness Madness,* Paramount, 1973; *Dark Places,* Cinerama, 1973; *State of Siege,* Cinema V, 1973; *Alfie Darling,* EMI, 1974; *I Don't Want to Be Born,* 1976; *The Bawdy Adventures of Tom Jones,* Universal, 1976; *The Devil within Her,* American International, 1976; *The Great Adventure,* Pacific International, 1976; *Empire of Ants,* American International, 1977; *The Stud,* 1978; *The Big Sleep,* Trans-American, 1978; *Sunburn,* 1979; *The Bitch,* Brent Walker, 1979; *Game for Vultures,* 1979; *Zero to Sixty,* 1979; *A Game for Vultures,* New Line Cinema, 1980; *Homework,* Jensen Farley, 1982; *Nutcracker,* Rank, 1982; *Georgy Porgy,* 1983; *Decadence,* 1993; *In the Bleak Midwinter,* Sony Pictures Classics, 1995; *Line King: Al Hirschfeld,* 1996; *The Clandestine Marriage,* 1999; *The Flintstones in Viva Rock Vegas,* 2000; *Ozzie,* 2001; and *Ellis in Glamourland,* 2004. Television performances include appearances in "The Galatea Affair," *The Man from U.N.C.L.E.,* National Broadcasting Company (NBC), 1966; "The Wail of the Siren," *Batman,* American Broadcasting Companies (ABC), 1967; "Ring around the Riddler," *Batman,* ABC, 1967; "The City on the Edge of Forever," *Star Trek,* NBC, 1967; "The Lady from Wichita," *The Virginian,* NBC, 1967; "Nicole," *Mission: Impossible,* ABC, 1969; "Five Miles to Midnight," *The Persuaders,* ABC, 1972; "The Man Who Came to Dinner," *Hallmark Hall of Fame,* NBC, 1972; "Hansel and Gretel," *The Persuaders,* ABC, 1972; *Drive Hard, Drive Fast,* NBC, 1973; "Five Miles to Midnight," *The Persuaders,* ABC, 1975; *Arthur Haily's The Moneychangers,* NBC, 1976; *Mission Impossible,* 1976; "The Trick Book," *Police Woman,* 1976; "Turnabout," *Fantastic Journey,* NBC, 1977; "Starsky and Hutch on Playboy Island," *Starsky and Hutch,* 1978; "Mission of the Dariens," *Space 1999,* 1979; "Georgy Porgy," *Tales of the Unexpected,* NBC, 1979; "My Fair Pharaoh/The Power," *Fantasy Island,* ABC, 1980; *Dynasty,* ABC, 1981-89; *Paper Dolls,* ABC, 1982; *The Making of a Male Model,* ABC, 1983; "The Captain's Crush/Off-Course Romance/Out of My Hair," *The Love Boat,* ABC, 1983; *My Life as a Man,* NBC, 1984; *The Cartier Affair,* NBC, 1984; *Sins,* Columbia Broadcasting System (CBS), 1985; *Monte Carlo,* CBS, 1986; *Fame, Fortune, and Romance,* syndicated, 1986; *To Tell the Truth,* NBC, 1990; *Dynasty: The Reunion,* ABC, 1991; *Tonight at 8:30,* 1991; *Mama's Back,* 1992; "Collins Meet Coward," *A&E Stage,* Arts & Entertainment, 1992; "First Question, Twice Removed," *Roseanne,* ABC, 1993; *Annie—A Royal Adventure,* 1995; *Two Harts in 3/4 Time,* 1995; "Me and Mrs. Joan," *The Nanny,* CBS, 1996; *Pacific Palisades,* 1997; *Sweet Deception,* Fox Broadcasting Company Family, 1998; "My Best Friend's Tush," *Will & Grace,* NBC, 2000; *These Old Broads,* 2000; and *Guiding Light,* CBS, 2002. Served as costume designer, *The Cartier Affair,* NBC, 1984; executive producer, *Sins,* CBS, 1986; executive producer (with Peter Holm), *Monte Carlo,* CBS, 1986; associate producer, "Collins Meet Coward," *A&E Stage,* Arts & Entertainment, 1992.

MEMBER: Actors' Equity Association, American Federation of Television and Radio Artists, Screen Actors Guild.

AWARDS, HONORS: Hollywood Women's Press Club Golden Apple Award, 1982, and 1983, for best actress in a TV drama for *Dynasty;* most popular actress, People's Choice Award, 1983, 1984; Golden Nymph Award, Monte Carlo Television Festival, 2001; named to Order of the British Empire, 2001; Annual Cable Excellence (ACE) Award, National Cable Television Association.

WRITINGS:

NOVELS

Prime Time, Simon & Schuster (New York, NY), 1988.
Love and Desire and Hate, Simon & Schuster (New York, NY), 1990.
Infamous, Dutton (New York, NY), 1996.
Star Quality, Hyperion (New York, NY), 2002.
Misfortune's Daughters, Hyperion (New York, NY), 2005.

BEAUTY BOOKS

Joan Collins' Beauty Book, Macmillan (New York, NY), 1980.
My Secrets, 1994.

My Friends' Secrets, 1999.
Joan's Way: Looking Good, Feeling Great, Robson Books (New York, NY), 2004.

OTHER

Past Imperfect: An Autobiography, W.H. Allen (London, England), 1978, revised edition, Simon & Schuster (New York, NY), 1984.
Katy: A Fight for Life (memoir), Gollancz (London, England), 1982.
Three Complete Books (contains novels *Prime Time* and *Love and Desire and Hate,* and autobiography *Past Imperfect*), Wings Books (New York, NY), 1994.
Second Act: An Autobiography, St. Martin's Press (New York, NY), 1997.
Memories from Mother, Benson Smythe (Wellsville, NY), 1998.

SIDELIGHTS: Actress Joan Collins grew up in a comfortable middle-class neighborhood in London, England. Attending the British Royal Academy of Dramatic Art for two years, she made her London stage debut in 1946 in *A Doll's House* and her British film debut in 1952 with *I Believe in You.* The teenage actress made ten more movies within the next three years—in most, playing an erring juvenile—and by the age of twenty she was offered a motion picture contract with Fox Studios in the United States. Collins signed and moved to Hollywood, becoming the sultry leading lady in a string of undistinguished movies. By the early 1970s she was appearing primarily in forgettable horror films. Yet Collins effected a career comeback later in the decade with her notable portrayals in *The Stud* and *The Bitch,* saucy B-movies adapted from novels written by her sister, Jackie Collins, and produced by her third husband, Ron Kass. In 1981, after capturing the interest of television producer Aaron Spelling, the actress was cast in the role of sexy, scheming, wicked, and sophisticated Alexis Carrington on his prime-time television drama *Dynasty.* Called "the woman America loves to hate" Collins is credited with adding to *Dynasty* a spark previously lacking in the show. Since taking the role of Alexis, Collins has attained the fame and professional security that eluded her on stage and screen for most of her acting career.

Collins recounts her life in *Past Imperfect: An Autobiography.* Although the performer relates much about her acting career in the best seller, her primary focus is on emotional passages and sexual adventures. She discusses parties, clothes, lovers, husbands, and children in a manner that *Times Literary Supplement* critic Anita Brookner called "cheerful and resilient." "In the present book [Collins] has achieved has a respectable account of a certain form of emancipation (so much more interesting than liberation) which is familiar to many women of her age and upbringing," the reviewer remarked. "What we really need from her is a second volume in about fifteen years time."

In 1980 Collins's daughter Katyana was hit by a car and became comatose. Collins relates this disaster and the subsequent battle to bring her daughter to health and consciousness in her 1982 book, *Katy: A Fight for Life.* Two years later, after proving a popular success in *Dynasty,* the actress published a revised version of her autobiography in the United States. Less explicit than the original, the 1984 *Past Imperfect* omits some expletives and romantic interludes, examines the disintegration of Collins's third marriage, and presents a behind-the-scenes look at *Dynasty* and its cast. American critics were appreciative of this second best-selling edition. In the *New York Times Book Review,* Chris Chase called the actress's revised chronicle "sheer heaven." Christopher Schemering, writing in the *Washington Post Book World,* labeled *Past Imperfect* "the fun book of the season."

Critics also noted that the woman who played the dastardly Alexis Carrington is actually a likable person with a self-effacing wit that saves *Past Imperfect* from the stuffy egotism often witnessed in Hollywood autobiographies. "The lady definitely commands respect," wrote Tom Ward in the *Voice Literary Supplement.* "Not cold but tough, levelheaded, she seems ruthlessly self-critical, not in the least agog at the trappings of stardom." *Los Angeles Times* reviewer Elaine Kendall commented that although "Collins' prose style seems directly derived from the romance novelists," filling "the gaps between all those perfect teeth are detailed accounts of the theatrical career, critical lumps taken in good spirits, successes celebrated and embarrassments noted."

About thirteen years after Collins published the revised version of *Past Imperfect,* she published another memoir titled *Second Act: An Autobiography.* She again writes about her life from childhood onward, touching on her marriages and long and varied career as an actress, and offering personal remembrances of her encounters with well-known stars. Collins also discusses her literary life, including a chapter on her court case involving Random House when the publisher tried to take back an advance given for one of her romantic novels because it deemed the manuscript of poor quality. Collins emerged victorious. Reviewing *Second Act* for *Booklist*, Ilene Cooper wrote: "As with so many other aspects of Collins' career, good or bad doesn't seem to matter . . . she'll [always] be laughing all the way to the bank."

Collins' romantic novels are mostly centered around the entertainment industry. *Infamous*, for example, focuses on an aging Hollywood actress, Katherine Bennet, who plays a character similar to Alexis Carrington on an American prime time soap opera. Bennet has a problematic life at work and at home when she begins a relationship with a questionable Frenchman, Jean-Claude Valmer. Writing in *People*, Alex Tresniowski commented that the novel, "a perfectly coherent if overripe showbiz saga, proves that Joan is fully capable of turning out readable junk."

Better received was *Star Quality*, a novel that follows the lives of three generations of women who become famous actresses. The story begins in World War I with Millie McClancey, who goes from being a maid in a manor house to a music hall star in both Great Britain and the United States. Her daughter Vickie becomes a famous Hollywood film actress in the 1940s. Vickie's daughter Lulu reaches stardom as both a model and soap opera star during the 1980s. Praising Collins' ability to capture the tone of each time period, *Booklist* contributor Mary Frances Wilkens called the book "a delicious romp."

Collins' *Misfortune's Daughters* only has an indirect relationship with Hollywood, but critics noted that it followed the formula of her other novels. Two rich sisters at the center of the plot are the daughters of a Hollywood star, Laura Marlowe, and her rich Greek husband, Nicholas Stephanopolis. Venetia looks like her mother, is favored by her father, and becomes self-destructive. Atlanta looks like her father, is ignored by him after her mother dies under suspicious circumstances, goes missing for a time, and reemerges to triumph after extensive cosmetic surgery. The pair lead somewhat tragic lives as they travel and live around the world. Atlanta eventually finds a successful career in publishing and attracts suitors, while Venetia continues to spiral downward. "Collins's patented glitz and overheated plotting keep the pages turning," attested a *Publishers Weekly* reviewer.

BIOGRAPHICAL AND CRITICAL SOURCES:

BOOKS

Collins, Joan, *Katy: A Fight for Life*, Gollancz (London, England), 1982.
Collins, Joan, *Past Imperfect: An Autobiography*, revised edition, Simon & Schuster (New York, NY), 1984.
Collins, Joan, *Second Act: An Autobiography*, St. Martin's Press (New York, NY), 1997.

PERIODICALS

Booklist, August, 1997, Ilene Cooper, review of *Second Act*, p. 1842; October 1, 2002, Mary Frances Wilkens, review of *Star Quality*, p. 275.
Los Angeles Times, April 10, 1984, Elaine Kendall, review of *Past Imperfect*, p. 16.
New York Times Book Review, May 6, 1984, Chris Chase, review of *Past Imperfect*, p. 28.
People, April 8, 1996, Alex Tresniowski, review of *Past Imperfect*, p. 33.
Publishers Weekly, February 14, 2005, review of *Misfortune's Daughters*, p. 55.
Spectator, October 30, 2004, Deborah Ross, "True to Herself: Deborah Ross Talks to Joan Collins about Lipstick and Ukip and Finds She Is as Glamorous and Game as Ever," p. 14.
Times Literary Supplement, Anita Bookner, review of *Past Imperfect*, July 7, 1978, p. 758.
Voice Literary Supplement, June, 1984, Tom Ward, review of *Past Imperfect*, p. 3.
Washington Post Book World, April 15, 1984, Christopher Schemering, review of *Past Imperfect*.

ONLINE

Joan Collins Home Page, http://www.joancollins.net (October 22, 2005).*

*   *   *

COLLINS, Joan Henrietta
   See COLLINS, Joan

COVILLE, Bruce 1950-
(Robyn Tallis)

PERSONAL: Born May 16, 1950, in Syracuse, NY; son of Arthur J. (a sales engineer) and Jean (an executive secretary; maiden name, Chase) Coville; married Katherine Dietz (an illustrator), October 11, 1969; children: Orion Sean, Cara Joy, Adam. *Education:* Attended Duke University and State University of New York at Binghamton; State University of New York at Oswego, B.A., 1974. *Politics:* "Eclectic." *Religion:* Unitarian.

ADDRESSES: Office—Oddly Enough, P.O. Box 6110, Syracuse, NY 13217. *Agent*—Ashley Grayson, 1342 18th Street, San Pedro, CA 90732.

CAREER: Author, playwright, and educator. Wetzel Road Elementary, Liverpool, NY, teacher, 1974-81. Cohost and coproducer of *Upstage,* a cable television program promoting local theater, 1983. Full Cast Audio, book recording company, owner, producer, and performer. Has also worked as a camp counselor, grave digger, assembly line worker, and toymaker.

MEMBER: Society of Children's Book Writers and Illustrators.

AWARDS, HONORS: California Young Reader Medal, 1996-97, for *Jennifer Murdley's Toad;* Knickerbocker Award, New York State Library Association, for entire body of work, 1997; over a dozen Children's Choice awards from various states, including Arizona, Hawaii, Maryland, and Nevada.

WRITINGS:

PICTURE BOOKS

The Foolish Giant, illustrated by wife, Katherine Coville, Lippincott (New York, NY), 1978.
Sarah's Unicorn, illustrated by Katherine Coville, Lippincott (New York, NY), 1979.
Sarah and the Dragon, illustrated by Beth Peck, Harper (New York, NY), 1984.
My Grandfather's House, illustrated by Henri Sorensen, BridgeWater (Mahwah, NJ), 1996.
The Prince of Butterflies, illustrated by John Clapp, Harcourt (San Diego, CA), 2000.

JUVENILE FICTION

The Brave Little Toaster Storybook, Doubleday (New York, NY), 1987.
Murder in Orbit, Scholastic (New York, NY), 1987.
Monster of the Year, Pocket (New York, NY), 1989.
Goblins in the Castle, Pocket (New York, NY), 1992.
The Dragonslayers, Pocket (New York, NY), 1994.
Oddly Enough (short stories), illustrated by Michael Hussar, Harcourt, 1994.
The World's Worst Fairy Godmother, illustrated by Katherine Coville, Pocket, 1996.
The Lapsnatcher, illustrated by Marissa Moss, Bridge-Water (Mahwah, NJ), 1997.
Odder Than Ever (short stories), Harcourt (San Diego, CA), 1999.
The Monsters of Morley Manor, Harcourt (San Diego, CA), 2001.
Odds Are Good: An Oddly Enough and Odder Than Ever Omnibus, Harcourt (San Diego, CA), 2005.
Thor's Wedding Day: By Thialfi, the Goat Boy; as Told to and Translated by Bruce Coville, illustrated by Matthew Cogswell, Harcourt (Orlando, FL), 2005.

YOUNG ADULT NOVELS

Space Station ICE III, Archway (New York, NY), 1985.
Fortune's Journey, BridgeWater (Mahwah, NJ), 1995.
(With Jane Yolen) *Armageddon Summer,* Harcourt (San Diego, CA), 1998.

"CHAMBER OF HORROR" SERIES; YOUNG ADULT NOVELS

Bruce Coville's Chamber of Horror: Amulet of Doom, Archway (New York, NY), 1983.
Bruce Coville's Chamber of Horror: Spirits and Spells, Archway (New York, NY), 1983.
Bruce Coville's Chamber of Horror: The Eyes of the Tarot, Archway (New York, NY), 1984.
Bruce Coville's Chamber of Horror: Waiting Spirits, Archway (New York, NY), 1985.

"A.I. GANG" SERIES

Operation Sherlock, NAL (New York, NY), 1986.
Robot Trouble, NAL (New York, NY), 1986.
Forever Begins Tomorrow, NAL (New York, NY), 1986.

"CAMP HAUNTED HILLS" SERIES

How I Survived My Summer Vacation, Pocket (New York, NY), 1988.
Some of My Best Friends Are Monsters, Pocket (New York, NY), 1989.
The Dinosaur That Followed Me Home, illustrated by John Pierard, Pocket (New York, NY), 1990.

"MY TEACHER" SERIES

My Teacher Is an Alien, Pocket (New York, NY), 1989.
My Teacher Fried My Brains, Pocket (New York, NY), 1991.
My Teacher Glows in the Dark, Pocket (New York, NY), 1991.
My Teacher Flunked the Planet, Pocket (New York, NY), 1992.

"MAGIC SHOP" SERIES

The Monster's Ring, illustrated by Katherine Coville, Pantheon (New York, NY), 1982.
Jeremy Thatcher, Dragon Hatcher, illustrated by Gary A. Lippincott, Harcourt (San Diego, CA), 1991.
Jennifer Murdley's Toad, illustrated by Gary A. Lippincott, Harcourt (San Diego, CA), 1992.
The Skull of Truth, illustrated by Gary A. Lippincott, Harcourt (San Diego, CA), 1997.
Juliet Dove, Queen of Love, Harcourt (Orlando, FL), 2003.

"NINA TANLEVEN" SERIES

The Ghost in the Third Row, Bantam (New York, NY), 1987.
The Ghost Wore Gray, Bantam (New York, NY), 1988.
Ghost in the Big Brass Bed, Bantam (New York, NY), 1991.

"SPACE BRAT" SERIES; CHAPTER BOOKS

Space Brat, illustrated by Katherine Coville, Pocket (New York, NY), 1992.
Blork's Evil Twin, illustrated by Katherine Coville, Pocket (New York, NY), 1993.

The Wrath of Squat, illustrated by Katherine Coville, Pocket (New York, NY), 1994.
Planet of the Dips, illustrated by Katherine Coville, Pocket (New York, NY), 1995.
The Saber-toothed Poodnoobie, illustrated by Katherine Coville, Pocket (New York, NY), 1997.

"ALIEN ADVENTURES" SERIES

Aliens Ate My Homework, illustrated by Katherine Coville, Pocket (New York, NY), 1993.
I Left My Sneakers in Dimension X, illustrated by Katherine Coville, Pocket (New York, NY), 1994.
The Search for Snout, illustrated by Katherine Coville, Pocket (New York, NY), 1995.
Aliens Stole My Body, illustrated by Katherine Coville, Pocket (New York, NY), 1998.

"UNICORN CHRONICLES" SERIES

Into the Land of the Unicorns, Scholastic (New York, NY), 1994.
The Song of the Wanderer, Scholastic (New York, NY), 1999.

"I WAS A SIXTH GRADE ALIEN" SERIES

I Was a Sixth-Grade Alien, illustrated by Tony Sansevero, Pocket (New York, NY), 1999.
The Attack of the Two-Inch Teacher, illustrated by Tony Sansevero, Pocket (New York, NY), 1999.
I Lost My Grandfather's Brain, illustrated by Tony Sansevero, Pocket (New York, NY), 1999.
Peanut Butter Lover Boy, illustrated by Tony Sansevero, Pocket (New York, NY), 2000.
Zombies of the Science Fair, illustrated by Tony Sansevero, Pocket (New York, NY), 2000.
Don't Fry My Veeblax!, illustrated by Tony Sansevero, Pocket (New York, NY), 2000.
Snatched from Earth, illustrated by Tony Sansevero, Minstrel (New York, NY), 2000.
There's an Alien in My Backpack, illustrated by Tony Sansevero, Pocket (New York, NY), 2000.
Too Many Aliens, illustrated by Tony Sansevero, Pocket (New York, NY), 2000.
Farewell to Earth, illustrated by Tony Sansevero, Pocket (New York, NY), 2001.
Revolt of the Miniature Mutants, illustrated by Tony Sansevero, Pocket (New York, NY), 2001.

"MOONGOBBLE AND ME" SERIES

Dragon of Doom, illustrated by Katherine Coville, Simon and Schuster (New York, NY), 2003.

The Evil Elves, illustrated by Katherine Coville, Simon and Schuster (New York, NY), 2004.

The Weeping Werewolf, illustrated by Katherine Coville, Simon and Schuster (New York, NY), 2004.

COMPILER AND EDITOR

The Unicorn Treasury, illustrated by Tim Hildebrandt, Doubleday (New York, NY), 1987.

Herds of Thunder, Manes of Gold: A Collection of Horse Stories and Poems, illustrated by Ted Lewin, Doubleday (New York, NY), 1991.

Bruce Coville's Book of Monsters, Scholastic (New York, NY), 1993.

Bruce Coville's Book of Aliens, Scholastic (New York, NY), 1994.

Bruce Coville's Book of Ghosts, illustrated by John Pierard, Scholastic (New York, NY), 1994.

Bruce Coville's Book of Nightmares, Scholastic (New York, NY), 1995.

Bruce Coville's Book of Spine Tinglers, Scholastic (New York, NY), 1996.

Bruce Coville's Book of Magic, Scholastic (New York, NY), 1996.

Bruce Coville's Book of Monsters II, illustrated by John Pierard, Scholastic (New York, NY), 1996.

Bruce Coville's Book of Aliens II, Scholastic (New York, NY), 1996.

Bruce Coville's Book of Ghosts II, illustrated by John Pierard, Scholastic (New York, NY), 1997.

Bruce Coville's Book of Nightmares II, illustrated by John Pierard, Scholastic (New York, NY), 1997.

Bruce Coville's Book of Spine Tinglers II, Scholastic (New York, NY), 1997.

Bruce Coville's Book of Magic II, Scholastic (New York, NY), 1997.

A Glory of Unicorns, illustrated by Alix Berenzy, Scholastic (New York, NY), 1998.

Bruce Coville's Strange Worlds, Avon (New York, NY), 2000.

Bruce Coville's UFOs, Avon (New York, NY), 2000.

Half-Human, illustrated by Marc Tauss, Scholastic (New York, NY), 2001.

RETELLER; PICTURE BOOKS

William Shakespeare, *William Shakespeare's The Tempest,* illustrated by Ruth Sanderson, Bantam (New York, NY), 1993.

William Shakespeare, *William Shakespeare's A Midsummer Night's Dream,* illustrated by Dennis Nolan, Dial (New York, NY), 1996.

William Shakespeare, *William Shakespeare's Macbeth,* illustrated by Gary Kelley, Dial (New York, NY), 1997.

William Shakespeare, *William Shakespeare's Romeo and Juliet,* illustrated by Dennis Nolan, Dial (New York, NY), 1999.

William Shakespeare, *William Shakespeare's Twelfth Night,* illustrated by Tim Raglin, Dial (New York, NY), 2003.

William Shakespeare, *William Shakespeare's Hamlet,* illustrated by Leonid Gore, Dial (New York, NY), 2004.

OTHER

(Author of book and lyrics) *The Dragon Slayers,* music by Angela Peterson, first produced at Syracuse Musical Theater, 1981.

(Author of book and lyrics) *Out of the Blue,* music by Angela Peterson, first produced at Syracuse Musical Theater, 1982.

(Author of book and lyrics with Barbara Russell) *It's Midnight: Do You Know Where Your Toys Are?,* music by Angela Peterson, first produced at Syracuse Musical Theater, 1983.

(With others) *Seniority Travel Directory,* Schueler Communications, 1986.

(With others) *The Sophisticated Leisure Travel Directory,* Schueler Communications, 1986.

The Dark Abyss (adult novel), Bantam (New York, NY), 1989.

Prehistoric People (nonfiction), illustrated by Michael McDermott, Doubleday (New York, NY), 1990.

Contributor to anthologies, including *Dragons and Dreams,* 1986, and *Read On! Two,* Books 4 and 6, 1987.

Author, under pseudonym Robyn Tallis, of two books in the "Planet Builder" series: *Night of Two New Moons,* 1985, and *Mountain of Stolen Dreams,* 1988.

Contributor to *Harper's Bookletter, Sesame Street Parent's Newsletter, Cricket,* and *Wilson Library Bulletin.* Associate editor, *Syracuse Business* and *Syracuse Magazine,* both 1982-83; editor and columnist, *Seniority,* 1983-84.

ADAPTATIONS: The Monster's Ring (cassette), Recorded Books, 1992; *The Ghost Wore Gray* (cassette), Recorded Books, 1993; *Jennifer Murdley's Toad* (cassette), Listening Library, 1996; *Jeremy Thatcher, Dragon Hatcher* (cassette), Listening Library, 1996; *Aliens Ate My Homework* (cassette), Listening Library, 1998; *Into the Land of the Unicorns: The Unicorn Chronicles Book I* (cassette), Listening Library, 1998; *The Skull of Truth* (cassette), Listening Library, 1998; *My Teacher Is an Alien* (cassette), Listening Library, 1998.

SIDELIGHTS: Bruce Coville is well known as a writer of juvenile fiction and the author of children's best-sellers such as *Jeremy Thatcher, Dragon Hatcher.* His novels draw heavily on mythic creatures, such as unicorns and dragons, and science-fiction traditions, such as aliens and space stations, often with a humorous twist. He has also contributed to and edited volumes of short stories and completed several musical plays for younger audiences. As he once commented, Coville cherishes memories of his childhood, noting that his early surroundings nurtured his vivid imagination: "I was raised in Phoenix, a small town in central New York. Actually, I lived well outside the town, around the corner from my grandparents' dairy farm, which was the site of my happiest childhood times. I still have fond memories of the huge barns with their mows and lofts, mysterious relics, and jostling cattle. It was a wonderful place for a child to grow up. In addition to the farm, there was a swamp behind the house, and a rambling wood beyond that, both of which were conducive to all kinds of imaginative games." It was during this period that Coville began to develop the heightened sensibility usually possessed by writers of fantasy.

Coville's father, not bookish himself, was instrumental in exposing the young Bruce to the delightful world of literature. Coville recalled: "Despite this wonderful setting, much of what went on at that time went on in my head, when I was reading, or thinking and dreaming about what I had read. I was an absolute bookaholic. My father had something to do with this." Coville went on to explain: "He was a traveling salesman, a gruff but loving man, who never displayed an overwhelming interest in books. But if anyone was to ask me what was the best thing he ever did for me I could reply without hesitation that he read me *Tom Swift in the City of Gold.* Why he happened to read this to me I was never quite certain, but it changed my

life. One night after supper he took me into the living room, had me sit in his lap, and opened a thick, ugly brown book (this was the *original* Tom Swift) and proceeded to open a whole new world for me. I was enthralled, listened raptly, waited anxiously for the next night and the next, resented any intrusion, and reread the book several times later on my own. It was the only book I can ever remember him reading to me, but it changed my life. I was hooked on books."

Coville may have loved books, but like many other authors, the realization that he wanted to be a writer came very abruptly. He explained, "I think it was sixth grade when I first realized that writing was something that I could do, and wanted to do very much. As it happened, I had spent most of that year making life miserable for my teacher by steadfastly failing to respond to the many creative devices she had to stimulate us to write. Then one day she simply (finally!) just let us write—told us that we had a certain amount of time to produce a short story of substance. Freed from writing topics imposed from without, I cut loose, and over several days found that I loved what I was doing. This may not be the first time that I knew I wanted to write, but it's the time that I remember." In addition to writing, Coville himself went on to be a teacher. He held a full-time position at Wetzel Road Elementary School, in Liverpool, New York, for seven years starting in 1974.

However, writing was always to be Coville's first love. He was introduced to the possibilities of writing for children by the woman who would later become his mother-in-law. He remembered that she "gave me a copy of *Winnie the Pooh* to read, and I suddenly knew that what I really wanted to write was children's books—to give to other children the joy that I got from books when I was young. This is the key to what I write now. I try, with greater or lesser success, to make my stories the kinds of things that I would have enjoyed myself when I was young; to write the books I wanted to read, but never found. My writing works best when I remember the bookish child who adored reading and gear the work toward him. It falters when I forget him."

As he developed into an experienced writer, Coville worked in different genres. He created musical plays, such as *The Dragon Slayers,* first produced at Syracuse Musical Theater. He contributed to anthologies of fantasy stories, such as *Dragons and Dreams.* But it was in the area of picture books, beginning with the publication of *The Foolish Giant* in 1978, that Coville made a significant mark. Illustrated by his wife, Katherine, that first tale for younger readers tells of a mild, clumsy giant who has difficulty being accepted by the ordinary people of his village until he saves them from an evil wizard. In the years since its publication, Coville has published numerous other tales for children, culminating in the appearance of several of his works on children's best-seller lists.

Many of Coville's books are jam-packed with the trappings of traditional mythic imagery: supernatural spirits, tarot cards, unicorns, prehistoric monsters, and futuristic creatures at the outer edge of the universe. He once related, "Myth is very important to me. My picture books have firm roots in basic mythic patterns. Hopefully, the patterns do not intrude, but provide a structure and depth that enhances my work." Coville often combines imaginary creatures with present-day people to create a tale of mystery or adventure. In *The Ghost in the Third Row,* for instance, a young character named Nina discovers a ghost haunting the theater where she is acting in a murder drama. Nina returns with her friend Chris in *The Ghost Wore Gray,* where the two try to discover the story behind the spirit of a Confederate soldier who appears in a New York hotel. "Despite the fantasy element of a ghost, this is a mystery," noted *School Library Journal* contributor Carolyn Caywood, who added that the tale "evokes real feeling."

Some of Coville's most popular books have been those that involve Mr. Elive's Magic Shop. In *Jeremy Thatcher, Dragon Hatcher,* young Jeremy escapes his tormenter Mary Lou only to find himself in a strange shop where he buys an unusual egg. When the egg hatches a baby dragon—that no one else but Mary Lou can see—Jeremy finds himself in the midst of adventure. "The book is filled with scenes that will bring laughter and near tears to readers," noted Kenneth E. Kowen in the *School Library Journal.* Reviewer Kathleen Redmond wrote in the *Voice of Youth Advocates* that the story is a good combination of real and fantasy worlds and "is right on target." Coville returns to the magic shop in *Jennifer Murdley's Toad,* where Jennifer purchases a lonely toad hatched from a witch's mouth. In aiding her new pet, Bufo, who seeks his lost love, Jennifer herself is turned into a toad and learns to appreciate her inner strengths. *School Library Journal* contributor Margaret C. How-

ell praised Coville's theme as "particularly well handled," adding that "the story moves well, with realistic characterizations."

Coville believes that a knowledge of mythic patterns and imagery can facilitate children's growth and social understanding. "This 'making sense' is a process that generally takes a lifetime and yet, sadly, it is all too often never even begun," he asserted. "To utilize myth as a guide in this quest one must be familiar with its patterns and structures, a familiarity that is best gained from reading or hearing myth and its reconstructions from earliest childhood on." Coville thinks that the literature he writes plays a part in exposing young people to the mythological realm. "I do not expect a child to read my picture books and suddenly discover the secret of the universe," he explained. "I do hope that something from my works will tuck itself away in the child's mind, ready to present itself as a piece of a puzzle on some future day when he or she is busy constructing a view of the world that will provide at least a modicum of hope and dignity."

Beyond his grounding in classic fantasy, Coville has filled many of his books with a zany, pungent humor aimed squarely at his young audience. In reviewing *Planet of the Dips, School Library Journal* critic Anne Connor referred to the book as "literary junk food" appealing to "beginning readers with a passion for weird words, stupid jokes and odd behavior." For his part, Coville defends the outrageous extremes of such stories. "There are those who want to keep children's books 'tasteful' and ten-year-old boys are not tasteful," he asserted. "One of the reasons we have this problem of reluctant readers, especially among boys, is that we're not writing to who and what we are. If you write a book that's a brilliant character study and is wonderfully tasteful and no kid ever reads it, you've failed. . . . There's another problem, where you publish to only the lowest common denominator, where you start with that and don't go anywhere else. If you do that, you've failed, too. To me, there's a sweet spot in between, where you start with boisterous energy that will engage, and then you take the reader somewhere else."

Coville acknowledges that he has a particular knack for fast-paced comedic storytelling, a talent borne out by the success of his four books in the "My Teacher" series, each of which sold over one million copies. But he also diversified into other types of books during the 1990s, including a series of retellings of Shakespeare's classic plays. Coville found the task of adapting *The Tempest, A Midsummer Night's Dream, Macbeth,* and other works a satisfying challenge. "I've learned little ways to squeeze in more and more of the language, but keep it accessible," he maintained. "Both my editor and I are aware of the hutzpah of what we are doing. We want to be respectful of the source and of the audience. We work really hard on these books." Reviewing *William Shakespeare's Romeo and Juliet* in *Booklist,* Michael Cart called the picture book "an accessible and entertaining introduction to one of Shakespeare's most popular works." Describing the text for *William Shakespeare's Macbeth* as being "true to the dark, brooding spirit of the play," *Booklist* contributor Hazel Rochman predicted that Coville's "dramatic narrative will keep [middle graders] reading." Reviewing Coville's *William Shakespeare's Twelfth Night* for the *School Library Journal,* Nancy Menaldi-Scanlan called it a "verbal and visual treat." Another *School Library Journal* contributor praised Coville's "taut, suspenseful prose" in *William Shakespeare's Hamlet,* while Graceanne DeCandido, reviewing the same title for the *Teacher Librarian,* felt Coville "made a coherent tale" of the Shakespeare classic.

Expanding further, Coville published several novels for young adults during the 1990s as well. *Fortune's Journey* combines action and romance in its tale of a resourceful teenage actress leading a theater troupe across the West during the Gold Rush era. The book received mixed reviews, with some critics praising the work strongly and others faulting the author for less-than-believable characters. "Part of it was, people complained that it was warped by a kind of contemporary mindset taking on these historical characters," Coville remarked. "But I'd done the research, and I knew there was a lot more that young women were doing back then than people now think." *Armageddon Summer* follows the story of two teenagers caught up in a religious cult with their parents. Cowritten with author Jane Yolen, the novel received more consistently favorable reviews. Writing in *Booklist,* Roger Leslie praised Coville and Yolen for "explor[ing] their rich, thought-provoking theme with the perfect balance of gripping adventure and understated pathos, leavened by a dollop of humor."

Coville has remained committed to educating as well as entertaining young people. He explained: "This may seem like a long-term goal and a minimal result for the work involved, but I am, after all, a teacher. This has always been our lot. We deal with a child for a year, pour our hearts and souls into his development, and then send him on his way with the scant hope that somehow, someday, some little of what we have tried to do may present itself to him when it is needed. . . . But this is idle speculation. The first and foremost job in writing is to tell a whacking good story. You just have to hope it might mean something before you're done."

Personal motivation and social idealism fuel Coville's commitment to children's literature. "There are two reasons that people go into writing for children," he declared. "It's either to heal a wounded childhood, or to celebrate a happy one. It's about nine to one (in favor of) the healing to the happy. But I had a happy childhood, and I love children's books. They're delicious . . . the writing is better, the stories are more interesting. I do it out of a sense of joy and excitement. But it's also a political choice. I feel that one of the ways I can have real impact is working for kids."

Coville has also branched out to audiobook production. As he explained to Candace Smith in a 2003 *Booklist* interview: "I took my daughter on a cross-country trip about 13 years ago, and we listened to audiobooks as we traveled. I fell in love with them. Tim Ditlow, from Listening Library, wanted to buy the rights to one of my books. We evolved our idea of producing full-cast-style recordings into a fantasy imprint." Then, when Listening Library was sold, the project ended, but not Coville's interest. "I missed it! I loved being in the studio. I loved directing and working with the actors, and I didn't want to let go. So I decided to start my own company." The result was the creation of Full Cast Audio, Coville's production company in which he serves as producer and sometimes performer. This commitment to audiobooks has not, however, slowed production of his own books. Returning to the picture book format with *The Prince of Butterflies,* Coville tells a tale of a youngster who helps migrating monarch butterflies find green spaces on their route. Later, as an adult, this friend of butterflies pursues political action to help the monarchs, and as an old man he is visited by his butterfly friends once more. Kathie Meizner, reviewing the title in the *School Library Journal,* felt "the narrative adopts a brisk, documentary tone," while a *Publishers Weekly* contributor characterized the same work as a "sometimes moving, but ultimately puzzling picture book."

Coville returns to magical adventures and silliness for middle-grade readers with several other titles. *The Monsters of Morley Manor* features a scary house and a pair of siblings who want to explore its reaches. Writing in the *Magazine of Fantasy and Science Fiction*, Michelle West called the book a "frenetic everything-but-the-kitchen-sink story." Coville adds to the "Magic Shop" series with his 2003 book *Juliet Dove, Queen of Love*. Shy Juliet attracts legions of boys wherever she goes since putting on a magic amulet. Finally she learns why she has been given the magic amulet: in order to bring Cupid and Psyche, mythological lovers, back together. Coville blends mythology and realism in this "story [that] has surprising depth, with musings on honor, power, strength, courage, and, above all, love," according to the *School Library Journal* contributor B. Allison Gray. Louise Brueggemann, reviewing the same title for *Booklist*, felt fans of the series "will enjoy this latest installment."

Coville launched a new series with "Moongobble and Me," whose first installment was *The Dragon of Doom*. The books feature the fractured magician Moongobble, and in the first book he must face the Dragon of Doom as a test in order to enter the coveted Magician's Guild. Teresa Bateman, reviewing the tale in the *School Library Journal*, found it a "humorous, off-beat story." *The Weeping Werewolf* finds Moongobble, aided by young Edward, facing his second test. Accompanying them are the Rusty Knight and Urk the toad, a rather abysmal crew for magical combat. Jenna Miller, writing in the *School Library Journal*, called the second book in the series a "lighthearted fantasy."

More humor is presented in the 2005 stand-alone title, *Thor's Wedding Day*, "a rare and funny tale from Norse mythology," according to a *Kirkus Reviews* critic. Coville presents a human narrator, Thor's goatherd Thialfi, at the center of this tale about a lost magical hammer and the trickery involved in getting it back from the giant Thrym. The *Kirkus Reviews* critic further felt that Coville's rendition provides a "hilarious alternative" to more traditional retellings of the myth.

BIOGRAPHICAL AND CRITICAL SOURCES:

PERIODICALS

Booklist, March 15, 1994, Karen Harris, review of *The Ghost Wore Gray*, p. 1385; October 1, 1994, Chris Sherman, review of *Into the Land of the Unicorns*, p. 325; December 1, 1994, Mary Harris Veeder, review of *The Dragonslayers*, p. 680; October 15, 1995, Susan Dove Lempke, review of *Fortune's Journey*, p. 401; November 1, 1995, Ellen Mandel, review of *Planet of the Dips*, p. 473; March 15, 1996, Barbara Baskin, review of *Jeremy Thatcher, Dragon Hatcher*, p. 1306; November 1, 1997, Hazel Rochman, review of *William Shakespeare's Macbeth*, p. 464; August, 1998, Roger Leslie, review of *Armageddon Summer*, p. 272; December 1, 1999, Michael Cart, review of *William Shakespeare's Romeo and Juliet*, p. 700; December 15, 2001, Frances Bradburn, review of *Half-Human*, p. 723; April 15, 2003, Candace Smith, "The Booklist Interview: Bruce Coville," p. 1485; January 1, 2004, Louise Brueggemann, review of *Juliet Dove, Queen of Love*, p. 854.

Bulletin of the Center for Children's Books, February, 1990, review of *Herds of Thunder, Manes of Gold*, p. 133; July, 1992, review of *Jennifer Murdley's Toad*, p. 292; July, 1996, review of *William Shakespeare's A Midsummer Night's Dream*, p. 385; January, 1998, review of *William Shakespeare's Macbeth*, p. 117.

Horn Book, March-April, 1990, Elizabeth S. Watson, review of *Herds of Thunder, Manes of Gold*, p. 200; September, 1996, review of *Jeremy Thatcher, Dragon Hatcher*, p. 566;

Kirkus Reviews, August 1, 2005, review of *Thor's Wedding*, p. 846.

Magazine of Fantasy and Science Fiction, March, 2002, Michelle West, review of *The Monsters of Morley Manor*, p. 34.

New York Times Book Review, October 31, 1982, Anne Jordan, review of *The Monster's Ring*, p. 27; October 23, 1994, Francine Prose, review of *Oddly Enough*, p. 30; April 23, 1995, Maxine Kumin, review of *William Shakespeare's The Tempest*, p. 27; July 28, 1996, Judith Viorst, review of *My Grandfather's House*, p. 21; December 19, 1999, review of *Song of the Wanderer*, p. 30.

Publishers Weekly, July 5, 1986, Diane Roback, review of *Operation, Sherlock*, p. 193; January 19, 1990, review of *The Foolish Giant*, p. 112; August 2, 1991, review of *The Unicorn Treasury*, p. 74; April 20, 1992, review of *Jennifer Murdley's Toad*, p. 57; July 27, 1992, review of *Space Brat*, p. 63; November 8, 1993, review of *Aliens Ate My Homework*, p. 77; August 22, 1994, review of *Into the Land of the Unicorns*, p. 56; August 21, 1995, review of *Fortune's Journey*, p. 66; August 11, 1997, review of *The Skull of Truth*, p. 402; May

10, 1999, review of *Odder Than Ever,* p. 69; November 15, 1999, review of *Into the Land of the Unicorns,* p. 69; March 18, 2002, review of *The Prince of Butterflies,* p. 104.

School Library Journal, September, 1988, Carolyn Caywood, review of *The Ghost Wore Gray,* p. 183; May, 1991, Kenneth E. Kowen, review of *Jeremy Thatcher, Dragon Hatcher,* p. 91; September, 1992, Margaret C. Howell, review of *Jennifer Murdley's Toad,* p. 250; December, 1994, Patricia A. Dolisch, review of *Oddly Enough,* p. 106; December, 1995, Anne Connor, review of *Planet of the Dips,* p. 79; December, 2001, Janet Hilburn, review of *Half-Human,* p. 133; May, 2002, Kathie Meizner, review of *The Prince of Butterflies,* p. 111; December, 2003, B. Allison Gray, review of *Juliet Dove, Queen of Love,* p. 148; February, 2004, Nancy Menaldi-Scanlan, review of *William Shakespeare's Twelfth Night,* p. 83; April, 2004, review of *William Shakespeare's Twelfth Night,* p. S47; October, 2004, Teresa Bateman, review of *The Dragon of Doom,* p. 84, Jenna Miller, review of *The Weeping Werewolf,* p. 111, and review of *William Shakespeare's Hamlet,* p. S50.

Teacher Librarian, February, 2005, Graceanne DeCandido, review of *William Shakespeare's Hamlet,* p. 31.

Voice of Youth Advocates, June, 1991, Kathleen Redmond, review of *Jeremy Thatcher, Dragon Hatcher,* p. 106; December, 1994, review of *Into the Land of the Unicorns,* p. 285; February, 1995, review of *Oddly Enough,* p. 344; February, 1996, review of *Fortune's Journey,* p. 369; April, 1998, review of *William Shakespeare's Macbeth,* p. 39.

ONLINE

Official Bruce Coville Web Site, http://www.brucecoville.com (November 8, 2005).*

*   *   *

CRAIG, Patricia 1949-

PERSONAL: Born January 16, 1949, in Belfast, Northern Ireland; daughter of W.A.T. (a mechanic) and Nora T. (a teacher; maiden name, Brady) Craig; married Jeffrey Morgan (a painter). *Education:* Attended Belfast College of Art, 1966-69, and Central School of Art, London, 1969-72; received diploma in art design.

ADDRESSES: Home—County Antrim, Ireland. *Agent*—Drury House, 34-43 Russell Street, London, WC2B 5HA, England; fax: 020-7836-9543.

CAREER: Writer and critic. Girls' school art teacher, 1972-73; freelance writer, 1976—.

MEMBER: Society of Authors.

WRITINGS:

(With Mary Cadogan) *You're a Brick, Angela!: A New Look at Girls' Fiction, 1839-1975,* Gollancz (London, England), 1976.

(With Mary Cadogan) *Women and Children First: The Fiction of Two World Wars,* Gollancz (London, England), 1978.

(With Mary Cadogan) *The Lady Investigates: Women Detectives and Spies in Fiction,* St. Martin's Press (New York, NY), 1982.

Elizabeth Bowen, Penguin (New York, NY), 1986.

(Editor) *The Oxford Book of English Detective Stories,* Oxford University Press (New York, NY), 1990, revised, 2002.

The Penguin Book of British Comic Stories, Viking (New York, NY), 1991.

(Editor) *The Rattle of the North: An Anthology of Ulster Prose,* Blackstaff Press (Belfast, Ireland), 1992.

(Editor) *The Oxford Book of Modern Women's Stories,* Oxford University Press (New York, NY), 1994.

(Editor) *The Oxford Book of Schooldays,* Oxford University Press (New York, NY), 1994.

(Editor) *The Oxford Book of Travel Stories,* Oxford University Press (New York, NY), 1996.

(Editor) *The Oxford Book of Ireland,* Oxford University Press (New York, NY), 1998.

(Compiler and author of introduction) *Twelve Irish Ghost Stories,* Oxford University Press (New York, NY), 1998.

(Editor) *The Oxford Book of Detective Stories,* Oxford University Press (New York, NY), 2000.

Brian Moore: A Biography, Bloomsbury (London, England), 2002.

Contributor to magazines and newspapers, including the *Times Literary Supplement, New Statesman & Society,* and the *Spectator.* Children's book editor of *Literary Review* (London, England), 1979-82.

SIDELIGHTS: In *The Lady Investigates: Women Detectives and Spies in Fiction,* Patricia Craig and her coauthor Mary Cadogan examine the careers of more than one hundred fictional women detectives and spies. The authors begin with a nineteenth-century widow, Mrs. Paschal, and include such recent characters as policewoman Charmian Daniels. The authors divide the characters into two major categories: women whose success was based on their feminine characteristics (on "women's intuition," for instance), and women who have transcended their gender and competed with men as equals. *The Lady Investigates* has been described as lighthearted, but critics emphasized that this is a work of solid scholarship. For example, T.J. Binyon wrote in the *Times Literary Supplement* that "obviously a great deal of careful research has gone into this book. Mistakes are few and far between." And the *Spectator* contributor Hugh Massingberd remarked that "it is an enjoyable nostalgic experience to be regaled with these well-researched snippets from a long-established genre."

Craig once told *CA:* "When we first met, Mary Cadogan and I found that we were each thinking about a study of girls' fiction with a slightly feminist bias, so it seemed sensible to collaborate. This first collaboration led to two others. When writing about not-very-elevated genres, our aim was always to entertain as well as (we hoped) to be informative. We couldn't help being struck by the humor of the stories, whether it was unconscious or conscious on the part of the writers."

The author has gone on to serve as the editor for numerous anthologies, such as *The Oxford Book of English Detective Stories,* which features a series of stories presented chronologically beginning with writer Sir Arthur Conan Doyle, creator of Sherlock Holmes. *Publishers Weekly* contributor Sybil Steinberg commented that the "anthology is chock-full of deductive reasoning, whimsy and that remarkable gift of the British: understatement." Craig gathers together a collection of British wit for *The Penguin Book of British Comic Stories.* An *Economist* contributor felt that Craig's primary objective as editor "is to have fun" and noted that Craig has "produced some refreshing novelties" in the book.

As editor of *The Rattle of the North: An Anthology of Ulster Prose,* Craig offers a broad collection of Irish writers, including the greats such as Oscar Wilde and James Joyce as well as lesser-known writers. Owen Dudley Edwards, writing in the *New Statesman & Society,* called the effort a "splendidly representative anthology." *The Oxford Book of Schooldays* presents a series of writings and stories about British schools by authors as diverse as Winston Churchill and Evelyn Waugh. An *Economist* contributor noted that the "book is presumably meant to be no more than an aid to nostalgia, and in this it succeeds admirably." Craig focuses on women's contributions to short story writing in the anthology *The Oxford Book of Modern Women's Stories,* which presents classics by such women writers as Willa Cather and stories by more recent writers such as Alice Munro. A *Publishers Weekly* contributor called the book "a splendid collection." Kathleen Hughes, writing in *Booklist,* noted, "This book is a stunning achievement that will linger in the mind of the reader long after the last story is read."

In *The Oxford Book of Travel Stories,* Craig gathers together travel tales from writers all over the world. Brad Hooper, writing in *Booklist,* noted that Craigs's "choices for inclusion are impeccable; treasures abound." In a review in London's *Guardian,* Ian Samson commented that "Craig's beautifully produced anthology is most definitely a book for the bedside table." Craig's anthology titled *The Oxford Book of Ireland* presents writings about Ireland and draws from sources dating back to the early Celtic writings on through to the late 1990s. *Library Journal* contributor Robert C. Moore noted that the editor's "challenge was to find fresh voices" and added: "To a degree she has succeeded."

Craig is also the author of *Brian Moore: A Biography.* The book explores the Irish novelist's life and works. Hermione Lee, writing in the *Times Literary Supplement,* noted that Moore "made meaning and power from his life out of a lasting love, long and warm friendships, a fine worldly pleasurable existence, and twenty magnificent novels, all of them remarkable, some of them great." Lee added, "If this honourable and generous biography keeps that success alive and sends readers back to those novels, it will have achieved what he would have wanted." In a review of the biography in the *Spectator,* Jonathan Keates noted that Craig "effortlessly conveys her subject's gift for friendship and his professional wizardry in always keeping several jumps ahead of both readers and critics" and also called the book a "sensitively weighed tribute." Seamus Deane commented in the *Guardian* that the biography is "a crisp and intelligent account of a man and a writer for whom Craig's clean and incisive approach seems perfectly appropriate."

BIOGRAPHICAL AND CRITICAL SOURCES:

PERIODICALS

Antioch Review, summer, 1995, Suzann Bick, review of *The Oxford Book of Modern Women's Stories,* p. 378.

Booklist, November 1, 1994, Kathleen Hughes, review of *The Oxford Book of Modern Women's Stories,* p. 478; September 1, 1996, Brad Hooper, review of *The Oxford Book of Travel Stories,* p. 63.

Economist, November 14, 1992, review of *The Penguin Book of British Comic Stories,* p. 112; March 5, 1994, review of *The Oxford Book of Schooldays,* p. 102.

Guardian (London, England), May 1, 1996, Ian Sansom, review of *The Oxford Book of Travel Stories,* p. 19; June 6, 1998, Steven Poole, review of *The Oxford Book of Ireland,* p. 10; December 14, 2002, Seamus Deane, review of *Brian Moore: A Biography,* p. 12.

Irish Literary Supplement, fall, 2004, Robert Lowery, review of *The Oxford Book of Ireland,* p. 32.

Library Journal, September 1, 1998, Robert C. Moore, review of *The Oxford Book of Ireland,* p. 198.

New Statesman & Society, January 29, 1993, Owen Dudley Edwards, review of *Rattle of the North: An Anthology of Ulster Prose,* p. 45.

Publishers Weekly, July 13, 1990, Sybil Steinberg, review of *The Oxford Book of English Detective Stories,* p. 44; January 11, 1991, Sybil Steinberg, review of *The Penguin Book of British Comic Stories,* p. 92; October 10, 1994, review of *The Oxford Book of Modern Women's Stories,* p. 60; August 5, 1996, review of *The Oxford Book of Travel Stories,* p. 432.

Spectator, April 11, 1981, Hugh Massingberd, review of *The Lady Investigates: Women Detectives and Spies in Fiction;* December 7, 2002, Jonathan Keates, review of *Brian Moore,* p. 46.

Sunday Telegraph (London, England), November 3, 2002, Anthony Thwaite, review of *Brian Moore.*

Times Literary Supplement, February 27, 1981, T.J. Binyon, review of *The Lady Investigates;* November 8, 2002, Hermione Lee, review of *Brian Moore,* p. 8.*

CREW, Gary 1947-

PERSONAL: Born September 23, 1947, in Brisbane, Queensland, Australia; son of Eric (a steam engine driver) and Phyllis (a milliner; maiden name, Winch) Crew; married Christine Joy Willis (a teacher), April 4, 1970; children: Rachel, Sarah, Joel. *Education:* Attended Queensland Institute of Technology; University of Queensland, Diploma (civil engineering drafting), 1970, B.A., 1979, M.A., 1984.

ADDRESSES: Home—P.O. Box 440, Maleny, Queensland, 4552, Australia. *Agent*—c/o Author Mail, Lothian Books, 11 Munro St., Port Melbourne, Victoria 3207, Australia.

CAREER: Writer for children and young adults, 1985—. McDonald, Wagner, and Priddle, Brisbane, Queensland, Australia, senior draftsman and drafting consultant, 1962-72; Everton Park State High School, Brisbane, English teacher, 1974-78; Mitchelton State High School, Brisbane, English teacher, 1978-81; Aspley High School, Brisbane, subject master in English, 1982; Albany Creek High School, Brisbane, subject master in English and head of English Department, 1983-88; Queensland University of Technology, creative writing lecturer, 1989—; Thomas Lothian (South Melbourne, Victoria, Australia), editor, 1990—. Lecturer, University of the Sunshine Coast.

MEMBER: Australian Society of Authors, Queensland Writers Centre (chair).

AWARDS, HONORS: Book of the Year Award for Older Readers, Children's Book Council of Australia (CCBA), 1991, for *Strange Objects,* and 1994, for *Angel's Gate;* Alan Marshall Prize for Children's Literature, and New South Wales Premier's Award, both 1991, both for *Strange Objects;* shortlist, Edgar Allan Poe Award, Mystery Writers of America, 1992, for *Strange Objects,* and 1995, for *Angel's Gate; Lucy's Bay* shortlisted for CCBA picture book of the year, 1993; National Children's Book of the Year citation, 1994, for *Angel's Gate;* Book of the Year Award for Picture Books, CCBA, 1994, for *First Light,* and 1995, for *The Watertower;* Bilby Children's Choice Award, 1995, for *The Watertower;* Ned Kelly Award for Crime Writing, 1996, for *The Well; The Blue Feather* shortlisted for West Australian Premier's

Award, 1997; CCBC Notable Book designation, 1997, for *Tagged;* CCBA Picture Book of the Year shortlist, 2000, for *Memorial.*

WRITINGS:

FICTION

The Inner Circle, Heinemann Octopus (Melbourne, Victoria, Australia), 1985.

The House of Tomorrow, Heinemann Octopus (Melbourne, Victoria, Australia), 1988.

Strange Objects, Heinemann Octopus (Melbourne, Victoria, Australia), 1990, Simon & Schuster (New York, NY), 1993.

No Such Country: A Book of Antipodean Hours, Heinemann Octopus (Melbourne, Victoria, Australia), 1991, Simon & Schuster (New York, NY), 1994.

Angel's Gate, Heinemann Octopus (Melbourne, Victoria, Australia), 1993, Simon & Schuster (New York, NY), 1995.

Inventing Anthony West, University of Queensland Press, 1994.

(With Michael O'Hara) *The Blue Feather,* Heinemann Octopus (Melbourne, Victoria, Australia), 1997.

Mama's Babies, 1998.

The Force of Evil, Lothian (South Melbourne, Victoria, Australia), 1998.

Gothic Hospital, Lothian (South Melbourne, Victoria, Australia), 2001.

The Diviner's Son, Pan (Sydney, New South Wales, Australia), 2002.

(With Declan Lee) *Automaton,* Lothian (South Melbourne, Victoria, Australia), 2004.

The Plague of Quentaris, Lothian (South Melbourne, Victoria, Australia), 2005.

Me and My Dog, Lothian (South Melbourne, Victoria, Australia), 2005.

The Lace Maker's Daughter, Pan (Sydney, New South Wales, Australia), 2005.

The Mystery of the Eilean Mor (mystery), illustrated by Jeremy Geddes, Lothian (South Melbourne, Victoria, Australia), 2005.

Sam Silverthorne: Quest, Hodder (Sydney, New South Wales, Australia), 2005.

PICTURE BOOKS

Tracks, illustrated by Gregory Rogers, Lothian (South Melbourne, Victoria, Australia), 1992, and Gareth Stevens (New York, NY), 1996.

Lucy's Bay, illustrated by Gregory Rogers, Jam Roll Press, 1993.

The Figures of Julian Ashcroft, illustrated by Hans DeHaas, Jam Roll Press, 1993.

First Light, illustrated by Peter Gouldthorpe, Lothian (South Melbourne, Victoria, Australia), 1993, Gareth Stevens (New York, NY), 1996.

Gulliver in the South Seas, illustrated by John Burge, Lothian (South Melbourne, Victoria, Australia), 1994.

The Watertower, illustrated by Steven Woolman, ERA Publishers (Adelaide, South Australia, Australia), 1994, Crocodile Books (New York, NY), 1998.

The Lost Diamonds of Killicrankie, illustrated by Peter Gouldthorpe, Lothian (South Melbourne, Victoria, Australia), 1995.

Caleb, illustrated by Steven Woolman, ERA Publishers (Adelaide, South Australia, Australia), 1996.

Bright Star, illustrated by Anne Spudvilas, Lothian (South Melbourne, Victoria, Australia), Kane Miller, 1997.

Tagged, illustrated by Steven Woolman, ERA Publishers (Adelaide, South Australia, Australia), 1997.

The Viewer, illustrated by Shaun Tan, Lothian (South Melbourne, Victoria, Australia), 1997.

Troy Thompson's Excellent Poetry Book, illustrated by Craig Smith, Lothian (South Melbourne, Victoria, Australia), 1998.

Memorial, illustrated by Shaun Tan, Lothian (South Melbourne, Victoria, Australia), 1999.

(With Annmarie Scott) *In My Father's Room,* Hodder (Sydney, New South Wales, Australia), 2000.

Beneath the Surface, Hodder (Sydney, New South Wales, Australia), 2004.

The Lantern, illustrated by Bruce Whatley, Hodder (Sydney, New South Wales, Australia), 2005.

The Mystery of Eileen Mor, illustrated by Jeremy Geddes, Lothian (South Melbourne, Victoria, Australia), 2005.

"AFTER DARK" SERIES; FICTION

The Windmill, Franklin Watts (London, England), 1998.

The Fort, Franklin Watts (London, England), 1998.

The Barn, Franklin Watts (London, England), 1999.

The Bent-back Bridge, Franklin Watts (London, England), 1999.

The Well, Franklin Watts (London, England), 1999.

NONFICTION

(With Mark Wilson) *The Castaways of the Charles Eaton,* Lothian (South Melbourne, Victoria, Australia), 2002.

(With Robert Ingpen) *In the Wake of the Mary Celeste,* Lothian (South Melbourne, Victoria, Australia), 2004.

Young Murphy: A Boy's Adventures (picture book biography), illustrated by Mark Wilson, Lothian (South Melbourne, Victoria, Australia), 2005.

Pig on the Titanic: A True Story, illustrated by Bruce Whatley, HarperCollins (New York, NY), 2005.

"EXTINCT" SERIES; NONFICTION; WITH MARK WILSON

I Saw Nothing: The Extinction of the Thylacine, Lothian (South Melbourne, Victoria, Australia), 2003.

I Said Nothing: The Extinction of the Paradise Parrot, Lothian (South Melbourne, Victoria, Australia), 2003.

I Did Nothing: The Extinction of the Gastric-Brooding Frog, Lothian (South Melbourne, Victoria, Australia), 2004.

OTHER

Contributor of short stories to anthologies, including *Hair Raising,* edited by Penny Matthews, Omnibus, 1992; *The Blue Dress,* edited by Libby Hathorn, Heinemann, 1992; *The Lottery,* edited by Lucy Sussex, Omnibus, 1994; *Family,* edited by Agnes Nieuwenhuizen, Reed, 1994; *Crossing,* edited by Agnes Nieuwenhuizen and Tessa Duder, Reed, 1995; *Nightmares in Paradise,* edited by R. Sheahan, Queensland University Press, 1995; and *Celebrate,* edited by M. Hillel and A. Hanzl, Viking, 1996. Compiling editor, *Dark House,* Reed, 1995, and *Crew's 13,* ABC Books, 1997. Contributor to books, including *At Least They're Reading!: Proceedings of the First National Conference of the Children's Book Council of Australia,* Thorpe, 1992; *The Second Authors and Illustrators Scrapbook,* Omnibus Books, 1992; and *The Phone Book,* Random House, 1995. Contributor to periodicals, including *Age, Australian Author, Imago, Magpies, Reading Time, Viewpoint,* and *World Literature Written in English.*

ADAPTATIONS: The story "Sleeping over at Lola's" was adapted as a radio play by the Australian Broadcasting Corporation.

SIDELIGHTS: The novels of Australian writer Gary Crew have received critical acclaim for achieving two qualities that are difficult to combine; they have been declared intricate and enriching examples of literary writing, and they are also accessible to young readers. "His novels epitomize young adult literature in Australia to date," wrote Maurice Saxby in *The Proof of the Pudding.* "They successfully combine popular appeal with intellectual, emotional, psychological and spiritual substance." Crew's books often explore the history of Australia, but he finds that it is his own personal history that often drives his fiction. "Perhaps more than other mortals, it is the writer of children's fiction who suffers most from the desire to return to the past," he wrote in an essay in *Magpies.* "I know I cannot entirely abandon my own past. Once I would have longed to; I would have given anything to at least redress, at best forget, the forces that shaped me—but, as I grow older, and more confident in my art, I am not so certain. . . . A writer who cannot remember must produce lean fare. And surely, a children's writer who cannot remember is no writer at all."

Crew's past begins in Brisbane, Australia, where he was born in 1947. In his *Magpies* essay, Crew recalled that he "spent most of my childhood with the local kids racing around the neighbourhood," but there was also a sadder aspect to the author's early years. Crew began to suffer from poor health as a youngster, describing himself in a speech published in *Australian Author* as "a sickly, puny child." As a result, his rambunctious adventures soon gave way to calmer pursuits. "My mother says that I was a very quiet child, and my earliest memories suggest that she is right," Crew once commented: "I was always happiest by myself, reading, drawing, or making models. I never did like crowds or noise." Crew's illness also forced him to spend a lot of time in hospitals or confined to the house, but this experience later benefited his writing in at least two ways. It first allowed him much time to read. In *Magpies,* Crew recalled that he and his sister read "anything," and this interest in books continued into adulthood, providing him with a solid literary background.

A second benefit of Crew's illness was that it brought him in closer contact with an influential setting that would later be featured in one of his books. "A significant period of my childhood had been spent at my great-grandmother's house in Ipswich, to the west of Brisbane," Crew related in *Australian Author.* "My great-grandmother was bedridden in this house; my widowed grandmother cared for her. Because I was always sick, there seemed to be some logic in packing me off to join them." Recalling the location in *The Second Authors and Illustrators Scrapbook,* Crew wrote that "this house was wonderful, with verandas all around, and a great big mango tree growing right up against it. We could climb over the rail and drop onto the branches of the mango. This house gave me the main idea for my second novel, *The House of Tomorrow.*" In that novel, Crew writes of Danny, a teenage boy who has difficulty coping with the increased pressures in his life. Searching for a means to order and understand the world around him, Danny finds solace in the house that is modeled on the home in Ipswich. As the author explained it in *Australian Author:* "In *The House of Tomorrow* my great-grandmother's house reestablished a sense of place and belonging in a young boy's life."

Crew's stays in Ipswich had other benefits, as well. "My first public attempts at writing were letters sent from my great-grandmother's house to my parents," he wrote in *The Second Authors and Illustrators Scrapbook,* and writing and drawing later became important elements in his life. "Until I went to high school, I never seemed to be especially good at anything," Crew once admitted, "but at fifteen years old, I realized that I could write and draw—but that was about all I could do well!"

Despite his desire to continue his studies, Crew's drawing abilities and his family's economic status soon led him in another direction. "My parents had very little money, so I left school at sixteen to become a cadet draftsman, working for a firm of engineers. I hated this, and at twenty-one I returned to college to matriculate by studying at night; then I went to university. All this time I was earning a living as a draftsman, but had decided to be a teacher of English because I loved books so much." Crew soon proved his abilities as a student, and he valued the opportunity to continue his delayed education. "I don't think anyone was ever more comfortable at uni[versity] than I was," he told *Scan* interviewer Niki Kallenberger, "It was most wonderful! I would have done all the assignments on the sheets! It was a feeling of being totally at home and I was a changed person."

It was not until after he became a high school English teacher that Crew began writing fiction, and then only at the urging of his wife. "Christine cut out a piece from the paper advertising a short story contest which I entered virtually as a joke," he told Kallenberger. The story placed in the contest and later won a best short story of the year contest. Crew then turned to novels for young adults and drew inspiration from the students in his English classes. "I guess my first novels came out of my experience as a high school teacher," he once said. "I saw so many teenagers who were confused and unhappy—about themselves and the world around them." His first book, *The Inner Circle,* focuses on the relationship between a black teenager named Joe, and a white teen named Tony, who form a bond despite their racial differences. Saxby, analyzing the novel in *The Proof of the Pudding,* found that *The Inner Circle* is "above all, a well-told story incorporating many of the concerns of today's teenagers. The theme of personal and racial reintegration and harmony is inherent in the plot and reinforced through symbolism." The book has enjoyed great popularity in Australia, and English and Canadian editions have also been published. Crew has been pleased by the book's success but believes the work contains several flaws. "I'm not a fool in regard to approaching the book critically myself and I know the book's got phenomenal weaknesses," he told Kallenberger. "But I also see it as being a remarkable publishing oddity because it's so accessible to kids and its use in the classroom continues to astound me."

Crew's enjoyment of academic study—and research in particular—has influenced his fiction-writing process. He is not an author who sits at a desk and waits for inspiration to visit him; instead, Crew actively seeks out information about a subject and collects the materials in a journal. As he told Kallenberger, a typical journal contains "clippings, drawings, scrappy notes I write to myself. I just keep it all in a carton and throw in anything, even books, that's broadly relevant. . . . It all goes in there and if it's a rainy day I'll look at it." Crew has also conducted computer searches to gain information on subjects, and he often employs his artistic skills in preparation for writing a book. "I think that drawing people and places before I write about them prevents me from having writer's block, and allows me to write smoothly without interruptions," he related in *The Second Authors and Illustrators Scrapbook.* "These jottings are quick and rough but they mean a great deal to me when I come to write the episode they represent; they serve as mental reminders."

Crew's explorations of Australian history began with his third novel, the award winning *Strange Objects.* The novel's hero, Stephen Messenger, is a sixteen year old who discovers a leather-bound journal and other mysterious objects in a cave. The relics are believed to have belonged to two survivors from the *Batavia,* a ship that wrecked off the coast of Australia in 1629. These relics provide Messenger with a direct link to his country's earliest European inhabitants, and they provide Crew with a means of addressing the relationship between the Europeans and the aboriginal peoples who were the original inhabitants of the Australian continent. As is the case in several of Crew's books, *Strange Objects* forces readers to consider some unpleasant aspects of the European conquest of the island and is often critical of the colonists who settled in Australia. Commenting on *Strange Objects* in *Reading Time,* Crew wrote that the book is "intended to challenge the reader to examine what has happened in our past, to reassess what forces shaped this nation— and the effect the white invasion has had on the original inhabitants of this country."

Crew finds that, like many other things, his interest in the past stems from his childhood. In his speech accepting the Book of the Year Award from the Children's Book Council of Australia for *Strange Objects,* Crew explained the influence of his early years. "The origins of *Strange Objects* are founded deep in my memory," he stated in the speech, later published in *Reading Time.* "During the never-ending sunshine of my childhood in the 50's, my parents would regularly take me and my sister Annita to the Queensland Museum. . . . Here we were able to stare goggle-eyed and open-mouthed at mummies stolen-away from the Torres Strait Islands, bamboo headhunters' knives complete with notches from every head taken and other so-called 'cannibal' artifacts. . . . When I had been made wiser by my studies, I began to understand the colonist's fear of the Indigene [or aborigines] as The Other, and to appreciate fully the fantastical and ever-changing phenomenon we call 'history.'"

Crew has further explored the legacy of Australia's past in his novel *No Such Country,* which takes place in the fictional setting of New Canaan and concerns the fate of the White Father, a priest who enjoys great power in the village. Joan Zahnleiter, writing about the book in *Magpies,* noted that "the Father uses his knowledge of a particularly evil event in the past of New Canaan to blackmail superstitious fisherfolk into accepting him as the Messiah who controls their lives with his great book." Zahnleiter also found that "the book has deeply religious concepts embedded in it so that a working knowledge of the Bible enriches the reading of it. However it is a story which works well for the reader without that knowledge."

As the editor of Lothian Books' "After Dark" series as well as the author of some of the titles in the series, Crew is no stranger to terrifying tales of gothic horror. Sometimes these stories come from history, such as *Mama's Babies.* Using actual nineteenth-century cases of women who would take on additional children for cash, only to later "dispose" of these children when they could, Crew tells the story of Sarah, the oldest adoptive child of Mama Pratchett. It seems as though each time a child has a mysterious accident, is hospitalized, or disappears, a new baby is brought into the family. When Sarah is forced to feed one of the younger children "medicine" that seems to make the child worse, she begins to develop suspicions about Mama Pratchett's behavior—but not soon enough to save the child. It is only with the help of her friend Will that Sarah is able to gain the courage to bring her suspicions to the authorities.

"Although the author wisely prepares readers for the horrific events well in advance, this gripping story isn't for the fainthearted," warned Kay Weisman in *Booklist,* adding in her review of *Mama's Babies* that horror lovers will be unable to put the book down. Sarah Applegate, writing for *Kliatt,* noted, "The story is disjointed and disconcerting but also morbidly fascinating to read." Kathryn A. Childs, in *Book Report,* found that the novel "will intrigue young adult readers who enjoy historical fiction as well as a good mystery."

Crew has also penned more traditional gothic horror stories, including *Gothic Hospital.* Narrated by the disturbed Johnny Doolan, a patient at a hospital situated in a dark castle on a mountain run by a mad doctor. Unlike most of the other children, who have lost their parents, Johnny's father is still alive, and Johnny has dreams that his father is being tortured somewhere inside the hospital. According to David Carroll, who reviewed the book for *Tabula-Rasa Online, Gothic Hospital* is "a mature, challenging, and ultimately fascinating work, and very much recommended."

In addition to his novels, Crew has published story books for young children such as *Tracks* and *Lucy's Bay,* both including illustrations by Gregory Rogers. In *Tracks,* a young boy ventures into the strange, night-time world of the jungle, making many unusual and beautiful discoveries. *Lucy's Bay* concerns a boy, Sam, whose sister drowns while he is taking care of her. Several years later, Sam returns to the scene of the tragedy in an attempt to come to terms with his feelings of sadness and guilt. A *Reading Time* review found *Lucy's Bay* to be "a beautiful piece of descriptive writing which places in perspective Sam's grief for his sister against the ceaseless rhythm of nature."

Crew is a consummate explorer who keeps a journal of ideas and "artifacts" to remind him of experiences and thoughts. He has drawn upon personal experiences, as well as fantasies born from reality to write children's stories. Some ideas, such as the fishing trip in *First Light,* come from his own life. Others, including the story presented in *The Watertower,* may have begun by remembering a childhood prank, and grew as the imagination took hold. The plot begins in a small town where two boys sneak a swim in an old watertower on a hot summer day. When one boy's pants blow away, the other leaves to get another pair. When he returns, his friend has a crazed, vacant stare and a strange new marking on his hand. Crew teamed up with illustrator Steve Woolman to enhance the mystery visually, making it "a genuinely eerie picture book, which is constructed as a kind of puzzle," according to a *Kirkus Reviews* critic. *School Library Journal* reviewer Patricia Lothrop-Green called *The Watertower* a "Twilight Zone-type picture book for older children . . . in which text and illustrations work inseparably to create a strange but compelling whole."

Crew also builds themes around ideas from criminology, science, and history as in *The Lost Diamonds of Killiecrankie.* Sometimes contemporary themes are woven into historically based fiction. *Bright Star* takes place in rural Australia in 1871. A school girl becomes frustrated because she does not have the same freedom as boys to choose what she studies. She dreams of learning astronomy rather than needlepoint, the curriculum usually offered to girls. An encounter with astronomer John Tebbutt, who lived in New South Wales and discovered "the Great Comet of 1861," along with her mother's support, helps her realize that she must choose her own destiny. Even though *Booklist* reviewer Carolyn Phelan found the girl's "longing for

freedom romanticized," she added that "the differences between the treatment of girls and boys in the 1800s are clearly set out, and picture books dealing with the history of astronomy are few."

Troy Thompson's Excellent Poetry Book features the poetry of fictional student Troy Thompson, a sixth grader competing in a poetry contest for his teacher, Ms. Kranke. Thompson's poetry covers silly topics, including gym locker rooms and talk show hosts, as well as serious issues, including the death of his father. The forms of poetry included in the book range from haiku to ballads to limericks, and the layout is designed to look like a student's notebook, as all of the poems are either handwritten, or typed and appear to be pasted into the notebook. "The title is complete with silliness and serious topics," noted Shawn Brommer, reviewing the title for the *School Library Journal.*

Crew has worked with artist Shaun Tan to produce two surreal tales, one about a dystopian future and the other about the nature of memory. In *The Viewer* Tristan discovers a strange box that contains a mask-like device which reveals visions of the past, including evil acts committed by humankind. Tristan watches scenes of war, torture, and slavery on his first day with the viewer, and when he returns to look through it on the second day, he finds that the pictures have changed into depictions of horrible possibilities for the future. On the third day when his mother goes to wake him for school, Tristan has disappeared, and the mysterious box is locked on his desk. Donna Ratterree called *The Viewer* an "eerie and disturbing story, while a critic for *Publishers Weekly* noted, "The audience can almost feel the power that the mask exudes in this unsettling walk through history."

Tan and Crew's second collaboration, *Memorial,* tells the story of a young boy who wants to save a living memorial, an overgrown tree that was planted the day that his great-grandfather came home from World War I. Though the boy loses his battle to stop the tree from being cut down, his great-grandfather teaches him that the important part to carry with him is the memory, and that by fighting against the city council, his acts—and the tree he was unable to save—will also be remembered. "Crew's words are simple and powerful and will resonate with both young and older readers," appraised Joanne de Groot in *Resource Links,* while Ellen Fader, writing for the *School Library Journal,* considered the book "undeniably a powerful package."

The story of the U.S.S. *Titanic* provided the plot for Crew's 2005 picture book *Pig on the Titanic: A True Story*. Edith Rosenbaum, a passenger on the *Titanic*'s ill-fated voyage, had a wonderful mechanical pig that played music. When Rosenbaum tried to give up her seat on a life boat, a member of the ship's crew mistook the pig she clutched in her arms for a baby, and forced the woman onto the boat. Told from the perspective of the marvelous machine, Maxine the musical pig, the book expresses her delight at being able to keep up the spirits of the children sharing the life boat with Rosenbaum. "Crew deftly captures the drama of that night," proclaimed Grace Oliff in her *School Library Journal* review. A critic for *Kirkus Reviews* commented that the book "lends the historical catastrophe immediacy . . . while downplaying its horrific aspects." A *Publishers Weekly* reviewer noted, "families and classrooms familiar with the *Titanic*'s story will be thrilled to find a book that tells the tale from a childlike perspective."

Crew believes that his personal experiences continue to play a large role in his books. "As a writer, I am not done with looking inward," he explained in *Australian Author*. "There is much for me still to find in my house of fiction; in those fantastical inner rooms of childhood from which, I imagine, some choose never to emerge." In each book he writes, he has definite aims regarding his young audience. "My main objective in writing is to open the minds of my readers," Crew once explained, "to say 'the world can be a wonderful place—its possibilities are open to you and your imagination.'"

BIOGRAPHICAL AND CRITICAL SOURCES:

BOOKS

At Least They're Reading!: Proceedings of the First National Conference of The Children's Book Council of Australia, 1992, Thorpe, 1992.

McKenna, Bernard, and Sharyn Peare, *Strange Journeys: The Works of Gary Crew*, Hodder, 1998.

Saxby, Maurice, *The Proof of the Pudding*, Ashton, 1993.

The Second Authors and Illustrators Scrapbook, Omnibus Books (London, England), 1992.

PERIODICALS

Australian Author, autumn, 1992, Gary Crew, "The Architecture of Memory," pp. 24-27.

Booklist, June 1, 1993, p. 1812; May 1, 1994, p. 1594; October 1, 1995, p. 303; August, 2002, Kay Weisman, review of *Mama's Babies*, p. 1948.

Book Report, November-December, 2002, Kathryn A. Childs, review of *Mama's Babies*, p. 45.

Horn Book, September-October, 1994, p. 596; March-April, 1996, p. 205; May, 1998, p. 330.

Kirkus Reviews, June 15, 1994, p. 842; August 15, 1995, p. 1186; January 1, 1998, review of *The Watertower*, p. 55; April 1, 2002, review of *Mama's Babies*, p. 489; March 1, 2005, review of *Pig on the Titanic: A True Story*, p. 285.

Kliatt, September, 2002, Sarah Applegate, review of *Mama's Babies*, p. 16.

Magpies, May, 1991, p. 22; July, 1991, p. 37; September, 1991, Joan Zahnleiter, "Know the Author: Gary Crew," pp. 17-19; March, 1992, p. 34; July, 1992, Gary Crew, "New Directions in Fiction," pp. 5-8; March, 1996, p. 12; October 15, 1997, Carolyn Phelan, review of *Bright Star*, p. 412; November, 1997, p. 21; May, 1998, p. 37; May, 2005, review of *The Plague of Quentaris*, p. 36.

Papers: Explorations in Children's Literature, August, 1990, pp. 51-58; April, 1992, pp. 18-26.

Reading Time, Volume 35, number 3, 1991, Gary Crew, essay on *Strange Objects*, pp. 11-12; Volume 35, number 4, 1991, Gary Crew, "Awards: The Children's Book Council of Australia Awards 1991 Acceptance Speeches," pp. 4-5; May, 1992, review of *Lucy's Bay*, p. 20.

Resource Links, October, 2004, Joanne de Groot, review of *Memorial*, p. 3.

Scan, November, 1990, Niki Kallenberger, interview with Crew, pp. 9-11.

School Librarian, spring, 2005, Joan Hamilton Jones, review of *I Did Nothing: The Extinction of the Gastric-Brooding Frog*, p. 44.

School Library Journal, May, 1993, p. 124; July, 1994, p. 116; October, 1995, p. 152; February, 1998, p. 79; March, 1998, Patricia Lothrop-Green, review of *The Watertower*, p. 168; June, 2002, Mary R. Hofmann, review of *Mama's Babies*, p. 136; January, 2004, Shawn Brommer, review of *Troy Thompson's Excellent Poetry Book*, p. 128; March, 2004, Donna Ratterree, review of *The Viewer*, p. 204; December, 2004, Ellen Fader, review of *Memorial*, p. 144; May, 2005, Grace Oliff, review of *Pig on the Titanic*, p. 80.

Voice of Youth Advocates, August 1993, p. 162; April, 1994, p. 19; April, 1996, p. 25.

ONLINE

Tabula-Rasa Online, http://www.tabula-rasa.info/ (July 31, 2005), David Carroll, review of *Gothic Hospital.*

*   *   *

CROWTHER, Peter 1949-
(Nick Hassam)

PERSONAL: Born July 4, 1949, in Leeds, England; son of Percival (an engineer) and Kathleen (Bowling) Crowther; married Nichola Hassam (a teacher), October 23, 1976; children: Oliver James, Timothy Nicholas. *Education:* Attended Leeds Metropolitan University, England. *Politics:* Socialist. *Religion:* "Lapsed Protestant."

ADDRESSES: Home and office—Bridgewood, 22 South Dr., Harrogate HG2 8AU, England. *Office*—PS Publishing, Grosvenor House, 1 New Road, Hornsea, East Yorkshire, HU18 1 PG, England. *Agent*—Susan Gleason, 325 Riverside Dr., New York, NY 10025.

CAREER: Writer and editor. Leeds Permanent Building Society, Leeds, England, communications manager, 1980-95; freelance writer and consulting editor, 1995—. PS Publishing, cofounder.

MEMBER: Horror Writers of America, Science Fiction and Fantasy Writers of America, Mystery Writers of America.

AWARDS, HONORS: Best Collection award, British Fantasy Society, 2000, for *Lonesome Roads;* Hugo Award, 2003, for editing.

WRITINGS:

EDITOR; FICTION ANTHOLOGIES

Narrow Houses: Tales of Superstition, Suspense and Fear, Little, Brown (London, England), 1992, Warner Books (New York, NY), 1994.

Touch Wood: Narrow Houses, Volume 2, Little, Brown (London, England), 1993, Warner Books (New York, NY), 1996.
Blue Motel: Narrow Houses, Volume 3, Little, Brown (London, England), 1994, White Wolf (Atlanta, GA), 1996.
Heaven Sent: An Anthology of Angel Stories, DAW Books (New York, NY), 1995.
(With Edward E. Kramer) *Tombs,* White Wolf (Atlanta, GA), 1995.
(With Edward E. Kramer) *Dante's Disciples,* White Wolf (Atlanta, GA), 1996.
Destination Unknown, White Wolf (Atlanta, GA), 1997.
Tales in Time, White Wolf (Atlanta, GA), 1997.
Taps and Sighs, Subterranean Press (Burton, MI), 2000.
Foursight, Victor Gollancz (London, England), 2000.
(And author of introduction) *Futures: Four Novellas,* Warner Books (New York, NY), 2001.
Mars Probes, Daw Books (New York, NY), 2002.
(And contributor) *Cities,* Four Walls Eight Windows (New York, NY), 2004.
Constellations, DAW (New York, NY), 2005.
Fourbodings (novellas), Cemetery Dance (Burton, MI), 2005.

Other anthologies edited include *Coast of Avon,* 1992; *Tales in Space,* 1995; *Moon Shots,* 1999; and *Infinities.* 2002. Also editor of the magazine *Postscripts 1,* spring, 2004.

EDITOR

A Single-Handed Sailing in Galway Blazer, Waterline Books, 1998.
(Editor) *The Diary of Robert Sharp of South Cave: Life in a Yorkshire Village 1812-1837,* Oxford University Press (New York, NY), 1998.
Gandalph Cohen and the Land at the End of the Working Day, Subterranean Press (Burton, MI), 1999.
Paleobiology, Blackwell Science, Inc. (Malden, MA), 2001.

OTHER

(With James Lovegrove) *Escardy Gap* (novel), Tor Books (New York, NY), 1996.
Forest Plains (story collection), Hypatia Press (Eugene, OR), 1996.

The Longest Single Note and Other Strange Compositions (story collection), CD Publications (Baltimore, MD), 1998.

Darkness, Darkness: Forever Twilight: Book One (novella), CD Publications (Baltimore, MD), 2002.

Songs of Leaving (short stories), Subterranean Press (Burton, MI), 2004.

Also author of the novels *Fugue on a G-String,* 1998; *The Hand that Feeds,* 1999; and *Happily Ever After,* 2000. Collections of short stories also include *Lonesome Roads,* 1999.

Contributor of short stories to numerous anthologies, including *First Contact,* 1987; *Dark Voices 4,* 1992; *Deathport,* 1993; *Celebrity Vampires,* 1995; *Monster Brigade 3000,* 1996; *Dancing with the Dar,* 1997; *Black Cats and Broken Mirrors,* 1998; *Alien Abductions,* 1999; *Perchance to Dream,* 2000; *Crimewave,* TTA (England), 2000; and *Single White Vampire Seeks Same,* 2001. Contributor to periodicals, sometimes under pseudonym Nick Hassam.

ADAPTATIONS: Author's stories have been adapted into audio format, including a collection titled *Cold Comforts and Other Fireside Mysteries,* Lone Wolf, 2001.

SIDELIGHTS: Peter Crowther has edited a number of popular anthologies of horror fiction, written horror novellas, and published a number of short stories in the genre as well. As an anthologist, Crowther edited the "Narrow Houses" series of anthologies. The series title comes from a traditional description of coffins as being "narrow houses for the dead." A critic for *Publishers Weekly* described the first volume in the "Narrow Houses" series as "an impressive variety of superb fiction." The anthology *Tombs,* coedited by Crowther and Edward E. Kramer, focuses on stories involving some sort of entombment, either in a literal or metaphoric sense. The collection includes works from such diverse writers as William F. Buckley, Jr., and Michael Moorcock. A *Publishers Weekly* reviewer dubbed *Tombs* an "agreeable grab bag of claustrophobic, mortifying pleasures." Writing in the *St. James Guide to Horror, Ghost and Gothic Writers,* a contributor called Crowther "a notable anthologist in the horror and dark fantasy fields."

Crowther's novel *Escardy Gap,* cowritten with James Lovegrove, concerns a visit to a small town by Jeremiah Rackstraw and the Company, a bizarre group of sideshow performers. The town is, according to Gilmore, "the sort of smug, ultra-folksy Midwestern rural community where everyone knows everyone else." Once Jeremiah and his performers gain the townspeople's confidence, they "set about the predictable mayhem, each in his/her own special way," wrote Gilmore. "It's handled as more than usually imaginative black farce with some fine bravura passages. . . . Most importantly the authors address a nagging wrongness found in almost all genre horror but very little fantasy, however dark: that the evil incursion is unsought and unearned. Horrid as the folk are, with their cracker-barrel wisdom, Mom's pie, regular churchgoing and long evenings gossiping on the porch, they deserve nothing than to be left to get on with it." Gilmore continued, "While the real world is full of injustice, the supernatural should effect a certain symmetry between what is sown and what is reaped. The [town's] Mayor expresses this forcefully enough to Rackstraw, only to be told that for all the torture and murder there is neither rationale nor justice, only the exercise of malign whimsy."

In his short-story collection *The Longest Single Note and Other Strange Compositions,* the author delivers a wide variety of twenty-six horror and fantasy stories, from a story about the humanism of vampires to ruminations on music and its impact on life and death. A *Publishers Weekly* contributor noted that "vigorous, genuinely fearsome work such as Crowther's demonstrates that the genre is decidedly undead." Crowther tells the story of the disappearance of a small-town populace only to have them reappear under the power of alien forces in his novel *Darkness, Darkness: Forever Twilight: Book One.* Soon the zombie-like people are after four members of a radio station who still are unsure of what has happened. A *Publishers Weekly* contributor noted that the author "evokes a range of creepy cinema classics." Don D'Ammassa, writing in the *Science Fiction Chronicle,* called the effort an "old fashioned SF horror movie."

Songs of Leaving is another short story collection, including stories about the abandonment of Earth due to an oncoming asteroid and the cloning of Abraham Lincoln, who finds himself lost in modern New York. A *Publishers Weekly* contributor noted: "The best [stories] . . . evoke a genuine sense of wonder and offer near-miraculous restoration of hope." The reviewer went on to write that the author "enchants as he tells deceptively simple tales of eternal truths."

Regina Schroeder, writing in *Booklist,* commented: "These lovely and thoughtful stories are speculative fiction at pretty much its best."

In addition to his own writings, the author has continued to serve as editor of numerous anthologies. In *Foursight,* Crowther presents four novellas by modern science fictions writers and, in the process, "has served up a lavish feast," according to Peter Ingham, writing in the *Times* of London. Crowther also served as editor of *Futures: Four Novellas,* which includes works by British science fiction writers Peter F. Hamilton, Stephen Baxter, Paul McAuley, and Ian McDonald. *Fourbodings* includes novellas by "some of the U.K.'s best practicing horror writers," noted a *Publishers Weekly* contributor. Writing in the *New York Times Book Review,* Gerald Jonas commented that the novellas in *Futures* present "satisfying changes on . . . classic science fiction themes." In *Constellations* Crowther as editor presents fifteen original stories by some of England's newest science fiction and fantasy writers. Aaron Hughes, writing on the *Fantastic Reviews* Web site, noted that the book "is ostensibly a theme anthology, with all the stories relating somehow to the constellations in the night sky." Hughes went on to comment that Crowther presents "readers [with] a chance to sample some of the great new British writers they may have missed."

BIOGRAPHICAL AND CRITICAL SOURCES:

BOOKS

St. James Guide to Horror, Ghost and Gothic Writers, St. James Press (Detroit, MI), 1998.

PERIODICALS

Booklist, November 15, 2001, Regina Schroeder, review of *Futures: Four Novellas,* p. 560; July, 2004, Regina Schroeder, review of *Songs of Leaving,* p. 1828.
Chronicle, September, 2004, Don D'Ammassa, review of *Postscripts 1,* p. 34.
Library Journal, August, 1997, p. 141; November 15, 2000, Michael Colford, review of *Crimewave,* p. 104; June 15, 2002, Jackie Cassada, review of *Mars Probes,* p. 100; January 1, 2005, Jackie Cassada, review of *Constellations,* p. 103.

Magazine of Fantasy & Science Fiction, May, 2002, James Sallis, review of *Futures,* p. 32.
New York Times Book Review, January 13, 2002, Gerald Jonas, review of *Futures,* p. 21.
Publishers Weekly, September 12, 1994, review of *Narrow Houses: Tales of Superstition, Suspense and Fear,* p. 86; May 15, 1995, review of *Tombs,* p. 61; June 21, 1999, review of *The Longest Single Note and Other Strange Compositions,* p. 61; May 29, 2000, review of *Taps and Sighs,* p. 57; August 26, 2002, review of *Darkness, Darkness: Forever Twilight: Book One,* p. 49; April 19, 2004, review of *Cities,* p. 45; May 10, 2004, review of *Songs of Leaving,* p. 41; January 3, 2005, review of *Fourbodings,* p. 41.
Science Fiction Chronicle, August, 2002, Don D'Ammassa, review of *Darkness, Darkness,* p. 40.
Times (London, England), April 8, 2000, Peter Ingham, review of *Foursight,* p. 22.

ONLINE

Fantastic Fiction, http://www.fantasticfiction.co.uk/ (October 5, 2005), brief profile of author and listing of works.
Fantastic Reviews, http://www.geocities.com/ fantasticreviews/ (November 14, 2005), Aaron Hughes, review of *Constellations.**

*   *   *

CUTLER, Jane 1936-

PERSONAL: Born September 24, 1936, in New York, NY; daughter of Emanuel (a manufacturer) and Beatrice (a homemaker; maiden name, Drooks) Cutler; children: Franny, David, Aaron. *Education:* Northwestern University, B.A., 1958; San Francisco State University, M.A., 1982. *Hobbies and other interests:* Reading, swimming, hiking, theater, art, music.

ADDRESSES: Agent—Gail Hochman, Brandt & Hochman Literary Agents, 1501 Broadway, Ste. 2310, New York, NY 10036. *E-mail*—janecutler@earthlink.net.

CAREER: Writer, editor, and writing teacher.

MEMBER: Authors Guild, Authors League of America, National Organization for Women, Society of Children's Book Writers and Illustrators.

AWARDS, HONORS: Herbert Wilner Award for short fiction, 1982; PEN prize for short fiction, 1987; Show Me Readers Award nomination, Missouri Association of School Librarians, for *Mr. Carey's Garden;* Nene Reading List for Hawaii Schools nomination, for *Rats!;* nominations for William Allen White Children's Book Award and Mark Twain Award; Best Children's Books of the Year designation, Bank Street College of Education, for *The Song of the Molimo;* Master List includee, New York Public Library, 1999, and Notable Social Studies Trade Book for Young Readers, Children's Book Council, Patterson Prize for Books for Young People, and Zena Sutherland Award for Children's Literature, all 2000, New Mexico Land of Enchantment Book Award, 2002-03, and Golden Kite Award nomination, all for *The Cello of Mr. O;* Lamplighter Award, 2002; featured author in Virginia Festival of the Book, 2005.

WRITINGS:

NOVELS; FOR CHILDREN

Family Dinner, Farrar, Straus & Giroux (New York, NY), 1991.
No Dogs Allowed ("Fraser Brothers" series), illustrated by Tracey Campbell Pearson, Farrar, Straus & Giroux (New York, NY), 1992.
My Wartime Summers, Farrar, Straus & Giroux (New York, NY), 1994.
Rats! ("Fraser Brothers" series), illustrated by Tracey Campbell Pearson, Farrar, Straus & Giroux (New York, NY), 1996.
Spaceman, Dutton (New York, NY), 1997.
The Song of the Molimo, Farrar, Straus & Giroux (New York, NY), 1998.
'Gator Aid ("Fraser Brothers" series), illustrated by Tracey Campbell Pearson, Farrar, Straus & Giroux (New York, NY), 1999.
Leap, Frog ("Fraser Brothers" series), illustrated by Tracey Campbell Pearson, Farrar, Straus & Giroux (New York, NY), 2001.
Commonsense and Fowls, illustrated by Lynne Barasch, Farrar, Straus & Giroux (New York, NY), 2005.

PICTURE BOOKS; FOR CHILDREN

Darcy and Gran Don't Like Babies, illustrated by Susannah Ryan, Scholastic (New York, NY), 1993.

Mr. Carey's Garden, illustrated by G. Brian Karas, Houghton (Boston, MA), 1996.
The Cello of Mr. O, illustrated by Greg Couch, Dutton (New York, NY), 1999.
The Birthday Doll, illustrated by Hiroe Nakata, Farrar, Straus & Giroux (New York, NY), 2001.
Rose and Riley, illustrated by Thomas F. Yezerski, Farrar, Straus & Giroux (New York, NY), 2005.
Rose and Riley Come and Go, illustrated by Thomas F. Yezerski, Farrar, Straus & Giroux (New York, NY), 2005.

OTHER

Contributor of adult short stories to periodicals, including *American Girl, Redbook, North American Review,* and the *Chicago Tribune;* editor and author of textbooks and encyclopedias; developer of remedial reading materials for children.

ADAPTATIONS: The Cello of Mr. O was adapted as a musical produced in Tokyo, Japan, 2004.

WORK IN PROGRESS: Guttersnipe, an illustrated picture book for older readers; a middle-grade novel about victims of the Holocaust who fled to Shanghai.

SIDELIGHTS: Born in New York, and raised in rural Missouri, Jane Cutler has created a number of well-received novels and picture books that focus on American family life. Her highly praised books for younger children range from picture books such as *The Birthday Doll* to beginning chapter books in the "Rosie and Riley" series to novels for older readers, such as the award-winning *The Cello of Mr. O,* which *Booklist* contributor Stephanie Zvirin dubbed a "touching story about hope, courage, and the way people surprise us."

Admitting to a love of writing that began in childhood, Cutler earned a master's degree in creative writing in 1982 before putting her writing career on the back burner for nearly a decade while raising her three children. Eventually returning to writing, she published her first juvenile novel, *Family Dinner,* in 1991, and followed that up two years later with her first picture book, *Darcy and Gran Don't Like Babies.* As Deborah Stevenson noted of Cutler's work in a review for the

Bulletin of the Center for Children's Books, her writing "is tender and thoughtful, humorous and sensitive, but never out of reach of her young readers."

A vole and groundhog who are the best of friends are introduced in the easy-reader *Rose and Riley.* In three stories, readers are treated to the kindness and concern shown by the happy-go-lucky Riley as he watches his friend Little Rose worry about all manner of things, even wasting sunny days waiting for rain. The duo's adventures continue in *Rose and Riley Come and Go,* which contains "intriguing" wordplay and an "unassuming but puckish text" that will entrance fledgling readers, according to a *Kirkus Reviews* writer.

For veteran bookworms, Cutler has written several novels that feature brothers Edward and Jason Fraser. Rambunctious, likable characters, the Fraser brothers find themselves embroiled in one humorous situation after another. They encounter the neighborhood bully, pretend to be a dog, take a camping trip, make the annual school clothes shopping trip, care for pet rats, and deal with pesky and over-attentive girls. Reviewing *No Dogs Allowed,* the first book in the "Fraser Brothers" series, a *Kirkus Reviews* critic commented that Cutler's "dialogue is on target, and the brothers make an entertaining pair," whose activities will appeal to readers who have enjoyed books by such well-known authors as Beverly Cleary and Johanna Hurwitz. Jana R. Fine also commented, in her review for the *School Library Journal,* on the realistic characters and "upbeat and lightweight" tone. A *Publishers Weekly* critic suggested that although the story's tone is "surprisingly funny," the "humor masks weightier matters."

Rats!, 'Gator Aid, and *Leap, Frog* continue the series about third grader Edward and his older brother Jason. The plots of the novels are lighthearted and full of typical childhood antics. Nancy Vasilakis, writing in *Horn Book,* praised *Rats!* for its "convincing characterizations" and "lighthearted humor that will appeal to those children who have read through Beverly Cleary and are looking for more." Although *Booklist* reviewer Ilene Cooper found Cutler's humor somewhat forced, she added that "there are still some very funny moments." *'Gator Aid* was described by *Horn Book* critic Vasilakis as an "undemanding, light read with characters a notch or two above stereotypes." *Booklist* critic Stephanie Zvirin cited the story's "pleasant comedy," and the story's "thought provoking undercurrent"

about the way casual statements quickly become outrageous rumors. In *Leap, Frog,* when overly active first grader Charley moves in next door and adopts the Fraser family for his own, Jason's school project—hatching eggs for a school sex-ed class—is derailed and the youngster's hyperactivity begins to affect even Edward and Jason's parents. *Leap, Frog* was praised by *School Library Journal* contributor Debbie Stewart for its "satisfying plot, . . . humorous characterizations, warm and realistic family interactions, and light mood," while Todd Morning predicted that middle-grade readers would enjoy the antics of Cutler's "loving (if slightly eccentric)" fictional family in *Booklist.* "What makes these stories so inviting," added Maggie McEwen of the series in the *School Library Journal,* "is Cutler's exceptional talent for describing events from the boys' rather literal point of view."

Other middle-grade novels include the historical fare *My Wartime Summers* and *The Song of the Molimo.* A first-person novel set in midwestern America during World War II, *My Wartime Summers* follows Ellen as she matures from a young girl into a teenager over three wartime summers during which she gradually becomes aware of the war and what it means in human terms. *The Song of the Molimo* takes place during the 1904 World's Fair in St. Louis, where Ota Benga (a real historical figure) and four other African Pygmies have been put on display in the anthropology exhibit. Twelve-year-old Harry Jones and his cousin Frederick, who is in charge of caring for the Pygmies, realize that these men deserve the same respect as other humans—an enlightened view in their prejudiced society—and plan to save their new friends.

Cultural misunderstanding are the focus of *Common Sense and Fowls,* which finds a small neighborhood in a turmoil. One of the residents, the foreign-born Mrs. Krnc, takes pity on the local pigeons and sets out food, which attracts more of the birds to the area. Led by Mr. Gioia, who finds the messy birds problematic, a plan is hatched to send Mrs. Krnc to a retirement home. Through the help of children Rachel and Brian, a more reasonable compromise is eventually reached in a book that a *Kirkus Reviews* writer dubbed "thought provoking." Praising the illustrations by Lynne Barasch, *School Library Journal* contributor Deanna Romriell cited Cutler for her "cast of likable and interesting characters," and praised the novel's "satisfying resolution."

Highly praised for its value to young readers with learning disabilities, *Spaceman* introduces fifth-grader Gary. Due to his learning disabilities, Gary earned the nickname "spaceman" because he "spaces out" when under pressure. After he is transferred to a special-needs classroom, he improves under the tutelage of a talented teacher. "Gary is a kid misunderstood and misplaced, and his dilemma is one with which many children can identify," asserted Janice M. Del Negro in her review of the novel for the *Bulletin of the Center for Children's Books*. Writing for the *School Library Journal*, Janet M. Bair suggested that classroom teachers could make good use of *Spaceman* due to the book's ability to "encourage discussion and promote empathy towards those who have different learning styles." "This compelling story . . . will help increase awareness and empathy," added Lauren Peterson in her *Booklist* review.

In addition to novels for middle-grade readers, Cutler has also penned several picture books. In *Darcy and Gran Don't Like Babies* she shows how one grandmother deals with her granddaughter's feelings of jealously toward the new baby in the house, while *Mr. Carey's Garden* treats a more unusual topic: snails eating holes in Mr. Carey's plants. When his gardening neighbors suggest various ways of killing the snails, they are baffled at his negative response, until one night they discover the snails' secret beauty. "A succinct but beautiful lesson in tolerance and understanding" is how Judith Constantinides described this work in the *School Library Journal*. Stephanie Zvirin also added praise in *Booklist*, called *Mr. Carey's Garden* "quiet" yet with "meaning that carries on beyond the confines of the story."

The recipient of numerous awards, *The Cello of Mr. O* describes the response of an elderly cellist to life in a war-ravaged community. By playing his cello amidst the ravages of war, Mr. O brings hope through his music. According to Ilene Cooper in *Booklist*, Cutler manages to "overlay the everyday horrors of war with a patina of hope." The author's "focus on turning calamity on its head will likely have an uplifting effect on readers young and old," enthused a *Publishers Weekly* critic. In *The Birthday Doll*, Franny receives both an old rag doll and a new, impressive talking doll as gifts from friends at her birthday party. The girl learns that a fancy exterior does not always have much depth. Calling *The Birthday Doll* "a surefire hit for doll lovers," *School Library Journal* reviewer Rosalyn

Pierini also praised Cutler's portrait of "a bouncy heroine and a loving home." A *Publishers Weekly* contributor deemed the picture book "a childlike and thoughtful offering."

About her works, Cutler once commented: "My own books are built around my characters: thoughtful characters, idiosyncratic characters, humorous characters. It is people who interest me most, and the books reflect this. But, like every writer, I need also to concern myself with plot—there has to be a story, after all! Fortunately, my characters have busy, active lives, which are, like most lives, full of stories."

BIOGRAPHICAL AND CRITICAL SOURCES:

PERIODICALS

Booklist, February 1, 1996, Ilene Cooper, review of *Rats!,* p. 932; March 15, 1996, Stephanie Zvirin, review of *Mr. Carey's Garden,* p. 1268; March 15, 1997, Lauren Peterson, review of *Spaceman,* p. 1242; October 15, 1998, p. 420; August, 1999, Stephanie Zvirin, review of *'Gator Aid,* p. 2056; December 15, 1999, Ilene Cooper, review of *The Cello of Mr. O,* p. 782; November 1, 2002, Todd Morning, review of *Leap, Frog,* p. 490.

Bulletin of the Center for Children's Books, May, 1997, Janice M. Del Negro, review of *Spaceman,* p. 318; October, 1998, Elizabeth Bush, review of *The Song of the Molimo,* pp. 55-56; August, 1999, Deborah Stevenson, "Jane Cutler."

Horn Book, May-June, 1996, Nancy Vasilakis, review of *Rats!,* pp. 334-335; September, 1999, Nancy Vasilakis, review of *'Gator Aid,* p. 609; September-October, 2002, Peter D. Sieruta, review of *Leap, Frog,* p. 569.

Kirkus Reviews, November 1, 1992, review of *No Dogs Allowed,* p. 1374; October 15, 2002, review of *Leap, Frog,* p. 1527; February 1, 2004, review of *The Birthday Doll,* p. 130; February, 2005, review of *Rose and Riley,* p. 227; March 1, 2005, review of *Common Sense and Fowls,* p. 285; July 1, 20005, review of *Rose and Riley Come and Go,* p. 733.

Publishers Weekly, November 9, 1992, review of *No Dogs Allowed,* p. 85; August 15, 1994, review of *My Wartime Summers,* p. 96; April 17, 1995, p. 62; February 24, 1997, review of *Spaceman,* p. 92; August, 16, 1999, review of *The Cello of Mr. O,* p. 84; February 2, 2004, review of *The Birthday Doll,* p. 76.

School Library Journal, December, 1992, Jana R. Fine, review of *No Dogs Allowed,* p. 80; November, 1994, Louise L. Sherman, review of *My Wartime Summers,* p. 102; April, 1996, Maggie McEwen, review of *Rats!,* p. 106; May, 1996, Judith Constantinides, review of *Mr. Carey's Garden,* p. 91; May, 1997, Janet M. Bair, review of *Spaceman,* p. 131; October, 2002, Debbie Stewart, review of *Leap, Frog,* p. 100; March, 2004, Rosalyn Pierini, review of *The Birthday Doll,* p. 156; March, 2005, Deanna Romriell, review of *Rose and Riley,* and Anne Knickerbocker, review of *Common Sense and Fowls,* p. 170.

Voice of Youth Advocates, June, 1999, Brenda Moses-Allen, review of *The Song of the Molimo,* p. 112.

ONLINE

Jane Cutler Web site, http://www.janecutler.com (July 5, 2005).

D

DANCER, Rex
   See KILIAN, Michael D.

*   *   *

DEE, Ed 1940-
   (Edward J. Dee, Jr.)

PERSONAL: Born February 3, 1940, in Yonkers, NY; son of Edward J., Sr. (a highway toll collector) and Ethel (a waiter and teletype operator; maiden name, Lawton) Dee; married Nancy Lee Hazzard, October 1, 1962; children: Brenda Sue Dee Crawford, Patricia Ann Dee Flanagan. *Education:* Rockland Community College, Suffern, NY, A.A.S., 1974; Fordham University, Bronx, NY, B.A., 1976, law student, 1977-78; Arizona State University, M.F.A., 1992. *Politics:* Independent. *Religion:* Roman Catholic.

ADDRESSES: Home—96 Henlopen Gardens, Lewes, DE 19958. *Agent*—Gail Hochman, Brandt & Hochman, 1501 Broadway, New York, NY 10036.

CAREER: Writer. New York Police Department (NYPD), New York, NY, police officer, 1962-82, retiring as lieutenant and supervisor of detectives in the Organized Crime Control Bureau. *Military service:* U.S. Army, 1958-60; U.S. Army Reserve, 1960-64.

MEMBER: Mystery Writers of America, Authors Guild, Superior Officers Association for Retirees.

WRITINGS:

14 Peck Slip, Warner Books (New York, NY), 1994.
Bronx Angel, Warner Books (New York, NY), 1995.
Little Boy Blue, Warner Books (New York, NY), 1997.
Nightbird, Warner Books (New York, NY), 1999.
The Con Man's Daughter, Mysterious Press (New York, NY), 2003.

SIDELIGHTS: Ed Dee's background as a twenty-year veteran of the New York Police Department (NYPD) lends a great deal of authenticity to his crime novels about NYPD detective Anthony Ryan and his partner, Joe Gregory. In the series opener, *14 Peck Slip,* the two men find a body floating in a barrel on the city's waterfront. It turns out to be that of a police officer who has been missing for ten years. Ryan and Gregory's investigation lead them to some shocking truths about corruption among their peers. Their story is told "in an authentic and powerful voice," wrote a *Publishers Weekly* reviewer. "Any writer who can sing NYPD blues like that is worth keeping an eye on." Marilyn Stasio of the *New York Times Book Review* also called attention to Dee's "drop-dead style and authenticity," and further commented that the author has "the eyes, the ears and especially the nose of a cop. You can see one character's fear in his jumpy movement, hear another's anger in his dirty talk. But you can smell the moral decay of the whole city."

Dee won further praise for his next novel, *Bronx Angel.* The story again concerns the murder of a policeman, apparently by a prostitute. With Ryan on the trail of the killer, "Mr. Dee takes us on a grand tour of the city the way it looks through Ryan's eyes," wrote Stasio in a review in the *New York Times Book Review,* "dirty, dangerous and so sad you wish you could look away. But you can't because you might miss something beautiful, or funny, or just plain nuts." *Booklist* contributor George Needham commented that Dee's "cops are tired and wary but not burned out. They still care about nailing the bad guys; they've just surrendered some of their quixotic notions to the realities of the street."

Dee's third effort, *Little Boy Blue,* was lauded as an "outstanding crime novel" by Wes Lukowsky in *Booklist.* The reviewer praised the author's "intelligent examination of modern families, . . . the extended family of cops; the loyalties exhibited by the Mafia; and the many unrelated groups who band together for companionship and support in an increasingly hostile, indifferent world." A *Publishers Weekly* writer also found that *Little Boy Blue* "crackles with authenticity," and declared: "There's a hard edge to everything and nearly everyone in this gripping novel, which plays some subtle improvisations on the theme of fathers and sons, and family and its obligations, even as Dee creates a tight mystery that emanates a gritty, world-weary air."

Although Dee has been successful at reaching his literary goals with the characters of Ryan and Gregory, he leaves them behind in his 2003 novel *The Con Man's Daughter.* Dee tells the story of ex-cop Eddie Dunn, who is kicked off New York's police force and becomes a courier for a Russian gangster. Dunn eventually retires from this "job," but when his own daughter is kidnapped, he suspects a connection with the Russian mafia. The violence escalates as Eddie fights the mob and his own past to rescue his daughter. A *Publishers Weekly* contributor wrote: "Down and dirty crime fiction doesn't get any better than this." Jane Jorgenson, writing in the *Library Journal,* commented, "At times graphic and gripping, and then bittersweet, Dee's latest is another solid offering." A *Kirkus Reviews* contributor noted: "Thriller fans who like their action down and dirty and their heroes thoughtful and flawed will welcome talented Dee's latest."

Dee once told *CA:* "After retiring from the New York Police Department, I wanted to write about the department in a way that no one had done before. After receiving my M.F.A. in creative writing, I submitted my first book. *Bronx Angel* is a sequel. I intend to use the same characters in a series of books that, I hope, get to the heart of the experience of being a cop in a city like New York. I hope they get at the *truth.*

"The book *The World according to Garp,* by John Irving, is what first got me interested in writing. I am most influenced by the stories of people of inner cities, the voices I heard all my life: the accents and humor of Italians, the Polish, the Jewish wit and mostly the soft musical brogue of my Irish grandmother.

"When I am writing, I write and rewrite as many times as needed. My favorite of my books are *14 Peck Slip* and *The Con Man's Daughter,* because both were new creative molds. I think the most surprising thing I have learned as a writer is that the normal hard edge a cop usually acquires never took hold."

BIOGRAPHICAL AND CRITICAL SOURCES:

PERIODICALS

Booklist, July, 1994, Wes Lukowsky, review of *14 Peck Slip,* p. 1925; July, 1995, George Needham, review of *Bronx Angel,* p. 1863; December 1, 1996, Wes Lukowsky, review of *Little Boy Blue,* p. 619.
Kirkus Reviews, September 15, 2003, review of *The Con Man's Daughter,* p. 1156.
Library Journal, July, 1994, Jo Ann Vicarel, review of *14 Peck Slip,* p. 125; October 15, 2003, Jane Jorgenson, review of *The Con Man's Daughter,* p. 96.
New York Times Book Review, July 17, 1994, Marilyn Stasio, review of *14 Peck Slip,* p. 19; December 4, 1994, review of *14 Peck Slip,* p. 69; August 20, 1995, Marilyn Stasio, review of *Bronx Angel,* p. 21; December 14, 2003, review of *The Con Man's Daughter,* p. 23.
Publishers Weekly, May 23, 1994, review of *14 Peck Slip,* p. 78; June 5, 1995, review of *Bronx Angel,* p. 49; November 11, 1996, review of *Little Boy Blue,* p. 54; September 8, 2003, review of *The Con Man's Daughter,* p. 52.
Wall Street Journal Western Edition, August 9, 1994, Tom Nolan, review of *14 Peck Slip,* p. A12(W), A10(E); September 8, 1995, Tom Nolan, review of *Bronx Angel,* p. A9(W), A7(E).
Wilson Library Bulletin, October, 1994, Gail Pool, review of *14 Peck Slip,* p. 90.

ONLINE

Ed Dee Home Page, http://www.eddeeauthor.com (November 11, 2005).

DEE, Edward J., Jr.
    See DEE, Ed

*   *   *

DiCAMILLO, Kate 1964-

PERSONAL: Born March 25, 1964, in Merion, PA; daughter of Adolph Louis (an orthodontist) and Betty Lee (a teacher; maiden name, Gouff) DiCamillo. *Education:* University of Florida, B.A., 1987.

ADDRESSES: Home—2403 West 42nd St., No. 3, Minneapolis, MN 55410.

CAREER: Writer. Bookman (book distributor), St. Louis Park, MN, former bookstore clerk.

AWARDS, HONORS: McKnight artist fellowship for writers, 1998; Newbery Honor Book award, and Hedgie Award, Hedgehogbooks.com, both 2000, and Dorothy Canfield Fisher Children's Book Award, 2002, all for *Because of Winn-Dixie;* finalist, National Book Award, for *Tiger Rising;* Newbery Medal, 2003, for *The Tale of Despereaux.*

WRITINGS:

Because of Winn-Dixie, Candlewick Press (Cambridge, MA), 2000.
The Tiger Rising, Candlewick Press (Cambridge, MA), 2001.
The Tale of Despereaux: Being the Story of a Mouse, a Princess, Some Soup, and a Spool of Thread, illustrated by Timothy Basil Ering, Candlewick Press (Cambridge, MA), 2003.
Mercy Watson to the Rescue, illustrated by Chris van Dusen, Candlewick Press (Cambridge, MA), 2005.
Mercy Watson Goes for a Ride, illustrated by Chris van Dusen, Candlewick Press (Cambridge, MA), 2006.
The Mysterious Journey of Edward Tulane, illustrated by Bagram Ibatoulline, Candlewick Press (Cambridge, MA), 2006.

Contributor of short fiction to periodicals, including *Jack and Jill, Alaska Quarterly Review, Greensboro Review, Nebraska Review,* and *Spider.*

ADAPTATIONS: Several of the author's books have been adapted as audio books; *Because of Winn-Dixie* was adapted for film, 2005.

SIDELIGHTS: Kate DiCamillo is "short. And loud," as she admitted on her Web site. Though she had trained to become an author, prior to 2000 DiCamillo had only published a few adult short stories in magazines. She worked in Minneapolis for The Bookman, a book distributor, in the children's department. It was during this time in Minneapolis, while she was missing the warm weather of Florida where she had spent much of her life, that DiCamillo began her first novel. Jennifer M. Brown, who interviewed the author for *Publishers Weekly,* reported: "This is what happened: she was just about to go to sleep when the book's narrator, India Opal Buloni, spoke to her, saying, 'I have a dog named Winn-Dixie.' DiCamillo says that after hearing that voice, 'the story told itself.'" From that moment, DiCamillo never stopped listening, and from India Opal Buloni in *Because of Winn-Dixie* to the mouse Despereaux in *The Tale of Despereaux: Being the Story of a Mouse, a Princess, Some Soup, and a Spool of Thread,* each of her narrators has given voice to a new story, different from the last. *Because of Winn-Dixie* was named a Newbery Honor Book after its publication, and three years later, *The Tale of Despereaux* was awarded the prestigious Newbery Medal.

Because of Winn-Dixie is the tale of a girl and her dog—only the dog in this case is Winn-Dixie, a stray mutt, a smelly, ugly dog who seems to have plenty of love to give. India Opal is in need of some of that love; she and her father just moved to Naomi, Florida, after her mother died, and she has been having trouble fitting in. "Rarely does salvation come in the form of a creature with as much personality as Winn-Dixie," wrote a *Horn Book* reviewer. Somehow, Winn-Dixie manages to open doors in her life that she had not even seen. "Readers will connect with India's love for her pet and her open-minded, free-spirited efforts to make friends and build a community," assured Gillian Engberg in her *Booklist* review. Helen Foster James, writing for the *School Library Journal,* asked if libraries really need another girl-and-her-dog book, then answered her own question: "Absolutely, if the protagonist is as spirited and endearing as Opal and the dog as loveable and charming as Winn-Dixie." A critic for *Publishers Weekly* noted that DiCamillo's "bittersweet tale of contemporary life in a Southern town will hold readers rapt," while Kathleen Odean wrote in *Book* that *Because of Winn-Dixie* is "a short, heartfelt book."

It took DiCamillo some time to get *Because of Winn-Dixie* to a publisher. She continued to work at The Bookman until she ran into a sales rep for Candlewick Press. "I told her, 'I love everything that Candlewick does, but I can't get in the door because I don't have an agent, and I've never been published, and they won't look at unsolicited manuscripts,'" DiCamillo explained to Kathleen T. Horning in an interview for the *School Library Journal.* The sales rep responded: "If you give me a manuscript, I'll get it to an editor." From there, it was not long until DiCamillo became a published children's author. "So that's how it happened," she explained, "great good fortune."

DiCamillo's second novel, *The Tiger Rising,* is aimed at a young-adult audience, but contains a similar setting to *Because of Winn-Dixie.* Rob and his father move to a small town in Florida, and Rob cannot figure out how to fit in. Rob has been dealing with pain for a long time, however, and he is good at keeping his emotions to himself. He manages to get a job with his father's boss, Beauchamp, taking care of a caged wild tiger Beauchamp keeps at an abandoned gas station. Ultimately, Rob meets Sistine, another new kid at school who is as openly angry at the world as Rob is secretive about his feelings, and things begin to change in Rob's life. Rob and Sistine come to believe they must free the tiger in order to liberate themselves.

The Tiger Rising "has a certain mythic quality" according to a reviewer in *Horn Book.* A critic for *Publishers Weekly* noted that, with her second novel, "DiCamillo demonstrates her versatility by treating themes similar to those of her first novel with a completely different approach." *School Library Journal* reviewer Kit Vaughan praised the "slender story" as "lush with haunting characters and spare descriptions, conjuring up vivid images." Claire Rosser, writing in *Kliatt,* complimented DiCamillo's text as "spare, poetic, [and] moving," while GraceAnne A. DeCandido, in a *Booklist* review, wrote that the author's "gorgeous language wastes not a single word."

In 2003, DiCamillo took a new path in her writing, publishing something entirely different with more than a little trepidation. In the acceptance speech for her

Newbery Medal, she explained: "Four years ago, when he was eight years old, my friend Luke Bailey asked me to write the story of an unlikely hero. I was afraid to tell the story he wanted told: afraid because I didn't know what I was doing; afraid because it was unlike anything I had written before; afraid, I guess, because the story was so intent on taking me into the depths of my own heart. But Luke wanted the story. I had promised him. And so, terrified and unwilling, I wrote *The Tale of Despereaux.*" DiCamillo need not have worried; the book was well received by critics and readers and earned her the Newbery Medal. The story, which has the subtitle *Being the Story of a Mouse, a Princess, Some Soup, and a Spool of Thread,* tells of Despereaux Tilling, a mouse more interested in reading books than eating them, who falls in love with a human princess. It also tells of a villainous rat, Roscuro, who longs to live in the light, and Miggery Sow, a serving girl who believes that someday she will become a princess. When Roscuro and Miggery kidnap the princess, it is up to Despereaux, small even for a mouse, to come to her rescue.

Narrated in a style that encourages reading aloud, *The Tale of Despereaux* contains "all the ingredients of an old-fashioned drama," according to a critic for *Kirkus Reviews.* Peter D. Sieruta, writing in *Horn Book,* noted that "DiCamillo tells an engaging tale. . . . Many readers will be enchanted by this story of mice and princesses, brave deeds, . . . and forgiveness." Miriam Lang Budin, writing in the *School Library Journal,* considered the book to be "a charming story of unlikely heroes whose destinies entwine to bring about a joyful resolution." Kathleen T. Horning wrote in *School Library Journal* that the book "contains a cast of quirky characters that would have made Dickens proud," while a *Publishers Weekly* critic, imitating the narrator's style, wrote: "I must tell you, you are in for a treat."

DiCamillo is also the author of a series of early chapter books about a pet pig named Mercy Watson, who has "personality a-plenty" according to a reviewer for *Publishers Weekly.* In the first book, *Mercy Watson to the Rescue,* Mercy manages to make her owners' bed start to fall through the floor of their room while they are on it; afraid to move, they cheer for Mercy as she leaves the room, convinced that she is going to find a way to rescue them. After a series of chaotic events, the neighbors eventually call the fire department, and when Mercy's owners are rescued, they give the pig all the credit. A *Publishers Weekly* critic felt that with *Mercy Watson to the Rescue,* DiCamillo "once again displays her versatility."

DiCamillo once commented: "I was a sickly child. My body happily played host to all of the usual childhood maladies (mumps and measles, chickenpox twice, and ear infections), plus a few exotic extras: inexplicable skin diseases, chronic pinkeye, and, most dreaded of all, pneumonia, recurring every winter for the first five years of my life. I mention this because, at the time, it seemed like such a senseless and unfair kind of thing to me, to be sick so often, to miss so much school, to be inside scratching or sneezing or coughing when everybody else was outside playing.

"Now, looking back, I can see all that illness for what it was: a gift that shaped me and made me what I am. I was alone a lot. I learned to rely on my imagination for entertainment. Because I was always on the lookout for the next needle, the next tongue depressor, I learned to watch and listen and gauge the behavior of those around me. I became an imaginative observer.

"Also, I suffered from chronic pneumonia at a time when geographical cures were still being prescribed. I was born near Philadelphia and, after my fifth winter in an oxygen tent, the doctor gave my parents this advice: take her to a warmer climate. We moved to central Florida. There I absorbed the speech patterns and cadences and nuances of life in a small southern town. I did not know it at the time, but Florida (and pneumonia) gave me a great gift: a voice in which to tell my stories.

"When I look back on childhood, I remember one moment with great clarity. I was three years old and in the hospital with pneumonia, and my father came to visit me. He arrived in a black overcoat that smelled of the cold outdoors, and he brought me a gift. It was a little, red net bag. Inside it there was a wooden village: wooden church, house, chicken, tree, farmer. It was as if he had flung the net bag out into the bright world and captured the essential elements and shrunk them down and brought them to me.

"He opened the bag and said, 'Hold out your hands.' I held out my hands. 'No,' he said, 'like this. Like you are going to drink from them.' I did as he said, and he poured the wooden figures, piece by piece, into my waiting hands. Then he told me a story about the chicken and the farmer and the house and the church. Something opened up inside me. There was the weight of the wooden figures in my hands, the smell of my father's overcoat, the whole great world hiding, waiting in the purple dusk outside my hospital room. And there was the story—the story.

"I think of that moment often. It was another gift of my illness. When I write, I sometimes stop and cup my hands, as if I am drinking water. I try, I want desperately to capture the world, to hold it for a moment in my hands."

BIOGRAPHICAL AND CRITICAL SOURCES:

PERIODICALS

Book, May, 2001, Kathleen Odean, review of *Because of Winn-Dixie,* p. 80; November-December, 2003, review of *The Tale of Despereaux,* p. 67.

Booklist, May 1, 2000, Gillian Engberg, review of *Because of Winn-Dixie,* p. 1665; June 1, 2001, GraceAnne A. DeCandido, review of *The Tiger Rising,* p. 1882, Patricia Austin, review of *Because of Winn-Dixie,* p. 1906; October 15, 2001, Lolly Gepson, review of audio book *The Tiger Rising,* p. 428; January 1, 2004, review of *The Tale of Despereaux,* p. 780; March 1, 2004, Patricia Austin, review of *The Tale of Despereaux* (audiobook), p. 1212.

Horn Book, July, 2000, review of *Because of Winn-Dixie,* p. 455; May, 2001, review of *The Tiger Rising,* p. 321, Kristi Beavin, review of *Because of Winn-Dixie* (audiobook), p. 359; September-October, 2003, Peter D. Sieruta, review of *The Tale of Despereaux,* p. 609; May-June, 2004, Kristi Elle Jemtegaard, review of *The Tale of Despereaux* (audiobook), p. 349; July-August, 2004, Kate DiCamillo, "Newbery Medal Acceptance Speech," pp. 395-400, Jane Resh Thomas, "Kate DiCamillo," pp. 401-404.

Kirkus Reviews, July 15, 2003, review of *The Tale of Despereaux,* p. 962.

Kliatt, November, 2002, Claire Rosser, review of *The Tiger Rising,* p. 18.

Publishers Weekly, February 21, 2000, review of *Because of Winn-Dixie,* p. 88; June 26, 2000, Jennifer M. Brown, "Kate DiCamillo," p. 30; January

15, 2001, review of *The Tiger Rising*, p. 77; April 9, 2001, review of *Because of Winn-Dixie* (audiobook), p. 28; July 9, 2001, review of *The Tiger Rising* (audiobook), p. 22; June 16, 2003, review of *The Tale of Despereaux*, p. 71; June 20, 2005, review of *Mercy Watson to the Rescue*, p. 77.

School Library Journal, June, 2000, Helen Foster, review of *Because of Winn-Dixie*, p. 143; March, 2001, Kit Vaughan, review of *The Tiger Rising*, p. 246; June, 2001, Lori Craft, review of *Because of Winn-Dixie* (audiobook), p. 74; August, 2001, Emily Herman, review of *The Tiger Rising* (audiobook), p. 90; August, 2003, Miriam Lang Budin, review of *The Tale of Despereaux*, p. 126; March, 2004, Barbara Wysocki, review of *The Tale of Despereaux* (audiobook), p. 88; April, 2004, Kathleen T. Horning, "The Tale of DiCamillo," pp. 44-48, review of *The Tale of Despereaux*, p. S28; April, 2005, "A Winn-Winn Situation," p. S7.

ONLINE

Kate DiCamillo Home Page, http://www.katedicamillo. com (July 31, 2005).*

*   *   *

DREIFUS, Claudia 1944-

PERSONAL: Born November 24, 1944, in New York, NY, daughter of Henry and Marianne (Willdorff) Dreifus. *Education:* New York University, B.S., 1966. *Politics:* "Radical feminist."

ADDRESSES: Home and office—158 9th Ave., New York, NY 10011. *Agent*—c/o Author Mail, Henry Holt and Company, Inc., 175 5th Ave., New York, NY 10010; fax: 212-633-0748.

CAREER: Journalist, writer, and educator. Organizer of drug and hospital workers union in New York, NY, 1967-68; freelance writer, 1968—. New York University, associate adjunct professor of journalism, 1974; New School for Social Research, instructor, 1975; New York University, New York, NY, associate visiting professor in the Department of Journalism,

1975, instructor in magazine writing in the School of Continuing Education, 1979; YWCA, New York, NY, lecturer in non-fiction writing, 1979-84; City College of New York, distinguished visiting professor, 1994-98; New School for Social Research, World Policy Institute, New York, NY, senior fellow, 1997; Columbia University School of International and Public Affairs, New York, NY, adjunct professor. Also served as a contributing writer at the *New York Times.*

MEMBER: American Society of Journalists and Authors, PEN, Society of Magazine Writers.

AWARDS, HONORS: Merit for Service to Women award, Young Women's Christian Association (YWCA), 1976; Outstanding Article award, 1987, American Society of Journalists and Authors; Simon Rockower Award for Distinguished Commentary, American Jewish Press Association, 1988; American Values Award, Community Action Association, 1996.

WRITINGS:

NONFICTION

Radical Lifestyles, Lancer (New York, NY), 1971.
Woman's Fate: Raps from a Feminist Consciousness-Raising Group, Bantam (New York, NY), 1973.
(Editor) *Seizing Our Bodies: The Politics of Women's Health Care*, Vintage Books (New York, NY), 1978.
Interview, Seven Stories Press (New York, NY), 1997.
Scientific Conversations: Interviews on Science from the New York Times, foreword by Natalie Angier, Times Books/Henry Holt (New York, NY), 2001.

Work is represented in anthologies, including *Radical Feminism, Women's Liberation Blueprint for the Future*, and *Seeing Through the Shuck*. Contributor to numerous periodicals, including *McCall's, Evergreen Review, Nation, New York Times Book Review, Rolling Stone, Realist, Family Circle, Ms., Newsday, Penthouse, New York Daily News Sunday Magazine, Signature, Social Policy, Viva, Glamour, Scientific American, SEED*, and *Progressive*. News editor, *East Village Other,* 1969-71.

SIDELIGHTS: Claudia Dreifus is a journalist whose forte is the interview. Her aptly titled book *Interview* presents interviews the author conducted with various people, including Toni Morrison, Dan Rather, and the Dalai Lama, all of which previously appeared in periodicals such as the *New York Times* and *Playboy.* "Not all the pieces are equally interesting, but the variety of the voices here makes irresistible reading," noted a *Publishers Weekly* contributor. Rebecca Wondriska, writing in the *Library Journal,* commented that the author's "questions are intelligent and frequently pointed." Writing in the *Columbia Journalism Review,* Neil Hickey noted: "Nuggets lurk in these transcripts and they're worth panning for." Hickey went on to write, "Altogether, Dreifus's book is a clinic on the interviewer's craft, a day at the races for tape cassette jockeys, and a treat for journalists everywhere who refuse to take no—or silence or evasion—for an answer." *Nation* contributor Miriam Schneir wrote that "Dreifus chooses her interview subjects in part for their capacity to astonish—and astonish they do."

Scientific Conversations: Interviews on Science from the New York Times presents interviews with scientists working in a wide range of fields and includes the well-known, such as Stephen Jay Gould, as well as those working on interesting projects but receiving little media attention. "The beauty of the book is that it allows one to see scientists as real people," wrote Amy Hark in *SB&F.* Hark went on to note: "For scientists or those simply fascinated by science, this collection is well worth a read." *Booklist* contributor Gilbert Taylor called the work "a lively reprise from the paper's science section."

BIOGRAPHICAL AND CRITICAL SOURCES:

PERIODICALS

Booklist, October 15, 2001, Gilbert Taylor, review of *Scientific Conversations: Interviews from the New York Times,* p. 363.

Columbia Journalism Review, September-October, 1997, Neil Hickey, review of *Interview* and interview with author, p. 62.

Library Journal, June 15, 1997, Rebecca Wondriska, review of *Interview,* p. 80.

Nation, October 20, 1997, Miriam Schneir, review of *Interview,* p. 36.

Publishers Weekly, May 19, 1997, review of *Interview,* p. 58.

SB&F, September-October, 2002, Amy Hark, review of *Scientific Conversations,* p. 499.*

DUGARD, Martin

PERSONAL: Married; children: three sons. *Education:* Graduated from college, 1986.

ADDRESSES: Home—Orange County, CA. *Agent*—c/o Author Mail, Little, Brown & Co., 1271 Avenue of the Americas, New York, NY 10020. *E-mail*—mjdugard@aol.com; ChasingLance7@aol.com.

CAREER: Writer. Involved in corporate marketing, c. 1986-93.

AWARDS, HONORS: Katie Award, Dallas Area Press Club, best magazine sports story, 1997.

WRITINGS:

On the Edge: Four True Stories of Extreme Outdoor Sports Adventure, Bantam (New York, NY), 1995.

In-line Skating Made Easy: A Manual for Beginners with Tips for the Experienced, Globe Pequot Press (Old Saybrook, CT), 1996.

Surviving the Toughest Race on Earth, Ragged Mountain Press (Camden, ME), 1998.

Knockdown: The Harrowing True Account of a Yacht Race Turned Deadly, Pocket Books (New York, NY), 1999.

(With Mark Burnett) *Survivor: The Ultimate Game: The Official Companion to the CBS Television Show,* TV Books (New York, NY), 2000.

Farther than Any Man: The Rise and Fall of Captain James Cook, Pocket Books (New York, NY), 2001.

Into Africa: The Epic Adventures of Stanley & Livingstone, Doubleday (New York, NY), 2003.

The Last Voyage of Columbus: Being the Epic Tale of the Great Captain's Fourth Expedition, including Accounts of Swordfight, Mutiny, Shipwreck, Gold, War, Hurricane, and Discovery, Little, Brown (New York, NY), 2005.

Also author of the screenplays *Be True* and *The Last Raid.* Contributor to periodicals, including *Competitor, ESPN: The Magazine, Esquire, GQ, Inside Sports-America, Outside,* and *Sports Illustrated.*

WORK IN PROGRESS: Chasing Lance, about the 2005 Tour de France.

SIDELIGHTS: Martin Dugard has produced books on sports and physical activities, as well as historical profiles of adventurers. His book *On the Edge: Four True Stories of Extreme Outdoor Sports Adventure,* for example, features tales of sporting adventures gone horribly awry. *On the Edge* "should be a winner with readers who like sports on the edge," declared Patrick Jones in *Kliatt.* Dugard's *In-line Skating Made Easy: A Manual for Beginners with Tips for the Experienced* is a primer for people learning to in-line skate and gives advice for skaters who want to improve their skills. It covers safety equipment, foot positions, and skating techniques, and its illustrations provide examples of how to put the tips into action. Another Dugard book, *Surviving the Toughest Race on Earth,* discusses his participation in the Raid Gauloises, a grueling race through mountains and rainforests. *Knockdown: The Harrowing True Account of a Yacht Race Turned Deadly* recounts the 1998 Sydney-Hobart race, which resulted in the death of six sailors in a torrential storm. A *Publishers Weekly* contributor noted that "Dugard pauses to give lay readers welcome explications of sailing jargon, as well as elementary lessons in the geometry—or perhaps it's really alchemy—of waveforms."

Dugard turns his attention to history in *Farther than Any Man: The Rise and Fall of Captain James Cook,* which probes the famous explorer's life, from his roots as a poor farm boy through his career in the British Royal Navy. "Well researched, with information from Cook's own journals, this fast-paced book brings to life the English explorer," attested a reviewer in *Publishers Weekly.* Margaret Flanagan, writing in *Booklist,* called the book a "stirring chronicle," adding that the author "paints an intriguing portrait of an extraordinary man."

In his book *Into Africa: The Epic Adventures of Stanley & Livingstone,* Dugard continues to mix history and adventure, providing an in-depth historical account of Henry Morton Stanley's search in the wilds of Africa for David Livingstone and their eventual meeting. Writing on the *BookReporter.com* Web site, Robert Finn observed that the author "tells the whole story in a work of historical recreation that reads like an adventure novel." Finn went on to write: "He puts the

tale in its historical setting, gives rounded pictures of the two men and a cast of fascinating supporting players, and leaves the reader with a strong sense of the incredible difficulties both men overcame on their separate roads to the village of Ujiji." "Fine entertainment for adventure buffs," according to one *Kirkus Reviews* contributor, the book is "solidly researched and fluently told."

Dugard provides a history of Columbus's harrowing fourth, and final, trip to the New World in the book *The Last Voyage of Columbus: Being the Epic Tale of the Great Captain's Fourth Expedition, including Accounts of Swordfight, Mutiny, Shipwreck, Gold, War, Hurricane, and Discovery.* As told by the author, the voyage included attacks by primitive natives, mutinies, and eventually a shipwreck that left Columbus and his crew in Jamaica for a year. Calling the historical account a "vivid narrative," a *Kirkus Reviews* contributor commented that the author offers "plenty to digest for the history-minded reader who enjoys a bracing story of courage and adventure on the uncharted high seas." Margaret Atwater-Singer, writing in the *Library Journal,* noted that the author's rendition of the story is "so compelling, that it is bound to capture the imagination of readers."

A longtime contributor of sports-related stories to various magazines, Dugard has participated in his own adventures, as well, including setting a global circumnavigation record. Flying aboard a French Concorde jet, he left New York City, traveled around the world, and returned to New York City in just thirty-one hours and twenty-eight minutes.

BIOGRAPHICAL AND CRITICAL SOURCES:

PERIODICALS

Booklist, February 1, 1998, Brenda Barrera, review of *Surviving the Toughest Race on Earth,* p. 892; June 1, 2001, Margaret Flanagan, review of *Farther than Any Man: The Rise and Fall of Captain James Cook,* p. 1828; June 1, 2003, Kristine Huntley, review of *Into Africa: The Epic Adventures of Stanley & Livingstone,* p. 1731.

Dallas Morning News, October 17, 2003, Larry Bleiberg, review of *Into Africa.*

Fort Worth Star Telegram, June 12, 2005, Jim Frisinger, review of *The Last Voyage of Columbus: Being the Epic Tale of the Great Captain's Fourth Expedition, including Accounts of Swordfight, Mutiny, Shipwreck, Gold, War, Hurricane, and Discovery.*

Geographical, April, 2004, Nick Smith, review of *Into Africa,* p. 87.

Hollywood Reporter, April 14, 2003, Gregory McNamee, review of *Into Africa,* p. 11.

Kirkus Reviews, February 1, 2003, review of *Into Africa,* p. 202; April 15, 2005, review of *The Last Voyage of Columbus,* p. 458.

Kliatt, September, 1995, Patrick Jones, review of *On the Edge: Four True Stories of Extreme Outdoor Sports Adventure,* p. 46; November, 2002, Raymond L. Puffer, review of *Farther than Any Man,* p. 30; January, 2004, Sunnie Grant, review of *Into Africa,* p. 53.

Library Journal, July, 2001, Stanley L. Itkin, review of *Farther than Any Man,* p. 100; March 1, 2003, Margaret Atwater-Singer, review of *Into Africa,* p. 98; May 15, 2005, Margaret Atwater-Singer, review of *The Last Voyage of Columbus,* p. 127.

Philadelphia Inquirer, July 10, 2005, Steve Weinberg, review of *The Last Voyage of Columbus.*

Pittsburgh Post-Gazette, June 12, 2005, Monika Kugemann, review of *The Last Voyage of Columbus.*

Publishers Weekly, January 12, 1998, review of *Surviving the Toughest Race on Earth,* p. 53; August 9, 1999, review of *Knockdown: The Harrowing True Account of a Yacht Race Turned Deadly,* p. 334; May 28, 2001, review of *Farther than Any Man,* p. 66; February 17, 2003, review of *Into Africa,* p. 63; March 21, 2005, review of *The Last Voyage of Columbus,* p. 44.

San Francisco Chronicle, June 26, 2005, Ben Cosgrove, review of *The Last Voyage of Columbus,* p. C1.

School Library Journal, November, 2003, Kathy Tewell, review of *Into Africa,* p. 172.

ONLINE

BookPage, http://www.bookpage.com/ (September 7, 2005), James Neal Webb, review of *The Last Voyage of Columbus.*

BookReporter.com, http://www.bookreporter.com/ (September 7, 2005), Robert Finn, review of *Into Africa.*

Martin Dugard Home Page, http://www.martindugard. com (February 24, 2000).

Martin Dugard Web log, http://blogs.active.com/ dugard (October 7, 2005).

Northern Rivers Echo Online, http://www.echonews. com/ (October 7, 2005), review of *Farther than Any Man.**

*   *   *

DUNANT, Peter
    See DUNANT, Sarah

*   *   *

DUNANT, Sarah 1950-
    (Peter Dunant, a joint pseudonym)

PERSONAL: Born August 8, 1950, in London, England; daughter of David (an airline manager) and Estelle (a teacher; maiden name, Joseph) Dunant; children: Zoe, Georgia. *Education:* Cambridge University, degree in history, 1972.

ADDRESSES: Home and office—17 Tytherton Rd., London N19 4QB, England. *Agent*—Aitken & Stone Ltd., 18-21 Cavaye Place, London SW10 9PT, England.

CAREER: BBC-Radio, London, England, producer, 1974-76; freelance writer and broadcaster, 1977—; *The Late Show,* BBC2, presenter; *Thin Air,* BBC1, co-writer; *Nightwaves,* BBC Radio 3, presenter. Also worked as a critic and writer for the *Guardian,* the *Times,* and the *Observer.*

AWARDS, HONORS: Golden Dragon Award nomination, Crime Writers Association, 1987, for *Intensive Care;* Dagger Award, British Crime Writers' Association, 1993, for *Fatlands.*

WRITINGS:

NOVELS; WITH PETER BUSBY, UNDER JOINT PSEUDONYM PETER DUNANT

Exterminating Angels, Deutsch, 1983.
Intensive Care, Deutsch, 1986.

NOVELS

Snow Storms in a Hot Climate, Random House (New York, NY), 1988.

Transgressions, Virago (London, England), 1997, ReganBooks (New York, NY), 1998.

Mapping the Edge, Virago (London, England), 1999, Random House (New York, NY), 2001.

The Birth of Venus, Little Brown (London, England), 2003, Random House (New York, NY), 2004.

In the Company of the Courtesan, Random House (New York, NY), 2006.

"HANNAH WOLFE MYSTERY" SERIES

Birth Marks, M. Joseph (London, England), 1991, Doubleday (New York, NY), 1992.

Fatlands, O. Penzler Books (New York, NY), 1994.

Under My Skin, Scribner (New York, NY), 1995, Thorndike Press (Thorndike, ME), 1996.

OTHER

Thin Air (television serial), broadcast by BBC-TV, 1988.

(Editor) *The War of the Words: The Political Correctness Debate,* Virago (London, England), 1994.

(Editor, with Roy Porter) *The Age of Anxiety,* Virago (London, England), 1996.

SIDELIGHTS: British author Sarah Dunant's first solo novel, *Snow Storms in a Hot Climate,* is a psychological thriller set in the United States. Michael Freitag, writing in the *New York Times Book Review,* noted: "While American readers may not find the settings—cramped, gritty New York City and the vast, sparkling California coast, among others—particularly exotic, they will find the writing refreshingly economical and astute." Oxford professor Marla, protagonist and narrator of the novel, travels to New York to come to the aid of an old friend who has become emotionally involved with a mysterious cocaine dealer who may also be a murderer. According to Freitag, Marla "finds that she too has become caught in a complex web of emotions: friendship, romance, curiosity, jealousy and revenge." Freitag found *Snow Storms in a Hot Climate* to be an "intelligent and rarely predictable" novel with

some "truly breathtaking" scenes. On the downside, he felt that Dunant "relies too heavily on secondhand storytelling to advance her plot."

In *Birth Marks* Dunant launched a mystery series featuring the female private detective Hannah Wolfe. Reviewing the novel for the *New York Times Book Review,* Marilyn Stasio called Dunant an "author with a streak of independence," and described Hannah as "entirely refreshing among her treacly peers . . . [a] coolly pragmatic London operative, [who] uses brains over charm, relies on psychology rather than intuition and does not confuse compassion with sentimentality." Hannah's first case involves a runaway ballerina who turns up floating in the Thames: dead, pregnant, and probably a suicide. The subsequent investigation reveals the woman's sad double life. The book's surprise ending, according to Stasio, leads to "a real education" for Hannah.

Hannah Wolfe returns in *Fatlands,* the tale of a scientist who uses animals in his experiments. The scientist's fourteen-year-old daughter is killed by a car bomb, probably meant for him and most likely planted by radical animal-rights activists. Hannah's investigation reveals corporate and scientific skulduggery fueled by runaway greed. Emily Melton of *Booklist* commented: "Dunant's writing is smooth, polished, funny, and sophisticated, with an inventive plot and some sharp-edged commentary about the ethics of the modern-day business/science community." A reviewer for *Publishers Weekly* found Hannah's observations to be "frequently funny, occasionally poignant and always insightful." The third Hannah Wolfe entry, *Under My Skin,* is set against the backdrop of an exclusive health and beauty spa. Someone is out to sabotage the spa and Hannah is hired to uncover the culprit. Melton was somewhat disappointed by the book, writing, "Not to say . . . [it] is a bad book. It just never quite reaches the pinnacle of excellence that *Fatlands* achieved." However, Melton concluded that the novel's "keep-'em-guessing plot, dry wit, and a revealing look at society's expectations about beauty and youth make this one an entertaining and educational read."

In *Transgressions,* a non-series mystery, Dunant explores the themes of sexual obsession, power, and violence. Elizabeth Skvorecky, deserted by her lover of eight years, isolates herself in her London mansion and spends her time translating a Czech police thriller that is rife with images of sadistic pornography. At first she finds the book disgusting, but then begins to realize it has "burrowed its way under her skin." When objects begin disappearing from the mansion, Elizabeth suspects either her former lover or a poltergeist, yet she is soon confronted by the real intruder, a serial rapist, whom she proceeds to seduce. Elizabeth subsequently "stalks" the rapist-stalker by baiting him with pornographic passages purportedly excerpted from the Czech police thriller, but which she has actually written herself. Much of this material appears in the text of the novel. Dunant's stated purpose with *Transgressions* was "to breathe life into the victims [of rape]." However, a *Publishers Weekly* reviewer felt that "it's hard to distinguish between what Lizzie writes and the ill-conceived, poorly disguised appeal to prurience Dunant has penned."

The Birth of Venus, Dunant's debut into the genre of historical fiction, has earned her critical acclaim. Set in Florence, Italy, in the late 1400s, *The Birth of Venus* begins with the death of a respected nun, Sister Lucrezia, whom the other sisters believed was suffering from a cancerous tumor. A postmortem examination of her body reveals not only a scandalous snake tattoo, but also that she had faked her illness. The rest of the book is a first-person account of Sister Lucrezia's secret history, beginning with her life as Alessandra Cecchi, the youngest daughter of a wealthy cloth merchant in Florence.

Coming of age during the Italian Renaissance, Alessandra is a clever, educated young woman who loves art and dreams of creating her own masterpiece. Entering into a marriage of convenience with an older man, Alessandra discovers her husband's dangerous secret on their wedding night, and seeks solace and fulfillment in the arms of a talented young artist.

Calling *The Birth of Venus* "a powerful and evocative novel," *Spectator* critic Alan Wall felt that Dunant "carries off the daring plot with considerable panache." Other critics were equally enthusiastic. A critic for *Publishers Weekly* termed the novel an "arresting tale of art, love and betrayal," and Bella Stander of *People* called it "a broad mural bursting with color, passion, and intrigue." Likewise, in a review for the *New Statesman,* Vicky Hutchings remarked, "Dunant has discovered her métier in the form of a historical melodrama."

Dunant is also the editor of and a contributor to *The War of the Words: The Political Correctness Debate,* a collection of essays that argues the relevance of gender and ethnic issues to any contemporary political debate, and attempts to put forth a methodology as to how these issues can best be raised.

Dunant, in a "Meet the Writers" interview on the *Barnes and Noble* Web site, revealed that the thing she finds most helpful to her writing is "terror." She went on, explaining that "the feeling that I will never write this book if I don't get up and type in some new words every morning" is her best motivation. She also remarked that to be a successful writer you "need a clear sense of determination." She said: "Writing is hard, rejection is harder, and both are necessary."

BIOGRAPHICAL AND CRITICAL SOURCES:

PERIODICALS

Booklist, November 1, 1994, Emily Melton, review of *Fatlands,* p. 480; September 15, 1995, Emily Melton, review of *Under My Skin,* p. 142; December 1, 2003, Elsa Gaztambide, review of *The Birth of Venus,* p. 645.

Bookseller, March 12, 2004, "'Pearl Earring' Factor for Dunant," review of *The Birth of Venus,* p. 33.

Kirkus Reviews, December 1, 2003, review of *The Birth of Venus,* p. 1371.

Kliatt, May, 2005, Nola Theiss, review of *The Birth of Venus,* p. 23.

Library Journal, December, 2003, Jean Langlais, review of *The Birth of Venus,* p. 165.

New Statesman, July 11, 1997, Vicky Hutchings, review of *Transgressions,* p. 49; April 14, 2003, Vicky Hutchings, review of *The Birth of Venus,* p. 51.

New Statesman & Society, October 21, 1994, Michael Rosen, review of *The War of the Words: The Political Correctness Debate,* p. 40.

Newsweek, May 3, 2004, Elise Soukup, "Books: Too Smart for Her Own Good?," review of *The Birth of Venus,* p. 14.

New York Times Book Review, January 1, 1989, Michael Freitag, review of *Snowstorms in a Hot Climate,* p. 14; October 25, 1992, Marilyn Stasio, review of *Birth Marks,* p. 29.

People, February 23, 2004, Bella Stander, review of *The Birth of Venus,* p. 46.

Publishers Weekly, October 17, 1994, review of *Fatlands,* p. 67; August 21, 1995, review of *Under*

My Skin, p. 49; February 16, 1998, review of *Transgressions,* p. 203; December 15, 2003, review of *The Birth of Venus,* p. 51.

Spectator, May 3, 2003, Alan Wall, "Feisty Renaissance Woman," review of *The Birth of Venus,* p. 44.

ONLINE

Barnes and Noble Web site, http://www.barnesand noble.com/ (September 29, 2005), "Meet the Writers: Sarah Dunant."*

E

ELLIOTT, David W. 1939-

PERSONAL: Born July 12, 1939, in New Haven, CT. *Politics:* "Peace."

ADDRESSES: Home—Brewster, NY. *Agent*—Perry Knowlton, Curtis Brown, Ltd., 60 E. 56th St., New York, NY 10022.

CAREER: Novelist.

WRITINGS:

Listen to the Silence, Holt (New York, NY), 1969.
Pieces of Night, Holt (New York, NY), 1973.*

*   *   *

ERSKINE, Thomas L. 1939-
(Thomas Leonard Erskine)

PERSONAL: Born June 2, 1939, in Waterville, ME; son of Chauncey Lee (in personnel) and Florence (a teacher; maiden name, Hapworth) Erskine: married Suzanne Fourcade (a teacher), August 19, 1961; children: Harden Peter, Jeffrey Louis. *Education:* Bowdoin College, B.A., 1961; University of Kansas, M.A., 1963; Emory University, Ph.D., 1969. *Religion:* Presbyterian.

ADDRESSES: Home—420 Elberta Ave., Salisbury, MD 21801. *Office*—Department of English, Salisbury State College, Salisbury, MD 21801.

CAREER: University of Delaware, Newark, instructor, 1965-69, assistant professor of English, 1969-71; Salisbury State College, Salisbury, MD, associate professor, 1971-72, professor of English, beginning 1972, became professor emeritus, chair of department, 1971-72, academic dean, 1972-76. Secretary of Ice World, Inc. Mid-Delmarva Young Men's Christian Association, president, 1976-77, former member of board of directors.

MEMBER: Modern Language Association of America, National Council of Teachers of English, Society for Cinema Studies, American Association for Higher Education, South Atlantic Modern Language Association, Maryland Association for Higher Education, Academic Affairs for Administrators, Rotary International.

WRITINGS:

(Editor, with Elaine Safer) *John Milton: "L'Allegro" and "Il Penseroso,"* C.E. Merrill (Columbus, OH), 1970.
(Editor, with W. Bruce Finnie) *Words on Words: A Language Reader,* Random House (New York, NY), 1971.
(Editor, with Gerald R. Barrett) *From Fiction to Film: Conrad Aiken's "Silent Snow, Secret Snow,"* Dickenson (Encino, CA), 1972.
(Editor, with Gerald R. Barrett) *From Fiction to Film: Ambrose Bierce's "An Occurrence at Owl Creek Bridge,"* Dickenson (Encino, CA), 1973.
(Editor) *From Fiction to Film: D.H. Lawrence's "Rocking-Horse Winner,"* Dickenson (Encino, CA), 1974.

(Editor, with Connie L. Richards) Charlotte Perkins Gilman, *The Yellow Wallpaper,* Rutgers University Press (New Brunswick, NJ), 1993.

(Editor, with James M. Welsh) *Video Versions: Film Adaptations of Plays on Video,* Greenwood Press (Westport, CT), 2000.

(Editor, with Chuck Berg) *The Encyclopedia of Orson Welles,* Facts on File (New York, NY), 2003.

Founder and editor of *Literature/Film Quarterly,* beginning 1973. Contributor to *The Encyclopedia of Hollywood,* second edition, Facts on File (New York, NY), 2005.

BIOGRAPHICAL AND CRITICAL SOURCES:

PERIODICALS

Booklist, September 1, 2000, review of *Video Versions: Film Adaptations of Plays on Video,* p. 181.

Choice, April, 2001, M. Lawler, review of *Video Versions,* p. 1436.

Library Journal, March 15, 2000, Kathy Breeden, review of *Video Versions,* p. 76.

Reference and Research Book News, August, 2000, review of *Video Versions,* p. 183.

Voice of Youth Advocates, October, 2000, review of *Video Versions,* p. 300.*

*   *   *

ERSKINE, Thomas Leonard
    See ERSKINE, Thomas L.

*   *   *

ETULAIN, Richard W. 1938-
    (Richard Wayne Etulain)

PERSONAL: Surname is pronounced "*Ed*-a-lane"; born August 26, 1938, in Wapato, WA; son of Sebastian (a rancher and businessman) and Mary (Gillard) Etulain; married Joyce Oldenkamp (a librarian), August 18, 1961; children: Jacqueline Joyce. *Education:* Northwest Nazarene College, B.A. (history and English), 1960; University of Oregon, M.A., 1962, Ph.

D., 1966; postdoctoral study at Dartmouth College, 1969-70, and University of Nevada, 1973-74. *Politics:* Independent. *Religion:* Church of the Nazarene. *Hobbies and other interests:* Travel, writing, book collecting.

ADDRESSES: Home—Portland, OR. *Office*—Department of History, University of New Mexico, Albuquerque, NM 87131-0001. *E-mail*—baldbasq@ unm.edu.

CAREER: High school teacher in Lowell, OR, 1961-62, and Eugene, OR, 1962-64; Lane Community College, Eugene, part-time instructor in history, 1965-66; University of Oregon, Eugene, assistant professor, 1966-68; Northwest Nazarene College, Nampa, ID, assistant professor of American studies, 1968-69; Idaho State University, Pocatello, associate professor, 1970-76, professor of history, 1976-79, chair of department, 1972-74; University of New Mexico, Albuquerque, NM, professor of history, beginning 1979, became professor emeritus. Member of European seminar at Gordon College, 1969; visiting associate professor, Eastern Nazarene College, 1968-69, and University of Oregon, 1973; visiting professor, University of California—Los Angeles, 1978, and University of Oregon, 1978; Hilliard Distinguished Professor of Humanities, University of Nevada, Reno, 1985; annual research lecturer, University of New Mexico, 1991; Pettyjohn Distinguished Lecturer, Washington State University, 1992; visiting professor, Pepperdine University, 1997. American Specialist Lecturer, U.S. Information Agency, 1977; lecturer in American western literature and culture, Falkenstein seminar, 1978; lecturer on American West in India, 1986.

MEMBER: Organization of American Historians, Western Literature Association (member of executive council, 1965-68, 1975-78; president, 1979-80), Western History Association (member of council, 1984-86; president, 1998-99).

AWARDS, HONORS: National Historical Publications Commission fellowship, 1969-70; National Endowment for the Humanities fellowship, 1973-74; Huntington Library fellow, summer, 1974 and 1984; Alumnus of the Year, Northwest Nazarene College, 1975; American Philosophical Society research grant, 1976-77; Louis Knott Koontz Award, 1976, for best article appearing in *Pacific Historical Review;* award for best journal article on western history, Western History Association, 1976; Alumni Achievement Award, University of Oregon, 1991; West Heritage Award, 1996; John Caughey Award, 1996; Best Book in Western History Award, Western History Association, 1997; Wrangler/Western Heritage Award, National Cowboy Hall of Fame, 1997; Excellence in Humanities Award, New Mexico Endowment for the Humanities, 1998.

WRITINGS:

Western American Literature: A Bibliography of Interpretive Books and Articles, University of South Dakota Press (Vermillion, SD), 1972.

(Editor, with others) *Interpretive Approaches to Western American Literature,* Idaho State University Press (Boise, ID), 1972.

Owen Wister, Boise State College (Boise, ID), 1973.

(Editor, with Bert W. Marley) *The Idaho Heritage: A Collection of Historical Essays,* Idaho State University Press (Boise, ID), 1974.

(Editor, with Michael T. Marsden) *The Popular Western: Essays toward a Definition,* Popular Culture Press (Bowling Green, OH), 1974.

(Editor, with Merwin R. Swanson) *Idaho History: A Bibliography,* Idaho State University Press (Boise, ID), 1974, second edition, 1979.

(Lecturer) *The Mountain Man in Literature* (sound recording), Everett/Edwards (Deland, FL), 1974.

(Editor) *The American West: The Frontier Era,* Everett/Edwards (Deland, FL), 1976.

(Lecturer) *The Closing Frontier* (sound recording), Everett/Edwards (Deland, FL), 1976.

(Editor, with Rodman W. Paul) *The Frontier and the American West,* AHM Publishing (Arlington Heights, IL), 1977.

(Editor, with W.A. Douglass and W. Jacobson) *Anglo-American Contributions to Basque Studies,* Desert Research Institute (Reno, NV), 1977.

(Editor) *The New Frontier: The Twentieth Century West,* Everett/Edwards (Deland, FL), 1979.

(Editor) *Jack London on the Road: The Tramp Diary and Other Hobo Writings,* Utah State University Press (Logan, UT), 1979.

(Lecturer) *The Modern Literary West* (sound recording), Everett/Edwards (Deland, FL), 1979.

(Editor) *The Basques* (bibliography), Gale (Detroit, MI), 1981.

(Editor, with Fred Erisman) *Fifty Western Writers: A Bio-Bibliographical Guide,* Greenwood Press (New York, NY), 1982.

(Editor) *A Bibliographical Guide to the Study of Western American Literature,* University of Nebraska Press (Lincoln, NE), 1982.

Conversations with Wallace Stegner on Western History and Literature, University of Utah Press (Salt Lake City, UT), 1983.

(Editor) *Western Films: A Short History,* Sunflower University Press (Manhattan, KS), 1983.

(Editor, with Noel Riley Fitch) *Faith and Imagination: Essays on Evangelicals and Literature,* Far West Books (Albuquerque, NM), 1985.

Ernest Haycox, Boise State University (Boise, ID), 1988.

(Coeditor) *The Twentieth-Century West: Historical Interpretations,* University of New Mexico Press (Albuquerque, NM), 1989.

(With Michael P. Malone) *The American West: A Twentieth-Century History,* University of Nebraska Press (Lincoln, NE), 1989.

(Editor) *Writing Western History: Essays on Major Western Historians,* University of New Mexico Press (Albuquerque, NM), 1991.

(Compiler) *Religion in the Twentieth-Century American West: A Bibliography,* University of New Mexico (Albuquerque, NM), 1991.

(Editor) *Contemporary New Mexico, 1940-1990,* University of New Mexico Press (Albuquerque, NM), 1994.

(Coeditor) *The American West in the Twentieth Century: A Bibliography,* University of Oklahoma Press (Norman, OK), 1994.

(Coeditor) *A Bibliographical Guide to the Study of Western American Literature,* University of New Mexico Press (Albuquerque, NM), 1995.

Reimagining the Modern American West: A Century of Fiction, History, and Art, University of Arizona Press (Tucson, AZ), 1996.

(Coauthor) *Stegner: Conversations on History and Literature,* University of Nevada Press (Reno, NV), 1996.

(Coeditor) James J. Rawls, *Chief Red Fox Is Dead: A History of Native Americans since 1945,* Harcourt (New York, NY), 1996.

(Coeditor) Henry C. Dethloff, *The United States and the Global Economy since 1945,* Harcourt (New York, NY), 1997.

(Editor, with Glenda Riley) *By Grit and Grace: Eleven Women Who Shaped the American West,* Fulcrum (Golden, CO), 1997.

(Editor, with Gerald D. Nash) *Researching Western History: Topics in the Twentieth Century,* University of New Mexico Press (Albuquerque, NM), 1997

(Editor, with Ferenc M. Szasz) *Religion in Modern New Mexico,* University of New Mexico Press (Albuquerque, NM), 1997.

(Editor) *Myths and the American West,* Sunflower University Press (Manhattan, KS), 1998.

(Coeditor) Hal K. Rothman, *The Greening of a Nation?: Environmentalism in the United States since 1945,* Harcourt (New York, NY), 1998.

(Coeditor) Mary Ann Watson, *Defining Visions: Television and the American Experience since 1945,* Harcourt (New York, NY), 1998.

(Coeditor) Philippa Strum, *Privacy: The Debate in the United States since 1945,* Harcourt (New York, NY), 1998.

(Coeditor) *With Badges and Bullets: Lawmen and Outlaws in the Old West,* Fulcrum (Golden, CO), 1999.

(Editor, with Jeronima Echeverria) *Portraits of Basques in the New World,* University of Nevada Press (Reno, NV), 1999.

(Compiler and author of introduction) *Does the Frontier Experience Make America Exceptional?,* Bedford/St. Martin's (New York, NY), 1999.

Telling Western Stories: From Buffalo Bill to Larry McMurtry, University of New Mexico Press (Albuquerque, NM), 1999.

(Coeditor) *The Hollywood West: Lives of Film Legends Who Shaped It,* Fulcrum (Golden, CO), 2000.

(Editor) Charles A. Siringo, *A Texas Cowboy; or, Fifteen Years on the Hurricane Deck of a Spanish Pony,* Penguin (New York, NY), 2000.

(Editor and author of introduction) *Cesar Chavez: A Brief Biography with Documents,* Palgrave (New York, NY), 2002.

(Editor) *Writing Western History: Essays on Major Western Historians,* foreword by Glenda Riley, University of Nevada Press (Reno, NV), 2002.

(Editor) *New Mexican Lives: Profiles and Historical Stories,* University of New Mexico Press (Albuquerque, NM), 2002.

(Editor, with Glenda Riley) *Wild Women of the Old West,* Fulcrum (Golden, CO), 2003.

(Editor, with Ferenc M. Szasz) *The American West in 2000: Essays in Honor of Gerald D. Nash,* University of New Mexico Press (Albuquerque, NM), 2003.

(Editor, with Glenda Riley) *Chiefs and Generals: Nine Men Who Shaped the American West,* Fulcrum (Golden, CO), 2004.

(Editor) *Western Lives: A Biographical History of the American West,* University of New Mexico Press (Albuquerque, NM), 2004.

Contributor of over 250 articles and reviews to scholarly journals. Editor, with Michael T. Marsden, of "Popular Western Writers" series (monographs), Bowling Green University Popular Press, 1977—. Editor, *The American Literary West,* special issue of *Journal of the West,* Sunflower University Press, 1980, and *Cultural History of the American West,* special issue of *Journal of American Culture,* Bowling Green University Popular Press, 1980. Editor, *New Mexico Historical Review,* 1979-85; member of editorial board, *Rendezvous,* 1976-79, *Pacific Historical Review,* 1976-79, *Idaho Yesterdays,* 1976-81, *Journal of the West,* 1978—, *Western Historical Quarterly,* 1978-80, *Journal of American Culture,* 1978—, *Great Plains Quarterly,* 1979—, *Journal of Regional Cultures,* 1981—, and *Montana: The Magazine of Western History,* 1985—.

SIDELIGHTS: Richard W. Etulain is a professor emeritus of history whose main interest is the history and literature of the American West. He has written and edited numerous books, approaching his subject from various angles. For example, in *Religion in Modern New Mexico* Etulain, working with Ferenc M. Szasz, edited a collection of essays by a number of experts on how various world religions have had an impact on New Mexican life and culture. "The cumulative result is informative and interesting," attested Eldon G. Ernst in the *Pacific Historical Review. Journal of Church and State* writer Jon Hunner commented that the book "engagingly depicts how the state's fertile environment has nurtured a rich mixture of Christian and non-Christian beliefs." Although Ernst felt the collection could have been more logically organized, he concluded that "the book contributes much to the generally neglected history of religion in the North American West."

Etulain focuses on the impact of women on Western history in another collection, edited with Glenda Riley, called *By Grit and Grace: Eleven Women Who Shaped the American West.* "This ambitious volume presents the state of the art in Western women's biography," according to Nancy Page Fernandez in a *Pacific Historical Review* article. The book covers the lives of well-known figures in history, such as Annie Oakley and Calamity Jane, as well as less well known but still important women, such as suffragist Abigail Scott and entrepreneur Mary Ellen Pleasant. "*By Grit and Grace* seeks to show the impact of women as pioneers and developers not only on the western United States but on the West as American history," explained Fernandez.

Etulain has also written a number of original works about the West for both students and general audiences. *Reimagining the Modern American West: A Century of Fiction, History, and Art* explains for general readers the three different cultural movements in the West, including the regionalists, postregionalists, and frontier schools, and how historians, writers, and artists figure into these movements. Although a *Publishers Weekly* contributor found the book to be well researched, the reviewer felt that the work was "not entirely successful" due to its heavy use of "academic jargon" that would not appeal to some readers. John Mort, writing in *Booklist,* noted that Etulain skips over some notables, such as Oakley Hall and Larry Woiwode, but added that "he is to be commended for naming many women and minority writers, and he has a good knowledge of the Beats."

Etulain's *Telling Western Stories: From Buffalo Bill to Larry McMurtry* earned warm reviews from critics. Here, the author draws on his extensive knowledge of Western literature to discuss such authors as Louis L'Amour, Owen Wister, and Leslie Marmon Silko, as well as the "untold stories" of famous Western heroes. "There is much to admire about this collection of essays," wrote Robert W. Rydell in the *Pacific Historical Review.* "It is refreshingly free from jargon; it offers new perspectives on canonical works in western American literature and history; and it demonstrates the ongoing power of narrative formulas to structure scholarly debates."

Etulain once told *CA:* "I find myself increasingly interested in the sociocultural life of the American West and the presentations of that region in American popular culture. As the son of an immigrant Basque, I grew up on a sheep ranch and experienced the West firsthand. But only in the last decade or so has the region become the focus of most of my research and writing. The history and culture of the modern West, particularly, are an unexplored frontier. At the same time, I am intrigued with evangelical America, especially with its influences on American history and literature, and intend to study these influences during the next few years."

BIOGRAPHICAL AND CRITICAL SOURCES:

PERIODICALS

American Literature, September, 2001, David Carpenter, review of *Telling Western Stories: From Buffalo Bill to Larry McMurtry,* p. 669.

Booklist, June 1, 1994, John Mort, review of *Contemporary New Mexico: 1940-1990,* p. 1767; September 15, 1996, John Mort, review of *Reimagining the Modern American West: A Century of Fiction, History, and Art,* p. 213.

Journal of American Ethnic History, winter, 2001, Linda White, review of *Portraits of Basques in the New World,* p. 142.

Journal of American History, December, 1990, Patricia Nelson Limerick, review of *The Twentieth-Century West: Historical Interpretations,* p. 1069; September, 1993, William Deverell, review of *The American West: A Twentieth-Century History,* p. 718; June, 1997, Nancy Shoemaker, review of *Reimagining the Modern American West,* p. 257; December, 2000, Fred Erisman, review of *Telling Western Stories,* p. 1066.

Journal of Church and State, winter, 1999, Jon Hunner, review of *Religion in Modern New Mexico,* p. 152.

Library Journal, December 1, 1982, review of *A Bibliographical Guide to the Study of Western American Literature,* p. 2248; October 15, 1994, Stephen L. Hupp, review of *The American West in the Twentieth Century: A Bibliography,* p. 50.

Pacific Historical Review, May, 1998, Walter Nugent, review of *Researching Western History: Topics in the Twentieth Century,* p. 300; August, 1998, Eldon G. Ernst, review of *Religion in Modern New Mexico,* p. 450; August, 1999, Nancy Page Fernandez, review of *By Grit and Grace: Eleven Women Who Shaped the American West,* p. 477; May, 2001, Robert W. Rydell, review of *Telling Western Stories,* p. 326.

Publishers Weekly, August 12, 1996, review of *Reimagining the Modern American West,* p. 80.

USA Today (magazine), January, 2005, Gerald F. Kreyche, review of *Western Lives: A Biographical History of the American West,* p. 80.

Wild West, June, 1998, Candy Moulton, review of *By Grit and Grace,* p. 67; October, 2000, Louis Hart, review of *With Badges and Bullets: Lawmen and Outlaws in the Old West,* p. 70.

Wilson Library Bulletin, December, 1982, James Rettig, review of *Fifty Western Writers: A Bio-Bibliographical Guide,* p. 348.*

*   *   *

ETULAIN, Richard Wayne
      See ETULAIN, Richard W.

*   *   *

EVANS, Nicholas 1950-

PERSONAL: Born 1950, in Worcestershire, England; married; wife's name Jennifer; children: three. *Education:* Oxford University, received law degree (with honors).

ADDRESSES: Home—London and Devon, England. *Agent*—c/o Penguin Publicity, Penguin UK, 80 Strand, London WC2R 0RL, England.

CAREER: Journalist, screenwriter, film producer, and writer. In early career, journalist for *Evening Chronicle,* Newcastle-upon-Tyne, England, for three years; worked as television film producer in the United States and Middle East, as well as on television series *Weekend World,* c. 1970s; documentary film producer, beginning 1982.

WRITINGS:

FICTION

The Horse Whisperer, Delacorte (New York, NY), 1995.
The Loop, Delacorte (New York, NY), 1998.
The Smoke Jumper, Bantam (New York, NY), 2001.
The Divide, Putnam (New York, NY), 2005.

Also author of screenplays, including *Just like a Woman* and *Murder by the Book.*

ADAPTATIONS: A film version of *The Horse Whisperer,* directed by and starring Robert Redford, and also starring Kristin Scott Thomas, was released

by Touchstone, 1998. Audiocassette recordings and numerous foreign-language versions of *The Horse Whisperer* have also been recorded. *The Loop* was made into an audiobook by Recorded Books, 1998, and *The Smoke Jumper* has been made into an audiobook by Bantam, 2001.

SIDELIGHTS: While struggling novelists often turn to screenwriting in search of a bigger pay day, Nicholas Evans took the opposite tack. Though he had enjoyed some success as a screenwriter for such films as *Just like a Woman,* by the early 1990s work was scarce and Evans was feeling stretched financially. He showed a friend the incomplete manuscript of a novel, *The Horse Whisperer,* that he had been writing, essentially as a side project. Soon major studios were competing for the movie rights, which went to Robert Redford's production company (Redford would later star in and direct the film) for three million dollars. Then Dell Publishing came up with the even larger sum— unprecedented for a first novel—of 3.15 million dollars for rights to the book in North America. With overseas rights added in, *The Horse Whisperer,* still unfinished at the time, had earned Evans over eight million dollars.

The Horse Whisperer is a story of emotional healing and self-discovery. Annie Graves, a British-born career woman who publishes a successful magazine in New York, has a daughter, Grace, who in turn has a horse named Pilgrim. When Grace and Pilgrim are both horribly injured in a riding accident, Annie comes to realize that her daughter's psychological recovery is in some way linked to the horse's recovery. Leaving her loyal husband, Robert, in New York, Annie takes Grace and Pilgrim to Montana ranch country, where she seeks the help of Tom Booker, a "horse whisperer" who reputedly cures mental illness in horses by talking to them. The proud and independent Tom reluctantly agrees to work with Pilgrim, and Annie, in the open spaces of Montana, begins to question her frenzied, career-driven lifestyle. As the damaged psyches of Pilgrim and Grace are repaired, Annie and Tom initiate a passionate affair that forces both to reevaluate their lives. Evans uses allusions to the seventeenth-century Christian allegory *Pilgrim's Progress* to develop his themes.

Horses had been a part of Evans' life growing up in rural Worcestershire in the west of England, and the idea for *The Horse Whisperer* evolved from a meeting with a blacksmith, who told him about a Gypsy reportedly able to control wild horses. Evans chose an American rather than an English setting for the book, though, partly under the lingering spell of old Western television series and Jack London adventure stories from his childhood, and partly because he felt class issues would make an English version of his love story unconvincing.

The Horse Whisperer justified the huge advances Evans had been paid by quickly becoming a major bestseller. Its critical reception was generally less enthusiastic, however. The book was frequently likened to *The Bridges of Madison County,* Robert James Waller's novel about an unfulfilled homemaker's liaison with a middle-aged roamer. *Los Angeles Times Book Review* critic Ruth Coughlin echoed a common grievance when she called the book's dialogue "so wooden you yearn to take an ax to it," but she noted that "Evans' descriptions of Big Sky country are richly detailed, and the knowledge he conveys about horses is both fascinating and oddly moving."

Evans used a virtually identical Montana setting for his follow-up novel, *The Loop.* When the government's program to reintroduce wolves to the area draws the ire of cattle ranchers, Fish and Wildlife man Dan Prior brings in Helen Ross, a government wolf expert, to monitor and protect the pack. However, the ranchers, led by the redoubtable Buck Calder, bring in their own wolf expert, an exterminator named J.J. Lovelace who kills wolves with a cruel device known as "the loop." Helen has a series of confrontations with the ranchers, but is aided by Buck's overshadowed, alienated son, Luke, who becomes her lover.

Though its locale and focus on animals recalls Evans' first book, *The Loop* is much more politically charged than *The Horse Whisperer.* Evans conducted extensive research on wolves, and consulted people on all sides of the real-life debate over the management of America's wolf population. Voices spanning the political spectrum are represented in *The Loop,* from eco-terrorists to anti-government militias. While a reviewer for *Publishers Weekly* felt that the novel's topicality made it "more a work of ideology than imagination," critical response on the whole has been relatively favorable. "*The Loop* is a tighter, cleaner and altogether better story" than its predecessor, wrote Linda Richards in the online *January Magazine.* "It's a more mature book that will ensure Evans a place among today's top storytellers."

In *The Smoke Jumper* Evans tells the story of forest fire fighters Connor Ford and Ed Tully, who become caught up in a love triangle with Ed's girlfriend, Julia. Although in love with Connor, who saves Julia from a forest fire, Julia marries Ed anyway. As a result, the disappointed and frustrated Connor leaves to pursue a career as a war photographer. Writing in the *New Statesman,* Rachel Cooke noted that "Evans knows how to twiddle all the right knobs. As a technician of the human response, he is second to none."

The Divide focuses on Abbie Cooper, a well-off young girl who becomes involved with an eco-terrorist and is found at the beginning of the novel frozen in ice in Montana. In flashbacks, the author recounts Abbie's young life, from her parent's divorce to her life as a terrorist hiding out from the FBI. "The most vivid thing in the book is the wrangling early on over Abbie's remains," wrote a reviewer in *Publishers Weekly.* A *Kirkus Reviews* contributor called the book an "effective, if melancholy portrait."

BIOGRAPHICAL AND CRITICAL SOURCES:

PERIODICALS

Booklist, August, 1995, George Needham, review of *The Horse Whisperer,* p. 1909; July, 1997, Whitney Scott, review of *The Horse Whisperer,* p. 1830; July, 1998, Donna Seaman, review of *The Loop,* p. 1828; January 1, 1999, review of *The Loop,* p. 781; September 1, 2001, Brad Hooper, review of *The Smoke Jumper,* p. 3.
Entertainment Weekly, September 8, 1995, L. S. Klepp, review of *The Horse Whisperer,* p. 72; October 11, 1996, review of *The Horse Whisperer,* p. 87; October 9, 1998, Alexandra Jacobs, review of *The Loop,* p. 78.
Kirkus Reviews, August 1, 2005, review of *The Divide,* p. 805.
Library Journal, August, 1998, Nancy Pearl, review of *The Loop,* p. 130; February 1, 1999, John Hiett, review of *The Loop,* p. 136; June 15, 1999, Kristin M. Jacobi, review of *The Loop,* p. 121.
Los Angeles Times Book Review, September 3, 1995, Ruth Coughlin, review of *The Horse Whisperer,* p. 7.
New Statesman, November 26, 2001, Rachel Cooke, review of *The Smoke Jumper,* p. 54.

New Statesman & Society, September 29, 1995, Boyd Tonkin, review of *The Horse Whisperer,* p. 57.

Publishers Weekly, June 12, 1995, review of *The Horse Whisperer,* p. 43; December 18, 1995, Daisy Maryles, "Behind the Bestsellers," review of *The Horse Whisperer,* p. 14; June 29, 1998, review of *The Loop,* p. 34; December 21, 1998, Daisy Maryles, "Delacorte's Double Hit," review of *The Loop,* p. 21; September 3, 2001, Daisy Maryles, "The List Jumper," p. 20; May 20, 2002, John F. Baker, "Evans Goes with Baron," p. 16; July 128, 2005, review of *The Divide,* p. 179.

Spectator, October 14, 1995, p. 46.

Time, October 16, 1995, p. 99; September 28, 1998, John Skow, review of *The Loop,* p. 90.

ONLINE

January Magazine, http://www.januarymagazine.com/ (October, 1998), Linda Richards, review of *The Loop.*

Random House Web site, http://www.randomhouse. com/ (September 7, 2005), author briefly discusses his work.*

F

FAGAN, Brian M. 1936-
   (Brian Murray Fagan)

PERSONAL: Born August 1, 1936, in Birmingham, England; naturalized U.S. citizen; son of Brian Walter and Margaret (Moir) Fagan; married Lesley Ann Newhart, March 16, 1985; children: Lindsay, Anastasia. *Education:* Pembroke College, Cambridge, B.A. (with honors), 1959, M.A., 1962, Ph.D., 1964. *Hobbies and other interests:* Sailing (since the age of eight), kayaking, bicycling, cooking, cats.

ADDRESSES: Home—Santa Barbara, CA. *Office*—Department of Anthropology, University of California, Santa Barbara, CA 93106. *E-mail*—brian@brianfagan. com.

CAREER: Livingstone Museum, Livingstone, Northern Rhodesia (now Zambia), keeper of prehistory, 1959-65; British Institute of History and Archaeology in East Africa, Nairobi, Kenya, director of Bantu studies project, 1965-66; University of Illinois at Urbana-Champaign, Urbana, IL, visiting associate professor of anthropology, 1966-67; University of California, Santa Barbara, Santa Barbara, CA, associate professor, 1967-68, professor of anthropology, 1968-2003, director of Center for the Study of Developing Nations, 1969-70, associate dean of research and graduate affairs, 1970-72, associate dean of College of Letters and Science, 1972-73, dean of instructional development, 1973-76, professor emeritus of anthropology, 2003—. University of Capetown, Capetown, South Africa, lecturer, 1960, visiting professor, 1982; Munro Lecturer, University of Edinburgh, Edinburgh, Scotland, 1967; Richard M. Nixon Visiting Scholar and Lecturer, Whittier College, 1976.

Zambia Monuments Commission, member, 1960-65, secretary, 1960-62; director of Kalomo/Choma Iron Age project, 1960-63, of Lochinvar research project, 1963-64, and of Bantu studies project in Kenya, Uganda, and Tanzania; conducted archaeological research in Zambia and Northern Nigeria, 1969-70. Evaluation of International Audio-Visual Resource Service, United Nations Fund for Population Activities, consultant to administrator and head of mission, 1976; Center for Democratic Institutions, director, 1979-80. Columnist for *Archaeology* (magazine), 1989-94; member of editorial board of the *Cambridge Archaeological Journal;* senior consultant for Time/Life Television's Emmy Award-winning series *Lost Civilizations,* 1996; lecturer on African history and archeological topics in the United States and abroad. *Military service:* Royal Navy, 1954-56.

MEMBER: Royal Geographical Society (fellow), Royal Anthropological Institute (fellow), Society for American Archaeology (board member, 1991-93), South African Archaeological Society, Santa Barbara Yacht Club.

AWARDS, HONORS: Grants from Wenner-Gren Foundation, 1967 and 1968, and National Science Foundation, 1968-70, 1970-71, and 1990; Guggenheim fellow, 1972-73; Gold Medal for nonfiction, Commonwealth Club, 1975, for *The Rape of the Nile: Tomb Robbers, Tourists, and Archaeologists in Egypt;* Hanson Cup, Cruising Association, 1975, for a cruise to Scandinavia; EDUCOM Award, 1990, for curriculum innovation in large undergraduate courses; Distinguished Service Award, Society of Professional Archaeologists, 1996; Presidential Recognition Award,

1996, and Public Education Award, 1997, both from Society for American Archaeology; Distinguished Teaching Award, University of California, Santa Barbara.

WRITINGS:

(Editor) *Victoria Falls: A Handbook to the Victoria Falls, the Batoka Gorge, and Part of the Upper Zambesi River,* 2nd edition, Commission for the Preservation of Natural and Historic Monuments and Relics (Lusaka, Northern Rhodesia), 1964.

(With G.C.R. Clay) *The Life and Work of David Livingstone: A Brief Guide to the Livingstone Collections in the Livingstone Museum* (revision of *Guide to the David Livingstone Centenary Exhibition*), National Museums of Zambia (Livingstone, Zambia), 1965.

Southern Africa during the Iron Age, F.A. Praeger (New York, NY), 1965.

(Editor) *A Short History of Zambia: From the Earliest Times until A.D. 1900,* Oxford University Press (Lusaka, Zambia), 1966.

Iron Age Cultures in Zambia, Humanities (Atlantic Highlands, NJ), Volume 1: *Kalomo and Kangila,* 1967, Volume 2 (with S.G.H. Daniels and D.W. Phillipson): *Dambwa, Ingombe Ilede, and the Tonga,* 1969.

(Editor) *Introductory Readings in Archaeology,* Little, Brown (Boston, MA), 1970.

(Author of introduction and editorial note) Randall MacIver, *Medieval Rhodesia,* Cass & Co. (London, England), 1971.

(With Francis L. van Noten) *The Hunter-Gatherers of Gwisho,* Musée Royal de l'Afrique Centralo (Tervuren, Belgium), 1971.

(Editor) Louis S.B. Leakey, *The Stone Age Cultures of Kenya Colony,* Cass & Co. (London, England), 1971.

In the Beginning: An Introduction to Archaeology, Little, Brown (Boston, MA), 1972, 11th edition, Prentice Hall (Upper Saddle River, NJ), 2005.

Ingombe Ilede: Early Trade in South Central Africa, Addison Wesley (Reading, MA), 1972.

A Cruising Guide to California Channel Islands, Capra (Santa Barbara, CA), 1972, 4th edition, Caractacus Corp. (Santa Barbara, CA), 1992.

(With J.T. Robinson and Melvin L. Fowler) *Human and Cultural Development,* Indiana Historical Society (Indianapolis, IN), 1974.

Men of the Earth: An Introduction to World Prehistory, Little, Brown (Boston, MA), 1974, 2nd edition published as *People of the Earth: An Introduction to World Prehistory,* 1977, 11th edition, Prentice Hall (Upper Saddle River, NJ), 2004.

(Editor) *Corridors in Time: A Reader in Introductory Archaeology,* Little, Brown (Boston, MA), 1974.

The Rape of the Nile: Tomb Robbers, Tourists, and Archaeologists in Egypt, Scribners (New York, NY), 1975, revised edition, Westview Press (Boulder, CO), 2004.

(With Roland Oliver) *Africa in the Iron Age, c. 500 B.C. to A.D. 1400,* Cambridge University Press (New York, NY), 1975.

(Author of introductions) *Avenues to Antiquity: Readings from Scientific American,* W.H. Freeman (San Francisco, CA), 1976.

Elusive Treasure: The Story of Early Archaeologists in the Americas, Scribners (New York, NY), 1977.

Quest for the Past: Great Discoveries in Archaeology, Addison Wesley (Reading, MA), 1977.

(Author of introductions) *Civilization: Readings from Scientific American,* W.H. Freeman (San Francisco, CA), 1978.

Archaeology: A Brief Introduction, Little, Brown (Boston, MA), 1978, 9th edition, Prentice Hall (Upper Saddle River, NJ), 2006.

World Prehistory: A Brief Introduction, Little, Brown (Boston, MA), 1979, 6th edition, Prentice Hall (Upper Saddle River, NJ), 2005.

Return to Babylon: Travelers, Archaeologists, and Monuments in Mesopotamia, Little, Brown (Boston, MA), 1979.

Cruising Guide to the Channel Islands, photographs by Graham Pomeroy, Capra Press (Santa Barbara, CA), 1979, revised edition, Western Marine Enterprises (Ventura, CA), 1983, revised edition published as *Cruising Guide to Southern California's Offshore Islands: With Sailing Directions for the Santa Barbara Channel's Mainland Coast,* Caractacus Corp. (Santa Barbara, CA), 1993.

California Coastal Passages: From San Francisco to Ensenada, Mexico, Capra Press (Santa Barbara, CA), 1981.

(Author of introductions) *Prehistoric Times: Readings from Scientific American,* W.H. Freeman (San Francisco, CA), 1983.

The Aztecs, W.H. Freeman (New York, NY), 1984.

Clash of Cultures, W.H. Freeman (New York, NY), 1984.

Bareboating, International Marine Publishing (Camden, ME), 1985.

The Adventure of Archaeology, National Geographic Society (Washington, DC), 1985, revised edition, 1989.

Anchoring, International Marine Publishing (Camden, ME), 1986, expanded edition published as *Staying Put!: The Art of Anchoring,* Caractacus Corp. (Santa Barbara, CA), 1993.

The Great Journey: The Peopling of Ancient America, Thames and Hudson (New York, NY), 1987, updated edition, University Press of Florida (Gainesville, FL), 2004.

New Treasures of the Past: Fresh Finds that Deepen Our Understanding of the Archaeology of Man, Barron's (New York, NY), 1987.

The Journey from Eden: The Peopling of Our World, Thames and Hudson (New York, NY), 1990.

Ancient North America: The Archaeology of a Continent, Thames and Hudson (New York, NY), 1991, 4th edition, 2005.

Kingdoms of Gold and Jade: The Americas before Columbus, Thames and Hudson (New York, NY), 1991.

Cruising Guide: San Francisco to Ensenada, Mexico, Caractacus Corp. (Santa Barbara, CA), 1994.

Time Detectives: How Archaeologists Use Technology to Recapture the Past, Simon & Schuster (New York, NY), 1995.

(With others) *Ancient America,* introduction by Karen Sinsheimer, edited by Patrick O'Dowd, R. Rinehart Publishers (Boulder, CO), 1995.

Snapshots of the Past, AltaMira Press (Walnut Creek, CA), 1995.

(With Charles E. Orser, Jr.) *Historical Archaeology,* HarperCollins (New York, NY), 1995.

(Editor) *The Oxford Companion to Archaeology,* Oxford University Press (New York, NY), 1996.

(Editor) *Eyewitness to Discovery: First-Person Accounts of More than Fifty of the World's Greatest Archaeological Discoveries,* Oxford University Press (New York, NY), 1996.

Catalina Cruising Guide, Caractacus Corp. (Santa Barbara, CA), 1997.

Into the Unknown: Solving Ancient Mysteries, National Geographic Society (Washington, DC), 1997.

(With Christopher Scarre) *Ancient Civilizations,* Longman (New York, NY), 1997.

Boating Guide, San Francisco Bay, photographs by Patrick Short, Caractacus Corp. (Santa Barbara, CA), 1998.

From Black Land to Fifth Sun: The Science of Sacred Sites, Addison Wesley (Reading, MA), 1998.

Floods, Famines, and Emperors: El Niño and the Fate of Civilizations, Basic Books (New York, NY), 1999.

Ancient Lives: An Introduction to Method and Theory in Archaeology, Prentice Hall (Upper Saddle River, NJ), 2000.

The Little Ice Age: How Climate Made History, 1300-1850, Basic Books (New York, NY), 2000.

Egypt of the Pharaohs, photographs by Kenneth Garrett, National Geographic Society (Washington, DC), 2001.

Grahame Clark: An Intellectual Life of an Archeologist, Westview Press (Boulder, CO), 2001.

The Cruising Guide to Central and Southern California: Golden Gate to Ensenada, Mexico, including the Offshore Islands, International Marine/McGraw Hill (Camden, ME), 2002.

(Editor) *The Seventy Great Mysteries of the Ancient World: Unlocking the Secrets of Past Civilizations,* Thames and Hudson (New York, NY), 2001.

The Discovery of Ancient Civilizations (sound recording), Teaching Co. (Chantilly, VA), 2002.

Archaeologists: Explorers of the Human Past, Oxford University Press (New York, NY), 2003.

Before California: An Archaeologist Looks at Our Earliest Inhabitants, Rowman & Littlefield (Lanham, MD), 2003.

(Editor) *The Seventy Great Inventions of the Ancient World,* Basic Books (New York, NY), 2004.

The Long Summer: How Climate Changed Civilization, Granta Books (London, England), 2004.

A Brief History of Archaeology: Classical Times to the Twenty-first Century, Pearson/Prentice Hall (Upper Saddle River, NJ), 2005.

Chaco Canyon: Archeologists Explore the Lives of an Ancient Society, Oxford University Press (New York, NY), 2005.

Fish on Friday: Feasting, Fasting, and the Discovery of the New World, Basic Books (New York, NY), 2005.

Also writer for *Patterns of the Past,* a National Public Radio (NPR) series on archaeology funded by the National Endowment for the Humanities. Contributor to *UNESCO History of Africa,* Volume 2, 1984. Contributor of numerous chapters to books and hundreds of articles and reviews to professional journals, popular magazines, and newspapers.

SIDELIGHTS: Anthropologist and archaeologist Brian M. Fagan's writings include many that are geared towards broad audiences and that are understandable to nonspecialists. One such book is the 1996 publication *The Oxford Companion to Archaeology,* a collection of 700 articles by 350 scholars that covers a wide range of topics. A *Booklist* reviewer referred to the volume as "the only recent work of its kind."

Eyewitness to Discovery: First-Person Accounts of More than Fifty of the World's Greatest Archaeological Discoveries spans 200 years of findings on all the continents, dating from 5,000 years ago to the more recent excavations of a Virginia colony and a Manhattan graveyard. An *Economist* reviewer wrote that "some of these accounts are as thrilling as a detective story (the discovery of the Dead Sea Scrolls); one or two are full of a strange, astonished poetry (John Lloyd Stephens's account of the jungle ruins of Copan in Honduras); others are full of gold." "Though many of these accounts come from the time of science," wrote Anthony Sinclair in *Antiquity,* "it is still the incidental and personal side that remains most revealing."

From Black Land to Fifth Sun: The Science of Sacred Sites is a study of cave paintings, burial mounds, pyramids, stone circles, and other sites Fagan has examined using modern technological methods in an attempt to understand the cultures with which they are associated. A *Publishers Weekly* reviewer commented that Fagan "takes us on an often gripping first-person tour of the world's past, and his excitement in surveying these areas for himself is almost palpable."

Fagan's *Floods, Famines, and Emperors: El Niño and the Fate of Civilizations* combines climatology with archaeology in examining the impact of ancient El Niños and other weather phenomena that have influenced weather over the Indian and South Pacific Oceans. Evidence of such activity has been detected in ice cores and lake sediments, indicating a contribution to the decline of pre-Columbian civilizations. "Fagan exhibits a conversant command of El Niño's history and its possible indications of global warming," wrote Gilbert Taylor in *Booklist.* In a *National Forum* review, James P. Kaetz noted that Fagan "beats the environmental drum, but not too heavily, and (at least from my lay perspective) his scientific information and historical detail are thorough and understandable."

In *The Little Ice Age: How Climate Made History, 1300-1850,* Fagan provides a history of the hard times that hit Europe beginning in 1315, when heavy rains prevented a spring planting. Centuries of cooling weather followed, with the Thames freezing regularly from 1650 through 1715. Fagan feels that these weather patterns contributed to food shortages, the breakup of Norse settlements in Greenland, the French Revolution, and the Irish famine. Climatologists believe the 500-year event was triggered by the North Atlantic Oscillation (NAO) and that its effect on history was undeniable. "This book is noteworthy for its chronological and geographical scope," wrote Nancy R. Curtis in the *Library Journal.*

Fagan has also published *Before California: An Archaeologist Looks at Our Earliest Inhabitants.* This time the author provides a history of the land of California from approximately 11,000 B.C. up to the arrival of the Spaniards in the sixteenth century. Fagan has also produced a revised edition of *The Rape of the Nile,* which Taylor, writing in *Booklist,* recommended as containing "exciting, colorful adventures for Indiana Jones admirers." Inspired and intrigued by the debates surrounding global warming, Fagan turns his attention to how climate has affected the earth's past in his book *The Long Summer: How Climate Changed Civilization.* The author focuses primarily on the periods between 18,000 B.C. to 1200 A.D. A *Contemporary Review* contributor noted that Fagan discusses how human beings' "relationship with . . . climate has always been 'in flux,'" adding "how man adapted to change is the theme" of the book.

Focusing on the world prior to 500 B.C., Fagan served as the editor of a book about early human innovations that changed the world. Titled *The Seventy Great Inventions of the Ancient World,* the volume includes various essays discussing such early technologies as ploughs and cloth-making tools. The various authors also look at early inventions dealing with transportation, as well as the development of adornments such as tattoos and jewelry. A *Contemporary Review* contributor noted that Fagan and the authors present "an entrancing story of man's development choc a bloc with bits of information." Writing in *MBR Bookwatch,* Diane C. Donovan called the effort "engagingly informative."

Fagan once told *CA:* "I became interested in popular writing about archaeology while working in Zambia during the 1960s. The early 1960s saw tumultuous and lasting political changes which resulted in the complete revamping of school and university history curricula.

We had to create national history from excavations rather than written records, compiling *A Short History of Zambia: From the Earliest Times until A.D. 1900,* from a patchwork of archaeology, oral history, and documents in 1966. The book remained the standard source in Zambian schools and at the University of Zambia for more than twenty years. I also became involved in radio and TV, as well as guidebook and newspaper article writing—a wonderful grounding for a working writer.

"Since coming to the United States in 1966, I have moved away from African archaeology and history and have worked on the complex issue of communicating archaeology to popular audiences. At the same time, I've been deeply involved in developing new approaches to teaching large university courses in archaeology for undergraduate audiences, also in much popular lecturing. Inevitably, these activities led me into textbook writing and eventually into trade books.

"I started textbook writing in 1967, and saw my first method and theory text, *In the Beginning: An Introduction to Archaeology,* published in 1972. Since then, I have published more than half a dozen college texts, all of which are in multiple editions. Many archaeologists have flattered me by calling them standard works. The experience of these books has given me a uniquely broad grip on world archaeology, a stimulating change in a world of acute specialization and narrowly focused writing and research.

"My trade career began with a chance letter from Scribners about an article I wrote for *Archaeology Magazine* on Giovanni Belzoni, the Egyptian tomb robber. Their inquiry led to *The Rape of the Nile: Tomb Robbers, Tourists, and Archaeologists in Egypt,* now in nine languages, and a whole new vista of writing opportunity. I have continued to write about archaeology for the general public ever since. Since the late 1980s, I have developed a special interest in American archaeology, where uncontrolled looting threatens the future both of archaeology and the Native American past. *Ancient North America: The Archaeology of a Continent,* a general account of North American archaeology, and *The Great Journey: The Peopling of Ancient America,* a description of the first settlement of the Americas, are the result. The National Geographic Society provided me with two unique opportunities to write books on archaeology for a very wide audience indeed. *The Adventure of Archaeology*

covers the history of archaeological discovery, while *Into the Unknown: Solving Ancient Mysteries* describes ways in which science is revolutionizing our knowledge of the remote past. I have also completed the mammoth task of editing *The Oxford Companion to Archaeology,* intended as a definitive statement on archaeology in the 1990s. An accompanying anthology, *Eyewitness to Discovery,* features firsthand accounts of major archaeological discoveries by those who have made them. I am continuing studies on ways in which archaeologists study ancient religions.

"I would describe myself as a day-to-day working writer, with feet in many camps. At one end of the spectrum lies the world of academic writing; at the other, highly popular works I have written for *National Geographic.* I've been very lucky, being one of the few professional archaeologists who writes for a general audience, enjoying frequent book club adoptions and foreign sales of most of my books. My ultimate objective in writing about the past is to communicate the enormous importance and fascination of scientific archaeology. I am NOT interested in mythic interpretations of the past, in ancient astronauts, conquering Egyptians crossing the Atlantic, or other forms of pseudo-archaeology. I'm a scientist who just happens to write for the public—and has fun doing it. The sheer diversity of writing opportunities which cross my desk make my life a constant fascination. And every day I sit at my computer, I realize just how much more I have to learn about the craft of writing."

BIOGRAPHICAL AND CRITICAL SOURCES:

PERIODICALS

American Journal of Archaeology, January, 1998, review of *The Oxford Companion to Archaeology,* p. 186.

Amicus Journal, summer, 2001, E.G. Vallianatos, review of *The Little Ice Age: How Climate Made History, 1300-1850,* p. 37.

Antiquity, June, 1997, Anthony Sinclair, review of *Eyewitness to Discovery: First-Person Accounts of More than Fifty of the World's Greatest Archaeological Discoveries,* p. 460, and review of *The Oxford Companion to Archaeology,* p. 464.

Atlantic, January, 1980, review of *Return to Babylon: Travelers, Archaeologists, and Monuments in Mesopotamia,* p. 88.

Booklist, December 1, 1994, Gilbert Taylor, review of *Time Detectives: How Archaeologists Use Technology to Recapture the Past,,* p. 642; March 15, 1997, review of *The Oxford Companion to Archaeology,* p. 1260; May 15, 1998, Donna Seaman, review of *From Black Land to Fifth Sun: The Science of Sacred Sites,* p. 1568; February 15, 1999, Gilbert Taylor, review of *Floods, Famines, and Emperors: El Niño and the Fate of Civilizations,* p. 1018; March 1, 2001, Gilbert Taylor, review of *The Little Ice Age,* p. 1214; September 15, 2001, Philip Herbst, review of *Grahame Clark: An Intellectual Life of an Archeologist,* p. 192; October 1, 2004, Gilbert Taylor, review of *The Rape of the Nile: Tomb Raiders, Tourists, and Archaeologists in Egypt,* p. 296.

Bookwatch, April, 1998, review of *Cruising Guide: San Francisco to Ensenada, Mexico,* p. 7; October, 1998, review of *From Black Land to Fifth Sun,* p. 3.

Choice, July, 1997, review of *The Oxford Companion to Archaeology,* p. 34; January, 1999, review of *From Black Land to Fifth Sun,* p. 929; July, 1999, review of *Floods, Famines, and Emperors,* p. 1971; July-August, 2001, H. N. Pollack, review of *The Little Ice Age,* p. 1994.

Chronicle of Higher Education, March 12, 1999, review of *Floods, Famines, and Emperors,* p. A19.

Contemporary Review, December, 2004, review of *The Long Summer: How Climate Changed Civilization,* p. 377; January, 2005, review of *The Seventy Great Inventions of the Ancient World,* p. 64.

Discover, February, 2001, Eric N. Nash, review of *The Little Ice Age,* p. 84.

Economist, May 17, 1997, review of *Eyewitness to Discovery,* p. S5.

History: Review of New Books, summer, 2001, Roger L. Cunniff, review of *The Little Ice Age,* p. 184.

History Today, April, 1997, review of *The Oxford Companion to Archaeology* and review of *Eyewitness to Discovery,* p. 56.

Isis, June, 1999, review of *From Black Land to Fifth Sun,* p. 357.

Kirkus Reviews, January 15, 1999, review of *Floods, Famines, and Emperors,* p. 118.

Kliatt, March, 1999, review of *Eyewitness to Discovery,* p. 38; September, 1999, review of *Eyewitness to Discovery,* p. 39; November, 1999, review of *From Black Land to Fifth Sun,* p. 39.

Library Journal, February 15, 1997, Joyce L. Ogburn, review of *The Oxford Companion to Archaeology,* p. 129; February 15, 2001, Nancy R. Curtis, review of *The Little Ice Age,* p. 196; September 1, 2004, Michael Rogers, review of *The Rape of the Nile,* p. 204.

MBR Bookwatch, March, 2005, Diane C. Donovan, review of *The Seventy Great Inventions of the Ancient World.*

National Forum, summer, 1999, James P. Kaetz, review of *Floods, Famines, and Emperors,* p. 38.

Natural History, May, 1997, review of *Eyewitness to Discovery,* p. 13; April, 1999, review of *Floods, Famines, and Emperors,* p. 23.

Nature, April 20, 1995, Paul G. Bahn, review of *Time Detectives,* p. 686; April 17, 1997, review of *Eyewitness to Discovery* and review of *The Oxford Companion to Archaeology,* p. 669; July 23, 1998, review of *From Black Land to Fifth Sun,* p. 335.

New Scientist, April 26, 1997, review of *Eyewitness to Discovery,* p. 43; June 28, 1997, review of *The Oxford Companion to Archaeology,* p. 42; September 5, 1998, Paul Bahn, review of *From Black Land to Fifth Sun,* p. 50.

Publishers Weekly, May 25, 1998, review of *From Black Land to Fifth Sun,* p. 72; February 12, 2001, review of *The Little Ice Age,* p. 196.

Reference & Research Book News, May, 1997, review of *The Oxford Companion to Archaeology* and review of *Eyewitness to Discovery,* p. 17; May, 1998, review of *Into the Unknown: Solving Ancient Mysteries,* p. 19.

Religious Studies Review, October, 1997, review of *The Oxford Companion to Archaeology,* p. 396.

Science, February 28, 1997, review of *The Oxford Companion to Archaeology,* p. 1276.

Science News, June 14, 2003, review of *Before California: An Archaeologist Looks at Our Earliest Inhabitants,* p. 383; January 15, 2005, review of *The Seventy Great Inventions of the Ancient World,* p. 47.

Scientific American, May, 2001, Keay Davidson, review of *The Little Ice Age,* p. 90.

SciTech Book News, June, 1999, review of *Floods, Famines, and Emperors,* p. 56.

Virginia Quarterly Review, spring, 1988, review of *The Great Journey: The Peopling of Ancient America,* p. 68; autumn, 1997, review of *The Oxford Companion to Archaeology,* p. 139.

Washington Post, May 20, 1999, David Laskin, "Extreme Weather and Human Catastrophes," p. C02.

Washington Post Book World, February 23, 1997, review of *Eyewitness to Discovery,* p. 13.

ONLINE

ONLINE

Brian Fagan Books Online Web site, http://www.brian fagan.com (November 11, 2005).

Globalist Web site, http://www.theglobalist.com/ (November 11, 2005), biography of Brian Fagan.

Society for California Archaeology Web site, http://www.scahome.org/ (November 11, 2005), Breck Parkman and C. Kristina Roper, 2002 interview with Brian Fagan.*

*　　*　　*

FAGAN, Brian Murray
　　See FAGAN, Brian M.

*　　*　　*

FAGAN, Cary 1957-

PERSONAL: Born June 29, 1957, in Toronto, Ontario, Canada; son of Maurice (a lawyer) and Belle (Menkes) Fagan; married Joanne Schwartz (a librarian), August 19, 1984. *Education:* University of Toronto, B.A., 1980, M.A., 1991. *Religion:* Jewish.

ADDRESSES: Home—Toronto, Ontario, Canada. *Office*—c/o Writers Union of Canada, 24 Ryerson Ave., Toronto, Ontario M5T 2P3, Canada.

CAREER: Canadian Forum, Toronto, Ontario, Canada, editorial assistant, 1980-82; *Seven News,* Toronto, editor, 1983; *Canadian Lawyer,* Toronto, assistant editor, 1983-84; Shaw Street Press, Toronto, co-owner, 1985—; *Paragraph,* Toronto, contributing editor, 1989—. Instructor at Toronto Writing Workshop.

MEMBER: Amnesty International, Writers Union of Canada, Canadian Bookbinders and Book Artists Guild.

AWARDS, HONORS: City of Toronto Book Award, 1990, for *Streets of Attitude: Toronto Stories;* Jewish Book Committee Prize for Fiction, 1994, for *The Animal's Waltz;* Sydney Taylor Honor Book for younger readers, 2000, for *The Market Wedding;* Norma Epstein Literary Award; Constance Nicholson Lee Prize.

WRITINGS:

Seeing, South Western Ontario Publishing (London, Ontario, Canada), 1983.

Two Stories, Piraeus Press (Toronto, Ontario, Canada), 1985.

Nora by the Sea, Shaw Street Press (Toronto, Ontario, Canada), 1988.

History Lessons: Stories and Novellas, Hounslow Press (Willowdale, Ontario, Canada), 1990.

City Hall and Mrs. God: A Passionate Journey through a Changing Toronto, Mercury Press (Stratford, Ontario, Canada), 1990.

(Editor, with Robert MacDonald) *Streets of Attitude: Toronto Stories,* Yonge & Bloor (Toronto, Ontario, Canada), 1990.

The Little Black Dress: Tales from France, Mercury Press (Stratford, Ontario, Canada), 1993.

The Fred Victor Mission Story, Wood Lake Books (Winfield, British Columbia, Canada), 1993.

The Animal's Waltz (novel), Lester Publishing (Toronto, Ontario, Canada), 1994, St. Martin's (New York, NY), 1996.

(Editor) *A Walk by the Seine: Canadian Poets on Paris,* Black Moss Press (Windsor, Ontario, Canada), 1995.

The Doctor's House (short stories), Paperplates Books (Toronto, Ontario, Canada), 1996.

Sleeping Weather, Porcupine's Quill (Erin, Ontario, Canada), 1997.

Gogol's Coat (for children; based on the story "The Overcoat" by Nikolai Gogol), illustrated by Regolo Ricci, Tundra Books (Montreal, Quebec, Canada), 1998.

Felix Roth (novel), Stoddart (Toronto, Ontario, Canada), 1999.

The Doctor's House and Other Fiction, Stoddart (Toronto, Ontario, Canada), 2000.

The Market Wedding (for children; based on the story "A Ghetto Wedding" by Abraham Cahan), illustrated by Regolo Ricci, Tundra Books (Montreal, Quebec, Canada), 2000.

Daughter of the Great Zandini (for children), illustrated by Cybele Young, Tundra Books (Montreal, Quebec, Canada), 2001.

(With Chan Hon Goh) *Beyond the Dance: A Ballerina's Life,* Tundra Books (Toronto, Ontario, Canada), 2002.

The Mermaid of Paris, Key Porter Books (Toronto, Ontario, Canada), 2003.

The Little Underworld of Edison Wiese, Hungry I Books (Montreal, Quebec, Canada), 2003.
The Fortress of Kaspar Snit, Tundra Books of Northern New York (Plattsburgh, NY), 2004.

Contributor to periodicals, including *Globe & Mail* and *Books in Canada.*

SIDELIGHTS: Canadian poetry critic Cary Fagan is also the author of fiction for adults and, more recently, children. His first novel, *The Animal's Waltz,* draws on his Jewish-Canadian heritage to tell the story of Sheila Hersh, a young woman leading a double life. During the day, she helps her father with his store in Toronto and appears to be a conservative and obedient daughter, but at night she visits dance clubs and even acts in a nude scene in a movie. Father and daughter are brought closer together, however, when Sheila becomes fascinated by a book of poems owned by her late mother. The poet, a fictitious Jewish pianist from Vienna named Charlotte Reissmann, killed herself at the age of twenty-three, and Sheila decides to translate the poems (verses from these "translated" poems begin each chapter in the novel). But Sheila feels she cannot truly understand Reissmann without actually traveling to Vienna, so she and her father decide to go together. Along the way, Sheila and her father try to resolve their feelings about the death of her mother. A *Publishers Weekly* critic enjoyed the first half of the novel, especially noting that the poems are "stunning," but felt that the sections about the journey to Vienna and the "neat coincidences" at the end of the book are somewhat of a "letdown." Nevertheless, the reviewer asserted that the author's debut novel proves Fagan to be "a wonderful writer with a rare comic gift."

More recently, Fagan has turned much of his attention to writing fiction for children. Some of these works, such as *Gogol's Coat* and *The Market Wedding,* are adapted from stories for adults by Nikolai Gogol and Abraham Cahan, respectively. In the first, an impoverished boy named Gogol scrimps and saves to pay for a coat only to have it stolen by a coworker. However, in what Carolyn Phelan of *Booklist* called a "melodramatic climax," the thief is revealed in the end and Gogol gets his coat back. In *The Market Wedding,* set in the 1920s in Toronto's Kensington Market, a fish seller named Morris falls in love with a milliner named Minnie. Deciding that she should have only the best, he convinces her that they should have the most

extravagant wedding possible so that their family and friends will feel obliged to buy them expensive gifts. But when those invited decide they cannot afford to come to such a lavish affair, Morris relents and has the wedding in their flat. "The tale's ironic humor socks home one of life's basic lessons," wrote Susan Scheps in the *School Library Journal.*

In 2002, Fagan's *Daughter of the Great Zandini* was published. Another story for children, the tale is about how the magician of the title wants his son, Theodore, to follow in his footsteps, even though Theodore has no desire to be a magician while his sister, Fanny, does and is very talented at prestidigitation. When Theodore flops at one of his father's shows, Fanny steps in, disguised as a boy, and wows the crowd. Set in the nineteenth-century, the story impressed critics with its accurate portrayal of life at the time. "There are several surprises in the plot," Linda Ludke noted in the *School Library Journal,* "and young readers will enjoy, as Zandini puts it, the 'Transformations, alterations, [and] manipulations.'"

BIOGRAPHICAL AND CRITICAL SOURCES:

PERIODICALS

Booklist, February 1, 1999, Carolyn Phelan, review of *Gogol's Coat,* p. 979; December 1, 2000, Michael Cart, review of *The Market Wedding,* p. 706; September 15, 2001, Stephanie Zvirin, review of *The Market Wedding,* p. 225.
Canadian Forum, October, 1993, Julie Mason, review of *The Little Black Dress: Stories from France,* p. 38.
Globe & Mail (Toronto, Ontario, Canada), December 8, 1990.
Library Journal, January, 1996, Marion Hanscom, review of *The Animal's Waltz,* p. 141.
New York Times Book Review, March 3, 1996, Sally Eckhoff, review of *The Animal's Waltz,* p. 18.
Publishers Weekly, December 18, 1995, review of *The Animal's Waltz,* p. 42.
School Library Journal, March, 2001, Susan Scheps, review of *The Market Wedding,* p. 208; April, 2002, Linda Ludke, review of *Daughter of the Great Zandini,* p. 109; April, 2003, Cheri Estes, review of *Beyond the Dance: A Ballerina's Life,* p. 182; August, 2004, Tim Wadham, review of *The Fortress of Kaspar Snit,* p. 121.*

FAIRCHILD, Bertram H., Jr.
   See FAIRCHILD, B.H.

*   *   *

FAIRCHILD, B.H. 1942-
   (Bertram H. Fairchild, Jr.)

PERSONAL: Born October 17, 1942, in Houston, TX; son of Bertram Harry (a machinist) and Locie Marie (Swearingen) Fairchild; married Patricia Lea Gillespie (a math teacher), October 12, 1968; children: Paul, Sarah. *Education:* University of Kansas, B.A., 1964, M.A., 1968; University of Tulsa, Ph.D., 1975. *Religion:* Episcopalian. *Hobbies and other interests:* Running, music, Kansas basketball.

ADDRESSES: Home—706 W. 11th St., Claremont, CA 91711. *Office*—California State University, 5500 University Parkway, San Bernardino, CA 92407. *E-mail*—Bhfairchil@aol.com; fairchld@csusb.edu.

CAREER: Poet and educator. C & W Machine Works, Liberal, KS, until 1966; Hercules, Inc., Lawrence, KS, 1966-67; Kearney State College (now University of Nebraska), Kearney, NE, instructor, 1968-70; University of Tulsa, Tulsa, OK, teaching fellow, 1970-73; Southwest Texas State University, assistant professor, 1973-76; Texas Woman's University, associate professor, 1976-83; California State University, San Bernardino, professor, 1983—. The Frost Place, Franconia, NH, poet in residence, summer, 2001.

MEMBER: Texas Institute of Letters.

AWARDS, HONORS: National Endowment for the Arts Fellowship in Poetry, 1988-89; National Book Award finalist, 1998; Capricorn Book Award, 1996, for *The Art of the Lathe: Poems* manuscript; Beatrice Hawley Award, 1997, National Book Award finalist, 1998, Natalie Ornish Award, Texas Institute of Letters, 1999, Kingsley Tufts Award, 1999, William Carlos Williams Award, Poetry Society of America, 1999, PEN Center West Award, 1999, California Book Award, 1999, and Poet's Prize honorable mention, 2000, all for *The Art of the Lathe: Poems;* Seaton Poetry Award, 1997; MacDowell Arts Colony fellowships, 1997, 1999; Guggenheim Fellowship, 1999; Rockefeller Fellowship, 2000;

National Book Critics Circle Award in poetry category, 2003, and Rebekah Johnson Bobbitt National Prize for Poetry, 2004, both for *Early Occult Memory Systems of the Lower Midwest;* Arthur Rense Poetry Award, American Academy of Arts and Letters.

WRITINGS:

POETRY; UNLESS OTHERWISE NOTED

Such Holy Song: Music as Idea, Form, and Image in the Poetry of William Blake (literary criticism), Kent State University Press (Kent, OH), 1980.
C & W Machine Works (chapbook), Trilobite Press (Denton, TX), 1983.
Flight (chapbook), Devil's Millhopper Press (Blythewood, SC), 1985.
The Arrival of the Future (poetry), illustrated by Ross Zirkle, Swallow's Tale Press (Norcross, GA), 1985, Livingston Publishing, 1985, 2nd edition, Alice James Books (Farmington, ME), 2000.
The System of Which the Body Is One Part (chapbook), State Street Press (Brockport, NY), 1988.
Local Knowledge (essay), Quarterly Review of Literature (Princeton, NJ), 1991, reprinted, Norton (New York, NY), 2005.
The Art of the Lathe: Poems, introduction by Anthony Hecht, Alice James Books/ University of Maine (Farmington, ME), 1998.
Early Occult Memory Systems of the Lower Midwest, Norton (New York, NY), 2003.

Contributor of poetry and articles to periodicals, including *Poetry, Southern Review, Hudson Review, TriQuarterly, Sewanee Review, Salmagundi, Threepenny Review, Prairie Schooner, Georgia Review, Thoth, Essays in Literature, Blake Studies,St. Louis Literary Supplement: A Review of Literature, Politics, and the Arts, Journal of Popular Film, Literature/Film Quarterly, Studies in American Humor,* and *Statements on Language and Rhetoric.*

WORK IN PROGRESS: Rave On, a book of poems.

SIDELIGHTS: Author and poet B.H. Fairchild's first published book was a critical study of another poet. *Such Holy Song: Music as Idea, Form, and Image in the Poetry of William Blake,* which saw print in 1980, looked at the influence of music on the work of the famed late eighteenth-century poet who pioneered Romanticism and created such masterpieces as *Songs of Innocence and of Experience* and *The Four Zoas.* In fact, it is primarily these two sets of poems by Blake that Fairchild uses to assert his premise that music is supremely important to Blake's poetic creations. As Brian Wilke pointed out in the *Rocky Mountain Review, Such Holy Song* itself "has a kind of simple ABA sonata form." The critic explained that chapter one provides a framework for the rest of the book. The next three chapters explore "the theoretical and mythic meaning of music for Blake," "melos" in the *Songs of Innocence and of Experience,* and the "sound effects, . . . musico-dramatic form, and . . . musical imagery" in *The Four Zoas.* The last chapter sums up the book. Fairchild also asserts that melody, in Blake's creative realm, is likened "to the visual . . . and the poetic line, . . . representing the right, healthy form of imagination." In addition, the author includes information about Blake's living conditions, which included a home near "pleasure gardens" where music was frequently performed.

Critical response to *Such Holy Song* was generally positive. Wilke noted that the chapter dealing with *The Four Zoas* is "the best part of the book." Wilke particularly appreciated the explanation "of the poem's sound effects, which Fairchild brings excitingly alive." A *Choice* contributor noted that Fairchild explores his subject matter and proves his points "clearly and effectively," and declared the volume to be "the first direct attempt to render as accurately as possible the musicality" of Blake's poetry.

Fairchild has also published volumes of his own poetry, including 1985's *The Arrival of the Future,* with illustrations by Ross Zirkle, and a volume titled *Local Knowledge,* which a *Publishers Weekly* reviewer noted for its "obvious strength." His collection of poems titled *The Art of the Lathe: Poems* was called "thoughtful and delicately crafted" by *Poetry* contributor John Taylor. The reviewer went on to note: "His images haunt with a sort of silent metaphysical immobility." Vince Gotera, writing in the *North American Review,* commented that the author provides "impeccably precise and fresh insight."

Fairchild received wide recognition and critical praise for his volume of poetry titled *Early Occult Memory Systems of the Lower Midwest.* Writing in *Poetry,* Bill Christophersen noted that the author "continues to mine the experience of growing up in various hard-scrabble towns of Oklahoma, Texas, and Kansas during the Fifties and Sixties." Christophersen went on to write: "Many of these poems, like their predecessors . . . are free verse narratives distinguished by their blue-collar settings and crisp detail." A *Publishers Weekly* contributor wrote that "fans of Fairchild's comforting excursions to the familiar isolated territory of machinists won't be disappointed." In a review in the *New York Times,* Michael Hainey wrote: "This is the American voice at its best."

BIOGRAPHICAL AND CRITICAL SOURCES:

BOOKS

Fairchild, B.H., *Such Holy Song: Music as Idea, Form, and Image in the Poetry of William Blake,* Kent State University Press (Kent, OH), 1980.

PERIODICALS

Booklist, November 15, 2002, Ray Olson, review of *Early Occult Memory Systems of the Lower Midwest,* p. 564; January 1, 2003, review of *Early Occult Memory Systems of the Lower Midwest,* p. 791.
Choice, January, 1981, review of *Such Holy Song: Music as Idea, Form, and Image in the Poetry of William Blake,* p. 658.
Houston Chronicle, January 12, 2003, Robert Phillips, review of *Early Occult Memory Systems of the Lower Midwest,* p. 21.
Hudson Review, spring, 1999, David Mason, review of *The Art of the Lathe: Poems,* p. 141; spring, 2001, Robert Phillips, review of *The Arrival of the Future,* p. 169; summer, 2004, David Mason, "Seven Poets," includes profile of author and work, p. 325.
New York Times, February 23, 2003, Michael Hainey, review of *Early Occult Memory Systems of the Lower Midwest,* p. 24.
North American Review, September-October, 2001, Vince Gotera, review of *The Art of the Lathe,* p. 45.
Poetry, October, 1984, pp. 29-30; January, 2001, John Taylor, review of *The Art of the Lathe,* p. 276; April, 2003, Bill Christophersen, review of *Early Occult Memory Systems of the Lower Midwest,* p. 35.

Publishers Weekly, November 4, 2002, review of *Early Occult Memory Systems of the Lower Midwest,* p. 79; August 15, 2005, review of *Local Knowledge,* p. 35.

Rocky Mountain Review, Volume 35, number 2, 1981, Brian Wilke, review of *Such Holy Song,* pp. 165-166.

San Francisco Chronicle, July 4, 1999, review of *The Art of the Lathe,* p. 11.

Sewanee Review, spring, 1999, Justin Quinn, review of "The Language of Our Emotions," brief mention of author's works, p. 289.

ONLINE

Poetry Daily, http://www.poetrydaily.net/ (March 28, 2003), includes various reviewers' comments about *Early Occult Memory Systems of the Lower Midwest.**

*   *   *

FALLON, Martin
    See PATTERSON, Harry

*   *   *

FARAH, Nuruddin 1945-

PERSONAL: Born November 24, 1945, in Baidoa, Somalia; son of Hassan (a merchant) and Aleeli (a poet; maiden name, Faduma) Farah; married Chitra Muliyil Farah (divorced); married Amina Mama (a physician), July 21, 1992; children: (first marriage) Koschin Nuruddin (son); (second marriage) Kaahiye (son). *Education:* Attended Punjab University, Chandigarh, India, 1966-70, University of London, 1974-75, and University of Essex, 1975-76. *Religion:* "Born Muslim."

ADDRESSES: Home—Kaduna, Nigeria. *Agent*—c/o Riverhead Publicity, 375 Hudson St., New York, NY 10014.

CAREER: Writer, translator, broadcaster, and educator. Clerk-typist for Ministry of Education in Somalia, 1964-66; teacher at secondary school in Mogadishu, Somalia, 1969-71; lecturer in comparative literature at Afgoi College of Education, and at Somali National University, Mogadishu, 1971-74; Royal Court Theatre, London, England, resident writer, 1976; University of Ibadan, Jos Campus, Jos, Nigeria, associate professor, 1981-83; Makerere University, Kampala, Uganda, professor, 1990—. Guest professor and lecturer at universities in the United States, Europe, and Africa.

MEMBER: Union of Writers of the African Peoples.

AWARDS, HONORS: United Nations Educational, Scientific and Cultural Organization (UNESCO) fellowship, 1974-76; literary award from English-Speaking Union, 1980, for *Sweet and Sour Milk;* Neustadt Award, 1998.

WRITINGS:

A Dagger in Vacuum (play), produced in Mogadishu, Somalia, 1970.

From a Crooked Rib (novel), Heinemann (London, England), 1970.

The Offering (play), produced in Colchester, Essex, England, 1975.

A Naked Needle (novel), Heinemann (London, England), 1976.

A Spread of Butter (radio play), 1978.

Sweet and Sour Milk (first novel in the "Variations on the Theme of an African Dictatorship" trilogy), Allison & Busby (London, England), 1979, Graywolf Press (St. Paul, MN), 1992.

Tartar Delight (radio play), broadcast in Germany, 1980.

Sardines (second novel in the "Variations on the Theme of an African Dictatorship" trilogy), Allison & Busby (London, England), 1981, Graywolf Press (St. Paul, MN), 1992.

Close Sesame (third novel in the "Variations on the Theme of an African Dictatorship" trilogy), Allison & Busby (London, England), 1982, Graywolf Press (St. Paul, MN), 1992.

Yussuf and His Brothers (play), produced in Jos, Nigeria, 1982.

Maps (novel), Pan Book (London, England), 1986, Pantheon (New York, NY), 1987.

Gavor (novel), 1990.

Secrets (novel), Little, Brown (Boston, MA), 1998.

Gifts, Arcade (New York, NY), 1999.

Yesterday, Tomorrow: Voices from the Somali Diaspora (nonfiction), Cassell (London, England), 2000.
Links, Riverhead (New York, NY), 2004.

Also author of short stories, including "Why Dead So Soon?," 1965. Contributor to periodicals, including *Suitcase: A Journal of Transcultural Traffic.*

SIDELIGHTS: An African writer best known for novels that champion the oppressed, particularly women, Nuruddin Farah sets his plots in twentieth-century Somalia, with most of the action occurring in the capital, Mogadishu. Farah is best known for the "Variations on the Theme of an African Dictatorship" trilogy about an African dictatorship led by the fictional Major General Muhammad Siyad, referred to as the "General," and the subsequent demise of democracy in Somalia. The first volume, *Sweet and Sour Milk,* focuses on a political activist who attempts to unravel the mysterious circumstances involving the death of his twin brother. The second novel, *Sardines,* depicts life under the General's repressive regime, while also examining the social barriers that limit Somalian women and their quest for individuality and equality. The novel's central character is Medina, a young woman who, after losing her job as editor of a state-run newspaper, refuses to support the General's domestic policies. The final volume in the trilogy is *Close Sesame,* the story of an elderly man who spent many years in prison for opposing both colonial and post-revolutionary governments. When the man's son plots to overthrow the General's regime, the man attempts to stop the coup himself.

Farah often portrays women's ability to take an active part in the environment which surrounds them. Because Farah presents his women from this perspective, he is unique among African creative writers. Farah's depiction of progress made by African women in their bid for personal freedom from outdated values is typified by Medina in *Sweet and Sour Milk.* Conscious that sacrifice is indispensable in any concerted struggle against established authority, Medina, despite a privileged background, rises up against the General in a blow for the silent majority. As an active member of a revolutionary group, Medina offers counsel and protection to young students who participate in protests of the General's tyrannical form of government. Another character in the same book, Qumman, also serves as an example of Farah's

portrayal of women taking an active role in the world. A suppressed, second-class citizen of traditional Muslim culture, Qumman is the typical mother, loving, all-caring, and patient. The victim of physical abuse by her husband, Qumman lives only for her children. But despite being cast in the traditional mold, Qumman organizes the religious rituals involved with her son Soyaan's funeral while arranging for the presence of the sheikhs watching over the corpse. Though such arrangements would be common in Western culture, this clearly exemplifies the changing role of women in African society.

In his 2004 novel, *Links,* the author tells the tale of Jeeblah, who is living in New York but returns after twenty years to Somalia, both to visit his recently deceased mother's grave and to help recover a friend's child who has been abducted. Back in Somalia, Jeeblah is nearly overwhelmed by the changes in his homeland, including the presence of warlords who prey on the citizenry. Nevertheless, Jeeblah is determined to bring about the return of his friend's daughter. "Farah writes of governmental and social unrest in chilling detail that hardly seems to be fiction at all," noted Christopher Korenowsky in the *Library Journal.* Writing in *Newsweek,* Malcolm Jones called the novel a "rough-hewn art, but art it surely is." The reviewer added, "Like Joseph Conrad and Graham Greene, writers to whom he can be favorably compared, Farah poses questions that, once asked, never go away."

Though sometimes criticized for substandard stylistic and technical writing, Farah is generally acknowledged—along with Sembene Ousmane and Ayi Kwei Armah, whose female characters also possess the same vision as Farah's women—as the African writers who have done the greatest justice in championing human rights. The political tone of his novels is evident as Farah attempts to show the pressure of the Somalian regime on individual psyches, but his writings concentrate on characters who, despite the system, slowly grow as individuals. Critics have praised the uniqueness of Farah's writing. "The novels are, in the widest sense, political but are never simplistic or predictable," declared Angela Smith in *Contemporary Novelists.* "Farah is not politically naive or specifically anti-Soviet; his implicit theme is the imprisoning effect of outside intervention in Somalian life."

Farah is also the author of the nonfiction work *Yesterday, Tomorrow: Voices from the Somali Diaspora.* This book, which is based on interviews with

Somali refugees conducted between 1991 and 1998, focuses on the refugees' lives, their sufferings at the hands of various overseers, and their attempts to build new lives. "Farah's courageous and unflinchingly honest book, sparing neither himself nor his subjects, helps us to understand the experiences of all peoples forced from their homelands into places where they have to start all over again," wrote Derek Wright in *World Literature Today*. "It is recommended reading for anyone working with refugees."

BIOGRAPHICAL AND CRITICAL SOURCES:

BOOKS

Alden, Patricia, and Louis Tremaine, *Nuruddin Farah,* Twayne (New York, NY), 1999.
Contemporary Novelists, St. James Press (Detroit, MI), 1996.
Little, Kenneth, *Women and Urbanization in African Literature,* Macmillan (New York, NY), 1981.
Wright, Derek, *The Novels of Nuruddin Farah,* Bayreuth University (Germany), 1994.

PERIODICALS

African Affairs, July, 1995, Stewart Brown, "The Novels of Nuruddin Farah," p. 413.
Africa News Service, November 1, 2004, Fanuel Jongwe, "Author Farah on Afro-Politics"; November 4, 2004, Sheuneni Kurasha, "Writers Have Role in Solving Problems"; November 16, 2004, "Farah Launches Novel in Zim"; November 23, 2004, Ron Charles, review of *Links.*
American Visions, February, 2000, Jennifer Hunt, "The 'Blood in the Sun' Trilogy: Maps, Gifts and Secrets," p. 36.
Booklist, May 15, 1998, Bonnie Johnston, review of *Secrets,* p. 1594; August, 1999, Bonnie Johnston, review of *Gifts,* p. 2023; March 15, 2004, Frank Caso, review of *Links,* p. 1264.
Economist, February 13, 1999, review of *The Secret.*
Entertainment Weekly, March 26, 2004, Ben Spier, review of *Links,* p. 77.
Journal of Asian and African Studies, October, 2004, Lee Cassanelli, review of *Yesterday, Tomorrow: Voices from the Somali Diaspora,* p. 484.
Kirkus Reviews, February 15, 2004, review of *Links,* p. 146.

Library Journal, May 1, 1998, Lisa Rohrbaugh, review of *Secrets,* p. 136; August, 1999, Ellen Flexman, reviews of *Maps,* and *Gifts,* p. 138; April 1, 2004, Christopher Korenowsky, review of *Links,* p. 120.
Newsweek, April 19, 2004, Malcolm Jones, review of *Links,* p. 65.
Newsweek International, April 19, 2004, Malcolm Jones, review of *Links,* p. 103.
Publishers Weekly, March 30, 1998, review of *Secrets,* p. 68; June 28, 1999, reviews of *Maps* and *Gifts,* pp. 52-53; August 23, 1999, Stephen Gray, "Nuruddin Farah: The Novelist and the Nomad," interview with Farah, p. 28; March 1, 2004, review of *Links,* p. 48.
Research in African Literature, spring, 2000, John C. Hawley, review of *Nuruddin Farah,* p. 198, Jacqueline Bardolph, "On Nuruddin Farah," p. 119; spring, 2005, Julia Praud, "Beyond Empire and Nation: Postnational Arguments in the Fiction of Nuruddin Farah and B. Kojo Laing," p. 130.
World Literature Today, autumn, 1994, Reed Way Dasenbrock, "The Novels of Nuruddin Farah," p. 868; autumn, 1998, Ngigi wa Thiong'o, "Nuruddin Farah: A Statement of Nomination to the 1998 Neustadt Jury," p. 715, "Chronology (Nuruddin Farah)," p. 716, "Selected Bibliography (Nuruddin Farah)," p. 723, Jacqueline Bardolph, "Brothers and Sisters in Nuruddin Farah's Two Trilogies," p. 727, Charles Sugnet, "Nuruddin Farah's Maps: Deterritorialization and 'The Postmodern,'" p. 739, and Reed Way Dasenbrock, "Nuruddin Farah: A Tale of Two Trilogies," p. 747; summer, 2000, Derek Wright, review of *Yesterday, Tomorrow: Voices from the Somali Diaspora,* p. 574, and Charlie Sugnet, review of *Nuruddin Farah,* p. 574.

ONLINE

Pegasos, http://www.kirjasto.sci.fi/ (September 7, 2005), biographical information on Farah.*

*   *   *

FARBER, Daniel A. 1950-

PERSONAL: Born July 16, 1950, in Chicago, IL; married Dianne S. Farber, March 25, 1972; children: Joseph, Sonia, Nora. *Education:* University of Illinois at Urbana-Champaign, B.A. (with high honors), 1971, M.A., 1972, J.D. (summa cum laude), 1975.

ADDRESSES: Home—25 E. Minnehaha Pkwy., Minneapolis, MN 55419. *Office*—University of California—Berkeley, School of Law, Boalt Hall, Rm. 894, Berkeley, CA 94270-7200; fax: 510-642-3728. *E-mail*—dfarber@law.berkeley.edu.

CAREER: Law clerk to Judge Philip W. Tone of U.S. Court of Appeals for the Seventh Circuit, 1975-76, and to Justice John Paul Stevens of the U.S. Supreme Court, 1976-77; Sidley & Austin, Washington, DC, associate, 1977-78; University of Illinois at Urbana-Champaign, assistant professor of law, 1978-81; University of Minnesota—Twin Cities, Minneapolis, associate professor, 1981-83, professor of law, 1983—, Julius E. Davis Professor of Law, 1983-84, Henry J. Fletcher Professor of Law, 1987, McKnight Presidential Professor of Public Law, 2000; University of California, Berkeley, Sho Sato professor of law, director of Environmental Law Program. Visiting professor at Stanford University, 1987-88, and at the University of Chicago Law School.

Also founder of the journal *Constitutional Commentary;* member of American Law Institute; member of advisory board of State and Local Legal Center, Washington, DC.

MEMBER: Association of American Law Schools (chair of contracts section, 1984; member of executive committee, 1987), American Economic Association.

WRITINGS:

(With Roger W. Findley) *Environmental Law: Cases and Materials,* West Publishing (St. Paul, MN), 1981, supplement, 1983, 2nd edition, 1985, supplement, 1988, also published as *Cases and Materials on Environmental Law,* West Publishing (St. Paul, MN), 1991, 1991 edition reprinted, Thomson/West (St. Paul, MN), 2005.

(With Roger W. Findley) *Environmental Law in a Nutshell,* West Publishing (St. Paul, MN), 1983, 5th edition, Thomson/West (St. Paul, MN), 2004.

(Contributor) P. Hay and M. Hoeflich, editors, *Essays on the Law of Property and Legal Education, in Honor of John E. Cribbet,* University of Illinois Press (Champaign, IL), 1988.

(With Suzanna Sherry) *A History of the American Constitution,* West Publishing (St. Paul, MN), 1990.

(With Philip P. Frickey) *Law and Public Choice: A Critical Introduction,* University of Chicago Press (Chicago, IL), 1991.

(With William N. Eskridge, Jr. and Philip P. Frickey) *Cases and Materials on Constitutional Law: Themes for the Constitution's Third Century,* West Publishing (St. Paul, MN), 1993.

(With Suzanna Sherry) *Beyond All Reason: The Radical Assault on Truth in American Law,* Oxford University Press (New York, NY), 1997.

The First Amendment, Foundation Press (New York, NY), 1998.

Eco-Pragmatism: Making Sensible Environmental Decisions in an Uncertain World, University of Chicago Press (Chicago, IL), 1999.

(With Suzanna Sherry) *Desperately Seeking Certainty: The Misguided Quest for Constitutional Foundations,* University of Chicago Press (Chicago, IL), 2002.

Lincoln's Constitution, University of Chicago Press (Chicago, IL), 2003.

Also contributor to *Sociological Concepts: A Literary Reader,* edited by R. Hardet, R. Cullen, and L. Hardet, 1986, and to *Research in Social Problems and Public Policy,* edited by M. Lewis and J. Miller, 1987. Contributor of articles and reviews to periodicals and law journals, including *Harvard Journal of Law and Public Policy, Washington Monthly,* and the *New Republic.* Past editor in chief of *University of Illinois Law Journal;* editor of Article Section, *Constitutional Commentary;* associate editor of *Sociological Perspectives.*

SIDELIGHTS: Daniel A. Farber has authored or coauthored numerous books focusing on law, including environmental and constitutional law, which are the author's primary areas of interest. In *Beyond All Reason: The Radical Assault on Truth in American Law,* which Farber coauthored with Suzanna Sherry, the authors discuss the legal scholarship surrounding the extreme law theories known as "radical multiculturism." According to the authors, purveyors of "radical multiculturism" essentially believe that a just society is impossible because there is no such thing as objective reality or truth. People that believe in this concept also state that any idea of objective truth or reality are merely used by those in power, which are white males, to keep their high-status positions. One of the results of such thinking is the belief that when minorities are taken to trial for a crime, they are actually victims of social discrimination whether they are guilty or not. Writing in *Commentary,* Heather MacDonald remarked that the authors "show in their new book, this movement is not just another expression of grievance politics. Rather it is a campaign against the very ideas that make possible the rule of law." In a review in the *New Republic,* Richard A. Posner called *Beyond All Reason* "a fine book, a work of intelligence and courage that will alter the terms of debate in academic law." *Constitutional Commentary* contributor Roderick M. Hills, Jr., called the book "a useful, well-written description of an unpromising trend in the legal academy."

The First Amendment provides a look at freedom of speech and religion in the United States and how the courts have analyzed this amendment over the years. The author also discusses how the amendment has worked in American society, exploring the complex doctrine and the many debates that have arisen around it, such as debates over hate speech and pornography. Writing in *Constitutional Commentary,* Alan E. Brownstein called the book "a concise, sophisticated, and probing text," adding: "I liked the book . . . [and] learned quite a bit in reading it."

In *Eco-Pragmatism: Making Sensible Environmental Decisions in an Uncertain World,* Farber sets out his ideas for a moderate, or pragmatic, approach for dealing with environmental problems and making decisions. "Farber uses key problems involved in making hard environmental decisions as his organizational tools," wrote Lynda L. Butler in *Ethics.* "Those problems include deciding how to make trade-offs between conflicting values, deciding how to deal with the time dimension of environmental problems, and deciding how to respond to uncertainty about risk." Butler went on to note that the book "can have a profound impact on the world of environmental decision making if readers recognize the masterful job Farber does of integrating theory and practice." Noting that the book "rewards the reader in many different ways," *Michigan Law Review* contributor Christopher H. Schroeder also wrote: "The book contains valuable discussions of . . . problems offering important insights into dealing with them." In a review in the *Yale Law Journal,* Richard A. Epstein commented that "the book does not fall prey to any of the excesses of environmental zealotry." Gilbert Whittemore, writing in the *Quarterly Review of Biology,* noted: "This is an

excellent introduction to the deeper issues of environmental poicy."

The author once again collaborated with Sherry to write about modern legal theorists' attempt to create a grand unified theory of constitutional interpretation. In their book *Desperately Seeking Certainty: The Misguided Quest for Constitutional Foundations,* the authors discuss the unconventional constitutional theories of several legal commentators and set forth their views of how problematic these theories are. Although he disagreed with some of the author's conclusions, Steven D. Smith, writing in *Constitutional Commentary,* commented: "The book's presentation of this . . . diagnosis is perceptive, good-natured, steadfastly (and even ostentatiously) commonsensical, sometimes entertaining, often insightful." *New York Times Book Review* contributor Garrett Epps wrote that the book "is at its best on the attack; the authors' criticisms are clear, sensitive and usually fair."

In his book *Lincoln's Constitution,* Farber examines the motivation and constitutionality of a series of decisions made by President Abraham Lincoln that seemed to defy the Constitution, including jailing dissidents, shutting down newspapers, and rescinding habeas corpus. The author argues that Lincoln's decisions had a basis in the Constitution and were necessary. Thomas W. McShane, writing in *Parameters,* noted, "Farber reviews the big themes underlying the Civil War: the nature of sovereignty; secession; presidential power; the nature of individual rights; and the rule of law." McShane went on to write: "This book illuminates current debates. Farber blends historical research with a pragmatic view of the Constitution, written in language non-lawyers will understand." *Michigan Law Review* contributor Craig S. Lerner noted that "Farber is generally balanced in his presentation of conflicting views, and measured and fair in his conclusions." Writing in the *New York Times Book Review,* Richard A. Posner commented: "Farber has written a timely and important book, which should provoke fruitful discussion of enduring issues of civil liberties and judicial philosophy."

Farber told *CA:* "When Roger Findley and I published our first environmental law book in 1981, Ronald Reagan had just been elected president. Friends told us that the field was dead and the book would only be useful to historians. But today environmental law is stronger than ever."

BIOGRAPHICAL AND CRITICAL SOURCES:

PERIODICALS

Commentary, October, 1997, Heather MacDonald, review of *Beyond All Reason: The Radical Assault on Truth in American Law,* p. 64.

Constitutional Commentary, summer, 1990, William M. Wiecek, review of *A History of the American Constitution,* pp. 441-447; summer, 1991, Herbert Hovenkamp, review of *Law and Public Choice: A Critical Introduction,* pp. 470-479; spring, 1998, Roderick M. Hills, Jr., review of *Beyond All Reason,* pp. 185-208; spring, 1999, Alan E. Brownstein, review of *The First Amendment,* p. 101; summer, 2002, Steven D. Smith, review of *Desperately Seeking Certainty: The Misguided Quest for Constitutional Foundations* p. 523; winter, 2003, Jim Chen, "Brilliance Remembered," testimonial to author, p. 717.

Ethics, January, 2001, Lynda L. Butler, review of *Eco-Pragmatism: Making Sensible Environmental Decisions in an Uncertain World,* p. 407.

Insight on the News, February 16, 1998, David Wagner, review of *Beyond All Reason,* p. 42.

Journal of the American Planning Association, spring, 2000, Rutherford H. Platt, review of *Eco-Pragmatism,* p. 212.

Michigan Law Review, May, 1992, William Dubinsky, review of *Law and Public Choice,* pp. 1512-1519; May, 1998, Daria Roithmayr, review of *Beyond All Reason,* pp. 1658-1684; May, 2000, Christopher H. Schroeder, review of *Eco-Pragmatism,* p. 1876; May, 2004, Craig S. Lerner, review of *Lincoln's Constitution,* p. 1263.

National Review, December 8, 1997, Mark Miller, review of *Beyond All Reason,* p. 52.

New Criterion, May, 1998, Marc M. Arkin, review of *Beyond All Reason,* p. 65.

New Republic, October 13, 1997, Richard A. Posner, October 13, 1997, review of *Beyond All Reason,* p. 40.

New York Times Book Review, August 25, 2002, Garrett Epps, review of *Desperately Seeking Certainty,* p. 17; August 24, 2003, review of *Lincoln's Constitution,* p. 10.

Parameters, autumn, 2004, Thomas W. McShane, review of *Lincoln's Constitution,* p. 160.

Publishers Weekly, April 26, 1999, review of *Eco-Pragmatism,* p. 71.

Quarterly Review of Biology, March, 2002, Gilbert Whittemore, review of *Eco-Pragmatism,* p. 88.

Yale Law Journal, May, 2000, Richard A. Epstein, review of *Eco-Pragmatism,* p. 1639.

ONLINE

University of California—Berkeley, School of Law Web site, http://www.law.berkeley.edu/ (November 3, 2005), faculty profile of author.*

*   *   *

FINCHLER, Judy 1943-

PERSONAL: Born March 28, 1943, in Paterson, NJ; daughter of Sidney (a postal worker) and Harriet (a teacher; maiden name, Schnittlich) Gold; married Jerome Finchler (an accountant), August 11, 1963; children: Todd, Lauren Finchler Fitch. *Education:* Montclair State University, B.A., 1964; William Paterson College of New Jersey, elementary school certification; Kean College of New Jersey, teacher-librarian certification. *Politics:* Independent. *Religion:* Jewish.

ADDRESSES: Home—23 Trouville Dr., Parsippany, NJ 07054. *E-mail*—finchler@intac.com.

CAREER: Educator, librarian, writer. School teacher in Paterson, NJ, 1964-67; supplemental instructor in Parsippany, NJ, 1977-81; Paterson Board of Education, teacher, 1981-86, teacher-librarian, 1986-2004.

MEMBER: National Education Association, New Jersey Education Association, Paterson Educational Association.

AWARDS, HONORS: Outstanding Service Award, Department of Instructional Services, Paterson Public Schools, 1994.

WRITINGS:

Miss Malarkey Doesn't Live in Room 10, illustrated by Kevin O'Malley, Walker (New York, NY), 1995.

Miss Malarkey Won't Be in Today, illustrated by Kevin O'Malley, Walker (New York, NY), 2000.

Testing Miss Malarkey, illustrated by Kevin O'Malley, Walker (New York, NY), 2000.

You're a Good Sport, Miss Malarkey, illustrated by Kevin O'Malley, Walker (New York, NY), 2002.

Miss Malarkey's Field Trip, illustrated by Kevin O'Malley, Walker (New York, NY), 2004.

Miss Malarkey Leaves No Child Behind, illustrated by Kevin O'Malley, Walker (New York, NY), 2006.

SIDELIGHTS: Judy Finchler's first book, *Miss Malarkey Doesn't Live in Room 10,* features a child narrator whose image of his teacher's life outside of school is dashed when she moves into his own apartment building. "Finchler's lively story destroys a typical misconception in wonderfully comic fashion, with an unnamed narrator trying to fit his teacher's after-hours life neatly into his own childhood frame of reference," noted *Booklist* reviewer Stephanie Zvirin. *School Library Journal* contributor Virginia Opocensky also offered a favorable assessment of *Miss Malarkey,* calling the book "an entertaining romp that's sure to elicit lots of chuckles."

In Finchler's *Miss Malarkey Won't Be in Today,* the teacher lets her imagination run away with her. When Miss Malarkey has to call in sick because she has the flu, she begins to worry about her class, the substitute teachers they might get to replace her, and how the students might misbehave in response. Wearing only a robe and slippers, she rushes off to school, only to find that everything is fine. Her students insist she go to the school nurse's office. While reviewers of *Miss Malarkey Won't Be in Today* thought the story was humorous, some of them questioned the negative portrayal of substitute teachers. For example, a *Publishers Weekly* contributor remarked that the story does "a great disservice to fill-in instructors." However, April Judge wrote in *Booklist* that the book could be used as an instructional tool for students "who may have more experience taking advantage of their substitute teachers," concluding that Finchler's book is a "robust story."

Students and parents will likely appreciate the situation in *Testing Miss Malarkey,* which is about standardized school tests. The entire school community is on edge as the big "Instructional Performance Through Understanding" examination approaches. Teachers drill their classes incessantly, and even the parents join in by quizzing their sons and daughters in their free time. As for Miss Malarkey, she is on the verge of becoming a nervous wreck, while her students, on the other hand, do not seem concerned in the least. In the end, all of the preparation pays off and the children all do well. *School Library Journal* critic Kate McClelland, ironically, found this conclusion to be a drawback to the story, saying that the author missed an opportunity to comment on the mass hysteria surrounding some standardized school tests. McClelland concluded that whether or not adult readers appreciate *Testing Miss Malarkey* depends on whether they feel "the laughs are at the expense of the testing process, society, or the teachers themselves." Nevertheless, *Booklist* reviewer Marta Segal concluded that "listeners will enjoy the silly humor and joyful, creative illustrations."

Finchler tackles another modern problem in schools with *You're a Good Sport, Miss Malarkey.* The bad behavior of parents attending school sporting events has become an increasing concern in recent years, and in this book the author points out just how this can have a negative effect on children's enjoyment of sport. Miss Malarkey takes on the role of soccer coach, and there is a great deal of silly fun as she tries to get her students organized for their games. But the parents in the stands put a damper on their fun by becoming increasingly loud and obnoxious, until, finally, Miss Malarkey cannot take it anymore and yells, "Are you people crazy?" The soccer game is cancelled, and the league is reorganized into a noncompetitive event so that children can just focus on having a good time and getting some exercise. Parents in the crowd are all given lollipops to enjoy. While reviewers appreciated the subject matter of *You're a Good Sport, Miss Malarkey,* Grace Oliff, writing in the *School Library Journal,* was disappointed that Malarkey resorts to screaming back at the parents "rather than trying to take a more reasoned approach." Still, critics generally felt that this fourth installment in the series is another humorous romp for readers. *Booklist* contributor Shelley Townsend-Hudson added that Kevin O'Malley's "lively illustrations . . . leaven a story about a subject of increasing concern to both parents and kids."

Finchler once commented: "I've always loved writing. Whether in a story, poem, letter, or even a grant proposal, words have always been my dearest friends. Finding the best word, the most appropriate phrase, arranging, rearranging, and expressing my ideas are all deeply satisfying. The experience of seeing my words in print in bookstores and libraries has greatly surpassed even what I envisioned it to be.

"As a lover of the written word, I am also a reader," Finchler once said. "It's hard to identify where one skill ends and the other begins. That is what I try to develop in my students: reading is so much more than what you have to do in school. A book is a lifelong companion that will enrich your life. The words you read become a part of you and will in some way be given back in what you write."

BIOGRAPHICAL AND CRITICAL SOURCES:

BOOKS

Finchler, Judy, *You're a Good Sport, Miss Malarkey,* illustrated by Kevin O'Malley, Walker (New York, NY), 2002.

PERIODICALS

Booklist, November 15, 1995, Stephanie Zvirin, review of *Miss Malarkey Doesn't Live in Room 10,* p. 563; September 1, 1998, April Judge, review of *Miss Malarkey Won't Be in Today,* p. 126; October 1, 2000, Marta Segal, review of *Testing Miss Malarkey,* p. 345; October 15, 2002, Shelley Townsend-Hudson, review of *You're a Good Sport, Miss Malarkey,* p. 411; September 15, 2004, Ilene Cooper, review of *Miss Malarkey's Field Trip,* p. 248.
Kirkus Reviews, August 15, 1995; July 1, 2004, review of *Miss Malarkey's Field Trip,* p. 628.
New York Times Book Review, March 11, 2001, review of *Testing Miss Malarkey,* p. 26.
Publishers Weekly, August 14, 1995, review of *Miss Malarkey Doesn't Live in Room 10,* p. 83; September 14, 1998, review of *Miss Malarkey Won't Be in Today,* p. 68; October 2, 2000, review of *Miss Malarkey Won't Be in Today,* p. 83; October 7, 2002, "Encore Performance," p. 75.
School Library Journal, December, 1995, Virginia Opocensky, review of *Miss Malarkey Doesn't Live in Room 10,* p. 80; October, 1998, Tom S. Hurlburt, review of *Miss Malarkey Won't Be in Today,* p. 98; October, 2000, Kate McClelland, review of *Test-*

ing Miss Malarkey, p. 124; October, 2002, Grace Oliff, review of *You're a Good Sport, Miss Malarkey,* p. 105; November, 2004, Grace Oliff, review of *Miss Malarkey's Field Trip,* p. 103.*

*   *   *

FINKELSTEIN, Norman G. 1953-

PERSONAL: Born December 8, 1953, in New York, NY; son of Harry and Maryla (Husyt) Finkelstein. *Education:* State University of New York— Binghamton, B.A., 1974; attended Ecole Pratique des Hautes Etudes, Paris, France, 1979; Princeton University, M.A., 1980, Ph.D., 1988.

ADDRESSES: Office—DePaul University, 990 W. Fullerton, Room 2217, Chicago, IL 60604. *E-mail*— normangf@hotmail.com.

CAREER: Rutgers University, New Brunswick, NJ, adjunct lecturer in international relations, 1977-78; Brooklyn College of the City University of New York, Brooklyn, NY, adjunct assistant professor of international relations and political theory, 1988-91; Hunter College of the City University of New York, New York, NY, adjunct associate professor of political theory, 1992-2001; New York University, New York, NY, adjunct associate professor of political science, 1992-2001; DePaul University, Chicago, IL, visiting professor, 2001-03, assistant professor of political science, 2003—.

MEMBER: Phi Beta Kappa.

AWARDS, HONORS: Excellence in Teaching Award, New York University, 1995; Golden Key National Honor Society Teaching Award, 2000; Fulbright Senior Specialist, 2002.

WRITINGS:

(Translator) Samir Amin, *The Future of Maoism,* Monthly Review Press (New York, NY), 1983.
Image and Reality of the Israel Palestine Conflict, Verso (New York, NY), 1995.

The Rise and Fall of Palestine: A Personal Account of the Intifada Years, University of Minnesota Press (Minneapolis, MN), 1996.

(With Ruth Bettina Birn) *A Nation on Trial: The Goldhagen Thesis and Historical Truth,* Holt (New York, NY), 1998.

The Holocaust Industry: Reflections on the Exploitation of Jewish Suffering, Verso (New York, NY), 2000.

Beyond Chutzpah: On the Misuse of Anti-Semitism and the Abuse of History, University of California Press (Berkeley, CA), 2005.

Also contributor to books, including *Blaming the Victims,* edited by Edward Said and Christopher Hitchens, Verso (New York, NY), 1988; and *Palestinian Refugees and Their Right of Return,* edited by Naseer Aruri, Pluto Press (London, England), 2001. Contributor to periodicals, including *Journal of Palestine Studies, New Left Review, Index on Censorship, London Review of Books, Christian Science Monitor, Middle East Report, Tikkun,* and *Al Ahram Weekly.*

SIDELIGHTS: Norman G. Finkelstein has built a reputation as a controversial figure on the topics of Zionism, Israeli-Palestinian relationships, and the Holocaust. Although some have labeled him a "self-hating Jew" for criticizing Israel's political policies and the way, as he claims, some Jewish organizations use the Holocaust to justify raising money for selfish purposes, Finkelstein is obdurate when he asserts that he is not dishonoring the lives of those who died during World War II. As he once told *CA:* "My mother and father were both survivors of the Warsaw Ghetto and the Nazi death camps. My main concern is upholding justice and truth. This means defending the oppressed (hence my two books documenting Israeli wrongs against the Palestinians) and opposing lies (hence my book *A Nation on Trial,* which documents that Daniel Jonah Goldhagen's much-acclaimed study, *Hitler's Willing Executioners,* is effectively a fraud)."

Finkelstein first made news with his book *Image and Reality of the Israel Palestine Conflict,* which was written in direct response to the best-selling, National Jewish Book Award-winning work by Joan Peters, *From Time Immemorial.* Peters' book claimed that the Arab peoples who were forced out of Palestine when it became the state of Israel had only been there since the nineteenth century, and that they, therefore, could not claim that they were indigenous to that land. Peters' theories were widely praised by book critics and the Jewish community as a way to justify Israel's treatment of the Palestinians. However, in *Image and Reality of the Israel Palestine Conflict,* Finkelstein suggested that *From Time Immemorial* was replete with flawed and misleading research. "Finkelstein exposed Peters's work as a tangle of fudged quotations, miscalculations, and distortions worthy of a professional propagandist," observed Eyal Press in the *Progressive.* Furthermore, as Press explained, the author exposes "what he sees as Zionism's basic incompatibility with democratic values. As Finkelstein shows, Zionism emerged as a subspecies of European romantic nationalism grounded in the notion that the state, and hence citizenship, belongs to one group. That is why Israel has no written constitution outlining civil rights for Jews and non-Jews."

Finkelstein also asserts in his book that the Holocaust and the oppression of the Jews by the Nazis do not justify Israeli oppression of and discrimination against the Palestinians. Finally, the author concludes that the on-again, off-again peace process in the Middle East actually aids the Zionist goal of separating the Arabs from the Jews, and that Israel, contrary to apologists such as Israeli historian Benny Morris, is actually orchestrating an organized plan to systematically rid itself of any significant Arab presence within its borders. Despite using facts to back up his attack on Peters, Finkelstein's theories were largely dismissed in America, where his book was barely reviewed. However, *Foreign Affairs* critic William B. Quandt felt that "this thoroughly documented book is guaranteed to stimulate and provoke."

To research his books, Finkelstein does not rely on printed documentation alone. He has made repeated trips to Palestinian towns in areas occupied by Israel, finding living conditions there, in his opinion, appalling. He wrote about these people in his second book, *The Rise and Fall of Palestine: A Personal Account of the Intifada Years.* Even after this work's publication, he continues to travel to the Middle East. "I stay in close touch with the families of whom I write in the book," he told Don Atapattu in a *Counterpunch* interview. "When I first went it was a moral test of the values that are meaningful to me, and I wanted to see if I could bridge the chasm between a Jew and a Palestinian based upon our common humanity and our shared commitment to justice and decency." Finkelstein found that the Palestinians he met were hardworking, good people who only wished to enjoy life and be afforded life's basic necessities. He was surprised when they accepted him, a Jew, into their homes openly. Finkelstein feels that accords such as the one reached in Oslo, Norway, in 1993 have only served to make the situation worse for Palestinians like those he has met, and events such as the intifadas can be seen as justified (he compares them to rebellions similar to the Warsaw ghetto uprising of Jews against the Germans). Although a *Publishers Weekly* reviewer felt that the author could, at times, be "sententious," the critic added that Finkelstein "brings a unique perspective to his subject."

Finkelstein's 1998 work, *A Nation on Trial: The Goldhagen Thesis and Historical Truth,* written with Ruth Bettina Birn, offers counter arguments to Daniel Goldhagen's *Hitler's Willing Executioners: Ordinary Germans and the Holocaust.* That book argued that all Germans shared responsibility for the persecution of the Jews during the Nazi regime. Finkelstein refuted this idea, as he explained to Atapattu: "In the case of Germany you were dealing with a fascist, terrorist state in which the population had, relatively speaking, no say in the making of policy and no say in the crimes committed." The authors received some negative feedback against their position. For example, Stanley Hoffmann wrote in *Foreign Affairs* that the authors of *A Nation on Trial* "repeatedly distort" Goldhagen's arguments. However, compared to Finkelstein's next book, reaction to *A Nation on Trial* was relatively meek.

With the 2000 release of *The Holocaust Industry: Reflections on the Exploitation of Jewish Suffering,* Finkelstein boldly maintains that the Jewish elite of today exploits the tragedy of the Holocaust for their own personal and political gain. It was for this position that many accused Finkelstein of being a "self-hating Jew" and anti-Semite. Given that his own parents lived through the Holocaust, the author contends that such declarations are patently ridiculous. Not to be misunderstood, the author asserts that the Jewish elite (he includes people such as those who run the World Jewish Congress and well-known Holocaust survivor Elie Wiesel) insist that the Holocaust was a unique historical event and not comparable to any other genocides that have occurred at any other time. They then exploit this position by extracting funds from governments, banks, and non-profit organizations in compensation while giving little in return to actual Holocaust survivors who might need the money. "They steal," Finkelstein said in his interview with Atapattu, "and I do use the word with intent. Ninety-five percent of the monies earmarked for victims of Nazi persecution [is kept by these organizations], and then [they] throw you a few crumbs while telling you to be grateful."

Finkelstein further maintained that recent efforts to extract money from Swiss banks and the German government for compensation is all a scam (for example, he says evidence shows that there is no hidden Nazi money in secret Swiss bank accounts). The Israeli government, too, uses the international community's guilt over the Holocaust as an excuse "to exempt Israel from criticism of its own oppressive treatment of the Palestinians," as Adam Newey explained in the *New Statesman.* According to Finkelstein's book: "Rationally comprehending The Holocaust amounts, in [Elie Wiesel's] view, to denying it. For rationality denies The Holocaust's uniqueness and mystery. And to compare The Holocaust with the sufferings of others constitutes, for Wiesel, a 'total betrayal of Jewish history.'" The author points out that many other people, including millions of Gypsies and those suffering from handicaps, were also executed by the Nazis, not to mention the many other genocides that have been perpetrated around the world.

In his interview with Atapattu, Finkelstein characterizes the attitude of the Jewish elite and their sympathizers this way: "Nothing compares to the Jews. Everything that the Jews endure, everything that the Jews achieve, is special, because we're the 'chosen people,' so don't compare us with garbage like the Tasmanian savages (the entire indigenous population of Tasmania were exterminated under British colonial rule), or don't compare us with the Gypsies. . . . You have to understand that the great tragedy of the Second World War was not that Jews per se were killed, but such a *cultured* people were killed—if you kill uncultured people, who cares?" Although he was castigated by many of his fellow Jews, as well as others in the liberal community, some reviewers asserted that his arguments have merit. Newey, for example, concluded that "this is . . . a lucid, provocative and passionate book. Anyone with an open mind and an interest in the subject should ignore the critical brickbats and read what Finkelstein has to say." An *Economist* reviewer, while maintaining that the author "exaggerates Israel's failings" and that he "is obsessive, and he rants," still felt that "his basic argument that memories of the Holocaust are being debased is serious and should be given its due."

BIOGRAPHICAL AND CRITICAL SOURCES:

BOOKS

Finkelstein, Norman G., *The Holocaust Industry: Reflections on the Exploitation of Jewish Suffering,* Verso (New York, NY), 2000.

PERIODICALS

Booklist, October 15, 2005, Bryce Christensen, review of *Beyond Chutzpah: On the Misuse of Anti-Semitism and the Abuse of History,* p. 9.
Contemporary Review, December, 2000, review of *The Holocaust Industry: Reflections on the Exploitation of Jewish Suffering,* p. 381.
Counterpunch, December 13, 2001, Don Atapattu, "A Conversation with Professor Norman Finkelstein: How to Lose Friends and Alienate People."
Economist, August 5, 2000, "Explosive Charges," p. 79.
Foreign Affairs, May-June, 1996, William B. Quandt, review of *Image and Reality of the Israel Palestine Conflict,* p. 152; July-August, 1998, Stanley Hoffmann, review of *A Nation on Trial: The Goldhagen Thesis and Historical Truth,* p. 128.
New Statesman, July 31, 2000, Adam Newey, "The One and Only," p. 42.
Progressive, April, 1996, Eyal Press, review of *Image and Reality of the Israel Palestine Conflict,* p. 42.
Publishers Weekly, November 11, 1996, review of *The Rise and Fall of Palestine: A Personal Account of the Intifada Years,* p. 70.
Race and Class, January-March, 1997, Edna Homa Hunt, review of *Image and Reality of the Israel Palestine Conflict,* p. 104.
Washington Report on Middle East Affairs, November, 2005, Sara Powell, review of *Beyond Chutzpah,* p. 42.

ONLINE

Norman G. Finkelstein Official Web Site, http://www.normanfinkelstein.com (February 7, 2002).*

FINNEY, Patricia 1958-
(P.F. Chisholm)

PERSONAL: Born May 12, 1958, in London, England; daughter of Jarlath John (an attorney) and Daisy (an attorney; maiden name, Veszy) Finney; married; children: three. *Education:* Wadham College, Oxford, B.A. (with honors), 1980. *Politics:* "Right-wing." *Religion:* Roman Catholic. *Hobbies and other interests:* Science, karate, embroidery, folk music.

ADDRESSES: Home—Spain. *Agent*—McIntosh & Otis, Inc., 475 Fifth Ave., New York, NY 10017. *E-mail*—patricia@patricia-finney.co.uk.

CAREER: Writer, 1977—.

AWARDS, HONORS: David Higham Award, David Higham Associates Literary Agency, 1977, for *A Shadow of Gulls;* Edgar Allan Poe Award nomination, Mystery Writers of America, 2005, for *Assassin.*

WRITINGS:

FOR CHILDREN

I, Jack, illustrated by Peter Bailey, Corgi Yearling (London, England), 2000, HarperCollins (New York, NY), 2004.
Jack and Police Dog Rebel, illustrated by Peter Bailey, Corgi Yearling (London, England), 2002.

"LADY GRACE MYSTERIES"; HISTORICAL FICTION; FOR YOUNG ADULTS

Assassin, Delacorte Press (New York, NY), 2004.
Betrayal, Delacorte Press (New York, NY), 2004.
Deception, Delacorte Press (New York, NY), 2005.

"DAVID BECKET AND SIMON AMES" SERIES; HISTORICAL FICTION; FOR ADULTS

Firedrake's Eye, St. Martin's (New York, NY), 1992.
Unicorn's Blood, Picador (New York, NY), 1998.
Gloriana's Torch, St. Martin's Press (New York, NY), 2003.

"SIR ROBERT CAREY MYSTERIES"; AS P.F. CHISHOLM; FOR ADULTS

A Famine of Horses, Hodder and Stoughton (London, England), 1994.

A Season of Knives, Hodder and Stoughton (London, England), 1995.

A Surfeit of Guns, Hodder and Stoughton (London, England), 1996.

A Plague of Angels, Hodder and Stoughton (London, England), 1998, with introduction by Diana Gabaldon, Poisoned Pen Press (Scottsdale, AZ), 2000.

OTHER

A Shadow of Gulls ("Lugh Mac Romain" series; historical fiction), Putnam (New York, NY), 1977.

The Flood (radio play), broadcast by British Broadcasting Corporation (BBC) Radio, 1977.

The Crow Goddess ("Lugh Mac Romain" series; historical fiction), Putnam (New York, NY), 1978.

Author of television preview column for London *Evening Standard;* author of unproduced screenplay *Saint Bridget.* Contributor of articles and stories to magazines and newspapers.

WORK IN PROGRESS: Jack and Old Chap, a sequel to *Jack and Police Dog Rebel;* "Reykiki," a fantasy trilogy for children; *Pushing a Pea up Your Nose,* a contemporary love story; *The Durable Fire,* an historical novel; *Queen's Shade,* a film script; and *A Quarrell of Lawyers,* a sequel to *A Plague of Angels.*

SIDELIGHTS: British-born writer Patricia Finney was only seventeen years old when she completed her first novel, *A Shadow of Gulls.* Set in second-century Ireland, the book is based on the Ulster cycle of Celtic hero tales. The hero of the story is Lugh the Harper, a warrior who participates in many bloody battles. In *The Crow Goddess* Finney continues the saga of Lugh the Harper and his adventures in ancient Ireland.

Finney has continued to write historical fiction, for both adults and young adults. Her adult series include the "David Becket and Simon Ames" series, about a pair of spies in the service of Queen Elizabeth I; and—

under the pseudonym P.F. Chisholm—the "Sir Robert Carey Mysteries," based on an actual, historical figure who lived in England in the late sixteenth century. Finney's young-adult series, the "Lady Grace Mysteries" are set in the same time period. Their protagonist, Lady Grace Cavendish, is a teenaged maid of honor to Queen Elizabeth I. The books are all written as entries in Lady Grace's journal, called a "day-booke" in the story's Renaissance parlance. In the first book in the series, *Assassin,* the queen arranges several suitors for the orphaned Lady Grace, and the girl must choose between them. Immediately after she does, at a regal St. Valentine's Day ball, one of the men Grace has rejected is found stabbed to death, and the man she chose is accused of being the murderer. Lady Grace believes that the man, Lord Robert Radcliffe, has been wrongly accused, and she is determined to investigate and exonerate him. "Action makes the story a page-turner," Cheri Dobbs wrote in the *School Library Journal,* "but Lady Grace's wit and personality are what readers will really enjoy." *BookLoons.com* contributor J.A. Kaszuba Locke also praised the tale, calling it "a sparkling combination of mystery and history, with surprising sidesteps, excellent momentum, and likable characters."

Lady Grace and her fellow sleuths Masou (a court acrobat and juggler) and Ellie (a laundry maid) return to investigate more strange happenings in *Betrayal* and *Conspiracy.* In the former title Lady Sarah Bartelmy, a maid of honor to the queen, disappears. She has eloped with Captain Francis Drake, according to a letter to the queen that is seemingly from Lady Sarah, but Lady Grace is suspicious. Disguised as a young man, she goes with Masou to Drake's ship to investigate and the two sleuths accidentally become stowaways. "Packed with grand adventure and frequent plot twists," according to a reviewer in *Looking GlassReview.com, Betrayal* "will delight those who relish tales of great deeds, foiled plots, and seafaring exploits."

Conspiracy takes place during the summer months, as Queen Elizabeth and her entourage travel throughout England visiting the manors of various nobles. Her majesty nearly falls victim to several potentially fatal accidents on this "progress," as the journey is called, and Lady Grace suspects a conspiracy against the controversial monarch. A reviewer for *Kidsreads.com* dubbed *Conspiracy* "not only a terrific read but also a fascinating and fun history lesson" due to Finney's inclusion of many details about life in the Elizabethan court.

Finney's novels about a big yellow Labrador dog named Jack are in a very different vein from her other works. The first book in this series, *I, Jack,* concerns the mutt's puppy love for Petra, a neighboring dog, and the difficulties the pair face when Petra has puppies. The book is written in Jack's voice, and the dog's "limited understanding of the human world and his funny names for things provide some droll humor," commented a *Kirkus Reviews* contributor. "Jack's sincere attempts to make sense of what people are telling him are particularly funny," wrote *School Library Journal* reviewer James K. Irwin. As *Booklist* contributor Michael Cart noted, additional amusement appears in the form of "acid commentary" provided by three cats and transcribed in the book's footnotes.

Finney once commented: "I write because I enjoy doing it. When it stops being fun I'll stop writing. I believe that writing is half talent, half skill—a writer should be able to turn her hand to anything that interests her. I particularly disagree with the idea that in order to be considered 'good' fiction must be 'highbrow' and literary. All the great writers have been bestsellers in their way, from Homer to Shakespeare to Dickens.

"As far as my future writing career is concerned, I would very much like to write screenplays. I intend to keep on writing historical novels but would also like to try my hand at publishing light nonfiction, science fiction, children's books, and history.

"To expand on my politics, I am a feminist, and am against all forms of totalitarian or authoritarian thought or government. As socialism and Communism seem to me at the moment greater threats to freedom than fascism or Nazism, I am right-wing."

BIOGRAPHICAL AND CRITICAL SOURCES:

PERIODICALS

Best Sellers, October, 1977, review of *A Shadow of Gulls,* p. 196.

Booklist, December 15, 2003, Michael Cart, review of *I, Jack,* p. 750.

Books and Bookmen, November, 1978, review of *The Crow Goddess,* p. 64.

Kirkus Reviews, September 15, 2003, review of *Gloriana's Torch,* p. 1144; January 15, 2004, review of *I, Jack,* p. 82.

Library Journal, January, 1998, Nancy Pearl, review of *Unicorn's Blood,* p. 139; October 1, 2003, Nancy Pearl, review of *Gloriana's Torch,* p. 116.

Listener, April 14, 1977.

Observer (London, England) June 5, 1977, review of *A Shadow of Gulls,* p. 29; September 3, 1978, review of *The Crow Goddess,* p. 26.

People, September 26, 1977.

Publishers Weekly, April 27, 1992, review of *Firedrake's Eye,* p. 253; November 24, 1997, review of *Unicorn's Blood,* p. 51; October 27, 2003, review of *Gloriana's Torch,* p. 44; February 23, 2004, review of *I, Jack,* p. 77; November 1, 2004, review of *Assassin,* p. 63.

School Library Journal, May, 2004, James K. Irwin, review of *I, Jack,* p. 147; October, 2004, Cheri Dobbs, review of *Assassin,* p. 158.

Times Literary Supplement, April 15, 1977, review of *A Shadow of Gulls,* p. 451.

ONLINE

BookLoons.com, http://www.bookloons.com/ (July 25, 2005), J.A. Kaszuba Locke, reviews of *Assassin, Betrayal,* and *Conspiracy;* Wesley Williamson, review of *Unicorn's Blood.*

Fantastic Fiction Web site, http://www.fantasticfiction.co.uk/ (July 6, 2005), "Patricia Finney."

Kidsreads.com, http://www.kidsreads.com/ (July 28, 2005), Shannon McKenna, review of "Lady Grace Mysteries"; reviews of *Assassin, Betrayal,* and *Conspiracy.*

LookingGlassReview.com, http://www.lookingglassreview.com/ (July 28, 2005), reviews of *Assassin, Betrayal,* and *Conspiracy.*

MysteryGuide.com, http://www.mysteryguide.com/ (July 25, 2005), review of *Firedrake's Eye.*

National Association for the Teaching of English Web site, http://www.nate.org.uk/ (July 28, 2005), Leanne Wood, review of *Assassin.*

Patricia Finney Home Page, http://www.patricia-finney.co.uk (July 6, 2005),

Shots: The Crime and Mystery Magazine Online, http://www.shotsmag.co.uk/ (July 25, 2005), Maureen Carlyle, review of *Gloriana's Torch.**

FONTENAY, Charles L. 1917-
  (Charles Louis Fontenay)

PERSONAL: Born March 17, 1917, in Sao Paulo, Brazil; son of Charles Robert and Miriam (Steel) Fontenay; married Glenda Lucille Miller, October 25, 1942 (marriage ended); married Martha Mae Howard (a social worker), September 30, 1962; children: (second marriage) Margarethe Louise, Charles Howard Blake. *Education:* Attended Vanderbilt University, 1966-68. *Hobbies and other interests:* Painting in watercolor and oil, chess, cooking Chinese foods, gardening, Korean karate, hypnotism.

ADDRESSES: Office—1708 20th Ave. N., Apt. D, St. Petersburg, FL 33713.

CAREER: Daily Messenger, Union City, TN, from reporter to sports editor to city editor, 1936-40; drug store soda-jerk in Washington, DC, 1940; Associated Press, editor in Nashville, TN, 1941-42; *Press-Chronicle,* Johnson City, TN, sports editor, 1946; *Tennessean,* Nashville, TN, political reporter, 1946-64, city editor, 1964-68, rewriter, 1968-87. *Military service:* U.S. Army, 1942-46; fought in the South Pacific; became captain.

AWARDS, HONORS: Southern Regional Education Board fellowship, 1966-67; Golden Duck Award, for *Kipton and the Tower of Time.*

WRITINGS:

Twice upon a Time (science fiction), Ace Books (New York, NY), 1958.
Rebels of the Red Planet (science fiction), Ace Books (New York, NY), 1961.
The Day the Oceans Overflowed (science fiction), Monarch Books (New York, NY), 1964.
Epistle to the Babylonians: An Essay on the Natural Inequality of Man (nonfiction), University of Tennessee Press (Knoxville, TN), 1969.
The Keyen of Fu Tze (nonfiction), Sherborne Institute, 1975.
Estes Kefauver: A Biography, University of Tennessee Press (Knoxville, TN), 1980.
Target: Grant, 1862 (science fiction), Silk Label (Unionville, NY), 1999.

Here, There and Elsewhen, Silk Label (Unionville, NY), 1999.
Modál: A Tale of Mind and Body, Love and Heroism, in a Possible Future World (science fiction), Silk Label (Unionville, NY), 2000.
Getting Back at Boo (science fiction), Silk Label (Unionville, NY), 2002.
Dionysos in Tears: A Tale of Destined Love . . . and Betrayal, iUniverse, 2003.

Contributor of science fiction short stories to periodicals, including *If* and the *Magazine of Fantasy and Science Fiction.*

"KIPTON CHRONICLES"; SCIENCE FICTION FOR YOUNG ADULTS

Kipton and the Ovoid, Royal Fireworks Press (Unionville, NY), 1996.
Kipton and the Tower of Time, Royal Fireworks Press (Unionville, NY), 1996.
Kipton in Wonderland, Royal Fireworks Press (Unionville, NY), 1996.
Kipton and the Voodoo Curse, Royal Fireworks Press (Unionville, NY), 1997.
Kipton and the Android, Royal Fireworks Press (Unionville, NY), 1997.
Kipton and the Christmas Gift, Royal Fireworks Press (Unionville, NY), 1997.
Kipton and the Caves of Mars, Royal Fireworks Press (Unionville, NY), 1998.
Kipton at the Martian Games, Royal Fireworks Press (Unionville, NY), 1998.
Kipton and the Martian Maidens, Royal Fireworks Press (Unionville, NY), 1999.
Kipton and the Delusions of Tante Else, Royal Fireworks Press (Unionville, NY), 1999.
Kipton and the Matter Transmitter, Royal Fireworks Press (Unionville, NY), 1999.
Kipton and the Monorail Murder, Royal Fireworks Press (Unionville, NY), 1999.
Kipton and the Riddle of Sandstone, Royal Fireworks Press (Unionville, NY), 1999.
Kipton on Phobos, Royal Fireworks Press (Unionville, NY), 1999.

SIDELIGHTS: Charles L. Fontenay is a former reporter who has been writing science fiction since the golden age of the genre back in the 1950s. His early works include *Twice upon a Time, Rebels of the Red*

Planet, and *The Day the Oceans Overflowed.* After *The Day the Oceans Overflowed,* he abandoned the genre temporarily to concentrate on nonfiction works, including *Epistle to the Babylonians: An Essay on the Natural Inequality of Man,* in which he discusses his ideas about the rise and fall of civilizations. He has also written a book on Eastern philosophy, *The Keyen of Fu Tze,* and a biography on a Tennessee senator, *Estes Kefauver: A Biography.*

In the 1990s, Fontenay returned to science fiction, first by writing a series of young adult mystery stories set on Mars called the "Kipton Chronicles," and then by writing a time-travel novel for adults called *Target: Grant, 1862* in which a twentieth-century man loyal to the memory of the Confederacy journeys back to the Civil War in order to assassinate General Ulysses S. Grant. This was followed by *Modál: A Tale of Mind and Body, Love and Heroism, in a Possible Future World.* Here, Fontenay describes a world in which civilization has been nearly destroyed because of the environmental effects of global warming called the "Great Change." The other central idea behind the novel, however, is based on a scientific theory that the human brain has several types of intelligence that are distinct from each other. The hero of the story must learn how to develop each of his "brains" in order to vanquish a despot who is holding the woman he loves. In the sequel to *Modál, Getting Back at Boo,* a guru named Soldier Boo has treasonous plans against the government, and it is left to two Modáls, Regal Stern and Coral Cordova, to hunt him down.

BIOGRAPHICAL AND CRITICAL SOURCES:

PERIODICALS

American History Illustrated, June, 1981, William Thomas Miller, review of *Estes Kefauver: A Biography,* p. 6.
Publishers Weekly, July 11, 1980, review of *Estes Kefauver,* p. 84.
School Library Journal, April, 2000, Lisa Prolman, review of *Kipton and the Matter Transmitter,* p. 134, and Elaine E. Knight, review of *Kipton and the Riddle of Sandstone,* p. 134.*

*   *   *

FONTENAY, Charles Louis
    See FONTENAY, Charles L.

FOWLER, Robert H. 1926-2002
    (Robert Howard Fowler)

PERSONAL: Born July 2, 1926, in Monroe, NC; died September 7, 2002; son of James Wiley and Stella (Mundy) Fowler; married Beverly Jeanne Utley (a research assistant), June 30, 1950; children: Wade Utley, Alyce Mundy, Robert Howard, Jr., Susanna Jeanne. *Education:* Attended Guilford College, Greensboro, NC, 1946-48; University of North Carolina, A.B., 1950; Columbia University, M.S., 1954. *Politics:* Democrat. *Religion:* Methodist.

CAREER: Journalist, publisher, and writer. *Reidsville Review,* Reidsville, NC, reporter, 1950; *Greensboro Daily News,* Greensboro, NC, reporter and assistant city editor, 1950-55; *St. Petersburg Times,* St. Petersburg, FL, city editor, 1955-56; *Harrisburg Patriot-News,* Harrisburg, PA, editorial writer, 1956-60; Historical Times, Inc., Harrisburg, PA, founder and member of board of directors, 1960-88, vice president and general manager, 1960-69, president, 1968-80, chairman of the board, 1980-88; Swank-Fowler Publications (included newspapers *Newport Sun* and the *Juniata Sentinel,* owner and publisher, 1984-2000; *Caribbean Travel & Life* magazine, part owner and director, until 1996. Also founding editor of *Civil War Times Illustrated,* 1959-73, and *American History Illustrated,* beginning 1966, and founder of *British History Illustrated.*

Served as member of board of directors of Commonwealth Communication Services, Inc.; director of People-to-People Book Drive, 1959; and president of the Pennsylvania Newspaper Foundation, 1999-2001; member of the Pennsylvania Historical and Museum Commission, beginning 1993; and a trustee of Albright College. *Military service:* U.S. Naval reserve, active duty, 1944-46.

MEMBER: American Society of Magazine Editors, National Historical Society (founder; president), Overseas Press Club, Company of Military Historians, Harrisburg Civil War Round Table, Pennsylvania Newspaper Association (president, 1989-90), Keystone Press Endowment Society, Sigma Delta Chi, Princeton Club, Savage Club.

AWARDS, HONORS: Prizes from Pennsylvania Newspaper Publishers Association, 1957-60, for editorial and public service.

WRITINGS:

Album of the Lincoln Murder (nonfiction), Stackpole (Mechanicsburg, PA), 1965.

(With Frederick Ray) *O, Say Can You See* (nonfiction), Stackpole (Mechanicsburg, PA), 1970.

Jim Mundy: A Novel of the American Civil War, Harper (New York, NY), 1977, reprinted, Stealth Press (Lancaster, PA), 2000.

Jason McGee, Harper & Row (New York, NY), 1979.

The Spoils of Eden (novel), Dodd, Mead (New York, NY), 1985.

Jeremiah Martin: A Revolutionary War Novel, St. Martin's Press (New York, NY), 1989.

Voyage to Honor: A Historical Novel: The War of 1812, Stackpole (Mechanicsburg, PA), 1996.

Annie Mundy (novel), Stealth Press (Lancaster, PA), 2001.

The Battle of Milroy Station: A Novel of the Nature of True Courage, Forge (New York, NY), 2003.

SIDELIGHTS: Robert H. Fowler once told *CA:* "*Jim Mundy* is my first published novel. I have written four detective novels based on the exploits of an ex-CIA man now a professor of American history and a Civil War buff, but have not offered them to a publisher. I pay a great deal of attention to accuracy in my historical novels. The writing of fiction is a hobby with me along with sculpting, tennis, and canoeing."

In *Jim Mundy: A Novel of the American Civil War,* Fowler tells the story of a Confederate patriot who serves in the Southern Army with little interest in slavery or the politics surrounding the war. Reviewing the 2000 reissue opf the novel, *Library Journal* contributor Michael Rogers noted that past critics placed *Jim Mundy* "on a level with *The Red Badge of Courage.*" Fowler's last book, *The Battle of Milroy Station: A Novel of the Nature of True Courage,* focuses on Andrew Jackson Mundy, who is asked to change parties and run as a vice-presidential candidate with Republican William McKinley. Mundy's ultimate refusal of the offer and the reasons behind his decision are Fowler's primary interest as the author delves into Mundy's past and his experience during an infamous Civil War battle. Writing in the *Library Journal,* Joel W. Tscherne noted that the author "fills his battle scenes with credible details and tactics." Also praising the battle scenes was a *Publishers Weekly* contributor, who went on to comment that the author "is able to

raise his characters, humble and mighty, above cliché." Wes Lukowsky, writing in *Booklist,* called the effort "a carefully researched and well-written historical novel."

BIOGRAPHICAL AND CRITICAL SOURCES:

PERIODICALS

America, May 3, 1980, Joseph Pusateri, review of *Jason McGee,* p. 388.

Booklist, January 1, 2003, Wes Lukowsky, review of *The Battle of Milroy Station: A Novel of the Nature of True Courage,* p. 846.

Library Journal, April 1, 1985, Lydia Burruel, review of *The Spoils of Eden,* p. 157; March 15, 2001, Michael Rogers, review of *Jim Mundy: A Novel of the American Civil War,* p. 112; February 1, 2003, Joel W. Tscherne, review of *The Battle of Milroy Station,* p. 116.

Publishers Weekly, February 8, 1985, review of *The Spoils of Eden,* p. 70; September 8, 1988, Sybil Steinberg, review of *Jeremiah Martin: A Revolutionary War Novel,* p. 120; January 6, 2003, review of *The Battle of Milroy Station,* p. 36.

OBITUARIES

PERIODICALS

Civil War Times Illustrated, December, 2002, Jim Kushlan, "Farewell to a Friend," p. 4.

ONLINE

Pennsylvania Newspaper Association Web site, http://www.pa-newspaper.org/ (November 16, 2005), "Members Share memories of Robert Fowler, His Legacy Contributions to PNA Are Noted."*

*   *   *

**FOWLER, Robert Howard
See FOWLER, Robert H.**

FRANK, Jeffrey 1942-

PERSONAL: Born April 10, 1942, in Baltimore, MD; son of Adam and Rachel (Brody) Frank; married Diana Crone, March 17, 1967; children: one son. *Education:* Attended Knox College, Galesburg, IL. *Hobbies and other interests:* Reading, music, hiking, and Oriental art; special interest in nineteenth-century Scandinavian literature.

ADDRESSES: Home—New York, NY. *Office*—c/o New Yorker, 4 Times Square, New York, NY 10036. *E-mail*—frankjeff@earthlink.net.

CAREER: Writer and editor. *New Yorker,* senior editor; *Letter from Washington* (Washington correspondents' newsletter), editor. Previous positions include writing and editing jobs at the *Washington Star, Buffalo Courier-Express, Washington Post,* and Random House.

WRITINGS:

The Creep (novel), Farrar, Straus (New York, NY), 1968.
The Columnist (novel), Simon & Schuster (New York, NY), 2001.
(Selector and translator, with wife, Diana Crone Frank) *The Stories of Hans Christian Andersen,* illustrations by Vilhelm Pedersen and Lorenz Frøelich, Houghton Mifflin (Boston, MA), 2003.
Bad Publicity: A Novel, Simon & Schuster (New York, NY), 2004.

SIDELIGHTS: New Yorker senior editor Jeffrey Frank wrote his first novel, *The Creep,* when he was just twenty-two years old. Upon the book's publication in 1968, a *Virginia Quarterly Review* contributor commented: "With an unheroic hero, bumbling, ineffectual, and evidently repulsive on sight, Mr. Frank has adroitly created for his character sketch the very portrait of a lonely man, introspective, adrift, and friendless in a large and underesponsive city. His . . . study is a pointed one, wringing with pathos one moment and slyly inducing derisive laughter the next." Frank, who has worked extensively in newspaper and magazine journalism since the publication of the *The Creep,* did not produce another novel for more than three decades. "But writing fiction has always been the thing I love most, and it's a completely different thing and different kind of energy," the author noted in an interview on the *Mediabistro.com* Web site.

In his 2001 novel *The Columnist,* Frank draws on his years of experience in reporting and publishing to tell the story of an aging Brandon Sladder, who has established his successful career as a Washington pundit by destroying others' careers. The story is revealed as Sladder writes his memoir and reminisces about his sordid past, from exacting revenge on his father to using prostitutes to get inside information from politicians. "*The Columnist* may not be the 'Gettysburg Address,' but it comes closer to perfectly satirizing a certain Washington type than anything else I've read," wrote Christopher Buckley in the *Washington Monthly.* A *Publishers Weekly* contributor commented, "The political material is enlightening and well delivered. . . . The result is a witty, racy and fast-moving novel that remains compelling despite its odious protagonist." Noting that the novel "packs a curiously subtle wallop," Eric Alterman, writing in the *Columbia Journalism Review,* also commented: "*The Columnist* is a marvelously fitting tribute to the men and women who make it—and remake it—every Sunday morning."

Frank's next novel, *Bad Publicity,* continues to examine the realms of power in Washington, DC. Washed-up former congressman Charlie Dingleman suddenly finds himself in line for a job in the White House—until he insults his junior law associate Judith Grust, who then sets out to destroy his new opportunity. Charlie's image consultants are there to help but are dealing with their own problems as Charlie's career appears doomed. "What brings this ship of fools to unforgettable life is Frank's heartlessly deadpan way of deflating their most cherished desires, from their petty scrabbling for 15 minutes of fame to their hilariously untitillating couplings," wrote a *Kirkus Reviews* contributor. A reviewer writing in *Publishers Weekly* noted that the author "pokes fun at power seekers on both sides of the aisle, political insiders for whom a sentence of 'obscurity without parole' is the worst possible fate." Barbara Conaty, writing in the *Library Journal,* called the novel a "satiric tour de force."

Frank, who is fluent in Danish, also collaborated with his wife, Diana Crone Frank, as selector and translator of *The Stories of Hans Christian Andersen,* which includes the original illustrations by Vilhelm Pedersen and Lorenz Frøelich.

BIOGRAPHICAL AND CRITICAL SOURCES:

PERIODICALS

Columbia Journalism Review, July, 2001, Eric Alterman, review of *The Columnist,* p. 62.

Harper's, May, 1968, review of *The Creep.*

Kirkus Reviews, November 1, 2003, review of *Bad Publicity,* p. 1288.

Library Journal, January, 2004, Barbara Conaty, review of *Bad Publicity,* p. 155.

Newsweek, October 6, 2003, Elise Soukup, review of *The Stories of Hans Christian Andersen,* p. 16.

Publishers Weekly, May 28, 2001, review of *The Columnist,* p. 49; November 3, 2003, review of *Bad Publicity,* p. 51; November 24, 2003, review of *The Stories of Hans Christian Andersen,* p. 66.

Saturday Review, January 6, 1968, review of *The Creep.*

Virginia Quarterly Review, spring, 1968, review of *The Creep.*

Washington Monthly, May, 2001, Christopher Buckley, review of *The Columnist,* p. 50.

ONLINE

Jeffrey Frank Web site, http://jeffreyfrank.com (November 20, 2005).

Mediabistro.com, http://www.mediabistro.com/ (October 28, 2005), David S. Hirschman, January 30, 2004 interview with the author.*

*   *   *

FRANKOWSKI, Leo 1943-

PERSONAL: Born February 13, 1943, in Detroit, MI; son of Leo Stanley (a bar owner) and Agnes (a bartender; maiden name, Kulczynski) Frankowski; married; children: one daughter. *Politics:* "Closet libertarian." *Religion:* "Born-again pagan."

ADDRESSES: Home—Tver, Russia. *Agent*—c/o Author Mail, Baen Books, P.O. Box 1403, Riverdale, NY 10471.

CAREER: Writer and businessperson. Sterling Manufacturing and Design, Utica, MI, owner, president, and designer, c. 1977-2001; *StarDate* magazine, owner; Reluctant Publishing Ltd., president and editor, Grand Duchy of Avalon Foundation, founder.

Previously worked in more than one hundred positions, including bartender, engineer, karate instructor, electrician, welder, janitor, mechanic, computer and real estate salesman, school administrator, gardener, and industrial controls designer. *Military service:* U.S. Air Force, 1963-66; became airman first class.

MEMBER: Mensa, Society for Creative Anachronism, Science Fiction Fandom, Science Fiction Writers of America, National Science Fiction Writers Exchange, Michigan Writers Guild.

AWARDS, HONORS: Waterloo Award, National Science Fiction Writer's Exchange, 1985, for "The Story of Thadeause Wolczynski"; Nebula Award nomination from Science Fiction Writers of America, 1986, for *The Cross-Time Engineer.*

WRITINGS:

"CONRAD STARGARD" SERIES; SCIENCE FICTION

The Cross-Time Engineer, Del Rey (New York, NY), 1986.

The High-Tech Knight, Del Rey (New York, NY), 1987.

The Radiant Warrior, Del Rey (New York, NY), 1987, published as *Conrad Stargard: The Radiant Warrior,* Baen (Riverdale, NY), 2004.

Conrad's Time Machine: A Prequel to the Adventures of Conrad Stargard, Baen (Riverdale, NY), 2002.

Conrad's Lady (includes the novels *The Flying Warlord, The Lord Conrad's Lady,* and *Conrad's Quest for Rubber*), Baen (Riverdale, NY), 2005.

Series includes the novels *The Flying Warlord,* 1989; *The Lord Conrad's Lady,* 1990; and *Conrad's Quest for Rubber,* 1998 (see above).

OTHER SCIENCE-FICTION NOVELS

Copernick's Rebellion, Del Rey (New York, NY), 1987.

A Boy and His Tank, Simon & Schuster (New York, NY), 1999.

The Fata Morgana, Simon & Schuster (New York, NY), 1999.

(With Dave Grossman) *The War with Earth,* Baen (Riverdale, NY), 2003.

(With Dave Grossman) *Kren of the Mitchegai,* Baen (Riverdale, NY), 2004.

(With Dave Grossman) *The Two-Space War,* Baen (Riverdale, NY), 2004.

SIDELIGHTS: Science-fiction writer Leo Frankowski told *CA:* "Writing is a pleasant trade. You can do it anywhere, any time. You don't have to put up with illiterate customers or rush-hour traffic. All sorts of things are deductible, and it is possible, once established, to make a decent living at it. My main motivation is to sell my work to satisfied readers."

Frankowski added: "Current history texts leave the student with the impression that the Americas didn't exist before 1492, that the Middle East was unpopulated between the Fall of Babylon and 1960, and that Eastern Europe somehow materialized in time for World War I. Well, my ancestors assure me that Eastern Europe was there all along.

"While the monarchs of England and France were fighting their senseless dynastic wars, Poland resisted invasions by the Huns, the Tartars, the Kipchaks, the Turks, and the Lithuanians—the roughest of the bunch. From the fourteenth through the seventeenth centuries, Poland was the largest country in Europe, with the largest military forces and the highest cultural standards. Some of my motivation for writing has been to get this across to the American public.

"I also want to show what engineering is about. What is it exactly that these engineers do? How do they do it, and what do they think about it? People seem to think that engineering has something to do with science. It doesn't. Science is an essentially religious endeavor, trying to find out how the world was made. Engineering concerns itself with small, practical problems. Scientists and engineers have been on speaking terms for only the last fifty years, and they still don't do it very often.

"Engineering has even less to do with mathematics. Oh, engineers have been trained in math for the last century, but they rarely use it unless experimentation is expensive—as in the space shuttle program. The pyramids, the cathedrals, and the automobile were largely built without anything more than arithmetic.

"All the engineers do is solve small problems, generally without much fanfare or even much planning, doing things in a mundane, work-a-day fashion. Yet cumulatively, their work has been ultimately responsible for all human progress, even that in politics, science, and the fine arts. Without the products designed by engineers, 98 percent of humanity would be dead—or rather, would never have existed at all. The few of us left would not find our lives to be very uplifting."

In his novel *A Boy and His Tank,* Frankowski sets his story on New Kashubia where Mickolai Derdowski gets his girlfriend pregnant, which leads to his arrest by the leaders of the planet and a death sentence unless he decides to fight in the New Kashubia military. The novel follows Mickolai's adventures as he fights in a tank controlled by a supercomputer that can also create virtual realities called the "Dream World" for those inside the tank. This virtual reality is used for training as well as the tank operator's own wished-for realities. As a result, it can be difficult for the tank's human operator to tell the difference between reality and virtual reality. Writing on the *SFSignal* Web site, a reviewer called the effort "a fun book well worth the read," adding, "By mixing virtual reality with military sf, the book had a distinctly likable flavor and Frankowski's to-the-point writing style was well suited to making this adventure story come alive." Frankowski collaborated with Dave Grossman for the sequel titled *The War with Earth,* in which Mickolai discovers that all his earlier battles were not real and all his fallen comrades are alive only to be sent this time into a real battle. Don D'Ammassa, writing in the *Chronicle,* called the book "a reasonably entertaining quasi-military SF novel."

The Fata Morgana tells the story of two engineering entrepreneurs who discover the island of Westria when their yacht gets caught in a storm. Once there, however, they are caught up in a battle among the island country's religious and scientific adherents. A *Publishers Weekly* contributor commented: "Frankowski has a knack for writing amenable prose with enjoyable characters." Frankowski collaborated with Grossman again for *The Two-Space War,* in which a crew that travels on wooden spaceships with sails find themselves caught between two warring space empires. D'Ammassa, writing in the *Chronicle,* gave the book "high points for creativity and wry humor."

Frankowski is also the author of a series of novels featuring Conrad Stargard, including *Conrad's Time Machine: A Prequel to the Adventures of Conrad Stargard.* The hero's real name is Conrad Schwartz and is an engineer and Air Force veteran. In this installment of his adventures, Conrad and friends discover the plans for a time machine. Writing in the *Library Journal,* Jackie Cassada wrote that the book is "raucously funny and thoughtfully sobering." *Booklist* contributor Regina Schroeder called the book "satisfying weekend reading." In *Conrad Stargard: The Radiant Warrior,* Conrad is sent back to 1231 AD and is chased by Teutonic knights in Poland. A *Library Bookwatch* contributor noted that in the book "medieval Poland comes alive."

BIOGRAPHICAL AND CRITICAL SOURCES:

PERIODICALS

Analog Science Fiction-Science Fact, February, 1988, Tom Easton, review of *Copernick's Rebellion,* p. 190.

Booklist, September 1, 2002, Regina Schroeder, review of *Conrad's Time Machine: A Prequel to the Adventures of Conrad Stargard,* p. 70.

Chronicle, October, 2003, Don D'Ammassa, review of *The War with Earth,* p. 40; June, 2004, Don D'Ammassa, review of *The Two-Space War,* p. 40.

Internet Bookwatch, February, 2005, review of *Conrad Stargard: The Radiant Warrior.*

Library Bookwatch, February, 2005, review of *Conrad Stargard: The Radiant Warrior.*

Library Journal, August, 1999, Jackie Cassada, review of *The Fata Morgana,* p. 148; September 15, 2002, Jackie Cassada, review of *Conrad's Time Machine,* p. 97.

Magazine of Fantasy and Science Fiction, January, 1990, Algis Budrys, review of *The Radiant Warrior,* p. 48; January, 1990, Algis Budrys, review of *The High-Tech Knight,* p. 48; May, 1990, Algis Budrys, review of *The Flying Warlord,* p. 48.

Publishers Weekly, February 22, 1999, review of *A Boy and His Tank,* p. 71; July 26, 1999, review of *The Fata Morgana,* p. 67; August 12, 2002, review of *Conrad's Time Machine,* p. 282.

Wilson Library Bulletin, June, 1989, Don Sakers, review of *The High-Tech Knight,* p. 108.

ONLINE

Fantastic Fiction, http://www.fantasticfiction.co.uk/ (November 3, 2005), information on author's works.

Leo Frankowski Home Page, http://leofrankowski.com (October 5, 2005).

SFSignal, http://www.sfsignal.com/ (October 5, 2005), review of *A Boy and His Tank.**

* * *

FRASER, David 1920-
(David William Fraser)

PERSONAL: Born December 30, 1920, in Camberley, England; son of William (a brigadier general) and Pamela (Maude) Fraser; married Anne Balfour, September 26, 1947 (marriage dissolved, 1952); married Julia Frances de la Hey, October 11, 1957; children: (first marriage) Antonia Fraser Hanbury; (second marriage) Arabella Fraser Birdwood, Alexander James, Simon, Lucy Fraser Baring. *Education:* Attended Christ Church, Oxford; British Army Staff College, 1949; and Imperial Defence College, 1966. *Religion:* Church of England. *Hobbies and other interests:* Shooting.

ADDRESSES: Home—Vallenders, Isington, Alton, Hampshire GU34 4PP, England. *Agent*—Michael Sissons, Peters, Fraser, and Dunlop Group, Drury House, 34-43 Russell St., London WC2B 5HA, England.

CAREER: British Army, career officer, 1941-80, served with Grenadier Guards in Northwest European Campaign and in Malaya, 1941-49, member of staff at War Office in London, England, 1950-51, assigned to regimental duty in Egypt and served as brigade major of First Guards Brigade, 1952-54, regimental adjutant in London, 1955-57, assigned to regimental duty in

Cyprus and Germany, 1958-60, commander of First Battalion of the Grenadier Guards in England and British Cameroons, 1960-62, member of general staff of London District, 1962-63, commander of 19th Infantry Brigade in England and Borneo, 1963-65, director of defense policy at Ministry of Defence, 1966-69, commander of 4th Division of the British Army of the Rhine, 1969-71, assistant chief of defense staff for policy, 1971-73, vice chief of general staff, 1973-75, British military representative to North Atlantic Treaty Organization (NATO) in Brussels, Belgium, 1975-77, commander of Royal College of Defence Studies, London, 1977-80, retired as general; writer, 1980—. Chairman of Treloar Trust and Governing Body of Lord Mayor Treloar College, 1982-93.

MEMBER: Society for Army Historical Research (president, 1980-93), Turf Club, Pratt's Club.

AWARDS, HONORS: Named Officer of Order of the British Empire, 1962; Grand Cross of Order of the Bath, 1980; D.Litt., University of Reading.

WRITINGS:

The Grenadier Guards ("Men-at-Arms" series), illustrated by Angus McBride, Osprey Publishing (London, England), 1978.

Alanbrooke, Atheneum (New York, NY), 1982.

And We Shall Shock Them: The British Army in the Second World War, Hodder & Stoughton (London, England), 1982.

August 1988 (novel), Collins (London, England), 1982.

(Editor) *The Christian Watt Papers,* Paul Harris (Edinburgh, Scotland), 1983.

The Fortunes of War (novel), Norton (New York, NY), 1983, published as *A Kiss for the Enemy,* Collins (London, England), 1983.

The Killing Times (novel), Collins (London, England), 1986.

The Dragon's Teeth (novel), Collins (London, England), 1987.

The Seizure (novel), Collins (London, England), 1988.

A Candle for Judas (novel), Collins (London, England), 1989.

In Good Company: The First World War Letters and Diaries of the Hon. William Fraser, Gordon Highlanders, Russell (Salisbury, England), 1990.

The Hardrow Chronicles, Penguin (New York, NY), Volume 1: *Adam Hardrow,* 1990, Volume 2: *Adam in the Breach,* 1993.

Codename Mercury (novel), Penguin (New York, NY), 1991.

Knight's Cross: A Life of Field Marshal Erwin Rommel, HarperCollins (New York, NY), 1993.

The Pain of Winning, Penguin (New York, NY), 1994.

Will: A Portrait of William Douglas Home, A. Deutsch (London, England), 1995.

Wellington and the Waterloo Campaign, University of Southampton (Southampton, Hampshire, England), 1995.

Frederick the Great: King of Prussia, A. Lane (New York, NY), 2000.

Wars and Shadows: Memoirs of General Sir David Fraser, A. Lane (London, England), 2002.

SIDELIGHTS: David Fraser is a retired British army general who has developed into a successful author, penning ten novels and several biographies since the 1980s. He has gained particular acclaim in the United States for his biographies of Erwin Rommel and Frederick II. *Knight's Cross: A Life of Field Marshal Erwin Rommel* is about the German military leader who became known as the "Desert Fox" during his World War II campaigns in northern Africa. Rommel had earned a reputation in World War I as a daring, brave, and brilliant soldier, and he was greatly admired and feared during World War II. Although he fought on the side of Hitler, he was known to be apolitical, until he was forced to drink poison by Nazi agents after it was discovered that he had helped in a plot to assassinate Hitler. "Many books have been written about Rommel," commented an *Economist* reviewer. "None has been more thoroughly researched nor examines his personality and character in more detail than this one." *Booklist* contributor Gilbert Taylor asserted that "Fraser presents what definitely will become the standard biography . . . as the author astutely traces the qualities of leadership which Rommel embodied."

Fraser was again praised for his 2000 biography, *Frederick the Great: King of Prussia.* The book's subject, Frederick II, is sometimes seen by historians only for his militaristic achievements—of which there were many—and as being a forerunner of even more militant expansionists, including Otto von Bismarck and Adolf Hitler. However, as Fraser points out, King Frederick was much more than a great military strategist. He was an artistic man who composed music and wrote verses, and who could name Voltaire as one of his best friends; he was also a great political leader who did much to reform his nation's laws to the benefit of the lower classes. "Frederick was blamed retrospectively for a German demonism he couldn't possibly have envisaged," noted *History Today* critic John F. Crossland. "This correction of the historical perspective is long overdue." Perhaps because of Fraser's military background, however, the author does tend to stress Frederick's achievements in war. During his reign, Prussia fought four wars to stave off pressures from Russia in the East and the Habsburg dynasties in the West and South, yet he successfully managed to keep Prussia an autonomous state while actually expanding its borders. Frederick's accomplishments thus made his kingdom a major power in Europe. Crossland added that "Fraser is particularly good in his battle sequences but gives us a rounded portrait of a monarch who at the same time could supervise the expansion of his poor country's economy and industry, build architectural jewels like [his castle] Sans Souci, and manage to write almost daily to his friend Voltaire." Barbara Walden added in the *Library Journal* that "this book will be the standard biography of this fascinating ruler for years to come."

BIOGRAPHICAL AND CRITICAL SOURCES:

PERIODICALS

Atlantic Monthly, December, 2002, Benjamin Schwarz, review of *Frederick the Great: King of Prussia,* p. 128.
Booklist, January 15, 1994, Gilbert Taylor, review of *Knight's Cross: The Life of Field Marshal Erwin Rommel,* p. 896.
Economist, December 4, 1993, review of *Knight's Cross,* p. 99; April 15, 2000, "Historical Biography," p. 6.
History Today, April, 1984, Christian Hesketh, review of *The Christian Watt Papers;* January, 1991, Christian Hesketh, review of *In Good Company: The First World War Letters and Diaries of the Hon. William Fraser, Gordon Highlanders,* p. 61; July, 2000, John F. Crossland, review of *Frederick the Great,* p. 56.
Library Journal, March 1, 1982, review of *Alanbrooke,* p. 52; April 1, 1985, Andrea Lee Shuey, review of *The Fortunes of War,* p. 157; May 15, 2001, Barbara Walden, review of *Frederick the Great,* p. 134.

Listener, April 22, 1982.
New Statesman, June 4, 1982.
New York Times Book Review, February 24, 1985, Russell F. Weigley, review of *And We Shall Shock Them: The British Army in the Second World War,* p. 12; March 6, 1994, Alistair Horne, review of *Knight's Cross,* p. 6.
Observer, May 9, 1982.
Publishers Weekly, January 22, 1982, Genevieve Stuttaford, review of *Alanbrooke,* p. 52; March 1, 1985, review of *The Fortunes of War,* p. 71; January 10, 1994, review of *Knight's Cross,* p. 54; April 30, 2001, review of *Frederick the Great,* p. 66.
Times Literary Supplement, May 7, 1981.*

*   *   *

FRASER, David William
   See FRASER, David

*   *   *

FRATKIN, Elliot 1948-

PERSONAL: Born June 22, 1948, in Philadelphia, PA; son of Ralph M. (an accountant) and Mildred L. (a homemaker) Fratkin; married Martha A. Nathan (a family physician), July 17, 1985; children: Leah Nathan. *Education:* University of Pennsylvania, B.A., 1970; London School of Economics and Political Science, London, England, M.Phil., 1972; Catholic University of America, Washington, DC, Ph.D., 1987. *Politics:* "Born Democrat, lived as a Socialist, will die a Democrat." *Religion:* "Jewish atheist." *Hobbies and other interests:* "Working on old tractors and jeeps, playing bluegrass and old-time music (mandolin, guitar, banjo), watching my daughter jump horses."

ADDRESSES: Office—Department of Anthropology, Smith College, Wright Hall 107, Northampton, MA 01063. *E-mail*—efratkin@smith.edu.

CAREER: Anthropologist, educator, and writer. University of Maryland, Baltimore County, Catonsville, instructor, 1979-85; University of Nairobi, Nairobi, Kenya, research associate, 1985-86; Duke University, Durham, NC, visiting assistant professor,

1987-89; Pennsylvania State University, University Park, assistant professor, 1989-94; Smith College, Northampton, MA, assistant professor of anthropology, beginning 1994, then professor of anthropology. Also served as consultant to the World Bank Inspection Panel on the Chad-Cameroon Oil Pipeline Project.

MEMBER: American Anthropological Association, Association for Africanist Anthropology, African Studies Association, National Organization for Women, Society for Economic Anthropology, Greenpeace, Greensboro Justice Fund.

AWARDS, HONORS: Fulbright fellow, University of Asmara, 2003; research grants from National Geographic Society, Social Science Research Council, and National Science Foundation.

WRITINGS:

Why Elephant Is an Old Woman: Animal Symbolism in Samburu, Institute of African Studies, University of Nairobi (Nairobi, Kenya), 1974.

Herbal Medicine and Concepts of Disease in Samburu, Institute of African Studies, University of Nairobi (Nairobi, Kenya), 1975.

Surviving Drought and Development, Westview (Boulder, CO), 1991.

(Editor, with Kathleen Galvin and Eric Abella Roth) *African Pastoralist Systems: An Integrated Approach,* Lynne Reinner Press (Boulder, CO), 1994.

Ariaal Pastoralists of Kenya: Surviving Drought and Development in Africa's Arid Lands, Allyn and Bacon (Boston, MA), 1998, 2nd edition published as *Ariaal Pastoralists of Kenya: Studying Pastoralism, Drought and Development in Africa's Arid Lands,* 2004.

(With Daniel G. Bates) *Cultural Anthropology,* Allyn and Bacon (Boston, MA), 1999.

(Editor, with Eric Abella Roth) *As Pastoralists Settle: Social, Health, and Economic Consequences of the Pastoral Sedentarization in Marsabit District, Kenya,* Kluwer Academic/Plenum Publishers (New York, NY), 2004.

Served as associate editor of *Human Ecology.* Contributor to professional journals and periodicals, including *American Anthropologist, Human Ecology, Natural History,* and *African Studies Review.* Contribu-

tor to books, including *Being Massai,* edited by Thomas Spear and Richard Waller, James Curry Publishers, 1993.

SIDELIGHTS: Cultural anthropologist Elliot Fratkin has written extensively about his research interests, including the book *Ariaal Pastoralists of Kenya: Surviving Drought and Development in Africa's Arid Lands.* According to Aneesa Kassam, writing in the *Journal of the Royal Anthropological Institute,* the author "examines the problems of social change and development among the Ariaal pastoralist." Noting that the book was written "for a . . . general readership," Kassam added that "the study raises some important questions for the future of pastoralism." *Africa* contributor Mario I. Aguilar commented: "This short book constitutes a first-class introduction to the world of pastoralism, in a cultural and wider perspective." Aguilar also recommended the book to "students interested not only in pastoralism but in wider issues of ecological and indeed developmental survival." Fratkin also served as a coeditor of and contributor to *African Pastoralist Systems: An Integrated Approach,* a collection of presentations from a 1991 American Anthropological Association meeting focusing on African pastoralists. Writing once again in *Africa,* Aguilar wrote that the author's own contribution to the book was among those that "deserve immense credit."

Fratkin told *CA:* "As a cultural anthropologist, I have been involved in a long-term study and friendship with Ariaal Rendille Camel pastoralists of Northern Kenya since 1974. I was adopted into a family of Maasai-speaking medicine-men (Loibonok) whom I continue to visit regularly. I have written a monograph on the Ariaal, which looks at their ecological adaptation to arid lands and their dealings with Christian missionaries and international development agencies, not all of which have been smooth.

"I am engaged in a long-term medical study of Ariaal and their changing lifestyle as they settle near growing towns of Kenya's north, a project with wife/collaborator/doctor Marty Nathan and demographer Eric Abella Roth."

BIOGRAPHICAL AND CRITICAL SOURCES:

PERIODICALS

Africa, fall, 1996, Mario I. Aguilar, review of *African Pastoralist Systems: An Integrated Approach,*

p. 612; summer, 1998, Mario I. Aguilar, review of *Ariaal Pastoralists of Kenya: Surviving Drought and Development in Africa's Arid Lands,* p. 440.

African Studies Review, April, 1999, review of *Ariaal Pastoralists of Kenya,* p. 135.

American Ethnologist, August, 1997, Philip Cal Salzman, review of *African Pastoralist Systems,* p. 692.

Journal of Royal Anthropological Institute, September, 2000, Aneesa Kassam, review of *Ariaal Pastoralists of Kenya,* p. 568.

ONLINE

Eldis, http://www.eldis.org/ (October 6, 2005), "Elliot Fratkin," profile of author's career.

Smith College Department of Anthropology Web site, http://www.smith.edu/anthro/ (October 6, 2005), faculty profile of author.*

*   *   *

FREEDMAN, David Noel 1922-

PERSONAL: Born May 12, 1922, in New York, NY; son of David (a writer) and Beatrice (Goodman) Freedman; married Cornelia Anne Pryor, May 16, 1944; children: Meredith Anne, Nadezhda, David Micaiah, Jonathan Pryor. *Education:* Attended City College (now City College of the City University of New York), 1935-38; University of California—Los Angeles, A.B., 1939; Princeton Theological Seminary, Th.B., 1944; Johns Hopkins University, Ph.D., 1948.

ADDRESSES: Office—Department of History, University of California—San Diego, 9500 Gilman Dr., Dept. 0104, La Jolla, CA 92093-5004. *E-mail*—dnfreedman@ucsd.edu.

CAREER: Ordained minister of Presbyterian Church, 1944; supply pastor in Acme, WA, and Deming, WA, 1944-45; Johns Hopkins University, Baltimore, MD, teaching fellow, 1946-47, assistant instructor, 1947-48; Western Theological Seminary, Pittsburgh, PA, assistant professor, 1948-51, professor of Hebrew and Old Testament literature, 1951-60; Pittsburgh Theological Seminary, Pittsburgh, PA, professor, 1960-62, James A. Kelso Professor of Hebrew and Old Testa-

ment Literature, 1962-64; San Francisco Theological Seminary, San Anselmo, CA, professor of Old Testament, 1964-70, Gray Professor of Hebrew Exegesis, 1970-71, dean of faculty, 1966-70, acting dean of seminary, 1970-71; Graduate Theological Union, Berkeley, CA, professor of Old Testament, 1964-71; University of Michigan, Ann Arbor, professor of Near Eastern studies and director of program on studies in religion, 1971-91, professor of biblical studies, 1984-92, professor emeritus, 1992—; University of California, San Diego, endowed chair in Hebrew Bible studies, 1987—, director of religious studies program, 1989-1997. Lecturer, Uppsala University, 1959, Johns Hopkins University, 1976, Loyola University, 1983, Society for Biblical Literature, 1983, Smithsonian Institution, 1984, Princeton Theological Seminary, 1989, Oslo University, 1991, Uppsala University, Sweden, 1991, Brigham Young Center for Near Eastern Studies, Jerusalem, 1993; visiting professor, International Christian University, Tokyo, Japan, 1967, Hebrew University, 1976-77, MacQuarie University, New South Wales, Australia, 1980, Texas Christian University, 1981, University of Queensland, 1982, 1984, and University of California—San Diego, 1985-87. Director of Ashdod excavation project, 1962-64, and Albright Institute for Archeological Research, 1969-70, 1976-77. Technical consultant, Milberg Productions, beginning 1961, including the films *Jacob and Joseph,* 1974, and *King David,* 1976.

MEMBER: Society of Biblical Literature (president, 1975-76), American Academy of Religion, Biblical Colloquium (secretary-treasurer, 1960-90), Archaeological Institute of America, American Oriental Society, American Schools of Oriental Research (vice president, 1970—; trustee, 1970—; director of publications, 1974—), Catholic Bible Association of America.

AWARDS, HONORS: Prize in New Testament exegesis, Princeton Theological Seminary, 1943; William H. Green fellow in Old Testament, 1944; William S. Rayner fellow, Johns Hopkins University, 1946-47; Guggenheim fellowship, 1959; American Association of Theological Schools fellowship, 1963; Carey-Thomas Award, *Publishers Weekly,* 1965, for "Anchor Bible" series; American Council of Learned Societies grants-in-aid, 1967, 1976; D.Litt., University of the Pacific, 1973; D.Sc., Davis and Elkins College, 1974; Johns Hopkins University Centennial Scholar, 1976;

Laymen's National Bible Committee Annual Award, 1978; three awards from Biblical Archaeology Society, 1993, for the "Anchor Bible."

WRITINGS:

(With Frank M. Cross, Jr.) *The Evolution of Early Hebrew Orthography: The Epigraphic Evidence,* 1948, revised edition published as *Early Hebrew Orthography,* American Oriental Society (New Haven, CT), 1952.

(With J.M. Allegro) *The People of the Dead Sea Scrolls,* Doubleday (New York, NY), 1958.

(With R.M. Grant) *The Secret Sayings of Jesus: The Gnostic Gospel of Thomas,* Doubleday (New York, NY), 1960.

(Editor) *The Biblical Archaeologist Reader,* Doubleday (New York, NY), Volume 1 (with G.E. Wright), 1961, Volume 2 (with Edward F. Campbell), 1964, Volume 3 (with Edward F. Campbell), 1970, Volume 4 (with Edward F. Campbell), 1983.

(With Moshe Dothan) *Ashdod I,* Department of Antiquities and Museums (Jerusalem, Israel), 1967.

The New World of the Old Testament, San Francisco Theological Seminary (San Anselmo, CA), 1968.

(With Jonas C. Greenfield) *New Directions in Biblical Archaeology,* Doubleday (New York, NY), 1969.

(With Frank M. Cross, Jr.) *Scrolls from Qumran Cave I,* Albright Institute of Archaeological Research (Jerusalem), 1972.

(Editor) *The Published Works of William Foxwell Albright: A Comprehensive Bibliography,* American Schools of Oriental Research (Cambridge, MA), 1975.

(With Frank M. Cross, Jr.) *Studies in Ancient Yahwistic Poetry,* Scholars Press (Atlanta, GA), 1975, revised edition, Dove/W.B. Eerdmans (Grand Rapids, MI), 1997.

(With Leona G. Running) *William Foxwell Albright: Twentieth-Century Genius,* Two Continents Publishing (New York, NY), 1975, second edition, 1991.

(With B. Mazar and Gaalyah Cornfeld) *The Mountain of the Lord,* Doubleday (New York, NY), 1975.

(With W. Phillips) *An Explorer's Life of Jesus,* Two Continents Publishing (New York, NY), 1975.

(Editor) *The Published Works of William Foxwell Albright: A Comprehensive Bibliography,* American Schools of Oriental Research (New Haven, CT), 1975.

(With Gaalyah Cornfeld) *Archaeology of the Bible: Book by Book,* Harper (New York, NY), 1976.

(Coeditor) Yehuda T. Radday, *An Analytical Linguistic Key-Word-in-Context Concordance to the Book of Judges,* Biblical Research Associates (Missoula, MT), 1977.

Excavation Reports, American Schools of Oriental Research (New Haven, CT), 1978.

(Editor) *Preliminary Excavation Reports: Bab edh-Dhra, Sardis, Meiron, Tell el Hesi, Carthage (Punic),* American Schools of Oriental Research (New Haven, CT), 1978.

(Editor) *Archeological Reports from the Tabqa Dam Project—Euphrates Valley, Syria,* American Schools of Oriental Research (New Haven, CT), 1979.

(Coeditor) Yehuda T. Radday, *An Analytical Linguistic Key-Word-in-Context Concordance to the Book of Genesis,* Biblical Research Associates (Missoula, MT), 1979.

(Author and editor, with F.I. Andersen) *Hosea: A New Translation with Introduction and Commentary* ("Anchor Bible" series), Doubleday (Garden City, NJ), 1980.

Pottery, Poetry, and Prophecy: Studies in Early Hebrew Poetry, Eisenbrauns (Winona Lake, IN), 1980.

(Coeditor) *Palestine in Transition: The Emergence of Ancient Israel,* Almond Press (Sheffield, England), 1983.

(With K.A. Mathews) *The Paleo-Hebrew Leviticus Scroll,* Eisenbrauns (Winona Lake, IN), 1985.

(Coeditor) *Backgrounds for the Bible,* Eisenbrauns (Winona Lake, IN), 1987.

(Author and editor, with F.I. Andersen) *Amos: A New Translation with Introduction and Commentary* ("Anchor Bible" series), Doubleday (New York, NY), 1989.

(Editor, with W.H. Propp and Baruch Halpern) *The Hebrew Bible and Its Interpreters,* Eisenbrauns (Winona Lake, IN), 1990.

The Unity of the Hebrew Bible, University of Michigan Press (Ann Arbor, MI), 1991.

(With A.D. Forbes and F.I. Andersen) *Studies in Hebrew and Aramaic Orthography,* Eisenbrauns (Winona Lake, IN), 1992.

(With Sara Mandell) *The Relationship between Herodotus' History and Primary History,* Scholars Press (Atlanta, GA), 1993.

(Coeditor) *Pomegranates and Golden Bells: Studies in Biblical, Jewish, and Near Eastern Ritual, Law, and Literature in Honor of Jacob Milgrom,* Eisenbrauns (Winona Lake, IN), 1995.

Divine Commitment and Human Obligation: Selected Writings of David Noel Freedman, two volumes, W.B. Eerdmans (Grand Rapids, MI), 1997.

(Coeditor) J. David Thompson and J. Arthur Baird, *A Critical Concordance to the Epistle of Barnabas,* Biblical Research Associates (Missoula, MT), 1997.

(Coeditor) J. David Thompson and J. Arthur Baird, *A Critical Concordance to the Epistle to Diognetus,* Biblical Research Associates (Missoula, MT), 1997.

(Coeditor) J. David Thompson and J. Arthur Baird, *A Critical Concordance to the Martyrdom of Saint Polycarp,* Biblical Research Associates (Missoula, MT), 1997.

(Coeditor) J. David Thompson and J. Arthur Baird, *A Critical Concordance to the Shepherd of Hermas,* Biblical Research Associates (Missoula, MT), 1998.

(Editor, with James A. Sanders, Marilyn J. Lundberg, and Astrid B. Beck) *The Leningrad Codex: A Facsimile Edition,* W.B. Eerdmans (Grand Rapids, MI), 1998.

(With Jeffrey C. Geoghegan and Andrew Welch) *Psalm 119: The Exaltation of Torah,* Eisenbrauns (Winona Lake, IN), 1999.

(Editor) *Eerdmans Dictionary of the Bible,* W.B. Eerdmans (Grand Rapids, MI), 2000.

(Author and editor, with F.I. Andersen) *Micah: A New Translation with Introduction and Commentary* ("Anchor Bible" series), Doubleday (New York, NY), 2000.

(With Jeffrey C. Geoghegan and Michael M. Homan) *The Nine Commandments: Uncovering a Hidden Pattern of Crime and Punishment in the Hebrew Bible,* edited by Astrid B. Beck, Doubleday (New York, NY), 2000.

(Editor, with Michael J. McClymond) *The Rivers of Paradise: Moses, Buddha, Confucius, Jesus, and Muhammad as Religious Founders,* W.B. Eerdmans (Grand Rapids, MI), 2001.

Also coauthor of *Jesus: The Four Gospels,* 1973, and (with T. Kachel) *Religion and the Academic Scene,* 1975. Contributor to books, including *The Bible and the Ancient Near East,* edited by G. Ernest Wright, Doubleday (New York, NY), 1961, and *Scripture and Ecumenism,* edited by L.J. Swidler, Duquesne University Press (Pittsburgh, PA), 1965. "Anchor Bible"

series, Doubleday (New York, NY), editor with W.F. Albright, 1956-71, editor in chief, 1971—; editor, with J.A. Baird, "Computer Bible" series, Biblical Research Associates, 1971—; editor for Reader's Digest books, including *Atlas of the Bible,* 1981, *Family Guide to the Bible,* 1984, *Mysteries of the Bible,* 1984, *Who's Who in the Bible,* 1994, *The Bible through the Ages,* 1996, and *The Complete Guide to the Bible,* 1998; editor, "Anchor Bible Reference Library," 1988—; editor in chief, *The Anchor Bible Dictionary,* six volumes, Doubleday (New York, NY), 1992; editor, "Eerdmans Critical Commentary" series. Consulting editor, *Interpreter's Dictionary of the Bible,* 1957-60, and *Theologisches Worterbuch des alten Testaments,* 1970-92. Editorial consultant to religious book departments, Doubleday, 1959-70, and Macmillan & Co., 1961-66, and to Genesis Project, 1973. Contributor to professional journals, including *Journal of Biblical Literature, Presbyterian Life, Near East Archaeological Society Bulletin,* and *Concordia Theological Quarterly. Journal of Biblical Literature,* associate editor, 1952-54, editor, 1955-59; editor, *American Schools of Oriental Research Bulletin,* 1974-78, and *Biblical Archaeologist,* 1976-82.

SIDELIGHTS: David Noel Freedman is an eminent biblical scholar whose work, especially as an editor of series such as the award-winning "Anchor Bible," has been valued by religious researchers going back to the 1950s. Decades later, he is still garnering respect from Bible experts for such works as the *The Anchor Bible Dictionary,* the compilation of which he supervised as editor in chief. Although noting some minor omissions in the six-volume reference work, Lawrence S. Cunningham, writing in *Commonweal,* called it "an extremely important reference tool both because of the solidity of the contributions and the abundant bibliographics. In that sense it will surely be the standard reference work on the shelf of every public and academic library." *Christian Century* writers Robert L. Brawley and Edward F. Campbell further remarked that the *The Anchor Bible Dictionary* bears witness to the fact that Freedman is "one of the most energetic, wide-ranging and creative figures in the current firmament of biblical scholarship."

Freedman received attention more recently for *The Nine Commandments: Uncovering a Hidden Pattern of Crime and Punishment in the Hebrew Bible,* which he wrote with Jeffrey C. Geoghegan and Michael M. Homan. In this work, Freedman makes the important assertion that it was not God who abandoned the Jews but rather the Jews who abandoned God because they repeatedly broke His commandments. (Freedman does not include "Thou shalt not covet" as the tenth commandment because covetous behavior is, in essence, according to Freedman, at the heart of several of the other commandments). *Library Journal* contributor Marcia Welsh called *The Nine Commandments* a "convincing and most stimulating new book." A *Publishers Weekly* critic praised the work even more highly, writing that it is a "rare example of a scholar who manages to say something new—new!—in an utterly accessible and engaging book about the Bible."

BIOGRAPHICAL AND CRITICAL SOURCES:

PERIODICALS

America, February 6, 1993, Daniel J. Harrington, review of *The Anchor Bible Dictionary,* p. 26; March 12, 2001, Daniel J. Harrington, "Books on the Bible: An Annual Roundup of Important Books on Scripture," p. 17.

Christian Century, April 21, 1993, Robert L. Brawley and Edward F. Campbell, review of *The Anchor Bible Dictionary,* p. 426; April 18, 2001, Leo D. Lefebure, review of *The Rivers of Paradise: Moses, Buddha, Confucius, Jesus, and Muhammad as Religious Founders,* p. 27.

Commonweal, November 20, 1992, Lawrence S. Cunningham, review of *The Anchor Bible Dictionary,* p. 28.

Journal of Near Eastern Studies, April, 2005, Kent Sparks, review of *The Rivers of Paradise,* p. 145; October, 2005, Dennis Pardee, review of *Eerdman's Dictionary of the Bible,* p. 285.

Library Journal, November 15, 2000, Marcia Welsh, review of *The Nine Commandments: Uncovering a Hidden Pattern of Crime and Punishment in the Hebrew Bible,* p. 74.

Publishers Weekly, October 16, 2000, review of *The Nine Commandments,* p. 68.*

*   *   *

FRIEDMAN, Norman 1925-

PERSONAL: Born April 10, 1925, in Boston, MA; son of Samuel and Eva (Nathanson) Friedman; married Zelda Nathanson, June 7, 1945; children: Michael, Janet. *Education:* Attended Brooklyn College (now Brooklyn College of the City University of New York), 1943, and Massachusetts Institute of Technology, 1943-44; Harvard University, A.B., 1948, A.M., 1949, Ph.D., 1952; Adelphi University, M.S.W., 1978; Gestalt Center for Psychotherapy and Training, certificate, 1978. *Politics:* Democrat. *Religion:* Jewish. *Hobbies and other interests:* Music, jogging, motorcycling.

ADDRESSES: Office—Gestalt Therapy Center of Queens, 33-54 164th St., Flushing, NY 11358-1442.

CAREER: Harvard University, Cambridge, MA, teaching fellow, 1950-52; University of Connecticut, Storrs, instructor, 1952-57, assistant professor, 1957-61, associate professor of English, 1961-63; Queens College of the City University of New York, Flushing, NY, associate professor, 1963-67, professor of English, 1968-88, professor emeritus, 1988—; part-time private practice in Gestalt therapy in Flushing, NY, beginning 1978; Gestalt Therapy Center of Queens, Flushing, NY, director, 1984—; Gestalt Center for Psychotherapy and Training, New York, NY, academic director, 1996-2000, executive codirector, 2000-03, academic consultant, 2003—. Fulbright lecturer in France, 1966-67. *Military service:* U.S. Navy, 1943-46, 1948; became lieutenant junior grade.

MEMBER: American Association of University Professors, Modern Language Association of America, National Council of Teachers of English, National Association of Social Workers, New York State United Teachers, New York State Association of Practicing Psychotherapists, Phi Beta Kappa.

AWARDS, HONORS: Bowdoin Essay Prize, Harvard University, 1948; American Council of Learned Societies grants, 1959, 1960; Annual Poetry Prize, *Northwest Review,* 1963; Borestone Mountain Poetry Award, 1964; winner of All-Nations Poetry Contest, 1977.

WRITINGS:

E.E. Cummings: The Art of His Poetry, Johns Hopkins Press (Baltimore, MD), 1960.

(With C.A. McLaughlin) *Poetry: An Introduction to Its Form and Art,* Harper (New York, NY), 1961, revised edition, 1963.

(With C.A. McLaughlin) *Logic, Rhetoric, and Style,* Little, Brown (Boston, MA), 1963.

E.E. Cummings: The Growth of a Writer, Southern Illinois University Press (Carbondale, IL), 1964.

(Editor) *E.E. Cummings: A Collection of Critical Essays,* Prentice-Hall (Englewood Cliffs, NJ), 1972.

Form and Meaning in Fiction, University of Georgia Press (Athens, GA), 1975.

The Magic Badge: Poems, 1953-1984, Slough Press (Austin, TX), 1984.

The Intrusions of Love: Poems, Mellen Poetry Press (Lewiston, NY), 1992.

(Re)valuing Cummings: Further Essays on the Poet, 1962-1993, University Press of Florida (Gainesville, FL), 1996.

Contributor to books, including *Perspectives,* edited by Leonard F. Dean, Harcourt (New York, NY), 1954; *The Red Badge of Courage: Text and Criticism,* edited by Lettis, McDonnell, and Morris, Harcourt (New York, NY), 1959; *Approaches to the Novel,* edited by Robert Scholes, Chandler Publishing, 1961; *A College Book of Modern Fiction,* edited by Rideout and Robinson, Row, Peterson, 1961; *The Bobbs-Merrill Reader,* edited by Kreuzer and Cogan, Bobbs-Merrill, 1962; *The Modern American Novel,* edited by Max Westbrook, Random House (New York, NY), 1966; *The Theory of the Novel,* edited by Philip Stevick, Macmillan (New York, NY), 1967; *The Novel: Modern Essays in Criticism,* edited by R.M. Davies, Prentice-Hall, 1969; *Forms of Rhetoric,* edited by Kakonis and Wilcox, McGraw, 1969; *Twentieth Century Interpretations of "A Farewell to Arms,"* edited by Jay Gellens, Prentice-Hall, 1970; *Virginia Woolf: "To the Lighthouse,"* edited by Morris Beja, Macmillan (New York, NY), 1970; *Kaleidoscope: Perspectives on Man,* edited by M. Weiss, Cummings, 1970; *Contemporary*

Poets of the English Language, edited by Rosalie Murphy, James Vinson, and D.L. Kirkpatrick, St. Martin's (New York, NY), 1970, second edition, 1975; *Die Amerikanische Short Story,* edited by Hans Burger, Wissenschaftliche Buchgesellschaft, 1972; *Essays on Metaphor,* edited by Warren Shibles, Language Press, 1972; *The Regeneration of the School,* edited by John De Cecco, Holt (New York, NY), 1972; *Short Story Theories,* edited by C.E. May, Ohio University Press, 1976; *Thomas Hardy, "The Mayor of Casterbridge": An Authoritative Text, Backgrounds, and Criticism,* edited by J.K. Robinson, Norton, 1977; and *Zur Struktur des Romans,* edited by Bruno Hillebrand, Wissenschaftliche Buchgesellschaft, 1978. Contributor to anthologies, including *New Voices 2: American Writing Today,* Hendricks House, 1955; *The National Poetry Anthology 1958,* National Poetry Association, 1958; *Lyrics of Love: Best New Love Poems, 1963,* Young Publishers, 1963; *Best Poems of 1963: Borestone Mountain Poetry Awards, 1964,* Pacific Books, 1964; *Best Poems of 1966: Borestone Mountain Poetry Awards, 1967,* Pacific Books, 1967; *May My Words Feed Others,* A.S. Barnes, 1974; *Passage IV,* Triton College Press, 1978; *The Magic Badge: Poems, 1953-1984,* Slough Press, 1984; and *The Intrusions of Love: Poems,* Mellen Poetry Press, 1992. Also contributor to *Encyclopedia Americana* and *Encyclopedia of Poetry and Poetics,* and to periodicals.

SIDELIGHTS: Norman Friedman once told *CA:* "I write literary criticism in order to know and understand others, and I write poems and stories in order to know and understand myself. So you can see, I will stop at nothing, having gone to great lengths to receive formal education and training in order to become a psychotherapist, as well as a teacher and writer. I find that psychology helps deepen and extend my literary criticism, and also my poems and stories."*

G

GABBARD, Krin 1948-

PERSONAL: Born January 29, 1948, in IL; son of Glendon (an actor) and Lucina (an actress; maiden name, Paquet) Gabbard; married Paula Beversdorf (a librarian), July 31, 1973. *Education:* University of Chicago, A.B., 1970; Indiana University—Bloomington, M.A., 1972, M.A., 1975, Ph.D., 1978.

ADDRESSES: Home—505 Court St., Apt. 4B, Brooklyn, NY 11236. *Office*—Department of Comparative Literature, State University of New York at Stony Brook, Stony Brook, NY 11794; fax: 631-632-5707. *E-mail*—kgabbard@notes.cc.sunysb.edu.

CAREER: University of South Dakota, Vermillion, assistant professor of comparative literature, 1977-79; Stephens College, Columbia, MO, assistant professor of comparative literature, 1979-81; State University of New York at Stony Brook, assistant professor, 1981-87, associate professor, 1987-96, professor of comparative literature, 1997—, chair of the department of comparative studies, acting director of Federated Learning Community, 1989-90. Visiting professor of film studies, Columbia University, 2001. Producer and announcer of "Jazz on the Air," WUSB-FM Radio. Member of advisory board, Forum for the Psychoanalytic Study of film, 1989.

MEMBER: Modern Language Association of America, American Comparative Literature Association, Society for Cinema Studies (member of executive council, 2003).

AWARDS, HONORS: George S. Kaufman Playwriting Prize, Dramatists Guild Fund, 1970; National Endowment for the Humanities fellowship, 1979; University Award, Stony Brook Foundation, 1982; State University at Stony Brook Exceptional Service to Undergraduate Education award, 1985, Merit Award for Excellence in Teaching, 1987, Merit Award for Teaching and Curriculum Development, 1995, and Presidential Mini-Grant for Innovative Teaching Projects, 1998; National Book Award nomination, 1996, for *Jammin' at the Margins.*

WRITINGS:

(With Glen O. Gabbard) *Psychiatry and the Cinema,* University of Chicago Press (Chicago, IL), 1987, second edition, American Psychiatric Press (Arlington, VA), 1999.

(Editor) *Jazz among the Discourses,* Duke University Press (Durham, NC), 1995.

(Editor) *Representing Jazz,* Duke University Press (Durham, NC), 1995.

Jammin' at the Margins: Jazz and the American Cinema, University of Chicago Press (Chicago, IL), 1996.

Black Magic: White Hollywood and African American Culture, Rutgers University Press (New Brunswick, NJ), 2004.

Also contributor of chapters to numerous books, including *Jazz in Mind: Essays on the History and Meanings of Jazz,* edited by Reginald T. Buckner and Steven Weiland, Wayne State University Press (Detroit, MI), 1991; *Screen Memories,* by Harvey R. Greenberg, Columbia University Press (New York, NY), 1993; *Jazz: A Century of Change,* edited by Lewis Porter, Schirmer (New York, NY), 1997; *The Louis Armstrong*

Companion: Eight Decades of Commentary, edited by Joshua Berett, Schirmer (New York, NY), 1999; *Music and Cinema,* edited by James Buhler, Caryl Flinn, and David Neumeyer, Wesleyan University Press (Westport, CT), 2000; *Cinesonic: Experiencing the Soundtrack,* edited by Philip Brothy, Australian Film Television and Radio School (North Ryde, Australia), 2001; *The Cambridge Companion to Jazz,* edited by Merwyn Cooke and David Horn, Cambridge University Press (Cambridge, England), 2002; and *The Other Side of Nowhere,* edited by Daniel Fischlin and Ajay Heble, Wesleyan University Press (Middletown, CT), 2004. Contributor to periodicals, including *Helios, Bucknell Review, Literature/Film Quarterly, Chronicle of Higher Education, Performing Arts: Broadcasting, Journal of Popular Musical Studies, Culture Front, American Music, Psychiatric Times, Menninger Perspective,* and *Psychoanalytic Review.* Book review editor, *Men and Masculinities,* 1994—; editorial board member, *Cinema Journal,* 1998-2003.

SIDELIGHTS: Krin Gabbard is a literature professor with a strong interest in film and music, especially jazz. In his book *Jammin' at the Margins: Jazz and the American Cinema* the author traces the history of jazz in film, beginning with jazz singer Al Jolson's appearance in the first talking movie, aptly titled *The Jazz Singer.* Writing in *Cineaste,* David Segal noted that "the book is not so much about jazz and the American cinema per se as it is about the representation of jazz in American film." Segal went on to comment, "This allows Gabbard to bring up questions of race, gender, sexual orientation, the jazz canon, 'art' vs. 'commercialism,' high art and popular culture, et al." Kathryn Kalinak, writing in the *Historical Journal of Film, Radio and Television,* called the effort "a wonderful book: well-researched, cogently argued and highly readable. That it accomplishes its goals in an area previously neglected in film (and music) scholarship clearly establishes it as the standard in the field."

In his *Black Magic: White Hollywood and African American Culture* the author examines Hollywood's representation of black culture and society in films, as well as how individual blacks have been portrayed in cinema. For example, he discusses movies in which black heavenly figures such as angels come to the aid of white people, "seeing them as an expression of the desire for racial healing without giving up white privilege,"as Vanessa Bush noted in *Booklist.*

BIOGRAPHICAL AND CRITICAL SOURCES:

PERIODICALS

Africa America Review, summer, 1997, Guthrie P. Ramsey, Jr., review of *Representing Jazz,* p. 348.

American Music, spring, 1997, Ingrid Monson, reviews of *Jazz among the Discourses* and *Representing Jazz,* p. 110; summer, 1998, Bernard Gendron, review of *Jammin' at the Margins: Jazz and the American Cinema,* p. 227.

Booklist, May 15, 2004, Vanessa Bush, review of *Black Magic: White Hollywood and African American Culture,* p. 1588.

Cineaste, fall, 1996, David Segal, review of *Jammin' at the Margins,* p. 67.

Entertainment Weekly, September 20, 1996, David Hajdu, review of *Jammin' at the Margins,* p. 74.

Historical Journal of Film, Radio and Television, March, 1997, Kathryn Kalinak, review of *Jammin' at the Margins,* p. 168.

Popular Music and Society, fall, 1991, Neil Lerner, review of *Jammin' at the Margins,* p. 122.

ONLINE

Columbia University Center for Jazz Studies Web site, http://www.jazz.columbia.edu/ (September 7, 2005), faculty profile of Gabbard.*

*   *   *

GADDIS, William 1922-1998

PERSONAL: Born 1922, in New York, NY; died December 16, 1998, in East Hampton, NY; children: one son, one daughter. *Education:* Attended Harvard College, 1941-45.

CAREER: Novelist. *New Yorker,* New York, NY, fact checker, 1946-47; lived in Latin America, Europe, and North Africa, 1947-52; freelance writer of filmscripts, speeches, and corporate communications, 1956-70. Also taught at universities, including a distinguished visiting professor at Bard College, 1977.

MEMBER: American Academy of Arts and Letters, American Academy of Arts and Sciences.

AWARDS, HONORS: National Institute of Arts and Letters grant, 1963; National Endowment for the Arts grants, 1967 and 1974; Rockefeller grant and National Book Award for fiction, both 1976, both for *JR;* Guggenheim Fellowship, 1981; MacArthur Foundation Fellowship, 1982; nomination for PEN/Faulkner Award, 1985, for *Carpenter's Gothic;* New York State Author, 1993-95; National Book Award, 1994, and National Book Critics' Circle Award, 1995, for *A Frolic of His Own.*

WRITINGS:

NOVELS

The Recognitions, Harcourt (New York, NY), 1955, corrected edition, Penguin Books (New York, NY), 1993.

JR, Knopf (New York, NY), 1975, corrected edition, Penguin Books, 1993.

Carpenter's Gothic, Viking (New York, NY), 1985.

A Frolic of His Own, Simon & Schuster (New York, NY), 1994.

Agape Agape, Viking (New York, NY), 2002.

OTHER

The Rush for Second Place: Essays and Occasional Writings, edited by Joseph Tabbi, Penguin Books (New York, NY), 2002.

Contributor to periodicals, including *Atlantic, Antaeus, New Yorker, New York Times,* and *Harper's.*

SIDELIGHTS: William Gaddis was one of the most highly regarded yet least read novelists in America. Although many readers remain unfamiliar with his work, certain critics have made extravagant claims for it. Richard Toney, in the *San Francisco Review of Books,* described Gaddis's first book, *The Recognitions,* as "a novel of stunning power, 956 pages of linguistic pyrotechnics and multi-lingual erudition unmatched by any American writer in this century— perhaps in any century." L.J. Davis, in the *National Observer,* wrote that Gaddis's second novel, *JR,* "is the equal of—if not superior to—its predecessor." With the publication in 1994 of *A Frolic of His Own,* which won a National Book Award, Gaddis's work received wider recognition.

Gaddis drew heavily on his own background for the settings of his novels. Born in Manhattan in 1922, he was raised in Massapequa, Long Island, in the house that was the model for the Bast home in *JR.* Like the Basts, Gaddis's maternal relatives were Quakers, though he himself was raised in a Calvinist tradition, as is Wyatt Gwyon in *The Recognitions.* Like Otto in the same novel and Jack Gibbs in *JR,* Gaddis grew up without a father. Haunting all four novels, in fact, is the spirit of a dead or absent father who leaves a ruinous state of affairs for his children, a situation that may be extrapolated to include Gaddis's literary vision of a world abandoned by God and plunged into disorder. The writer's fifth through thirteenth years were spent at a boarding school in Berlin, Connecticut, which not only furnished the fictional Jack Gibbs with the bleak memories recalled in *JR* but also provided the unnamed New England setting for the first chapter of *The Recognitions.* Returning to Long Island to attend Farmingdale High School, Gaddis contracted the illness that debilitates Wyatt in the first novel and that kept Gaddis out of World War II. Instead he attended Harvard University and edited the *Harvard Lampoon* until circumstances required him to leave in 1945 without a degree.

Back in New York, Gaddis worked as a fact checker at the *New Yorker,* a job that he later recalled as "terribly good training, a kind of post-graduate school for a writer, checking everything, whether they were stories or profiles or articles." The author once noted that he got the intricacies associated with high finance for his novel *JR* while working at the *New Yorker.* At this time he also mingled in the Greenwich Village milieu recreated in the middle section of *The Recognitions.* Here he became acquainted with future Beat writers William Burroughs, Allen Ginsberg, Alan Ansen, Chandler Brossard, and Jack Kerouac. (In fact, Kerouac converted Gaddis into a character named Harold Sand in his 1958 novel *The Subterraneans.*) In 1947 Gaddis set off on five years of wandering through Mexico, Central America, Spain, France, and North Africa until, in 1952, he returned to America to complete his first novel.

Published in 1955, *The Recognitions* is an account of personal integration amid collective disintegration, of an individual finding himself in a society losing itself.

Protagonist Wyatt Gwyon, a failed seminarian, turns to forging Old Masters in an earnest but misguided attempt to return to an era when art was authentic and sanctioned by God. Gaddis sets Wyatt in stark contrast to most of the other artist figures in the novel: Otto, the playwright; Esme, the poet; Max, the painter; Sinisterra, the counterfeiter—all of whom plagiarize, falsify, or discredit the artistic process. These personages, along with the rest of the novel's large cast of characters, are representative of a society crumbling in a shoddy world so encrusted with counterfeit that "recognitions" of authenticity are nearly impossible.

The action in *The Recognitions* runs on two narrative planes that occasionally intersect. On one plane lives Wyatt, whom Frederick Karl in *Conjunctions* called "an avenging Messiah . . . because he perceives himself as bringing a purifying and cleansing quality, a 'recognition,' to a society that has doomed itself with corruptive sophistication." Wyatt, however, is hobbled in his pursuit of a "vision of order" (as it is later defined in *Carpenter's Gothic*) by a psychologically crippling boyhood that has instilled in him a mixture of guilt, secrecy, and alienation. The author exposes the compromised worlds of religion and art in the first two chapters, and Wyatt's brief fling with conventionality (complete with wife and nine-to-five job) fails by chapter three, leaving him open to the temptations of the novel's Mephistopheles, Recktall Brown, a corrupt art dealer. Selling his soul to the devil, Wyatt retreats offstage for the entrance of his parodic counterpart, Otto Pivner, whose comic misadventures in Central America and Greenwich Village constitute the second narrative plane of the novel.

Here the "corruptive sophistication" mentioned by *Conjunctions* reviewer Karl appear as endless discussions of art and religion are carried on through endless parties and bar conversations by those whom Gaddis lampoons as "the educated classes, an ill-dressed, underfed, overdrunken group of squatters with minds so highly developed that they were excused from good manners, tastes so refined in one direction that they were excused for having none in any other, emotions so cultivated that the only aberration was normality, all afloat here on sodden pools of depravity calculated only to manifest the pricelessness of what they were throwing away, the three sexes in two colors, a group of people all mentally and physically the wrong size."

With the realization that the major cause for the godless condition embodied by and surrounding modern humanity may be attributed to the absence of love, Wyatt abandons forgery, travels to Spain (where his mother is entombed), and finds the love necessary to baptize his new life. Spurning love, the rest of the novel's characters are last seen rushing headlong into death, madness, or disintegration.

The Recognitions presents a multi-layered complexity necessary to dramatize the novel's themes of imitation versus reality. As Tony Tanner pointed out in the *New York Times Book Review:* "If at times we feel lost, displaced, disoriented as we move through the complicated edifice of the book, we are only experiencing analogically a lostness that is felt in varying ways by all the characters in the book." Often eschewing traditional narrative exposition, Gaddis abandons the reader at the various scenes of action, forcing him instead to overhear the confused gropings, deliberate lies, and mistaken notions of the characters, to sort them out as best he can. In other words, the reader must participate in the novel and make the same "recognitions" demanded of its characters by the title. An immense network of allusions, references, motifs, and gestures are introduced and repeated in countless convoluted permutations, demanding much more than casual attention from the reader. The novel is also very erudite, but any negative effects of this characteristic have often been overemphasized; the sense, if not the literal meaning, of Gaddis's hundreds of references, allusions, and foreign language phrases is usually clear enough from the context.

The Recognitions had little immediate critical impact upon publication. A few readers recognized its greatness immediately, but only in later years did a historical perspective allow critics to gauge its importance. In his 1975 *Saturday Review* assessment of Gaddis's second novel, John W. Aldridge, an early champion, wrote from such a perspective: "As is usually the case with abrasively original work, there had to be a certain passage of time before an audience could begin to be educated to accept *The Recognitions*. The problem was not simply that the novel was too long and intricate or its vision of experience too outrageous, but that even the sophisticated reading public of the mid-Fifties was not yet accustomed to the kind of fiction it represented."

Little was heard of Gaddis in the decade and a half after 1955. Denied the life of a "successful" novelist, he began a long line of jobs in industry, working first in publicity for a pharmaceutical firm, then writing films for the army, and later writing speeches for corporate executives (as does Thomas Eigen in *JR*, who has also published an important but neglected novel). With the 1970 appearance in the *Dutton Review* of what would later become the opening pages of his second novel, Gaddis broke his fifteen-year silence. Two more fragments from *JR* appeared, in *Antaeus* and *Harper's*, before the novel was published in the fall of 1975 to much stronger reviews than those received by *The Recognitions*. *JR* won the National Book Award for the best fiction of the year and has since earned the praise of such writers as Saul Bellow, Mary McCarthy, William H. Gass, Stanley Elkin, Joseph McElroy, and Don DeLillo.

Although this intricate, 726-page novel resists easy summary, it is essentially a satire of corporate America, a "country" so obsessed with money that failure is all but inevitable for anyone who does not sell his soul to Mammon. The first word of the novel is "money," a word that reappears throughout the novel as its debasing touch besmirches everything from education to science, from politics to marriage, from the arts to warfare. At the center of the novel is eleven-year-old J.R. Vansant, a slovenly but clever boy who transforms a small "portfolio" of mail order acquisitions and penny stocks into an unwieldy paper empire in an improbably short time. The most radical feature of the novel is its narrative mode: except for an occasional transitional passage, the novel is composed entirely of dialogue. While novels composed totally of dialogue had been written before, none followed Gaddis's extreme format. For his dialogue is not the literary dialogue of most novels, tidied up and helpfully sprinkled with conversational conventions and explanatory asides by the author helping to clarify what the characters actually mean. Instead, *JR* reads like a tape-recorded transcription of real voices: ungrammatical, often truncated, with constant interruptions by other characters (and by telephones, radios, and televisions), with rarely an identifying or interpretive remark by the author.

Such a literary mode makes unusual demands upon the reader; it requires that he read actively with involvement and concentration, rather than passively, awaiting entertainment. Jack Gibbs, a major character, pinpoints this problem during a drunken conversation with Edward Bast, a young composer: ". . . problem most God damned readers rather be at the movies. Pay

attention here bring something to it take something away problem most God damned writing's written for readers perfectly happy who they are rather be at the movies, come in empty-handed go out the same God damned way I told him Bast. Ask them to bring one God damned bit of effort want everything done for them they get up and go to the movies."

Just as everyone in the counterfeit cultural world of *The Recognitions* moves in relation to Wyatt, everyone in the phony paper world of *JR* moves in relation to the young title figure, who embodies ignorance in its happy, greedy pursuit of money. J.R. gleefully accepts the corrupt civilization handed down to him, wanting only to know how fast he can get his share. By following the letter of the law at the expense of its spirit, he is able to build his "family of companies" with the assistance of adults as amoral as he is.

The only adults who attempt to infuse a moral sense into J.R. are his teacher, Amy Joubert, and his reluctant business associate, Edward Bast, a struggling musician. But Amy is too preoccupied with her own problems to be of much help, and Bast causes more problems than he solves. Although one of the major conflicts in the novel is between such outwardly directed people as J.R. and such inwardly directed people as the book's artists, all of the latter figures have largely themselves to blame for their artistic failures rather than the crass business world to which they belong. Despite their failures, however, most are seen at work on new art projects at the novel's end, representing their only chance to break away from the worship of materialism.

The term "entropy" is introduced in the novel almost as early as "money," and this concept—the tendency for any system to move from a state of order to one of disorder—operates throughout the novel. Nearly everyone in Gaddis's novel is caught up in a desperate attempt to hold things together in the face of encroaching disorder and dissolution. But the attempts are largely futile: families break up, artists burn out and/or commit suicide, businesses close or are swallowed up by conglomerates, children are abandoned, coitus is interrupted, and communication breaks down. In *JR*, everyone's life is chaotic, and the exclusive use of dialogue creates what Thomas LeClair described in *Modern Fiction Studies* as "a massive consistency in which characters with different backgrounds, money-men and artists alike, come to have the same rushed habits of speech, the inability to complete a message or act." As *Saturday Review* contributor Aldridge concluded about *JR:* "It is undoubtedly inevitable that the novel promises at almost every point to fall victim to the imitative fallacy, that it is frequently as turgid, monotonous, and confusing as the situation it describes. Yet Gaddis has a strength of mind and talent capable of surmounting this very large difficulty. He has managed to reflect chaos in a fiction that is not itself artistically chaotic because it is imbued with the conserving and correcting power of his imagination. His awareness of what is human and sensible is always present behind his depiction of how far we have fallen from humanity and sense."

Like its predecessor, *JR* is primarily a comic novel. As Alicia Metcalf Miller wrote in the Cleveland *Plain Dealer:* "If Gaddis is a moralist, he is also a master of satire and humor. *JR* is a devastatingly funny book. Reading it, I laughed loudly and unashamedly in public places, and at home, more than once, I saw my small children gather in consternation as tears of laughter ran down my face."

Gaddis's underground reputation surfaced somewhat following the publication of *JR* in 1975. The National Book Award for fiction was followed by a steady stream of academic essays and dissertations about him, culminating in 1982 with the first book on Gaddis's work, a special issue of the *Review of Contemporary Fiction,* and his receipt of a MacArthur Foundation Fellowship. Two years later, the second book on his work appeared, Gaddis was elected to the American Academy and Institute of Arts and Letters, and he finished his third novel.

For this novel—originally titled *That Time of Year: A Romance* but published in the summer of 1985 as *Carpenter's Gothic*—Gaddis turned away from the "mega-novel" and set out to write a shorter (262 pages), different sort of book. As he explained in a *Washington Post Book World* interview with Lloyd Grove: "I wanted it to move very fast. Everything that happens on one page is preparing for the next page and the next chapter and the end of the book. When I started I thought, 'I want 240 pages'—that was what I set out for. It preserved the unity: one place, one very small amount of time, very small group of characters, and then, in effect, there's a nicer word than 'cliche,' what is it? Staples. That is, the staples of the marriage, which is on the rocks, the obligatory adultery, the locked room, the mysterious stranger, the older man and the younger woman, to try to take these and make them work."

Gaddis restores to worn-out literary clichés some of their original drama and intensity, particularly in *Carpenter's Gothic.* Like *The Recognitions,* his third novel is concerned with the ambiguous nature of reality; "there's a very fine line between the truth and what really happens" is an oft-repeated line in *Carpenter's Gothic.* It also attacks the perversions done in the name of religion. From *JR* it takes its narrative technique—an almost total dependence on dialogue—and its contempt for the motivating factor of capitalism. Sometimes seen by critics as a smaller, less important reflection of the author's two preceding novels, this novel presents Gaddis's most characteristic themes and techniques with economy and flair.

Carpenter's Gothic is rooted in a specific time and place: the action takes place over a month's time (internal references date it October-November, 1983) in a "carpenter gothic" style Victorian house in a small Hudson River Valley town. (Gaddis owned just such a house on Ritie Street in Piermont, New York.) Almost continuously on stage is Elizabeth Booth: "Bibbs" to her brother Billy, "Liz" to her husband Paul, and "Mrs. Booth" to McCandless, the house's owner and a failed novelist. These men subject Liz to the bullying, self-serving dialogue that makes up the bulk of the novel and that brings the outside world onto Gaddis's one-set stage. With newspapers and telephone calls filling the roles of messengers, a complicated plot quickly unfolds concerning Christian fundamentalism, political chicanery, African mineral rights, and a half-dozen family disputes. Long-suffering Liz endures it all, helpless to prevent her men from rushing headlong into—and even creating—the Armageddon that looms on the final pages of the novel.

In *Carpenter's Gothic,* as in all of Gaddis's novels, the males do most of the talking and create most of the problems. Like Esme in *The Recognitions* and Amy in *JR,* Liz is the still point in a frantic male world, "the only thing that holds things together," as her brother Billy admits. Though flawed, she is perhaps the most sympathetic figure in all three of Gaddis's novels.

Liz's husband Paul, a Vietnam veteran once attacked by his own men, is in one sense a grown-up J.R. Vansant—an identification Gaddis encourages when someone dismisses Paul for "know[ing] as much about finance as some snot nosed sixth grader." Like J.R., Paul simply does what people do to "make it" in

America, never examining for an instant the ethics or morality of his questionable dealings. But the man who brings the greatest disorder into Liz's life is McCandless, the mysterious owner of the house, whom she transforms into a wearily romantic figure out of Charlotte Bronte's *Jane Eyre* (a movie version of which serves as a backdrop to Liz and Paul's joyless lovemaking). McCandless, no longer feeling any connection between his world and himself and outraged at the stupidity that has severed that connection, can only envision a bleak future.

This vision of deep disorder and empty outlook belonged to Gaddis as well, for *Carpenter's Gothic,* as Peter Prescott declared in his *Newsweek* article, "is surely Gaddis's most pessimistic, his most savage novel." No one in the novel demonstrates any possibility of sidestepping, much less overcoming, Gaddis's vision of the world's crushing stupidity. An escape hatch through which characters such as Wyatt and Bast can save themselves is present in the first two novels, but no such option exists in *Carpenter's Gothic.* As Robert Kelly noted in *Conjunctions,* Gaddis does not seem to have "an optimistic bone in his body—at least not in his writing hand." This pessimism bothers many readers, but Kelly explains: "We are foolish if we expect the skilful anatomist who excoriates vicious folly to provide a cure for it too— and doubly foolish if we credit any panacea he does trick himself into prescribing."

In a 1986 *Listener* article, Peter Kemp described the work as Gaddis's "grimmest book," observing, "A scathing, exacerbated tour de force, *Carpenter's Gothic* seems the last word on a society whose doomed babble it so vehemently transmits." In the *Nation,* Terrence Rafferty mentioned the book's "sour, contemptuous tone and its formal bad faith," adding: "The real story of *Carpenter's Gothic* isn't the end of the world, it's the end of the imagination, the world gone dark in the writer's head." Carol Iannone remarked in *Commentary* that "Gaddis means to show us the consequences of stupidity . . . . *Carpenter's Gothic* shows that Gaddis was not so much an artist as an anti-artist, working with cartoon characters and disembodied ideas."

Even art, the panacea prescribed in the first two novels, is suspect in the third book. On one level, *Carpenter's Gothic* is a meditation on fiction, specifically on the dubious motives for writers' fiction-making impulses.

For Liz—as perhaps for the younger Gaddis—fiction offers "some hope of order restored, even that of a past life in tatters, revised, amended, fabricated in fact from its very outset to reorder its unlikelihoods, what it all might have been." But McCandless insists on the suspect, compromised nature of art in his commentary on the carpenter gothic style of his house, a passage which doubles as a description of the novel itself: "All they had were the simple dependable old materials, the wood and their hammers and saws and their own clumsy ingenuity bringing those grandiose visions the masters had left behind down to a human scale with their own little inventions, . . . a patchwork of conceits, borrowings, deceptions, the inside's a hodgepodge of good intentions like one last ridiculous effort at something worth doing even on this small a scale." In this sense, any reader who flees the disorder of life for the order of art will find cold comfort in *Carpenter's Gothic.*

Throughout Gaddis's novels there is a sense of bitter disappointment at America for not fulfilling its potential, for events not working out as planned. In this regard Gaddis resembles his beloved Russian novelists of the nineteenth century. In the third novel, however, America seems to have reached the bottom of the psychosocial abyss. *Carpenter's Gothic* implies that it is too late to reverse the tide, to restore the promise of the American dream, too late for anything more than "one last ridiculous effort at something worth doing."

Emphasizing litigiousness and greed as characteristics of contemporary American society, Gaddis's award-winning novel *A Frolic of His Own* focuses on Oscar Crease, his family, his friends, and the various lawsuits in which they are all enmeshed. Employing elements of humor and farce, Gaddis exhaustively details the absurdities of his characters' suits and subsequent countersuits. For example, Oscar is plaintiff in a plagiarism case he has brought against Constantine Kiester, a top Hollywood producer whose real name is Jonathan Livingston Siegal. Oscar is also, paradoxically, plaintiff and defendant in a suit concerning a hit-and-run accident in which he was hit by his own car—a Sosumi ("so sue me"). Taking its title from a British legal phrase used to describe an employee's actions which, though they resulted in on-the-job injuries, do not entitle the employee to compensation, *A Frolic of His Own* is largely noted for its satire of justice and law in contemporary American society and for its unusual narrative structure.

Except for the inclusion of excerpts from Oscar's writings, legal documents, and court opinions, the novel is told primarily through dialogue that is unattributed and only lightly punctuated. Critics praised Gaddis's realistic depiction of everyday speech—complete with pauses, interruptions, and unfinished thoughts—and stressed the difficulty such a narrative technique, reminiscent of stream-of-consciousness writing, places on readers. Steven Moore observed in the *Nation:* "*A Frolic of His Own* is both cutting-edge, state-of-the-art fiction and a throwback to the great moral novels of Tolstoy and Dickens. That it can be both is just one of the many balancing acts it performs: It is bleak and pessimistic while howlingly funny; it is a deeply serious exploration of such lofty themes as justice and morality but is paced like a screwball comedy; it is avant-garde in its fictional techniques but traditional in conception and in the reading pleasures it offers; it is a damning indictment of the United States, Christianity and the legal system." Zachary Leader in the *Times Literary Supplement* called *A Frolic of His Own* a "bleak, brilliant, exhausting novel."

Gaddis's novel *Agape Agape* was published posthumously nearly four years after the author's death in 1998. The novel is made up of the monologue of a man on his deathbed, reflecting the fact that Gaddis himself was dying when he wrote the book. At less than a hundred pages, *Agape Agape* represents a different approach for the author as the dying unnamed character explains his efforts to bring together notes and other jottings to tell his story. His story involves the invention of the player piano and its representation as the mechanization of society and the loss of the real artist. Writing in the *Library Journal,* David W. Henderson commented: "The fertility of Gaddis's own mind is evident." *Booklist* contributor Donna Seaman called the book an "incisive, caustically elegiac final novel." Peter Kemp, writing in London's *Sunday Times,* noted that the novel is "Beckett-like in its minimalism." In an article in the *Daily Telegraph* of London, Alan Marshall noted that the book contains "many fine passages"and also wrote: "It's not a book to rush through but to savour."

The Rush for Second Place: Essays and Occasional Writings presents a broad spectrum of the author's writings, primarily focusing on nonfiction essays and including notes, tributes, a movie treatment, and other work. In this collection the author addresses many of the same themes he discusses in his fiction, such as corporate greed, the military industrial complex, and the overemphasis in America on work and money that often leads to hypocrisy. Donna Seaman commented in *Booklist* that the author "wrote tonic critical essays spiked with a parodic wit." A *Kirkus Reviews* contributor wrote: "Sometimes dense, but always discerning: essential for Gaddis fans and those seeking an offbeat critique of American civilization." *Book* contributor Tom Leclair noted: "The best essays produce objective sociological and political evidence for their author's outrage."

BIOGRAPHICAL AND CRITICAL SOURCES:

BOOKS

Aldridge, John W., *In Search of Heresy,* McGraw (New York, NY), 1956.

Comnes, Gregory, *The Ethics of Indeterminacy in the Novels of William Gaddis,* University Press of Florida (Gainesville, FL), 1994.

Contemporary Literary Criticism, Gale (Detroit, MI), Volume 1, 1973, Volume 3, 1975, Volume 6, 1976, Volume 8, 1978, Volume 10, 1979, Volume 19, 1981, Volume 43, 1987, Volume 86, 1995.

Dictionary of Literary Biography, Volume 2: *American Novelists since World War II,* Gale (Detroit, MI), 1978.

Gaddis, William, *The Recognitions,* Harcourt (New York, NY), 1955, corrected edition, Penguin Books (New York, NY), 1985.

Gaddis, William, *JR,* Knopf (New York, NY), 1975, corrected edition, Penguin Books (New York, NY), 1985.

Gaddis, William, *Carpenter's Gothic,* Viking (New York, NY), 1985.

Gardner, John, *On Moral Fiction,* Basic Books (New York, NY), 1978.

Knight, Christopher J., *Hints and Guesses: William Gaddis's Fiction of Longing,* University of Wisconsin Press (Madison, WI), 1997.

Kuehl, John, and Steven Moore, editors, *In Recognition of William Gaddis,* Syracuse University Press (Syracuse, NY), 1984.

Madden, David, *Rediscoveries,* Crown (New York, NY), 1971.

Magill, Frank N., editor, *Survey of Contemporary Literature,* supplement, Salem Press, 1972.

Magill, Frank N., editor, *Literary Annual,* Salem Press, 1976.

McCaffery, Larry, editor, *Postmodern Fiction,* Greenwood Press (Westport, CT), 1986.

Moore, Steven, *A Reader's Guide to William Gaddis's "The Recognitions,"* University of Nebraska Press (Lincoln, NE), 1982.

Tanner, Tony, *City of Words,* Harper (New York, NY), 1971.

Wiener, Norbert, *The Human Use of Human Beings,* Houghton Mifflin (Boston, MA), 1954.

Wolfe, Peter, *A Vision of His Own: The Mind and Art of William Gaddis,* Fairleigh Dickinson University Press (Madison, NJ), 1996.

PERIODICALS

Book, November-December, 2002, Tom Leclair, review of *The Rush for Second Place: Essays and Occasional Writings,* p. 81.

Booklist, September 15, 2002, Donna Seaman, reviews of *Agape Agape* and *The Rush for Second Place,* p. 194.

Boston Globe, March 16, 2003, John Freeman, review of *Agape Agape,* p. D9.

Commentary, December, 1985, Carol Iannone, review of *Carpenter Gothic,* pp. 62-65.

Conjunctions, spring, 1985, Frederick Karl, *American Fictions: The Mega Novel;* fall, 1985, Robert Kelly, "Elegy."

Contemporary Literature, winter, 2001, Christopher J. Knight, "The New York State Writers Institute Tapes: William Gaddis," transcript, p. 666.

Denver Post, January 5, 2003, John Freeman, "Gaddis Deserves to Be Read, Not Just Dissected and Discussed," p. EE-02.

Guardian (London, England), December 21, 2002, Peter Dempsey, "Left on the Shelf," review of authors' works, p. 26.

Irish Times, January 11, 2003, Eileen Battersby, review of *Agape Agape,* p. 60.

Kirkus Reviews, August 1, 2002, review of *Agape Agape,* p. 1053; August 15, 2002, review of *The Rush for Second Place,* p. 1193.

Library Journal, September 15, 2002, David W. Henderson, review of *Agape Agape,* p. 89.

Listener, March 13, 1986, Peter Kemp, review of *Carpenter's Gothic,* pp. 28-29.

Modern Fiction Studies, Number 27, 1981-82, Thomas LeClair, review of *JR.*

Nation, April 30, 1955; November 16, 1985, Terrence Rafferty, review of *Carpenter's Gothic,* p. 496; April 25, 1994, Steven Moore, review of *A Frolic of His Own,* pp. 569-571.

National Observer, October 11, 1975, L.J. Davis, review of *JR.*

New England Review, summer, 1995, Anatole Broyard, "Remembering William Gaddis in the Nineteen-Fifites," p. 13.

Newsweek, July 15, 1985, Peter Prescott, review of *Carpenter's Gothic.*

New York Times Book Review, July 14, 1974, Tony Tanner, review of *The Recognitions,* p. 27; November 9, 1975, review of *JR,* p. 62; January 9, 1994, Robert Towers, review of *A Frolic of His Own,* pp. 1, 22.

Plain Dealer (Cleveland, OH), October, 1975, Alicia Metcalf Miller, review of *JR;* December 22, 2002, John Freeman, reviews of *Agape Agape* and *The Rush for Second Place,* p. 19.

Publishers Weekly, January 6, 1997, Judy Quinn, "Gaddis's First Nonfiction," p. 22; September 23, 2002, review of *Agape Agape,* p. 48.

San Francisco Review of Books, February, 1976, Richard Toney, review of author's works.

Saturday Review, March 12, 1955; October 4, 1975, John W. Aldridge reviews of *The Recognitions* and *JR.*

Sunday Times (London, England), January 19, 2003, Peter Kemp, review of *Agape Agape,* p. 44.

Times Literary Supplement, June 3, 1994, Zachary Leader, review of *A Frolic of His Own,* p. 22.

Washington Post Book World, July 7, 1985, Lloyd Grove, interview with author, p. 1.

ONLINE

Complete Review, http://www.complete-review.com/ (March 26, 2003), review of *Agape Agape.*

Gaddis Annotations, http://www.williamgaddis.org/ (March 26, 2003), Web site devoted to author and his work.

New York State Writers Institute Web site, http://www.albany.edu/writers-inst/ (March 27, 2003), profile of author and his works.

SFGate.com, http://www.sfgate.com/ (March 26, 2003), reviews of *Agape Agape* and *The Rush for Second Place.*

OBITUARIES

PERIODICALS

Chicago Tribune, December 19, 1998, p. 23.

Independent (London, England), December 24, 1998, Malcolm Bradbury.

Los Angeles Times, December 18, 1998, Elaine Woo, "William Gaddis; Noted but Little-Read Author," p. 2.

New York Times, December 17, 1998, p. B15.

Times (London, England), January 14, 1999.

Washington Post, December 19, 1998, p. B6.*

*   *   *

GARROW, David J. 1953-
(David Jeffries Garrow)

PERSONAL: Born May 11, 1953, in New Bedford, MA; son of Walter J. (in business) and Barbara (Fassett) Garrow; married Susan Foster Newcomer, December 18, 1984. *Education:* Wesleyan University, B.A. (magna cum laude), 1975; Duke University, M.A., 1978, Ph.D., 1981.

ADDRESSES: Agent—c/o Author Mail, The University of Chicago Press, 1427 E. 60th St., Chicago, IL 60637; fax: 773-702-9756.

CAREER: Historian, educator, and writer. Institute for Advanced Study, Princeton, NJ, visiting member, 1979-80; University of North Carolina, Chapel Hill, assistant professor of political science, 1980-84; Joint Center for Political Studies, Washington, DC, visiting fellow, 1984; City University of New York, College and the Graduate Center, New York, NY, associate professor, 1984-87, professor of political science, 1987-91; Cooper Union, New York, NY, visiting distinguished professor of history, 1992-93; College of William and Mary, Williamsburg, VA, Harrison professor of history, 1994-95; American University, distinguished historian in residence, 1995-96; Emory University School of Law, presidential distinguished professor, c. 1979-2003.

MEMBER: Author's Guild, Phi Beta Kappa.

AWARDS, HONORS: Pulitzer Prize for biography and Robert F. Kennedy Book Award, both 1987, both for *Bearing the Cross;* Gustavus Myers Human Rights Book Award, 1987. Also recipient of numerous grants, including grants from the Ford Foundation, 1979-80,

Lyndon B. Johnson Foundation, 1979-80, National Endowment for the Humanities, 1984-85, and the Eisenhower World Affairs Institute, 1985-86.

WRITINGS:

Protest at Selma: Martin Luther King, Jr. and the Voting Rights Act of 1965, Yale University Press (New Haven, CT), 1978.

The FBI and Martin Luther King, Jr.: From "Solo" to Memphis, W.W. Norton (New York, NY), 1981, new and enlarged edition, Yale University Press (New Haven, CT) 2001.

Bearing the Cross: Martin Luther King, Jr., and the Southern Christian Leadership Conference, Morrow (New York, NY), 1986.

(Editor) *The Montgomery Bus Boycott and the Women Who Started it: The Memoir of Jo Ann Gibson Robinson,* University of Tennessee Press (Knoxville, TN), 1987.

(Editor) *Centers of the Southeastern Struggle,* University Publications of America (Frederick, MD), 1988.

(Editor and author of preface) *Atlanta, Georgia, 1960-1961: Sit-ins and Student Activism,* Carlson (Brooklyn, NY), 1989.

(Editor and author of preface) *Birmingham, Alabama, 1956-1963: The Black Struggle for Civil Rights,* Carlson (Brooklyn, NY),1989.

Chicago 1996: Open Housing Marches, Summit Negotiations, and Operations Breadbasket, Carlson (Brooklyn, NY),1989.

(Editor and author of preface) *Martin Luther King, Jr.: Civil Rights Leader, Theologian, Orator,* Carlson (Brooklyn, NY), 1989.

(Editor and author of preface) *St. Augustine, Florida, 1963-1964: Mass Protest and Racial Violence,* Carlson (Brooklyn, NY),1989.

(Editor and author of preface) *Walking City: The Montgomery Bus Boycott, 1955-1956,* Carlson (Brooklyn, NY),1989.

(Editor and author of preface) *We Shall Overcome: The Civil Rights Movement in the United States in the 1950's and 1960's,* Carlson (Brooklyn, NY), 1989.

Liberty and Sexuality: The Right to Privacy and the Making of Roe v. Wade, Maxwell Macmillan International (New York, NY), 1994, updated edition with a new epilogue, University of California Press (Berkeley, CA), 1998

(Editor and author of foreword and afterword, with Dennis J. Hutchinson) *The Forgotten Memoir of John Knox: A Year in the Life of a Supreme Court Clerk in FDR's Washington,* University of Chicago Press (Chicago, IL), 2002.

Author of introduction to *Louis Martin and the Rise of Black Political Power,* by Alex Poinsett, Madison, 1997; member of the editorial board for *Reporting Civil Rights,* Library of America, 2003. Contributor to numerous journals and periodicals, including the *New York Times, Washington Post, Dissent, Journal of American History,* and *Constitutional Commentary.*

ADAPTATIONS: Bearing the Cross has been adapted as an audio book, Blackstone Audiobooks, 1998.

SIDELIGHTS: David J. Garrow is a historian of politics with an interest in such areas as American legal history, the Supreme Court, African-American political history and the civil rights movement, and reproductive rights politics. Garrow once told CA: "*Protest at Selma: Martin Luther King, Jr. and the Voting Rights Act of 1965* began as my undergraduate honors thesis. It argues that Dr. King should be viewed as an insightful and pragmatic political strategist whose foremost goal was winning the enactment of federal civil rights laws, and not simply as the charismatic orator the media have portrayed him as."

According to *Social Science Quarterly* contributor James Button, *Protest at Selma* "is a thorough and astute analysis of the crucial role of black protest in the emergence of the revolutionary Voting Rights Act of 1965." Specifically, Garrow examines both the dynamics of protest and what he calls "nonviolent coercion," the tactic "used to induce white southern officials to brutalize black demonstrators and thereby gain publicity and nationwide support for the cause," Button observed. Francis M. Wilhoit, writing in the *American Historical Review,* wrote that the book "merits high marks for its excellent integration of a wide variety of data into a unified explanation of what contributes to the success or failure of protest appeals in an open society. . . . The strengths of the work are, in fact, so considerable that the book could well serve as a model of scholarly insight and research design implementation."

In *The FBI and Martin Luther King, Jr.: From "Solo" to Memphis,* the author recounts the U.S. Federal Bureau of Investigation's secret surveillance of the civil rights leader as well as their ultimate harassment of him. The author details how the FBI garnered the authority in the early 1960s to conduct surveillance on King and then passed on damaging information to political officials, newspapers, and magazines, and even other civil rights leaders in an effort to discredit King. Writing in *Time,* Jack E. White and Richard Zoglin noted that some of King's admirers and past associates were unhappy about Garrow's book, which reveals the FBI's discovery of King's philandering; but the reviewers went on to write that some approved of the book and regarded the effort as "an unvarnished understanding of the complex man and his struggles with the FBI—and with himself—[that] provides a deeper appreciation of the larger crusade he waged." The reviewers added: "The book does not diminish the heroic nature of his struggle, but instead makes it more real."

Garrow continues his interest in King with the biography titled *Bearing the Cross: Martin Luther King Jr. and the Southern Christian Leadership Conference.* Based on more than 700 interviews of King's colleagues, friends, and enemies, the book focuses primarily on King's leadership of the conference as the basis of his civil rights activities. Writing in the *New Republic,* David Brion Davis commented that the author "relies on skillful narrative almost devoid of overt analysis, interpretation, or moralizing." Davis also noted that the author "in no way minimizes King's weaknesses" in what Davis called a "monumental biography." *Nation* contributor William H. Chafe noted that the book represents "a singularly impressive piece of research," adding that "Garrow has greatly enhanced our appreciation of King and his contribution to history." Michael Rogers, writing in the *Library Journal,* called the biography "definitive and essential."

In his book *Liberty and Sexuality: The Right to Privacy and the Making of Roe v. Wade,* Garrow focuses on the women and men who played key roles in the legal and political efforts that eventually led to the U.S. Supreme Court's 1973 landmark decision to legalize abortion. Among the people profiled are a 1930s Connecticut activist (actress Katherine Hepburn's mother) who defiantly opened birth control clinics, and another Connecticut woman who took her case to the Supreme Court to wipe out her earlier conviction for running the Connecticut Planned Parenthood clinic. Throughout the book, the author details many cases of litigation that contributed to the abortion rights cause. Mary Carroll, writing in *Booklist,* noted that the author "has an important, largely unacknowledged story to tell." In a review in the *Atlantic Monthly,* Jeffrey Rosen called the effort an "impressively researched and useful book." *New Republic* contributor Kathleen M. Sullivan noted that the book should be "valued as an exhaustively researched historical account that enables the patient reader to discern from his raw material both the power and the limits of arguments for reproductive or sexual liberty." James R. Kelley noted in *America* that the book "is likely to become the indispensable account of how abortion became legal in America."

Garrow also collaborated with Dennis J. Hutchinson as editor of *The Forgotten Memoir of John Knox: A Year in the Life of a Supreme Court Clerk in FDR's Washington.* The book presents Knox's diary writings covering the time he served as a law clerk in 1936-1937 to Justice James McReynolds and provides an inside look at the reactions of conservative justices to the New Deal legislation passed under President Franklin Delano Roosevelt's administration, as well as an insider's view of McReynolds, who was a known racist and anti-Semite. Writing in the *Michigan Law Review,* Laura Krugman Ray commented that "the memoir . . . records a young man's progressive disillusionment with the Justice he serves." *New York Times Book Review* contributor Adam Clymer called the book "a strangely compelling account of an incomplete voyage of discovery by a lonely, self-absorbed and utterly naïve young man in a world stranger to him than it would seem to any of us."

BIOGRAPHICAL AND CRITICAL SOURCES:

PERIODICALS

America, December 31, 1994, James R. Kelley, review of *Liberty and Sexuality: The Right to Privacy and the Making of Roe v. Wade,* p. 26.

American Historical Review, June, 1979, Francis M. Wilhoit, review of *Protest at Selma: Martin Luther King, Jr. and the Voting Rights Act of 1965.*

Atlantic Monthly, April, 1994, Jeffrey Rosen, review of *Liberty and Sexuality,* p. 121.

Black Issues in Higher Education, June 27, 1996, Gwendolyn Glenn, "Bringing King to the Classroom," interview with author, p. 12.

Booklist, February 15, 1994, Mary Carroll, review of *Liberty and Sexuality,* p. 1036.

Columbia Journalism Review, January-February, 2003, James Boylan, review of *Reporting Civil Rights,* p. 55.

Human Life Review, summer, 1994, Robert A. Destro, review of *Liberty and Sexuality,* p. 28.

Journal of Interdisciplinary History, fall, 1995, Mark V. Tushnet, review of *Liberty and Sexuality,* p. 356.

Journal of Social History, spring, 2001, Stanley Cohen, review of *The FBI and Martin Luther King, Jr.: From "Solo" to Memphis,* p. 703.

Lancet, June 18, 1994, Simon Heller, review of *Liberty and Sexuality,* p. 1555.

Library Journal, February 15, 2004, Michael Rogers, review of *Bearing the Cross: Martin Luther King, Jr. and the Southern Christian Leadership Conference,* p. 168.

Michigan Law Review, May, 1995, Neal Devins, review of *Liberty and Sexuality,* pp. 1433-1459; May, 2003, Laura Krugman Ray, review of *The Forgotten Memoir of John Knox: A Year in the Life of a Supreme Court Clerk in FDR's Washington,* p. 2103.

Nation, February 21, 1987, William H. Chafe, review of *Bearing the Cross,* p. 221; July 4, 1987, Alexander Cockburn, review of review of *Bearing the Cross,* p. 9.

National Review, December 23, 1983, Joseph Sobran, review of *The FBI and Martin Luther King Jr.,* p. 1617.

New Republic, January 5, 1987, David Brion Davis, review of *Bearing the Cross,* p. 34; May 23, 1994, Kathleen M. Sullivan, review of *Liberty and Sexuality,* p. 42; August 5, 2002, Jeffrey Rosen, review of *The Forgotten Memoir of John Knox,* p. 25.

New York Times Book Review, October 6, 2002, Adam Clymer, review of *The Forgotten Memoir of John Knox,* p. 35.

Progressive, January, 1995, Linda Rocawich, review of *Liberty and Sexuality,* p. 44.

Publishers Weekly, January 10, 1994, review of *Liberty and Sexuality,* p. 50.

Reviews in American History, December, 1994, Laura Kalman, review of *Liberty and Sexuality,* p. 725.

Social Science Quarterly, June, 1979, James Button, review of *Protest at Selma.*

Society, September-October, 1996, Robert J. McKeever, review of *Liberty and Sexuality,* p. 81.

Time, January 19, 1987, Jack E. White and Richard Zoglin, review of *The FBI and Martin Luther King, Jr.,* p. 24.*

*   *   *

GARROW, David Jeffries
   See GARROW, David J.

*   *   *

GEESLIN, Campbell 1925-

PERSONAL: Born December 5, 1925, in Goldthwaite, TX; son of Edward (an engineer) and Margaret Lee (Gaddis) Geeslin; married Marilyn Low (a teacher of English as a second language), 1951; children: Seth, Meg Melillo, Ned. *Education:* Columbia College, A.B., 1949; University of Texas, M.A., 1950.

ADDRESSES: Home—209 Davis Ave., White Plains, NY 10605. *Agent*—Robert Lescher, 47 E. 19th St., New York, NY 10003.

CAREER: Houston Post, Houston, TX, began as reporter, became assistant managing editor, 1950-64; worked for Gannett Newspapers in Cocoa Beach, FL, White Plains, NY, and Rochester, NY, 1964-68; *This Week,* New York, NY, managing editor, 1968-71; *Parade,* New York, NY, managing editor, 1970-71; New York Times Syndicate, New York, NY, editor, 1971-73; *Cue,* New York, NY, editor, 1973-75; *People,* New York, NY, senior editor, 1975-78; *Life,* New York, NY, text editor, 1978-89. Trustee, White Plains Public Library. *Military service:* U.S. Navy, 1943-46.

AWARDS, HONORS: Parents Foundation award, and Comstock Book Award for Best Picture Book, 2004, both for *Elena's Serenade.*

WRITINGS:

The Bonner Boys: A Novel about Texas, Simon & Schuster (New York, NY), 1981.
In Rosa's Mexico, illustrated by Andrea Arroyo, Knopf (New York, NY), 1996.

On Ramón's Farm: Five Tales of Mexico, illustrated by Petra Mathers, Atheneum (New York, NY), 1998.
Big Ears: Growing up in West Texas (autobiography), White Pine Press (White Plains, NY), 1998.
How Nanita Learned to Make Flan (also see below), illustrated by Petra Mathers, Atheneum (New York, NY), 1999.
Elena's Serenade, illustrated by Ana Juan, Atheneum (New York, NY), 2004.

Author of libretto for *How Nanita Learned to Make Flan,* music by Enrique Gonzalez-Medina, produced in Cincinnati, OH, 2000. Columnist for *Authors Guild Bulletin.*

Author's works have been translated into Japanese and Korean.

ADAPTATIONS: Elena's serenade was optioned for an animated film produced in Japan, and was adapted for CD-ROM.

WORK IN PROGRESS: Clara and Señor Frog.

SIDELIGHTS: Campbell Geeslin published his first book shortly before his retirement from the world of print journalism, where he had worked for more than three decades as a reporter and editor. Although Geeslin and his family were centered for many years in and around New York City, the author retains vivid memories of his youth in rural west Texas in the 1930s, and the vacations he and his family took to an even more exotic locale—across the border into Mexico. Geeslin draws on his familiarity with the Texas-Mexico border area in his writing, which includes picture books such as *Elena's Serenade* and *How Nanita Learned to Make Flan.*

Geeslin's first book, *The Bonner Boys: A Novel about Texas,* was written primarily for adult readers. A saga of five brothers who come of age on a West Texas ranch in the 1930s, the novel follows the siblings through the decisive experiences of World War II and its aftermath, as each must weigh a wide array of choices as he ponders his future. One brother becomes a musician, another an entrepreneur of questionable conduct, the third a journalist, and the last two begin careers as corporate executive and attorney. The brothers' lives are contrasted when they eventually return to the Texas capital of Austin for a reunion and a visit with their aged mother. A *Publishers Weekly* critic dubbed *The Bonner Boys* "a warm and satisfying novel" that solidly evokes life in the American Southwest of the 1930s.

Geeslin moved from novels to picture books in the mid-1990s. As he once commented: "After I retired from a job as an editor at *Life* magazine, I wrote and hand-printed from woodcuts an illustrated story for my twin granddaughters. An editor at Knopf wanted to buy the story, *In Rosa's Mexico,* but hired a professional illustrator to do the pictures." The book was published in 1996 with illustrations by Andrea Arroyo.

Written for beginning readers, *In Rosa's Mexico* presents three tales centered on a Mexican girl and her encounters with fabled characters from Mexican folklore. In the first story, "Rosa and El Gallo," Rosa is distressed when ash from a nearby volcano ruins the local violet crop because she sells these flowers at the market to earn money for her impoverished family. When the hungry family decides to cook their rooster for food, the bird begins to cough up lovely violet petals in an effort to save himself. Rosa now has something to sell at the market, and she earns enough money to feed her family and postpone the clever rooster's demise. In the book's second tale, when Rosa's beloved burro becomes sick, she rides up to the night sky and retrieves a remedy from "las estrellas"; the burro recovers and now wears the mark of heaven on his head. The final story centers on Rosa and her discovery of a missing wedding ring that had been stolen by a fox. Her honest actions save El Lobo, the wolf, who rewards her with a magic pillow.

Geeslin narrates all the stories included in *In Rosa's Mexico* in a limited vocabulary that incorporates many Spanish terms. Arroyo's drawings provide easy clues to these words' meaning for non-Spanish speakers, and a glossary of Spanish words precedes the text as well. *New York Times Book Review* contributor Kathleen Krull termed the language and action of *In Rosa's Mexico* somewhat "idiosyncratic," adding that the spare prose works very well for the bilingual, magical-themed format. A *Publishers Weekly* contributor noted that Geeslin crafts a "simply stated yet musical text." Praising Arroyo's illustrations, Janice M. Del Negro asserted in the *Bulletin of the Center for Children's*

Books that the book's pictures reveal "a place and time more magical than mundane."

Other books by Geeslin have continued to focus on children living in Mexico, and all contain a bilingual text, created with the help of the author's wife, a Spanish teacher. *On Ramón's Farm: Five Tales of Mexico* follows a day in the life of a young boy as he goes about his farm chores. As he cleans up the barnyard and feeds its varied residents, Ramon is entertained by the friendly animals, and in return he creates poems about them. In *Elena's Serenade* a young girl hopes to become a glass-blower like her father, but when he disapproves of such a life for his daughter, she takes her glass-blowing pipe and runs away, disguised as a boy. On the way to the city, Elena gains a special skill—she can produce sweet music as well as beautiful glass from her pipe—and when she returns home her father learns to appreciate his daughter's special creative talent. In the *School Library Journal,* Tracy Bell praised *Elena's Serenade* as "a fascinating adventure that explores issues of gender roles, self-confidence, and the workings of an artist's heart," while a *Publishers Weekly* critic wrote that Geeslin presents young readers with a "magical-realist fable with a girl-power message."

BIOGRAPHICAL AND CRITICAL SOURCES:

PERIODICALS

Booklist, May 1, 1981, p. 1186; November 15, 1996, p. 594; March 1, 2004, Jennifer Mattson, review of *Elena's Serenade,* p. 1194.

Bulletin of the Center for Children's Books, January, 1997, Janice M. Del Negro, review of *In Rosa's Mexico,* p. 169.

Kirkus Reviews, January 15, 2004, review of *Elena's Serenade,* p. 82.

New York Times Book Review, May 11, 1997, Kathleen Krull, review of *In Rosa's Mexico,* p. 24.

Publishers Weekly, February 20, 1981, review of *The Bonner Boys: A Novel about Texas,* pp. 90-91; November 18, 1996, review of *In Rosa's Mexico,* p. 74; October 12, 1998, p. 75; January 26, 2004, review of *Elena's Serenade,* p. 253.

School Library Journal, December, 1996, p. 92; March, 2004, Tracy Bell, review of *Elena's Serenade,* p. 158.

GILL, Graeme 1947-

PERSONAL: Born December 10, 1947, in Melbourne, Victoria, Australia; son of Joseph Harold Francis (a storekeeper) and Gwyneth Florence Mary (a homemaker; maiden name, Sherriff) Gill; married Heather Pomroy (a teacher), January 8, 1972; children: Fiona Jane, Lachlan David. *Education:* Monash University, Victoria, Australia, B.A. (with first class honors), 1970, M.A., 1973; London School of Economics and Political Science, Ph.D., 1976. *Hobbies and other interests:* Reading, music, and sports.

ADDRESSES: Home—14 Werona St., Pennant Hills, New South Wales 2120, Australia. *Office*—University of Sydney, H04-Merewether Building, Sydney, New South Wales 2006, Australia. *E-mail*—g.gill@econ. usyd.edu.au.

CAREER: University of Tasmania, Hobart, Australia, tutor, 1976-77, lecturer, 1978-81; University of Sydney, Sydney, New South Wales, Australia, began as lecturer, became senior lecturer, 1981-88, associate professor, 1988-90, professor of government and public administration, 1990—, has also served as associate dean of the faculty of economics, deputy chair of the Academic Board, and acting pro vice-chancellor (research), and head of the School of Economics and Political Science. Served as visiting fellow at the London School of Economics and the Moscow State University.

MEMBER: Australasian Political Studies Association, Australian Association for the Study of Socialist Countries, American Association for the Advancement of Slavic Studies.

AWARDS, HONORS: Academy of Social Sciences fellow; Australian Research Council grantee, 1989-93, 1994-96, 1997-99, and 1999-2000.

WRITINGS:

Peasants and Government in the Russian Revolution, Macmillan (New York, NY), 1979.
Twentieth-Century Russia, Thomas Nelson (Nashville, TN), 1987.

(Editor) *The Rules of the Communist Party of the Soviet Union,* M.E. Sharpe (Armonk, NY), 1988.
Stalinism, St. Martin's Press (New York, NY), 1990.
The Origins of the Stalinist Political System, Cambridge University Press (New York, NY), 1990.
(With Stephen White and Darrell Slider) *The Politics of Transition: Shaping a Post-Soviet Future,* Cambridge University Press (New York, NY), 1993.
The Collapse of a Single-Party System: The Disintegration of CPSU, Cambridge University Press (New York, NY), 1995.
Power in the Party: The Organization of Power and Central-Republican Relations in the CPSU, St. Martin's Press (New York, NY), 1997.
(Editor and contributor) *Elites and Leadership in Russian Politics,* St. Martin's Press (New York, NY), 1999.
The Dynamics of Democratization: Elites, Civil Society, and the Transition Process, St. Martin's Press (New York, NY), 2000.
(With Roger D. Markwick) *Russia's Stillborn Democracy?: From Gorbachev to Yeltsin,* Oxford University Press (New York, NY), 2000.
Democracy and Post-Communism: Political Change in the Post-Communist World, Routledge (New York, NY), 2002.
The Nature and Development of the Modern State, Palgrave Macmillan (New York, NY), 2003.

Member of editorial board, *Journal of Communist Politics and Transition Studies* and *Current Affairs Bulletin.*

Contributor to numerous professional journals, including *Perspectives on European Politics and Society, Acta Politica, Government and Opposition,* and *World Politics.*

SIDELIGHTS: Graeme Gill has written widely about politics and communism. In his book *Stalinism,* Gill looks at the twenty-five-year dictatorship of Joseph Stalin and delves into how the system he created led to numerous abuses and horrors. The author explores what he considers to be the four primary components of Stalinism, that is, its economic, cultural, social, and political sides. Writing in *Demokratizatsiya,* Desiree R. Hopkins called the book "remarkably comprehensive, considering its brevity" and also noted: "Gill's overall analysis is certainly extremely valuable."

Gill collaborated with Stephen White and Darrell Slider to write *The Politics of Transition: Shaping a Post-Soviet Future*. The 1993 book examines the Soviet Union with a focus on the years between 1988-1991 and discusses its future political landscape and chances for democracy. The authors draw extensively on various Soviet news sources and write about such issues as the need for representation of ethnic minorities, trade unions, and public opinion. A *Publishers Weekly* contributor called the book "an informative academic resource."

Gill examines the fall of the Communist Party of the Soviet Union (CPSU) in his book *The Collapse of a Single-Party System: The Disintegration of CPSU*. The book focuses primarily on the internal processes within the CPSU that led to its loss of power. Writing in *Europe-Asia Studies,* E.A. Rees noted that the book "is intended as a contribution to our understanding of the collapse of communism in the USSR," adding that the book has "significant merits." John P. Wilerton, writing in the *American Political Science Review,* commented that the author's "especially detailed analysis of Gorbachevian institutional reforms, combined with a more selective treatment of the changing political leadership and evolving policy debates, yields a useful illumination of late Soviet period political causes for the collapse of the USSR."

Gill also served as editor of *Elites and Leadership in Russian Politics*. The book is primarily a collection of papers presented at the 1995 Fifth World Congress of Central and East European Studies. Commenting on Gill's own contribution, *Europe-Asia Studies* contributor David Lane noted that Gill "addresses the important question of elite conflict and consensus in Russia." The reviewer went on to note that "there are important articles in this collection and many of the chapters could usefully be used in teaching contemporary Russian politics."

In *Russia's Stillborn Democracy?: From Gorbachev to Yeltsin,* Gill and coauthor Roger D. Markwick write about their belief that democracy has little real life in Russia and identify the reasons for this belief with a focus primarily on the issue of civil society forces, groups that are dedicated to political and social issues. "Russia's 'stillborn democracy' is explained not by the importation of inappropriate models of economic and political development from abroad but by the very nature of Russian society—its incapacity to absorb

democratic change and to curb the ambitions of elites and leaders, largely due to the unitarist, bureaucratic character of the Soviet polity and the ways in which subsequent leaders built upon this legacy," wrote Mark R. Beissinger in the *American Political Science Review.* Beissinger also commented that the authors "provide a useful chronicle of the momentous changes in Russia." *Europe-Asia Studies* contributor Catherine J. Danks wrote that they "provide a forceful and coherent argument to support their contention that Russia's democracy has been stillborn."

Democracy and Post-Communism: Political Change in the Post-Communist World examines the differences between the various post-communist states and how these differences helped some to achieve a stable democracy following the collapse of the Soviet Union. Focusing on twenty-six countries, the author writes that while some have achieved democracies, others have only put on the façade of a democratic system, while still others have essentially rejected democracy. "The book's central argument that the strength of civil society and the role it played at the time of regime crisis determines whether a country will become a democracy is plausible and compelling," wrote Oxana Shevel in the *Political Science Quarterly.* Writing in *Choice,* E. Pascal noted that the author "makes a significant contribution to the literature on postcommunism."

Gill told *CA:* "I have been interested in Russia and the USSR since I was a child. This interest was strengthened at university in Australia and consolidated in the United Kingdom, where I studied under the late Professor Leonard Schapiro. I have visited the country numerous times, both the USSR and independent Russia. I am fascinated by how such a political system as the Soviet could emerge, develop, and ultimately collapse. This involves not just an interest in the last seventy years, but both the historical antecedents of the state and the more basic question of why people adopt particular sorts of political structures to rule themselves."

BIOGRAPHICAL AND CRITICAL SOURCES:

PERIODICALS

American Political Science Review, March, 1996, John P. Willerton, review of *The Collapse of a Single-Party System: The Disintegration of CPSU,* p. 215;

September, 1999, Thomas F. Remington, review of *Democracy and Post-Communism: Political Change in the Post-Communist World,* p. 729; June, 2001, Mark R. Beissinger, review of *Russia's Stillborn Democracy?: From Gorbachev to Yeltsin,* p. 494.

Choice, May, 1995, R. J. Mitchell, review of *The Collapse of a Single-Party System,* p. 1519; May, 2001, P. Rutland, review of *Russia's Stillborn Democracy?,* p. 1688; November, 2002, E. Pascal, review of *Democracy and Post-Communism,* p. 545.

Demokratizatsiya, summer, 1999, Desiree R. Hopkins, review of *Stalinism,* p. 453.

Europe-Asia Studies, July, 1995, E.A. Rees, review of *The Collapse of the Single-Party System,* p. 897; December, 1998, review of *Stalinism,* p. 1513; March, 1999, David Lane, review of *Elites and Leadership in Russian Politics,* p. 353; January, 2001, Catherine J. Danks, review of *Russia's Stillborn Democracy?,* p. 171; June, 2001, Mark R. Beissinger, review of *Russia's Stillborn Democracy?,* p. 494.

Political Science Quarterly, fall, 2003, Oxana Shevel, review of *Democracy and Post-Communism,* p. 513.

Publishers Weekly, August 30, 1993, review of *The Politics of Transition: Shaping a Post-Soviet Future,* p. 88.

ONLINE

University of Sydney Faculty of Economics and Business Web site, http://www.econ.usyd.edu.au/ (October 6, 2005), faculty profile of author.*

*   *   *

GILLISON, Samantha 1967-

PERSONAL: Born April 7, 1967, in Melbourne, Australia; daughter of David (an artist) and Gillian (an anthropologist) Gillison; married Duncan Bork (a writer and editor), 1997; children: Henry. *Education:* Brown University, B.A.

ADDRESSES: Home—Brooklyn, NY. *Agent*—Sloan Harris, ICM, 40 W. 57th St., New York, NY 10019-4001. *E-mail*—finghal@aol.com.

CAREER: Writer, 1988—.

AWARDS, HONORS: Philadelphia City Paper Fiction contest winner, 1995; "The Best Fiction of 1998" designation, *Los Angeles Times,* 1998, for *The Undiscovered Country;* Whiting Writers' Award for fiction, Giles Whiting Foundation, 2000.

WRITINGS:

The Undiscovered Country, Grove Press (New York, NY), 1998.

The King of America, Random House (New York, NY), 2004.

WORK IN PROGRESS: The Furies, a book of short stories which examines the lives of seven women in different places and at different times of their lives.

SIDELIGHTS: In Samantha Gillison's first novel, *The Undiscovered Country,* a young couple tries to repair their marriage with disastrous results. Peter Campbell is a Harvard doctoral student who has failed to find funding for his research project. Believing in his research, Peter's wealthy wife, June, funds the project, and together the family travels to Papua New Guinea to carry out the intended research: the study of a blood-borne parasite that has impacted a remote village. June also secretly hopes that living outside of civilization will repair the rift that has established itself in their shaky marriage.

The family arrives in New Guinea to face the skepticism of local scientists, but they are helped to their new home in the village of Albini, where they stay in a hut until their house is erected. They face hardships immediately: the locale is full of insects and infectious diseases, and the primitive conditions make it hard to keep anything clean. After the initial relocation, June remains in a state of culture shock and feels extremely self-conscious, convinced the villagers consider her an oddity. Initially obsessed by his research, Peter eventually drifts off to spend time on men-only hunting expeditions. The biggest surprise to the couple is the reaction of their seven-year-old daughter, Taylor, who quickly learns the native language and spends more time with her new native friends than she does with her mother. Both parents fear that in the jungle, Taylor will lose all traces of her Boston upbringing. June finds herself increasingly isolated, spending time alone in their hut and trying to complete her husband's research while her resentment of both the research and of Peter grows.

Elizabeth Gaffney, reviewing *The Undiscovered Country* for the *New York Times,* remarked on the vivid descriptions of the landscape of New Guinea and noted the ironic contradiction of "a journey to the center of this exceptional story that is less scenic and more harrowing than any of the characters expect." A contributor to *Publishers Weekly,* remarking on the "terrible, beautiful economy" of Gillison's descriptions of a disintegrating marriage, enjoyed the "strikingly original" plot, which contrasted the lush New Guinea jungle with a darker story being played out within its shadows. A *Detroit Free Press* critic called *The Undiscovered Country* "a novel to admire, if not exactly love—there are no happy endings." *Boston Phoenix* writer Jennifer Coogan complimented Gillison for creating an "engaging and unforgettable portrait" of a Western couple who arrive together but find themselves increasingly split by circumstances.

In *The King of America* Gillison fictionalizes the story of Michael Rockfeller, who disappeared in Dutch New Guinea in the 1960s. In the novel, Stephen Hesse, the son of a millionaire, struggles to establish his own identity and seeks a career in anthropology that leads him to conduct research focusing on headhunters. The book follows Hesse as he experiences an awakening on the way to his inevitable disappearance. "Gillison is a quietly commanding writer who has some extremely provocative and important things to say about wealth, indigenous cultures, and the domination of Western civilization," wrote Donna Seaman in *Booklist.* A *Publishers Weekly* contributor noted that the author "skips nimbly through time and space to create a moving portrait of an intellectual, enthusiastic young man." Alex Abramovich added in *People* that the novel "is smart and beautiful and contains a great deal to admire."

BIOGRAPHICAL AND CRITICAL SOURCES:

PERIODICALS

Booklist, February 1, 2004, Donna Seaman, review of *The King of America,* p. 950.

Boston Phoenix, June 4, 1998, Jennifer Coogan, review of *The Undiscovered Country.*
Detroit Free Press, August 2, 1998, review of *The Undiscovered Country,* p. 7H.
Kirkus Reviews, April 1, 1998, review of *The Undiscovered Country,* p. 421.
Library Journal, April 15, 1998, review of *The Undiscovered Country,* p. 112.
New York Times Book Review, September 13, 1998, Elizabeth Gaffney, review of *The Undiscovered Country,* p. 27.
People, April 5, 2004, Alex Abramovich, review of *The King of America,* p. 47.
Publishers Weekly, March 23, 1998, review of *The Undiscovered Country,* p. 75; February 16, 2004, review of *The King of America,* p. 150.

ONLINE

BookPage.com, http://www.bookpage.com/ (October 28, 2005), Alden Mudge, "Samantha Gillison Weaves Fact and Fiction in a Mesmerizing New Novel,"interview with author.*

* * *

GOLDBERG, Steven 1941-

PERSONAL: Born October 14, 1941, in New York, NY; son of I.J. and Claire Goldberg. *Education:* Ricker College, B.A., 1965; University of New Brunswick, M.A., 1968; Graduate Center, City University of New York, Ph.D, 1978. *Religion:* Jewish.

ADDRESSES: Home—205 E. 78th St., No. 17D, New York, NY 10021-1242. *E-mail*—nighttrain@nyc.rr.com.

CAREER: Writer. City College of the City University of New York, New York, NY, sociology teacher, 1970-2005, and past department head. *Military service:* U.S. Marine Corps, 1963-69.

MEMBER: American Sociological Association.

WRITINGS:

The Inevitability of Patriarchy, Morrow (New York, NY), 1973.

When Wish Replaces Thought: Why So Much of What You Believe Is False, Prometheus Books (Buffalo, NY), 1991.

Why Men Rule: A Theory of Male Dominance, Open Court (Chicago, IL), 1993.

Fads and Fallacies in the Social Sciences, Humanity Books (Amherst, NY), 2003.

Contributor to *Chronicles, Gender Issues, International Journal of Sociology and Social Policy, Journal of Recreational Mathematics, National Review, Society, Psychiatry, Ethics, Yale Review,* and *Saturday Review.*

WORK IN PROGRESS: Simply Beautiful: Elegance in Mathematics.

SIDELIGHTS: In *When Wish Replaces Thought: Why So Much of What You Believe Is False,* Steven Goldberg states that the discussions of highly emotional social topics "[tend] to rely on beliefs derived from emotions . . . rather than beliefs based on empirical study," according to Geoffrey Morris in the *National Review.* Daniel Seligman's *Fortune* review of the book noted that Goldberg attributes "a lot of validity" to stereotypes and "tells us stereotypes are 'statistical approximations,' not meant to be applicable to every last member of the class," and therefore should not be negated based on the existence of exceptions to the stereotypes.

In two different books, Goldberg argues that men, based on physiology, "are driven to attain 'dominance'" outside familial situations, and as such "they will invariably hold most of the top positions in the political and other hierarchies that set society's basic direction," reported Seligman in the *National Review.* Goldberg discusses this position in *Why Men Rule: A Theory of Male Dominance,* published in 1993, and *The Inevitability of Patriarchy,* published two decades earlier, after being rejected sixty-nine times (once a record in *The Guinness Book of World Records.*) Seligman noted in his review of *Why Men Rule:* "Although the earlier work is here substantially rewritten, its point remains the same: To explain why men, rather than women, have always run things and will continue to do so." Seligman cited the book for an unclear definition of dominance and for being "repetitive and disorganized, featuring innumerable digressions in which Mr. Goldberg hammers away at logical fallacies committed by critics of the earlier

version, all of which might seem excessive to readers who don't have *The Inevitability of Patriarchy* committed to memory." However, Seligman summarized that it is a "one of a kind [book that is]. . . . persuasive about most matters," and further stated: "Readers will instantly sense that they are in the hands of a writer who is brilliant, enormously interesting, and utterly maddening."

BIOGRAPHICAL AND CRITICAL SOURCES:

PERIODICALS

Commentary, December, 1973.

Fortune, September 7, 1992, Daniel Seligman, review of *When Wish Replaces Thought: Why So Much of What You Believe Is False.*

National Review, October 19, 1992, Geoffrey Morris, review of *When Wish Replaces Thought;* April 4, 1994, Daniel Seligman, review of *Why Men Rule: A Theory of Male Dominance.*

*   *   *

GOMEZ-JEFFERSON, Annetta L. 1927-
(Annetta Louise Gomez-Jefferson)

PERSONAL: Born December 5, 1927, in Detroit, MI; daughter of Joseph (a bishop) and Hazel (Thompson) Gomez; married Curtis F. Jefferson, 1950 (divorced, 1971); children: Curtis A. Gomez, Joseph Jefferson. *Ethnicity:* "African American." *Education:* Paul Quinn College, B.A. (magna cum laude), 1957; Western Reserve University (now Case-Western Reserve University), M.A., 1959; also attended John Carroll University; studied drama with Erwin Piscator at Dramatic Workshop, New York City, 1948-50. *Politics:* Democrat. *Religion:* African Methodist Episcopal. *Hobbies and other interests:* Reading, oil painting (portraits), music.

ADDRESSES: Home—2631 Tanglewood Dr., Wooster, OH 44691. *E-mail*—gomezjefferson@aol.com.

CAREER: Writer. Teacher of English and drama at public junior and senior high schools in Cleveland, OH, 1959-66; Educational Research Council of

America, Cleveland, writer, 1966-67; producer and hostess of the television series *Black Journal: Cleveland Response, Brother Man,* and *Blackpeoplehood,* between 1967 and 1974; College of Wooster, Wooster, OH, teacher of theater and department head, 1974-95, professor emeritus, 1995—, and director of more than forty plays. WVIZ-TV, producer of television series, including *Inside/Out, Individualization of Instruction, Behavior Modification,* and *Reflections in Black;* producer and narrator of the series *The History of Black Americans.* Stage Right Repertory Company, founder and director, summers, 1982-86. Oberlin College, visiting lecturer in residence, 1972; Cuyahoga Community College, guest director for Humanist Theater at Karamu House; gives poetry readings at colleges and universities.

MEMBER: National Association for the Advancement of Colored People, Ohioana.

AWARDS, HONORS: Martha Holden Jennings grant for the television series *Reflections in Black;* Ford Foundation grant for the television series *Blackpeoplehood;* Luce grants, 1986-87, 1990-91; citation for distinguished service to Ohio in the field of theater, Ohioana, 2000.

WRITINGS:

Mazes (poetry), Ramaka Press (Cleveland, OH), 1957.
(Editor) *Through Love to Light: Excerpts from the Sermons, Addresses, and Prayers of Joseph Gomez, a Bishop in the African Methodist Episcopal Church,* Christian Education Department, African Methodist Episcopal Church (Nashville, TN), 1997.
In Darkness with God: The Life of Joseph Gomez, a Bishop in the African Methodist Episcopal Church, Kent State University Press (Kent, OH), 1998.
The Sage of Tawawa: Reverdy Cassius Ransom, 1861-1959, Kent State University Press (Kent, OH), 2002.

Writer of the television series *Black Journal: Cleveland Response, Brother Man,* and *Blackpeoplehood,* between 1967 and 1974; writer for television series, including *Inside/Out, Individualization of Instruction, Behavior Modification,* and *Reflections in Black,* all WVIZ-TV; writer of the series *The History of Black*

Americans. Work represented in anthologies, including *Classical and Modern Narratives of Leadership,* edited by Vivian Holiday, Bolchazy-Carducci (Wauconda, IL), 2000. Contributor of poetry to magazines, including *Black Scholarship, A.M.E. Church Review,* and *Free Lance.*

WORK IN PROGRESS: Cinnamon Secrets, poetry, publication expected in 2006; *Born Alive,* an autobiography, 2007.

SIDELIGHTS: Annetta L. Gomez-Jefferson once told *CA:* "I have always wanted to express myself through writing. When I was a small girl, I would sit on my father's lap and listen to him read from the renowned authors, past and present; and I dreamed that some day I would be able to transport people to another realm as those writers did me. Although I have a special love for poetry, I am most inspired by biographies, the events in the lives of real people, their strengths, weaknesses, and aspirations. Perhaps that is also why, when I paint, I am most interested in the human face. To me there is nothing more revealing. The faces are an expression of people's lives—their evolution—their struggle up out of the darkness toward the divine."

"Since retiring from the College of Wooster in 1995, I have had time at last to concentrate fully on my writing. I wanted to write biographies of African Americans who paved the way for the civil rights leaders of the sixties and today. So many people believe that the movement only started during that period. But there are many valiant men and women who clawed their way from slavery, Jim Crowism, and racism in the late 1800s and early 1900s, whose stories have never been told. I wanted to tell their story. My father, Joseph Gomez, was one of them, as was his mentor, Reverdy Cassius Ransom. The biographies of my father and Ransom have been published by Kent State University Press. Now I am in the process of telling my own story and writing a book of poetry.

"I begin writing by amassing all the available material I can find about a subject that especially interests me. I gather letters, newspaper articles, journals, pictures, programs, minutes, speeches and sermons, books; and I conduct interviews. In addition, most of the time, I have rich personal memories of the personalities about whom I write. Then I put the events in chronological order on cards and see what parallels, what themes emerge. After that I sit at my computer and begin to write, keeping the outline in mind. For the most part, if I have done my research carefully, the story writes itself. My retirement has been most enlightening. Seemingly, at the age of seventy-one, I began to carve out a second career for myself. At seventy-seven, I am still going. Every day I learn more, and I believe I am making a contribution to African American history, a history ignored for so long. It is good to have a small part in its evolution."

*   *   *

GOMEZ-JEFFERSON, Annetta Louise
      See GOMEZ-JEFFERSON, Annetta L.

*   *   *

GRAHAM, James
      See PATTERSON, Harry

*   *   *

GRIFFIN, Merv 1925-
      (Mervyn Edward Griffin, Jr.)

PERSONAL: Born July 6, 1925, in San Mateo, CA.; son of Mervyn Edward (a stockbroker) and Rita (Robinson) Griffin; married Julann Elizabeth Wright (a comedienne), May 18, 1958 (divorced, June, 1976); children: Anthony Patrick. *Education:* Attended San Mateo College, 1942-44.

ADDRESSES: Office—Merv Griffin Entertainment, 130 S. El Camino Dr., Beverly Hills, CA 90212. *E-mail*—Ask_Merv@griffgroup.com.

CAREER: Businessperson, writer, actor, television producer, composer, singer, and bandleader. KFRC-Radio, San Francisco, CA, host of "Merv Griffin Show," 1945-48; vocalist with Freddy Martin's Orchestra, 1948-52; contract actor for Warner Brothers Studios, 1952-55; entertainer in night clubs and on television and radio programs, 1955-62; host of "Merv Griffin Show," National Broadcasting Co., 1962-63,

Westinghouse Broadcasting Co., 1965-69, Columbia Broadcasting System, 1969-71, and Metro Media Productions, 1972-86; television performer, 1962-65; Merv Griffin Enterprises, Hollywood, CA, owner, creator and producer of television programs, including *Jeopardy!, Wheel of Fortune,* and *Dance Fever,* 1963-86; Griffin Group, Beverly Hills, CA, founder and chairman, 1987—.

Business career has included ownership of numerous hotels, including Beverly Hilton Hotel, Beverly Hills, CA; Blue Moon Hotel, South Beach, Miami Beach, FL; Wickenburg Inn, Arizona; and currently Scottsdale Hilton, Arizona and Cleran's Manor House, Galway, Ireland. Also owner of Teleview Racing Patrol Inc., Miami, FL. Real estate developer, 2005—. Breeds racehorses.

Actor in films, theater and television, including roles in *Cattle Town,* 1952; *By the Light of the Silvery Moon,* 1953; *The Beast from 20,000 Fathoms,* 1953; *So This Is Love,* 1953; *Three Sailors and A Girl,* 1953; *The Boy from Oklahoma,* 1954; *Phantom of the Rue Morgue,* 1954; *Finian's Rainbow* (Broadway production), 1955; *Saturday Prom* (television series), 1960; *One Trick Pony,* 1980; *Slapstick (Of Another Kind),* 1982; *The Funny Farm,* 1983; *Alice in Wonderland* (television), 1985; and *Murder at the Cannes Film Festival* (television), 2000. Has also made numerous television appearances as himself and directed the television series *Saturday Prom,* 1960.

Composer of music for numerous television series, including *Jeopardy!, Wheel of Fortune, The All New Jeopardy!,* and *Super Jeopardy!* Released numerous music recordings.

AWARDS, HONORS: Actor of the Year Award from Catholic Actors Guild, 1966; L.H.D. from Emerson College, 1981; Michael Landon Award, 1994; President's Award, BMI Film and TV Awards, 2003; honorary doctorate degree, National University of Ireland, 2005. Has won 17 Emmy awards for television work, including a Lifetime Achievement Emmy, 2005. Has a star on the Hollywood Walk of Fame.

WRITINGS:

(With Peter Barsocchini) *Merv: An Autobiography,* Simon & Schuster (New York, NY), 1980.

(With Peter Barsocchini) *From Where I Sit: Merv Griffin's Book of People*, Arbor House (New York, NY), 1982.

(With Alex Trebek) *The Jeopardy! Challenge: The Toughest Games from America's Greatest Quiz Show!; Featuring the Teen Tournament, the College Tournament, the Seniors Tournament, and the Tournament of Champions*, HarperPerennial (New York, NY), 1992.

(With David Bender) *Merv: Making the Good Life Last*, Simon & Schuster (New York, NY), 2003.

Credited as writer/creator for television series *Jeopardy!*, 1964; *Wheel of Fortune*, 1975; *The All New Jeopardy!*, 1978; *Dance Fever*, 1979; *Jeopardy!*, 1984; *Super Jeopardy!*, 1990; and *Monopoly*, 1990.

SIDELIGHTS: Television executive Merv Griffin achieved popularity as host of his own talk show for various networks beginning in the early 1960s. Also an accomplished musician, Griffin learned to play the piano at age four and was singing in a church choir by age ten. As a teenager he played the piano at local dances. His first professional job was at a San Francisco radio station, where his baritone voice was discovered by bandleader Freddy Martin. Griffin went on to make six records with Martin's band and eight on his own, including the albums *A Tinkling Piano in the Next Apartment* (released by MGM Records) and *Merv Griffin's Dance Party!* (released by Carlton).

In the early 1950s Griffin worked as a film extra at Warner Brothers and had a starring role in *So This Is Love*. In the mid to late 1950s Griffin sang in night clubs, made his stage debut in New York City in *Finian's Rainbow,* and appeared frequently on television and radio programs such as *Look Up and Live,* which he hosted in 1955, and *Morning Show,* where he was the guest of Robert Q. Lewis in 1956. In 1957 Griffin hosted the Miami-based television program *Going Places*. A year later the entertainer had his own radio program for American Broadcasting Companies.

Griffin's television fame began to grow in 1959 when he appeared on *Play Your Hunch* and later on the talk show *Keep Talking*. In 1962 the National Broadcasting Company chose him as the replacement for Jack Paar on the *Tonight Show*. Griffin went on to establish a career as a television host and personality before moving on to the business side and becoming a producer of successful television programs leading to numerous other businesses.

In 1980 Griffin published his memoirs as *Merv: An Autobiography*. The book, written with Peter Barsocchini, recalls Griffin's early life as well as his ascent to stardom. Some of the memorable events he discusses in the volume include dating actress Elizabeth Taylor, singing to deaf people on Broadway, and introducing singer Barbra Streisand to President John F. Kennedy. Dale Pollock wrote in the *Los Angeles Times* that Griffin "emerges as an affable, conscientious entertainer," and *Washington Post* contributor Christopher Schemering called Griffin's book a "sleek, carefully written autobiography . . . [that] displays the same smart, disarming charm that has always distinguished his show."

Griffin has remained active in his many pursuits long past the retirement age, leading to his second autobiography, titled *Merv: Making the Good Life Last.* The first half focuses on Griffin's career in entertainment and television, with the second detailing his business life. Although critics generally liked the book, most noted that Griffin talked far more about the famous and successful people he has known than about himself. A *Publishers Weekly* contributor wrote, "The book's chatty style is reminiscent of a talk show, and beneath its light tone are suggestions of a complex, enthralling person." Writing for the *Knight Ridder/ Tribune News Service,* John Smyntek wrote that the author "simply knows how to condense a good tale into three or four sentences." Syntek added, "Relentlessly optimistic, mean only to a few people . . . there are worse ways to spend an afternoon or evening." In a review in *Booklist,* Kathleen Hughes wrote, "A light read that fans of Merv Griffin or anyone interested in the entertainment industry as a whole will enjoy."

BIOGRAPHICAL AND CRITICAL SOURCES:

BOOKS

Griffin, Merv, with Peter Barsocchini, *Merv: An Autobiography,* Simon & Schuster (New York, NY), 1980.

Griffin, Merv, with David Bender, *Merv: Making the Good Life Last,* Simon & Schuster (New York, NY), 2003.

PERIODICALS

America's Intelligence Wire, January 24, 2005, Greta Van Susteren, "Interview with Merv Griffin."

Book, March-April, 2003, Eric Wargo, review of *Merv: Making the Good Life Last,* p. 77.

Booklist, January 1, 2003, Kathleen Hughes, review of *Merv: Making the Good Life Last,* p. 804.

Knight Ridder/Tribune News Service, March 19, 2003, John Smyntek, review of *Merv: Making the Good Life Last,* p. 6564.

Los Angeles Times, September 11, 1980, Dale Pollock, review of *Merv: An Autobiography.*

PR Newswire, March 15, 2005, "Merv Griffin Establishes Griffin & Company, LLC: A Real Estate Investment Banking Firm."

Publishers Weekly, January 6, 2003, review of *Merv: Making the Good Life Last,* p. 55.

TV Guide, June 9, 2001, Hilary De Vries, "Simply Marvelous," interview with Merv Griffin.

Vanity Fair, June, 1998, Matt Tyrnauer, "'S Wonderful, 'S Mervlous," p. 202.

Washington Post, September 6, 1980, Christopher Schemering, review of *Merv: An Autobiography.*

ONLINE

Griffin Group, http://www.merv.com/ (December 21, 2005), biography of author.

Internet Movie Database, http://www.imdb.com/ (October 6, 2005), information on author's entertainment career.

*   *   *

GRIFFIN, Mervyn Edward, Jr.
See GRIFFIN, Merv

*   *   *

GRUNWALD, Lisa 1959-

PERSONAL: Born June 1, 1959, in New York, NY; daughter of Henry Anatole (an editor) and Beverly (a writer; maiden name, Suser) Grunwald; married Stephen Adler (writer and editor); children: one son, one daughter. *Education:* Harvard University, B.A., 1981.

ADDRESSES: Home—105 W. 70th St., New York, NY 10023. *Agent*—Liz Darhansoff, 1220 Park Ave., New York, NY 10028.

CAREER: Journalist, writer, and editor. *Vineyard Gazette,* Martha's Vineyard, MA, reporter, summers, 1975-80; *Avenue,* New York, NY, managing editor, 1981-85; *Esquire,* New York, NY, former associate editor, beginning 1985.

WRITINGS:

Summer (novel), Knopf (New York, NY), 1986.

The Theory of Everything (novel), Knopf (New York, NY), 1991.

Now, Soon, Later (picture book), illustrated by Jane Johnson, Greenwillow (New York, NY), 1996.

New Year's Eve (novel), Crown (New York, NY), 1997.

(Editor, with husband, Stephen J. Adler) *Letters of the Century: America, 1900-1999,* Dial Press (New York, NY), 1999.

(Editor, with Stephen J. Adler) *Women's Letters: America from the Revolutionary War to the Present,* Dial Press (New York, NY), 2005.

Whatever Makes You Happy (novel), Random House (New York, NY), 2005.

Former contributing editor, *Life* magazine.

SIDELIGHTS: Former journalist turned author Lisa Grunwald has published several novels that deal with family relationships. Her first novel, *Summer,* tells the story of the prominent Burke family and their summer vacation on an island off Cape Cod, Massachusetts. Milo Burke, a well-known sculptor, his wife, Lulu, and their daughters, Jennifer and Hilary, have always spent their summers on the island. The vacation described in *Summer* is very different, however, because Lulu reveals that she is dying of cancer. Narrated by eighteen-year-old Jennifer, *Summer* examines how the Burke family copes with Lulu's declaration and the changing relationships involved with such an ordeal. Jennifer, for example, becomes angry with her mother because she continues to live her life as if nothing is wrong. While Jennifer is terrified by the thought of losing her mother, her mother remains cheerful. "She would not act like a dying woman," Jennifer explains in *Summer.* She "would not grant us the haven of feeling sympathy and outrage and pity and sorrow."

Noting that Grunwald's own mother died of cancer in 1981, *Detroit News* critic Ruth Pollack Coughlin suggested that "autobiography and a minimal plot are undeniable components of *Summer*." She declared that nonetheless "the novel is beautifully constructed and richly textured." Coughlin added that *Summer* is "an accomplished and moving first novel," calling Grunwald "an extremely talented young woman."

In her second novel, *The Theory of Everything*, the author tells the story of Alexander Simon, a physicist who may be close to establishing a unifying "theory of everything," that explains the fundamental science behind the existence of mass, energy, and space-time. Despite his work, Alexander deals with inner struggles involving abandonment by his mother, who had introduced Alexander to New Age beliefs. Noting that the novel "displays the conflict between the opposing worlds of science and magic," *Publishers Weekly* contributor Sybil Steinberg commented on the author's "lyrical and sensitive prose." Commenting on the novel's central themes of the battle between science and metaphysics, Stefan Kanfer wrote in *Time* magazine that "Grunwald offers no final answers, but her chart of genius in extremis is witty and sympathetic."

Grunwald's next novel, *New Year's Eve* focuses on twin sisters Erica and Heather, who have children only weeks apart in age. After Heather's son, David, dies in a car accident, Sarah, Erica's daughter, believes she can talk with him as an angel. Heather encourages Sarah's devotion to her departed son and, as a result, begins to break the family apart. Theresa Ducato, writing in *Booklist*, noted that the author "understands her characters and subtly guides their emotions as they shift and collide throughout this perceptive novel." *People* contributor Paula Chin complimented the author for being "strong in her portrayal of sibling rivalry" and added that "she spins her story briskly." In a review for *World and I*, Maude McDaniel concluded that the novel is "a delicate filigree of a story that is as pleasing in its parts as in its pattern."

Whatever Makes You Happy spins a tale around Sally Farber, who seemingly has it all, including a contract to write a book about happiness. Despite a loving husband and two lovely daughters, Sally is approaching middle age and is restless. Her personal idea of happiness is soon tested when she finds herself drawn to an artist. In a review in *Time*, Pico Iyer wrote that the author "tells the story with a wit . . . that never quite conceals the sting of wisdom just below." Cathleen Medwick attested in *O, The Oprah Magazine* that the novel is "a dictionary of delights."

In addition to her novels, Grunwald has also written a picture book, *Now, Soon, Later*, which provides a series of illustrated vignettes about the meaning of these words both in the long and short term. "This gentle book is a wonderful tool to teach young children . . . the concept of how time passes," according to a *Publishers Weekly* contributor.

Grunwald has also edited several letter collections with her husband, Stephen J. Adler. For example, *Letters of the Century: America, 1900-1999* includes more than four hundred letters from the twentieth century by American writers as diverse as social leaders and criminals. Jesse Birnbaum, writing in *Time*, called the book "an exceptional bedside companion." In a similar book, *Women's Letters: America from the Revolutionary War to the Present*, the editors provide readers with a look at American history through women's eyes; topics cover everything from notable events to the matters of going about everyday life. "This is a delightful collection of belles letters in the most literal sense of the term," observed a *Publishers Weekly* contributor.

BIOGRAPHICAL AND CRITICAL SOURCES:

BOOKS

Grunwald, Lisa, *Summer*, Knopf (New York, NY), 1986.

PERIODICALS

Booklist, December 1, 1994, Donna Seaman, review of *The Theory of Everything*, p. 645; July, 1996, Donna Seaman, review of *Now, Soon, Later*, p. 1829; November 1, 1996, Theresa Ducato, review of *New Year's Eve*, p. 481.

Detroit News, February 23, 1986, Ruth Pollack Coughlin, review of *Summer*.

Good Housekeeping, November, 1996, Lisa Grunwald, "New Year's Eve," p. 179.

Kirkus Reviews, May 1, 2005, review of *Whatever Makes You Happy*, p. 495.

Library Journal, May 15, 2005, Maureen Neville, review of *Whatever Makes You Happy*, p. 105.

New Republic, April 21, 1986, Ivan Kreilkamp, review of *Summer*, p. 40.

O, The Oprah Magazine, June, 2005, Cathleen Medwick, review of *Whatever Makes You Happy,* p. 162.

People, February 3, 1986, Campbell Geeslin, review of *Summer,* p. 16; January 20, 1997, Paula Chin, review of *New Year's Eve,* p. 33; June 6, 2005, review of *Whatever Makes You Happy,* p. 50.

Publishers Weekly, February 1, 1991, Sybil Steinberg, review of *The Theory of Everything,* p. 68; July 15, 1996, review of *Now, Soon, Later,* p. 73; October 14, 1996, review of *New Year's Eve,* p. 62; September 13, 1999, review of *Letters of the Century: America, 1900-1999,* p. 68; November 1, 1999, review of *Letters of the Century,* p. 50; May 2, 2005, review of *Whatever Makes You Happy,* p. 175; July 18, 2005, review of *Women's Letters: America from the Revolutionary War to the Present,* p. 199.

Time, February 17, 1986, Stefan Kanfer, review of *Summer,* p. 77; April 15, 1991, Stefan Kanfer, review of *The Theory of Everything,* p. 66; November 8, 1999, Jesse Birnbaum, review of *Letters of the Century,* p. 152; May 30, 2005, Pico Iyer, review of *Whatever Makes You Happy,* p. 75.

W, July, 2005, Jenny Comita, review of *Whatever Makes You Happy,* p. 60.

World and I, April, 1997, Maude McDaniel, review of *New Year's Eve,* p. 292.

*　　*　　*

GUELZO, Allen C. 1953-
(Allen Carl Guelzo)

PERSONAL: Born February 2, 1953, in Yokohama, Japan; son of Carl Martin Jr. and Leila (Kerrigan) Guelzo; married Debra K. Hotchkiss, June 27, 1981; children: Jerusha, Alexandra, Jonathan. *Education:* University of Pennsylvania, M.A., Ph.D., 1986; Philadelphia Theological Seminary, M.Div.

ADDRESSES: Home—526 Foxwood Ln., Paoli, PA 19301-2009. *Office*—Gettysburg College, Campus Box 0413, 300 North Washington St., Gettysburg, PA 17325. *Agent*—Michele Rubin, Writer's House, Inc., 21 E. 26th St., New York, NY 10010. *E-mail*—aguelzo@gettysburg.edu.

CAREER: Eastern College, St. Davids, PA, Grace F. Kea Professor of American History, beginning 1991, dean of Templeton Honors College, beginning 1998;

Gettysburg College, Gettysburg, PA, currently Henry R. Luce Professor of the Civil War Era and Professor of History. Visiting fellow, Philadelphia Center for Early American Studies, University of Pennsylvania, 1992-93; fellow, Charles Warren Center for Studies in American History, Harvard University, 1994-95. Board of directors member, Abraham Lincoln Institute of the Mid-Atlantic; advisory board member, Knox College, Lincoln Studies Center; member, Easttown Township Planning Commission, c. 2000; member, Union League of Philadelphia.

MEMBER: American Historical Association, Organization of American Historians, Abraham Lincoln Association (member of board of directors).

AWARDS, HONORS: Choice Award, American Library Association, 1989, for *Edwards on the Will;* National Endowment for the Humanities grant, 1990-91; American Council of Learned Societies fellowship, 1991-92; American Philosophical Society grant, 1992; F.B. Artz grant, Oberlin College, 1992; Albert C. Outler Prize, American Society of Church History, 1994; Lincoln Prize, Lincoln and Soldiers' Institute, 2000, for *Abraham Lincoln: Redeemer President,* 2005, for *Lincoln's Emancipation Proclamation: The End of Slavery in America;* Book Prize, Abraham Lincoln Institute of the Mid-Atlantic, 2000, for *Abraham Lincoln: Redeemer President,* 2005, for *Lincoln's Emancipation Proclamation.* Honorary doctorate, Lincoln College.

WRITINGS:

(With Timothy Clark Lemmer) *Making God's Word Plain: One Hundred and Fifty Years in the History of Tenth Presbyterian,* edited by James Montgomery Boice, The Church (Philadelphia, PA), 1979.

(Editor) *Ambitious to be Well-Pleasing: A Festschrift for the Centennial of the Theological Seminary of the Reformed Episcopal Church, 1886/87-1986/87,* foreword by Jay Adams, postscript by Joni Eareckson Tada, Reformed Episcopal Publication Society: Trinity Foundation (Philadelphia, PA), 1986.

Edwards on the Will: A Century of American Philosophical Debate, 1750-1850, Wesleyan University Press (Middletown, CT), 1989.

(Editor) Manning Ferguson Force, *From Fort Henry to Corinth,* reprint edition, Broadfoot Publishing (Wilmington, NC), 1989.

For the Union of Evangelical Christendom: The Irony of the Reformed Episcopalians, Pennsylvania State University Press (University Park, PA), 1994.

The Crisis of the American Republic: A History of the Civil War and Reconstruction Era, St. Martin's (New York, NY), 1995.

(Editor) Josiah Gilbert Holland, *Life of Abraham Lincoln,* reprint edition, University of Nebraska Press (Lincoln, NE), 1998.

Abraham Lincoln: Redeemer President, Eerdmans (Grand Rapids, MI), 1999.

(Editor, with Sang Hyun Lee) *Edwards in Our Time: Jonathan Edwards and the Shaping of American Religion,* Eerdmans (Grand Rapids, MI), 1999.

(With Gary W. Gallagher and Patrick N. Allitt) *The History of the United States* (sound recording), second edition, Teaching (Chantilly, VA), 2003.

Lincoln's Emancipation Proclamation: The End of Slavery in America, Simon & Schuster (New York, NY), 2004.

Contributor to books, including *Jonathan Edwards's Writings: Text, Context, and Interpretation,* edited by Stephen J. Stein, Indiana University Press (Bloomington, IN), 1996; *The Civil War: A Research Handbook,* edited by Steven E. Woodworth, Greenwood Press (Westport, CT), 1996; *New Horizons in American Religious History,* edited by H. S. Stout and D.G. Hart, Oxford University Press (New York, NY), 1998; *The Evangelical Engagement with Science,* edited by David Livingston and Mark A. Noll, Oxford University Press (New York, NY), 1999; *The Human Tradition in the Civil War and Reconstruction,* edited by Steven E. Woodworth, Scholarly Resources (Wilmington, DE), 1999; *The Lincoln Enigma,* edited by Gabor Boritt, Oxford University Press (New York, NY), 2001; and *Tenth Presbyterian Church of Philadelphia: 175 Years of Thinking and Acting Biblically,* edited by Philip Graham Ryken, P & R (Phillipsburg, NJ), 2004. Contributor to encyclopedias, and of articles and reviews to academic journals, including *Journal of the Abraham Lincoln Association, Journal of the Early Republic, Journal of the History of Ideas, Anglican and Episcopal History,* and *William and Mary Quarterly.*

ADAPTATIONS: Abraham Lincoln: Redeemer President has been made into a recorded book by Blackstone Audio Books, c. 1999.

SIDELIGHTS: Historian Allen C. Guelzo is best known for his works on American history, many of which are about his favorite subject, President Abraham Lincoln. Holding a master's degree in divinity, in addition to his history degrees, he has also written books on philosophy and theology, most notably on American theologian Jonathan Edwards. One of these works, *Edwards in Our Time: Jonathan Edwards and the Shaping of American Religion,* is a book he edited with Sang Hyun Lee. David Bebbington, in a *Journal of Ecclesiastical History* review, noted that "the essays represent a dialogue between the voice of the theologian and the present day." Beggington went on to comment on the author's own contribution to the volume, writing that it "perceptively reveals the differences between Edwards on the free will debate and subsequent writings on the subject."

Guelzo has earned awards for his books about Lincoln. In *Abraham Lincoln: Redeemer President,* the author delves into everything from Lincoln's initial forays into politics to his presidency and assassination. Noting that there has been a glut of books about Abraham Lincoln, Benjamin Schwarz, writing in the *Atlantic Monthly,* commented that the author's biography "is quite simply the best book on Lincoln to be published in a generation." Schwarz went on to note: "It treats every aspect of its subject's public and private life with intelligence and penetration . . . but this is primarily a study of Lincoln's ideas and outlook." The reviewer concluded that the book is a "masterpiece."

Guelzo once again turned his attention to Lincoln in *Lincoln's Emancipation Proclamation: The End of Slavery in America.* Since the early years after Lincoln made the Emancipation Proclamation, debate has focused on the importance of the proclamation, with many thinking that it had little effect on the state or idea of slavery in the United States and that it reveals an unwillingness on Lincoln's part to take on the slavery issue in full. In his book, Guelzo sets out his case for the proclamation being the foundation of the destruction of American slavery and, contrary to some beliefs, a risky political move.

George McKenna, writing in *First Things: A Monthly Journal of Religion and Public Life,* commented that the author "lays out his case methodically," adding that Guelzo reveals "Lincoln's underlying principles, then the way he applied them in the rapidly shifting landscape between 1861 and 1865." McKenna also noted that "Guelzo presents a well-documented account of a president who stretched his powers as far as the Constitution and the climate of the times permitted in order to set the nation on a course leading to what he had hoped for many years earlier: the 'ultimate extinction' of slavery. I do not know whether that is still taught in our public schools. Guelzo makes a persuasive case that it should be." Silvana R. Siddali, writing in the *Journal of Southern History,* commented: "The overarching theoretical framework for this book rests on the author's use of the eighteenth-century definition of good statesmanship." The reviewer later added: "One of the book's most significant contributions is its methodology. Guelzo weaves a close reading of primary sources with a meticulous retelling of historical narrative. He insists throughout on a strict nineteenth-century understanding of the scope, purpose, and power of public documents such as proclamations and public letters." In a review in the *Christian Century,* Ronald C. White, Jr., wrote that *Lincoln's Emancipation Proclamation* "leads us into contested territory." Calling the author "a guide who can be trusted to navigate fairly a whole series of questions and issues," White concluded: "This book, and the story it tells with great erudition, deserves a wide reading."

BIOGRAPHICAL AND CRITICAL SOURCES:

PERIODICALS

Atlantic Monthly, June, 2003, Benjamin Schwarz, review of *Abraham Lincoln: Redeemer President,* p. 88.

Christian Century, October 19, 2004, Ronald C. White, Jr., review of *Lincoln's Emancipation Proclamation: The End of Slavery in America,* p. 58.

First Things: A Monthly Journal of Religion and Public Life, June-July, 2004, George McKenna, review of *Lincoln's Emancipation Proclamation,* p. 49.

Journal of Ecclesiastical History, October, 2001, David Bebbington, review of *Edwards in Our Time: Jonathan Edwards and the Shaping of American Religion,* p. 762.

Journal of Southern History, May, 2005, Silvana R. Siddali, review of *Lincoln's Emancipation Proclamation,* p. 468.*

*   *   *

GUELZO, Allen Carl
    See GUELZO, Allen C.

H

HARRIS, Anne L. 1964-

PERSONAL: Born 1964. *Education:* Oakland University, Rochester, MI, degree in computer science.

ADDRESSES: Home—Detroit, MI. *Agent*—c/o Author Mail, Tor Books, 175 5th Ave., 14th Fl., New York, NY 10010.

CAREER: Writer. Has held numerous jobs, including working as an operations research analyst for the U.S. Department of Defense, and as a vegetarian cook, dry-cleaner, book store clerk, small-town reporter, and public relations writer.

AWARDS, HONORS: Spectrum Award for best novel dealing with gay, lesbian, bisexual, transgendered rights, for *Accidental Creatures.*

WRITINGS:

SCIENCE-FICTION NOVELS

The Nature of Smoke, Tor Books (New York, NY), 1996.
Accidental Creatures, Tor Books (New York, NY), 1998.
Inventing Memory, Tor Books (New York, NY), 2004.

SIDELIGHTS: A science-fiction writer from the Detroit suburb of Royal Oak, Michigan, Anne L. Harris has made Detroit an important locale in her novels.

Harris uses what she knows about Detroit to create the eerily transformed setting for her science fiction. Her debut, *The Nature of Smoke,* follows Magnolia from Detroit's devastation to the chaos of New York, where the teen soon falls into the hands of Dano, a sleazy pornography producer. Dano plans to broadcast a sex scene with Magnolia that will climax with her real-life murder; but Magnolia is less vulnerable than her years imply. During the live broadcast of Dano's snuff scene, she takes his knife and manages to kill him. Remus Rahul, a powerful scientist who has produced artificial life, sees Magnolia on television and wants to use her as a prototype for a cutting-edge android robot. Magnolia escapes him as well, but when she makes it to his Siberian industrial complex, she meets the pinnacle of his creations, Tumcari, a sort of aqua-man—part human and part aquatic. She also meets Cid, Tumcari's female co-creator. Ruhal tracks Magnolia to Siberia, discovering in the process that Cid has been experimenting in unsanctioned directions. Reviewers lauded *The Nature of Smoke* for its well-developed characterizations and interesting plot twists. A *Kirkus Reviews* contributor called the novel an "encouraging debut—flawed, furious, fizzing with ideas, and with a plot that bangs and crashes like boxcars in a switching yard." A *Publishers Weekly* critic considered the book to be "impressive," its plot "strong" and characters "substantial."

Harris followed *The Nature of Smoke* two years later with *Accidental Creatures.* The story takes place in Detroit in the middle of the twenty-first century, when imported "magnetic-levitation transports" have taken the place of gasoline-burning cars. As a result, the economy of the city has hit bottom. The fifty percent unemployment rate and gutted factories make Detroit a fine site for GeneSys, which manufactures biopolymers used for a vast range of materials out of huge vats filled with "growth medium." The trouble is that the growth medium is so rich in nutrients that it is toxic to the human workers who must dive into it to harvest the polymers. The workers wear special suits that are supposed to protect them, but they leak and leave them with life-threatening mutations and deformities. When the workers try to organize to demand better conditions, their leader, Ada, dies mysteriously. Ada's mutant sister, Chango, refuses to dive, even though it is the only paying job in town. But after her sister dies, she gets involved in GeneSys. Another key character is Helix, the adopted daughter of an important research scientist at GeneSys. Helix is a "sport," the mutant daughter of divers, who leaves home to try to test her independence and come to terms with her deformities. Paul Kershaw, reviewing the novel for the *Detroit Free Press*, called *Accidental Creatures* "darkly convincing." Chris Donner, who reviewed the novel online for the *SF Site* applauded its "powerful and believable story. . . . [Harris's] ability with language is obvious, and she quickly creates interesting characters and a riveting plot, all while taking a realistic look at what the future may hold."

In *Inventing Memory* the author tells the dual stories of two girls: Shula, a Mesopotamian slave girl from Erech who is chosen for a task by the goddess Inanna, and modern day Wendy, a bullied girl who designs a computer simulation of the city of Erech for her research into matriarchal societies. In the final "book" of the novel, the two worlds collide in what turns out to be a very dangerous experiment. Writing in the *Library Journal*, Jackie Cassada called *Inventing Memory* a "good choice for . . . fans of speculative fiction." *Booklist* contributor Regina Schroeder observed that "the teen ostracism that motivates Wendy's scholarship will resonate with many YA girls." A *Publishers Weekly* contributor concluded that the author "makes questing for the inner goddess look like child's play in this intriguing but sometimes uneasy mix of SF, romance and feminist fantasy."

BIOGRAPHICAL AND CRITICAL SOURCES:

PERIODICALS

Booklist, June 1, 1996, Carl Hays, review of *The Nature of Smoke*, p. 1682; July, 1998, John Mort, review of *Accidental Creatures*, p. 1867; March 1, 2004, Regina Schroeder, review of *Inventing Memory*, p. 1146.

Detroit Free Press, August 16, 1998, Paul Kershaw, review of *Accidental Creatures*, p. 7H.
Kirkus Reviews, April 15, 1996, review of *The Nature of Smoke*, p. 568; January 1, 2004, review of *Inventing Memory*, p. 18.
Library Journal, March 15, 2004, Jackie Cassada, review of *Inventing Memory*, p. 110.
Publishers Weekly, May 27, 1996, review of *The Nature of Smoke*, p. 69; August 24, 1998, review of *Accidental Creatures*, p. 54; February 9, 2004, review of *Inventing Memory*, p. 62.

ONLINE

SF Site, http://www.sfsite.com/ (November 11, 1998), Chris Donner, review of *Accidental Creatures*.*

*   *   *

HASSAM, Nick
  See CROWTHER, Peter

*   *   *

HAVILL, Steven 1945-

PERSONAL: Born June 22, 1945, in Penn Yan, NY; son of Edward (a writer) and Margaret (Nasset) Havill; married Kathleen Murphey (a writer and artist), February 4, 1969. *Education:* University of New Mexico, B.A., 1969, M.A., 1982.

ADDRESSES: Home—Albuquerque, NM. *Agent*—St. Martin's Press, Attn: Publicity Dept., 175 5th Ave., New York, NY 10010.

CAREER: Writer and educator. Greenhow Newspapers, Inc., Penn Yan, NY, reporter and editor, 1973-76; Grants High School, Grants, NM, teacher of biology and English, 1979—.

WRITINGS:

WESTERN NOVELS

The Killer, Doubleday (New York, NY), 1981.
The Worst Enemy, Doubleday (New York, NY), 1982.

Leadfire, Doubleday (New York, NY), 1984.
Timber Blood, Doubleday (New York, NY), 1986.

"BILL GASTNER" DETECTIVE NOVELS

Heartshot, St. Martin's Press (New York, NY), 1991.
Bitter Recoil, St. Martin's Press (New York, NY), 1992.
Twice Buried, St. Martin's Press (New York, NY), 1994.
Before She Dies, St. Martin's Press (New York, NY), 1996.
Privileged to Kill, St. Martin's Press (New York, NY), 1997.
Prolonged Exposure, St. Martin's Press (New York, NY), 1998.
Out of Season, Thomas Dunne Books (New York, NY), 1999.
Dead Weight, Thomas Dunne Books (New York, NY), 2000.
Bag Limit, Thomas Dunne Books/St. Martin's Minotaur (New York, NY), 2001.

"POSADAS COUNTY" MYSTERIES

Scavengers, Thomas Dunne Books/St. Martin's Minotaur (New York, NY), 2002.
A Discount for Death, Thomas Dunne Books (New York, NY), 2003.
Convenient Disposal, Thomas Dunne Books (New York, NY), 2004.
Statute of Limitations, Thomas Dunne Books/St. Martin's Minotaur (New York, NY), 2006.

SIDELIGHTS: Steven Havill began his fiction career with such unconventional westerns as *The Killer* and *Leadfire.* Havill once commented to *CA:* "I believe there must be a market for slightly off-genre westerns, where characters use their heads, and not every hero is flinty-eyed and steely-nerved, with speed-of-light reflexes. I enjoy writing stories where physicians are dominant characters. Medicine played a critical part on the frontier. *The Killer* was prompted by my love of writing for storytelling's sake. The main character is a basically good person who must face the consequences of a grave mistake—a mistake prompted more by immaturity than anything else."

The author cemented his success with his "Bill Gastner" mystery series. Gastner is a portly insomniac who serves as undersheriff of Posadas County, New Mexico. *Booklist* contributor Wes Lukowsky found that the first Gastner novel set a "high standard," which was successfully met in later books. "Gastner is an incisive investigator," wrote Lukowsky in a review of Havill's second Gastner mystery, *Twice Buried.* "Unlike other fictional detectives who approach murder as personal affront, Gastner sees himself as the victims' advocate, striving to even the scales of justice for those no longer able to do it themselves."

Reviewing *Before She Dies,* the fourth Gastner book, Lukowsky called it the best thus far, noting that this accomplishment is "no small feat in a series as strong as this one." Lukowsky added: "Gastner is compassionate, intelligent, bulldog tough, and painfully aware of all his limitations, both physical and emotional. The same inward eye that provides insights into his own soul can quickly swivel outward to discern others' hidden traits." A unique feature of the series is the ongoing subplot of Gastner's health. Overweight, seemingly addicted to chili, and apparently unwilling to do anything about his unhealthy habits, Gastner is constantly badgered by his deputy Estelle and her physician spouse to take better care of himself.

Prolonged Exposure, the fifth title in the series, finds Gastner in Michigan recuperating from heart surgery at his daughter Camille's house. His wish to return home is answered when he is notified that his house has been burglarized. He is soon drawn into a much more serious problem—the kidnapping of small children and the discovery of a black-market child exploitation ring. Lukowsky called this book "another small-town caper in which common sense, compassion, loyalty, and decency are law enforcement's primary tools against an increasingly brutal world. It's a good thing Gastner has had his heart mended because it may be the biggest in contemporary crime fiction."

In *Out of Season,* Gastner discovers that the death of Sheriff Martin Holman in a plane crash might not have been an accident; an autopsy reveals that the pilot had been shot. Further rousing Gastner's suspicions is the fact that Holman had stepped out behind the administrator's desk to investigate a case on his own. Bill Ott, writing in *Booklist,* noted that the author "writes crisp, marvelously detailed police procedurals." A *Publishers Weekly* contributor wrote that *Out of Season* "again demonstrates Havill's talent for combining amiable characters with believable suspense."

Dead Weight finds Gastner nearing the age of seventy and now serving as sheriff of Posadas County. Gastner struggles with the fact that his rural surroundings are slowly succumbing to development as he deals with a deputy accused of harassing Mexicans and a murder involving sex and politics that is bound to bring even more attention to his small town. To further complicate matters, he is facing an election year. In a review in *Booklist,* Bill Ott wrote: "Quiet yet powerful human drama resting comfortably within the procedural formula." A *Publishers Weekly* contributor commented: "Gastner is surely one of the most appealing heroes to come along in a while."

With a hero facing impending retirement, Havill focuses on Gastner's last two days in office as sheriff in his book *Bag Limit*. Despite the fact that he is leaving, Gastner is not taking his final days in office easy as he investigates the death of a teenager killed in traffic while trying to escape being arrested for drunk driving. Bill Ott, writing in *Booklist,* called the novel a "transitional episode in the saga."

With *Scavengers*, Havill features the new Posadas County undersheriff, who turns out to be Gastner's long-time top detective Estelle Reyes-Guzman, who had been living in Minnesota. Havill calls the book "A Posadas County Mystery," and places Reyes-Guzman on the case of two murders as she deals with the pressure of being the new head cop and caring for her aging mother. Reyes-Guzman's former boss Gastner also plays a supporting role in the action. Rex E. Klett, writing in the *Library Journal,* commented: "Solid groundwork for a new series." *Booklist* contributor Bill Ott wrote that the new undersheriff "brings a different dynamic to the series, but the human drama remains equally satisfying."

The series continues with *A Discount for Death,* in which Reyes-Guzman deals with the circumstances surrounding the motorcycle death of a single mother while looking into the disappearance of an insurance agent who had been charged with fraud. Noting that Havill has left behind the "lumbering, methodical approach" of Gastner for the new undersheriff's "frenetic

balancing of family and profession," *Booklist* contributor Ott wrote that the author's "attention to both personal and procedural detail continues to drive the action." Writing in *Publishers Weekly,* a reviewer noted: "The author renders his characters as artfully as ever."

In *Convenient Disposal,* Reyes-Guzman is on the case of a murdered teenage girl who was beaten and stabbed with a hatpin. The undersheriff already has a lead stemming from her visit to a group of feuding teenage girls earlier at their middle school. During her talk with the girls, Reyes-Guzman had noticed that one of them had a hatpin attached to her jeans. The disappearance of the county manager further complicates the case as Reyes-Guzman suspects it may have something to do with the murder. Wes Lukowsky, in a *Booklist* review, called the book part of "an outstanding series on all levels." A *Kirkus Reviews* contributor remarked: "Literate, lively, and sharply observed as ever."

BIOGRAPHICAL AND CRITICAL SOURCES:

PERIODICALS

Booklist, March 1, 1994, Wes Lukowsky, review of *Twice Buried,* p. 1184; March 1, 1996, Wes Lukowsky, review of *Before She Dies,* p. 1125; February 15, 1997, Wes Lukowsky, review of *Privleged to Kill,* p. 1006; February 15, 1998, Wes Lukowsky, review of *Prolonged Exposure,* p. 988; August, 1999, Bill Ott, review of *Out of Season,* p. 2034; May 1, 2000, Bill Ott and Brad Hooper, review of *Prolonged Exposure,* p. 1595; August, 2000, Bill Ott, review of *Dead Weight,* p. 2120; October 15, 2001, Bill Ott, review of *Bag Limit,* p. 385; September 15, 2002, Bill Ott, review of *Scavengers,* p. 210; October 1, 2003, Bill Ott, review of *A Discount for Death,* p. 304; November 1, 2004, Wes Lukowsky, review of *Convenient Disposal,* p. 466.

Kirkus Reviews, October 1, 2001, review of *Bag Limit,* p. 1383; September 1, 2002, review of *Scavengers,* p. 1268; September 15, 2003, review of *A Discount for Death,* p. 1156; October 1, 2004, review of *Convenient Disposal,* p. 941.

Library Journal, October 1, 2002, Rex E. Klett, review of *Scavengers,* p. 132; November 1, 2003, Rex E. Klett, review of *A Discount for Death,* p. 128.

Publishers Weekly, June 8, 1992, review of *Bitter Recoil,* p. 56; September 20, 1999, review of *Out of Season,* p. 78; September 11, 2000, review of *Dead Weight,* p. 73; October 29, 2001, review of *Bag Limit,* p. 39; September 9, 2002, review of *Scavengers,* p. 46; October 6, 2003, review of *A Discount for Death,* p. 65.

ONLINE

AllReaders.Com, http://www.allreaders.com/ (October 6, 2005), Harriet Klausner, review of *Convenient Disposal.*

BookBrowser, http://www.bookbrowser.com/ (January 22, 2003), Harriet Klausner, reviews of *Out of Season, Scavengers, Dead Weight,* and *Bag Limit.*

Crescent Blues, http://www.crescentblues.com/ (January 22, 3003), Patricia White, review of *Out of Season.*

Fantastic Fiction, http://www.fantasticfiction.co.uk/ (October 6, 2005), brief profile of author.

Mystery Reader, http://www.themysteryreader.com/ (January 22, 2003), Jennifer Monahan Winberry, review of *Dead Weight.*

* * *

HAYDEN, Torey L. 1951-
(Torey Lynn Hayden)

PERSONAL: Born May 21, 1951 in Livingston, MT; daughter of Joyce Jansen (a secretary); married, 1982; children: one daughter. *Education:* Whitman College, B.A., 1972; Eastern Montana College, M.S., 1973; doctoral study at University of Minnesota, 1975-79. *Hobbies and other interests:* Opera, classical theatre, classical music, ancient history, archaeology, farming, cosmology, physics.

ADDRESSES: Home—Northern Wales, United Kingdom. *Agent*—P. Ginsberg, Curtis Brown Associates, Inc., 10 Astor Place, New York, NY 10003.

CAREER: Writer and educator. Has worked as a special-education teacher for the emotionally disturbed, a university lecturer, a graduate lecturer, a research coordinator, a child psychologist, and a child-abuse consultant. Former archaeological site supervisor; sheep breeder.

AWARDS, HONORS: Christopher Award, 1981, for *One Child;* New York Times Public Library Books for the Teen Age selection, 1981, for *One Child,* and 1982, for *Somebody Else's Kids;* American Library Association Best Young-Adult Book selection, and *School Library Journal* Best Young-Adult Book selection, both 1983, both for *Murphy's Boy.*

WRITINGS:

One Child (nonfiction), Putnam (New York, NY), 1980.

Somebody Else's Kids (nonfiction), Putnam (New York, NY), 1981.

Murphy's Boy (nonfiction), Putnam (New York, NY), 1983.

The Sunflower Forest (fiction), Putnam (New York, NY), 1984.

Just Another Kid (nonfiction), Putnam (New York, NY), 1988.

Ghost Girl (nonfiction), Putnam (New York, NY), 1991.

The Tiger's Child (nonfiction), Scribner (New York, NY), 1995.

The Mechanical Cat (fiction), 1999.

Beautiful Child (nonfiction), HarperCollins Publishers (New York, NY), 2002.

The Very Worst Thing (fiction), HarperCollins Publishers (New York, NY), 2003.

Twilight Children: Three Voices No One Heard until a Therapist Listened (nonfiction), William Morrow (New York, NY), 2005.

Contributor to professional journals.

ADAPTATIONS: Murphy's Boy was adapted as a television movie titled *Trapped in Silence,* starring Marsha Mason, 1986; *One Child, Somebody Else's Kids,* and *Murphy's Boy* were adapted to audio cassette for the visually impaired.

SIDELIGHTS: Torey L. Hayden described herself in an interview posted on her Home Page as "very active, very curious, and inclined to get into everything just to find out what it was like" as a child. "Also, I liked being different, so I didn't mind making a fool of myself. I liked being alone a lot because I had an extraordinary fantasy life." Hayden's vivid imagination has helped inspire several of her books for young readers, including *The Mechanical Cat* and *The Very Worst Thing*. In addition, her advocacy efforts have inspired works such as *Twilight Children: Three Voices No One Heard until a Therapist Listened.* An account of Hayden's experience in a juvenile psychiatric crisis unit, the book was praised by *School Library Journal* reviewer Lynn Nutwell for presenting, with "compelling grace and compassion," a realistic and "valuable perspective" on the crisis intervention field that would be valuable to "students considering career options."

Born in 1951 in Montana, Hayden was a fan of the original *Star Trek* television series, and as an adult she developed a keen interest in computers, learning how to both repair and build them. If she had not grown up to be a teacher and author, Hayden explained in her interview that she "would . . . have been an astrophysicist or a cosmologist."

Much of Hayden's inspiration as an author has come from her work with young people, particularly students she has known and helped. In *Ghost Girl* she focuses on eight-year-old Jadie Ekdahl, a troubled girl who, when Hayden meets her, is electively mute: she is able to talk, but chooses to remain silent. "Jadie might as well have been a ghost," Hayden wrote in the book; she talked to no one, and no one talked to her. To make matters worse, she had unusual behaviors, such as always walking hunched over, and drawing strange markings on her papers. Hayden has a special interest in children with elective mutism, and with her skills and knowledge she is finally able to convince Jadie to start talking. When the girl reveals horrifying stories of abuse and possible involvement in a satanic cult, Hayden is unsure whether the girl's stories are true or new manifestations of serious psychological problems. After deciding to contact the authorities, Hayden's concerns are found to be justified, and Jadie is rescued from a terrible situation.

A reviewer in *Books* called *Ghost Girl* "fascinating," and Genevieve Stuttaford, writing in *Publishers Weekly,* remarked that "ultimately Jadie's is a success story, and a testament to the powers of caring and commitment." Also praising Hayden's book, a *Kirkus Reviews* critic observed that *Ghost Girl* is "suspenseful, compelling, and offering welcome insights into troubled children and how a gifted and compassionate professional treats them."

In *One Child* Hayden describes the day-to-day occurrences in her classroom of emotionally disturbed children, "kids with whom nobody else wants to deal,"

as Bonnie J. Dodge described them in a review for *English Journal.* Included are a shy boy who speaks only to repeat weather forecasts; a child so abused by his parents that the beatings have caused brain damage; and Sheila, a violent, autistic, electively mute girl with a genius-level IQ. "The reader is left with a profound sense of respect and admiration for the courage, patience, and most of all, the love it takes to be such a special teacher," Dodge remarked.

As a sequel of sorts to *One Child, The Tiger's Child* picks up Sheila's story, following her through her teenage and adult years as Hayden continues to help the autistic genius adjust to the changing world around her. Sheila's early story is more fully told: she was pushed out of a car and abandoned on the side of the road by her mother at age four; her drug-addict father abused her; and she once set fire to a younger boy. When Hayden encounters Sheila in a clinical setting after a span of several years, the emotionally troubled girl is a fourteen-year-old punk rocker, sexually precocious, but still desperately in need of help. After a few months the two develop a shaky friendship outside of the professional arena. Hayden watches as Sheila ages and matures further; eventually, she graduates from high school and finds a job that offers her a stability and contentment she never had before. A *Publishers Weekly* reviewer called *The Tiger's Child* "an inspirational testament to the healing power of love," and remarked that "this authentic tearjerker resonates with drama." Nancy E. Zuwiyya, writing in the *Library Journal,* observed that Hayden's "book is not only interesting as a biography of a seriously disturbed child but as a portrayal of a working psychologist." Readers "learn about the limitations on therapy and the slow, often painful process of healing," wrote Claire Rosser in *Kliatt,* while a *Kirkus Reviews* critic called *The Tiger's Child* "An effective chronicle of a relationship full of potholes that nonetheless brings both student and teacher further along the road to maturity."

Beautiful Child follows Hayden through another academic year with another class of "fascinating, difficult, and immensely appealing" special-needs children, wrote Francine Prose in *O.* The students include a boy with Tourette's syndrome, a girl who spouts sophisticated elliptical poetry when under stress, and a set of twins with the telltale signs of fetal alcohol syndrome. The "beautiful child" of the title is seven-year-old Wanda Fox, an "unwashed, smelly, drastically neglected girl," Prose noted, who is so steadfastly mute and disinterested that she is almost catatonic. Hayden wonders if Wanda is also deaf, or developmentally disabled in some way. "Though Hayden seems almost endless resourceful, dedicated, resilient, and patient, none of the tried-and-tested techniques developed in her career with special-needs children—singing, games, behavior modification, even physical force—succeed" with this child, Prose added. Hayden's narrative describing her experiences with these children "takes on a timeless quality," observed a *Kirkus Reviews* critic. "As well as representing all special-needs children, the students come into focus as individuals about whom the reader cares deeply." Throughout the book, Hayden "shares her own thoughts, worries, and strained relationship with a mismatched classroom aide, creating a rich tapestry of the dynamics of a group of special needs youngsters and the adults who try to help them," commented a *Publishers Weekly* reviewer. David Carr, writing in *Booklist,* concluded that *Beautiful Child* "ultimately shows this kind of teaching to be the tireless embrace of the vulnerable by the devoted."

Hayden took a break from her real-world experience to write the novel *The Very Worst Thing.* The only stable part of twelve-year-old David's life is his sister. Bounced from one foster home to another, David repeatedly finds himself the "new kid," ridiculed because of his stutter and academic problems. Worse, his sister is in juvenile hall. In a rage over his situation, David destroys an owl's nest, but regrets his action almost immediately. He takes the single remaining egg from the nest and raises the owl that hatches from it. When the owl ultimately declines in health due to being held in captivity, David learns about "losing something you love," according to a *Kirkus Reviews* critic. Calling Hayden's protagonist "a believable child with many obstacles to mount," the critic called *The Very Worst Thing* "a well-wrought problem novel for the younger set." While Faith Brautigam wrote in the *School Library Journal* that "the hatching and development of the owl keep the story moving and help to compensate for some of the plot details that seem tacked on," she ultimately conceded David's story is "adequately told."

Hayden once commented: "I don't remember when I first became interested in writing. It seems like it has been something that has been with me, been a part of me, for as long as I have memories, but I have a very

clear recollection of when the magic of writing took hold. I was eight, a none-too-enthusiastic third-grader in Miss Webb's class. . . . I was supposed to be at my desk doing my reading workbook, but I wrote instead on the back of an old math paper. Miss Webb came down the aisle unexpectedly, caught me, and confiscated the story.

"That wasn't a particularly traumatic event. In fact, I forgot all about it until some days later when she was cleaning out her desk and found the story, which she returned to me. . . . Among all the memories of my childhood, that particular moment is one of the clearest. I remember the exhilaration of reading that story and finding it every bit as exciting to me as the day I wrote it. For the first time I discovered that, like a camera, words can capture the complexity, the beauty, the subtlety of life so precisely that one can return to them the next day, the next week, or years later and feel the experience they have created as powerfully as the moment it happened. That to me is magic of the first order.

"Writing remains an affair of the heart for me. . . . [and] each time I sit down to the typewriter to start a new book, I write it for me. I *love* the process of writing, the nudge and jiggle of words until that ripe moment when *snap!* the emotional photograph is taken and all the complex beauty of being human is captured.

"How did I come to write the books I did? In the case of the five nonfiction books, I think it was simply a desire to share my experiences, to open up to others a world that most people do not encounter firsthand and, if I'm honest, to open minds. All the stories told in these books are true; all the characters in them exist. They did the hard part by living; I did the easy part by writing about it."

On her Home Page, Hayden offered the following advice to young writers: "Know that only you can write your own story. No one else can teach you how. They can teach you the mechanics of writing, like grammar and punctuation, but only you will have your particular style. So, while it is all right to read lots of books to see how other authors write or to take creative writing classes or listen to writers speak, let your own style develop."

BIOGRAPHICAL AND CRITICAL SOURCES:

PERIODICALS

Booklist, August, 2002, David Carr, review of *Beautiful Child,* p. 1896.

Books, March, 1992, review of *Ghost Girl,* p. 20.

English Journal, September, 1993, Bonnie J. Dodge, review of *One Child,* p. 96.

Kirkus Reviews, March 15, 1991, review of *Ghost Girl,* p. 377; January 1, 1995, review of *The Tiger's Child,* p. 47; May 15, 2002, review of *Beautiful Child,* p. 717; May 15, 2003, review of *The Very Worst Thing,* p. 751.

Kliatt, July, 1996, Claire Rosser, review of *The Tiger's Child,* p. 27.

Library Journal, March 15, 1984; January 15, 1995, Nancy E. Zuwiyya, review of *The Tiger's Child,* p. 122; July, 2002, Terry Christner, review of *Beautiful Child,* p. 94.

Los Angeles Times, April 24, 1980.

Los Angeles Times Book Review, May 26, 1991, review of *Ghost Girl,* p. 8.

New York Times Book Review, May 4, 1980; April 26, 1981; March 6, 1988.

O, June, 2002, Francine Prose, review of *Beautiful Child,* p. 73.

Publishers Weekly, March 22, 1991, review of *Ghost Girl,* p. 66; January 16, 1995, review of *The Tiger's Child,* p. 448; May 13, 2002, review of *Beautiful Child,* p. 58.

School Library Journal, October, 2003, Faith Brautigam, review of *The Very Worst Thing,* p. 166; July, 2005, Lynn Nutwell, review of *Twilight Children,* p. 133.

Voice of Youth Advocates, February, 1991, Pam Spencer, review of *Just Another Kid,* pp. 347-348.

Washington Post, May 8, 1981; July 6, 1984; April 19, 1988.

Washington Post Book World, August 15, 1982.

Wilson Library Bulletin, February, 1985.

ONLINE

Torey Hayden Home Page, http://www.torey-hayden.com (July 15, 2005).*

*   *   *

HAYDEN, Torey Lynn
See HAYDEN, Torey L.

HENG, Liu 1954-

PERSONAL: Born 1954, in Beijing, China.

ADDRESSES: *Agent*—c/o Author Mail, Grove/Atlantic Inc., 841 Broadway, 4th Fl., New York, NY 10003-4793.

CAREER: Novelist and screenwriter. Former laborer for Beijing Motor Factory; *Beijing Literature,* editor, beginning 1979. *Military service:* Served in Chinese Navy.

AWARDS, HONORS: Recipient of writing awards, including China's national Prize for Novelettes, 1987.

WRITINGS:

The Obsessed (includes *"The Obsessed," "Whirlpool,"* and *"Unreliable Witness"*), translated by David Kwan, Chinese Literature Press, 1991.

Black Snow (novel), translated by Howard Goldblatt, Atlantic Monthly (New York, NY), 1993.

Green River Daydreams: A Novel, translated by Howard Goldblatt, Grove (New York, NY), 2001.

SCREENPLAYS

Ju Dou, Miramax, 1990.

Also writer or cowriter of the screenplays for *Red Sorghum,* directed by Zhang Yimou, 1987; *Black Snow,* 1990; *The Story of Qiu Ju,* based on short story by Chen Yuanbin, directed by Zhang Yimou, 1991; *Sishi Buhuo,* 1992; *Red Rose, White Rose,* 1994; *The Great Conqueror's Concubine,* 1994; *Piaoliang Mama,* 2000; and *Meishi Touzhe Le,* 2000.

OTHER

Quan sheng, [Beijing, China], 2000.
Liu Heng, [Beijing, China], 2000.

Also author of the book *Meishi Touzhe Le,* 2000.

SIDELIGHTS: Liu Heng's career rose along with that of Chinese director Zhang Yimou when Heng joined the highly regarded director to write screenplays for the films *Red Sorghum, Ju Dou,* and *The Story of Qiu Ju. Red Sorghum* and *Ju Dou* both deal with unwilling brides. *Red Sorghum,* set in the 1920s and 1930s in a time of cultural change and impending war against Japan, a girl becomes the head of a sorghum-wine distillery after a series of bloody and suspenseful adventures.

Ju Dou, the first Chinese film ever nominated for an Academy Award, was controversial in China and denounced by the government, which found the story offensive. The film, also set in the 1920s, is about an old man, the owner of a dye factory, who purchases a wife and treats her, as he himself admits, "like an animal." As time passes, the wife, Ju Dou, becomes more rebellious and stubborn, and eventually has an affair with her husband's nephew, with whom she has a son, who turns out to be mute and insane.

For his screenplay *The Story of Qiu Ju,* Heng teamed up again with internationally recognized film director Zhang Yimou. The main character, a woman whose husband is kicked "where it hurts" by the village chief, dedicates her life to revenging this humiliation. Her first step is to approach the local public-security bureau agent, who fines the chief two hundred yuan. When Qui Ju comes to receive the payment, the chief tosses twenty ten-yuan bills on the ground, saying: "You'll bow your head to me twenty times, and then we'll be even." "I'll decide when we're even," responds the proud Qiu Ju, leaving without the money. But the price of such pride for a poor country woman is high. Qiu Ju's pursuit of justice takes her from one level of a seemingly limitless bureaucracy to another. Using gifts of fruit to try to influence officials, she merely underlines her own inexperience and lack of clout. *Time* reviewer Richard Corliss appreciated the film's vision because it offers "a rare glimpse into the last communist monolith, it has the fascination of an individual's—and a People's—tragedy."

Black Snow, Heng's second novel, follows the struggles of twenty-five-year-old Li Huiquan, who has just been released after three years in a Chinese forced-labor camp. Abandoned as an infant, Huiquan grew up an angry loner, and things have not improved during his time in prison. He returns to a seamy, gritty side of Beijing and tries to set his life in order. But his bad luck has followed him: one of his friends has died in a motorcycle crash, another is in prison for life, and his childhood crush has married another man.

Huiquan tries to be respectable: he sells clothes from a stall on the street and falls in love with a singer at a fashionable club, but he cannot sustain the relationship, and falls back into bitterness and despair. He tries to kill himself, but instead is killed by two teenaged robbers. *Booklist* contributor Mary Ellen Sullivan wrote that the book is "bleak in tone and outlook . . . but engrossing." *Publishers Weekly* reviewer Sybil Steinberg found the book "disturbing and richly alive."

Like director Zhang Yimou, Heng is often caught between his creative principles and the expectations of the Chinese communist government, which frequently denounces his work for focusing on unpleasant issues in modern Chinese life. Heng is part of a development in Chinese literature in which writers contradict the official portrayal of Chinese society and explore aspects of Chinese life that were previously censored or forbidden.

In his novel *Green River Daydreams,* Heng tells the story of Ears the Slave in early twentieth-century China. The centenarian narrates his own tale to an auditor, revealing his life as a personal servant to the master of the Cao family. A faithful servant, Ears tries to save the self-absorbed family from disaster when the young Guanghan joins a rebellion against the Qing dynasty. When Guanghan discards the wife of his arranged marriage, she starts an affair with one of her husband's co-workers and sends the family into turmoil. Writing in the *Library Journal,* Tom Cooper called the novel "a masterly blending of character and story in a compelling historical setting." A *Publishers Weekly* contributor wrote, "The frank, unprettified voice of Heng's narrator immediately imparts vigor and urgency to this dramatic story of tragic love."

BIOGRAPHICAL AND CRITICAL SOURCES:

PERIODICALS

Booklist, March 1, 1993, Mary Ellen Sullivan, review of *Black Snow,* p. 1156; June 1, 2001, Bonnie Johnston, review of *Green River Dreams,* p. 1842.

Kirkus Reviews, July 15, 2001, review of *Green River Dreams,* p. 979.

Library Journal, June 15, 2001, Tom Cooper, review of *Green River Daydreams,* p. 104.

Publishers Weekly, February 1, 1993, Sybil Steinberg, review of *Black Snow,* p. 70; June 11, 2001, review of *Green River Dreams,* p. 55.

Time, April 26, 1993, Richard Corliss, review of *The Story of Qiu Ju,* pp. 68-69.

ONLINE

College of Wooster Web site, http://www.wooster.edu/ (November 5, 2005), brief profile of author.*

*   *   *

HESLAM, Peter S. 1963-

PERSONAL: Born June 12, 1963, in the Netherlands; British citizen; son of David S. (a chartered civil engineer), and Johanna (Groenendijk) Heslam; married Judith Schultink (a medical doctor), July 9, 1994; children: Samuel, Benjamin. *Ethnicity:* "Anglo-Saxon." *Education:* University of Hull, B.A. (with honors), 1989; Oxford University, D. Phil., 1993; Cambridge University, B.A. (with honors), 1996, M.A., 1999. *Religion:* Church of England.

ADDRESSES: Home—64a Glebe Rd., Cambridge, Cambridgeshire CB1 7SZ, England.

CAREER: Commonwealth House, Oxford, England, deputy warden, 1990-92; ordained minister and curate of Church of England, 1996-99; Cambridge Theological Federation, Cambridge, England, director of studies, 1999-2000, tutor, 1999—. London Institute for Contemporary Christianity, director of capitalism project, 2000-04, associate lecturer in social and economic ethics, 2004—; Cambridge University, tutor at Ridley Hall, 2000—, director of transforming business project, 2005—.

AWARDS, HONORS: British Academy scholar, 1989; research scholar, Free University of Amsterdam, 1990, 1992, Institute of Historical Research, University of London, 1990, and Netherlands Ministry of Education and Science, 1991.

WRITINGS:

Creating a Christian Worldview: Abraham Kuyper's Lectures on Calvinism, Eerdmans (Grand Rapids, MI), 1998.

Globalization: Unravelling the New Capitalism, Grove Books (Cambridge, England), 2002.

(Editor) *Globalization and the Good,* Eerdmans (Grand Rapids, MI), 2004.

Contributor to books. Contributor to scholarly journals, including *Theology, Anvil, European Journal of Theology,* and *Themelios.*

SIDELIGHTS: Creating a Christian Worldview: Abraham Kuyper's Lectures on Calvinism is Peter S. Heslam's first book, based on his Oxford doctoral dissertation of 1993; its publication was timed to coincide with the centennial of Kuyper's famous Stone Lectures, given at Princeton University in 1898. In these lectures, which under the title *Lectures on Calvinism* have been reprinted numerous times, Kuyper argues that Christianity is not simply the subject of church, doctrine, and evangelism, but encompasses the whole of life; it is a worldview relevant to culture, society, politics, education, the arts, and so forth. Kuyper embodied much of this ideal in his own career, as journalist, university founder, professor, politician and prime minister of the Netherlands. Although a committed Reformed believer, he was remarkably successful in his efforts to cooperate with Roman Catholics in the political sphere and headed a Catholic-Reformed coalition cabinet. Kuyper was also an extremely prolific writer, with 223 publications in addition to his newspaper editorials.

Heslam chose the Stone Lectures as the focus of his analysis of Kuyper's work for a number of reasons; he states in the book that the lectures are a summary of Kuyper's thought that, because they were given to a foreign audience, required a broader and more comprehensible language. Heslam calls the lectures the "manifesto of Kuyperian Calvinism" and "the most complete, cogent, and visionary expression of Kuyperian thought." His book offers not only an analysis of the Stone Lectures, stated David W. Hall of the Kuyper Institute in the periodical *Covenant Syndicate,* but "a lively biography of Kuyper based on primary sources, along with pertinent discussions of religious and cultural factors at the time, and . . . the context of American evangelism and the Princeton tradition." Hall wrote approvingly of Heslam's book in *Covenant Syndicate:* "Such analysis of a Dutch Calvinist by a British Anglican [Heslam] must surely bring a smile to Kuyper in Abraham's bosom as a vindication of his belief in common grace. It also will become necessary material for discussions about the future of Calvinism. . . . [The book is a] contribution that will help unveil one of the most influential hidden hands of our time."

Heslam once told *CA* that his book is "a scholarly and critical analysis of Kuyper's ideas and it aims to place him firmly within the context of his times. It is written, however, from the conviction that his legacy has much to offer succeeding generations of Christian thinkers who seek to engage with socio-political and cultural issues from a biblically-informed standpoint.

"A century after the Stone Lectures were given, Kuyper's influence is growing in many parts of the world, not least in the author's own country, Great Britain. Having introduced Kuyper more widely in the English-speaking world, I am keen to develop some of the themes in Kuyper's work more fully, and thus to contribute to the contemporary debate on the relationship between gospel and present-day culture. This is what I have sought to do as director of the capitalism project at the London Institute for Contemporary Christianity, and I intend to continue this as director of the transforming business project at the faculty of divinity at Cambridge University."

BIOGRAPHICAL AND CRITICAL SOURCES:

BOOKS

Heslam, Peter S., *Creating a Christian Worldview: Abraham Kuyper's Lectures on Calvinism,* Eerdmans (Grand Rapids, MI), 1998.

ONLINE

Cambridge University Faculty of Divinity Web site,, http://www.divinity.cam.ac.uk/ (November 12, 2005).

Covenant Syndicate Web site, http://capo.org/ (April 7, 1999), David W. Hall, review of *Creating a Christian Worldview: Abraham Kuyper's Lectures on Calvinism.*

*　　*　　*

HIGGINS, Aidan 1927-

PERSONAL: Born March 3, 1927, in Celbridge, Kildare, Ireland; son of Bartholomew Joseph and Lillian Ann (Boyd) Higgins; married Jill Damaris Anders, November 25, 1955; children: Carl, Julien, Elwin. *Education:* Attended Clongowes Wood College.

ADDRESSES: Home—Cork, Ireland. *Agent*—c/o Author Mail, Dalkey Archive Press, ISU Campus 8905, Normal, IL 61790-8905.

CAREER: Writer. Laborer in light industry in and around London, England, for about two years; copywriter for Domas Advertising, early 1950s; John Wright's Marionette Co., puppeteer in Europe, South Africa, and Rhodesia, 1958-60; Filmlets, Johannesburg, South Africa, scriptwriter, 1960-61.

MEMBER: Aosdána.

AWARDS, HONORS: Somin Trust Award, 1963, for *Felo de Se;* James Tait Black Memorial Prize, 1967, and Irish Academy of Letters Award, 1970, both for *Langrishe, Go Down;* DAAD scholarship of Berlin, 1969; American-Irish Foundation grant, 1977; D.D.L., National University of Ireland, 2001; Booker Prize shortlist, for *Balcony of Europe;* British Arts Council grants.

WRITINGS:

NOVELS

Langrishe, Go Down, Grove Press (New York, NY), 1966.
Balcony of Europe, Delacorte (New York, NY), 1973.
Scenes from a Receding Past, Riverrun Press (New York, NY), 1977.

Bornholm Night-Ferry, Allison and Busby (London, England), 1983.

Lions of the Grunewald, Secker & Warburg (London, England), 1993.

RADIO PLAYS

Assassination, 1973.
Imperfect Sympathies, 1977,
Discords of Good Humour, 1982.
Vanishing Heroes, 1983.
Texts for the Air, 1983.
Winter Is Coming, 1983.
Tomb of Dreams, 1984.
Zoo Station, 1985.
Boomtown, 1990, published as *As I Was Riding down Duval Boulevard with Pete La Salle,* Anam Press (Kinsale, Ireland), 2002.

OTHER

Felo de Se (short stories), Calder (London, England), 1960, published as *Killachter Meadow,* Grove (New York, NY), 1960, revised edition published as *Asylum, and Other Stories,* Calder (London, England), 1978, Riverrun Press (New York, NY), 1979.

Images of Africa: Diary (1956-60), Calder (London, England), 1971.

(Editor and author of introduction) *A Century of Short Stories,* Cape (London, England), 1977.

(Editor) Julien Carl and Elwin Higgins, *Colossal Gongorr and the Turkes of Mars,* Cape (London, England), 1979.

Ronda Gorge and Other Precipices: Travel Writings, 1959-1989, Secker & Warburg (London, England), 1989.

Helsingor Station and Other Departures: Fictions and Autobiographies, 1956-1989, Secker & Warburg (London, England), 1989.

Donkey's Years: Memories of a Life as Story Told (autobiographical fiction; also see below), Secker & Warburg (London, England), 1995.

Samuel Beckett, Secker & Warburg (London, England), 1995.

Flotsam and Jetsam (short stories), Minerva (London, England), 1997, Dalkey Archive Press (Chicago, IL), 2002.

Dog Days (autobiographical fiction; also see below), Secker & Warburg (London, England), 1998.

Whole Hog: A Sequel to Donkey's Years and Dog Days (autobiographical fiction; also see below), Secker & Warburg (London, England), 2000.

A Bestiary (autobiographical fiction; contains *Donkey's Ears, Dog Days,* and *The Whole Hog*), Dalkey Archive Press (Normal, IL), 2004.

Windy Arbours (literary criticism), Dalkey Archive Press (Normal, IL), 2005.

Contributor to *X Magazine, Art & Literature, Evergreen Review, Les Letters nouvelles, Transatlantic Review, Malahat Review,* and *Tri-Quarterly. Killachter Meadow* has been published in France, Germany, Italy, Holland, Portugal, and Denmark. A collection of Higgins's manuscripts are housed at the University of Victoria, British Columbia.

ADAPTATIONS: Harold Pinter adapted *Langrishe, Go Down* for BBC Television, 1978. The film starred Pinter, Jeremy Irons, and Judi Dench.

SIDELIGHTS: Aidan Higgins is part of a rich history of Irish writers, and is often mentioned as a successor to such great Irish writers of the twentieth century as Frank O'Connor, Samuel Beckett, James Joyce, and Brian O Nuallain. Yet Higgins has resisted being hemmed in by his origins and has revealed the influence of literary figures from other cultures, such as Jorge Luis Borges and T.S. Eliot. As Peter G.W. van de Kamp pointed out in *Contemporary Novelists,* "In his attempt to escape the traditional constraints of Irish fiction, Aidan Higgins has emerged as an Irish internationalist, firmly grounded in his Irish experience and yet devoted to an extensive view." Reflecting this extensive view, Higgins's novels and short stories often involve Irish characters in foreign landscapes or in relationships with non-Irish characters.

The family "as a kind of collective neurosis, imprisoning its members inextricably in a welter of obsessions and delusions" is the subject of *Langrishe, Go Down,* according to Bill Grantham in the *Dictionary of Literary Biography.* The novel focuses on the women of the Langrishe family, specifically "on the affair in 1932 between Imogen Langrishe, a spinster from a declining line of the Irish landed middle class, and Otto Beck, a German research student," Grantham explained. The setting is Ireland during the years leading up to World War II, and as Grantham observed, "While the action is confined to a debilitated section of Ireland and its culture, the dramatic sweep encompasses the vast upheavals on the European scene." This type of setting, a cloistered locale vexed by rumblings in the distance, is a device characteristic of Higgins's stories, according to Grantham. The critic described it as a "depiction of localized, personal events being held in suspension by outside matters which at once appear beyond the reach of the characters of the story and yet hold them completely in thrall."

Langrishe, Go Down captures the slow deterioration of isolated lives. As a *Times Literary Supplement* reviewer commented: "Mr. Higgins clearly feels his responsibilities towards prose rather acutely, but his style is sustained not so much by ambition as by an unremitting attention, and although his particularities can verge on the gratuitous, they do make you see. The relation of the bits of the novel to the whole piece is not always convincing . . . but [the book] certainly reveals a promising talent."

Balcony of Europe, set in Spain in the early 1960s, introduces the character of Dan Ruttle, an Irish painter married to a New Zealander. Ruttle moves in expatriate circles, and the characters he meets form a "panorama of grotesques and misfits," as Grantham explained, "all distillations of aspects of the European societies rent asunder by the war and finding it impossible to put back together what has been lost." In this context, Ruttle begins an affair with the American wife of a friend. In creating yet another isolated community where personal tensions are influenced by events happening on the larger scale, "plot is largely sacrificed for a number of cognitive tableaux," commented van de Kamp, "held together by cross-references and a distinctively idiosyncratic voice. As a result," the critic continued, "the novel is dominated by a technique of Beckettian repetitions, ellipses, and grammatical distortions to which are added spices of [Laurence] Sterne and numerous quotations from [William Butler] Yeats." Through this approach, "Higgins manages to produce a work again similar to a historical novel, but not quite in that category," Grantham suggested. "History itself is the issue here—its status, its theory, its influence."

Scenes from a Receding Past offers more of Dan Ruttle's personal history, following the Irish artist from his early childhood through his marriage to Olivia, the

girl from New Zealand, past his experiences in Spain. The novel is "constructed primarily through the use of a montage effect: events and moments blend with newspaper reports, scorecards from cricket matches, and other ephemera from Ruttle's life," related Grantham. Though not as well received as Higgins's two previous novels, *Scenes from a Receding Past* provides a logical bridge between those works and *Bornholm Night-Ferry,* according to van de Kamp. The "epistolary form" of this novel, set in northern Europe, "enables Higgins to combine successfully post-modernism and his timeless gift for detail," added the critic.

With the publication of *Asylum, and Other Stories,* a revised version of 1960's *Felo de Se,* Higgins placed himself in the company of another great twentieth-century Irish short story writer, William Trevor. Each of these stories deals with characters that live quiet, desperate lives on the fringe of society. The major achievement in these writings may be the intensity in which the author captures the raw emotions of his characters.

Flotsam and Jetsam is another collection of short fiction and prose. Spanning the author's entire career, it is a primary introduction for those unfamiliar with his body of work. Published between 1960 and 1989, the stories in this volume are scrupulously crafted and challenge the reader with a sense of wonder and astonishment about language and literature. Annie Proulx stated in her review of the work for the *Washington Post:* "To read *Flotsam and Jetsam* is to be introduced to complex and masterly prose of striking richness." The range of emotions and subjects covered in the collection is nothing less than "dizzying," according to John Green in *Booklist.* Both humor and poignant sadness are achieved by the author, who portrays his situations and people "with quick lyrical bursts." Many of the stories are set in Berlin during the Cold War era, and Green noted that like Ireland and Berlin, Higgins's characters are in a near-constant struggle to reconcile the past with the present. A *Publishers Weekly* reviewer noted the author's affinity for a certain type of character, one who is "eccentric, sexually tormented and pathetic." One example is the protagonist of the story "Catchpole," in which a married man tells the narrator the strange tale of his life and his many sexual misadventures, including being discovered in a compromising position with the best man at his own wedding. The reviewer called the author's work "determinedly odd and aesthetically uncompromising," while acknowledging that it was not likely to have broad appeal. Still, concluded the reviewer, "this collection will amply satisfy the discerning few who savor his work."

In *Donkey's Years: Memories of a Life as Story Told* Higgins fictionalizes the lives of a Catholic family in his birthplace, County Kildare. The hilarious autobiography examines the mysteries of lost love and coming-of-age during World War II. "It seems that for most of his writing career, Aidan Higgins has been preparing for *Donkey's Years,*" according to Jack Byrne in the *Review of Contemporary Fiction.* Higgins followed *Donkey's Years* with *Dog Days* and then *Whole Hog: A Sequel to Donkey's Years and Dog Days. Whole Hog* is an honest look at one man's struggle to build relationships with members of the opposite sex. The author's candid talk about sex is built upon a lifetime of experiences that started in his school days and lasted through over twenty years of marriage. Penny Perrick, writing in the London *Times,* called the dialogue "dazzling," and *Sunday Times* contributor Phil Baker referred to the author's writing in this memoir as an "intoxication with language."

Donkey's Ears, Dog Days, and *Whole Hog* were brought together into one volume in 2004 titled *A Bestiary.* Commenting on the numerous stories of the amorous conquests, *Library Journal* reviewer William D. Walsh found that "the most interesting woman in Higgins's life is his mother," and the author's "unflinching" description of her death is "a sad yet virtuoso piece of writing." *Booklist* commentator Brendan Driscoll commented that the trilogy is "a modernist adventure to the bone and not for the prudish."

BIOGRAPHICAL AND CRITICAL SOURCES:

BOOKS

Contemporary Novelists, seventh edition, Gale (Detroit, MI), 2000.
Dictionary of Literary Biography, Volume 14: *British Novelists since 1960,* Gale (Detroit, MI), 1983.
Higgins, Aidan, *Donkey's Years: Memories of a Life as Story Told,* Secker & Warburg (London, England), 1995.

Higgins, Aidan, *Dog Days,* Secker & Warburg (London, England), 1998.
Higgins, Aidan, *Whole Hog: A Sequel to Donkey's Years and Dog Days,* Secker & Warburg (London, England), 2000.
Higgins, Aidan, *A Bestiary,* Dalkey Archive Press (Normal, IL), 2004.
Modern British Literature, second edition, St. James Press (Detroit, MI), 2000.

PERIODICALS

Booklist, March 1, 2002, John Green, review of *Flotsam and Jetsam,* p. 1092; July, 2004, Brendan Driscoll, review of *A Bestiary,* p. 1811.
Herald (Glasgow, Scotland) September 23, 1999, review of *Dog Days,* p. 22.
Kirkus Reviews, January 1, 2002, review of *Flotsam and Jetsam,* p. 17.
Library Journal, February 15, 2002, Philip Santo, review of *Flotsam and Jetsam,* p. 180; August, 2004, William D. Walsh, review of *A Bestiary,* p. 76.
New Statesman, November 21, 1980, Judy Cooke, review *Scenes from a Receding Past,* p. 23; June 17, 1983, Angela McRobbie, review of *Bornholm Night-Ferry,* p. 26.
New York Times Book Review, June 16, 2002, Michael Porter, review of *Flotsam and Jetsam,* p. 24.
Publishers Weekly, June 28, 1985, review of *Bornholm Night-Ferry,* p. 61; February 18, 2002, review of *Flotsam and Jetsam,* p. 75; June 14, 2004, review of *A Bestiary,* p. 55.
Review of Contemporary Fiction, summer, 1990, Eamonn Wall, review of *Ronda Gorge and Other Precipices: Travel Writings, 1959-1989,* p. 260; spring, 1996, Jack Byrne, review of *Donkey's Years: Memories of a Life as Story Told,* p. 147; fall, 1998, George O'Brien, review of *Dog Days,* p. 258; fall, 2003, Neil Murphy, "Aidan Higgins," p. 49.
Spectator, October 14, 2000, Patrick Skene Catling, review of *Whole Hog: A Sequel to Donkey's Years and Dog Days,* p. 53.
Sunday Times (London, England), January 7, 2001, Phil Baker, review of *Whole Hog,* p. 39.
Times (London, England), January 5, 2002, Penny Perrick, review of *Whole Hog,* p. 16.
Times Literary Supplement, March 3, 1966, review of *Langrishe, Go Down;* December 29, 2000, John Kenny, review of *Whole Hog,* p. 19.
Washington Post, June 16, 2002, Annie Proulx, review of *Flotsam and Jetsam,* p. T07.

ONLINE

University College Cork Web site, http://www.ucc.ie/ (October 6, 2005), biographical information on Aidan Higgins.*

*   *   *

HIGGINS, Jack
    See PATTERSON, Harry

*   *   *

HOBB, Robin
    See OGDEN, Margaret Lindholm

*   *   *

HOOVER, Kenneth R. 1940-
    (Kenneth Ray Hoover)

PERSONAL: Born September 15, 1940, in Marshalltown, IA; son of Lee and Margaret (Whitcomb) Hoover; married Judith Maybee, 1963; children: two. *Education:* Beloit College, B.Sc., 1962; University of Wisconsin—Madison, M.Sc., 1965, Ph. D., 1970.

ADDRESSES: Office—c/o Department of Political Science, Western Washington University, Bellingham, WA 98225.

CAREER: Johnson Foundation, assistant to the president, 1962-64; University of Wisconsin—Whitewater, Whitewater, instructor, 1964-65, assistant professor of political science, 1965-69; College of Wooster, Wooster, OH, assistant professor, 1970-76, associate professor of political science, 1976-78; University of Wisconsin—Parkside, Kenosha, associate professor, 1978-85, professor of political science, 1985-88; Western Washington University, Bellingham, professor of political science, 1988-2004, professor emeritus, 2004—, department chair, 1988-95, president of faculty senate, 1995-96. University of London, academic visitor at London School of Economics and

Political Science, 1996-97; Oxford University, member of Senior Common Room, St. Catherine's College, 1996-97; Seattle University, visiting professor, 2005.

MEMBER: American Political Science Association, American Association of University Professors, Pacific Northwest Political Science Association (president, 2005).

AWARDS, HONORS: Distinguished Teaching Award, University of Wisconsin—Parkside, 1984; Eugenio Battisti Award, 1992, for article published in *Utopian Studies;* Paul J. Olscamp Faculty Research Award, Western Washington University, 2004.

WRITINGS:

A Politics of Identity: Liberation and the Natural Community, University of Illinois Press (Urbana, IL), 1975.
The Elements of Social Scientific Thinking, St. Martin's Press (New York, NY), 1976, 6th edition (with Todd Donovan), 1995, 8th edition, Thomson/Wadsworth (Belmont, CA), 2004.
Ideology and Political Life, Brooks/Cole Publishing (Monterey, CA), 1986, 3rd edition (with Vernon Johnson and others), Harcourt College Publishers (Fort Worth, TX), 2001.
(With Raymond Plant) *Conservative Capitalism in Britain and the United States: A Critical Appraisal,* Routledge (New York, NY), 1989.
(With James Marcia and Kristen Parris) *The Power of Identity: Politics in a New Key,* Chatham House Publishers (Chatham, NJ), 1997.
Economics as Ideology: Keynes, Laski, Hayek, and the Creation of Contemporary Politics, Rowman & Littlefield (Lanham, MD), 2003.
(Editor) *The Future of Identity: Centennial Reflections on the Legacy of Erik Erikson,* Lexington Books (Lanham, MD), 2004.

Contributor to political science journals, including *American Journal of Political Science, Comparative Studies in Society and History,* and *Western Political Quarterly.*

SIDELIGHTS: Kenneth R. Hoover told *CA:* "My article 'What Should Democracies Do about Identity?' presents my view of a new basis for progressive politics." The article is available at the author's Internet Home Page.

BIOGRAPHICAL AND CRITICAL SOURCES:

ONLINE

Western Washington University Web site: Kenneth R. Hoover Home Page,, http://www.wwu.edu/~khoover (November 12, 2005).

*   *   *

HOOVER, Kenneth Ray
    See HOOVER, Kenneth R.

*   *   *

HORNE, Alistair 1925-
    (Alistair Allan Horne)

PERSONAL: Born November 9, 1925, in London, England; son of Sir James Allan and Auriel Camilla (Hay) Horne; married Renira Margaret Hawkins, November 28, 1953 (divorced, 1982); children: Camilla, Alexandra, Vanessa. *Education:* Jesus College, Cambridge, M.A., 1949. *Politics:* "Nonconformist but anti-Communist." *Religion:* Church of England. *Hobbies and other interests:* Skiing, painting, shooting, fishing, travel.

ADDRESSES: Home—Cambridge, England. *Agent*—c/o Author Mail, Knopf Publicity, 1745 Broadway, New York, NY 10019.

CAREER: Writer and historian. *Cambridge Daily News,* Cambridge, England, journalist, 1950-51; *Daily Telegraph,* London, England, staff correspondent in Germany, 1952-55; freelance writer, 1955—; John W. Kluge Center, Library of Congress, Washington, DC, senior distinguished scholar, 2005—. Has also served as director of Mombasa Investment Trust, Ltd., and member of the Committee of Management, Royal Literary Fund, 1969-90.

Work-related activities include Imperial War Museum, trustee, 1975-82; Woodrow Wilson Center, Washington, DC, fellow; St. Antony's College, Oxford, England, honorary fellow, 1988—, and Jesus College,

Cambridge, England, honorary fellow, 1996—. *Military service:* Royal Air Force, 1943-44; British Army, Coldstream Guards, 1944-47, attached to Counter-Intelligence; became captain.

MEMBER: Royal Institute of International Affairs, Garrick Club (London), Beefsteak.

AWARDS, HONORS: Hawthornden Prize, 1963, for *The Price of Glory;* Yorkshire Post Book of the Year Prize and Wolfson Literary Award, both 1978, both for *A Savage War of Peace: Algeria 1954-1962;* French Légion d'Honneur, 1993, for work on French history; Commander of the British Empire (CBE), 2003.

WRITINGS:

Back into Power, Parrish, 1955, published as *Return to Power,* Praeger (New York, NY), 1956.
The Land Is Bright, Parrish, 1958.
Canada and the Canadians, Macmillan (London, England), 1961.
The Price of Glory: Verdun, 1916 (first book in trilogy), St. Martin's Press (New York, NY), 1962.
The Fall of Paris: The Seige and the Commune, 1870-1871 (second book in trilogy), St. Martin's Press (New York, NY), 1965.
To Lose a Battle: France, 1940 (third book in trilogy), Little, Brown (Boston, MA), 1969.
Death of a Generation: From Neuve and Chapelle to Verdun and the Somme, Heritage Press, 1970.
The Terrible Year: The Paris Commune, 1871, Viking (New York, NY), 1971.
Small Earthquake in Chile: Allende's South America, Viking (New York, NY), 1972, published in England as *Small Earthquake in Chile: A Visit to Allende's South America,* Macmillan (London, England), 1972.
A Savage War of Peace: Algeria, 1954-1962, Macmillan (London, England), 1977, Viking (New York, NY), 1978.
Napoleon, Master of Europe, 1806-1807, Morrow (New York, NY), 1979.
The French Army and Politics, 1870-1970, Peter Bedrick Books (New York, NY), 1984.
Harold Macmillan, Penguin Books (New York, NY), 1991, published in England as *Harold Macmillan, Politician, 1894-1956,* (two volumes), 1989.

Monty: The Lonely Leader, 1944-1945, HarperCollins (New York, NY), 1994.

A Bundle from Britain, St. Martin's Press (New York, NY), 1994.

How Far from Austerlitz?: Napoleon, 1805-1815, St. Martin's Press (New York, NY), 1996.

(Editor and contributor) *Telling Lives,* Macmillan (London, England), 2000.

Seven Ages of Paris, Knopf (New York, NY), 2002.

The Age of Napoleon, Modern Library (New York, NY), 2004.

Friend or Foe: An Anglo-Saxon History of France, Orion (London, England), 2004.

La Belle France: A Short History, Knopf (New York, NY), 2005.

Also author of script, *The Terrible Year,* based on book of same title, for BBC *Chronicle,* 1971. Contributor to periodicals, including *Times Literary Supplement, Observer, Spectator, New York Times, Time and Tide,* and *Sunday Telegraph.*

SIDELIGHTS: Alistair Horne is a "distinguished historian whose trilogy on Franco-German conflict from 1870 to 1940 could hardly be bettered," John Leonard wrote in the *New York Times.* Horne's studies of revolutionary movements, especially his award-winning analysis of the Algerian insurrection, have also received critical acclaim. Horne's books, critics have observed, are marked by a balanced presentation of warring parties, strong narrative hold, and extensive research.

The Price of Glory: Verdun, 1916, the first volume of Horne's trilogy, is "a battle saga which rises above mere narrative to achieve the status of veritable drama," according to L.F. Eliot in the *National Review.* It is "one of the most scrupulously documented war (or anti-war) books of our time," Leon Wolff wrote in the *New York Times Book Review.* "No historian of our times has so poignantly recaptured the malignancy of war on the Western Front." Barbara Tuchman praised *The Fall of Paris: The Seige and the Commune, 1870-1871,* the trilogy's second volume. In a *New York Times Book Review* article, she wrote that "Horne tells the story . . . with such vivid verisimilitude that the reader feels he is inside the beleaguered city and turns the pages anxiously to learn what will be his fate. . . . As a historian, [Horne] is honest, meticulous, consistently interesting and readable, with an eye for the colorful and informative detail, the telling picture and dramatic episode."

The third volume of the trilogy, *To Lose a Battle: France, 1940,* chronicles the six-week rout of France by the German Army in 1940 and examines the reasons behind the collapse of the French Army, regarded at the time as the strongest military unit in Europe. "Horne's superbly readable narrative explores this question in its political, military, economic, and moral ramifications," Jack Beatty commented in the *New Republic.* "Horne's pen gives instant life to everything in its path; like the German army, he sweeps easily before him the political contortions of the Third Republic, with its giddy succession of premiers, its government by crony and mistress, and its deep and virulent social divisions between left and right." An *Economist* critic observed: "All the details are there: the small, fleeting triumphs, the cowardice, the stupidity and the intelligence. Horne's great gift is his ability to hold his readers in the grip of such feelings, constantly shifting his focus . . . without mystifying or fatiguing them." And Keith Eubank of *Library Journal* noted that *To Lose a Battle* "should become one of the great classic accounts of this terrible disaster which befell France . . . . It is a magnificent book."

Horne's study, *A Savage War of Peace: Algeria, 1954-1962,* was called "as full and objective a history of the Algerian war as we are likely to see" by James Joll in the *New York Times Book Review.* On November 4, 1954, the Algerian revolutionary army *Front de Liberation Nationale* (F.L.N.) attacked a police station in the city of Biskra to begin its campaign against French colonial rule. Eight years later the French withdrew and the undeclared war ended, with two million soldiers and civilians dead or exiled.

"The terror, mutilation, counterterror, torture and murder took place on both sides. There was no middle," John Leonard wrote in the *New York Times.* "The criminal difference between the 19th century and the 20th," Leonard added, "is that in the 20th there are no civilians." "It is a frightful story—begotten in the blood of innocents," Priscilla L. Buckley commented in the *National Review.* "[The war has been] much written about but never as skillfully or even-handedly as in this book." In the *Spectator,* Raymond Carr commented: "Occasionally an epic subject encounters a fine historian. This was the case with the Algerian war and Mr. Horne. The result is a book of compelling power, written with compassion and understanding." *A Savage War of Peace* "is a magnificent book," Carr continued. "It has the poetic sense of place without which no great work of history can be written. It is more than a narrative, skillfully distilled from a mountain of sources, often difficult to follow because of its complexity, but which nevertheless holds the reader."

Several reviewers commented on the fairness of Horne's account of the conflict, a great achievement "given that the sources are so polemical, that the passions of the participants have not died down, and that so many indeed still refuse to say much about their roles," Theodore Zeldin observed in the *Listener.* Zeldin noted that Horne "tells his story—and it is a gripping story—not quite with detachment, because he is too appalled by the cruelty of it all, but with fairness and lucidity, showing that horrific violence was used by almost all the parties involved." "For Mr. Horne, after talking to everybody he could find and reading everything he could get his hands on, nobody is a hero. He merely does his considerable best to understand," Leonard observed. And Richard Cobb wrote in the *New Statesman:* "Horne's book is quite unsurpassed, and is likely to remain so. . . . He has a word of understanding for all the protagonists, even the most fanatical and cruel." Cobb added, "Such a repetitive account of daily killings, of mindless violence, could be merely sickening; yet, thanks to the author's ever-alert compassion, to his eye for each pathetic detail, it attains a sort of sombre beauty and a dignity that illuminates the whole book." *A Savage War of Peace,* Cobb wrote, is "a work of great beauty and insight."

Horne is also the author of the biography *Harold Macmillan,* which was published in two volumes in England as *Harold Macmillan, Politician, 1894-1956.* Macmillan was a British politician who became the prime minister of England and directly requested Horne to write his authorized biography. "It was an inspired choice: Horne carries none of the baleful ballast of a psychobiographer, who would have had an oedipal field day exploring Macmillan's relationships," wrote John P. Roche in the *New Leader.* Roche went on to note: "Horne has brought Macmillan to life, has removed the masks he seemed wont to don, and in doing so has written a superb book."

In his book *Monty: The Lonely Leader, 1944-1945.* Horne focuses on British World War II General Bernard Montgomery as the Allies neared victory and Montgomery develops the "master plan" for the inva-

sion of Normandy. Horne achieves his goal through the recounting of a 1992 trip he made with Montgomery's son David, as they retraced the general's travels from one headquarters to another leading up to the invasion. The book also includes a brief account of the general's early life. Writing in *History Today,* M.R.D. Foot noted that the author "disposes of several myths, and enhances understanding of the recent past." Fritz Stern, writing in *Foreign Affairs,* commented that, for the most part, he found the book to be a "brilliant and authoritative study."

In his memoir, *A Bundle from Britain,* Horne describes his life growing up in Great Britain and reflects on the years he spent in America beginning at the age of fifteen. His British parents had sent him to live with the Cutler family in Ganison, NY, to protect him from the bombing of England during World War II. Horne describes in detail his life in America and his time at a boarding school, where he befriended the young William F. Buckley, Jr., who would go on to gain fame as a noted conservative political commentator. A *Publishers Weekly* contributor noted that the author "recalls his American adolescence with prim, sometimes cloying affection and gratitude." Writing in *Booklist,* Alice Joyce called the book "an appealing reminiscence of historical significance."

How Far from Austerlitz?: Napoleon, 1805-1815 focuses on the French leader's military career and also discusses his non-military accomplishments, such as his influence on the institution of the metric system, the layout of Paris, and French legal codes. William F. Buckley, Jr., commented in the *National Review* that the book is "an engrossing work by a master historian."

In the *Seven Ages of Paris,* Horne traces the history of Paris by examining seven important epochs in the city's life, beginning with its days as a Roman colony and island in the middle of the Seine. "A rich, vigorously fresh study for history lovers," wrote Brad Hooper in *Booklist.* A *Publishers Weekly* contributor noted that the book "is sure to delight Francophiles everywhere." Writing in the *Spectator,* Douglas Johnson commented that Horne "has produced a work of great scholarship, which, as Maurice Duron states in his preface, combines the art of synthesis with that of detail."

Horne continued to write about France in *The Age of Napoleon,* in which he focuses on Napoleon's nonmilitary achievements and life, including his character and private life. A *Publishers Weekly* contributor called the book a "picturesque social history." Marc Arkin, writing in the *New Criterion,* noted that the short book "is intended to be the historian's version of a beach book, a niche it fits splendidly."

Friend or Foe: An Anglo-Saxon History of France delves into the long history of Anglo-French relations. Calling Horne "perhaps the most accessible and—occasionally—authoritative writer on French affairs in English," *New Statesman* contributor Andrew Hussey went on to note, "Horne's prose is entertaining, elegant and crisp, and his acerbic views on the great men and moments of French history are always bracing." In a review in *History Today,* Glen Richardson noted, "He writes with brio and has an engaging, readable, style with touches of humour throughout."

Horne provides a quick look at the past 200 or so years of French history in his book *La Belle France: A Short History.* "His work is enriched by examples from contemporary observers and by his focus on cultural and intellectual development," wrote Marie Marmo Mullaney in the *Library Journal.* A *Kirkus Reviews* contributor called the book "a sweeping, literate history" and also commented that it was "a pleasure for Francophile readers, balancing the recent spate of dim-witted screeds against a nation that dares to go its own way." A *Publishers Weekly* contributor wrote: "It's the compellingly subjective treatment of modern France, and the irreverent appraisal of its icons, that makes this book so worth reading."

BIOGRAPHICAL AND CRITICAL SOURCES:

BOOKS

Horne, Alistair, *A Bundle from Britain,* St. Martin's Press (New York, NY), 1994.

PERIODICALS

Booklist, August, 1994, Alice Joyce, review of *A Bundle from Britain,* p. 2018; October 15, 2002, Brad Hooper, review of *Seven Ages of Paris,* p. 383.
Business Week, August 9, 2004, Hardy Green, review of *The Age of Napoleon,* p. 11.

Denver Post, November 24, 2002, Brian Richard Boylan, review of *Seven Ages of Paris.*
Economist, April 19, 1969, review of *To Lose a Battle: France, 1940;* July 1, 1989, review of *Harold Macmillan, Politician, 1894-1956,* volume 2, 73; June 4, 1994, review of *Monty: The Lonely Leader, 1944-45,* p. 91; November 16, 2002, review of *Seven Ages of Paris.*
Foreign Affairs, November-December, 1994, Fritz Stern, review of *Monty,* p. 170.
History Today, June, 1995, M. R. D. Foot, review of *Monty,* p. 47; May, 2005, Glen Richardson, review of *Friend or Foe: An Anglo-Saxon History of France,* p. 85.
Kirkus Reviews, October 1, 2002, review of *Seven Ages of Paris,* pp. 1446-1447; May 15, 2005, review of *La Belle France: A Short History,* p. 575.
Library Journal, May 15, 1969, Keith Eubank, review of *To Lose a Battle;* November 15, 2002, Marie Marmo Mullaney, review of *Seven Ages of Paris,* p. 85; August 2, 2005, Marie Marmo Mullaney, review of *La Belle France,* p. 100.
Listener, January 26, 1978, Theodore Zeldin, review of *A Savage War of Peace: Algeria, 1954-1962.*
Los Angeles Times, December 22, 2002, Victor Brombert, review of *Seven Ages of Paris,* p. R-4.
National Review, February 26, 1963, L. F. Eliot, review of *The Price of Glory;* June 23, 1978, Priscilla L. Buckley, review of *A Savage War of Peace,* p. 785; April 21, 1989, John O'Sullivan, review of *Harold Macmillan, Politician, 1894-1956,* volume 1, p. 48; June 30, 1997, William F. Buckley, Jr., review of *How Far from Austerlitz?: Napoleon, 1805-1815,* p. 54.
New Criterion, June, 2004, Marc Arkin, review of *The Age of Napoleon,* p. 78.
New Leader, June 12, 1989, John P. Roche, review of *Harold Macmillan, Politician, 1894-1956,* volume 1, p. 17; February 5, 1990, John P. Roche, review of *Harold Macmillan, Politician, 1894-1956,* volume 2, p. 23.
New Republic, January 19, 1969, Jack Beatty, review of *To Lose a Battle;* March 20, 1989, Henry Fairlie, review of *Harold Macmillan, Politician, 1894-1956,* volume 1, p. 42.
New Statesman, November 18, 1977, Richard Cobb, review of *A Savage War of Peace;* July 10, 2000, John Colvin, review of *Telling Lives,* p. 59; November 29, 2004, review of *Friend or Foe,* p. 46; December 6, 2004, Andrew Hussey, review of *Friend or Foe,* p. 48.

New York Times, March 23, 1978, John Leonard, review of *A Savage War of Peace,* p. 31; December 22, 2002, review of *Seven Ages of Paris,* p.22.

New York Times Book Review, April 7, 1963, Leon Wolff, review of *The Price of Glory;* January 30, 1966, Barbara Tuchman, review of *The Fall of Paris: The Seige and the Commune, 1870-1871,* p. 1; July 20, 1969, review of *To Lose a Battle,* p. 3; March 19, 1978, James Joll, review of *A Savage War of Peace,* p. 31.

Publishers Weekly, June 20, 1994, review of *A Bundle from Britain,* p. 87; October 21, 2002, review of *Seven Ages of Paris,,* p. 61; April 5, 2004, review of *The Age of Napoleon,* p. 51; April 18, 2005, review of *La Belle France,* p. 50.

Spectator, October 22, 1977, Raymond Carr, review of *A Savage War of Peace;* November 9, 2002, Douglas Johnson, review of *Seven Ages of Paris,* p. 81; July 17, 2004, Robert Stewart Castlereagh, review of *The Age of Napoleon,* p. 35.

Sunday Telegraph (London, England), October 27, 2002, Munro Price, review of *Seven Ages of Paris.*

Times (London, England), November 27, 2002, Jonathan Fenby, review of *Seven Ages of Paris,* p. 19.

ONLINE

Library of Congress Web site, http://www.loc.gov/ (March 28, 2005), "Alistair Horne Named Senior Distinguished Scholar at the John W. Kluge Center" (news release).*

*   *   *

HORNE, Alistair Allan
    See HORNE, Alistair

*   *   *

HUMMER, Terence Randolph
    See HUMMER, T.R.

*   *   *

HUMMER, T.R. 1950-
    (Terence Randolph Hummer)

PERSONAL: Born August 7, 1950, in Macon, MS; son of Charles Vernon (a postal worker and farmer) and Marion Kate (a homemaker; maiden name, Slocum) Hummer; second wife's name Stephanie; children: (first marriage) Theo (daughter); (second marriage) Jackson (daughter). *Education:* University of Southern Mississippi, B.A. (English), 1972, M.A. (English), 1974; University of Utah, Ph.D. (American literature and creative writing), 1980. *Hobbies and other interests:* Playing the saxophone.

ADDRESSES: Office—Georgia Review, University of Georgia, Athens, GA 30602-9009. *E-mail*—garev@ uga.edu.

CAREER: Oklahoma State University, Stillwater, OK, assistant professor of English, 1980-84; Kenyon College, Gambier, OH, assistant professor of English, 1984-89; Middlebury College, Middlebury, VT, assistant professor of English and editor of *New England Review,* 1989-93; University of Oregon, Eugene, OR, professor and director of M.F.A. program in creative writing, 1993-97; Virginia Commonwealth University, Richmond, VA, senior poet, 1997-2001; University of Georgia, Athens, editor of *Georgia Review* and professor of English, 2001—. Visiting professor, Exeter College, England; writer in residence, University of California—Irvine.

AWARDS, HONORS: National Endowment for the Arts poetry fellowships, 1987, 1992-93; Guggenheim fellowship, 1992-93; Pushcart Prize, 1990 and 1992; Hanes Poetry Prize, 1999; Richard Wright Award for Literary Excellence, 2003; Phi Beta Kappa Poetry Prize finalist.

WRITINGS:

Translation of Light (poetry chapbook), Cedar Creek Press (Stillwater, OK), 1976.

The Angelic Orders (poetry), Louisiana State University Press (Baton Rouge, LA), 1982.

The Passion of the Right-Angled Man (poetry), University of Illinois Press (Urbana, IL), 1984.

(Editor and author of introduction, with Bruce Weigl) *The Imagination of Glory: The Poetry of James Dickey,* University of Illinois Press (Urbana, IL), 1984.

Lower-Class Heresy (poetry), University of Illinois Press (Urbana, IL), 1987.

The Eighteen-Thousand-Ton Olympic Dream (poetry), Morrow (New York, NY), 1990.

(Editor, with Devon Jersild) *The Unfeigned Word: Fifteen Years of New England Review,* University Press of New England (Hanover, NH), 1993.

Walt Whitman in Hell: Poems, Louisiana State University Press (Baton Rouge, LA), 1996.

Useless Virtues (poetry), Louisiana State University Press (Baton Rouge, LA), 2001.

The Infinity Sessions (poetry), Louisiana State University Press (Baton Rouge, LA), 2005.

The Muse in the Machine: Essays on Poetry and the Anatomy of the Body Politic, University of Georgia Press (Athens, GA), 2006.

Contributor of poems to periodicals, including *New Yorker, Harper's, Atlantic Monthly, Paris Review,* and *Georgia Review.* Also former associate editor and editor in chief of *Quarterly West,* 1979; editor of *Cimarron Review,* 1980-84, and *Kenyon Review,* 1984-89; contributing editor, *Kenyon Review,* 1989—, and *Manoa: A Literary Journal of the Pacific Rim;* former guest editor of *Bread Loaf Quarterly.*

WORK IN PROGRESS: Bluegrass Wasteland: New and Selected Poems.

SIDELIGHTS: T.R. Hummer is a respected critic, scholar, and poet who is the recipient of two Pushcart Prizes for his verses. Born and raised in Mississippi, his early poetry was naturally reflective of modern Southern poets, and his first verses have been compared to those of James Dickey, about whom he coedited the book *The Imagination of Glory: The Poetry of James Dickey,* and Dave Smith, who was Hummer's mentor while he attended the University of Utah. Furthermore, as a *Contemporary Poets* contributor noted, Hummer explored "pain, suffering, and regret" in his early poems: "The argument of his poetry is that we are shaped by our losses. What we lose becomes our emotional heritage."

However, with the exception of his very first poems, Hummer has said that he would not classify his poetry as Southern. "I think it is inaccurate to paint me as so unreconstructed a Southern poet," he told *CA.* "The real story is more vastly more complicated than that, and my last three books at least have not been Southern in the least, insofar as I understand that word to mean anything (take a look at *Useless Virtues* and see if it ain't so—I haven't been compared with Dickey since the early 80s)."

Among Hummer's current poetic themes are human sexuality, birth versus death, and political concerns. The latter theme especially comes to the fore in his collection *The Eighteen-Thousand-Ton Olympic Dream,* in which the poet laments the current state of America's working classes and environment. Although Penny Kaganoff, writing in *Publishers Weekly,* felt that Hummer "is sometimes given to superfluities of language and a rambling narrative," she praised his "startling imagery and lyrical descriptions."

BIOGRAPHICAL AND CRITICAL SOURCES:

BOOKS

Contemporary Poets, 7th edition, St. James Press (Detroit, MI), 2001.

PERIODICALS

Kenyon Review, spring, 2000, David Baker, "Heresy and the American Ideal: On T.R. Hummer," p. 131.

Publishers Weekly, April 13, 1990, Penny Kaganoff, review of *The Eighteen-Thousand-Ton Olympic Dream,* p. 59.*

*   *   *

HUSTON, James W. 1953-
(James Webb Huston)

PERSONAL: Born October 26, 1953, in Lafayette, IN; son of James Alvin and Florence (Webb) Huston; married Dianna Suzanne Henry, February 2, 1980; children: Stephanie, Paul, Shannon, Colleen, Scott. *Education:* Attended University of Warwick, Coventry, England; University of South Carolina, B.A., 1975; University of Virginia, J.D., 1984. *Politics:* Republican. *Religion:* Presbyterian.

ADDRESSES: Home and office—P.O. Box 270072, San Diego, CA 92198-2071. *Office*—Gray, Cary, Ware & Freidenrich LLP, 401 B St., Ste. 1700, San Diego, CA 92101. *E-mail*—jwh@jameshuston.com..

CAREER: Attorney and writer. Admitted to the California Bar, 1984; Gray, Cary, Ames & Frye (now Gray, Cary, Ware & Freidenrich LLP), San Diego, CA, attorney, 1984-90, partner, 1990—. *Military service:* U.S. Navy, lieutenant, 1975-81; U.S. Naval Reserve, commander, 1981—.

MEMBER: American Bar Association, Americans United for Life, San Diego USO (member of board of directors).

AWARDS, HONORS: Warwick Scholar, 1974.

WRITINGS:

NOVELS

Balance of Power: A Novel, William Morrow (New York, NY), 1998.
The Price of Power (sequel to *Balance of Power: A Novel*), William Morrow (New York, NY), 1999.
Flash Point: A Novel, William Morrow (New York, NY), 2001.
Fallout: A Novel, William Morrow (New York, NY), 2001.
The Shadows of Power: A Novel, William Morrow (New York, NY), 2002.
Secret Justice: A Novel, William Morrow (New York, NY), 2003.

ADAPTATIONS: Author's works have been made into audiobooks, including *Balance of Power: A Novel,* Blackstone, 2001; *The Shadows of Power: A Novel,* Sound Library, BBC Audiobooks America, 2002; and *Secret Justice,* Blackstone, 2003.

SIDELIGHTS: James W. Huston is an attorney practicing in San Diego, California, who specializes in litigation, specifically product liability, insurance bad faith and coverage, aviation, and contracts. He applies his experience in law and the military to the fiction realm in his first novel, *Balance of Power: A Novel,* a work called "a heart-stopping story of military action combined with Washington politics and law" by Katherine E.A. Sorci in the *Library Journal.* The protagonist is Jim Dillon, aide to Speaker of the House John Stanbridge, a hawkish Republican serving during the administration of President Edward Manchester, a "dove" who opposes military aggression. The action of the novel begins when an American cargo vessel is attacked by Indonesian pirates in the South China Sea. The torture of the crew is captured on videotape and

released for television viewing, the ship is destroyed, and the captain is taken hostage to an Indonesian island. When the president refuses to act, Stanbridge begins impeachment proceedings. Molly Vaughan, the president's aide and love interest of Dillon, tells Dillon that the Constitution allows Congress to issue a letter of reprisal to authorize military action by a private vessel on behalf of the United States. Dillon passes this information on to Stanbridge and soon finds himself taking the order to the U.S.S. *Constitution* and Admiral Billings, who commands a battle group. Billings has two sets of orders, the one from the president to leave the area, and the Congressional order to attack.

Lev Raphael wrote in the *Detroit Free Press* that "Huston's battle scenes do work." "Not a bad debut performance, not bad at all," wrote Gilbert Taylor in *Booklist.* A *Kirkus Reviews* contributor deemed the book "a debut military thriller that delivers the requisite guts and glory while making a meaningful statement about the ambiguous role of violence in America."

In *The Price of Power,* the author brings back Dillon, who is involved in the court martial of an admiral who disregarded an order from the President of the United States. Meanwhile, the president himself faces impeachment for dereliction of duty. A *Publishers Weekly* contributor noted that readers "should be impressed . . . by the authenticity of the author's procedural details." *Flash Point: A Novel* is a military thriller that focuses on the terrorist murder of a Navy pilot in training on the aircraft carrier *George Washington.* The pilot's roommate, Sean Woods, seeks revenge. During a flight, Woods joins an Israeli air attack designed to kill the terrorist group's leader. Although the attack fails, Woods goes on to convince the higher-ups in Washington to make another attempt to kill the leader with Woods flying the plane that will drop the bomb on a hideout in Iran. A *Publishers Weekly* contributor noted that the author "does craft a well-conceived subplot about Arab-Israeli relations in the American spy community and a hair-raising finale." Jane Jorgenson, writing in the *Library Journal,* noted that in the description of flying and law "the details are all there—and they are nicely handled."

In *Fallout: A Novel,* Huston tells the story of Luke Henry, a Navy pilot, who is forced to leave the Navy after being wrongly accused of being responsible for a fatal aircraft accident. Henry decides to start his own private "Top Gun" school and soon has a secret contract with the government to train pilots. Henry, however, finds himself in trouble once again when he realizes that he has been set up by terrorists. Gilbert Taylor, writing in *Booklist*, noted: "The action culminates in a well-sketched aerial battle." A *Publishers Weekly* contributor noted: "The aviation scenes are best."

The Shadows of Power: A Novel introduces Navy SEAL Kent Rathman, known as Rat. Rathman finds himself seeking out Algerian terrorists after one of them vows revenge on a former colleague who shot down the terrorist's brother. A *Publishers Weekly* contributor noted that the book has "plenty of action." Rathman returns in *Secret Justice: A Novel* and captures a stand-in for Osama bin Laden named Wahamed Duar but is in trouble after a terrorist he was interrogating dies. Rathman eventually faces a court battle while trying to stop a terrorist plot involving a freighter rigged to blow up Washington, DC. A *Publishers Weekly* contributor wrote, "The plot is ripped from the pages of tomorrow's newspapers, the military action is authentic, the [l]egal scenes believable."

BIOGRAPHICAL AND CRITICAL SOURCES:

PERIODICALS

Booklist, March 15, 1998, Gilbert Taylor, review of *Balance of Power: A Novel*, p. 1180; June 1, 2000, Gilbert Taylor, review of *Fallout: A Novel*, p. 1842.

Detroit Free Press, August 9, 1998, Lev Raphael, review of *Balance of Power*, p. 7F.

Kirkus Reviews, May 1, 1998, review of *Balance of Power*, p. 604; May 15, 2001, review of *Fallout*, p. 686; May 15, 2003, review of *Secret Justice: A Novel*, p. 703.

Library Journal, April 15, 1998, Katherine E. A. Sorci, review of *Balance of Power*, p. 112; May 15, 2000, Jane Jorgenson, review of *Flash Point: A Novel*, p. 125.

Publishers Weekly, April 27, 1998, review of *Balance of Power*, p. 44; May 10, 1999, review of *The Price of Power*, p. 57; May 15, 2000, review of *Flash Point*, p. 87; July 2, 2001, review of *Fallout*, p. 53; June 3, 2002, review of *The Shadows of Power: A Novel*, p. 66; May 15, 2003, review of *Secret Justice*, p. 199.

ONLINE

James W. Huston Home Page, http://www.jameswhuston.com (November 6, 2005).*

* * *

HUSTON, James Webb
See HUSTON, James W.

I

IDLE, Eric 1943-

PERSONAL: Born March 29, 1943, in South Shields, Durham, England; son of Ernest (a Royal Air Force sergeant) and Norah (a health visitor; maiden name, Sanderson) Idle; married Lyn Ashley (an actress), July 7, 1969 (divorced, 1978); married Tania Kosevich (a model), 1981; children: (first marriage) Carey (son); (second marriage) Lily. *Education:* Pembroke College, Cambridge, degree (with honors), 1965.

ADDRESSES: Agent—William Morris Agency, 1325 Avenue of the Americas, New York, NY 10019.

CAREER: Actor, writer, composer, and director. British Broadcasting Corp. (BBC) television programs, writer, 1960s; writer and performer with Graham Chapman, John Cleese, Terry Gilliam, Terry Jones, and Michael Palin as Monty Python comedy troupe, beginning 1969; cofounder and president of Prominent Features (production company). Cambridge Footlights, president, 1964-65.

Actor in television series, including *Do Not Adjust Your Set,* BBC, 1968-69; *Monty Python's Flying Circus,* BBC, 1969-74, Public Broadcasting Service (PBS), 1974-82; *Rutland Weekend Television,* BBC, 1975-76; *Nearly Departed,* National Broadcasting Company (NBC), 1989; *Hercules* (animated; also known as *Disney's Hercules*), 1998; *Suddenly Susan,* NBC, 1999-2000. Actor in television miniseries, including *Around the World in Eighty Days,* NBC, 1989. Actor in television movies, including *Ken Russell's Isadora the Biggest Dancer in the World,* BBC, 1966; *Jonathan Miller's Alice in Wonderland,* BBC, 1966; *No, That's Me over Here,* London Weekend Television, 1967; *We Have Ways of Making You Laugh,* London Weekend Television, 1968; *Pythons in Deutschland,* Bavaria Atelier, 1971; *Monty Python's Fliegende Zircus,* Bavaria TV, 1971, 1972; (and director) *The Rutles* (also known as *All You Need Is Cash*), NBC, 1978; *The Mikado,* Thames TV, 1987; *Parrot Sketch Not Included,* 1989; *Thirty Years of Python: A Revelation,* 1999; and *The Scream Team,* Disney, 2002.

Actor in films, including *Albert Carter Q.O.S.O.,* Dormer, 1968; *And Now for Something Completely Different,* Columbia, 1971; *Monty Python and the Holy Grail,* Cinema V, 1975; *Side by Side,* 1976; *Life of Brian* (also known as *Monty Python's The Life of Brian*), Warner Bros., 1979; *Monty Python Live at the Hollywood Bowl,* Paramount, 1982; *Group Madness,* 1983; *Monty Python's The Meaning of Life,* Universal, 1983; *Yellowbeard,* Orion, 1983; *The Secret Policeman's Private Parts,* 1984; *European Vacation* (also known as *National Lampoon's European Vacation*), Warner Bros., 1985; *The Transformers: The Movie,* DEG, 1986; *The Adventures of Baron Munchausen,* Columbia/TriStar, 1988; *Nuns on the Run,* Twentieth Century-Fox, 1990; *Missing Pieces,* HBO Home Video, 1991; *Too Much Sun,* RCA/Columbia Home Video, 1991; *Mom and Dad Save the World,* Warner Bros., 1992; *Splitting Heirs,* Universal, 1993; *Honey, I Shrunk the Audience,* 1995; *Casper,* Universal, 1995; *The Wind in the Willows* (also known as *Mr. Toad's Wild Ride*), Columbia, 1996; *An Alan Smithee Film: Burn, Hollywood, Burn,* Buena Vista, 1997; *Quest for Camelot,* Warner Bros., 1998; *Rudolph the Red-nosed Reindeer: The Movie,* Legacy Releasing,

1998; *The Secret of NIMH 2: Timmy to the Rescue,* MGM/UA Home Video, 1998; *Journey into Your Imagination,* 1999; *South Park: Bigger, Longer, and Uncut,* Paramount, 1999; *Dudley Do-Right,* Universal, 1999; *102 Dalmations,* 2000; *Pinocchio,* Miramax, 2002; *Hollywood Homicide,* 2003; and *Ella Enchanted,* Miramax, 2003.

Actor in theatre, including *Footlights '63,* Edinburgh Festival, 1963; *My Girl Herbert,* Lyric Hammersmith Theatre, London, 1963; *I'm Just Wild about Harry,* Henry Miller Theatre, Edinburgh Festival, 1963; *The Tempest,* Edinburgh Festival, 1964; *Footlights '64,* Edinburgh Festival, 1964; *One for the Pot,* Leicester Phoenix Theatre, 1965; *Oh What a Lovely War,* Leicester Phoenix Theatre, 1965; Coventry Festival, 1972; *Monty Python's First Farewell Tour,* Canada, then United Kingdom, 1973; *Monty Python Live at Drury Lane,* 1974; *Monty Python Live at City Centre,* 1976; and *Monty Python Live at the Hollywood Bowl,* 1980. Also performed in opera, including *The Mikado,* English National Opera, 1987, then Houston Grand Opera, 1989.

Performed voice-over work for video games and computer games, including *Monty Python's Complete Waste of Time,* 1994; *Discworld,* 1995; *Discworld II: Mortality Bytes,* 1996; *Monty Python and the Quest for the Holy Grail,* 1996; and *Monty Python's The Meaning of Life,* 1997.

AWARDS, HONORS: Silver Rose, Montreux Television Festival, 1971, for *Monty Python's Flying Circus;* ACE Cable Award for Best Cable Show of the Year, 1982, for "The Frog Prince"; Grand Prix Special du Jury award, Cannes Film Festival, 1983, for *Monty Python's The Meaning of Life;* Michael Balcon Award for Outstanding British Contribution to Cinema (with Monty Python), British Academy of Film and Television Arts, 1987; Tony Award for best musical, Outer Critics Circle best Broadway musical award, and Drama Desk best musical award, all 2005, all for *Monty Python's Spamalot.*

WRITINGS:

Hello, Sailor (novel), Weidenfeld & Nicolson (London, England), 1974.
The Rutland Dirty Weekend Book, Methuen (London, England), 1976.

Pass the Butler (play; produced at Globe Theatre, London, 1982), Methuen (London, England), 1982.
The Quite Remarkable Adventures of the Owl and the Pussycat (children's fiction; based on the works of Edward Lear), illustrated by Edward Lear and Wesla Weller, Dove Kids (Los Angeles, CA), 1996.
The Road to Mars: A Post Modem Novel, Pantheon Books (New York, NY), 1999.
Eric Idle Live at the Getty (stage show), 1999.
Eric Idle Exploits Monty Python (touring stage show), 2000.
The Greedy Bastard Diary: A Comic Tour of America, HarperEntertainment (New York, NY), 2005.

Also author, with Neil Innes, of recording *Rutland Dirty Weekend Songbook,* 1975.

SCREENPLAYS

Albert Carter Q.O.S.O., Dormer, 1968.
Splitting Heirs, Universal, 1992.
Welcome to the Family, Savoy, 1994.
The Remains of the Piano, Miramax, 1995.

TELEPLAYS

(With Graham Chapman and Cryer) *No, That's Me over Here,* London Weekend Television, 1967.
The Frost Report, British Broadcasting Company (BBC-TV), 1967.
Twice a Fortnight, BBC-TV, 1967.
Frost on Sunday, Wednesday, Thursday, Friday, etc. (series), London Weekend Television, 1967–1968.
Marty Feldman, BBC-TV, 1968–1969.
Rutland Weekend Television (series), BBC-TV, 1975–1976.
All You Need Is Cash (movie), National Broadcasting Company (NBC), 1978, televised in Britain as *The Rutles,* BBC-TV, 1978.
(And director) *"The Frog Prince,"* Faerie Tale Theatre, Showtime, 1982.
Nearly Departed, NBC, 1989.

RADIO PLAYS

I'm Sorry I'll Read that Again, British Broadcasting Company (BBC), 1966, 1968.
(With John Du Prez) *Behind the Crease,* BBC, 1990.

Also author of *Radio Five* (two series), c. 1970s.

And Now for Something Completely Different (adapted from *Monty Python's Flying Circus*), Columbia, 1972.

Monty Python and the Holy Grail (also see below), Cinema V, 1975.

Monty Python's Life of Brian (also see below), Warner Bros., 1979.

Monty Python Live at the Hollywood Bowl, Columbia, 1982.

Monty Python's The Meaning of Life (also see below), Universal, 1983.

(And editor) *Monty Python's Big Red Book,* Methuen (London, England), 1972, Warner Books (New York, NY), 1975.

(And editor) *The Brand New Monty Python Bok,* illustrations by Terry Gilliam (under pseudonym Jerry Gillian) and Peter Brookes, Methuen (London, England), 1973, published as *The Brand New Monty Python Papperbok,* 1974.

Monty Python and the Holy Grail (also published as *Monty Python's Second Film: A First Draft*), Methuen (London, England), 1977.

(And editor) *Monty Python's Life of Brian* [and] *Montypythonscrapbook,* Grosset (New York, NY), 1979.

The Complete Works of Shakespeare and Monty Python: Volume One—Monty Python (contains *Monty Python's Big Red Book* and *The Brand New Monty Python Papperbok*), Methuen (London, England), 1981.

Monty Python's The Meaning of Life, Grove Press (New York, NY), 1983.

The Complete Monty Python's Flying Circus: All the Words, two volumes, Pantheon (New York, NY), 1989.

Monty Python Speaks!: John Cleese, Terry Gilliam, Eric Idle, Terry Jones, and Michael Palin Recount an Amazing, and Silly, Thirty-Year Spree in Television and Film—in Their Own Words, Squire!, interviewed by David Morgan, Spike (New York, NY), 1999.

Do Not Adjust Your Set, British Broadcasting Company (BBC-TV), 1968–1969.

Pythons in Deutschland (movie), Bavaria Atelier, 1971.

Monty Python's Flying Circus (series), BBC-TV/Public Broadcasting Service (PBS), 1974–82.

Monty Python's Flying Circus, British Broadcasting Company (BBC), 1970.

Another Monty Python Record, Charisma, 1970.

Monty Python's Previous Record, Charisma, 1972.

Monty Python Matching Tie and Handkerchief, Charisma, 1973.

Monty Python Live at the Theatre Royal, Drury Lane, Charisma, 1974.

The Album of the Soundtrack of the Trailer of the Film of Monty Python and the Holy Grail (film soundtrack; includes additional material), Charisma, 1975.

Monty Python Live at City Center, 1976.

The Worst of Monty Python, 1976.

The Monty Python Instant Record Collection, Charisma, 1977.

(And coproducer) *Monty Python's Life of Brian* (film soundtrack), WEA, 1979.

(And producer) *Monty Python's Contractual Obligation Album,* Charisma, 1980.

Monty Python's The Meaning of Life (film soundtrack), CBS, 1983.

Monty Python's the Final Ripoff (compilation), Virgin, 1987.

(And producer) *Monty Python Sings,* Virgin, 1989.

Always Look on the Bright Side of Life (single), Virgin, 1991.

The Rutland Isles (recording), Artist Direct, 2003.

Monty Python's Spamalot (musical adaptation of the film *Monty Python and the Holy Grail*), produced in Chicago, IL, at Shubert Theatre, 2005, produced on Broadway, 2005.

Also conceived the idea for the musical *Seussical,* based on the works of Theodore Seuss Geisel, first produced on Broadway at the Richard Rogers Theater, November 30, 2000.

SIDELIGHTS: Eric Idle is one of six members of Monty Python, a group of British comedians whose absurd humor earned them a large following in Europe and North America. The group first appeared together in 1969 in the television series *Monty Python's Flying Circus,* which regularly featured such offbeat skits as "Hell's Grannies," in which Idle and cohorts play obscene and rowdy old women, and "The Upper Class Twit of the Year," in which aristocratic morons compete on an obstacle course. Among Idle's most memorable roles on the show are leering rogues, obsequious television hosts, and fussy old women. Idle has also undertaken a number of successful solo projects in writing and acting.

Many of the Python troupe's most renowned skits from the *Flying Circus*'s first two seasons, including "Hell's Grannies" and the twit contest, have been collected in the film *And Now for Something Completely Different.* This work contains such celebrated Python material as the "Dead Parrot" sketch, in which a pet store proprietor and a customer debate the state of a recently purchased parrot, and "The Lumberjack Song," which begins with a lumberjack boastfully singing the virtues of manly work but ends with him confessing he is a transvestite. Blaine Allen, reviewing the film in *Take One,* called it "one of the most hilarious and original movies to come along in a while."

As *Monty Python's Flying Circus* became increasingly popular, the Pythons began recording and publishing some of their material. Idle edited many of the Python books, including *Monty Python's Big Red Book* (which has a blue cover) and *The Brand New Monty Python Bok,* incorporating new and old material with graphics and stills from the series and films. The results provided Python fans with hard copy of their favorite sketches while giving the Pythons themselves enough additional revenue to work independently.

Their first independent venture was the 1975 movie *Monty Python and the Holy Grail,* which follows the legendary King Arthur and his knights on their quest to find the sacred cup of Christ. Idle is particularly memorable as Sir Robin the Not-So-Brave, who wets his armor at the first sign of danger and is accompanied by a troupe of minstrels who sing odes to his cowardice. While "there are the usual sillies—phrases repeated endlessly, nonsense syllables, and sight gags plentiful enough to warm the cockles of a hitter's heart," Richard Goldstein commented in the *Village*

Voice, there is also "a great deal of gratuitous cruelty, much of it occasioned by the presence of poverty and plague. The film's anger at these occurrences adds dimension to its anarchy, and makes it matter more than the TV show."

After the last season of *Flying Circus* was broadcast in 1974, Idle persuaded the BBC to air his program *Rutland Weekend Television,* a parody of a small independent television station. The show only ran for two seasons, but provided the idea for the "Rutles," a takeoff of the Beatles. With the assistance of Neil Innes, a regular contributor of music to Python projects, Idle constructed a thorough "re-creation" of a pop music group's trials and triumphs. After the group appeared with Idle on an episode of *Saturday Night Live* in 1977, NBC offered Idle the chance to make a Rutles television movie. *All You Need Is Cash* features cameos by such recording stars as Mick Jagger, Paul Simon, and even former Beatle George Harrison. "The growth of the ersatz quartet's career and ultimate breakup is followed in a take-off of that you-are-actually-making-history-this-very-moment approach to documentary reporting," *Village Voice* writers Howard Smith and Leslie Harlib noted. The reviewers also found that the program has a "sneaky power" to its satire and praise in particular its "fifteen slyly brilliant parody songs of well-known Beatles tunes."

Idle rejoined the Pythons to film *Monty Python's Life of Brian,* a satire along biblical lines. The title character is a poor fellow who is mistaken for the messiah and spends his life frantically trying to evade his "followers." Notable among the Monty Python members—each of whom portrays numerous characters in the film—is Idle as a nonchalant crucifixion victim who jokes with his executioners and leads his fellow convicts in a sing-along of "Always Look on the Bright Side of Life" (a song written by Idle) while dangling from a cross. The film, with its irreverent portrayal of religion and its followers, drew protesters in many places. But "Jesus isn't singled out for ridicule," Gene Siskel of the *Chicago Tribune* observed, explaining that *Life of Brian* "is simply the Python response to such pompous pictures as *King of Kings.*" The critic added that "the protests of religious groups against the film, however well-intentioned, are simply missing the point of the picture." Many people clearly agreed, since the film proved a success at the box office.

After appearing in fellow Python member Graham Chapman's film *Yellowbeard,* in 1983 Idle and the rest of the Pythons completed another celebrated film, *Monty Python's The Meaning of Life.* There were problems getting the script together, for the group had grown unaccustomed to writing in collaboration. Nevertheless, the difficulties helped to produce a stronger film. As Idle pointed out to George Perry in *The Life of Python,* the group's self-criticism was essential: "I think it's the important thing—we do all keep a strong critical eye on what everyone else is doing. It's healthy, and if you're reading scripts out to everyone and something doesn't work, it's better to get that sort of criticism while you're still making the film than when it is out—at least you have a chance to make it better."

Monty Python's The Meaning of Life, which was honored at the Cannes Film Festival, is comprised of sketches on topics such as birth, sex, and death. As in the previous films, members of the troupe play several characters, with Idle most striking as he emerges, clad in a pink long-tailed tuxedo, from a refrigerator to disrupt a "live" organ transplant by serenading the unwilling donor with facts about the universe. Siskel described the film as "fresh and original and delightfully offensive," while *Newsweek* reviewer Katrine Ames called it "the best movie to date from England's satirical sextet." The critic further praised the group's humor as "never . . . more incisive—they've become savagely hilarious observers of the human condition." *Time* writer Richard Schickel believed that *The Meaning of Life* overcomes any minor flaws: "In their assaults on conventional morality, [the Pythons] generate a ferocious and near Swiftian moral gravity of their own," the critic concluded. "It is this quality that distinguishes their humor from the competition, rescues it from its own excesses and makes braving it an exhilarating experience."

Idle ha undertaken solo writing projects, as well, since the 1970s. *Hello Sailor,* published in 1974, is his first novel. Frank Pike, writing in the *Times Literary Supplement,* described the novel "as 'rude' and 'silly' as the [Monty Python] detractors would expect." In 1976, Idle released *The Rutland Dirty Weekend Book. Listener* contributor D.A.N. Jones felt that the book was not as funny as it intends to be: "*The Rutland Dirty Weekend Book* is based on the television show and has many panto-dame jokes about sex—that is, 'sexy' sexlessness." More recently, in 1996 Idle published the children's work *The Quite Remarkable Adventures of the Owl and the Pussycat.* The book is a

mixture of the familiar and the novel; Idle's Monty Python antics infiltrate the classic story in a much more subdued form appropriate for children.

In another medium, an *Amusement Business* article by Tim O'Brien regarding Idle's "3-D Pirates Stranded at Sea World" revealed what Sea World and Renaissance Entertainment and Creative Services Production stated about the fifteen-minute film written by and featuring Idle and Leslie Nielsen. Eric Miles, corporate manager of production for Busch Entertainment Company and executive producer of the film, said in the article, "This film is instant magic. The energy between Eric Idle and Leslie Nielsen is amazing." The article reports that Jim Timon of Renaissance Entertainment and Creative Services Production and the executive heading the production of this film concurs with Miles: "Unlike many 3-D films, this one has a progressive plot and is not used strictly to 'wow' viewers with effects."

Pursuing his solo work again, Idle published *The Road to Mars: A Post-Modem Novel* in 1999. Gary Kamiya, reviewing the title for the *New York Times,* commented that Idle's adept physical comedy makes an inadequate comic novel, but recognized the more favorable aspects in the book: "Idle handles plot competently, even displaying some genuine narrative quirkiness." For Kamiya, the basic problem of *The Road to Mars* is the fact that an actor wrote the book, rather than a writer: "His terse prose lacks the robust, cunning, luxurious stupidity that comedy needs." A reviewer for *Publishers Weekly* felt the writing was lacking as well: "The narrative meanders for long stretches with scene after scene whose only point is to set up a weak joke— the sort of thing that works so well as TV farce but when passed off as a novel, is tedious." Devon Thomas, writing in the *Library Journal,* however, had a different view: "Idle . . . has written an engaging and amusing work of speculative fiction with fully developed characters, a taut plot, and a thoughtful and entertaining analysis of humor's part in human development. A joy to read; highly recommended."

Idle had one of the bigger hits of his solo career with the creation of *Monty Python's Spamalot,* a Broadway musical adaptation of *Monty Python and the Holy Grail.* The award-winning musical expands the territory of the original film, spoofing not only the King Arthur legends but also the film itself, other Python sketches, and Broadway musicals in general. After Sir

Robin (played on Broadway by David Hyde Pierce rather than Idle) insists that "You Won't Succeed on Broadway (If You Haven't Any Jews)," the cast takes a detour through *Fiddler on the Roof;* another song, "The Song that Goes Like This," pokes fun at the formulaic power-ballads of famed Broadway composer Andrew Lloyd Webber. *Monty Python's Spamalot* also retains many of the most popular bits from the original film, including the Knights Who Say Ni, the hacked-to-bits but still fighting Black Knight, the French Taunter, and the killer rabbit. The result, Don Shewey commented in the *Advocate,* "is a frothy frappe of pop-cultural references that's tastier but no more substantial than the canned slab of processed pork from which it takes its title." "It gives off such irrepressible energy, it's contagious," Cathleen McGuigan commented in *Newsweek,* adding: "Whether it's actually nutritious—well, who cares?" At the same time that *Monty Python's Spamalot* debuted, Idle published *The Greedy Bastard Diary: A Comic Tour of America,* which recounts a backstage view of one of Idle's comedy tours and also discusses some of the creation of *Monty Python's Spamalot.* Idle's "take on Hollywood is refreshingly unjaded" in the book, noted a *Variety* reviewer.

Despite his solo success, Idle looks back fondly at his days as a Python. Expressing amazement at the enduring popularity of the group, he told *People* interviewer Susan Schindehette: "It's astounding. Here we are . . . years on, and people are still watching the same silly stuff. They're fascinated by the program."

BIOGRAPHICAL AND CRITICAL SOURCES:

BOOKS

Contemporary Literary Criticism, Volume 21, Gale (Detroit, MI), 1982.

Hewison, Robert, *Monty Python: The Case Against,* Methuen (London, England), 1981.

Hewison, Robert, *Footlights!,* Methuen (London, England), 1983.

Johnson, Kim Howard, *The First 200 Years of Monty Python,* St. Martin's (New York, NY), 1989.

Perry, George, *The Life of Python,* Pavilion, 1983.

Thompson, John O., editor, *Monty Python: Complete and Utter Theory of the Grotesque,* University of Illinois Press (Champaign, IL), 1982.

Wilmut, Roger, *From Fringe to Flying Circus,* Methuen (London, England), 1980.

PERIODICALS

Advocate, May 10, 2005, Don Shewey, review of *Monty Python's Spamalot,* p. 67.

Amusement Business, March 17, 1997, Tim O'Brien, "Eric Idle's 3-D Pirates Stranded at Sea World," p. 26.

Chicago Tribune, September 21, 1979, Gene Siskel, review of *Monty Python's Life of Brian;* April 1, 1983, Gene Siskel, review of *Monty Python's The Meaning of Life.*

Entertainment Weekly, September 6, 1996, Erin Richter, review of *Missing Pieces,* p. 84.

Library Bookwatch, June, 2005, review of *The Greedy Bastard Diary: A Comic Tour of America.*

Library Journal, August, 1999, Devon Thomas, review of *The Road to Mars,* p. 139.

Listener, December 23, 1976, D.A.N. Jones, review of *The Rutland Dirty Weekend Book.*

Nation, March 27, 1989, Stuart Klawans, review of *The Adventures of Baron Munchausen,* p. 427.

New Criterion, May, 2005, Mark Steyn, review of *Monty Python's Spamalot,* p. 38.

New Republic, April 16, 1990, Stanley Kauffmann, review of *Nuns on the Run,* p. 27; June 7, 1993, Stanley Kauffmann, review of *Splitting Heirs,* p. 27.

Newsweek, April 4, 1983, Katrine Ames, review of *The Meaning of Life;* January 24, 2005, Cathleen McGuigan, review of *Monty Python and the Holy Grail,* p. 64.

New York Times, September 19, 1999, Gary Kamiya, review of *The Road to Mars: A Post-Modem Novel,* p. 21.

People, July 11, 1983, review of *Yellowbeard,* p. 10; April 17, 1989, John Stark, review of *Around the World in Eighty Days,* p. 13; April 24, 1989, Susan Schindehette, "Puzzling out His Post-Python Life Leaves Eric Idle with Hands Full," p. 59; February 11, 1991, Ralph Novak, review of *Too Much Sun,* p.12; August 10, 1992, Ralph Novak, review of *Mom and Dad Save the World,* p. 20; July 1, 1996, Stanley Young, "Older and Wiseacre," p. 35.

Publishers Weekly, July 19, 1999, review of *The Road to Mars,* p. 188.

Take One, May-June, 1971, Blaine Allen, review of *And Now for Something Completely Different.*

Time, March 28, 1983, Richard Schickel, review of *The Meaning of Life;* June 12, 1995, Richard Corliss, review of *Casper,* p. 68.

Times Literary Supplement, March 21, 1975, Frank Pike, review of *Hello, Sailor.*

Variety, October 6, 1997, Deborah Young, review of *An Alan Smithee Film—Burn, Hollywood, Burn*, p. 54; November 3, 1997, Todd McCarthy, review of *The Wind in the Willows*, p. 99; May 11, 1998, Joe Leydon, review of *Quest for Camelot*, p. 58; March 7, 2005, review of *The Greedy Bastard Diary*, p. 53.

Village Voice, May 5, 1975, Richard Goldstein, review of *Monty Python and the Holy Grail*; March 20, 1978, Howard Smith and Leslie Harlib, review of *All You Need Is Cash*.

ONLINE

Welcome to PythOnline!, http://www.pythonline.com/ (June 6, 2000).

William Morris Agency Web site, http://www.wma.com/ (October 11, 2005), "Eric Idle."*

*   *   *

ILES, Greg 1961(?)-

PERSONAL: Born 1961 (some sources say 1960), in Stuttgart, West Germany (now Germany); married; children: one daughter, one son. *Education:* University of Mississippi, earned degree, 1983. *Hobbies and other interests:* Music, song writing.

ADDRESSES: Home—Natchez, MS. *Agent*—c/o Author Mail, Simon & Schuster, Inc., 1230 Avenue of the Americas, New York, NY 10020. *E-mail*—greg@gregiles.com.

CAREER: Writer.

AWARDS, HONORS: Mississippi Author's Award for Fiction, for *Black Cross*.

WRITINGS:

NOVELS

Spandau Phoenix, Dutton (New York, NY), 1993.
Black Cross, Dutton (New York, NY), 1995.
Mortal Fear, Dutton (New York, NY), 1997.

The Quiet Game, Dutton (New York, NY), 1999.
24 Hours, Putnam (New York, NY), 2000.
Dead Sleep, Putnam (New York, NY), 2001.
Sleep No More, Putnam (New York, NY), 2002.
The Footprints of God, Scribner, (New York, NY), 2003.
Blood Memory, Scribner, (New York, NY), 2005.
Turning Angel, Scribner, (New York, NY), 2005.

Iles's novels have been translated into more than a dozen languages.

SCREENPLAYS

24 Hours, Columbia Pictures, 2002.
Trapped, 2002.

ADAPTATIONS: Sleep No More has been made into a sound recording by Brilliance Audio, 2002.

SIDELIGHTS: Greg Iles is a writer of mystery and suspense novels who has mined his childhood in East Germany, where he grew up as the son of a U.S. embassy official, to find inspiration for some of his works. Iles's earliest novels feature latter-day Nazis and cold war-era international intrigue, and more recent works have included serial killers, kidnappers, and psychopaths. All of his works are noted for their intricate plotting, quick pace, and surprising endings. *Booklist* contributor Vanessa Bush echoed the sentiments of many critics with regard to Iles's books when she called his *24 Hours* "a fast-paced, gripping novel of suspense and action." A longtime resident of Mississippi, Iles has also utilized the deep South as a setting for many of his books, and many critics have noted elements of the Southern Gothic style in his writing.

Iles's first novel, *Spandau Phoenix*, was a *New York Times* bestseller. It tells of a young German police sergeant's discovery of some yellowed old documents uncovered during the demolition of Spandau prison. In reality, the prison had housed Rudolph Hess, the infamous Nazi-era war criminal, who died in 1987. In Iles's tale, the real Hess remained free, carrying on Hitler's legacy while hiding in South Africa; a highly trained double was imprisoned in his place. The found papers reveal a plot dating back to 1941 but having modern-day ramifications, including the possible eradication of Israel by a neo-Nazi brotherhood. The sergeant's wife, along with a historian, translate the mysterious papers and embark on a mission to thwart the Nazi plot.

"Iles does a credible job of managing his large cast of characters and maintaining suspense," Mary Ellen Quinn wrote in a *Booklist* review of *Spandau Phoenix*. *Library Journal* contributor V. Louise Saylor, however, remarked that the novel "loses its impact long before the end of the drawn-out plot." Although finding fault with the story's "stock characters and melodramatic plot," a reviewer for *Publishers Weekly* called this debut novel "clearly written, with some entertaining speculation."

A contributor to *Kirkus Reviews* judged Iles's second bestseller, *Black Cross,* to be "a swift historical thriller of such brutal accomplishment that it vaporizes almost every cliché about the limits of the genre." Set during World War II, this novel revolves around a secret Allied mission to infiltrate a Nazi concentration camp, where the Reich is developing poison gases in a secret lab. The two men assigned to infiltrate the camp are to release a British poison gas, code-named "Black Cross," which is available to the Allies in only a limited amount. The action is devised as a warning to the Nazis to stop their research and prevent them from ever using their own supply of nerve gases against Allied troops. Because the raid is likely to kill everyone in the camp, including the prisoners and the British agents, the operatives modify the mission's original strategy—with harrowing results.

Praising *Black Cross* as "full of runaway-train excitement," a *Kirkus Reviews* contributor regarded it as "good enough to read twice." A *Publishers Weekly* writer concluded that *Black Cross* is "an unusually resonant, gripping thriller" deserving a place on any "recommended reading list of thrillers." John F. Harvey, writing in *Armchair Detective,* deemed the plot "more complex than those of most thrillers. . . . The novel makes the reader feel that he/she has been through a significant, emotionally rending and bitterly educational experience." Harvey added, "The work poses several life vs. death philosophical questions and discusses them in the heat of extreme wartime conditions." Emily Melton called the author and the story "remarkable" in a *Booklist* review. "This stunning, horrifying, mesmerizing novel will keep readers transfixed from beginning to end," she maintained.

Iles's third novel, *Mortal Fear,* is about the race to find a serial killer who stalks female victims on the Internet. The systems operator for an erotic online service becomes a suspect in the murders of subscribers around the country, then goes online himself, posing as a woman and potential victim in order to trap the real murderer. A contributor to the *New York Time Book Review* called *Mortal Fear* "more complicated than it needs to be," but labeled the technology involved in the computer chase "fascinating." "Iles scores high with this psychological thriller," Lori Dunn wrote in *Library Journal,* "easily accessible even to the computer-semiliterate." A reviewer for *Publishers Weekly* concluded, "Iles uses rich first-person narration and clever plotting to tell a sizzler of a thriller."

Natchez, Mississippi, is the setting for *The Quiet Game,* in which Penn Cage, an attorney-turned-author as well as a recent widower, returns to his home town from Houston and begins an investigation into a thirty-year-old murder case with racial overtones. Penn has personal reasons for conducting his investigation; he suspects the culprit is a former judge who is blackmailing his father in an attempt to ruin his medical practice. But the small Southern town does not take kindly to Penn's plans to dig into the past and upset their precarious social order. The FBI proves to be a hindrance as well, and soon enough Penn's family is endangered. Urged on by the family of the murdered man, Penn's quest becomes an obsession as he discovers cover-ups and lies that stretch all the way to J. Edgar Hoover. *Booklist* critic Brad Hooper praised *The Quiet Game* as a "deliciously complicated tale," and *Library Journal* contributor Thomas L. Kilpatrick called the book a "Southern superthriller that rivals John Grisham's best."

In *24 Hours* the best laid plans of kidnappers Joe and his wife, Cheryl, go awry when they kidnap Abby, the diabetic five-year-old daughter of Dr. William Jennings and his wife, Karen. The kidnappers' goal is to receive ransom money and release the child within twenty-four hours, before federal authorities can investigate the crime—a scenario they have successfully carried out numerous times in the past. But Karen, who is being held hostage by Joe's lumbering and mentally incompetent cousin, and William, who is intercepted at a medical convention by the alluring Cheryl, fight back in order to save their daughter, who may die if she does not receive her daily insulin injection. As in other Iles stories, the FBI proves to be of little use, and William and Karen must outsmart the criminals on their own. Kilpatrick praised the book as a "thriller that will mesmerize to the bitter end." A *Publishers Weekly* contributor wrote that *24 Hours* is a "brilliantly plotted tale [that] walks the razor's edge between cinematic excess and bone-chilling suspense."

Dead Sleep features Jordan Glass, an award-winning, New Orleans-based photojournalist who is traumatized by the disappearance of her twin sister. While on a vacation in Hong Kong, Jordan discovers a painting of her sister in a museum exhibition devoted to the works of an anonymous artist. The startling paintings all depict sleeping (or possibly dead) nude women; all the women are known to be missing. Shocked, Jordan must confront secrets from her past as she recognizes her sister may have been the victim of a serial killer. The trail leads to an eccentric art professor at Tulane University, a Vietnam-based French art collector, and the possibility that Jordan's father, a famous photographer himself, may not have been killed in Cambodia as she has long believed. The characters Daniel Baxter and Dr. Lenz from *Mortal Fear* figure into the plot as well. A reviewer for *Publishers Weekly* called Iles a writer with "incredible range," and *Dead Sleep* a book with a "double surprise ending" and a "perfect final payoff." The book proved to transcend the genre of the murder mystery as well. *Booklist* critic Stephanie Zvirin called the work "atmospheric, sexy, and provocative in its depiction of the duality of human nature."

In *Sleep No More*, Iles tells the story of John Waters, a geologist in Natchez who suddenly finds himself attracted to a younger woman who knows everything about an affair he had years ago with a murdered woman. When this new woman is murdered as well, John begins to suspect that someone, possibly even his wife, may be out to ruin his life. A *Publishers Weekly* contributor noted that the author's "fans will certainly enjoy the way he once again brings to piquant life his home turf—Natchez and the Mississippi Delta—and creates a character with an actual job."

More recent thrillers by Iles include *The Footprints of God* and *Blood Memory*. In the former, the author presents David Tennant, a government scientist working on an intelligent machine. When one of his colleagues dies, Tennant suspects foul play and thinks he may be next. He decides to run, with the help of his psychiatrist. Edward Karam, writing in *People*, com-

mented that the author "addresses serious issues in popular form, and the pursuits are plenty hot." Iles tells the story of Dr. Catherine (Cat) Ferry in his thriller *Blood Memory*. Cat is an alcoholic forensic odontologist who discovers that she is pregnant by her married boyfriend, a cop. Cat also finds herself working on a series of murder cases in which the murderer bites and chews the victims after they are dead. There is something about this case, however, that sends Cat back home to Natchez with a sense that these murders are connected to the shooting death of her father when she was eight years old. Calling the novel "as southern Gothic as it gets," a *Kirkus Reviews* contributor wrote: "It's clearly Cat's meow."

BIOGRAPHICAL AND CRITICAL SOURCES:

PERIODICALS

Armchair Detective, spring, 1995, John F. Harvey, review of *Black Cross*, pp. 220-221.

Booklist, May 1, 1993, Mary Ellen Quinn, review of *Spandau Phoenix*, pp. 1569, 1576; November 1, 1994, Emily Melton, review of *Black Cross*, p. 459; July, 1999, Brad Hooper, review of *The Quiet Game*, p. 1894; July, 2000, Vanessa Bush, review of *24 Hours*, p. 1974; June 1, 2001, Stephanie Zvirin, review of *Dead Sleep*, p. 1852; September 1, 2001, Ted Hipple, review of *The Quiet Game*, p. 126.

Entertainment Weekly, August 15, 2003, Wook Kim, review of *The Footprints of God*, p. 83.

Kirkus Reviews, November 1, 1994, review of *Black Cross*, pp. 1431-1432; February 1, 2005, review of *Blood Memory*, p. 139.

Library Journal, April 15, 1993, V. Louise Saylor, review of *Spandau Phoenix*, p. 126; January, 1997, Lori Dunn, review of *Mortal Fear*, p. 146; August, 1999, Thomas L. Kilpatrick, review of *The Quiet Game*, p. 140; August, 2000, Thomas L. Kilpatrick, review of *24 Hours*, p. 157; May 15, 2001, Michael Adams, review of *The Quiet Game*, p. 18; July, 2001, Jane Jorgenson, review of *Dead Sleep*, p. 123; February 15, 2005, Jeff Ayers, review of *Blood Memory*, p. 119.

New York Times Book Review, February 16, 1997, review of *Mortal Fear*, p. 28.

People, September 22, 2003, Edward Karam, review of *The Footprints of God*, p. 58.

Publishers Weekly, March 15, 1993, review of *Spandau Phoenix*, p. 67; October 9, 1995, review of *Black Cross*, p. 83; December 9, 1996, review of *Mortal*

Fear, p. 59; July 5, 1999, review of *The Quiet Game,* p. 55; July 31, 2000, review of *24 Hours,* p. 71; June 11, 2001, review of *Dead Sleep,* p. 58; July 23, 2001, Daisy Maryles and Dick Donahue, "A True 'Sleep'-er," p. 20; June 17, 2002, review of *Sleep No More,* p. 43.

ONLINE

Greg Iles Web site, http://www.gregiles.com (April 1, 2002).

Internet Movie Database, http://www.Imdb.com/ (October 30, 2005), filmography of Iles' work.*

J

JACKSON, Alison 1953-

PERSONAL: Born August 22, 1953, in Alhambra, CA; daughter of Samuel (a physician) and Lorayne (a musician; maiden name, Swarthout) Coombs; married Stephen Jackson (a computer analyst), September 10, 1983; children: Kyle, Quinn. *Ethnicity:* "Caucasian." *Education:* University of California, Irvine, B.A., 1975; San Jose State University, M.L.S., 1977. *Politics:* Democrat. *Religion:* Protestant. *Hobbies and other interests:* Travel, snow skiing, water skiing.

ADDRESSES: Home—6213 Wynfield Ct., Orlando, FL 32819. *Office*—Seminole County Public Library, 245 Hunt Club Blvd., North Longwood, FL 32779.

CAREER: Long Beach Public Library, Long Beach, CA, children's librarian, 1977-80; Newport Beach Public Library, Newport Beach, CA, children's librarian, 1980-87; Fullerton Public Library, Fullerton, CA, children's librarian, 1987-97; Seminole County Public Library, Longwood, FL, children's librarian, 1997—.

MEMBER: American Library Association, Society of Children's Book Writers and Illustrators, California Library Association, Southern California Council on Literature for Children and Young People, Florida Library Association.

WRITINGS:

CHILDREN'S BOOKS

My Brother the Star, illustrated by Diane Dawson Hearn, Dutton (New York, NY), 1990.

Crane's Rebound, illustrated by Diane Dawson Hearn, Dutton (New York, NY), 1991.

Blowing Bubbles with the Enemy, Dutton (New York, NY), 1993.

I Know an Old Lady Who Swallowed a Pie, illustrated by Judith Byron Schachner, Dutton (New York, NY), 1997.

If the Shoe Fits, illustrated by Karla Firehammer, Henry Holt (New York, NY), 2001.

The Ballad of Valentine, illustrated by Tricia Tusa, Dutton (New York, NY), 2002.

Rainmaker, Boyds Mills (Honesdale, PA), 2005.

SIDELIGHTS: Alison Jackson once told *CA:* "I grew up in South Pasadena, California. I was always interested in writing as a child, and I served on the staff of both my school newspaper and yearbook while attending South Pasadena High School.

"I only began writing seriously after entering college in 1971. I enrolled in the creative writing program at the University of California, Irvine, where I took a number of writing courses and learned many of the basic techniques necessary in writing fiction. At that time I had written a few short stories, but I had never attempted a novel-length work. And I certainly wouldn't have dared to send anything in for publication. I didn't think I had enough talent!

"In fact, it was not until 1988 (seventeen years later) that I summoned up enough courage to submit a manuscript to a major publisher. At that time I had been working as a professional children's librarian for over ten years and was married with a tiny baby of my own at home. I decided that I had read enough good children's books in the past ten years to try writing one myself. And by that time there was no doubt in my mind that I wanted to write for children—not adults.

"The problem was . . . I needed something to write about. As luck would have it, a workshop was being conducted in our library. The class was titled 'How to Get Your Child into Television Commercials,' and I thought this would be a wonderful subject to write about. Why not?, I decided. I'll write about a kid on TV.

"So I did. I invented the character of Cameron Crane, a six-year-old terror who stars in television commercials. Then I came up with the idea of an older brother, Leslie, who feels overshadowed by his brother and ignored by his parents—until he himself is given a chance to star on a county-wide basketball team. The result was *My Brother the Star,* which was published by Dutton Children's Books."

School Library Journal contributor Trish Ebbatson called *My Brother the Star* a "nicely written first novel. . . . Leslie is a likable and believable central character." Also voicing approval of Jackson's first novel, a *Kirkus Reviews* critic observed that "the author writes with unforced fluidity." "This is light fare," commented Denise Wilms in *Booklist,* "but it moves easily." Wilms recommended *My Brother the Star* as "one for the popular reading shelf."

Talking about her next endeavor, Jackson continued: "I enjoyed writing about these two characters [Leslie and Cameron] so much that I created a sequel, *Crane's Rebound,* which came out the following year. *Crane's Rebound* recounts Leslie's adventures at a summer sports camp. Unfortunately, competition on the basketball court is not all Les is forced to contend with. He also has an obnoxious roommate, who happens to be a bully—and the best player on the team. In *Crane's Rebound,* I also feature a character who was introduced in my first novel. Her name is Bobby Lorimer. She is a feisty basketball-playing tomboy who develops a huge crush on Leslie while continuing to be one of his main adversaries on the court." *Booklist* critic Kay Weisman called Jackson's portrayal of Leslie's insecurities "right on target." She also noted Jackson's "comic touch that will appeal to sports fans and problem-novel enthusiasts alike."

Jackson commented: "The feisty character, Bobby Lorimer, proved to be so popular that I decided to write a third novel, just about her. Titled *Blowing Bubbles with the Enemy,* this third book in the series deals with Bobby's instant unpopularity when she chooses to try out for the boys' basketball team at her junior high school. Not only does her tryout anger the boys at her school, but when Bobby is unjustly denied a spot on the team, the girls take up a crusade in her honor, nearly creating a civil war at Jefferson Junior High." A *Kirkus Reviews* critic noted that female readers will "enjoy Bobby's breezy voice, admire her gumption, and share her confusion over the awkwardness of boy-girl relationships." *School Library Journal* contributor Renee Steinberg also appreciated the "likeable, well-drawn heroine" of *Blowing Bubbles with the Enemy.* "Jackson's smooth prose style and believable characters make this an enjoyable read," wrote Steinberg.

Reflecting on her goals as an author, Jackson said: "I have always enjoyed writing books for children. I especially feel that there is a need for good, funny stories that can be enjoyed by boys in the middle (third through fifth) grades. In the future, I intend to write more books about Leslie, Cameron, and Bobby. But I would also like to branch out and create new characters with other interests."

Jackson branched out with the title character of her picture book, *I Know an Old Lady Who Swallowed a Pie.* The elderly lady seems to have one interest—eating everything. In this humorous take off on the traditional folk song, "I Know an Old Lady Who Swallowed a Fly," a woman, who has been invited to share a family's Thanksgiving feast, proceeds to devour not only a pie, but an entire feast, down to the roasting pan. The result is "an amusingly successful variation" on the original, commented Gahan Wilson in the *New York Times Book Review.* Several reviewers complimented Jackson on her inventive, holiday-appropriate conclusion, in which the family finally trusses up the old lady with ropes and throws her out the door, where she floats away among the other enormous balloons in the Thanksgiving Day parade. Told in whimsical rhymes that mimic the original, the story prompted *Bulletin of the Center for Children's Books* critic Elizabeth Bush to predict: "Sing it once, and kids'll beg for seconds."

Responding to those cries for more from her youngest fans, Jackson said: "After seeing the immense popularity of *I Know an Old Lady Who Swallowed a Pie,* I plan to continue writing picture books in addition to chapter books. Takeoffs on familiar songs and stories are of particular interest to me."

Jackson later added: "My next two books were indeed takeoffs on familiar songs and rhymes. *If the Show Fits* tells the story of the old woman in the shoe, moving a multicultural cast of children into other recognizable nursery rhymes. In another humorous takeoff, *The Ballad of Valentine* replaces the heroine of 'Clementine' with a dreamy girl named Valentine, whose unnamed admirer tries to send her various love notes, only to have all of his letters go astray.

"After moving to Florida in 1997, I wanted to write a book about the state and its unique history. This effort resulted in a novel for upper-grade children, *Rainmaker.* The story tells of a Depression-era farmer and his family during one of the state's most devastating droughts. In an act of desperation, he sends for the rainmaker, an elderly woman from Mississippi, who arrives bringing hopes and doubts in equal measure." A *School Library Journal* contributor noted that "All the story lines converge at the end to reinforce the theme: accepting change as a part of life, even when one doesn't like it."

In commenting on her writing style, Jackson said "When writing a novel or picture book, I first create an outline, plus personal sketches of each character. I then proceed to 'fill in the outline' as I write the first draft. Subsequent drafts embellish the text and flesh out the characters. Lastly, I read the text aloud to see if it flows, and most especially to test out the dialogue."

Jackson's writings are the product of various influences, as she once commented to *CA:* "A number of sources have influenced my writing. One University of California, Irvine professor in particular, by the name of Oakley Hall, gave me much encouragement and advice. He taught me some of the finer points of plotting and characterization, and he continually emphasized the use of realistic detail.

"My children continue to be a source of humorous material for me. They have a logic and sense of perspective that is always fresh and entirely unique. In fact, as they grow older, I can already see a number of potential books in the works.

"I also pay close attention to the students who come into the library every day, either to do homework or just to chat with each other. I find that children will talk about almost anything, if I simply stay in the background. And I have already used quite a few of their inspirational conversations in my books.

"I think this is the real reason why I want to continue writing for children. They are so uninhibited and funny that I find them irresistible, not only as subjects in my work, but as members of my potential audience. So I feel safe in saying that as long as kids keep on reading . . . I will continue writing books for them."

BIOGRAPHICAL AND CRITICAL SOURCES:

PERIODICALS

Booklist, January 1, 1990, Denise Wilms, review of *My Brother the Star,* p. 917; September 15, 1991, Kay Weisman, review of *Crane's Rebound,* pp. 151-152; November 1, 1993, pp. 521-523; September 1, 1997, p. 139; October 1, 2001, Kathy Broderick, review of *If the Shoe Fits,* p. 325; March 15, 2005, Shelle Rosenfeld, review of *Rainmaker,* p. 1292.

Bulletin of the Center for Children's Books, November, 1997, Elizabeth Bush, review of *I Know an Old Lady Who Swallowed a Pie,* p. 87; November 15, 2002, Julie Cummins, review of *The Ballad of Valentine,* p. 602.

Kirkus Reviews, September 1, 1989, review of *My Brother the Star,* p. 1328; November 1, 1993, review of *Blowing Bubbles with the Enemy,* p. 1392; March 15, 2005, review of *Rainmaker,* p. 353.

New York Times Book Review, November 16, 1997, Gahan Wilson, review of *I Know an Old Lady Who Swallowed a Pie,* p. 56.

Publishers Weekly, August 27, 2001, review of *If the Shoe Fits,* p. 83; December 2, 2002, review of *The Ballad of Valentine,* p. 52.

School Library Journal, January, 1990, Trish Ebbatson, review of *My Brother the Star,* p. 104; January, 1994, Renee Steinberg, review of *Blowing Bubbles with the Enemy,* p. 114; November, 1997, p. 84; December, 2001, Piper L. Nyman, review of *If the Shoe Fits,* p. 104; December, 2002, Shawn Brommer, review of *The Ballad of Valentine,* p. 98; April, 2005, Diana Pierce, review of *Rainmaker,* p. 134.

Alison Jackson Web site,, http://www.alison-jackson.
com (November 12, 2005).

*   *   *

JACKSON, Jacqueline 1928-
(Jacqueline Dougan Jackson)

PERSONAL: Born May 3, 1928, in Beloit, WI;
daughter of Ronald Arthur (a dairy farm owner) and
Vera (Wardner) Dougan; married Robert S. Jackson,
June 17, 1950 (divorced, 1973); children: Damaris
Lee, Megan Trever, Gillian Patricia, Jacqueline
Elspeth. *Education:* Beloit College, B.A., 1950;
University of Michigan, M.A., 1951.

ADDRESSES: Home—816 N. 5th St., Springfield, IL
62702. *Office*—University of Illinois at Springfield,
Springfield, IL 62701.

CAREER: Educator and writer. Kent State University,
Kent, OH, lecturer in children's literature, 1964-68;
Teacher Development Center, Rockford, IL, consultant
in creative writing, 1968-70; University of Illinois at
Springfield (formerly Sangamon State University),
Springfield, IL, associate professor of literature, 1970-
83, professor, then professor emeritus, 1983—.
Developed series of creative writing programs for
University of Wisconsin, 1969—; teacher in workshops
on children's creativity; radio lecturer for *The Author
Is You,* WHA of the University of Wisconsin, 1969-78,
and *Reading and Writing and Radio,* WSSU,
Springfield, IL, 1975-94.

MEMBER: Modern Language Association of America,
Children's Reading Round Table, Phi Beta Kappa.

AWARDS, HONORS: Notable Book citation from
American Library Association, 1966, and Dorothy
Canfield Fisher children's book award, 1967, both for
The Taste of Spruce Gum; honorary degrees include:
D.Litt. from MacMurray College, 1976, and D.H.L.
from Beloit College, 1977.

WRITINGS:

FOR CHILDREN

Julie's Secret Sloth, Little, Brown (Boston, MA), 1953.

(And illustrator) *The Paleface Redskins,* Little, Brown
(Boston, MA), 1958.
The Taste of Spruce Gum, Little, Brown (Boston, MA),
1966.
Missing Melinda, Little, Brown (Boston, MA), 1967.
Chicken Ten Thousand (Junior Literary Guild
selection), Little, Brown (Boston, MA), 1968.
(And illustrator) *The Ghost Boat,* Little, Brown
(Boston, MA), 1969.
Spring Song, Kent State University Press (Kent State,
OH), 1969.
The Orchestra Mice, Reilly & Lee (Chicago, IL), 1970.
The Endless Pavement, Seabury, 1973.
Turn Not Pale, Beloved Snail (also for adults), Little,
Brown (Boston, MA), 1974.
James R. Jackson: Art Was His Life, Bay Books
(Sydney, New South Wales, Australia), 1991.

OTHER

(Illustrator) Chad Walsh, *Knock and Enter,* Morehouse
(New York, NY), 1952.
(As Jacqueline Dougan Jackson) *Stories from the
Round Barn* (memoir), TriQuarterly Books
(Evanston, IL), 2000.
(As Jacqueline Dougan Jackson) *More Stories from
the Round Barn* (memoir), TriQuarterly Books
(Evanston, IL), 2001.

Also author of *The Cloudlanders,* published in a
newspaper. Contributor of about forty short stories and
poems to magazines, including *Highlights, Grade
Teacher, Instructor, American Farm Youth, Episcopal
Churchnews, Journal of the National Federation of
Music Clubs, Top 'o' the News, Episcopalian, Writer,
Publishers Weekly,* and *Classmate.*

SIDELIGHTS: Jacqueline Jackson's first story was
published when she was ten years old; and her first
novel, *The Cloudlanders,* was published in a local
newspaper shortly after that. Jackson has written
and/or illustrated several children's books since then.
In 2001, her memoir *Stories from the Round Barn* was
published. Jackson recounts her experiences growing
up on the family dairy farm, including learning about
sex from the farm's artificial inseminator, and recalls
her family history from the early 1900s. Carolyn
Maddux, writing in the *Antioch Review,* commented
that the author "offers an affectionate, no-holds-barred
look at dairy farm life." A *Publishers Weekly* contribu-

tor noted that the book is "rich in human warmth and rural detail" and went on to call the effort "heartfelt." Irwin Weintraub, writing in the *Library Journal,* commented, "Jackson's delightful recollections will arouse readers' curiosity about Midwestern life in a bygone era." The author continued her recollections in her follow-up memoir *More Stories from the Round Barn.* "These earnest sketches capture the sounds and rhythms of early and mid-20th-century rural life," wrote a *Publishers Weekly* contributor in a review of the second memoir. The reviewer went on to call the book "quaint, warm and sincere."

BIOGRAPHICAL AND CRITICAL SOURCES:

BOOKS

Jackson, Jacqueline Dougan, *Stories from the Round Barn,* TriQuarterly Books (Evanston, IL), 2000.
Jackson, Jacqueline Dougan, *More Stories from the Round Barn,* TriQuarterly Books (Evanston, IL), 2001.

PERIODICALS

Antioch Review, winter, 1999, Carolyn Maddux, review of *Stories from the Round Barn,* p. 115.
Kirkus Reviews, August 1, 1967, review of *Missing Melinda,* p. 878; April 15, 1969, review of *The Ghost Boat,* p. 441; December 1, 1974, review of *Turn Not Pale, Beloved Snail,* p. 1261; August 15, 1997, review of *Stories from the Round Barn,* p. 1277.
Library Journal, October 15, 1966, review of *The Taste of Spruce Gum,* p. 5252; May 15, 1970, review of *The Orchestra Mice,* p. 1943; October 1, 1997, Irwin Weintraub, review of *Stories from the Round Barn,* p. 109.
Publishers Weekly, July 22, 1968, review of *Chicken Ten Thousand,* p. 63; September 17, 1973, review of *The Endless Pavement,* p. 56; September 1, 1997, review of *Stories from the Round Barn,* p. 85; June 3, 2002, review of *More Stories from the Round Barn,* p. 80.

ONLINE

University of Illinois—Springfield, http://www.uis.edu/ (January 24, 2003), faculty profile of author.*

JACKSON, Jacqueline Dougan
  See JACKSON, Jacqueline

*   *   *

JENCKS, Charles 1939-
  (Charles Alexander Jencks)

PERSONAL: Born June 21, 1939, in Baltimore, MD; son of Gardner Platt (a composer) and Ruth (Pearl) Jencks; married Pamela Balding, June 20, 1961 (marriage ended, July, 1973); married Margaret ("Maggie") Keswick, 1978 (deceased), partner with Louisa Lane Fox; children: (first marriage) Ivor Cosmo, Justin Alexander; (second marriage) John Keswick, Lily-Clare. *Education:* Harvard University, B.A., 1961, M.A., 1965; University of London, Ph.D., 1970.

ADDRESSES: Office—c/o Architectural Association, 36 Bedford Sq., London W.C.1, England. *Agent*—c/o Author Mail, Rizzoli/Universe International Publications, 30 Park Avenue S., 3rd Floor, New York, NY 10010; fax: 212-387-3535.

CAREER: Architect, designer, writer, and educator. Architectural Association, London, England, senior lecturer in architectural history, 1968-88; University of California—Los Angeles, adjunct professor of architecture, then visiting professor, 1974-92; writer. Visiting lecturer at numerous universities worldwide, including Ecole des Beaux-Arts, Paris, and Yale University. Architect and builder of Gargagia Rotunda, Truro, 1976-77; The Thematic House, London, with Terry Farrell, 1979-84, and The Elemental House, Santa Monica, with Buzz Yudell, 1983. Also served on the Committee for the Selection of Architects, Biennale, Venice, 1980.

Has lectured at more than forty universities throughout the world; also served on numerous exhibition juries; has also appeared on numerous television and radio programs and in documentary films, including *Rebuilding the Palace.*

MEMBER: Architectural Association (London, England), Royal Society of Arts (London, England), Broucho, Athenaeum, Chelsea Arts.

AWARDS, HONORS: Fulbright scholarship to England, 1965-67; Melbourne Oration, Australia, 1974; Bosom Lectures, Royal Society of Arts, London, 1980; Gold Medal recipient from RIBA, 1983; NARA Gold Medal for Architecture, 1992; Country Life Gardener of the Year, 1998; Bulbenkian Prize for Museum of the Year, with the Scottish National Gallery of Modern Art, 2004, for landscaping project titled "Landform"; honorary degree from the University of Glasgow, 2005.

WRITINGS:

(Editor, with George Baird) *Meaning in Architecture,* Braziller (New York, NY), 1967.

Architecture 2000: Predictions and Methods, Praeger (New York, NY), 1971.

(With Nathan Silver) *Adhocism,* Doubleday (New York, NY), 1973.

Modern Movements in Architecture, Doubleday (New York, NY), 1973.

Le Corbusier and the Tragic View of Architecture, Harvard University Press (Cambridge, MA), 1973.

The Language of Post-Modern Architecture, Rizzoli (New York, NY), 1977, revised edition published as *The New Paradigm in Architecture: The Language of Post-Modern Architecture,* Yale University Press (New Haven, CT), 2002.

The Daydream Houses of Los Angeles, Rizzoli (New York, NY), 1978.

Bizarre Architecture, Rizzoli (New York, NY), 1979.

(Editor, with Richard Bunt and Geoffrey Broadbent) *Signs, Symbols and Architecture,* Wiley (New York, NY), 1980.

Skyscrapers—Sky Cities, Rizzoli (New York, NY), 1980.

Late-Modern Architecture: Selected Essays, Rizzoli (New York, NY), 1980.

Post-Modern Classicism, Rizzoli (New York, NY), 1980.

Free-Style Classicism, Rizzoli (New York, NY), 1982.

Architecture Today, Abrams (New York, NY), 1982, revised edition, 1988.

Abstract Representation, St. Martin's Press (New York, NY), 1983.

Kings of Infinite Space: Frank Lloyd Wright and Michael Graves, St. Martin's Press (New York, NY), 1983.

Towards a Symbolic Architecture: The Thematic House, Rizzoli (New York, NY), 1985.

Charles Platt: The Artist as Architect, MIT Press (Boston, MA), 1985.

(With Terry Farrell) *Designing a House: An Architectural Design Profile,* St. Martin's Press (New York, NY), 1986.

Post-Modernism & Discontinuity, St. Martin's Press (New York, NY), 1987.

Post-Modernism: The New Classicism in Art and Architecture, Rizzoli (New York, NY), 1987.

The Prince, the Architects and New Wave Monarchy, Rizzoli (New York, NY), 1988.

(Editor) *The Architecture of Democracy,* St. Martin's Press (New York, NY), 1988.

The New Moderns: From Late to Neo-Modernism, Rizzoli (New York, NY), 1990.

What Is Post-Modernism?, St. Martin's Press (New York, NY), 1990.

Post-Modern Triumphs in London, St. Martin's Press (New York, NY), 1991.

(Editor) *A Post-Modern Reader: Elements of a New Cultural Synthesis,* St. Martin's Press (New York, NY), 1992.

Heteropolis: Los Angeles, the Riots and the Strange Beauty of Hetero-Architecture, Academy Editions: Ernst & Sohn (London, England), 1993.

(Editor) *Frank O. Gehry: Individual Imagination and Cultural Conservatism,* St. Martin's Press (New York, NY), 1995.

The Architecture of the Jumping Universe: A Polemic: How Complexity Science Is Changing Architecture and Culture, Academy Editions/National Book Network (New York, NY), 1995.

(Editor, with Karl Kropf) *Theories and Manifestos of Contemporary Architecture,* Wiley (New York, NY), 1997.

Ecstatic Architecture: The Surprising Link: From a Debate of the Academy International Forum at the Royal Academy, Wiley (New York, NY), 1999.

(Editor, with Maggie Toy) *Millennium Architecture,* Wiley (New York, NY), 1999.

Architecture 2000 and Beyond (critique of earlier book, see above), Wiley-Academy (New York, NY), 2000.

Le Corbusier and the Continual Revolution in Architecture, Monacelli Press (New York, NY), 2000.

The Garden of Cosmic Speculation, Frances Lincoln (London, England), 2003.

The Iconic Building, Rizzoli (New York, NY), 2005.

Author of television scripts for programs on Le Corbusier and on "adhocism," for British Broadcasting

Corporation (BBC); contributor to *Hopkins2: The Work of Michael Hopkins and Partner,* by Colin Davies, Phaidon (London, England), 2001, and to *The Chinese Garden: History, Art, and Architecture,* by Maggie Keswick, Harvard University Press (Cambridge, MA), 2003.

Contributor to numerous magazines and journals, including *Architectural Design, Architectural Forum, Domus, Encounter, Times Literary Supplement, Observer,* and the *Independent.*

SIDELIGHTS: Charles Jencks, an architectural historian and theoretician, is often recognized for his books questioning Modern architecture and describing and defending Post-Modern architecture. Jencks is widely considered one of the shapers of the Post-Modern movement and is certainly among the writers and essayists who helped to define the style. "If there has been any single catalyst for the new, it has been the work of Charles Jencks, by far the most articulate and productive apostle of postmodernism from its beginnings," wrote Ada Louise Huxtable in the *New York Review of Books.* "To an acute sense of what is new, he adds that most important critical faculty, a very good eye." Through books ranging from scholarly and polemical to popular and picture-strewn, Jencks has helped to publicize late Modern and Post-Modern buildings and their builders.

Jencks began publishing in the early 1970s, when architects of his generation began to question the Modern movement with its "less is more" emphasis on utility and austerity. Jencks and others conceived the Post-Modernist movement as a "multivalent" style that could use coded design elements to convey double meanings, project symbolism, and even reflect irony and humor. Jencks's prolific writings on the subject have influenced at least two generations of architects, including those who will be working well past the year 2000. Huxtable wrote: "At a time when architectural commentary is at its most pretentious, turgid, and murky, Jencks is an intelligent, stylish, and provocative polemicist. An able manipulator of facts and opinions, a master of architectural hat tricks with styles and substyles, an expert maker of elaborate charts and graphs of cosmic, disembodied logic, he entertains at the same time that he outrages—something he does with a calculated consistency. You don't have to be a postmodernist to enjoy Jencks's books."

Throughout his oeuvre, Jencks has expressed dissatisfaction with the Modern architectural genre, which tends to eliminate the symbolic value of buildings in favor of the purely functional. In a *New York Times* review of *The Language of Post-Modern Architecture,* Paul Goldberger wrote: "Architecture is language and communication, [Jencks] argues, not abstract form-making or pure functionalism. We need towers on churches because churches are supposed to play a symbolic role in our lives—they are not supposed to look like boiler houses, and Mies van der Rohe's notion of a universal architectural vocabulary is, to Mr. Jencks, naively simplistic at best, destructively inhuman at worst." Jencks believes that a building should reflect both its environment and symbolic value and terms his preferred style "radical eclecticism." Goldberger commented: "'radical eclecticism' is not basically different from the style other 'post-modernists' have proclaimed—an architecture that eschews theories and formal order in favor of something looser, something more reflective of both historical values and human needs."

Post-Modernism: The New Classicism in Art and Architecture encompasses "art and culture as well as architecture," observed reviewer Sam Hall Kaplan in the *Los Angeles Times Book Review.* In a *New York Review of Books* review of *Post-Modernism: The New Classicism in Art and Architecture,* critic Hugh Honour cast Jencks as "an internationally aware Post-Modernist, the inventor of the term so far as architecture is concerned and its first theorist," adding: "For him Post-Modern classicism is not simply a negation of functional minimalism and the machine aesthetic, still less the result of a swing in the pendulum of taste, but "a wider social protest against modernisation, against the destruction of local culture by the combined forces of rationalisation, bureaucracy, large-scale development and, it is true, the Modern International Style." As for Jencks's analysis of art, Honour claimed: "It is the product of overlapping sets of preoccupations, including 'a commitment to anamnesis (i.e., the memory of past forms),' which Jencks detects in the work of many contemporary painters and sculptors as well as architects."

Often finding himself in the position of an historian who was covering events even as they unfolded, Jencks became an "apologist for a generation of symbiotic stylists," noted Kaplan. Even those critics who have reservations about post-modern style generally agree that Jencks has served the movement well as its "most voluble spokesman and chief public relations counsel," as noted by *Times Literary Supplement* reviewer Martin Filler. *New York Times Book Review* contributor Goldberger wrote that Jencks is "surely our time's most energetic compiler and classifier of architectural events," adding that the author's body of work is "as good a catalogue as exists of the kinds of architecture that have provoked serious thought over the last decade."

In his book *Heteropolis: Los Angeles, the Riots and the Strange Beauty of Hetero-Architecture*, Jencks focuses in on the post-modern architecture of Los Angeles, describing the style in what he calls "heteroarchitecture," which he states is an expression of cultural pluralism. The author brings physics into the discussion of postmodern architecture and landscaping in his book *The Architecture of the Jumping Universe: A Polemic: How Complexity Science Is Changing Architecture and Culture*. Writing in *New Statesman & Society*, Conrad Jameson explained the author's attempt to engage physics in the discussion of post-modern architecture, noting that the author "realizes that a larger postmodern movement is in dreadful straits for relying on a nihilistic form of relativism, based on the opposite conclusions about disorder: that behind disorder is only more disorder, that even our human attempts to build constructs of meaning are doomed."

In *Le Corbusier and the Continual Revolution in Architecture*, Jencks gives the reader a critical biography of noted architect and artist Charles-Edouard Jeanneret, who used the pseudonym Le Corbusier. Writing in the *Library Journal*, Paul Glassman noted that the author looks at "Le Corbusier's growth into the role of master architect and innovator through detailed, original and illuminating analyses." In a review in *Architecture*, Brian Brace Taylor called the author "a gifted storyteller who makes his subject come alive." He also wrote, "Jencks is true to his signature method of interpretation, which proceeds by analogy and metaphor, with limitless imagination." George Maurios, writing in *Architectural Review*, commented, "Right from the first lines of the introduction we understand the originality of Jencks' book: showing, through the writing of L.C., the importance and the extent of his work."

In a revision of his 1977 book *The Language of Post-Modern Architecture*, published as *The New Paradigm in Architecture: The Language of Post-Modern Architecture*, the author includes two new chapters to a book that has become a classic through its six previous editions and is used in many architecture classrooms. "He is such a readable writer that almost any library collection would benefit from this book," wrote Peter McKee Kaufman in the *Library Journal*. Writing in *Building Design*, Kenneth Powell noted that the book presents the author's "recent thinking" about postmodernism and went on to call the book "hugely impressive," later adding: "Combining scholarship with speculation and polemic, it is indispensable reading."

Jencks discusses the garden he and his late wife Maggie Keswick developed over the years at their home in Scotland in his book *The Garden of Cosmic Speculation*. Writing in the *Library Journal*, Edward J. Valauskas noted that the author "explains the gestation of this locale and its meaning on an altogether different plane from any other garden on the planet." *Architectural Review* contributor Michael Spens wrote, "This book provides a worthy documentation of a determined, thoroughly researched venture into the redefinition of meaning for landscape." *Spectator* contributor Kim Wilkie commented: "The garden is a unique exploration of one man's mission to understand the universe." Wilkie went on to write that the book "is beautifully illustrated, and the descriptions of the way in which the garden evolved are absorbing."

The Iconic Building presents his theories about the emergence of a new architecture type, namely the building as an icon. For example, he discusses the evolving plans for the memorial building to be built at the site of the World Trade Center following its bombing by terrorists. "Neither a pious jeremiad nor a jargon-ridden manifesto, Jencks's volume is more interested in outsize buildings and personalities than in prescriptions and complaints," wrote a *Publishers Weekly* contributor. The reviewer went on to note that the book is "brimming with critical energy," calling the book "absolutely the chronicle of our age." *Building Design* contributor Kester Rattenbury went on to mark the book as "a classic" adding, "Love or hate iconic buildings, the book is a must-read, stuffed full of good meaty material."

BIOGRAPHICAL AND CRITICAL SOURCES:

PERIODICALS

Architectural Review, September, 1995, Peter Davey, "The Scientific American," discusses author's work, p. 84; July, 2000, "Jencks's Theory of Evolution an Overview of Twentieth-Century Architecture;" May 1, 2001, George Maurios, review of *Le Corbusier and the Continual Revolution in Architecture*, p. 99; April, 2004, Michael Spens, review of *The Garden of Cosmic Speculation*, p. 97.

Architecture, May, 2001, Brian Brace Taylor, review of *Le Corbusier and the Continual Revolution in Architecture*, p. 93.

Building Design, September 6, 2002, Kenneth Powell, review of *The New Paradigm in Architecture: The Language of Post-Modern Architecture*, p. 17; April 29, 2005, Kester Rattenbury, "Metaphor Writ Large," interview with author about the book *The Iconic Building*, p. 18; July 8, 2005, announcement of honorary degree for author, p. 2.

Guardian (London, England), December 22, 2001, Jonathan Glancey, "Saturday Review: Arts 2002: Architecture: High Anxiety," briefly mentions author, p. 5.

Interior Design, January, 1994, Stanley Abercrombie, review of *Heteropolis: Los Angeles, The Riots and the Strange Beauty of Hetero-Architecture*, p. 51.

Library Journal, February 1, 2001, Paul Glassman, review of *Le Corbusier and the Continual Revolution in Architecture*, p. 85; October 1, 2002, Peter McKee Kaufman, review of *The New Paradigm in Architecture: The Language of Post-Modern Architecture*, p. 90; January, 2004, Edward J. Valauskas, review of *The Garden of Cosmic Speculation*, p. 103.

Los Angeles Times Book Review, July 19, 1987, Sam Hall Kaplan, *Post-Modernism: The New Classicism in Art and Architecture*, p. 14.

New Statesman & Society, May 27, 1994, Conrad Jameson, review of *Heteropolis*, p. 45; June 2, 1995, Conrad Jameson, review of *The Architecture of the Jumping Universe: A Polemic: How Complexity Science Is Changing Architecture and Culture*, p. 41.

New York Review of Books, December 22, 1983, Ada Louise Huxtable, "Architecture Today," pp. 55-61; September 29, 1988, Hugh Honour, review of *Post-Modernism: The New Classicism in Art and Architecture*, pp. 27-33.

New York Times, November 5, 1977, Paul Goldberger, review of *The Language of Post-Modern Architecture*, p. 19.

New York Times Book Review, December 12, 1982, Paul Goldberger, review of *Architecture Today*, p. 22; December 6, 1987, Paul Goldberger, review of *Post-Modernism: The New Classicism in Art and Architecture*, p. 22.

Publishers Weekly, September 19, 2005, review of *The Iconic Building*, p. 58.

Spectator, December 6, 2003, Kim Wilkie, review of *The Garden of Cosmic Speculation*, p. 56.

Times Literary Supplement, March 24-30, 1989, Martin Filler, "What Is Post-Modernism," p. 295; December 4, 1992, p. 13.

ONLINE

Charles Jencks Home Page, http://www.charlesjencks.com (November 6, 2005).

24 Hour Museum, http://www.24hourmuseum.org.uk/ (October 6, 2005), announcement of Gulbenkian Prize.*

*   *   *

**JENCKS, Charles Alexander
See JENCKS, Charles**

*   *   *

JUSTER, Norton 1929-

PERSONAL: Born June 2, 1929, in Brooklyn, NY; son of Samuel H. (an architect) and Minnie (Silberman) Juster; married Jeanne Ray (a graphic designer), August 15, 1964; children: Emily. *Education:* University of Pennsylvania, B.Arch. (Bachelor of Architecture), 1952; University of Liverpool, 1953. *Hobbies and other interests:* Gardening, bicycling, reading, making pickles and preserves, being a grandfather.

ADDRESSES: Home—259 Lincoln Ave., Amherst, MA 01002-2010. *Agent*—c/o Gail Hochman, Brandt & Hochman, 1501 Broadway, New York, NY 10036.

CAREER: Writer, teacher, architect. Juster & Gugliotta, New York, NY, architect, 1960-68; Pratt Institute, Brooklyn, NY, professor of environmental design, 1960-70; Juster Pope Frazier (an architectural firm), Shelburne Falls, MA, founder and architect, 1969-99;

Hampshire College, Amherst, MA, professor, 1970-92, professor emeritus of design, 1992—. *Military service:* U.S. Naval Reserve, Civil Engineer Corps, active duty, 1954-57.

AWARDS, HONORS: Fulbright fellowship, 1952-53; Ford Foundation grant, 1960-61; National Academy of Arts and Sciences award for outstanding achievement, 1968-69; Guggenheim fellowship, 1970-71; George G. Stone Center for Children's Books Seventh Recognition of Merit, 1971; *Boston Globe/Horn Book* Award Honor Book, 2005, for *The Hello, Goodbye Window.*

WRITINGS:

FOR CHILDREN

The Phantom Tollbooth, illustrated by Jules Feiffer, Random House (New York, NY), 1961.

The Dot and the Line: A Romance in Lower Mathematics, Random House (New York, NY), 1963.

Alberic the Wise and Other Journeys, illustrated by Domenico Gnoli, Pantheon (New York, NY), 1965, illustrated by Leonard Baskin, Picture Book Studios (Saxonville, MA), 1992.

Otter Nonsense, illustrated by Eric Carle, Philomel (New York, NY), 1982, illustrated by Michael Witte, Morrow (New York, NY), 1994.

As: A Surfeit of Similes, illustrated by David Small, Morrow (New York, NY), 1989.

As Silly as Knees, as Busy as Bees: An Astounding Assortment of Similes, Beech Tree (New York, NY), 1998.

The Hello, Goodbye Window, illustrated by Chris Raschka, Michael di Capua Books/Hyperion (New York, NY), 2005.

FOR ADULTS

Stark Naked: A Paranomastic Odyssey, illustrated by Arnold Roth, Random House (New York, NY), 1969.

(Editor) *So Sweet to Labor: Rural Women in America, 1865-1895,* Viking (New York, NY), 1979, published as *A Woman's Place: Yesterday's Rural Women in America,* Fulcrum Publishing (Golden, CO), 1996.

Author of libretto, with Sheldon Harnick, for an opera version of *The Phantom Tollbooth,* 1995.

ADAPTATIONS: The Dot and the Line: A Romance in Lower Mathematics was produced as an animated short film by Metro-Goldwyn-Mayer (MGM) in 1965; *The Phantom Tollbooth* was produced as an animated full-length feature film by MGM in 1970.

SIDELIGHTS: Norton Juster, an architect and professor of design, is best known to children and adults alike as the author of *The Phantom Tollbooth,* a work which *New York Times Book Review* critic Diane Manuel recalled "turned children's librarians on their ears" when it was published in 1961. At the beginning of the twenty-first century, *The Phantom Tollbooth* remained a modern classic of children's literature.

In *The Phantom Tollbooth,* the main character, Milo, experiences an awakening of his indifferent and lazy mind. He is bored by just about everything—his toys, his house, and especially his schoolwork. After class one day, Milo finds a large package waiting for him. It is labeled "One Genuine Turnpike Tollbooth," for use by "Those Who Have Never Traveled in Lands Beyond." Intrigued, he sets up the tollbooth and, driving his small electric car, passes through. In an instant, Milo is transported to an unfamiliar road in the Kingdom of Wisdom.

The kingdom, discovers Milo, is made up of Dictionopolis, the land of words, and Digitopolis, the land of numbers. These lands are ruled by feuding brothers named King Azaz the Unabridged and the Mathemagician. The pair argue constantly over which are better: words or numbers. Peace in the Kingdom of Wisdom has been maintained by the kings' adopted sisters, Rhyme and Reason. However, the sisters have recently been exiled from the kingdoms and are being held captive in the Mountains of Ignorance. Milo is persuaded by the only slightly malevolent witch Faintly Macabre to bring Rhyme and Reason back to the kingdom.

The creatures and colleagues Milo encounters in the Kingdom of Wisdom humorously demonstrate the many quirks of the English language: there are his traveling companions, the giant, insectile Humbug, and the watchdog Tock (whose body is a large alarm clock); there are the noisy Dischord and Dynne, and the insidious Terrible Trivium; as well as the Gross Exaggeration, the Threadbare Excuse, and the Overbearing Know-It-All. The travelers dine on "ragamuf-fins" and "rigamarolls" in Dictionopolis, while in Digi-topolis they nibble on plus signs to fill up and minus signs to become hungry again. *Atlantic Monthly*'s Charlotte Jackson noted that *The Phantom Tollbooth*, "besides being very amusing, has a quality that will quicken young minds and encourage readers to pursue pleasures that do not depend on artificial stimulation." With its wordplay and fantastic characters, Juster's book has often been compared to another classic, Lewis Carroll's *Alice in Wonderland*. But Emily Maxwell stressed in her *New Yorker* review that *The Phantom Tollbooth* "remains triumphantly itself, lucid, humorous, full of warmth and real invention." Maxwell described her initial reading of *The Phantom Tollbooth* as "my first experience of opening a book with no special anticipation and gradually becoming aware that I am holding in my hands a newborn classic."

Because it is a modern morality play in the vein of the "Everyman" dramas, many critics have argued that *The Phantom Tollbooth* is too sophisticated for young readers. "The ironies, the subtle play on words will be completely lost on all but the most precocious children," commented Miriam Mathes in the *Library Journal*, while a critic for the *Saturday Review* stated: "I'm inclined to think it is largely an adult book [for it] goes above the head of its intended audience." *New York Times Book Review* critic Ann McGovern, however, believed in the universal appeal of *The Phantom Tollbooth*: "To those who might wonder whether children will grasp Mr. Juster's subtleties, I can only quote one well-read eleven-year-old who reported it 'the cleverest book I've ever read.' Youngsters who drive through the tollbooth with Milo will probably, in the midst of their laughter, digest some important truth of life."

Juster has delivered over the years several more allegorical children's tales, including *The Dot and the Line: A Romance in Lower Mathematics* and *Alberic the Wise and Other Journeys*. As: *A Surfeit of Similes* is probably closest to *The Phantom Tollbooth* in style. In this book, two gentlemen travel the world by any means available in order to collect similes; some (like "slow as ketchup" and "hot as a griddle") are relatively mundane, while others ("clever as paint," "tight as a suture," and "reassuring as a dentist's smile") are refreshingly original. Though she described its premise

as "slim as an isthmus," Manuel called Juster's As "the kind of book that could help to sell youngsters on the devilish delights of well-turned phrases."

Alberic the Wise and Other Journeys, originally published in 1965, is a "fable on the nature of wisdom and success," stated a reviewer in *Horn Book Magazine*. Alberic is a stolid country lad with no particular talents, but he yearns to have wisdom. A story of the world beyond his rural home prompts him to set out on a journey of his own. He serves as apprentice to numerous tradesmen but excels at none of the skilled trades he tries. Still, years later, his riveting stories of his own search for knowledge and wisdom earn him a most-desired name: Alberic the Wise. Wisdom, he learns, often comes simply from seeking it. A *Publishers Weekly* contributor felt that the "author's compelling prose, elevated without being lofty, will draw in advanced readers."

Prior to 1980, Juster and his family lived on a rural farm. While working to restore and run their property, Juster was taken aback by the amount of sheer labor involved in maintaining a farm. He became curious as to how early American farmers—and, in particular, farm women—managed the burdens of farm work. His research into the subject yielded 1979's *So Sweet to Labor: Rural Women in America, 1865-1895*, a collection of essays, letters, and poetry written by, to, and about farm women. This collection "evokes the concrete struggles, deeply held cultural values and the blind spots of nineteenth-century rural women," commented Milton Cantor in the *Nation*. Juster's documents "tell us something about the fragility and chanciness of life in rural America and about the part played by those whom history has swept into the darkened corners of our national past." Though Sharon Congdon of the *Washington Post Book World* pointed out that *So Sweet to Labor* "is plagued with problems," such as poor editing and a too-heavy reliance upon the late 1800s periodical *The Household* as a source, she asserted that Juster's "message is sound." Cantor concluded: "Juster's collection is a realistic and balanced sampling, and enlarges our understanding of the still mostly uncharted history of farm women." *So Sweet to Labor* was re-released as *A Woman's Place: Yesterday's Rural Women in America* in 1996.

The Hello, Goodbye Window is a "paean to loving grandparents" and their special relationship with their grandchildren, wrote reviewer Martha V. Parravano in

Horn Book Magazine. When the young female narrator and her parents arrive to drop her off for an overnight visit, Nanna and Poppy are watching eagerly for them out the large kitchen window—the Hello, Goodbye Window of the title. While there, she counts stars with her grandmother, listens to her grandfather give an impromptu harmonica performance, looks for raisins hidden in her cereal, naps contentedly, and considers the peril of the tiger (actually, a striped cat) in the garden, all under the watchful eye of her doting and loving grandparents. When her parents return to pick her up, she sees them coming through the Hello, Goodbye Window, and realizes that it is possible to be happy (over reuniting with her parents) and sad (over leaving her grandparents' house) at the same time.

In a 2005 interview with Nathalie Op De Beeck in *Publishers Weekly,* Juster admitted that there was a real-life Hello, Goodbye Window in his house. "Our granddaughter stays over one night a week," Juster commented. "The main life in our house revolves around the kitchen, as in many houses, and we always used to play little games with that window. Almost everything that happens in the book either was suggested or almost literally given through things we did a couple years ago." Another notable element of the book is that the parents are an interracial couple, like Juster, who is white, and his wife, Jeanne, who is black. Juster noted in the *Publishers Weekly* interview that he wanted the book's illustrations "to reflect that, but I didn't want to say anything in the book to drive it home as a message. I just wanted it to be there as a fact of life. I think [illustrator' Chris [Raschka] did that wonderfully too." *Booklist* reviewer Ilene Cooper commented that the book "speaks to the real lives of children and their experiences." A *Publishers Weekly* critic observed that Juster creates "a gently humorous account of a family's conversations and games, all centered on the special window." A *Kirkus Reviews* contributor commented that the story's "present-tense narration is just right," while *School Library Journal* reviewer Angela J. Reynolds observed that the "text is both simple and sophisticated, conjuring a perfectly child-centered world."

BIOGRAPHICAL AND CRITICAL SOURCES:

BOOKS

St. James Guide to Fantasy Writers, St. James Press, 1996.

Twentieth-Century Children's Writers, 3rd edition, St. James Press, 1989.

Twentieth-Century Young-Adult Writers, St. James Press, 1994.

PERIODICALS

Atlantic Monthly, December, 1961, Charlotte Jackson, review of *The Phantom Tollbooth,* p. 120.

Book, July-August, 2003, Adam Langer, "Where Are They Now?," profile of Norton Juster, p. 34.

Booklist, March 15, 2005, Ilene Cooper, review of *The Hello, Goodbye Window,* p. 1286.

Building Design, June 7, 2002, Alan Powers, "Milo the Mindbender," review of *The Phantom Tollbooth,* p. 15.

Horn Book Magazine, March-April, 1993, review of *Alberic the Wise and Other Journeys,* p. 231; July-August, 2005, Martha V. Parravano, review of *The Hello, Goodbye Window,* p. 451.

Kirkus Reviews, March 1, 2005, review of *The Hello, Goodbye Window,* p. 289.

Library Journal, January 15, 1962, Miriam Mathes, review of *The Phantom Tollbooth,* p. 332.

Nation, September 8, 1979, Milton Cantor, review of *So Sweet to Labor: Rural Women in America, 1865-1895,* p. 187.

New Yorker, November 18, 1961, Emily Maxwell, review of *The Phantom Tollbooth,* pp. 222-224.

New York Times Book Review, November 12, 1961, Diane Manuel, review of *The Phantom Tollbooth,* p. 35; November 14, 1982, Karla Kuskin, review of *Otter Nonsense,* p. 43; October 22, 1989, Diane Manuel, review of *As: A Surfeit of Similes,* p. 35.

Publishers Weekly, November 30, 1992, review of *Alberic the Wise and Other Journeys,* p. 55; January 8, 2001, "Great Comebacks," review of *The Dot and the Line: A Romance in Lower Mathematics,* p. 69; February 21, 2005, review of *The Hello, Goodbye Window,* p. 173; February 21, 2005, Nathalia Op De Beeck, "On Comings and Goings," interview with Norton Juster, p. 174.

Saturday Review, January 20, 1962, review of *The Phantom Tollbooth,* p. 27.

School Library Journal, April, 1989, Michael Cart, review of *As,* p. 112; March, 2005, Angela J. Reynolds, review of *The Hello, Goodbye Window,* p. 174.

Washington Post Book World, February 3, 1980, Sharon Congdon, review of *So Sweet to Labor,* p. 10.

ONLINE

Absolute Write Web site, http://www.absolutewrite. com/ (October 5, 2005), RoseEtta Stone, "Interview with Norton Juster."

Powells Books Web site, http://www.powells.com/ (October 5, 2005), Dave Weich, "Norton Juster, Beyond Expectations," interview with Norton Juster.

Salon.com, http://www.salon.com/ (March 12, 2001), Laura Miller, "The Road to Dictionopolis," interview with Norton Juster.

Underdown.org, http://www.underdown.org/ (October 5, 2005), RoseEtta Stone, "An Interview with Norton Juster, Author of *The Phantom Tollbooth.*"*

K

KARWOSKI, Gail 1949-
(Gail Langer Karwoski)

PERSONAL: Surname pronounced "car-*woh*-ski"; born March 16, 1949, in Boston, MA; daughter of Farley (a hardware store owner) and Esther (a homemaker) Langer; adopted mother, Charlotte Langer (a homemaker); married Chester John Karwoski (a university professor), 1970; children: Leslie, Geneva. *Education:* University of Massachusetts—Amherst, B.A., 1970; University of Minnesota—Minneapolis, M.A., 1972; earned teaching certificates from University of Georgia—Athens.

ADDRESSES: Home—1040 Sweet Gum Way, Watkinsville, GA 30677. *E-mail*—gailkarwoski@hotmail.com.

CAREER: Teacher in Athens and Watkinsville, GA, 1974-98; writer, 1998—. Also worked as a newspaper reporter and as an editor for the Carl Vinson Institute of Government at the University of Georgia.

MEMBER: Society for Children's Book Writers and Illustrators (and regional branch, the Southern Breeze), Four at Five Writers (founding member), Athens Rock and Gem Club.

AWARDS, HONORS: Individual Artist Grant, Georgia Council for the Arts, 1994-95; Georgia Author of the Year for Children's Literature, Georgia Writers Inc., 1996; winner, Tellable Story, 1997 Storytelling World Awards, for "Mammy Kate Uses Her Head", and honor, for "War Woman!"; American Booksellers Association Children's Pick of the Lists, 1999, for *Seaman: The Dog Who Went Exploring with Lewis and Clark;* Bank Street College Best Children's Books of the Year, 2001, for *Surviving Jamestown;* Maxwell Medal for Best Children's Book, Dog Writers Association of America, and Sydney Taylor Award, Association of Jewish Libraries Notable Books for Older Readers, both 2004, Pennsylvania School Librarians Association Young Adult Top Forty, 2004, all for *Quake!;* Georgia Children's Young Adult Author of the Year, Georgia Writers Association, 2004, Junior Library Guild literary selection, 2004, 2005 featured title, National Book Festival Pavilion of States, 2005, *St. Louis Post-Dispatch* Best Books for Young Readers, 2005, all for *Miracle;* Most Outstanding Author of the Year, a Mom's Choice Award, Just for Moms Foundation, 2005, for *Water Beds; Sleeping in the Ocean.*

WRITINGS:

HISTORICAL FICTION; FOR YOUNG READERS

(With Loretta Johnson Hammer) *The Tree that Owns Itself and Other Adventure Tales from Georgia's Past,* illustrated by James Watling, Peachtree (Atlanta, GA), 1996.

Seaman: The Dog Who Explored the West with Lewis and Clark, illustrated by James Watling, Peachtree (Atlanta, GA), 1999.

Surviving Jamestown: The Adventures of Young Sam Collier, illustrated by Paul Casale, Peachtree (Atlanta, GA), 2001.

Quake!: Disaster in San Francisco, 1906, illustrated by Robert Papp, Peachtree (Atlanta, GA), 2003.

Miracle: The True Story of the Wreck of the Sea Venture (nonfiction), illustrated by John MacDonald, Darby Creek (Plain City, OH), 2004.

OTHER

(With Mary Hepburn and Ann Blum) *City Government in Georgia,* Institute of Government, University of Georgia (Athens, GA), 1980.

Water Beds; Sleeping in the Ocean (picture book), illustrated by Connie McLennan, Sylvan Dell (Mt. Pleasant, SC), 2005.

Contributor to periodicals including *Athens* and *Cobblestone.*

SIDELIGHTS: Young adult book author Gail Karwoski once commented to *CA:* "When I was a youngster, my absolute favorite pastime was playing with paper dolls. I had a shoe box full of them, and when I came upon a cartoon figure or magazine photo that appealed to me, I clipped it out and added it to my paper doll collection. Usually, I played by myself, because I didn't have sisters and my only brother was much older than me. I made up relationships and problems for my paper dolls, dressed them, and moved them around in houses and cars and yards that were actually scatter rugs and bedspreads. I liked to imagine what each character would say and do. As a writer, I'm still playing with paper dolls!

"I was born in Jamaica Plain, which is part of Boston, Massachusetts. My family lived above my father's hardware store until I was eight. Then we moved to the suburb of Brookline. When I was very young, my dad told me bedtime stories that he made up, about the imaginary mice who lived in the store's warehouse and outwitted local alley cats. My whole family worked in the store during busy seasons. Neither of my parents went to college. My dad moved to the United States from Poland with his family when he was seven years old. His formal education ended before high school.

"I'm eight years younger than my brother, Bob. As a child, I was short and small for my age, so I was my parents' darling. I adored my mother and tried hard to

be a good little girl to please her. I played quietly, read a lot, and created stories. My mother died of cancer when I was around ten; her death was the most painful thing that ever happened to me. After her death, I saw myself as different from other children, and part of me became an outsider. Although I had friends at school, I interacted with only part of myself—the other part of me kept a distance and watched warily for signs of danger. I learned to be a clown so I could conceal my worries and hurts.

"I went to college at the University of Massachusetts in Amherst and majored in English because I loved reading and talking about books. I got my teaching certificate so I would have a way to earn money and stay close to books. I met my husband, Chester, in college, and we applied to graduate schools together. I got my master's degree at the University of Minnesota in Minneapolis, while he got his Ph.D. After I finished graduate school, I worked as a reporter for a small community newspaper. In 1974, we moved to Georgia, where Chester became a professor at the University of Georgia in Athens. I taught high school English and drama until Leslie, our first daughter, was born. When Leslie was a toddler, I became an editor for the Carl Vinson Institute of Government at the University of Georgia. Then I returned to teaching, this time as the gifted education teacher in middle schools, until Chester got a six-month research appointment in Geneva, Switzerland. After our second daughter, Geneva, was born, I returned to the classroom. We spent one year in San Francisco, again for Chester's research, then I began teaching the gifted classes for grades three to five.

"I wrote my first published book with a teaching colleague, Lori Hammer. *The Tree that Owns Itself and Other Adventure Tales from Georgia's Past* is a collection of twelve historical fiction stories. We tried to arrange them so every child in the state would feel close to Georgia's history—no matter where you are in the state, you're within an hour or two drive of a good story!

"When I received a contract for my second book, *Seaman: The Dog Who Explored the West with Lewis and Clark,* I resigned from my teaching position to become a full-time writer. I worked so hard to finish this historical novel that my paws ached! But it was worth the effort. Writing is the most satisfying work I've ever done.

"Now I return to classrooms as an author-in-schools. I tell students that writing, like teaching, is all about communicating—sharing information, insights, and feelings with people. Except, as a writer, my classroom is for students all over the world. Actually, writing is my rebirth, and it brings me back to the quiet activities of my childhood. It's a grownup version of playing with paper dolls. I move interesting characters around in places that I've imagined. I create relationships between my characters, give them problems to solve, and let them talk to each other. Like the good little girl I was, I'm still eager to please. But writing is more satisfying than playing with paper dolls because it's a game that I can share with thousands of readers. It's my way of enriching and improving the world where children grow up."

Though Karwoski once commented that she and her coauthor, Loretta Johnson Hammer, chose to emphasize the geographical range of the stories they selected for *The Tree that Owns Itself and Other Adventure Tales from Georgia's Past,* it was the historical range of the stories that impressed Jacqueline Elsner, a reviewer for the *School Library Journal.* Elsner noted that in a mere twelve stories, the authors manage to touch upon pivotal moments in three centuries of Georgia's, and the nation's, history, including the Revolutionary War and the era of pirates in the eighteenth century, the Industrial Revolution, the Civil War, the Trail of Tears, and the gold rushes of the nineteenth century, and World War II and the Olympics in the twentieth. The authors effectively blend historical and fictional characters in each story, and "energetic pacing and keen plot development pull readers in," Elsner added. Each story concludes with additional information about the facts behind the tale. "This title reaches far beyond regional interest," wrote Elsner.

Karwoski returned to the historical record for her next book, *Seaman: The Dog Who Explored the West with Lewis and Clark.* Karwoski's story focuses on Seaman, a real dog of Newfoundland breed who accompanied the famous explorers on their historic trek across the continent, and who is mentioned in the explorers' journals numerous times. Karwoski's focus on Seaman helps bring out the human side of the larger-than-life participants in this historic adventure, noted *School Library Journal* contributor Dona J. Helmer. Karwoski "is guilty of trying to soften the historical realities," this critic added, however, referring to her treatment of the young Indian guide, Sacagawea, and of the slave

among Clark's servants. Nevertheless, Helmer concluded, once the story of *Seaman* is begun, readers "will be caught up in the drama and action and even reluctant readers will find it just too good to put down." *Booklist* reviewer Carolyn Phelan dubbed *Seaman* "an effective, fictional introduction to the Lewis and Clark expedition."

The early American colonies provide the setting for Karwoski's next work, *Surviving Jamestown: The Adventures of Young Sam Collier.* Serving as a page to Captain John Smith, twelve-year-old Sam Collier relates his story as he and his fellow English settlers leave Europe, hoping to establish a colony in the New World. In her story, the author relates the terrible the conditions the colonists endured as they carved a settlement out of the wilderness. Though the other colonists dislike the low-born Smith, the Captain remains the head of the group until he is burned badly in a fire and must return to England. Smith offers Sam the choice of staying in America or accompanying him on the voyage home. Realizing that though the life is harsh, the young colonist decides the opportunities are better for him in the new country. "The story flows well," according to *School Library Journal* contributor Patti Gonzales, who found the book "a good fictional introduction to Jamestown."

In *Miracle: The True Story of the Wreck of the Sea Venture* Karwoski tells the true story of the *Sea Venture,* which encountered a hurricane on the high seas and got separated from a small fleet on the way to the Jamestown Colony in America in 1609. The ship ends up in the Bermuda islands, where the passengers wonder at the paradise that supports them for the next ten months. Eventually, they move on to bring much needed supplies to Jamestown. The book includes maps, wood engravings, and other illustrations. Writing in *Booklist,* John Peters noted that "this tale of shipwreck, discovery, and radical reversals of fortune will leave young readers marveling." Rita Soltan, writing in the *School Library Journal,* called the book "an engaging account" and also noted, "Karwoski offers a wealth of historical information through a well-researched narrative detailing highlights of the key players."

Karwoski returns to fictional history with *Quake!: Disaster in San Francisco, 1906.* Jacob Kaufman is thirteen years old when the infamous San Francisco earthquake hits. Separated from his family, he saves the life of a Chinese boy and the two go off on an adventure of survival as they search for their respective families. In the process Jacob learns about the mistreatment of and hatred for Chinese immigrants, which is much like the anti-Semitism he himself has experienced. Noting that the author provides "many vivid details of life after the earthquake," *Booklist* contributor Carolyn Phelan went on to comment that readers will be drawn by "the developing stories of the sympathetic characters." In a review in the *School Library Journal,* Coop Renner wrote that the novel "combines disaster and family longing for a sturdily constructed and affecting look at the past."

BIOGRAPHICAL AND CRITICAL SOURCES:

PERIODICALS

Booklist, August, 1999, Carolyn Phelan, review of *Seaman: The Dog Who Explored the West with Lewis and Clark,* p. 2058; May 15, 2004, Carolyn Phelan, review of *Quake!: Disaster in San Francisco, 1906,* p. 1631; November 15, 2004, John Peters, review of *Miracle: The True Story of the Wreck of the Sea Venture,* p. 576.
School Library Journal, July, 1996, Jacqueline Elsner, review of *The Tree that Owns Itself,* p. 85; October, 1999, Dona J. Helmer, review of *Seaman,* p. 152; August 8, 2001, Patti Gonzales, review of *Surviving Jamestown: The Adventures of Young Sam Collier;* June, 2004, Coop Renner, review of *Quake!,* p. 144; January, 2005, Rita Soltan, review of *Miracle,* p. 149.
Voice of Youth Advocates, August, 2001, Pam Carlson, review of *Surviving Jamestown.*

ONLINE

Gail Karwoski Home Page, http://www.gailkarwoski. com (November 1, 2005).

*   *   *

KARWOSKI, Gail Langer
See KARWOSKI, Gail

KAZAN, Frances 1946-

PERSONAL: Born November 18, 1946, in Brighton, England; daughter of Joseph Charles (an accountant) and Rita Doris (a social service worker) Wright; married Peter David Rudge (a manager), April 5, 1969 (divorced); married Elia Kazan (a film director), June 28, 1982; children: (first marriage) Joseph Daniel, Charlotte. *Education:* Hockerill Teachers College, teaching degree, 1968; attended New York University, 1980-81. *Religion:* Church of England.

ADDRESSES: Agent—c/o Author Mail, Random House, 299 Park Ave., New York, NY 10171-0002.

CAREER: Schoolteacher in London, England, 1968-72; writer.

WRITINGS:

Good Night, Little Sister (novel), Stein & Day (New York, NY), 1986.
Halide's Gift (novel), Random House (New York, NY), 2001.

Also contributor to *Self.*

SIDELIGHTS: The wife of well-known film director Elia Kazan, Frances Kazan is a former school teacher who later turned to writing fiction. Her novel *Halide's Gift* is set in Constantinople at the beginning of the twentieth century and features a young woman raised in a traditional Muslim home at a time when Western influences are beginning to encroach. The central character, Halide Edib, is the daughter of an administrator for the last Ottoman sultan. Living in a privileged home, she receives a Western-style education from her governess and is later sent to an American school. Despite this educational influence, however, Halide still has strong ties to family tradition, and she possesses an unusual gift, as well: the ability to hear the voices of her ancestors, which she inherited from her grandmother.

As Halide becomes caught between the intellectual and the spiritual, the East and the West, the novel describes the dramatic social changes that occurred in Turkey with the decline of the Ottoman Empire.

Although a *Publishers Weekly* critic called this effort by Kazan "old fashioned" and "undistinguished," the reviewer asserted that "its portrayal of an Islamic world on the brink of change is carefully detailed and convincing." Writing in *Booklist*, Elsa Gaztambide asserted that *Halide's Gift* is a "uniquely stylized novel with a subject matter that is refreshingly untrodden."

Kazan once told *CA*, "I travel between New York, the Bahamas, and England, where my family still lives. Living on two continents has, I hope, given my work a broader perspective."

BIOGRAPHICAL AND CRITICAL SOURCES:

PERIODICALS

Booklist, June 1, 2001, Elsa Gaztambide, review of *Halide's Gift*, p. 1842.
Publishers Weekly, January 3, 1986, review of *Goodnight, Little Sister*, p. 41; June 18, 2001, review of *Halide's Gift*, p. 55.*

*   *   *

KEHRET, Peg 1936-

PERSONAL: Surname is pronounced "carrot"; born November 11, 1936, in LaCrosse, WI; daughter of Arthur R. (a food company executive) and Elizabeth M. (a homemaker) Schulze; married Carl E. Kehret (a player-piano restorer), July 2, 1955; children: Bob C., Anne M. *Education:* Attended University of Minnesota, 1954-55. *Hobbies and other interests:* Reading, gardening, antiques, watching baseball games, animals, cooking.

ADDRESSES: Home—Box 303, Wilkeson, WA 98396. *Agent*—Emilie Jacobson, Curtis Brown Ltd., 10 Astor Pl., New York, NY 10003.

CAREER: Writer, 1973—. Humane Society volunteer.

MEMBER: Authors Guild, Authors League of America, Society of Children's Book Writers and Illustrators, Mystery Writers of America.

AWARDS, HONORS: Forest Roberts Playwriting Award, Northern Michigan University, 1978, Best New Play of 1979, Pioneer Drama Service, and Best Plays for Senior Adults, American Theater Association, 1981, all for *Spirit!;* Children's Choice Award, International Reading Association and Children's Book Council (IRA-CBC), 1988, for *Deadly Stranger;* Service Award, American Humane Association, 1989; Young Hoosier Book Award, Association for Indiana Media Educators, 1992, Nebraska Golden Sower Award and Iowa Children's Choice Award, both 1993, and Maud Hart Lovelace Award, 1995, all for *Nightmare Mountain;* Maud Hart Lovelace Award for *Cages;* Achievement Award, Pacific Northwest Writer's Conference, 1992; Pacific Northwest Young Reader's Choice Award and Iowa Children's Choice Award, both for *Terror at the Zoo;* Sequoyah Award and Indiana Young Hoosier Book Award, both for *Horror at the Haunted House;* Golden Kite Award, Society of Children's Book Writers and Illustrators, 1996, award for children's literature from PEN Center U.S.A. West, 1997, Dorothy Canfield Fisher Award, 1998, Mark Twain Award, 1999, and Young Hoosier Award, 2001, all for *Small Steps: The Year I Got Polio;* Children's Crown Award, National Christian Schools Association, and West Virginia Children's Book Award, both 1998, and Utah Children's Choice Award, all for *Earthquake Terror;* Edgar Allan Poe Award nomination, Mystery Writers of America, 2005, for *Abduction!* Florida Sunshine Award, 2000, for *The Volcano Disaster;* Henry Bergh Award, American Society for the Prevention of Cruelty to Animals, 2001, for *Saving Lilly;* Lamplighter Award, National Christian Schools Association, 2003, for *I'm Not Who You Think I Am!* Nevada Young Readers' Award and Oklahoma Sequoyah Award, both 2005, both for *The Stranger Next Door.*Cited among recommended books for reluctant young adult readers, American Library Association (ALA), 1989, for *The Winner,* and 1992, for *Cages;* cited among books for the teen age, New York Public Library, 1992, for *Cages* and *Winning Monologs for Young Actors: 65 Honest-to-Life Characterizations to Delight Young Actors and Audiences of All Ages;* cited in Texas Lone Star list, 1992; cited as young adult's choice, International Reading Association (IRA), for *Cages,* and 1992, for *Sisters, Long Ago,* and for *Terror at the Zoo;* cited among quick picks for reluctant young adult readers, ALA, and cited among children's choices, IRA, both for *Danger at the Fair;* cited among children's books of the year, Child Study Children's Book Committee, 1995, for *The Richest Kids in Town;* notable book citation, ALA, 1997, for *Small Steps.*

WRITINGS:

FOR CHILDREN

Winning Monologs for Young Actors: 65 Honest-to-Life Characterizations to Delight Young Actors and Audiences of All Ages, Meriwether Publishing (Colorado Springs, CO), 1986.

Deadly Stranger, Dodd, Mead (New York, NY), 1987.

Encore!: More Winning Monologs for Young Actors: 63 More Honest-to-Life Monologs for Teenage Boys and Girls, Meriwether Publishing (Colorado Springs, CO), 1988.

The Winner, Turman (Seattle, WA), 1988.

Nightmare Mountain, Dutton (New York, NY), 1989.

Sisters, Long Ago, Cobblehill (New York, NY), 1990.

Cages, Cobblehill (New York, NY), 1991.

Acting Natural: Monologs, Dialogs, and Playlets for Teens, Meriwether Publishing (Colorado Springs, CO), 1991.

Terror at the Zoo, Cobblehill (New York, NY), 1992.

Horror at the Haunted House, Cobblehill (New York, NY), 1992, 2nd edition, Puffin Books (New York, NY), 2002.

Night of Fear, Cobblehill (New York, NY), 1994.

The Richest Kids in Town, Cobblehill (New York, NY), 1994.

Danger at the Fair, Cobblehill (New York, NY), 1995.

Don't Go Near Mrs. Tallie, Pocket Books (New York, NY), 1995.

Desert Danger, Pocket Books (New York, NY), 1995.

Cat Burglar on the Prowl, Pocket Books (New York, NY), 1995.

Bone Breath and the Vandals, Pocket Books (New York, NY), 1995.

Backstage Fright, Pocket Books (New York, NY), 1996.

Earthquake Terror, Cobblehill (New York, NY), 1996.

Screaming Eagles, Pocket Books (New York, NY), 1996.

Race to Disaster, Pocket Books (New York, NY), 1996.

Small Steps: The Year I Got Polio, Albert Whitman (Morton Grove, IL), 1996.

The Ghost Followed Us Home, Pocket Books (New York, NY), 1996.

Searching for Candlestick Park, Cobblehill (New York, NY), 1997.

The Volcano Disaster, Pocket Books (New York, NY), 1998.

The Blizzard Disaster, Pocket Books (New York, NY), 1998.

I'm Not Who You Think I Am, Dutton (New York, NY), 1999.

Shelter Dogs: Amazing Stories of Adopted Strays, Albert Whitman (Morton Grove, IL), 1999.

The Flood Disaster, Pocket Books (New York, NY), 1999.

The Secret Journey, Pocket Books (New York, NY), 1999.

My Brother Made Me Do It, Pocket Books (New York, NY), 2000.

Don't Tell Anyone, Dutton (New York, NY), 2000.

The Hideout, Pocket Books (New York, NY), 2001, 2nd edition, Aladdin Paperbacks (New York, NY), 2002.

Saving Lilly, Aladdin Paperbacks (New York, NY), 2002.

Five Pages a Day: A Writer's Journey, Albert Whitman (Morton Grove, IL), 2002.

The Stranger Next Door, Dutton (New York, NY), 2002.

Escaping the Giant Wave, Simon & Schuster (New York, NY), 2003.

Spy Cat, Dutton (New York, NY), 2003.

Abduction!, Dutton (New York, NY), 2004.

The Ghost's Grave, Dutton (New York, NY), 2005.

PLAYS

Cemeteries Are a Grave Matter, Dramatic Publishing (Woodstock, IL), 1975.

Let Him Sleep 'till It's Time for His Funeral, Contemporary Drama Service (Colorado Springs, CO), 1977.

Spirit!, Pioneer Drama Service (Englewood, CO), 1979.

Dracula, Darling, Contemporary Drama Service (Colorado Springs, CO), 1979.

Charming Billy, Contemporary Drama Service (Colorado Springs, CO), 1983.

Bicycles Built for Two (musical), Contemporary Drama Service (Colorado Springs, CO), 1985.

FOR ADULTS

Wedding Vows: How to Express Your Love in Your Own Words, Meriwether Publishing (Colorado Springs, CO), 1979, 2nd edition, 1989.

Refinishing and Restoring Your Piano, Tab Books (Blue Ridge Summmit, PA), 1985.

Contributor to periodicals.

SIDELIGHTS: Peg Kehret is the author of over two dozen children's novels; most of them, such as award-winners *Deadly Stranger, Nightmare Mountain,* and *Earthquake Terror,* serve up heavy doses of suspense and danger. Kehret has also written nonfiction for adults as well as for children. *Winning Monologs for Young Actors: 65 Honest-to-Life Characterizations to Delight Young Actors and Audiences of All Ages* and *Acting Natural: Monologs, Dialogs, and Playlets for Teems* both reflect her own commitment to theater; Kehret is also a playwright. *Small Steps: The Year I Got Polio* documents her own fight with a childhood case of polio that left her temporarily paralyzed. In a *Booklist* review of Kehret's *Earthquake Terror,* Stephanie Zvirin summed up the author's career to date: "Prolific author Kehret has a well-deserved reputation for writing good, solid thrillers for middle-graders."

Kehret formed an early passion for words and writing. Paid three cents a story by her grandfather, she wrote, published, and sold her own newspaper about the dogs in her neighborhood. From this experience she gained valuable knowledge about pleasing an audience: her youthful broadsheet soon went out of business because she continually featured her own dog on the front page.

Kehret's idyllic childhood was shattered when she contracted polio in the seventh grade. As a result, she was paralyzed from the neck down and told that she would never walk again. "Much to everyone's surprise," Kehret once said, "I made almost a complete recovery. I vividly remember the time when I got sick and my months in the hospital and my eventual return to school. Maybe that's why I enjoy writing books for young people; I recall exactly how it felt to be that age. I remember my friends and the books I liked and even what programs I listened to on the radio. When I write, it is easy for me to slip back in my imagination and become twelve years old again."

As a teen, Kehret dreamed of being either a veterinarian or writer, finally opting for the wordsmith business. "I'm glad I chose writing," Kehret said, "but two of the main characters in my books want to be veterinarians. Dogs, llamas, and elephants have played important parts in my books." With high school came a new direction for Kehret's interest in words: theater.

Cast as a hillbilly in a one-act play as a freshman, Kehret was seriously bit by the theater bug, working backstage or in acting roles in every production she could. Kehret briefly attended the University of Minnesota before marrying in 1955. Children soon followed and she lived the busy life of mother and homemaker, alsoserving as a volunteer with the Humane Society.

Kehret began writing in the early 1970s, spurred on by further work in community theater as well as her interest in research of various sorts. She began selling magazine stories, eventually logging over 300 of them before turning her hand to lengthier works. One-act and full-length plays followed, including the award-winning *Spirit!,* as well as two adult nonfiction titles, before she began writing books for young people. Her initial juvenile title, *Winning Monologs for Young Actors,* appeared in 1986 and was followed by her first novel for young people, *Deadly Stranger.* The story of a kidnapping, this novel was dubbed a "cliffhanger" by a *Kirkus Reviews* contributor. "As soon as I tried writing from a youthful point of view," Kehret continued, "I knew I had found my place in the writing world."

Another popular early title from Kehret is *Nightmare Mountain,* a thriller involving young Molly and her visit to her aunt's ranch at the foot of Mount Baker. The fun visit turns into a nightmare when her Aunt Karen falls into a coma and three valuable llamas are stolen. *Booklist* reviewer Denise Wilms observed that Kehret delivered "a fast-paced mystery-adventure tale with a heroine who, when forced to deal with disaster, shows courage and resourcefulness." Jeanette Larson concluded in the *School Library Journal* that the book is a "satisfying novel that will keep readers guessing until the end." Reincarnation informs Kehret's next book, *Sisters, Long Ago.* When Willow comes close to drowning, she sees herself in another life in ancient Egypt. The girl who saves her seems to be her sister from Egyptian days, while her own sister, Sarah, is fighting a losing battle with leukemia. Bruce Anne Shook, writing in the *School Library Journal,* noted that "suspense is maintained up to the very end, making this a page-turner."

One of Kehret's personal favorites, *Cages,* allowed her to write about a passion of hers, the Humane Society. When young Kit—who has an alcoholic stepfather and a mother in denial—gives in to a momentary urge and shoplifts a bracelet, she sets off a train of events that has lasting repercussions in her life. Caught, she is sentenced to community service at the Humane Society. There she falls in love with the homeless dogs and learns lessons about personal responsibility and facing her problems. As Andrea Davidson noted in the *Voice of Youth Advocates,* the book "will appeal to young teen readers interested in getting out of the 'cages' represented by their problems." *School Library Journal* reviewer Sylvia V. Meisner concluded that Kit's determination to set herself free from "the cages of alcohol enablement, jealousy, and, ultimately, the secret of her crime make her an appealing protagonist."

Terror at the Zoo is the story of an overnight camp-out at the zoo which goes very wrong. *Horror at the Haunted House* continues the adventures of Ellen and Corey from *Terror at the Zoo.* This time around, they help with a Halloween haunted-house project at the local historical museum, only to discover that the house really is haunted. Overcoming her fear of ghosts, Ellen helps find out who is stealing from the museum's collection. Donna Houser noted in the *Voice of Youth Advocates* that this "fun, fast-paced novel can be read in an evening," while *Booklist* contributor Chris Sherman concluded that readers "will be waiting in line for this action-packed novel, which combines a good mystery with an exciting ghost story, a little danger, and a satisfying ending that ties everything up neatly." Ellen and Corey appear again in *Danger at the Fair,* "this time sharing a thrill-a-minute adventure set at a county fair," according to *Booklist* contributor Zvirin. Atop the Ferris wheel, Corey spies a pickpocket at work, but when Corey subsequently trails the thief, he is trapped inside the "River of Fear" ride. Zvirin concluded that the mystery-suspense components of the story, plus "a pair of enthusiastic, heroic, quite likable" protagonists all added up to a book "that won't stay on the shelf for long."

Two other personal favorites of Kehret are *The Richest Kids in Town* and *Searching for Candlestick Park.* The former title represents a departure for Kehret; it is a comic novel about a boy's money-making ventures that all go wrong. New in town, Peter desperately wants to save up enough money for a plane ticket to go back and visit his best friend. Peter enlists the help of some other kids, including Wishbone Wyoming, in some of his crazy money-making schemes. Their plans range from an alternative health club to a rubber-duck race, and all fail miserably and rather humorously. Finally Peter comes to see that he no longer needs to make money for a ticket; he has a new best friend in Wishbone. A critic for *Kirkus Reviews* concluded that there were "clever antics in this fun book," while a reviewer in *Horn Book* dubbed it a "read-aloud comedy." In *Searching for Candlestick Park,* twelve-year-old Spencer is trying to find the father who left him and his mom three years before. Sure that his dad works for the San Francisco Giants, Spencer sets off on his bicycle from Seattle, accompanied by his cat, Foxey. Lauren Peterson noted in *Booklist* that Spencer's "honesty and integrity are repeatedly tested" in this "fast-paced, exciting adventure." A *Kirkus Reviews* contributor commented that "Spencer's impulsive escapade may give readers infatuated with the notion of running away some second thoughts."

With *Earthquake Terror,* Kehret returned to her more usual thriller format. When an earthquake destroys the only bridge to the mainland from the tiny island where Jonathan and his disabled sister Abby are staying, the young boy is pitted against nature. With no food or supplies, and unable to contact help, Jonathan must single-handedly save Abby, his dog, and himself. With displaced waters from the quake beginning to flood the island, the clock is ticking on Jonathan's efforts. "It will be a rare thriller fan who won't want to see what happens," Zvirin commented in her *Booklist* review. Roger Sutton, writing in the *Bulletin of the Center for Children's Books,* noted that Kehret's "focus on the action is tight and involving," while Elaine E. Knight concluded in the *School Library Journal* that "Jonathan is a sympathetic and realistic character," and that this "exciting tale is a fine choice for most collections."

Kehret has also authored several titles in the "Frightmare" series, a competitor to the popular "Goosebumps" books. Her books feature friends Rosie and Kayo who get involved in adventures and mysteries, from solving a kidnapping in Arizona in *Desert Danger* to solving a possible poisoning in *Don't Go Near Mrs. Tallie* to discovering vandals in the school with the help of a pet in *Bone Breath and the Vandals.* Using youthful protagonists Warren and Betsy, Kehret has also employed time travel to set up thrilling stories, as in *The Volcano Disaster,* in which Warren must survive the eruption of Mount St. Helens. *Booklist* contributor Peterson, reviewing *Bone Breath and the Vandals,* noted that "Kehret delivers some likable characters and a thrilling plot that won't disappoint suspense fans."

Nonfiction for children has also received the Kehret touch. Of her several books of monologues for young actors, one of the most popular is *Acting Natural.* "A wide range of topics is addressed in this sourcebook of 60 original scenes and monologues," noted Dianne G. Mahony in the *School Library Journal.* Donna Houser commented in the *Voice of Youth Advocates* that "all sections have their own merit because they deal with problems that are relevant to today's youth."

Kehret details her own battle with the paralyzing after-effects of polio in her award-winning *Small Steps.* "This heartfelt memoir takes readers back to 1949 when the author, at age 12, contracted polio," noted Zvirin in *Booklist.* Kehret describes the progress of the illness, the paralysis, and her slow recovery. Christine A. Moesch concluded in the *School Library Journal* that Kehret's memoir was an "honest and well-done book." Yet another nonfiction title is Kehret's *Shelter Dogs: Amazing Stories of Adopted Strays,* stories of dogs that found a second life after being taken from Humane Society shelters. A *Kirkus Reviews* critic called the book "an amiable collection of short anecdotes," concluding that there was "a ready audience to cry over and gasp at the tale behind every dog."

Kehret has amassed a large body of work and a legion of loyal fans—both girls and boys—for her middle-grade thrillers. Blending exciting action, likable characters, and "hi-lo" language, Kehret writes books that lead her readers on to more difficult fiction and nonfiction.

In *Abduction!* five-year-old Matt is kidnapped by the birth-father he has never met, and it is up to his twelve-year-old half-sister Bonnie to come to his rescue, despite the danger to herself. In addition to offering readers a suspenseful page-turner, *Abduction!* also provides an education about the ruses that kidnappers can use to lure children, the appropriate steps that even a child can take to find a missing youngster, and the procedures in place (both formal and casual) to locate and save a kidnapping victim. A *Kirkus Reviews* contributor observed that Kehret "demonstrates a deft touch in maintaining suspense while keeping her narrative light enough" to avoid intimidating the middle-grade readers for whom she writes. *School Library Journal* reviewer Diana Pierce also noted the level of suspense in *Abduction!,* adding that "the story is resolved happily but with a twist."

The Ghost's Grave is another suspense novel, one in which danger is leavened by an element of the fantastic. Young Josh is sent to spend the summer with an eccentric old aunt who turns out to be more interesting than he expected her to be. He roams the woods of Washington state coal-mining country until he finds a dilapidated tree house that is not as abandoned as it appears to be. Its resident ghost is one-legged Willy, who begs Josh to find his missing leg and bury it with the rest of his body. Josh finds a lot more than a buried leg: there is treasure and real-world danger in abundance. A *Kirkus Reviews* contributor called it "a solidly plotted ghost story." Michele Winship went further in her *Kliatt* review, calling *The Ghost's Grave* "a warm-hearted novel of the relationship between a boy, an old woman, and a ghost."

Kehret recently told *CA:* "When I began writing books for kids, my purpose was to entertain. I soon realized that I could be entertaining and share my values at the same time. One underlying theme in all of my work is that violence is never a solution. I show my characters using their brains to get out of trouble, rather than relying on a gun or some other weapon.

"Since I'm an animal lover, animals play a part in all of my books. Some, such as *Saving Lilly* and *Don't Tell Anyone* and Shelter Dogs, have an animal welfare theme as the main plot; others, such as *The Hideout* and *Searching for Candlestick Park,* use animals in a sub-plot. I always show my protagonists acting with compassion in the hope that readers who identify with those characters will learn to be more compassionate, too."

BIOGRAPHICAL AND CRITICAL SOURCES:

BOOKS

Science Fiction and Fantasy Literature, 1975-1991, Gale (Detroit, MI), 1992.

PERIODICALS

Booklist, September 15, 1989, Denise Wilms, review of *Nightmare Mountain,* p. 184; February 15, 1990, p. 1166; May 15, 1992, p. 1672; September 1, 1992, Chris Sherman, review of *Horror at the*

Haunted House, p. 254; September 1, 1994, p. 41; December 1, 1994, p. 664; January 1, 1995, Stephanie Zvirin, review of *Danger at the Fair,* p. 830; May 1, 1995, p. 1573; October 1, 1995, p. 314; January 1, 1996, Stephanie Zvirin, review of *Earthquake Terror,* p. 834; November 1, 1996, Stephanie Zvirin, review of *Small Steps: The Year I Got Polio,* pp. 492-493; August, 1997, Lauren Peterson, review of *Searching for Candlestick Park,* p. 1901; August, 1998, Lauren Peterson, review of *Bone Breath and the Vandals,* p. 2005.

Bulletin of the Center for Children's Books, February, 1995, pp. 202-203; March, 1996, Roger Sutton, review of *Earthquake Terror,* p. 231; November, 1996, pp. 100-101; November, 1997, pp. 88-89.

Horn Book, spring, 1995, review of *The Richest Kid in Town,* p. 78.

Kirkus Reviews, March 1, 1987, review of *Deadly Stranger,* p. 373; August 15, 1994, review of *The Richest Kid in Town,* p. 1131; June 1, 1997, review of *Searching for Candlestick Park,* p. 874; April 1, 1999, review of *Shelter Dogs: Amazing Stories of Adopted Strays,* p. 535; November 1, 2005, review of *Abduction!,* p. 1090; July 1, 2005, review of *The Ghost's Grave,* p. 737.

Kliatt, July, 1993, p. 10; March, 1997, p. 40; July, 2005, Michele Winship, review of *The Ghost's Grave.* p. 12.

School Library Journal, October, 1989, Jeanette Larson, review of *Nightmare Mountain,* p. 120; March, 1990, Bruce Anne Shook, review of *Sisters, Long Ago,* pp. 218-219; June, 1991, Sylvia V. Meisner, review of *Cages,* p. 126; August, 1992, Dianne G. Mahony, review of *Acting Natural: Monologs, Dialogs, and Playlets for Teens,* p. 182; September, 1994, p. 218; May, 1995, p. 108; December, 1995, p. 104; February, 1996, Elaine E. Knight, review of *Earthquake Terror,* p. 100; November, 1996, Christine A. Moesch, review of *Small Steps,* p. 114; July, 1998, p. 96; December, 2004, Diana Pierce, review of *Abduction!,* p. 149.

Voice of Youth Advocates, June, 1991, Andrea Davidson, review of *Cages,* pp. 97-98; June, 1992, Donna Houser, review of *Acting Natural,* pp. 126-127; October, 1992, Donna Houser, review of *Horror at the Haunted House,* p. 224; February, 1996, p. 373.

ONLINE

Kids Love Books by Peg Kehret, http://www.pegkehret.com (November 12, 2005).

KILIAN, Michael D. 1939-2005
(Rex Dancer)

PERSONAL: Born July 16, 1939, in Toledo, OH; died October 26, 2005, of complications from liver disease; son of D. Frederick and Laura Casmere (Dulski) Kilian; married Pamela H. Reeves, October 17, 1970; children: Eric, Colin. *Education:* Attended the New School for Social Research, 1957-58, and University of Maryland, 1964. *Religion:* Presbyterian. *Hobbies and other interests:* Flying.

CAREER: KNTV, San Jose, CA, writer, 1960-63; City News Bureau, Chicago, IL, reporter, 1965-66; *Chicago Tribune,* Chicago, IL, reporter and assistant political editor, 1966-71, member of the editorial board, 1971-2005, editorial writer, 1971-86, editorial page columnist, 1974-86, Washington, DC, columnist and cultural commentator, 1986-2005. CBS Radio, WBBM, Chicago, IL, commentator, 1973-82; WTTW Channel 11, Chicago, IL, commentator, 1975-78; National Public Radio, commentator, 1978-79; CLTV News, host of "DC Journal," 1995; WGN, Chicago, IL, correspondent for the *Roy Leonard Show,* 1996-99; commentator for CBC, 1996; commentator for Irish Radio. Board of directors, Fund for Animals, beginning 1976. *Military service:* U.S. Army, 1963-65; U.S. Air Force Civil Air Patrol, 1976; became captain.

MEMBER: White House Correspondents Association, English Speaking Union (life member), National Press Club.

AWARDS, HONORS: Humor Writing Award, United Press International, 1971.

WRITINGS:

NOVELS

The Valkyrie Project, St. Martin's (New York, NY), 1981.

Northern Exposure, St. Martin's (New York, NY), 1983.

Blood of the Czars, St. Martin's (New York, NY), 1984.

By Order of the President, St. Martin's (New York, NY), 1986.

Dance on a Sinking Ship, St. Martin's (New York, NY), 1988.

Looker, St. Martin's (New York, NY), 1991.

The Last Virginia Gentleman, St. Martin's (New York, NY), 1992.

The Big Score, St. Martin's (New York, NY), 1993.

(As Rex Dancer) *Bad Girl Blues,* Simon & Schuster (New York, NY), 1994.

(As Rex Dancer) *Postcard from Hell,* Simon & Schuster (New York, NY), 1995.

Major Washington, St. Martin's (New York, NY)/ Thomas Dunne (New York, NY), 1998.

Deep Kill, Berkley (New York, NY), 2005.

"HARRISON RAINES" SERIES; CIVIL WAR HISTORICAL MYSTERIES

Murder at Manassas, Berkley Prime Crime (New York, NY), 2000.

A Killing at Ball's Bluff, Berkley Prime Crime (New York, NY), 2001.

The Ironclad Alibi, Berkley Prime Crime (New York, NY), 2002.

A Grave at Glorieta, Berkley Prime Crime (New York, NY), 2003.

The Shiloh Sisters, Berkley Prime Crime (New York, NY), 2003.

Antietam Assassins, Severn House (Brooklyn, NY), 2005.

"JAZZ AGE" MYSTERY SERIES

The Weeping Woman, Berkley Prime Crime (New York, NY), 2001.

The Uninvited Countess, Berkley Prime Crime (New York, NY), 2002.

A Sinful Safari, Berkley Prime Crime (New York, NY), 2003.

OTHER

(With Connie Fletcher and F. Richard Ciccone) *Who Runs Chicago?,* St. Martin's (New York, NY), 1979.

(With Arnold Sawislak) *Who Runs Washington?,* St. Martin's (New York, NY), 1982.

(With James Coates) *Heavy Losses: The Dangerous Decline of American Defense,* Viking (New York, NY), 1985.

Flying Can Be Fun (humor), illustrated by Dick Locher, Pelican Publishing (Gretna, LA), 1985.

Author, with Dick Locher, of comic strip *Dick Tracy,* 1993-2005. Also served as the sports editor for the *Encyclopaedia Britannica Book of the Year,* Encyclopaedia Britannica (Chicago, IL).

SIDELIGHTS: A journalist for the *Chicago Tribune,* Michael D. Kilian authored political thrillers and mystery series, collaborated with others to pen books about American politics and defense, and took over the writing of the *Dick Tracy* comic strip in 1993, a position he held until his death in 2005. A *Chicago Tribune* correspondent from Washington, DC, the versatile author covered topics ranging from politics to arts and culture.

Early in his book publishing career, Kilian wrote the 1979 book *Who Runs Chicago?* with university professor Connie Fletcher and *Chicago Tribune* journalist F. Richard Ciccone. In *Who Runs Chicago?* Kilian, Fletcher, and Ciccone examine nineteen interest groups—ranging from city politicians to society matrons to street gangs—that held power in Chicago at the time of the book's writing. A *Kirkus Reviews* contributor noted that the authors "have compiled a Who's Who of Chicago power-brokers." Washington, DC, gets a similar treatment from Kilian and United Press International correspondent Arnold Sawislak in *Who Runs Washington?,* which a *Publishers Weekly* reviewer called an "informative if somewhat irreverent guide to Washington's political and social scene." A *Booklist* contributor pronounced it an "antic but informed guidebook to life in the nation's capital."

As a novelist, Kilian preferred to write political thrillers and mysteries. His first, *The Valkyrie Project,* takes place in Iceland on the eve of national elections that might lead to a Communist victory and upset the balance of power between the United States and the Soviet Union. Jack Spencer, an American intelligence agent and former journalist, has been assigned to sabotage the Valkyrie Project, a Soviet attempt to build a defense system that can strike down American nuclear missiles. *Library Journal* contributor John North wrote that "the action zips along with the requisite doses of sex, violence, and duplicity." A *Publishers Weekly* reviewer remarked that the novel contains "a twisting plot, engaging characters, and picturesque backgrounds," while a *Booklist* contributor deemed *The Valkyrie Project* "a stylish spy tale."

Another Kilian novel, *Northern Exposure,* concerns a plot to secure the province of Quebec's independence from Canada. The responsibility for preventing Canada's disintegration falls to American diplomat Dennis Showers, who becomes trapped in a deadly cauldron of intrigue involving the CIA, the KGB, the Royal Canadian Mounted Police, and others. A *Publishers Weekly* reviewer commented that *Northern Exposure* has a "fast-moving plot" as well as "fairly interesting characters," concluding that the story "fizzles out at the end, but it's pretty good fun while it lasts." *Library Journal* contributor Necia A. Musser observed that *Northern Exposure* "provides lively entertainment."

In Kilian's *The Big Score* the corpse of a young woman is found wrapped in a painting. Police chief Zane Rawlings investigates the death and finds himself in ever-increasing danger. A *Publishers Weekly* contributor wrote that although some of the characters "are a little broad," the author "has a great feel for plot," concluding that *The Big Score* "is a thoroughly entertaining thriller." Writing in the *Library Journal,* Beth Ann Mills said that while *The Big Score* is "entertainingly long on plot, it is unfortunately short on characterization."

Major Washington is a historical novel about three crucial years (1753 through 1755) in the life of George Washington, as told by Washington's fictional associate, Thomas Morley, a young ship owner and adventurer. During these years, the French and Indian War began, with Great Britain and France fighting for control of the North American interior. Washington, then in his early twenties, established his reputation as a military leader based on his actions in the conflict. *Booklist* contributor Brad Hooper praised Kilian's "careful and copious research" and declared: "We see a truly human Washington here, deeper than a frozen-in-ice icon." Writing in the *Library Journal,* Bettie Alston Shea also enjoyed the novel, calling *Major Washington* "well done but demanding reading."

After *Major Washington* Kilian wrote several mystery novels set during the Civil War, featuring his character Harrison Raines, a Virginian who dabbles in gambling and horse trading. Although Raines is a Southerner, his anti-slavery sentiments lead him to work for the U.S. Secret Service in the first book in the series, *Murder at Manassas.* Taking place during the first year of the Civil War, this tale follows Raines as he sets out to prove that a young officer who died at Manassas was actually a murdered hero, and not a coward killed while leading a Union retreat. What follows is a mix of spy intrigue, as Raines conducts his investigation in both the South and the North, with guest appearances from famous figures such as Allan Pinkerton, Clara Barton, and Abraham Lincoln. While a *Publishers Weekly* reviewer felt that the plot in *Murder at Manassas* was somewhat convoluted and that "the narrative never seems to find a pace it's comfortable with," *Booklist* contributor Jay Freeman called Raines "an interesting and attractive sleuth" and noted that Kilian "effectively handles the irony of a quest for justice in the midst of mass killing."

Throughout the series, the author uses an important historical event in the Civil War as the backdrop of each Harrison Raines book. Kilian's next installment, *A Killing at Ball's Bluff,* consequently features the battle of the title and involves the real-life mystery of the murder of Abraham Lincoln's friend Colonel Edward Baker. While Raines works on the case, Kilian touches on some of the issues of the time, including abolition and the consequences of war, but the main focus is on "picaresque adventure" with much "spy vs. spy" action, as one *Publishers Weekly* contributor described it. Both enthusiasts of Civil War novels and mysteries "will appreciate Kilian's grasp of the genres of historical fiction and mystery," according to Freeman in *Booklist.*

The threat of attack on Washington, DC, from a new ironclad Confederate warship, the *C.S.S. Virginia* (formerly the Union ship *Merrimac*) is a central concern in Raines' next escapade, *The Ironclad Alibi.* But even more worrying for him on a personal level is that his friend, a freed slave named Caesar Augustus, is accused of murdering a woman in Raines' room. Certain that Caesar is innocent, the sleuth gets permission from Robert E. Lee himself to solve the case—but he only has one week in which to do it. His investigation leads him to link the real killer to the *Virginia* itself. "A colorful and exciting climax caps a book that entertains from start to finish," said a *Publishers Weekly* writer about *The Ironclad Alibi.*

In addition to his historical Civil War mystery series, Kilian also began a new series of books before his death, the "Jazz Age" mysteries, and he had also been writing comic strips for *Dick Tracy. Dick Tracy* was originally started in 1931 by Chester Gould and features the square-jawed crime fighter of the title. When Gould retired in 1977, other writers and artists kept the strip going, with Kilian and editorial cartoonist Dick Locher taking the torch in 1993. Although *Dick Tracy* is much less popular than it once was, it is still carried in fifty U.S. newspapers and has many diehard fans. "[Dick Tracy] is the cop in America," said Kilian in a *Denver Business Journal* article. "He is part of the language," he added as explanation for the character's longevity. "I can't think of another comic strip where the character is as identifiable as Dick Tracy."

BIOGRAPHICAL AND CRITICAL SOURCES:

PERIODICALS

Best Sellers, February, 1980.

Booklist, December 1, 1981, p. 483; June 15, 1982, pp. 1344-1345; March 15, 1983, p. 946; September 1, 1986, p. 33; January 1, 1991, p. 909; April 15, 1992, Denise Perry Donavin, review of *The Last Virginia Gentleman,* p. 1507; October 1, 1993, Richard Paul Snyder, review of *The Big Score,* p. 253; January 1, 1998, Brad Hooper, review of *Major Washington,* p. 777; December 1, 1999, Jay Freeman, review of *Murder at Manassas,* p. 687; December 15, 2000, Jay Freeman, review of *A Killing at Ball's Bluff,* p. 792; October 15, 2005, Emily Melton, review of *Antietam Assassins,* p. 33.

Business Week, October 14, 1985, Dave Griffiths, review of *Heavy Losses: The Dangerous Decline of American Defense,* p. 14.

Chicago, January, 1993, pp. 80-86.

Denver Business Journal, October 12, 2001, L. Wayne Hicks, "Dick Tracy Going Strong at 70," p. 33A.

Kirkus Reviews, September 15, 1979, p. 1112; January 1, 1984, p. 9; August 15, 1993, p. 1020; August 15, 2005, review of *Antietam Assassins,* p. 886.

Library Journal, December 1, 1981, review of *The Valkyrie Project,* p. 2332; March 15, 1983, Necia A. Musser, review of *Northern Exposure,* p. 601; November 15, 1985, Dennis Felbel, review of *Heavy Losses,* p. 85; March 1, 1988, p. 77; December, 1990, Patricia Y. Morton, review of *Looker,* p. 164; June 1, 1992, Barbara Conaty,

review of *The Last Virginia Gentleman,* p. 177; September 15, 1993, Beth Ann Mills, review of *The Big Score,* p. 104; January, 1998, Bettie Alston Shea, review of *Major Washington,* p. 142.

New York Times Book Review, April 10, 1983, Dean Flower, review of *Northern Exposure,* p. 30; September 15, 1985, Harry G. Summers, Jr., review of *Heavy Losses,* p. 11; March 15, 1998, David Walton, review of *Major Washington,* p. 27.

Publishers Weekly, October 30, 1981, Barbara A. Bannnon, review of *The Valkyrie Project,* p. 56; May 28, 1982, review of *Who Runs Washington?,* p. 62; January 7, 1983, review of *Northern Exposure,* pp. 61-62; January 6, 1984, p. 77; December 6, 1985, Sybil Steinberg, review of *Blood of the Czars,* p. 74; August 1, 1986, Sybil Steinberg, review of *By Order of the President,* pp. 67-68; July 10, 1987, p. 65; January 8, 1988, Sybil Steinberg, review of *Dance on a Sinking Ship,* p. 72; November 16, 1990, Sybil Steinberg, review of *Looker,* p. 44; April 13, 1992, review of *The Last Virginia Gentleman,* pp. 41-42; September 27, 1993, p. 46; January 5, 1998, review of *Major Washington,* pp. 59-60; December 13, 1999, review of *Murder at Manassas,* p. 68; December 4, 2000, review of *A Killing at Ball's Bluff,* p. 56; December 24, 2001, review of *The Ironclad Alibi,* p. 46; December 22, 2003, review of *The Shiloh Sisters,* p. 41; August 29, 2005, review of *Antietam Assassins,* p. 37.

School Library Journal, January, 1999, Carol Clark, review of *Major Washington,* p. 159.

Tribune Books (Chicago, IL), October 19, 1986, p. 6; March 20, 1988, p. 7; June 28, 1992, p. 7; October 17, 1993, p. 7.

Virginia Quarterly Review, autumn, 1982, p. 124.

Washingtonian, May, 1982, review of *Who Runs Washington?,* p. 19.

Washington Monthly, February, 1986, pp. 52-55.

West Coast Review of Books, May-June, 1984, p. 29.

OBITUARIES

PERIODICALS

Chicago Tribune, October 27, 2005, William Neikirk and Glen Elsasser, "Michael Kilian, 1939-2005," p. 13.*

KIRBY, David K. 1944-
(David Kirk Kirby)

PERSONAL: Born November 29, 1944, in Baton Rouge, LA; son of Thomas Austin (a professor) and Josie (a school teacher; maiden name, Dyson) Kirby; married Judy Kates (a high school French teacher), March 21, 1969 (divorced); married Barbara Hamby (a poet), 1981; children: William, Ian. *Education:* Louisiana State University, B.A., 1966; Johns Hopkins University, Ph.D., 1969.

ADDRESSES: Home—1168 Seminole Dr., Tallahassee, FL 32301-4656. *Office*—Department of English, 420 Williams Bldg., Florida State University, Tallahassee, FL 32306-1580; fax: 850-644-0811. *E-mail*—dkirby@ english.fsu.edu.

CAREER: Poet, critic, writer, and educator. Florida State University, Tallahassee, FL, assistant professor, 1969-74, director of writing program, 1973-77, associate professor, 1974-79, professor, 1979-89, McKenzie Professor of English, 1989-2003, Robert O. Lawton Distinguished Professor, 2003-04, assistant executive vice-president, 1975-77; Florida State University Study Center in Florence, Italy, faculty member, 1973; also taught in other Florida State University international programs in England, France, and Spain. Has conducted workshops and seminars for groups, including elementary school children and prison inmates; member of Board of Directors of the National Book Critics Circle.

MEMBER: Associated Writing Programs, Modern Language Association of America, Melville Society, National Book Critics Circle, National Council of Teachers of English, College English Association, South Atlantic Modern Language Association.

AWARDS, HONORS: Pushcart Prize Outstanding Writer Citations, 1978, 1984, for poetry, and 1987, for nonfiction; grants from Florida Arts Council, 1983, 1989, 1996, and 2002; National Endowment for the Arts grant, 1985; Brittingham Prize in Poetry, 1987, for *Saving Young Men of Vienna;* W. Guy McKensie Professorship, 1989; College of Arts and Sciences Teaching Award, Florida State University, 1990; University Teaching Awards, Florida State University, 1992, 1997; Pushcart Prize, 2001; Guggenheim Fellow, 2003.

WRITINGS:

POETRY

The Opera Lover: Poems, Anhinga Press (Tallahassee, FL), 1977.
Sarah Bernhardt's Leg: Poems, Cleveland State University Poetry Center (Cleveland, OH), 1983.
Diving for Poems, World Beat Press (Tallahassee, FL), 1985.
Saving the Young Men of Vienna, University of Wisconsin Press (Madison, WI), 1987.
Big Leg Music, Orchises (Alexandria, VA), 1995.
My Twentieth Century: Poems, Orchises (Washington, DC), 1999.
The House of Blue Light: Poems, Louisiana State University Press (Baton Rouge, LA), 2000.
The Travelling Library: Three Poems, Orchises (Washington, DC), 2001.
The Ha-Ha: Poems, Louisiana State University Press (Baton Rouge, LA), 2003.
I Think I Am Going to Call My Wife Paraguay: Selected Early Poems, Orchises (Washington, DC), 2004.

CHILDREN'S FICTION

(With Allen Woodman) *The Cows Are Going to Paris,* illustrated by Chris L. Demarest, Caroline House (Honesdale, PA), 1991.
(With Allen Woodman) *The Bear Who Came to Stay,* illustrated by Harvey Stevenson, Bradbury Press (New York, NY), 1994.

NONFICTION/CRITICISM

(Editor, with Kenneth H. Baldwin) *Individual and Community: Variations on a Theme in American Fiction,* Duke University Press (Durham, NC), 1975.
American Fiction to 1900: Guide to Information Sources, Gale (Detroit, MI), 1975.
America's Hive of Honey: or, Foreign Influences on American Fiction through Henry James, Scarecrow Press (Metuchen, NJ), 1980.
Grace King, Twayne (Boston, MA), 1980.

The Sun Rises in the Evening: Monism and Quietism in Western Culture, Scarecrow Press (Metuchen, NJ), 1982.

Dictionary of Contemporary Thought, Macmillan (London, England), 1984.

The Plural World: An Interdisciplinary Glossary of Contemporary Thought, Garland (New York, NY), 1984.

Writing Poetry: Where Poems Come from and How to Write Them, Writer (Boston, MA), 1989, revised edition, 1997.

Mark Strand and the Poet's Contemporary Culture, University of Missouri Press (Columbia, MO), 1990.

Boyishness in American Culture: The Charms and Dangers of Social Immaturity, E. Mellen Press (Lewiston, NY), 1991.

The Portrait of a Lady and The Turn of the Screw: Henry James and Melodrama, Macmillan (Houndmills, Basingstoke, Hampshire, England), 1991.

Herman Melville, Continuum (New York, NY), 1993.

What Is a Book?, University of Georgia Press (Athens, GA), 2002.

Contributor of poems, reviews, and essays to numerous journals and periodicals, including the *New York Times Book Review, Times Literary Supplement, Village Voice, Writer, Quarterly, Southern Review, Sewanee Review, Ploughshares, College English, Virginia Quarterly Review, Christian Science Monitor,* and the *Gettysburg Review.*

SIDELIGHTS: David K. Kirby is the author and coauthor of numerous books of literary criticism, two children's books, and several volumes of poetry. As a poet, Kirby often incorporates humor into his poems, which are known for their conversational style. "The words and the rhythm are conversational, despite their velocity, creating the illusion of everybody speech— even though it's safe to say that nobody really talks like that," noted Steve Macqueen in *Florida Trend.* "Kirby has his own term for the style—'ultra-talk.'" Kirby told Macqueen: "I wanted to make my poetry conversational but take out the 'uhs' and 'ums,' give it a cup of coffee, and just make it smart and funny and fast." In a review of Kirby's *My Twentieth Century: Poems, Library Journal* contributor Graham Christian noted that the author "writes verse closer to the rhythms of popular culture . . . than the traditional sources of lyric poetry."

In *The House of Blue Light: Poems,* Kirby's fifth collection of poetry, the poet reflects on his own middle-aged life and circumstances. Writing in *Booklist,* Ray Olson noted that "the dominant motif in these brilliantly prattling poems is his own bozohood." A *Publishers Weekly* contributor called the poems "disarming in their lack of pretense and posturing." In his next effort, *The Travelling Library: Three Poems,* Kirby writes about a trip he took to Europe. Frank Allen, writing in the *Library Journal,* called the book "a beautiful and sane feat of poems."

In *The Ha-Ha: Poems,* Kirby presents whimsical poems, such as one about a man who suddenly is able to see himself in the past and wishes he could change things based on his current experience and knowledge of life. *Library Journal* contributor Diane Scharper noted that the poems are "a combination of anecdotes, repartee, and verbal wit." *I Think I Am Going to Call My Wife Paraguay: Selected Early Poems* presents Kirby writing about a variety of topics, from literature to his personal life to rock music. Writing in *Booklist,* Olson noted that the "early Kirby is wilder, smarter-assed, more sentimental."

In addition to his poetry, Kirby has collaborated with Allen Woodman on children's books. *The Cows Are Going to Paris* features bovines who decide to take a train to Paris and act like tourists. In *The Bear Who Came to Stay,* a bear visits a family and takes on their life of watching television and brushing its teeth while the family goes out to live in the forest and sleep in a cave. A *Publishers Weekly* contributor noted the book's "high quotient of cuteness."

Among Kirby's books of criticism is *What Is a Book?,* in which the author explores literature though seventeen essays, including essays about such writers as Hermann Melville, Henry James, and Charles Wright. Writing in *Booklist,* Donna Seaman commented that *What Is a Book?* "radiantly celebrates our unceasing love and need for books." *Library Journal* contributor Paul D'Alessandro wrote: "An important and useful book that is also surprisingly pleasurable and entertaining to read."

Kirby told CA: "As a writer and a teacher of writing I have two principles: (1) reverence toward language and (2) irreverence toward everything else, including myself and my own writing. I'm addicted to poetry readings, workshops, professional meetings, conferences, lectures—any situation which is likely to result in wit, brilliance, animated conversation, and perhaps a congenial glass or two among friends. I appreciate anyone who writes anything that interests me, no matter how they do it or what form it takes."

BIOGRAPHICAL AND CRITICAL SOURCES:

PERIODICALS

Booklist, January 15, 1994, review of *The Bear Who Came to Stay,* p. 940; September 1, 2000, Ray Olson, review of *The House of Blue Light,* p. 58; March 15, 2001, Ray Olson, review of *The House of Blue Light: Poems,* p. 1349; November 1, 2002, Donna Seaman, review of *What Is a Book?,* p. 468; December 15, 2003, Ray Olson, review of *I Think I Am Going to Call My Wife Paraguay: Selected Early Poems,* p. 721.
Childhood Education, winter, 2002, Colleen McAndrew, review of *The Cows Are Going to Paris,* p. 110.
Choice, April, 1994, M.S. Stephenson, review of *Herman Melville,* p. 940.
Florida Trend, February, 2004, Steve Macqueen, "Sho' Like to Ball," interview with author, p. S12.
Library Journal, May 15, 1999, Graham Christian, review of *My Twentieth Century: Poems,* p. 99; September 1, 2000, Ann K. van Buren, review of *The House of Blue Light,* p. 214; January, 2002, Frank Allen, review of *The Travelling Library: Three Poems,* p. 109; November 15, 2002, Paul D'Alessandro, review of *What Is a Book?,* p. 71; October 1, 2003, Diane Scharper, review of *The Ha-Ha: Poems,* p. 80.
Ploughshares, fall, 2004, review of *The Ha-Ha,* p. 215.
Publishers Weekly, December 20, 1993, review of *The Bear Who Came to Stay,* p. 70; October 30, 2000, review of *The House of Blue Light,* p. 72.
School Library Journal, May, 1994, Lisa S. Murphy, review of *The Bear Who Came to Stay,* p. 105.

ONLINE

David Kirby Home Page, http://www.davidkirby.com/ (November 7, 2005).

*   *   *

KIRBY, David Kirk
  See KIRBY, David K.

KORELITZ, Jean Hanff 1961-

PERSONAL: Born May 16, 1961, in New York, NY; daughter of Burton I. (a doctor) and Ann (a therapist in social work) Korelitz; married Paul Muldoon (a writer), August 30, 1987; children: one daughter, one son. *Education:* Dartmouth College, B.A. (cum laude), 1983; Clare College, Cambridge, M.A., 1985.

ADDRESSES: Home—Princeton, NJ. *Agent*—c/o Suzanne Gluek, William Morris Agency, 1325 Avenue of the Americas, New York, NY 10019.

CAREER: Writer, novelist, poet, and educator. Freelance writer, 1979—. Farrar, Straus & Giroux, Inc. (publisher), New York City, editorial assistant, 1987-88; University of Massachusetts, Amherst, instructor in Division of Continuing Education, 1990—. Editorial intern for *Seventeen* magazine, summer, 1979; summer intern of American Society of Magazine Editors for *Glamour* magazine, 1982.

AWARDS, HONORS: Named among "top ten college women for 1983" by *Glamour* magazine; Marguerite Eyer Wilbur Foundation fellow, 1985; Harper-Wood Studentship for Creative Writing and Chancellor's Medal for Poetry, both from Cambridge University, both 1985; resident at MacDowell Colony, 1988 and 1989.

WRITINGS:

NOVELS

A Jury of Her Peers, Crown Publishers (New York, NY), 1996.
The Sabbathday River, Farrar, Straus (New York, NY), 1999.
Interference Powder, Marshall Cavendish (New York, NY), 2003.
The White Rose, Miramax Books (New York, NY), 2005.

OTHER

The Properties of Breath (poems), Bloodaxe Books (Newcastle upon Tyne, England), 1988.

Contributor of articles to magazines and periodicals, including *Vogue, Real Simple, More, Organic Style, Newsweek, O, Redbook, New York Times,* and *Lifetime.*

SIDELIGHTS: Jean Hanff Korelitz is a novelist, poet, and educator. Her first novel, *A Jury of Her Peers,* is a "fast-moving legal thriller," noted a *Publishers Weekly* contributor. Sybylla Muldoon, a legal aid attorney in New York, is assigned to defend Trent, a homeless man accused in the vicious stabbing death of a seven-year-old girl. Trent tells a fanciful story of being kidnapped and held against his will in a hospital. Though committed to the defense of her clients, Sybylla finds the story difficult to believe. However, when a mysterious implant is removed from Trent's arm, it is discovered to be a time-release device full of LSD, lending credibility to Trent's story and possibly explaining the once-gentle man's seeming mental illness and descent into murder. Before she can use this information, however, Trent dies, and Sybylla becomes aware that she is in danger herself. Worse, her predicament seems linked to a recent nominee to the U.S. Supreme Court—Sybylla's own father. The *Publishers Weekly* reviewer called the book an "accomplished first novel." *Booklist* contributor Margaret Flanagan concluded that the work is "a suspenseful and tautly rendered legal drama." Korelitz's "convincing characterization, vigorous prose and rapid-fire pacing deliver thoughtful entertainment along with the promised thrills," the *Publishers Weekly* reviewer stated.

When Naomi Roth, the protagonist of *The Sabbathday River,* moved to Goddard, New Hampshire, in the 1970s, she was a VISTA volunteer looking to make a difference in the world. She stayed on to found a crafts cooperative. Decades later, she is still in Goddard and the cooperative is flourishing. Most popular among the cooperative's products is the extraordinary embroidery work of Heather Pratt, a local girl haunted by an affair with a married man, Ashley Deacon, and the illegitimate child she had by him. When Naomi finds the stabbed body of an infant floating in the Sabbathday River, the townsfolk are quick to assume that it is Heather's, and that she has slain her unwanted second child. Naomi steps forward to assist and defend Heather, convincing a newly arrived attorney, Judith Friedman, to defend the young woman in court. Heather is not the only one, however, who will be seared by the shocking and emotionally wrenching case. Korelitz touches on many themes in the novel,

noted Emily Melton in *Booklist,* including friendship, Judaism, and the unique experience of being a modern woman, but "it all works together brilliantly as a combination suspense thriller, courtroom drama, and cautionary morality tale." "Smart and engrossing, this thriller addresses the complex morality behind its characters' behavior with gravity and deep humanity," observed a *Publishers Weekly* critic. Melton called the novel a "powerful tale of obsession and murder with a searing examination of human nature."

Interference Powder is a fanciful tale about what happens when a young girl acquires the ability to rework the world as she chooses. When Nina Zabin receives a low grade on her social studies test, she copes by painting a picture of herself getting a perfect score. Finding a bottle of interference powder—ground-up mica that artists sometimes use to add shimmer to paintings—among her substitute teacher's art supplies, she adds a bit of the substance to the painting of herself, and finds her world transformed. Her test score morphs into the perfect result found in her painting. To her surprise, Nina learns that her superior test performance now means she must represent her class in an all-school history contest. She thinks the powder will help her through, and it does, to a point, with unexpected and undesired results. Among the effects: Nina's sudden inability to speak without the words coming forth in song, and the ability to cause a flood merely by crying. A child psychologist advises Nina to use the magic powder one last time, to fix all the problems it has caused. "Despite the magical element, this is largely realistic fiction about knowing oneself and being true to one's dreams," observed Barbara Auerback in the *School Library Journal. Booklist* contributor Todd Morning commented that "the novel has a winning central character and some funny scenes that many young readers will enjoy."

In *The White Rose,* forty-eight-year-old Marian Kahn is married, a successful history professor at Columbia University, and the author of a bestselling book of popular history. Middle-aged steadfastness gives way to youthful indiscretion when she plunges into a sultry affair with twenty-six-year-old Oliver Stern, son of Marian's oldest friend. Oliver, the owner of a popular flower shop called The White Rose, is thoroughly smitten with Marian, but when he meets Sophie Klein, a graduate student and heiress, his emotions and commitments clash. Complicating matters is the fact that Sophie is engaged to Barton Ochstein, Marian's arrogant cousin. Marian and Oliver must contend with the disintegration of their still-strong emotional attachments while Sophie and Barton reconsider their commitment. A *Kirkus Reviews* contributor called the novel "elegant and melancholy yet surprisingly optimistic, warmed by full-bodied characterizations and expert delineation of complex emotions." A *Publishers Weekly* writer concluded that, "even when their own comfort is at stake, Korelitz's characters succumb to generous impulses, making this a satisfying, emotionally rich read."

BIOGRAPHICAL AND CRITICAL SOURCES:

PERIODICALS

Booklist, March 1, 1996, Margaret Flanagan, review of *A Jury of Her Peers,* p. 1121; March 15, 1999, Emily Melton, review of *The Sabbathday River,* p. 1291; October 15, 2003, Todd Morning, review of *Interference Powder,* p. 412.

Kirkus Reviews, September 15, 2004, review of *The White Rose,* p. 884.

Publishers Weekly, February 5, 1996, review of *A Jury of Her Peers,* p. 76; February 8, 1999, review of *The Sabbathday River,* p. 193; November 15, 2004, review of *The White Rose,* p. 39.

School Library Journal, December, 2003, Barbara Auerbach, review of *Interference Powder,* p. 153.

Times Literary Supplement, August 4, 1989, Tim Dooley, review of *The Properties of Breath,* p. 850.

ONLINE

Pan Macmillan, http://www.panmacmillan.com/ (October 31, 2005), biography of Jean Hanff Korelitz.

L

LAMBERT, Gavin 1924-2005

PERSONAL: Born July 23, 1924, in East Grinstead, Sussex, England; naturalized U.S. citizen, 1964; died of pulmonary fibrosis, July 17, 2005, in Los Angeles, CA; son of Mervyn and Vera (Pembroke) Lambert. *Education:* Attended St. George's Windsor, Cheltenham College, and Magdalen College, Oxford. *Hobbies and other interests:* Reading, music, travel.

CAREER: Editor, *Sight and Sound* (film magazine), 1950-56; freelance writer, 1950-2005.

MEMBER: Writers Guild of America West.

AWARDS, HONORS: Thomas R. Coward Memorial Award, 1966, for *Norman's Letter.*

WRITINGS:

The Slide Area: Scenes of Hollywood Life, Viking Press (New York, NY), 1959, Serpent's Tail (New York, NY), 1998.
Inside Daisy Clover, Viking Press (New York, NY), 1963, Serpent's Tail (New York, NY), 1996.
Norman's Letter, Coward-McCann (New York, NY), 1966.
A Case for the Angels, Dial Press (New York, NY), 1968.
The Goodby People, Simon & Schuster (New York, NY), 1971, published as *The Goodbye People,* Serpent's Tail (London, England), 2000.

On Cukor (interviews), W.H. Allen (London, England), 1972, Putnam (New York, NY), 1973, Rizzoli (New York, NY), 2000.
GWTW: The Making of "Gone with the Wind," Little, Brown (Boston, MA), 1973.
The Dangerous Edge, Barrie & Jenkins (London, England), 1975, Grossman Publishers (New York, NY), 1976.
In the Night All Cats Are Grey, W.H. Allen (London, England), 1976.
Running Time, Macmillan (New York, NY), 1983.
Norma Shearer: A Life, Knopf (New York, NY), 1990.
(Author of introduction) *Dear Paul, Dear Ned: The Correspondence of Paul Bowles and Ned Rorem,* Elysium Press (North Pomfret, VT), 1997.
Nazimova: A Biography, Knopf (New York, NY), 1997.
Mainly about Lindsay Anderson (biographical memoir), Knopf (New York, NY), 2000.
Natalie Wood: A Life, Knopf (New York, NY), 2004.
(Editor and author of foreword and afterword) *The Ivan Moffat File: Life among the Beautiful and Damned in London, Paris, New York, and Hollywood,* Pantheon Books (New York, NY), 2004.

SCREENPLAYS

"The Road to Edinburgh," *General Electric Theater,* Columbia Broadcasting System (CBS), 1953.
"Strange Witness," *General Electric Theater,* Columbia Broadcasting System (CBS), 1953.
Another Sky, Edward Harrison, 1954.
(Uncredited, with others) *Bigger than Life,* Twentieth Century Fox, 1956.

Bitter Victory, Columbia, 1957.

"The Closed Set," Startime, National Broadcasting Company (NBC), 1960.

Sons and Lovers, Twentieth Century-Fox, 1960.

The Roman Spring of Mrs. Stone, Warner Brothers, 1961.

Inside Daisy Clover (based on his novel of same title), Warner Brothers, 1965.

Interval, AVCO Embassy Pictures, 1973.

I Never Promised You a Rose Garden, New World, 1977.

Second Serve (television screenplay), Columbia Broadcasting System (CBS) Television, 1986.

Caftan d'amour, Centre Cinematographique Morocain, 1988.

Liberace: Behind the Music, 1988.

Sweet Bird of Youth (television screenplay; adaptation of Tennessee Williams play), National Broadcasting Company (NBC), 1989.

Dead on the Money (television screenplay), Turner Pictures, 1991.

Also author and director of *Another Sky,* 1956. Also author of screenplays for television. Contributor of articles to *New Statesman, Observer, Harper's Bazaar,* and other periodicals. Founder, *Sequence* (magazine).

SIDELIGHTS: Although he was born and raised in England, Gavin Lambert spent most of his life in the United States—more specifically, in Hollywood. Hired as a screenwriter in 1958, Lambert became better known as an observer and biographer of the film industry. Both his fiction and nonfiction speak candidly about the pleasures and pitfalls of stardom and the devastating effects a movie career can have upon sensitive people. Lambert's best-known novel, *Inside Daisy Clover,* charts the mental collapse of an exploited teen star, played in the film version by Natalie Wood. Another Lambert novel, *Running Time,* follows a child screen star from her earliest years as a sensation to her later years as a television talk show host. As Elizabeth Jakab put it in the *New York Times Book Review,* "Hollywood's a glamorous place, even when it isn't, and nobody understands that better than Gavin Lambert."

In the latter part of his career, Lambert focused on producing biographies of film and theater artists. Two of these biographies, *Nazimova: A Biography* and *Norma Shearer: A Life,* cover the lives and work of two actresses who were well known in their time but who have since almost lost their places in film history. Alla Nazimova was a Russian immigrant who did her best work on the stage, and Shearer, while one of the biggest stars of her era, stopped working in movies in the early 1940s. In a *People* review of *Norma Shearer,* Leah Rozen wrote: "Lambert, blending thorough research with able prose, gives Norma her due without overstating her talent, or intellectual or emotional depth." *New York Times Book Review* correspondent Arthur Lubow called *Nazimova* "a gracefully written, highly entertaining, surprisingly poignant biography" in which Lambert is able to "evoke the thrill that her audiences felt."

Mainly about Lindsay Anderson is a combination biography-memoir in which Lambert muses about his relationship with the brilliant British director Lindsay Anderson. Close friends in their teens in England, Lambert and Anderson pursued different paths in the theater and film industry, with Lambert moving to California and Anderson staying in England. According to Stanley Kauffmann in the *New York Times Book Review,* "from his long friendship and from Anderson's extensive diaries, Lambert is able to paint a full portrait of his friend, even though he spent his own life out of England." *Booklist* contributor Ray Olson noted of the work: "Anderson is fascinating, and Lambert describes his work with the keen insight of a fine critic." A *Publishers Weekly* reviewer likewise found the work a "thoughtful meditation on art, politics and sexuality" that "deftly elucidates Anderson's troubled . . . life." Kauffmann observed that Lambert "writes a fluent, wry, purring prose," and the critic concluded that *Mainly about Lindsay Anderson* is a "candid yet affectionate book."

Lambert served as editor and author of the foreword and afterword for *The Ivan Moffat File: Life among the Beautiful and Damned in London, Paris, New York, and Hollywood.* The book contains "curious and evocative fragments of autobiography by boulevardier and screenwriter Moffat, gathered and embellished by Lambert," remarked a *Kirkus Reviews* critic. Moffatt was a "sophisticate, socialite, and appreciator of beautiful women" whose life as a bon vivant in Hollywood "is arguably more fascinating than his filmography," observed a *Publishers Weekly* reviewer. The son of renowned actress Iris Tree and the grandson of prominent actor Sir Robert Beerbohm, Moffatt remained true to his own Hollywood roots and carved out his own personal and professional life there. His own work includes such films as *They Came to Cordura, Shane,* and *Tender Is the Night,* all critically praised but also considered to be flawed. Moffat also wrote the movie that cemented James Dean's image as a cinema icon, *Giant.* Moffat was known as a womanizer who lived in luxury, and his account reveals that he had as much of both as he could manage. But Moffatt also lived many years in the wan glow of fading glory, constantly near financial ruin, but maintaining the facade of elegance and gregariousness that had served him his entire life. Lambert "matches Moffat's beautiful, polished style with his own chapters, penned after Moffat's death," noted the *Publishers Weekly* reviewer.

Once again turning to biography, Lambert wrote *Natalie Wood: A Life,* "a sympathetic telling of the short and often unhappy life of actress Wood," noted *Library Journal* reviewer Nann Blaine Hilyard. Lambert was also a personal friend of Wood and her husband, Robert Wagner, who urged Lambert to write the biography. Lambert covers Wood's early childhood, her dominating mother, her intermittently abusive father, the origins of many of the actress's fears and insecurities, and her rise to stardom. He covers the time period in which Wood worked in film, including the political climate and the other film notables Wood counted as friends and business associates. He also closely examines Wood's death by drowning, and attempts to dispel long-time speculation that the actress was the victim of foul play. Lambert's "riveting biography of Natalie Wood is sure to surprise and enlighten even veteran industry insiders as well as neophytes, film buffs and social anthropologists," commented reviewer Beatrice Williams-Rude in *Variety.* "It's an honest, meticulously researched work."

BIOGRAPHICAL AND CRITICAL SOURCES:

PERIODICALS

Advocate, June 10, 1997, review of *Nazimova: A Biography,* p. 77.

Artforum International, January, 2001, "Gary Indiana," review of *Mainly about Lindsay Anderson,* p. 30.

Back Stage, July 22, 1983, George L. George, review of *Running Time,* p. 18.

Booklist, April 15, 1997, Jack Helbig, review of *Nazimova: A Biography,* p. 1374; September 15, 2000, Ray Olson, review of *Mainly about Lindsay*

Anderson, p. 201; June 1, 2001, Ray Olson, review of *Mainly about Lindsay Anderson,* p. 1815; December 15, 2003, Ray Olson, review of *Natalie Wood: A Life,* p. 718.

Choice: Current Reviews for Academic Libraries, October, 1997, review of *Nazimova: A Biography,* p. 308.

Christian Science Monitor, August 3, 1990, Nat Segaloff, review of *Norma Shearer: A Life,* p. 10.

Cineaste, winter, 2002, review of *Mainly about Lindsay Anderson,* p. 60.

Film Quarterly, summer, 1973; spring, 2002, Linda A Robinson, review of *Mainly about Lindsay Anderson,* p. 65.

Films in Review, January, 1992, review of *Norma Shearer: A Life,* p. 61.

Kirkus Reviews, August 15, 2000, review of *Mainly about Lindsay Anderson,* p. 1169; November 15, 2003, review of *Natalie Wood: A Life,* p. 1352; August 15, 2004, review of *The Ivan Moffat File,* p. 791.

Library Journal, February 15, 1983, review of *Running Time,* p. 412; April 1, 1990, John Smothers, review of *Norma Shearer: A Life,* p. 117; November 15, 1996, review of *Inside Daisy Clover,* p. 93; April 15, 1998, Michael Rogers, review of *The Slide Area,* p. 120; August, 2000, Neal Baker, review of *Mainly about Lindsay Anderson,* p. 107; January, 2004, Rosellen Brewer, review of *Natalie Wood: A Life,* p. 116; July, 2004, Nann Blaine Hilyard, review of *Natalie Wood: A Life,* p. 126.

Los Angeles Times, August 7, 1983, Elaine Kendall, review of *Running Time,* p. 10; August 5, 1997, Mary Susan Herczog, "Sunset Blvd.," review of *Nazimova: A Biography,* p. E1; December 14, 1997, Eric Lax, review of *Nazimova: A Biography,* p. 12.

New Republic, November 20, 2000, David Thomson, "Fool Britannia," review of *Mainly about Lindsay Anderson,* p. 38.

New York, November 21, 1988, John Leonard, television review of *the Closed Set,* p. 128; October 2, 1989, John Leonard, television review of *Sweet Bird of Youth,* p. 76.

New Yorker, April 25, 1983, review of *Running Time,* p. 153; August 11, 1997, review of *Nazimova: A Biography,* p. 79; April 25, 1983, review of *Running Time,* p. 153.

New York Review of Books, January 15, 2004, John Gregory Dunne, "Star!," review of *Natalie Wood: A Life,* p. 35.

New York Times, May 1, 1983, Elisabeth Jakab, review of *Running Time,* p. 14; June 12, 1983, review of

Running Time, p. 37; October 8, 1988, John J. O'Connor, film review of *Liberace: Behind the Music,* p. 52; July 30, 1989, Stephen Farber, television review of *Sweet Bird of Youth,* p. H27; June 17, 1991, John J. O'Connor, television review of *Dead on the Money,* p. C14.

New York Times Book Review, May 1, 1983, Elisabeth Jakab, review of *Running Time,* p. 14; June 12, 1983, review of *Running Time,* p. 37; April 27, 1997, Arthur Lubow, "Sunset Boulevard," review of *Nazimova: A Biography,* p. 12; November 12, 2000, Stanley Kauffmann, "Angry Young Man: The Life of the British Director Lindsay Anderson as Seen by an Old Friend," p. 9; December 3, 2000, review of *Mainly about Lindsay Anderson,* p. 80; January 18, 2004, Stephanie Zacharek, "A Star is Born," review of *Natalie Wood: A Life,* p. 8.

Opera News, January 3, 1998, F. Robert Schwartz, review of *Dear Paul, Dear Ned: The Correspondence of Paul Bowles and Ned Rorem,* p. 50.

People, June 25, 1990, Leah Rozen, review of *Norma Shearer: A Life,* p. 29; January 19, 2004, Arion Berger, review of *Natalie Wood: A Life,* p. 46.

Publishers Weekly, January 21, 1983, review of *Running Time,* p. 70; April 6, 1990, Genevieve Stuttaford, review of *Norma Shearer: A Life,* p. 108; February 24, 1997, review of *Nazimova: A Biography,* p. 72; July 3, 2000, review of *Mainly about Lindsay Anderson,* p. 56; December 8, 2003, review of *Natalie Wood: A Life,* p. 57; August 23, 2004, review of *The Ivan Moffat File,* p. 44.

Sight and Sound, October, 2002, John Wrathall, interview with Gavin Lambert, p. 12.

Spectator, June 28, 1978; May 27, 2000, Helen Osborne, review of *Mainly about Lindsay Anderson,* p. 36; November 18, 2000, review of *Mainly about Lindsay Anderson,* p. 53.

Times Higher Education Supplement, June 16, 2000, Mamoun Hassan, review of *Mainly about Lindsay Anderson,* p. 22.

Times Literary Supplement, June 30, 2000, Patrick O'Connor, review of *Mainly about Lindsay Anderson,* p. 21; July 2, 2004, Philip French, "Splendour on the Screen: Child Stardom, Adult Glamour, a Mysterious Accident: The Troubled Life and Death of Natalie Wood," p. 16.

Variety, October 19, 1988, film review of *Liberace: Behind the Music,* p. 496; November 23, 1988, television review of *The Closed Set,* p. 90B; October 25, 1989, television review of *Sweet Bird of Youth,* p. 65; June 20, 1990, review of *Norma Shearer: A Life,* p. 75; September 11, 2000,

Jonathan Bing, review of *Mainly about Lindsay Anderson,* p. 30; February 9, 2004, Beatrice Williams-Rude, review of *Natalie Wood: A Life,* p. 95.

Video Business, November 20, 2000, Samantha Clark, "A Book of a Legend," review of *On Cukor,* p. 24.

Vogue, June, 1983, Leo Lerman, review of *Running Time,* p. 51.

Women's Review of Books, September, 1997, Susan Manning, review of *Nazimova: A Biography,* p. 6.

ONLINE

Beatrice, http://www.beatrice.com/ (November 10, 2005), Ron Hogan, two interviews with Gavin Lambert.

Books Unlimited, http://www.booksunlimited.co.uk/ (May 20, 2000), Brian Cox, review of *Mainly about Lindsay Anderson.*

Internet Movie Database Web site, http://www.imdb.com/ (October 31, 2005), biography of Gavin Lambert.

OBITUARIES

PERIODICALS

Advocate, August 30, 2005, p. 30.

Daily Variety, July 25, 2005, p. 11.

Hollywood Reporter, July 19, 2005, Gregg Kilday, "*Clover* Author Lambert Dies," p. 8.

New York Times, July 19, 2005, Sharon Waxman, "Gavin Lambert, 80, Writer Who Chronicled Hollywood Life," p. B7.

Time, "Milestones," p. 19.

Time Canada, "Milestones," p. 9.

Variety, July 25, 2005, p. 55.*

*　　　*　　　*

LANSING, Gerrit 1928-
(Gerrit Yates Lansing)

PERSONAL: Born February 25, 1928, in Albany, NY. *Education:* Harvard University, B.A.; Columbia University, M.A.

ADDRESSES: Home—Gloucester, MA. *Office*—c/o Granary Books, 307 7th Ave., Ste. 1401, New York, NY 10001.

CAREER: Columbia University Press, New York, NY, editorial assistant, 1955-60. Writer.

WRITINGS:

The Heavenly Tree Grows Downward (poetry), Matter Books (Gloucester, MA), 1966.
Heavenly Tree, Soluble Forest, Talisman (Jersey City, NJ), 1995.
(With Reese Ligorano) *Turning Leaves of Mind,* limited edition, Granary Books (New York, NY), 2002.
A February Sheaf, Pressed Wafer Press (Boston, MA), 2003.

Work represented in anthologies, including *A Controversy of Poets,* Doubleday (New York, NY), 1965, and *Poems Now,* Kulchur Press, 1966. Contributor of poems to *Tomorrow, Caterpillar,* and *Io.* Editor, *SET* (poetry magazine).

SIDELIGHTS: On the themes and subjects of his poetry, Gerrit Lansing once commented, "I favor love, the wedding of the natural and supernatural, and visible things." Lansing has traveled extensively in the United States and Europe.*

*   *   *

LANSING, Gerrit Yates
    See LANSING, Gerrit

*   *   *

LASHNER, William 1956(?)-

PERSONAL: Born c. 1956, in Philadelphia, PA; son of Melvin (an attorney) and Marilyn (Auerbach) Lashner; married Pam Ellen Stern, June 11, 1989; children: Nora, Jack, Michael. *Education:* Swarthmore College, B.A., 1979; New York University Law School, J.D.; graduate of University of Iowa Writer's Program, 1991.

ADDRESSES: Home—Philadelphia, PA. *Agent*—c/o Author Mail, William Morrow Publishers, 10 E. 53rd St., New York, NY 10022.

CAREER: Attorney and writer. Law clerk for Honorable James B. Moran, Chicago, IL, 1983-85; U.S. Department of Justice, Criminal Division, Washington, DC, trial attorney, 1985-86; Lashner & Lashner, Philadelphia, PA, partner, 1987-95.

MEMBER: Writer's Guild.

WRITINGS:

NOVELS

Hostile Witness, HarperCollins/Regan Books (New York, NY), 1995.
Veritas, HarperCollins/Regan Books (New York, NY), 1997.
Bitter Truth, HarperTorch (New York, NY), 2003.
Fatal Flaw, William Morrow (New York, NY), 2003.
Past Due, William Morrow (New York, NY), 2004.
Falls the Shadow, William Morrow (New York, NY), 2005.

Lashner's work has been translated into nine languages.

SIDELIGHTS: Philadelphia native William Lashner used his own experiences as a lawyer to write what would become his first published novel. Like attorneys-turned-authors John Grisham and Scott Turow, Lashner chalked up several years' experience in private practice after graduating from New York University Law School. He also worked for the Justice Department in Washington, DC, before returning to Philadelphia to work for his father's firm. He had penned two unpublished novels, and based on the lack of interest aroused by these more literary-minded works, decided to write a crime thriller. The result was 1995's *Hostile Witness.*

Hostile Witness's protagonist is Victor Carl, a Philadelphia attorney on a permanent losing streak. His resentful attitude is often targeted at the city's monied class, represented by the venerable and prestigious law firms that are his more successful opponents in the courtroom. "We weren't quite as down-and-out as Victor is," Lashner told a *Publishers Weekly* reviewer about the similarities between his family's firm and Victor's two-man office. "But we were always going up against big firms that had a dozen lawyers assigned cases while I was running around doing everything myself." As *Hostile Witness* gets underway, one such blueblood firm asks Victor Carl to serve as outside counsel for a defendant, an African-American aide to a scandal-plagued Philadelphia councilman. The two have been charged with extortion, but Carl soon realizes that his 15,000 dollar retainer fee is actually his reward for allowing the aide to get railroaded so that the councilman will walk free. Drug dealers, organized crime, a Hasidic detective, and a love interest all enter the fray. While faulting the book for "a shallow fascination with surfaces and types," Bill Kent in the *New York Times Book Review* noted that "Lashner's depictions of violence are appropriately nasty and unsettling, and his courtroom scenes achieve an echo of truth." *People* contributor Joanne Kaufman noted that the debut novel "has a good, gritty feel and a sardonic . . . protagonist who grows on you." The *Publishers Weekly* contributor wrote that the book "is suspenseful" and "a promising debut." Resounding praise for the book came from Emily Melton, who wrote in *Booklist:* "Lashner has written a dark, gut-wrenching thriller. . . . In the tradition of his highly successful colleagues, Grisham and Turow, Lashner has written an absorbing legal thriller. What sets this one apart, though, is the dark, despairing view it takes of human nature. A superb, disturbing read."

Victor Carl appeared again in Lashner's next book, *Veritas.* In this "appealing noir murder mystery," as a *Publishers Weekly* writer described it, Carl helps Caroline Shaw, heiress to the Reddman pickle fortune. Caroline's sister Jackie recently died, and though the death appeared to be a suicide, Caroline believes her sister was killed by the Mafia in revenge for their brother's overdue gambling debts. Naturally, she is worried that she might be next. As Victor investigates the case and the Redmann family's history, many layers of nasty business are exposed, and he discovers that their entire fortune may have been built on a dishonest deal. "Energized by crisp and delightfully venal first-person narration, this guided tour through the lifestyles of the rich and nasty teems with clever plot twists and (literally) buried secrets, with greed and revenge running neck and neck as the winning motive of a patient murderer," noted the *Publishers Weekly* contributor. *Booklist* contributor Wes Lukowsky

compared Lashner to top-notch suspense author Ross Macdonald. Lukowsky wrote that, like Macdonald, "Lashner invents a past that never relinquishes its hold on the present, wreaking havoc in subtle, often deadly fashion." Lukowsky went on to note that, unlike Macdonald's Lew Archer, however, who is an "empathetic hero," Victor Carl is "blind to both present and past in his quest for profound wealth. This unique updating of the Macdonald formula offers extremely entertaining reading."

Lashner has continued to write courtroom thrillers featuring Carl, including *Bitter Truth,* in which Carl gets mixed up with the mob as he tries to prove that a Philadelphia heiress did not commit suicide but was murdered. In *Fatal Flaw,* Carl takes on the case of lawyer Guy Forrest, who is accused of murdering his fiancée. The evidence is stacked against Forrest, who is Carl's good friend. Further complicating matters is the fact that Carl also had a relationship with the murdered woman. Nevertheless, Carl is convinced of Forrest's innocence and sets out to find the real killer, which takes him from Las Vegas to West Virginia, where he learns that the dead woman's high school sweetheart was also murdered. "It's the tallest of tall tales . . . but it's got robust drive," noted a *Kirkus Reviews* contributor. David Pitt, writing in *Booklist,* commented: "This startling legal thriller is very, very good."

In *Past Due,* Lashner has Carl listening to a confession by one of his clients about a murder that took place twenty years earlier. When the client turns up shortly afterwards with his throat slashed, Carl is suspicious and sets out to find out who the murder victim was and who was the perpetrator. He soon finds that many of the potential suspects have achieved success in politics and law. "This is an extremely good crime novel, and it vaults Lashner into the upper reaches of the hardboiled universe," wrote Wes Lukowsky in *Booklist.* A *Publishers Weekly* contributor noted, "Lashner's writing . . . gains depth and richness with every installment."

In *Falls the Shadow,* Carl finds himself defending Francois Dube, a chef, for the murder of his wife, even though Dube has already been convicted and has spent three years in jail. Although Carl thinks Dube is probably guilty, he takes the case and works with fellow lawyer Beth Derringer as they uncover the chef's unseemly past and try to come to terms with each other and their different views of the law. David Pitt, writing in *Booklist,* called the book "great fun and a wonderful antidote to the high seriousness of too many legal thrillers." A *Publishers Weekly* contributor commented that "the well-staged plot twists and Carl's amusingly amoral narration make for good beach reading."

BIOGRAPHICAL AND CRITICAL SOURCES:

PERIODICALS

Booklist, March 15, 1995, Emily Melton, review of *Hostile Witness,* p. 1284; December 15, 1996, Wes Lukowsky, review of *Vertitas,* p. 692; March 15, 2003, David Pitt, review of *Fatal Flaw,* p. 1253; January 1, 2004, Wes Lukowsky, review of *Past Due,* p. 790; March 15, 2005, David Pitt, review of *Falls the Shadow,* p. 1247.
Entertainment Weekly, April 28, 1995, Mark Harris, review of *Hostile Witness,* p. 56.
Kirkus Reviews, March 15, 2003, review of *Fatal Flaw,* p. 420; February 1, 2004, review of *Past Due,* p. 102; April 1, 2005, review of *Falls the Shadow,* p. 376.
Library Journal, March 15, 2004, Craig Shufelt, review of *Past Due,* p. 107.
New York Times Book Review, August 20, 1995, Bill Kent, review of *Hostile Witness,* p. 20.
People, May 22, 1995, Joanne Kaufman, review of *Hostile Witness,* pp. 34-35; June 23, 2003, Arion Berger, review of *Fatal Flaw,* p. 43; May 10, 2004, Edward Karam, review of *Past Due,* p. 58.
Publishers Weekly, February 20, 1995, review of *Hostile Witness,* p. 193; December 9, 1996, review of *Veritas,* p. 59; March 3, 1997, review of *Veritas,* p. 30; April 21, 2003, review of *Fatal Flaw,* p. 37; February 2, 2004, review of *Past Due,* p. 56; April 18, 2005, review of *Falls the Shadow,* p. 43.
Texas Lawyer, June 6, 2005, Michael P. Maslanka, review of *Falls the Shadow.*

ONLINE

Bookreporter.com, http://www.bookreporter.com/ (January 9, 2004), "William Lashner," interview with author.
William Lashner Home Page, http://www.william lashner.com (November 7, 2005).*

LEBSOCK, Suzanne 1949-
   (Suzanne Dee Lebsock)

PERSONAL: Born December 1, 1949, in Williston, ND; married Richard L. McCormick (a university president); children: Betsy, Michael. *Education:* Carleton College, B.A., 1971; University of Virginia, M.A., 1973, Ph.D., 1977.

ADDRESSES: Office—Department of History, Rutgers University, 111 Van Dyck Hall, 16 Seminary Pl., New Brunswick, NJ, 08901. *E-mail*—lebsock@history.rutgers.edu.

CAREER: Writer and professor. Rutgers University, New Brunswick, NJ, assistant professor, became professor of history, 1977-93, acting director of women's studies, 1986-87, Board of Governors professor of history, 2003—; University of North Carolina at Chapel Hill, Chapel Hill, NC, 1993-95; University of Washington, Seattle, WA, professor of history, 1995-c. 2003. Woodrow Wilson International Center for Scholars, Washington, DC, fellow, 1985.

MEMBER: American Historical Association, Organization of American Historians, American Studies Association, Berkshire Conference of Women Historians, Sisters in Crime, Southern Association for Women Historians, Southern Historical Association, Association of Women Historians.

AWARDS, HONORS: Grant from American Council of Learned Societies, 1978; Bancroft Prize, Columbia University, 1985, for *The Free Women of Petersburg: Status and Culture in a Southern Town, 1784-1860;* John D. and Catherine T. MacArthur Foundation Fellowship, 1992; Francis Parkman Prize for literary distinction in the writing of American history, and Library of Virginia Literary Award, nonfiction winner, both 2004, both for *A Murder in Virginia: Southern Justice on Trial.*

WRITINGS:

NONFICTION

"A Share of Honour": Virginia Women, 1600-1945 (essays), Project (Richmond, VA), 1984.

The Free Women of Petersburg: Status and Culture in a Southern Town, 1784-1860, W.W. Norton & Co. (New York, NY), 1984.

(With Anne Firor Scott) *Virginia Women: The First Two Hundred Years,* Colonial Williamsburg Foundation (Williamsburg, VA), 1988.

(Contributor) Louise Tilly and Patricia Gurrin, editors, *Women and Politics in the Twentieth Century,* Russell Sage Foundation (New York, NY), 1990.

(Editor, with Nancy A. Hewitt) *Visible Women: New Essays on American Activism,* University of Illinois Press (Urbana, IL), 1993.

A Murder in Virginia: Southern Justice on Trial, W.W. Norton & Co. (New York, NY), 2003.

Contributor to periodicals, including the *Journal of Southern History* and *Georgia Historical Quarterly.*

SIDELIGHTS: Suzanne Lebsock is a historian known for her expertise on the history of southern American women. Among her writings is *The Free Women of Petersburg: Status and Culture in a Southern Town, 1784-1860,* which documents the lives of women in a slaveholding town during the period between the American Revolution and the Civil War. Wendy Kaminer, writing in the *New York Times Book Review,* called Lebsock's book "a lively and illuminating review," showing that "the women of Petersburg . . . enjoyed increasing personal autonomy and economic independence" during what was in many ways an era of "strident domesticity."

In 2003, Lebsock published a second award-winning historical volume *A Murder in Virginia: Southern Justice on Trial.* The book examines an event which occurred in a small, segregated town in Virginia in 1895. Three black women—Mary Barnes, her daughter Pokey Barnes, and Mary Abernathy—were arrested and tried several times for using an ax to murder a white woman, Lucy Pollard, and robbing her husband, Edward, a wealthy farmer. The African-American women were accused by the first person arrested for the crime, a black man named Solomon Marable. In the community, many citizens, white and black, believed the women were innocent. There was a movement, primarily among African Americans, to free them. Lebsock draws on both primary sources, such as letters, and secondary sources, like court documents from the many related trials and newspaper stories, to tell the multi-faceted story. The historian

argues that these women received justice that was at least somewhat fair despite the expectations of time and place. She also examines race relations in this part of post-Civil War America. Reviewing *A Murder in Virginia* in *Southern Cultures,* S. Willoughby Anderson commented: "By showing us engaged black citizens, divided whites, and the myriad daily interactions that took place beneath the veneer of a codifying racial system, Lebsock opens the window onto a remarkable moment of ambiguity and lost possibility in the South."

BIOGRAPHICAL AND CRITICAL SOURCES:

PERIODICALS

New York Times Book Review, February 26, 1984, Wendy Kaminer, review of *The Free Women of Petersburg: Status and Culture in a Southern Town, 1784-1860,* p. 23.

Southern Cultures, summer, 2004, S. Willoughby Anderson, review of *A Murder in Virginia: Southern Justice on Trial,* p. 110.

ONLINE

Rutgers University Web site, http://ur.rutgers.edu/ (July 24, 2003), "Noted Scholar Dr. Suzanne Lebsock Named Board of Governors Professor of History at Rutgers," biography of Suzanne Lebsock.*

*   *   *

LEBSOCK, Suzanne Dee
  See LEBSOCK, Suzanne

*   *   *

LEFKOWITZ, Mary R. 1935-
  (Mary Rosenthal Lefkowitz)

PERSONAL: Born April 30, 1935, in New York, NY; daughter of Harold L. and Mena G. (Weil) Rosenthal; married Alan L. Lefkowitz, July 1, 1956 (divorced, 1981); married Hugh Lloyd-Jones (a professor), March 26, 1982; children: (first marriage) Rachel Greil, Hannah Weil. *Education:* Attended the Brearley School, New York, NY (graduated); Wellesley College, B.A. (summa cum laude), 1957; Radcliffe College, M.A., 1959, Ph.D., 1961.

ADDRESSES: Home—15 West Riding, Wellesley, MA 02181. *E-mail*—mlefkowi@wellesley.edu.

CAREER: Wellesley College, Wellesley, MA, instructor, 1959-63, assistant professor, 1963-69, associate professor, 1969-75, professor of Greek and Latin, 1975-79, chair of department, 1970-72, 1975-78, 1981-87, 1991-94, and 1997-2001, director of educational research, 1978-79, Andrew W. Mellon Professor in the Humanities, 1979-2005, Mellon Professor Emerita, 2005—. Visiting professor at University of California, Berkeley, 1978; Sacher visiting fellow at St. Hilda's College, Oxford, 1979-80, honorary fellow, 1994—, Pembroke College, Oxford, 1986-87, and Corpus Christi College, Oxford, 1990-91. Director, National Endowment for the Humanities seminars for college teachers, 1984, 1985, and Pew Foundation Grant, 1986-91. Guest on television programs such as *60 Minutes.*

MEMBER: American Philological Association (member of national board of directors, 1974-77), Phi Beta Kappa, American School of Classical Studies in Athens (member of board of trustees, 2004—).

AWARDS, HONORS: Woodrow Wilson fellow, 1957-58; Radcliffe Institute fellow, 1966-67, 1972-73; American Council of Learned Societies fellow, 1972-73; National Endowment for the Humanities fellow, 1979-80, 1990-91; Mellon Grant, Wellesley Center for Research on Women, 1980-81; Radcliffe Graduate Society Medal, 2004; recipient of honorary degrees from Trinity College (Hartford, CT), University of Patras (Greece), and Grinnell College (Grinnell, IA).

WRITINGS:

The Victory Ode: An Introduction, Noyes Press (Park Ridge, NJ), 1976.
(Editor with Maureen B. Fant) *Women in Greece and Rome,* Samuel Stevens (Sarasota, FL), 1977, revised edition published as *Women's Life in Greece and Rome,* Johns Hopkins University Press (Baltimore, MD), 1982, 3rd edition, 2005.

Heroines and Hysterics, St. Martin's Press (New York, NY), 1981.
The Lives of the Greek Poets, Johns Hopkins University Press (Baltimore, MD), 1981.
Women in Greek Myth, Johns Hopkins University Press (Baltimore, MD), 1986.
First-Person Fictions: Pindar's Poetic "I", Clarendon Press (New York, NY), 1991.
Not Out of Africa: How Afrocentrism Became an Excuse to Teach Myth as History, Basic Books (New York, NY), 1996.
(Editor, with Guy MacLean Rogers) *Black Athena Revisited,* University of North Carolina Press (Chapel Hill, NC), 1996.
Greek Gods, Human Lives: What We Can Learn from Myths, Yale University Press (New Haven, CT), 2003.

Contributor of articles and reviews to periodicals, including *Times Literary Supplement, New York Times Book Review, New Republic, Partisan Review,* and *American Scholar.* New England editor, *Classical Journal,* 1977-83; member of editorial board, *American Journal of Philology,* 1986-89, and *American Scholar,* 1988—.

SIDELIGHTS: Classical scholar Mary R. Lefkowitz is the author of works on the lives of the Greek poets, women in Greek myth, and the status and treatment of women in ancient Greece and Rome. One of her books, *Women's Life in Greece and Rome,* coedited with Maureen B. Fant, is considered "the standard source book in the field," noted a biographer on the *Wellesley College* Web site.

Lefkowitz has willingly courted controversy in her career. With *Not Out of Africa: How Afrocentrism Became an Excuse to Teach Myth as History,* Lefkowitz entered into the conflict regarding Martin Bernal's theory that African influences helped shape early Greek culture. Bernal argued that "linguistic, technological and intellectual contributions of Egyptian (i.e., African) and Phoenician (i.e., Semitic) provenance played a significant role in the genesis and subsequent development of ancient Greek civilization," reported Jacques Berlinerblau in the *Nation.* This suggestion rang loudly in the halls of classical academia, causing many classicists to dispute the suggestion and call Bernal's scholarly credentials into question (he has a Ph.D. in Oriental Studies, but specializing in China).

Lefkowitz sees adherence to Bernal's position as a symptom of modern universities' "subordination of genuine scholarship to fashionable causes and politically correct ideologies," commented reviewer Graeme Voyer in the *Alberta Report*. In other words, Bernal's argument is not scholarship but political correctness, and to Lefkowitz, it cannot be allowed to permeate the field and take root in Classical studies. In her book, Lefkowitz "assails the Afrocentric view and thoroughly demolishes it, revealing it as based on faulty reasoning and misuse of evidence," stated Voyer.

In *Black Athena Revisited,* edited by Lefkowitz and Guy MacLean Rogers and published shortly after *Not Out of Africa,* Lefkowitz attempts to establish a scholarly framework for further examining Bernal's assertion that African civilization had a profound influence on the development of early European and Classical civilization. If Bernal's volume has "captured the imagination of the public, it has earned the author the enmity of many of his fellow scholars," observed Elizabeth Sherman in the *Wilson Quarterly*. In approaching Bernal's argument, two questions must be answered, Sherman stated. "First, is there any truth to Bernal's bold claim that the real cradle of Western civilization was not classical Greece but Africa? And second, what is the standard of truth by which such scholarly (some would say pseudoscholarly) claims can be measured?" The contributors in Lefkowitz's volume analyze those questions and conclude that Bernal's hypothesis does not withstand careful scrutiny. Voyer stated that the Afrocentrism at the heart of Bernal's work "is only one manifestation of a deeper problem. It could only have emerged in the contemporary anti-intellectual climate—a climate which denies the reality of objective truth, claiming that all 'perspectives' are equally valid."

With *Greek Gods, Human Lives: What We Can Learn from Myths,* Lefkowitz offers an intriguing intellectual question: How could the Greeks, whose society, technology, and intellect were the exemplars of the time and the basis for much of Western science, worship gods who were spiteful, capricious, and at most times unworthy of worship? Lefkowitz "advances a convincing answer to such questions and in the process provides an intriguing look at our own cultural presuppositions about the nature of God and the world," commented Paula L. Reimers in *Journal of Church and State*. The answer, she concludes, is found in the way that Classical myths and stories have been translated and retold over the years. The translated stories focus on the perspective of the humans in the story; in the ancient texts, however, the focus was more on the lives of the gods. Works such as the *Iliad* and the *Odyssey* take on a profoundly new slant when retold from this perspective. "No longer tales of humans affected by the gods, they were shown to be stories of the lives, loves, and rivalries of the gods that happened to intersect human affairs," Reimers noted. Humans were interested in the gods because of their superiority, and because they did not have to endure the same privations and hardships as even the most influential human leader. In most cases, the gods tended to their own affairs and left humans alone. But humans sometimes forgot their position in relation to the gods; failure to accord them the honor and respect they felt they deserved would cause the gods' wrath to fall on humans, individually and collectively. In the original stories, Lefkowitz reveals, the gods did not exist for the benefit of humans, they tended to favor only those who could somehow help advance their interests, and human-god interaction was often catastrophic. Lefkowitz's "treatment is both accessible to the general reader interested in mythology and stimulating to the specialist," stated *Library Journal* reviewer T.L. Cooksey. Reimers concluded that "Lefkowitz's work is an absorbing study for those who wish to understand the worldview of the ancient Greeks and to meditate on the meaning of their own faith."

BIOGRAPHICAL AND CRITICAL SOURCES:

PERIODICALS

Alberta Report, May 26, 1997, Graeme Voyer, review of *Out of Africa: How Afrocentrism Became an Excuse to Teach Myth as History,* p. 42.

Journal of Church and State, summer, 2004, Paula L. Reimers, review of *Greek Gods, Human Lives: What We Can Learn from Myths,* p. 652.

Journal of World History, fall, 2000, Maghan Keita, review of *Not out of Africa,* p. 337.

Library Journal, November 1, 2003, T. L. Cooksey, review of *Greek Gods, Human Lives,* p. 83.

Nation, October 28, 1996, Jacques Berlinerblau, review of *Out of Africa,* p. 42.

Research in African Literatures, spring, 1998, Molefi Kete Asante, review of *Black Athena Revisited,* p. 206.

Wilson Quarterly, spring, 1996, Elizabeth Sherman, review of *Black Athena Revisited,* p. 79.

ONLINE

Wellesley College, http://www.wellesley.edu/ (October 31, 2005), biography of Mary R. Lefkowitz.

* * *

LEFKOWITZ, Mary Rosenthal
See LEFKOWITZ, Mary R.

* * *

LEHMAN, John F., Jr. 1942-
(John Francis Lehman, Jr.)

PERSONAL: Born September 14, 1942, in Philadelphia, PA; son of John Francis, Sr. (an executive) and Grace Constance (Cruice) Lehman. Education: St. Joseph's College, B.S., 1964; Cambridge University, B.A. (with honors), M.A., 1967; University of Pennsylvania, M.A., Ph.D., 1974. Politics: Republican. Religion: Catholic.

ADDRESSES: Office—J.H. Lehman & Company, 450 Park Ave., 6th Fl., New York, NY 10022; 2001 Jefferson Davis Hwy., Ste. 607, Arlington, VA 22202.

CAREER: Intercollegiate Review, Philadelphia, PA, assistant editor, 1964-66; Bendix-University of Pennsylvania Third International Arms Control Symposium, executive director, 1966; University of Pennsylvania, Philadelphia, Foreign Policy Research Institute, staff member, 1967-69, chair of Defense Task Force, 1996-2000, member of board of trustees; National Security Council, Washington, DC, staff member, 1969-71, senior staff member and special counsel, 1971-74; member of U.S. Delegation to Mutual Balance Force Reduction Talks, Vienna, Austria, 1974; Arms Control and Disarmament Agency, Washington, DC, deputy director, 1975-77; Abington Corp. (defense consulting firm), president, 1977-81; Secretary of the U.S. Navy, Washington, DC, 1981-87; Paine Webber, Inc. (investment banking corp.), New York, NY, managing director, 1988-91; Sperry Marine, Inc., New York, NY, chair, 1993-96; J.F. Lehman & Company (investment firm), New York, NY, founding partner, managing partner, and chair, c. 1990s—; OAO Technology

Solutions, Greenbelt, MD, chair, 2001. Defense Advisory Committee, Republican National Committee, chair, 1977-80; Ball Corporation, Broomfield, CO, director, 1987—; National Commission on Terrorist Attacks upon the United States, Washington, DC, commissioner, 2002-04; Insurance Services Office, Jersey City, NJ, director; SDI Inc., Huntsville, AL, director; Elgar, Inc., San Diego, CA, director. Paribas Affaires Industrielles, member of advisory board; Prince Grace Foundation, U.S.A., chair; University of Pennsylvania School of Engineering, Philadelphia, PA, member of board of overseers; honorary fellow of Gonville and Caius College, Cambridge University, Cambridge, England. Military service: U.S. Navy Reserve.

WRITINGS:

NONFICTION

(Editor, with James E. Dougherty) The Prospects for Arms Control, MacFadden-Bartell Corp. (New York, NY), 1965.
(Editor, with James E. Dougherty) Arms Control for the Late Sixties, Van Nostrand (Princeton, NJ), 1967.
The Executive, Congress, and Foreign Policy: Studies of the Nixon Administration, Praeger (New York, NY), 1974.
Aircraft Carriers: The Real Choices, Sage Publications (Beverly Hills, CA), 1978.
(With Seymour Weiss) Beyond the SALT II Failure, foreword by Richard Perle, Praeger (New York, NY), 1981.
The Launching of the U.S.S. Ohio (sound recording), Encyclopedia Americana/CBS News Audio Resources Library (New York, NY), 1981.
Maritime Strategy in the Defense of NATO: The Fourth David M. Abshire Endowed Lecture, September 25, 1986, Center for Strategic and International Studies, Georgetown University (Washington, DC), 1986.
Command of the Seas (memoir), Scribner's (New York, NY), 1988.
Making War: The 200-Year-Old Battle between the President and Congress over How America Goes to War, Scribner's (New York, NY), 1992.
On Seas of Glory: Heroic Men, Great Ships, and Epic Battles of the American Navy, Free Press (New York, NY), 2001.

(Editor, with Harvey Sicherman) *America the Vulnerable: Our Military Problems and How to Fix Them,* Foreign Policy Research Institute (Philadelphia, PA), 2002.

Also member of commission for report *The 9/11 Commission Report: Final Report of the National Commission on Terrorist Attacks Upon the United States,* W.H. Norton & Co. (New York, NY), 2004.

SIDELIGHTS: John F. Lehman, Jr., was born into a prominent Philadelphia, Pennsylvania, family and has served in various governmental and executive positions throughout his career. A long-time member of the U.S. Naval Reserve, he was the secretary of the U.S. Navy during the two terms of Ronald Reagan's presidency in the 1980s. After leaving government service, Lehman worked in investment banking, including as chair of J.F. Lehman & Company, a firm he founded. Even while focusing on banking, however, Lehman has served the federal government on occasion, most notably as a member of the National Commission on Terrorist Attacks upon the United States (commonly known as the 9/11 commission), which looked into the causes and conditions surrounding the terrorist attacks of September 11, 2001.

Many of Lehman's books focus on his experiences working in the federal government and the U.S. Navy. A Republican, he did not support the United States' ratification of the SALT II (Strategic Arms Limitations Treaty II) nor did he back President Jimmy Carter's budget cuts in the area of defense. *Aircraft Carriers: The Real Choices* is his argument for America buying and using more ships, especially nuclear-powered aircraft carriers. When Lehman served as Secretary of the U.S. Navy, he worked to increase the size of America's fleet.

The memoir *Command of the Seas* recalls Lehman's background and experiences as the U.S. Secretary of the Navy. In addition to his fight to add more ships to the U.S. Navy, he discusses personal battles with Paul Thayer, the deputy secretary of defense, and Admiral Rickover, who was eventually fired. While finding moments of poor editing of the book problematic, a reviewer for the *Economist* commented that "for those who care about how the American defense establishment really works and, more important, how it fails to work, this book must on no account be missed."

In *Making War: The 200-Year-Old Battle between the President and Congress over How America Goes to War* Lehman considers the history of declaring war in the United States, both legally and politically. Two events are particularly significant to Lehman's book: a very early Supreme Court decision that drew a distinction between "imperfect" and "solemn" wars and the passage of the 1972 War Powers Act during the administration of President Richard M. Nixon. The author also looks at the increasing importance of covert action and the strangling effect of an ever-growing bureaucracy since the Vietnam War.

Lehman offers a history of the United States Navy from the Revolutionary War to the present in *On Seas of Glory: Heroic Men, Great Ships, and Epic Battles of the American Navy.* The topic has captivated Lehman since childhood. As Lehman told Fred L. Schultz in *Naval History:* "My interest began when I was sitting around the dinner table, hearing stories that my dad would tell about his grandfather, who was in the Civil War Navy. . . . A few times, although he spoke rarely about it, he recalled his own adventures in the Navy. I've always been fascinated, obviously, with naval history. But more important, I developed an appreciation of naval people." In Lehman's book, he analyzes technological innovations, strategic changes, the role of the navy in U.S. history, and significant personalities in the development of naval forces in America. A *Publishers Weekly* reviewer commented: "This is, simply put, old-fashioned drums and trumpets military writing. Lehman knows his subject, and his folksy writing style is easy to read and comprehend."

BIOGRAPHICAL AND CRITICAL SOURCES:

BOOKS

The Cold War, 1945-1991, edited by Benjamin Frankel, Gale (Detroit, MI), 1992.
Lehman, John F., Jr., *Command of the Seas,* Scribner's (New York, NY), 1988.

PERIODICALS

Economist, February 18, 1989 review of *Command of the Seas,* p. 96.

Naval History, February, 2002, Fred L. Schultz, "An Interview with John Lehman: 'Captivated by the American Spirit,'" p. 22.

Publishers Weekly, September 10, 2001, review of *On Seas of Glory: Heroic Men, Great Ships, and Epic Battles of the American Navy,* p. 81.

ONLINE

John F. Lehman Home Page, http://www.johnflehman. com (October 22, 2005).

National Commission on Terrorist Attacks upon the United States Web site, http://www.9-11 commission.gov/ (October 7, 2005), biography of John F. Lehman, Jr.

Right-Web, http://rightweb.irc-online.org/ (October 7, 2005), biography of John F. Lehman, Jr.

* * *

LEHMAN, John Francis, Jr.
See LEHMAN, John F., Jr.

* * *

LENTRICCHIA, Frank 1940-
(Frank Lentricchia, Jr.)

PERSONAL: Surname is pronounced Len-*trick*-ya; born May 23, 1940, in Utica, NY; son of Frank John and Ann (Yacovella) Lentricchia; married Karen Young (a teacher), June 24, 1967 (divorced, 1973); married Melissa Christensen, 1973; married Jody McAuliffe (theatre director and educator); children: two. *Education:* Utica College of Syracuse University, B.A., 1962; Duke University, M.A., 1963, Ph.D., 1966.

ADDRESSES: Office—Duke University, 119 Art Museum, Durham, NC 27708. *E-mail*—frll@duke.edu.

CAREER: Writer, novelist, educator, and critic. University of California, Los Angeles, assistant professor of English and comparative literature, 1966-68; University of California, Irvine, assistant professor, 1968-70, associate professor, 1970-76, professor, 1976-82; Rice University, Houston, TX, Autrey Professor of Humanities, 1982-84; Duke University, Durham, NC, professor, 1984—, named Katherine Everett Gilbert Professor of English and Literature.

MEMBER: Modern Language Association of America.

WRITINGS:

The Gaiety of Language: An Essay on the Radical Poetics of W.B. Yeats and Wallace Stevens, University of California Press (Berkeley, CA), 1968.

Robert Frost: Modern Poetics and the Landscapes of Self, Duke University Press (Durham, NC), 1975.

(Compiler, with Melissa Christensen Lentricchia) *Robert Frost: A Bibliography, 1913-1974,* Scarecrow (Metuchen, NJ), 1976.

After the New Criticism, University of Chicago Press (Chicago, IL), 1980.

Criticism and Social Change, University of Chicago Press (Chicago, IL), 1983.

Ariel and the Police: Michel Foucault, William James, Wallace Stevens, University of Wisconsin Press (Madison, WI), 1988.

(Editor, with Thomas McLaughlin) *Critical Terms for Literary Study,* University of Chicago Press (Chicago, IL), 1990, 2nd edition, 1995.

(Editor) *Introducing Don DeLillo,* Duke University Press (Durham, NC), 1991.

(Editor) *New Essays on White Noise,* Cambridge University Press (New York, NY), 1991.

(With Edward W. Said) *Situational Tensions of Critic-Intellectuals: Thinking through Literary Politics with Edward W. Said and Frank Lentricchia,* Peter Lang (New York, NY), 1992.

The Edge of Night: A Confession, Random House (New York, NY), 1994.

Modernist Quartet, Cambridge University Press (New York, NY), 1994.

Johnny Critelli; and, The Knifemen, Scribner (New York, NY), 1996.

The Music of the Inferno (novel), State University of New York Press (Albany, NY), 1999.

Lucchesi and the Whale, Duke University Press (Durham, NC), 2001.

(With wife, Jody McAuliffe) *Crimes of Art + Terror,* University of Chicago Press (Chicago, IL), 2003.

(Editor, with Stanley Hauerwas) *Dissent from the Homeland: Essays after September 11,* Duke University Press (Durham, NC), 2003.

(Editor, with Andrew DuBois) *Close Reading: The Reader,* Duke University Press (Durham, NC), 2003.

The Book of Ruth (novel), Ravenna Press (Seattle, WA), 2005.

Contributor to *Poetry, Yale Review,* and other journals. Former editorial chair, *South Atlantic Quarterly.*

SIDELIGHTS: Frank Lentricchia is "a star in the galaxy of cultural theory," as a *Publishers Weekly* reviewer put it. The son of a house painter, Lentricchia has become one of the best known literary critics in the United States, and has received notice for writing novels and fiction/criticism hybrids unique to his pen. *National Review* contributor Jeffrey Hart wrote of Lentricchia: "He is a denizen of the infamous Duke University English Department, a major center of the brand of literary 'theory' allied with ideology that a large and aggressive segment of the professoriate has substituted for literature. Indeed, Mr. Lentricchia has been known as one of the foremost exponents of theory."

According to Terence Hawkes in the *Times Literary Supplement,* Lentricchia's book, *After the New Criticism,* is "a tough-minded account of some of the major theoretical preoccupations of literary criticism [of the late twentieth century] . . . . Its anti-idealist commitment, openly presented and tellingly deployed, gives it an attractive bite. The result is a demanding and compelling work, spirited in its deflation of a number of established reputations, and implacable in its raising of the crucial questions concerning historical consciousness which any new New Criticism must be prepared to answer." Peter Rudnytsky observed in *World Literature Today* that *After the New Criticism* "is a landmark book. Combining a masterful gift for exposition with incisive analytical rigor . . . Lentricchia offers a mapping of the contemporary critical scene on axes at once historical and theoretical."

In *Crimes of Art + Terror,* Lentricchia and his wife and coauthor, Jody McAuliffe, explore the motivations behind those who committed the September 11th terrorist attacks on the United States. Disturbingly, the authors pinpoint an "incestuous relationship between killers and writers" and that such acts are often "governed by a logic that grows out of the romantic tradition and that real terrorists take their inspiration

from books," stated reviewer Aparna Zambare in the *Library Journal.* The two authors ponder whether "Western art's post-Romantic veneration of the destructive, alienated outsider" can be "in any way answerable for the real destruction our culture brings into being," noted a *Publishers Weekly* contributor. They look at writers such as Bret Easton Ellis, Joseph Conrad, Thomas Mann, and Dostoyevsky, as well as such filmmakers as Francis Ford Coppola and Martin Scorsese, to determine how fictional and cultural concepts inspire real-life violence. The *Publishers Weekly* reviewer commented that the book's "accessible combination of conceptual daring and moral seriousness places it well above the common run of lit crit."

In addition to his numerous critical works, Lentricchia has written several works of fiction that reveal "the once-detached scholar no longer hiding, or hiding behind, his judgments and values," in the words of a *Kirkus Reviews* critic. Lentricchia bases his fiction closely on his youth in Utica, New York, but he is also well versed in a postmodern aesthetic that revels in crossing genres and bending the rules of character, plot, and purpose. A *Publishers Weekly* contributor candidly noted that *The Edge of Night: A Confession* "may be indigestible for the average reader." According to other critics, more demanding readers can find rewards in Lentricchia's work. In his *New York Times Book Review* piece on *The Edge of Night,* John Sutherland maintained that the book is "absorbing . . . because Mr. Lentricchia is an interesting and ultimately rather elusive man. In a competitive field where traditionally the cards are stacked against sons of Italian-American house painters, he has succeeded brilliantly. . . . He has refused to conform, assimilate or show his origins. It is a remarkable achievement." Writing in the *Review of Contemporary Fiction,* Irving Malin deemed *Johnny Critelli; and, The Knifemen* "an ambitious attempt to use language as matter to make it bleed." A *Publishers Weekly* reviewer noted that Lentricchia's fiction displays "a rousing capacity for language and a gritty sense of the contemporary male mind."

In *Lucchesi and the Whale,* Lentricchia combines a contemplative rumination on Melville's classic *Moby Dick* with metafictional episodes surrounding Thomas Lucchesi, a fictional reader of the novel. The author uses as a starting point the fact that the novel's title was originally hyphenated, while the whale's name is unhyphenated. Luccesi, acting as his own literary critic, goes on to present a deep reading of Melville and the novel, as well as offering sage commentary on such topics as writers and writing, sons and fathers, and the nature of death. "Lucchessi's take on *Moby-Dick* may be profound revelation or deconstructionist over-reading, but it is most definitely a pleasure," commented T.J. Gerlach in the *Review of Contemporary Fiction.*

Lucchesi reappears in Lentricchia's novel, *The Book of Ruth.* In the book, Ruth Cohen is a forty-six-year-old photographer who still bitterly regrets events that happened to her in Cuba years before. Visiting Cuba to take pictures of the daily lives of ordinary Cubans, Ruth is deceived by two Cuban double agents working for the United States. As a result, an assassination attempt on Cuban dictator Fidel Castro is botched and an innocent young girl is killed. Though Ruth's photographic portraits catapulted her to later fame, she still feels guilty for the girl's death. Almost thirty years later, she meets and marries Lucchesi and goes off to live in a remote part of the Adirondacks. In 2002, she is pulled from obscurity and is sent to Iraq to photograph Saddam Hussein in the build-up to the Iraq War. The photographs are a success, but Lucchesi is apprehended by Saddam's henchmen. A *Kirkus Reviews* critic called the novel "an extravagantly far-fetched novel that ogles celebrity even as it professes artistic detachment."

For Sutherland, both Lentricchia's fiction and his critical work reveal a unique mind at work. The critic declared: "Think of 'college professor' or 'Eliot scholar' and a tweedy, pipe-puffing, upper-class WASP (or would-be WASP) comes to mind. Mr. Lentricchia is a new breed—one for whom 'don' evokes Al Pacino playing Michael Corleone rather than C.S. Lewis."

BIOGRAPHICAL AND CRITICAL SOURCES:

BOOKS

Lentricchia, Frank, and Edward W. Said, *Situational Tensions of Critic-Intellectuals: Thinking through Literary Politics with Edward W. Said and Frank Lentricchia,* Peter Lang (New York, NY), 1992.

PERIODICALS

America, May 7, 1994, Paul Wilkes, review of *The Edge of Night: A Confession,* p. 18.

Kirkus Reviews, December 15, 2000, review of *Lucchesi and the Whale,* p. 1710; September 15, 2005, review of *The Book of Ruth,* p. 996.

Library Journal, June 15, 1980, George Rallis, review of *After the New Criticism,* p. 1389; November 1, 2003, Aparna Zambare, review of *Crimes of Art + Terror,* p. 83.

National Review, November 21, 1994, Jeffrey Hart, review of *Modernist Quartet,* p. 68.

New York Times Book Review, February 6, 1994, John Sutherland, review of *The Edge of Night,* p. 24; December 29, 1996, Lorna Sage, review of *Johnny Critelli; and, The Knifemen,* p. 7.

Publishers Weekly, January 10, 1994, review of *The Edge of Night: A Confession,* p. 51; November 4, 1996, review of *Johnny Critelli; and, The Knifemen,* p. 64; December 11, 2000, review of *Lucchesi and the Whale,* p. 62; October 27, 2003, review of *Crimes of Art + Terror,* p. 57.

Review of Contemporary Fiction, summer, 1997, Irving Malin, review of *Johnny Critelli; and, The Knifemen,* p. 294; spring, 2002, T.J. Gerlach, review of *Luccesi and the Whale,* p. 139.

Times Literary Supplement, April 17, 1981, Terence Hawkes, review of *After the New Criticism.*

World Literature Today, spring, 1981, Peter Rudnytsky, review of *After the New Criticism.*

ONLINE

Duke University, http://www.duke.edu/ (October 31, 2005), biography of Frank Lentricchia.

*   *   *

LENTRICCHIA, Frank, Jr.
   See LENTRICCHIA, Frank

*   *   *

LETTS, Billie 1938-

PERSONAL: Born May 30, 1938, in Tulsa, OK; daughter of Bill and Virginia (a secretary; maiden name, Barnes) Gipson; married Dennis Letts (a professor of English); children: Shawn, Tracy (son). *Education:* Attended Northeastern State College (now

Northeastern Oklahoma State University), 1956-58; Southeast Missouri State College (now University), B.A., 1969; Southeastern Oklahoma State University, M.A., 1974.

ADDRESSES: Home—Durant, OK. *Agent*—Elaine Markson, Elaine Markson Literary Agency, Inc., 44 Greenwich Ave., New York, NY 10011.

CAREER: Has worked variously as a waitress, window washer, dance instructor, dishwasher roller-skating car hop, secretary to a private detective, an English teacher in Cairo and Paxton, IL, a journalism teacher at Southeastern Oklahoma State, an elementary school teacher in Durant and Fillmore, OK, and as a teacher of English as a second language.

MEMBER: Writers Guild of America, Authors Guild, Oklahoma Federation of Writers.

AWARDS, HONORS: Walker Percy Award, 1994, for *Where the Heart Is;* Oklahoma Book Award, 1995, for *Where the Heart Is,* and 1998, for *The Honk and Holler Opening Soon.*

WRITINGS:

Where the Heart Is (novel), Warner Books (New York, NY), 1995.
The Honk and Holler Opening Soon (novel), Warner Books (New York, NY), 1998.
Shoot the Moon, Warner Books (New York, NY), 2004.

Contributor of stories to magazines, including *Good Housekeeping* and *North American Review.*

ADAPTATIONS: Where the Heart Is was adapted as a feature film.

SIDELIGHTS: Novelist Billie Letts is an Oklahoma native who learned early the power that words can have. The first in her class to learn how to read, she was capable of tackling more advanced books even at an early age, she related in an autobiography on the *Time Warner Bookmark* Web site. Her parents did not have a great deal of money for extras, and there were only two books in the house: the *Holy Bible* and a copy of Erskine Caldwell's *God's Little Acre.* She used the latter as the subject for a fourth-grade book report, "which caused such a stir that I knew I was on to something," she related in the online autobiography. "If I had the power to agitate a language-arts teacher in Tulsa, Oklahoma, by simply writing about someone else's writing, how much power might I have in telling my own stories? I suspect it was then, at age nine, that the idea of becoming a writer took hold."

Letts's first novel originated in a screenplay she showed to agent Elaine Markson at a writers conference in New Orleans. This prompted Markson to ask to see some short fiction Letts had written, which included a short story about an abandoned seventeen-year-old girl living at a Wal-Mart. Markson suggested that the story seemed like the beginning of a novel, and it evolved into *Where the Heart Is.* "The first time I walked into a bookstore and saw my book with my name on the cover, I was finally ready to deliver the line I'd been saying in my head since I was a kid: 'Now, at last, I'm a real writer,'" Letts remarked in her autobiography. "But I didn't say it because I suddenly knew that I'd been a real writer for almost fifty years." Letts was propelled into higher levels of success when the book was chosen for inclusion in Oprah Winfrey's Book Club, a Midas touch for a book that practically guarantees bestseller status. The novel has also been adapted as a feature film, starring popular actresses Natalie Portman and Ashley Judd.

In *Where the Heart Is* Novalee Nation, who is seventeen years old and seven months pregnant, looks forward to a better life with her boyfriend, Willy Jack Pickens. Instead of taking care of her and buying her a house, however, Willy Jack abandons her in front of a Wal-Mart Store in Sequoyah, Oklahoma. For the next two months, Novalee carefully hides out in the Wal-Mart, until the birth of her "Wal-Mart Baby" makes her a local star. The community, touched by her plight, reaches out to help. Sister Husband, an eccentric local, gives them a place to stay; photographer Moses Whitecotton sees raw talent in Novalee, and teaches her all the photographic skills he knows; Lexie Coop becomes her best friend. Even billionaire Sam Walton appears to offer her a job. The novel follows five years in the eventful, even charmed life of Novalee and her daughter. *Booklist* reviewer Kathleen Hughes observed that the novel's "emotional manipulation may be distasteful to some, others may find its soap-opera plot and Forrest Gump-ish optimism appealing." A *Publishers Weekly* reviewer commented that "Letts's wacky characters are depicted with humor and hope, as well as an earnestness that rises above the story's uneven conceits."

The Honk and Holler Opening Soon is Letts's "gently humorous second novel" that "confirms the promise of her debut," commented a reviewer in *Publishers Weekly.* Caney Paxton, a Vietnam veteran confined to a wheelchair, has never left his restaurant in Sequoyah, Oklahoma. The café, known by a signmaker's error as the Honk and Holler Opening Soon, has been stable enough to make Caney a living. Molly O, a waitress with four ex-husbands and a daughter looking to make it big in country music, serves the food without much noticing the romantic interest of a café regular. Meanwhile, Caney still regrets his part in the war, and the loss of the use of his legs, which happened not from combat but from a fall from a helicopter. During the Christmas season of 1985, things look bleak at the Honk and Holler. Bills are piling up, business is down, and the roof has a leak. Then, two remarkable new employees arrive. Crow Indian Vena Takes Horse becomes a carhop, while Vietnamese refugee Bui Khanh takes on cooking chores and handyman duties. Both Vena and Bui are hiding some secrets of their own, but they find a welcome at the Honk and Holler. Business picks up, and Vena and Caney discover a mutual attraction. The group grows even closer when an act of violence threatens Bui.

Together, the characters "create a sense of warmth and community in which reconciliation and love can flourish," noted *Library Journal* contributor Kimberly G. Allen. "This is a warm-hearted, humorous, and sometimes tear-inducing look at friendships and tolerance," commented another *Library Journal* reviewer. "Vena and Bui are sparkling creations, fresh and involving, and Letts tells the story of their impact on the town with a wonderfully light touch," noted Donna Seaman in *Booklist.* A *Publishers Weekly* contributor commented: "Even a few unresolved loose ends can't diminish the cumulative effect of this warm, sentimental tale, abundant with quirky detail and homespun wisdom," romance, and community togetherness.

In *Shoot the Moon,* the author's third novel, California veterinarian Mark Albright, born Nicky Jack Harjo, learns that he is adopted and returns to his Oklahoma home town to find out about his early life and his mother. To his sadness, he discovers that his mother, a lovely Cherokee woman named Gaylene Harjo, was murdered when he was ten years old. However, the local authorities do not seem very interested in helping him with his inquiries or giving him details about his mother's life or death. The murder was blamed on local preacher Joe Dawson, but very few in town believe that Dawson was capable of such an act. With his own investigation causing conflict with belligerent deputy Oliver Daniels, Nicky Jack becomes more and more determined to find out what happened during the tragic days of his infancy. "A great cast of small-town Oklahoma characters peppers this story with human interest, intrigue, suspense, murder, a cover-up, and a love interest," stated *Kliatt* contributor Sue Rosenzweig. *Booklist* reviewer Allison Block called the novel a "memorable tale of love, loss, humanity, and hope."

BIOGRAPHICAL AND CRITICAL SOURCES:

BOOKS

Griffis, Molly Levite, *You've Got Mail, Billie Letts,* Eakin Publications (Austin, TX), 1999.

PERIODICALS

Booklist, September 1, 1995, Kathleen Hughes, review of *Where the Heart Is,* p. 41. May 1, 1998, Donna Seaman, review of *The Honk and Holler Opening Soon,* p. 1478; August, 1999, review of *Where the Heart Is,* p. 2025; June 1, 2001, Neal Wyatt, review of *The Honk and Holler Opening Soon,* p. 1841; June 1, 2004, Allison Block, review of *Shoot the Moon,* p. 1701; November 15, 2004, Whitney Scott, review of *Shoot the Moon,* p. 606.
Chicago Tribune, August 12, 1998, review of *The Honk and Holler Opening Soon.*
Daily Times (Maryville, TN), August 11, 2005, Melanie Tucker, "Where Her 'Heart Is'—Author Billie Letts Keeps Success in Perspective."
Entertainment Weekly, July 16, 2004, Allyssa Lee, review of *Shoot the Moon,* p. 82.
Kirkus Reviews, May 15, 1998, review of *The Honk and Holler Opening Soon;* May 15, 2004, review of *Shoot the Moon,* p. 462.

Kliatt, November, 2004, Sue Rosenzweig, review of *Shoot the Moon,* p. 50.

Library Journal, July, 1995, Barbara E. Kemp, review of *Where the Heart Is,* p. 121; June 1, 1998, Kimberly G. Allen, review of *The Honk and Holler Opening Soon,* p. 154; November 15, 1998, review of *The Honk and Holler Opening Soon,* p. 124.

New York Times Book Review, August 6, 1995, Dwight Garner, review of *Where the Heart Is,* p. 20.

People Weekly, February 22, 1999, Peter Ames Carlin and Carlton Stowers, "Never Too Late: At 60, Small-Town Novelist Billie Letts Knows Success Was Worth Waiting For," p. 101.

Publishers Weekly, May 15, 1995, review of *Where the Heart Is,* p. 55; May 11, 1998, review of *The Honk and Holler Opening Soon,* p. 50.

School Library Journal, April, 1996, Pamela B. Rearden, review of *Where the Heart Is,* p. 168; January, 1999, Carol Clark, review of *The Honk and Holler Opening Soon,* p. 160.

Southern Living, August, 1998, Carly L. Price, review of *The Honk and Holler Opening Soon,* p. 48.

ONLINE

Time Warner Bookmark Web site, http://www.tw bookmark.com/ (October 8, 2005), Billie Letts, "On Billie Letts."*

*   *   *

LINDHOLM, Megan
    See OGDEN, Margaret Lindholm

*   *   *

LOMAX, Pearl
    See CLEAGE, Pearl

*   *   *

LOMAX, Pearl Cleage
    See CLEAGE, Pearl

LOTT, Bret 1958-

PERSONAL: Born October 8, 1958, in Los Angeles, CA; son of Wilman Sequoia (a corporative executive) and Barbara (a banker; maiden name, Holmes) Lott; married Melanie Kai Swank (an office manager), June 28, 1980; children: Zebulun Holmes, Jacob Daynes. *Education:* California State University, B.A., 1981; University of Massachusetts—Amherst, M.F.A., 1984. *Religion:* Christian.

ADDRESSES: Home—1215-A Meadow Park Ln., Mt. Pleasant, SC 29464. *Office*—Department of English, College of Charleston, Charleston, SC 29424. *Agent*—c/o The Puchala Agency, 595 W. Church St., #237, Orlando, FL 32805.

CAREER: Writer, novelist, educator, and editor. Big Yellow House, Santa Barbara, CA, cook's trainer, 1977-79; RC Cola, Los Angeles, CA, salesman, 1979-80; *Daily Commercial News,* Los Angeles, reporter, 1980-81; Ohio State University, Columbus, instructor in remedial English, 1984-86; College of Charleston, Charleston, SC, assistant professor of English, 1986—.

MEMBER: Associated Writing Programs, Poets and Writers.

AWARDS, HONORS: Syndicated fiction project award from PEN/National Endowment for the Arts, for "I Owned Vermont"; Ohio Arts Council fellow in literature, 1986; South Carolina Arts Commission fellow in literature, 1987-88; South Carolina syndicated fiction project award, 1987, for "Lights."

WRITINGS:

The Man Who Owned Vermont (novel), Viking (New York, NY), 1987.

A Stranger's House (novel), Viking (New York, NY), 1988.

A Dream of Old Leaves (short stories), Viking (New York, NY), 1989.

Jewel (novel), Pocket Books (New York, NY), 1991.

Reed's Beach, Pocket Books (New York, NY), 1993.

How to Get Home (novella and stories), John F. Blair (Winston-Salem, NC), 1996.

Fathers, Sons, and Brothers: The Men in My Family (essays), Harcourt (New York, NY), 1997.

The Hunt Club (novel), Villard (New York, NY), 1998.

(Editor, with W. Scott Olsen) *A Year in Place*, University of Utah Press (Salt Lake City, UT), 2001.

A Song I Knew by Heart (novel), Random House (New York, NY), 2004.

The Difference between Men and Women (short stories), Random House (New York, NY), 2005.

Before We Get Started: A Practical Memoir of the Writer's Life, Ballantine Books (New York, NY), 2005.

Short stories represented in anthology *Twenty Under Thirty*, Scribner, 1986. Contributor of fiction to periodicals, including *Missouri Review, Michigan Quarterly Review, Iowa Review, Yale Review, Yankee, Seattle Review, Redbook,* and *Confrontation;* contributor of literary reviews to periodicals, including *New York Review of Books, Los Angeles Times,* and *Michigan Quarterly Review.* Editor, *Southern Review.*

SIDELIGHTS: Bret Lott is a writer of short stories and novels, as well as the editor of *Southern Review.* Lott has also worked in sales, experience which he brings to bear in his first novel, *The Man Who Owned Vermont.* Rick Wheeler, a Massachusetts soft drink salesman who both knowingly and unknowingly sabotages his marriage, is the protagonist of the book. With a life and marriage that fall short of his expectations, Rick is often sullen and self-defeating. On one occasion he refuses to stop the car to let his pregnant wife find a bathroom, and her subsequent miscarriage—along with the guilt and blame—trigger a growing breach that culminates in separation. Only then, as Rick tries to connect with others in order to fill the emptiness, does he recognize his complicity in the gradual disintegration of the relationship. "It is the story of the unwitting betrayals that slowly erode his marriage . . . that eventually leads him to greater self-knowledge—and back to his wife," commented Lori B. Miller in the *New York Times Book Review.* "Mr. Lott knows how ordinary people work and love (or try to love), and knows how intractable, even perverse, human feelings can be," wrote Michiko Kakutani in the *New York Times.* "He shows us how small lies and resentments can fester into something ugly and irrevocable, and he shows us, as well, the redemptive powers of love."

Writing in *Time* magazine, one critic perceived Wheeler's story as a tale of ordinary human courage.

"Given every reason to surrender, he struggles on," the reviewer reflected. "*The Man Who Owned Vermont* is a vivid example of mind and spirit grappling with oppressive fates." Carolyn See, writing in the *Los Angeles Times,* made similar comments when she stated: "What makes this narrative so engrossing is the pure familiarity of it. If Brett Lott isn't lying, this is one of the most interesting stories on the sadness of American men that's out there in our world." Discussing *The Man Who Owned Vermont* in the *Washington Post,* Dennis Drabelle found in the "unrelieved dreariness" of Wheeler's world "surprising vividness, even a kind of stark beauty." "This novel manages to capture ordinary life's poetic—and tragic—moments," Miller similarly observed. "Mr. Lott's . . . storytelling . . . is subtle but powerful; his prose, uncluttered and simple. Yet the story he chooses to tell demonstrates a profound understanding of human interaction and the precarious condition called marriage."

Lott presents a different kind of family dynamic in his first thriller novel, *The Hunt Club.* Fifteen-year-old Huger Dillard, the protagonist, helps his blind uncle run a primitive backwoods hunting club for wealthy patrons, largely physicians, from Charleston, SC. Huger serves as his uncle's eyes, but nothing prepares them for the Saturday when they find a headless corpse, labeled with a cardboard sign identifying the deceased as Dr. Charles Middleton Simons, and identifying the murderer as his wife. But she is later found hanged in a hotel room. From this harrowing beginning, the story proceeds as Huger and his uncle find themselves in real danger, with someone after their apparently worthless Carolina swampland. *Booklist* reviewer Joanne Wilkinson noted that the book is promoted as a thriller, but "at the heart of this wonderfully well written novel is a haunting coming-of-age story." Thomas L. Kilpatrick, writing in the *Library Journal,* called the book "a good read with action, suspense, and a hint of Southern folklore."

In 1999, Lott's literary career, for many years low-key, received a tremendous boost when his novel, *Jewel,* was selected as part of Oprah Winfrey's TV book club. The novel tells the story of Jewel Hilburn, a devoted Mississippi wife and mother of three sons and a daughter. When her sixth child, Brenda Kay, is born, the infant girl suffers from Down's syndrome, and a once-tranquil family life is thrown into turmoil. Jewel is fiercely determined that Brenda Kay will have the best care possible, and the girl becomes the family's entire focus. Many of the other characters' own dreams and ambitions wither in the face of this new reality, including husband Leston's hopes of owning a lumber yard. Jewel's decision to move the family to California to ensure Brenda Kay's education, however, ignites conflict between her and Leston that even love and compassion for the child cannot overcome. Lott "expertly realizes a stubborn, faithful mother and her phenomenally unselfish, supportive family," commented a *Publishers Weekly* reviewer.

A Song I Knew by Heart is a "highly emotional depiction of grief and its aftermath," commented Joanne Wilkinson in *Booklist*. Naomi, a widow in her seventies, has already suffered the profound grief of the loss of her spouse, Eli, whom she had known since childhood. She is devastated when her son, Mahlon, is killed in a car accident. As Naomi and widowed daughter-in-law Ruth endure the bitter pain together, Naomi decides to return to her childhood home in South Carolina. Ruth, with no ties left to keep her in the north, accompanies her. Together, the two women, bound by death, face aspects of their pasts, endure the dreadful present, and look toward a better future. Wilkinson called the book "a radiant, achingly tender portrait of the grieving process."

In his collection *The Difference between Men and Women*, "the universe of Bret Lott's stories is the uncertainty of family life," noted reviewer Edith Alston in the *Weekly Standard*. In one story, a man uses an unfortunate turn of phrase while traveling in a car with his wife. Upon reaching home, he discovers that his marriage of twenty-seven years is now in jeopardy. "Most of the stories eerily border the edge of an alternate universe," Alston commented. When a man admits an affair to his wife in another story, he is confident that the two of them will be able to get through the difficult situation. However, he is unaware that, in his wife's view and in reality, he has already begun to vanish, bit by bit. "The Train, the Lake, the Bridge" is the "real jewel" of the collection, Alston stated, "a memory piece, and a ghost story without ghosts" in which haunting events from the narrator's Depression-era boyhood in New England figure prominently. In "Rose," Lott revisits the characters, settings, and events of William Faulkner's extraordinary short story, "A Rose for Emily." The "characters Lott plays witness to inhabit today's world, where marriage and parenthood are fragile states, never very far removed from disintegration," Alston observed.

As a writer of essays, novels, and short stories, Lott has considerable experience in the literary world. With *Before We Get Started: A Practical Memoir of the Writer's Life,* he offers a collection of advice and insight geared toward the neophyte writer. Lott "takes on the art of writing by focusing on creativity and guiding the writer to certain realities of the craft," noted Loree Davis in the *Library Journal.* A combination of memoir and instruction, Lott's book recounts the difficulties from his early days as a writer, prior to being selected as an Oprah writer, when he had to balance the needs of his family with a teaching job that drained time from his writing schedule. He encourages writers to pay attention to the weight and importance of every word in a story, and to work hard to make time to write even in a frenetically busy life. "Beginning writers will appreciate the heartfelt supportiveness of his counsel as he imparts encouragement and insight," noted a *Publishers Weekly* critic, and as he speaks about writing and publishing "with resounding candor and sincerity."

Lott told *CA:* "Though I'd always enjoyed writing—whether letters, or essays for school—the idea of being a writer never really occurred to me until I was a senior in college, after first having been a forestry major, then a marine biology major, then quitting school to work as a salesman, then coming back to school with the notion of teaching high school. But finally, in my senior year, my teacher John Herman suggested I go on for a master's degree, which I did. At the University of Massachusetts—Amherst I studied under Jay Neugeboren and James Baldwin, and my first stories started appearing in *Writer's Forum,* the *Yale Review,* and the *Iowa Review.* After graduation I got a job teaching five sections of remedial English each quarter at Ohio State University. Even though we had our first child then, and even though I was teaching so much, I managed to sneak down to the basement of our apartment each morning at about 4:30 to write for a couple of hours before my wife, Melanie, and Zeb woke up. In that way I was able to complete *The Man Who Owned Vermont.*

"All my writings, whether short stories or novels, are about working people—people who have to sort through their personal lives and problems while working to pay bills and put food in the refrigerator. I think this comes from the fact that my family is a working one (I was the first person to go to college in the Lott family in three generations). My brothers and sister and wife and in-laws and most friends all work forty hours a week; that seems real to me—not a professor's life or a writer's life that so many people imagine is glamorous and full of interesting activities. And so writing is for me my own work, my job, what I do. And though it is work, I still have a blast every time I sit down at my desk, imagining the lives of other people and putting them down on paper. In the *Georgia Review,* Steven Corey called *The Man Who Owned Vermont* 'a delicate and wise view of working and loving in modern America.' These are indeed the themes I want to write about, the concerns I want to capture in my fiction."

BIOGRAPHICAL AND CRITICAL SOURCES:

PERIODICALS

Booklist, August, 1996, Jim O'Laughlin, review of *How to Get Home,* p. 1882; May 1, 1997, Brian McCombie, review of *Fathers, Sons, and Brothers: The Men in My Family,* p. 1474; February 1, 1998, Joanne Wilkinson, review of *The Hunt Club,* p. 899; February 15, 2004, Joanne Wilkinson, review of *A Song I Know by Heart,* p. 1003.

Books & Culture, September-October, 2005, Susan Wise Bauer, review of *The Difference between Women and Men,* p. 31.

Library Journal, June 1, 1987, James B. Hemesath, review of *The Man Who Owned Vermont,* p. 129; June 15, 1997, William Gargan, review of *Fathers, Sons, and Brothers,* p. 69; January, 1998, Thomas L. Kilpatrick, review of *The Hunt Club,* p. 142; March 1, 2004, Robin Nesbitt, review of *A Song I Know by Heart,* p. 108; January 1, 2005, Loree Davis, review of *Before We Get Started,* p. 112.

Los Angeles Times, July 6, 1987, Carolyn See, review of *The Man Who Owned Vermont.*

New York Times, June 6, 1987, Michiko Kakutani, review of *The Man Who Owned Vermont,* p. 12.

New York Times Book Review, July 12, 1987, Lori B. Miller, review of *The Man Who Owned Vermont,* p. 20.

Publishers Weekly, May 1, 1987, Sybil Steinberg, review of *The Man Who Owned Vermont,* p. 54; August 23, 1991, review of *Jewel,* p. 46; August 16, 1993, review of *Reed's Beach,* p. 85; June 17, 1996, review of *How to Get Home,* p. 48; January 25, 1999, Daisy Maryles, "A Jewel of a Pick," p. 20; November 22, 2004, review of *Before We Get Started,* p. 52.

Time, July 27, 1987, review of *The Man Who Owned Vermont,* p. 65.

Tribune Books, August 7, 1988, review of *A Stranger's House,* p. 6.

Washington Post, August 14, 1987, Dennis Drabelle, review of *The Man Who Owned Vermont.*

Weekly Standard, August 15, 2005, Edith Alston, review of *The Difference between Women and Men,* p. 39.

Wilson Library Bulletin, September, 1987, Ben Davis, review of *The Man Who Owned Vermont,* p. 101.

ONLINE

Bret Lott Home Page, http://www.bretlott.com (October 31, 2005).*

*　　*　　*

LUBIN, David M. 1950-

PERSONAL: Born November 24, 1950, in Columbus, OH; son of Samuel (a businessman) and Louise (a writer; maiden name, Stone) Lubin; married Elizabeth Warner (a writer), May 7, 1977; children: Molly, Gus. *Education:* Attended Principia College, 1968-70, and University of Southern California, 1971-72; Ohio State University, B.A., 1973; Yale University, M.A., 1980, Ph.D., 1983.

ADDRESSES: Home—Fairfield, ME. *Office*—Department of Arts History, Wake Forest University, 101 Scales Fine Art Center, 1834 Wake Forest Rd., Winston-Salem, NC 27106. *Agent*—Gail Hochman, Brandt & Brandt, 1501 Broadway, New York, NY 10036. *E-mail*—lubin@wfu.edu.

CAREER: UNESCO, Paris, France, administrative assistant, 1974-75; Colby College, Waterville, ME, assistant professor of art and American studies, 1983-99; Wake Forest University, Winston-Salem, NC, C. Weber Professor of Art, 1999—.

MEMBER: American Studies Association, College Art Association of America, Society for Cinema Studies.

AWARDS, HONORS: Fellow of American Council of Learned Societies and Andrew W. Mellon fellow, Standard Humanities Center, both 1986-87; Charles C. Eldredge Prize, Smithsonian American Art Museum, 2004, for outstanding scholarship in American art.

WRITINGS:

Act of Portrayal: Eakins, Sargent, James, Yale
    University Press (New Haven, CT), 1985.
*Picturing a Nation: Art and Social Change in
    Nineteenth-Century America,* Yale University
    Press (New Haven, CT), 1994.
Titanic, BFI Publishing (London, England), 1999.
Shooting Kennedy: JFK and the Culture of Images,
    University of California Press (Berkeley, CA),
    2003.

Contributor to periodicals, including *Rolling Stone.*

WORK IN PROGRESS: A study of modern visual
culture in Europe and the United States from 1830s to
the present.

SIDELIGHTS: Art historian David M. Lubin addresses
areas in his books where art and culture meet, and
how art influences social issues and the basic fabric of
American culture. *Picturing a Nation: Art and Social
Change in Nineteenth-Century America* contains six
essays by Lubin, each dedicated to a single artist or
particular work of art, that are "sustained inquiries
into the relationship between visual images and the
personal, social and historical issues that have shaped
experience within our particular culture," commented
reviewer Angela Miller in *Art in America.* "Lubin's
approach is unusual," Miller further observed. "Historically grounded, theoretically informed and often
wonderfully intelligent, it is also speculative, allusive
and open-ended in its readings." He discusses artists
such as George Caleb Bingham, whose painting *Emigration of Daniel Boone* represents early settlers'
willing, even eager, entry into the wilderness to
discover the riches there. Lubin suggests that the painting expresses Bingham's ambivalence toward slavery.
Though slaves were important to Boone's expedition,
they are absent from the painting. However, critics
such as *Art Bulletin* contributor Eric M. Rosenberg
indicated that it is "just as likely that they are assumed
to be in the background. unavailable to the eye trained
on that part of the wilderness experience reserved for
dominance, patriarchy," and other subjects informing
the painting. Lubin interprets the realistic trompe l'oeil
paintings of William Harnett as "a fascinating explica-
tion of commodity fetishism and male identity formation in late 19th-century New York," Rosenberg also

noted. By including consideration of a female artist
and an African-American artist, "Lubin lays claim to a
new inclusiveness, bringing the contemporary concerns
of multiculturalism to his reading of the past while
also providing historical evidence for his insistence
upon the multivocal nature of American culture,"
Miller stated. "This is a challenging and provocative
text," Rosenberg concluded. "It should not and cannot
be ignored. It must, however, be read critically,
subjected to the same barrage of questions to which it
in turn subjects its material. Lubin wouldn't have it
any other way; he says as much and we can only take
him at his word, a word that is often fascinating but as
frequently deserves argument."

With *Shooting Kennedy: JFK and the Culture of
Images,* which *Winterthur Portfolio* contributor James
C. Curtis called "a masterpiece of material culture
scholarship," Lubin analyzes images from one of the
twentieth century's signal events: the assassination of
President John F. Kennedy. He "examines some of the
twentieth century's most unforgettable images and
through them fashions a fascinating and fresh appraisal
of modern American culture," Curtis remarked. Lubin
"provides a series of provocative essays about how
perceptions of the Kennedys have become part of our
national memory," noted *Library Journal* reviewers
Karl Helicher and Michael A. Genovese. John and Jacqueline Kennedy "became such dominant personalities
because the public associated them with enduring
themes of classical and popular culture," Helicher and
Genovese commented. For example, both the
Kennedys and the most popular television show of the
day, *The Beverly Hillbillies,* tended to take an amused,
even satirical approach to the foibles of the rich.
Kennedy himself cultivated a masculine, macho image,
polished by his fondness for James Bond novels. The
comparison of Kennedy's era to the fabled land of
Camelot was easily accepted by an American public
shocked and grief-stricken by the president's violent
death. Through it all, the popular perception was
enhanced by visual images that supported the message
that the Kennedys wanted to get across in photographs
and portraits. "At once stodgy and delirious, unexpectedly brilliant and brilliantly spurious, appropriately
world historical and facetiously ahistoric, *Shooting
Kennedy* is a book that, Lubin suggests, advances its
own conspiracy theory" by looking at and considering
previously unnoticed connections between the visual
representation of the Kennedy legend and the reality
of his life and death, commented reviewer J. Hoberman in *Artforum International.* "The daring of Lubin's

approach is as instructive as his often startling results" and conclusions, wrote a *Publishers Weekly* reviewer. Curtis concluded that "gathered together, intertwined and animated by a lyrical narrative, these [visual] manifestations of material culture help us understand the media-made world we live in."

Lubin once told *CA:* "My writing is concerned not only with specific works of art and literature but also with the historical, philosophic, and social issues that these works embody. In *Act of Portrayal* I applied a formal, compositional analysis to three works of American portraiture ('character depiction') from the 1880's and discovered how each of these works concerns itself with matters such as the tension between masculine and feminine characteristics, the connections between verbal and visual types of expression, and the underlying conflicts between traditional authority (social, familial, artistic) and the desire to be free of that authority.

"Two of the works I studied are paintings (Thomas Eakins's 'The Agnew Clinic' and John Singer Sargent's 'The Boit Children'), while one is a novel (*The Portrait of a Lady* by Henry James), but in each instance, the portrait is more than simply a portrait. It is also a portrait *about* portraiture, or, in other words, about the ways in which we look at each other and make 'portraits' of one another. Thus *Act of Portrayal* deals not only with art and society of a century ago but also with that of today, inasmuch as it devotes considerable attention to how our perception of people in the real world is related to our perception of characters in fiction and painting, and is determined by many of the same social forces.

"While the *Virginia Quarterly* was impressed by the book's procedure, the *American Art Journal* found *Act of Portrayal* 'quite a nasty, irresponsible piece of work—and an X-rated one at that.' Indeed, *Act of Portrayal* has raised controversy by its insistent analysis of three classic works of American art and literature in terms of sexual politics, psychoanalysis, class conflict, and deconstruction."

BIOGRAPHICAL AND CRITICAL SOURCES:

PERIODICALS

Art Bulletin, September, 1995, Eric M. Rosenberg, review of *Picturing a Nation: Art and Social Change in Nineteenth-Century America,* p. 507.

Artforum International, January, 2004, J. Hoberman, "President's Day," review of *Shooting Kennedy: JFK and the Culture of Images,* p. 29.

Art in America, February, 1995, Angela Miller, review of *Picturing a Nation,* p. 31.

Library Journal, November 1, 2003, Karl Helicher and Michael A. Genovese, "Forty Years from Dallas," review of *Shooting Kennedy,* p. 96

Publishers Weekly, October 27, 2003, review of *Shooting Kennedy,* p. 57.

Winterthur Portfolio, spring, 2004, James C. Curtis, review of *Shooting Kennedy,* p. 97.

ONLINE

Wake Forest University Department of Art History Web site, http://www.wfu.edu/academics/art/ (October 5, 2005), biography of David Lubin.*

M

MARIN, Cheech 1946-
(Richard Anthony Marin)

PERSONAL: Born Richard Anthony Marin, July 13, 1946, in Los Angeles, CA; son of Oscar and Elsa (Meza) Marin; married Rikki Mae Morley, November 1, 1975 (divorced); married Patti Heid (a painter), 1984; children: three. *Education:* California State University, Northridge, B.A.

ADDRESSES: Home—San Francisco, CA. *Agent*—c/o Author Mail, Bulfinch Press, 1271 Avenue of the Americas, New York, NY 10020.

CAREER: Comedian, actor, and screenwriter, beginning c. 1969; formed improvisational theater group City Works, and comedy team Cheech and Chong with Tommy Chong, and performed in clubs and concert halls throughout the United States and Canada. Appeared in films, including *Up in Smoke,* 1978, *Cheech and Chong's Next Movie,* 1980, *Cheech and Chong's Nice Dreams,* 1981, *Things Are Tough All Over,* 1982, *It Came from Hollywood,* 1982, *Still Smokin',* 1983, *Yellowbeard,* 1983, *Cheech and Chong's "The Corsican Brothers,"* 1984, *After Hours,* 1985, *Echo Park,* 1986, *Born in East L.A.,* 1987, *Fatal Beauty,* 1987, *Ghostbusters II,* 1989, *Rude Awakening,* 1989; *Troop Beverly Hills,* 1989, *Far Out Man,* 1991, *The Shrimp on the Barbie,* 1990, *Desperado,* 1995, *Tin Cup,* 1996, *The Great White Hype,* 1996, *From Dusk Till Dawn,* 1996, *Paulie,* 1998, *Picking Up The Pieces,* 2000, *Spy Kids, Spy Kids 2: Island of Lost Dreams,* 2002, *Spy Kids 3-D: Game Over,* 2003, *Once upon a Time in Mexico,* 2003, and *Christmas with the Kranks,* 2004.

Provided voice work for films, including *Oliver & Company,* 1988, *Ferngulley: The Last Rainforest,* 1993, *The Lion King,* 1994, *It's Tough to Be a Bug,* 1999, and *The Lion King 1 1/2,* 2004. Director of films, including *Born in East L.A.,* 1987. Appeared on television series, including *The Tracey Ullman Show,* 1987, *The Golden Palace,* 1992, *Nash Bridges,* 1996, and *Judging Amy,* 2004-05; appeared in television specials, including *Get Out of My Room,* 1985, and *Charlie Barnett—Terms of Enrollment,* 1986; appeared in television films, including *The Cisco Kid,* 1994. Director of television specials, including *Get Out of My Room,* 1985. Producer of six episodes of a comedy series for Fox Television starring Latino comedy team Culture Clash, 1991; narrator for audio books, including *The Milagro Beanfield War* by John Nichols.

AWARDS, HONORS: Grammy Award (with Tommy Chong) from National Academy of Recording Arts and Sciences, Best Comedy Record, 1973, for *Los Cochinos;* ALMA Community Service Award, National Council of La Raza, 1999; Creative Achievement Award, Imagen Foundation, 2000.

WRITINGS:

SCREENPLAYS

(With Tommy Chong) *Up in Smoke,* Paramount, 1978.
(With Tommy Chong) *Cheech and Chong's Next Movie,* Universal, 1980.
(With Tommy Chong) *Cheech and Chong's Nice Dreams,* Columbia, 1981.

(With Tommy Chong) *Things Are Tough All Over,* Columbia, 1982.

(With Tommy Chong) *Still Smokin',* Paramount, 1983.

(With Tommy Chong) *Cheech and Chong's "The Corsican Brothers,"* Orion, 1984.

(And director) *Born in East L.A.,* Universal, 1987.

COMEDY RECORDINGS

(With Tommy Chong) *Cheech and Chong,* Ode, 1972.

(With Tommy Chong) *Los Cochinos,* Warner Brothers, 1973.

(With Tommy Chong) *Wedding Album,* Warner Brothers, 1974.

(With Tommy Chong) *Sleeping Beauty,* Warner Brothers, 1976.

(With Tommy Chong) *Up in Smoke,* Warner Brothers, 1978.

(With Tommy Chong) *Get Out of My Room,* MCA, 1985.

My Name Is Cheech, the School Bus Driver (for children), Ode to Kids, 1992.

OTHER

(Contributor) *The Latino Holiday Book: From Cinco de Mayo to Dia de los Muertos—the Celebrations and Traditions of Hispanic-Americans,* Publishers Group West (New York, NY), 2000.

Chicano Visions: American Painters on the Verge, Little, Brown (Boston, MA), 2002.

Also recorded *Big Bambu, Let's Make a New Dope Deal,* and *Greatest Hits,* all with Tommy Chong; wrote and recorded the hit single, "Born in East L.A.," MCA, 1985.

SIDELIGHTS: Comedy writer and performer Cheech Marin is famous for his albums and films with early comedic partner Tommy Chong. Together Cheech and Chong became renowned for their drug-related humor, prompting an *American Film* critic reviewing their first motion picture, *Up in Smoke,* to hail them as "the Laurel and Hardy of dope." The duo saw their popularity rise during the 1970s, winning a 1973 Grammy Award for Best Comedy Record for *Los Cochinos.* They collaborated on the screenplays for several other films following *Up in Smoke,* including *Things Are*

Tough All Over, Still Smokin', and *Cheech and Chong's "The Corsican Brothers."* After Cheech and Chong went their separate ways, Marin wrote, directed, and starred in the successful motion picture comedy *Born in East L.A.;* he has also performed in more mainstream television and film roles, and used his voice talent for several animated features, including Disney's *The Lion King.*

Marin began his association with Chong during the late 1960s. At first Marin and Chong formed a small theater group with others called "City Works"; then they decided to split off on their own as a comedy duo. Their recorded comedy albums, featuring jokes about smoking pot and using hallucinogens, eventually brought them a large enough following—particularly among teenagers and college students—to encourage them to take their act to the big screen. In 1978 Cheech and Chong released *Up in Smoke.* Critical opinion has varied on this project, and on all of the pair's movie efforts. Some deplored the advocation of drug use, others lambasted the low bathroom humor that Cheech and Chong mixed with their marijuana jokes. Others found the films uneven and lacking professional polish, but extremely funny. Fans and detractors alike called the plots minimal. In *Up in Smoke,* Marin picks up hitchhiker Chong after the latter is kicked out of the home of his well-to-do parents. The two decide to form a rock band, but persecution by the police lead them to travel to Tijuana. They must return, however, in time to enter their band in a contest; the only available transportation back from Mexico proves to be a fantastic vehicle composed solely of marijuana compressed into something called "fibreweed." *Up in Smoke* was made on a very small budget, yet managed to gross twenty-eight million dollars at the box office.

Marin and Chong's next screenwriting collaboration, released in 1980, bore the title *Cheech and Chong's Next Movie.* The plot concerns the pair's involvement with a stand-up comic and a rich spinster. The cast also included Marin's wife, Rikki, whom he married in 1975. She continued to play roles in the comedy team's subsequent motion pictures. The following year brought *Cheech and Chong's Nice Dreams* to the screen—this vehicle featured the duo as ice cream vendors who also dole out drugs to their customers.

In 1982's *Things Are Tough All Over,* Marin and Chong each take dual roles—as themselves, and as a pair of rich Arabs who hire their other personas to drive a limousine secretly stuffed with cash. *Things Are Tough All Over* is something of a departure in that it contains only one instance of drug usage—Chong eating a peyote button. *Still Smokin'*, which was released in 1983, however, re-established Cheech and Chong as commentators on the drug culture. This film includes a large quantity of concert footage, as well as a connecting plot concerning the Amsterdam Film Festival.

An even bigger departure from their usual subject matter came with 1984's *Cheech and Chong's "The Corsican Brothers."* Marin and Chong took the classic short story by Alexandre Dumas—about twin brothers during the French Revolution who each feel physical pain when the other is wounded—and played it strictly for laughs. *The Corsican Brothers*, however, proved to be the last screenwriting collaboration between Marin and Chong. The pair occasionally appeared together in the films of others, as in 1983's *Yellowbeard*, but creatively they went their separate ways. Of the characters he created with Chong, Marin explained to Susan King in the *Los Angeles Times*: "I didn't want to keep doing that and he did . . . We had grown out of those guys. At some point, it becomes pathetic and not funny."

Marin's first solo screenwriting effort grew out of a musical video parody he did of rock singer Bruce Springsteen's hit, "Born in the U.S.A." He got the original idea when he read of a case in which a fourteen-year-old Hispanic, born a U.S. citizen, was accidentally deported in an Immigration and Naturalization Services (INS) round-up of illegal aliens. Marin then expanded his adapted spoof into the 1987 film *Born in East L.A.*, which he also directed and starred in. Marin's character in the film, Rudy Robles, is a third-generation American citizen of Mexican descent. Summoned by his more recently immigrated cousin to give him a ride home from work, Robles leaves the house without his wallet. When the factory where his cousin works is raided by the INS, his cousin escapes, but Robles is sent to Tijuana. His somewhat naive cousin interprets his call for help as a message from Jesus Christ, while his more competent relatives are vacationing elsewhere in California.

Once in Tijuana, Robles must work in order to pay a smuggler of illegal aliens to take him back to the United States. He raises the money by playing in a mariachi band, giving tattoos, providing fake passports,

and selling oranges. During this process, he meets many memorable characters who share his desire to enter the United States, including an El Salvadoran woman with whom he falls in love.

New York Times reviewer Caryn James did not especially like the film, but lauded "Marin's appealing performance as . . . a straight-arrow cousin of the laid-back, dope-smoking character he usually plays." She further declared that "Marin may be a greatly underrated actor."

Since *Born in East L.A.*, Marin has been involved in an acting capacity in several projects devoted to furthering the opportunities and bettering the image of Hispanics in the arts. He performed in a public television presentation of the Spanish miracle play *La Pastorella*, and starred as Pancho in an updated, less stereotypical cable version of *The Cisco Kid*. Marin described Pancho in the *New York Times* as "a true revolutionary who represents Mexico trying to regain its independence. He's very volatile, very loyal, very stubborn." Marin has also done several projects for children in recent years, including a record album called *My Name Is Cheech, the School Bus Driver*. He has created voice roles in animated films for Disney, in addition to working with Chong again in the animated *Ferngulley: The Last Rainforest*. Marin has also acted in a number of popular movies, including the *Spy Kids* trilogy, *Once Upon a Time in Mexico*, and *Christmas with the Kranks*. Because of his work, Marin was the recipient of the 2000 Creative Achievement Award from the Imagen Foundation.

Beyond Marin's work in film, the actor and comedian is one of the largest collectors of Chicano art. This is the subject of his 2002 book, *Chicano Visions: American Painters on the Verge*. Chicano artwork is noted for its combination of traditional Mexican images and styles with American pop. The book features the work of more than thirty artists, including John Valadez, Gronk, Diane Gamboa, and Adan Hernandez. Marin writes the book's introduction, and art critic Max Benavidez provides essays on the works.

Critics lauded Marin's work in publishing *Chicano Visions*. Many found this art movement to be under-represented in literature, and welcomed Marin's contribution. "Marin is . . . a pioneer in recognizing the vibrancy and significance of Chicano art," wrote

Booklist contributor Donna Seaman. Others enjoyed Marin's specific selections and believed that the author highlighted each piece thoughtfully. "Short essays provide historical context, but *Chicano Visions* is primarily an art book, with gorgeous, full-page reproductions," noted Robert Ito in a review for *Los Angeles Magazine.*

BIOGRAPHICAL AND CRITICAL SOURCES:

BOOKS

Almanac of Famous People, 7th edition, Gale (Detroit, MI), 2000.
Contemporary Theatre, Film, and Television, Volume 45, Gale (Detroit, MI), 2002.
Dictionary of Hispanic Biography, Gale (Detroit, MI), 1996.
Newsmakers 2000, Issue 1, Gale (Detroit, MI), 2000.

PERIODICALS

Adweek Western Edition, July 15, 1990, Shelly Garcia, "Cheech Marin Turns on to Advertising," p. 6; September 24, 1990, Dan Cray, "Cheech Marin's New Stash," p. 4.
American Film, November, 1990, Frank Thompson, review of *Up in Smoke,* p. 56.
America's Intelligence Wire, August 27, 2003, "Interview with Katie Roiphe, Rick Marin;" February 13, 2005, "Cheech and Chong Played It Straight on the Movie Set"; August 1, 2005, "Chicano Art"; August 9, 2005, "American Voices"; August 12, 2005, "Chicano Art."
Back Stage, June 15, 1990, Robert Goldrich, "Comedian Cheech Marin to Direct Spots," p. 6.
Booklist, November 15, 2002, Donna Seaman, review of *Chicano Visions: American Painters on the Verge,* p. 560.
Christian Science Monitor, December 17, 1991, Alan Bunce, review of *La Pastorela,* p. 10.
Daily Variety, May 12, 2003, Scott Hettrick, "Goldberg, Marin Roar Back in 'Lion,'" p. 21; September 9, 2003, "Helmer Leads 'Mexico' Jam," p. 15; February 8, 2005, Deborah Netburn, "Back in Smoke," p. 1.
Entertainment Weekly, February 4, 1994, Bruce Fretts, "To Cheech his Own," p. 44; May 6, 1994, Glenn Kenny, review of *Ring of the Musketeers,* p. 70;

July 29, 1994, Michael Sauter, review of *The Cisco Kid,* p. 64; August 25, 1995, Owen Gleiberman, review of *Desperado,* p. 90; August 16, 1996, Owen Gleiberman, review of *Tin Cup,* p. 44; September 27, 1996, Michale Sauter, review of *Oliver and Company,* p. 88; December 20, 1996, Ira Robbins, review of *Tin Cup,* p. 82; April 23, 1998, review of *Paulie,* p. 58; September 9, 2005, Lisa Schwarzbaum, review of *Underclassman,* p. 127.
Family Circle, September 20, 1994, Jeffrey Lyons, review of *The Lion King,* p. 148.
Film Journal International, September, 2003, "New Line," p. 32.
Glamour, September, 1989, David Denicolo, review of *Rude Awakening,* p. 210.
GQ, January, 1990, Patrice Serrani, "Splendor without Grass," p. 28.
Hispanic, September, 1996, Valerie Menard, "Cheech Enjoys Second Career in TV," p. 12; October, 2001, Cathy Areu Jones, "Cheech Marin's New Mission," p. 48.
Hollywood Reporter, November 11, 2002, Nellie Andreeva, "Marin Plays Pop on NBC's 'Ortegas,'" p. 3; July 23, 2003, Cynthia Littleton, "Cheech and Chong Take Another Hit," p. 1; September 10, 2003, "Marin Cops Role as Police Boss in 'Underclassman,'" p. 4; September 15, 2003, Ray Richmond, "Latin Kings of Comedy," p. 18.
In Style, January 15, 2004, John Griffiths, "It Takes a Village," p. 422.
Knight Ridder/Tribune News Service, December 2, 1996, Steve Hall, "Cheech Marin's Career Is Hardly up in Smoke."
Los Angeles Magazine, August, 1996, Peter Rainer, review of *Tin Cup,* p. 145; November, 2002, Robert Ito, "Art Nuevo," p. 136; April, 2003, Abel Salas, "Comic Drive: On the Greens with George Lopez and Cheech Marin," p. 17.
Los Angeles Times, May 11, 1983, Linda Gross, "Cheech and Chong Still Smokin," p. 6; August 24, 1985, Chris Willman, "Cheech and Chong Enjoy Rebirth 'In East L.A.,'" p. 1; September 19, 1992, Susan King, interview with Marin, p. 1; December 1, 2002, review of *Chicano Visions,* p. 8.
National Review, September 16, 1996, John Simon, review of *Tin Cup,* p. 67.
Newsweek, June 29, 1981, David Ansen, review of *Cheech and Chong's Nice Dreams,* p. 71; September 4, 1989, David Ansen, review of *Rude Awakening,* p. 68.

New York, August 11, 1980, David Denby, review of *Cheech and Chong's Next Movie,* p. 40; February 7, 1994, John Leonard, review of *The Cisco Kid,* p. 60; June 20, 1994, David Denby, review of *The Lion King,* p. 79; August 26, 1996, David Denby, review of *Tin Cup,* p. 117.

New Yorker, August 12, 1996, Terrence Rafferty, review of *Tin Cup,* p. 78.

New York Times, August 9, 1982, Janet Maslin, review of *Things Are Tough All Over,* p. 14; May 7, 1983, Vincent Canby, review of *Still Smokin',* p. 12; September 13, 1985, Vincent Canby, review of *After Hours,* p. 20; August 24, 1987, Caryn James, review of *Born in East L.A.,* p. 14; May 22, 1988, Patricia T. O'Conner, review of *Born in East L.A.,* p. 30; August 16, 1989, Vincent Canby, review of *Rude Awakening,* p. 19; December 23, 1991, Jon Pareles, review of *La Pastorela,* p. 11; January 30, 1994, p. 32; February 5, 1994, John O'Connor, review of *The Cisco Kid,* p. 17; March 29, 1996, Caryn James, "Nash Bridges," p. 20.

People, September 22, 1980, Gail Buchalter, "Cheech and Chong's Joint Career Is a Smoke Screen," p. 85; July 20, 1981, review of *Cheech and Chong's Nice Dreams,* p. 15; July 11, 1983, Jack Friedman, "A Tale of Two Musketeers," p. 26; September 14, 1987, Tom Cunneff, review of *Born in East L.A.,* p. 14; November 21, 1988, Peter Travers, review of *Oliver and Company,* p. 17; October 12, 1992, David Hiltbrand, review of *The Golden Palace,* p. 9; February 7, 1994, David Hiltbrand, review of *The Cisco Kid,* p. 16; August 5, 1996, Michael A. Lipton, review of *Nash Bridges,* p. 15; August 19, 1996, Leah Rozen, review of *Tin Cup,* p. 19; April 24, 1998, "Puff Daddy," p. 125; December 6, 2004, review of *Christmas with the Kranks,* p. 32.

Premiere, March, 1996, Maximillian Potter, "Idol Chatter," p. 46.

PR Newswire, July 21, 2004, "Twin Cities to Host Cheech Marin's Personal Chicano Art Collection."

Rolling Stone, July 14, 1994, Peter Travers, review of *The Lion King,* p. 98.

School Library Journal, March, 1990, Marilyn Higgins, "Birthwrite: Growing Up Hispanic," p. 171; February, 1998, Penny Peck, review of *My Name Is Cheech, the School Bus Driver,* p. 74.

Smithsonian, October, 2002, Frank B. Phillippi, "The Cheech Marin Collection," p. 45.

Sport, December, 1997, Randy Williams, "Smokin' Again," p. 92.

Time Canada, February 21, 2005, Barbara Kiviat, "Re-Upped in Smoke," p. 47.

TV Guide, February 5, 1994, Jeff Jarvis, review of *The Cisco Kid,* p. 39; February 12, 1994, review of *The Cisco Kid,* p. 28; May 17, 1997, Jeff Jarvis, review of *Nash Bridges,* p. 14.

UPI NewsTrack, October 1, 2004, "Cheech Marin Wants to Educate through Art"; February 14, 2005, "Cheech and Chong Plan New Movie."

Variety, June 3, 1981, review of *Cheech and Chong's Nice Dreams,* p. 14; May 11, 1983, review of *Still Smokin',* p. 20; May 23, 1984, review of *Cheech and Chong's "The Corsican Brothers,"* p. 13; August 26, 1987, review of *Born in East L.A.,* p. 15; November 16, 1988, review of *Oliver and Company,* p. 19; August 16, 1989, review of *Rude Awakening,* p. 23; April 13, 1992, Todd McCarthy, review of *Ferngully,* p. 64; September 21, 1992, Hoyt Hilsman, review of *The Golden Palace,* p. 88; January 31, 1994, Todd Everett, review of *The Cisco Kid,* p. 70; May 29, 1995, Todd McCarthy, review of *Desperado,* p. 53; March 25, 1996, John P. McCarthy, review of *Nash Bridges,* p. 30; August 5, 1996, Todd McCarthy, review of *Tin Cup,* p. 47; April 20, 1998, Todd McCarthy, review of *Paulie,* p. 43; February 21, 2005, "Inhaling Laughs," p. 45.

Wall Street Journal Western Edition, December 23, 1991, Robert Goldberg, review of *La Pastorela,* p. 7.

Washingtonian, July, 1981, Dan Rottenberg, review of *Cheech and Chong's Nice Dreams,* p. 46.

ONLINE

Chicano, http://www.chicano-art-life.com/ (September 12, 2005), biography of Cheech Marin.

E Online, http://www.eonline.com/ (July 24, 2003), fact sheet on Cheech Marin.

Internet Movie Database, http://www.imdb.com/ (September 12, 2005), fact sheet and filmography of Cheech Marin.

MSN Entertainment, http://entertainment.msn.com/ (July 24, 2003), biography of Cheech Marin.

Time Warner Books, http://www.twbookmark.com/ (July 24, 2003), description of *Chicano Visions.* *

*   *   *

MARIN, Richard Anthony
See MARIN, Cheech

MARLOWE, Hugh
  See PATTERSON, Harry

*   *   *

MASO, Carole 1955(?)-

PERSONAL: Born c. 1955, in NJ; father a musician, mother a nurse; companion of Helen Lange; children: Rose. *Education:* Vassar College, B.A., 1977.

ADDRESSES: Office—Brown University, Box 1920, Providence, RI 02912. *E-mail*—Carole_Maso@brown. edu.

CAREER: Illinois State University, Normal, IL, writer-in-residence, 1991-92; George Washington University, Washington, DC, writer-in-residence, 1992-93; Columbia University, New York, NY, associate professor, 1993; Brown University, Providence, RI, professor of English and director of creative writing, 1995—. Has worked as a waitress, an artist's model, and a fencing instructor.

AWARDS, HONORS: CAPS grant for fiction, New York State Council on the Arts, 1983; W.K. Rose fellowship in the creative arts, Vassar College, 1985; New York Foundation for the Arts grant, 1987; National Endowment for the Arts literature grant, 1988; Lannan Literary fellowship for fiction, Lannan Foundation, 1993.

WRITINGS:

NOVELS

Ghost Dance, Perennial Library (New York, NY), 1987.
The Art Lover, North Point Press (San Francisco, CA), 1990.
Ava, Dalkey Archive Press (Normal, IL), 1993.
The American Woman in the Chinese Hat, Dalkey Archive (Normal, IL), 1994.
Defiance, Dutton (New York, NY), 1998.

OTHER

Aureole: An Erotic Sequence (short stories) Ecco Press (Hopewell, NJ), 1996.

Break Every Rule: Essays on Language, Longing, and Moments of Desire, Counterpoint (Washington, DC), 2000.
The Room Lit by Roses: A Journal of Pregnancy and Birth (memoir), Counterpoint (Washington, DC), 2000.
Beauty Is Convulsive: The Passion of Frida Kahlo (prose and poetry), Counterpoint (Washington, DC), 2001.

Also author of screenplay *Pandora's Box,* 1993. Contributor to anthologies, including *Tasting Life Twice: Literary Lesbian Fiction by New American Writers,* edited by E.J. Levy, Avon Books (New York, NY), 1995; and *Tolstoy's Dictaphone: Technology and the Muse,* edited by Sven Birkerts, Graywolf Press (St. Paul, MN), 1996. Contributor periodicals, including *American Periodical Review, Common Knowledge, Review of Contemporary Fiction, Bomb, Nerve,* and *Conjunctions.*

SIDELIGHTS: Carole Maso is a professor of English and author whose first novel, *Ghost Dance,* is the story of a family's disintegration and an exploration of loss. "Carole writes beautifully, with a depth of imagination and fine descriptive power—but plot, continuity, and climax generally conceded to a novel are most difficult to pull from the thick cloudy contest of ephemeral memories," stated Alicia Dulac in *Best Sellers.* A critic in *Publishers Weekly* commented: "Comparable more to musical than to literary forms, this first novel resembles a tone poem."

The novel is not organized into chapters but rather into five parts that are further divided. "*Ghost Dance*'s unconventional structure is not a pretentious, arty overlay," claimed Leslie Lawrence in *Sojourner.* "The structure is born of necessity; the story could be told no other way. This is not a novel about character development or about how one event leads to another. It is a novel that succeeds in conveying the enormity and fertility of one woman's mind." *Library Journal* reviewer Jeanne Buckley called Maso's prose "repetitious and dreamlike, and her poetic images are sharp and evocative." A critic in *Kirkus Reviews* felt that Vanessa tells the story "in an emotion-charged and montage-like narrative that roams freely from deep in the past right up to the present."

The narrator of *Ghost Dance* is Vanessa Turin, daughter of the distinguished, beautiful, and mad poet Christine Wing. Vanessa's father is a quiet man, devoted to his wife. Fletcher, Vanessa's brother, is an activist, and her grandfather travels west to learn from the Native Americans. "The children observe marriages of opposites, parents and grandparents," explained E.M. Broner in the *Women's Review of Books*. "Their father is silent, their mother's life and living are words. Their Italian grandmother is practical; her husband is a visionary, a moralist. . . . The children are the heirs of these symbiotic traits. Vanessa, the eldest, inherits her mother's physical form, and, like the mother, writes. Fletcher, the brother, a year younger, speaks out for the silent things that have no speech themselves, flora, fauna, the environment." As the novel progresses, Vanessa loses her mother to an automobile accident and her father when he departs on an unannounced pilgrimage. Fletcher journeys to remote places and sends Vanessa postcards with muddled messages.

Ron Burnett remarked in the *Christian Science Monitor* that *Ghost Dance* is not so much a story as it is "a mode of recall by a narrator who really isn't telling a story at all but trying to build a rationale for her own existence." Vanessa becomes addicted to cocaine and then heroin. She has an affair with her mother's female lover of over two decades. The sections of the book are connected by imagery. "Snow, for example, is at once cocaine, the asbestos in a worker's lungs, and the setting for the massacre of Native Americans at Wounded Knee," observed Meredith Sue Willis in the *New York Times Book Review*. Cyra McFadden, in her assessment for the *Los Angeles Times Book Review,* characterized the language of the novel as "dense" and "lyrical" and contended that Maso "takes enormous risks, juggling level upon level of metaphor. . . . The book's strengths are greater than its flaws, however, and the flaws are honorable, born of ambition and abundant talent. I can't remember a more striking depiction of madness, or the labyrinth of family ties." *Booklist* reviewer Joanne Wilkinson called *Ghost Dance* a "stunning debut."

Maso's second novel, *The Art Lover,* is dedicated to Gary Falk, a friend of hers who died of AIDS. Linda L. Rome, writing in the *Library Journal,* said that the "nontraditional novel presents an experimental face to the reader." The main character, Caroline, is a poet and writer who returns to New York from an artists' colony to settle the estate of her father, an art historian who had told her that art is everything. She accepts his belief but feels that her mother's suicide may have

been linked to her father's philosophy. As Caroline's childhood friend is dying of AIDS, "Caroline begins to feel that retreating into art may in fact be nothing but an exquisite form of betrayal," explained William Ferguson in the *New York Times Book Review*. At one point, Caroline is replaced by Maso's persona, describing her work on the novel as her own friend is dying. Photographs of art, reviews, start charts, poems, and newspaper clippings are scattered throughout the story, "often as ironic counterpoint," said Ferguson. He maintained that although the book contains many "imaginative levels," *The Art Lover* "is fully coherent, moving and elegiac, a genuine consolation."

The Art Lover "is more a deconstructionist art gallery of the author's sensibility than a conventional novel," wrote Carol Muske Dukes in the *Los Angeles Times Book Review*. "These 'pieces' form a puzzle, an album of memories, though the style is in no way retrospective; it is as contemporary and self-conscious as a style can get in our post-structuralist age." Dukes characterized the images as "sensual, obsessed—with long passages of intoxicating beauty. . . . Maso has found an innovative way to see, like a laser, into the human heart." A reviewer in *Publishers Weekly* pointed out that Maso "brings to life a 'bombardment of images and sounds,' fashioning a pattern of astonishing complexity and beauty."

A critic for *Publishers Weekly* compared Maso's third novel, *Ava,* to James Joyce's *Ulysses* in that the protagonist, Ava Klein, recalls her past on the last day of her life as she dies from a rare cancer of the blood. The reviewer contended that *Ava* "presents heartbreakingly familiar emotions in an utterly original form." L. Winters suggested in *Choice* that *Ava* is "mysterious and richly allusive. . . . Maso contributes new insights into women's inner life."

In the novel, Ava is a thirty-nine-year-old professor of literature at Hunter College who reflects upon her marriages to an Italian film director, a French pilot, and a Latin American. Her current partner is a Czech writer. Wendy Smith observed in the *New York Times Book Review* that references to Ava's literary mentors (such as Nabokov and Neruda) "signal that this novel's goals are modernist: to stimulate new kinds of thinking through new kinds of writing, to refract reality through the prism of an individual consciousness rather than mimicking it with an omniscient, third-person narration." Smith noted Ava's memories of New York as it had been and said that "her memories of vanished amenities are not just sentimental expressions of the typical complaint . . . but mirror Ava's sense of her own vital forces ebbing away. . . . Although Ava's memories come to her on the eve of death, they all celebrate life." "Maso has written another spellbinder in this current novel," commented Cherry W. Li in the *Library Journal.*

The title of Maso's fourth novel, *The American Woman in the Chinese Hat,* refers to the central character, Catherine, a young American writer traveling on a grant whose female lover decides not to join her on the French Riviera. Rejected, Catherine writes and cries in cafes and engages in sexual adventures with a variety of men, including a seventeen-year-old artist's model. "This book may shock the genteel reader, but others will be enthralled," observed Jim Dwyer in the *Library Journal.* "Language is the shape of her pain and her desire: she continually inscribes her life . . ., reinventing herself in the pages of her notebook," contended a reviewer in *Publishers Weekly.* Tom Sleigh maintained in the *New York Times Book Review* that "Ms. Maso seems to identify passionately with her narrator's plight, but as the novel cycles through pickups and love affairs, devolving eventually into Catherine's madness, the relationship between the wily Ms. Maso and her first-person narrator grows steadily more complex . . . forcing us to assess and reassess not only our attitudes toward Catherine but Ms. Maso's own attitude toward her narrator." Sleigh noted Maso's "sophisticated use of verbal collage" and movement "from internal monologue to fragmentary perception" and praised her "rigorous associative logic"; she added that "there is nothing slack or frenzied about Ms. Maso's writing: despite the overheated plot and setting, the depiction of Catherine's suffering is provocatively cool."

A *Publishers Weekly* reviewer called Maso's fifth book, *Aureole: An Erotic Sequence,* "a lesbian erotic fantasia so drunk with language games, impressionistic imagery and self-referential play as to be almost plotless." The book is composed of poetry and vignettes in mainly French settings, often on the beach, and sometimes involving food. Barbara Hoffert maintained in *Library Journal* that Maso has entered "rarefied territory" in this "extended prose poem . . . with only a hint of character and plot to guide the reader."

"For Maso, *Defiance* is definitely a new thing," remarked Matthew Debord in *Publishers Weekly;* he

concluded that Maso's sixth novel "employs a recognizable structure and manages to live up to its billing as a thriller by suspensefully manipulating a reader's expectations until its brutal, macabre conclusion." *Defiance*'s protagonist, Bernadette O'Brien, is a former Harvard physics professor awaiting execution on death row in a Georgia prison for the murder of two of her male students. Bernadette keeps a journal, which Elizabeth Bukowski described in the *Wall Street Journal* as "a dizzying swirl of memories and mathematics, black humor and hallucinatory voices." Bukowski called *Defiance* "a sharp exploration of new extremes of cynicism and darkness." Bernadette had been a child prodigy in a working-class Irish family; she had been mistreated and had witnessed her father's abuse of her mother and his infidelities. She does not see herself as a victim and rejects the social workers and feminists who urge her to plead mental illness to win a stay of execution. *Library Journal* contributor Faye A. Chadwell considered Maso's "unsympathetic, explicit" treatment of her central character's dark side "the novel's greatest strength."

In addition to novels, Maso has also written books in other genres, including literary criticism, memoir, and poetic works. *Break Every Rule: Essays on Language, Longing, and Moments of Desire,* for example, consists of ten individual works in which the author critiques the creative process and encourages pushing the boundaries of literary conventions, language, and genre. A *Publishers Weekly* critic noted: "Some will find her advice to 'break every rule' of narrative truly subversive, while others may find it stuck in the adolescent fantasy that rebellion against authority is inherently liberating."

In 2001, Maso chronicled her quest to have a child, her pregnancy, and the birth of her daughter, Rose, in *The Room Lit by Roses: A Journal of Pregnancy and Birth.* "*The Room Lit by Roses,*" wrote Sonja Franeta in *Gay & Lesbian Review,* "is not like any book you've read. The gentle incantations and rhythms of her prose are a banquet of sound and meaning." Written in diary form, the text takes a sometimes poetic style and tone while describing the effect her pregnancy and the events surrounding it had on her life and body. A critic for *Publishers Weekly* felt that "her dreamlike treatment of pregnancy, birth, mothering and writing should enchant mothers, mothers-to-be and writers with a poetic bent."

In *Beauty Is Convulsive: The Passion of Frida Kahlo* Maso combines prose and poetry to imaginatively describe painful events in the life of Kahlo, the famous Mexican painter. She draws on firsthand sources, including Kahlo's diary and related letters, as well as biographies about Kahlo, to construct the images of the artist. In a writing style that a reviewer for *Publishers Weekly* described as "impressionistic," Maso relates how the bus accident that impaled Kahlo affected her life, including the many years of agonizing treatments, subsequent related injuries, failure to carry a child to term, and her paintings. The reviewer noted that "despite the grim goings-on, Maso, like her subject, is not without a sense of humor . . . which helps her to capture" the absurdity of the situation.

BIOGRAPHICAL AND CRITICAL SOURCES:

BOOKS

Contemporary Literary Criticism, Volume 44, Gale (Detroit, MI), 1987, pp. 57-61.
Contemporary Novelists, seventh edition, St. James Press (Detroit, MI), 2001.
Maso, Carole, *The Room Lit by Roses: A Journal of Pregnancy and Birth,* Counterpoint (Washington, DC), 2000.

PERIODICALS

Best Sellers, September, 1986, Alicia Dulac, review of *Ghost Dance,* p. 204.
Booklist, May 1, 1986, Joanne Wilkinson, review of *Ghost Dance,* p. 1283.
Choice, September, 1993, L. Winters, review of *Ava,* p. 121.
Christian Science Monitor, July 18, 1986, Ron Burnett, review of *Ghost Dance,* p. 22.
Gay & Lesbian Review, March, 2001, Sonja Franeta, "The Mother of the Woman," review of *The Room Lit by Roses,* p. 121.
Kirkus Reviews, April 15, 1986, review of *Ghost Dance,* p. 572; March 1, 1994, review of *The American Woman in the Chinese Hat,* pp. 237-38; August 15, 1996, review of *Aureole: An Erotic Sequence,* p. 1179.
Library Journal, July, 1986, Jeanne Buckley, review of *Ghost Dance,* p. 110; May 15, 1990, Linda L. Rome, review of *The Art Lover,* p. 95; April 1, 1993, Cherry W. Li, review of *Ava,* p. 132; February 1, 1994, Jim Dwyer, review of *The American

Woman in the Chinese Hat,* p. 113; November 1, 1996, Barbara Hoffert, review of *Aureole: An Erotic Sequence,* p. 108; April 1, 1998, Faye A. Chadwell, review of *Defiance,* p. 124.
Los Angeles Times Book Review, July 27, 1986, Cyra McFadden, review of *Ghost Dance,* p. 3; July 1, 1990, Carol Muske Dukes, review of *The Art Lover,* p. 2.
New York Times Book Review, July 20, 1986, Meredith Sue Willis, review of *Ghost Dance,* p. 18; June 24, 1990, William Ferguson, review of *The Art Lover,* p. I20; December 12, 1993, Wendy Smith, review of *Ava,* p. 23; May 15, 1994, Tom Sleigh, review of *The American Women in the Chinese Hat,* p. 31.
Publishers Weekly, April, 25, 1986, review of *Ghost Dance,* p. 66; March 23, 1990, review of *The Art Lover,* p. 64; March 15, 1993, review of *Ava,* p. 67; March 28, 1994, *The American Woman in the Chinese Hat,* pp. 83-84; September 30, 1996, review of *Aureole: An Erotic Sequence,* p. 63; April 27, 1998, Matthew Debord, "Carole Maso: From Margins to Center," interview with Carole Maso, pp. 38-39; May 1, 2000, review of *Break Every Rule: Essays on Language, Longing, and Moments of Desire,* p. 65; November 27, 2000, review of *The Room Lit by Roses,* p. 67; November 25, 2002, review of *Beauty Is Convulsive,* p. 42.
Sojourner, December, 1986, Leslie Lawrence, review of *Ghost Dance,* pp. 38-39.
Wall Street Journal, April 24, 1998, Elizabeth Bukowski, review of *Defiance,* p. W4.
Women's Review of Books, September, 1986, E.M. Broner, review of *Ghost Dance,* p. 13.

ONLINE

Absolute Write, http://www.absolutewrite.com/ (October 7, 2005), interview with Carole Maso.
Barcelona Review Online, http://www.barcelonareview. com/ (April 17, 2003), Jill Adams, interview with Carole Maso.*

*   *   *

McGLATHERY, James M. 1936-
(James Melville McGlathery)

PERSONAL: Born November 22, 1936, in New Orleans, LA; son of Samuel Lyon and Mary Jackson (Garrott) McGlathery; married Nancy Judith Beyer,

June 16, 1963; children: Samuel, Daniel, Benjamin, Andrew. *Education:* Princeton University, B.A., 1958; Yale University, M.A., 1959, Ph.D., 1964. *Politics:* Democrat. *Hobbies and other interests:* Cooking.

ADDRESSES: Home—1204 Thomas Dr., Champaign, IL 61821-1632. *Office*—Department of Germanic Languages, University of Illinois at Urbana-Champaign, 707 S. Mathews, Urbana, IL 61801-3675; fax: 217-244-3242. *E-mail*—nmcglath@yahoo.com.

CAREER: German teacher at a private boys' school in Andover, MA, 1959-60; Harvard University, Cambridge, MA, began as lecturer, became instructor in German, 1963-65; University of Illinois at Urbana-Champaign, Urbana, assistant professor, 1965-71, associate professor, 1971-84, professor of German, 1984-2000, professor emeritus, 2000—, department head, 1985-95. *Journal of English and Germanic Philology,* managing editor, 1972-2000.

MEMBER: North American Heine Society, American Society for Eighteenth-Century Studies, E.T.A. Hoffmann-Gesellschaft, East-central Society for Eighteenth-Century Studies, South Central Society for Eighteenth-Century Studies.

WRITINGS:

(Editor, with Lathrop P. Johnson) *German Source Readings in the Arts and Sciences,* Stipes Publishing (Champaign, IL), 1974.
Mysticism and Sexuality: E.T.A. Hoffmann, Peter Lang Verlag (Bern, Switzerland), Part 1: *Hoffmann and His Sources,* 1981, Part 2: *Interpretations of the Tales,* 1985.
Desire's Sway: The Plays and Stories of Heinrich von Kleist, Wayne State University Press (Detroit, MI), 1983.
(Editor) *The Brothers Grimm and Folktale,* University of Illinois Press (Urbana, IL), 1988.
Fairy Tale Romance: The Grimms, Basile, Perrault, University of Illinois Press (Urbana, IL), 1991.
(Editor) *Music and German Literature: Their Relationship since the Middle Ages,* Camden House (Columbia, SC), 1992.
Grimm's Fairy Tales: A History of Criticism on a Popular Classic, Camden House (Columbia, SC), 1993.

E.T.A. Hoffmann, Twayne (New York, NY), 1997.
Wagner's Operas and Desire, Peter Lang (New York, NY), 1998.

*   *   *

McGLATHERY, James Melville
   See McGLATHERY, James M.

*   *   *

McGRATH, Patrick 1950-

PERSONAL: Surname is pronounced "McGraw"; born February 7, 1950, in London, England; son of Patrick (a psychiatrist and hospital superintendent) and Helen (O'Brien) McGrath; married; wife's name Maria Aitken. *Education:* University of London, B.A. (with honors), 1971; attended Simon Fraser University.

ADDRESSES: Home and office—21 E. 2nd St., #10, New York, NY 10003. *Agent*—Eric Ashworth, 231 W. 22nd St., New York, NY 10011.

CAREER: Writer. Media Dimensions, New York City, managing editor of *Speech Technology* magazine, 1982-87. Worked at Broadmoor mental institution in England; worked at mental institution in Canada; taught in British Columbia.

AWARDS, HONORS: Bram Stoker Award nomination, Horror Writers of America, 1998, for *Asylum.*

WRITINGS:

The Lewis and Clark Expedition (nonfiction), Silver Burdett (Morristown, NJ), 1985.
Blood and Water and Other Tales, Poseidon Press (New York, NY), 1988.
The Grotesque (novel), Poseidon Press (New York, NY), 1989.
Spider (novel), Poseidon Press (New York, NY), 1990.
(Editor with Bradford Morrow) *The New Gothic: A Collection of Contemporary Gothic Fiction,* Random House (New York, NY), 1991, published as *The Picador Book of the New Gothic,* Picador (London, England), 1992.

Dr. Haggard's Disease (novel), Poseidon Press (New York, NY), 1993.

The Angel and Other Stories, Penguin (London, England), 1995.

Asylum, Random House (New York, NY), 1997.

Martha Peake: A Novel of the Revolution, Random House (New York, NY), 2000.

Port Mungo, Knopf (New York, NY), 2004.

Ghost Town: Tales of Manhattan Then and Now (short stories), Bloomsbury (New York, NY), 2005.

SCREENPLAYS

The Grotesque (based on his novel), J&M Entertainment, 1995.

Spider (based on his novel), Sony Pictures Classics, 2002.

Author of introduction to *Moby Dick* by Herman Melville, Oxford University Press (New York, NY), 1999. Work appears in anthologies, including *Between C & D: New Writing from the Lower East Side Fiction Magazine,* Penguin, 1988. Contributor to *Confrontation, New York Times, Missouri Review, The Quarterly,* and other periodicals. Contributing editor to the magazines *Bomb* and *Between C and D.*

SIDELIGHTS: Patrick McGrath is the author of a number of Neo-Gothic novels and stories that have earned him comparisons to such notable writers as H.P. Lovecraft, Ian McEwan, and Edgar Allan Poe. The grotesque and macabre fascinate McGrath, as does mental pathology of all sorts; his central characters are often quite familiar with psychosis and obsessive longing, and they may act upon their most bizarre beliefs. A *Publishers Weekly* correspondent cited McGrath for "a mind that revels in the toxic side of things." Tim Woods, writing in *Contemporary Novelists,* found that McGrath "is a novelist whose fiction interestingly explores a wide range of ideas in a condensed space, and he has breathed new and vigorous life into the well-trodden paths of the Gothic and mystery genres."

Born in London, England, McGrath grew up on the grounds of Broadmoor, an institution for the criminally insane where his father was a superintendent. In a *Publishers Weekly* interview, Michael Coffey noted: "Broadmoor is home to England's most violent and disturbed killers, and yet McGrath recalls the trustees working in the family garden, with his mother delivering tea in the afternoon. He remembers playing with some of the patients and endlessly watching others." When asked by Coffey about his affinity for the Gothic style, McGrath mused: "At first I think I was attracted purely to the furniture of [G]othic fiction, . . . the crumbling mansions, the dripping cellars, the gloomy attics . . . . Quite why it clicked I don't know. Certainly as I began to work in the genre the interest in purely [G]othic effects began to fade and I became much more intrigued in the application of [G]othic mood to states of mind, to extreme states of psychological disturbance."

McGrath's first book, *Blood and Water and Other Tales,* illustrates his penchant for mixing the grotesque and the comic. Parodies of the typical Gothic tale—distinguished by mysterious or bizarre episodes and remote, gloomy settings—McGrath's stories are populated by characters such as a miniature Sigmund Freud who drives a man mad, people with pernicious anemia who crave human blood, and a proper English gentleman who is eventually strangled by a hand that grows out of his head. *New York Times* critic Michiko Kakutani commented: "Severed hands, dead monkeys, swarming insects, pickled body parts and menacing pygmies proliferate in *Blood and Water.*" The reviewer went on to compare McGrath's stories to Brian DePalma's horror movies, because "not only do they share those movies' baroque romanticism and their tendency to mix up narrative conventions in an expressionistic, post-modern stew, but they also share a similar preoccupation with sex and guilt, violence and death." In the *Georgia Review,* Greg Johnson declared that McGrath's tales "collectively offer a brilliant pastiche not only of the conventional Gothic but of such modern obsessions as sexuality, psychoanalysis, and the nature of storytelling." McGrath was also praised for his prose, which, according to *New York Times Book Review* contributor Stephen Schiff, "gushes and twirls, winding around itself in thick, wordy coils." Although some reviewers found the collection to be of uneven quality, Chicago *Tribune Books* contributor John Blades concluded: "At their grotesque best, they are diabolically funny parables about the bestial excesses of modern life, which stalk the narrow border dividing man from animal, civilization from savagery." And, according to Kakutani, McGrath has "an ability to invest his narratives with a disturbing psychological subtext. Combined with his Gothic imagination and dark, splenetic humor, the result is fiction that can be as powerful as it is strange."

McGrath incorporated many of the same elements from his stories—gruesome images, Gothic settings, and dark humor—into his first novel, *The Grotesque*. The title is derived from the narrator, Sir Hugo Coal, an Englishman who is rendered quadriplegic and unable to speak after an accident. Susan Kenney quoted one of Sir Hugo's musings in the *New York Times Book Review:* "I have come to believe that to be a grotesque is my destiny. For a man who turns into a vegetable—isn't that a grotesque?" Sir Hugo, a paleontologist who theorizes that dinosaurs are closely related to birds, feels that his misfortune is due to the arrival of his new butler, Fledge, and his wife, Doris. Sir Hugo believes that Fledge, in an attempt to become master of the house, seduced Lady Coal and tried to kill him, accounting for his current state. He also contends that Fledge murdered his daughter's fiance and fed the corpse's bones to the pigs, a murder that Sir Hugo is accused of committing.

Reviewers observed that the reader begins to doubt Sir Hugo's reliability as a narrator—has the accident affected his memory? Is he mad? Or is he lying? *Washington Post* critic Michael Dirda commented on McGrath's approach: "Though a shivery whodunit on the surface, *The Grotesque* really thrills as a study in narrative technique." Kakutani called the book "a coy yet compelling horror story that functions as a superb example of the [Gothic] genre, even as it's sending that genre up." Writing in the *St. James Guide to Horror, Ghost & Gothic Writers,* Chris Morgan judged that *The Grotesque* "is also a black comedy and comes close to being a farce that parodies the gothic."

Like *The Grotesque, Spider* is told by an unreliable narrator. He is Dennis "Spider" Cleg, a schizophrenic who is released from a mental hospital after twenty years and returns to his childhood neighborhood in London's East End. In this environment, memories of an abusive, adulterous father and loving mother come flooding back to him. Though he is accused of killing his mother, Spider recounts in his journal how his father and a prostitute committed the crime and tried to kill him as well. As his journal progresses, a portrait of a fragile, disturbed man emerges—and what is truth and what is delusion becomes unclear. "McGrath's interest is not in guilt or innocence," Chicago *Tribune Books* contributor Margot Mifflin noted, "but in the grim reality of Spider's tangled mind, which is precisely where the author's most arabesque talents are employed." The author commented on his approach

in the interview with Coffey: "I would say that my working model in all my books is that we don't see clearly, we don't see objectively, and the reason is that perception is always biased by guilt or desire or madness. I'm interested in characters whose negotiations with reality are disturbed."

Critics noted that *Spider* is quite different from McGrath's earlier works; it is less darkly humorous, and "absent are the ambiguous sexual orientations, fantastic appendages, the meditations on the sex lives of flies," remarked Coffey. McGrath concentrates little on the macabre; he explained in the interview with Coffey that "the horror [of *Spider*] is somehow implicit in the illness rather than being present in formal terms." Some critics, however, felt the novel was not horrific enough; "*Spider* is a thriller, of sorts, as well as a psychological case study and a gem of self-conscious prose. The only thing it lacks, to give it true thriller status, is the thrill of terror," commented Wendy Lesser in the *Washington Post Book World.* But Kakutani praised *Spider:* "The writing is spare, direct and understated—an approach that actually serves to heighten the narrative's grisly effects. *Spider* is a small classic of horror—a model of authorial craft and control."

A macabre tale of obsessional love unfolds in McGrath's novel *Dr. Haggard's Disease.* Dr. Edward Haggard, a morphine-addicted general practice doctor in a seaside community, relives his adulterous passion for a colleague's wife when the woman's son comes to call. Dr. Haggard becomes convinced that his lover's spirit has inhabited her son's body—especially after the son begins to show signs of sexual androgyny. "This wonderful and ghastly novel . . . sends us once more into a world as grisly and swollen with malignant intent as the background of a Francis Bacon painting," declared Liza Pennywitt Taylor in the *Los Angeles Times Book Review.* "*Dr. Haggard's Disease* abounds with creepy, kinky details which, if they had been turned up a degree or two higher in camp intensity, could have been hilarious, as they are in *Grotesque.* . . . In this new book they subtly work to create a world of dark apprehension."

A number of reviewers cited *Dr. Haggard's Disease* for its exploitation of the Gothic, including a crumbling cliffside manor and the narrator's willed descent into madness. To quote Ann Arensberg in the *New York Times Book Review,* McGrath "feels no compulsion to invent a better mousetrap: the Gothic horror tale is a proven vehicle for exploring the perversities of the human mind and heart and for portraying extreme states of feeling. Its atmosphere of gloom, its structure that builds to a calamity, are well suited to the author's enterprise: the study of a diseased passion." Arensberg concluded: "As *Dr. Haggard's Disease* demonstrates, the Gothic genre, far from being restrictive, is as capacious as the mind of the writer employing it. Patrick McGrath has produced a myth of the creator sacrificed to his creation, a novel in which—as in its Gothic predecessors—the terrible and the beautiful are melded, one and the same." In the *Times Literary Supplement,* M. John Harrison likewise observed that *Dr. Haggard's Disease* "is a rapid, elegant tour of the New Gothic sensibility, 'horror, madness, monstrosity, death, disease, terror, evil, and weird sexuality,' each landmark given an impeccable sense of its historical niche and significance."

With his novel *Asylum,* McGrath muted his Gothic instincts to produce a story that—while still shocking and grisly—deals with irrational passion and its consequences. Narrated by a state psychiatrist who has his own dubious role in the tale, *Asylum* describes an illicit affair between a doctor's wife and a criminally insane hospital inmate. Needless to say, the affair produces nightmare results for the woman, who winds up committed to an institution. In the *New Statesman,* Julie Wheelwright called *Asylum* "a subtly menacing portrait of 1950s hospital life gone desperately wrong." The reviewer continued: "With its pared-down plot, attention to period detail and focus on internal events, the novel creates powerful suspense. . . . The pleasure of McGrath's fiction lies, however, in his refusal to be predictable. He pulls the tension taut until the final page and creates that rare thing, a chillingly good read."

"It is part of McGrath's bemusing artfulness in *Asylum* that he can make the reader suffer the fate of all of his characters . . .," wrote Adam Phillips in a *London Review of Books* piece on the novel. "But what makes *Asylum* so compelling—both gripping and horribly funny—is McGrath's mordant knowingness about the obvious points. . . . It is McGrath's acute sense that everyone's language is the archest rhetoric, a performance bristling with intent, that makes *Asylum* so tricky and unsettling." Kakutani also praised the work in her *New York Times* review, noting that *Asylum* "not only emerges as [McGrath's] most polished perfor-

mance to date, but also stands as a distillation of his preoccupations: his Freudian equation of sex and death, of control and obsession, and his fascination with the morbid and grotesque." Kakutani concluded: "By pushing familiar passions to extremes and by glossing familiar psychological concepts with religious notions of sin and guilt and redemption, Mr. McGrath has managed to construct a chilling story that works as both a Freudian parable and an old-fashioned gothic shocker."

Martha Peake: A Novel of the Revolution is, according to Wilda Williams in the *Library Journal,* another of the author's "twisted neo-Gothic tales of psychological suspense." The novel opens on a storm-tossed night in 1825 within Drogo Hall, an imposing gothic mansion falling into ruin on the outskirts of London. As the night progresses, narrator Ambrose Tree listens to his uncle, William, tell the grotesque story of Harry Peake and his sixteen-year-old daughter, Martha. Harry is an ex-smuggler whose spine has been hideously twisted and crushed in an accident; he makes a meager living showing off his deformities as the Cripplegate Monster in the lower pubs of London. Harry's exhibitions draw the attention of Lord Drogo, previous lord of the manor, an anatomist interested in Harry not for his showmanship or his fledgling talent with song, but for his skeleton, which would make a prize research piece. Meanwhile, Drogo's assistant, the current Uncle William, develops a deep infatuation with Martha Peake, which is not returned. When Harry attacks Martha in a drunken rage, she flees to Drogo Hall, where William is happy to protect her, locked in a room in a remote turret. Eventually, he helps her escape London and flee to the American colonies, where she becomes involved in the American Revolution and is made into a symbol of the independence of the new America. Turning on the device of the unreliable narrator, the novel leaves many questions unanswered as Ambrose finds himself courting madness through speculating on the unresolved history related by his uncle, who may have other plans of his own for his nephew and the family manse. Rex Roberts, writing in *Insight on the News,* called the novel "a fascinating book, as are all of McGrath's, if only for the sheer pleasure of watching a masterful writer work his craft."

McGrath's *Port Mungo* is the "psychologically suspenseful story" of Jack Rathbone, who departs his native England, Gaugin-like, to take up a career as a painter and pursue a relationship with artist Vera

Savage. Told in a series of flashbacks by Rathbone's sister, Gin, the story tells how Jack settled in Port Mungo, a Honduran seaside town, and developed his unique style of painting. When Jack and Vera's daughter, Peg, is born, the child's arrival threatens their marriage. When Peg dies a mysterious death sixteen rocky years later, the couple's relationship is destroyed, and Jack moves in with his sister in New York. As the story unfolds, the truth of Peg's death is revealed, and Jack's role in the tragedy becomes clear. Elaina Richardson, writing in *O, the Oprah Magazine,* observed that "the outstanding feature of McGrath's storytelling is his ability to write with tranquil, evocative beauty about the vilest of subjects." The story is haunting, Richardson observed, because "we see so completely how damaging the most basic human emotions can be."

Ghost Town: Tales of Manhattan Then and Now attempts to "capture the restless spirit of New York City through the ages in an elegant and compact trio of spooky stories," noted reviewer Jennifer Reese in *Entertainment Weekly.* In "Year of the Gibbet," a boy in the Revolutionary era must watch as his mother is forced to strip for a haughty British soldier, who later hangs her. The main character in "Julius" is an art-class model whose appearance in the nude sparks an unhealthy obsession in an unstable student and leads to the downfall of his once-powerful family. "Ground Zero" features a psychiatrist, another of McGrath's unreliable narrators, who tells the story of a patient's bizarre affair with a prostitute following the 9/11 terrorist attacks. The three works explore McGrath's trademark themes of "obsession, madness, and transgression," observed *Library Journal* contributor Patrick Sullivan, who called the book a "dark, ambitious portrait of a complex and storied city" where millions of tales can be found.

In an interview with the *Guardian,* McGrath said he tended not to take the "New Gothic" label too seriously. The Gothic, he observed, is "generally all about power." With its emphasis on secrecy, its dependence upon nighttime action, its subversion of good and noble impulses, the genre is interested in "states of mind that are other than sober, thrifty, and industrious." McGrath once told *CA:* "I am interested in the dark and hidden areas of human nature and how they have been represented in fiction. My work comments upon the Gothic fiction of the past while using the genre as a vehicle for my own ideas."

BIOGRAPHICAL AND CRITICAL SOURCES:

BOOKS

Contemporary Literary Criticism, Volume 55, Gale (Detroit, MI), 1989.
Contemporary Novelists, 7th Edition, St. James Press (Detroit, MI), 2001.
McGrath, Patrick, *The Grotesque,* Poseidon Press (New York, NY), 1989.
St. James Guide to Horror, Ghost & Gothic Writers, St. James Press (Detroit, MI), 1998.

PERIODICALS

Booklist, April 15, 1993, William Beatty, review of *Dr. Haggard's Disease,* p. 493; December 1, 1996, Donna Seaman, review of *Asylum,* p. 620.
Christian Science Monitor, January 29, 1991, Thomas D'Evelyn, review of *Spider,* p. 14.
Entertainment Weekly, May 28, 1993, Margot Mifflin, review of *Dr. Haggard's Disease,* p. 61; March 7, 1997, Margot Mifflin, review of *Asylum,* p. 60; August 26, 2005, review of *Ghost Town,* p. 64.
Georgia Review, winter, 1988, Greg Johnson, review of *Blood and Water,* p. 840.
Guardian, May 8, 1993, Patrick Wright, "A Night in a Ghoulish Tunnel," profile of Patrick McGrath, p. 28.
Insight on the News, March 12, 2001, Rex Roberts, review of *Martha Peake: A Novel of the Revolution,* p. 26.
Library Journal, April 15, 1993, Lawrence Rungren, review of *Dr. Haggard's Disease,* p. 126; February 1, 1997, Starr E. Smith, review of *Asylum,* p. 106; October 1, 2000, Wilda Williams, review of *Martha Peake,* p. 148; July 1, 2005, Patrick Sullivan, review of *Ghost Town,* p. 74.
London Review of Books, October 31, 1996, Adam Phillips, review of *Asylum,* p. 7.
Los Angeles Times Book Review, June 20, 1993, Liza Pennywitt Taylor, review of *Dr. Haggard's Disease,* p. 3.
New Statesman, October 16, 1992, pp. 39-40; September 13, 1996, July Wheelwright, review of *Asylum,* p. 48.
New Statesman & Society, October 16, 1992, Robert Carver, review of *The Picador Book of the New Gothic,* p. 39; May 21, 1993, p. 37.

Newsweek, May 31, 1993, David Gates, review of *Dr. Haggard's Disease,* p. 55.

New Yorker, January 27, 1997, John Lanchester, review of *Asylum,* p. 78; February 24, 1997, Liesl Schillinger, "Letting the Snakes Out," profile of Patrick McGrath, p. 52.

New York Times, February 24, 1988, Michiko Kakutani, review of *Blood and Water,* p. C25; April 21, 1989, Michiko Kakutani, review of *The Grotesque,* p. B4; October 9, 1990, Michiko Kakutani, review of *Spider,* p. 17; February 14, 1997, Michiko Kakutani, review of *Asylum,* p. C38.

New York Times Book Review, March 6, 1988, Steven Schiff, review of *Blood and Water,* p. 6; May 28, 1989, Susan Kenendy, review of *The Grotesque,* p. 7; March 8, 1992, Jack Sullivan, review of *The New Gothic,* p. 12; May 2, 1993, Ann Arensberg, review of *Dr. Haggard's Disease,* p. 7; February 23, 1997, Michael Wood, review of *Asylum,* p. 6.

O, the Oprah Magazine, June, 2004, Elaina Richardson, "Too Close for Comfort: *Port Mungo* Brilliantly Explores Family, Love, and Lust, p. 146.

People, March 31, 1997, Adam Begley, review of *Asylum,* p. 37.

Publishers Weekly, September 28, 1990, Michael Coffey, "Patrick McGrath: A Purveyor of the Fantastic Makes a Foray into Madness," interview with Patrick McGrath, pp. 82-83; March 22, 1993, review of *Dr. Haggard's Disease,* p. 70; December 16, 1996, review of *Asylum,* p. 41; June 7, 2004, review of *Port Mungo,* p. 31.

Review of Contemporary Fiction, fall, 1989, Irving Malin, review of *The Grotesque,* p. 221; spring, 1991, Irving Malin, review of *Spider,* p. 329.

School Library Journal, March, 2003, Renee Steinberg, review of *The Lewis and Clark Expedition,* p. 172.

Spectator, August 17, 1996, Philip Hensher, review of *Asylum,* p. 24.

Times Literary Supplement, April 26, 1991, Tim Gooderham, review of *Spider,* p. 18; October 9, 1992, M. John Harrison, review of *The Picador Book of the New Gothic,* p. 23; May 14, 1993, M. John Harrison, review of *Dr. Haggard's Disease,* p. 22; August 23, 1996, David Flusfeder, review of *Asylum,* p. 22.

Tribune Books (Chicago, IL), October 14, 1990, review of *Spider,* p. 6.

Variety, February 21, 2005, Eddie Cockrell, film review of *Asylum,* p. 26.

Washington Post, June 5, 1989, Michael Dirda, review of *The Grotesque.*

Washington Post Book World, October 14, 1990, Wendy Lesser, review of *Spider,* p. 6.*

MONNINGER, Joseph 1953-

PERSONAL: Born October 28, 1953, in Baltimore, MD; married Amy Short (marriage ended). *Education:* Temple University, A.B., 1975; University of New Hampshire, M.A., 1982. *Hobbies and other interests:* Fly fishing.

ADDRESSES: Office—17 High St., Plymouth, NH 03264-1595. *E-mail*—joem@plymouth.edu; joe@joe manninger.com.

CAREER: Peace Corps, Upper Volta, West Africa, well digger, 1975-77; American Agency for International Development, Mali, West Africa, well digger, 1977-79; University of New Hampshire, Durham, NH, instructor in freshman composition, 1980-82; Lincoln School, Providence, RI, English teacher, 1982-84; American International School, Vienna, Austria, teacher, 1984-86; Plymouth State University, Plymouth, NH, associate professor of English. Certified New Hampshire fishing guide.

MEMBER: Authors Guild, Authors League of America.

AWARDS, HONORS: National Endowment for the Arts fellow, 1987.

WRITINGS:

NOVELS

The Family Man, Atheneum (New York, NY), 1982.
Summer Hunt, Atheneum (New York, NY), 1983.
New Jersey, Atheneum (New York, NY), 1986.
Second Season, Atheneum (New York, NY), 1987.
Incident at Potter's Bridge, D.I. Fine (New York, NY), 1991.
The Viper Tree, Simon & Schuster (New York, NY), 1991.
Mather, D.I. Fine (New York, NY), 1995.

OTHER

(With T.L. Taigen) *Biology Write Now!,* McGraw-Hill (New York, NY), 1992.

Home Waters: Fishing with an Old Friend (memoir), Chronicle Books (San Francisco, CA), 1999.

A Barn in New England: Making a Home on Three Acres (memoir), Chronicle Books (San Francisco, CA), 2001.

Also contributor to periodicals, including *Sports Illustrated.*

SIDELIGHTS: Joseph Monninger's novels, while not completely autobiographical, often involve thoughts, feelings, and locations from the author's past. *The Family Man,* Monninger's first novel, depicts a family on summer vacation in Maine, where the father's feelings of discontentment with his routine life lead to domestic tragedy. Monninger's second book, *Summer Hunt,* is set in West Africa, where the author worked for the Peace Corps. The protagonist, Noel Simpson, is a hydrologist stationed in a desolate area with his wife, Kathy. After growing accustomed to the violent harshness of this environment, Noel returns to New Hampshire. He renews his relationship with his brother Grant and becomes involved in the mercy killing of his father, who is dying of cancer.

Monninger grew up in New Jersey, which provides the locale for his third novel. *New Jersey* concerns an adolescent boy named Max whose mother died in his first year and whose father is crazy. After turning their backyard into a huge pit to search for historical artifacts, Max's father leaves him with an aunt and uncle near Stockton, New Jersey. There Max finds friends to grow up with—Martin, Stu, and Chris. His romantic relationship with Chris is shattered when he goes out with her sister, and he shares his friend's pain when Martin gets his girlfriend pregnant. As Gary Krist pointed out in the *New York Times Book Review,* *New Jersey* is primarily "a collection of telling scenes from a colorful American adolescence." Krist also pointed out "Monninger's extraordinary ability to write evocative scenes that shimmer on the page." Richard Edler concluded in the *Los Angeles Times Book Review* that *New Jersey* is an "affecting and subtle novel."

Monninger has also written nonfiction works, including two memoirs: *Home Waters: Fishing with an Old Friend* and *A Barn in New England: Making a Home on Three Acres.* In the former, the author describes what he thinks is the last trip he took with his beloved golden retriever, Nellie. The eleven-year-old dog prob-

ably has cancer and Monninger decides to enjoy what he believes will be her final days by taking her west, where they hike and fish in places they have visited before. The trip also helps Monninger connect to his past and allow him to reflect on what he truly enjoys in life. Writing in *Publishers Weekly,* a reviewer called it a "touching account of fishing and hiking" that "is both a fly-fisher's engaging daybook and a wonderfully affecting probe of the human-pet bond."

In *A Barn in New England* the author discusses his purchase and renovation of an old barn into a home for him, his companion, Wendy, and her young son. Including vignettes about the ups and downs of the construction process, Monninger also describes the help given by members of the local community, especially indispensable handyman Clarence. This assistance ensures that the trio can make the old barn their primary, year-round residence. In addition, Monninger uses the experience as a means of exploring history and traditions of the area, as well as the lifestyle he will embrace. "Neither plaything nor conceit," noted a *Kirkus Reviews* critic, "Monninger's rural idyll is very much a lived experience: genuine, well-earned, and downright enviable."

BIOGRAPHICAL AND CRITICAL SOURCES:

BOOKS

Monninger, Joseph, *Home Waters: Fishing with an Old Friend,* Chronicle Books (San Francisco, CA), 1999.

Monninger, Joseph, *A Barn in New England: Making a Home on Three Acres,* Chronicle Books (San Francisco, CA), 2001.

PERIODICALS

Kirkus Reviews, August 1, 2001, review of *A Barn in New England,* p. 1096.

Los Angeles Times Book Review, July 27, 1986, Richard Edler, review of *New Jersey,* p. 3.

New York Times Book Review, August 10, 1986, Gary Krist, review of *New Jersey,* p. 18.

Publishers Weekly, May 31, 1999, review of *Home Waters,* p. 79.

ONLINE

Joseph Monninger Home Page, http://www.joe monninger.com (July 25, 2003).*

*   *   *

MORTON, Patricia 1945-

PERSONAL: Born 1945; Canadian citizen; children: two. *Education:* University of Toronto, Ph.D.

ADDRESSES: Home—39-300 Franmor Dr., Peterborough, Ontario K9H 7R2, Canada. *E-mail*—dmort05@att.global.net.

CAREER: Trent University, Peterborough, Ontario, Canada, worked as professor of history, now professor emeritus.

WRITINGS:

Disfigured Images: The Historical Assault on Afro-American Women, Greenwood Press (New York, NY), 1991.
(Principal editor and author of introduction) *Discovering the Women in Slavery: Emancipating Perspectives on the American Past,* University of Georgia (Athens, GA), 1996.

SIDELIGHTS: As a professor of history at Trent University in Canada, Patricia Morton was instrumental in the publication of two works dealing with the way African-American women have been portrayed in the writing of American history. In 1991, Morton, who specialized in the history of women, authored *Disfigured Images: The Historical Assault on Afro-American Women,* a work in which she explains how stereotypical images of African-American women were created historically and why they have continued to be promulgated in prominent books and journals. She points out that most of these slavery-and-segregationist-era stereotypes were constructed and perpetuated by white, male historians and social scientists, but she also maintains that many white women, as well as some black male scholars, espoused opinions about black women that were just as damaging. Morton also discusses the case of mulatto women, who she argues are tragic figures because they could not escape the influential, negative images of their racial heritage. J.R. Feagin of *Choice* called the work a "detailed analysis." Sheila L. Skemp, reviewing the book for the *American Historical Review,* assessed it as "useful." Despite this praise, Skemp did find some structural problems with the book, and wrote that it "tends to be extremely repetitive and is badly in need of an editor."

In 1996, Morton was the compiler and principal editor of *Discovering the Women in Slavery: Emancipating Perspectives on the American Past,* a work for which she also wrote the introduction. Both books garnered their share of critical praise for adding a fresh perspective to the evolving historical analysis of the African-American woman's place in this nation's past. Critical opinion of *Discovering the Women in Slavery* was generally favorable. Susan Westbury, reviewing the book for the *William and Mary Quarterly,* called it "wide-ranging and stimulating," and felt it was an indication of "the breadth and depth of current research on the issue of women in slavery." Hilary McD. Beckles, writing in the *Journal of American History* had a similar assessment of the work, stating that it "serves to move us along, and certainly closer to a settlement of the contest between historians of women and historians of gender." J. Wishnia in *Choice* characterized the volume as "an excellent introduction," though one "clearly meant to appeal to a wide readership."

BIOGRAPHICAL AND CRITICAL SOURCES:

PERIODICALS

American Historical Review, December, 1992, Sheila L. Skemp, review of *Disfigured Images: The Historical Assault on Afro-American Women,* p. 1585.
Choice, November, 1991, J.R. Feagin, review of *Disfigured Images,* p. 510; June, 1996, J. Wishnia, review of *Discovering the Women in Slavery: Emancipating Perspectives on the American Past,* p. 1711.
Journal of American History, June, 1997, Hilary McD. Beckles, review of *Discovering the Women in Slavery,* pp. 219-220.

William and Mary Quarterly, October, 1997, Susan Westbury, review of *Discovering the Women in Slavery,* pp. 863-866.

*   *   *

MOYERS, Bill 1934-

PERSONAL: Original given name Billy Don; name legally changed; born June 5, 1934, in Hugo, OK; son of John Henry (a laborer) and Ruby (Johnson) Moyers; married Judith Suzanne Davidson, December 18, 1954; children: William Cope, Alice Suzanne, John Davidson. *Education:* Attended North Texas State University, 1952-54; University of Texas, Austin, B.J. (with honors), 1956; attended University of Edinburgh, 1956-57; Southwestern Baptist Theological Seminary, B.D., 1959.

ADDRESSES: Agent—c/o Author Mail, Anchor Books, 1745 Broadway, New York, NY, 10019.

CAREER: News Messenger, Marshall, TX, reporter and sports editor, 1949-54; KTBC Radio and Television, Austin, TX, assistant news editor, 1954-56; assistant pastor of churches in Texas and Oklahoma, 1956-59; special assistant to Senator Lyndon B. Johnson, 1959-60; executive assistant for vice presidential campaign, 1960-61; Peace Corps, Washington, DC, director of public affairs, 1961, deputy director, 1962-63; special assistant to President Lyndon B. Johnson, 1963-65, White House press secretary, 1965-67; *Newsday,* Garden City, NY, publisher, 1967-70; television executive and series host, beginning 1970; host of "This Week," National Educational Television, 1970, and of "Bill Moyers' Journal," Educational Broadcasting Corp., 1971-76, 1978-81; editor and chief correspondent, "CBS Reports," Columbia Broadcasting System (CBS), 1976-80, senior news analyst and commentator, "CBS News," 1981-86; executive editor, Public Affairs TV, Inc., beginning 1987; commentator on "NBC Nightly News," National Broadcasting Company (NBC), 1995-2004; host and editor of "Now with Bill Moyers," PBS, 2002-04; host of *Wide Angle,* 2002-04; host of *Now,* 2002-04. Founder, Public Affairs Television (independent production company), 1986. Creator of programs "The Fire Next Door," and "The Vanishing Family." Host or creator of public television series: *The Arab World,*

Public Affairs Television, April, 1991; and *Listening to America with Bill Moyers,* April, 1992. Also host or creator of the following public television specials: "All Our Children," 1991; "Moyers: Project Censored," 1991; "The Home Front," 1991; "Sports for Sale," 1991; "Moyers: Beyond Hate," Public Affairs Television, May, 1991; "Special Report: After the War with Bill Moyers," Public Affairs Television, June, 1991; "Moyers: Hate on Trial," 1992; "Minimum Wages: The New Economy," 1992; "What Can We Do about Violence?: A Bill Moyers Special," 1995; and "Trade Secrets," PBS, 2001. President, Rockefeller Foundation and Florence and John Schumann Foundation and Schumann Foundation of New Jersey.

AWARDS, HONORS: Emmy Award, National Academy of Television Arts and Sciences for outstanding broadcaster, 1974, 1978, 1980, and 1982-87; Silver Gavel Award, American Bar Association (ABA), 1974, for distinguished service to the American law system; Certificate of Merit, ABA, 1975; Ralph Lowell Medal for contributions to public television, 1975; George Peabody Awards, 1976, 1980, 1985, 1986-89, 1998-99, and 2004; Monte Carlo Television Festival Grand Prize, Jurors Prize, and Nymph Award, all 1977, all for "The Fire Next Door"; Robert F. Kennedy Journalism Grand Prize, 1978, 1988; Christopher Award, 1978; Sidney Hillman Prize for Distinguished Service, 1978, 1981, and 1987; Distinguished Urban Journalism Award, National Urban Coalition, 1978; George Polk awards, 1981, 1986, and 1987; Alfred I. du Pont-Columbia University Award, 1981, 1987, 1988, 1991, and 1992; Medal of Excellence from University of the State of New York, 1984; Overseas Press Award, 1986; fellow, American Academy of Arts and Sciences, 1991; Gold Baton, Alfred I. du Pont-Columbia University, 1992, for the body of work; Silver Baton, Alfred I. du Pont-Columbia University, 1992, for documentaries; Global Environmental Citizen Award, Center for Health and Global Environment, Harvard Medical School, 2004; Outstanding Informational Series distinction, Academy of Arts and Sciences.

WRITINGS:

Listening to America: A Traveler Rediscovers His Country, Harper Magazine Press, 1971.

Genesis: A Living Conversation, Doubleday (New York, NY), 1996.

(Editor) *Fooling with Words: A Celebration of Poets and Their Craft,* Morrow (New York, NY), 1999.

Genesis and the Millennium: An Essay on Religious Pluralism in the Twenty-First Century, J.M. Dawson Institute of Church-State Studies, 2000.

Moyers on America: A Journalist and His Times, edited by Julie Leininger Pycior, Anchor Books (New York, NY), 2005.

Contributing editor, *Newsweek.*

TELEVISION SERIES

Creativity, first broadcast by the Public Broadcasting System (PBS), January, 1982.

A Walk through the Twentieth Century, first broadcast by PBS, January, 1984.

In Search of the Constitution, first broadcast by PBS, April, 1987.

Joseph Campbell and the Power of Myth, first broadcast by PBS, 1987.

The Secret Government: The Constitution in Crisis (first broadcast by PBS, 1987), Seven Locks Press (Washington, DC), 1988.

Facing Evil, first broadcast by PBS, March, 1988.

A World of Ideas, Volume 1: *Conversations with Thoughtful Men and Women about American Life Today and the Ideas Shaping Our Future* (first broadcast by PBS, 1988), Doubleday (New York, NY), 1989, Volume 2: *Public Opinions from Private Citizens,* Doubleday, 1990.

Moyers: The Power of the Word, first broadcast by PBS, September, 1989.

Global Dumping Ground: The International Traffic in Hazardous Waste (first broadcast by PBS, 1990), Seven Locks Press (Washington, DC), 1990.

Healing and the Mind (first broadcast by PBS, February, 1993), Doubleday (New York, NY), 1993.

The Language of Life: A Festival of Poets (first broadcast by PBS, 1995), Doubleday (New York, NY), 1995.

America's First River: Bill Moyers on the Hudson, broadcast on WNET, 2002.

Becoming American: The Chinese Experience, first broadcast by PBS on March 25, 2003.

SIDELIGHTS: Retired broadcast journalist Bill Moyers is well known for the decades he spent providing American television audiences with "news of the mind." His erudite political commentaries, historical essays, and series on such subjects as myth and evil challenged the limits of television programming and offered educational alternatives to standard prime-time fare. "The conventional wisdom is that ideas and intelligent conversation make bad TV," Geoffrey C. Ward once wrote in *American Heritage* magazine. "Within the industry, human beings with something to say are dismissed as 'talking heads.' Moyers knows better and has proved it time and again. His is an earnest presence . . . but it is also intelligent, humane, and intensely curious. He seems genuinely affected by what he sees and hears, and more important, he possesses the mysterious power to pass along his amusement or astonishment or horror intact to the viewer." Many of Moyers's work, including his series *Creativity: A Walk through the Twentieth Century,* and *Facing Evil,* have appeared on public television, a forum well-suited to his intellectual style and scope. He has also served as a commentator and investigative reporter for CBS Television, both on the nightly news and in specials. According to *Saturday Review* contributor Katherine Bouton, Moyers "asks the questions we ourselves would like to [ask] and, unlike most of us, never interrupts the answer. His passing comment seems designed not to draw attention to himself, . . . but to bring out something in the interviewee that a direct question might not evoke. . . . He's an intellectual. . . . He's a man of political acuity. . . . He's moral but not a preacher, political but not a politician."

Moyers was born in 1934 and christened Billy Don. The younger of two sons, he grew up in Marshall, Texas, where his father held a variety of blue collar jobs. In *People* magazine, Moyers reminisced about his youth. Marshall, he said, "was a wonderful place to be poor if you had to be poor. It was a genteel poverty in which people knew who you were and kind of looked after you. Status was important in Marshall, but more important was being part of the community." As a child during the World War II, Moyers was particularly drawn to the overseas broadcasts of journalist Edward R. Murrow. "This stout voice coming across the ocean night after night, describing the horrors of war," he told *People.* "He brought history alive for me." A good student who also found time to work and engage in extracurricular activities, Moyers began his own journalism career at the Marshall *News Messenger* in 1949. He changed his name to Bill because he thought the name more appropriate for a budding sports writer. After graduating from high school, he enrolled at North Texas State University, where he met his future wife, Judith Suzanne Davidson.

In the spring of his sophomore year of college, Moyers wrote to Senator Lyndon B. Johnson, offering to help with Johnson's reelection campaign. Johnson hired Moyers for a summer internship, then, impressed with the young man's work habits, persuaded Moyers to transfer to the University of Texas at Austin. There Moyers studied journalism and theology, worked as assistant news director at KTBC-TV, and preached at two small Baptist churches two Sundays per month. He received his bachelor's degree in journalism in 1956 and spent the following year at the University of Edinburgh in Scotland as a Rotary International fellow. In 1957 he entered the Southwestern Baptist Theological Seminary to train for the ministry, and he earned another bachelor's degree with honors in 1959. Moyers never served as a full-time minister, however. He told *People:* "I knew I couldn't be a preacher. I thought that my talents lay elsewhere." Apparently Lyndon Johnson agreed with that assessment, offering Moyers a position as special assistant in Washington, DC. Soon after Johnson was elected vice president, Moyers was appointed associate director of public affairs of the newly created Peace Corps. He was made deputy director in 1962—one of the youngest presidential appointees ever approved by Congress.

Moyers returned to the White House in 1963, when John F. Kennedy's assassination elevated Johnson to the presidency. Moyers first served as one of Johnson's advisors on domestic affairs, overseeing the far-reaching Great Society legislation. Then, in 1964, he became White House chief of staff, and in 1965 he assumed the position of press secretary. As the *Saturday Review* reporter noted, the Washington press corps "was fascinated by the young man who seemed to have Lyndon Johnson's full confidence. Part of the appeal was his background—son of an East Texas dirt farmer, former divinity student, and ordained Baptist teacher. Part was his age—30. Part was his already impressive political credentials. . . . And part was his character—he was bright, and he was calm and efficient. This inner fortitude took its toll. Moyers suffered from a chronic ulcer when he worked for Johnson, and the strain is obvious even in photographs, which show a tense, skinny young man with heavy, black-rimmed glasses." Indeed, Moyers became increasingly disillusioned as Johnson intensified America's military involvement in Southeast Asia while placing less stress on domestic improvements. In 1967 he left public service, over Johnson's strenuous objections, to become publisher of *Newsday,* one of the nation's largest suburban daily newspapers.

Under Moyers's tenure at *Newsday,* the paper garnered thirty-three major journalism awards, including two Pulitzer Prizes. Still, Moyers quit *Newsday* in the summer of 1970 for a more leisurely adventure. He boarded a bus with a notebook and tape recorder and embarked on a 13,000-mile trip across the United States. Claiming that he had been out of touch with Americans for too long, he interviewed numerous ordinary folk from all walks of life and described his subjects in *Listening to America: A Traveler Rediscovers His Country,* published in 1971. The book became a best-seller, as well as a critical success.

Moyers also began his long association with public television in 1970. He recognized the then-fledgling medium as the perfect forum for a free and unhurried discussion of important issues. "You know that your [public television] viewer has a tolerance for ideas, a willingness to be patient, a mind that wants to be stretched," Moyers commented in *Saturday Review.* "Commercial television paces itself so rapidly that it's hard to absorb. It's racing—it wants to keep the action flowing like the Indianapolis speedway. . . . My work on public broadcasting wants to almost infiltrate—to insinuate itself into the consciousness of the viewer." In 1971 Moyers became host of *Bill Moyers' Journal,* a weekly show that addressed the political and social issues of the time. To quote the *Saturday Review* reporter, the program "epitomized public-affairs broadcasting at its best"; it won its host a total of five Emmy Awards. After a decade in commercial television at CBS, he returned to public television.

Returning to public television, Moyers worked through PBS and Public Affairs TV, a production company, to create programs that focus on ideas and issues. These programs often involve an interview format in which Moyers engaged, questioned, provoked, and listened to thinkers, experts, policy-makers, and others. As James Gardner observed in *Commentary,* "The popular success of . . . projects with which Bill Moyers has been associated over the years, evidently results from the distinctive chemistry generated among the three parts in the equation—Moyers, his subjects, and his audience." Programs which have used this interview format include series such as *Joseph Campbell and the Power of Myth, A World of Ideas with Bill Moyers, The Arab World, Listening to America with Bill Moyers,* and *The Language of Life: A Festival of Poets.* Moyers was also the host or driving force for numerous documentaries and special reports aired on PBS on subjects such as government excess, toxic pollution, violence, and hate crimes.

Several of Moyers's television projects had a more permanent impact and reach a wider audience through books published as companions to the television series. Among these, *Joseph Campbell and the Power of Myth,* the two volumes of *A World of Ideas, Healing and the Mind,* and *The Language of Life: A Festival of Poets* have received significant audience attention.

A World of Ideas is just the kind of project that Bill Moyers is known for creating. The first volume, subtitled *Conversations with Thoughtful Men and Women about American Life Today and the Ideas Shaping Our Future,* contains over forty interviews with authors, poets, scientists, social scientists, policy-makers, and other thinkers and doers from a variety of social groups, countries, and walks of life. The second volume, subtitled *Public Opinions from Private Citizens,* adds almost thirty similar interviews. "Although Mr. Moyers imposes few constraints, he does have an overall agenda, albeit a broad one," noted Alison Friesinger Hill in the *New York Times Book Review.* "He is inquiring into contemporary values and concerns, within the United States and in global society." Characteristically, in exploring these issues "Moyers doesn't lower the level of the dialogue for TV."

Publishing the transcripts of these interviews in a book form not only made them permanent, but also gave the reader a chance to savor some of the comments and Moyers a chance to further highlight some of the issues. "This new format is generally more satisfying than the original broadcasts because it permits us to study more closely those arguments that possess real substance, and to skip over much cant and attitudinizing," Gardner pointed out. "Thus, while the broadcasts were generally duller than polite people were willing to concede at the time, these transcripts do provide some moments of genuine intelligence and illumination."

In *Healing and the Mind* Moyers explores Chinese medicine, psychoneuroimmunology, meditation, and other unconventional approaches to healing, as well as old-fashioned, personal, and humane medicine in traditional settings. Moyers's investigation of the growing interest in alternative approaches to healing

"frequently reinforces Western medicine's domination and underscores how little is really known about the mind's effect on the body," admitted M.S. Mason in the *Christian Science Monitor.* "He is scrupulously careful not to undermine the biomedical model. Yet implicit in all the information provided is an important challenge to the medical establishment's mechanistic approach to curing: A human being is more than a 'ghost in a machine.'" Mason concluded that "the most important insights *Healing and the Mind* has to offer concern the importance of community, the importance of respect for the whole person, and the direct effect of thought on the body."

The Language of Life is Moyers's celebration of poetry and its place in American life. The book brings together Moyers's public television series of the same name with two television specials, one on Rita Dove and another on Donald Hall and Jane Kenyon. Here again Moyers employs his characteristic interviewing style to probe the issues, public and personal, on the minds and in the poetry of twenty-nine poets. He also includes short speeches given by five other poets at the Doge Poetry Festival, a regular gathering in Stanhope, New Jersey. Helen Vendler found fault with the companion book in a *New York Times Book Review* piece. "Mr. Moyers's earnestly proclaimed love for poetry turns out to be a love of its human narratives, its therapeutic power and its unifying messages," she observed. "The poets themselves try to return Mr. Moyers to what he is missing: to imagination, to language, to rhythms, to structure," she added. "But these are not grist for television, with its abhorrence of analytic talk. So each interview is relentlessly diverted from the discussion of poetry itself to human-interest topics, which usually produce statements of thoughtless banality." Vendler also found that "the poems quoted are strikingly uneven in worth," but she admitted "everyone will find something to like."

In *Moyers on America,* the distinguished journalist "offers a thoughtful and caustic look at American politics," commented Vanessa Bush in *Booklist.* In his collection of essays, speeches, and related material, Moyers covers a wide breadth of topics that have concerned him over the years, and that he still considers of critical importance today. He provides essays on subjects such as the increasing influence of the wealthy at the expense of the poor; how a more progressive government of the past took a more active and genuine interest in protecting the welfare of citizens; and how journalists were more dedicated to breaching the smokescreen surrounding business and government corruption. "Moyers's ability to communicate history, philosophy and personal experience simultaneously is impressive," commented a *Publishers Weekly* reviewer. He tells personal stories of his boyhood in Texas and of his role in the Lyndon Johnson presidency. He points out that Johnson, brusque and pugnacious though he might have been, knew the difference between right and wrong and sought to ensure that right was done, as when he integrated the Faculty Club of the University of Texas in 1964. The *Publishers Weekly* critic concluded that "Moyers's wisdom, common sense and deeply felt principles should inspire and energize many readers in the very best way."

Critical acclaim and viewer support from a surprising cross-section of the population has assured Moyers will have a lasting impression on journalism and public television. He retired from broadcasting in 2004 to focus on writing projects that most interest him, as well as to "think about the Last Act—capital L, capital A—of my life," Moyers commented to Frazier Moore in *America's Intelligence Wire*. *Newsweek* contributor Harry F. Waters wrote that Bill Moyers "looks at America and sees freeways of the mind connecting great and complex issues, a landscape of ethical cloverleafs that affords a natural habitat for the journalist as moralist. . . . Along with his gifts of insight and eloquence, this Texas populist and former Baptist preacher possesses a special knack for bringing big issues down to human dimension." Waters concluded, "Besides choosing fertile thematic terrain, Moyers always brings a point of view to his craft that . . . at least dares to challenge and provoke. Agree with him or not, he never leaves your mind in neutral."

BIOGRAPHICAL AND CRITICAL SOURCES:

PERIODICALS

American Film, June, 1990, interview with Bill Moyers, p. 16.

American Heritage, December, 1983, Geoffrey C. Ward, review of *A Walk through the Twentieth Century,* p. 12.

America's Intelligence Wire, December 10, 2004, Frazier Moore, "Prominent American TV Journalist to Retire, Blasts 'Right-Wing Media' for Pro-Bush Propaganda," profile of Bill Moyers.

Booklist, May 1, 2004, Vanessa Bush, review of *Moyers on America: A Journalist and His Times,* p. 1482.

Business Wire, April 18, 2005, "From Religion to Revolution, Epidemics to Economics, *Wide Angle* Returns for its Fourth Season of In-Depth Documentaries on the Critical Issues Shaping the World Today."

Christian Science Monitor, February 19, 1993, M. S. Mason, review of *Healing and the Mind,* p. 13.

Commentary, October, 1989, James Gardner, review of *A World of Ideas,* p. 70.

Esquire, October, 1989, David Zurawik, "The Following Myth Is Made Possible by a Grant from Bill Moyers: On the Road with the Hero of a Thousand Televisions," profile of Bill Moyers, p. 139.

Hollywood Reporter, March 24, 2003, Irv Letofsky, review of *The Chinese Experience,* p. 38.

National Review, March 10, 1989, Tod Lindberg and Hadley Arkes, "The World According to Moyers," profile of Bill Moyers, p. 22.

New Republic, August 19, 1991, Andrew Ferguson, "The Power of Myth: Bill Moyers, Liberal Fraud," profile of Bill Moyers, p. 22.

Newsweek, July 4, 1983, Harry F. Waters, "Travels with Charlie and Bill," profile of Bill Moyers, p. 74.

New York Times Book Review, June 4, 1989, Alison Friesinger Hill, "A World of Ideas: Conversations with Thoughtful Men and Women about American Life Today and the Ideas Shaping Our Future," interview with Bill Moyers, p. 23; November 25, 1990, Robert H. Boyle, review of *Global Dumping Ground: The International Traffic in Hazardous Waste,* p. 14; May 23, 1993, Eric Cassell, review of *Healing and the Mind,* p. 29; June 18, 1995, Helen Vendler, review of *The Language of Life: A Festival of Poets,* p. 14.

People, February 22, 1982, Lisa E. Smith, "Bill Moyers: A Colossus from Texas Is Bestriding Two Networks—at PBS He Explores 'Creativity'; at CBS He's the New Eric Sevareid," p. 47; August 1, 1983, "Marshall, Texas Is Deep in the Heart of TV Newsman Bill Moyers—and Vice Versa," profile of Bill Moyers, p. 41.

Publishers Weekly, April 19, 2004, review of *Moyers on America,* p. 55.

Saturday Review, February, 1982, Katherine Bouton, "Bill Moyers: The Quest for Quality TV," p. 16.

Texas Monthly, June, 2004, Evan Smith, "Bill Moyers: The Seventy-Year-Old Journalist—Whose New Collection of Speeches and Essays Arrives in

Bookstores This Month—on Why He's Parting Ways with PBS, What It Was Like to Work for LBJ, and Whether Objectivity Is All It's Cracked up to Be," interview with Bill Moyers, p. 92.

Times Literary Supplement, November 8, 1991, review of *Global Dumping Ground*, p. 32.

ONLINE

Lucidcafe.com, http://www.lucidcafe.com/ (October 8, 2005), biography of Bill Moyers.

Salon.com, http://www.salon.com/ (April 7, 2003), Andrew O'Hehir, interview with Bill Moyers.*

*   *   *

MÜLLER, Herta 1953-

PERSONAL: Born August 17, 1953, in Nitzkydorf, Romania; immigrated to Germany, 1987; married Richard Wagner. *Education:* Attended the University of Timisoara.

ADDRESSES: Agent—c/o Author Mail, Picador, 175 5th Ave., New York, NY 10010.

CAREER: Writer. Worked as a teacher and as a translator in a machine factory, both in Romania.

AWARDS, HONORS: Marieluise-Fleißer Prize, 1990; Kranichsteiner Literary Prize, Darmstadt, 1991; Kleist Prize, Germany, 1994; European Literary Prize, 1991; International IMPAC Dublin Literary Award (with Michael Hoffman), 1997, for *The Land of Green Plums*.

WRITINGS:

Niederungen (stories), 1982, translation by Sieglinde Lug published as *Nadirs*, University of Nebraska Press (Lincoln, NE), 1999.

Drückender Tango (stories), c.1984.

Barfuessiger Februar: Prosa (title means "Barefoot February"), Rotbuch-Verlag (Berlin, Germany), 1987.

Reisende auf einem Bein, Rotbuch-Verlag (Berlin, Germany), 1989.

Die Teufel sitzt im Speigel: Wie Wahrnehmung sich erfindet, Rotbuch-Verlag (Berlin, Germany), 1991.

Der Fuchs war damals schon der Jager (novel), Rowohlt (Reinbek bei Hamburg, Germany), 1992.

(Editor, with Verona Gerasch) *Beitrage zum Kolloquium, Jans von Bulow, Leben, Wirken und Vermachtnis: Veranstaltet von der Abteilung Musikgeschichte der Staatlichen Museen Meiningen am 6. und 7. Mai 1994 im Rahmen der Meininger Landesmusiktage zum 100*, Staatliche Museen (Meiningen, Germany), 1994.

Herztier (novel), Rowohlt (Reinbek bei Hamburg, Germany), 1994, translation by Michael Hoffman published as *The Land of Green Plums*, Metropolitan Books (New York, NY), 1996.

Hunger und Seide: Essays, [Germany], 1995.

In der Falle, Wallstein (Gottingen, Germany), 1996.

Heute wär ich mir lieber nicht begegnet (novel), Rowohlt (Reinbek bei Hamburg, Germany), 1997, translation by Michael Hulse and Philip Boehm published as *The Appointment: A Novel*, Metropolitan Books (New York, NY), 2001.

Reisende auf einem Bein, [Germany], translation by Valentina Glajar and Andre Lefevere published as *Traveling on One Leg*, Northwestern University Press (Evanston, IL), 1998.

(Author of epilogue) Theodor Kramer, *Die Wahrheit ist, man hat mir nichts getan: Gedichte*, (title means "This Truth, It Has Not Hurt Me: Poems"), P. Zsolnay (Wien, Austria), 1999.

Im Haarknoten wohnt eine Dame, (title means "A Lady Lives in the Hair-Knot"), Rowohlt (Reinbek bei Hamburg, Germany), 2000.

Beobachtungen, Alb-Donau-Kreis (Ulm, Germany), 2000.

(Contributor of essay) Kent Klich, *Children of Ceausescu*, photographs by Kent Klich, Umbrage Editions (New York, NY), 2001.

(With Yoko Tawada and Alissa Walser) *Wenn die ein Pferd wäre, könnte man durch die Bäume reiten: Prosa*, Swiridoff (Künzelsau, Germany), 2001.

Die Handtasche: Prosa, Lyrik, Szenen & Essays, Swiridoff (Künzelsau, Germany), 2001.

Der König Verneigt Sich und Tötet, C. Hanser (Munich, Germany), 2003.

Die Blassen Herren mit den Mokkatassen, C. Hanser (Munich, Germany), 2005.

SIDELIGHTS: Herta Müller was described by a critic in the *Times Literary Supplement* as "one of the most gifted writers in the German language." Müller grew up in Romania, where she was a member of the German-speaking minority, and left her village to attend the University of Timisoara, where she studied German and Romanian literature. She also joined a group of Romanian-German writers who, despite the rule of the repressive regime of Nicholai Ceausescu, believed in freedom of expression. Her short stories, novels, and essays describe the Romanian dictatorship and the ruin it has brought to that country, as well as the rootlessness of political exiles. Müller has garnered prestigious awards for her writing, including the coveted German Kleist Prize and the 1997 IMPAC Dublin Literary Award, which she shared with Michael Hoffman, for her 1996 novel *The Land of Green Plums.*

After graduating from school, Müller worked as a translator in a machine factory, but was fired because she would not cooperate with the secret police. During this time she wrote *Niederungen,* a collection of short stories, but could not get permission from the government censors to publish it in its complete form. Two years later she wrote another collection, *Drückender Tango.* Both of these works show the hypocrisy of life in Romania's German-speaking villages and their zealous oppression of nonconformists. In a review in *World Literature Today,* Rita Terras described the village in *Niederungen* as "a landscape of the soul . . . the battered existence of a narrator wallowing in despair. . . . There is no end to the list of unfortunate incidents, and the village idyll turns into a nightmare populated by black-garbed, backward, superstitious, German-speaking farmers dwelling among the tattered white flowers of death and harvests of corn."

Romanians criticized her for ruining their image, but when *Niederungen* was smuggled out of Romania, it was published in Germany and won instant acclaim. Müller traveled to Germany, where she spoke against the Romanian government, and after that was forbidden to publish anything in Romania. Despite this, she continued to write, and in 1987, after two years of waiting for permission, left Romania and immigrated to Berlin with her husband, Richard Wagner.

Müller's *The Land of Green Plums* (originally published in 1994 in Germany as *Herztier*) begins with the student narrator describing Lola, her roommate who, like the narrator, has come from a small village and is unprepared for city life. Lola is promiscuous, and finally hangs herself; after her death, she is expelled from the Communist party. Suspicion is contagious: soon the narrator is under suspicion too, and ends up leaving the university. Larry Wolff wrote in the *New York Times Book Review* that the book is "a novel of graphically observed detail in which the author seeks to create a sort of poetry out of the spiritual and material ugliness of life in Communist Romania." Margaret Walter noted in the *Sunday Times Books* that the narrator "has no real stories to tell: she can offer only heartbreaking glimpses" of her family, the city she lives in, and her own troubled life.

The novel's title comes from a scene in which the narrator watches the police stealing green plums from the trees. "They knew where the plum trees were in every precinct they policed," Müller writes. "The green plums made them stupid. They ate themselves away from their duty. They reverted to childhood, stealing plums." Wolff remarked: "Ms. Müller's vision of a police state manned by plum thieves reads like a kind of fairy tale on the mingled evils of gluttony, stupidity and brutality. . . . As the narrator ponders Lola's pathetic fate, the novel encompasses not only the political persecution of dissidents and the harassment of a national minority but also the particular kinds of oppression and vulnerability that women experience under a regime of policemen." He also asserted that the book "addresses issues of vampirish complicity in the bloody rituals of an oppressive regime, whose hungry subjects, whether stealing fresh offal or green plums, ingest political poisons with historically protracted, corrosive consequences."

The next significant novel published by Müller is *Heute wär ich mir lieber nicht begegnet,* published in English as *The Appointment: A Novel.* With thematic concerns similar to *The Land of Green Plums, The Appointment* looks at how the repressive culture in Romania under Ceausescu affects one factory worker. Using the first person voice and a stream-of-conscious narrative style, this female factory worker reflects on her life, the people she is close to, those who have betrayed her, and friends and family members that are no longer living. The now-unemployed worker has been charged with prostitution because she has been putting her name, address, and plea to marry her in the men's suits she sews. The suits are being sent to Italy and she hopes someone there will help her escape her current existence. Writing in the *Chicago Review,* Jason M. Baskin commented: "Müller's psychological acuity makes *The Appointment* both more and less a fable: it is a disturbingly precise representation of individual consciousness under siege, yet it lacks the kind of discernable architecture that would allow the reader analytical distance." Summarizing the novel's appeal, a *Kirkus Reviews* critic concluded that *The Appointment* was "sensitive, observant, unrelenting—and compelling."

BIOGRAPHICAL AND CRITICAL SOURCES:

BOOKS

Müller, Herta, *The Land of Green Plums,* translated by Michael Hoffman, Metropolitan Books (New York, NY), 1996.

PERIODICALS

Chicago Review, Jason M. Baskin, review of *The Appointment: A Novel,* p. 138.
Kirkus Reviews, July 15, 2001, review of *The Appointment,* p. 969.
New York Times Book Review, December 1, 1996, Larry Wolff, review of *The Land of Green Plums,* p. 38.
Sunday Times Books (London, England), August 2, 1998, Margaret Walter, review of *The Land of Green Plums,* p. 9.
Times Literary Supplement, October 6, 1989, review of *Reisende auf einem Bein,* p. 19.
World Literature Today, autumn, 1985, Rita Terras, review of *Niederungen,* p. 586.

ONLINE

Dickinson College Web site, http://www.dickinson.edu/ (October 30, 2005), Beverley Driver Eddy, biography of Herta Müller.*

*   *   *

MUNHALL, Edgar 1933-

PERSONAL: Born March 14, 1933, in Pittsburgh, PA; son of Walter (an engineer) and Anna (a teacher; maiden name, Burns) Munhall. *Education:* Yale University, B.A. (with high honors), 1955, Ph.D., 1959; New York University, M.A., 1957; also attended Arts Student League. *Religion:* Episcopalian.

ADDRESSES: Agent—c/o Author Mail, Scala Books, 141 Wooster St., New York, NY 10012. *E-mail*—munhall@frick.org.

CAREER: Writer and professor. Yale University, New Haven, CT, instructor, 1959-64, assistant professor, 1964-65, assistant curator of prints and drawings at the university art gallery, 1959-64; Frick Collection, New York, NY, curator, 1965-99; organized touring exhibit of drawings by Jean-Baptiste Greuze, 2002. Columbia University, New York, NY, adjunct professor, 1979, 1981; *du,* contributing editor, 1980-84; lecturer.

AWARDS, HONORS: Decorated Chevalier, 1989, Decorated Officier, 2002, French Ordre des Arts et des Lettres; Phi Beta Kappa.

WRITINGS:

NONFICTION

Ingres and the Comtesse d'Haussonville, Frick Collection (New York, NY), 1985.
Whistler and Montesquiou: The Butterfly and the Bat, Abbeville Press (New York, NY), 1995.
(With Susan Grace Galassi and Ashley Thomas) *The Frick Collection: A Tour,* Scala Books (New York, NY), 1999.
Greuze the Draftsman (exhibition catalog), Merrell (New York, NY), 2002.

Contributor to periodicals, including *Apollo, Arts Quarterly, Burlington Magazine, Gazette des Beaux-Arts,* and *L'Oeil.* Author of exhibition catalogs. Prime author of the "ArtPhone" INFORM tour by Acoustiguide, 1998.

SIDELIGHTS: An aspiring artist who found his niche in art history early in life, Edgar Munhall was the first curator of the Frick Collection of major works in Western art and held that position for nearly thrity-five years. Before his retirement from the Frick Collection, Munhall played a role in the major acquisitions purchased by the collection and organized some of its special exhibitions.

After his departure in 1999, Munhall organized a touring exhibit of drawings by Jean-Baptiste Greuze, a popular and highly regarded eighteenth-century French painter, and wrote the accompanying catalog, *Greuze the Draftsman.* Munhall had become a recognized expert on Greuze after writing his Ph.D. dissertation on him in the late 1950s. Though Greuze was primarily a portrait artist and genre painter, he also created many drawings. Some of these drawings were studies used in preparation for paintings; others were created as independent works of art. In addition to detailing the background and importance of many of Greuze's drawings, Munhall also includes an introduction to Greuze as well as a short biography in *Greuze the Draftsman.* Praising the comprehensive nature of the book, Katherine Rook Lieber wrote in a review published on *ArtScope.net*, "*Greuze the Draftsman* represents the cream of fine art books: superb works, solid scholarship, and a subtle excellence of graphic layout that presents both at their elegant best."

BIOGRAPHICAL AND CRITICAL SOURCES:

PERIODICALS

Booklist, April 15, 1995, Donna Seaman, review of *Whister and Montesquiou: The Butterfly and the Bat,* p. 1465.
Library Journal, November 15, 2002, Sandra Rothenberg, review of *Greuze the Draftsman,* p. 69.
New York Times Book Review, June 4, 1995, John Russell, review of *Whister and Montesquiou,* p. 20.

ONLINE

ArtScope.net, http://www.artscope.net/ (April 17, 2003), Katherine Rooke Lieber, review of *Greuze the Draftsman.*
Frick Collection Web site, http://www.frick.org/ (April 17, 2003), "Edgar Munhall, the First Curator of the Frick Collection, Retires; Edgar Munhall Organizes a Touring Exhibition of Drawings by Greuze to Open at the Frick Collection in 2002," biography of Edgar Munhall.

*   *   *

MURGUÍA, Alejandro 1949-

PERSONAL: Born 1949. *Education:* San Francisco State University, B.A., M.F.A.

ADDRESSES: Office—1600 Holloway Ave., San Francisco, CA 94132. *E-mail*—gmurguia@sfsu.edu.

CAREER: Writer and professor. San Francisco State University, College of Ethnic Studies, San Francisco, CA, associate professor and faculty advisor to *Cipactli: Raza Studies Journal of Literature and Art.* Mission Central Cultural Center for Latino Arts, San Francisco, CA, founding member and former director; worked on *Tin Tan* (a Chicano literary magazine), San Francisco, CA, c. late 1970s.

AWARDS, HONORS: American Book Award, Before Columbus Foundation, 1991, for *Southern Front,* and 2003, for *This War Called Love: Nine Stories; The Medicine of Memory: A Mexican Clan in California* was nominated for the Victor Turner Prize in ethnographic writing.

WRITINGS:

Farewell to the Coast (stories), Heirs Press (San Francisco, CA), 1980.
(Editor, with Barbara Paschke) *Volcan: Poems from Central America; A Bilingual Anthology,* City Lights (San Francisco, CA), 1983.
Southern Front (historical fiction), Bilingual Press (Tempe, AZ), 1990.
(Translator) Rosario Murillo, *Angel in the Deluge* (poetry), City Lights (San Francisco, CA), 1994.
This War Called Love: Nine Stories, City Lights (San Francisco, CA), 2002.
The Medicine of Memory: A Mexican Clan in California (memoir), University of Texas Press (Austin, TX), 2002.

SIDELIGHTS: Alejandro Murguía is a Chicano writer and professor who has published two collections of short stories, *Farewell to the Coast* and *This War Called Love: Nine Stories,* both which look at life as a Latino. In the first, many of the stories are set in the city of San Francisco, while in the second, international settings, such as Mexico, Costa Rica, and Nicaragua, are also employed.

Many of the stories in the second collection feature characters trying to improve their lot in life, often unsuccessfully. In *This War Called Love,* three stories, including "Boy on a Wooden Horse" and "Of rendas," feature a character named Reymundo, his many difficulties and losses.

Murguía's memoir, *The Medicine of Memory: A Mexican Clan in California,* is not just his autobiography of life in California and Mexico, it is also a discussion of his family's past and his perspective on a number of events in the history of Hispanics in the United States from the 1700s onward. Gwen Gregory in the *Library Journal* observed that *The Medicine of Memory,* which was nominated for the Victor Turner Prize in ethnographic writing, features "Murguía's spirited writing."

BIOGRAPHICAL AND CRITICAL SOURCES:

BOOKS

The Medicine of Memory: A Mexican Clan in California, University of Texas Press (Austin, TX), 2002.

PERIODICALS

Library Journal, November 15, 2002, Gwen Gregory, review of *The Medicine of Memory,* p. 91.

ONLINE

San Francisco Reader, http://www.sanfranciscoreader. com/ (October 7, 2005), Jeff Troiano, "Raising the Chicano Voice," interview with Alejandro Murguía.

San Francisco State University Web site, http://www. sfsu.edu/ (October 30, 2005), biography of Alejandro Murguía.*

N

NEATE, Patrick 1970-

PERSONAL: Born 1970, in Putney, London, England. *Education:* Earned a degree at Cambridge University; attended City University, London.

ADDRESSES: Home—Hammersmith, England. *Agent*—Simon Trewin, PFD, Ltd., Drury House, 34-43 Russell St., London WC2B 5HA, England.

CAREER: Disc jockey and novelist. Worked as a teacher in Zimbabwe; founder of an Internet company; freelance journalist in England. Participant in conference on ethical tourism, 2001.

AWARDS, HONORS: Betty Trask Award, 2001, for *Musungo Jim and the Great Chief Tuloko;* Whitbread Novel Award, 2001, for *Twelve Bar Blues;* National Book Critics Circle Award for criticism, 2004, for *Where You're At: Notes from the Frontline of a Hip-Hop Planet.*

WRITINGS:

Musungo Jim and the Great Chief Tuloko, Penguin (London, England), 2000.
Twelve Bar Blues, Penguin (London, England), 2001.
The London Pigeon Wars, Farrar, Straus & Giroux (New York, NY), 2004.
Where You're At: Notes from the Frontline of a Hip-Hop Planet, Riverhead Books (New York, NY), 2004.
City of Tiny Lights (mystery novel), Viking (New York, NY) 2005.

Contributor to periodicals, including *Washington Post, The Face, Tatler, Fabric Magazine, Quintessentially Magazine, Mixmag, Q, Guardian* (London), *Harper's Magazine, Sunday Tribune, Standard, Tatler, Time Out, Hospital Doctor, Times* (London), *Telegraph* (London), *Sky,* and *Marie-Claire.*

WORK IN PROGRESS: A book on hip-hop for Bloomsbury; a novel for Penguin; a screenplay adaptation of *The Tesseract* by Alex Garland.

SIDELIGHTS: British journalist and part-time disc jockey Patrick Neate reacted with surprise to the announcement that he had won his country's coveted Whitbread Novel Award for his second novel, *Twelve Bar Blues.* In fact, he expressed astonishment that he was even considered for the prestigious award, especially with noted British novelist Ian McEwan also in the running. "When you're up against Ian McEwan, someone I've read since university and loved and think is incredibly amazing in a way I never will be, you find it incredibly humbling and embarrassing to have won," Neate admitted to Louise Jury in the online *Independent.* "I was short-listed with a lot of grown-up writers, and then there's little you. When I found I'd won, I thought it was a bit of a joke."

Born in southwest London in 1970, Neate attended St. Paul's School in Barnes, England, before enrolling at Cambridge University, where he majored in social anthropology. As Neate once explained to *CA,* he "might have got a first if I hadn't been so put off by the tie-dye hippies with dogs on bits of string" then in vogue in British academia. After graduating from university, finding his degree opened no doors to employment, he decided to spend some time teaching in Africa. He spent a year teaching at a small school in Mashonaland West, Zimbabwe, which made a lasting impression on him. Neate would later participate in a national conference on ethical travel in which he discussed being a wealthy westerner in an impoverished country, as a way of helping tourists and other young teachers appreciate and respect cultural and economic differences. Upon returning from Africa, he took a journalism course at City University, London, then set up a dot.com company, made some money, and left the business. Following this foray into the business world, Neate focused on writing about black musical forms such as jazz and hip-hop as a freelance journalist. Working as a part-time disc jockey, Neate also began writing fiction.

Neate published his first novel, *Musungo Jim and the Great Chief Tuloko,* in 2000. The story features Jim Tulloh, an English teacher in Zambawi, a fictional small postcolonial republic in sub-Saharan Africa. In the midst of the political unrest that is often typical in such African republics, Tulloh becomes involved in a military coup and, through a series of comic convolutions, ends up leading the revolution. Several critics noted the similarity between the fictitious "Zambawi" and the country of Zimbabwe, and found *Musungo Jim and the Great Chief Tuloko* a political satire of a corrupt postcolonial government.

While his first novel received relatively little attention in the British press, with his second novel, *Twelve Bar Blues,* Neate suddenly found himself the talk of the literary world. In the *Daily Telegraph,* Helen Brown commented: "If I could choose one current British writer to tell tall tales around my fantasy campfire, it would be Patrick Neate." *Twelve Bar Blues,* while not a sequel to *Musungo Jim,* does include some of the same characters. The story opens in 1790 in Africa, beginning with a "brief tale of music and betrayal," according to Brown. The novel fast-forwards to the Louisiana Bayou of 1899, offering the life story of Fortis "Lick" Holden, history's forgotten man of jazz. Lick is searching for his stepsister in turn-of-the-twentieth-century New Orleans, and eventually Jim Tulloh—the protagonist of Neate's first novel—appears. Jim forms a casual friendship with Sylvia diNapoli, a retired prostitute, while his plane is departing Heathrow for a flight to New York City. James

Urquhart, in his review for the *Independent,* noted that, "by JFK, they are tentative friends," and quoted from the novel: "'What an odd couple they must make,' Sylvia muses as Jim eagerly presses his nose to the Manhattan skyline streaming past the cab's window: 'a pasty-faced kid and a knackered old whore.'" Chief Tongo, another character from *Musungo Jim* returns as well. "Neate's laconic humor bridges the tongue-in-cheek ribaldry of Tongo's post-colonial chiefdom and the steamy jazz vernacular of Louisiana honky-tonks," commented Urquhart, adding that "thorough research and Neate's delicious dialogue fuse into a compelling genealogy, mostly of jazz musicians and prostitutes, all seeking their destinies."

In *The London Pigeon Wars,* a bored group of thirty-something London urbanites is reinvigorated after the return of their old friend, Murray, a charming con man and philanderer. His group includes Tom Dare, whom he met at Mass one Sunday; Tom's girlfriend, Karen, who works in the mayor's office; and Tariq Khan and wife Emma, owners of a computer-software firm. As the Khans' business begins to flounder, Murray steps up to organize a plan to keep them from losing their home. Murray's schemes in the past usually led to little more than entertainment, but his new idea is grimly serious, very illegal, and potentially deadly. Still, his charm and persistence sway the others. As Murray puts his plan into operation, the city becomes plagued by a peculiar phenomenon: flocks of killer pigeons sweep through the skies, fighting each other over apparent territorial rights, and routinely swooping down on the helpless human population. No one knows what motivates the birds, but in the end, Murray is involved. A *Kirkus Reviews* critic called the book "amusing, and just credible enough to be read straight" without making fantasy or horror-genre allowances for the inexplicable behavior of the birds. "Neate casts his satirical eye on a bleak urban landscape where the search for identity haunts both the earth-bound and the winged," observed *Booklist* reviewer Allison Block.

Where You're At: Notes from the Frontline of a Hip-Hop Planet explores the international influence of hip-hop and how it has become infused in modern musical styles worldwide. Neate chronicles an international trip he took to places around the world where hip-hop music thrives and flourishes, sometimes evolving to suit the local culture. In New York, Japan, South Africa, and Brazil, he notes how hip-hop remains "a powerful voice of protest against the status quo," commented a *Publishers Weekly* reviewer, and how it is critical for hip-hop artists to regain control of their music from the big media and record companies. For Neate, hip-hop represents a different type of globalism, one in which various cultures across the world create their own individual processes. "Black America is assimilated by different cultures on many different continents," commented *Booklist* critic Carlos Orellana. Neate "displays a sympathy and sensitivity to the musical genre many American critics would be hard-pressed to match," the *Publishers Weekly* contributor noted. Orellana called the book "a persuasive examination of the worldwide hip-hop phenomenon."

In *City of Tiny Lights,* Tommy Akhtar is a private investigator in London whose ethnicity is Pakistani, Ugandan, Indian, and British. Many of his clients and cases also involve people who are racially and culturally diverse. Tommy is a rough sort, an amphetamine user and heavy drinker, depressed and using drugs to try to forget his mother's premature death. Early one morning, a black woman, Melody, arrives at Tommy's office. Melody—who says she saw Tommy's ad in the Yellow Pages—is there to hire him to find her missing roommate, a Russian woman named Natasha, who disappeared after a date with a member of parliament who was later found with his skull bashed in. Tommy locates Natasha with little difficulty, but realizes that Melody has not been completely honest with him. Though he is warned off the case, and a vigorous beating by thugs punctuates that warning, Tommy continues, intent on finding out what happened. Eventually his path crosses that of a megalomaniac Saudi Arabian, Azmat al-Dubayan, who plans a series of devastating suicide bombings across London. Tommy's priorities shift as he works to stop al-Dubayan's plans. In the structure of the story, Neate gives each character a distinctive voice, reserving one "like an English version of Raymond Chandler" for Tommy, commented Alaistair Sooke in *New Statesman.* Because Tommy is a "hard-boiled private dick who hangs out with sleazy lowlife and busty hustlers," his characterization both pays homage to and carries on the tradition of such genre icons as Raymond Chandler. However, Sook observed that Tommy's basic characterization "is constructed from second-hand, faux-American idioms" rather than English traits and mannerisms. Despite this caveat, Sook concluded that the novel is a "diverting thriller."

Neate was quoted on the *BBC News* Web site: "A good novel should keep you hooked from start to finish and then make you feel a little better about the world we live in at the end." The Whitbread judges may have agreed, as they were quoted in the *Guardian* as calling *Twelve Bar Blues* "a sprawling and unusual extravaganza of a novel. The ranginess of the story mirrors the arbitrariness of life," the judges added, "while the electrifying prose brings to life characters whose experiences span one century, several cultures and many colours."

Despite his Whitbread success, Neate spends little time resting on his laurels. He has a screenplay and several book-length works underway. "I write very fast and very prolifically," he told Jury in the *Independent* interview. "I've got millions of stories I haven't done anything with at home."

BIOGRAPHICAL AND CRITICAL SOURCES:

PERIODICALS

Booklist, May 1, 2004, Allison Block, review of *The London Pigeon Wars,* p. 1547; July, 2004, Carlos Orellana, review of *Where You're At: Notes from the Frontline of a Hip-Hop Planet,* p. 1809.

Daily Telegraph (London, England), May 12, 2001, Helen Brown, "A Hephelant Blows Its Nose."

Guardian (London, England), January 4, 2002, Fiachra Gibbons, "Whitbread Winner's Ring of Absolute Truth"; January 7, 2002, "Justine Jordon on Books."

Independent (London, England), May 13, 2001, James Urquhart, review of *Twelve Bar Blues,* p. 45.

Kirkus Reviews, April 1, 2004, review of *The London Pigeon Wars,* p. 292.

New Statesman, July 11, 2005, Alastaire Sooke, review of *The City of Tiny Lights,* p. 55.

Newsweek International, July 25, 2005, Shailaja Neelakantan, review of *The City of Tiny Lights,* p. 87.

New York Times, January 3, 2002, "Novel with All That Jazz Takes Whitbread Prize."

Observer (London, England), December 23, 2001, Clover Hughes, review of *Musungo Jim and the Great Chief Tuloko,* p. 18.

Publishers Weekly, July 5, 2004, review of *Where You're At,* p. 47.

Times (London, England), December 12, 2001, Anthea Lawson, review of *Twelve Bar Blues,* p. 12; January 4, 2002, Dalya Alberge, "Writer Is a Winner in Black and White."

ONLINE

BBC News, http://www.bbc.co.uk/ (January 4, 2002), "Surprise Winner for Whitbread Novel" and "Patrick Neate: All That Jazz."

Independent Digital, http://enjoyment.independent.co.uk/ (January 4, 2002), Louise Jury, "McEwan Loses Again as Jazz Novel Claims Top Prize."

Patrick Neate Home Page, http://www.patrickneate.com (October 31, 2005).

Varsityonline, http://www.varsity.cam.ac.uk/ (April 27, 2000), James Knight, "A Neate Touch."*

*   *   *

NORMAN, Barry 1933-

PERSONAL: Born August 21, 1933, London, England; son of Leslie (a film producer and director) and Elizabeth (a film editor) Norman; married, December 10, 1957; wife's name, Diana (a novelist); children: Samantha Norman Clifford, Emma. *Politics:* "Liberal-Democrat." *Religion:* Church of England. *Hobbies and other interests:* Politics, current affairs, and most sports.

ADDRESSES: Agent—c/o Author Mail, Simon & Schuster, 1230 Avenue of the Americas, New York, NY 10020.

CAREER: Writer and television show host. *London Daily Mail,* London, England, show business editor, ended 1971; *The Guardian,* London, England, humorous columnist, beginning 1971; British Broadcasting Corporation-Television (BBC-TV), London, England, writer and presenter of the weekly film review show *Film,* 1972-98, writer and presenter of television show *Omnibus,* 1982, writer and host of *The Hollywood Greats* and *Talking Pictures,* 1977-79; presenter of television show *Barry Norman's Film Night,* Sky Premier, 1998-c.2001; *Radio Times,* London, England, columnist, c. 2003. Appeared on other television programs, including *Night of a Thousand Faces,* 2001; *Best Ever Bond,* 2002; *Countdown,* 2003-05; and *The Unseen Eric Morecambe,* 2005. Radio appearances include: *Going Places; The News Quiz; Breakaway;* and *The Chip Shop.* National Film Finance Corp., director, 1980-84; British Film Institute, member of board of governors, 1996—.

AWARDS, HONORS: Honorary doctorate from University of East Anglia, England; Richard Dimbleby Award, British Academy of Film and Television Arts, for "outstanding personal contributions to factual television."

WRITINGS:

NOVELS

The Matter of Mandrake, W.H. Allen (London, England), 1967.

The Hounds of Sparta, W.H. Allen (London, England), 1968.

End Product, Quartet (London, England), 1976.

A Series of Defeats, Quartet (London, England), 1977.

To Nick a Good Body, Quartet (London, England), 1978.

Have a Nice Day, Quartet (London, England), 1981.

Sticky Wicket, Hodder & Stoughton (London, England), 1984.

The Birddog Tape, St. Martin's Press (New York, NY), 1992.

The Mickey Mouse Affair, Orion (London, England), 1995, published as *The Butterfly Tattoo,* St. Martin's Press (New York, NY), 1996.

Death on Sunset, Orion (London, England), 1998.

NONFICTION

Tales of the Redundance Kid, Van Nostrand (New York, NY), 1975.

The Hollywood Greats, Hodder & Stoughton (London, England), 1979.

The Movie Greats, Hodder & Stoughton (London, England), 1981.

The Film Greats, Hodder & Stoughton (London, England), 1985.

Talking Pictures, Hodder & Stoughton (London, England), 1987.

One Hundred Best Films of the Century, Chapman (London, England), 1992.

(With daughter, Emma Norman) *Barry Norman's Video Guide,* Mandarin (London, England), 1993, 3rd edition, 1995.

(With Emma Norman) *The Radio Times Family Video Guide,* BBC Publications (London, England), 1995.

And Why Not?: Memoirs of a Film Lover, Simon & Schuster (London, England), 2002.

SIDELIGHTS: Barry Norman provided film reviews and interviews with film stars for British television audiences as the host of several programs from the early 1970s until the early 2000s. In addition to being one of the most recognizable film critics in England because of his television appearances, Norman is the author of books about film and novels, primarily thrillers. In 2002, he published his memoir *And Why Not?: Memoirs of a Film Lover.* Though the text covers the whole of Norman's life, it focuses on his many experiences in the entertainment industry and the celebrities he interacted with over the course of his life. While Philip Kerr of the *New Statesman* found the book "a fascinating read," he also wrote: "Barry always struck me as a very fair kind of film critic, too good-humored to nurture a grudge . . . too decent ever to yield to the flashy . . . . Which is all quite at odds with this rather prickly book." In contrast, Jon Barnes of the *Times Literary Supplement* found the book "endearing," noting: "Enormously enjoyable . . . are his tweedy English jibes at Tinseltown and its pretensions."

BIOGRAPHICAL AND CRITICAL SOURCES:

BOOKS

And Why Not?: Memoirs of a Film Lover, Simon & Schuster (London, England), 2002.

PERIODICALS

New Statesman, September 30, 2002, Philip Kerr, "Print the Legend," review of *And Why Not?: Memoirs of a Film Lover,* p. 77.
Times Literary Supplement, November 8, 2002, Jon Barnes, review of *And Why Not?: Memoirs of a Film Lover,* pp. 34-35.

ONLINE

Guardian Unlimited, http://film.guardian.co.uk/ (July 25, 2003), Libby Brooks, "So I Said to Liz Taylor . . .," interview with Barry Norman.*

*   *   *

NUTTALL, A.D. 1937-
(Anthony David Nuttall)

PERSONAL: Born April 25, 1937, in Hereford, England; son of Kenneth (a schoolmaster) and Hilda Mary (Addison) Nuttall; married May Donagh, July 1, 1960; children: William James, Mary Addison. *Education:* Merton College, Oxford, B.A., 1959, M.A., 1962, B.Litt., 1963.

ADDRESSES: Home—175 Divinity Rd., Oxford OX4 1LP, England. *Office*—New College, Oxford OX1 3BN, England. *Agent*—c/o Writer's Representatives, 116 W. 14th St., 11th Fl., New York, NY 10011-7305. *E-mail*—anthony.nuttall@new.ox.ac.uk.

CAREER: University of Sussex, lecturer, 1962-70, reader in English, 1970-73, professor of English, 1973-84, pro-vice chancellor, 1978-81; New College, Oxford, fellow, 1984—; Oxford University, Oxford, England, reader in English, 1990-92, professor of English, 1992—.

AWARDS, HONORS: South East Arts literature prize, 1980, for *Overheard by God.*

WRITINGS:

William Shakespeare: The Winter's Tale, Edward Arnold (London, England), 1966.
Two Concepts of Allegory: A Study of Shakespeare's "The Tempest" and the Logic of Allegorical Expression, Barnes & Noble (New York, NY), 1967.
(Editor, with D. Bush) John Milton, *The Minor Poems in English,* Macmillan (London, England), 1972.
A Common Sky: Philosophy and the Literary Imagination, University of California Press (Berkeley, CA), 1974.
Dostoevsky's "Crime and Punishment": Murder as Philosophic Experiment, Scottish Academic Press for Sussex University Press (Edinburgh, Scotland), 1978.
Overheard by God: Fiction and Prayer in Herbert, Milton, Dante and St. John, Methuen (London, England), 1980.
A New Mimesis: Shakespeare and the Representation of Reality, Methuen (London, England), 1983.
Pope's Essay on Man, Allen & Unwin (London, England), 1984.
Timon of Athens, Twayne Publishers (Woodbridge, CT), 1989.
The Stoic in Love: Selected Essays on Literature and Ideas, Barnes & Noble, (New York, NY), 1990.

Openings: Narrative Beginnings from the Epic to the Novel, Clarendon Press (Oxford, England), 1992.

Why Does Tragedy Give Pleasure?, Clarendon Press (Oxford, England), 1996.

The Alternative Trinity: Gnostic Heresy in Marlowe, Milton, and Blake, Clarendon Press (Oxford, England), 1998.

Dead from the Waist Down: Scholars and Scholarship in Literature and the Popular Imagination, Yale University Press (New Haven, CT), 2003.

Also author, with Arthur Raleigh Humphreys, of phonotape, "Coriolanus," BFA Educational Media, 1972. Contributor to *Critical Quarterly, Review of English Studies,* and other publications.

SIDELIGHTS: A.D. Nuttall's work often combines religious scholarship with literary criticism, as in his books *Overheard by God: Fiction and Prayer in Herbert, Milton, Dante and St. John* and *The Alternative Trinity: Gnostic Heresy in Marlowe, Milton, and Blake.* He has written studies of Shakespeare's works and John Milton's poems, and on such topics such as philosophy and the literary imagination, murder, and the uses of tragedy.

Openings: Narrative Beginnings from the Epic to the Novel examines in depth how epics, long stories, novels, and other lengthy works begin, and how those beginnings affect readers' reaction to and relation with the story. Nuttall looks at formal and natural types of openings, and discusses how some writers tend to start their stories *in medias res*—in the middle of the action—while others prefer to begin at the beginning. In his work, Nuttall evinces a "graceful display of classical and modern scholarship" throughout his analysis, noted critic Avrom Fleishman in the *Journal of English and Germanic Philology.*

Why Does Tragedy Give Pleasure? finds Nuttall analyzing the seeming contradiction that readers derive pleasure from tragedy. Based on a series of lectures he gave in 1992, Nuttall's chapters offer these topics: "Aristotle and After," "Enter Freud," "The Game of Death," and "King Lear." He considers Aristotle's ideas of katharsis, and provides discussions of major works of literature, the works of philosophers such as Nietzsche, and the role tragedy plays in creating a satisfying experience for the reader. Ultimately, the pleasure that readers take from works of tragedy is "a

pleasure qualified but also intensified by the fact that we are learning to recognize something terrible, important, and probable," observed Lars Engle in *Studies in English Literature, 1500-1900.*

The Alternative Trinity: Gnostic Heresy in Marlowe, Milton, and Blake explores Nuttall's theory that Gnosticism gave Christopher Marlowe, John Milton, and William Blake "a refuge from oppressive Christian orthodoxies" that affected their writing and what they could write about, commented John Rumrich in *Modern Philology.* Nuttall identifies a basic tenet of Gnosticism, that the Father is a tyrannical force opposed by the Son. This antagonism and conflict with traditional Christian doctrine formed the atmosphere in which the authors' greatest works were created. Rumrich called the study "a wonderfully informative and provocative series of insights into the theology, poetry, and culture of early modern England."

In *Dead from the Waist Down: Scholars and Scholarship in Literature and the Popular Imagination,* Nuttall approaches a topic he knows well, academia and scholarship, and how practitioners are often stereotyped as being so intent on poring through dusty books and manuscripts that they have no time for anything else—not even sex and relationships with other humans. In contrast, noted Patrick Henry in *Christian Century,* the scholar once enjoyed the "Renaissance ideal of the swashbuckling voyager, the potent and alluring man" of means and ability. Nuttall analyzes how this image of the scholar began to transform in the nineteenth century, and how scholarship became equated with a dry, dusty lifestyle that was itself a sort of death of normal human interaction. For Nuttall, however, this is not a reason to grieve missed opportunities to consort with one's fellows. Sheldon Rothblatt, writing in *Victorian Studies,* concluded that Nuttall's book is "an old-fashioned tribute to scholars and to scholarship, to the pleasures of reading classics or encountering classical ideas, to the fine points and the small things, the footnotes and the indices, the apparatus and scaffolding of learning." *Library Journal* reviewer Felicity D. Walsh called the book a "valuable scholarly work."

Nuttall told *CA:* "The only language I speak easily is English, but I enjoy reading Latin verse (especially Horace). Am interested primarily in the connection between the study of literature and the study of philosophy. Have in addition a less articulate passion for the art and architecture of Italy."

BIOGRAPHICAL AND CRITICAL SOURCES:

PERIODICALS

Christian Century, February 24, 2004, Patrick Henry, review of *Dead from the Waist Down: Scholars and Scholarship in Literature and the Popular Imagination,* p. 56.

Criticism, winter, 1969, review of *Two Concepts of Allegory,* p. 106.

Journal of English and Germanic Philology, January, 1994, Avrom Fleishman, review of *Openings: Narrative Beginnings from the Epic to the Novel,* p. 134.

Library Journal, October 15, 2003, Felicity D. Walsh, review of *Dead from the Waist Down,* p. 70.

Modern Language Review, April, 2001, David Loewenstein, review of *The Alternative Trinity: Gnostic Heresy in Marlow, Milton, and Blake,* p. 465.

Modern Philology, November, 2001, John Rumrich, review of *The Alternative Trinity,* p. 306.

Studies in English Literature, 1500-1900, spring, 1997, Lars Engle, review of *Why Does Tragedy Give Pleasure?,* p. 428.

Times Literary Supplement, April 24, 1981, review of *Overheard by God,* p. 458.

Victorian Studies, winter, 2004, Sheldon Rothblatt, review of *Dead from the Waist Down,* p. 327.

*   *   *

NUTTALL, Anthony David
    See NUTTALL, A.D.

O-P

OGDEN, Margaret Astrid Lindholm
   See OGDEN, Margaret Lindholm

*   *   *

OGDEN, Margaret Lindholm 1952-
   (Robin Hobb, Megan Lindholm, Margaret Astrid Lindholm Ogden)

PERSONAL: Born 1952, in Oakland, CA; daughter of George (a chemist) and Phyllis Lindholm; married; children: four. *Education:* Attended Denver University.

ADDRESSES: Agent—c/o Author Mail, Bantam Books, 1540 Broadway, New York, NY 10036.

CAREER: Writer. Wrote for newspapers in Alaska.

AWARDS, HONORS: Alaska State Council for the Arts grant, 1979, for "The Poaching"; Readers' Award, *Asimov's Science Fiction,* 1989; Nebula Award finalist, Science Fiction and Fantasy Writers of America, for *Wizard of the Pigeons.*

WRITINGS:

"WINDSINGER" SERIES; UNDER PSEUDONYM MEGAN LINDHOLM

Harpy's Flight, Ace (New York, NY), 1983.
The Windsingers, Ace (New York, NY), 1984.

The Limbreth Gate, Ace (New York, NY), 1984.
The Windsingers (omnibus; contains *Harpy's Flight, The Windsingers,* and *The Limbreth Gate*), Corgi (London, England), 1986.
Luck of the Wheels, Ace (New York, NY), 1989.

NOVELS; UNDER NAME MEGAN LINDHOLM

The Wizard of the Pigeons (fantasy), Ace (New York, NY), 1986.
The Reindeer People ("Reindeer People" series), Ace (New York, NY), 1988.
Wolf's Brother ("Reindeer People" series), Ace (New York, NY), 1988.
Cloven Hooves, Bantam (New York, NY), 1991.
(With Steven Brust) *The Gypsy,* Tor (New York, NY), 1992.
Alien Earth (science fiction), Bantam (New York, NY), 1992.

"FARSEER" SERIES; UNDER PSEUDONYM ROBIN HOBB

Assassin's Apprentice, Bantam (New York, NY), 1995.
Royal Assassin, Bantam (New York, NY), 1996.
Assassin's Quest, Bantam (New York, NY), 1997.

"LIVESHIP TRADERS" SERIES; UNDER PSEUDONYM ROBIN HOBB

Ship of Magic, Bantam (New York, NY), 1998.
The Mad Ship, Bantam (New York, NY), 1999.
Ship of Destiny, Bantam (New York, NY), 2000.

"THE TAWNY MAN" SERIES; UNDER PSEUDONYM ROBIN HOBB

Fool's Errand, Bantam (New York, NY), 2002.
Golden Fool, Bantam (New York, NY), 2003.
Fool's Fate, Bantam (New York, NY), 2004.

FANTASY NOVELS; UNDER PSEUDONYM ROBIN HOBB

Shaman's Crossing, Eos (New York, NY), 2005.

Contributor to periodicals and anthologies, including *Space and Time,* edited by Gordon Linzner, 1979; *Amazons!,* edited by Jessica Amanda Salmonson, Daw Books (New York, NY), 1981; the "Liavek" anthologies, edited by Will Shetterly and Emma Bull, 1985-88.

SIDELIGHTS: Margaret Lindholm Ogden wrote her first fantasy novels as Megan Lindholm, a variation of her maiden name. In an interview in *Locus,* she said she assumed a second pseudonym, Robin Hobb, for her "Farseer" series, since booksellers orders based on previous sales, and hers had been decreasing. "Taking a new name kind of erased that part," she said. *Assassin's Quest,* the last book in the "Farseer" saga, was described by a contributor to *Kirkus Reviews* as "an enthralling conclusion to this superb trilogy displaying an exceptional combination of originality, magic, adventure, character, and drama." Roland Green wrote in *Booklist* that the final installment "will please readers and probably whet their appetites for more from Hobb."

In 1998, the first of the "Liveship Traders" series was published, *Ship of Magic.* The story is set in Bingtown, a port city where Trader families pilot "liveships" built from wizardwood that become intelligent as they absorb the spirits of their owners after three generations have died. When Ephron Vestrit dies, his widow, Ronica, passes his liveship, *Vivacia,* to her son-in-law, Kyle Haven, with the hope that his experience in trading will save the family business. Ronica's daughter, Althea, disappointed because she had expected to take command, disguises herself as a boy and goes off to sea. There she is threatened by a pirate, Captain Kennit, who would like to take over the *Vivacia.* Other characters include Althea's younger sister, Malta, and Kyle's son, Wintrow, who is kidnapped from a

monastery and forced into service on the *Vivacia.* The ship has come alive, but she is unstable under the rule of the ambitious Kyle. Wintrow is the only person Althea trusts. A reviewer for *Publishers Weekly* believed the new series is "sure to please fantasy fans." Jackie Cassada wrote in the *Library Journal* that the author "excels in depicting complex characters; even her villains command respect."

Cassada described *The Mad Ship,* the second book in the series, as "imaginative and compelling." A reviewer for *Publishers Weekly* wrote that it "solidifies the series' promise as a major work of high fantasy, reading like a cross between [J.R.R.] Tolkien and Patrick O'Brian." Althea is now an experienced sailor, and she restores the *Paragon,* the male ship of the title, with the help of her lover, Brashen Tell, and a woodcarver named Amber. Althea's mission is to rescue the *Vivacia,* now taken over by the pirate Captain Kennit, who has turned it into a slave ship. Also on board the *Vivacia* are Etta, the Captain's mistress, and Kyle and his son, who are held captive. Wintrow makes a deal with Captain Kennit, promising to heal his wounds in exchange for their lives. The secrets of the liveships, wizardwood, sea serpents, and the dragons of the Rain Wild River's forests are revealed. In *Booklist,* Green wrote that "with [Hobb's] hands on the wheel, high fantasy is going to sea magnificently."

In the third installment, *Ship of Destiny,* Etta is pregnant with Captain Kennit's child, and Wintrow is destined to become king of the Pirate Isles. Ronica rallies Bingtown's inhabitants to resist new invaders, while Althea continues her quest to recover the *Vivacia,* and the mad ship *Paragon* is plotting his own form of revenge. A reviewer for *Publishers Weekly* wrote that "one has to use a jeweler's loupe to find a flaw or a dull moment in this splendid conclusion to one of the finest fantasy sagas to bridge the millennium."

Lindholm Ogden followed the "Live Ship Traders" series with another three-novel series published under the Robin Hobb pseudonym. Called "The Tawny Man" series, these novels are a sequel to the "Farseer" series and are set in the same world. In *Fool's Errand,* the adventures of a now-mature FitzChivalry Farseer are followed, first describing his recent past and now quiet life with his wolf bondmate, Nighteyes, and a foster son. Drawn out of retirement by his friend the Fool, FitzChivalry goes on a new quest to find and escort the badly behaved Prince Dutiful, the heir to the local throne, back to his home. In *Booklist,* Green commented positively on the novel, especially the characters, noting "all of them [are] drawn in exquisite detail, particularly the women."

The next part in the series, *Golden Fool,* finds Fitz-Chivalry dealing with the death of Nighteyes while obediently agreeing to act as the skill-master and train Prince Dutiful at Buckkeep Castle. Though FitzChivalry really wants to embrace solitude and be away from the castle, he is forced to deal with many difficult crises in the kingdom of the Six Duchies. The problems only grow in difficulty as FitzChivalry makes many poor decisions along the way. The critic in *Publishers Weekly* commented: "The writing might not be quite as fine as that in Hobb's 'Assassins' series . . ., but this latest nonetheless shows why she ranks near the top of the high fantasy field."

"The Tawny Man" series concludes with *Fool's Fate.* FitzChivalry and his friend the Fool, now known as Lord Golden, are part of a nearly impossible quest led by Prince Dutiful. The prince made a promise to his fiancée to bring her the head of a certain dragon frozen in ice on a faraway island. The journey is fraught with peril and struggles, both physical and diplomatic. A critic in *Kirkus Reviews* found the book "a winning combination of strong characters and colorful societies." Summarizing the appeal of the whole trilogy, a reviewer in *Publishers Weekly* commented that, "with its carefully modulated tension, wonderful final revelation, and strong characters who remain true to themselves throughout, this series may well become a classic in the Fantasy field."

BIOGRAPHICAL AND CRITICAL SOURCES:

BOOKS

St. James Guide to Fantasy Writers, St. James Press (Detroit, MI), 1996.

PERIODICALS

Booklist, February 1, 1997, Roland Green, review of *Assassin's Quest,* p. 929; March 1, 1998, Roland Green, review of *Ship of Magic,* p. 1098; April 1,

1999, Roland Green, review of *The Mad Ship,* p. 1388; December 15, 2001, Roland Green, review of *Fool's Errand,* p. 709.

Kirkus Reviews, February 1, 1997, review of *Assassin's Quest;* December 1, 2003, review of *Fool's Fate,* p. 1386.

Library Journal, February 15, 1998, Jackie Cassada, review of *Ship of Magic,* p. 173; March 15, 1999, Jackie Cassada, review of *The Mad Ship,* p. 112; March 1, 2000, review of *Ship of Destiny,* p. S9; August 1, 2000, Jackie Cassada, review of *Ship of Destiny,* p. 167.

Locus, January, 1998, interview with Margaret Lindholm Ogden.

Publishers Weekly, January 26, 1998, review of *Ship of Magic,* p. 74; March 22, 1999, review of *The Mad Ship,* p. 75; July 31, 2000, review of *Ship of Destiny,* p. 76; November 18, 2002, review of *Golden Fool,* p. 46; December 8, 2003, review of *Fool's Fate,* p. 50.

ONLINE

Megan Lindholm Home Page, http://www.meganlindholm.com (October 22, 2005), biography of Megan Lindholm.*

*   *   *

PARTHASARATHY, R. 1934-
(Rajagopal Parthasarathy)

PERSONAL: Born August 20, 1934, in Tirupparaiturai, near Tiruchchirappalli, Tamil Nadu, India; married Shobhan Koppikar, 1969; children: two sons. *Ethnicity:* "Asian." *Education:* University of Bombay, M.A., 1959; University of Leeds, postgraduate diploma in English studies 1964; University of Texas at Austin, Ph.D., 1987.

ADDRESSES: Office—Department of English and Program in Asian Studies, Skidmore College, 815 N. Broadway, Saratoga Springs, NY 12866-1632. *E-mail*—rparthas@skidmore.edu.

CAREER: Ismail Yusuf College, Bombay, India, lecturer in English, 1959-62; Mithibai College, Bombay, lecturer in English, 1962-63, 1964-65; British Council, Bombay, lecturer in English language teaching, 1965-66; Presidency College, Madras, India, assistant professor of English, 1966-67; South Indian Education Society College, Bombay, lecturer in English, 1967-71; Oxford University Press, Oxford England, regional editor in Madras, 1971-78, editor in Delhi, India, beginning 1978; University of Iowa, Iowa City, member of international writing program, 1978-79; University of Texas at Austin, Austin, assistant instructor in English, 1982-86; Skidmore College, Saratoga Springs, NY, assistant professor, 1986-92, associate professor of English and Asian studies, 1992—, director of Asian studies program, 1994-98. National Academy of Letters, New Delhi, member of the advisory board for English, 1978-82.

MEMBER: Association for Asian Studies.

AWARDS, HONORS: Ulka poetry prize, *Poetry India,* 1966; translation prize, National Academy of Letters (New Delhi, India), 1995, and A.K. Ramanujan Book Prize for translation, Association for Asian Studies, 1996, both for *The Cilappatikaram of Ilanko Atikal: An Epic of South India;* British Council scholar at University of Leeds.

WRITINGS:

POETRY

(Editor, with J.J. Healy) *Poetry from Leeds,* Writers Workshop (Calcutta, India), 1968.
(Editor) *Ten Twentieth-Century Indian Poets,* Oxford University Press (New Delhi, India), 1976.
Rough Passage, Oxford University Press (New Delhi, India), 1977.
(Translator) *The Cilappatikaram of Ilanko Atikal: An Epic of South India,* Columbia University Press (New York, NY), 1991, also published as *The Cilappatikaram: The Tale of an Anklet,* Penguin Books India (New Delhi, India), 2004.

Also author of *A House Divided: Poems of Love and War* and *The Forked Tongue: The Indian Writer and Tradition;* translator of *The Earliest Tamil Poems.*

SIDELIGHTS: R. Parthasarathy is an Indian poet who writes in English. He is the author of *Rough Passage,* a three-part, autobiographical poem which addresses

the poet's own background of both Indian and English cultures. "The dilemma, simply stated," wrote S. Nagarajan in *Contemporary Poets,* "is how an Indian writer can be himself when he writes in a language which is not his mother tongue or the language of his community or his tradition."

In *Rough Passage,* Parthasarathy attempts to reconcile his two backgrounds by imposing Indian—specifically, Tamil, elements—on English poetic structures. The poems explore the poet's years abroad, his returns home, and his general growth as an artist. Nagarajan suggests in *Contemporary Poets* that Parthasarathy's method proved "only partially successful" in *Rough Passage,* and he mentions that the verse is less impressive than some poems translated into English from other languages.

Parthsarathy told *CA:* "One of the realities of the literary scene in our time is that of the exile as writer who takes his language and homeland abroad with him or writes in a language other than his own. Exile is seen as a rite of passage he must go through before he earns the right to speak. *Rough Passage* is in the tradition of the literature of exile, where the English language and residence abroad are in the nature of attempts to situation myself more firmly at home. The dominance of English in India made us exiles in our own homeland, and no Indian writer of the last 150 years has escaped the bewitchment of English. Modern Indian literature is unthinkable without the English language. It is within the framework of exile that *Rough Passage* should be read. Exile, I repeat, is not a prison house: it is in exile that a writer is most at home.

"One of the problems that the Indian poet writing in English faces is the problem of trying to relate himself meaningfully to a living tradition. The poet who writes only in English is unable to relate himself to any specific tradition. He cannot relate himself, for instance, to the tradition of English verse, and he should not. Nor can he relate himself to a tradition of verse in any one of the Indian languages. From the beginning, I saw my task as one of acclimatizing the English language to an indigenous tradition. In fact, the tenor of *Rough Passage* is explicit: to initiate a dialogue between myself and my Tamil past. The poem attempts a redefinition of myself as a Tamil—what it means to be a Tamil after having whored after English gods. Part three of the work, 'Homecoming,' in particular, tries to derive its sustenance from grafting itself on to whatever I find usable in the Tamil tradition. I was eventually able to 'nativize' in English something that had eluded me over the years—the flavor, the essence or Tamil mores.

"I am aware of the hiatus between the soil of the language I use and my own roots. Even though I am Tamil-speaking and yet write in English, there is the overwhelming difficulty of using images in a linguistic tradition that is quite other than that of my own. I believe that an Indian poet who thinks long and hard enough on his own use of language, even if it is English, will sooner or later, through the English language, try to come to terms with himself as an Indian, with his Indian past and present, and that the language will become acclimatized to the Indian environment. Further, if the poet has access to an Indian language, even though he may not write in it himself, he can gradually try to appropriate the tradition of that language. This would mean reconciling ourselves to Tamil English verse, Kannada English verse, Marathi English verse, and so on—all segments of a pan-Indian mosaic that we recognize as the literatures of India. When that happens, the severed head (Indian English verse) will no longer 'choke/to speak another tongue.'

"*A House Divided: Poems of Love and War* is a long poem rooted in the Tamil and Sanskrit literary traditions, whose resonances it tries to convey in English verse. It is set against the turbulent history of the Indian subcontinent. It draws upon myths to explore the paradox of India since the Raj and to reinforce the survival and continuity of Indian civilization in spite of the ebb and flow of conquests, striking in the process a truly epic note. The poems are located in the social and political realities of India today, in the heart of South Asia, and may be read as notes toward the story of a civilization.

"The book contains one hundred poems arranged in two parts: the inner (personal) world and the outer (public) world. The two worlds are not exclusive; they often overlap. Each part includes several sequences that focus on specific aspects of the personal and public worlds. The opening sequences in part one celebrates the erotic in the tradition of Sanskrit poetry. The erotic is seen as the creative source of poetry. It also informs three other sequences that mediate between the two worlds.

"Five of the poems investigate the uneasy relationship between Hindus and Muslims that has its origin in the Muslim conquest of India in 1192. The Revolt of 1857 and its aftermath were a watershed that further polarized that relationship. Even after independence in 1947, conflicts between the two communities continued to surface, often erupting into violence, as in 1992, when Babur's Mosque in the northern city of Ayodhya was destroyed. Two other sequences also contribute to the dialogue on the politics of conquest.

"The closing sequence, 'Srirangam,' a poem of pilgrimage to a sacred place, explores the transformative potential of the journey as a passage from individuality to community. In the book as a whole, individual and national histories blend together to tell the story of a troubled land. *A House Divided* is a testament that bears witness to the political uncertainties of the times in which we live. It opposes those uncertainties with the human need for community."

BIOGRAPHICAL AND CRITICAL SOURCES:

BOOKS

Contemporary Indian Poetry in English: With Special Reference to the Poetry of Nissim Ezekiel, Kamala Das, A.K. Ramanujan, and R. Parthasarathy, P.K.J. Kurup (New Delhi, India), 1991.
Contemporary Poets, 8th edition, St. James Press (Detroit, MI), 2001.
Das, Bijay Kumar, editor, *Perspectives on the Poetry of R. Parthasarathy,* Prakash Book Deposit (Bareilly, India), 1983.
King, Bruce, *Modern Indian Poetry in English,* revised edition, Oxford University Press (Delhi, India), 2001, pp. 231-243.
Kulshrestha, Chirantan, *Contemporary Indian English Verse: An Evaluation,* Arnold-Heinemann (New Delhi, India), 1980, pp. 250-274.
Walsh, William, *Indian Literature in English,* Longman (London, England), 1990, pp. 136-140.

PERIODICALS

Choice, February, 1979.
Times Literary Supplement, February 3, 1978.
World Literature Today, winter, 1978.

*   *   *

PARTHASARATHY, Rajagopal
   See PARTHASARATHY, R.

PATTERSON, Harry 1929-
(Martin Fallon, James Graham, Jack Higgins, Hugh Marlowe, Henry Patterson)

PERSONAL: Some sources list given name as Henry; born July 27, 1929, in Newcastle-on-Tyne, England; holds dual English and Irish citizenship; son of Henry (a shipwright) and Henrietta Higgins (Bell) Patterson; married Amy Margaret Hewitt, December 27, 1958 (marriage ended, 1984); married Denise Lesley Anne Palmer, 1985; children: (first marriage) Sarah, Ruth, Sean, Hannah. *Education:* Beckett Park College for Teachers, certificate in education, 1958; London School of Economics and Political Science (external student), B.Sc. (honors), 1962. *Politics:* "Slightly right of center." *Religion:* Presbyterian.

ADDRESSES: Agent—c/o Author Mail, G.P. Putnam's Sons, 345 Hudson St., New York, NY 10014.

CAREER: Writer. Worked at a variety of commercial and civil service posts, ranging from clerk to circus tent laborer, 1950-58; Allerton Grange Comprehensive School, Leeds, England, history teacher, 1958-64; Leeds College of Commerce, Leeds, England, lecturer in liberal studies, 1964-68; James Graham College, New Farnley, Yorkshire, England, senior lecturer in education, 1968-70; Leeds University, Leeds, England, tutor, 1971-73; Manchester University, Manchester, England, professor. Former member of Leeds Art Theatre. *Military service:* British Army, Royal Horse Guards, 1947-50.

MEMBER: Royal Economic Society (fellow), Royal Society of Arts (fellow), Crime Writers' Association.

AWARDS, HONORS: D. Univ., Leeds Municipal University, 1995.

WRITINGS:

Sad Wind from the Sea, Long (London, England), 1959.
Cry of the Hunter, Long (London, England), 1960.
The Thousand Faces of Night, Long (London, England), 1961.
Comes the Dark Stranger, Long (London, England), 1962.

Hell Is Too Crowded, Long (London, England), 1962, reprinted under pseudonym Jack Higgins, Fawcett (New York, NY), 1977.
Pay the Devil, Barrie Rockliff (London, England), 1963.
The Dark Side of the Island, Long (London, England), 1963, reprinted under pseudonym Jack Higgins, Fawcett (New York, NY), 1977.
A Phoenix in the Blood, Barrie Rockliff (London, England), 1964.
Thunder at Noon, Long (London, England), 1964.
Wrath of the Lion, Long (London, England), 1964, reprinted under pseudonym Jack Higgins, Fawcett (New York, NY), 1977.
The Graveyard Shift, Long (London, England), 1965.
The Iron Tiger, Long (London, England), 1966, reprinted under pseudonym Jack Higgins, Fawcett (New York, NY), 1979.
Brought in Dead, Long (London, England), 1967.
Hell Is Always Today, Long (London, England), 1968, reprinted under pseudonym Jack Higgins, Fawcett (New York, NY), 1979.
Toll for the Brave, Long (London, England), 1971 (London, England), reprinted under pseudonym Jack Higgins, Fawcett (New York, NY), 1976.
The Valhalla Exchange, Stein and Day (New York, NY), 1976.
To Catch a King: A Novel, Stein and Day (New York, NY), 1979.
Dillinger: A Novel, Stein and Day (New York, NY), 1983.

UNDER PSEUDONYM MARTIN FALLON

The Testament of Caspar Shultz, Abelard (New York, NY), 1962, reprinted under pseudonym Jack Higgins, Fawcett (New York, NY), 1978.
Year of the Tiger, Abelard (New York, NY), 1964.
The Keys of Hell, Abelard (New York, NY), 1965, reprinted under pseudonym Jack Higgins, Fawcett (New York, NY), 1976.
Midnight Never Comes, Long (London, England), 1966, reprinted under pseudonym Jack Higgins, Fawcett (New York, NY), 1975.
Dark Side of the Street, Long (London, England), 1967, reprinted under pseudonym Jack Higgins, Fawcett (New York, NY), 1974.
A Fine Night for Dying, Long (London, England), 1969, reprinted under pseudonym Jack Higgins, Arrow (London, England), 1977.

(Editor) *The Sketches of Erinensis: Selections of Irish Medical Satire, 1824-1836,* Skilton and Shaw (London, England), 1979.

UNDER PSEUDONYM JAMES GRAHAM

A Game for Heroes, Doubleday (Garden City, NY), 1970.

The Wrath of God, Doubleday (Garden City, NY), 1971.

The Khufra Run, Macmillan (London, England), 1972, Doubleday (Garden City, NY), 1973.

The Run to Morning, Stein and Day (New York, NY), 1974, published in England as *Bloody Passage,* Macmillan (London, England), 1974.

Cancer Selection: The New Theory of Evolution, Aculeus Press (Lexington, VA), 1992.

Vessels of Rage, Engines of Power: The Secret History of Alcoholism, Aculeus Press (Lexington, VA), 1994.

UNDER PSEUDONYM JACK HIGGINS

East of Desolation, Hodder & Stoughton (London, England), 1968, Doubleday (Garden City, NY), 1969.

In the Hour before Midnight, Hodder & Stoughton (London, England), 1969, published as *The Sicilian Heritage,* Lancer (New York, NY), 1970.

Night Judgment at Sinos, Hodder & Stoughton (London, England), 1970, Doubleday (Garden City, NY),1971.

The Last Place God Made, Collins (London, England), 1971, Holt (New York, NY), 1972.

The Savage Day, Holt (New York, NY), 1972.

A Prayer for the Dying, Collins (London, England), 1973, Holt (New York, NY), 1974.

The Eagle Has Landed, Holt (New York, NY), 1975, revised edition, Run (London, England), 1982.

Storm Warning, Holt (New York, NY), 1976.

Day of Judgment, Collins (London, England), 1978, Holt (New York, NY), 1979.

The Cretan Lover, Holt (New York, NY), 1980.

Solo, Stein and Day (New York, NY), 1980.

Luciano's Luck, Stein and Day (New York, NY), 1981.

Touch the Devil, Stein and Day (New York, NY), 1982.

Exocet, Stein and Day (New York, NY), 1983.

Confessional, Stein and Day (New York, NY), 1985.

A Jack Higgins Trilogy, Scarborough House (New York, NY), 1986.

Night of the Fox, Collins (London, England), 1986, Simon & Schuster (New York, NY), 1987.

A Season in Hell, Simon & Schuster (New York, NY), 1989.

Memoirs of a Dance Hall Romeo, Simon & Schuster (New York, NY), 1989.

Cold Harbour, Simon & Schuster (New York, NY), 1990.

The Eagle Has Flown: A Novel, Simon & Schuster (New York, NY), 1991.

Eye of the Storm, G.P. Putnam's Sons (New York, NY), 1992.

Thunder Point, G.P. Putnam's Sons (New York, NY), 1993.

Three Complete Novels (contains *The Last Place God Made, The Savage Day,* and *A Prayer for the Dying*), G.P. Putnam's Sons (New York, NY), 1994.

Three Complete Novels (contains *The Eagle Has Landed, The Eagle Has Flown,* and *Night of the Fox*), G.P. Putnam's Sons (New York, NY) 1994.

On Dangerous Ground, G.P. Putnam's Sons (New York, NY), 1994.

Angel of Death, G.P. Putnam's Sons (New York, NY), 1995.

Drink with the Devil, G.P. Putnam's Sons (New York, NY), 1996.

The President's Daughter, G.P. Putnam's Sons (New York, NY), 1997.

Flight of Eagles, G.P. Putnam's Sons (New York, NY), 1998.

The White House Connection, G.P. Putnam's Sons (New York, NY), 1999.

Day of Reckoning, G.P. Putnam's Sons (New York, NY), 2000.

Edge of Danger, G.P. Putnam's Sons (New York, NY), 2001.

Midnight Runner, G.P. Putnam's Sons (New York, NY), 2002.

Bad Company, G.P. Putnam's Sons (New York, NY), 2003.

Dark Justice, G.P. Putnam's Sons (New York, NY), 2004.

Without Mercy, G.P. Putnam's Sons (New York, NY), 2005.

UNDER PSEUDONYM HUGH MARLOWE

Seven Pillars to Hell, Abelard (New York, NY), 1963, revised edition published as *Sheba,* G.P. Putnam's Sons (New York, NY), 1994.

Passage by Night, Abelard (New York, NY), 1964, reprinted under pseudonym Jack Higgins, Fawcett (New York, NY), 1978.

A Candle for the Dead, Abelard (New York, NY), 1966, published in England under pseudonym Jack Higgins as *The Violent Enemy,* Hodder & Stoughton (London, England), 1969.

OTHER

Also author of stage plays, including *Walking Wounded,* 1987, and of radio plays, including *The Island City,* 1987, and *Dead of Night,* 1990.

ADAPTATIONS: Several of Patterson's novels have been adapted for film, including *The Violent Enemy,* 1968; *The Wrath of God,* 1972; *The Eagle Has Landed,* Columbia, 1977; *Confessional,* 1985; and *A Prayer for the Dying,* Samuel Goldwyn Co., 1987. Television movies have been made of Patterson's novels, including *To Catch a King,* Home Box Office (HBO), 1984; *Night of the Fox,* 1990; *Midnight Man* (based on the novel *Eye of the Storm*), 1995; *On Dangerous Ground,* 1995; *Windsor Protocol,* 1996; and *Thunderpoint,* 1998. An unabridged version of *A Fine Night for Dying* was adapted for audio cassette, read by Nicholas Ball, Dove Audio (Beverly Hills, CA), 1992; an unabridged version of *The Graveyard Shift* was adapted for audio cassette, read by Patrick MacNee, New Millennium, 2002.

SIDELIGHTS: Harry Patterson has written more than sixty novels, many of which have been best sellers. His work has been translated into more than forty languages, making his work accessible to a worldwide audience. Patterson is perhaps best known for the adventure novel *The Eagle Has Landed,* published under the name Jack Higgins. The novel tells of a secret Nazi plot during the Second World War to kidnap British leader Winston Churchill. First published in 1975, the book became an international bestseller and was made into a successful film. Patterson followed the book with many other popular thriller novels, including *Storm Warning, The Valhalla Exchange, To Catch a King, Night of the Fox,* and *A Season in Hell.* "A Higgins book," noted George Kelley in the *St. James Guide to Crime and Mystery Writers,* "features adventure, action, strong characters, and breathless excitement."

Patterson began writing while still teaching school in England. "While I was a struggling schoolmaster," he told Edwin McDowell of the *New York Times,* "I was

struggling very much to make some kind of living by writing, but I couldn't because the return on each book was so small. That meant I had to publish books one after the other, so I used several names." When he decided to focus on adventure fiction, he adopted the Higgins pseudonym, based on the name of a militant Irish uncle.

Many of Higgins's novels are set during the Second World War and feature a mix of real and fictional characters. *The Eagle Has Landed,* for instance, features a group of Nazi paratroopers who have landed in Britain in 1943 with orders to kidnap Winston Churchill. "The suspense," Kelley commented, "is generated by the novel's realism in depicting World War II and historical events."

Storm Warning relates the story of several Germans and five nuns who try to cross the Atlantic late in the war to rejoin their families in war-torn Europe. "The war," Kelley remarked, "is only a backdrop to the real action of the struggle of the characters against the sea. In the powerful conclusion, allegiances are forgotten as the English and Germans join forces to battle the sea. *Storm Warning* is a classic tale of epic proportions."

The novel *Exocet* concerns a Russian plot to supply Argentina with missiles during the Falklands War with England. Gabrielle Legrand, a reluctant spy for the British who is in love with an Argentine air force pilot, must prevent the Argentines from getting the Russian missiles. "*Exocet* is a complicated but compelling novel," according to Larry Jones in the *West Coast Review of Books.* "Higgins' style is graceful, his dialogue is natural, and his story-telling gripping." Kelley found that, with *Exocet,* Patterson proves he can write a "novel with a contemporary setting as realistic and exciting as his bestselling World War II books."

While some critics complain about Higgins's later works, others praise his ability to continue writing exciting novels. In a review of *The White House Connection* for *Booklist,* Budd Arthur commented: "When it comes to thrillers, Jack Higgins wrote the book. . . . And this is one of the best." A critic for *Publishers Weekly* remarked in a review of *Edge of Danger:* "After 31 Higgins thrillers, nearly all first-rate, fans know that this author is as reliable as a Rolls. His 32nd novel proves no letdown. . . . This is Higgins near the top of his game." In another *Publishers Weekly* review, a critic wrote that *Midnight Runner*—a sequel to the "electrifying" *Edge of Danger*—is "swift and coursing with dark passion."

Patterson continued to publish adventure novels under the Higgins pseudonym in the early 2000s. *Bad Company*, a sequel to *Midnight Runner*, links the vast wealth of a rogue Nazi officer, Baron Max von Berger, from the end of World War II to present day Arabia. British investigator Sean Dillon and his team become the target of von Berger's wrath because of Dillon's defensive killing of Lady Kate Rashid, a love interest of the baron. *Bad Company* was followed by *Dark Justice* and *Without Mercy*. The former concerns Dillon's investigation into an assassination attempt on the president of the United States, while the latter is set amidst the aftermath of a shootout between Dillon's people and a group of underhanded Russians. In a *Publishers Weekly* review of *Dark Justice*, a critic praised "the author's high-speed narration and the mesmerizing hard edges of heroes and villains alike"

Patterson once told *CA:* "I look upon myself primarily as an entertainer. Even in my novel *A Phoenix in the Blood*, which deals with the colour-bar problem in England, I still have tried to entertain, to make the events interesting as a story—not just the ideas [and] ethics of the situation. I believe that at any level a writer's only success is to be measured by his ability to communicate."

BIOGRAPHICAL AND CRITICAL SOURCES:

BOOKS

St. James Guide to Crime and Mystery Writers, 4th edition, St. James Press (Detroit, MI), 1996.

PERIODICALS

Booklist, April 15, 1999, Budd Arthur, review of *The White House Connection*, p. 1478.
Kirkus Reviews, May 15, 2003, review of *Bad Company*, p. 702.
Library Journal, June 1, 1999, Roland Person, review of *The White House Connection*, p. 174; December, 2000, Roland Person, review of *Edge of Danger*, p. 188.

New York Times, July 28, 1982, Edwin McDowell, "Higgins Odyssey: Potboiler to Best Seller," biography of Harry Patterson, p. C22.
Publishers Weekly, March 23, 1998, review of *Flight of Eagles*, p. 78; October 25, 1999, review of *Pay the Devil*, p. 78; February 28, 2000, review of *Day of Reckoning*, p. 61; January 22, 2001, review of *Edge of Danger*, p. 303; February 11, 2002, review of *Midnight Runner*, p. 162; July 26, 2004, review of *Dark Justice*, p. 40.
West Coast Review of Books, September, 1983, Larry Jones, review of *Exocet*, p. 34.*

* * *

PATTERSON, Henry
  See PATTERSON, Harry

* * *

PEARS, Tim 1956-

PERSONAL: Born November 15, 1956, in Tonbridge Wells, Kent, England; son of W.S. Pears (an Anglican priest) and Jill (Charles-Edwards) Scurfield; married; children: two. *Education:* Graduated from National Film and Television School, London, England, 1993. *Politics:* "As liberal as possible in a cruel world." *Religion:* "Still searching."

ADDRESSES: Home—Oxford, England. *Agent*—AM Heath & Co. Ltd., 79 St. Martin's Ln., London WC2N 4RE, England.

CAREER: Writer. Worked variously as a construction laborer, nurse in a mental hospital, bodyguard, house painter, security guard, farm worker, house decorator, night porter, and manager of an art gallery.

MEMBER: Ebony International.

AWARDS, HONORS: Ruth Hadden Memorial Award, 1993, and Hawthornden Prize, Hawthornden Trust, 1994, both for *In the Place of Fallen Leaves;* Lannan Literary Award (fiction), Lannan Foundation, 1996.

WRITINGS:

NOVELS

In the Place of Fallen Leaves, Hamish Hamilton (London, England), 1993.

In a Land of Plenty, Doubleday (New York, NY), 1997.

A Revolution of the Sun, Doubleday (New York, NY), 2001.

Wake Up, Bloomsbury (London, England), 2002.

ADAPTATIONS: The novel *In a Land of Plenty* was filmed for the British Broadcasting Corporation ten-part television drama series and broadcast in 2001.

SIDELIGHTS: Tim Pears is the author of *In the Place of Fallen Leaves,* which he described to *CA* as a novel "about home and leaving home, about being at home and being in exile," and, more specifically, as the story of "an adolescent coming to understand her world and her place in it." The novel's heroine is thirteen-year-old Alison, who lives in a farming community with her family, including an eccentric grandmother and a somewhat deranged father. During the particularly hot summer of 1984, Alison befriends Jonathan, son of an impoverished aristocrat living nearby. While troubles develop among striking miners and similarly dissatisfied teachers, Alison and Jonathan prosper in the rural countryside, where they share experiences, thoughts, and feelings.

In the Place of Fallen Leaves also abounds with memorable secondary characters. Alison's father, for instance, is an endearing amnesiac whose brain has rotted from alcohol, and Alison's grandmother is a similarly loveable sort who holds some rather peculiar beliefs about time and magnetic fields. Also significant is Pam, Alison's sister, who forsakes the countryside for academic pursuits. Pam, as Giles Foden reported in the *Independent,* "presents a kind of sexual example for Alison or, maybe, a warning."

Upon its publication in 1993, *In the Place of Fallen Leaves* won widespread acclaim in England, where it was hailed as a significant literary debut. London *Times* reviewer Penny Perrick described the novel as "astounding," and A.S. Byatt asserted in the London *Telegraph* that Pears's story "is entirely satisfying." Byatt added that the work is "comic, and wry, and elegiac, and shrewd and thoughtful all at once." Foden declared that *In the Place of Fallen Leaves* is "technically sophisticated" and "an unusually well-made novel." Martyn Bedford wrote in the *Oxford Times* that with *In the Place of Fallen Leaves* Pears has produced "a moving and beautifully written book."

Pears's novel, Bedford concluded, "is an utterly convincing portrayal of the life and times of the Devon countryside, deeply evocative and rich with sensuous imagery—sad and funny . . . but never mawkish."

In a Land of Plenty also uses the concept of home as part of its plot. Pears's book centers on the Freemans, headed by Charles and Mary (nee Wyndham) Freeman. Beginning with their wedding in 1952 and purchase of an old mansion, Pears constructs an epic story. The mansion overlooks a small town in Great Britain where the often difficult Charles runs a factory that he inherits. The factory employs many who live in the community and affords a privileged life for the family. Pears explores the lives and relationships of the children, James, Simon, Robert, and Alice, their friends, relatives, and townspeople in the text. Particular attention is paid to James, who has a physical deformity and becomes interested in photography. This hobby is used to illuminate some of the themes of the novel. Barbara Love in the *Library Journal* commented: "In this great big novel . . . Pears . . . affords his characters the luxury of time and space to become fully realized."

Pears explores a very different topic in *Wake Up:* genetic engineering and the concept of progress through science. In the short novel, narrator John Sharpe has taken his family potato company and made a deal with a genetics firm to develop vaccines in plants that can be eaten. Unfortunately, people being used in secret human trials on the vaccines have been dying, creating dilemmas for John. While dealing with this crisis by driving in circles and avoiding his workplace, John reflects on his past. During his reflections, he continually admits to lying about certain aspects of his life and corrects himself over and over again. Emma Tristram of the *Times Literary Supplement* concluded: "Tim Pears has created an impressive, subtle and serious book, lifted from a preaching tone by the personality of its narrator—a combination of poet, Ancient Mariner, and pub bore."

Pears told *CA:* "I left school at sixteen knowing only that I wanted to be a poet. For ten years I did all kinds of jobs and wrote a lot of awful poetry. Then one day I transposed a poem into a short story and set it in the tiny Devon village in which I'd grown up. It was a moment of liberation: Writing was no longer simply an intellectual process; it became physical, the world of my adolescence vividly recalled—I could smell the lanes after the rain, hear a mother calling her children in for tea, touch the sharp blades of grass we blew notes from through our fingers.

"I wrote no more poems but many stories and set them all in this small village. I found that there was nothing that interested me which couldn't be adapted to fit into this world. The stories developed eventually into *In the Place of Fallen Leaves.*

"I think human beings are preoccupied by the same things they've always been preoccupied with: Where do we come from, why are we here, where are we going? How should we live our lives? What are our hopes, responsibilities, dreams? How can we love and be loved? The things that spring us from sleep at night in a state of misery or joy. I want to create characters I love and explore their lives."

BIOGRAPHICAL AND CRITICAL SOURCES:

PERIODICALS

Independent (London, England), April 4, 1993, Giles Foden, review of *In the Place of Fallen Leaves.*
Library Journal, December, 1997, Barbara Love, review of *In a Land of Plenty,* p. 155.
Oxford Times, April 23, 1993, Martyn Bedford, review of *In the Place of Fallen Leaves.*
Telegraph (London, England), March 27, 1993, A.S. Byatt, review of *In the Place of Fallen Leaves.*
Times (London, England), March 28, 1993, Penny Perrick, review of *In the Place of Fallen Leaves.*
Times Literary Supplement, August 16, 2002, Emma Tristram, "Monster on the Ring Road," review of *Wake Up,* p. 20

ONLINE

Bloomsbury Web Site, http://www.bloomsbury.com/ (October 7, 2005), biography of Tim Pears.
British Council Arts Contemporary Writers Web Site, http://www.contemporarywriters.com/ (October 7, 2005), biography of Tim Pears.

*   *   *

PEDERSON, William D. 1946-
(William David Pederson)

PERSONAL: Born March 17, 1946, in Eugene, OR; son of Jon M. and Rose Marie (Ryan) Pederson. *Education:* University of Oregon, B.S., 1967, M.A., 1972, Ph.D., 1979. *Hobbies and other interests:* Reading, jogging, collecting foreign Abraham Lincoln stamps.

ADDRESSES: Home—5734 Roma Dr., Shreveport, LA 71105-4225. *Office*—Department of History and Social Sciences, 321BH, Louisiana State University in Shreveport, 1 University Pl., Shreveport, LA 71115-2301; fax: 318-795-4203. *E-mail*—wpederso@pilot.lsus.edu.

CAREER: Lamar University, Beaumont, TX, teacher, 1977-79; Westminster College, Fulton, MO, teacher, 1979-80; Yankton College, Yankton, SD, teacher, 1980-81; Louisiana State University in Shreveport, Shreveport, professor of political science, 1981—, founding director of American Studies Program, 1982-91, 1995—, and International Lincoln Center for American Studies, 1982—, founder of presidential conference series, 1992, holder of American studies chair in liberal arts, 1999. Georgetown University, professor, 1997—; Centenary College of Louisiana, teacher, 1999, 2005; also taught at University of Oregon, American University, and Southern University in Shreveport. Louisiana Endowment for the Humanities, member of executive committee for Cross-Currents Series, 1997—. Lincoln Forum, member of board of directors and national advisory board, 1996—; Smithsonian Institution, resident associate; member of Center for the Study of the Presidency and Presidency Research Group. Shreveport Mayor's Committee on the Bicentennial of the U.S. Constitution, member, 1986-89. *Military service:* U.S. Army, 1968-70.

MEMBER: International Lincoln Association (president, 1990-92; chair of board of directors, 1998—), International PEN (Center USA West), International Society of Political Psychology (founding member), International Studies Association, Association of Third World Studies (life member), American Association for the Advancement of Slavic Studies, American Society of Public Administration, German Studies Association, Abraham Lincoln Association (member of board of directors, 1994-95), Academy of Criminal Justice Sciences (life member), Washington Semester and Internship Association (founding member), Southern Historical Association (life member), Louisiana Historical Association (life member; member of board of directors, 2001-04),

Lincoln Fellowship of Wisconsin (life member), North Louisiana Historical Association (life member), Amnesty International, Phi Kappa Phi (life member; president-elect of local chapter, 1998), Pi Sigma Alpha (founder of Nu Chi chapter, 1983).

AWARDS, HONORS: National Endowment for the Humanities, fellow at New York University, 1981, fellow at Harvard University, 1985; Louisiana Endowment for the Humanities, winner of essay competition, 1987, for a column on the bicentennial of the U.S. Constitution, and Special Humanities Award, 1998; Annual Achievement Award, Abraham Lincoln Association, 1994; Regional Award in Humanities, Cultural Olympiad, 1995-96; Association of Third World Studies, distinguished leadership award and appreciation award, 2003, and presidential award, 2004; grants from Kosciuszko Foundation, Community Foundation of Shreveport-Bossier, and Louisiana Endowment for the Humanities.

WRITINGS:

(Editor, with Ann M. McLaurin, and contributor) *The Rating Game in American Politics,* Irvington (New York, NY), 1987.

(Editor, with Norman W. Provizer, and contributor) *Grassroots Constitutionalism: Shreveport, the South, and the Supreme Law of the Land,* University Press of America (Lanham, MD), 1988.

(Editor and contributor) *The "Barberian" Presidency,* Peter Lang (New York, NY), 1989.

(Editor) *Governmental Gridlock: Congressional-Presidential Relations in the U.S.,* Edwin Mellen Press (Lewiston, NY), 1991.

(Editor) *Lincoln and Leadership: A Model for a Summer Teachers Institute,* Louisiana Lincoln Group (Shreveport, LA), 1993.

(Editor, with Norman W. Provizer) *Great Justices of the U.S. Supreme Court,* Peter Lang (New York, NY), 1993.

(Editor, with Frank J. Williams, and contributor) *Abraham Lincoln: Sources and Style of Leadership,* Greenwood Press (Westport, CT), 1994.

(Editor, with Frank J. Williams, and author of preface) *Abraham Lincoln: Contemporary,* Savas Woodbury (Campbell, CA), 1995.

(Editor, with Mark J. Rozell) *FDR and the Modern Presidency: Leadership and Legacy,* Praeger Publishers (Westport, CT), 1997.

(Editor, with Byron W. Daynes) *The New Deal and Public Policy,* St. Martin's Press (New York, NY), 1998.

(Editor, with John Y. Simon) *Abraham Lincoln, Gettysburg, and the Civil War,* Savas Woodbury (Campbell, CA), 1999.

(Editor, with Mark J. Rozell and Frank J. Williams) *George Washington and the Origins of the American Presidency,* Praeger Publishers (Westport, CT), 2000.

(Editor, with Kevin Cope) *George Washington's Image in American Culture,* AMS Press (New York, NY), 2001.

(Editor, with Nancy Beck Young and Byron W. Daynes) *Franklin D. Roosevelt and the Shaping of American Culture,* M.E. Sharpe (Armonk, NY), 2001.

(Editor, with Thomas P. Wolf and Byron W. Daynes) *Franklin D. Roosevelt and Congress: The New Deal and Its Aftermath,* M.E. Sharpe (Armonk, NY), 2001.

(Editor, with Ethan Fishman and Mark J. Rozell) *George Washington: Foundation of Leadership and Character,* Praeger Publishers (Westport, CT), 2001.

(Editor, with Norman W. Provizer) *Classic Cases in American Constitutional Law,* WestGroup (St. Paul, MN), 2001.

(Editor, with Thomas C. Howard) *Franklin D. Roosevelt and the Formation of the Modern World,* M.E. Sharpe (Armonk, NY), 2003.

(Editor, with Frank J. Williams) *Franklin D. Roosevelt and Abraham Lincoln: Competing Perspectives on Two Great Presidencies,* M.E. Sharpe (Armonk, NY), 2003.

(Editor, with Norman W. Provizer, and contributor) *Leaders of the Pack: Polls and Case Studies of Great Supreme Court Justices,* Peter Lang (New York, NY), 2003.

(Editor, with Stephen K. Shaw and Frank J. Williams) *Franklin D. Roosevelt and the Transformation of the Supreme Court,* M.E. Sharpe (Armonk, NY), 2004.

The FDR Years, Facts on File (New York, NY), 2006.

(With Marilyn R. Bedgood) *Theodore Roosevelt's Bear Hunt in Louisiana,* 2006.

Contributor to books, including *Dimensions of the Modern Presidency,* edited by Edward N. Kearny, Forum Press, 1981; *Morality and Conviction in American Politics,* edited by Martin Shann and Susan

Duffy, Prentice-Hall (Englewood Cliffs, NJ), 1990; *Theodore Roosevelt: Many-Sided American,* edited by Natalie A. Naylor, Douglas Brinkley, and John Allen Gable, Heart of the Lakes Publishing (Interlaken, NY), 1992; *The Presidency and Domestic Policies of Jimmy Carter,* edited by Herbert D. Rosenbaum and Alexej Ugrinsky, Greenwood Press (Westport, CT), 1994; and *Debating the Issues: America's Government and Politics.* edited by Robert P. Watson, Longman Publishers (New York, NY), 2005. Contributor of more than 150 articles and reviews to history and political science journals and newspapers, including *Shreveport Journal, Presidential Studies Quarterly,* and *Social Science Quarterly.* Guest editor, *Quarterly Journal of Ideology,* 1994, and *White House Studies;* editor, *Political Science Educator,* 1996-98, and *International Abraham Lincoln Journal,* 2000—; coeditor, *Journal of Contemporary Thought,* 1997—. Founding editor, *Abraham Lincoln Abroad, International Lincoln Association Newsletter, Lincolnator, Abraham Lincoln at Home,* and *Washington Semesters and Internships,* all 1998—.

WORK IN PROGRESS: Editing *Lincoln Lessons: Essays Commemorating Abraham Lincoln's Birthday Bicentennial,* with Frank J. Williams.

SIDELIGHTS: William D. Pederson once told *CA:* "Although I have contributed numerous political commentary columns to newspapers, most of my writing has been published in journals and volumes intended for academic audiences. Underlying themes in my work reflect both my career research interest in the political psychology of leaders and the causes of revolts in prison camps, as well as my experiences as a university political science professor and director of a multidisciplinary American studies program. Based upon my interest in political leaders, in 1992 I founded the first presidential conference series in the South at Louisiana State University in Shreveport. This triennial conference series follows the rank order of America's greatest presidents as selected by scholars. Abraham Lincoln was the subject of the first conference of the series, which also was the first academic conference on the sixteenth president ever to be held in the Deep South. The next year I offered the first Summer Institute on Lincoln for secondary teachers ever held in the nation. The conference resulted in two edited volumes and two newsletters for which I am the founding editor. In addition to my continuing editorship of the two Lincoln newsletters, I also edit

Washington Semesters and Internships, a newsletter that grew from my interest as the resident director of the first independent Washington semester at a public university in the South."

* * *

PEDERSON, William David
    See PEDERSON, William D.

* * *

POLIKOFF, Barbara G. 1929-
    (Barbara Garland Polikoff)

PERSONAL: Born May 13, 1929; daughter of Joseph M. Garland and Julia Garland (a homemaker); married Alexander Polikoff (a lawyer), June 28, 1951; children: Deborah, Daniel, Joan. *Education:* University of Michigan, B.A., 1950; University of Chicago, M.A., 1952 *Hobbies and other interests:* Back-packing, gardening, photography.

ADDRESSES: Home—848 Broadview Ave., Highland Park, IL 60035. *Agent*—Jane Jordan Browne, 410 S. Michigan, Chicago, IL 60605. *E-mail*—barbarapol@ aol.com.

CAREER: Von Steuben Public High School, Chicago, IL, teacher, 1951-52; Chicago Natural History Museum, Chicago, associate editor of museum bulletin, 1952-55; writer. Sullivan House (alternative school for poor and troubled inner-city kids), board member, 1970-90; Chicago Public Schools, volunteer teacher for writing workshops, 1973-93.

MEMBER: Society of Midland Authors, Amnesty International, American Civil Liberties Union, Sierra Club, Nature Conservancy.

AWARDS, HONORS: Best Books citation, *School Library Journal,* 1992, and Maryland Black-eyed Susan Award nomination, 1995-96, both for *Life's a Funny Proposition, Horatio;* Carl Sandburg Award for best children's book, Friends of the Chicago Public Library, 1993; Notable Book citation, American Library Association.

WRITINGS:

(And photographer) *My Parrot Eats Baked Beans: Kids Talk about Their Pets,* Albert Whitman (Niles, IL), 1987.

James Madison: Fourth President of the United States (biography), Garrett Publishing Company (Ada, OK), 1988.

Herbert C. Hoover: Thirty-first President of the United States (biography), Garrett Publishing Company (Ada, OK), 1990.

Life's a Funny Proposition, Horatio (novel), Holt (New York, NY), 1992.

Riding the Wind (companion novel to *Life's a Funny Proposition, Horatio*), Holt (New York, NY), 1995.

With One Bold Act: The Story of Jane Addams, Boswell (Chicago, IL), 1999.

Why Does the Coquí Sing?, Holiday House (New York, NY), 2004.

SIDELIGHTS: Barbara G. Polikoff is a writer of biographies and novels for young adults. Though her first book was not published until 1987, she once commented that "I can't remember a time that I wasn't writing something: poetry, articles, stories, or memoirs. I have been happiest writing books." Polikoff's first novel, *Life's a Funny Proposition, Horatio,* first gained her critical acclaim, winning awards and best-book citations. The novel tells of twelve-year-old Horatio, whose father has died from lung cancer. Horatio has been adjusting to his new life in Wisconsin with his mother and his ill grandfather, but his efforts are now complicated by his mother's new boyfriend; the death of his grandfather's dog soon makes his grief resurface. Turning to his friend Erik and Erik's sister, Angie, Horatio finds ways to deal with his sadness.

Polikoff once explained "*Life's a Funny Proposition, Horatio* grew out of a conversation I had with my neighbor in the tiny town of Palmyra, Wisconsin. My husband and I have backpacked in the wilderness with our children since they were very young. Five years ago, we built a house in the Wisconsin woods, just one hour and forty-five minutes from our Chicago suburban home, so that we can enjoy living out in nature every weekend. Horatio lives in a town patterned after Palmyra, and the woods he loves are the woods I love. He has a beloved Siberian husky, Silver Chief, and I also have two of those dogs. Horatio's father died when Horatio was very young, as did my father when I was young. Part of his struggle is to accept death and move on with an open heart to what lies in the future. I understand his struggle and I wrote about it because I feel that many children today have to learn to live with loss and grief. The book is serious, but filled with humor, because I believe humor is one of our best tools for survival. Laughter is a great healer."

"Effervescing with humor . . . this little book packs quite a wallop," wrote a *Publishers Weekly* reviewer of *Life's a Funny Proposition, Horatio.* Brian E. Wilson, reviewing the novel for the *School Library Journal* felt that Polikoff's book "provides a worthwhile look at grief." Popular with readers, protagonists Angie and Horatio reappear in *Riding the Wind,* in which Angie nurses an abused Arabian horse back to health. "What's best here is the sense of connection between friends and the woods around them," commented Hazel Rochman in *Booklist.*

Returning to biography with her next title, Polikoff focuses on a noted nineteenth-century social worker in *With One Bold Act: The Story of Jane Addams.* Polikoff explained "The book is about Sadie Garland Dreikers, my ninety-three-year-old aunt, who first went to Hull House as an eleven-year-old child of poor immigrant parents to take painting lessons. She remained at the settlement house, training in social work under Jane Addams until Addams's death in 1935. With the training she received at Hull House as an artist and social worker, she went on to pioneer the field of art therapy worldwide. Much of the book is based on recorded memories of my aunt that I made over an eight-year period." Previous to the publication of Polikoff's biography, very few books had been written on Jane Addams's earlier life, and Polikoff's broad biography offers perspective into Addams' younger years without going into the philosophies underlying the noted reformer's liberal programs. A *Publishers Weekly* reviewer concluded: "This illustrated account is a useful introduction to Addams's life."

Why Does the Coquí Sing?, Polikoff's next novel, is a different type of coming-of-age story than her novels about Horatio and Angie. Luz, who was raised in Chicago, has to move with her family to Puerto Rico, her mother and stepfather's homeland. However, the place does not feel like home to a Chicago-born girl, and she and her brother, Rome, both feel like outsiders.

As Luz begins to adjust to her new life, however, she also learns to deal with issues that have been troubling her since before the move: her hatred of a long scar on her face, and the knowledge that her birth father did not seem to care about her. "Polikoff makes the sights, smells, and sounds of Puerto Rico come to life," praised a *Publishers Weekly* reviewer. A *Kirkus Reviews* contributor noted that "this unique coming-of-age story is comforting without becoming predictable." Gillian Engberg, writing in *Booklist,* complimented Luz's "sensitive, sometimes lyrical voice that's always true to her age." *School Library Journal* reviewer Carol A. Edwards considered the novel "useful emigrant fiction that shows some of the adjustment required" in moving to a new country.

Polikoff once commented: "I've always loved language. When I was very young I collected pretty words the way some children collect rocks or shells. I remember thinking that 'chartreuse' was a particularly beautiful word and that 'porch' was quite an ugly one. As I grew older I collected funny names—a dairy bar called 'The Udder End' and a florist called 'Plant Parenthood.' I began spoken wordplay with my children when they were three years old. By the time they were five, they began putting words on paper. They haven't stopped. Each of them, two daughters and a son, went on to college and earned degrees in literature. My youngest daughter, upon completing a poem, confided that the only feeling comparable to the pleasure of writing a good poem is falling in love. 'Or writing a book that comes out the way you wanted it to,' I responded.

"After teaching English in a Chicago high school for a year, it became clear that if I were to be the kind of teacher that I wanted to be, I would never have time for my own writing. I resigned as a teacher and did editorial work for awhile, and then I began working as a volunteer in a Chicago public elementary school, teaching writing one day a week. I've been doing this for twenty years. At first, I taught because I loved it, but during the last decade an urgency has been added to that love and now I teach because I want to help inner-city children gain the full and exciting use of language. In so doing, I want to help them find the key to who they are, and also to help them become literate, productive adults.

"I write books that I hope children will want to read because they will involve them emotionally in things that matter to them: family relationships, the struggle to find and be oneself in spite of social pressures, and love and respect for the natural world and for each other.

"Some people ask when I'm going to write a novel for adults, as if books for children were not as important or as difficult to write. Right now, I know that I derive great pleasure from writing for children. Who loves their favorite books the way children do, hiding them under their pillows and re-reading them? Who lives with the characters in books as passionately as children? When my grown daughters come home to visit, they will often pull a book off the shelf that they loved as children and read it from cover to cover. If grown children do that with my books, I will be content."

BIOGRAPHICAL AND CRITICAL SOURCES:

PERIODICALS

Booklist, September 15, 1988, p. 164; June 15, 1992, p. 1826; June 1, 1995, Hazel Rochman, review of *Riding the Wind,* p. 1772; April 15, 2002, Anna Rich, "Award Winners," p. 1424; May 15, 2004, Gillian Engberg, review of *Why Does the Coquí Sing?,* p. 1620.
Bulletin of the Center for Children's Books, November, 1988, p. 82; September, 1992, p. 21.
Kirkus Reviews, August 1, 1988, p. 1155; July 1, 1992, p. 853; March 15, 2004, review of *Why Does the Coquí Sing?,* p. 275.
Publishers Weekly, June 22, 1992, review of *Life's a Funny Proposition, Horatio,* p. 62; July 26, 1999, review of *With One Bold Act: The Story of Jane Addams,* p. 72; May 10, 2004, review of *Why Does the Coquí Sing?,* p. 59.
School Library Journal, November, 1988, p. 121; August, 1992, p. 156; April, 2002, Brian E. Wilson, review of *Life's a Funny Proposition, Horatio,* p. 85; June, 2004, Carol A. Edwards, review of *Why Does the Coquí Sing?,* p. 148.*

*　　　*　　　*

POLIKOFF, Barbara Garland
See POLIKOFF, Barbara G.

PUSHKER, Gloria 1927-
(Gloria Teles Pushker)

PERSONAL: Born January 12, 1927, in New Orleans, LA; daughter of Abraham (a retail merchant) and Rose (Pesses) Teles; married Benjamin Pushker (a retail merchant), 1948 (died, June 7, 1992); children: Judy, Elizabeth, Gail. *Education:* Loyola University, B.A., 1982; University of New Orleans, M.Ed., 1987.

ADDRESSES: Home—302 West Gatehouse Dr., Metairie, LA 70001.

CAREER: Storyteller, based in New Orleans, LA, beginning 1983. Also worked variously as a retail store manager, fashion coordinator, and Sunday school teacher.

MEMBER: National Association for the Preservation and Perpetuation of Storytelling, Coalition for the Advancement of Jewish Education.

WRITINGS:

Toby Belfer Never Had a Christmas Tree, Pelican (Gretna, LA), 1990.

Toby Belfer's Seder: A Passover Story Retold, Pelican (Gretna, LA), 1994.

A Belfer Bar Mitzvah, Pelican (Gretna, LA), 1995.

Toby Belfer and the High Holy Days, Pelican (Gretna, LA), 2001.

Toby Belfer Visits Ellis Island, Pelican (Gretna, LA), 2003.

SIDELIGHTS: Gloria Pushker is the author of a children's book series focusing on a girl named Toby Belfer that seeks to educate children about the Jewish faith. In *Toby Belfer and the High Holy Days* Toby surprises her friend Donna when she apologizes for any wrongs she may have committed against her. At first confused, Donna later understands why Toby is apologizing after Toby explains that during the High Holy Days, Jewish people must reflect on their actions and make amends for their wrongs. Ilene Cooper commented in *Booklist* that "Toby often sounds more like she's giving a speech than having a conversation with a friend, but the story does get across the meaning of these Jewish holidays and the requisite introspection that accompanies them."

In *Toby Belfer Visits Ellis Island* young readers are once again educated regarding the Jewish heritage, this time with an immigration story. Toby is told the story of her family's immigration by her great-grandmother, who explains how she and her own family escaped the soldiers in her small Polish village and made the flight to safety in America. After safely arriving in New York City, the new immigrants were faced with the daunting and intrusive inspections and tests at Ellis Island before they were able to successfully enter their new country. Hazel Rochman, writing in *Booklist,* stated that Pushker's "account of a contemporary child's visit to the museum makes this a useful first book for young readers wanting to trace their own European immigrant roots."

Pushker once commented: "In 1971, I had a conversation with my sister about people who were jealous. She added that I don't have a jealous bone in my body. My reply was 'Yes, I have. I sincerely wish I had a master's degree and a flat tummy.' Her reply was, 'If you wanted either one badly enough you could have them both!' I heard an ad on the radio the same day about continuing education for women at Loyola University in New Orleans. I thought that must be some kind of omen, so I registered the very next day for one course in English with the understanding that if I passed, I would continue. I was forty-four years old." Pushker has since earned her B.A. from Loyola with a concentration in psychology and sociology, and a master's degree in education from the University of New Orleans with a concentration in children's literature, and also pursued postgraduate work in children's literature and a teaching career.

Pushker dedicated her first book to "my 'magnificent seven' grandchildren, my major professor, and one of my sisters." "I have had great fun being a storyteller-author," she added, "my goal being to make storytellers out of my audiences. My repertoire includes stories from literature, Southern classics, Jewish tales, as well as original poems and stories." Pushker has served as a guest speaker at many book fairs, from San Diego, California to the Cayman Islands. "I love to tell stories, my own and others," she explained, noting her enjoyment in performing before audiences at schools, churches, and synagogues.

BIOGRAPHICAL AND CRITICAL SOURCES:

PERIODICALS

Booklist, October 1, 2001, Ilene Cooper, review of *Toby Belfer and the High Holy Days,* p. 338; January 1, 2004, Hazel Rochman, review of *Toby Belfer Visits Ellis Island,* p. 880.
School Library Journal, January, 2002, Amy Kellman, review of *Toby Belfer and the High Holy Days,* p. 108.

ONLINE

Loyola University Web site, http://www.loyno.edu/ (June 11, 2005).

*   *   *

PUSHKER, Gloria Teles
See PUSHKER, Gloria

Q-R

QUIN, Ann 1936-1973
(Ann Marie Quin)

PERSONAL: Born March 17, 1936, in Brighton, Sussex, England; died from drowning, August, 1973; daughter of Nicholas Montague (former opera singer) and Ann (Reid) Quin. *Education:* Attended Convent of the Blessed Sacrament, Brighton, Sussex, and Hillcroft College, 1972.

CAREER: Secretary to foreign rights manager, Hutchinson & Co., London, England, two and one half years; manuscript reader for New Authors, Ltd., 1956-58; Royal College of Art, London, secretary to Professor Corel Weight, 1960-62.

MEMBER: PEN, LAMDA Theatre Club, Academy Cinema Club.

AWARDS, HONORS: Harkness Commonwealth fellowship, 1964-67; D.H. Lawrence fellowship, 1964.

WRITINGS:

Berg (novel), J. Calder (London, England), 1964, Scribner (New York, NY), 1965, Dalkey Archive Press (Chicago, IL), 2001.
Three (novel), Scribner (New York, NY), 1966, Dalkey Archive Press (Chicago, IL), 2001.
Passages (novel), Calder & Boyars (London, England), 1969, Boyars (Salem, NH), 1979, Dalkey Archive Press (Chicago, IL), 2003.

Tripticks, illustrated by Carol Annand, Calder & Boyars (London, England), 1972, Boyars (Salem, NH), 1979, Dalkey Archive Press (Chicago, IL), 2002.

Also contributor to *Signature Anthology,* Calder & Boyars (London, England), 1975; and *Beyond the Words: Eleven Writers in Search of a New Fiction,* edited by Giles Gordon, Hutchinson (London, England), 1975. Contributor to periodicals, including *Nova, London Magazine,* and *Transatlantic Review.* Quin's manuscripts and publishers' correspondence are held in the Lilly Library, University of Indiana, Bloomington; other manuscripts and letters are in the Robert David Cohen Papers, Modern Literary Manuscripts Collection, Special Collections, Washington University Libraries, St. Louis, Missouri.

ADAPTATIONS: Berg was adapted as the movie *Killing Dad,* 1989; *Berg, Three,* and *Passages* were the basis for the 1997 play *Ann Quin—A Turn of Tides,* 1997.

SIDELIGHTS: A novelist whose experimentations in literature were considered far ahead of her time when she first started publishing in the 1960s, English author Ann Quin was both praised and criticized for a writing style that some found refreshing and others found too obfuscating. The four novels she published use non-linear narration, multiple viewpoints, stream of consciousness, an often poetic style, and dream and fantasy sequences, among other techniques, to explore a wide variety of themes, including the search for identity, the influence of the past on the present, and the pressures that parents put on their children.

Quin experienced a troubled childhood that would later influence her writing, as well as her mental health. She suffered from several breakdowns during her lifetime, and when she drowned in 1973 many of her friends and family suspected she had actually committed suicide. After her father, an opera singer, abandoned her family, Quin was raised by her mother. She spent part of her education at a convent, where, not being Catholic herself, she felt alienated and alone. She retreated into her own world of fantasy and books, briefly toying with the idea of becoming an actress before discovering that she suffered from severe stage fright. With theater being out of the question as a means of expressing herself, Quin decided to become a writer. She began by composing poetry while taking on a variety of odd jobs, including being a secretary and a manuscript reader, in order to earn an income.

Deciding to try her hand at a novel, her first effort was rejected by publishers. She started a second novel while working at a hotel, but the combination of work and writing proved too much for her, and she suffered her first breakdown. She recovered after seeing a psychiatrist, but for the rest of her life she would have recurring bouts of what Judith Mackrell, writing in the *Dictionary of Literary Biography,* speculated to be "probably some form of schizophrenia."

Quin's second novel, like the first, was rejected, but her third attempt, *Berg,* was successfully published in 1964. Mackrell described *Berg* as a "highly autobiographical [novel] in its underlying emotional impulse if not in particular detail. (Here the underlying impulse relates to Quin's absent father, about whom she wove an intense fantasy life.)" The main character in the book is Alistair Berg, who determines to murder his father, Nathaniel, as revenge for the way he abandoned his family. Traveling to the seaside boardinghouse where his father is staying, Berg does practically everything *but* kill his father. Instead, he finds revenge in other ways, including having an affair with his father's lover, destroying things that are dear to his father, and, in one scene that might actually be a dream sequence, humiliating his father when he tries to seduce Berg, who is dressed as a woman in an attempt to hide from the police. At one point, Berg even kills a different man whom he substitutes for his actual father.

All through the book, it becomes clear that Berg is doing these things in order to assert his own self-image as distinct from his father; however, he is unsuccessful in the attempt, and at times even takes on the role of his father, becoming more like him. Many scenes in the book are farcical, such as one scene where Berg dresses up as his father's lover and when he seems to believe that a ventriloquist's dummy is his father's body, which he must hide before it is discovered. The "black humor . . . also conveys a sense of the strange world that Berg's consciousness creates for itself," wrote Mackrell. And Quin uses shifts in style to convey the shifts between sanity and insanity that Berg seems to go through.

Berg was well received by critics, especially those in England who felt that Quin's novel had helped to revitalize English literature, which had remained overly literal and realistic while literature in other countries had become more innovative. A *Times Literary Supplement* reviewer, for one, called *Berg* "a most impressive debut," and the novel won Quin two fellowships.

Quin followed *Berg* with *Three,* the complex tale of a middle-aged, childless couple whose marital problems are revealed when a young woman enters their lives while she recovers from an abortion. The couple, Leonard and Ruth, are financially well off, but their marriage is a sterile relationship in which husband and wife merely seem to tolerate one another. "S," as the young woman is known, attempts to break Leonard and Ruth out of their rut and self-delusion, and the three form an awkward relationship laced with sexual tension. "In a sense," commented Nicolas Tredell in the *Dictionary of Literary Biography,* "S functions as the couple's surrogate child, as Ruth's confidante, and as a kind of fantasy outlet for the thwarted sexuality of both Ruth and Leonard." But after some time, S determines that she cannot open the couple's eyes, and she departs, leaving a note that appears to indicate that she has gone to drown herself. Much of the rest of the novel consists of passages from S's tape recordings, which she has left behind and which Ruth and Leonard analyze in an attempt to find out why S has decided to kill herself. But although S had thought that she could never shake up the stagnant marriage, her departure and possible suicide have done just that, and the novel ends with Ruth and Leonard finally reexamining their relationship.

While *Three* was praised by a number of critics, it was less warmly received than Quin's *Berg.* The experimental format Quin employs, in which blocks of text are set off as different views, as well as the mix of memories, impressions, and dreams, led a *New Statesman* reviewer to call the book "alternately irritating and fascinating."

Passages, Quin's third novel, has even less of a distinct plot than her earlier books. The basic framework of the story involves a woman's quest to find her missing brother in Greece; he may have died during the coup there in 1967. She is accompanied by her lover, and the novel alternates between their two viewpoints. However, as Mackrell pointed out, "despite the frequent interweaving of consciousnesses, the two characters in *Passages* cease very quickly to be discernible individuals." Again, the theme of the unsuccessful quest for self-identity is part of the novel, as it becomes clear that the two characters find that they cannot escape each other, even if they desired. Quin again blends fantasy and reality as she explores "not simply the confused and fragmented workings of her characters' minds but showing, too, the ways in which they reflect and are part of each other and how they are bound together in what seems to be a shifting sadomasochistic relationship." Although Mackrell called *Passages* a "much more ambitious novel than the previous two" that addresses the author's thematic concerns "with much greater literary originality," the book confused many reviewers. A number of critics felt that Quin was more interested in showy literary techniques than in conveying a story to her audience. For example, David Haworth, writing in *New Statesman,* charged Quin with "the elevation of technique above content." However, a *Times Literary Supplement* contributor said the "fusion between what is experience, dreamt of and thought . . . is well suggested."

As Quin's writing career progressed, her books continued to become more and more difficult to interpret, and Tredell called her last complete novel, *Tripticks,* "her most scrambled text." The main character is a thrice-divorced man who believes that he is being pursued by his first wife and her lover, but it also might be that he is actually pursuing them. "During his journey," as Mackrell described it, "the series of bizarre incidents that occur and fantasies [the protagonist] experiences are juxtaposed with flashbacks from the past, all of which have a dual purpose. On the one hand, they reveal the hero's erotic obsessions and paranoia; on the other hand, they satirize, either through style or theme, some aspect of American

culture: its materialism; its uncritical acceptance of fashionable ideas and jargon; its crass notion of psychology; and the loss of individual contact and humanity within a mass-produced ideology." Many critics of *Tripticks* thought the book to be a thinly veiled excuse for the author to express her dislike of American culture, and of New York City in particular. A *New Statesman* reviewer, according to Mackrell, labeled it a "piece of self-gratification." Reviewed more recently in the *Publishers Weekly,* however, a critic lauded the book for being so far ahead of its time that it "still feels fresh and exciting and should win [Quin] some new fans."

Quin was working on a fifth novel, "The Unmapped Country," when she died in 1973. The fragments of the book were later published in the collection *Beyond the Words: Eleven Writers in Search of a New Fiction.* "The Unmapped Country" strongly reflects Quin's own experiences in recovering from the last mental breakdown she had before her death, telling of a young woman named Sandra who is convalescing from just such a collapse. Unlike her earlier books, however, this last effort is much more realistically told. Tredell called it "an accomplished piece of work, and the novel might have brought Quin a wider audience had she lived to complete it."

BIOGRAPHICAL AND CRITICAL SOURCES:

BOOKS

Dictionary of Literary Biography, Gale (Detroit, MI), Volume 14: *British Novelists since 1960,* 1983, pp. 608-614, Volume 231: *British Novelists since 1960, Fourth Series,* 2000, pp. 230-238.
Dunn, Nell, *Talking to Women,* MacGibbon & Kee (London, England), 1965, pp. 126-153.

PERIODICALS

Choice, July, 1967.
Library Journal, July, 2002, Eleanor J. Bader, review of *Tripticks,* p. 122.
London Magazine, June, 1969.
New Statesman, May 27, 1966, review of *Three;* March 21, 1969, David Haworth, review of *Passages.*

New York Times Book Review, October 31, 1965;
    October 9, 1966.
Poetry, August, 1968.
Publishers Weekly, July 1, 2002, "July Publications,"
    p. 56.
Review of Contemporary Fiction, summer, 2003, Brian
    Evenson and Joanna Howard, "Ann Quin," p. 50.
Times Literary Supplement, June 25, 1964, review of
    Berg; April 3, 1969, review of *Passages.**

*   *   *

QUIN, Ann Marie
    See QUIN, Ann

*   *   *

REYNOLDS, Roger 1934-
    (Roger Lee Reynolds)

PERSONAL: Born July 18, 1934, in Detroit, MI; son
of George Arthur (an architect) and Katherine (a
teacher; maiden name, Butler) Reynolds; married Sandra Byers (divorced, 1963); married Karen Jeanne Hill
(a musician), April 11, 1964; children: (second
marriage) Erika Lynn, Wendy Claire. *Education:*
University of Michigan, Ann Arbor, B.S.E.
(engineering physics), 1957, B.M. (music literature),
1960, M.M. (music composition), 1961.

ADDRESSES: Office—Department of Music 0326,
University of California—San Diego, La Jolla, CA
92093.

CAREER: University of California—San Diego, La
Jolla, associate professor, 1969-73, professor of music,
beginning 1973, founder and director of Center for
Music Experiment, 1971-77, chair of music
department, 1979-81. Visiting professor, University of
Illinois, 1971, Yale University, 1983, and Amherst
College, 1988; visiting composer, IRCAM, Paris,
France, 1981-83; Institute for Studies in American
Music, Brooklyn College, NY, senior fellow, 1985;
Peabody Conservatory of Music, Baltimore, MD,
Rothschild composer in residence, 1992-93. Cofounder
of the ONCE festival, Ann Arbor, MI, 1961; co-
organizer of the Cross Talk concerts and festival in
Tokyo, Japan, 1967-70. Member of Institute of Cur-

rent World Affairs, 1972-76; member of Broadcast
Music, Inc.; member of board of directors, American
Music Center and Fromm Foundation. Guest composer
and lecturer.

AWARDS, HONORS: Fulbright fellowship, 1962-63;
Guggenheim fellowship, 1963-64; Rockefeller Founda-
tion grant, 1965-66; Institute of Current World Affairs
fellowship, 1967-70; awards from Fromm Foundation,
1968, National Institute of Arts and Letters, 1971, and
Ford Foundation, 1972; Koussevitsky Prize, Berkshire
Music Center, 1970; National Endowment for the Arts
awards, 1975, 1978, 1979, and 1986; Pulitzer Prize in
Music, 1989, for *Whispers Out of Time for Strings;*
Suntory Foundation commission, 1990; Koussevitsky
Foundation commission, 1991-92.

WRITINGS:

Mind Models: New Forms of Musical Experience,
    Praeger (New York, NY), 1974, Routledge (New
    York, NY), 2005.
A Searcher's Path: A Composer's Ways, Brooklyn Col-
    lege of the City of New York (Brooklyn, NY),
    1987.
Form and Method: Composing Music ("Contemporary
    Music Studies" series), Routledge (New York,
    NY), 2002.

Contributor to books, including *John Cage,* Peters
(New York, NY), 1962; *Contemporary Composers on
Contemporary Music,* edited by Schwartz and Childs,
Holt (New York, NY), 1967; *Thoughts about Music:
John Cage's World,* Asahi Shuppan-sha (Tokyo,
Japan), 1981; *A Celebration of American Music: Words
and Music in Honor of H. Wiley Hitchcock,* edited by
R. Crawford, R.A. Lott, and C.J. Oja, University of
Michigan Press (Ann Arbor, MI), 1990; *Musically
Incorrect,* edited by H. Biggs and S. Orzel, Peters
(New York, NY), 1998; and *Samuel Beckett and Music,*
edited by Mary Bryden, Clarendon Press, 1998.
Contributor to journals, including *Perspectives of New
Music, Generation Magazine, Musical Quarterly,
Asian Art and Culture, American Music,* and *Contem-
porary Music Review.*

MUSICAL COMPOSITIONS

110: A Ritual (musical drama), first performed in
    Pasadena, CA, January 24, 1971.

The Emperor of Ice Cream (music-theater), first performed in New York, NY, March, 1975.

A Merciful Coincidence (Voicespace II) (music-theater), first performed in Bourges, France, June 9, 1976.

The Red Act Arias (selections from the forthcoming opera *The Red Act*), first performed on BBC-TV, 1997.

Also author of incidental music for Shakespeare's *The Tempest,* performed in Lenox, MA, July 30, 1980, and Anton Chekhov's *Ivanov,* performed in Mito, Japan, January, 1992. Author of symphonies and orchestral works, including *Graffiti 1964,* 1965, *Fiery Wind,* 1968, *Archipelago,* 1983, *The Dream of the Infinite Rooms,* 1986, *Whispers Out of Time,* 1988, and *Symphony: Myths,* 1990; also author of numerous chamber, instrumental, vocal, and choral works. Published musical scores include *The Serpent-Snapping Eye: Trumpet, Percussion, Piano, and Four-Channel Computer Synthesized Sound,* Peters (New York, NY), 1980; *The Palace: Baritone Voice and Computer-Generated Tape,* Peters (New York, NY), 1981; *Shadowed Narrative,* Peters (New York, NY) 1982; *Transfigured Wind II,* Peters (New York, NY), 1984; *Transfigured Wind III,* Peters (New York, NY), 1984; *Islands from Archipelago: II, Autumn Island: Marimba Solo,* Peters (New York, NY), 1989; *Whispers Out of Time: String Orchestra: Pulitzer Prize 1989,* Peters (New York, NY), 1989; *Symphony (Myths): Orchestra,* Peters (New York, NY), 1991; *Personae: The Vanity of Words,* Neuma Records (Acton, MA), 1992; *Variation: Piano Solo,* Peters (New York, NY), 1993; *Visions: String Quartet,* Peters (New York, NY), 1994; *Transfigured Wind I/IV,* Peters (New York, NY), 1995; and *Ariadne's Thread: String Quartet and Computer Synthesized Sound,* Peters (New York, NY), 2000. A number of Reynolds' compositions have been recorded, including *Arditti String Quartet Plays Roger Reynolds,* Auvidis/Naive (France), 2000.

SIDELIGHTS: Roger Reynolds is a Pulitzer Prize-winning composer who has been at the forefront of American music since the 1960s. Freely experimenting, and at times creating, new syntaxes in Western music, such as diatonic scales, micro-tone procedures, and computer-generated sounds, he "has created a body of work that encompasses nearly every major musical development in the 20th century," according to Ciro G. Scotto in *Contemporary Composers.* His influence can be seen in such works as *The*

Emperor of Ice Cream, which, according to Scotto, "became the model for a new genre." For inspiration for his work, Reynolds often looks to literature, drawing on such authors as Milan Kundera, Samuel Beckett, and Jorge Luis Borges.

Reynolds also uses computers in many of his pieces, a technique that has sometimes been criticized for its lack of immediacy but which he has staunchly defended. As he argued in an interview with Stephen Pettitt in the *Financial Times:* "A composer doesn't work in real time. He's free of time and can invent history and the future. The computer allows the realm of imagination to be converted into the realm of experience, and that's a very important thing for an artist. It's also a lot of fun." Reynolds' theories about musical composition can be studied in his books *Mind Models: New Forms of Musical Experience* and *A Searcher's Path: A Composer's Ways.*

BIOGRAPHICAL AND CRITICAL SOURCES:

BOOKS

Contemporary Composers, St. James Press (Detroit, MI), 1992.

PERIODICALS

American Music, fall, 1997, Marshall Bialosky, "Sonor Ensemble of the University of San Diego," p. 415.
Financial Times, August 1, 1997, Stephen Pettitt, "Music Fit for the Gods: Stephen Pettitt Talks to US Composer Roger Reynolds about His Proms Commission," p. 17.
Perspectives of New Music, winter, 2002, John Rahn, "Worth Noting: Roger Reynolds's Form and Method," p. 241.
Times (London, England), August 6, 1997, John Allison, "Encore, Maestro; Arts," p. 14.

ONLINE

Library of Congress, http://www.loc.gov/ (November 19, 2005), "The Roger Reynolds Collection."
Roger Reynolds Web site, http://www.rogerreynolds.com (November 19, 2005).*

REYNOLDS, Roger Lee
    See REYNOLDS, Roger

*   *   *

ROBINSON, Sharon 1950-

PERSONAL: Born January 13, 1950, in New York, NY; daughter of Jackie (a baseball player) and Rachel (Isum) Robinson; married twice (both marriages ended); children: Jesse Simms. *Education:* Harvard University, B.S.; Columbia University, M.S. *Hobbies and other interests:* Sports, reading.

ADDRESSES: Home—Norwalk, CT. *Agent*—Marie Brown, Marie Brown Associates, 625 Broadway, New York, NY 10012.

CAREER: Nurse midwife, 1975—; writer. Yale University, New Haven, CT, assistant professor of nursing; also taught at Columbia University, Howard University, and Georgetown University. Jackie Robinson Foundation, member of board of directors. Appointed director of educational programming for major-league baseball.

MEMBER: American College of Nurse-Midwives (member of board of directors).

WRITINGS:

Stealing Home: An Intimate Family Portrait by the Daughter of Jackie Robinson, HarperCollins (New York, NY), 1996.
Jackie's Nine: Jackie Robinson's Values to Live By, Scholastic (New York, NY), 2001.
Still the Storm, Genesis Press, Inc. (Columbus, MS), 2002.
Promises to Keep: How Jackie Robinson Changed America, Scholastic (New York, NY), 2004.

Contributor to a women's health textbook; contributor of articles to *Essence* magazine and to professional journals.

SIDELIGHTS: Sharon Robinson was born in 1950 to a famous father: Jackie Robinson, the first African American to play major-league baseball. She recounts what it was like for her and her brothers to grow up in the public environment that came with their father's pioneering achievement in the world of sports in her 1996 book, *Stealing Home: An Intimate Family Portrait by the Daughter of Jackie Robinson.* As Robinson reveals, her father tried very hard to be a good family man, and to give time and attention to his children. Nevertheless, she and her brothers, Jackie, Jr. and David, felt the strain of having to share their dad with his many admiring fans. As an adult, Sharon became a nurse midwife, and survived two failed marriages. In addition to the details of her life and her family's life in *Stealing Home,* Robinson also includes a collection of family photographs that follow her father's career and his growing family. A *Publishers Weekly* critic responded favorably to the volume, predicting that Sharon Robinson's "loving biography" of her father "will add to his stature."

In *Jackie's Nine: Jackie Robinson's Values to Live By* Robinson presents a collection of essays on nine inspiring character traits that shaped her while growing up under her father's tutelage, including: courage, determination, teamwork, persistence, integrity, citizenship, justice, commitment, and excellence. As Robinson notes, *Jackie's Nine* "presents values as principles by which to shape a life, rather than as mere buzz worlds." The text also describes the ways the elder Robinson attempted to embody those same values, prompting readers "to nurture those same values within their own lives," according to Daniel R. Beach in *Book Report.*

Promises to Keep: How Jackie Robinson Changed America provides readers with insight into the active role the baseball legend played in fueling the civil rights movement. Robinson chronicles her father's legendary career and the trials he faced while growing up. "In captivating words and pictures," the daughter includes telling glimpses into Robinson's life that reveal "information on the post-Civil War world, race relations, and the struggle for civil rights," commented Tracy Bell in the *School Library Journal.* Gillian Engberg stated in *Booklist* that "there are numerous biographies about Robinson available for young people, but none have this book's advantage of family intimacy."

BIOGRAPHICAL AND CRITICAL SOURCES:

BOOKS

Robinson, Sharon, *Jackie's Nine: Jackie Robinson's Values to Live By,* Scholastic (New York, NY), 2001.

PERIODICALS

Booklist, June 1, 1996, p. 1628; July, 2001, John Peters, review of *Jackie's Nine: Jackie Robinson's Values to Live By,* p. 2004; February 15, 2004, Gillian Engberg, review of *Promises to Keep: How Jackie Robinson Changed America,* p. 1077.

Book Report, September-October, 2001, Daniel R. Beach, review of *Jackie's Nine,* p. 72.

Emerge, October, 1996, p. 73.

Kirkus Reviews, January 15, 2004, p. 88.

Library Journal, June 15, 1996, p. 72.

Newsweek, February 9, 2004, Elise Soukup, review of *Fast Chat: Humble Heroics* p. 12.

New York Times Book Review, November 3, 1996, p. 18.

Publishers Weekly, May 13, 1996, p. 66; May 14, 2001, review of *Jackie's Nine,* p. 84; February 9, 2004, review of *Promises to Keep,* p. 82; March 1, 2004, review of *Promises to Keep,* p. 34.

School Library Journal, October, 1996, p. 166; June, 2001, review of *Jackie's Nine,* p. 180; March, 2004, Tracy Bell, review of *Promises to Keep,* p. 242; October, 2004, review of *Promises to Keep,* p. 32.

Sports Illustrated, July 8, 1996, p. 5.

ONLINE

BookPage.com, http://www.bookpage.com/ (June 11, 2005), "Sharon Robinson."*

*   *   *

ROGERS, Kenneth Ray
See ROGERS, Kenny

*   *   *

ROGERS, Kenny 1938-
(Kenneth Ray Rogers)

PERSONAL: Born August 21, 1938, in Houston, TX; son of Floyd and Lucille (Hester) Rogers; married first wife (marriage ended); married Janice Gordon, 1957 (divorced, 1959); married third wife, 1964 (divorced, 1976); married Marianne Gordon (an actress), October 2, 1977 (divorced, 1993); married Wanda Miller (a production assistant), June 1, 1997; children: (second marriage) Carolee; (third marriage) Kenneth Jr.; (fourth marriage) Christopher Cody. *Education:* Attended University of Houston. *Hobbies and other interests:* Softball, tennis.

ADDRESSES: Agent—c/o Author Mail, HarperCollins Publishers, 10 E. 53rd St., New York, NY 10022.

CAREER: Musician. The Scholars (rockabilly band), member, c. 1956; Bobby Doyle Trio (jazz band), bass fiddle player, 1959-66; New Christy Minstrels (pop and funk band), member, 1966-67; First Edition (rock 'n' roll band; later known as Kenny Rogers and the First Edition), 1967-74; solo musician, 1974—; United Artists, recording artist, 1975-83; RCA Records, New York, NY, recording artist, 1983-88; Dreamcatcher Entertainment (record company), Nashville, TN, founder, 1999. Photographer, c. 1980s. Hands Across America (charity fundraiser), participant, 1985.

Singer on numerous albums, including (with First Edition) *Something's Burning,* Reprise, 1970; (with First Edition) *Ballad of Calico,* Reprise, 1972; *Kenny Rogers,* United Artists, 1976; *Lucille,* United Artists, 1977; *Daytime Friends,* United Artists, 1977; (with Dottie West) *Every Time Two Fools Collide,* United Artists, 1978; *Love or Something Like It,* United Artists, 1978; (with Dottie West) *Kenny Rogers and Dottie West—Classics,* United Artists, 1979; *The Gambler,* United Artists, 1979; *Kenny,* United Artists, 1979; *Ten Years of Gold,* EMI America, 1979; *Classics,* United Artists, 1979; *Gideon,* United Artists, 1980; *Love Lifted Me,* United Artists, 1980; *Greatest Hits,* EMI America, 1980; *Share Your Love,* Liberty, 1981; *Christmas,* Liberty, 1981; *Love Will Turn You Around,* Liberty, 1982; *We've Got Tonight,* Liberty, 1983; *Twenty Greatest Hits,* Liberty, 1983; *Eyes that See in the Dark,* RCA, 1983; *What about Me?,* RCA, 1984; *Duets: Kenny Rogers with Kim Carnes, Sheena Easton, and Dottie West,* Capitol, 1984; (with Dolly Parton) *Once upon a Christmas,* RCA, 1984; *Love Is What We Make It,* Liberty, 1985; *Short Stories,* Liberty, 1985; *The Heart of the Matter,* RCA, 1985; *They Don't Make Them like They Used To,* RCA, 1986; *Twenty-Five Greatest Hits,* EMI America, 1987; *I Prefer the Moonlight,* RCA, 1987; *Greatest Hits,* RCA, 1988; *Lucille and Other Classics,* EMI/Capitol, 1989; *Something Inside So Strong,* Reprise, 1989; *Christmas in*

America, 1989; *Twenty Great Years*, Reprise, 1990; *Greatest Country Hits*, 1990; *Love Is Strange*, Reprise, 1990; *Back Home Again*, WEA/Warner Bros. Records, 1991; *Very Best*, Quicksilver Records, 1991; *Best of Kenny Rogers*, EMI/Capitol, 1992; *If Only My Heart Had Voice*, 1993; *TimePiece*, Atlantic, 1994; *All-Time Greatest Hits*, Cema, 1996; *Greatest Hits*, Hipp, 1996; *Vote for Love*, QMusic, 1996; *The Gift*, Magnatone, 1996; *A Decade of Hits*, Reprise, 1997; *Across My Heart*, Magnatone, 1997; *King of Country*, Spotlight On, 1997; *Songs You Know by Heart*, Boomerang, 1997; *Vol. 1—Greatest Hits*, Public Music, 1997; *Branson City Limits*, Unison/Navarre, 1998; *Original Hits*, Forever Classic, 1998; *With Love*, 1998; *Christmas from the Heart*, Dreamcatcher, 1998; *A&E Biography—A Musical Anthology*, Cema/Capitol, 1999; *She Rides Wild Horses*, Dreamcatcher, 1999; *Kenny Rogers*, Classic World, 1999; *Love Collection*, Madacy Records, 1999; *Love Songs*, EMD/Capitol, 1999; *Through the Years—A Retrospective*, Cema/Capitol, 1999; *Forever Love*, 2000; *There You Go Again*; (with Dolly Parton) *Dolly Parton and Kenny Rogers Gold*.

Actor in television series, including *Rollin' on the River*, syndicated, 1971-73; and *The Real West*, Arts and Entertainment (A&E), 1993. Actor in television miniseries, including *The Luck of the Draw: The Gambler Returns*, National Broadcasting Company, Inc. (NBC), 1991; and *The Gambler V: Playing for Keeps*, Columbia Broadcasting System, Inc. (CBS), 1994. Actor in television movies, *The Dream Makers*, NBC, 1975; *The Gambler*, CBS, 1980; *Coward of the County*, CBS, 1981; *Kenny Rogers as The Gambler, Part II—The Adventure Continues*, CBS, 1983; *Wild Horses*, CBS, 1985; *Kenny Rogers as the Gambler, Part III—The Legend Continues*, CBS, 1987; *Rio Diablo*, CBS, 1993; *MacShayne: Winner Takes All*, NBC, 1994; *MacShayne: Final Roll of the Dice*, NBC, 1994; *Big Dreams and Broken Hearts: The Dottie West Story*, CBS, 1995; and *Get to the Heart*, CBS, 1997.

Actor in television specials, including *The World's Largest Indoor Country Music Show*, NBC, 1978; *The Kenny Rogers Special*, CBS, 1979; *A Special Kenny Rogers*, CBS, 1981; *Roy Acuff—Fifty Years the King of Country Music*, NBC, 1982; *Kenny Rogers in Concert*, Home Box Office (HBO), 1983; *Glen Campbell and Friends: The Silver Anniversary*, HBO, 1984; *Kenny and Dolly: A Christmas to Remember*, CBS, 1984; *Kenny Rogers and Dolly Parton: Together*, 1985; *Kenny Rogers: Working America*, CBS, 1987; *Kenny*

Rogers Classic Weekend, 1988; *Kenny, Dolly, and Willie: Something Inside So Strong*, 1989; *Kenny Rogers in Concert: A Holiday Special for Public Television*, Public Broadcasting Service (PBS), 1989; *Christmas in America: A Love Story*, NBC, 1989; *Kenny Rogers: Keep Christmas with You*, CBS, 1992; *A Day in the Life of Country Music*, CBS, 1993; *The American Music Awards 20th Anniversary Special*, American Broadcasting Companies, Inc., (ABC), 1993; *Kenny Rogers: Going Home*, Disney Channel, 1995; *The Life and Times of Kenny Rogers*, The Nashville Network (TNN), 1996; *Kenny Rogers: The Gift*, Family Channel, 1996; *Live by Request*, A&E, 1999.

Actor in television episodes, including *American Bandstand*, ABC, 1958; *The Andy Williams Show*, NBC, 1969; *The Muppet Show*, syndicated, 1979; *Evening Shade*, CBS, 1990; "The Portrait," *Dr. Quinn, Medicine Woman*, CBS, 1993; *Cybill*, CBS, 1995; and *Touched by An Angel*, CBS, 2000. Actor in films, including *Six Pack*, Twentieth Century-Fox, 1982. Actor in stage productions, including *Christmas from the Heart Featuring the Toy Shoppe*, Beacon Theatre, New York, NY, 1998, then touring U.S. cities. Executive producer of television movie *A Different Affair*, 1987; executive producer of television special *Kenny Rogers in Concert*, HBO, 1983.

AWARDS, HONORS: Album of the Year, Academy of Country Music Awards, 1977, for *Kenny Rogers;* named "Cross-Over Artist of the Year" by *Billboard*, 1977; Grammy Award for best male vocalist (country) from National Academy of Recording Arts and Sciences, Academy of Country Music Award best single, and Academy of Country Music Award best song, all 1977, and American Music Award for country favorite singer from Dick Clark Productions, 1978, all for "Lucille"; Academy of Country Music Award for best male vocalist, 1977; Academy of Country Music Award for entertainer of the year, 1978; three awards from America's Juke Box Operators Association, 1978; Academy of Country Music Awards (with Dottie West) for vocal duo of the year, 1978, 1979; Country Music Association Awards for male vocalist of the year and album of the year, both 1979; Grammy Award for best male country vocalist, National Academy of Recording Arts and Sciences, and The Nashville Network *Music City News* Country Award for best single, both 1979, both for "The Gambler"; *Music City News* Country Award for male artist of the year, The

Nashville Network, 1979; Country Music Association Award (with Dottie West), vocal duo of the year, and The Nashville Network *Music City News* Country Award (with Dottie West), best vocal duo, both 1979; named *People Weekly*'s top male vocalist, 1979, 1980, and most popular male singer, 1981, 1982, and 1983; American Music Awards for country favorite male vocalist, Dick Clark Productions, 1979, 1980, 1981, 1983, and 1985; American Music Awards for favorite album, Dick Clark Productions, 1979, 1980, 1981, and 1985; American Music Award for country favorite single, Dick Clark Productions, and *Music City News* Country Award for best single, The Nashville Network, both 1981, both for "Coward of the County"; American Music Awards for pop/rock favorite male vocalist, Dick Clark Productions, 1981, 1982; People's Choice Awards for best male musical performer, 1981, 1982, 1983, and for best country/western musical performer, 1982, 1983, 1984, 1985, 1986, and 1987; American Music Award for pop/rock favorite album, Dick Clark Productions, 1982, for *Greatest Hits;* American Music Awards for special award of merit and country favorite single, Dick Clark Productions, 1983, both for "Love Will Turn You Around"; Academy of Country Music Awards single of the year and best vocal group and/or duet (with Dolly Parton), both 1983; song of the year, American Society of Composers, Authors, and Publishers Award, 1983; Presidential End Hunger Award (celebrity category), Agency for International Development, 1983; *Music City News* Award (with Dolly Parton) for best vocal duo, The Nashville Network, 1984; *Rolling Stone* Readers' Poll Award for country artist of the year, 1984; Record Industry Association of the America Award for most awarded artist, 1984, for number of gold and platinum albums; American Music Awards (with Dolly Parton) for country favorite single, Dick Clark Productions, 1984, 1985, both for "Islands in the Stream"; Roy Acuff Award, Country Music Foundation, 1985; named "Favorite Singer of All Time," *PM Magazine/USA Today* poll, 1986; Grammy Award (with Ronnie Milsap) for best country vocal collaboration, National Academy of Recording Arts and Sciences, 1987, for "Make No Mistake, She's Mine"; People's Choice Award for best male musical performer, 1988; Harry Chapin Award for Humanitarianism, American Society of Composers, Authors, and Publishers, 1988; People's Choice Award (with Randy Travis) for best country/western performer, 1990; Horatio Alger Award, Horatio Alger Association of Distinguished Americans, 1990; Diamond Award, Recording Industry Association of America, 1999; named a "hero of public housing," United States Department of Housing and Urban Development; United Nations Peace Award.

WRITINGS:

(With Len Epand) *Making It with Music* (nonfiction), HarperCollins (New York, NY), 1978.

Kenny Rogers' America (photography), forward by Yousuf Karsh, Little, Brown (Boston, MA), 1986.

Your Friends and Mine: A Collection of 80 Photographs, Little, Brown (Boston, MA), 1987.

The Gift: An Original Short Story, T. Nelson (Nashville, TN), 1996.

Kenny Rogers Presents the Greatest (based on a song written by Don Schlitz), Addax Publishing Group (Lenexa, KS), 2000.

(With Kelly Junkermann) *Kenny Rogers Presents the Toy Shoppe,* Addax Publishing Group (Lenexa, KS), 2000.

(With Donald Davenport) *Christmas in Canaan* (for children), HarperCollins (New York, NY), 2002.

Author of numerous songs, including "Sweet Music Man." Author of songs for television movies, including *The Dream Makers,* NBC, 1975; *Wild Horses,* CBS, 1985; *MacShayne: Final Roll of the Dice,* 1994. Author of songs for specials, including *From the Heart . . . The First International Very Special Arts Festival,* NBC, 1989. Author of songs for television miniseries, including *The Gambler V: Playing for Keeps,* CBS, 1994. Author of songs for films, including *Urban Cowboy,* Paramount, 1980; *Tough Guys,* Buena Vista, 1986; *Light of Day,* TriStar, 1987; and *The Big Lebowski,* Gramercy Pictures, 1998. Wrote story with Kelly Junkermann, and co-wrote songs for stage production *Christmas from the Heart Featuring the Toy Shoppe,* Beacon Theatre, New York, NY, 1998.

ADAPTATIONS: An unabridged version of *Christmas in Canaan* was adapted for audio cassette, HarperCollins, 2002; The single "The Greatest" was adapted as a children's book.

SIDELIGHTS: A tireless performer, Kenny Rogers devotes equal time to touring and recording. He has recorded numerous gold records, as well as given concerts throughout the United States, Canada, New Zealand, and Scotland. His many awards testify to his talents as both a singer and songwriter. Rogers' career took off after he formed the band the First Edition with other members of the New Christy Minstrels. A basic rock 'n' roll group, the First Edition peaked in the late 1960s with a string of hits, including "Just Dropped in to See What Condition My Condition Was In," "Ruby (Don't Take Your Love to Town)," and "Something's Burnin." "I loved the First Edition," Rogers once recalled. "There never was one minute I didn't feel proud of its success." Rogers soon tired of the repetition involved in touring and recording with the group, though, so the band broke up. "One day we realized doing the same thing over and over just didn't excite us," he said. "There were no hard feelings. We just left the stage one night and never came back."

Embarking on a solo career, Rogers seemed content to stay out of the limelight for a while. Within two years, however, he was back with another popular song, "Lucille." "I was going along just fine with my quiet little career," Rogers mused, "when someone screwed up and got me a hit." "Lucille" was not his first solo hit, however. He had already made the country music charts with three singles: "Home-made Love," "Laura," and "While the Feeling's Good."

Rogers followed the success of "Lucille" with another popular tune, "Every Time Two Fools Collide." From the album of the same title, "Every Time Two Fools Collide" was recorded with another country music artist, Dottie West. "Dottie is a very good friend of mine and the thing I enjoyed most about doing the album is that it was all so genuine," claimed Rogers. "It was done for the right reason; we really enjoy singing together." The resulting collaboration was such a success with music fans that Rogers and West decided to record a second album together.

While working with West, Rogers also was busy writing a book, *Making It with Music*. "The reason I decided to write the book is that I've been barraged constantly, throughout my career, with questions from aspiring young musicians," said Rogers. "The book heavily stresses what one should do to get started in the business. It's not designed to make a star out of someone who is not capable of or interested in becoming a star. It's designed to help a person with an average amount of talent who just wants to make a decent living in a very lucrative business." Rogers has done more than just make a living for himself. He reached the top of his field in two distinctly different forms of music: country and rock 'n' roll. Although he never regretted his years playing rock 'n' roll, Rogers noted: "It's interesting. I had to become a country artist to buy a tuxedo."

Rogers expanded his career beyond music and advice for aspiring musicians when he published a number of books containing his photographs as well as fictional works. One of his published collections of photographs is *Kenny Rogers' America*. Including photographs he took all around the United States, the book incorporates images of churches, national parks, and prisons. While *People Weekly* contributor Campbell Geeslin called the pictures "technically sharp," the reviewer also commented that Rogers "has not yet found a subject or way or presentation that would make his images unique."

The children's novel *Christmas in Canaan*, which Rogers wrote with screenwriter Donald Davenport, takes on the theme of overcoming racial prejudice through the tale of two young boys in the Texas town of Canaan in the early 1960s. DJ is white, while Rodney is African American. After a conflict between the two on the school bus, DJ is forced to confront his racist attitude towards Rodney through a unique punishment devised by their families. The two boys eventually become friends. Shelley Townsend-Hudson noted in *Booklist* that "the gentle narrative chronicles a sweet, lifelong bond."

BIOGRAPHICAL AND CRITICAL SOURCES:

BOOKS

St. James Encyclopedia of Popular Culture, St. James Press (Detroit, MI), 2000.

PERIODICALS

Booklist, November 1, 2002, Shelley Townsend-Hudson, review of *Christmas in Canaan*, pp. 497, 499.
People Weekly, November 3, 1998, Campbell Geeslin, review of *Kenny Rogers' America*, p. 20.

ONLINE

Kenny Rogers Home Page, http://www.kennyrogers. com (October 10, 2002), biography of Kenny Rogers.*

ROGOW, Roberta 1942-

PERSONAL: Born March 7, 1942; daughter of Stanley (a lawyer and actor) and Shirley (a psychologist; maiden name, Heller) Winston; married Murray Rogow (a press agent and writer), November 3, 1963 (died, September 22, 2002); children: Miriam Ann (a mystery writer), Louise Katherine. *Education:* Queens College of the City University of New York, B.A., 1962; Columbia University, M.L.S., 1971. *Politics:* Democrat. *Religion:* Jewish. *Hobbies and other interests:* Needlework, science fiction costuming, songwriting, singing in choir, science fiction conventions.

ADDRESSES: Office—Union Free Public Library, Friberger Park, Union, NJ 07083.

CAREER: Writer and librarian. Paterson Free Public Library, Paterson, NJ, various positions, 1971-82; Ridgefield Public Library, Ridgefield, NJ, children's librarian, 1982-87; Union Free Public Library, Union, NJ, children's librarian, 1987—. Other Worlds Books, Fair Lawn, NJ, editor, publisher, and owner, 1978-95.

MEMBER: Science Fiction Writers of America, New Jersey Library Association, Science Fiction Association of Bergen County.

WRITINGS:

MYSTERY NOVELS; FEATURING CHARLES DODGSON AND ARTHUR CONAN DOYLE

The Problem of the Missing Miss, St. Martin's Press (New York, NY), 1998.
The Problem of the Missing Hoyden, Robert Hale (London, England), 1999.
The Problem of the Spiteful Spiritualist, St. Martin's Press (New York, NY), 1999.
The Problem of the Evil Editor: A Charles Dodgson/ Arthur Conan Doyle Mystery, St. Martin's Minotaur (New York, NY), 2000.
The Problem of the Surly Servant: A Charles Dodgson/ Arthur Conan Doyle Mystery, St. Martin's Minotaur (New York, NY), 2001.

OTHER

Trexindex: An Index to Star Trek Fanzines, Other Worlds Books (Fair Lawn, NJ), 1976.

FutureSpeak: A Fan's Guide to the Language of Science Fiction, Paragon House (New York, NY), 1991.

Also author of five supplements to *Trexindex,* c. 1976-87. Contributor to anthologies, including *Merovingen Nights #3: Troubled Waters,* DAW Books (New York, NY), 1988; *Merovingen Nights #4: Smuggler's Gold,* DAW Books (New York, NY), 1988; *Merovingen Nights #5: Divine Right,* DAW Books (New York, NY), 1989; *Merovingen Nights #6: Flood Tide,* DAW Books (New York, NY), 1990; *The Resurrected Holmes: New Cases from the Notes of John H. Watson,* 1990; and *Don't Open This Book!,* 1998. Author of column, "Child's Play," *Mystery Scene Magazine. Beyond . . . Science Fiction and Fantasy,* editor, 1987-91; *GRIP,* editor, beginning 1978. Contributor of stories to periodicals.

SIDELIGHTS: While pursuing a primary career as a librarian and a secondary career in science fiction fan-related writing, Roberta Rogow also became a mystery novelist. Her first series of mysteries is set in Victorian England and features the creator of Sherlock Holmes, Arthur Conan Doyle, working in conjunction with Charles Dodgson, the real name of Lewis Carroll, author of *Alice in Wonderland.* (In real life, however, the pair never met.) Rogow uses a relatively young Doyle in her novels, one who has recently completed medical school, as the Watson-type character while Dodgson is aged and wise, the senior partner of the tandem. GraceAnne A. DeCandido in *Booklist* called the books an "utterly charming series."

In the first novel, *The Problem of the Missing Miss,* Doyle and Dodgson have an accidental meeting in 1885 in a Brighton, England, train station. The pair become involved with the case of a young girl, Alicia Marbury, kidnapped by those political forces working in opposition to her father, Lord Richard, a member of Parliament. The father was once a student of Dodgson's, and Alicia was coming to visit Dodgson. Rogow also ties in historical fact from the time period; the kidnappers have taken Alicia because they want her father to stop his sponsorship of a bill intended to deter child prostitution. Writing in *Publishers Weekly,* a critic commented positively on "Rogow's engaging tale."

The Problem of the Evil Editor: A Charles Dodgson/ Arthur Conan Doyle Mystery has the pair directly involved in an investigation into the murder of a children's magazine editor, Samuel Bassett, who has wronged Dodgson by selling books intended for charity at a profit. After a visit to Bassett's office by Dodgson and Doyle, they find themselves caught up in a London workers' riot and briefly held by the police. Throughout the series, Rogow works in relevant literary and history figures, and this book is no exception. The two are released when noted author Oscar Wilde helps them out. A reviewer in *Publishers Weekly* noted: "While the playful tone may be a bit at odds with the murderer's sad and sordid motives, Rogow's sly in-jokes and seamless blend of fact and fiction should delight many."

Rogow told *CA:* "I have two full-time careers. By day I am a municipal librarian in New Jersey, as I have been since 1971. Weekends and vacations are devoted to the subculture of science fiction in all its manifestations. The union of librarianship and science fiction led to the writing of *FutureSpeak: A Fan's Guide to the Language of Science Fiction,* published by Paragon House in 1991.

"I grew up in an upper-middle class Jewish suburban household; my mother was a psychologist and my father was a corporation lawyer. I went through the New York City school system and graduated from Queens College of the City University of New York with a degree in music and theater in 1962. After a decade of musical and acting studies and 'working in show biz' with a variety of fringe groups, I abandoned the elusive dream of stardom. I married Murray Rogow, a theatrical press agent, and temporarily hung up my costumes to give birth to Miriam in 1964 and Louise in 1968.

"I resumed my studies in 1969 at the Columbia School of Library Science, where I earned my master's degree in 1971. My theatrical and musical talents were utilized at the Paterson Free Public Library, Ridgefield Public Library, and Union Free Public Library, where I held positions in the children's and young adults' departments. I also served on several committees of the New Jersey Library Association.

"My second career in science fiction began when I discovered the early novels of Robert Heinlein and the story collections of C.L. Moore. The lure of faraway worlds and strange people drew me into science fiction in its 'silver age.' However, I remained a 'passifan' who only read the stories—until I discovered the world of *Star Trek.* I got hooked and devoured each weekly episode and rerun. A 'Trekker' had been born. At a library convention I met two fellow Trekkers who were active in the committee that ran the first *Star Trek* conventions. I attended my first convention in 1973, where I found hundreds of devotees who could spend a whole weekend talking 'Trek.' I also discovered 'fanzines,' those non-commercial publications produced by amateur publishers or on copying machines and sold at conventions. In the fanzines, writers could take the *Star Trek* characters and put them in new situations and universes.

"I had always wanted to share my stories. Now I had an audience. There was little or no money to be made from this, but there was the light at the end of the tunnel—I might someday see my writing in print. Two years later, in 1976, one of my stories was accepted and printed; the second career was begun. I plunged into fandom with both feet. I felt that if I could write for fanzines, I could also edit them. My own fanzine, *GRIP,* was begun in 1978. Between 1978 and 1987, I was involved with two other fanzines. I not only published my own magazines, I sold them at conventions. I extended my efforts to promoting items on consignment from other fanzine publishers all over the country.

"Once, after reading the first part of a two-part story in a fanzine, I was unable to find the second half of the continued story. In trying to solve this problem, the librarian in me took over, and I began compiling and publishing *Trexindex: An Index to Star Trek Magazines.* It was a massive effort in which I indexed, by story and author, over 500 titles from the previous ten years. Five supplements of *Trexindex* followed, the last appearing in 1987, when other demands on my time caused me to turn the project over to Bill Hupe, who has since done two more supplements.

"My songwriting, guitar playing, and folksinging talents also found their way into my science fiction life. I began writing and performing parodies about the Star Trek characters, science fiction books and films, and the 'fannish' life (such parodies are called 'filk' songs, from a misprint on a convention songsheet). I have published nine collections of my 'filk' songs and have recorded and produced six audiocassettes, which are sold at science fiction conventions across the United States.

"My writing found a paying market when C.J. Cherryh accepted my story 'Nessus' Shirt' for the 'Shared Universe' anthology *Merovingen Nights #3: Troubled Waters.* More sales followed. I have had stories in four of the *Merovingen Nights* anthologies.

"In addition to my writing and singing activities, I have participated in many other areas of the science fiction world. I have entered my original needlepoints in science fiction convention art shows. I have participated in masquerades, wearing homemade costumes based on science fiction characters that have earned me a wall full of trophies. I have even served on convention committees, running the dealer's room or assisting backstage at the masquerades. All this experience has been distilled into *FutureSpeak,* which uses a dictionary format to clarify the mysterious subculture of science fiction fandom by explaining the words and phrases of its many worlds. Fannish jargon, writers' terminology, and the scientific background materials that make up the 'science' in science fiction are all part of this 'language.' Both 'fans' and 'mundanes' have found *FutureSpeak* both fascinating and informative."

BIOGRAPHICAL AND CRITICAL SOURCES:

PERIODICALS

Booklist, July, 2001, GraceAnne A. DeCandido, review of *The Problem of the Surly Servant: A Charles Dodgson/Arthur Conan Doyle Mystery,* p. 1989.
Publishers Weekly, March 9, 1998, review of *The Problem of the Missing Miss,* p. 51; May 8, 2000, review of *The Problem of the Evil Editor: A Charles Dodgson/Arthur Conan Doyle Mystery,* p. 208.
Writer's Digest, September, 1998, Peter Blocksom, "First Novelist Profile: Roberta Rogow," interview with Roberta Rogow.*

*   *   *

RUBENSTEIN, Joshua 1949-

PERSONAL: Born July 18, 1949, in New Britain, CT; son of Bernard Alfred (a furrier) and Ruth (Ruden) Rubenstein. *Education:* Columbia University, B.A., 1971.

ADDRESSES: Office—Center for Government and International Studies, 1730 Cambridge St., 3rd Fl., Cambridge, MA 02138. *E-mail*—jrubenst@aiusa.org.

CAREER: Writer, teacher, and director. Worked as teacher of English in Jerusalem, Israel, 1971-72; teacher of Hebrew in Swampscott, MA, 1972-74; Polaroid Corp., Cambridge, MA, teacher of English, 1974-75; teacher of Hebrew in Chestnut Hill, MA, 1974-79; Amnesty International U.S.A., Northeast Regional Director, 1975—. Mendeleev Institute, Moscow, Russia, lecturer, 1990-91; Davis Center for Russian and Eurasian Studies, Harvard University, Cambridge, MA, fellow.

WRITINGS:

NONFICTION

(Editor and author of introduction) Anatoly Marchenko, *From Tarusa to Siberia,* Strathcona Publishing (Royal Oak, MI), 1980.
Soviet Dissidents: Their Struggle for Human Rights, Beacon Press (Boston, MA), 1980.
Adolf Hitler, F. Watts (New York, NY), 1982.
Tangled Loyalties: The Life and Times of Ilya Ehrenburg (biography), Basic Books (New York, NY), 1996.
(Editor, with V.P. Naumov, and author of introductions) *Stalin's Secret Pogrom: The Postwar Inquisition of the Jewish Anti-Fascist Committee* (history), Yale University Press (New Haven, CT), 2001.
(Editor, with Alexander Gribanov, and author of introductions) *The KGB File of Andrei Sakharov* (history), Yale University Press (New Haven, CT), 2005.

Author of educational filmstrips. Contributor to magazines and newspapers, including *Art News, New York Times Book Review, Commentary, New Republic, Canto, Moment, New York Times, Wall Street Journal, Boston Globe, Nation,* and *Columbia Journalism Review.*

SIDELIGHTS: A human rights activist and long-time employee of Amnesty International, Joshua Rubenstein is also a writer with expertise on Russian and Soviet affairs and history. Rubenstein spent thirteen years researching and writing a comprehensive biography of

Ilya Ehrenburg, a journalist and author in the Soviet Union. Titled *Tangled Loyalties: The Life and Times of Ilya Ehrenburg,* Rubenstein conducted interviews with at least one hundred people associated with Ehrenburg to flesh out his complicated story.

Ehrenburg, a Russian Jew, was a famous war correspondent during World War II, supporting Soviet leader Josef Stalin in his virulent anti-German reporting. Ehrenburg remained a public supporter and official state writer for Stalin for many years, despite Stalin's anti-Jewish sentiment and regular purges of those who dared to challenge him in any way. Yet over time, Ehrenburg became more in touch with his Jewish roots, was friends with many dissidents, became a respected intellectual force, and was sometimes indirectly critical of Stalin's regime. As Vladimir Tismaneanu wrote in *Society:* "In the end, the story of his life is one of a mutilated mind and amputated intellect. Rubenstein does an excellent job in documenting Ehrenburg's public and private life and highlighting the intrigues within the Soviet literary world."

Rubenstein coedited and wrote the introduction to *Stalin's Secret Pogrom: The Postwar Inquisition of the Jewish Anti-Fascist Committee* The primary text consists of a translation of the transcripts from the secret trial of the fifteen defendants. The fifteen, all Soviet Jewish writers who wrote in Yiddish, were accused of conspiracy because they were members of the Jewish Anti-Fascist Committee during World War II. They were interrogated, beaten, and tortured for acting against the Soviet Union in the late 1940s and early 1950s. However, many of them had actually supported communism and Stalin while working against Nazi Germany in their Yiddish-language writings several years earlier. Reviewing the book in *Midstream,* Arnold Ages wrote: "The one simple truth that emerges from this extraordinary volume is that the 13 Yiddish writers who were executed at Lubianka prison in 1952 died not because of the patently ridiculous accusations hurled against them—but because they were Jews."

Rubenstein told *CA:* "I happened on the subject of Soviet dissent almost by accident. I spent my first year in Boston living in a small, run-down apartment in the North End, trying to write fiction. Having produced one-half of a worthless novel and several mediocre short stories, I was in such a profound rut that I longed for something new to do. During my year in Israel I had managed to produce an article on a young artist I had met in Leningrad (in the summer of 1970) who

had since immigrated to Jerusalem and then Paris. His name was William Brui. With his help, I was able to write an article about him and his work that appeared in *Art News* in December 1971. Entitled "Refreezing the Thaw," it described William's efforts to revive the traditions of Constructivism and Suprematism, artistic movements that flourished in the early years of the Soviet regime only to be extinguished by Stalin.

"Armed with this article, I was able to show book review editors, first at the *Boston Phoenix,* then the *New Republic* and *Commentary,* that I could write about Russia. By 1975, I managed to place reviews in *The New York Times Book Review* as well and wrote my first extended piece on the Soviet dissident movement and the Jewish emigration movement for *Moment.* This article later served as the basis for a chapter of my book.

"Meanwhile, after teaching Hebrew school Sunday mornings and four afternoons a week for two years, I was able to relinquish the afternoon commitment in favor of a position teaching at Polaroid Corporation. This job, unfortunately, lasted only about half a year when the effects of the recession limited the company's willingness to provide classes for their employees on company time. My classes were simply dissolved and I was left with regular work only on Sunday mornings. For a time, my writing was able adequately to supplement my income. I wrote my first set of filmstrips that year for Guidance Associates, at the time a subsidiary of Harcourt Brace Jovanovich.

"It was during this period that I joined Amnesty International. I clipped a membership form from *The New York Review of Books* and sent in a donation. By April 1975, I formed a local chapter in Cambridge, and our efforts began on behalf of Prisoners of Conscience. In the fall, the woman who had been serving as New England coordinator resigned to join the Foreign Service. I immediately applied for the position and was hired in October 1975.

"I work part time for Amnesty as New England coordinator and field organizer. Aside from my responsibilities in the Northeast, where I do a good deal of organizing and public speaking, I also help to organize Amnesty chapters in the Midwest and South. Between 1976 and 1978, I took numerous trips to areas of the country, like Indiana, Texas, Iowa, Ohio, Tennessee, and Georgia, where there was no organized Amnesty International activity but where a number of contributors to Amnesty International lived.

"I don't have the facility to describe how lucky I am to be able to work for Amnesty International and still have the time to pursue my interests as a writer."

BIOGRAPHICAL AND CRITICAL SOURCES:

PERIODICALS

Midstream, July, 2001, Arnold Ages, review of *Stalin's Secret Pogrom: The Postwar Inquisition of the Jewish Anti-Fascist Committee,* p. 45.

Society, July-August, 1998, Vladimir Tismaneau, review of *Tangled Loyalties: The Life and Times of Ilya Ehrenburg,* p. 95.

ONLINE

Davis Center for Russian and Eurasian Studies Web site, http://daviscenter.fas.harvard.edu/ (October 10, 2005).
Joshua Rubenstein Home Page, http://www.joshua rubenstein.com (October 10, 2005).*

S

SAFIRE, William 1929-

PERSONAL: Born William Safir, December 17, 1929, in New York, NY; name legally changed to Safire; son of Oliver C (a thread merchant) and Ida (Panish) Safir; married Helene Belmar Julius (a jewelry maker), December 16, 1962; children: Mark Lindsey, Annabel Victoria. *Education:* Attended Syracuse University, 1947-49. *Politics:* Libertarian conservative.

ADDRESSES: Office—New York Times,, 1627 I St. N.W., Washington, DC 20006. *Agent*—Morton Janklow, 598 Madison Ave., New York, NY 10036.

CAREER: New York Herald-Tribune Syndicate, reporter, 1949-51; WNBC-WNBT, correspondent in Europe and Middle East, 1951; WNBC, New York, NY, radio-TV producer, 1954-55; Tex McCrary, Inc., vice president, 1955-60; Safire Public Relations, Inc., New York, NY, president, 1961-68; The White House, Washington, DC, special assistant to the President and speechwriter, 1968-73; *New York Times,* New York, NY, columnist in Washington, DC, 1973-2005. Member of Pulitzer Prize board, 1995-2004; Dana Foundation (a philanthropic organization in neuroscience), chairman and chief executive officer, 2000—. *Military service:* U.S. Army, 1952-54.

AWARDS, HONORS: Pulitzer Prize for distinguished commentary, 1978, for articles on Bert Lance.

WRITINGS:

The Relations Explosion, Macmillan (New York, NY), 1963.

(With M. Loeb) *Plunging into Politics,* McKay (New York, NY), 1964.

The New Language of Politics, Random House (New York, NY), 1968, third edition published as *Safire's Political Dictionary: The New Language of Politics,* 1978, revised and enlarged edition published as *Safire's New Political Dictionary: The Definitive Guide to the New Language of Politics,* 1993.

Before the Fall, Doubleday (New York, NY), 1975, published as *Before the Fall: An Inside View of the Pre-Watergate White House,* Da Capo Press (New York, NY), 1988.

Safire's Washington, Times Books (New York, NY), 1980.

What's the Good Word?, Times Books (New York, NY), 1982.

(Compiler, with brother, Leonard Safir) *Good Advice,* Times Books (New York, NY), 1982.

You Could Look It Up: More on Language, Times Books (New York, NY), 1988.

(Compiler and editor, with Leonard Safir) *Words of Wisdom,* Simon & Schuster (New York, NY), 1989.

Fumblerules: A Light-hearted Guide to Grammar and Good Usage, 1990.

(Compiler and editor, with Leonard Safir) *Leadership,* Simon & Schuster (New York, NY), 1990

The First Dissident: The Book of Job in Today's Politics, Random House (New York, NY), 1992.

(Compiler and author of introduction) *Lend Me Your Ears: Great Speeches in History,* Norton (New York, NY), 1992.

(Compiler, with Leonard Safir) *Good Advice on Writing: Writers Past and Present on How to Write Well,* Simon & Schuster (New York, NY), 1992.

Let a Simile Be Your Umbrella, illustrations by Terry Allen, Crown Publishers (New York, NY) 2001.

How Not to Write: The Essential Misrules of Grammar, Norton (New York, NY), 2005.

Author of political column "Essay," in *New York Times,* and "On Language" column in *New York Times Magazine,* 1979—. Contributor to *Harvard Business Review, Cosmopolitan, Playboy, Esquire, Reader's Digest, Redbook,* and *Collier's.*

COLLECTED COLUMNS

On Language, Times Books (New York, NY), 1980.

I Stand Corrected: More on Language, Times Books (New York, NY), 1984.

Take My Word for It: More on Language, Times Books (New York, NY), 1986.

Language Maven Strikes Again, Holt (New York, NY), 1990.

Coming to Terms, Doubleday (New York, NY), 1991.

Quoth the Maven, Random House (New York, NY), 1993.

In Love with Norma Loquendi, Random House (New York, NY), 1994.

Watching My Language, Random House (New York, NY), 1996.

Spread the Word, Times Books (New York, NY), 1999.

No Uncertain Terms: More Writing from the Popular "On Language" Column in the New York Times Magazine, Simon & Schuster (New York, NY), 2003.

The Right Word in the Right Place at the Right Time: Wit and Wisdom from the Popular "On Language" Column in the New York Times Magazine, Simon & Schuster (New York, NY), 2004.

FICTION

Full Disclosure, Doubleday (New York, NY), 1977, limited edition with illustrations by George Jones, Franklin Library, 1977.

Freedom, Doubleday, 1987.

Sleeper Spy, Random House (New York, NY), 1995.

Scandalmonger, Simon & Schuster (New York, NY), 2000.

SIDELIGHTS: William Safire has worn several hats in his varied career: speechwriter for President Richard Nixon, language commentator for the Sunday *New York Times Magazine,* political commentator for the *New York Times,* novelist, and historian. Safire does not pull his punches, and he has made both friends and enemies on all sides of political and linguistic issues. According to John A. Barnes in the *National Review,* "whether you love [Safire] or you hate him, you cannot afford to skip over him." *Time* contributor Paul Gray appreciated Safire's lack of rigidity: "William Safire has largely made his reputation through epigrammatic feistiness and hit-and-run repartee. . . . His twice-a-week columns continue to display reportorial zeal and refreshing unpredictability." Safire is also quick to alert his readers to governmental figures who run amuck. When speaking of his commentaries on English-language usage, some critics view Safire as an institution. David Thomas observed in the *Christian Science Monitor* that "Safire may be the closest we have to a clearinghouse for hearing, seeing, and testing how we're doing with the language."

Safire began his career as a public relations writer, took a job as speechwriter for Spiro Agnew in the 1968 presidential campaign, and eventually became a senior speechwriter for President Richard M. Nixon. He left his position, however, before the infamous bugging of Watergate and was finishing his memoir of the Nixon White House when the president resigned. Because of the timing of its completion, *Before the Fall* almost missed publication entirely. The book painted a fairly positive view of the administration and was rejected by William Morrow, who also demanded back the royalty advance they had paid the author. But eventually the book was published by Doubleday.

Newsweek critic Walter Clemons called *Before the Fall* "a puffy, lightweight concoction, served up for the faithful." Clemons noted that "Safire is protective of Nixon, reserving his harshest judgment for the deviousness and drive for power he attributes to Henry Kissinger." But *Atlantic* contributor Richard Todd gave the book credit for being "full of interesting data on the theme that Safire identifies as crucial to the Nixon Administration: its sense of the world as 'us' against 'them.rsquo;" And Daniel Schorr recounted in the *New York Times Book Review,* Safire's description of Nixon's desire for "understanding and perspective," and noted: "If Nixon gets the kind of understanding he wants, this book will surely have helped a lot. In any event [*Before the Fall*] . . . will still be an enormous contribution to understanding the phenomenon called Nixon."

Safire's first novel, *Full Disclosure,* also deals with a president in danger of losing his office. His fictional leader, Sven Ericson, has been blinded after a bump on the head received while closeted in a Pullman berth with a female member of the White House press corps. The plot concerns whether the Twenty-fifth Amendment, which addresses disabled presidents, will be used to oust Ericson. *New Republic* contributor Stephen Hess commented that *Full Disclosure*'s strength comes from the fact that it "is about presidential politics by a man who intimately knows presidential politics." But a *Saturday Review* contributor questioned the work's literary value, claiming that the story's political puzzle is "the book's one redeeming feature." The critic added, however, that by exploring Ericson's uncertain position, "Safire not only cooks up a fiery stewpot of political ambitions, but produces a dramatic warning of the [Twenty-fifth Amendment's] possible abuse."

Safire's columns on language for the *New York Times Magazine* are widely read and enjoyed. In several books, he has reprinted column selections and his readers' replies. *On Language,* the first of these collections, gives examples of correct and incorrect language usage and explores word origins as well. Several reviewers enjoyed Safire's interaction with his readers. "Although what Safire has discovered about word origins and their current usage made good reading, the inclusion of what his readers have to add makes them even more so," stated *Christian Science Monitor* contributor Maria Lenhart. And, according to D.J. Enright in the *Encounter,* "Safire's relations with his Irregulars are highly interesting, and help to generate much of the comedy in this almost continuously entertaining book."

Freedom, a heavily detailed historical novel, is the author's longest work. When Safire submitted the manuscript to his publisher after working on it for seven years, the triple-spaced copy ran 3,300 pages. When Doubleday found the book too large to bind, Safire had to cut at least one section; still, the final product was 1,152 pages long. In *Freedom* Safire again uses his Washington experience to describe the capital between June of 1861 and January 1, 1863. The story opens with Lincoln's issue of the Emancipation Proclamation and focuses on the president's role during the early Civil War years. *New York Review of Books* contributor C. Vann Woodward described Safire's Lincoln as "a Lincoln racked by debilitating depression (which he called melancholia), agonizing over the daily choice of evils, and seeking relief in one of his that-reminds-me stories. He is by turns Saint Sebastian, Machiavelli, Pericles, and an oversize, countrified Puck."

Safire explained his attitude toward Lincoln to Alvin P. Sanoff for *U.S. News & World Report:* "It's impossible to approach Lincoln honestly with a spirit of reverence and awe. He is a secular and not a religious figure. He wasn't martyred; he was assassinated. Approaching Lincoln as a political figure, which is what he was, you can appreciate him." Still, Safire concluded that "I've come to the conclusion that he was, indeed, the greatest President, with the possible exception of Washington, because he was so complex and so purposeful. When you see him with all the warts, when you see his drawbacks and his failures and his shortcomings, then you see his greatness." The author explained to *Publishers Weekly* contributor Trish Todd that one of the greatest issues facing the U.S. government at that time was the contemporary problem of "how much freedom must be taken away from individuals in order to protect the freedom of the nation."

While *Freedom* has received much popular and critical acclaim, some reviewers dislike the book's focus. Woodward felt Safire has almost neglected the presence of blacks in the Civil War: "One book of the nine into which the novel is divided is indeed entitled 'The Negro,' but it is largely concerned with other matters, with only four or five pages on blacks, and most of that is what whites said or did about them, not what they said and did themselves." Woodward added, "as a whole [blacks] are granted fewer than twenty-five lines of their own to speak. None of their prominent leaders are introduced, and Frederick Douglass is not mentioned. . . . Nowhere does this huge book face up squarely to the impact of slavery and the complexities of race." Other critics have found the book too lengthy and detailed. Chicago *Tribune Books* contributor John Calvin Batchelor, furthermore, called *Freedom* "a mountain to dazzle and assault," and stated that it is "loving, cogent, bottomlessly researched, [and] passionately argued." He also claimed that the book "is guaranteed to exhaust the reader like no other intellectual endeavor, yet in the end it delivers a miracle."

Safire ventured further into new writing territory with *The First Dissident: The Book of Job in Today's Politics.* Safire had long been fascinated by Job, the

Biblical figure whose faith was tested by his many troubles and who sought an explanation from God. Published in a U.S. presidential election year, 1992, the book led Kenneth L. Woodward to report in *Newsweek:* "In this campaign season's most improbable political meditation, Safire has published . . . a sometimes wise and frequently witty demonstration of how Job's confrontation with Ultimate Authority can illuminate the power struggles in Washington and vice versa." Safire's interpretation of Job is a far cry from the most widely held view of him. He is usually held up as a model of long-suffering patience, but Safire views him as a righteous, rebellious, "even blasphemous" figure "who demands that God explain himself or stand guilty of abusing his own authority," explained Woodward. "He is in short, the original political contrarian, a fellow who, in another era, might just find work as a brave, truth-telling columnist."

Christian Science Monitor contributor Marshall Ingwerson noted that extensive study informs the book, and he remarked that "Safire's own concept of God is of a powerful—but not all-powerful—creator who leaves it to man to carve out justice in the world." But while Ingwerson and Woodward both credited the author with serious theological intent, another reviewer, Jonathan Dorfman, found *The First Dissident* a disappointing, superficial book. Writing in the *Washington Post Book World,* he found promise in Safire's stated premise, "to discern political lessons in Job and the book's relevance to modern politics," but goes on to say: "You begin the book with high expectations. Five minutes later, you realize that the author reduces the gravity of Job to a trifle with all the moral freight of *Larry King Live.*" Dorfman further criticized Safire for trivializing Job's suffering by comparing him to politicians such as Gary Hart and Bert Lance. The reviewer deemed Safire's discussion of Job and Lincoln more appropriate, though: "In his meditation on Lincoln and Job, Safire drops his street-smart style; the tone is somber, fit for the gravity of the subject. . . . [The essay is] an elegiac lament that atones for much of his frivolity on the angry howl of Job."

Safire tried another new genre in 1995 with *Sleeper Spy,* a novel of espionage. *New Yorker* reviewer David Remnick characterized it as "an old-fashioned Washington-Moscow thriller. It features a hundred billion dollars, a sexy network newsie, a K.G.B. mole, lots of secret agents, and a hero who is . . . 'the world's greatest reporter.'" In the story, a Russian spy who has been working in finance in the United States is given a small fortune to invest and increases it many times over. With the breakup of the Soviet Union and the deaths of his spymasters, however, the agent is left on his own to be pursued by various factions. Reviewers were mixed in their assessment of Safire's skill in handling this type of thriller. "Interesting as all this is conceptually, it makes for a highly cerebral and talky novel—a mind game," remarked Morton Kondracke in the *New York Times Book Review,* adding, "Toward the end the reader is made to feel that the writer is having most of the fun, some of it at the expense of the reader, who's suddenly told without warning that things presumed to be facts simply aren't." Yet Kondracke allowed that *Sleeper Spy* "certainly does engage the mind and, on a few occasions, stir the pulse." *New York Times* reviewer George Stade was critical of Safire's handling of plot and dialogue, asserting that the author "has the skills of a reporter but not those of a storyteller." Remnick was more generous, however, calling *Sleeper Spy* "a great big ice-cream cone of a book: predictable, sweet fun."

Safire attracted considerable media attention himself in 1996, after he made a comment in his *New York Times* column about the firing of the travel workers in the White House by First Lady Hillary Rodham Clinton. Safire wrote in his column that Mrs. Clinton was a "congenital liar" for claiming that she "hadn't personally insisted on firing the seven-man White House Travel staff," reported William F. Buckley Jr. in the *National Review.* "In fact, according to her ex-employee and Clinton pal Mr. Watkins, she did want them fired." President Clinton took umbrage at Safire's remarks and responded (through White House spokesman Mike McCurry) that, were he not president, he would punch Mr. Safire in the nose. "What fascinates is that this episode and a few others . . . invite the formal scrutiny of investigating panels, and theoretically, the courts themselves, because perjury is contingently involved," Buckley explained. "To get to the White House one promises one thing, does another. Or else one reaffirms on Monday what one repudiates on Tuesday? Some would go so far as guess that if he were simply 'Mr.' Clinton even then he wouldn't actually go to Mr. Safire's office and poke him in the Republican Party, or Congress, or the voters who vote for the wrong people."

The author reexamined some of the same issues surrounding the Clintons and their relationship with the media in his historical novel *Scandalmonger.* The book details the life and career of journalist James Thomson Callender, who at Thomas Jefferson's instigation first broke the story of Alexander Hamilton's extramarital affair, then a few years later released the story of Jefferson's decades-long affair with his slave Sally Hemings. "In light of the recent White House brouhaha," declared a *Publishers Weekly* reviewer, "it's fascinating to learn that in the days of the founding fathers, politicians were just as licentious and newspapermen even more scurrilous than some players in contemporary media." "Drawing on letters and historical records," Daisy Maryles and Dick Donahue stated in *Publishers Weekly,* "Safire shows how media invasion of private lives—as well as politicians' manipulation of the press—are as old as the Constitution itself." *Booklist* contributor Brad Hooper wrote, "For any who still believe that sexual scandalmongering is something new in Washington, DC, or that bitter partisanship did not exist in those hollowed days of the Founding Fathers, or that First Amendment issues are something only we in the present day wrestle with, let them read this novel and think again." "This meaty, profoundly engrossing novel," Barbara Conaty commented in *Library Journal,* "vividly illustrates episodes in the history of American journalism and government."

Safire's collections of his language columns continued to be popular with readers as the millennium drew to a close and the new one opened. *Spread the Word,* published in 1999, celebrates the twentieth anniversary of his "On Language" column. Among the terms and concepts Safire grapples with are alpha male; the new feminist power of the word "babe"; and how words related to cleaning, such as "ethnic cleansing," can stand in for genocide. Safire also considers the political metaphor of "left wing and right wing" and how it does not have much relation to birds. The proper use of among, betwixt, and between can also be found in these pages. "With energy and wit, he takes us for a spin around the linguistic turf of politics, the media, and popular culture," observed *Booklist* reviewer Philip Herbst.

Let a Simile Be Your Umbrella finds Safire "in fine form," noted Herbst in another *Booklist* review. With a diverse range of resources "he dissects curious coinages, trends, and flubs in English usage," Herbst stated. Much of the language in this volume concerns political terminology and concepts from the Bill Clin-

ton presidency and Newt Gingrich's tenure as speaker of the house. As much as Safire delights in pointing out the linguistic gaffes of others, particularly politicians, he is equally demanding of himself, and demonstrates several instances in which his precision of language was in need of calibration. Although *Library Journal* reviewer Paul D'Allessandro felt the author's analysis of political terms is better than of popular phrases, he declared, "Safire never fails to prick the interest of word lovers." A *Publishers Weekly* contributor noted that Safire "proves that there is no wittier, more gracious stickler for correct usage and grammar" than himself.

No Uncertain Terms: More Writing from the Popular "On Language" Column in the New York Times Magazine concentrates on words and word usage from the last years of the Clinton presidency and the beginning of the Bush era. There are terms that figured large in Clinton's impeachment proceedings, as well as words that were important to Al Gore's ultimately failed presidential campaign, Safire points out. He covers word misuse, the development of slang terms, the evolutions of words and their meanings over time, and particularly creative uses of words or phrases. He also continues to print letters and feedback from his readers, establishing communications between himself and those who peruse his column. Collections of Safire's columns permit readers to "move from essay to essay and get a full sense of the breadth and depth of his work," observed Necia Parker-Gibson in the *Library Journal.* "If you are a fan of language or worried about your grammar, William Safire is your touchstone, whatever your political persuasion," commented Bob Trimble in the *Dallas Morning News.*

The Right Word in the Right Place at the Right Time: Wit and Wisdom from the Popular "On Language" Column in the New York Times Magazine once again collects a series of "On Language" columns, with Safire's crisp commentary. In this edition, however, "he does more than elucidate the origins of slang or correct common grammatical mistakes: he alerts readers to the rhetorical maneuvers of our politicians and public figures as only a former speechwriter can," observed a reviewer in *Publishers Weekly.* The subtle meaning of the Bush doctrine of "No Child Left Behind" is methodically analyzed, as are the important distinctions between "antiterrorism" and "counterterrorism" functions. Safire also looks carefully at the wording of a number of Supreme Court rulings, which resulted in a spirited response from Justice Antonin Scalia. "There is a lot to think about here for the language lover, for there is much subtlety in Satire's examinations of word usage," noted *Booklist* reviewer Brad Hooper.

Safire further indulges his love for words in *Safire's New Political Dictionary: The Definitive Guide to the New Language of Politics,* a collection of 1,100 definitions covering 1,800 terms in common use in politics and related pursuits. "It is a treasury of practical, curious, incidental and entertaining knowledge," commented Jay W. Stein in the *Defense Counsel Journal.* The words and phrases covered in the book consist largely of material that were notably used or introduced by presidents. From the Reagan years, Safire gleans evil empire, star wars, and Reaganomics. The first President Bush introduced America to voodoo economics, read my lips, and a thousand points of light. The end of the Cold War and the collapse of the Soviet empire brought to prominence words such as glasnost and perestroika. Each brief definition also includes a longer and more detailed word history. "For working journalists, the appeal of Safire's book isn't so much the definitions but its rich array of anecdotes and quotes that beg for use in one's next feature, column, or editorial," observed James E. Casto in *American Journalism Review.* A *Booklist* reviewer called the book a "highly readable, informative work."

BIOGRAPHICAL AND CRITICAL SOURCES:

BOOKS

Contemporary Literary Criticism, Volume 10, Gale (Detroit, MI), 1979.

PERIODICALS

American Journalism Review, March, 1993, Dennis McCann, review of *The First Dissident: The Book of Job in Today's Politics,* p. 49; May, 1994, James E. Casto, review of *Safire's New Political Dictionary,* p. 46.

America's Intelligence Wire, November 15, 2004, Pat Milton, "*The New York Times*' William Safire Announces Retirement as Op-ed Page Columnist."

Ascribe Higher Education News Service, September 13, 2002, "Pulitzer Prize Winning Essayist William Safire to Launch Fall 2002 University Lectures at Syracuse University."

Atlantic, July, 1975, Richard Todd, review of *Before the Fall.*

Booklist, January 15, 1994, review of *Safire's New Political Dictionary,* p. 971; August, 1994, Denise Perry, review of *In Love with Norma Loquendi,* p. 2004; September 1, 1995, George Needham, review of *Sleeper Spy,* p. 47; September 1, 1997, Alice Joyce, review of *Watching My Language,* p. 43; October 15, 1999, Philip Herbst, review of *Spread the Word,* p. 401; December 15, 1999, Brad Hooper, review of *Scandalmonger,* p. 739; October 15, 2000, Leah Sparks, review of *Scandalmonger,* p. 472; April 1, 2001, Karen Harris, review of *Scandalmonger,* p. 1490; October 15, 2001, Philip Herbst, review of *Let a Simile Be Your Umbrella,* p. 363; May 15, 2003, Gavin Quinn, review of *No Uncertain Terms: More Writing from the Popular "On Language" Column in the New York Times Magazine,* p. 1623; April 15, 2004, Brad Hooper, review of *The Right Word in the Right Place at the Right Time: Wit and Wisdom from the Popular "On Language" Column in the New York Times Magazine,* p. 1404.

Business Wire, November 15, 2004, "*The New York Times* to Run Final Op-ed Column by William Safire."

Christian Science Monitor, January 12, 1981, Maria Lenhart, review of *On Language,* p. B3; December 31, 1984, David Thomas, review of *I Stand Corrected: More "On Language,"* p. 16; January 11, 1993, Marshall Ingwerson, review of *The First Dissident,* p. 15.

Columbia Journalism Review, January, 2000, Evan Cornog, review of *Scandalmonger,* p. 77; November-December, 2001, "The Rise of the Conservative Voice: William Safire, George Will Win Pulitzer Prizes for Column-Writing," p. 84.

Commentary, April, 1993, Edward N. Luttwak, review of *The First Dissident,* p. 56.

Daily News (New York, NY), November 16, 2004, Paul D. Colford, profile of William Safire.

Dallas Morning News, July 24, 2003, Bob Trimble, review of *No Uncertain Terms.*

Defense Counsel Journal, October, 1994, Jay W. Stein, review of *Safire's New Political Dictionary,* p. 597.

Economist, November 21, 1992, review of *Lend Me Your Ears: Great Speeches in History,* p. 107.

Encounter, April, 1981, D.J. Enright, review of *On Language..*

Entertainment Weekly, November 10, 1995, Gene Lyons, review of *Sleeper Spy,* p. 55.

Forbes, October 26, 1992, Steve Forbes, review of *The First Dissident,* p. 26.

Insight on the News, February 12, 1996, Alan L. Anderson, "The White House and the Liberal, Lawyer, Liar Label," p. 30.

Kirkus Reviews, April 15, 2003, review of *No Uncertain Terms,* p. 594; April 1, 2005, review of *How Not to Write: The Essential Misrules of Grammar,* p. 407.

Library Journal, June 1, 1997, Peter A. Dollard, review of *Lend Me Your Ears,* p. 90; July, 1997, Cathy Sabol, review of *Watching My Language,* p. 83; November 15, 1999, Lisa J. Cihlar, review of *Spread the Word,* p. 78; January, 2000, Barbara Conaty, review of *Scandalmonger,* p. 162; February 15, 2001, Joseph L. Carlson, review of *Scandalmonger,* p. 217; October 1, 2001, Paul D'Allessandro, review of *Let a Simile Be Your Umbrella,* p. 99; June 15, 2003, Necia Parker-Gibson, review of *No Uncertain Terms,* p. 81.

Nation, June 21, 1999, David Sarasohn, "On Safire's Language," p. 10.

National Catholic Reporter, February 5, 1993, Michael J. Farrell, review of *The First Dissident,* p. 25.

National Review, November 28, 1980, John A. Barnes, review of *Safire's Washington,* p. 1472; March 29, 1993, Jerold S. Auerbach, review of *The First Dissident,* p. 66; February 12, 1996, William F. Buckley, Jr., "This 'Liar' Business," p. 62; December 13, 2004, "After More than Thirty Years, William Safire Is Relinquishing His Spot on the *New York Times* Op-ed Page," p. 14.

New Republic, July 9, 1977, Stephen Hess, review of *Full Disclosure.*

Newsweek, March 3, 1975, Walter Clemons, review of *Before the Fall;* November 9, 1992, Kenneth L. Woodward, review of *The First Dissident,* p. 81; January 31, 1994, Jonathan Alter, "Where There's Smoke, There's Safire," profile of William Safire, p. 41.

New York, December 21, 1992, William F. Buckley, Jr., "Right from the Start," profile of William Safire, p. 107.

New Yorker, August 21, 1995, David Remnick, "Spy Anxiety," review of *Sleeper Spy,* p. 116.

New York Review of Books, September 24, 1987, C. Vann Woodward, review of *Freedom,,* p. 23.

New York Times, November 5, 1992, Nicholas Lemann, review of *The First Dissident,* p. C20; September 4, 1995, George Stade, review of *Sleeper Spy,* p. A15.

New York Times Book Review, February 23, 1975, Daniel Schorr, review of *Before the Fall;* July 21, 1991, review of *Coming to Terms,* p. 18; November 8, 1992, Geoffrey Hodgson, review of *The First Dissident,* p. 14; October 31, 1993, Martin Walker, review of *Safire's New Political Dictionary,* p. 9; September 18, 1994, review of *In Love with Norma Loquendi,* p. 20; September 17, 1995, Morton Kondracke, review of *Sleeper Spy,* p. 15.

People, December 4, 1995, p. 36; January 29, 1996, Kim Cunningham, "Hell from the Chief," p. 94.

Publishers Weekly, April 30, 1982, Stella Dong, interview with William Safire, p. 12; March 29, 1987, Trish Todd, "William Safire Talks about *Freedom,* His New Novel," interview with William Safire; August 10, 1992, review of *The First Dissident,* p. 61; July 11, 1994, review of *In Love with Norma Loquendi,* p. 70; July 31, 1995, review of *Sleeper Spy,* p. 67; June 30, 1997, review of *Watching My Language,* p. 59; December 20, 1999, review of *Scandalmonger,* p. 53; February 14, 2000, Daisy Maryles and Dick Donahue, "A Scandalous Newcomer," p. 85; October 8, 2001, *Let a Simile Be Your Umbrella,* p. 52; April 21, 2003, review of *No Uncertain Terms,* p. 49; May 10, 2004, review of *The Right Word in the Right Place at the Right Time,* p. 44; May 2, 2005, review of *How Not to Write,* p. 185.

Saturday Review, July 9, 1977, review of *Full Disclosure.*

Time, August 31, 1987, Paul Gray, review of *Freedom,* p. 61; February 12, 1990, Walter Shapiro, "Prolific Purveyor of Punditry: As Comfortable with Wordplay as with Politics, William Safire Is the Country's Best Practitioner of the Art of Columny," p. 62; December 11, 1995, Belinda Luscombe, "Tinker, Tailor, Soldier, Critic," p. 95; January 22, 1996, "Pugilistic Main Event of the Week," p. 11; March 18, 1996, "Verbatim," p. 33.

Tribune Books (Chicago, IL), August 9, 1987, John Calvin Batchelor, review of *Freedom,* p. 1; October 17, 1993, review of *Good Advice on Writing,* p. 8; September 17, 1995, review of *Sleeper Spy,* p. 6.

UPI Newstrack, November 15, 2004, "William Safire Ending *NY Times* Column."

U.S. News & World Report, August 24, 1987, Alvin P. Sanoff, "A Modern Vote for Abraham Lincoln," interview with William Safire, p. 57.

Vanity Fair, November, 1992, Marjorie Williams, "Safire and Brimstone," profile of William Safire, p. 148.

Washingtonian, August, 1991, Victor Gold, "Strong Words: Bill Safire on Truth, Consequences, and Winning in Washington," interview with William Safire, p. 66.

Washington Post, December 1, 1995, Howard Kurtz, "The Mole in the Hill: a Spy Story; How Aldrich Ames Became a Literary Critic," p. F1.

Washington Post Book World, August 27, 1995, Jonathan Dorfman, review of *The First Dissident,* p. 5.

Weekly Standard, November 22, 2004, Elaine Margolin, review of *Lend Me Your Ears,* p. 43.

Wilson Library Bulletin, March, 1994, James Rettig, review of *Safire's New Political Dictionary,* p. 95.

ONLINE

New York Times Online, http://www.nytimes.com/ (October 8, 2005), biography of William Safire.

Salon.com, http://www.salon.com/ (November 22, 2004), Eric Boehlert, "William Safire's Dubious Legacy."*

*   *   *

SAIL, Lawrence 1942-
  (Lawrence Richard Sail)

PERSONAL: Born October 29, 1942, in London, England; son of Helmut Gustav (a painter) and Barbara (Wright) Sail; married Teresa Luke, September 18, 1965 (divorced, August, 1981); married Helen Bird, 1994; children: (first marriage) Matthew Charles, Erica Jocelyn; (second marriage) Rose Arlette and Grace Romola (twins). *Education:* St. John's College, Oxford, B.A. (with honors), 1964. *Hobbies and other interests:* Music, sailing.

ADDRESSES: Home—Richmond Villa, 7 Wonford Rd., Exeter, Devon EX2 4LF, England.

CAREER: Greater London Council, London, England, administrative officer, 1964-65; teacher of modern languages at schools in Nairobi, Kenya, and in England, 1966-90; writer. Blundell's School, visiting

writer, 1980-81. Oxford University, member of Senior Common Room of St. John's College; South West Arts Literature Panel, member, 1978-85; Arvon Foundation, chair, 1990-94; Cheltenham Festival of Literature, program director, 1991, codirector, 1999.

AWARDS, HONORS: Hawthornden fellow, 1992; Arts Council writer's bursary, 1993; Cholmondeley Award, 2004.

WRITINGS:

POETRY

Opposite Views, Dent (London, England), 1974.

The Drowned River, Mandeville Press (Hitchin, Hertfordshire, England), 1978.

The Kingdom of Atlas, Secker & Warburg (London, England), 1980.

Devotions, Secker & Warburg (London, England), 1987.

Aquamarine, Gruffyground Press (Sidcot, Somerset, England), 1988.

Out of Land: New and Selected Poems, Bloodaxe Books (Newcastle upon Tyne, England), 1992.

Building into Air, Bloodaxe Books (Newcastle upon Tyne, England), 1995.

The World Returning, Bloodaxe Books (Newcastle upon Tyne, England), 2002.

Eye-Baby, Bloodaxe Books (Newcastle upon Tyne, England), 2006.

EDITOR

South West Review: A Celebration, South West Arts (Exeter, England), 1985.

First and Always: Poems for the Great Ormond Street Children's Hospital, Faber (London, England), 1988.

One Hundred Voices: A Century of County Councils (children's poetry), Wheaton (Exeter, England), 1989.

(With Kevin Crossley-Holland) *The New Exeter Book of Riddles,* Enitharmon Press (London, England), 1999.

(With Kevin Crossley-Holland) *Light Unlocked: Christmas Card Poems,* Enitharmon Press (London, England), 2005.

OTHER

Cross-currents: Essays, Enitharmon Press (London, England), 2005.

Author of a radio play titled *Death of an Echo,* 1980. Contributor of articles and reviews to periodicals, including *Poetry Review, Poetry Nation Review,* and *Stand.* Editor, *South West Review,* 1980-85.

SIDELIGHTS: Lawrence Sail told *CA:* "Over many years I've appreciated the force of W.H. Auden's injunction at the close of his poem in memory to Yeats. A close second to this, as an aim at least, might be Robert Frost's suggestion that a poem should begin with delight and end in wisdom.

"For me the possibilities of poems remain as challenging as ever. On one level you are only as good as the poem you are about to write. Nothing illustrates this better, as emblem or image, than the sea, to whose perspectives I return again and again. Protean, it is never the same as it was: look at it, then away and back, and already it has escaped the words you might have formed for it. Much of experience seems to have something of the same slipperiness, while also encouraging the urge to commute between it and meaning.

"As to the world my poems inhabit, it's a borderland which straddles dreams and history, discovery and concealment, doubt and belief."

BIOGRAPHICAL AND CRITICAL SOURCES:

BOOKS

Contemporary Poets, 6th edition, St. James Press (Detroit, MI), 1996.

PERIODICALS

Books, December, 1988, p. 30.
Encounter, March, 1987, p. 61.
Listener, March 5, 1987, p. 28.
London Review of Books, April 20, 1989, p. 22.

New Statesman and Society, August 11, 1995, p. 41.
Observer, October 16, 1988, p. 43.
Stand, winter, 1993, p. 22.
Times Literary Supplement, April 10, 1981; December 25, 1987, p. 1435; May 5, 1989, p. 495; January 22, 1993, p. 21.

*   *   *

SAIL, Lawrence Richard
    See SAIL, Lawrence

*   *   *

SAVILLE, Andrew
    See TAYLOR, Andrew

*   *   *

SAXTON, Martha 1945-

PERSONAL: Born September 3, 1945, in New York, NY; daughter of Mark (a writer and editor) and Josephine (an editor; maiden name, Stocking) Saxton; married Enrico Ferorelli (a photographer), July 11, 1977. *Education:* University of Chicago, B.A., 1967; Columbia University, Ph.D. *Hobbies and other interests:* Playing the piano, jogging.

ADDRESSES: Home—New York, NY. *Office*—111 Chapin Hall, Amherst College, Amherst, MA 01002-5000. *E-mail*—msaxton@amherst.edu.

CAREER: Writer and professor. Massachusetts Historical Society, Boston, MA, editorial assistant, 1967-68; Rand McNally & Co., New York, NY, editorial assistant, 1969; Literary Guild, New York, NY, editor, 1970-73; freelance writer, beginning 1973; Amherst College, Amherst, MA, assistant professor of history and women's and gender studies, 1997—.

MEMBER: Authors Guild, Authors League of America.

WRITINGS:

NONFICTION

Jayne Mansfield and the American Dream, Houghton Mifflin (Boston, MA), 1975.

Louisa May Alcott: A Modern Biography, Houghton Mifflin (Boston, MA), 1977.

(Contributor) Geoffrey C. Ward, *Not for Ourselves Alone: The Story of Elizabeth Cady Stanton and Susan B. Anthony: An Illustrated History,* Knopf (New York, NY), 1999.

Being Good: Women's Moral Values in Early America, Hall and Wang (New York, NY), 2003.

OTHER

(With Rupert Holmes) *The Forties,* edited by Jeffrey Weiss, Consolidated Music Publishers (New York, NY), 1975.

The Fifties, edited by Jeffrey Weiss, Consolidated Music Publishers (New York, NY), 1975.

The Twenties, edited by Jeffrey Weiss, Consolidated Music Publishers (New York, NY), 1976.

(With Gordon Williams) *Love Songs,* Consolidated Music Publishers (New York, NY), 1976.

Contributor to periodicals, including *Quest, New Yorker, American Heritage, History Today,* and *Viva.*

SIDELIGHTS: After a career as a writer and editor that included the publication of several biographies of prominent American women, Martha Saxton became a college professor teaching history and women's and gender studies. She continued to write about women, publishing the nonfiction title *Being Good: Women's Moral Values in Early America* in 2003. In the book, Saxton explores the moral values imposed on girls and women in the United States, how the values affected them, and the ways in which these values changed over time. Saxon limits her focus to three times and places in the United States: Boston, Massachusetts, in the 1600s; Virginia in the 1700s; and St. Louis, Missouri, in 1900s. Saxton believes that as the United States became bigger in size and economy, white women had an increased moral value, at least on a symbolic basis. However, black women saw their moral value decrease over the years, especially as slavery became more widespread. Writing in the *Journal of Social History,* Linda W. Rosenzweig commented, "Martha Saxton has written an intriguing and complex book that offers much for the reader who is interested in women's and gender history, emotions history, and behavioral history."

Saxton once commented: "Good biography, like good fiction, seems to me the best way to understand as completely as possible another person's point of view.

History and travel are the other two ways I prefer for changing perspective. I read and write history, and travel as often as possible."

BIOGRAPHICAL AND CRITICAL SOURCES:

PERIODICALS

History: Review of New Books, summer, 2003, Frederick M. Beatty, review of *Being Good: Women's Moral Values in Early America,* p. 148.

Journal of Social History, winter, 2004, Linda W. Rosenzweig, review of *Being Good,* p. 550.

Publishers Weekly, January 6, 2003, review of *Being Good,* p. 49.

ONLINE

Amherst College Web site, http://www.amherst.edu/ (July 28, 2003), biography of Martha Saxton.

*　　*　　*

SCHARFSTEIN, Ben-Ami 1919-

PERSONAL: Born April 12, 1919, in New York, NY; son of Zevi (a writer, educator, and publisher) and Rose (a publisher; maiden name, Goldfarb) Scharfstein; married Ghela Efros, June 15, 1952; children: Doreet. *Education:* Brooklyn College (now of the City University of New York), B.A., 1939; Harvard University, M.A., 1940; Jewish Theological Seminary, B.J.P., 1941; Columbia University, Ph.D., 1942.

ADDRESSES: Home—Gluskin St. 1, Tel-Aviv, Israel.

CAREER: Brooklyn College (now of the City University of New York), Brooklyn, NY, fellow, 1942-43, tutor, 1944, instructor in philosophy, 1945-49; Columbia University, New York, NY, lecturer in philosophy, 1949-50; Reali School and Teachers Seminary, Haifa, Israel, teacher of English, history, and education, 1950-51; Hunter College (now of the City University of New York), New York, NY, instructor in philosophy, 1953-54; University of Utah, Salt Lake City, assistant professor of philosophy, 1954-55;

Tel-Aviv University, Tel-Aviv, Israel, associate professor, 1955-76, professor of philosophy, 1976-88, professor emeritus, 1988—, head of department, 1955-72, vice rector, 1969-72. Jewish Theological Seminary of America, guest lecturer at Teachers Institute, 1946-47.

MEMBER: International Society for the Comparative Study of Civilization, American Philosophical Association, New Israeli Philosophical Association, Israeli Association for Aesthetics.

AWARDS, HONORS: Citation for outstanding academic book, *Choice,* 1998, for *A Comparative History of World Philosophy: From the Upanishads to Kant;* Israel Prize for philosophy, 2005.

WRITINGS:

Roots of Bergson's Philosophy, Columbia University Press (New York, NY), 1943.

(With Mortimer Ostow) *The Need to Believe,* International Universities Press (New York, NY), 1954.

(With Raphael Sappan) *English-Hebrew Dictionary,* edited by Zevi Scharfstein, Shilo (New York, NY), 1961.

Mystical Experience, Bobbs-Merrill (New York, NY), 1972.

(With mother Rose Scharfstein and father Zevi Scharfstein) *New Comprehensive Shilo Pocket Dictionary, Hebrew-English, English-Hebrew,* Shilo (New York, NY), 1973.

The Mind of China, Basic Books (New York, NY), 1974.

(Editor, with Yoav Ariel, Shlomo Biderman, and others, and contributor) *Philosophy East/Philosophy West,* Oxford University Press (New York, NY), 1978.

The Philosophers, Oxford University Press (New York, NY), 1980.

Of Birds, Beast, and Other Artists: An Essay on the Universality of Art, New York University Press (New York, NY), 1988.

The Dilemma of Context, New York University Press (New York, NY), 1989.

(Editor, with Shlomo Biderman) *Rationality in Question: On Eastern and Western Views of Rationality,* E.J. Brill (New York, NY), 1989.

(Editor, with Shlomo Biderman) *Interpretation in Religion,* E.J. Brill (New York, NY), 1992.

Ineffability: The Failure of Words in Philosophy and Religion, State University of New York Press (Albany, NY), 1993.

(Editor, with Shlomo Biderman) *Myths and Fictions,* E.J. Brill (New York, NY), 1993.

Amoral Politics: The Persistent Truth of Machiavellism, State University of New York Press (Albany, NY), 1995.

A Comparative History of World Philosophy: From the Upanishads to Kant, State University of New York Press (Albany, NY), 1998.

IN HEBREW

Ha´Oman B´Tarbuyot Ha´Olam (title means "The Artist in World Art"), Am Oved (Tel-Aviv, Israel), 1970.

Toldot ha-filosofyah: Meha-Renesans ve-ad Kant, Matkal (Tel Aviv, Israel), 1978.

Ha-Omanut: Keshet be-anan, Masadah (Ramat-Gan, Israel), 1988.

Keshet: Kovets le-tsiyun Yovel ha-araba`im le-reshit hofa`ato shel "Keshet," ha-riv`on le-sifrut, `iyun u-viokoret (1958-1976), Hed Artsi (Sifriyat Maariv, Israel), 1998.

Other publications in Hebrew include *Spontaneity in Art* and *Prehuman Art,* both 2005.

OTHER

Associate editor, *Keshet.*

SIDELIGHTS: Ben-Ami Scharfstein is a respected scholar who has written books on art, philosophy, and other subjects, in both English and Hebrew. In his first published work, *Roots of Bergson's Philosophy,* he proposed that the famous philosopher was not a great innovator, but rather a great synthesizer of ideas that had come before him. A *Christian Century* reviewer noted: "The ideas which converged were some meta-scientific speculations concerning time, various theories based upon 'depth psychology,' evolutionism and vitalism, and certain sociological interpretations of morality and religion. Scharfstein shows that Bergson's most famous sentences are quite similar to the opinions expressed by many nineteenth century philosophers."

Reviewing *Roots of Bergson's Philosophy* for *Crozer Quarterly,* G.W. Davis commented: "This small volume is an interesting disclosure of the roots of the thinking of one of our most vivid contemporary philosophers. It discloses the dependence of even the great thinker upon the world about him and the thoughts of his past and present. Surely it reveals the requirement that every philosopher seek to understand the cultural milieu of his world before he sets down his conclusions about life and human destiny."

The author took a skeptical view of his subject in *Mystical Experience,* in which he analyzes mysticism in Christianity, Taoism, Buddhism, Suffism, Hinduism, and other religions. A *Times Literary Supplement* writer believed that Scharfstein noted: "The reader who has read [this book] attentively . . . will have sensed throughout that despite the best of intentions the author dislikes the whole murky business of mysticism."

Scharfstein examined Eastern literary culture in *The Mind of China.* A reviewer for *Choice* called it "a superb study of the life and thought of the scholar-officials who dominated traditional Chinese society." Noting that there were few new insights in the book, the critic nevertheless praised it for "its organization of material, its judicious use of quotations from the Chinese literati themselves and, above all, in the author's beautiful style which reanimates the culture of China's greatest days." F.W. Drake concurred in *Library Journal* that *The Mind of China* was "a convenient and stimulating introduction to 'Confucian culture.'"

In *A Comparative History of World Philosophy: From the Upanishads to Kant,* Scharfstein compares major philosophers from European, Indian and Chinese traditions. Paul J. Griffiths noted, in a review for *Iyyun: The Jerusalem Philosophical Quarterly,* that the author separates each chapter by philosophical viewpoint as opposed to tradition or timeframe, observing that this method of combining thinkers from different areas works "by juxtaposing them and permitting them to enter into philosophical discussion one with another." Griffiths felt that "there is no book like this in English. Works with comparable (or greater) scope lack Scharfstein's attention to detail, and those with comparable or greater detail almost always lack the comparative emphasis and broad range found here."

Scharfstein once commented to *CA:* "I have a passionate interest in art (I paint), in philosophy, in comparative culture, and in learning generally. In writing, I'm apparently attracted to difficult syntheses, the difficulty of which is increased by my attempt to balance the claims of good writing against those of accuracy of scholarship and of some elusive general truth.

"My generalizing passion—contained, I hope, within scholarly bounds—inspired *A Comparative History of World Philosophy: From the Upanishads to Kant,* and is now asserting itself even more strongly in an almost finished manuscript with the not immodest title of *AESTHETICS WITHOUT LIMITS* of Place, Time, or Culture. Two of its chapters have mutated into short independent books. One has the name *Spontaneity in Art,* and the other, called *Prehuman Art: An Essay in Interspecies Aesthetics,* extends the conception of art, or at least of the basic impulses that in humans lead to art, to other, nonhuman animals. In the course of writing these books, I have come to see that art has been invented everywhere to satisfy humans' boundless hunger for experience in all of its real, imagined, and imaginable variations. In trying to understand how appreciation might cross temporal and cultural boundaries, I have learned to weaken aesthetic dichotomies by adding intermediate possibilities and by denying, implicitly or not, that we are forced to choose between opposite positions. 'Yes and/or no,' I'm now likely to say. This is because the sharp distinction into opposites that helps to make our thinking clear deprives us of the ability to perceive whatever it has a priori excluded from thought by omitting its possibility. Thinking that is too flagrantly dichotomous sets us at odds with ourselves, with others, and, most seriously, with the reality whose elusiveness has provoked us into such thinking. (When faced by a rigidly logic-bound argument I'm apt to remember the words of the poet who said, 'If only philosophers could learn a single thing from poet—how not to have opinions.')

'It's hard for me to choose which of my books I like best. I like *The Philosophers* for the richness of the individual experience it embodies and its success, in my opinion, in grasping that almost all philosophies are incomplete by their own philosophical standards, so that an understanding of the formally irrelevant psychological characteristics of a philosopher can help to close the gaps or explain the odd turns in his or her thought. I like *The Dilemma of Context* because it joins the exotic descriptions of anthropology with the analytic energies of philosophy, and because its argument seems to me to succeed in constructing arguments in which abstract ideas and empirical examples lend one another mutual support, and because it is so clearly constructed and so elegantly brief. I like *A Comparative History of World Philosophy* because it seems to me to join clarity and exactness of exposition, and because its basic categories and comparisons seem to me original and revealing. And I like my current writing on art because it has led me to learn so much about the world at large and about myself, has helped me to solve the major problems of aesthetics to at least my own satisfaction. Because it is a textbook for a seminar, in which the students are encouraged to question what it says, I learn how to improve it, and because it challenges me to try to turn a philosophical book on esthetics into a work of art of the kind not unlike the art is meant to explain. While I've suffered some brutal reviews, my books have brought me many emotional rewards, not only in their writing, but in the spontaneous appreciation of strangers, which is now usually a gift brought me by the Internet. Like the other forms of art, writing is by itself able to create immediate emotional and intellectual bonds between perfect strangers."

BIOGRAPHICAL AND CRITICAL SOURCES:

PERIODICALS

Choice, July, 1974, review of *The Mind of China;* October, 1980, review of *The Philosophers,* p. 264; January, 1999, J. Bussanich, review of *A Comparative History of World Philosophy: From the Upanishads to Kant.*

Christian Century, October 6, 1943, review of *Roots of Bergson's Philosophy.*

Critic, January, 1981, review of *The Philosophers,* p. 7.

Crozer Quarterly, October, 1943, G. W. Davis, review of *Roots of Bergson's Philosophy.*

Economist, October 25, 1980, review of *The Philosophers,* p. 129.

Iyyun: The Jerusalem Philosophical Quarterly, January, 2001, Paul J. Griffiths, review of *A Comparative History of World Philosophy,* p. 85.

Journal of Religion, July, 2000, Matthew T. Kapstein, review of *A Comparative History of World Philosophy,* p. 526.

Library Journal, December 1, 1973, review of *Mystical Experience,* p. 3568; August, 1974, F. W.

Drake, review of *The Mind of China;* June 1, 1998, Terry C. Skeats, review of *A Comparative History of World Philosophy,* p. 113.

Philosophy East and West, January, 1999, review of *A Comparative History of World Philosophy,* p. 96.

Times Literary Supplement, November 30, 1973, review of *Mystical Experience,* p. 1349.

*   *   *

SCHWARTZ, Elliott S. 1936-
(Elliott Shelling Schwartz)

PERSONAL: Born January 19, 1936, in Brooklyn, NY; son of Nathan (a physician) and Rose (Shelling) Schwartz; married Dorothy Feldman (an artist and art instructor), June 26, 1960; children: Nina, Jonathan. *Education:* Columbia University, A.B., 1957, M.A., 1958, Ed.D., 1962; studied composition at Bennington Composers Conference, summers, 1961-66; studied piano under Alton Jones. *Hobbies and other interests:* All sports, chess, travel, unusual cuisine, films, and the theater.

ADDRESSES: Home—P.O. Box 451, 10 Highview Rd., South Freeport, ME 04078-0451. *Office*—Department of Music, Bowdoin College, Brunswick, ME 04011. *E-mail*—elliott@schwartzmusic.com.

CAREER: University of Massachusetts, Amherst, instructor in music, 1960-64; Bowdoin College, Brunswick, ME, assistant professor, 1964-70, associate professor, 1970-75, professor of music, 1975—, chairman of music department, 1975-87, founder of Bowdoin College of Music and Bowdoin Music Festival. Visiting professor, Trinity College of Music, 1967, University of California—Santa Barbara, 1970, 1973, 1974, and Robinson College, Cambridge, 1993-94, 1999; Ohio State University, Columbus, OH, visiting professor, 1985-86, part-time professor of composition, 1989-92. Vice president of the American Music Center, 1982-88; cofounder and president of Maine Composers Forum, 1995. Member of board of directors, American Composers Alliance, 1996. British Broadcasting Corp., London, England, composer, pianist, and commentator, 1972, 1974, 1978, and 1983. Music consultant for publishing companies, including Holt, Rinehart & Winston, Random House, Schirmer Books, and Oxford University Press, 1977.

MEMBER: National Association for American Composers and Conductors, Music Teachers National Association, American Society of Composers, Authors and Publishers, College Music Society (president, 1989-90), American Society of University Composers (chairman, 1983-88).

AWARDS, HONORS: MacDowell Colony fellowships, 1964, 1965; American Society of Composers, Authors and Publishers award, 1965; Ford Foundation travel grants, 1969, 1972; Gaudeamus Foundation Prize (the Netherlands), 1970; Maine State Award, Maine Commission for the Arts and Humanities, 1970; National Endowment for the Arts grants, 1974, 1976, 1982; Yaddo residence fellowship, 1977; Rockefeller Foundation fellowships, 1980, 1989; McKim Commission Award, 1986.

WRITINGS:

The Symphonies of Ralph Vaughan Williams, University of Massachusetts Press (Amherst, MA), 1965.
(Editor, with Barney Childs) *Contemporary Composers on Contemporary Music,* Holt (New York, NY), 1967, revised edition with Jim Fox, Da Capo Press (New York, NY), 1998.
Electronic Music: A Listener's Guide, Praeger (New York, NY), 1973, revised edition, Da Capo Press (New York, NY), 1989.
Music: Ways of Listening, Holt (New York, NY), 1982.
(With Daniel Godfrey) *Music since 1945: Issues, Materials, Literature,* Macmillan (New York, NY), 1993.

Contributor to periodicals, including *Yale Journal of Music Theory, American Music, Musical Quarterly, Massachusetts Review, Notes, Music and Musicians, Natida Musik,* and *Composer.*

SOUND RECORDINGS

Music for Instruments and Tape, Orion (Malibu, CA), 1980.
Dream Music with Variations: For Violin, Viola, Violoncello, and Piano (with *On Light Wings: For Violin, Viola, Violoncello, and Piano* by Gunther Schuller), Orion (Malibu, CA), c. 1986.
Chamber Works, CRI (New York, NY), 1991.

Music for Strings and Mallet Percussion, GM Recordings (Newton Centre, MA), 1993.
Variations, Metier (Dorset, England), 2000.
Equinox, New World Records (New York, NY), 2000.

MUSICAL COMPOSITIONS

Composer of orchestral pieces, including *Magic Music,* 1967, *Island,* 1970, *Janus,* 1978, *Zebra,* 1980, *Celebrations/Reflections: A Time Warp,* 1985; *Equinox,* 1994, revised, 1997; *Rainbow,* 1996; *Mehitabel's Serenade,* 2000; and *Voyager,* 2002. Chamber orchestra works include *Pastorale,* 1960, *Texture,* 1966, *Eclipse III,* 1975, *Chamber Concerto I-IV,* 1977-78, *Four American Portraits,* 1986, *Timepiece 1794,* 1994, *Jack-o-Lantern,* 2000, and *Water Music,* 2002. Also composer of band/wind ensemble and chamber ensemble music, and theatrical pieces.

Author of published scores, including *Areas: Music for Dancers and Small Chamber Ensemble,* C. Fischer (New York, NY), 1977; *Cycles and Gongs: For Organ, Bb Trumpet, and Tape,* Hinshaw Music (Chapel Hill, NC), 1977; *Five Mobiles: For Flute, Organ, Harpsichord, and Tape,* Hinshaw Music (Chapel Hill, NC), 1977; *Dream Music with Variations: For Violin, Viola, Cello & Piano,* T. Presser (Bryn Mawr, PA), c. 1984; *Chamber Concerto II: For Clarinet and Nine Players,* Margun Music (Newton Centre, MA), 1986; *Souvenir: For Bb Clarinet & Piano,* Margun Music (Newton Centre, MA), 1990; *Memorial in Two Parts: For Violin and Piano,* Fallen Leaf Press (Berkeley, CA), 1991; and *Travelogue: For Flute and Contrabass,* Fallen Leaf Press (Berkeley, CA), 1991. Musical works also published by General Music, Carl Fischer, Alexander Broude, Media Press, and Bowdoin College Music Press.

SIDELIGHTS: Elliott S. Schwartz is a highly respected composer, educator, and author whose music is comprised primarily of instrumental works. A longtime professor at Bowdoin College, he founded the college of music there and also started a music festival and press. The result of this work, according to Russell Kane in *Contemporary Composers,* is that he "has had a significant impact on new music performance in northern New England."

As an author, Schwartz has written a number of books on music that seek to demystify the subject for readers. *Music: Ways of Listening,* for example, is a college textbook for students with no musical background. While being a survey of Western concert music, it also instructs readers on how to develop their listening skills. Similarly, *Electronic Music: A Listener's Guide* guides readers toward ways of better appreciating recent technical developments in music. In both books, according to Kane, Schwartz "wishes to break down some of the more oppressive hierarchies in an effort to open music out to an audience which may not ordinarily consider itself musically literate."

Schwartz has also written and edited surveys of American music, including *Contemporary Composers on Contemporary Music* and *Music since 1945: Issues, Materials, Literature.* The first work, edited with Barney Childs, includes essays by important composers such as Aaron Copland, Igor Stravinsky, and John Cage, as well as writings by less prominent composers, in an effort to provide an overview of the evolution of music in the twentieth century. *Music since 1945,* as the title indicates, is a survey of post-war music, but it also is an attempt by Schwartz to defray cultural and aesthetic assumptions about musical works of the second half of the twentieth century.

BIOGRAPHICAL AND CRITICAL SOURCES:

BOOKS

Contemporary Composers, St. James Press (Detroit, MI), 1992.

PERIODICALS

ASCAP Newsletter, fall, 1965.
Carl Fischer Newsletter, no. 1, 1972.

ONLINE

Schwartz Music, http://www.schwartzmusic.com/ (December 16, 2002).*

*   *   *

SCHWARTZ, Elliott Shelling
    See SCHWARTZ, Elliott S.

SEWELL, Lisa 1960-

PERSONAL: Born March 9, 1960, in Hollywood, CA; daughter of George and Edith Sewell. *Education:* University of California—Berkeley, B.A., 1984; New York University, M.A., 1988; Tufts University, Ph.D., 1998.

ADDRESSES: Office—Department of English, Villanova University, 800 Lancaster Ave., Villanova, PA 19085. *E-mail*—lisa.sewell@villanova.edu.

CAREER: New York University, New York, NY, instructor in English, 1987-88; Texas Christian University, Fort Worth, visiting lecturer in English, 1997-98; Villanova University, Villanova, PA, began as assistant professor, became associate professor of English and creative writing, 1998—. Goldwater State Hospital for the Severely Disabled, instructor in creative writing, 1987-88; speaker at educational institutions, libraries and museums, and writers' gatherings.

MEMBER: Academy of American Poets, Poetry Society of America, Modern Language Association of America, American Literature Association, Associated Writing Programs.

AWARDS, HONORS: Resident at Millay Colony for the Arts, 1992, Virginia Center for the Creative Arts, 1993, 1994, 1996, and Blue Mountain Center, 1994, Pushcart Prize nominations, Academy of American Poets, 1994, 1996, 1998, 2002; poetry grant, Massachusetts Cultural Council, 1994; scholar's fellow, Bread Loaf Writers' Conference, 1994; Yaddo fellow, 1996, 1999, 2003; National Prize in Poetry from the Loft (Minneapolis, MN), 1996, for "The Miraculous"; poetry fellow, Fine Arts Work Center (Provincetown, MA), 1996-97; fellow, MacDowell Colony, 1997-98; creative writing fellow, National Endowment for the Arts, 1999; resident at Fundación Valparaíso (Spain), 2000; international exchange fellow, Schloss Wiepersdorf (Germany), 2001; achievement grant in poetry, Leeway Foundation, 2001; international exchange fellow, Tyrone Guthrie Centre (Ireland), 2002; poetry fellow, Pennsylvania Council on the Arts, 2002.

WRITINGS:

The Way Out: Poems, Alice James Books (Farmington, ME), 1998.

(Editor, with Claudia Rankine) *American Poets in the 21st Century: The New Poetics,* Wesleyan University Press (Middletown, CT), 2006.

Name Witheld (poetry), Four Way Books (New York, NY), 2006.

Work represented in anthologies, including *American Poetry: The Next Generation,* Carnegie-Mellon University Press (Pittsburgh, PA), 2000. Contributor of poetry to periodicals, including *Indiana Review, Michigan Quarterly Review, Pequod, Passages North, Massachusetts Review, Third Coast, American Poetry Review, Paris Review, Ploughshares,* and *Gulf Coast.* Former assistant poetry editor, *Descant.*

WORK IN PROGRESS: A memoir of the author's father, tentatively titled *Century; Autobibliography,* a poetry manuscript.

SIDELIGHTS: Lisa Sewell studied genetics and marine biology at the University of California—Berkeley and creative writing at New York University. While continuing her education, she wrote her first collection, *The Way Out: Poems.* David Daniel wrote in *Ploughshares* that Sewell's poetry "explores territory that's not fit for the timid; whether she's writing about the body's generation or its decay, or of love, or sex, or of abortions, she does so with a precise, lidless eye. One welcomes her careful charting of the fleshy world and all of its difficulties."

The poems in *The Way Out* reflect such diverse worlds as those of Italian poet Dante Alighieri, the mythologic figure of Persephone, and German philosopher Friedrich Wilhelm Nietzsche. Some are Sewell's observations, and others offer insights to the poet herself. In "Evolution," Sewell writes of the way an unexpected negative word or phrase, spoken on the phone, can change the perception of life. "Maybe this sourness and spastic stomach are what the first amphibian tasted the day its gills sprouted into lungs." In "Human Nature" Sewell questions her willingness to respond to a kiss and wonders whether it is part of her nature. "What if wired into me, part of the helical strands of code that made my hair brown and my elbows bony, is the kiss?" On the *Alice James Poetry Cooperative* Web site, reviewer Frank Bidart called *The Way Out* a "ferocious book" containing poems of "great weight and power." Bidart declared that the collection "dares to enter the many underworlds of hu-

man existence." Deborah Digges added to the Web site dialogue on Sewell's work, noting that the poems "enact a lyric muscle that explodes narrative." And Mark Doty found the collection to be an "engaging quarrel with the fact of flesh."

Sewell once told *CA:* "I write poems out of a desire to understand experience—and to put pressure on the truths that inform that experience, to ask if myth or history can help me shed light on it, to ask if memory can be relied upon."

BIOGRAPHICAL AND CRITICAL SOURCES:

BOOKS

Sewell, Lisa, *The Way Out: Poems,* Alice James Books (Farmington, ME), 1998.

PERIODICALS

Boston Review of Books, November, 1998.
Colorado Review, spring, 1999.
Ploughshares, fall, 1998, David Daniel, review of *The Way Out.*
Quarterly West, spring-summer, 1999.

ONLINE

Alice James Poetry Cooperative Web site, http://gladiola.umfacad.maine.edu/~ajb (March 15, 1999), commentary on *The Way Out.**

*   *   *

SHAW, Nancy 1946-

PERSONAL: Born 1946, in Pittsburgh, PA; daughter of Walter Mark (a graphic-arts purchasing agent and accountant) and Dorothy L. (a medical secretary) Shaw; married D. Scott Shaw (an engineer), November 11, 1972; children: Allison, Daniel. *Education:* University of Michigan, A.B., 1968; Harvard University, M.A.T., 1970. *Hobbies and other interests:* Gardening.

ADDRESSES: Agent—c/o Author Mail, Houghton Mifflin Co., 222 Berkeley, Boston, MA 02116.

CAREER: Writer and homemaker. Author of radio scripts for "Senior Sounds," University of Michigan Institute of Gerontology, Ann Arbor, 1978-81.

MEMBER: Authors Guild, Authors League of America, American Association of University Women, Society of Children's Book Writers, Phi Beta Kappa, Herb Study (Ann Arbor, MI).

AWARDS, HONORS: Jules and Avery Hopwood Award, University of Michigan, 1968; Fanfare citation, *Horn Book,* 1987, for *Sheep in a Jeep;* Best Books citation, *School Library Journal,* and Reading Magic Award, *Parenting* magazine, both 1991, both for *Sheep in a Shop.*

WRITINGS:

Sheep in a Jeep, illustrated by Margot Apple, Houghton (Boston, MA), 1986.
Sheep on a Ship, illustrated by Margot Apple, Houghton (Boston, MA), 1989.
Sheep in a Shop, illustrated by Margot Apple, Houghton (Boston, MA), 1991.
Sheep out to Eat, illustrated by Margot Apple, Houghton (Boston, MA), 1992.
Sheep Take a Hike, illustrated by Margot Apple, Houghton (Boston, MA), 1994.
Sheep Trick or Treat, illustrated by Margot Apple, Houghton (Boston, MA), 1997.
Raccoon Tune, illustrated by Howard Fine, Henry Holt (New York, NY), 2003.

ADAPTATIONS: Sheep in a Jeep and *Sheep on a Ship* were produced as school readers; *Sheep in a Jeep* was adapted as an audiobook.

SIDELIGHTS: According to Nancy Shaw, a boring car trip inspired her first book, *Sheep in a Jeep.* "I have a long history of getting bored on trips, going back to my childhood. We used to take very long ones to my grandparents' house," Shaw once explained. "One time, when my kids were fairly young, we were on a trip to their grandparents' house and we had been reading a rhyming book. I tried making more rhymes and

once I hit upon 'sheep' and 'Jeep,' I felt I wanted to extend that and see what else went with it. Pretty soon a fair amount did go with it." In addition to *Sheep in a Jeep,* Shaw has penned a number of related works featuring fleeced characters, and has more recently mined the wild-animal kingdom for her 2003 picture book *Raccoon Tune.*

Born in Pittsburgh, Pennsylvania, Shaw eventually moved to the Midwest and attended the University of Michigan. During college she worked at the nearby Ann Arbor Public Library, and became interested in the work of picture-book author/artist Maurice Sendak while shelving children's books. She went on to write an essay about Sendak that earned her the University of Michigan's Hopwood Award.

Shaw had ideas for children's books before *Sheep in a Jeep,* but "I just had not had one that I pursued as doggedly as I did this," she said. She began by reading books on how to write and sell picture books, then gathered publishers' addresses from *Writers' Market* and *Literary Marketplace.* "I just thought about the different publishers that I enjoyed," she recalled. "I read a whole lot of books to my children so I chose publishers who I thought would have views similar to mine or who had published books I liked a lot." From its genesis during that fateful car trip, *Sheep in a Jeep* took Shaw two-and-a-half years, working off and on. During that time she discovered one of the challenges of writing children's books: to tell her story in very few words, and, in her case, words that rhyme. "A lot of it is a process of putting the words together and then stripping away what doesn't belong," she said.

Sheep in a Jeep tells the tale of five sheep out for a drive. When their jeep breaks down, calamity ensues, ending with a crash and, ultimately, the sale of their jeep. Reviewing the text for *Publishers Weekly,* a reviewer commented that "Shaw demonstrates a promising capacity for creating nonsense rhymes," while *School Library Journal* contributor Nancy Palmer called the book "a great choice for . . . beginning readers who want a funny story."

Shaw was fortunate in her publisher's choice of illustrator for her first picture-book effort; she and Margot Apple have gone on to create several more "Sheep" books. *Sheep in a Shop* finds the sheep out shopping for a birthday gift, and the five animals cause a host of problems for shopkeepers during their hunt for the perfect present. Once they have their gift picked out, the sheep realize they do not have enough money to pay for it, but this problem is solved when they barter with their fleece—"a neat nod to Mother Goose and tradition," according to *Horn Book* reviewer Mary M. Burns, who also called the book "irresistible."

In *Sheep out to Eat* the five run into trouble when they decide to enjoy a meal at a local tea room. Inexperienced at out-of-pasture dining, the sheeps' table manners are woefully lacking, and as a result, they salt their custard and pepper their cake, all the while disturbing their fellow diners. When the sheep are finally asked to leave, they locate a field of green grass—and a far more suitable lunch. *Booklist* reviewer Carolyn Phelan commented that the tale "will fascinate preschoolers with the understated humor of its pithy, rhyming text," and a *Publishers Weekly* critic called Shaw's "tongue-twisting rhymes . . . as simply clever as ever." Additional titles in the series include *Sheep Trick or Treat* and *Sheep Take a Hike*, the latter of which Burns termed "a delightful book for young audiences that will also appeal to the adults who read to them."

While illustrator Apple was responsible for the drawings in *Sheep in a Jeep,* Shaw also had input into decisions regarding the illustrations for her text, and actually made up a dummy copy showing her ideas as to what the pictures should be and where they should be placed. The dummy is useful to Shaw because it reminds her to include "drawable" scenes and allows her to "see that the story is proceeding at the right pace. There has to be so much text per page turned; if the text is a little bit skimpy on a certain action, it might be possible for a picture to fill in for it. On the other hand, it can't be too skimpy; you can't ask pictures to do things that aren't there."

Regarding her method of creating rhyme sequences, Shaw once commented: "I don't like it if a book maintains the same rhythm in a sing-song fashion. I prefer to switch from very short couplets to longer ones." She noted that it takes more than simple rhymes to make her books work. "A lot of what I'm doing in writing is following sounds as well as following meaning. I find that it's often quite stiff if I just take an idea and go looking for the rhymes for it. I have to do that, too, but the best rhymes seem to come together with a strong sound component. With *Sheep in a Jeep*

I was just challenging myself to see if I could get all the sounds to work together and make something, so it's a little bit choppier. In the later books, the actions are a little more complex. And the sheep start learning how to solve problems, thank goodness!"

Shaw considers several elements to be important to writing children's books. "I don't like preachy books, but I think a good book has some kind of a lesson in life as its core," she commented. "The lesson in the 'Sheep' books is, 'Look before you leap.' Also, I think that there is a very important place for slapstick and silliness in helping very small children sort out what's sensible and what isn't. There is a strong place for humor in kids' books."

Shaw has continued to mine her sense of humor beyond sheep; *Raccoon Tune* spotlights the chaos that ensues during a raccoon clan's nighttime invasion of a quiet suburban neighborhood in search of garbage-can delights. In Shaw's "catchy verses," four raccoons "morph from suburban menaces to cute critters on a mission," noted a *Publishers Weekly* contributor, while in *Kirkus Reviews* a writer called the book "perfect from start to finish and impossible to read only once."

BIOGRAPHICAL AND CRITICAL SOURCES:

PERIODICALS

Booklist, September 15, 1992, Carolyn Phelan, review of *Sheep out to Eat*, p. 157; September 1, 1997, Stephanie Zvirin, review of *Sheep Trick or Treat*, p. 141.

Childhood Education, April, 1987, Tina L. Burke, review of *Sheep in a Jeep*, p. 379.

Horn Book, November-December, 1986, Karen Jameyson, review of *Sheep in a Jeep*, p. 739; May-June, 1991, Mary M. Burns, review of *Sheep in a Shop*, p. 323; November-December, 1994, Mary M. Burns, review of *Sheep Take a Hike*, p. 726; September-October, 1997, Martha V. Parravano, review of *Sheep Trick or Treat*, p. 563.

Kirkus Reviews, May 15, 2003, review of *Raccoon Tune*, p. 756.

Parents, May, 1992, Liz Rosenberg, review of *Sheep in a Jeep*, p. 239.

Publishers Weekly, September 26, 1986, review of *Sheep in a Jeep*, p. 78; April 14, 1989, review of *Sheep on a Ship*, p. 66; January 25, 1991, review of *Sheep in a Shop,* p. 56; July 6, 1992, review of *Sheep out to Eat,* p. 53; July 4, 1994, review of *Sheep Take a Hike,* p. 60; April 28, 2003, review of *Raccoon Tune,* p. 69.

School Library Journal, December, 1986, Nancy Palmer, review of *Sheep in a Jeep,* p. 124; June, 1989, Nancy Palmer, review of *Sheep on a Ship,* p. 95; February, 1991, Luann Toth, review of *Sheep in a Shop,* p. 75; September, 1992, Lauralyn Persson, review of *Sheep out to Eat,* p. 210; September, 1997, Dina Sherman, review of *Sheep Trick or Treat;* July, 2003, Louise L. Sherman, review of *Raccoon Tune,* p. 106.*

*   *   *

SHEEHAN, Aurelie 1963-

PERSONAL: Born June 16, 1963, in Verdun, France; U.S. citizen; daughter of Laurence Sheehan (a writer) and Valerie Harms (a writer). *Education:* Hampshire College, B.A., 1984; City College of the City University of New York, M.A., 1990. *Politics:* Democrat.

ADDRESSES: Office—Department of English, University of Arizona, P.O. Box 210067, Tucson, AZ 85721. *Agent*—Ellen Levine, Trident Media Group, 41 Madison Ave., 36th Fl., New York, NY 10010. *E-mail*—aurelie@aureliesheehan.com.

CAREER: Radcliffe College, Cambridge, MA, administrative assistant at Mary Ingraham Bunting Institute, 1984-86; *Child* (magazine), New York, NY, assistant editor, 1987-90; City College of the City University of New York, New York, NY, administrative assistant, 1987-92, adjunct instructor in humanities, 1989-92; Ucross Foundation, Clearmont, WY, program coordinator of Artists' Residency Program, 1993-96; Johns Hopkins University, Washington, DC, lecturer in arts and sciences, 1997-98; University of Arizona, Tucson, assistant professor, 2000-05, associate professor of English and director of creative writing program, 2005—. Sheridan College, instructor, 1995; Folger Shakespeare Library, ex officio member of poetry board, 1997-2000, coordinator of poetry and lectures, 1997-2000; gives readings from her works; judge of writing contests.

MEMBER: Authors Guild, Associated Writing Programs.

AWARDS, HONORS: Resident, Ucross Foundation, 1992; Jack Kerouac Literary Award, Jack Kerouac Historical Society, 1993; Camargo Foundation fellow in Cassis, France, 1993; resident, Tyrone Guthrie Centre, Annaghmakerrig, Ireland, 1996, and Sanskriti Kendra, New Delhi, India, 1997; Pushcart Prize in creative nonfiction, 1999; grant from Arizona Commission on the Arts, 2005.

WRITINGS:

Jack Kerouac Is Pregnant (short stories), Dalkey Archive Press (Normal, IL), 1994.
The Anxiety of Everyday Objects (novel), Penguin Books (New York, NY), 2004.
History Lesson for Girls (novel), Viking (New York, NY), 2006.

Work represented in anthologies, including *The Pushcart Prize XXIII: Best of the Small Presses,* edited by Bill Henderson, Pushcart Press (Wainscott, NY), 1999; and *Weavings: The Maryland Millennial Anthology,* edited by Michael S. Glaser, Forest Woods Media Productions, 2000. Contributor of short stories, poetry, nonfiction, and reviews to periodicals, including *Critical Quarterly, Alaska Quarterly Review, American Voice, Florida Review, New England Review, Confrontation, Gargoyle, Epoch, Shenandoah, New Orleans Review,* and *Fiction International.*

BIOGRAPHICAL AND CRITICAL SOURCES:

ONLINE

Aurelie Sheehan Home Page, http://www.aurelie sheehan.com (November 14, 2005).

*   *   *

SHERMER, Michael 1954-
(Michael Brant Shermer)

PERSONAL: Born September 8, 1954, in Glendale, CA; son of Richard and Lois Shermer; married Kim Ziel, July 7, 1990; children: Devin. *Education:* Pepperdine University, B.A., 1976; California State

University, Fullerton, M.A., 1978; Claremont Graduate School, Ph.D., 1991. *Politics:* Libertarian. *Religion:* Atheist. *Hobbies and other interests:* "Cycling, skiing, basketball, reading, reading, and reading."

ADDRESSES: Office—P.O. Box 338, Altadena, CA 91001. *E-mail*—mshermer@skeptic.com; drmichael shermer@aol.com.

CAREER: Writer, professor, and publisher. Glendale College, Glendale, CA, psychology instructor, 1980-86, assistant professor, 1986-91; *Skeptic* magazine, founder and publisher, beginning 1991, founding publisher; KPCC 89.3 FM, Pasadena, CA, host of *Science Talk* radio program and science correspondent, 1998—. Occidental College, Los Angeles, CA, adjunct professor, 1989-98; California State University, Los Angeles, CA, adjunct professor, 1991-93; *Exploring the Unknown,* Fox Family Channel, co-host and producer. Skeptic Society, director, beginning 1991, then executive director; the Skeptics Distinguished Lecture Series, California Institute of Technology, Pasadena, CA, host.

Appeared on television shows, including *20/20, Dateline, Charlie Rose, Tom Snyder, Donahue, Oprah, Sally, Lezza,* and *Unsolved Mysteries;* appeared on documentaries that aired on Arts and Entertainment, Discovery Channel, Public Broadcasting Corporation, the History Channel, the Science Channel, and the Learning Channel.

AWARDS, HONORS: Alumni of the Year, California State University, Fullerton, 1997.

WRITINGS:

NONFICTION

Sport Cycling: A Guide to Training, Racing, and Endurance, Contemporary Books (Chicago, IL), 1985.
Cycling: Endurance and Speed, Contemporary Books (Chicago, IL), 1987.
Teach Your Child Science: Making Science Fun for the Both of You, Lowell House (Los Angeles, CA), 1989.

(With George Yates) *Meet the Challenge of Arthritis: A Motivational Program to Help You Live a Better Life,* Lowell House (Los Angeles, CA), 1990.
(With Arthur Benjamin) *Teach Your Child Math: Making Math Fun for the Both of You,* Lowell House (Los Angeles, CA), 1991.
(With Arthur Benjamin) *Mathemagics: How to Look like a Genius without Really Trying,* Lowell House (Los Angeles, CA), 1993.
Race across America, WRS Publishing (Waco, TX), 1993.
(Editor, with Benno Maidhof-Christig and Lee Traynor) *Argumente und Kritik: Skeptisches Jahrbuch. Rassiismus, die Leugnung des Holocaust, AIDS ohne HIV und andere fragwuerdige Behauptungen,* IBDK Verlag (Berlin, Germany), 1997.
Why People Believe Weird Things: Pseudoscience, Superstition, and Other Confusions of Our Time, W.H. Freeman (New York, NY), 1997, revised and expanded edition, W.H. Freeman/Owl Books (New York, NY), 2002.
(Editor, with Benno Maidhof-Christig and Lee Traynor) *Endzeittaumel: Propheten, Prognosen, Propaganda,* IBDK Verlag (Berlin, Germany), 1998.
How We Believe: The Search for God in an Age of Science, W.H. Freeman (New York, NY), 2000, revised 2nd edition, Henry Holt (New York, NY), 2003.
(With Alex Grobman) *Denying History: Who Says the Holocaust Never Happened and Why Do They Say It?,* foreword by Arthur Hertzberg, University of California Press (Berkeley, CA), 2000.
The Borderlands of Science: Where Sense Meets Nonsense, Oxford University Press (New York, NY), 2001.
In Darwin's Shadow: The Life and Science of Alfred Russel Wallace: A Biographical Study on the Psychology of History, Oxford University Press (New York, NY), 2002.
The Skeptic Encyclopedia of Pseudoscience, ABC-CLIO (Santa Barbara, CA), 2002.
The Science of Good and Evil: Why People Cheat, Gossip, Share, Care, and Follow the Golden Rule, Henry Holt/Times Books (New York, NY), 2004.
Science Friction: Where the Known Meets the Unknown (essays), Henry Holt/Times Books (New York, NY), 2005.

Contributing editor and monthly columnist for *Scientific American;* reviews books for periodicals, including *Los Angeles Times, New York Times, Washington Post, Scientific American, American Scientist,* and *Skeptic;* contributor to periodicals, including *Los Angeles Times, Complexity, Nonlinear Science,* and *Skeptic.*

WORK IN PROGRESS: Why Darwin Matters: Evolution, Intelligent Design, and the Battle for Science and Religion for Henry Holt/Times Books.

SIDELIGHTS: As founder of the Skeptic Society and holder of degrees in psychology and the history of science, Michael Shermer has written a number of books on scientific, psychological, and historical subjects which incorporate his diverse background. He has questioned such assorted topics as the roots of religious belief, pseudoscience, and why certain groups do not believe the Holocaust occurred. Shermer's first books look at the inner workings of the mind. Whether in sports training, coaching kids in math and science, or teaching science and critical thinking, Shermer offers how-to advice to allow readers to understand better how to motivate and understand themselves and others.

Sport Cycling: A Guide to Training, Racing, and Endurance details a series of long-distance road races—three trips from Seattle to San Diego and the Great American Bike Race across America, which was broadcast on American Broadcasting Companies, Inc.'s (ABC) *Wide World of Sports.* Along with the information about the physical training, Shermer includes "his positive point of view on hypnosis, chiropractors, mental imaging, and massage," according to Thomas K. Fry in the *Library Journal.*

Teach Your Child Science: Making Science Fun for the Both of You is a how-to guide for parents who want to cultivate their children's curiosity. Shermer contends that children lose much of their innate curiosity due to "school and social pressure," according to a reviewer in *Astronomy* magazine. By working together with their children on special science projects, parents can prevent their potential geniuses from becoming workaday drones. The book "provides good advice and sensible projects," where parents and children can both have fun, according to the critic in *Astronomy.*

In *Why People Believe Weird Things: Pseudoscience, Superstition, and Other Confusions of Our Time,* Shermer analyzes the underlying reasons that humans sometimes "entertain the most fantastic notions," as Diane White in the *Boston Globe* put it. The root cause, according to Shermer, is a basic desire to feel good; and strange phenomena can provide comfort to some. "From psychic telephone hot lines to theories of racial supremacy," observed White, Shermer runs the gamut of topics. She concluded that the book "deserves a wide audience, perhaps among readers who think they're too smart to believe weird things."

Shermer continues to look at the development of belief system in *How We Believe: The Search for God in an Age of Science.* In this book, Shermer explains what he believes are the roots of the phenomenon of religion. He also lays out his theory for why humanity believes in God. A critic in *Publishers Weekly* explained: "Shermer wonders why religious belief . . . remains widespread in contemporary America, confounding expectations that progress in science and technology should bring a corresponding decline in faith." Included in the text are the results and analysis of a survey he conducted on these subjects. Jim Walker of *Nobeliefs.com* concluded: "Encyclopedic in scope, yet eminently readable, *How We Believe* gives us fresh insights on the nature of belief and finding meaning in a meaningless universe."

Cowritten with Alex Grobman, Shermer analyzes another religious-related topic in *Denying History: Who Says the Holocaust Never Happened and Why Do They Say It?* In this book, the authors look at those who believe the Holocaust did not occur and why. The coauthors also outline the facts that support the idea that the Holocaust did happen, consider other events in history which have also been denied or distorted over time, and offer a methodology for counteracting such revisionism. Reviewing the book in *CLIO,* Michael Bernard-Donals stated: "As good as it is as a strong antidote for the deniers' arguments, it does not go to the heart of why the deniers should be able to make their case in the first place."

Shermer takes on a scientific subject in a different way in the biography, *In Darwin's Shadow: The Life and Science of Alfred Russel Wallace: A Biographical Study on the Psychology of History.* Independent of Charles Darwin, the nineteenth-century naturalist Wallace developed a theory of natural selection and evolution and was considered a co-discoverer of the theories. Shermer spent fifteen years researching the book, which covers the whole of Wallace's long life and takes a psychological approach to understanding Wallace. A *Kirkus Reviews* contributor stated: "Along with the basic facts of Wallace's life and thought, Shermer explores the process of creative thought, the politics of science, and the sociology of scholarly communication."

Like Darwin, Wallace made a number of harrowing journeys to collect samples to prove his theory of natural selection. However, Wallace's journeys were financed at great personal cost: he sold precious pieces of his personal collection. Despite having nearly lost his life several times in the process and earning respect from many scientists for his work, Wallace's scientific credibility among his peers was eventually undermined because he believed in phrenology (the study of bumps on the skull) and spiritualism. Gloria Maxwell of *Library Journal* commented: "[Shermer's] expertise in analyzing the life and paradoxical beliefs of this complex man elevate 'the last great Victorian' to a position of prominence as one of the significant leaders in modern science."

The Science of Good and Evil: Why People Cheat, Gossip, Share, Care, and Follow the Golden Rule looks at the idea of ethics, including where morals and morality come from and how they have evolved over time. Shermer takes a Humanist perspective, arguing that people have needed morality since the beginning of existence, especially as they formed bigger social groups for social control. Shermer also believes that morality should be provisional and not a single, comprehensive system. Jende Huang in the *Humanist* explained: "By grounding morals outside of the individual but still focusing on actual human need, *The Science of Good and Evil* helps make another case for why morality can and should exist outside of a theistic framework." Summarizing the books's appeal, Garrett Eastman of the *Library Journal* called it "Challenging but engaging reading."

Shermer collects fourteen of his essays that have previously appeared in periodicals in *Science Friction: Where the Known Meets the Unknown*. Covering diverse topics, many essays analyze controversial subjects in science and pseudoscience using scientific methods. For example, Shermer offers his disbelieving appraisal of the concept of intelligent design in one essay, while sharing how easy it was to be an accurate television psychic in another. A few of the essays touch on personal topics such as the death of Shermer's mother and how he better understands athletes because of his own professional bike racing activities. A reviewer in *Science News* noted that the essays "can be extremely entertaining." While the critic in *Publishers Weekly* found the amount of detail included sometimes overwhelming, the critic also noted: "Shermer furthers the cause of skepticism and makes a great case for its role in all aspects of human endeavor."

BIOGRAPHICAL AND CRITICAL SOURCES:

BOOKS

Encyclopedia of Occultism and Parapsychology, 5th edition, Gale (Detroit, MI), 2001.

PERIODICALS

Astronomy, January, 1991, review of *Teach Your Child Science: Making Science Fun for the Both of You,* pp. 96-97.
Boston Globe, April 24, 1997, Diane White, review of *Why People Believe Weird Things: Pseudoscience, Superstition, and Other Confusions of Our Time.*
CLIO, summer, 2001, Michael Bernard-Donals, review of *Denying History: Who Says the Holocaust Never Happened and Why Do They Say It?,* p. 475.
Humanist, November-December, 2004, Jende Huang, review of *The Science of Good and Evil: Why People Cheat, Gossip, Care, Share, and Follow the Golden Rule,* p. 38.
Kirkus Reviews, July 1, 2002, review of *In Darwin's Shadow: The Life and Science of Alfred Russel Wallace,* p. 941.
Library Journal, July, 1985, Thomas K. Fry, review of *Sport Cycling: A Guide to Training, Racing, and Endurance,* p. 89; October 1, 2002, Gloria Maxwell, review of *In Darwin's Shadow,* p. 124; February 15, 2004, Garrett Eastman, review of *The Science of Good and Evil,* p. 158.
Publishers Weekly, September 27, 1999, review of *How We Believe,* p. 95; November 8, 2004, review of *Science Fiction: Where the Known Meets the Unknown,* p. 42.
Science News, January 8, 2005, review of *Science Fiction,* p. 31.

ONLINE

American Scientist Online, http://www.american scientist.org/ (October 10, 2005), interview with Michael Shermer.

CONTEMPORARY AUTHORS • *New Revision Series, Volume 148*   **SIERRA**

Nobeliefs.com, http://www.nobeliefs.com/ (March 20, 2003), Jim Walker, review of *How We Believe: The Search for God in an Age of Science.*

Skeptic Magazine Web site, http://www.skeptic.com/ (October 10, 2005), biography of Michael Shermer.

*   *   *

SHERMER, Michael Brant
    See SHERMER, Michael

*   *   *

SIERRA, Judy 1945-

PERSONAL: Born Judy Strup, June 8, 1945, in Washington, DC; name legally changed, 1985; daughter of Joseph L. (a photographer) and Jean (a librarian; maiden name, Law) Strup; married Robert Walter Kaminski (a puppeteer and elementary schoolteacher); children: Christopher Robin Strup. *Education:* American University, B.A., 1968; California State University—San Jose (now San Jose State University), M.A., 1973; University of California—Los Angeles, Ph.D.

ADDRESSES: Home—4913 Indian Wood Rd., No. 507, Culver City, CA 90230.

CAREER: Puppeteer and storyteller, 1976—. Part-time librarian at Los Angeles Public Library, 1986—; teacher of children's literature and storytelling at Extension of University of California—Los Angeles. Artist-in-residence at Smithsonian Institution, 1984.

MEMBER: National Association for the Preservation and Perpetuation of Storytelling, American Folklore Society, California Folklore Society.

AWARDS, HONORS: Best Books designation, *Publishers Weekly,* 1996, Fanfare List includee, *Horn Book,* 1997, and Notable Books for Children designation, American Library Association (ALA), 1997, all for *Nursery Tales around the World;* Notable Book citation, ALA, 2005, for *Wild about Books.*

WRITINGS:

FOR YOUNG READERS

The Elephant's Wrestling Match, illustrated by Brian Pinkney, Lodestar (New York, NY), 1992.

The House that Drac Built, illustrated by Will Hillenbrand, Harcourt Brace (San Diego, CA), 1995.

Good Night, Dinosaurs, illustrated by Victoria Chess, Clarion (New York, NY), 1996.

(Reteller) *Wiley and the Hairy Man,* illustrated by Brian Pinkney, Lodestar (New York, NY), 1996.

(Reteller) *The Mean Hyena: A Folktale from Malawi,* illustrated by Michael Bryant, Lodestar (New York, NY), 1997.

Counting Crocodiles, illustrated by Will Hillenbrand, Harcourt Brace (San Diego, CA), 1997.

Antarctic Antics: A Book of Penguin Poems, illustrated by Jose Aruego and Ariane Dewey, Harcourt Brace (San Diego, CA), 1998.

Tasty Baby Belly Buttons: A Japanese Folktale, illustrated by Meilo So, Alfred A. Knopf (New York, NY), 1998.

The Dancing Pig, illustrated by Jesse Sweetwater, Harcourt Brace (San Diego, CA), 1999.

(Reteller) *The Beautiful Butterfly: A Folktale from Spain,* illustrated by Victoria Chess, Clarion (New York, NY), 2000.

The Gift of the Crocodile: A Cinderella Story, illustrated by Reynold Ruffins, Simon & Schuster (New York, NY), 2000.

There's a Zoo in Room 22, illustrated by Barney Saltzberg, Harcourt Brace (San Diego, CA), 2000.

Preschool to the Rescue, illustrated by Will Hillenbrand, Harcourt Brace (San Diego, CA), 2001.

Monster Goose, illustrated by Jack E. Davis, Harcourt Brace (San Diego, CA), 2001.

'Twas the Fright before Christmas, illustrated by Will Hillenbrand, Harcourt Brace (San Diego, CA), 2002.

Coco and Cavendish: Circus Dogs, illustrated by Paul Meisel, Random House (New York, NY), 2003.

Coco and Cavendish: Fire Dogs, illustrated by Paul Meisel, Random House (New York, NY), 2004.

What Time Is It, Mr. Crocodile?, illustrated by Doug Cushman, Gulliver (Orlando, FL), 2004.

Wild about Books, illustrated by Marc Brown, Knopf (New York, NY), 2004.

STORY COLLECTIONS

(With Robert Kaminski) *Twice upon a Time: Stories to Tell, Retell, Act Out, and Write About,* H.W. Wilson (Bronx, NY), 1989.

(With Robert Kaminski) *Multicultural Folktales: Stories to Tell Young Children,* Oryx Press (Phoenix, AZ), 1991.

(Compiler) *Cinderella,* illustrated by Joanne Caroselli, Oryx Press (Phoenix, AZ), 1992.

(Editor and annotator) *Quests and Spells: Fairy Tales from the European Oral Tradition,* Bob Kaminski Media Arts (Ashland, OR), 1994.

Mother Goose's Playhouse: Toddler Tales and Nursery Rhymes, with Patterns for Puppets and Feltboards, Bob Kaminski Media Arts (Ashland, OR), 1994.

(Selector and reteller) *Nursery Tales around the World,* illustrated by Stefano Vitale, Clarion (New York, NY), 1996.

Multicultural Folktales for the Feltboard and Readers' Theater, Oryx Press (Phoenix, AZ), 1996.

Can You Guess My Name?: Traditional Tales around the World, illustrated by Stefano Vitale, Clarion (New York, NY), 2002.

Silly and Sillier: Read-Aloud Tales from around the World, illustrated by Valeri Gorbachev, Knopf (New York, NY), 2002.

Schoolyard Rhymes, illustrated by Melissa Sweet, Knopf (New York, NY), 2005.

Gruesome Guide to World Monsters, illustrated by Henrik Drescher, Candlewick (Cambridge, MA), 2005.

NONFICTION

The Flannel Board Storytelling Book, H.W. Wilson (Bronx, NY), 1987.

Storytelling and Creative Dramatics, H.W. Wilson (Bronx, NY), 1989.

Fantastic Theater: Puppets and Plays for Young Performers and Young Audiences, H.W. Wilson (Bronx, NY), 1991.

(With Robert Kaminski) *Children's Traditional Games: Games from 137 Countries and Cultures,* Oryx Press (Phoenix, AZ), 1995.

Storytellers' Research Guide: Folktales, Myths, and Legends, Folkprint (Eugene, OR), 1996.

Celtic Baby Names: Traditional Names from Ireland, Scotland, Wales, Brittany, Cornwall, and the Isle of Man, Folkprint (Eugene, OR), 1997.

Spanish Baby Names: Traditional and Modern First Names of Spain and the Americas, Folkprint (Eugene, OR), 2002.

Editor of *Folklore and Mythology Journal,* 1988—.

ADAPTATIONS: Antarctic Antics was adapted as an animated film and as a sound recording.

SIDELIGHTS: Interested in storytelling and puppetry arts from childhood, Judy Sierra has built a career as a writer in two areas: she has published numerous books about storytelling and related subjects, working closely with her husband, Robert Kaminski; and since the publication of *The Elephant's Wrestling Match* in 1992, she has also emerged as a writer of stories, many of them adaptations of folk tales from other countries.

The original story inspiring *The Elephant's Wrestling Match,* for instance, comes from the African nation of Cameroon. In Sierra's retelling, the mighty elephant challenges all the other animals to a test of strength, and each fails: "The leopard, crocodile, and rhinoceros all respond," Linda Greengrass reported in the *School Library Journal,* "only to be easily thwarted by the mighty beast. Each time, Monkey beats out the results on the drum." In a surprising twist, a small but clever bat turns out to be the winner, although that is not the resolution of the story. The tale concludes by explaining that, because of his anger at Monkey for spreading the news of his defeat, Elephant smashes Monkey's drum; for this reason, "you don't see monkeys playing the talking drum." A reviewer in *Publishers Weekly* noted that "Sierra's staccato retelling of this lively African tale crackles with energy," and Greengrass added that "listeners can almost hear the beating of the drum." As Betsy Hearne, reviewing the book for the *Bulletin of the Center for Children's Books,* maintained: "The drama is simple enough for toddlers to follow but sturdy enough to hold other kids' attention as well."

In *The House that Drac Built* Sierra takes on literary and folk symbols more familiar to American children, inserting the character of Dracula into the nursery rhyme "The House that Jack Built." Thus, as Nancy Vasilakas recounted in *Horn Book:* "Young audiences are introduced to the bat that lived in the house that Drac built, then to the cat that bit the bat, the werewolf that chased the cat that bit the bat, and so on through 'fearsome' manticore, coffin, mummy, zombie, and fiend of Bloodygore." Ghoulish as all this sounds, the story has a humorous twist, as a group of trick-or-treaters enters the house and puts everything right, re-wrapping the mummy and tending to the bitten bat. Noting its appeal at Halloween, *School Library Journal* contributor Beth Irish called the book "a definite hit for holiday story programs."

Whereas *The House that Drac Built* may not exactly be bedtime reading, *Good Night, Dinosaurs* certainly is. The book depicts a family of dinosaurs getting ready for bed, brushing their teeth and then listening to lullabies and stories from their parents. "Young dinosaur fanciers will be charmed and undoubtedly claim this as their favorite go-to-sleep book," concluded Ann A. Flowers in *Horn Book*. Beth Tegart, writing in the *School Library Journal*, dubbed *Good Night, Dinosaurs* "a pleasant read at bedtime for dinosaur fans as well as those who need a chuckle at the end of the day."

With *Wiley and the Hairy Man*, Sierra retells another folk tale, this one from the American South. Frightened by the Hairy Man, Wiley enlists the help of his mother to trick the monster three times, and thus forces him to leave them alone. "Through the use of dialogue without dialect and a lissome narration," commented Maria B. Salvadore in *Horn Book*, "Sierra captures the cadence of the oral language of Alabama."

Like *The Elephant's Wrestling Match*, *The Mean Hyena* comes originally from Africa, in this case the country of Malawi, where Nyanja people tell how the turtle got his revenge on the title character after the hyena played a cruel trick on him. *School Library Journal* contributor Marilyn Iarusso called *The Mean Hyena* "a must for all folk-tale collections."

Counting Crocodiles takes place in a tropical location, although its setting is perhaps even more fanciful than that of Sierra's earlier tales. An unfortunate monkey finds herself on an island with nothing to eat but lemons, and longs to make her way to a nearby island with banana trees. There is only one problem: the Sillabobble Sea, which separates the two pieces of land, is filled with crocodiles. But the monkey, like many another small but clever creature in Sierra's stories, devises an ingenious plan to trick the crocodiles and obtain not only a bunch of bananas, but a sapling from which she can acquire fruit in the future. "The whimsical rhyme . . . and the lively alliteration ('crusty croc, feasting fearlessly on fishes') add to the appeal," wrote Kathleen Squires in *Booklist*. A reviewer in *Publishers Weekly* also praised Sierra's collaboration with illustrator Will Hillenbrand: "Working with traditional materials, author and artist arrive at an altogether fresh presentation."

After retelling a tale from Japan with *Tasty Baby Belly Buttons*, spinning a story about two girls who are able to evade a witch due to their kindness to animals in *The Dancing Pig*, and creating poems about penguins for *Antarctic Antics*, Sierra returned to crocodiles with a story set in Indonesia. In *The Gift of the Crocodile: A Cinderella Story* no fairy godmother comes to Damara's rescue when her stepmother shows her cruelty; instead, Grandmother Crocodile rewards the girl for her honesty and good heart. When the prince announces plans to host a lavish ball, Damara goes to the generous Grandmother Crocodile for Cinderella-type assistance. "Sierra's unadorned retelling is straightforward" wrote a *Horn Book* reviewer, who concluded: "This Southeast Asian variation adds some tropical zest to the oft-told tale." Hazel Rochman, writing for *Booklist*, simply called the tale "a storytelling treat."

Leaving fairy tales behind and heading for the playground, Sierra shows how a giant mud puddle is thwarted in *Preschool to the Rescue*. The mud puddle lurks, waiting until it can capture anything that passes through it—which, over the course of the story, includes a pizza van and four other vehicles. Only the preschoolers know how to deal with the mud: by making it into mud pies until the sun comes out and dries it away. "In a feast of unbridled mud-food making, the heroic preschoolers completely consume the rogue puddle," explained a *Publishers Weekly* reviewer. Marlene Gawron commented in the *School Library Journal* on the onomatopoeia Sierra uses in her text: "What a wonderful noisy book this is." Gawron concluded: "The fun doesn't stop until the book is closed." As a *Horn Book* contributor recommended: "This uncomplicated story . . . has rainy-day read-aloud written all over it."

Twisted versions of Mother Goose's rhymes fill the pages of *Monster Goose*. Featuring such characters as Little Miss Mummy, Cannibal Horner, and the Zombie who lives in a shoe, the revisions of familiar Mother Goose rhymes might be too much for particularly young readers, according to a reviewer for *Kirkus Reviews*, commenting: "But it's a fiendishly good time for everyone else." A critic for *Publishers Weekly* noted that "the Goose has been spoofed before, but this volume strikes a nice balance between goofy and ghastly," while *School Library Journal* reviewer Gay Lynn Van Vleck advised school librarians to keep extra copies of the title for students, "since teachers may hoard it for themselves." Gillian Engberg, writing in *Booklist*, recommended the book as "perfect for rowdy Halloween read-alouds."

With her next book on monsters, Sierra and artist Will Hillenbrand made reference to their previous *The House that Drac Built* collaboration in *'Twas the Fright before Christmas*. Trouble starts when Santa Mouse, who delivers presents in a sleigh pulled by eight bats, tickles a dragon's nose. A werewolf finds himself at the end of the chain of events with a pinched and sore tail, and tries to figure out just what started the mess. Once the mystery is solved, Santa Mouse apologizes and suggests they all read a story, which, in Hillenbrand's illustration, is *The House that Drac Built*. Mummies and other monsters fill the pages of the book, which a *Kirkus Reviews* contributor considered "another innovation on a well-known text."

Wild about Books is a celebration of zoos, libraries, and Dr. Seuss. Sierra teamed up with award-winning illustrator Marc Brown to tell the story of a librarian who accidentally takes the bookmobile into the zoo, and finds that all of the animals want to learn to read. She begins to read to them, picking out the perfect books for each species (tall books for the giraffes, featuring basketball and skyscrapers, books written in Chinese for the pandas, and dramas for the llamas). But for many of the animals, reading is not enough: the dung beetles write haiku and a hippo wins the "Zoolitzer" prize. The book is "both homage to and reminiscent of Dr. Seuss's epic rhyming sagas," praised *School Library Journal* reviewer Marge Loch-Wouters. A *Publishers Weekly* contributor called the tale a "winning paean to reading and writing," while a *Kirkus Reviews* critic considered it "a storytime spectacular."

Crocodiles and mischievious monkeys appear again in *What Time Is It, Mr. Crocodile?* Mr. Crocodile has a list of things to accomplish during his day, one of which is to capture and dine on the pesky monkeys who constantly pester him for the time of day. However, due to monkey meddling, things do not quite go as Mr. Crocodile planned, and he decides to make peace with the monkeys instead. A *Kirkus Reviews* contributor found that "any time [is] the right time for this irresistible rhyme." A *School Library Journal* reviewer warned readers to be ready for "some memorable monkey business in this entertaining tale," while Ilene Cooper, writing for *Booklist,* noted that "the best part of the book is Sierra's handy way with a rhyming text." Lauren Peterson, also writing for *Booklist,* praised the book, adding that "Sierra's bouncy rhyming text will make this a fun read-aloud."

Sierra is also the collector of silly tales, traditional tales, and bedtime stories in her books *Nursery Tales from around the World, Can You Guess My Name?: Traditional Tales around the World,* and *Silly and Sillier: Read-Aloud Tales from around the World.* With *Can You Guess My Name?* Sierra collects similar tales that appear in different cultures around the world, comparing versions of the "Three Little Pigs," "The Brementown Musicians," and "Rumplestiltskin." A *Kirkus Reviews* contributor noted that "this beautifully illustrated volume presents readable examples that just might send readers to the shelves to search for single editions" of the stories included. Lee Bock, writing in the *School Library Journal,* noted that "each section is fascinating for both the similarities among the tales, and the differences," and added that the book "can open doors to other cultures" for its readers. John Peters, writing in *Booklist,* considered the book to be a "handsome, horizon-expanding collection," while Mary M. Burns, in *Horn Book,* called *Can You Guess My Name?* "an outstanding example of what folklore collections for children can and should be."

Silly and Sillier brings together funny tales from around the world, including a trickster tale from Argentina, a story of an exploding mitten from Russia, and tales from countries including Bangladesh, Ireland, and Mexico. "Balancing nonsense capers and trickster tales, Sierra occasionally integrates words from the language of the country of origin," a *Publishers Weekly* reviewer pointed out, while Hazel Rochman noted in her *Booklist* review that "it's fun to see trickster tales from around the world." Carol L. MacKay, in her *School Library Journal* review, commented on the lessons given in many of the tales: "Children will discover that these themes of justice are as universal as laughter," she concluded.

Sierra explained on her Web site that when she retells folktales, she does research by collecting stories from people she meets. "Most of the folktales I've published are mixtures of several versions from the same culture or region," she wrote. When she begins to collect versions of different tales, she puts them all into a file folder until she has enough variations to turn it into a book. When asked if it is fun to be a writer, Sierra responded: "Yes, but not all of the time. Writing is a job, and there are many difficult and frustrating times. The most enjoyable part of being a writer is spending time with children and adults who love to read."

BIOGRAPHICAL AND CRITICAL SOURCES:

PERIODICALS

Booklist, August, 1992, p. 2019; September 15, 1995, p. 173; March 1, 1997, p. 1177; April 1, 1997, p. 1306; September 1, 1997, Kathleen Squires, review of *Counting Crocodiles,* p. 135; April 15, 2001, Amy Brandt, review of *Preschool to the Rescue,* p. 1566; July, 2001, Stephanie Zvirin, review of *The Gift of the Crocodile,* p. 2011; September 15, 2001, Gillian Engberg, review of *Monster Goose,* p. 237; January 1, 2002, Hazel Rochman, review of *The Gift of the Crocodile: A Cinderella Story,* p. 962; November 15, 2002, John Peters, review of *Can You Guess My Name?: Traditional Tales around the World,* p. 599; December 15, 2002, Hazel Rochman, review of *Silly and Sillier: Read-Aloud Tales from around the World,* p. 765; January 1, 2004, Ilene Cooper, review of *Coco and Cavendish: Circus Dogs,* p. 882; September 1, 2004, Ilene Cooper, review of *What Time Is It, Mr. Crocodile?* p. 123; September 15, 2004, Lauren Peterson, review of *What Time Is It, Mr. Crocodile?* p. 254.

Bulletin of the Center for Children's Books, February, 1993, Betsy Hearne, review of *The Elephant's Wrestling Match,* pp. 190-191.

Children's Book Watch, November, 1992, p. 6; May, 1996, p. 3.

Horn Book, November-December, 1995, Nancy Vasilakas, review of *The House that Drac Built,* pp. 730-731; May-June, 1996, Maria B. Salvadore, review of *Wiley and the Hairy Man,* pp. 343-344; July-August, 1996, Ann A. Flowers, review of *Good Night, Dinosaurs,* pp. 474-475; January, 2001, review of *The Gift of the Crocodile,* p. 104; May, 2001, review of *Preschool to the Rescue,* p. 317; January-February, 2003, Mary M. Burns, review of *Can You Guess My Name?,* p. 87.

Instructor, September, 2001, Judy Freeman, review of *The Gift of the Crocodile,* p. 28; April, 2003, Judy Freeman, review of *Can You Guess My Name?,* p. 55.

Kirkus Reviews, July 15, 1992, p. 930; August 1, 1997, p. 1228; August 1, 2001, review of *Monster Goose,* p. 1131; September 15, 2002, review of *Silly and Sillier,* p. 1400; October 15, 2002, review of *Can You Guess My Name?,* p. 1538; November 1, 2002, review of *'Twas the Night before Christmas,* p. 1625; July 1, 2004, review of *Wild about Books* and *What Time Is It, Mr. Crocodile?,* p. 636.

Library Talk, May-June, 2002.

Parenting, September, 1996, p. 209; December, 1996, p. 252.

Publishers Weekly, July 13, 1992, review of *The Elephant's Wrestling Match,* p. 55; November 4, 1996, p. 48; June 30, 1997, review of *Counting Crocodiles,* p. 75; March 19, 2001, review of *Preschool to the Rescue,* p. 98; August 13, 2001, review of *Monster Goose,* p. 312; September 30, 2002, review of *Silly and Sillier,* p. 71; June 14, 2004, review of *Wild about Books,* p. 62.

School Library Journal, September, 1992, Linda Greenglass, review of *The Elephant's Wrestling Match,* p. 211; September, 1995, Beth Irish, review of *The House that Drac Built,* p. 186; April, 1996, Beth Tegart, review of *Good Night, Dinosaurs,* p. 118; April, 1997, p. 51; June, 1997, p. 39; October, 1997, Marilyn Iarusso, review of *The Mean Hyena,* pp. 123-124; December, 2000, review of *The Gift of the Crocodile,* p. 55; May, 2001, Marlene Gawron, review of *Preschool to the Rescue,* p. 135; September, 2001, Gay Lynn Van Vleck, review of *Monster Goose,* p. 254; October, 2002, Eva Mitnick, review of *'Twas the Fright before Christmas,* p. 63; November, 2002, Lee Bock, review of *Can You Guess My Name?,* p. 148, Carol L. MacKay, review of *Silly and Sillier,* p. 150; October, 2003, review of *Can You Guess My Name?,* p. S53; August, 2004, Marge Loch-Wouters, review of *Wild about Books,* p. 94; September, 2004, review of *What Time Is It, Mr. Crocodile?,* p. 180.

Science-Fiction Chronicle, June, 1995, p. 36.

ONLINE

Judy Sierra's Home Page, http://www.judysierra.net (July 18, 2005).*

*   *   *

SILBER, Joan 1945-

PERSONAL: Born June 14, 1945, in Millburn, NJ; daughter of Samuel S. (a dentist) and Dorothy (a teacher; maiden name, Arlein) Silber. *Education:* Sarah Lawrence College, B.A., 1967; New York University, M.A., 1979.

ADDRESSES: Home—43 Bond St., New York, NY 10012. Office—Sarah Lawrence College, 1 Mead Way, Bronxville, NY 10708. Agent—Geri Thoma, Elaine Markson Literary Agency, 44 Greenwich Ave., New York, NY 10011.

CAREER: Holt, Rinehart & Winston, New York, NY, copy editor, 1967-68; New York Free Press, New York, NY, reporter, 1968; waitress, 1968-71; salesclerk, 1971-72; assistant teacher in day-care centers in New York, NY, 1972; Ideal Publishing, New York, NY, editor of fan magazines Movie Stars and Movie Life, 1975; Kirkus Service, New York, NY, reviewer, 1976; Warner & Gillers, New York, NY, lawyer's assistant, 1977-78; Women's Action Alliance, New York, NY, legal proofreader, 1981; Sarah Lawrence College, Bronxville, NY, member of faculty, 1985-90, 1994—. Visiting assistant professor, University of Utah, 1988; visiting lecturer, Boston University, 1992; writer-in-residence, Vanderbilt University, 1993. Also affiliated with New York University School of Continuing Education, 1981-84, Warren Wilson College M.F.A. Program for Writers, 1986—, Aspen Writers Conference, 1988, 92nd Street Y, 1987-90, 1994-99, Indiana University Writers Conference, 1987, 1989-90, 1994, and 1997, Manhattanville Writers Conference, 1996 and 1999, and Bread Loaf Writers Conference, 2001, Napa Valley Writers Conference, 2005.

MEMBER: PEN, Authors Guild, Authors League of America.

AWARDS, HONORS: PEN/Hemingway Award for best first novel, 1981, for Household Words; Guggenheim fellowship, 1984-85; New York Foundation for the Arts grant and National Endowment for the Arts grant, both 1986; Pushcart Prize, 2000; O. Henry Prize; National Book Award finalist, 2004, for Ideas of Heaven: A Ring of Stories.

WRITINGS:

Household Words (novel), Viking (New York, NY), 1980, reprint, W.W. Norton (New York, NY), 2005.
In the City (novel), Viking (New York, NY), 1987.
In My Other Life (short stories), Sarabande (Louisville, KY), 2000.

Lucky Us (novel), Algonquin (Chapel Hill, NC), 2001.
Ideas of Heaven: A Ring of Stories, W.W. Norton (New York, NY), 2004.

Contributor to books, including Writer's Digest Handbook of Short Story Writing, Writers Digest, 1977; An Inn Near Kyoto: Writing by American Women Abroad, New Rivers Press, 1998; and Pushcart Prize XXV, Pushcart Press, 2000. Contributor of short stories to periodicals, including Redbook, New Yorker, Ploughshares, Boulevard, Witness, Paris Review, and Aphra, and of book reviews to Ms., New York Times Book Review, Yale Review, Newsday, and Village Voice.

WORK IN PROGRESS: A novel about travel and the lure of solitude for Norton; a book on time in fiction for Graywolf's "Craft of Fiction" series.

SIDELIGHTS: Joan Silber has published novels and short stories marked by a subtle use of language and focused on the everyday experiences of her characters. Her first novel, Household Words, depicts the life of Rhoda Taber, a middle-class homemaker living in New Jersey in the 1940s and 1950s. After her pharmacist husband dies, Rhoda determinedly cares for her family and "goes on" for "where else is there to go?" Her "life is relatively unremarkable," explained Susan Isaacs in the New York Times Book Review. "There are no thunderous confrontations here. . . . Rhoda's consciousness never rises, her horizons never soar. Instead she stays in New Jersey, raises her two daughters, visits with friends, works, vacations, suffers." Isaacs continued: "The heroine exhibits strength and integrity under the most mundane circumstances—comforting a wailing baby, presiding over a lonely Thanksgiving dinner."

Marilyn Murray Wilson maintained in the Los Angeles Times, though, that the lack of drive on the part of the main character is the novel's weakness. "What Rhoda does not have—and I can't help but perceive it as a flaw in the book—is a goal of some sort. . . . She . . . floats from day to day, year to year, with no plan, no dream, no real reason for living. . . . Her life has no urgency." Isaacs, however, felt that Household Words "is about ordinary life. There is no zippy dialogue, no literary razzle-dazzle. People live, die, raise children, put on girdles and teach school. But the details add up to a novel full of dignity and humanity." Linda B. Osborne similarly commented in the

Washington Post Book World: "Silber's writing is strong and richly detailed, spotlighting the drama inherent in ordinary lives without sentiment or pretension."

In Silber's *In the City,* a young Jewish girl from Newark moves to 1920s New York City, hoping to find friends more suitable to her artistic tastes. The story focuses on what *New York Times Book Review* contributor Joyce Johnson called "the tension between freedom and vulnerability that rebellious young women have typically experienced." Pauline easily gains access to the trendy circles she yearns for, adapting herself to their manners and language, and experiences new love. Silber told Laurel Graeber in the *New York Times Book Review* that she had originally intended to set her novel in the 1960s, but opted instead for the 1920s: "To transfer it to the 1920s was a way of saying that I wanted it to be about youth, not just a particular time frame," she explained.

Lucky Us features "an unlikely couple [who] weather a crisis in this forthright novel about love and accommodation," observed a *Publishers Weekly* reviewer. Elisa is an artist in New York; she is in her late twenties and not sure what she wants to do with her life. Another character, Gabe, is a camera shop clerk who is about fifteen years older than Elisa. The two meet while working at the camera shop and, against the odds, fall in love. Bookish and companionable Gabe is a former drug dealer and ex-con who learned his lesson during his brush with the law. Elisa still flirts with the wild side, exploring drugs and promiscuity. Still, the relationship between the two advances, and eventually they talk marriage. On a whim, Elisa takes an AIDS test before their wedding and discovers that she is HIV positive. Gabe tries to be supportive, but Elisa breaks off their relationship, returning to the abusive Jason, who originally infected her, but with whom sex is animalistic and raw. Eventually, when Elisa falls ill, Jason tires of her and she leaves. Reunited with Gabe at a wedding of two AIDS patients, "the story closes on a gently hopeful but indeterminate note," commented a *Kirkus Reviews* contributor. *Booklist* reviewer Danise Hoover called the book "a timely and wonderful tale." Ann H. Fisher, writing in the *Library Journal,* concluded: "It's difficult to imagine that such a simple plot could yield such a profound, engaging tale."

The author has also published a couple of short story collections, including *In My Other Life* and *Ideas of*

Heaven: A Ring of Stories. In the former, Silber gathered together twelve short stories focusing on characters who took wild chances in their youth and have lived to see their later lives play out. One story tells of a woman moving to the country with her lesbian lover and their mixed-race adopted child, against the nagging objections of an ex-junkie friend; another follows a woman who was in a rock band in her younger days but now works with inner-city children. "Some of these reflective characters can hardly believe they've outlived their perilous youth," a *Publishers Weekly* critic noted. Donna Seaman, writing in *Booklist,* called Silber's stories "carefully rendered documentaries of lives in transition."

Ideas of Heaven is a collection of six short stories, each linked to the other so that minor characters and events in one story enlarge to central themes and protagonists in the next. In this way, the plots of the stories follow a circular pattern until the final tale is connected to the first. "The overlapping . . . gives this slender book the weight and breadth of a novel," commented Jennifer Reese in *Entertainment Weekly.* In the first story, "My Shape," Alice, a woman whose teenage years were influenced by her large and shapely breasts, meets her husband on a cruise ship and lives with him in France, but she abandons him to pursue a dancing career. A failure at dance, she is humiliated and insulted by her gay dance teacher, Duncan. In the second story, "The High Road," Duncan takes center stage and shows a softer side to the bully of the first tale when he falls in love with Andre, a man he cannot have. After visiting Andre in later life, Duncan once again falls into platonic love with Carl, a young singer performing works by Italian poet Gaspara Stampa. Stampa figures in the self-titled third story, in which Silber explores what the life of the renaissance poet might have been like."Ashes of Love" follows carefree and footloose couple Tom and Peggy as they travel freely, until Peggy's pregnancy changes their lives forever. "Ideas of Heaven" concentrates on a pair of missionaries in China—Tom's wife's great-great-grandparents—who are so devoted to their religious work that they fail to notice the danger around them during the Boxer Rebellion. In the final tale, Alice, now middle aged, reappears as the woman with whom Giles, the narrator, falls in love.

"Wonderfully evocative of time and place, this is a collection to be read and savored by all," commented *Booklist* reviewer Danise Hoover about *Ideas of*

Heaven. "Big ideas come in lovely, small packages in this collection" of short stories, remarked a writer for *Publishers Weekly.* "Silber travels the globe and the centuries with ease," observed a *Kirkus Reviews* contributor, who concluded, "If more collections were like this one, readers would gladly abandon the novel."

Silber told *CA:* "I've always been interested in getting long spans of time into my fiction—my first novel, written before I knew any better, covered twenty years in a woman's life. Recently I've been writing short stories that pretty much cover characters' whole lives. Alice Munro has been a great influence in this. And Chekhov, whom I read early on, showed me how fiction could suddenly light up a character who'd been unlikable. The patern of *Ideas of Heaven,* in which a minor person in one story is major in the next, comes from a similar impulse. I'd like to think a recent interest in Buddhism has added coherence to these long-held learnings. The novel I'm working on now hos parts set in Thailand and Vietnam and shows the marks of travel to Asia in recent years."

BIOGRAPHICAL AND CRITICAL SOURCES:

BOOKS

Silber, Joan, *Household Words,* Viking (New York, NY), 1980.

PERIODICALS

Atlantic Monthly, June, 2005, Christina Schwarz, "A Close Read: What Makes Good Writing Good," review of *Ideas of Heaven: A Ring of Stories,* p. 117.
Booklist, April 15, 2000, Donna Seaman, review of *In My Other Life,* p. 1525; September 1, 2001, Danise Hoover, review of *Lucky Us,* p. 53; February 15, 2004, Danise Hoover, review of *Ideas of Heaven,* p. 1038.
Christian Century, December 14, 2004, review of *Ideas of Heaven,* p. 22.
Entertainment Weekly, April 23, 2004, Jennifer Reese, review of *Ideas of Heaven,* p. 86.
Kirkus Reviews, March 15, 2000, review of *In My Other Life,* pp. 328-329; August 1, 2001, review of *Lucky Us,* p. 1062; February 15, 2004, review of *Ideas of Heaven,* p. 152.

Library Journal, April 1, 2000, Christine DeZelar-Tiedman, review of *In My Other Life,* p. 134; July, 2001, Ann H. Fisher, review of *Lucky Us,* p. 126; February 1, 2004, Leann Isaac, review of *Ideas of Heaven,* p. 127.
Los Angeles Times, March 6, 1980, Marilyn Murray Wilson, review of *Household Words.*
New York Times Book Review, February 3, 1980, Susan Isaacs, review of *Household Words;* March 29, 1987, Joyce Johnson, review of *In the City,* p. 8, and Laurel Graeber, "Everyone's 1920s Are Different," review of *In the City,* p. 9; June 11, 2000, Carmela Ciuraru, review of *In My Other Life,* p. 17.
Philadelphia Inquirer, September 11, 2000, Rita Giordano, review of *In My Other Life.*
Publishers Weekly, March 20, 2000, review of *In My Other Life,* p. 71; September 3, 2001, review of *Lucky Us,* p. 55; March 15, 2004, review of *Ideas of Heaven,* p. 54.
Washington Post, November 11, 2004, Carole Burns, "Off the Page: Joan Silver and Houck Smith," transcript of online chat with Joan Silber and Carol Houck Smith.
Washington Post Book World, January 31, 1980, Linda B. Osborne, review of *Household Words.*
Westchester County Business Journal, November 29, 2004, "Two Sarah Lawrence Faculty Members Named National Book Award Finalists," p. 26.
Women's Review of Books, July, 2004, "Paradises Lost," review of *Ideas of Heaven,* p. 20.

ONLINE

BookReporter.com, http://www.bookreporter.com/ (October 19, 2001), interview with Joan Silber; (October 5, 2005), Chuck Leddy, review of *Lucky Us.*
National Book Foundation Web site, http://www.nationalbook.org/ (October 5, 2005), biography of Joan Silber.
Sarah Lawrence College Web site, http://www.slc.edu/ (October 5, 2005), biography of Joan Silber.*

*   *   *

SILVERMAN, Al 1926-

PERSONAL: Born April 12, 1926, in Lynn, MA; son of Henry and Minnie (Damsky) Silverman; married Rosa Magaro, September 9, 1951; children: Thomas, Brian, Matthew. *Education:* Boston University, B.S., 1949.

ADDRESSES: Home—15 Woods Way, White Plains, NY 10605-5446. *Agent*—c/o Author Mail, The Overlook Press, One Overlook Dr., Woodstock, NY 12498.

CAREER: Sport, New York, NY, associate editor, 1951-52; *True,* New York, NY, sports editor, 1952-54; *Argosy* magazine, New York, NY, assistant editor, 1954-55; freelance writer for magazines, 1955-60; Macfadden-Bartell Corp., New York, NY, editor-in-chief of magazines *Sport, Sport Library, Impact,* and *Saga,* 1960-72; Book-of-the-Month Club, New York, NY, executive vice president and editorial director, 1972-81, president and chief operating officer, 1981-85, chair and chief executive officer, 1985-88; Viking Penguin, New York, NY, vice president and contributing editor, 1989-92, senior vice president of publications and editor in chief, 1992-94, senior vice president and editor at large, 1994-97, editorial advisor, 1998.

MEMBER: Society of Magazine Writers, Authors Guild, Authors League of America, PEN (member of board of directors).

AWARDS, HONORS: Litt.D., Boston University, 1986.

WRITINGS:

SPORTS BIOGRAPHY

Warren Spahn, Immortal Southpaw, Bartholomew House (New York, NY), 1961.
Mickey Mantle, Mister Yankee, Putnam (New York, NY), 1963.
Joe DiMaggio: The Golden Year, 1941, Prentice-Hall (Englewood Cliffs, NJ), 1969.
(With Gale Sayers) *I Am Third,* Viking (New York, NY), 1970, published with a new introduction as *I Am Third: The Inspiration for Brian's Song,* Penguin (New York, NY), 2001.

SPORTS NONFICTION

(With Phil Rizzuto) *The "Miracle" New York Yankees,* Coward (New York, NY), 1962.
(Editor) *The World of Sport: The Best from Sport Magazine,* Holt (New York, NY), 1962.
Heroes of the World Series, Putnam (New York, NY), 1964.

(With Paul Hornung) *Football and the Single Man,* Doubleday (Garden City, NY), 1965.
Sports Titans of the 20th Century, Putnam (New York, NY), 1965.
(Editor) *The Specialist in Pro Football* (article collection), Random House (New York, NY), 1966.
(With Frank Robinson) *My Life Is Baseball,* Doubleday (Garden City, NY), 1968.
More Sports Titans of the 20th Century, Putnam (New York, NY), 1968.
(Editor) *Best of Sport,* Viking (New York, NY), 1971.
(Editor, with Brian Silverman) *The Twentieth Century Treasury of Sports,* Viking (New York, NY), 1992.
It's Not Over 'Til It's Over: Stories behind the Most Magnificent, Heart-Stopping Sports Miracles of Our Time, Overlook Press (Woodstock, NY), 2002.

OTHER NONFICTION

(Editor) *John F. Kennedy Memorial Album,* Macfadden (New York, NY), 1964.
(Editor) *Churchill: A Memorial Album,* Macfadden (New York, NY), 1965.
Foster and Laurie, Little, Brown (Boston, MA), 1974.
(Editor) *The Book of the Month: Sixty Years of Books in American Life,* Little, Brown (Boston, MA), 1986.

SIDELIGHTS: In conjunction with a long career as a sports writer for periodicals and editor of sports magazines, Al Silverman has written a number of books that are primarily about sports-related topics. *It's Not Over 'Til It's Over: The Stories behind the Most Magnificent, Heart-Stopping Sports Miracles of Our Time,* for example, features the stories of thirteen sporting events in the twentieth century that the author has deemed extraordinary. Silverman includes accounts of the 1971 boxing match between Muhammad Ali and Joe Frazier, the U.S. Women's soccer team's victory over China in the 1999 Women's World Cup, the so-called "Miracle on Ice" hockey match-up between the United States and the Soviet Union at the 1980 Winter Olympics, and the 1908 heartbreaking loss of the New York Giants to the Chicago Cubs which ruined the Giants' season. Calling the book "engaging reading," a reviewer for *Publishers Weekly* noted, "He often tracks down and interviews event participants to provide perspective . . ., giving the book its greatest authority."

BIOGRAPHICAL AND CRITICAL SOURCES:

PERIODICALS

Publishers Weekly, September 30, 2002, review of *It's Not Over 'Til It's Over: The Stories behind the Most Magnificent, Heart-Stopping Sports Miracles of Our Time,* p. 63; September 30, 2002, Ed Nawotka, "A Publishing Career Ain't Over 'Til It's Over," interview with Al Silverman, p. 64.*

*   *   *

SPENCER, Scott 1945-

PERSONAL: Born September 1, 1945, in Washington, DC; son of Charles (a steelworker and union organizer) and Jean (Novick) Spencer; married Claire Joubert Dupuy, January 24, 1979; children: Celeste, Asher. *Education:* University of Wisconsin—Madison, B.A., 1969; attended University of Illinois.

ADDRESSES: Home—Rhinebeck, NY. *Agent*—c/o Author Mail, HarperCollins Publishers, Inc., 10 E. 53rd St., New York, NY 10022.

CAREER: Writer. Worked variously in an employment agency and as an evaluator for federal education programs.

MEMBER: PEN American Center (member of executive board, 1979-85; member of Freedom to Write Committee), Authors Guild, National Writers Union (member of executive board, 1986-92).

AWARDS, HONORS: National Book Award nominations, Before Columbus Foundation, 1981, for *Endless Love,* and 2003, for *A Ship Made of Paper.*

WRITINGS:

NOVELS

Last Night at the Brain Thieves Ball, Houghton Mifflin (Boston, MA), 1973.
Preservation Hall, Knopf (New York, NY), 1976.

Endless Love, Knopf (New York, NY), 1979.
Waking the Dead, Knopf (New York, NY), 1986.
The Magic Room, Harmony Books (New York, NY), 1987.
Secret Anniversaries, Knopf (New York, NY), 1990.
Men in Black, Knopf (New York, NY), 1995.
The Rich Man's Table, Knopf (New York, NY), 1998.
A Ship Made of Paper, HarperCollins (New York, NY), 2003.

OTHER

Act of Vengeance (screenplay), Home Box Office (HBO), 1985.

Contributor of stories and articles to periodicals, including *Esquire, Harper's, Film Comment, Ladies' Home Journal, New York Times Book Review, Redbook, Rolling Stone,* and *Vanity Fair.*

ADAPTATIONS: Endless Love was adapted for film by Judith Rascoe and released by Universal, 1981.

SIDELIGHTS: Noted for the intensity of his prose and his acute understanding of character and situation, Scott Spencer first received widespread critical attention and popularity following the publication of his third novel, *Endless Love.* Writing in the *Dictionary of Literary Biography Yearbook,* a contributor stated that "Spencer has said . . . he writes one book at a time; so, while his books do have elements in common, most notably characters whose desires place them in opposition to society, each is unique." The plot and subject matter for Spencer's first novel, *Last Night at the Brain Thieves Ball,* for instance, is a far cry from the story in *Endless Love.* Told in the form of a journal, *Last Night at the Brain Thieves Ball* centers on Paul Galambos, a psychology professor who takes a job with NESTER—a secret company that hopes to use brain implants to control people's desires. Growing dissatisfaction with his employers leads Paul to begin keeping a journal with which he hopes to expose NESTER. Eventually Paul escapes from the company's complex but is returned after being captured. On the day Paul's supervisor releases him from his contract, he informs Paul that his work for NESTER was part of a plan to rehabilitate him, that he was a danger to society, and that all his experiments were fake. The supervisor then cuts off Paul's hand.

"Like Paul Galambos," Mullen wrote, "the main character in *Preservation Hall*, Virgil Morgan, is not sure who he is or what his place in the world is, and to learn these things, he must pay a price for them." The main action of the novel takes place at a secluded country house in Maine, where Virgil and his wife are spending the New Year's holiday with Virgil's stepbrother and his stepbrother's girlfriend. While destroying a dresser they plan to burn in the fireplace, Virgil, who despises his father, kills his stepbrother. Mullen stated that Virgil's uncertainty over the extent to which his stepbrother's death was accidental forces him "to come to terms with what is good and bad in himself . . . [and] to reevaluate his relationship with his father in an attempt to expiate the guilt he still feels about killing his stepbrother." In a review for the *New York Times Book Review,* Katha Pollitt commented positively on Spencer's characterization of Virgil and his father Earl. "It's a mark of Spencer's skill that although we hear the whole story from Virgil's point of view, ultimately Earl's resentment of his son's success seems less mean-spirited than Virgil's shame at his father's failure. . . . Spencer deserves a good deal of praise for having the imagination to know more about his characters than they do themselves."

Spencer also created such complex characterizations in his next novel, *Endless Love.* Set in the 1960s, *Endless Love* traces the relationship of seventeen-year-old David Axelrod, sixteen-year-old Jade Butterfield, and her pot-smoking, permissive parents. David cherishes the Butterfields' laissez-faire lifestyle and leaves his own parents to live with Jade's family. Although Mr. and Mrs. Butterfield encourage David, who develops an obsessive love for Jade, to sleep with their daughter, they eventually deem the young couple's relationship too intense and banish David from the house, forbidding him to return for thirty days. In his desperation to see the family, David ignites the Butterfields' newspaper on their porch, hoping the small fire will bring the family out of the house where he can see them. The fire, however, rages out of control, and David must rescue the Butterfields from the blazing structure. As punishment for starting the fire, David is sent to a private mental institution for three years, during which time the Butterfield family deteriorates, beginning with the divorce of Jade's parents. After his release from the hospital, David tries to rekindle his relationship with Jade and reunite the Butterfield family, but all his efforts prove futile.

Critics claimed that Spencer's book is not concerned so much with the actions of its characters as with the psychological conflicts underlying their actions. Edward Rothstein, writing in the *New York Times Book Review,* noted that "Mr. Spencer has an acute grasp of character and situation. He gives us details that make these often tormented people uncommonly convincing. There are the erotic ties within the Butterfield family that are threatened by David's intrusion; the absence of such ties in his own parents; his mother's confused pain at his obsession; his father's active interest in it."

Rothstein considered David the "true heart of the book," and stated: "He tells his story with such ardent conviction that we begin to share his obsession. He constantly surprises us, too, because he takes himself by surprise. . . . But the world in this novel is as unpredictable as David, and just as threatening; unexpected encounters, sudden partings, deaths and punishments assault him. They beset us as well, for we are in the grip of an expert storyteller." Summarizing the book's appeal, Christopher Lehmann-Haupt stated in the *New York Times:* "If you've ever been wildly and impractically in love, you won't stop to look at it objectively. You'll soar and sink with David, and ache for him. . . . Reading Mr. Spencer's novel, you'll remember for a while when it seemed possible to die of love."

Obsessive love is also a theme in Spencer's next work, *Waking the Dead.* The story centers on Fielding Pierce, a lawyer who loses his girlfriend, Sarah Williams, to a violent act of terrorism. After Fielding has apparently put his life back together and embarked on a promising political career, he begins to imagine that his dead girlfriend has come back to life. His obsession with recapturing his lost love threatens his stability and his nomination as a Congressional candidate.

Critical response to the novel was not as positive as for his previous books. A reviewer in the *New Yorker* observed that while Spencer is sometimes "excessive" and has moments of "uncomfortable sentimentality," he is also "a writer of great intensity, of imagery in the Graham Greene manner." For other critics, the novel lacked a narrative coherence that ultimately proves crippling. According to Judith Levine in the *Village Voice,* the trouble starts with the death of Sarah, a left-wing activist from a wealthy family who becomes embroiled in Chilean politics. "The violent event around which much of the action, including Fielding's advancing madness, turns is not all that believable," Levine argued. The reviewer also noted some inconsistencies in how Spencer develops his characters and wondered whether Fielding is meant to be seen as a "a true man of the people," "a naive puppet of the powers that be," or "a self-serving creep using *them*." Similarly, Michiko Kakutani of the *New York Times* wrote: "Given Fielding's calculating nature, we never completely believe in his love for Sarah," and the story's tragic end "seems so arbitrary and unnecessary." Kakutani also noted that the evocative and lyrical prose that marked the speech of *Endless Love*'s teenaged hero becomes awkward and embarrassing for the middle-aged Fielding. "We often have the feeling that Fielding is giving a campaign speech," she commented.

Spencer's next work, *Secret Anniversaries,* pivots on a bold young girl named Caitlin. The action begins in the 1930s, when Caitlin is forced to leave her quiet hometown in rural upstate New York after her employers find her in bed with their son. Caitlin moves to Washington, DC, where she begins working for a pro-German, isolationist Congressman who wants to keep the United States out of World War II. Caitlin's sympathies are torn between loyalty to her boss and love for an investigative reporter who is working to uncover pro-Fascist sympathizers in the government. The culmination of Caitlin's political consciousness, which includes exposure to 1960s radicalism in New York City's Greenwich Village and work for the World Refugee Alliance following World War II, reaches its apogee when she visits the enshrined home of Anne Frank in Amsterdam. "*Secret Anniversaries* is a strange novel, layered, cleverly woven," commented Carol Muske in the *New York Times Book Review.* In a review for the *New York Times,* Kakutani wrote that Caitlin is "a finely observed portrait of a woman . . . who has lived most of her life on the margins of conventionality." However, Kakutani lamented, *Secret Anniversaries* places its heroine in "such a crudely drawn cartoon world of political villains that it manages to almost completely ruin the reader's sense of credulity."

A lighter tone prevails in Spencer's next work, *Men in Black,* which probes the troubled life of Sam Holland, a serious writer whose literary works have failed to gain a following. Responding to pressure to finally make some money, he gives up his calling and moves to a small rural town to write popular nonfiction on such topics as traveling with a pet and avoiding the hazards of too much salt. To Sam's astonishment, his

book on UFOs brings him enormous success and catapults him to the national stage. While his career soars, his family life heads in a downward spiral. His wife finds out that he has a lover, while his son runs away from home and becomes a criminal. Sam also learns that his pseudonym matches the name of an anti-Semitic extremist, whose followers flock to Sam's nationwide book tour.

"Sam's experiences on the road [doing a book tour] are uncommonly hilarious and terrifying, handled with tremendous verve," observed Elaine Kendall in the *Los Angeles Times.* Robert Chatain stated in the *Tribune Books* that "*Men in Black* is a good story—a speedy time-lapse image of evasive struggle. Its rummage through the debris of a life lived by taking the easier course among available alternatives doesn't uncover much wisdom, merely a talent for survival." The novel loses power, Chatain argued, because Sam is too self-pitying, especially when pondering his fate should his wife discover his infidelity. "His frustrated dreams, his past failures, his old temptations are held up to brooding condemnation, but his close-at-hand present and future actions escape the kind of reasoned weighing of alternatives that is a familiar, even necessary ethical dimension of life," Chatain wrote. However, Christopher Lehmann-Haupt, writing in the *New York Times,* found *Men in Black* "charmingly funny-sad" and argued that "Mr. Spencer . . . has a charming way of capturing the banal side of the antic and the antic side of the banal."

Fame also plays a role in Spencer's next novel, *The Rich Man's Table.* This book follows Billy Rothschild's search for Luke Fairchild, a world-famous 1960s folk rock superstar based on Bob Dylan. Billy is the son of Luke, born to Luke's girlfriend Esther Rothschild just as he was hitting the big time, though Luke has never acknowledged him as such. Though Billy is an adult, he has not had much of a life, holding only temporary jobs, such as substitute teacher, in part because of who his father is. His mission to find Luke, understand him in his many paradoxes by interviewing those close to him, and be acknowledged as his son, is a means for Billy to begin his own life again. Spencer uses the novel to explore the meaning of having a public life and persona, and the effect it has had on Luke and those around him. Steve Brzezinski in the *Antioch Review* wrote: "The ending is rather melodramatic and forced, but the precision of the writing, the evocation of the period, and in particular the portrait of Luke Fairchild make this a compelling and absorbing novel."

Spencer returns to familiar territory in *A Ship Made of Paper.* The novel looks at a love affair from the point of view of the two parties involved. It also considers the affect their illicit romance has on their lives and those of the people around them. Daniel Emerson is a successful lawyer living with his girlfriend Kate and her young daughter Ruby in his New York State hometown of Leyden. The family has left New York City to escape the danger caused by his losing a major case. It becomes more complicated when Daniel gets involved with Iris Davenport, a married graduate student. The couple meets at Ruby's daycare center where Iris's son is also enrolled. The passionate affair leads to a social and economic downfall for Daniel. In the novel, Spencer also looks at issues of race and racism that emerge because Daniel is white while Iris is black. Noting that "*A Ship Made of Paper* rocks with suspense and daring," Suzy Hansen in *Salon.com* also commented: "Spencer . . . is an enchanting writer. The steady, expanding intensity of his sentences do spellbinding justice to the misery and joy of romantic obsession."

BIOGRAPHICAL AND CRITICAL SOURCES:

BOOKS

Dictionary of Literary Biography Yearbook 1986, Gale (Detroit, MI), 1987, pp. 329-334.

PERIODICALS

Antioch Review, fall, 1998, Steve Brzezinski, review of *The Rich Man's Table,* p. 498.
Los Angeles Times, May 16, 1995, Elaine Kendall, review of *Men in Black,* p. E5.
New Yorker, July 21, 1986, review of *Waking the Dead,* pp. 93-94.
New York Times, September 6, 1979, Christopher Lehmann-Haupt, review of *Endless Love,* p. C19; May 7, 1986, Michiko Kakutani, review of *Waking the Dead,* p. C28; May 8, 1990, Michiko Kakutani, review of *Secret Anniversaries,* p. C19; April 17, 1995, Christopher Lehmann-Haupt, review of *Men in Black,* p. C13.

New York Times Book Review, September 16, 1973, Katha Pollitt, review of *Last Night at the Brain Thieves Ball,* p. 32; January 2, 1977, Katha Pollitt, review of *Preservation Hall,* p. 12; September 23, 1979, Edward Rothstein, review of *Endless Love,* p. 13; July 22, 1990, Carol Muske, review of *Secret Anniversaries,* p. 12.
Publishers Weekly, March 31, 2003, Amy Boaz, "Scott Spencer: Affairs of the Heart and Soul," interview with Scott Spencer, p. 36.
Tribune Books (Chicago, IL), May 21, 1995, Robert Chatain, review of *Men in Black,* pp. 3, 5.
Village Voice, June 17, 1986, Judith Levine, review of *Waking the Dead,* p. 49.

ONLINE

Salon.com, http://www.salon.com/ (July 28, 2003), Suzy Hansen, review of *A Ship Made of Paper.**

*   *   *

STARR, Jason 1966-

PERSONAL: Born November 22, 1966, in New York, NY; married; children: one daughter. *Education:* Binghampton University, B.A., 1988; Brooklyn College, M.F.A., 1990. *Hobbies and other interests:* Movies, sports, travel.

ADDRESSES: Home—New York, NY. *Agent*—c/o Author Mail, Orion House, 5 Upper St. Martin's Ln., London WC2H 9EA, England. *E-mail*—crimeflix@yahoo.com.

CAREER: Writer. *Richmond Review* (online literary magazine), editor. Has worked as a telemarketer.

AWARDS, HONORS: Barry Award for best paperback, 2004, for *Tough Luck;* Anthony Award, Boucheron World Mystery, 2005, for *Twisted City.*

WRITINGS:

NOVELS

Cold Caller, Norton (New York, NY), 1998.
Nothing Personal, No Exit Press (Harpenden, England), 1998.

Fake I.D., No Exit Press (Harpenden, England), 2000.
Hard Feelings, Vintage (New York, NY), 2002.
Tough Luck, Vintage (New York, NY), 2003.
Twisted City, Vintage (New York, NY), 2004.
Lights Out, St. Martin's Press (New York, NY), 2006.
(With Ken Bruen) *Bust,* Hard Case Crime, 2006.

OTHER

October Squall (screenplay), 2004.

Contributor to business magazines, including *Financial World* and *Crain's New York Business;* short stories have appeared in the *Barcelona Review, Richmond Review, Shots,* and *Crime Time,* as well as in anthologies in England, Italy, and France; playwright for several theatre groups in New York, NY.

SIDELIGHTS: Jason Starr worked as a successful telemarketer for years before writing his first novel, and he used the experience for the basis of his debut story. In *Cold Caller* protagonist Bill Moss gives the reader insight into the life of a downsized American professional. Moss had previously held a high-level job as an advertising executive but was dismissed when he was suspected of sexual harassment. Faced with extremely high rent and unable to find any job of equal quality, he is forced to work as a telemarketer who makes cold calls for a failing long-distance phone company. For the next two years, Moss works in this new and mediocre job environment, where he must put up with riding the subway, working out of a cubicle, and dealing with an incompetent and alcoholic boss who takes the credit for Moss's work.

A particularly bad day, which includes getting assaulted on the subway and getting locked out of his bedroom by his girlfriend, sends Moss over the edge. He enters the new territory of insanity, killing someone in the process. A reviewer for *Publishers Weekly* called *Cold Caller* a "stylish pulp throwback" reminiscent of the 1930s "Black Mask" series.

Starr's second novel, the thriller *Nothing Personal,* looks at how crime drives two very different couples together and apart. The poor DePinos struggle with compulsive gambler husband Joey's gambling debts and a failing marriage. He decides to solve the problem by kidnapping the daughter of his wife's friends, the wealthy Sussmans. Husband David is a successful advertising executive, who has a mistress out to get him and his wife. Because of Joey and David's situations, they end up killing and committing blackmail in an attempt to solve their problems. "Starr just never lets up as he twists the plot in ever more sinister directions," observed *Booklist* critic Joanne Wilkinson, "and his deadpan tone is a perfect match for his material."

Moving towards black comedy, Starr's *Tough Luck* finds the main character, down-on-his luck Mickey Prada, getting drawn deeper into the criminal world in the 1980s. While working at a seafood market in Brooklyn and trying to earn enough to go to college, he deals with an ailing father and is compelled to place bets for his customer Angelo Santoro. Angelo's bets are bad, so Mickey finds both the bookie and Angelo after him because Angelo refuses to pay. To get out of this difficulty, he agrees to go on a home robbery job with best friend Chris. Though the crime was supposed to be a sure thing, it does not go well and Mickey finds himself spiraling downward. A *Publishers Weekly* reviewer noted: "Starr moves deftly through his milieu, twisting expectations and producing a grim comedy."

Twisted City is a noir novel that revolves around David Miller, who has an unsatisfying life both personally and professionally. When his wallet is lost one day, David goes to the tenement apartment of Charlotte, a prostitute with a drug problem, to retrieve the missing item. Instead, he finds himself with problems that may cost him his life. A *Publishers Weekly* contributor praised the author for creating an ordinary character who finds himself "calmly accepting a ticket to hell, where an ending worthy of Charles Willeford at his most absurd awaits him."

Starr once told *CA:* "Some of my favorite writers, such as Ernest Hemingway, Paul Bolos, Jim Thompson, and Patricia Highsmith, have been major influences for me. I write for several hours every day and try to complete at least one new book each year."

BIOGRAPHICAL AND CRITICAL SOURCES:

PERIODICALS

Booklist, May 1, 2000, Joanne Wilkinson, review of *Nothing Personal,* p. 1625.

Publishers Weekly, March 16, 1998, review of *Cold Caller,* p. 54; October 28, 2002, review of *Tough Luck,* p. 47; June 28, 2004, review of *Twisted City,* p. 32.

ONLINE

Jason Starr Home Page, http://www.jasonstarr.com (December 21, 2005).

* * *

STEWIG, John Warren 1937-

PERSONAL: Born January 7, 1937, in Waukesha, WI; son of John G. and Marguerite W. Stewig. *Education:* University of Wisconsin at Madison, B.S., 1958, M.S., 1962, Ph.D., 1967. *Religion:* Episcopalian.

ADDRESSES: Home—1717 W. Greentree Rd., No. 201, Glendale, WI 53209. *Office*—Lentz Hall, Rm. E328, Carthage College, 2001 Alford Park Rd., Kenosha, WI 53140. *E-mail*—jstewig@carthage.edu.

CAREER: Elementary-school teacher in Monona Grove, WI, 1958-64; Purdue University, West Lafayette, IN, assistant professor, 1967-72, associate professor of curriculum and instruction, 1972-77; University of Wisconsin, Milwaukee, professor of language arts, 1977-2001; Carthage College Center for Children's Literature, Kenosha, WI, director, 2001—. Faculty member and workshop leader at colleges and universities in the United States and Canada, including Indiana University, Bloomington, School of the Ozarks, Western Montana State University, Northern Montana State University, University of Denver, and University of Victoria; speaker at schools and professional gatherings. Worked as a music teacher at a hospital school for school-age patients. Member of Wisconsin State Literacy Assessment advisory committee, 1974; Madison Cooperative Children's Book Center, member of advisory board, 1974-78, 1989-92.

MEMBER: International Reading Association (member of children's book award committee, 1984-86), International Visual Literacy Association, Association for Childhood Education International, National Council of Teachers of English (president, 1982-83; member of standing committee against censorship), American Library Association (chair of Caldecott committee, 1997), Wisconsin Council of Teachers of English (board member, 1977-79; president, 1980-81), Milwaukee Association for the Education of Young Children, English Association of Greater Milwaukee (board member, 1973-81).

AWARDS, HONORS: Grants from U.S. Office of Education, 1973, and State of Wisconsin, 1981; Creative Drama for Human Awareness Award, American Association of Theatre for Youth, 1987; Distinguished Elementary Education Award, University of Wisconsin, Madison, 1987; Aesop Honor designation, American Folklore Society, for *Princess Florecita and the Iron Shoes: A Spanish Fairy Tale.*

WRITINGS:

FOR CHILDREN

Sending Messages, photographs by Richard D. Bradley, Houghton (Boston, MA), 1978.

(Reteller) *The Fisherman and His Wife,* illustrated by Margaret Tomes, Holiday House (New York, NY), 1988.

(Reteller) *Stone Soup,* illustrated by Margaret Tomes, Holiday House (New York, NY), 1991.

The Moon's Choice, illustrated by Jan Palmer, Simon & Schuster Books for Young Readers (New York, NY), 1993.

Princess Florecita and the Iron Shoes: A Spanish Fairy Tale, illustrated by K. Wendy Popp, Knopf (New York, NY), 1995.

(Reteller) *King Midas,* illustrated by Omar Rayyan, Holiday House (New York, NY), 1999.

Clever Gretchen, illustrated by Patricia Wittmann, Marshall Cavendish (New York, NY), 2000.

Mother Holly: A Retelling from the Brothers Grimm, illustrated by Joanna Westerman, North/South Books (New York, NY), 2001.

Making Plum Jam, illustrated by Kevin O'Malley, Hyperion (New York, NY), 2002.

Whuppity Stoorie, illustrated by Preston McDaniels, Holiday House (New York, NY), 2004.

OTHER

Spontaneous Drama: A Language Art, C.E. Merrill (Columbus, OH), 1973.

Exploring Language with Children, C.E. Merrill (Columbus, OH), 1974.

Read to Write: Using Literature as a Springboard to Writing, Hawthorn (New York, NY), 1975, 3rd edition published as *Read to Write: Using Literature as a Springboard for Teaching Writing,* Richard C. Owen Publishers (Katonah, NY), 1990.

Children's Language Acquisition, Department of Public Instruction (Madison, WI), 1976.

(Editor with Sam L. Sebesta, and contributor) *Using Literature in the Elementary Classroom* (monograph), National Council of Teachers of English (Urbana, IL), 1978 2nd edition, 1989.

Children and Literature, Rand McNally (Chicago, IL), 1980, 2nd edition, Houghton (Boston, MA), 1988.

Teaching Language Arts in Early Childhood, Holt (New York, NY), 1982.

Exploring Language Arts in the Elementary Classroom, Holt (New York, NY), 1983.

Informal Drama in the Elementary Language-Arts Program, Teachers College (New York, NY), 1983.

(With Carol Buege) *Dramatizing Literature in Whole-Language Classrooms,* Teachers College (New York, NY), 1994.

(With Mary Jett-Simpson) *Language Arts in the Early Childhood Classroom,* Wadsworth, 1995.

(With Beverly Nordberg) *Exploring Language Arts in the Elementary Classroom,* Wadsworth, 1995.

Looking at Picture Books, Highsmith (Fort Atkinson, WI), 1995.

Contributor to books on reading and elementary education; contributor of articles and reviews to periodicals. Member of editorial board, *Childhood Education,* 1972-74, *Advocate,* 1983-86, Children's Literature Association *Quarterly,* 1987-93, and *Writing Teacher,* 1992-99; associate editor, *Children's Theatre Review,* 1985-86.

SIDELIGHTS: Beginning his teaching career in elementary education, reading, and literacy, John Warren Stewig worked as a professor at the University of Wisconsin for many years. In addition to many other professional activities, including writing articles and teacher guides and serving as chair of the 1998 Caldecott Medal committee, Stewig has also found the time to write quality books for younger readers. Beginning with 1978's *Sending Messages,* he has produced retellings of stories such as *The Fisherman and His Wife* and *Clever Gretchen.* In addition, he is the author of

Making Plum Jam, an original story drawn from the author's childhood in which the transgressions of three elderly women—Stewig's own aunts, who steal plums from a nearby farmer to make jam—are made right by the women's young nephew. In *Booklist,* Kathy Broderick dubbed the work "a fond reminiscence of another era," while *School Library Journal* critic Barbara Buckley called *Making Plum Jam* "a summertime treat" featuring "quirky, colorful" illustrations by Kevin O'Malley.

The Fisherman and His Wife is the first book in which Stewig draws upon a classic from children's literature. His retelling, based on an European fairy tale attributed to the Brothers Grimm, is accompanied by illustrations by Margaret Tomes. The story involves a humble fisherman who catches a magical flounder; his greedy wife discovers the fish will grant all her wishes, but in the end, the flounder finds a clever way to punish the wife for her materialistic ways. Kenneth Marantz, reviewing *The Fisherman and His Wife* for the *School Library Journal,* found that "Stewig does such a full job that there seems little for Tomes' gentle, chromatically subdued illustrations to do." In a critique of the book, *Booklist* reviewer Denise M. Wilms termed it "a clean, direct retelling."

Stewig's *Stone Soup* is an adaptation of another classic tale for young readers. Also illustrated by Tomes, the tale features a young, impoverished girl named Grethel who decides to try her luck at finding food for herself and her starving mother in a distant village. At first, the village people treat her, a stranger, with hostility, but Grethel cleverly charms them into providing the ingredients for a special soup she promises to make with her magic stone. The dish is a delicious success, and in the end Grethel returns to her mother with some useful knowledge. "Stewig's brisk prose is well suited to reading aloud," opined Carolyn Phelan in *Booklist,* while a *Kirkus Reviews* critic termed *Stone Soup* "a pleasing new version of a popular favorite."

Princess Florecita and the Iron Shoes: A Spanish Fairy Tale, another retelling of an old European tale, was cited by *Books in Canada* writer Alison Sutherland as "evidence that authentic folklore has always been aware that women are just as heroic as men." The story's heroine learns, by birdsong, of an enchanted sleeping prince who only wakes once a year; the woman who wears out a pair of iron shoes to get to his castle and touches him with a special black feather will awaken the prince forever. When a black feather drops at Princess Florecita's feet, she orders a pair of iron shoes to be made and then sets off to meet her destiny. Along the way, she meets three fierce but kindly older women, mothers of the East, West, and North winds, who provide the young woman with the necessary knowledge to complete her journey successfully. Stewig's version, with illustrations by K. Wendy Popp, won strong praise from reviewers. Donna L. Scanlon, writing in the *School Library Journal,* found the text "rich in imagery," Stewig's "rhythm and pacing . . . just right, and the storytelling . . . at once traditional and fresh." *Booklist* reviewer Chris Sherman praised the author for presenting the heroine in truly heroic terms, noting that "Stewig captures perfectly the romantic nature of the story."

Stewig's picture book *King Midas,* with illustrations by Omar Rayyan, presents to young readers the story of the ancient Mediterranean king to whom a creature appears and grants the power to turn all that the king touches into gold. Midas excitedly makes use of his new power, but is devastated when he inadvertently turns his beloved daughter Marygold into a frozen gold statue. All ends well when the creature reappears and offers to take back the gift, and Midas realizes that there are things in life more valuable than gold. Writing in the *School Library Journal,* Patricia Lothrop-Green commended Stewig's "deft, direct language" as well as the humorous touches added to the classic tale.

Other retellings by Stewig include *Mother Holly,* a retelling of a less-familiar Brothers Grimm story, and *Whuppity Stoorie,* a tale based on a Scottish variant of "Rumplestiltskin." In *Mother Holly* Rose and Blanche are stepsisters, Rose gentle and hardworking and Blanche the complete opposite. When Rose's spindle falls down a deep well, she tumbles in after it and ends up in a strange land where she shows herself to be caring and compassionate. Meeting the old, infirm, and ugly Mother Holly, Rose takes pity on the woman and stays with her. When she leaves to return to her actual home, she is given a wealth of gold. When Blanche sees Rose's largesse, she jumps down the well, but because her behaviors are selfish and cruel, she is rewarded with thorns. Unlike the original ending, which found Blanche stewing in pitch forever, in Stewig's version Rose and Mother Holly help Blanche to improve her character by teaching the selfish young woman to care for others. Although noting that children would prefer an ending where good triumphs over evil rather than helping it, *Booklist* contributor Ilene Cooper dubbed *Mother Holly* "an engaging retelling that captures the cadence of fairy tales." Giving special praise to the artwork by Johanna Weserman, Mirian Lang Budin added in the *School Library Journal* that Stewig's alternative ending serves as "a reassuring departure from the harsh traditional ending" of the original.

Stewig once commented: "One of the greatest pleasures of my professional life has been the variety of writing opportunities which have come to me. Each of several general categories of writing have come, with their own sets of parameters, providing very different challenges and satisfactions.

"When I began, I wrote professional journal articles and books for teachers. I enjoyed the challenge of working, usually alone, to craft ideas and then find an editor willing to publish them. Finding an editor who thought my work was worthy was followed by intense contact reshaping the writing under the guidance of the editor. Back then, periodical editors had the time to actually edit, rather than simply publish as many do today, and it wasn't unusual for the exchanges of letters to take up to a year before the article appeared. A book involved close work for a long period of time, and in either format I learned much from editors who cared about my work and wanted it to be better.

"Later, I was asked, and subsequently became—with a valued professional colleague—the coauthor of a language-arts textbook series for children in kindergarten through eighth grades. This entailed working with several editors and a number of authors over an extended period of time, to produce a large quantity of related materials intended for audiences which differed not only in age but also in ability. Group meetings, which included designers, layout and sales personnel, often involved dozens of people and stretched over several days. Many different ideas had to be reconciled and then written into a firmly prescribed format. In all, a very different kind of writing than I had done previously.

"Still later, I was fortunate to move into doing trade picture-books for children, yet another very different kind of writing. Here economy of expression, conciseness, is paramount. Here, every word has to fit into the prescribed 32-page final format. So as an author I work alone, crafting words and re-crafting, eliminating, and changing until everything seems right to me. While my first picture book was informational, I've subsequently done fairytale retellings, and . . . a personal childhood reminiscence. Each has involved very different kinds of preparation before writing.

"One rare opportunity I've had is some involvement with the art in my books. Years ago, a gracious editor agreed to see a naive young writer, without a scheduled appointment, on a Friday afternoon. I sold her on using a photographer friend to do the illustrations. Not a smart approach, as I now know! Since then I've kept suitably quiet about the art in my books, realizing how jealously editors guard their decision-making in this area. In the meantime, I've studied and then spoken and written extensively about children's-book illustration generally. So, editors have come to involve me in some of the decisions made, including the kind of pine tree to include, and the color of the hero's hair. I thank each of those editors for the involvement they've allowed me.

"My understanding of the nature of writing has greatly expanded since my first published article appeared over forty years ago. My understanding of revision has been enhanced by interactions with a myriad of editors who have helped me make my work stronger. And great is the satisfaction of having communicated through fiction and nonfiction with readers, preschool through adult, most of whom I'll never meet in person. Having influenced the growth and development of children, both directly and through their teachers, parents, and librarians, is the delight of being a writer."

BIOGRAPHICAL AND CRITICAL SOURCES:

PERIODICALS

Booklist, November 1, 1988, Denise M. Wilms, review of *The Fisherman and His Wife,* p. 487; March 15, 1991, Carolyn Phelan, review of *Stone Soup,* p. 1495; October 15, 1995, Chris Sherman, review of *Princess Florecita and the Iron Shoes,* p. 312; February 15, 1999, p. 1073; September 15, 1999, John Peters, review of *Clever Gretchen,* p. 251; July, 2001, Ilene Cooper, review of *Mother Holly,* p. 2015; August, 2002, Kathy Broderick, review of *Making Plum Jam,* p. 1977.

Books in Canada, December, 1995, Alison Sutherland, "Children and Myths," pp. 18-19.
Bulletin of the Center for Children's Books, September, 1978, review of *Sending Messages,* pp. 19-20.
Horn Book, August, 1978, p. 414; April 15, 1991, review of *Stone Soup,* p. 540.
Kirkus Reviews, May 15, 1978, p. 550; February 1, 2004, review of *Whuppity Stoorie,* p. 139.
Publishers Weekly, September 30, 1988, p. 68.
Quill & Quire, November, 1995, p. 47.
School Library Journal, December, 1988, Kenneth Marantz, review of *The Fisherman and His Wife,* p. 102; April, 1991, p. 114; January, 1996, Donna L. Scanlon, review of *Princess Florecita and the Iron Shoes,* p. 107; March, 1999, Patricia Lothrop-Green, review of *King Midas,* p. 201; October, 2000, Ginny Gustin, review of *Clever Gretchen,* p. 153; September, 2001, Miriam Lang Budin, review of *Mother Holly,* p. 215; June, 2002, Barbara Buckley, review of *Making Plum Jam,* p. 112; March, 2004, Grace Oliff, review of *Whuppity Stoorie,* p. 200.

ONLINE

Carthage College Center for Children's Literature Web site, http://www3.carthage.edu/childliturature/ (July 20, 2005), "John Warren Stewig."

*   *   *

ST. GEORGE, Judith 1931-

PERSONAL: Born February 26, 1931, in Westfield, NJ; daughter of John H. (a lawyer) and Edna (maiden name, Perkins) Alexander; married David St. George (an Episcopal minister), June 5, 1954; children: Peter, James, Philip, Sarah. *Education:* Smith College, B.A., 1952. *Religion:* Episcopalian.

ADDRESSES: Home—8 Binney Rd., Old Lyme, CT 06371.

CAREER: Suburban Frontiers (re-locating service), Basking Ridge, NJ, president, 1968-71; writer, 1970—. Rutgers University, Rutgers, NJ, instructor in children's writing and member of advisory council on children's literature; Brooklyn Bridge Centennial Commission, commissioner; York Correctional Institution, Niantic, CT, instructor in creative writing.

MEMBER: Authors Guild, Mystery Writers of America.

AWARDS, HONORS: Best books for spring list, *Saturday Review*, 1976, for *By George, Bloomers!;* runner-up, Edgar Allan Poe Award, Mystery Writers of America, 1979, for *The Halloween Pumpkin Smasher;* Children's Choice book, Children's Book Council (CBC)/International Reading Association, and *New York Times* Best Mystery designation, both 1980, both for *Haunted;* named American Library Association (ALA) Notable Book, American Book Award Honor Book, Golden Kite Honor Book, and *New York Times* notable book, all 1982, and New York Academy of Sciences award, 1983, all for *The Brooklyn Bridge: They Said It Couldn't Be Built;* New Jersey Institute of Technology children's literature award, 1983, for *Do You See What I See?*, 1988, for *Who's Scared? Not Me!*, 1989, and Golden Kite Nonfiction Award, and ALA Notable Book designation, all for *Panama Canal: Gateway to the World;* Notable Children's Trade Book in the Field of Social Studies, National Council on the Social Studies/CBC, ALA Notable Book designation, and Golden Kite Honor Book designation, all 1985, and Christopher Award, and Claremont Graduate School Recognition of Merit Award, both 1986, all for *The Mount Rushmore Story;* best juvenile novel award, *Voice of Youth Advocates*, 1986, for *What's Happening to My Junior Year?;* Recommended Books for Teenagers, 1992, for *Mason and Dixon's Line of Fire;* Notable Book in the Field of Social Studies, William Allen White Book Award, 1993-94, and Young Hoosier Book Award, 1994-95, all for *Dear Dr. Bell . . . Your Friend Helen Keller;* Young Adult's Choices, IRA/CBC, 1998, for *To See with the Heart: The Life of Sitting Bull;* New York State Book Award, Sons of the American Revolution, 1998, for *Betsy Ross: Patriot of Philadelphia;* Caldecott Medal, 2000, and ALA Notable Book designation, 2001, both for *So You Want to Be President.*

WRITINGS:

FOR YOUNG PEOPLE; FICTION

Turncoat Winter, Rebel Spring, Chilton, 1970.
The Girl with Spunk, Putnam (New York, NY), 1975.

By George, Bloomers!, Coward (New York, NY), 1976.
The Chinese Puzzle of Shag Island, Putnam (New York, NY), 1976.
The Shad Are Running, Putnam (New York, NY), 1977.
The Shadow of the Shaman, Putnam (New York, NY), 1977.
The Halloween Pumpkin Smasher, Putnam (New York, NY), 1978.
The Halo Wind, Putnam (New York, NY), 1978.
Mystery at St. Martin's, Putnam (New York, NY), 1979.
Haunted, Putnam (New York, NY), 1980.
Call Me Margo, Putnam (New York, NY), 1981.
The Mysterious Girl in the Garden, Putnam (New York, NY), 1981.
Do You See What I See?, Putnam (New York, NY), 1982.
In the Shadow of the Bear, Putnam (New York, NY), 1983.
What's Happening to My Junior Year?, Putnam (New York, NY), 1986.
Who's Scared?: Not Me!, Putnam (New York, NY), 1987.

NONFICTION

The Amazing Voyage of the New Orleans, Putnam (New York, NY), 1980.
The Brooklyn Bridge: They Said It Couldn't Be Built, Putnam (New York, NY), 1982.
The Mount Rushmore Story, Putnam (New York, NY), 1985.
Panama Canal: Gateway to the World, Putnam (New York, NY), 1989.
The White House: Cornerstone of a Nation, Putnam (New York, NY), 1990.
Mason and Dixon's Line of Fire, Putnam (New York, NY), 1991.
Dear Dr. Bell . . . Your Friend, Helen Keller, Putnam (New York, NY), 1992.
Crazy Horse, Putnam (New York, NY), 1994.
To See with the Heart: The Life of Sitting Bull, Putnam (New York, NY), 1996.
Sacagawea, Putnam (New York, NY), 1997.
Betsy Ross: Patriot of Philadelphia, Holt (New York, NY), 1997.
In the Line of Fire: President's Lives at Stake, Holiday House (New York, NY), 1999.

So You Want to Be President?, Philomel Books (New York, NY), 2000.

John and Abigail Adams: An American Love Story, Holiday House (New York, NY), 2001.

So You Want to Be an Inventor?, Philomel Books (New York, NY), 2002.

You're on Your Way, Teddy Roosevelt, Philomel Books (New York, NY), 2004.

So You Want to Be an Explorer?, Philomel Books (New York, NY), 2005.

Take the Lead, George Washington, Philomel Books (New York, NY), 2005.

The One and Only Declaration of Independence, Philomel Books (New York, NY), 2005.

SIDELIGHTS: Judith St. George writes both historical fiction and nonfiction, blending elements of mystery and exciting action along with closely detailed research to come up with such award-winning titles as *Haunted, The Halloween Pumpkin Smasher, In the Shadow of the Bear, The Brooklyn Bridge: They Said It Couldn't Be Built,* and *The Mount Rushmore Story.* Employing elements of personal experience in both her fiction and nonfiction, St. George often writes of young girls confronting challenging situations, and of the importance of friendship and family history.

Born in Westfield, New Jersey, in 1931, St. George was raised during the Great Depression and had close contact with grandparents on both sides. Her childhood was, as she typified it in an essay for *Something about the Author Autobiography Series* (SAAS), "idyllic." Raised in a close and loving family, St. George did not greatly feel the effects of the Depression years. Instead, her childhood memories are filled with the escapades of her four best friends on Maple Street in quiet Westfield, of hopscotch and roller skating in the summer months, and of making snow angels and playing hockey on a frozen pond in winter. Her older brother, Jack, and younger sister, Anne, both influenced these early years as well, and they also found their way into the pages of her fiction. In her *SAAS* entry, St. George recalled herself being "terribly shy" and a "worrier" as a child. Though she was a slight, gangly girl, she excelled at sports; "I have to admit that being selected as the only girl to play on the boys' sixth-grade baseball team still remains a high moment of my school career," the author recalled in *SAAS*.

St. George's parents were a strong influence in her life. High school sweethearts, her parents remained married for sixty-one years. Her father was an inveter-

ate reader who "always had his nose in a book," and was the one who taught St. George the importance of ethics and integrity, the two words most often used to describe him. Her mother devoted her life to her family and provided a nurturing and secure environment. Another "powerful factor in the growing up years was having two sets of grandparents, who also lived in Westfield," St. George noted in *SAAS*. Her paternal grandfather, "rather foreboding," was the model for the stern father figures in her fiction, while her maternal grandparents, the Perkinses, were "another set of warm, loving, and caring parents." St. George spent a weekly overnight with the Perkinses, listening to the tales of her mother's grandfather, who had been a sea captain for thirty-five years. These stories have also found their way into her fiction.

"I have no recollection of when I learned to read," St. George wrote in *SAAS*, "probably in the first grade like everyone else." Once started, she coursed through everything from "Nancy Drew" mysteries to movie magazines and comics. "There was no question that reading became a permanent habit," St. George recalled in *SAAS*, "and to this day, if I'm not in the middle of a book, I feel a distinct void in my life." If she is vague about when she learned to read, St. George is very exact about when she first began writing: In October of 1941 she composed a play for her sixth-grade class, a reflective drama featuring four matrons sitting around a tea table reminiscing about their classmates of fifty years before. From a very early age, friendship formed a core to her life, and it takes on equally great importance in the pages of her books.

If her years at elementary school were serene, those spent at "fortress-like" Roosevelt Junior High were less so. Placed in different classes from her old friends, St. George reverted to shyness. The same year she began junior high, her paternal grandfather died, and her family moved into his large, imposing home in Westfield. Always afraid of the dark, St. George's fears were compounded in this draughty old house with its five exterior doors and several unused rooms on the second floor.

She continued her reading and sports—adding tennis to her favorite competitions—and at age fifteen was sent to boarding school. The next two years were, according to St. George in *SAAS*, "among my unhappiest." Not only did she have trouble making friends, but she also had an English teacher who made her feel "truly hopeless." All these experiences would provide grist for St. George's literary mill, however, and furnish her with scene, character, and incident for her fiction.

In 1948 St. George entered Smith College and experienced "the most wonderful and fulfilling" four years "any college student could ask for," she noted in *SAAS*. She formed close friendships and was fortunate to study English in a department full of world-class instructors. She also wrote for and edited the college humor magazine, the *Campus Cat,* and continued her enjoyment of athletics. After graduation, she moved in with several friends in Cambridge, Massachusetts. Two years later she married David St. George, who was studying to become an Episcopal minister. St. George then "lapsed into the 50's syndrome of house-keeping with a capital H," as she once commented. After her first child, she and her husband moved to Eastern Oregon for his ministry, serving a population of less than 6,000 in a county the size of New Jersey. St. George soon found friends and settled into her new life. Another son was born, and then her husband received a ministry in New Jersey, where her next two children were born. "Those were baby years for me," St. George noted in *SAAS,* "filled with pregnancies, diapers, mumps, measles, chicken pox, colds, and little else." In New Jersey she was close to her parents again, as well as to her grandparents, who all took an active role in helping with her children.

By the time her youngest child was three years old, St. George began "to feel a definite itch," desiring to do more with herself than parenting. Another move, this time to Millington, New Jersey, near Morristown, set her researching the Revolutionary War, for it was there that George Washington and his troops once wintered. As a young reader, St. George had been hooked on historical fiction; now she began creating it herself, working on her old college typewriter. Soon she had a book, *Turncoat Winter, Rebel Spring,* the story of a fourteen-year-old patriot boy in the winter of 1779-80 who is torn between protecting a friend who saved him and turning him in as a British spy. After nine rejections, she finally sold the book. Now the typewriter came out of hiding. But the second book went unpublished, and it was not until her third, *The Girl with Spunk,* that she began publishing regularly.

Set in 1848 in a town in New York, *The Girl with Spunk* tells the story of fourteen-year-old Josie, who loses her job due to gossip and finds help in the fledgling women's rights movement. In the end, she has hopes that maybe she can eventually become a naturalist in a world controlled by men. Barbara Elleman, writing in *Booklist,* felt that the book is a "memorable recreation of a young girl's struggles against the attitudes of the times," while a *Kirkus Reviews* critic noted that there "is a sprinkling of ginger in Josie; her trials are realistic . . . and those who take their adventures on the tame side and their consciousness raising in small stages can share her growing imagination." Josie's habit of stuttering when faced with a threatening situation is a direct writing from life. The use of such real-life material became a hallmark for St. George's work.

St. George continued with historical fiction for her next title, *By George, Bloomers!,* set in the mid-nineteenth century and dealing with the disapproval that eight-year-old Hannah suffers when she wants to wear a pair of the new and daring lady's apparel, bloomers. She eventually wins the right to wear these pants after rescuing her brother from the roof in a story that "gives historical perspective" and that is both "pleasantly told and illustrated," according to a reviewer in the *Bulletin of the Center for Children's Books.*

St. George employs both her maternal grandfather's reminiscences of a seafaring life and the domineering character of her paternal grandfather, and even indulges in her love for mysteries and spooky ghosts, in *The Chinese Puzzle of Shag Island.* Young Kim Laudall goes to her family's ancestral home, Shag Island off the coast of Maine, to visit her supposedly senile ninety-three-year-old great-grandfather. He protests against selling his imposing mansion, and soon Kim is involved in a "Yankee gothic, with clues and curios," according to a critic in *Kirkus Reviews.* Some of these "curios" are the ghosts of Chinese pirates who may be haunting the house, though, according to a reviewer for *Publishers Weekly,* "Everything is satisfactorily explained at the end of a fresh, entertaining mystery for young buffs of the genre."

St. George's paternal grandfather also inspires the demanding father figure in *The Shad Are Running,* an historical novel that is partly based on the sport of racing Hudson River steamboats in the 1830s. Young Corny Van Loon overcomes his fear of water and of his stern fisherman father when he alerts his village to the collision of steamboats and participates in the subsequent rescue process. Patricia S. Butcher, writing in the *School Library Journal,* noted that the "plot moves along at a good clip, climaxed by a well described rescue scene."

With her fiction, St. George has continued to explore her twin loves: history and mystery. In *The Halo Wind,* set along the Oregon Trail in 1845, St. George describes a mystery surrounding a young Chinook girl who joins a group of settlers. She details the actual hardships such a journey involved in "a nicely balanced and well-written novel," according to Ann Flowers in *Horn Book.* Blending a contemporary setting with fantasy time-travel, St. George evoked nineteenth-century England in *The Mysterious Girl in the Garden* and the life of the naturalist painter, James Audubon, in *Who's Scared?: Not Me!*

Other St. George fiction titles remain firmly planted in contemporary times and deal with adventure and suspense, as in the award-winning *Haunted,* the story of sixteen-year-old Alex, who is hired to house-sit an estate which was recently the scene of a murder-suicide. Drew Stevenson, writing in the *School Library Journal,* found the book to be "St. George's suspense at its best." Young male protagonists star in the mystery-adventures *The Shadow of the Shaman,* set in Oregon, and *Do You See What I See?,* set on Cape Cod. The former involves mysterious Indian charms and a rickety old lodge in a story with a "brisk" pace and "colorful" scenery, according to a *Kirkus Reviews* contributor, while the latter is, as Judith Geer noted in the *Voice of Youth Advocates,* "an excellently written story with firm characterization and suspense enough to curl your toes." Church business and counterfeit money come into play in *Mystery at St. Martin's,* an opportunity for St. George to use material drawn from her husband's career, while adventures in Alaska involving a wilderness-trek and U.S.-Soviet relations form the core of the thriller *In the Shadow of the Bear.* In *Call Me Margo* and *What's Happening to My Junior Year?* St. George tackles material dealing with her own boarding-school years.

More recently, St. George's fiction has given way to nonfiction. Starting with her first factual book, *The Amazing Voyage of the New Orleans,* she has created award-winning titles dealing with everything from a history of the Brooklyn Bridge to biographies of Native Americans and a profile of the U.S. presidency. Writing in *SAAS,* St. George noted that she began to

realize that "nonfiction was a whole new field for me, a field in which I felt very much at ease."

In *The Amazing Voyage of the New Orleans,* St. George tells the story of the first steamboat to travel down the Ohio and Mississippi Rivers in 1811. *Booklist* critic Elleman noted that the book "is recounted in an amiable, amusing narrative." In *The Brooklyn Bridge: They Said It Couldn't Be Built* she hit her stride with nonfiction, and much of her best creative effort has been devoted to that genre since 1982. The book's publication coincided with the centennial of the Brooklyn Bridge, and the work relates the seemingly impossible job of building a bridge over the East River in the nineteenth century, focusing on the Roebling family, two of whose members were chief engineers on the project. "The author touches gently upon the personal trials and torments of this remarkable family, celebrating instead their public triumphs," Shirley Wilton stated in the *School Library Journal.* Writing in *Horn Book,* Karen Jameyson called the book a "fascinating history."

Other famous man-made structures—both imaginary and real—are described in *The Mount Rushmore Story, Panama Canal: Gateway to the World, The White House: Cornerstone of a Nation, Mason and Dixon's Line of Fire,* and *Dear Dr. Bell . . . Your Friend, Helen Keller.* For the award-winning book about Mount Rushmore, St. George climbed atop the Black Hills monument for her own personal up-close look, and blended stories of the sculptor Gutzon Borglum with those of the Sioux Indians for whom the Black Hills of South Dakota are a spiritual home. "*The Mount Rushmore Story* is a fine acquisition for basic general information and details," concluded George Gleason in a *School Library Journal* review of the work.

More recent nonfiction works by St. George have examined the lives of notable Native Americans, including the Oglala warrior, Crazy Horse, the Hunkpapa Sioux chief, Sitting Bull, and Sacagawea of Lewis and Clark fame. Daniel Menaker, writing in the *New Yorker,* called St. George's *Crazy Horse* a "soundly written biography," while a *Publishers Weekly* critic noted that *To See with the Heart: The Life of Sitting Bull* is "a biography of unusual depth."

In the Line of Fire: President's Lives at Stake tells the stories of those presidents who have been the victims of assassination or targets of assassination attempts.

The four presidents to have been killed by assassins— Lincoln, Garfield, McKinley, and Kennedy—are given a full chapter each. The motives of their killers, the medical treatment they received in an effort to save their lives, and their accomplishments while in office are highlighted. The book's concluding section covers seven presidents who were violently attacked but survived, including Theodore Roosevelt and Ronald Reagan. Randy Meyer in *Booklist* called the book "a thorough account of our history of presidential assassinations."

St. George examines the top job in the United States in the Caldecott Medal-winning *So You Want to Be President?* She begins by presenting the job's advantages and disadvantages. St. George then considers qualifications for the job, comparing forty-one presidents on the basis of upbringing, personality, physical appearance, educational background, and other factors. The book closes with the presidential oath of office and includes an appendix that chronologically lists the presidents, along with biographical data, terms of office, and brief summaries of their tenures. Carolyn Phelan, writing in *Booklist,* stressed the book's "sense of the significance and dignity of the office and the faith that children still aspire to be president." A reviewer for *Horn Book* found the book to be "positively inspiring," while a critic for *Publishers Weekly* dubbed it "a clever and engrossing approach to the men who have led America."

So You Want to Be an Inventor? takes a similar approach to another childhood career aspiration. Here St. George tells the stories of many famous inventors, including Alexander Graham Bell, Henry Ford, and Clarence Birdseye, to illustrate the qualities it takes to be a successful inventor. Among those qualities are persistence, stubbornness, and the ability to dream. Dona Ratterree, writing in the *School Library Journal,* called the book "a skewed, funny, and informative look at the history of inventions and their inventors," while a critic for *Publishers Weekly* praised the book's "lighthearted style."

St. George recounts a real-life love story in her book *John and Abigail Adams: An American Love Story.* John Adams was America's second president and a leading figure in the events that led up to the American Revolution. He and his wife Abigail were married for fifty-four years. Much of their voluminous correspondence has survived, and St. George makes use of this material to present the details of their long and happy relationship. "The history is solid," according to Randy Meyer in *Booklist,* and "there's a good deal of information here." "Readers will enjoy this look at the romance of these two patriots who worked so tirelessly for their country," a critic for *Publishers Weekly* maintained. Kitty Flynn, writing in *Horn Book,* found that "St. George succeeds in humanizing her subjects and in fleshing out complicated social and political events."

While finding research to be "fun," as she noted in her *SAAS* entry, St. George concluded that "it's the writing that's hard. Writing *is* hard for me. Is that because I make more demands on myself with each new book? I hope that's the reason, but I'm not sure. All I know is that I want my readers to care as much about the outcome of historical events as if they were reading today's headlines."

BIOGRAPHICAL AND CRITICAL SOURCES:

BOOKS

Something about the Author Autobiography Series, Volume 12, Gale (Detroit, MI), 1991.

PERIODICALS

Booklist, February 15, 1976, Barbara Elleman, review of *The Girl with Spunk,* p. 857; March 15, 1977, p. 1101; October 15, 1978, p. 386; January 1, 1980, p. 669; May 1, 1980, Barbara Elleman, review of *The Amazing Voyage of the New Orleans,* pp. 1298-1299; November 1, 1980, p. 401; January 1, 1982, p. 599; January 15, 1982, p. 668; December 15, 1986, p. 642; November 15, 1987, p. 555; March 1, 1996, p. 1174; August, 1997, Lauren Peterson, review of *Sacagawea,* p. 1896; January 1, 1998, Carolyn Phelan, review of *Betsy Ross: Patriot of Philadelphia,* p. 807; December 1, 1999, Randy Meyer, review of *In the Line of Fire,* p. 692; July, 2000, Carolyn Phelan, review of *So You Want to Be President?,* p. 2034; November 1, 2001, Randy Meyer, review of *John and Abigail Adams: An American Love Story,* p. 466; August, 2002, GraceAnne A. DeCandido, review of *So You Want to Be an Inventor?,* p. 1954; March 1, 2005, Ilene Cooper, review of *The One and Only Declaration of Independence,* p. 1201.

Bulletin of the Center for Children's Books, June, 1976, p. 163; September, 1976, review of *By George, Bloomers!,* p. 17; October, 1976, pp. 30-31; December, 1977, p. 68; February, 1979, p. 105; February, 1980, p. 118; March, 1981, p. 138; September, 1981, p. 15; January, 1983, p. 96; January, 1987, p. 99; February, 1993, pp. 192-193; December, 1994, pp. 145-146; January, 1998, p. 178.

Horn Book, February, 1979, Ann Flowers, review of *The Halo Wind,* p. 66; August, 1980, p. 430; August, 1982, Karen Jameyson, review of *The Brooklyn Bridge: They Said It Couldn't Be Built,* pp. 425-426; July, 2000, review of *So You Want to Be President?,* p. 476; January-February, 2002, Kitty Flynn, review of *John and Abigail Adams,* p. 107; September-October, 2002, Betty Carter, review of *So You Want to Be an Inventor?,* p. 601; September-October, 2004, Betty Carter, review of *You're on Your Way, Teddy Roosevelt,* p. 608.

Kirkus Reviews, December 1, 1975, review of *The Girl With Spunk,* p. 1336; February 1, 1976, p. 132; May 15, 1976, review of *The Chinese Puzzle of Shag Island,* p. 594; January 15, 1978, review of *The Shadow of the Shaman,* p. 47; May 1, 1982, pp. 557-558; November 1, 1983, p. 207; October 1, 2001, review of *John and Abigail Adams,* p. 1434; July 15, 2002, review of *So You Want to Be an Inventor?,* p. 1044; August 15, 2004, review of *You're on Your Way, Teddy Roosevelt,* p. 813; December 15, 2004, review of *Take the Lead, George Washington,* p. 1208.

New Yorker, December 12, 1994, Daniel Menaker, review of *Crazy Horse,* p. 118.

Publishers Weekly, May 3, 1976, review of *The Chinese Puzzle of Shag Island,* p. 64; November 9, 1992, p. 88; May 27, 1996, review of *To See with the Heart: The Life of Sitting Bull,* p. 80; June 30, 1997, review of *Sacagawea,* p. 77; December 13, 1999, review of *In the Line of Fire,* p. 84; July 17, 2000, review of *So You Want to Be President?,* p. 193; October 1, 2001, review of *John and Abigail Adams,* p. 62; July 1, 2002, review of *So You Want to Be an Inventor?,* p. 77; September 13, 2004, review of *You're on Your Way, Teddy Roosevelt,* p. 78.

School Library Journal, September, 1977, Patricia S. Butcher, review of *The Shad Are Running,* p. 137; August, 1980, p. 70; December, 1980, Drew Stevenson, review of *Haunted,* p. 74; December, 1981, p. 68; February, 1983, Shirley Wilton, review of *The Brooklyn Bridge: They Said It Couldn't Be Built,* p. 92; February, 1984, p. 85; October, 1985, George Gleason, review of *The Mount Rushmore Story,* p. 188; February, 1987, p. 85; November, 1994, p. 117; July, 1996, pp. 96-97; February, 1998, p. 124; March, 1998, p. 242; December, 2001, Shauna Yusko, review of *John and Abigail Adams,* p. 171; September, 2002, Dona Ratterree, review of *So You Want to Be an Inventor?,* p. 251; March, 2003, Renee Steinberg, review of *Sacagawea,* p. 173; October, 2003, review of *So You Want to Be President?* (audiobook), p. S23; October, 2004, Margaret Bush, review of *You're on Your Way, Teddy Roosevelt,* p. 150; January, 2005, Ann Welton, review of *Take the Lead, George Washington,* p. 114.

Voice of Youth Advocates, December, 1982, Judith Geer, review of *Do You See What I See?,* pp. 35-36.

*   *   *

STOLLMAN, Aryeh Lev 1954-

PERSONAL: Born 1954, in Windsor, Ontario, Canada; father, a rabbi. *Education:* Graduated from Yeshiva University and Albert Einstein College of Medicine.

ADDRESSES: Agent—c/o Author Mail, Riverhead Books, 345 Hudson St., New York, NY 10014.

CAREER: Writer. Mount Sinai Medical Center, New York, NY, resident in radiology, then neuroradiologist; New York University, New York, NY, fellowship in neuroradiology.

AWARDS, HONORS: American Library Association Notable Book, 1997, *Los Angeles Times Book Review* Recommended Book of the Year, Wilbur Award, Religion Communicator Council, and Lambda Award, Lambda Literary Foundation, all for *The Far Euphrates;* Chaim Potok Literary Award, Jewish Community Centers of Greater Philadelphia.

WRITINGS:

The Far Euphrates (novel), Riverhead Books (New York, NY), 1997.

The Illuminated Soul (novel), Riverhead Books (New York, NY), 2002.

The Dialogues of Time and Entropy (short stories), Riverhead Books (New York, NY), 2003.

Contributor of short stories to journals, including *American Short Fiction, Story, Southwest Review, Foreword, Tikkun,* and *Yale Review.*

The Far Euphrates has been translated into Dutch, German, Italian, and Portuguese. *The Illuminated Soul* has been translated into German, Dutch, and Italian.

SIDELIGHTS: With his debut effort, *The Far Euphrates,* novelist Aryeh Lev Stollman tells of a young Jewish boy whose Holocaust-surviving parents have sheltered him from the outside world in an effort to protect him from its many dangers. Set in the quiet backdrop of Windsor, Ontario, the story leads the boy, Aryeh Alexander ben Shelomo (Alexander), on a journey of discovery, both about himself and the history of the Holocaust, which is intertwined with his own family's history.

Not only are Alexander's parents survivors of the horrible tragedy, but his next-door neighbor, Bernard Seidengarn, and Bernard's twin sister Hannalore are as well. Growing up in this insulated world, Alexander finds himself caught between the powerful forces of his protective parents. Alexander feels pulled by "my mother's uncontrollable fears and my father's unanswerable intellectual and spiritual pursuits," a direct reflection of the personality traits of each of his parents. When Alexander begins to make a habit of daydreaming while cooped-up in his little world, his mother Sarah seeks out a gypsy "prophetess" for advice. His father, on the other hand, is constantly immersed in his inexhaustible search for knowledge. He is particularly hungry to find the origins of human existence, which in his opinion had roots in the valley of "the far Euphrates with its source in Eden." At one point he tells Alexander, "it's human nature to seek out patterns wherever they may present themselves."

Alexander's search for his own identity leads him through a courtship with a girl who simultaneously entices and shuns him, and an episode where he has a flood of sexual feelings for a handsome boy. Although these events are important in Alexander's development, it is the history of his people that most effects the impressionable boy. Alexander particularly agonizes when he learns the "secret" of Bernard and Hannalore's past imprisonment in the death camp of Auschwitz, where they suffered through the twisted experiments of Nazi doctor Josef Mengele. Bernard is also the family's cantor (a religious official of the Jewish faith who leads the musical aspects of a service) and is very much a part of Alexander's upbringing. Because of this fact, the impact of the discovery is even greater on Alexander. This teaches the disillusioned Alexander that innocence is always susceptible to the cruelty of the world.

Stollman's style in writing *The Far Euphrates* was noted by critics. "Highly recommended for all fiction collections," wrote Molly Abramowitz of the *Library Journal.* A contributor for *Publishers Weekly* was impressed with the book's "deceptively quiet, gentle tone" and believed it "works on its readers most visceral sympathies and fears." In like manner, a contributor in *Kirkus Reviews* called the book a "ruminative and wonderfully moving first novel." The reviewer went on to write that the story is "an affirmation of our right and need to believe in the essential permanence of things and of the spirit."

Stollman's second novel, *The Illuminated Soul,* was also somewhat influenced by his childhood. A *Publishers Weekly* reviewer wrote of the book: "Stollman illuminates the mysteries of life with the clear eye of a scientist and the faith of a believer." Told from the point of view of Dr. Joseph Ivri, a Jewish neuroanatomist, *The Illuminated Soul* looks back at a summer in his childhood home in Windsor in the late 1940s when he was fourteen years old. Eva Laquedem Higashi, a Jewish refugee from Prague who has traveled from place to place since the 1930s, rented a room from Joseph's mother, Adele, a recent widow who was starting a catering business to support Joseph and his brother.

A scientist who also speaks seven languages, Eva tells many stories and charms the family with her exotic nature. She also possesses an illuminated Hebrew manuscript, which has been in her family for several centuries. The manuscript, the Augsburg Miscellany, and its importance are revealed over the course of the book. Eva opens Joseph's eyes to the world and affects his future. *New York Times* contributor Nell Freudenberger noted: "Stollman is one of those writers who can not only create a convincing child but can crawl into his skin, unlearning the things adults know and becoming, again, a kind of foreigner in the world." Of the novel as a whole, a critic in *Kirkus Reviews* wrote: "Stollman is a writer of rare skill, every line molded and sculpted to perfection, and life in a small

Canadian Jewish community is well rendered. The sense of loss pervading these Holocaust-stricken pages is almost overwhelming."

Stollman next published a collection of short stories featuring Jewish characters, *The Dialogues of Time and Entropy.* The title story is about a woman, Ahuvah, who works as a physicist and has an autistic daughter. She leaves her husband Paul in Canada and takes her daughter to an Israeli settlement in Palestine that is about to be returned to the Palestinians. While Ahuvah hopes to find help, perhaps in the form of a miracle, for her daughter and herself, the reality is more complicated. Another story, "If I Have Found Favor in Your Eyes," concerns a Jewish teenager whose unconventional parents are divorcing. He becomes fascinated by his neighbors, Hasidic Jews. A *Kirkus Reviews* contributor noted of the collection: "An expert weaver, Stollman brings together themes of religion, science, and love into an emotional whole."

BIOGRAPHICAL AND CRITICAL SOURCES:

BOOKS

Stollman, Aryeh Lev, *The Far Euphrates,* Riverhead (New York, NY), 1997.

PERIODICALS

Kirkus Reviews, July 1, 1997, review of *The Far Euphrates,* p. 980; December 15, 2001, review of *The Illuminated Soul,* p. 1717; January 1, 2003, review of *The Dialogues of Time and Entropy,* p. 23.
Library Journal, September 1, 1997, Molly Abramowitz, review of *The Far Euphrates,* p. 221.
New York Times, April 28, 2002, Nell Freudenberger, "A Woman without a Past," review of *The Illuminated Soul,* sec. 7, p. 15.
Publishers Weekly, July 7, 1997, review of *The Far Euphrates,* p. 46; January 28, 2002, review of *The Illuminated Soul,* p. 269.

ONLINE

Aryeh Lev Stollman Home Page, http://www.aryehlev stollman.com (October 10, 2005).
BOMB, http://www.bombsite.com/ (October 10, 2005), Betsy Sussler, interview with Aryeh Lev Stollman.*

T

TALLIS, Robyn
See COVILLE, Bruce

*   *   *

TAYLOR, Andrew 1951-
(Andrew Saville, Andrew John Robert Taylor, John Robert Taylor)

PERSONAL: Born October 14, 1951, in Stevenage, England; son of Arthur John (a teacher and minister) and Hilda (a physiotherapist; maiden name, Haines) Taylor; married Caroline Silverwood (a librarian), September 8, 1979; children: Sarah Jessica, William John Alexander. *Education:* Emmanuel College, Cambridge, B.A. (with honors), 1973, M.A., 1976; University of London, M.A., 1979.

ADDRESSES: Agent—Sheil Land Associates, 43 Doughty St., London WC1N 2LF, England. *E-mail*—ataylor@lydmouth.demon.co.uk.

CAREER: Borough of Brent, London, England, librarian, 1976-78, 1979-81; freelance writer and sub-editor for London area publishers, 1981—.

MEMBER: Crime Writers Association, Society of Authors.

AWARDS, HONORS: John Creasey Memorial Award, Crime Writers Association, 1982, and Edgar Award nomination, Mystery Writers of America, both for *Caroline Minuscule;* Gold Dagger nomination, Crime Writers Association, 1985, for *Our Fathers' Lies;* Ellis Peters Historical Dagger Award, Crime Writers Association, 2001, for *Office of the Dead,* 2003, for *The American Boy;* Audie Award, for *The American Boy.*

WRITINGS:

"DOUGAL" SERIES

Caroline Minuscule, Gollancz (London, England), 1982, Dodd (New York, NY), 1983.
Waiting for the End of the World, Dodd (New York, NY), 1984.
Our Fathers' Lies, Dodd (New York, NY), 1985.
An Old School Tie, Dodd (New York, NY), 1986.
Freelance Death, Gollancz (London, England), 1987, Dodd (New York, NY), 1988.
Blood Relation, Gollancz (London, England), 1990, Doubleday (New York, NY), 1991.
The Sleeping Policeman, Gollancz (London, England), 1992.
Odd Man Out, Gollancz (London, England), 1993.

"THE BLAINES" TRILOGY

The Second Midnight, Dodd (New York, NY), 1987.
Blacklist, Collins (London, England), 1988.
Toyshop, Collins (London, England), 1990.

"LYDMOUTH" SERIES

An Air that Kills, Hodder and Stoughton (London, England), 1994, St. Martin's (New York, NY), 1995.

The Mortal Sickness, Hodder and Stoughton (London, England), 1995, St. Martin's (New York, NY), 1996.

The Lover of the Grave, St. Martin's (New York, NY), 1997.

The Suffocating Night, Hodder and Stoughton (London, England), 1998.

Where Roses Fade, Hodder and Stoughton (London, England), 2000.

Death's Own Door, Hodder and Stoughton (London, England), 2001.

Call the Dying, Hodder and Stoughton (London, England), 2004.

"ROTH" TRILOGY

The Four Last Things, St. Martin's (New York, NY), 1997.

The Judgment of Strangers, St. Martin's (New York, NY), 1998.

The Office of the Dead, St. Martin's (New York, NY), 2000.

"BERGERAC" SERIES; UNDER PSEUDONYM ANDREW SAVILLE

Bergerac, Panther (London, England), 1985.

Bergerac Is Back!, Severn House (London, England), 1985.

Bergerac and the Fatal Weakness, Severn House (London, England), 1988.

Bergerac and the Jersey Rose, Penguin (London, England), 1988.

Bergerac and the Moving Fever, Penguin (London, England), 1988.

Bergerac and the Traitor's Child, Severn House (London, England), 1989.

CRIME AND THRILLER NOVELS

(Under name John Robert Taylor) *Hairline Cracks* (young adult), Dutton/Lodestar (New York, NY), 1988.

(Under name John Robert Taylor) *The Private Nose* (juvenile), Walker (London, England), 1989, Candlewick (New York, NY), 1993.

Snapshot (young adult), Collins (London, England), 1989.

Double Exposure (young adult), Collins (London, England), 1990.

The Raven on the Water, HarperCollins (New York, NY), 1991.

Negative Image (young adult), HarperCollins (New York, NY), 1992.

The Barred Window, Sinclair Stevenson (London, England), 1993.

The Invader (young adult), HarperCollins (New York, NY), 1994.

The American Boy, Flamingo (London, England), 2003, published as *An Unpardonable Crime,* Theia (New York, NY), 2004.

ADAPTATIONS: Caroline Minuscule was adapted for radio by the British Broadcasting Corp.

SIDELIGHTS: Andrew Taylor has written mysteries, espionage thrillers, and young adult novels. His best-known works are the novel, *Caroline Minuscule,* and the "Roth Trilogy," in which Taylor tells his story in reverse order, beginning with the present day and moving backwards in time to the 1950s.

Taylor's first novel, *Caroline Minuscule,* tells the story of university graduate student William Dougal, who decides not to report a murder in order that he may profit from it. Although a crime story, the novel is also a portrait of a young man unexpectedly drawn into an amoral way of dealing with the world. "Much of the appeal," noted a writer in the *St. James Guide to Crime and Mystery Writers,* "lies in the way that our everyday world so swiftly comes to seem so bizarre and richly comic. . . . Taylor's quick intelligent eye notes the comic oddities of a society from which William and [his girlfriend] Amanda become more and more detached until they are mere visitors, sharks drifting past." Dougal has gone on to appear in a number of other Taylor novels.

In the "Roth Trilogy," which consists of *The Four Last Things, The Judgment of Strangers,* and *The Office of the Dead,* Taylor begins his story with the 1995 kidnapping of a young girl, then traces his characters back in time to discover the reasons behind the crime. In *The Four Last Things,* Sally and Michael Appleyard's four-year-old daughter, Lucy, is kidnapped by a female serial killer. Told through shifting points of view, the story follows the desperate efforts of the police to track down the criminals. The story continues in *The Judgment of Strangers,* which is set some twenty-five years earlier. It traces Appleyard's childhood visit to his godfather, the vicar of a suburb of London, and the morbid consequences of that visit. *The Office of the Dead,* set in the late 1950s, ties the criminal events of the present to those of the distant past. A *Kirkus Reviews* critic dubbed the "Roth Trilogy," "an uncommonly rich tour de force."

An Unpardonable Crime, which was originally published in England as *The American Boy,* is set in London of 1819, a particularly squalid period and an especially seedy section of the city. The book also has a distinct connection to the literary legend of Edgar Allan Poe. In the novel, Thomas Shield is a former soldier who has turned to teaching to make his living. His position teaching Latin to groups of bored schoolboys is unsatisfying and stultifying. One of Shield's students, an American named Edgar Allan (not yet Poe), befriends one of the bullies' favorite targets, Charlie Frant, the son of a banker. As the story progresses, Shield becomes reluctantly involved in Charlie's turbulent home life. However, other elements of the Frant household are more attractive, including Charlie's mother, Sophie, and cousin Flora. When Charlie's father is brutally murdered, he becomes even more involved in the family's affairs after being called upon to identify the body. Shield has to contend, too, with the appearance of Edgar's father, David, an actor and a menacing and unpredictable presence. With Henry Frant dead, it seems that Shield has no obstacles to his courting of the beautiful Sophie, but he has strong suspicions that the body that was supposed to be Frant's was, in fact, someone else's.

The novel stands as a "carefully constructed Gothic mystery, whose layered intrigues encompass inheritance, romance, treason, incest, and fraud," noted Michael Carlson in the *Spectator.* Taylor "knits his considerable skills as a crime writer and as a master of historical detail into a smooth, agreeably complex solution of two mysteries in the life of the real-life Poe," noted a *Kirkus Reviews* contributor, these being the early disappearance his actor father and Poe's own disappearance years later. Taylor "does an excellent job in portraying early 19th-century London and writes in a clear, consistent period style," commented a reviewer in *Publishers Weekly.* "Despite the shopworn elements, Taylor constructs an entertaining, sometimes enchanting, world," stated *People* reviewer Ron Givens. Carlson concluded that the novel "should

satisfy those drawn to the fictions of the 19th century, or Poe, or indeed to crime writing at its most creative."

Taylor once told *CA:* "The urge to write fiction is mysterious, but you ignore it at your peril. For most of my twenties I was one of those writers who managed to avoid actually writing anything. One lunchtime on a grey February in 1980, I realized that a lifetime of undemanding and unsatisfying jobs stretched before me: if I didn't start writing now, I never would. Then and there, I pushed aside the sandwich crumbs and scribbled the first few pages of what eventually became *Caroline Minuscule.* Long before I'd finished the first draft, I knew I was hooked. Before the book had been accepted by a publisher, I left my safe, sensible job and became precariously self-employed.

"I chose to write a crime novel because I knew and liked the genre. Although my work has broadened out—I have written adventure thrillers, psychological novels and espionage, as well as mysteries—crime remains a constant ingredient. Patricia Highsmith remarked in her *Plotting and Writing Suspense Fiction* that a wise author knows what makes his or her creative juices flow. For me, crime in fiction offers a way of revealing and examining both character and society: under stress we show ourselves as we really are. I am fascinated, too, by the long shadows cast by events in the past, and by the way in which family life acts on personality as an emotional hothouse, forcing strange growths.

"Since 1981 I have been fortunate enough to make my living as a writer. In that time I have written over twenty books, including some for children. I see myself primarily as a storyteller whose medium happens to be the written word. My novels sell in English and in translation. Writing fiction is hard work and still financially precarious; it's both a business and a vocation; and I would not happily do anything else. In writing fiction there are no rules, only precedents you may or may not follow. When I talk to writers' classes, I can give only one piece of advice with absolute confidence. And that is: write."

BIOGRAPHICAL AND CRITICAL SOURCES:

BOOKS

St. James Guide to Crime and Mystery Writers, 4th edition, St. James Press (Detroit, MI), 1996.

PERIODICALS

Booklist, January 1, 2004, Connie Fletcher, review of *An Unpardonable Crime,* p. 835; July, 2004, Candace Smith, review of *An Unpardonable Crime,* p. 1856.

Bookseller, December 5, 2003, "Andrew Taylor," p. 29.

Kirkus Reviews, July 15, 1997, review of *The Lover of the Grave,* p. 1072; November 1, 1997, review of *The Four Last Things,* p. 1610; September 15, 1998, review of *The Judgment of Strangers,* p. 1336; June 15, 2000, review of *The Office of the Dead,* p. 839; December 15, 2003, review of *An Unpardonable Crime,* p. 1421.

Library Journal, November 1, 1998, Rex E. Klett, review of *The Judgment of Strangers,* p. 128; January, 2004, Laurel Bliss, review of *An Unpardonable Crime,* p. 166.

M2 Best Books, October 27, 2003, "Andrew Taylor Wins Ellis Peters Dagger for Second Time"; January 5, 2004, "Crime Writer Signs to Penguin."

New York Times Book Review, July 21, 1996, Marilyn Stasio, review of *The Mortal Sickness,* p. 25; August 10, 1997, review of *The Lover of the Grave,* p. 18; December 28, 1997, Marilyn Stasio, review of *The Four Last Things,* p. 18.

People, April 19, 2004, Ron Givens, review of *An Unpardonable Crime,* p. 50.

Publishers Weekly, June 3, 1996, review of *The Mortal Sickness,* p. 66; November 10, 1997, review of *The Four Last Things,* p. 59; August 24, 1998, review of *The Judgment of Strangers,* p. 52; November 10, 2003, review of *An Unpardonable Crime,* p. 39.

Spectator, May 6, 1995, review of *An Air that Kills,* p. 45; December 16, 1995, review of *The Mortal Sickness,* p. 76; August 2, 2003, Michael Carlson, "The Haunting Presence of Poe," review of *The American Boy,* p. 31; October 23, 2004, Harriet Waugh, review of *Call the Dying,* p. 58.

Times Literary Supplement, January 29, 1993, review of *The Barred Window,* p. 20; July 31, 1998, review of *The Judgment of Strangers,* p. 20; February 4, 2000, review of *The Office of the Dead,* p. 22.

ONLINE

Andrew Taylor's Home Page, http://www.lydmouth.demon.co.uk (October 14, 2005).

TAYLOR, Andrew John Robert
    See TAYLOR, Andrew

*   *   *

TAYLOR, John Robert
    See TAYLOR, Andrew

*   *   *

TEAGUE, Mark 1963-
    (Mark Christopher Teague)

PERSONAL: Born February 10, 1963, in La Mesa, CA; son of John Wesley (an insurance agent) and Joan (Clay) Teague; married Laura Quinlan (an insurance claims examiner), June 18, 1988; children: Lily, Ava. *Education:* University of California, Santa Cruz, B.A., 1985. *Politics:* Democrat. *Religion:* Christian.

ADDRESSES: Home—Coxsackie, NY. *Agent*—c/o Author Mail, Scholastic Trade Division, 557 Broadway, New York, NY 10012.

CAREER: Illustrator and writer. Freelance illustrator and writer, 1989—. Worked at Barnes & Noble, New York, NY.

MEMBER: Authors Guild, Authors League of America.

AWARDS, HONORS: Christopher Award, 2000, for *How Do Dinosaurs Say Good Night?,* and in books for young people category, 2003, for *Dear Mrs. LaRue: Letters from Obedience School.*

WRITINGS:

FOR CHILDREN; SELF-ILLUSTRATED

The Trouble with the Johnsons, Scholastic (New York, NY), 1989.

Moog-Moog, Space Barber, Scholastic (New York, NY), 1990.

Frog Medicine, Scholastic (New York, NY), 1991.

The Field Beyond the Outfield, Scholastic (New York, NY), 1992.

Pigsty, Scholastic (New York, NY), 1994.

How I Spent My Summer Vacation, Crown Publishers (New York, NY), 1995.

The Secret Shortcut, Scholastic (New York, NY), 1996.

Baby Tamer, Scholastic (New York, NY), 1997.

The Lost and Found, Scholastic (New York, NY), 1998.

One Halloween Night, Scholastic (New York, NY), 1999.

Dear Mrs. LaRue: Letters from Obedience School, Scholastic (New York, NY), 2002.

Detective LaRue: Letters from the Investigation, Scholastic (New York, NY), 2004.

FOR CHILDREN; ILLUSTRATOR

What Are Scientists, What Do They Do?, Scholastic (New York, NY), 1991.

Adventures in Lego Land, Scholastic (New York, NY), 1991.

Chris Babcock, *No Moon, No Milk!* Crown (New York, NY), 1993.

Dick King-Smith, *Three Terrible Trins,* Crown (New York, NY), 1994.

Tony Johnston, *The Iguana Brothers, a Tale of Two Lizards,* Blue Sky Press (New York, NY), 1995.

Dick King-Smith, *Mr. Potter's Pet,* Hyperion (New York, NY), 1996.

Audrey Wood, *The Flying Dragon Room,* Blue Sky Press (New York, NY), 1996.

Audrey Wood, *Sweet Dream Pie,* Blue Sky Press (New York, NY), 1998.

Cynthia Rylant, *The Great Gracie Chase,* Blue Sky Press (New York, NY), 2001.

Anne Isaacs, *Toby Littlewood,* Scholastic (New York, NY), 2006.

"POPPLETON" SERIES, ILLUSTRATED BY TEAGUE

Cynthia Rylant, *Poppleton,* Blue Sky Press (New York, NY), 1997.

Cynthia Rylant, *Poppleton and Friends,* Blue Sky Press (New York, NY), 1997.

Cynthia Rylant, *Poppleton Forever,* Blue Sky Press (New York, NY), 1998.

Cynthia Rylant, *Poppleton Everyday,* Blue Sky Press (New York, NY), 1998.

Cynthia Rylant, *Poppleton in Fall,* Blue Sky Press (New York, NY), 1999.

Cynthia Rylant, *Poppleton in Spring,* Scholastic (New York, NY), 1999.

Cynthia Rylant, *Poppleton Has Fun,* Blue Sky Press (New York, NY), 2000.

Cynthia Rylant, *Poppleton in Winter,* Blue Sky Press (New York, NY), 2001.

"FIRST GRADERS FROM MARS" SERIES, SELF-ILLUSTRATED

Shana Corey, *First Graders from Mars. Episode 1, Horus's Horrible Day,* Scholastic (New York, NY), 2001.

Shana Corey, *First Graders from Mars. Episode 2, The Problem with Pelly,* Scholastic (New York, NY), 2002.

Shana Corey, *First Graders from Mars. Episode 3, Nergal and the Great Space Race,* Scholastic (New York, NY), 2002.

Shana Corey, *First Graders from Mars. Episode 4, Tera, Star Student,* Scholastic (New York, NY), 2003.

"DINOSAURS" SERIES, SELF-ILLUSTRATED

Jane Yolen, *How Do Dinosaurs Say Goodnight?,* Scholastic (New York, NY), 2000.

Jane Yolen, *How Do Dinosaurs Get Well Soon?,* Blue Sky Press (New York, NY), 2003.

Jane Yolen, *How Do Dinosaurs Clean Their Rooms?,* Blue Sky Press (New York, NY), 2004.

Jane Yolen, *How Do Dinosaurs Count to Ten?,* Blue Sky Press (New York, NY), 2004.

Jane Yolen, *How Do Dinosaurs Eat Their Food?,* Blue Sky Press (New York, NY), 2005.

SIDELIGHTS: An illustrator of children's books, Mark Teague has also written a number of his own books for which he has provided illustrations. In all his work, Teague displays an unusual sense of humor, reflected in his pictures, the names of his characters, and in the topics of his books.

Teague's first three books share a common character, a young boy named Elmo Freem. In *The Trouble with the Johnsons,* Elmo has moved with his family from the country to a large metropolis. Elmo and his cat decide to return to their old home, but discover a dinosaur family is living there. The second book, *Moog-Moog, Space Barber,* finds Elmo dealing with aliens and, even worse, a dreadful haircut just as school is starting. In the last, *Frog Medicine,* Elmo becomes so stressed over a book report that he grows the feet of a frog. A reviewer in *Publishers Weekly* noted of *Frog Medicine:* "Teague again demonstrates his knack for dealing with the kinds of predicaments that loom large on children's horizons in a fresh and funny way."

Teague continued to feature children and animal characters in *Pigsty.* The story focuses on young Wendell Fultz, who has been forced to clean his messy room by his mother. As he goes to his room, he finds a pig on his bed. Over time, more pigs show up. Wendell plays with them, but comes to realize that his room might really need to be cleaned. A reviewer in *Publishers Weekly* found the book "fun," and commenting positively on "his idiosyncratic brand of sly humor."

Two of Teague's children's books are mysteries featuring Ike, a dog who writes letters to his owner, Mrs. LaRue, about his experiences. Ike is not always truthful in his notes, providing a humorous challenge for young readers as they compare what Ike says with Teague's more accurate pictures. Teague uses color illustrations to depict the reality of the situation, while black-and-white pictures display what Ike believes is real. In *Dear Mrs. LaRue: Letters from Obedience School,* Ike has been left at an obedience school, Igor Brotweiler Canine Academy, that he believes is exactly like jail. Through his letters, Ike addresses what got him sent to obedience school in the first place and complains about his current situation. Ike escapes the school, but emerges as a hero when he saves Mrs. LaRue's life. Ilene Cooper of *Booklist* felt that "the wonderfully arch text is matched with Teague's sly pictures."

In *Detective LaRue: Letters from the Investigation,* two cats have managed to break out of a neighborhood apartment and Ike is the prime suspect in their disappearance. He tells his spa-visiting owner that he has been put in jail himself, but escapes to look for the cats, who seem to be on a bird-attacking rampage. The wronged dog becomes a detective himself to prove his innocence. Ike emerges as the hero when he finds the cats and brings them home. Steven Engelfried of

the *School Library Journal* noted: "The contrast between the melodrama of Ike's imagined world and the comfort of his true experiences should elicit many smiles." Summarizing the book's appeal, a critic in *Kirkus Reviews* commented: "Teague's innovative approach to storytelling is fun, but educational as well, skillfully imparting some valuable lessons in . . . reading between the lines."

Among the works by other authors for which Teague has provided illustration is the "First Graders from Mars" series by Shana Corey. For Corey's humorous take on some young students on another planet, Teague created vivid pictures of Martian students like Tera and the alien teacher, Ms. Vortext, who has many eyes. Reviewing *First Graders from Mars: Episode 4: Tera, Star Student,* Lauralyn Persson of the *School Library Journal* wrote: "Teague's bright pictures are perfect, adding all sorts of wonderfully zany touches." Teague also illustrated Jane Yolen's "Dinosaur" series. Each book chronicles the experiences of human parents with dinosaur children. Noting that Teague "wrings every last drop of comedy" from the premise, a critic for *Publishers Weekly* concluded that "Teague's droll artwork heightens the humor of Yolen's verse."

Teague once commented: "I managed to graduate from college without having any idea what I was going to do with my life. My degree was in U.S. history but I wasn't interested in teaching. I enjoyed art but had no formal training. I liked to write but was unsure how to make it pay. So I took a job as a waiter in San Diego and when I couldn't stand it any longer I loaded up my 1969 Dodge and headed East. A few months later, in the spring of 1986, I was in New York with my brother John, who helped me get a job at Barnes & Noble in Manhattan. I worked in the display department, making signs and window displays for the Rockefeller Center bookstore. The job provided a sort of crash course in design and graphic arts techniques and exposed me to a lot of new books. Looking at children's books in the store reminded me of how much I had enjoyed picture books as a child and how much fun it had been to write and illustrate my own stories at that age.

"*The Trouble with the Johnsons,* about a boy who wishes to return to his home in the country after moving to the city, came out of my experience living in Brooklyn. The theme was somewhat melancholy, but I tried to offset this with humor and a plot which was energetic and bizarre.

"Scholastic accepted the book in 1988. That same year my wife, Laura, and I were married and moved upstate. My next project, *Moog-Moog, Space Barber,* was in some ways a sequel to the first, though both the characters and my illustration style had changed somewhat. The book was not inspired by any particular event. It found its drama in the apparently universal horror inspired by a bad haircut. The book contains a touch of science fiction and fantasy too—with a taste of upstate New York in the illustrations.

"*Frog Medicine* is the last book with these characters. It involves that dreaded subject: homework—as well as giant frogs, and things of that sort."

BIOGRAPHICAL AND CRITICAL SOURCES:

PERIODICALS

Booklist, November 1, 2002, Ilene Cooper, review of *Dear Mrs. LaRue: Letters from Obedience School,* p. 494.
Kirkus Reviews, August 15, 2004, review of *Detective LaRue: Letters from the Investigation,* p. 814.
Publishers Weekly, October 4, 1991, review of *Frog Medicine,* p. 88; July 11, 1994, review of *Pigsty,* p. 78; December 23, 2002, review of *How Do Dinosaurs Get Well Soon?,* p. 68.
School Library Journal, August, 2003, Lauralyn Persson, review of *First Graders from Mars: Episode 4: Tera, Star Student,* p. 124; October, 2004, Steven Engelfried, review of *Detective LaRue: Letters from the Investigation,* p. 135.

ONLINE

Scholastic Web site, http://www.scholastic.com/ (October 10, 2005), biography of Mark Teague.

*   *   *

TEAGUE, Mark Christopher
See TEAGUE, Mark

*   *   *

THAYLER, Carl 1933-

PERSONAL: Born April 29, 1933, in Los Angeles, CA; son of Ben and Jean (Rosensweig) Thayler; married Marcia Ann Katz, March 28, 1964 (divorced); children: Emily Margaret. *Education:* Attended Los Angeles City College; Kenyon College, B.A., 1968; University of Wisconsin, graduate study, 1968-72; also attended Bowling Green State University's writing program.

CAREER: Writer. During the early 1950s, actor for the Folksay Theater troupe; actor in films, including *The True Story of Jesse James.* Has participated in Wisconsin Poetry-in-the-Schools program. *Military service:* Served in the U.S. Navy.

WRITINGS:

The Drivers (poems), Perishable Press (Mount Horeb, WI), 1969.
Some Ground (poems), Modine Gunch Press, 1970.
The Mariposa Suite (poems), Tetrad (London, England), 1971.
The Providings: Poems, 1963-1971, Sumac Press (Fremont, MI), 1971.
Goodrich and the Haggard Ode and the Disfiguration (poems), Capricorn Press (Santa Barbara, CA), 1972.
The Drivers, Second Series (poems), Bloody Twin Press (Stout, OH), 1988.
Poems from Naltsus Bichidin, Skanky Possum Press (Austin, TX), 1999.
The Tailgunner's Song (poetry chapbook), Skanky Possum Press (Austin, TX), 2000.
Shake Hands (poems), Pavement Saw Press (Columbus, OH), 2001.

Also author of a play, "Graill."

WORK IN PROGRESS: Poetry collection titled *3 Lives Country.*

SIDELIGHTS: Poet Carl Thayler claims that even as a preverbal child he knew the power of language. "I navigated by language through the seclusion that silence imposed upon me," he recalled in the *Contemporary Authors Autobiography Series* (*CAAS*). "It lessened the gloom of nap time. I listened to older children on the stairs, and still older ones in the schoolyard across the street, and to Mother and the neighbor girl discussing whether or not to sin and eat chocolate. I understood the arrangements each made, and why. I understood firm decisions and feeble songs. I felt like a spy and liked the feeling. Language was a big deal, and mine."

During his high school years, Thayler fought with other students, did his best to "evade an education," and read the works of Henry Miller, Kenneth Rexroth, and Kenneth Patchen. Thayler wrote in *CAAS* that upon discovering the work of poet William Carlos Williams, "I decided I'd been a poet all along. . . . But my immediate desire was to race cars." He pursued that ambition, did odd jobs, and eventually began working in the film industry while also sporadically writing. "Language was as obstinate as a cowlick, as unmanageable as a libido," he said of his early efforts to master his craft.

After decades of eking out a living and occasionally publishing a volume of poetry, Thayler said in *CAAS:* "It's fitting for me to be writing in a rented room with my belongings, mostly manuscripts and books, in boxes. In two days I'll move across the hall. It will be cooler there. I like those manuscripts, the stories and the poetry, they read OK to me. Publishers don't care for them, although they claim to admire the writing. They claim also to be puzzled, and they ask why I'm 'perverse.' They talk about an admixture of 'realism' and 'surrealism.' Whatever they mean, there's no room in their theology for my brand of hermeticism. Well, far be it for me to discourage perversity."

BIOGRAPHICAL AND CRITICAL SOURCES:

BOOKS

Contemporary Authors Autobiography Series, Volume 11, Gale (Detroit, MI), 1990.

ONLINE

Carl Thayler Home Page, http://www.possibilityx. com/ct/lobby.htm (December 27, 2002).*

*   *   *

TOMPKINS, Ptolemy 1962(?)-
(Ptolemy Christian Tompkins)

PERSONAL: Born c. 1962, in Washington, DC; son of Peter (a journalist, editor, and writer) and Jerree Lee Talbot (Smith) Tompkins. *Education:* Attended Vassar College, early 1980s.

ADDRESSES: Agent—c/o Author Mail, HarperCollins Publishers, 10 E. 53rd St., New York, NY 10022.

CAREER: Writer and illustrator.

WRITINGS:

NONFICTION

This Tree Grows Out of Hell: Mesoamerica and the Search for the Magical Body, HarperCollins (San Francisco, CA), 1990.
Color the Ancient Forest (juvenile), Living Planet Press (Venice, CA), 1991.
(Editor) Patrick Bowe, *Gardens in Central Europe,* photographs by Nicolas Sapieha, Scala Books (New York, NY), 1991.
The Monkey in Art, Sotheby's Books (New York, NY), 1994.
(With Nicolas Sapieha) *A Dog Lover's Collection,* Scala Books (New York, NY), 1995.
Paradise Fever: Growing Up in the Shadow of the New Age (autobiography), Avon (New York, NY), 1997.
The Beaten Path: Field Notes on Getting Wise in a Wisdom-crazy World, HarperCollins (New York, NY), 2001.

Tompkins's works have been translated into Spanish.

ILLUSTRATOR; JUVENILE NONFICTION

Big Cats, Little Cats, Living Planet Press (Venice, CA), 1991.
Bartleby Nash, *Mother Nature's Greatest Hits: The Top 40 Wonders of the Animal World,* Living Planet Press (Venice, CA), 1991.

SIDELIGHTS: Ptolemy Tompkins has written and illustrated a variety of nonfiction works about the natural world of plants and animals, and he has illustrated a number of titles for young audiences as well. He wrote the book *Color the Ancient Forest* for the Wilderness Society, and illustrated the World Wildlife Fund's *Mother Nature's Greatest Hits: The Top 40 Wonders of the Animal World* by Bartleby Nash.

Tompkins's autobiography, *Paradise Fever: Growing Up in the Shadow of the New Age,* traces his life as the son of guru Peter Tompkins, author of the cult best-seller, *The Secret Life of Plants* and other works. A *Kirkus Reviews* critic observed that *Paradise Fever* "is best in its details, from a young person's perspective, of the brave new world Tompkins, Sr., tried to create." This "new world" included Peter Tompkins's communal living with a wide variety of people and his extramarital affairs, including a mistress who remained a permanent fixture in the household. In an effort to deal with the lifestyle his father created, Ptolemy Tompkins turned to alcohol and other drugs. Reviewing *Paradise Fever,* a *Publishers Weekly* critic noted that "Tompkins's writing is vivid throughout, but particularly so in describing daily life caught in the viselike grip of addiction."

In *Paradise Fever* Tompkins recalls: "From the very beginning, my father's books dealt with secrets of one sort or another—with things hidden, ignored, unspoken, or outright denied by the world at large." The culmination, Tompkins revealed, came "in 1973—after several years of especially intensive research" when "my father and his friend Christopher Bird finished writing *The Secret Life of Plants,* a book which made the claim that plants were conscious beings capable of communicating with humans. Plants were such spiritually evolved organisms, my father argued, that if we listened to them attentively they could teach us how to live more happily and harmoniously on earth—so harmoniously that our frayed and tired planet could be transformed into a new Eden."

Tompkins also explains in his autobiography that "by the mid-1970s, my father had become a kind of walking, talking, concatenation of his revelation-hungry way of thinking, as well as the experimental lifestyle that tended to go along with it." He reminisces: "Bearded, bald, and with a perpetually intense and preoccupied expression on his face (as a child I suspected that he must have lost his hair from thinking too much), my father was in appearance and in character perfectly suited for his role as unveiler of the dawning age. With little in the way of conscious calculation," Tompkins continues, "he became the definitive model of the Fringe Investigator: the mysteriously authoritative figure with whitening beard, khaki bush jacket, and unfazably open mind who was forever lurking on the outer edges of accepted science and conventional thinking." He concludes of his father:

"From Peter Tompkins, you could always count on learning that the impossible wasn't really impossible."

Tompkins did not foreswear the religious and metaphysical elements he had been exposed to, and his life still contained a search for knowledge. In *The Beaten Path: Field Notes on Getting Wise in a Wisdom-crazy World* Tompkins describes his search for wisdom through popular books, religious experience, and various forms of physical and spiritual exploration. A student at Vassar in the early 1980s, Tompkins dropped out of school to pursue his spiritual course. He traveled to various places around the world, including Colombia and the American West, all with his family's approval. Tompkins explains how he looked to famed spiritual works such as the *Tao Te Ching* and the *Bhagavad-Ghita;* how he delved into the writings of mystics and teachers such as Carlos Castaneda, Aldous Huxley, and Alan Watts; and how the experience of Buddhism was not the mind-expanding experience he expected it to be.

Tompkins found, to his dismay, that many of the gurus he had known and followed were actually shallow and, in some cases, fraudulent, and that their teachings were not guaranteed roadmaps to wisdom. He describes his mounting frustration at remaining "unenlightened" and relates the conclusion he ultimately reaches: acquiring wisdom is a process, not an end result. Writing in *Booklist* reviewer Donna Seaman called the book a "charmingly offhanded and refreshingly critical memoir," while a *Publishers Weekly* reviewer described it as "witty" and "provocative."

BIOGRAPHICAL AND CRITICAL SOURCES:

BOOKS

Tompkins, Ptolemy, *Paradise Fever: Growing Up in the Shadow of the New Age,* Avon (New York, NY), 1997.

PERIODICALS

Booklist, August, 2001, Donna Seaman, review of *The Beaten Path: Field Notes on Getting Wise in a Wisdom-crazy World,* p. 2058.

Entertainment Weekly, October 24, 1997, Margot Mifflin, review of *Paradise Fever,* p. 60.

Kirkus Reviews, September 15, 1997, review of *Paradise Fever;* June 1, 2001, review of *The Beaten Path,* p. 792.

Publishers Weekly, October 6, 1997, review of *Paradise Fever,* p. 66; August 6, 2001, review of *The Beaten Path,* p. 81.*

*   *   *

TOMPKINS, Ptolemy Christian
See TOMPKINS, Ptolemy

*   *   *

TOWNLEY, Rod
See TOWNLEY, Roderick

*   *   *

TOWNLEY, Roderick 1942-
(Rod Townley)

PERSONAL: Born June 7, 1942, in Orange, NJ; son of William Richard (a businessman) and Elise (Fredman) Townley; married Libby Blackman, April 4, 1970 (divorced, 1980); married Wyatt Baker (a poet and yoga instructor), February 15, 1986; children: (first marriage) Jesse Blackman; (second marriage) Grace Whitman. *Education:* Attended Hamilton College, 1960-61, and University of Chicago, 1961-62; Bard College, A.B., 1965; Rutgers University, M.A., 1970, Ph.D., 1972.

ADDRESSES: Home—Kansas City, MO. *Agent*—c/o Writers House, 21 W. 26th St., New York, NY 10010. *E-mail*—rodericktownley@everestkc.net.

CAREER: Writer. Passaic County Community College, Paterson, NJ, associate professor of world literature, 1972-73; *TV Guide,* New York, NY, former editorial writer, beginning 1980. Visiting professor, University of Concepcion, Chile, 1978-79.

AWARDS, HONORS: Fulbright fellowship, 1978-79.

WRITINGS:

Safe and Sound: A Parent's Guide to Child Protection, Simon & Schuster (New York, NY), 1985.

Final Approach (poetry), Countryman Press (Woodstock, VT), 1986.

(Translator) Rene Escudie, *Paul and Sebastian* (for children), Kane/Miller Books (La Jolla, CA), 1988.

(Editor) *Night Errands: How Poets Use Dreams,* University of Pittsburgh Press (Pittsburgh, PA), 1998.

The Great Good Thing (novel; for young readers), Atheneum Books for Young Readers (New York, NY), 2001.

Into the Labyrinth (sequel to *The Great Good Thing;* novel; for young readers), Atheneum Books for Young Readers (New York, NY), 2002.

Sky: A Novel in Three Sets and an Encore, Atheneum Books for Young Readers (New York, NY), 2004.

The Constellation of Sylvie (novel), Atheneum Books for Young Readers (New York, NY), 2005.

Contributor to periodicals, including *Studies in Short Fiction, Philadelphia, New York Times, Washington Post, Village Voice,* and the *Detroit Free Press.*

UNDER NAME ROD TOWNLEY

Blue Angels Black Angels (poetry), privately printed, 1972.

The Early Poetry of William Carlos Williams (criticism), Cornell University Press (Ithaca, NY), 1975.

Summer Street (chapbook), The Smith (New York, NY), 1975.

Minor Gods (novel), St. Martin's Press (New York, NY), 1976.

Three Musicians (poetry), The Smith (New York, NY), 1978.

The Year in Soaps: 1983, Crown (New York, NY), 1984.

Contributor to books, including *University and College Poetry Prizes: 1967-1972,* edited by Daniel Hoffman, Academy of American Poets (New York, NY), 1974; *Eleven Young Poets: The Smith Seventeen,* edited by Ray Boxer, The Smith (New York, NY), 1975; *William Carlos Williams: Man and Poet,* edited by Carroll F. Terrell, National Poetry Foundation

(Orono, ME), 1983; *Conversations with Ralph Ellison,* edited by Maryemma Graham and Amritjit Singh, University Press of Mississippi (Jackson, MS), 1995; and *Ravishing Disunities,* edited by Agha Shahid Ali, Wesleyan University Press (Hanover, NH), 2000.

SIDELIGHTS: Roderick Townley has published several books of poetry as well as works of literary criticism, including books on poet William Carlos Williams, but among his better known works are several novels for younger readers. *The Great Good Thing,* for one, follows Princess Sylvie and her numerous friends as they reenact their story each time the book is read. Princess Sylvie and her comrades exist within the pages of an old, almost forgotten book, *The Great Good Thing.* In it, Sylvie yearns to do "one great good thing" before she submits to marriage, and the story follows her swashbuckling adventures in pursuit of that thing, whatever it may be. When young Claire reads the book, the same copy that her grandmother had also read and loved, the characters return to life, acting out each part of the story anew. The book is destroyed by Claire's vile brother, however, and with nowhere else to go the characters cross into Claire's mind, where they live in her dreams. The sheer passage of time threatens them because Claire may forget them and their story completely. Sylvie rescues herself and her friends when she crosses into the mind of Lily, Claire's daughter, and Lily is inspired to retell and republish the story, giving the storybook characters a renewed life. *School Library Journal* reviewer Debbie Whitbeck commented that Townley's approach is "an extremely clever and multilayered concept," but questioned whether younger readers will be able to grasp its multiple levels. A *Publishers Weekly* reviewer called it a "clever, deftly written" novel for younger readers.

Into the Labyrinth finds Princess Sylvie and her cohorts busily reenacting their story in the wake of a fresh printing, as Sylvie continues searching for her "one great good thing" to do before marriage. When their story is published on the Internet, however, the pace becomes exhausting. The story must be reenacted again and again as new readers come to the tale. Not only must the characters get used to a frenzied pace, they also have to come to terms with new threats and phenomena unique to the online world, including wordpools, unexpected changes to their stories, the loss of sections of the text, and deliberate changes by readers with access to electronic versions of the story.

When a dragonlike "bot" appears, created by a descendent of the original author, it seems its mission is simply to destroy the story, ripping out chunks of text and bringing in characters from other stories. However, Princess Sylvie and her friends are not going to passively sit by and be destroyed, and they mount an expedition to confront and delete the dangerous electronic dragon-bot. A *Kirkus Reviews* critic called the book a "brilliantly imagined sequel" to *The Great Good Thing.* that explores concepts of how stories happen and how fiction affects readers. *Booklist* contributor John Peters called the novel a "grand, tongue-in-cheek adventure." Beth L. Meister, writing in the *School Library Journal,* commented: "Sylvie is an appealing, thoughtful, and involving heroine, pulling the fast-paced plot to its satisfying conclusion."

Sky: A Novel in Three Sets and an Encore centers on fifteen-year-old jazz pianist Alex "Sky" Schuyler. Though his private-school classmates think little of him, Sky is a driving force in his jazz band, consisting of drummer Max, bass player Larry, and manager Suze. Along with his jazz, Sky also has an eye for Suze. Unfortunately for Sky, his conservative, workaday father sees jazz music as a waste of time and wants Sky to quit his band for something more practical. As punishment for sneaking out to a Count Basie concert, Sky's father takes away his piano, which had belonged to his mother. Pushed beyond endurance, Sky runs away to make a life on the street. When he meets Art Olmedo, a blind jazz pianist in rapidly declining health, Sky bonds instantly with the weathered musician. Through Olmedo, he learns important lessons about music and about life. The book "brings the beatnik era to life while expressing timeless, universal themes about the generation gap," observed a *Publishers Weekly* reviewer. Paula Rohrlick, writing in *Kliatt,* called the novel an "appealing coming-of-age tale about finding yourself and finding your calling."

BIOGRAPHICAL AND CRITICAL SOURCES:

PERIODICALS

Booklist, November 1, 2002, John Peters, review of *Into the Labyrinth,* p. 499.

Guardian (London, England), April 26, 2003, Jan Mark, "The Never-Ending Story," review of *The Great Good Thing.*

Kirkus Reviews, September 15, 2002, review of *Into the Labyrinth,* p. 1402; July 1, 2004, review of *Sky: A Novel in Three Sets and an Encore,* p. 638.

Kliatt, July, 2004, Paula Rohrlick, review of *Sky,* p. 13.

Library Journal, September 1, 1998, Kim Woodbridge, review of *Night Errands: How Poets Use Dreams,* p. 181.

Publishers Weekly, May 21, 2001, review of *The Great Good Thing,* p. 108; August 30, 2004, review of *Sky,* p. 56.

School Library Journal, July, 2001, Debbie Whitbeck, review of *The Great Good Thing,* p. 114; October, 2001, Louise T. Sherman, review of *The Great Good Thing,* p. 89; October, 2002, Beth L. Meister, review of *Into the Labyrinth,* p. 174; July, 2004, Susan Riley, review of *Sky,* p. 113.

ONLINE

Books for Sleepless Nights, http://www.sleephomepage. org/ (November 5, 2005), review of *Night Errands.*

Kidsreads.com, http://www.kidsreads.com/ (November 5, 2005), Lisa Marx, review of *The Great Good Thing.*

*   *   *

TURNER, Tom 1942-

PERSONAL: Born April 2, 1942, in Oakland, CA; son of James Oliver (an engineer) and Elizabeth (Setze) Turner; married Mary Catherine Jorgensen (a professor of French), August 4, 1979; children: Kathryn and Bret (twins). *Education:* University of California—Berkeley, B.A., 1965. *Politics:* "Green."

ADDRESSES: Home—1288 Campus Dr., Berkeley, CA 94708. *Office*—Earthjustice, National Headquarters, 426 17th St., 6th Fl., Oakland, CA 94812-2820; fax: 510-550-6740. *E-mail*—tturner@earthjustice.org.

CAREER: Writer, environmental activist, and editor. U.S. Peace Corps, volunteer near Trabzon, Turkey, 1965-67; Sierra Club, San Francisco, CA, editor and administrative assistant, 1968-69; Friends of the Earth, San Francisco, editor, 1969-86; Sierra Club Legal Defense Fund (now Earthjustice), Oakland, CA, staff writer, 1986—, currently advocate and senior editor.

WRITINGS:

Wild by Law: The Sierra Club Legal Defense Fund and the Places It Has Saved, Sierra Books (San Francisco, CA), 1990.

Sierra Club: One Hundred Years of Protecting Nature, Abrams (New York, NY), 1991.

(With John Sparks, John Goepel and Alison Moore) *The Spirit of the Road: One Hundred Years of the Californian State Automobile Association,* Welcome Enterprises (New York, NY), 2000.

Justice on Earth: Earthjustice and the People It Has Served, Chelsea Green Publishing Company (White River Junction, VT), 2002.

Contributor to books, including *The Encyclopedia of the Environment,* 1994. Contributor to periodicals, including *Wilderness, E, Amicus Journal,* and *Defenders.* Editor of *Not Man Apart,* 1969-86. Columnist, *Sierra.*

SIDELIGHTS: Tom Turner is an environmental activist with a lengthy career working for such organizations as the Sierra Club, Friends of the Earth, and the Sierra Club Legal Defense Fund (now Earthjustice). Earthjustice represents both large and small public interest clients, without charge, and uses litigation and other legal means to safeguard public lands, conserve endangered species and wildlife habitat, and reduce air and water pollution. His job, Turner noted on the *Earthjustice* Web site, is that of "opinionated journalist, describing issues and strategies and techniques that society must understand and adopt if the environment is to be preserved and restored."

A number of Turner's books have focused on the mission and successes of the Sierra Club and Earthjustice. *Wild by Law: The Sierra Club Legal Defense Fund and the Places It Has Saved* provides full-color photographs and detailed descriptions of more than three hundred environmental victories that the Sierra Club's Legal Defense Fund has enjoyed through the years. Turner writes in detail about the conflict between industries that want to use nature for economic gain and environmentalists, who want to preserve nature and spare it from exploitation. Turner provides biographical detail on the participants in the cases, and he identifies organizations that are ostensibly on the side of the environment but which have actually been at odds with environmental preservation. An account of the group's successful attempt to stop Walt Disney's plans to destroy a high-altitude valley in California for a ski resort explains how litigation has become a key weapon in the environmentalist arsenal. The book is a "worthy tribute to environmentalists waging the good fight," commented Genevieve Stuttaford in *Publishers Weekly.*

Sierra Club: One Hundred Years of Protecting Nature is an illustrated history of the most prominent environmental group in the United States. Turner provides a "lively history" of the group and its more than a century's worth of struggle to protect and preserve the environment, noted a *Publishers Weekly* contributor. Reviewer John Garrity, writing in *Sports Illustrated,* called the book an "elegant history," adding that "Turner's text, while free of polemics, clearly embraces the Sierra Club's mission." The *Publishers Weekly* critic labeled the book an "important addition to the environmentalist's library."

Turner's *Justice on Earth: Earthjustice and the People It Has Served* "consists of ten can't-put-down stories in which—by the time you're halfway through—you feel you know the storyteller as if he were your closest neighbor," observed a reviewer in *World Watch.* These ten cases have been litigated successfully by the Earthjustice organization. The stories include that of Waiahole Ditch, an irrigation channel on Oahu that, for years, had been used to unjustly transfer fresh water from native farmers to organized sugar growers and tourism developers. Even after laws were passed to correct the injustice, lawyers for the sugar growers and developers insisted on their rights to the fresh water for use in "diversified agriculture," until it was discovered that their idea of diversified agriculture meant golf courses. With tenacity Earthjustice finally ensured that the water was returned where it belonged. *Library Journal* contributor Noemie Maxwell called the book "readable and aesthetically beautiful."

BIOGRAPHICAL AND CRITICAL SOURCES:

PERIODICALS

Ecologist, May, 2003, review of *Justice on Earth: Earthjustice and the People It Has Served,* p. 60.
Library Journal, November 15, 2002, Noemie Maxwell, review of *Justice on Earth,* p. 87.
Publishers Weekly, August 31, 1990, Genevieve Stuttaford, review of *Wild by Law: The Sierra Club Legal Defense Fund and the Places It Has Saved,* p. 55; September 20, 1991, review of *Sierra Club: One Hundred Years of Protecting Nature,* p. 115.
Sports Illustrated, December 16, 1991, John Garrity, review of *Sierra Club: One Hundred Years of Protecting Nature,* p. 132.
World Watch, March-April, 2003, "Because the Earth Needs a Good Lawyer," review of *Justice on Earth,* p. 26.

ONLINE

Earthjustice Web site, http://www.earthjustice.org/ (November 5, 2005).

* * *

TYSON, Timothy B. 1959-

PERSONAL: Born 1959, in Raleigh, NC; son of Vernon Tyson (a minister) and a teacher; married Perri Morgan; children: Hope, Sam. *Education:* Emory University, B.A., 1987; Duke University, Ph.D., 1994.

ADDRESSES: Office—Department of Afro-American Studies, University of Wisconsin, White Hall, Helen C 4137, 600 North Park St., Madison, WI 53706. *E-mail*—tbtyson@facstaff.wisc.edu.

CAREER: University of Wisconsin—Madison, associate professor of Afro-American Studies.

MEMBER: Organization of American Historians.

AWARDS, HONORS: James R. Rawley Prize and corecipient of Frederick Jackson Turner Award, Organization of American Historians, both 2000, both for *Radio Free Dixie: Robert F. Williams and the Roots of Black Power;* National Book Critics Circle Award nomination, 2004, for *Blood Done Sign My Name: A True Story;* Organization of American Historians Distinguished Lecturer, 2005-06; Outstanding Book Award, Gustavus Myers Center for the Study of Human Rights, for *Democracy Betrayed.*

WRITINGS:

(Editor, with David S. Cecelski) *Democracy Betrayed: The Wilmington Race Riot of 1898 and Its Legacy,* foreword by John Hope Franklin, University of North Carolina Press (Chapel Hill, NC), 1998.

Radio Free Dixie: Robert F. Williams and the Roots of Black Power, University of North Carolina Press (Chapel Hill, NC), 1999.

Blood Done Sign My Name: A True Story, Crown Publishers (New York, NY), 2004.

Contributor to periodicals, including *Southern Cultures.* Editorial advisor for *The Black Power Movement. Part Two, the Papers of Robert F. Williams* (microform), University Publications of America (Bethesda, MD), 2001.

ADAPTATIONS: Blood Done Sign My Name was adapted as an audiobook, Unabridged Books on Tape, 2004.

SIDELIGHTS: Timothy B. Tyson is a scholar of Afro-American studies who has published several books related to the subject. His first work, *Democracy Betrayed: The Wilmington Race Riot of 1898 and Its Legacy,* was edited with David S. Cecelski and contains a collection of articles and essays on the 1898 race riots in Wilmington, North Carolina, and their aftermath. Wilmington served as the Confederacy's major port during the Civil War, and it was the state's largest city at the time of the riots. Government leaders throughout the south did not want to openly exclude and disenfranchise blacks because they wanted to avoid federal enforcement of the Fifteenth Amendment. Prejudice and racial hatred, however, still existed in abundance. Political turmoil was common, and as Democrats faced mounting political losses, they launched a statewide campaign of white supremacy in 1898. As Democrats planned violent takeovers in Wilmington, the party's terrorist arm, the Red Shirts, moved from South Carolina into North Carolina, intimidating blacks and their white supporters.

When black newspaperman Alex Manly reacted to a call by Rebecca Felton in Georgia to "lynch a thousand times a week if necessary" to protect white female virtue, he provoked the wrath of an already belligerent white population. Manly's suggestion that "not every liaison between black men and white women was forced" was considered "vile and slanderous," noted reviewer James W. Loewen in *Southern Cultures.* Democrats demanded that Manly's paper cease publication and that he leave town, but their reaction went far beyond such a demand. More than two thousand whites marched through downtown Wilmington and destroyed the newspaper office, missing Manly, who had already fled. Gunfights erupted, and the rioters moved into black sections of town, looking for targets. The mob forced the city's republican mayor and alderman to resign. "By 1900 Wilmington was majority white," Loewen noted. "In that year, under Aycock's leadership, Democrats disfranchised blacks statewide." The riot showed that Southern Republicans could not stand against determined racist Democrats. Wilmington tried to forget about the riot, but in 1998, the city formed the 1998 Centennial Foundation, which finally publicly addressed Wilmington's racist history and started a process of education and reconciliation for wrongdoings a century old. "Because it shows national trends and social processes with local concreteness, *Democracy Betrayed* will be useful in courses on southern history or U.S. race relations," Loewen stated.

Tyson expanded on his graduate research on the radical civil rights leader Robert F. Williams to write *Radio Free Dixie: Robert F. Williams and the Roots of Black Power.* Williams served in the U.S. Army during World War II, then returned home to Monroe, North Carolina, where he formed a militant chapter of the National Association for the Advancement of Colored People (NAACP). He rejected the nonviolent approach to civil rights advocated by Martin Luther King, Jr., instead calling for blacks to arm themselves in their fight for self determination. In the late 1950s, Williams and his followers confronted Ku Klux Klan vigilantes with machine guns and dynamite. Targeted by the Federal Bureau of Investigation and the Klan, Williams fled to revolutionary Cuba with his family in 1961. There he broadcast his *Radio Free Dixie* through Radio Havana. His music and politics were picked up from as far away as New York City and Los Angeles. He talked about life in the South from the 1940s through the 1960s. *Radio Free Dixie* is the first full-length biography of Williams ever published.

Tyson's study contains quotes by Williams from interviews, radio show tapes, and Williams's unpublished autobiography. A *Publishers Weekly* reviewer averred that "Tyson's firecracker text crackles with brilliant and lasting images. . . . The book is imbued with the man's voice and his indefatigable spirit." *Library Journal* reviewer Charles C. Hay called Tyson's work "groundbreaking, skillfully written," and added, "Tyson resuscitates Williams as an important forefather of Black Power."

The author's next book, *Blood Done Sign My Name: A True Story,* is about a racially motivated murder that occurred in Oxford, North Carolina, in 1970, but it also addresses Tyson's own maturation and the development of his views on race. When he was ten years old, Tyson experienced a traumatic "racial awakening," noted reviewer Fred Hobson in *Southern Cultures.* One May morning, Tyson's friend Gerald Teel declared that his father and brother had killed a black man. Shocked, Tyson found that the story was true. Robert and Roger Teel had indeed shot twenty-three-year-old Vietnam veteran Henry "Dickie" Marrow, for the dubious transgression of making a flirtatious remark to Robert Teel's daughter-in-law. When the woman's husband erupted with rage, the disturbance alerted the Teels, who shot at the fleeing Marrow with shotguns. Infuriated and determined, the men caught up with Marrow, beating and kicking him as he lay helpless on the ground. Without warning, fury gave way to murder when one of the men shot and killed Marrow. The incident sparked racial violence and rioting throughout Oxford. Marches and protests degenerated into mob violence and firebombing, with much property destroyed throughout the city, including two tobacco warehouses with millions of dollars worth of product inside. When the Teels were tried three months later, they were acquitted by an all-white jury.

Tyson and his family also felt the heat of the racial furor. His father, a pastor at the First Methodist Church of Oxford, encouraged racial understanding among the members of his congregation. However, this idea proved to be too radical for most Oxford residents. Vernon Tyson and his family were forced to leave the area when the local bishop transferred Tyson to another church well away from Oxford. The unspoken threat in Tyson's book is that his family, even though they were white, might well have also fallen victim to racial vindictiveness if they had not left when they did. Some thirteen years later, Tyson returned to his old home town as a freshman at the University of North Carolina at Greensboro. He was seeking not only closure to a traumatic episode in his past but also the material for an academic analysis of the events as he began his career as a historian. He researched newspaper reports and police records. He interviewed several participants, including Robert Teel himself, as well as Ben Chavis, a young black militant who lived in Oxford at the time. What Tyson found was that the City of Oxford continued to harbor guilt over the event and that officials of the time recognized that they had made grave mistakes, but Teel remained unrepentant. However, he also realized that there was probably little chance that the tragic scenario could have played out differently given the cultural and racial climate of the day. In the years following, Tyson credits militants and radicals of the 1970s with helping black Americans achieve greater social gains. "The indisputable fact was that whites in Oxford did not even consider altering the racial caste system until rocks began to fly and buildings began to burn," Tyson commented.

Library Journal contributor Stephen L. Hupp called the book "a significant work of memoir and social history." Traci Todd, writing in *Booklist,* described it as "a riveting memoir." Tyson's "avoidance of stereotypes and simple answers brings a shameful recent era in our country's history to vivid life," commented a *Publishers Weekly* reviewer, who concluded that "this book deserves the largest possible audience."

BIOGRAPHICAL AND CRITICAL SOURCES:

BOOKS

Tyson, Timothy B., *Blood Done Sign My Name: A True Story,* Crown Publishers (New York, NY), 2004.

PERIODICALS

Booklist, October 1, 2004, Traci Todd, review of *Blood Done Sign My Name* (audiobook), p. 350.
Christian Century, November 2, 2004, Eugene H. Winkler, review of *Blood Done Sign My Name,* p. 37.
Emerge, October, 1999, Mark Anthony Neal, "The Southern Roots of Black Power," p. 67.
Entertainment Weekly, May 21, 2004, "A Clear 'Sign'; In a Powerful New Book, a White Southerner Examines a 1970 Lynching," review of *Blood Done Sign My Name,* p. 83.

Historian, summer, 2001, review of *Radio Free Dixie: Robert F. Williams and the Roots of Black Power,* p. 808.

Journal of Negro History, spring, 2001, review of *Radio Free Dixie,* p. 193.

Journal of Southern History, November, 2001, Lance Hill, review of *Radio Free Dixie,* p. 900.

Kirkus Reviews, March 1, 2004, review of *Blood Done Sign My Name* (audiobook), p. 216.

Library Journal, October 1, 1999, Charles C. Hay, review of *Radio Free Dixie,* p. 104; March 15, 2004, Stephen L. Hupp, review of *Blood Done Sign My Name,* p. 90.

Michigan Historical Review, fall, 2000, Mark D. Higbee, review of *Radio Free Dixie,* p. 186.

Publishers Weekly, September 27, 1999, review of *Radio Free Dixie,* p. 82; April 19, 2004, review of *Blood Done Sign My Name,* p. 56, and Leonard Packer, "Celebrating Rather than Understanding," interview with Timothy B. Tyson, p. 56.

Southern Cultures, fall, 2000, James W. Loewen, review of *Democracy Betrayed,* p. 90; winter, 2004, Fred Hobson, review of *Blood Done Sign My Name,* p. 86.

Touching History: A Journal of Methods, fall, 2001, Paul Gaffney, review of *Radio Free Dixie,* p. 107.

ONLINE

BookReporter.com, http://www.bookreporter.com/ (October 5, 2005), Barbara Bamberger Scott, review of *Blood Done Sign My Name.*

Organization of American Historians Web site, http://www.oah.org/ (October 5, 2005), biographical information on Tyson.*

V

VARGAS LLOSA, Jorge Mario Pedro
    See VARGAS LLOSA, Mario

*   *   *

VARGAS LLOSA, Mario 1936-
    (Jorge Mario Pedro Vargas Llosa)

PERSONAL: Born March 28, 1936, in Arequipa, Peru; became Spanish citizen, 1994; son of Ernesto Vargas Maldonaldo and Dora Llosa Ureta; married Julia Urquidi, 1955 (divorced); married Patricia Llosa, 1965; children: (second marriage) Alvaro, Gonzalo, Morgana. *Education:* Attended University of San Marcos, 1953-57; University of Madrid, Ph.D., 1959. *Politics:* Liberal. *Religion:* Agnostic. *Hobbies and other interests:* Films, jogging, football.

ADDRESSES: Agent—Algaguara, Torrelaguna, 60, 28043 Madrid, Spain.

CAREER: Writer and journalist. Journalist with *La Industria,* Piura, Peru, and with Radio Panamericana and *La Cronica,* both in Lima, Peru, c. 1950s; worked in Paris, France, as a journalist with Agence France-Presse, as a broadcaster with the radio-television network L'Office de radiodiffusion télévision française (ORTF), and as a language teacher; Queen Mary College and Kings College, London, England, faculty member, 1966-68; Washington State University, Seattle, writer-in-residence, 1968; University of Puerto Rico, visiting professor, 1969; *Libre,* Paris, cofounder, 1971; Columbia University, New York, NY, Edward Laroque Tinker Visiting Professor, 1975; Harvard University, Cambridge, MA, Robert Kennedy Professor, beginning 1992. Former fellow, Woodrow Wilson Center, Washington, DC; former host of Peruvian television program *The Tower of Babel;* Peruvian presidential candidate, Liberty Movement, 1989-90.

MEMBER: PEN (president 1976-79), Academy Peruana de la Lengua, Modern Language Association of America (honorary fellow), American Academy and Institute of Arts and Letters (honorary member).

AWARDS, HONORS: Prize of the *Revue Française,* 1957, for *The Challenge;*; Premio Leopoldo Alas, 1959, for *Los jefes;* Premio Biblioteca Breve, 1962, for *La ciudad y los perros;* Premio de la Critica Española, 1963, for *La ciudad y los perros;* Premio de la Critica Española,1967, for *La casa verde;* Premio Nacional de la Novela, Peru, and Premio Internacional Literatura Romulo Gallegos, both 1967, both for *La casa verde;* annual prize for theater (Argentina), 1981; Congressional Medal of Honor, Peruvian government, 1981; Instituto Italo Latinoamericano Iila prize (Italy), 1982, for *La tia Julia y el escribidor;* Ritz Paris Hemingway Award, 1985, for *The War of the End of the World;* Legion of Honor, France, 1985; Principe de Asturias Prize for Letters, 1986; Scanno Prize, Rizzoli Libri (Italy), 1989; Castiglione Prize of Sicily, 1990; Legion of Freedom, the Cultural Institute Ludwig von Mises, Mexico, 1990; T.S. Eliot Prize, Ingersoll Foundation, the Rockford Institute, 1991, for creative writing; Golden Palm Award of INTAR, Hispanic American Arts Center of New York, 1992; named Chevalier de l'Ordre des Arts et des Lettres, France,

1993; Miguel de Cervantes prize for literature, Ministry of Culture, Spain, 1994; Jerusalem prize, 1995; Prize of La Paz, Booksellers of Germany, 1996; Prize Mariano de Cavia, 1997; Golden PEN Award, PEN Executive Committee, 1997; Medal and Diploma of Honor, Catholic University of Santa Maria of Arequipa, Peru, 1997; National Book Critics Circle Award for Criticism, 1997, for *Making Waves;* Medal from the University of California, Los Angeles, 1999; Jorge Isaacs Prize, 1999; Prize Américas, Foundation of the Américas, 2000-01; Gold Medal, city of Genoa, Italy, 2002; Nabokov Prize, PEN American Center, 2002; Medal of Honor, Peruvian Congress, 2003; Prize Roger Caillos, Paris, France, 2003; Prize Budapest, Budapest, Hungary, 2003; Konex Prize, Konex Foundation, 2004. Honorary degrees from Florida International University, Miami, FL, 1990; Dowling College, 1993; University Francisco Marroquiín, 1993; Georgetown University, 1994; Yale University, 1994; University of Rennes II, 1994; University of Murcia, Spain, 1995; University of Valladolid, Spain, 1995; University of Lima, Peru, 1997; and Harvard University, 1999; also D.H.L., Connecticut College, 1991, and honorary doctorates from Boston University and University of Genoa, Italy, both 1992.

WRITINGS:

NOVELS

La ciudad y los perros, Seix Barral (Barcelona, Spain), 1963, translation by Lysander Kemp published as *The Time of the Hero,* Grove (New York, NY), 1966, 2nd edition, Alfaguara (Madrid, Spain), 1999.

La casa verde, Seix Barral (Barcelona, Spain), 1966, translation by Gregory Rabassa published as *The Green House,* Harper (New York, NY), 1968, reprinted, Rayo (New York, NY), 2005.

Conversacion en la catedral, two volumes, Seix Barral (Barcelona, Spain), 1969, translation by Gregory Rabassa published as *Conversation in the Cathedral: A Novel,* Harper (New York, NY), 1975, reprinted, Rayo (New York, NY), 2005.

Pantaleon y las visitadoras, Seix Barral (Barcelona, Spain), 1973, translation by Ronald Christ and Gregory Kolovakos published as *Captain Pantoja and the Special Service,* Harper (New York, NY), 1978.

La tia Julia y el escribidor, Seix Barral (Barcelona, Spain), 1977, translation by Helen Lane published as *Aunt Julia and the Scriptwriter,* Farrar, Straus, and Giroux (New York, NY), 1982.

La guerra del fin del mundo, Seix Barral (Barcelona, Spain), 1981, translation by Helen Lane published as *The War of the End of the World,* Farrar, Straus, and Giroux (New York, NY), 1984.

Historia de Mayta, Seix Barral (Barcelona, Spain), 1985, translation by Alfred MacAdam published as *The Real Life of Alejandro Mayta,* Farrar, Straus, and Giroux (New York, NY), 1986.

Quien mato a Palomino Molero?, Seix Barral (Barcelona, Spain), 1986, translation by Alfred MacAdam published as *Who Killed Palomino Molero?,* Farrar, Straus, and Giroux (New York, NY), 1987.

El hablador, Seix Barral (Barcelona, Spain), 1987, translation by Helen Lane published as *The Storyteller,* Farrar, Straus, and Giroux (New York, NY), 1989.

Elogio de la madrastra, Tusquets (Barcelona, Spain), 1988, translation by Helen Lane published as *In Praise of the Stepmother,* Farrar, Straus, and Giroux (New York, NY), 1990.

Lituma en los Andes, Planeta (Barcelona, Spain), 1993, translation by Edith Grossman published as *Death in the Andes,* Farrar, Straus, and Giroux (New York, NY), 1996.

OTHER FICTION

Los jefes (story collection; title means "The Leaders" see also below), Rocas (Barcelona, Spain), 1959, translation by Ronald Christ and Gregory Kolovakos published in *The Cubs and Other Stories,* Harper (New York, NY), 1979.

Los cachorros (novella; title means "The Cubs"; also see below), Lumen (Barcelona, Spain), 1967.

Los cachorros; Los jefes, Peisa (Lima, Peru), 1973.

Los cuadernos de don Rigoberto, Alfaguara (Madrid, Spain), 1997, translation by Edith Grossman published as *The Notebooks of Don Rigoberto,* Farrar, Straus, and Giroux (New York, NY), 1998.

Obra reunida. Narrativa breve (short stories), Alfaguara (Madrid, Spain), 1999.

La fiesta del chivo, Alfaguara (Madrid, Spain), 2000, translation by Edith Grossman published as *The Feast of the Goat,* Farrar, Straus, and Giroux (New York, NY), 2002.

El paraíso en la otra esquina, Alfaguara (Lima, Peru), 2003, translation by Natasha Wimmer published as *The Way to Paradise,* Farrar, Straus, and Giroux (New York, NY), 2003.

PLAYS

La senorita de Tacna (produced as *Senorita from Tacna* in New York, NY, 1983; produced as *The Young Lady from Tacna* in Los Angeles, CA, 1985), Seix Barral (Barcelona, Spain), 1981, translation by David Graham-Young published as *The Young Lady from Tacna* in *Mario Vargas Llosa: Three Plays* (also see below), 1990.

Kathie y el hipopotamo: Comedia en dos actos (translation by Kerry McKenny and Anthony Oliver-Smith produced as *Kathie and the Hippopotamus* in Edinburgh, Scotland, 1986), Seix Barral (Barcelona, Spain), 1983, translation by David Graham-Young published in *Mario Vargas Llosa: Three Plays* (also see below), 1990.

La chunga (translation by Joanne Pottlitzer first produced in New York, NY, 1986), Seix Barral (Barcelona, Spain), 1986, translation by David Graham-Young published in *Mario Vargas Llosa: Three Plays* (also see below), 1990.

Mario Vargas Llosa: Three Plays (contains *The Young Lady from Tacna, Kathie and the Hippopotamus,* and *La chunga*), Hill & Wang (New York, NY), 1990.

El señor de los balcones (title means "Lord of the Balconies"), Seix Barral (Barcelona, Spain), 1993.

Also author of play *Le Huida* (title means "The Escape"), produced in Piura, Peru.

ESSAYS

La verdad de las mentiras (title means "The Truth of Lies"), Seix Barral (Barcelona, Spain), 1990.

Making Waves, edited by and translation by John King, Farrar, Straus, and Giroux (New York, NY), 1997.

Cartas a un joven novelista, Ariel/Planeta (Barcelona, Spain), 1997, translation by Natasha Wimmer published as *Letters to a Young Novelist,* Picador (New York, NY), 2003.

El lenguaje de la pasion, El Pais (Madrid, Spain), 2001, translation by Natasha Wimmer published as *The Language of Passion: Selected Commentary,* Farrar, Straus, and Giroux (New York, NY), 2003.

Ce cahier a été dirigé par Albert Bensoussan, Editions de l'Herne (Paris, France), 2003.

OTHER

La novela, Fundacion de Cultura Universitaria (Montevideo, Uruguay), 1968.

(With Gabriel García Márquez) *La novela en America Latina,* Milla Batres (Lima, Peru), 1968.

(Editor, with G. Brotherston) *Seven Stories from Spanish America,* Pergamon Press (Oxford, NY), 1968.

Antologia minima de M. Vargas Llosa, Tiempo Contemporaneo (Buenos Aires, Argentina), 1969.

Letra de batalla per "Tirant lo Blanc," Edicions 62, 1969, published as *Carta de batalla por Tirant lo Blanc,* Seix Barral (Barcelona, Spain), 1991.

(With Oscar Collazos and Julio Cortazar) *Literatura en la revolucion y revolucion en la literatura,* Siglo Veintiuno (Mexico City, Mexico), 1970.

Los cachorros; El desafio; Dia domingo, Salvat (Barcelona, Spain), 1970, *Dia domingo* published separately, Amadis (Buenos Aires, Argentina), 1971.

García Márquez: Historia de un deicidio (title means "García Márquez: The Story of a Deicide"), Seix Barral (Barcelona, Spain), 1971.

La historia secreta de una novela, Tusquets (Madrid, Spain), 1971.

(With Martin de Riquer) *El combate imaginario: Las cartas de batalla de Joanot Martorell,* Seix Barral (Barcelona, Spain), 1972.

(With Angel Rama) *García Márquez y la problematica de la novela,* Corregidor-Marcha (Buenos Aires, Argentina), 1973.

Obras escogidas: novelas y cuentos, Aguilar (Madrid, Spain), 1973.

La orgia perpetua: Flaubert y "Madame Bovary," Taurus (Madrid, Spain), 1975, translation by Helen Lane published as *The Perpetual Orgy: Flaubert and "Madame Bovary,"* Farrar, Straus, and Giroux (New York, NY), 1986.

Conversacion en la catedral; La orgia perpetua; Pantaleon y las visitadoras, Aguilar (Madrid, Spain), 1978.

Jose Maria Arguedas, entre sapos y halcones, Ediciones Cultura Hispanica del Centro Iberoamericano de Cooperacion (Madrid, Spain), 1978.

La utopia arcaica, Centre of Latin American Studies, University of Cambridge (Cambridge, England), 1978.

The Genesis and Evolution of "Pantaleon y las visitadoras," City College (New York, NY), 1979.

Art, Authenticity, and Latin-American Culture, Wilson Center (Washington, DC), 1981.

Entre Sartre y Camus, Huracan (Rio Piedras, Puerto Rico), 1981.

Contra viento y marea (journalism; title means "Against All Odds"), three volumes, Seix Barral (Barcelona, Spain), 1983–1990.

La cultura de la libertad, la libertad de la cultura, Fundacion Eduardo Frei (Santiago, Chile), 1985.

El debate, Universidad del Pacifico, Centro de Investigacion (Lima, Peru), 1990.

A Writer's Reality, Syracuse University Press (Syracuse, NY), 1991.

El pez en el agua: Memorias, Seix Barral (Barcelona, Spain), 1993, translation by Helen Lane published as *A Fish in the Water: A Memoir,* Farrar, Straus, and Giroux (New York, NY), 1994.

Desafios a la libertad, Aguilar (Madrid, Spain), 1994.

Ojos bonitos, cuadros feos, Peisa (Lima, Peru), 1996.

Una historia no oficial, Espasa Calpe (Madrid, Spain), 1997.

(With Paul Bowles) *Claudio Bravo: Paintings and Drawings,* Abbeville Press (New York, NY), 1997.

(With others) *Los desafios a la socieda abierta: A fines del siglo XX* (title means "Challenges to the Open Society: At the End of the Twentieth Century"), Ameghino (Buenos Aires, Argentina), 1999.

(Author of introduction) Plinio Apuleyo Mendoza and Carlos Alberto Montaner, *Guide to the Perfect Latin-American Idiot,* translation by Michaela Lajda Ames, Madison Books, distributed by National Book Network (Lanham, MD), 2000.

(Author of text) Pablo Corral Vega, *Andes* (photographs), National Geographic Society (Washington, DC), 2001.

Literatura y politica, Technical School of Monterrey (Monterrey, Mexico), 2001.

Palma, Valor nacional, Universidad Ricardo Palma (Lima, Peru), 2003.

(Author of text) Morgana Vargas Llosa, *Diario de Irak* (photographs), Aguilar (Buenos Aires, Argentina), 2003.

(Author of preface) Flora Tristan, *Flora Tristan, la paria et son rêve: Correspondence,* second revised edition, Presses Sorbonne nouvelle (Paris, France), 2003.

Entretien avec Mario Vargas Llosa: Suivi de, Ma parente d'Arequipa: Nouvelle inédite (interviews), Terre de brume (Rennes, France), 2003.

Entrevistas escogidas: Selección (interviews), edited by Jorge Coaguila, Fondo Editorial Cultura Peruana (Lima, Peru), 2004.

La tentación de lo imposible: Victor Hugo y Los miserables, Alfaguara (Madrid, Spain), 2004.

Contributor to *The Eye of the Heart,* 1973. Contributor to periodicals, including *Commentary, Harper's, National Review, New Perspectives Quarterly, New York Times Book Review, New York Times Magazine, UNESCO Courier,* and *World Press Review.* Syndicated columnist, *El Paiís,* 1977—.

ADAPTATIONS: The Cubs was filmed in 1971; *Captain Pantoja and the Special Service* was filmed in 1976, directed by Vargas Llosa; *Aunt Julia and the Scriptwriter* was adapted as a television series in Peru, as a screenplay written by William Boyd and directed by Jon Amiel in 1989, and as a motion picture titled *Tune in Tomorrow,* c. 1990; *The Feast of the Goat* was adapted for the stage by Veronia Triana and Jorge Ali Triana and directed by Jorge Ali Triana at the Gramercy Arts Theater, New York, NY, 2003. Selected works have been recorded by the Library of Congress Archive of Recorded Poetry and Literature.

SIDELIGHTS: Peruvian writer Mario Vargas Llosa often draws from his personal experiences to write of the injustices and corruption of contemporary Latin America. At one time an admirer of communist Cuba, since the early 1970s Vargas Llosa has been opposed to tyrannies of both the political left and right. He advocates democracy, a free market, and individual liberty and cautions against extreme or violent political action, instead calling for peaceful democratic reforms. In 1989 Vargas Llosa was chosen to be the presidential candidate of Fredemo, a political coalition in Peru; though at one point he held a large lead in election polls, in the end he lost the election to Alberto Fujimori. Through his novels, which are marked by complex structures and an innovative merging of dialogue and description in an attempt to recreate the actual feeling of life, Vargas Llosa has established himself as one of the most important of contemporary writers in the Spanish language.

As a young man, Vargas Llosa spent two years at the Leoncio Prado Military Academy. Sent there by his father, who had discovered that his son wrote poetry and was therefore fearful for the boy's masculinity, Vargas Llosa found the school insufferable and horrendous. His years at the school inspired his first novel, *The Time of the Hero,* originally published in Spanish as *La ciudad y los perros.* The novel's success was assured when the school's officials objected to Vargas Llosa's portrayal of their institution. The school went as far as to burn a thousand of copies of the book.

Vargas Llosa wrote *The Time of the Hero* after leaving Peru for Europe in 1958, when he was twenty-two. In embracing Europe and entering into self-imposed exile from his native land, he was following in the footsteps of numerous Latin-American writers, including Jorge Luis Borges, Julio Cortazar, and Carlos Fuentes. Vargas Llosa was to stay in Europe for thirty years, not returning to Peru until the late 1980s after the country had slipped into political chaos and economic impoverishment. These conditions prompted Vargas Llosa's decision to seek the presidency of Peru. During his three decades in Europe, Vargas Llosa became an internationally celebrated author.

Though Vargas Llosa had attracted widespread attention with his first novel, it was his second that cemented his status as a major novelist. In the award-winning *La casa verde* (*The Green House*), the author draws upon another period from his childhood for inspiration. For several years his family lived in the Peruvian jungle town of Piura, and his memories of the gaudy local brothel, known to everyone as the Green House, form the basis of his novel. The book's several stories are interwoven in a nonlinear narrative revolving around the brothel and the family that owns it, the military that runs the town, a dealer in stolen rubber in the nearby jungle, and a prostitute who was raised in a convent. "Scenes overlap, different times and places overrun each other . . . echoes precede voices, and disembodied consciences dissolve almost before they can be identified," Luis Harss and Barbara Dohmann wrote in *Into the Mainstream: Conversations with Latin-American Writers.* Gregory Rabassa, writing in *World Literature Today,* noted that the novel's title "is the connective theme that links the primitive world of the jungle to the primal lusts of 'civilization' which are enclosed by the green walls of the whorehouse." Rabassa saw, too, that Vargas Llosa's narrative style "has not reduced time to a device of measurement or location, a practical tool, but has conjoined it with space, so that the characters carry their space with them too . . . inseparable from their time." Harss and Dohmann found that *The Green House* "is probably the most accomplished work of fiction ever to come out of Latin America. It has sweep, beauty, imaginative scope, and a sustained eruptive power that carries the reader from first page to last like a fish in a bloodstream."

With *Conversacion en la catedral,* published in translation as *Conversation in the Cathedral,* Vargas Llosa widened his scope. Whereas in previous novels he had sought to recreate the repression and corruption of a particular place, in *Conversation in the*

Cathedral he attempts to provide a panoramic view of his native country. As John M. Kirk stated in the *International Fiction Review,* this novel "presents a wider, more encompassing view of Peruvian society. . . . [Vargas Llosa's] gaze extends further afield in a determined effort to incorporate as many representative regions of Peru as possible." Set during the dictatorship of Manuel Odria in the late 1940s and 1950s, the book, according to Penny Leroux in a *Nation* review, is "one of the most scathing denunciations ever written on the corruption and immorality of Latin America's ruling classes."

The nonlinear writing of *Conversation in the Cathedral* was seen by several critics to be the culmination of Vargas Llosa's narrative experimentation. Kirk explained that Vargas Llosa is "attempting the ambitious and obviously impossible plan of conveying to the reader all aspects of the reality of [Peruvian] society, of writing the 'total' novel." By interweaving five different narratives, the author forces audiences to study the text closely, making the reader an "accomplice of the writer [which] undoubtedly helps the reader to a more profound understanding of the work." Kirk concluded that *Conversation in the Cathedral* is "both a perfect showcase for all the structural techniques and thematic obsessions found in [Vargas Llosa's] . . . other work, as well as being the true culmination of his personal anguish for Peru."

Ronald de Feo pointed out in the *New Republic* this and other early novels by Vargas Llosa explore "with a near-savage seriousness and single-mindedness themes of social and political corruption." However, in *Captain Pantoja and the Special Service* (*Pantaleon y las Visitados*) "a new unexpected element entered Vargas Llosa's work: an unrestrained sense of humor," de Feo reported. A farcical novel involving a military officer's assignment to provide prostitutes for troops in the Peruvian jungle, *Captain Pantoja and the Special Service* is "told through an artful combination of dry military dispatches, juicy personal letters, verbose radio rhetoric, and lurid sensationalist news reports," Gene Bell-Villada reported in *Commonweal.* Vargas Llosa also mixes conversations from different places and times, as he did in previous novels. Like these earlier works, *Captain Pantoja and the Special Service* "sniffs out corruption in high places, but it also presents something of a break, Vargas Llosa here shedding his high seriousness and adopting a humorous ribald tone," Bell-Villada concluded. The novel's satirical attack is aimed not at the military, a *Times Literary Supplement* reviewer wrote, but at "any institution which channels instincts into a socially acceptable ritual. The humor of the narrative derives less from this serious underlying motive, however, than from the various linguistic codes into which people channel the darker forces."

The humorous tone of *Captain Pantoja and the Special Service* is also found in *Aunt Julia and the Scriptwriter* (*La tia Julia y el escribidor*). The novel concerns two characters based on people in Vargas Llosa's own life: his first wife, Julia, who was his aunt by marriage, and a writer of radio soap opera whom the author names Pedro Camacho in the novel. The eighteen-year-old narrator, Mario, has a love affair with the thirty-two-year-old Julia. Their story is interrupted in alternate chapters by Camacho's wildly complicated soap opera scripts. As Camacho goes mad, his daily scripts for ten different soap operas become more and more entangled, with characters from one serial appearing in others and all of his plots converging into a single unlikely story. The scripts display "fissures through which are revealed secret obsessions, aversions and perversions that allow us to view his soap operas as the story of his disturbed mind," Jose Miguel Oviedo wrote in *World Literature Today*. "The result," explained Nicholas Shakespeare in the *Times Literary Supplement*, "is that Camacho ends up in an asylum, while Mario concludes his real-life soap opera by running off to marry Aunt Julia."

Although *Aunt Julia and the Scriptwriter* is as humorous as *Captain Pantoja and the Special Service*, "it has a thematic richness and density the other book lacked," de Feo concluded. This richness is found in the novel's exploration of the writer's life and of the relationship between a creative work and its inspiration. In the contrasting of soap opera plots with the real-life romance of Mario and Julia, the novel raises questions about the distinctions between fiction and fact. In a review for *New York*, Carolyn Clay called *Aunt Julia and the Scriptwriter* "a treatise on the art of writing, on the relationship of stimuli to imagination." It is, de Feo observed, "a multilayered, high-spirited, and in the end terribly affecting text about the interplay of fiction and reality, the transformation of life into art, and life seen and sometimes even lived as fiction."

In *The War of the End of the World* (*La guerra del fin del mundo*) Vargas Llosa for the first time sets his story outside of his native Peru. He turns instead to Brazil and bases his story on an apocalyptic religious movement that gained momentum toward the end of the nineteenth century. Convinced that the year 1900 would mark the end of the world, these zealots, led by a man named the Counselor, set up the community of Canudos. Because of the Counselor's continued denunciations of the Brazilian government, which he called the "antichrist" for its legal separation of church and state, the national government sent in troops to break up this religious community. The first military assault was repulsed, as were the second and third, but the fourth expedition involved a force of some four thousand soldiers. They laid waste to the entire area and killed nearly forty thousand people.

Vargas Llosa told Wendy Smith in *Publishers Weekly* that he was drawn to write of this bloody episode because he felt the fanaticism of both sides in this conflict is exemplary of late-twentieth-century Latin America. "Fanaticism is the root of violence in Latin America," he explained. In the Brazilian war, he believes, is a microcosm of Latin America. "Canudos presents a limited situation in which you can see clearly. Everything is there: a society in which on the one hand people are living a very old-fashioned life and have an archaic way of thinking, and on the other hand progressives want to impose modernism on society with guns. This creates a total lack of communication, of dialogue, and when there is no communication, war or repression or upheaval comes immediately," he told Smith. In an article for the *Washington Post*, Vargas Llosa explained to Curt Suplee that "in the history of the Canudos war you could really see something that has been happening in Latin American history over the nineteenth and twentieth centuries—the total lack of communication between two sections of a society which kill each other fighting *ghosts*, no? Fighting fictional enemies who are invented out of fanaticism. This kind of reciprocal incapacity of understanding is probably the main problem we have to overcome in Latin America."

Not only is *The War of the End of the World* set in the nineteenth century, but its length and stylistic approach are also reminiscent of that time. A writer for the London *Times* called it "a massive novel in the nineteenth-century tradition: massive in content, in its ambitions, in its technical achievement." *Times Literary Supplement* contributor Gordon Brotherston described the book as being "on the grand scale of the nineteenth century," while Salman Rushdie, writing in the *New Republic,* similarly defined the novel as "a modern tragedy on the grand scale." Richard Locke wrote in the *Washington Post Book World* that *The War of the End of the World* "overshadows the majority of novels published . . . in the past few years. Indeed, it makes most recent American fiction seem very small, very private, very gray, and very timid."

Vargas Llosa's political perspective in *The War of the End of the World* exhibits a marked change from his earlier works. He does not attack a corrupt society, instead treating both sides in the Canudos war ironically. The novel ends with a character from either side locked in a fight to the death. As Rushdie observed, "This image would seem to crystallize Vargas Llosa's political vision." This condemnation of both sides in the Canudos conflict reflects Vargas Llosa's view of the contemporary Latin-American scene, where rightist dictatorships often battle communist guerrillas. Suplee described Vargas Llosa as "a humanist who reviles with equal vigor tyrannies of the right or left (is there really a difference, he asks, between 'good tortures and bad tortures'?)."

Although his political views have changed during the course of his career, taking him from a leftist supporter of communist Cuba to a strong advocate of democracy, Vargas Llosa's abhorrence of dictatorship, violence, and corruption has remained constant. He sees Latin-American intellectuals as participants in a continuing cycle of "repression, chaos, and subversion," as he told Philip Bennett in the *Washington Post.* Many of these intellectuals, Vargas Llosa explained further, "are seduced by rigidly dogmatic stands. Although they are not accustomed to pick up a rifle or throw bombs from their studies, they foment and defend the violence." Speaking of the late-twentieth-century conflict in Peru between the government and the Maoist guerrilla movement the Shining Path, Vargas Llosa clarified to Suplee that "the struggle between the guerrillas and the armed forces is really a settling of accounts between privileged sectors of society, and the peasant masses are used cynically and brutally by those who say they want to 'liberate' them."

Vargas Llosa believes that a Latin-American writer is obligated to speak out on political matters. "If you're a writer in a country like Peru," he told Suplee, "you're a privileged person because you know how to read and write, you have an audience, you are respected. It is a moral obligation of a writer in Latin America to be involved in civic activities." This belief led Vargas Llosa in 1987 to speak out when the Peruvian government proposed to nationalize the country's banks. His protest quickly led to a mass movement in opposition to the plan, and the government was forced to back down. Vargas Llosa's supporters went on to create Fredemo, a political party calling for democracy, a free market, and individual liberty. Together with two other political parties, Fredemo established a coalition group called the Liberty Movement. In June of 1989 Vargas Llosa was chosen to be the coalition's presidential candidate for Peru's 1990 elections. Visiting small rural towns, the urban strongholds of his Marxist opponents, and the jungle villages of the country's Indians, Vargas Llosa campaigned on what he believes is Peru's foremost problem: creating democracy in the face of the rightist military and extreme Leftists. Opinion polls in late summer of 1988 showed him to be the leading contender for the presidency, with a 44-to-19-percent lead over his nearest opponent. By the time of the election, however, Vargas Llosa's lead had eroded, and he ended up losing the election to Alberto Fujimori.

Vargas Llosa chronicles his experience as a presidential candidate in *A Fish in the Water: A Memoir* (*El pez en el agua: Memorias*). In addition to discussing the campaign, however, the author also offers a memoir of his early years in Peru. "One string of alternating chapters in the book ends with the young writer's departure for France in 1958," noted Rockwell Gray in Chicago's *Tribune Books;* "the other recreates the exhausting and dangerous [presidential] campaign that carried him to every corner of Peru." Alan Riding added in the *New York Times Book Review* that the book "serves as [Vargas Llosa's] . . . mea culpa: he explains why the aspiring writer of the 1950's became a politician in the late 1980's and why, in the end, this was a terrible mistake." Vargas Llosa's account of his childhood and young adulthood includes his ambivalent relationship with his father, whom he met for the first time at age eleven and toward whom he had an intense dislike. Mark Falcoff, writing in the *Times Literary Supplement,* stated: "The pages of this book dealing with the father-son relationship are among the most violent and passionate Vargas Llosa has ever written."

In discussing his failed presidential campaign in *A Fish in the Water,* Vargas Llosa portrays the political backstabbing, unavoidable compromises, and character attacks that tainted the campaign against Fujimori. He also writes about his alienation from the majority of Peruvians: as a white, wealthy, educated, expatriate intellectual, he had little in common with poor Peruvians of Indian descent, many of whom do not speak Spanish. Riding commented: "Tall, white and well dressed, he invariably looked out of place." Falcoff explained that "the chapters dealing with the presidential campaign suggest an impressive knowledge of Peruvian society at all levels and in the several regions, particularly the needs of its humblest groups." Gray, however, remarked: "Much of this book is engaging and informative, but it becomes at times slack, even gossipy, and assumes an interest in the nuances of Peruvian political and literary life shared by very few American readers."

After losing the campaign, Vargas Llosa returned to Europe—this time to Spain, where he assumed Spanish citizenship. His first novel after running for president, *Death in the Andes* (*Lituma en los Andes*), is set in his homeland amid the modern political and social strife evidenced by the rebellion of the Shining Path guerrilla movement. In part a murder mystery, the novel follows Corporal Lituma as he ventures from his home in Peru's coastal region to a mountain village to investigate the disappearance of three men. In addition to the story line of the missing men, Vargas Llosa intersperses tales of violence committed by the Shining Path as well as a romantic story involving Tomas Carreño, Lituma's guide and partner. Critics commented positively on Vargas Llosa's skill in creating a technically ambitious novel, although some reviewers remarked that the author failed to integrate the various plot lines into a coherent story line. *New York Times Book Review* contributor Madison Smartt Bell, for instance, wrote that "amid this multiplicity of plot potential, the reader may share Lituma's difficulty in finding any central focus, or even in identifying a single continuous thread." Similarly, Rockwell Gray, again writing in Chicago's *Tribune Books,* felt that "for all the author's adroit weaving of shifts in viewpoint, voice and time—his attempt to grasp Peru's dilemma from many angles—this technically interesting novel is not on a par with his best work." In contrast, Marie Arana-Ward wrote in the *Washington Post Book World:* "This is well-knit social criticism as trenchant as any by [Honore de] Balzac or [Gustave] Flaubert—an ingenious patchwork of the conflicting mythologies that have shaped the New World psyche since the big bang of Columbus's first step on shore."

Vargas Llosa's next novel, *The Notebooks of Don Rigoberto* (*Los cuadernos de don Rigoberto*), is also set in Peru. In this dreamlike narrative, Don Rigoberto has separated from his beautiful wife, Doña Lucrecia, because of a sexual encounter between her and her stepson, Fonchito, a precocious boy who has yet to reach puberty. Don Rigoberto misses his wife terribly, and to appease his loneliness he imagines, and writes about, Lucrecia's erotic life—with him as well as with other lovers. It is unclear how much of the narrative is meant to be true and how much is a fantasy. This book lacks the political overtones of much of Vargas Llosa's work, but it does provide "grand, sexy reading for sophisticated audiences," reflected Barbara Hoffert in the *Library Journal*. A writer in *Publishers Weekly* remarked: "As in much of his writing, Vargas Llosa creates a certain timelessness, a dream-like play on the present. The more he leaves sex to the imagination, the more erotic and beautifully suggestive it becomes."

The author mixes fiction and fact in his novel *The Feast of the Goat* (*La fiesta del chivo*), which concerns Dominican dictator Rafael Trujillo. Trujillo was assassinated in 1961, and his death remains a cause for celebration in the Dominican Republic. Despite his cruelty and perversions, Trujillo was supported by the U.S. government since he was seen as being strongly against communism. Vargas Llosa tells the story of Urania Cabral, a successful New York City lawyer who was victimized by her father and Trujillo shortly before the dictator's death. Moving forward and back in time, in the author's trademark style, the novel gives a detailed portrait of Trujillo and his frustration with the one enemy he could not conquer: his own advancing age. Obsessive about his habits and grooming, he is unable to do a thing about his increasing incontinence and sexual impotence. The methods he used to victimize individuals and, in fact, his entire country are laid out here, while the stories of Urania, her father, and the men who killed Trujillo are also presented with empathy. "This is an impressively crafted novel," commented Sebastian Shakespeare in the *New Statesman*. "The set pieces are magnificent . . . but it's the small details that you recall: the smell of cheap perfume sprayed on to electric chairs to conceal the stench of urine, excrement and charred flesh." Noting that the Trujillista era was characterized by its vileness, Liliana Wendorff added in the *Library Journal* that Vargas Llosa "skillfully uses language to demystify subjects that could easily offend." Jonathan Heawood concluded in the *Guardian Unlimited* that "*The Feast of the Goat* is as dark and complicated as a Jacobean revenge tragedy; but it is also rich and humane."

Vargas Llosa continues to blend reality in fiction in *The Way to Paradise (El paraíso en la otra esquina)*. In this novel, he contrasts, chapter by chapter, the rebellious lives of the painter Paul Gaugin with that of his maternal grandmother, Flora Tristán. Both Gaugin and Tristán chose to live outside of the norms of European middle-class society. As Richard Lacayo wrote in *Time:* "Both of them rejected the world as they found it—repressed, greed, deaf to the higher (or lower) impulses." A stockbroker by trade, Gaugin left his life behind to live and paint in remote areas of the South Pacific, returning to France only twice in the last twelve years of his life. After his death from syphilis, his paintings became extremely influential in the art world. Similarly, Tristán left behind her violent husband to travel through France with her young daughter, Aline. Tristán actively championed women's liberation, cooperatives, and working-class causes. She went from town to town to accomplish her goals. The pair never met; Tristán died about four years before Gaugin was born. Summarizing the novel's appeal, a critic for *Kirkus Reviews* noted that "there isn't a page of this magnificently imagined and orchestrated story that does not vibrate with the energy and mystery of felt, and fully comprehended, life."

Vargas Llosa analyzes the novel itself in *Letters to a Young Novelist (Cartas a un joven novelista)*. The book consists of eleven letters/essays written by a successful novelist to an aspiring author and fan. Ulrich Baer in the *Library Journal* noted that "his consistently brilliant observations constitute critical revelations in their own right." In the pieces, the author offers his advice and theories on writing and literature. He also discusses the merits of certain prominent novelists from several Western traditions, such as Ernest Hemingway, Jorge Luis Borges, and Gustave Flaubert. Often compared to Rainer Maria Rilke's *Letters to a Young Poet, Letters to a Young Novelist* is "neither a survey course in what to read nor a practical guide to writing," according to a *Publishers Weekly* critic, who added that "the book finally is a meditation on writing and its proper relationship to life."

Vargas Llosa has also published collections of his essays, many of which originally appeared in his newspaper column in *El País*. Though composed with journalistic objectivity, many of these works are about topics on which the author has strong personal feelings. Like *Making Waves* before it, *The Language of Passion: Selected Commentary* includes many pieces on such political topics as democracy in Latin America and globalization, as well as on cultural topics. Included in *The Language of Passion* are pieces on a romance writer who endowed an award for her fellow writers, everyday existence in a small community in Palestine, and an homage to Bob Marley. Commenting positively on the "clear, crisp manner" in which the essays are written, Neal Wyatt noted in the *Library Journal* that many of the essays "are imbued with a wit and an intellect that make them instantly engaging."

"A major figure in contemporary Latin American letters," as Locke explained in the *Washington Post Book World,* Vargas Llosa is usually ranked with Jorgé Luis Borges, Gabriel García Márquez, and other writers in what has been called the Latin American "Boom" of the 1960s. His body of work set in his native Peru, Suzanne Jill Levine explained in the *New York Times Book Review,* is "one of the largest narrative efforts in contemporary Latin American letters. . . . [He] has begun a complete inventory of the political, social, economic and cultural reality of Peru. . . . Very deliberately, Vargas Llosa has chosen to be his country's conscience."

BIOGRAPHICAL AND CRITICAL SOURCES:

BOOKS

A Marxist Reading of Fuentes, Vargas Llosa, and Puig, University Press of America (Lanham, MD), 1994.

Booker, Keith M., *Vargas Llosa among the Postmodernists,* University Press of Florida (Gainesville, FL), 1994.

Contemporary Hispanic Biography, Volume 1, Gale (Detroit, MI), 2002.

Dictionary of Literary Biography, Volume 145: *Modern Latin-American Fiction Writers, Second Series,* Gale (Detroit, MI), 1994.

Encyclopedia of World Biography, 2nd edition, Gale (Detroit, MI), 1998.

Encyclopedia of World Literature in the Twentieth Century, St. James Press (Detroit, MI), 1999.

Feal, Rosemary Geisdorfer, *Novel Lives: The Fictional Autobiographies of Guillermo Cabrera Infante and Mario Vargas Llosa,* University of North Carolina Press (Chapel Hill, NC), 1986.

Gallagher, D.P., *Modern Latin-American Literature,* Oxford University Press (New York, NY), 1973.

Gerdes, Dick, *Mario Vargas Llosa,* Twayne (Boston, MA), 1985.

Harss, Luis, and Barbara Dohmann, *Into the Mainstream: Conversations with Latin-American Writers,* Harper (New York, NY), 1967.

Hispanic Literature Criticism, Gale (Detroit, MI), 1994.

Köllman, Sabine, *Vargas Llosa's Fiction and the Demons of Politics,* P. Lang (New York, NY), 2002.

Kristal, Efrain, *Temptation of the Word: The Novels of Mario Vargas Llosa,* Vanderbilt University Press (Nashville, TN), 1998.

Lewis, Marvin A., *From Lime to Leticia: The Peruvian Novels of Mario Vargas Llosa,* University Press of America (Lanham, MD), 1983.

Moses, Michael Valdez, *The Novel and the Globalization of Culture,* Oxford University Press (New York, NY), 1995.

Muñoz, Braulio, *A Storyteller: Mario Vargas Llosa between Civilization and Barbarism,* Rowman & Littlefield (Lanham, MD), 2000.

Reference Guide to World Literature, 2nd edition, Gale (Detroit, MI), 1995.

Rossmann, Charles, and Alan Warren Friedman, editors, *Mario Vargas Llosa: A Collection of Critical Essays,* University of Texas Press (Austin, TX), 1978.

Williams, Raymond Leslie, *Mario Vargas Llosa,* Ungar (New York, NY), 1986.

PERIODICALS

American Enterprise, June, 2005, Mario Vargas Llosa, "Confessions of an Old-fashioned Liberal," p. 40.

Commonweal, June 8, 1979, Gene Bell-Villada, review of *Captain Pantoja and the Special Service,* p. 346.

International Fiction Review, January, 1977, John M. Kirk, review of *Conversation in the Cathedral.*

Kirkus Reviews, October 1, 2003, review of *The Way to Paradise,* p. 1200.

Library Journal, April 1, 1998, Barbara Hoffert, review of *The Notebooks of Don Rigoberto,* p. 126; June 1, 2001, Liliana Wendorff, review of *The Feast of the Goat,* p. S31; April 1, 2002, Ulrich Baer, review of *Letters to a Young Novelist,* p. 110; April 1, 2003, Neal Wyatt, review of *The Language of Passion: Selected Commentary,* p. 99.

Nation, November 22, 1975, Penny Leroux, review of *Conversation in the Cathedral.*

New Republic, August 16, 1982, Ronald de Feo, review of *Aunt Julia and the Scriptwriter,* p. 39; October 8, 1984, Salman Rushdie, review of *The War of the End of the World,* pp. 25-27.

New Statesman, March 25, 2002, Sebastian Shakespeare, review of *The Feast of the Goat,* p. 57; November 24, 2003, Jonathan Heawood, review of *The Way to Paradise,* p. 55.

Newsweek International, November 3, 2003, Joseph Contreras, interview with Mario Vargas Llosa, p. 68.

New York, August 23, 1982, Carolyn Clay, review of *Aunt Julia and the Scriptwriter,* p. 90.

New York Times Book Review, November 4, 1984, Suzanne Jill Levine, review of *Conversation in the Cathedral,* p. 42; May 15, 1994, Alan Riding, review of *A Fish in the Water,* p. 10; October 1, 1995, p. 36; February 18, 1996, Madison Smartt Bell, review of *Death in the Andes,* p. 7.

New York Times Magazine, November 20, 1983, Alan Riding, "Revolution and the Intellectual in Latin America," interview with Mario Vargas Llosa, p. 28; November 5, 1989, Gerald Marzoratti, "Can a Novelist Save Peru?," p. 44.

Publishers Weekly, October 5, 1984, Wendy Smith, interview with Mario Vargas Llosa, p. 98; March 23, 1998, review of *The Notebooks of Don Rigoberto,* p. 76; April 22, 2002, review of *Letters to a Young Novelist,* p. 57.

Time, December 1, 2003, Richard Lacayo, "Kindred Spirits: Mario Vargas Llosa Weaves a Vivid Tale of Gaugin's and His Grandmother's Lives," review of *The Way to Paradise,* p. 93.

Times (London, England), May 13, 1985, review of *The War of the End of the World.*

Times Literary Supplement, October 12, 1973, review of *Pantaleon y las Visitados,* p. 1208; June 9, 1978, Nicholas Shakespeare, review of *La tia Julia y el escribidor,* p. 638; May 17, 1985, Gordon Brotherston, review of *The War of the End of the World,* p. 540; June 17, 1994, Mark Falcoff, review of *A Fish in Water,* p. 11.

Tribune Books (Chicago, IL), September 11, 1994, Rockwell Gray, review of *A Fish in Water,* p. 7; March 3, 1996, Rockwell Gray, review of *Death in the Andes,* p. 6.

Washington Post, August 29, 1983, Philip Bennett, "Conscience of His Country; '19th-century Novelist' Mario Vargas Llosa and his 20th-century Solutions for Peru," interview with Mario Vargas Llosa, p. C1; October 1, 1984, Curt Suplee, "Voice from the End of the World; Novelist Mario Vargas

Llosa: Peru's Prolific Political Conscience, Fighting Tyrannies Left and Right," interview with Mario Vargas Llosa, p. B1.

Washington Post Book World, August 26, 1984, Richard Locke, review of *The War of the End of the World,* p. 1; February 25, 1996, Marie Arana-Ward, review of *Death in the Andes,* p. 1.

World Literature Today, winter, 1978, Gregory Rabassa, review of *The Green House;* spring, 1978, Jose Miguel Oviedo, review of *La tia Julia y el escribidor,* p. 261.

ONLINE

Books and Writers, http://www.kirjasto.sci.fi/ (October 10, 2005), biography of Mario Vargas Llosa.

Guardian Unlimited, http://books.guardian.co.uk/ (May 1, 2002), Jonathan Heawood, review of *The Feast of the Goat.*

January Magazine Online, http://www.january magazine.com/ (August 16, 2004), Heidi Johnson-Wright, interview with Mario Vargas Llosa.

Mario Vargas Llosa Home Page, http://www.mvargas-llosa.com (October 10, 2005).

OTHER

Sklodowska, Elzbieta, *An Interview with Mario Vargas Llosa,* American Audio Prose Library, 1994.*

*   *   *

VISSER, Margaret 1940-

PERSONAL: Surname is pronounced "*Fiss*-ser"; born May 11, 1940, in Germiston, South Africa; naturalized Canadian citizen; daughter of John Holland (an engineer) and Ruby Margaret Agar (a teacher; maiden name, O'Connell) Barclay-Lloyd; married Colin Wills Visser (a professor), June 8, 1962; children: Emily, Alexander. *Education:* University of Toronto, B.A. (with honors), 1970, M.A., 1973, Ph.D., 1980. *Religion:* Roman Catholic. *Hobbies and other interests:* Music, film, theater, reading, painting, architecture.

ADDRESSES: Home—Toronto, Ontario, Canada. *Agent*—Westwood Creative Artists, 94 Harbord St., Toronto, Ontario, Canada M5S 1G6; and The Wylie Agency, 250 W. 57th St., Ste. 2114, New York, NY 10107. *E-mail*—visser@retemail.es.

CAREER: Writer, educator, journalist, and broadcaster. *Mansfield Chronicle-Advertiser,* Mansfield, England, reporter, 1958-60; British Council, London, England, schoolteacher in Baghdad, Iraq, 1962-64; University of Rochester, Rochester, NY, secretary, 1964-66; York University, Toronto, Ontario, Canada, lecturer in classics, 1974-79, course director and lecturer in classics, 1982-88, Canada Research fellow in department of classics, 1988-93. Canadian Broacasting Corp. (CBC-Radio), Toronto, broadcaster, 1980—, including for such programs as *Morningside,* 1982-91, and *The Arts Tonight,* 1991-96; also appeared on series *Lifetime,* CFTO-TV, 1986-89; *A comme Artiste,* TVO, 1992; *Women's Channel,* 1995; and radio series *A Tale of Six Cities,* British Broadcasting Corp. (BBC), 1998.

AWARDS, HONORS: Gold Medal for Classics, University of Toronto, 1970; Glenfiddich Award, Foodbook of the Year, 1989, for *Much Depends on Dinner;* International Association of Culinary Professionals' Literary Food Writing Award and Jane Grigson Award for Scholarly Distinction, both 1992, both for *The Rituals of Dinner;* Sweeney Award, 2004. Honorary degree, Brescia University College of the University of Western Ontario.

WRITINGS:

Much Depends on Dinner: The Extraordinary History and Mythology, Allure and Obsessions, Perils and Taboos of an Ordinary Meal, McClelland & Stewart (Toronto, Ontario, Canada), 1986, Collier (New York, NY), 1988.

The Rituals of Dinner: The Origins, Evolution, Eccentricities, and Meaning of Table Manners, Grove Weidenfeld (New York, NY), 1991.

The Way We Are, HarperCollins (Toronto, Ontario, Canada), 1994, Faber (Boston, MA), 1996.

More than Meets the Eye, 1996.

The Geometry of Love: Space, Time, Mystery, and Meaning in an Ordinary Church, HarperFlamingo Canada (Toronto, Ontario, Canada), 2000.

Beyond Fate, House of Anansi Press (Toronto, Ontario, Canada), 2002.

Writer for "Siblings," a feature on CBC-Radio program *Ideas,* 1983. Contributor to book *Greek Tragedy and Its Legacy,* edited by Martin Cropp, Elaine Fantham, and S.E. Scully, University of Cal-gary Press, 1986. Contributor to journals, including *Journal of the History of Ideas* and *Harvard Theological Review*. Contributing editor and author of monthly column "The Way We Are," *Saturday Night* magazine, 1988-94; contributing editor and writer, *Compass* magazine, 1994-96.

Visserr's works have been translated into French, German, Dutch, Spanish, Italian, and Portuguese.

ADAPTATIONS: The Geometry of Love is being made into a documentary film.

SIDELIGHTS: Margaret Visser is a university professor of classics, a columnist, and the author of several well-received books. She has also worked in radio and television. "Visser's forte is to take the ordinary and turn it into the extraordinary by providing a cultural history of its evolution," according to a *Publishers Weekly* reviewer. Accepting a last minute invitation to speak on the CBC-Radio program *Morningside,* "Visser, seldom at a loss for something to say, came right over and delivered an authoritative and captivating recitation on just why it is that North Americans don't eat insects," reported *Los Angeles Times* contributor Mary Williams Walsh. According to Walsh, the audience loved Visser, who later became a regular on the well-known radio show, and "the essay on insect-eating was the prototype for what would ultimately become Visser's stock-in-trade: Learned but accessible explanations of commonplace items and practices that most North Americans take for granted."

Encouraged by the requests of radio listeners, Visser wrote a book. *Much Depends on Dinner: The Extraordinary History and Mythology, Allure and Obsessions, Perils and Taboos of an Ordinary Meal,* begins with a simple, generic dinner menu: corn with salt and butter, chicken with rice, lettuce with olive oil and lemon juice, and ice cream. The rest of the work is devoted to a history of the food items contained in such a meal. "In a discursive way, she examines the historical, mythological, religious, medicinal, agricultural, and social aspects of each" food item, noted Janet Fetherling in *Quill & Quire.* Fetherling further remarked that the book "offers fascinating trivia, yet it is also a serious project, leavened with [an appealing] voice." *New York Times Book Review* contributor Laura Shapiro called the book "a lively and perceptive guide" and commented: "Despite a fascinating subject and Mrs.

Visser's graceful writing style, *Much Depends on Dinner* never quite comes to life, a problem that may be called the no-primary-sources syndrome. . . . [She] has relied almost entirely on secondary sources, ignoring those unmediated voices from the past that give focus, immediacy and a human dimension to scholarship. . . . Still [her unconvincing] assertions inspire the sorts of arguments for which one should thank Mrs. Visser, not bury her." Keith Jeffrey, writing in the *Times Literary Supplement,* recommended the book, however, even though he also noted that it has "no detailed source references." Jeffrey elaborated: "The approach, however, is so infectious, and the writing generally so engaging and stimulating that passing references prompt one to further speculation."

Visser's second book, *The Rituals of Dinner: The Origins, Evolution, Eccentricities, and Meaning of Table Manners,* "is, for all its good-naturedness, a scary work, devoted as it is to the mystery and menace of entertaining, the politics that underlie each decision confronting a host, the risks borne in each seemingly innocent gesture of hospitality," related Walsh. Called a "fascinating work" by P.N. Furbank in the *London Review of Books,* it "is crammed to overflowing with things that one would want to know . . . [ranging] as widely as possible, both in space and time, and [Visser] explores her theme in a logical progression." Hilary Mantel was not alone when she clearly noted in a *Spectator* review that, unlike many books involving etiquette, this one is "descriptive not prescriptive." Mantel attested, "Visser's style seems heavy, for a page or so; then you notice the subterranean drollness seeping through. Her book is a learned, fascinating and wide-ranging survey of eating customs from prehistoric times to the present day; it is one of those rare books that, because it touches on the essence of everyday experience, transforms your world while you are reading it. . . . There is something quotable, interesting or alarming on every page of this book." In the *New York Times Book Review* Molly O'Neil commented that Visser's "dense learned patter could ground a frivolous cocktail hour, but it might become a little pedantic over the course of a long meal. Read [*The Rituals of Dinner*] in small doses. But read it, because you'll never look at a table knife the same way again."

A critic for *Kirkus Reviews* similarly warned that *The Way We Are* should be read "at random and in short bursts" so that "Visser's warmth and humor" can overcome "a tendency to the pedantic, which . . . in larger swallows becomes almost overwhelming." Comments on food are part, but not all, of what comprise *The Way We Are*. Visser's third publication is a compilation of about fifty short essays previously published in the popular Canadian magazine *Saturday Night*. The book's topics vary widely and, according to Thomas Blaikie in *Spectator*, "There will be readers who will protest that too much of the material is incidental, that the open-minded, suggestive approach leads nowhere . . . [but] it can be said unequivocally that in Margaret Visser's hands to read a history of knitting or of Christmas Pudding is pure pleasure." Positively highlighting the book, Sandra Martin called it "witty, erudite, and succinct" and stated in *Quill & Quire*: "If I have one complaint . . . it is that Visser does tend to circle the same ground . . . more than once, but can a columnist ignore Christmas or spring just because she covered it last year?"

In *The Geometry of Love: Space, Time, Mystery, and Meaning in an Ordinary Church* Visser brings her precise and focused analysis of the ordinary to the study of a small Italian church. "Seeking to open the springs of the spirit, Margaret Visser has written an ascetic, private, devotional meditation on Christian history, embodied in a church and its bones and stones, which she lovingly numbers," commented Marina Warner in the *New York Times*. Sant Agnese Furore le Mure (St. Agnes Outside the Walls) is a very old church in Rome that has been open to worshipers for more than 1,350 years. Within it are buried the remains of Saint Agnes, a twelve-year-old girl who died a martyr's death in 305 C.E. for refusing to marry the governor of Rome. Visser provides a deep consideration not only of the church itself, but of the history, ritual, and meaning of Catholic religion, and what the architecture of the church can reveal to a modern pilgrim who experiences it. She describes the layout of the church and the various sections within, such as the nave, and what they mean in the context of Catholicism in particular and religion in general. She explains the meaning of the catacombs and Christian burial traditions, the power of relics and martyrs, the origins of words relevant to Christian religion, and the symbolism represented by depictions of St. Agnes and the structural elements of the church.

"What is astonishing is the depth of Visser's knowledge of the Bible and church history as well as the depth of her theological reflections," remarked Arthur Van Seters in a *Presbyterian Record* article on *The Geometry of Love*. Visser "brings an enormous breadth—literary, archaeological, anthropological, theological—to her study," observed John Savant in *America*. *Christian Century* reviewer Ronald Goetz named Visser "a first-rate collector and reporter of the history and legends that make up the folklore of St. Agnes." Sally Cunneen, writing in *Christian Century*, commented that Visser's "remarkable book is something to savor and reread," concluding that the book is a "clear-eyed, generous introduction to Christianity as it has existed in time and aspires to eternity."

A Canadian citizen, Visser was raised in what is now Zambia, and she has lived in Iraq, France, England, and the United States, as well as Canada. She once told *CA:* "My intention, in my radio and television work as well as in my books, is to celebrate the 'ordinary' in such a way that people who listen, watch, or read it will never feel quite the same about everyday things again. After all, the word 'ordinary' derives from 'order'; the more you take a thing or a custom for granted, the more it organizes you and directs your actions. Nothing 'ordinary' can be unimportant.

"My academic training is in ancient Greek and Latin, with a specialty in Greek drama, mythology, and religion. The ideas and methods I learned from this scholarly pursuit have formed the basis of my work outside the university." Visser's scholarly research is conducted in French, German, and Italian, as well as in the classical languages.

BIOGRAPHICAL AND CRITICAL SOURCES:

PERIODICALS

America, September 17, 2001, John Savant, "Agnes and Beyond," review of *The Geometry of Love: Space, Time, Mystery, and Meaning in an Ordinary Church*, p. 23.

Booklist, March 15, 1996, Donna Seaman, review of *The Way We Are*, p. 1227.

Christian Century, May 23, 2001, Ronald Goetz, review of *The Geometry of Love*, p. 28; January 2, 2002, Sally Cunneen, review of *The Geometry of Love*, p. 42.

Kirkus Reviews, January 1, 1996, review of *The Way We Are*, p. 58.

Library Journal, August, 1991, Eric Hinsdale, review of *The Rituals of Dinner: The Origins, Evolution, Eccentricities, and Meaning of Table Manners,* p. 108.

London Review of Books, December 3, 1992, P.N. Furbank, review of *The Rituals of Dinner,* p. 27.

Los Angeles Times, August 6, 1992, Mary Williams Walsh, profile of Margaret Visser.

New York, July 22, 1991, Rhoda Koenig, review of *The Rituals of Dinner,* p. 50.

New York Times, June 3, 2001, Marina Warner, "Where Heaven Touches Down," review of *The Geometry of Love,* p. 48.

New York Times Book Review, February 21, 1988, Laura Shapiro, review of *Much Depends on Dinner,* p. 18; July 28, 1991, Molly O'Neill, review of *The Rituals of Dinner,* p. 7; August 18, 2002, Scott Veale, review of *The Geometry of Love,* p. 20.

Presbyterian Record, July, 2001, Arthur Van Seters, review of *The Geometry of Love,* p. 45.

Psychology Today, November, 1988, Judith Klein, review of *Much Depends on Dinner,* p. 70.

Publishers Weekly, May 17, 1991, p. review of *The Rituals of Dinner,* 49; January 8, 1996, review of *The Way We Are,* p. 52; February 26, 2001, review of *The Geometry of Love,* p. 79.

Quill & Quire, October, 1986, Janet Fetherling, review of *Much Depends on Dinner,* p. 46; July, 1994, Sandra Martin, review of *The Way We Are,* p. 57.

Spectator, September 5, 1992, Hilary Mantel, review of *The Rituals of Dinner,* p. 27; January 6, 1996, Thomas Blaikie, review of *The Way We Are,* p. 30.

Times Literary Supplement, July 27, 1990, Keith Jeffrey, review of *Much Depends on Dinner,* p. 809.

Wilson Library Bulletin, June, 1988, Barbara Scotto, review of *Much Depends on Dinner,* p. 133.

ONLINE

Domestic-Church.com Web site, http://www.domestic-church.com/ (November 5, 2005), Catherine Fournier, review of *The Geometry of Love.*

Margaret Visser Home Page, http://www.margaret visser.com (November 5, 2005).

Rebecca's Reads, http://rebeccasreads.com/ (November 5, 2005), review of *The Geometry of Love.*

Spirituality & Health, http://www.spiritualityhealth.com/ (November 5, 2005), Frederic and Mary Ann Brussel, review of *The Geometry of Love.* *

---

von HOFFMAN, Nicholas 1929-

PERSONAL: Born October 16, 1929, in New York, NY; son of Carl (an explorer) and Anna (a dentist; maiden name, Bruenn) von Hoffman; married Ann Byrne, 1950 (divorced); married Patricia Bennett, 1979 (divorced); children (first marriage): Alexander, Aristodemus, Constantine. *Education:* Graduated Fordham Prep School, 1948.

ADDRESSES: Office—c/o King Features, 235 E. 45th St., New York, NY 10017. *Agent*—Virginia Barber, 44 Greenwich Ave., New York, NY 10011. *E-mail*—nvonhoffman@observer.com.

CAREER: Industrial Area Foundation, Chicago, IL, associate director, 1954-63; *Chicago Daily News,* Chicago, staff member, 1963-66; *Washington Post,* Washington, DC, staff member and columnist, 1966-76; *Spectator,* London, England, Washington correspondent, beginning 1976; free-lance writer; *Point-Counterpoint* commentator on CBS's *60 Minutes; New York Observer,* New York, NY, columnist.

AWARDS, HONORS: Friends of Literature Journalism Award, 1965, for *Mississippi Notebook.*

WRITINGS:

Mississippi Notebook, David White (New York, NY), 1964.

The Multiversity: A Personal Report on What Happens to Today's Students at American Universities, Holt (New York, NY), 1966.

We Are the People Our Parents Warned Us Against, Quadrangle (Chicago, IL), 1968.

Two, Three, Many More: A Novel, Quadrangle (Chicago, IL), 1969.

Left at the Post, Quadrangle (Chicago, IL), 1970.

(With Garry Trudeau) *The Fireside Watergate,* Sheed (New York, NY), 1973.

(With Garry Trudeau) *Tales from the Margaret Mead Taproom: The Compleat Gonzo Governorship of Doonesbury's Uncle Duke,* Sheed (New York, NY), 1976.

Make-Believe Presidents: Illusions of Power from McKinley to Carter, Pantheon (New York, NY), 1978.

Organized Crimes, Harper (New York, NY), 1984.

Citizen Cohn, Doubleday (New York, NY), 1988.

Capitalist Fools: Tales of American Business, from Carnegie to Forbes to the Milken Gang, Doubleday (New York, NY), 1992.

A Devil's Dictionary of American Business, Texere (New York, NY), 2003.

Hoax: Why Americans Are Suckered by White House Lies, Nation Books (New York, NY), 2004.

Author of syndicated column "Poster." Contributor of numerous articles to periodicals, including the *New Republic, Esquire,* and *GQ.*

ADAPTATIONS: Citizen Cohn was adapted as a film for HBO.

SIDELIGHTS: Nicholas von Hoffman began his career in Chicago, where he worked for nine years as associate director of the Industrial Areas Foundation under the tutelage of Saul Alinsky. A grass-roots organizer and social activist, Alinsky's spirited defense of underdog causes made him a Chicago institution. Alinsky's notoriety helped von Hoffman get a job in 1963 as labor reporter for the *Chicago Daily News,* a position he held until 1966. At that point, Ben Bradlee of the *Washington Post* offered von Hoffman a job. As a reporter for the *Post,* von Hoffman covered a wide range of stories, from the civil rights movement to Watergate. It was also while at the *Post* that von Hoffman began writing a column entitled "Poster" for King Features Syndicate. According to Chalmers M. Roberts, author of *The Washington Post: The First Hundred Years,* von Hoffman's column rarely failed to elicit response: "His vivid prose, often intentionally provocative, produced more angry letters to the editor than the work of any other single reporter in the paper's history. In the late 1960s and early 1970s, von Hoffman became a favorite of the New Left and of some youth cults. At the *Post* some adored him; others considered him a menace to journalism. . . . By the very power of his words, the details of his reporting, and the outrage of his expressed beliefs he forced uncounted *Post* readers to examine a life style that repelled them, especially when it became that of their own middle-class offspring."

Von Hoffman's gift for voicing the concerns, problems, and aspirations of the young has been apparent in much of his writing, most notably *The Multiversity: A Personal Report on What Happens to Today's Students at American Universities* and *We Are the People Our Parents Warned Us Against.* The latter became a watershed of sorts due to its unflinching portrait of discord among America's youth. The book began as an assignment for the *Washington Post* about the 1967 "summer of love," with von Hoffman centering his focus on San Francisco's Haight-Ashbury district. Included were gritty and sometimes grim details of the drug/counter-culture scene as it really was, the provocative contents angering and shocking many people. It was not, however, the only time von Hoffman dealt with potentially incendiary topics in his writings. Both his novels, such as *Two, Three, Many More* (about a college revolt), and nonfiction, such as *Mississippi Notebook,* which was concerned with the civil rights movement, engendered strong reaction. Von Hoffman further aroused public sentiment with his *Point-Counterpoint* appearances on *60 Minutes,* where he vocally embraced the views of the far left.

After leaving the *Washington Post* in 1976, von Hoffman worked on two books with political satirist Garry Trudeau, acted as the Washington correspondent for London-based *Spectator* magazine, and continued writing commentary. Von Hoffman's prodigious output slowed a bit as the 1980s began. In 1984, however, von Hoffman received critical attention for his novel *Organized Crimes.* Set in Chicago during the Depression, the novel tells the story of several notorious gangsters and the "better" moneyed people who both supported and decried their activities. The central character of the story is Allan Archibald, a wealthy, handsome student doing sociological field research about the Chicago underworld. Allan's meetings with various criminals are tempered by his love affair with another student, the beautiful but poor Irena Giron. Their relationship blooms amid gang warfare, political manipulation, and social upheavals. As Allan becomes more and more involved in gang associations, his father's fortunes reverse, and young Archibald finds himself driven into the arms of a gangster's moll. All is resolved in a climax that is violent, shocking, and sudden.

Critics were impressed with von Hoffman's ability to re-create an era and populate it with colorful characters. "It is historical fiction of a kind: although the period it deals with is just fifty years past," *Washington Post* writer Bruce Cook said, *Organized Crimes* "is crammed with accurate and fascinating social detail of the kind usually lavished on novels dealing with periods more distant in time. . . . This is one of the best Chicago novels in quite a while." *Time* reviewer William Henry III compared von Hoffman's *Chicago* to turn-of-the-century New York in E.L. Doctorow's *Ragtime,* praising the author's "ruefully comic invention." In the *New York Times Book Review,* Jan Herman stressed the novel's "clever blend of anecdotal history and sentimental history" remarking that von Hoffman "sketches a fascinating era with disarming ease."

Much of the detail von Hoffman introduced into *Organized Crimes* was the result of his reportorial skills. These skills were integral to von Hoffman's next project, a biography of attorney Roy Cohn. Entitled *Citizen Cohn,* the text is an unflinching look at a controversial figure. Cohn died of AIDS in August of 1986, leaving behind a perplexing legacy. During the course of his career, Cohn was a political manipulator, wheeler-dealer, and confidant of the rich and famous. Best known for his role as chief counsel to Senator Joseph R. McCarthy during the infamous "red scare" of the 1950's, Cohn was also involved in the espionage trial of Julius and Ethel Rosenberg. His private law practice was very lucrative, but its profits were largely based on Cohn's ability to exploit the legal system. At the time of his death, he faced government scrutiny of his business affairs and disbarment action.

Ironically, von Hoffman's 1988 Cohn biography was released simultaneously with Sidney Zion's *Autobiography of Roy Cohn.* As a result, many critics reviewed the books concurrently, noting that while von Hoffman and Zion shared the same subject matter, their treatment of it differed. Zion was a close friend of Cohn, and had taken over the transcription of his memoirs when Cohn was no longer physically able to continue. As a result, Zion's transcription has a more personal, sympathetic emphasis. Von Hoffman assumed a more analytical stance, concentrating on the facts (such as were available) of Cohn's life, beginning with his death from AIDS-related ailments (a condition Cohn denied until the very end) and concluding with his ongoing battles with the IRS and New York State Bar Association.

Critical reaction to *Citizen Cohn* was mixed. Christopher Lehmann-Haupt of the *New York Times* felt that von Hoffman was not always clear in identifying his source references, but still managed to offer the reader a "richer, more rounded, better balanced view of his subject's life" than Zion. In the *Times Literary Supplement,* Gary Wills noted that von Hoffman had a good grasp of the political ramifications of Cohn's activities, but "misses the deeper ironies and betrayals" while maintaining a "whimsically clinical" attitude toward his subject that makes for a sometimes rambling discourse.

Peter Collier of the *Washington Post Book World* observed that von Hoffman's emphasis on prurient trivia indicates he has "picked through Cohn's life with a kind of repelled fascination." Collier found muddled passages and haphazard editing distracting, yet maintained that one "begins the book with disdain for the subject, but ends with a distant sympathy. . . . While von Hoffman is far from preaching forgiveness, what he writes does remind us once again of the truth in H.L. Menken's observation that this would be a dull world if it were not for the sinners." Writing in the *New York Times Book Review,* Tom Wolfe concluded that *Citizen Cohn* is a fast, entertaining read that eventually "bogs down," not so much for literary reasons, but because the book concerns "the depressing spectacle of a prodigy who grew old without overcoming the childhood fevers that inflamed him."

In the book *Capitalist Fools: Tales of American Business, from Carnegie to Forbes to the Milken Gang,* von Hoffman provides a study of capitalism in the United States and the transformations it has undergone over the course of a few generations. The author began the book as a straightforward biography of businessman Malcolm Forbes, but he soon expanded his subject. As Wendy Smith reported in *Publishers Weekly,* von Hoffman's book "scathingly criticizes contemporary American business leaders as shortsighted scavengers who make money by leveraging and conglomerating rather than manufacturing useful products." Although the author paints the business tycoons of yesteryear as unashamedly greedy and unresponsive to the needs of workers, he nevertheless sees the ways in which they truly contributed to the building of the United States. Today's business captains have the same failings but less leadership and vision. "Whole chapters of *Capitalist Fools* read like the anguish of a middle-aged elitist who despairs of modern times. Von Hoffman berates the trashing of children's minds by an entertainment culture which has turned them into couch potatoes." stated Robert Dawson in *Management Today.* Dawson found that any generation could be subject to the same criticisms von Hoffman directs at the modern era, but concluded that "*Capitalist Fools* is a thoughtful book containing many persuasive insights and startling prescriptions."

Von Hoffman analyzed the rationale behind the invasion of Iraq by U.S. forces in his book *Hoax: Why Americans Are Suckered by White House Lies.* The author's stance on the issue is clear from his title, and he discusses not only the strategies used to build up support for the Iraq invasion, but for other foreign policies as well. Noting that many books on similar subjects came out at about the same time, a *Publishers Weekly* reviewer called von Hoffman's offering "a smart, elegant standout," which "relies on subtle, nuanced cultural analyses to examine the peculiarity of America's hermetic view of itself." The reviewer concluded that while this penetrating critique of American actions would not please "the blindly patriotic," it would be of great interest to those who question the foreign policy decisions of the Bush administration. *Booklist* reviewer Vanessa Bush also predicted that while some would agree with the author's conclusions and others would find them "harsh . . . all will find them provocative."

BIOGRAPHICAL AND CRITICAL SOURCES:

BOOKS

Roberts, Chalmers M., *The Washington Post: The First 100 Years,* Houghton (Boston, MA), 1977.

PERIODICALS

Booklist, July, 2004, Vanessa Bush, review of *Hoax: Why Americans Are Suckered by White House Lies,* p. 1806.

Economist, May 7, 1988, review of *Citizen Cohn,* p. 85.

Kirkus Reviews, April 1, 2004, review of *Hoax,* p. 321.

Management Today, July, 1993, Robert Dawson, review of *Capitalist Fools: Tales of American Business, from Carnegie to Forbes to the Milken Gang,* p. 74.

Nation, May 21, 1988, Robert Sherrill, review of *Citizen Cohn,* p. 719.

National Review, June 24, 1988, review of *Citizen Cohn,* p. 44.

New Leader, May 16, 1988, David M. Oshinsky, review of *Citizen Cohn,* p. 17.

New Republic, December 7, 1992, Michael Lewis, review of *Capitalist Fools,* p. 43.

New York Times Book Review, October 21, 1984, Jan Herman, review of *Organized Crimes.*

People, May 2, 1988, Mary Vespa, review of *Citizen Cohn,* p. 25.

Publishers Weekly, September 21, 1992, Wendy Smith, interview with Nicholas von Hoffman, p. 72; April 19, 2004, review of *Hoax,* p. 48.

Time, December 3, 1984, William A. Henry III, review of *Organized Crimes.*

Washington Post, October 22, 1984, Bruce Cook, review of *Organized Crimes.**

W

WAKEMAN, Frederic Evans, Jr.
See WAKEMAN, Frederic, Jr.

* * *

WAKEMAN, Frederic, Jr. 1937-
(Frederic Evans Wakeman, Jr.)

PERSONAL: Born December 12, 1937, in Kansas City, KS.; son of Frederic Evans (an author) and Margaret (Keyes) Wakeman; married Nancy Schuster, December 28, 1957 (divorced January, 1974); married Carolyn Huntley, December 31, 1974; children: Frederic Evans III, Matthew Clark. Education: Harvard University, A.B., 1959; Institut d'Etudes Politiques, graduate study, 1959-60; University of California, Berkeley, M.A., 1962, Ph.D., 1965.

ADDRESSES: Home—56 Arlington Ct., Kensington, CA 94704. Office—3220 Dwinelle Hall, University of California—Berkeley, CA 94720-2550. E-mail—jingcha@socrates.berkeley.edu.

CAREER: University of California—Berkeley, CA, assistant professor, 1965-67, associate professor, 1968-70, professor of Chinese history, 1971-79, currently Haas Professor of Asian Studies; Inter-University Program for Chinese Language Studies, Taipei, Taiwan, director, 1967-68. Visiting scholar at Corpus Christi College, Cambridge University, and Beijing University.

MEMBER: American Historical Association, Association for Asian Studies, Society for Ch'ing Studies.

AWARDS, HONORS: Harvard National Scholar, 1955-1959; Center for Chinese Studies (Berkeley, CA) junior fellowship, 1960-62; National Defense Foreign Language fellowship, 1962-63; John Simon Guggenheim fellowship, 1973-74; National Book Award nomination, 1974, for History and Will; National Research Council fellow.

WRITINGS:

NONFICTION, EXCEPT AS NOTED

Seventeen Royal Palms Drive (novel), New American Library (New York, NY), 1962.
Strangers at the Gate: Social Disorder in South China, 1839-1861, University of California Press (Berkeley, CA), 1966.
Nothing Concealed: Essays in Honor of Liu Yuyun, Chinese Materials and Research Aids Service Center (Taiwan), 1970.
(With Thomas Metcalf and Edward Tannenbaum) A World History, Wiley (New York, NY), 1973.
History and Will: Philosophical Perspectives of the Thought of Mao Tse-tung, University of California Press (Berkeley, CA), 1973.
(Editor) Conflict and Control in Late Imperial China, University of California Press (Berkeley, CA), 1975.
The Fall of Imperial China, Free Press (New York, NY), 1975.
(Editor) Ming and Qing Historical Studies in the People's Republic of China, University of California at Berkeley Center for Chinese Studies (Berkeley, CA), 1980.

The Great Enterprise: The Manchu Reconstruction of Imperial Order in Seventeenth-Century China, University of California Press (Berkeley, CA), 1985.

(Editor, with Wen-hsin Yeh) *Shanghai Sojourners,* University of California at Berkeley Center for Chinese Studies (Berkeley, CA), 1992

Policing Shanghai, 1927-1937, University of California Press (Berkeley, CA), 1995.

The Shanghai Badlands: Wartime Terrorism and Urban Crime, 1937-1941, Cambridge University Press (New York, NY), 1996.

(With Wang Xi) *China's Quest for Modernization: A Historical Perspective,* University of California Press (Berkeley, CA), 1997.

(Editor, with Richard Louis Edmonds) *Reappraising Republican China,* Cambridge University Press (New York, NY), 2000.

Spymaster: Dai Li and the Chinese Secret Service, University of California Press (Berkeley, CA), 2003.

Author of foreword to *Poisoned Arrows: The Stalin-Choibalsan Mongolian Massacres, 1921-1941,* by Shagdariin Sandag and Harry H. Kendall, Westview (Boulder, CO), 2000. Contributor to books, including *From Ming to Ch'ing,* edited by Jonathon Spence and John Wills, Yale University Press (New Haven, CT), 1979; and *The Cambridge History of China,* Volume 10, Cambridge University Press, 1979. Contributor of articles and reviews to scholarly journals. *Spymaster: Dai Li and the Chinese Secret Service* has been translated into Chinese.

SIDELIGHTS: Frederic Wakeman, Jr., "is one of the brightest of the middle generation of American historians of China," according to a reviewer in the *Times Literary Supplement.* He praised Wakeman's first study of the Chinese, *Strangers at the Gate: Social Disorder in South China, 1839-1861,* for being "one of the few Western studies of nineteenth-century Chinese history that can be recommended . . . to readers not accustomed to . . . sinological writing." Wakeman's subsequent work has been similarly praised.

History and Will: Philosophical Perspectives of the Thought of Mao Tse-tung, which was nominated for the 1974 National Book Award, is Wakeman's analysis of the influence of various Chinese and European political, philosophical, and cultural traditions on Mao Tse-tung's thought. *Library Journal* reviewer Leo Ou-fan Lee commented that *History and Will* "presents a mosaic of documentation, insights, and reflections on a variety of historical and philosophical subjects . . . which provide the intellectual background of Maoism." Although the *Times Literary Supplement* critic pointed to certain structural and thematic flaws and suggested that Wakeman may have "tried to cover too much ground," he considered the book a "bold effort" and concluded: "The faults of this interesting book do not cancel out its achievements, which are considerable. Dr. Wakeman has opened up new perspectives on modern Chinese intellectual history and sown some ideas that will yield fruit in the future. It is not often that a book on China makes one think hard, and so long as *History and Will* is treated neither as a textbook nor as an authoritative work it is to be welcomed."

In *Policing Shanghai: 1927-1937,* Wakeman provides an analysis of a crucial decade in Chinese history, focusing on the city of Shanghai. The threat of Japanese expansion was imminent, and the country's national identity was weak due to various factors. Wakeman examines the Chinese Nationalists' plans for renewing the nation. He also charts the powerful influences of the Shanghai underworld, which was filled with casinos, brothels, and drug rings. *Policing Shanghai* offers "a magisterial slice of modern Chinese history," according to Kellee S. Tsai in the *Journal of International Affairs. Journal of Asian and African Studies* contributor Richard J. Smith found the picture Wakeman painted to be depressing, but presented with "color and clarity." Smith further commented that the book will "dazzle us with its brilliant narrative and convince us that even without the invasion of the Japanese in the 1930s, the Nationalists were doomed to failure." Wakeman delves further into the history of Shanghai in *The Shanghai Badlands: Wartime Terrorism and Urban Crime, 1937-41.*

The author focuses on twentieth-century espionage in *Spymaster: Dai Li and the Chinese Secret Service.* Reviewing the book for the *Canadian Journal of History,* Ryan Dunch recommended it as a "masterful" depiction of "the secretive world of kidnappers, torturers, spies, and smugglers in government employ." He outlines the development of the secret police system, as carried out during that period by General Dai Li. Dunch advised, "The book is difficult reading, both for its subject matter and for the depth of detail it contains, but it is by the same token a tour de force and richly instructive for any modern historian in illuminating the hidden politics of Republican China, which gave rise to a veritable army of agents and assassins." Dai Li's complex personality mirrored the complexities of life in China at that time, and Wakeman's portrait of him won praise from critics. "Minutely researched, richly contextualized, and lucidly written," remarked Yu Shen in *Historian,* "Wakeman produces an amazingly evenhanded account of Dai Li, a man better known for his evil reputation than historical consequence." Shen concluded that after reading this book the figure of Dai Li "will remain on our conscience and challenge us to stare into his eyes and try to comprehend the complexity of both his life and his time."

BIOGRAPHICAL AND CRITICAL SOURCES:

PERIODICALS

Canadian Journal of History, December, 2004, Ryan Dunch, review of *Spymaster: Dai Li and the Chinese Secret Service,* p. 648.
China Journal, July, 2004, Brian G. Martin, review of *Spymaster,* p. 219.
Choice, January, 1974, review of *History and Will: Philosophical Perspectives of the Thought of Mao Tse-tung,* p. 1788.
Historian, winter, 1999, Arif Dirlik, review of *The Shanghai Badlands: Wartime Terrorism and Urban Crime, 1937-1941,* p. 446; spring, 2005, Yu Shen, review of *Spymaster,* p. 139.
Journal of Asian and African Studies, December, 1996, Richard J. Smith, review of *Policing Shanghai, 1927-1937,* p. 259; November, 1998, Tzi-Ki Hon, review of *China's Quest for Modernization: A Historical Perspective,* p. 388.
Journal of Asian Studies, February, 1974, review of *History and Will,* p. 310.
Journal of Interdisciplinary History, summer, 1997, Lillian M. Li, review of *Policing Shanghai, 1927-1937,* p. 177.
Journal of International Affairs, winter, 1996, Kellee S. Tsai, review of *Policing Shanghai, 1927-1937,* pp. 606-612.
Library Journal, April 15, 1973, Leo Oufan Lee, review of *History and Will,* p. 1289.
Times Literary Supplement, March 15, 1974, review of *History and Will,* p. 251.

WALSH, George 1931-
   (George William Walsh)

PERSONAL: Born January 16, 1931, in New York, NY; son of William Francis and Madeline (Maass) Walsh; married Joan Mary Dunn, May 20, 1961; children: Grail, Simon. *Education:* Fordham University, B.S., 1952; Columbia University, M.S., 1953. *Religion:* Roman Catholic.

ADDRESSES: Home and office—35 Prospect Park, W. Brooklyn, NY 11215-2370. *E-mail*—edchief@earthlink.net.

CAREER: Cape Cod Standard-Times, Hyannis, MA, copy editor and reporter, 1955; International Business Machines Corp. (IBM), New York, NY, communications specialist, 1955-58; Time, Inc., New York, NY, editorial trainee, 1958-59; *Sports Illustrated,* New York, NY, writer-reporter, 1959-62; *Cosmopolitan,* New York, NY, book editor, 1962-65, managing editor, 1965-74; Random House, Inc., New York, NY, vice-president and editor in chief of Ballantine Books division, 1974-79; Macmillan Publishing Co., New York, NY, vice-president and editor in chief of general books division, 1979-85; publishing consultant and writer, 1985—. *Military service:* U.S. Army, 1953-55.

MEMBER: Association of American Publishers, University Club (New York, NY), Pamet Harbor Yacht and Tennis Club (Truro, MA).

WRITINGS:

Gentleman Jimmy Walker: Mayor of the Jazz Age, foreword by Robert Moses, Praeger (New York, NY), 1974.
Public Enemies: The Mayor, the Mob, and the Crime that Was, Norton (New York, NY), 1980.
Damage Them All You Can: Robert E. Lee's Army of Northern Virginia, Forge (New York, NY), 2002.
"Whip the Rebellion": Ulysses S. Grant's Rise to Command, Tom Doherty Associates (New York, NY), 2005.

WORK IN PROGRESS: The third volume in the author's Civil War trilogy, *Those Damn Horse Soldiers—True Tales of the Civil War Cavalry.*

SIDELIGHTS: George Walsh frames *Gentleman Jimmy Walker: Mayor of the Jazz Age,* his political biography of flamboyant New York mayor James J. Walker, with a social history of the city in the Roaring Twenties. Lavish celebrity receptions, glamorous theatrical life, Ziegfeld Follies showgirls, and such notorious gangland figures as "Dutch" Schultz and "Mad Dog" Coll colored the era in which Walker flourished. Elected to office in 1926 with the support of the local Democratic party organization called Tammany Hall, "Gentleman Jimmy," as he was known to legions of admiring voters, presided over one of the most openly corrupt municipal administrations in New York City history. Nevertheless, according to Walsh, the debonair mayor managed to charm nearly everyone he met, from visiting dignitaries to show business personalities like Follies star Betty Compton, who became his mistress.

The onset of the Great Depression foreshadowed the end of Walker's political career. In 1930 the state of New York mounted an investigation of corruption in New York City's municipal courts, and the following year a judicial commission was formed to probe allegedly rampant malfeasance throughout Walker's administration. The commission uncovered evidence that many city officials had taken bribes and payoffs for political favors, and it surfaced that Walker himself kept secret bank and brokerage accounts totaling almost one million dollars, supplied by illegal payoffs from businessmen and contractors. At a removal hearing before Governor Franklin Delano Roosevelt in 1932, Walker defended the acceptance of what he called "beneficences." He nevertheless resigned his position before a judgment on the case was rendered.

New York Times critic Herbert Mitgang praised the Walker biography for getting "a great deal of information on the record without changing any past impressions about the charming rogue." Contrasting Walsh's treatment of the subject with two earlier, less formal biographies of Walker, the critic observed that "by playing it straight Mr. Walsh indirectly provides a case history of how not to govern New York City." And *New York Times Book Review* critic Richard F. Shepherd remarked that Walsh "accepts Walker as a very fallible man and chronicles his life, with little moralizing."

The subject of Walsh's *Public Enemies: The Mayor, the Mob, and the Crime that Was* is another Tammany-backed New York mayor, William O'Dwyer, who was first elected in 1945. The author probes the nature of O'Dwyer's relationship with organized crime boss Frank Costello, relying in part on transcripts from the Kefauver Crime Investigation Committee hearings held by the U.S. Senate, for which both men testified. The book recounts how the two, each ambitious immigrants who started at the bottom, fought their way to high position: Costello by means of the gangland wars of the 1920's and 1930's, and O'Dwyer as a young district attorney who prosecuted Murder Incorporated. The seemingly natural antagonists cemented an alliance brokered by Tammany Hall when O'Dwyer decided to run for mayor. The political machine controlled key votes and the crime syndicate backed Tammany, supplying goons to marshal illegal votes and threaten opponents. Walsh quotes O'Dwyer's explanation that "there are things you have to do politically, if you want cooperation." When the crime connection scandal broke, O'Dwyer resigned his second term as mayor to become ambassador to Mexico.

In the *New York Times Book Review,* Jeff Greenfield judged *Public Enemies* to be "a lively account of the immense political influence wielded by gangsters in the biggest city in America." Similarly *Los Angeles Times* critic Robert Kirsch wrote that "Walsh has written a cool and crisp case study of the way a genial, sociable mayor sought to exploit—and was used by—organized crime. There are elements of Damon Runyon and Lincoln Steffens in the account."

Walsh turns his attention to the American Civil War in *Damage Them All You Can: Robert E. Lee's Army of Northern Virginia.* Under the broader scope of the Civil War, Walsh narrows his focus to a variety of everyday citizens—laborers, craftsmen, farmers, teachers, and other professionals—who made up the officers and enlisted soldiers of the Army of Northern Virginia. With an eye toward the human side of Lee's army, Walsh covers numerous critical battles that involved the Army of Northern Virginia, including Manassas, Chancellorsville, and Gettysburg. He describes in detail the toll on soldiers taken by the elements, the lack of supplies, constant disease, and the stress of battle. At Second Manassas, the troops were so short of supplies that they were reduced to throwing rocks at their enemies. Walsh explores how Lee's tendency to issue vague orders led to confusion; how field-grade officers practiced the art of blame-fixing and scapegoating; and how the personalities of the major officers affected the outcome of the battles. Though their experiences were harsh, the Army of Northern Virginia's "bravery and tenacity . . . held right through the closing hours of the war," noted a *Kirkus Reviews* critic. *Library Journal* contributor John Carver Edwards called it a "persuasively detailed work," and *Booklist* reviewer Roland Green commented favorably on Walsh's "real virtues of intelligibility, balance, and narrative skill."

In *"Whip the Rebellion": Ulysses S. Grant's Rise to Command* Walsh looks at Lee's northern counterpart, Ulysses S. Grant, and offers "a good, but not great, overview of Grant's military prowess," commented Gayla Koerting in the *Library Journal*. He provides an analysis of Grant's evolution as a military leader and commander. With additional material on William Tecumseh Sherman and Philip Sheridan, Walsh examines how the three generals created strategy and issued important decisions that helped shape the outcome of the Civil War. In his work Walsh "attains a very high level of popular historiography," commented Green in another *Booklist* review.

BIOGRAPHICAL AND CRITICAL SOURCES:

PERIODICALS

Booklist, November 15, 2002, Roland Green, review of *Damage Them All You Can: Robert E. Lee's Army of Northern Virginia,* p. 567; March 1, 2005, Roland Green, review of *"Whip the Rebellion": Ulysses S. Grant's Rise to Command,* p. 1135.

Civil War Times Illustrated, February, 2003, Kevin M. Levin, review of *Damage Them All You Can,* p. 61.

Kirkus Reviews, October 1, 2002, review of *Damage Them All You Can,* p. 1454.

Library Journal, November 15, 2002, John Carver Edwards, review of *Damage Them All You Can,* p. 86; March 1, 2005, Gayla Koerting, review of *"Whip the Rebellion",* p. 99.

Los Angeles Times, March 7, 1980, Robert Kirsch, review of *Public Enemies: The Mayor, the Mob, and the Crime that Was.*

Military Images, July-August, 2003, Thomas Boaz, review of *Damage Them All You Can,* p. 4.

New York Times, December 18, 1974, Herbert Mitgang, review of *Gentleman Jimmy Walker.*

New York Times Book Review, February 16, 1975, Richard F. Shepherd, review of *Gentleman Jimmy Walker;* February 10, 1980, Jeff Greenfield, review of *Public Enemies,* p. 16.

*   *   *

WALSH, George William
See WALSH, George

*   *   *

WHITEHEAD, Barbara Dafoe 1944-

PERSONAL: Born November 10, 1944, in Rochester, MN; daughter of William A. (a surgeon) and Muriel (a nurse) Dafoe; married Ralph Watson Whitehead, Jr., June 17, 1967; children: Ann, Sarah, John. *Education:* University of Wisconsin, B.A., 1966; University of Chicago, M.A., 1972, Ph.D., 1976. *Politics:* Democrat. *Religion:* Protestant.

ADDRESSES: Home—15 Forest Edge Rd., Amherst, MA 01002. *Office*—The National Marriage Project, Rutgers, The State University of New Jersey, 25 Bishop Pl., New Brunswick, NJ 08901-1181; fax 732-932-2957.

CAREER: Institute for American Values, New York, NY, vice president; National Marriage Project, Rutgers University, Camden, NJ co-director. Serves on the Massachusetts Commission for Responsible Fatherhood and the Religion and Public Values Task Force of the National Campaign to Prevent Teen Pregnancy.

AWARDS, HONORS: Woodrow Wilson fellowship, 1967-68; Exceptional Merit in Media Award, National Women's Political Caucus and Radcliffe College, 1993, for article "Dan Quayle Was Right"; Editorial Excellence Award, *Folio* Magazine and The Cowles Foundation, 1994, for "The Failure of Sex Education."; D.H.L., Lawrence University.

WRITINGS:

The Divorce Culture, Alfred A. Knopf (New York, NY), 1997.

(With David Popenoe) *Should We Live Together?: What Young Adults Need to Know about Cohabitation before Marriage: A Comprehensive Review of Recent Research,* National Marriage Project (New Brunswick, NJ), 1999.

Why There Are No Good Men Left: The Romantic Plight of the New Single Woman, Broadway Books (New York, NY), 2003.

Also contributor to periodicals, including *Atlantic Monthly, American Enterprise, Commonweal, Wilson Quarterly, Times Literary Supplement, New York Times, Reader's Digest, Boston Globe, Los Angeles Times, Slate, Washington Post,* and *Wall Street Journal.*

SIDELIGHTS: Barbara Dafoe Whitehead is a writer, sociologist, and advocate of family and marriage. She serves as the codirector of the National Marriage Project at Rutgers University and is active in state and national organizations that encourage family solidarity, responsible fatherhood, and public values. Her first book, *The Divorce Culture,* analyzes the tremendous rise in divorce in America, searches for reasons behind it, and looks at the effects of divorce on children and society in general. Based on a controversial article Whitehead published in 1993 in the *Atlantic Monthly,* the book endorses the traditional nuclear family arrangement and affixes blame for a variety of social ills squarely on divorce, and by extension those who put their interests above those of family by seeking divorce. Her work makes clear that Whitehead is not a supporter of divorce, particularly in relationships that have produced children. She maintains that it is the institution of marriage that creates the strongest parent-child bonds, and that other forms of family arrangement such as single-parent, cohabiting parent, and step-parent families cannot provide equivalent levels of love, nurturing, socialization, and structure.

Whitehead provides considerable evidence to support her stance, including the results of scientific studies, a variety of statistics, and other material. She traces the rise of divorce to the increased female participation in the paid workforce, but also ascribes the high divorce rate to national changes in attitudes during the 1960s, particularly the idea that divorce is an individual issue and personal decision unrestricted by the needs or interests of other members of the family. "Divorce became 'expressive,' not a failure or an occasion for guilt but an opportunity for growth, the signature of a mature, accomplished identity, a validation leading to greater self-knowledge," as Eric P. Olsen explained in the *World and I.* "Whitehead's basic argument is both unsurprising and, in light of the increasing frequency of divorce, distressing," observed Corinna Vallianatos in the *Washington Monthly.*

Despite the book's earnestness, critics such as Vallianatos report that elements of Whitehead's argument veer toward the extreme, such as her suggestion that out-of-wedlock fathering is a potential precursor to child sexual abuse, and that single and cohabiting parents who bring new lovers into a home environment create a dangerous and erotically charged atmosphere antithetical to the sedate and affectionate environment of a traditional household. In the end, Whitehead endorses a widespread change in consciousness and in perceptions of divorce, in the hopes that those changes in thinking will illuminate the dangers of divorce and reawaken in people the desire for a traditional family household. The book's "main value is simply its existence, for if nothing else, *The Divorce Culture* is an invitation to truly serious reflection on a deeply problematic institution," commented Leslie Gerber in *NWSA Journal.* Robert L. Plunkett, writing in the *National Review,* concluded that the book is "potentially a seminal work. It should change the thinking of many who favor or are neutral on divorce. It will be a valuable source book for those who oppose divorce."

Whitehead explores the modern-day realities of dating and finding a stable, marriage-minded relationship in *Why There Are No Good Men Left: The Romantic Plight of the New Single Woman.* Though her research and interview subjects belong to a certain type of person—young, educated, good-looking, professional white women—Whitehead extrapolates from their experiences a representative experience for women in the early part of the twenty-first century. It is becoming more and more difficult for single women to find a suitable mate and establish a stable marriage, Whitehead notes. She identifies two major reasons for this evolution of marriage patterns in the post-baby-boomer generations. First, many woman are taking greater control of their own lives, particularly in terms of career and education. Woman are focusing on finishing school and establishing their professional careers before considering marriage. By then, however, they have left one of the most fruitful environments for mate-finding—school—and are left in a world where it is more difficult to meet and evaluate potential mates. Second, new methods of dating and courtship have evolved that did not exist before, such as Internet dating, paid matchmaking services, and speed-dating, in which men and women spend ten minutes or so with each other, getting acquainted and making preliminary assessments, before switching round-robin style to another potential suitor, where the process begins again. These new systems, according to Whitehead, have the potential to replace the traditional spouse-finding methods that seem to have faded away in the new millennium. A *BookPage* Web site reviewer called the book a "highly readable account of the single woman's plight," while *Library Journal* reviewer Margaret Cardwell declared it "an intriguing study of the culture in which young, well-educated women find themselves today." A *Publishers Weekly* contributor concluded: "Her engaging cultural assessment, while not novel, sheds light on a current problem many women now face."

BIOGRAPHICAL AND CRITICAL SOURCES:

PERIODICALS

Atlantic Monthly, December, 2002, Caitlin Flanagan, "Hothouse Flowers," review of *Why There Are No Good Men Left: The Romantic Plight of the New Single Woman,* p. 150.
Booklist, January 1, 1997, Patricia Hassler, review of *The Divorce Culture,* p. 792; December 1, 2002, Kristine Huntley, review of *Why There Are No Good Men Left,* p. 624.
Christian Century, February 1, 1995, Don Browning, "On Values: Talking with Peggy Noonan," p. 121.
International Herald Tribune, January 8, 2003, Patricia Cohen, review of *Why There Are No Good Men Left.*
Library Journal, February 15, 1997, Janice Dunham, review of *The Divorce Culture,* p. 152; January, 2003, Margaret Cardwell, review of *Why There Are No Good Men Left,* p. 136.
National Review, March 24, 1997, Robert L. Plunkett, review of *The Divorce Culture,* p. 52.
New Republic, April 14, 1997, Margaret Talbot, review of *The Divorce Culture,* p. 30.
New York, February 10, 1997, Walter Kirn, review of *The Divorce Culture,* p. 52.
New York Times Book Review, January 26, 1997, Fred Miller Robinson, review of *The Divorce Culture,* p. 21.

NWSA Journal, spring, 1998, Leslie Gerber, review of *The Divorce Culture,* p. 189.
Public Interest, spring, 1997, Midge Decter, review of *The Divorce Culture,* p. 115.
Publishers Weekly, December 2, 1996, review of *The Divorce Culture,* p. 48; November 25, 2002, review of *Why There Are No Good Men Left,* p. 56.
Reason, October, 1997, Nick Gillespie, review of *The Divorce Culture,* p. 63.
Tribune Books (Chicago, IL), February 9, 1997, review of *The Divorce Culture,* p. 6.
Washington Monthly, April, 1997, Corinna Vallianatos, review of *The Divorce Culture,* p. 52.
World and I, May, 1997, Eric P. Olsen, review of *The Divorce Culture,* p. 253.

ONLINE

Ashbrook Center for Public Affairs Web site, http://www.ashbrook.org/ (November 5, 2005), brief biography on Barbara Dafoe Whitehead.
Atlantic Online, http://www.TheAtlantic.com/(October 5, 1994), review of *The Divorce Culture.*
BookPage.com, http://www.bookpage.com/ (November 5, 2005), Lynn Green, "Is Cohabitation All It's Cracked up to Be?," review of *Why There Are No Good Men Left.*
Mother Jones Online, http://www.mojones.com/ (November 6, 2005).
National Review Online, http://www.nationalreview.com/ (February 14, 2003), Kathryn Jean Lopez, "Single Hope," interview with Barbara Dafoe Whitehead.
Public Broadcasting Service, http://www.pbs.org/ (November 6, 2005).
Salon.com, http://www.salon.com/ (November 6, 2005), "Salon Daily Clicks/Sneak Peeks."*

*   *   *

WILEY, Ralph 1952-2004

PERSONAL: Born April 12, 1952, in Memphis, TN; died of heart failure, June 13, 2004, in Orlando, FL; son of Ralph H. (a night watchman) and Dorothy Brown (a professor; maiden name, Taylor) Wiley; married Brenda Joysmith (divorced, 1978); married Brenda Joysmith, 1978 (divorced); married Holly Anne Cypress (in marketing), 1982; children: Colen Cypress Wiley. *Education:* Knoxville College, B.S., 1975.

CAREER: *Oakland Tribune,* Oakland, CA, reporter, 1975-76, beat writer for professional and collegiate sports, 1976-79, columnist, 1979-82; article and feature writer for *Sports Illustrated,* 1982-91; Heygood Images Productions, Inc., Landover, MD, founder and chair, 1987-2004. National Broadcasting Company, Inc., *NFL Live,* commentator.

WRITINGS:

Serenity: A Boxing Memoir, Holt (New York, NY), 1989, reprinted with new afterword, University of Nebraska Press (Lincoln, NE), 2000.

Why Black People Tend to Shout: Cold Facts and Wry Views from a Black Man's World (essays), Carol Publishing Group (Secaucus, NJ), 1991.

(With Spike Lee) *By Any Means Necessary: The Trials and Tribulations of the Making of Malcolm X,* Hyperion (New York, NY), 1992.

What Black People Should Do Now: Dispatches from near the Vanguard, Ballantine Books (New York, NY), 1993.

Dark Witness: When Black People Should Be Sacrificed (Again), Ballantine Books (New York, NY), 1996.

(With Spike Lee) *Best Seat in the House: A Basketball Memoir,* Crown Publishers (New York, NY), 1997.

(With Eric Davis) *Born to Play: The Eric Davis Story: Life Lessons in Overcoming Adversity On and Off the Field,* Viking (New York, NY), 1999.

(With Dexter Scott King) *Growing Up King: An Intimate Memoir,* IPM (New York, NY), 2003.

Also author of television documentary *The Other Side of Victory,* three-act play *Cardinals,* and screenplay *Knuckle Down.* Contributor of essays to periodicals.

SIDELIGHTS: Ralph Wiley was a biographer and frequent collaborator with a number of black celebrities, including filmmaker Spike Lee and baseball player Eric Lee. Wiley, who died in 2004, was also the author of several collections of provocative and controversial essays that examined the African American experience.

In *Serenity: A Boxing Memoir* Wiley profiles both the renowned and the unsung fighters who have defined boxing over the years. As the grandson and nephew of two prizefighters and a seasoned sportswriter for both the *Oakland Tribune* and *Sports Illustrated,* the author relies upon his personal and professional background to present an intimate look at the sport. Wiley offers insights on such pugilists as Muhammad Ali, Joe Louis, and Mike Tyson, and speaks of the satisfaction that boxers experience in boldly living up to challenges both inside and outside of the ring.

In his next book, *Why Black People Tend to Shout: Cold Facts and Wry Views from a Black Man's World,* Wiley employs thirty-three essays to discuss problems facing his fellow African Americans. In addition to surveying a wide variety of social and cultural issues, Wiley presents opinions on such diverse figures as Klansman-turned-politician David Duke, pop star Michael Jackson, and former Harlem Globetrotter Meadowlark Lemon. Notable among the author's observations is a discussion of novelist Alice Walker, whom Wiley faults for negatively portraying black men in *The Color Purple.* A writer for the *Los Angeles Times Book Review* praised Wiley as "a bold new voice."

What Black People Should Do Now: Dispatches from near the Vanguard contains a collection of twenty-three essays that offer "a vigorous, mordant perspective on the African American experience," noted a *Publishers Weekly* reviewer. Several of the essays originally appeared in publications such as the *Washington Post* and *Los Angeles Times.* Wiley covers topics such as Magic Johnson and his struggle with AIDS; the various reactions to the Rodney King case; and his sadness at how his son, then attending a well-integrated public school, will eventually learn about racial division. In a humorous essay, Wiley explores the myth that black people do not buy books. Readers "will find Wiley sometimes engaging or amusing," noted Frederick D. Robinson in *Black Enterprise. American Visions* contributor Gary A. Puckrein called the book a "fast-paced work of contemporary social commentary."

Continuing to write about the condition of the African American with *Dark Witness: When Black People Should Be Sacrificed (Again)* Wiley "mixes current trends and topics of debate over Black America with a uniquely American Question: Who is Black?," noted Zachary Dowdy in *Emerge.* Wiley "launches his satirical barbs high," noted a *Publishers Weekly* reviewer, as he considers topics as diverse as the speech syntax of NAACP leader Ben Chavis; the surreal life led by

O.J. Simpson, and the musical prowess of Wynton Marsalis. He wonders why the attack on Waco, Texas, was more important to American militia members than the bombing of the black group MOVE in Philadelphia in 1987. He also offers a perspective on the Hughes brothers' film *Dead Presidents*. "Something here should energize or offend (or both) all readers," observed Mary Carroll in *Booklist*. Dowdy concluded: "Wiley brings to the debate his own inimitable style, a bold perspective that is without compromise, and a voice that provokes laughter about society's weightiest dilemmas."

Best Seat in the House: A Basketball Memoir provides an autobiographical slant on filmmaker, basketball lover, and top-flight New York Knicks fan Spike Lee. In what a *Publishers Weekly* contributor called a "disjointed but high-spirited memoir," Lee reflects on his childhood when he sneaked into Madison Square Garden to watch a 1970 playoff game from the rafters. Lee also relates how he became a famed writer and director with a thousand-dollar courtside seat for Knicks games, where he encourages the players, harangues the coaches, and reviles the referees. Lee includes his own memories of significant games and prominent players with material from his own personal highlights, including his breakout movie, *Do the Right Thing,* his marriage and fatherhood, and his meeting with Jackie Robinson. *Booklist* reviewer Bonnie Smothers called the work "the sweetest book about sports to be published in a long time."

Born to Play: The Eric Davis Story: Life Lessons in Overcoming Adversity On and Off the Field covers Davis's promising early career, the physical injuries and hardships he suffered, and the strength that allowed him to overcome his obstacles and remain a major-league player. Davis came from a difficult life in South Central Los Angeles, where poverty, violence, and drugs were rampant. When he came to the major leagues, Davis demonstrated a combination of phenomenal speed and tremendous power that had last been noticed in legend Willie Mays. He played on the World Series champion Cincinnati Reds in 1991, and on the 1997 contender team, the Baltimore Orioles. Several health problems nearly cost him both his ability to play and his life, however. While making a diving catch during the 1990 World Series, he lacerated a kidney, an injury that was life-threatening. Then, in 1997, Davis was diagnosed with colon cancer during the season. He endured surgery and chemotherapy and

returned to play by that September. The death of his brother, who had gravitated toward the gangster lifestyle, dealt another stunning emotional blow during his cancer treatment. Despite his troubles, Davis maintained the spirit and the desire to play. Davis and Wiley tell the story of how Davis overcame his life's toughest problems. The team of Davis and Wiley moved *New York Times Book Review* critic Allen Barra to write that the book "differs from many baseball memoirs in that it has a player who can think and a writer who can write." Barra called it a "superior sports autobiography." *Library Journal* reviewer John M. Maxymuk commented that Davis's story "is a fascinating tale, at times grippingly told."

Moving from sports to even larger issues, *Growing Up King: An Intimate Memoir* is an "honest and telling autobiography" of Dexter Scott King, the youngest son and third child of legendary civil rights leader Dr. Martin Luther King, Jr. The son who most closely resembles his father, Dexter King has lived beneath a giant's shadow, doing his best to live up to a legacy that followed him through every step of his life. He describes what it was like to grow up with such a famous father. The authors include details and remembrances from King's early childhood, of his father and mother, and of his father's assassination. The death of their father profoundly affected Dexter and all his siblings, but his legacy also placed a great strain on the children as they grew up and searched for their own identity. King and Wiley candidly relate some of King's travails and shortcomings, including his failure to complete a degree at Morehouse College, which had graduated men in his family since 1898, and his sometimes aimless pursuit of a professional career. They discuss his tumultuous years as chief executive officer and president of the King Center in Atlanta and the battles between King and the center's board of directors. King also describes the difficulties of securing the intellectual property rights to his father's speeches and writings. Finally, he comments on his family's struggle to make sense of a number of conspiracy theories surrounding his father's death. *Booklist* contributor Vanessa Bush declared the book "a fascinating biography."

BIOGRAPHICAL AND CRITICAL SOURCES:

BOOKS

Contemporary Black Biography, Volume 8, Gale (Detroit, MI), 1994.

PERIODICALS

American Visions, October-November, 1993, Gary A. Puckrein, review of *What Black People Should Do Now: Dispatches from near the Vanguard,* p. 35.

Black Collegian, February, 2003, Corinne Nelson, review of *Growing Up King: An Intimate Memoir,* p. 120.

Black Enterprise, March, 1994, Frederick D. Robinson, review of *What Black People Should Do Now,* p. 93.

Booklist, May 15, 1996, Mary Carroll, review of *Dark Witness: When Black People Should Be Sacrificed (Again),* p. 1553; April 1, 1997, Bonnie Smothers, review of *Best Seat in the House: A Basketball Memoir,* p. 1267; January 1, 2003, Vanessa Bush, review of *Growing Up King,* p. 815.

Ebony, January, 2003, review of *Growing Up King,* p. 16.

Emerge, June, 1996, Zachary Dowdy, "To Be or Not to Be—Black," review of *Dark Witness,* p. 71.

Kirkus Reviews, November 15, 2002, review of *Growing Up King,* p. 1675.

Kliatt, July, 2004, Nola Theiss, review of *Growing Up King,* p. 37.

Library Journal, April 1, 1999, John M. Maxymuk, review of *Born to Play,* p. 105.

Los Angeles Times Book Review, March 31, 1991, review of *Why Black People Tend to Shout,* p. 6.

New York Times, June 8, 1997, Lena Williams, review of *Best Seat in the House,* p. 24.

New York Times Book Review, May 30, 1999, Allen Barra, review of *Born to Play,* p. 16.

People, May 19, 1997, Alex Tresniowski, review of *Best Seat in the House,* p. 38.

Publishers Weekly, November 16, 1992, review of *By Any Means Necessary,* p. 56; August 30, 1993, review of *What Black People Should Do Now,* p. 85; March 25, 1996, review of *Dark Witness,* p. 73; April 28, 1997, review of *Best Seat in the House,* p. 61; March 8, 1999, review of *Born to Play,* p. 60; December 2, 2002, review of *Growing up King,* p. 45.

ONLINE

Large Print Reviews Web site, http://www.largeprint reviews.com/ (February 5, 2003), Leo Johnston, review of *Growing Up King.*

Salon.com, http://www.salon.com/ (May, 1997), Rob Spillman, review of *Best Seat in the House.*

OBITUARIES

PERIODICALS

Los Angeles Times, June 16, 2004, p. B8.
New York Times, June 17, 2004, p. A27.
Washington Post, June 16, 2004, p. B6.

ONLINE

ESPN.com, http://sports.espn.go.com/ (June 14, 2004).
New York Times Online, http://www.nytimes.com/ (June 17, 2004).*

* * *

WILLIAMS, Raymond 1921-1988
(Raymond Henry Williams)

PERSONAL: Born August 31, 1921, in Llanfihangel Crocorney, Monmouthshire, Wales; died January 26, 1988, in London, England; son of Henry Joseph (a railway worker) and Gwendolene (Bird) Williams; married Joyce Mary Dalling, June 19, 1942; children: Merryn, Ederyn, Gwydion Madawc. *Education:* Trinity College, Cambridge, M.A., 1946, Litt.D., 1969. *Politics:* Socialist.

CAREER: Oxford University Delegacy for Extra-Mural Studies, Oxford, England, staff tutor in literature, 1946-61; Cambridge University, Cambridge, England, lecturer, 1961-68, fellow of Jesus College, 1961-88, reader, 1968-74, professor of drama, 1974-83; visiting professor of political science at Stanford University, 1973, and Open University, 1975; member of the Arts Council, 1976-78. *Military service:* British Army, Guards Armored Division, 1941-45; became captain.

AWARDS, HONORS: Welsh Arts Council prize for fiction, 1979, for *The Fight for Manod;* honorary D.Litt. degrees from University of Wales, Open University, and University of Kent.

WRITINGS:

NONFICTION

Reading and Criticism, Muller (London, England), 1950.

Drama from Ibsen to Eliot, Chatto & Windus (London, England), 1952, Oxford University Press (New York, NY), 1953, revised as *Drama from Ibsen to Brecht,* Chatto & Windus (London, England), 1968, Oxford University Press (New York, NY), 1969.

(With Michael Orrom) *Preface to Film,* Film Drama (London, England), 1954.

Drama in Performance, Muller (London, England), 1954, Dufour (Chester Springs, PA), 1961, 3rd edition, Penguin (New York, NY), 1973, published with a new introduction and bibliography by Graham Hoderness, Open University Press (Buckingham, England), 1991.

Culture and Society, 1780-1950, Columbia University Press (New York, NY), 1958, published with a new postscript by Williams, Penguin/Chatto & Windus (Harmondsworth, England), 1963, Columbia University Press (New York, NY), 1983.

The Long Revolution, Columbia University Press (New York, NY), 1961.

Communications, Penguin (Harmondsworth, England), 1962, 2nd edition, 1976.

The Existing Alternatives to Communications, Fabian Society (London, England), 1962.

Modern Tragedy, Stanford University Press (Stanford, CA), 1966, revised edition, Verso (London, England), 1979.

The English Novel from Dickens to Lawrence, Oxford University Press (New York, NY), 1970.

Orwell, Viking (New York, NY), 1971, revised and enlarged edition, Fontana (London, England), 1984.

The Country and the City, Oxford University Press (New York, NY), 1973.

Television: Technology and Cultural Form, Fontana (London, England), 1973, Schocken (New York, NY), 1975, revised edition, 1992.

Drama in a Dramatized Society, Cambridge University Press (New York, NY), 1975.

Keywords: A Vocabulary of Culture and Society, Oxford University Press (New York, NY), 1976, revised and enlarged edition, Fontana (London, England), 1983, Oxford University Press (New York, NY), 1985, new revised edition published as *New Keywords: A Revised Vocabulary of Culture and Society,* Blackwell (Malden, MA), 2005.

Marxism and Literature, Oxford University Press (Oxford, England), 1977.

Politics and Letters: Interviews with New Left Review, Schocken (New York, NY), 1979.

The Welsh Industrial Novel: The Inaugural Gwyn Jones Lecture, University College Cardiff Press (Cardiff, Wales), 1979.

Problems in Materialism and Culture: Selected Essays, Verso (London, England), 1980, Schocken (New York, NY), 1981.

Culture, Fontana (London, England), 1981, published as *The Sociology of Culture,* Schocken (New York, NY), 1982.

Democracy and Parliament, introduction by Peter Tatchell, Socialist Society (London, England), 1982.

Socialism and Ecology, Socialist Environment and Resources Association (London, England), c. 1982.

Cobbett, Oxford University Press (New York, NY), 1983.

Towards 2000, Chatto & Windus (London, England), 1983, published as *The Year 2000,* Pantheon (New York, NY), 1984.

Writing in Society, Verso (London, England), 1983.

(With Maureen Williams) *The Defenders of Malta,* Raymond Williams (Newby Bridge, England), 1988.

Raymond Williams on Television, 1921-1987, edited by Alan O'Connor, Routledge (New York, NY), 1989.

Resources of Hope: Culture, Democracy, Socialism, edited by Robin Gable, Verso (London, England, and New York, NY), 1989.

The Politics of Modernism: Against the New Conformists, edited by Tony Pinkney, Verso (London, England, and New York, NY), 1989.

What I Came to Say, Hutchinson Radius (London, England), 1989.

The Raymond Williams Reader, edited by John Higgins Oxford, Blackwell (Malden, MA), 2001.

NOVELS

Border Country, Chatto & Windus (London, England), 1960, Horizon (New York, NY), 1962.

Second Generation, Chatto & Windus (London, England), 1964, Horizon (New York, NY), 1965.

The Volunteers, Methuen (London, England), 1978, Hogarth (New York, NY), 1986.

The Fight for Manod, Chatto & Windus (London, England), 1979.

Loyalties, Chatto & Windus (London, England), 1985.

The People of the Black Mountains, Chatto & Windus (London, England), Volume 1: *The Beginning,* 1989, Volume 2: *The Eggs of the Eagle,* 1990.

EDITOR

May Day Manifesto 1968, Penguin (Harmondsworth, England), 1968.

Pelican Book of English Prose, Volume 2: *From 1780 to the Present Day,* Penguin (Harmondsworth, England), 1969.

(With Joyce Williams) *D.H. Lawrence on Education,* Penguin Educational (Harmondsworth, England), 1973.

George Orwell: A Collection of Critical Essays, Prentice-Hall (Englewood Cliffs, NJ), 1974.

(With Marie Axton) Charles Dickens, *Dombey and Son,* Cambridge University Press (Cambridge, England), 1977.

(With Marie Axton) *English Drama: Forms and Development; Essays in Honour of Muriel Clara Bradbrook,* Cambridge University Press (Cambridge, England), 1978.

Contact: Human Communication and Its History, Thames & Hudson (London, England), 1981.

Roger Sales, *English Literature and History, 1780-1830: Pastoral and Politics,* St. Martin's (New York, NY), 1983.

(With Merryn Williams) *John Clare: Selected Poetry and Prose,* Methuen (New York, NY), 1986.

OTHER

A Letter from the Country (teleplay), British Broadcasting Corporation (BBC), 1966.

Public Inquiry (teleplay), BBC, 1967.

Also author of *The Country and the City* (television documentary), produced for the *Where We Live Now* series. Author of introductions to books, including *Dombey and Son,* by Charles Dickens, Penguin (Harmondsworth, England), 1970; *Racine,* by Lucien Goldmann, Rivers (Cambridge, England), 1972; and *Visions and Blueprints: Avant-Garde Culture and Radical Politics in Early Twentieth-Century Europe,* edited by Edward Timms and Peter Collier, Manchester University Press (Manchester, England), 1988; author of foreword to *Languages of Nature: Critical Essays on Science and Literature,* edited by L.J. Jordanova,

Free Association Books (London, England), 1986. Editor of *Politics and Letters,* 1946-47; general editor, *New Thinkers' Library,* 1962-70. Contributor to *Revue des Langues Vivantes* and *Science Fiction Studies.*

SIDELIGHTS: In the *Dictionary of Literary Biography,* an essayist described Raymond Williams as "a major figure in the world of English letters," and cited his "rare combination of right-of-center Marxism and a moral passion akin to that of F.R. Leavis" as the explanation for why the author's "massive interdisciplinary output [had] commanded the respect of both the New Left and the traditional literary establishment." For Robert Christgau of the *Voice Literary Supplement,* Williams was not "just a fecund and significant and immensely useful writer. [He was] an enjoyable and even exciting one." Among the writings for which Williams will be remembered are the sociological studies *Culture and Society, 1780-1950* and *The Long Revolution;* his widely studied text of dramatic theory, *Drama from Ibsen to Brecht* (originally published as *Drama from Ibsen to Eliot*); and the trilogy of popular novels *Border Country, Second Generation,* and *The Fight for Manod.*

Often considered one of the founding fathers of the field of cultural studies, Williams was governed by certain consistent principles in his sociological and political writings. His *The Sociology of Culture* explores an idea the author termed "cultural materialism"—a way of analyzing art that mandates the analysis of the process behind the production of that art, as well as the recognition of the art as product, in order to understand its social significance. "One of the distinguishing features of Williams's 'cultural materialism,'" Anthony Giddens wrote in the *Times Literary Supplement,* was "his uncompromising insistence upon the diversity of cultural forms, that always have to be studied in the contexts of their creation and reception." Among the forms Williams insisted must be studied were television and other examples of popular art that had traditionally been shunned in studies of "culture."

Williams also discussed cultural materialism in several of the essays collected in *Problems in Materialism and Culture: Selected Essays,* along with another issue of central importance to his life and work: Marxism. In the *Times Literary Supplement,* Robert Hewison offered an explanation of the notion of "structure of feeling," one of the tenets of the Marxism Williams espoused: "The term describes the empirical and imaginative perception of the world by a group or class, but not an individual, and though this collective world picture finds its most coherent expression in the highest works of literature, the ideas, images and values these express permeate all perceptions of the world, thus constituting a particular ideology. The great works are created, of course, by individuals, but they reflect the group consciousness." While Hewison felt that Williams's prose made his complex ideas even more difficult to comprehend, the reviewer noted that *Problems in Materialism and Culture* did "demonstrate that culture is a material product and therefore economically and politically is as significant as the organization of the steel industry," thus lending greater meaning to the term "cultural revolution."

In a London *Times* review, Richard Holmes described *Contact: Human Communication and Its History* as "an admirable and provocative compilation" of essays. Of the texts—which range from explorations of the fundamentals of communication to the authoritarian element of radio—Holmes found special favor with the piece Williams, the book's editor, contributed to the collection, an analysis of the future of telecommunications that Holmes called "a masterly essay of summary." Williams's essays, lectures, and reviews collected in 1983's *Writing in Society* explore the study of literature and the changing role of literary criticism from the perspective of Marxism. For Christgau, five of the collection's essays were "superb."

The Year 2000, originally published as *Towards 2000,* picks up where *Culture and Society* and *The Long Revolution* leave off, continuing what Bryan Appleyard called in the London *Times* "the drive . . . towards a benevolent, free socialism in which production will once again be directed towards use rather than consumption." It was Appleyard's opinion that, in *The Year 2000,* Williams had ceased to be "a critic, tossing his socio-political nets over art," and had become instead "a prophet, making unfashionable attempts to make his mind the compass of the world"—attempts the critic felt to be very persuasive. Reviewer Janet Morgan was not quite as convinced, however. Despite writing in the *Times Literary Supplement* that she found Williams's "anecdotes . . . so endearing, [his] speculations about trends and relations so interesting and his effort to explore contemporary vocabulary so admirable an enterprise," Morgan took great exception

to the methodology behind the author's argument. For her, the methods Williams proposed for analyzing his subject were inconsistently followed through and bore little connection to the author's ensuing proposals, ultimately raising more questions than Williams could answer by the book's end. Robert Bendiner expressed a similar opinion in the *New York Times Book Review,* asserting that though Williams's goals were admirable (the author "would remake world politics along . . . gentler lines"), his proposals were unrealistic at best.

Resources of Hope, published the year after Williams's death, gathers writings from the last thirty years of the author's life. Peter Ackroyd described its contents in the London *Times* as being representative of "the kind of life that can essentially be defined in parochial terms. . . . Very much a life built upon exclusion, within a small community which implicitly or actively denies the values of the larger world beyond." Critics like Ackroyd and *Times Literary Supplement* writer Denis Donaghue felt that though this final collection was lacking in spots, "Williams's work [is] indeed already honourably if not impeccably complete."

Williams's fiction, however, was left incomplete at the time of his death. His final writings were collected in the two posthumously published volumes that made up *The People of the Black Mountains* (*The Beginning* and *The Eggs of the Eagle*), which were well received by critics. The success of Williams's fiction with the public began with the 1960 publication of *Border Country.* The first of a trio of linked novels sometimes referred to as his "Welsh Trilogy" (*Second Generation* and *The Fight for Manod* followed in 1964 and 1979, respectively), *Border Country* tells the story of Matthew Price, a lecturer in London who returns to the Welsh border village of his birth when his father falls ill. Considered autobiographical by some, the novel took as its theme "the conflict between alienation and reintegration," according to Weis, a theme revealed in Price's struggle to link his working-class past to his intellectual present. *Second Generation* picked up its predecessor's border imagery, tracing the lives of two generations of a family relocated from a Welsh border town to a university city. For Weis, *Second Generation* suffered in comparison to its predecessor, though the critic saw a poignancy in the "depiction of the emotional struggle" of the main characters. Matthew Price returns to the trilogy in its final volume, *The Fight for Manod,* in which he is caught up in a battle over a government project that would forever alter the border country. Weis called it "a strange, almost nightmarish, evocation of what happens when the connections between economic figures and human beings are ignored." According to Patricia Craig in the *Times Literary Supplement,* the three novels amounted to "a densely written, thoughtful and evocative trilogy."

In the London *Times,* Elaine Feinstein described Williams's *Loyalties* as "one of his best novels." The story of Norman Braose and the socialism and espionage into which he is swept over the course of fifty years, *Loyalties* met with a largely positive critical response. Howard Jacobson, who called it "a novel of ideas; more specifically a novel of socialist ideas" in the *Times Literary Supplement,* found the book "altogether more gripping" than a novel of ideas should be. "Altogether a tough, thoughtful, haunting novel" was the way Seon Manley described it in the *New York Times Book Review.* Williams's next novel, *The Volunteers,* was also an intellectual study beneath its tale of murder and political intrigue. For one *Washington Post Book World* reviewer, this was a successful combination: "Like all really good thrillers, [*Volunteers*] deals . . . with man's inward life and the difficulties of moral choice."

The People of the Black Mountains moves episodically from a modern narrative to times in Wales's history ranging from 82 A.D. to 1415 A.D. (Williams had planned to take the unfinished text into the twentieth century as well). In a review of *The Eggs of the Eagle,* the second volume, Terence Hawkes wrote in the *Times Literary Supplement* that "Raymond Williams devoted much of his academic effort to changing the nature of 'English' by undermining the reductive boundaries which it constructed across a complex history and culture." The critic explained what he saw as the consistent idea underlying the "borders" that recurred in Williams's fiction: that "although walls father cultural restriction they must also be the mothers of creative transgression." For Hawkes, Williams managed to achieve his goal of transgressing those borders with *The People of the Black Mountains,* mounting "his final assault on the political and cultural walls."

BIOGRAPHICAL AND CRITICAL SOURCES:

BOOKS

Contemporary Literary Critics, 2nd edition, Gale (Detroit, MI), 1982.

Dictionary of Literary Biography, Gale (Detroit, MI), Volume 14: *British Novelists since 1960,* 1982, Volume 231: *British Novelists since 1960, Fourth Series,* 2000, Volume 232: *Twentieth-Century European Cultural Theorists, First Series,* 2001.

Inglis, Fred, *Raymond Williams,* Routledge (New York, NY), 1995.

Prendergast, Christopher, editor, *Cultural Materialism: On Raymond Williams,* University of Minnesota Press (Minneapolis, MN), 1995.

Stevenson, Nick, *Culture, Ideology and Socialism: Raymond Williams and E.P. Thompson,* Avebury (Brookfield, VT), 1995.

Wallace, Jeff, Rod Jones, and Sophie Nield, editors, *Raymond Williams Now: Knowledge, Limits, and the Future,* St. Martin's (New York, NY), 1997.

PERIODICALS

Art Journal, fall, 1997, Jonathan Harris, "Art Education and Cyber-Ideology: Beyond Individualism and Technological Determination," p. 39.

New York Times Book Review, May 6, 1984, p. 27; March 22, 1987.

Times (London, England), January 7, 1982; October 20, 1983; September 26, 1985; February 23, 1989.

Times Literary Supplement, February 27, 1981, pp. 215, 239; December 10, 1982, p. 1362; November 4, 1983, p. 1223; January 13, 1984, p. 29; February 8, 1985, p. 147; October 11, 1985, p. 1125; February 12-18, 1988, p. 172; March 3-9, 1989, p. 217; November 3-9, 1989, p. 1205; October 19, 1990, pp. 1131, 1137.

Voice Literary Supplement, November, 1982, p. 10; April, 1985, p. 1.

Washington Post Book World, February 23, 1986, p. 12.

ONLINE

New Criterion Online, http://www.newcriterion.com/ (February 7, 2003), Maurice Cowling, "Raymond Williams in Retrospect."

OBITUARIES

PERIODICALS

New York Times, January 29, 1988.
Times (London, England), January 27, 1988.*

WILLIAMS, Raymond Henry
  See WILLIAMS, Raymond

*   *   *

WILSON, John Morgan 1945-

PERSONAL: Born 1945, in Tampa, FL. *Education:* Attended Michigan State University; San Diego State University, B.A., 1968.

ADDRESSES: Home—West Hollywood, CA. *Agent*—c/o Publicity Department, Minotaur Books, 175 5th Ave., New York, NY 10010. *E-mail*—john@johnmorganwilson.com.

CAREER: Former police reporter for *Los Angeles Herald-Examiner;* University of California, Los Angeles, Extension Writers' Program, instructor, 1980—; *Los Angeles Times,* Los Angeles, CA, assistant editor, 1985-92; *Easy Reader* (newspaper), Hermosa Beach, CA, founder. Has also worked as a freelance writer and staff reporter for numerous newspapers and magazines.

MEMBER: Sisters in Crime, Mystery Writers of America (former board member, Southern California Chapter).

AWARDS, HONORS: Certificate of Excellence for Reporting on Media, Los Angeles Press Club, 1987, for work published in the *Los Angeles Times;* Edgar Allan Poe Award for best first mystery novel, Mystery Writers of America, 1997, for *Simple Justice;* Lambda Literary Award for Best Gay Men's Mystery, 2000, for *Justice at Risk,* 2001, for *Limits of Justice,* and 2003, for *Blind Eye.*

WRITINGS:

(As John M. Wilson) *The Complete Guide to Magazine Article Writing,* Writer's Digest Books (Cincinnati, OH), 1993.

Inside Hollywood: A Writer's Guide to the World of Movies and TV, Writer's Digest Books (Cincinnati, OH), 1998.

Blue Moon (novel; "Philip Damon" mystery series), Berkley Prime Crime (New York, NY), 2002.

Good Morning, Heartache (novel; "Philip Damon" mystery series), Berkley Prime Crime (New York, NY), 2003.

Has also written for numerous television programs and networks, including Fox, the Discovery Channel, the History Channel, Court TV, and the Learning Channel. Served as supervising writer for documentary series *Anatomy of Crime,* and writer and co-producer for documentary series *Video Justice,* both for Court TV. Contributor to periodicals, including the *New York Times, Washington Post, Los Angeles Times, Chicago Tribune Magazine, Los Angeles Magazine, TV Guide, Surfer, Entertainment Weekly,* and *Advocate.* Columnist for *Writer's Digest.* Editor of Mystery Writers of America newsletter, *The March of Crime.* Has published short stories in *Ellery Queen Mystery Magazine* and *Blithe House Quarterly.*

"BENJAMIN JUSTICE" SERIES; MYSTERY NOVELS

Simple Justice, Doubleday (New York, NY), 1996.

Revision of Justice, Doubleday (New York, NY), 1997.

Justice at Risk, Doubleday (New York, NY), 1999.

The Limits of Justice, Doubleday (New York, NY), 2000.

Blind Eye, St. Martin's Minotaur (New York, NY), 2003.

Moth and Flame, St. Martin's Minotaur (New York, NY), 2004.

Rhapsody in Blood, St. Martin's Minotaur (New York, NY), 2006.

SIDELIGHTS: Freelance journalist and author John Morgan Wilson scored a critical hit with his first crime novel, *Simple Justice.* The 1996 story introduced a mystery series featuring amateur sleuth Benjamin Justice. Justice, a gay journalist, had won a Pulitzer Prize for a story about a dying couple's struggle against AIDS six years prior to the novel's opening. However, he was forced to return the prestigious award—and was forced from his job as well—after it was discovered that he had invented the entire story. Now, mourning the death of his lover from AIDS—and drinking too much—the disgraced reporter is recruited by his former editor (who also lost his *Los Angeles Times* job over the fraudulent story) to do research on the murder of a gay man outside a Los

Angeles bar. A Hispanic gang member has confessed to the killing, but his story sounds fishy to the editor; when Justice investigates he finds that no one involved is what they first seem to be. Suspects and interviewees include such diverse characters as a senator and his son and a lesbian tennis player and her publicist.

Richard Lipez, reviewing *Simple Justice* for the *Washington Post Book World,* noted: "Little of this is original, but Wilson writes with such skill, pluck, and conviction that it becomes both suspenseful and moving." *Library Journal* reviewer Rex E. Klett assessed the novel similarly, finding that the murderer's identity was not hard to guess but that the pathway to the guessing was an enjoyable one, including lots of "LA local color." An enthusiastic review came from *Booklist* contributor Charles Harmon, who called *Simple Justice* "an exceptionally fine debut," adding that "Wilson has created a most compelling lead character in Justice . . . a more human and real character than most mystery sleuths."

Following the success of *Simple Justice,* which won an Edgar Award in 1997, Wilson authored the second Benjamin Justice book. *Revision of Justice* is set in the Hollywood world of screenwriting. When a young screenwriter is found dead at a party, Justice decides to investigate the lives of the party guests to determine who might have wanted him dead. A reviewer for *Booklist* called *Revision of Justice* a "tightly paced page-turner filled with memorable scoundrels." Though a reviewer for *Publishers Weekly* found Justice's character hard to like, the critic commented that "Wilson offers a stark, absorbing and seemingly authentic tour of the Hollywood fringes."

In *Justice at Risk* Justice finds himself with a chance at a new career when documentary film producer Cecile Change hires him to work on a segment for a film about AIDS. His interest is also sparked by handsome associate producer Peter Groff, who has been taking up the slack on the production caused by director Tom Callahan's disappearance. When Justice and Groff look for the missing director, they find an empty apartment and traces of a struggle in the blood-spattered bedroom. The director's body is later found in a section of Los Angeles known for homosexual cruising, but soon connections arise between Callahan's and that of another filmmaker. Justice discovers a link between those murders and a police cover-up of a brutality case that suggests political cor-

ruption and a system-wide police prejudice. A *Publishers Weekly* reviewer called the novel "a startlingly complex and refreshingly sophisticated mystery." The "atmosphere is foreboding and bleak, yet Justice manages to survive with his humanity intact," commented Margaret Hanes in the *Library Journal. Booklist* contributor Whitney Scott noted that "Wilson explores wealth, power, and corruption in considerable depth and concludes Justice's third caper with a cliffhanger that will have fans lining up for the next."

"Rivetingly dark and brooding," *The Limits of Justice* finds Justice recovering from a bout with alcoholism and taking on a new writing gig, noted Scott in another *Booklist* review. Justice has been hired by Charlotte Preston, the daughter of late Hollywood star Rod Preston, to write a biography of her famous father in response to a recent tell-all biography. Charlotte feels that the biography is scandalously wrong in its contention that her father was guilty of systematic predation of young boys. Though she gives Justice a substantial advance, he decides he does not want to work on the project. When he goes to see Charlotte to return the advance, he finds her dead, apparently from suicide. Justice, however, does not believe she killed herself, and his investigation uncovers a group of predatory Hollywood denizens that victimize young boys in a mansion in the desert. "Amazingly, within this obvious and often ludicrous premise, Wilson is able to nourish many moments of effective art," observed a *Publishers Weekly* reviewer.

Wilson's *Blind Eye* uncovers another layer of Justice's deep character, revealing that the writer-turned-sleuth was molested by a Catholic priest, Father Blackley, when he was twelve years old. The recipient of a 150,000 dollar advance for his autobiography, Justice determines to locate the priest, but learns that he died in a hiking accident years before. He has difficulty finding out more about Blackley's death, and in response he lets *Los Angeles Times* columnist Joe Soto run an exposé on Blackley's history. Hours after his column appears, however, Soto is killed in a hit and run. The identity of the killer is unknown, but Justice has several suspects: a freelance assassin who was due to be the subject of a book by Soto; a shady police detective who longs for Soto's fiancée, Alexandre; and a church-connected person determined to suppress scandal. Lawrence Schimel, reviewing the book inthe *Lambda Book Report,* noted that "Wilson handles admirably Justice's complexly flawed character."

Wilson "writes meditations on repentance and forgiveness as well as whodunits, giving discerning readers reason to rejoice," commented Scott in *Booklist*.

In *Moth and Flame* Justice takes on the task of finishing a book on West Hollywood that was begun by actor-cum-writer Bruce Bibby, who was recently murdered. As Justice works through the project, he discovers that Bibby's murder is related to a shady real estate development deal and the decades-old mysterious disappearance of a local handyman. The book is "another first-rate, increasingly engrossing, multilayered novel" in the Justice series, Scott concluded in *Booklist*.

Critics have often commented on the dark, depressing nature of Wilson's Justice novels. A *Publishers Weekly* reviewer called Wilson a "sensitive and powerful writer." In an interview on NPR's "All Things Considered," Wilson commented: "As I write these, I cry along with the characters. Sometimes I laugh along with the characters, but not so often in these books."

In a collaborative effort with Peter Duchin, Wilson opens a new series with *Blue Moon*. The book draws upon the musical experience of bandleader Duchin to tell the story of sleuth and high-society bandleader Peter Damon. In 1963 Damon returns to San Francisco to play at the Fairmont Hotel's Venetian Room. It is an important gig, but one filled with conflicting emotions, as the Fairmont is where Damon met his wife, who was later brutally murdered in an unsolved case. More bewildering is that he sees a woman who looks remarkably like his wife around the hotel, until he spots her on the dance floor during his band's performance, dancing with seedy real estate mogul Hamilton Collier III. Abruptly, the lights go out, and when they are restored, Collier is found on the floor dead, an ice pick in his chest. Damon is inexplicably linked to Collier's death, and he must work to uncover the identity of his wife's seeming twin, find out who killed Collier and why, and clear his own name of suspicion of murder. "This collaboration marks a promising debut in a new series," commented Rex E. Klett in the *Library Journal*. A *Publishers Weekly* contributor stated: "Expect applause and an encore for bandleader sleuth, Philip Damon."

The second music-themed mystery from Wilson and Duchin, *Good Morning, Heartache*, finds Damon working at the prestigious Cocoanut Grove. Unfortunately, his band is incomplete because the singer is temporarily sidelined by a cold. Damon offers the fill-in gig to trumpeter and vocalist Buddy Bixby. It is a risky proposition: though Bixby has more than enough talent to make the fill-in work perfectly, he is notorious for unreliability brought on by a taste for drugs. When Bixby fails to show up for his gig this time, however, it is because he has been killed. Damon, along with bandmate, ex-cop, and sax player Hercules Platt (once the Los Angeles Police Department's only black inspector), piece together the reasons behind Bixby's death. Jenny McLarin, writing in *Booklist*, commented that Wilson and Duchin "brilliantly combine bits of film and music history with a thought-provoking account of bigotry against gays and blacks in a city known for its liberal excesses."

BIOGRAPHICAL AND CRITICAL SOURCES:

PERIODICALS

Advocate, September 17, 1996, review of *Simple Justice*, p. 60.

Booklist, June 1, 1996, Charles Harmon, review of *Simple Justice*, p. 1643; November 15, 1997, Whitney Scott, review of *Revision of Justice*, April 15, 1998, Ted Leventhal, review of *Inside Hollywood: A Writer's Guide to the World of Movies and TV*, p. 1410; June 1, 1998, Ray Olson, review of *Revision of Justice*, p. 1681; June 1, 1999, Whitney Scott, review of *Justice at Risk*, p. 1787; June 1, 2000, Ray Olson, review of *Justice at Risk*, p. 1808; July, 2000, Whitney Scott, review of *The Limits of Justice*, p. 2014; June 1, 2001, Ray Olson, review of *The Limits of Justice*, p. 1815; October 1, 2002, Barbara M. Bibel, review of *Blue Moon*, p. 303; September 15, 2003, Whitney Scott, review of *Blind Eye*, p. 216; November 15, 2003, Jenny McLarin, review of *Good Morning, Heartache*, p. 584; February 1, 2005, Whitney Scott, review of *Moth and Flame*, p. 947.

Kirkus Reviews, June 15, 1996, review of *Simple Justice*, p. 863; August 15, 2002, review of *Blue Moon*, p. 1176; August 15, 2003, review of *Blind Eye*, p. 1050; October 15, 2003, review of *Good Morning, Heartache*, p. 1253.

Lambda Book Report, November-December, 2002, Jameson Currier, review of *Blue Moon*, p. 48; March-April, 2004, Lawrence Schimel, "Redeeming Justice," review of *Blind Eye*, p. 24.

Library Journal, July 1996, Rex E. Klett, review of *Simple Justice,* p. 168; May 1, 1998, Marty D. Evensvold, review of *Inside Hollywood,* p. 112; March 15, 2000, Margaret Hanes, review of *Justice at Risk,* p. 156; June 1, 2000, Rex E. Klett, review of *The Limits of Justice,* p. 208; October 1, 2002, Rex E. Klett, review of *Blue Moon,* p. 132; Rex E. Klett, review of *Moth and Flame,* p. 71.

Publishers Weekly, June 24, 1996, review of *Simple Justice,* p. 48; October 20, 1997, review of *Revision of Justice,* p. 58; June 28, 1999, review of *Justice at Risk,* p. 58; June 12, 2000, review of *The Limits of Justice,* p. 57; September 23, 2002, review of *Blue Moon,* p. 53; August 25, 2003, review of *Blind Eye,* p. 42; November 17, 2003, review of *Good Morning, Heartache,* p. 49; January 10, 2005, review of *Moth and Flame,* p. 42.

Washington Post Book World, September 15, 1996, Richard Lipez, review of *Simple Justice,* p. 6.

ONLINE

All about Romance, http://www.likesbooks.com/ (November 5, 2005), Anthony D. Langford, review of *The Limits of Justice.*

Books for a Buck, http://www.booksforabuck.com/ (November 5, 2005), review of *Blue Moon.*

Books 'n' Bytes, http://www.booksn bytes.com/ (November 5, 2005), Harriet Klausner, reviews of *Limits of Justice* and *Blue Moon.*

John Morgan Wilson Home Page, http://www.john morganwilson.com (November 5, 2005).

Mystery Reader, http://www.themysteryreader.com/ (November 5, 2005), Andy Plonka, review of *Justice at Risk.*

National Public Radio Web site, http://www.npr.com/ (December 31, 2003), Karen Grigsby Bates, "All Things Considered," transcript of interview with John Morgan Wilson.

*   *   *

WYATT, David M. 1948-

PERSONAL: Born October 7, 1948, in Lynwood, CA; son of James (an artist) and Joy Wyatt; married Libby Ortiz, June 9, 1970 (divorced, August, 1983); married Ann Porotti, May 4, 1991; children: Luke. *Education:* Yale University, B.A., 1970; University of California—Berkeley, Ph.D., 1975.

ADDRESSES: Office—Department of English, University of Maryland at College Park, College Park, MD 20742. *E-mail*—dw58@umail.umd.edu.

CAREER: University of Virginia, Charlottesville, assistant professor of English, 1975-82; Virginia Foundation for the Humanities, Charlottesville, program associate, 1982-84 and 1985-87; Princeton University, Princeton, NJ, visiting lecturer in English, 1984-85; University of Maryland at College Park, College Park, associate professor, 1987-89, professor of English, 1989—.

WRITINGS:

Prodigal Sons: A Study in Authorship and Authority, Johns Hopkins University Press (Baltimore, MD), 1980.

The Fall into Eden: Landscape and Imagination, Cambridge University Press (New York, NY), 1986.

(Editor) *New Essays on "The Grapes of Wrath,"* Cambridge University Press (New York, NY), 1990.

Out of the 'Sixties: Storytelling and the Vietnam Generation, Cambridge University Press (New York, NY), 1993.

Five Fives: Race, Catastrophe, and the Shaping of California, Addison Wesley (Reading, MA), 1997.

And the War Came: An Accidental Memoir, Terrace Books (Madison, WI), 2004.

SIDELIGHTS: David M. Wyatt once told *CA:* "I am interested in careers, regions, generations—in categories of understanding that honor the contexts in which literature is produced."

BIOGRAPHICAL AND CRITICAL SOURCES:

BOOKS

Wyatt, David M., *And the War Came: An Accidental Memoir,* Terrace Books (Madison, WI), 2004.

PERIODICALS

Los Angeles Times Book Review, August 24, 1986.
Times Literary Supplement, February 6, 1981.
Virginia Quarterly Review, winter, 1981; winter, 1998.

Y-Z

YANG, Philip Q. 1955-

PERSONAL: Born July 27, 1955, in Guangdong Province, China; naturalized U.S. citizen; son of Yuan and Xuan (Ma) Yang; married Jianling Li, 1984; children: Ming, William. *Ethnicity:* "Chinese." *Education:* Zhongshan University, B.A., 1982; University of California—Los Angeles, M.A., 1988, Ph.D., 1993.

ADDRESSES: Office—Department of Sociology and Social Work, Texas Woman's University, Denton, TX 76204-5887; fax: 940-898-2067. *E-mail*—pyang@mail.twu.edu.

CAREER: Zhongshan University, Canton, China, assistant professor of demography, 1982-86; University of California, Los Angeles, lecturer in sociology, 1994-95; California Polytechnic State University, San Luis Obispo, began as assistant professor, became associate professor of ethnic studies, 1995-99; Texas Woman's University, Denton, associate professor of sociology, 1999—.

MEMBER: North American Chinese Sociologists Association, American Sociological Association, Population Association of America, National Association for Ethnic Studies, Association for Asian American Studies, Association of Chinese Professors of Social Sciences in the United States, Southwestern Social Science Association.

AWARDS, HONORS: United Nations fellow, 1986-87; National Science Foundation grantee, 2001-2003; Texas Woman's University Chancellor's Research Fellow, 2001-01, and 2002-03.

WRITINGS:

Post-1965 Immigration to the United States: Structural Determinants, Praeger Publishers (Westport, CT), 1995.

Introduction to Ethnic Studies: A Reader, Kendall/Hunt (Dubuque, IA), 1999.

Ethnic Studies: Issues and Approaches, State University of New York Press (Albany, NY), 2000.

Contributor to books, including *Ethnic Los Angeles,* edited by Roger Waldinger and Mehdi Bozorgmehr, Russell Sage Foundation, 1996; *The Psychology of Ethnic and Cultural Conflict: Looking through American and Global Chaos or Harmony,* edited by Yueh-Ting Lee, Clark McCauley, and others, Praeger Publishers (Westport, CT), 2004; and *Asian Americans: Contemporary Trends and Issues,* edited by Pyong Gap Min, 2nd edition, Pine Forge Press, 2005. Contributor to periodicals, including *International Migration Review, Ethnic and Racial Studies, Journal of Asian American Studies, Diaspora, Journal of Ethnicity in Substance Abuse, International Journal of Comparative and Applied Criminal Justice, Educational Studies, International Journal of Social Welfare, Ethnic Studies Review,* and *Population and Environment.*

*   *   *

YELLIN, Jean Fagan 1930-

PERSONAL: Born September 19, 1930, in Lansing, MI; daughter of Peter (an editor) and Sarah (an editor; maiden name, Robinson) Fagan; married Edward Yellin (a biomedical engineer), December 17, 1948;

children: Peter, Lisa, Michael. *Education:* Attended Michigan State University and University of Michigan; Roosevelt University, B.A., 1951; University of Illinois, M.A., 1963, Ph.D.,1969.

ADDRESSES: Home—38 Lakeside Dr., New Rochelle, NY 10801. *Office*—Department of English, Pace University, 1 Pace Plaza, New York, NY 10038. *E-mail*—jyellin@pace.edu; jeanfagan@yellin.net.

CAREER: Pace University, New York, NY, assistant professor, 1968-74, associate professor of English, beginning 1974; currently professor emeritus.

MEMBER: Modern Language Association of America, College Language Association, American Studies Association, Association for the Study of Afro-American Life and History, Melville Society, Society for the Study of Multi-Ethnic Literature, Northeast Modern Language Association.

AWARDS, HONORS: American Association of University Women fellowship; Pace University scholarly research awards; National Endowment for the Humanities younger humanist fellowship and summer fellowship; National Humanities Institute fellowship; National Collection of Fine Arts-Smithsonian fellowship; W.E.B. DuBois Institute for Afro-American Research fellowship; Ethnic Scholar of the Year award; scholar-in-residence, Shomburg Center for Research in Black Culture; Pulitzer Prize nomination; Frederick Douglass Book Prize, 2004; D.H.L., Pace University, 2005.

WRITINGS:

NONFICTION

The Intricate Knot: Black Figures in American Literature, 1776-1863, New York University Press (New York, NY), 1972.
(Editor) *Criticisms of American Culture: A Reader,* Pace and Pace (New York, NY), 1982.
(Editor) Harriet A. Jacobs, *Incidents in the Life of a Slave Girl: Written by Herself,* Harvard University Press (Cambridge, MA), 1987.
Women & Sisters: The Antislavery Feminists in American Culture, Yale University Press (New Haven, CT), 1989.

(Compiler, with Cynthia D. Bond) *The Pen Is Ours: A Listing of Writings by and about African-American Women before 1910 with Secondary Bibliography to the Present,* Oxford University Press (New York, NY), 1991.
(Editor, with John C. Van Horne) *The Abolitionist Sisterhood: Women's Political Culture in Antebellum America,* Cornell University Press (Ithaca, NY), 1994.
Harriet Jacobs: A Life, Civitas/Basic Books (New York, NY), 2004.

Also author of *Afro-American Women Writers, 1800-1910,* G.K. Hall. Author of introduction, *Clotel,* by William W. Brown, Arno (New York, NY), 1969. Contributor to *Black Women's Studies,* coedited by Gloria T. Hull, Feminist Press (New York, NY), 1979. Contributor of articles and reviews to *American Quarterly, CLA Journal, Massachusetts Review, Criticism,* and *Freedomways.*

SIDELIGHTS: Jean Fagan Yellin has spent many years researching the life of Harriet Jacobs, a slave in the American South. Jacobs was born into slavery, but she learned to read as a child with the help of her first mistress. When that kindly woman died, Harriet became the property of a Dr. James Norcom. As she approached womanhood, she did what she could to deflect the unwanted sexual attentions from this owner; she even entered into a romantic liaison with a neighbor in the hopes of turning her owner away. She was just fifteen years old at the time. Her ploy was not successful, though, so Harriet then resorted to hiding out in a cubbyhole at her grandmother's house. For nearly seven years, she spent most of her time in a room that was only nine feet long and three feet high. In 1842, she escaped to the North, where she worked as a domestic, taught at a school for poor black children, and worked with refugees from the Civil War. Her memoir *Incidents in the Life of a Slave Girl: Written by Herself,* published in 1861, became a classic of slave narrative literature. Yet, for many years, there was doubt that Jacobs had really written the book herself. Yellin dedicated herself to authenticating the narrative, and edited a reissue of the book.

Yellin added to Jacob's own story with the biography *Harriet Jacobs: A Life.* She added details and background to the well-known story of Jacob's life, and continued it beyond where Jacob's own narrative ended. "Yellin offers moving insights into Jacob's feelings at crucial junctures," reported Jennifer Fleischner in *Legacy: A Journal of American Women Writers.* "Overall, Yellin triumphs in recovering the person behind the best-known woman's slave narrative in American literature." A *Kirkus Reviews* writer called the book a "graceful, honorable portrait, extensively documented and annotated," and concluded: "Yellin's fine reconstruction of an impressive personality should firmly embed Jacobs in American cultural history."

BIOGRAPHICAL AND CRITICAL SOURCES:

PERIODICALS

Chronicle of Higher Education, December 8, 1993, Liz McMillen, "A Slave Girl's Authentic Life," p. A8.
College English, February, 1990, Maryemma Graham, S.B. Dietzel, and R.W. Bailey, review of *Incidents in the Life of a Slave Girl: Written by Herself,* p. 194.
Journal of Negro History, spring, 2001, review of *Incidents in the Life of a Slave Girl,* p. 192.
Kirkus Reviews, November 15, 2003, review of *Harriet Jacobs: A Life,* p. 1356.
Legacy: A Journal of American Women Writers, January, 2005, Jennifer Fleischner, review of *Harriet Jacobs,* p. 78.
Publishers Weekly, December 1, 2003, review of *Harriet Jacobs,* p. 52.
Reviews in American History, September, 1993, Jerome Nadelhaft, review of *Women and Sisters: The Antislavery Feminists in American Culture,* p. 407.
Time, February 9, 2004, Lev Grossman, review of *Harriet Jacobs,* p. 75.
Women's Review of Books, December, 2004, Joyce Moody, review of *Harriet Jacobs,* p. 4.

ONLINE

Jean Fagan Yellin's Home Page, http://jeanfagan. yellin.net (November 11, 2005).*

                    *   *   *

ZIMLER, Richard 1956-
(Richard C. Zimler)

PERSONAL: Born January 1, 1956, in Roslyn Heights, NY; son of Robert and Ruth (Goodkind) Zimler. *Ethnicity:* "Many." *Education:* Duke University, B.A., 1977; Stanford University, M.A., 1982. *Hobbies and other interests:* Gardening.

ADDRESSES: Agent—c/o Author Mail, Constable & Robinson Ltd., 3 The Lanchesters, 162 Fulham Palace Rd., London W6 9ER England. *E-mail*—rczimler@ hotmail.com.

CAREER: Worked as a journalist in the San Francisco Bay Area, 1982-90. College of Journalism and University of Porto, Porto, Portugal, journalism instructor, 1990—

AWARDS, HONORS: Fellow in fiction, National Endowment for the Arts, 1994; first prize, *Panurge* Short Fiction Contest, 1994; *The Last Kabbalist of Lisbon* was named one of thirty "literary events," *LER* magazine, 1997; Herodotus Award, International Mystery Society, 1998, for *The Last Kabbalist of Lisbon; The Last Kabbalist of Lisbon* was also named book of the year by the London *Daily Telegraph, Gay Times,* and *Spectator,* all 1998.

WRITINGS:

NOVELS

Unholy Ghosts, GMP Publishers (London, England), 1996.
(And translator of Portuguese edition) *The Last Kabbalist of Lisbon,* Quetzal Editores (Lisbon, Portugal), 1996, Overlook Press (New York, NY), 1998.
The Angelic Darkness, Norton (New York, NY), 1999.
Hunting Midnight, Delacorte Press (New York, NY), 2003.
Guardian of the Dawn, Delta Trade Paperbacks (New York, NY), 2005.
The Search for Sana, Constable (London, England), 2005.

TRANSLATOR

A Portuguese Museum (museum exhibition catalog), Fundacao de Serralves (Oporto, Portugal), 1992.

Images for the 1990s (museum exhibition catalog), Fundacao de Serralves (Oporto, Portugal), 1993.

Al Berto, *Days without Anyone and Other Poems*, Mediterraneans (Paris, France), 1995.

Noah's Ark (museum exhibition catalog), Fundacao de Serralves (Oporto, Portugal), 1995.

Helena Almeida (museum exhibition catalog), Fundacao de Serralves (Oporto, Portugal), 1995.

The Garden of Fire (museum exhibition catalog), [Funchal, Portugal], 1996.

Marta Seixas (museum exhibition catalog), [Barcelona, Spain], 1996.

Nuno Judice, *Kidnappings* (poetry), 1998.

Agustina Bessa-Luis, *Oporto's Many Sides* (photography), [Lisbon, Portugal], 1998.

Al Berto, *The Secret Life of Images* (poetry), [Dublin, Ireland], 1998.

Also translated a photobiography of Jose Saramago, sonnets and other poems by Pedro Tamen, and stories by Clara Pinto Correia. Translated poems for periodicals, including *Element, James White Review, Literary Review,* and *Puerto del Sol.*

OTHER

Contributor to books, including *The Book of Eros,* Harmony Books (New York, NY), 1995; *His 2,* Faber (Boston, MA), 1997; *Men on Men: 6,* Plume (New York, NY), 1997; *Seven Hundred Kisses,* HarperCollins (San Francisco, CA), 1997; and *Voices from Home,* Avisson Press (Greensboro, NC), 1997. Contributor to periodicals, including *Los Angeles Times, San Francisco Chronicle, African American Review, Blue Light Red Light, Bronte Street, Element, Guys, Il Caffe, James White Review, Lactuca, LER, Literal Latte, London Magazine, Madison Review, Margin, Panurge, Puerto del Sol, RE Arts and Letters, San Miguel Writer, Santa Barbara Review, Sunk Island Review, Yellow Silk,* and *Z Miscellaneous.*

Zimler's books have been published in several languages, including Portuguese, Italian, Spanish, German, Dutch, Croatian, Greek, and Turkish.

SIDELIGHTS: American author Richard Zimler mixes aspects of Jewish philosophy and elements of a murder mystery in his novel *The Last Kabbalist of Lisbon.* In the preface, Zimler claims that the manuscript was found inside an old ceremonial chest in Istanbul, Turkey. He writes that the manuscript was found among other documents relating to the kabbalah (also spelled cabala), a mystical Jewish philosophy. According to Richard Bernstein in the *New York Times Book Review,* this claim is "clever," but not entirely believable because the sensibility of the characters is eminently modern. Although this book is a work of fiction, its setting does have an historical basis. It occurs during the 1506 Lisbon Inquisition, when the Portuguese government killed thousands of Jews. Fearing similar fates, other Jews converted to Christianity or practiced Judaism in secrecy.

In *The Last Kabbalist of Lisbon* the family of protagonist Berekiah Zarco secretly follows Jewish rites and explores the kabbalah. Berekiah, a young manuscript illuminator and fruit seller, returns home one night in 1506 to discover the nude bodies of his beloved uncle and a young girl dead in the family's secret prayer cellar. Berekiah must determine who killed the couple, as well as learn the killer's motive. His investigation leads the reader on a tour of sixteenth-century Lisbon and introduces omens, portents, more dead bodies, and the intricacies of the kabbalah. Other characters include Berekiah's companion, a highly perceptive Muslim, as well as a priest, a group of religious text smugglers, and the real-life Jewish historian Solomon Ibn Verga. Berekiah's trail leads to clues in the illustrations of a Haggadah, the Passover prayer book.

A *Publishers Weekly* reviewer commented that the book has an "artificial, labyrinthine plot," but added that "its aura of constant menace and its startling, beautiful imagery steeped in Jewish mysticism" create a "memorable and haunting" novel. Bernstein observed, "I'm not sure how deep your understanding of cabala will become, but you will find yourself drawn into a moody, tightly constructed historical thriller that is both entertaining and instructive." A *Kirkus Reviews* contributor concluded that *The Last Kabbalist of Lisbon* is "a bit attenuated, but, on balance, one of the more unusual and interesting first novels of recent vintage."

Well familiar with Portugal because he has taught journalism there since the 1990s, Zimler also set his novel *Unholy Ghosts* in that country. This time, however, the story occurs in the present day. It is the story of an American classical guitar teacher who looks for a lifestyle change in Portugal after some of his close friends die of AIDS. Yet he cannot escape the specter of AIDS, as his gifted student, Antonio, discovers he also has the disease.

Zimler's *The Angelic Darkness* mixes the occult with concepts of androgyny as it reveals the "mystical account of a divorced man's struggle for personal transformation in 1980s San Francisco," according to a writer in *Publishers Weekly.* Bill Ticino is a womanizer whose constant philandering has finally destroyed his marriage. Emotionally weary, psychically fragile, and inexplicably afraid of the dark, Bill cannot sleep and deteriorates physically and emotionally. To ameliorate the loneliness of his newly empty home, he takes in a housemate, the inscrutable, androgynous, but handsome Peter. Bill develops a thorough fascination, even infatuation, for Peter that is fueled by Peter's poetic mode of speech, his strange stories, his seeming ability to read Bill's mind, and his peculiar collection of talismans and Holocaust relics. Bill finds himself falling further into a world he had never known before, a landscape of sexual ambiguity, prostitution, transvestitism, teenage runaways, and androgyny. Zimler "excels at suspenseful depictions of such heightened states," commented *Booklist* reviewer Donna Seaman. As Bill works through issues surrounding his own androgyny, he finds the keys to his own transformation. *Library Journal* reviewer Robert E. Brown called the book "interesting, quirky fiction for curious readers susceptible to the curious."

Hunting Midnight offers a "rich blend of insight and imagination" in a "dazzling new novel," commented Elizabeth Rosner in *Tikkun.* The novel begins in 1798 Porto, Portugal, when the protagonist, John Zarco Stewart, is seven years old. He is the son of a Scottish father and a Portuguese mother who is a Marrano, or hidden Jew. When he is nine years old, John is cursed by a necromancer, a disturbing event for a young boy. The curse appears to be genuine to John, whose best friend drowns in an accident, while another friend, Violeta, is abruptly taken away by her parents who apparently have been abusing her. A surprising guest in his home appears able to help John deal with his problems. Midnight, an African bushman, becomes John's trusted companion and teacher, but tragedy descends again as Midnight is shot by a local landowner for poaching.

In the novel's second half, John is an adult who has discovered an act of treachery in his father's past. He

travels to Antebellum America to search for Midnight, who survived the shooting. There, he sees firsthand the horrors of slavery in its fullest form. John's search becomes a determined effort to right a tremendous wrong visited upon the man who taught him life's most important lessons as he was growing up. The narrative also intertwines around the life of the teenage slave Morri, as her life and John's slowly begin to intersect, with Midnight as the connecting point. "The bridge she creates between the two worlds is testimony to the talents of this novelist," Rosner observed. "There are profound glimpses here of the solidarity possible between Jews and blacks, among those who are able to recognize in one another's suffering the potential for collaboration and liberation," Rosner stated. Ilene Cooper, writing in *Booklist,* remarked that Zimler is a "superbly talented historical novelist." A *Publishers Weekly* contributor observed that "the narrative has a vintage flavor that becomes absorbing."

Guardian of the Dawn tells the story of Tiago Zarco, a half-Jewish, half-Indian man who finds himself betrayed by a member of his family and subjected to the cruelties of the Inquisition. A talented graphic artist, Tiago's comfortable life in Goa, Portugal, is shattered when he and his father are captured and imprisoned by the Inquisition. In order to save himself, Tiago professes Christianity, and he is imprisoned in Lisbon, where he spends many bleak years. Steeped in unrelenting fury during his imprisonment, Tiago constructs an elaborate plan for revenge against the person who betrayed him and against the priest who sentenced him and his father to their dismal fates. When Tiago is eventually released, he puts his deadly plan on hold after discovering that the person who betrayed him is someone much closer to home than he suspected. "Moody, atmospheric and at times ink-black with pain, Zimler's writing conjures vivid pictures of Portuguese Goa, of imprisonment and of personal devastation," observed Jessica Mulley on the *Virtual Bookshelf* Web site. "The weird contrast of Christianity at its most murderous and India at its most sumptuous jars the senses as crime and punishment work their usual spell in this deeply absorbing work," commented a *Kirkus Reviews* critic.

BIOGRAPHICAL AND CRITICAL SOURCES:

PERIODICALS

Booklist, April 15, 1998, Bill Ott, review of *The Last Kabbalist of Lisbon,* p. 1395; September 1, 1999,

Donna Seaman, review of *The Angelic Darkness,* p. 70; August, 2003, Ilene Cooper, review of *Hunting Midnight,* p. 1960.

Guardian (London, England), January 29, 2005, Elena Seymenliyska and Alfred Hickling, "Busy Dying," review of *Guardian of the Dawn.*

Kirkus Reviews, March 1, 1998, review of *The Last Kabbalist of Lisbon,* p. 297; May 15, 2003, review of *Hunting Midnight,* p. 714; May 15, 2005, review of *Guardian of the Dawn,* p. 563.

Library Journal, March 1, 1998, Margee Smith, review of *The Last Kabbalist of Lisbon,* p. 130; August, 1999, Robert E. Brown, review of *The Angelic Darkness,* p. 144.

New Leader, June 29, 1998, Tova Reich, review of *The Last Kabbalist of Lisbon,* p. 30.

New York Times Book Review, July 19, 1998, Erik Burns, review of *The Last Kabbalist of Lisbon,* p. 18; August 28, 1998, Richard Bernstein, review of *The Last Kabbalist of Lisbon.*

Publishers Weekly, January 26, 1998, review of *The Last Kabbalist of Lisbon,* p. 68; August 2, 1999, review of *The Angelic Darkness,* p. 73; June 2, 2003, review of *Hunting Midnight,* p. 31.

Tikkun, September-October, 2003, Elizabeth Rosner, review of *Hunting Midnight,* p. 78.

ONLINE

Virtual Bookshelf, http://www.thevirtualbookshelf.com/ (November 5, 2005), Jessica Mulley, review of *Guardian of the Dawn.*

*   *   *

ZIMLER, Richard C.
See ZIMLER, Richard